JEWELS OF THE IMAGINATION

JEWELS OF THE IMAGINATION

Mariah Hourihan, Editor

Amanda D'Wynter, Associate Editor

THE INTERNATIONAL LIBRARY OF POETRY

Jewels of the Imagination

ISBN 1-57553-182-8

Printing and Binding by
BPC Wheatons Ltd, Exeter, UK

Editor's Note

Imagine.

Standing alone the mere word "imagine" is liberating. Any words that follow it become an immediate possibility, where before they were only words: imagine a world without conflict; imagine communicating through telepathy; imagine flying among the birds. Imagination gives form and shape to things unknown. As Keats defined it, poetry, most simply, is "the expression of the imagination"(*A Defence of Poetry*). In Wordsworth's opinion, imagination is

> . . . *another name for absolute power*
> *And clearest insight, amplitude of mind,*
> *And Reason in her most exalted mood* (*The Prelude*, bk. xiv, l. 190).

The poets in *Jewels of the Imagination* channel this imaginative power to create works that entertain, delight, and often inform.

Some poetic forms, in their regulation of line and meter, require the imagination to manoeuvre between carefully-laid boundaries. The sonnet is one of these complex forms. The imagination must move shrewdly to weave images into a delicate framework of fourteen-lines, usually of iambic pentameter. Catesby Allers has woven an impressive tapestry of language in his poem, "A Sonnet of Quiescent Love" (p.451) in which the persona's love is likened to a "dormant dove". In the tradition of the Elizabethan sonneteers, Mr. Allers divides his poem into sections through the use of rhyme and imagery. The first and third lines rhyme, as do the second and fourth, creating a pattern which is then repeated twice more. In the first section Mr. Allers presents the image of a dove resting, then bursting into flight, as does his heart at the thought of love. Desiring some sign of affection, in the second section the dove lands at the feet of its lover "a-craving crumb". The persona imagines his behaviour if his lover were to reciprocate:

> *Then timidly, should you but morsel cast,*
> *'twould weigh askance and sidle to partake*
> *A peck from Aphrodite's sweet repast . . .*

This dream of love is quickly displaced in the third section by apparitions of her more attractive suitors:

> *But your lorn pigeon's crop you'd not replete,*
> *For soon, to gleam your eye and blush your bloom,*
> *Some vainglorious, strutting beau you'd meet*
> *And ne'er could fantail best a peacock's plume.*

In the final couplet, the persona is resigned to keeping his love unspoken, rather than to "coo love-lost's plaint from life's forsaken sill". Carefully and cleverly constructed, "A Sonnet to Quiescent Love" is an exceptional display of language and imagination.

Another familiar poetic form is the characteristically Romantic lyric, in which the poet engages in some form of personal meditation, often in a natural setting. The assumption is that in communing with nature, one can leave the civilized world, go to a benevolent place and thereby rediscover one's soul. "Monday", (p.373) a poem by Anderson Desir, seems to play on this tradition.

The poem opens with poignant images of a natural world alive with joy and activity. The poet is lost in the motion of morning as "wind rock[s] the wading cattle / stirring a surge of egrets" and "the sun [is] a great flower, spindling pollen". This reverie is violently interrupted, however, as the flow of morning and the flow of the poem itself are broken by the mechanical reality of urban existence:

> *this morning came, vivid as sliced oranges*
> *and the unmanned, unmaneouvred world scape*
> *broken open suddenly . . . Living.*
> *Inhaling a.m. . . . . Exhaling p.m.*
> *workers waiting at the terminus.*

Days begin and end unremarkably. Instead of drawing their strength from nature, the workers are powered by "the engines of the clock in Moffat's office" and the beautiful morning, "owned by no one", has fallen from sight. The persona must face a morning of work, of being owned by the clock, as he feels the clock's "hired hands . . . reach out and strangle [him] for profit."

The natural setting of a beach has always been a favourite place for people to escape the daily grind. Populated by countless bodies in summer and often deserted in winter, the beach is the subject of Andrea Fairweather's poem, "Coast" (p.169). Memories of warm days spent on the prom and in the sand speed through her mind as she visits the coast in the off-season. The arcades are empty, hollow and in the absence of merrymakers have become macabre:

> *Sticky, singed carpet tugs at my sole*
> *as I enter the den of inequity.*
> *Eyes flash, grimace past the dancing puppet box,*
> *limp corpses strung up, aching for the old 5p.*
> *The seedy clown stares his paedophile smile*
> *lusting for young laughter.*

The machines are forgotten, lost souls in a junkyard with only a "tale [to tell] of 1000 thumb prints." With the return of eager fingers in summer, the cycle of life will continue as it always has. A new footstep will be placed in the sand, only to be washed away:

> *Oh, if each grain could talk of what it saw,*
> *the dog's cocked leg, dropped ice-cream,*

sweethearts heaving.
Do they remember the Victorian foot, the Viking stomp,
do they recall? Do they?

These grains of sand have silently witnessed the passing of many footsteps, many lifetimes.

The recollection of one man's profound experience is the subject of a powerful poem by Andrew Ford called "V.E. Day: Observing Silence" (p.349). From the eyes of a veteran's grandson, the poem expresses the spiritual isolation both he and his grandfather feel amidst the family's celebration of the World War II victory in Europe. The family joyously gathers for lunch, while the grandfather, the old soldier and man of the hour, can only muster a half smile, which he "bequeaths" to the occasion. "Bequeath" is a term ordinarily reserved for funerals and wills, and by using it in this context, Mr. Ford creates the sense that the grandfather is somehow absent—that he is not a participant in the celebration around him:

> *He says nothing—his half smile has much to say.*
> *Stooped in warm new sun, he remembers the burn.*
> *Far off, his eyes rifle through valleys that stay*
> *Dug out in his face by Time's stealthy advance.*

The war reverberates in the poem's subtle rhyme and language: the family "rallies to the cause"; his eyes "rifle through valleys"; time "advances" on him like a foe on a battle ground. Despite the years, the war still haunts the grandfather. The marks of war have not healed upon his face, but have become "dug out" and fixed in time.

The focus moves in the second stanza as the description shifts from the grandfather to the gathering around him. He is the centrepiece but remains reticent while society's lessons, not his own, are passed on:

> *Such respectful beauties shall know how to treat*
> *Forefathers, heroes, killers of tyranny.*
> *They'll learn their freedom, know the bastard he beat*

The children will "learn their freedom"; they will learn who were the 'heroes' and who were the 'enemies'. They will learn to see and to celebrate the victory, but they will never see what their grandfather has seen, nor experience his inner demons. The grandson, however, has demons of his own. As he comes of age, he has his own, new battles to fight and issues with which to wrestle, and the tired soldier cannot show him the way:

> *. . . I'm still watching him, entreating prayer*
> *To appease my new monsters that rage within.*
> *He sees in my eyes that torment lives on*
> *But his wisdom is muted behind that grin—*
> *They stop, see our eyes locked across Time, screaming.*

Cutting through the celebration, the suffering eyes of the young and the old fighters meet in torment. "V.E. Day: Observing Silence" adds a new dimension to the tradition of 'observing silence' in memorial to those who gave their lives in military service. It is an intriguing depiction of war and what lies beneath it.

There are a number of other poems which merit careful reading: Spend "An Afternoon at the Tate" with Penny Insole (p.24). Enjoy the mystical golden end of day in "Kilmalooda" by Mayhew Connelly (p.387). Hear the whack of the cricket ball in John Eden's poem "Uppish But Safe" (p.35). Meet the "Poet" in Jean Crowther's poem (p.457). Feel the void left by "Father's Day" by Archie Wilson (p.174).

I encourage you to take the time to delve into these and the many other excellent poems contained in *Jewels of the Imagination*. I am confident you will find many interesting and entertaining works of imagination to inspire you as you read this anthology. Congratulations to all the poets included in this work on their creative achievements.

Jewels of the Imagination is the culmination of the efforts of many talented and dedicated individuals. I would like to thank the editors, assistant editors, customer service representatives, data entry, administrative staff, post-production personnel and all of those who brought their respective talents to bear on this project.

Mariah Hourihan, Editor

Featured Poetry

Hold The Candle Away

"Hold the candle away from you, gel."
My Mother would say as we climbed the stair
To the chamber where the apples lay,
Spread on the floor on a bed of straw.

She climbed the last step as I stood by
Holding the guttering candle high.
Stooping to choose from the rosy store
Filling her apron with apples galore.

The stars looked down through the small sky-light
And the Winter winds moaned round our house of a night
But round the hearth so snug and bright
We sampled the bounty of Autumn's warm light.

Now the apple room's changed
And there is no sky-light, a larger window lets in the light
But I often think of Mother and me climbing the stairs and
Hearing her tell. "Hold the candle away from you, gel."

Grace Palin

Water Of Life

Night covers day, day covers night,
As night eclipse day every minute passes away.
The babbling brook flows underneath
the bridge of thought,
The feelings in which I contain are
the ones that I have brought.
To sell my soul to the water of life,
I must forgive the ones that I dislike.
The sounds of nature echo throughout my ears,
As water is released from my eyes
to form my tears.

Angela Lewis

The Girl In Gossamer Wings

His smiley face glowed happiness
As arm in arm they skipped the sand
 And up the stairs

I turned away because I thought they'd see
 My words for them weren't true
And she held him, and he loved her
But as I looked I had to smile too
At their sunshine—syrup, summer love
 While through the door
 The specks of velvet light
Honeyed into deep and dusky eventide
And one by one the stars flecked black eternities
And glittered down
 While his cherry–lipped love
 Danced away through gossamer mists
And I watched him
As he turned
 And she led him
 To a copper–plated haven
Where I could see him no more.

Rachel Gosnall

Celestial Mirror

Awaken. Open your eyes. See.
 Black mists obscure vision.
Focus. Threads of silver entwine
 you in the stars.
Up there, somewhere, our threads converge,
 as I gaze at the same sky.
Which star is our meeting place,
 in this galaxy of rendez-vous?
Concentrate. In that star
 my reflection you see, and I yours,
though ocean and mountain separate us,
 take comfort in this celestial mirror.
Till dawn at least, are we together,
 then will the sun our looking-glass destroy
and till the Silver Orb stirs, we must part.
 So fare thee well, keeper of my soul, till Dusk.

James Thompson

Soldier Of Fortune

Soldier of fortune, soldier of fame.
Don't go to battle you've nothing to gain.
Leaders will tell you it's for a good cause,
Surely they're mistaken, please stop and pause.

They're somebody's brother, husband or son,
I beg you dear soldier please put down your gun.
For thousands lie dying, such a dreadful sight,
Please tell me dear brother, who is wrong or right.

You see bodies scattered, all over the ground.
Lying quite still with never a sound,
Please look at them closely they're just like you and I.
Who gives you the right, to say they must die.

They're somebody's brother, husband or son,
I beg you dear soldier please put down your gun.
For thousands lie dying, such a dreadful sight,
Please tell me dear brother, who is wrong or right.

Leaders continue, to do what they think is right.
They send all young soldiers into battle to fight,
When people stop hating, the anger will cease,
And maybe the world, can then live in peace.

Margaret Cook

Circle Of Care

Direct care, NVQ,
Relaxation, exercise too.
Effective communication is the key,
Encouraging clients with mobility.
Lifting safely from bed to chair,
Assisting client with personal care.
Privacy, dignity and toilet routine,
Keeping care setting impeccably clean.
Choice of menu, protective clothing, long hair.
Seating client comfortably in chair.
Appetizing food—right texture—amount,
Illnesses—allergies—taken into account.
Good observation, pressure aids and cream,
Working together as part of a team.
Two hourly turning, prolonged bed rest,
Praising your client is always best.

Christine Hannabuss

Rufus

I miss you waiting by the gate for me,
I miss the way you turn yourself round to
 cuddle me as I pick you up.
I miss the vibration of your purring against my skin,
I miss the way you roll on the sunny hot
 soil and flatten the flower beds
I miss the way you look at me and follow my every move
I miss the way you play with a leaf or a stone, always happy,
I miss your contented dribble as you lay snuggled in my arms,
I miss the touch of your silky fur and soft cuddly body,
I miss you as you expected nothing and gave everything
I just miss you, because I love you,
 and because you loved me in return.

Shirley Ann Jarvis

Reconciliation

Pick up the cords that bind Humanity and Love
 Weave a wondrous pattern
 of care and understanding
Entwine every heart, and un-pick all the hatred
 Sewn in former years

When all the patterns of Peace have been created
 Let the World rejoice in the joy that's been restored
The hungry have been fed. The guns have now been silenced
 And for a child—there's a future once more

Leaders meet with their enemies and talk
 Until there is full agreement
Everyone shake their hand in the hope of total reconciliation
 And pray for Peace throughout the World for evermore.

F. M. Wright

War

As we pray for our lives,
They plan their next move.
What will they do?
They're dropping bombs from the sky,
But they can't see the terror in our eyes.

Nobody cares and no one helps,
They just keep destroying and killing.
They say they care, that's why they are slaying!
They say that everything will be fine,
But it's just another of their lies and they can't see the pain in
    our eyes.

They're loosing the war,
They think that's all that matters.
We're loosing our lives, and our loved ones,
But still, they can't see the tears in our eyes.

Why can't they give up and sign a treaty,
Bring peace to the land of our country.
Stop taking what is rightfully ours,
Stop bringing all this pain and suffering.
I know they can, so please tell me . . . Why are they so blind?

Deborah Piercy

The New Religion

I gaze at the screen in mesmerised stupor, the TV images drift l
    like vapour.
I lose my mind within the mass, of facets of the world at large.
Every night when I've had tea, I take my seat to watch TV.
My wife, who's not as keen as me, prefers to do embroidery.

The range of programmes I now see, has made an addict out of me.
The Beechgrove Garden, with Bill Torrence, which I regard
with some abhorrence.
To her a show, she will not miss.
It isn't even on my list.

The 'soaps', like Coronation Street, become an overwhelming weight.
They make concerns within their plot, so our lives don't seem
    worth a lot.
Bay Watch leaves us in a daze, no wonder it's the latest craze.
With scanty costumes in abundance, enhancing virtual
decadence.

Television's our new religion, controlling people by the million,
Manipulated by the pathos, persuade some even to buy a Playtex.
I see the world in all its glory, the Bible couldn't tell these stories,
With all the detail shown to us, my life seems very commonplace.

Jeff Robertson

Despair To Bliss

She had been married for many years,
Enduring hardship and many tears.

Life had improved as she had got older,
But her errant husband had become somewhat colder.

Career and ambition had been his main-stay,
But when this ended he yearned to be away.

Vain and cruel and self–opinionated,
He left one day, leaving the life he hated.

The very first woman who flattered and cajoled him,
Ensnared his affection, as he indulged in his every whim.

She told him that his wife was a shrew,
And his family, who had loved him once were a drain on him too.

Divorce was quick to suit his purpose,
Leaving the faithful wife impoverished and cursed.

Very soon she began to realize how precious was her independence,
That life was good away from his unremitting domineering
presence.

Times were hard at first without financial support,
But with ingenuity, and an awful lot of thought,

She set up business on her own,
Glad at last that she was now alone.

Jean Thomas

Poor Player

Been a poor player now for so long,
Wouldn't know what to do,
Should good times come my way.
Wouldn't know that I would care,
Could so easily kiss it all goodbye.

Been told I go from one extreme to another,
What's that supposed to mean?
Didn't care when I was told.
Don't care now.

Been a dreamer all my life.
Couldn't reach out and hold those dreams,
Fear of falling weighed so heavy on my soul.

Been a poor player now for so long.
Wouldn't know what to do,
Should good times come my way.

K. Pattar

My Favourite Colour

What would we do without the colour green
Our life, I'm sure, would never seem serene
The trees and grasses, coloured light and dark
The subtle tinges shadowed in the park
Take time today to open wide your eyes
The blue greens, sea greens reaching to the skies
Just think how lovely nature has really been
To give us all the many shades of green

Gwendolene Duffell

A Day In The Life

It was a late night
Which was beyond your control,
You woke to an early morning
To face a hard day.
You're tired, you're weary,
Aching and dreary.
But as the day drags on,
You put on a brave face.
You're expected to be happy,
Not allowed to hurt.
But you feel the pain of the words spoken
See your dreams all shattered and broken.
The sun goes down, preparing for tomorrow
Which you know will bring hurt and sorrow.
Why is life so hard, is it a test?
You don't know but you're trying your best.
But take any more and that's the limit,
You can't think why, but you're in it.
That thing called life.

Rehanah Hussain

"Remember Me"

Remember me like the mist on the water,
And sailing free with the birds on the wing.
Remember me like the ships at the quay side.
Think of me when the bell-buoy rings.
Remember me when the North wind blowest,
And when you take a walk on the shore.
Remember me like the summer breezes,
Look out to sea, and you'll see me once more.

Remember me like the flowing rivers,
Think of me with every ebbing tide.
Remember me when you weigh up anchor,
Imagine me standing by your side.

Remember me like the five great oceans,
And when you see the pale moonlight.
Remember me when you're safe in the harbour,
In your thoughts and in your prayers tonight.

Remember me on a cold frosty morning,
When it snows or rains on thee.
Remember me as the sun is setting.
And remember, the sea has been good to me.

Michael Stanforth Jr.

Loved One Lost

As death's icy fingers settle around his heart
I now know the time has come to part.
And I feel so helpless,
As I haven't even cried, only shuddered, only sighed.
I can still remember out first night of love,
And I can still taste his last sweet kiss
"You're the girl I love" he said holding me close.
Now his ashes are scattered,
And the last of him is gone.
Now please don't be sad, if my tears start to fall.
And do take care up there with Our Lord,
Though you've gone it isn't the end.
I love you still and I'll see you again.
Now the painful tears spill,
God takes your hands and leads you away.
I dry my eyes, promise to remember our good times.
Walk away with my head held high,
Though my heart is breaking inside.

Fleur Nixon

Remembering The Innocent

As we sit and think about what did part
Knowing deep down they'll always be in our heart.
We can't help but think how lucky we are
Condolences sent from near and far.

We will remember them as victims of crime.
We will never forget even in time,
The coldness of the chilling screams.
I only wish this was a dream.

Innocence was to be your end
A son, a daughter, a very special friend.
Life in itself is so unfair
What can we do to show we care?

Remembering together the nation links
A minute's silence where we all think.
The price of life that you must pay
You are in our thoughts throughout the day.

No words can describe what we feel
Or what would possess a man to kill.
Never again will it be the same
The haunting memories of Dunblane.

Suzy Martin

The Rising Of The Foal

The birth of the foal is so soft and so sweet,
As the foal's eyes open they look so deep.
The mother's protection of this tiny child,
And the foal takes its first steps so tiny and mild,
The child is suckling from its very own mother,
It gives no care to any other.
The hair on the foal is its small kind of cover.
This bond that they have between one another.
And that is the poem of foal and its mother.

Dawn McCormick

Life

We wake in the morning full of hope
What will life throw at us will we cope
The trial's of life come large and small
Will we survive to climb or fall
We stride to make our mark in life
Be it an Actor or a thoughtful wife
Whatever life throws we cope some how
Some of us bad or holier than though
Do we know what tomorrow might bring
Will we feel happy wanting to sing
My wish each day is to do the best I can
Not because I'm a woman and not a man
It's still a man's world of this I'm sure
But being a woman as usual I want more
They say that behind every good man
A woman puts the seed there, and eventually a plan!

Elaine Marjorie Meyern

If I Didn't Have To Care

If I didn't have to care what others thought of me
I'd lock my kitchen door and throw away the key

I'd only wash up my cup the rest can do their own
I'd spend my days just eating and talking on the phone

I'd wear odd shoes and stuff my bra
and drive a bright pink little car

If I didn't have to care.

I'd sit in the doctor's surgery and ask strangers what's
wrong with you?
When asked for my opinion I wouldn't have a clue

If I didn't have to care what others thought of me
I'd go swimming in the summer and learn to climb a tree

I'd always dress up sexy and leave my midriff bare
I'd learn to drive a moped and dye my orange hair

But care I do and must you see
Has anyone seen my kitchen door key

Teresa Harding

Domestic Bliss

The winds of change blow in silence
and gently tease long–awaited dreams.
By the wayside you and I
pick our way carefully
over the shattered shards of promises
and sorry remains of quarrels
to the lanes of bitterness crossed and recrossed
and hopes laid to rest in routine.

Kalpana Vijayavarathan

In My Head

As I lie here in this hospital bed
Dozens of things go round in my head
I think of my family
And friends by the score
And thank God for them
To love and adore.

As I lie here in this hospital bed
Hundreds of things whirl around in my head
I think of all the things I have seen
Then think again of the places I've been.

As I still lie in this hospital bed
Millions of things whiz around in my head
I think of the loved ones
And friends gone before
Waiting for us on the far distant shore
And as I believe in a God of true love
I know we will meet in His heaven above.

Beaty Roberts

To Danny

I've seen the start of a wonderful venture
By a man who is strong and near to nature
To build a home which will forever remain
A symbol of love on his own terrain
Each tree felled, a step nearer his dream
Strip the bark sons, we'll work as a team
Spurred on by ideas, and womanly whims
Must have the softness that comes with the trims
To add to the magic when all is complete
When the moon is high, sit on your log seat
Listen to the waves lapping on the shore
Your achievement will satisfy more
When you have time to contemplate
Away from thing's that irritate
Inside, the wood will mellow with years
With joys and love, passion and tears
Boys grow to men, and someday leave home
But whatever they do, wherever they roam
That home in the forest will always be
A symbol of strength, infinite as the sea

Doris Fenion

All Alone

I wandered lonely as a cloud,
    Was what I muttered quite aloud;
I pondered as to what came next,
    What mystery lay in the text.

And then it rained and I knew well,
    The cloud had been too shy to tell;
It never was alone at all,
    And that is why the rain did fall.

Now these are mysteries you see,
    Because of ignorance in me;
But someone somewhere can explain,
    The Met men strive to make it plain.

But with some charts upon the wall,
    Giving details I can't recall;
I realize I'm still alone,
    I'll call my wife, she has her phone!

So I will call I know not where,
    The phone can find her anywhere;
It's sure to interrupt her day,
    I think I like it well that way.

Eric Wood

"Sunlight Streamed Through Casting Shadows Across"

Sunlight streamed through casting shadows across the street.
In the branches of the tree tops up above the little birds did tweet.
While further down the street, outside the front door of his home,
a little boy sat on the step all alone,
waiting for his friend to call, unaware that his friend had had a fatal fall.
The little boy looked anxiously all around at every footfall
every sound. He heard the other children's running feet,
their laughter as they played up and down the street.
People smiled as they passed by,
at the little boy on the step, they wondered why
the little lad looked so sad.
As days passed by each day he sat in vain waiting for the
friend that never came. In the house he stared out through
the window at the falling rain.
Then one day he cried, and plaintively asked his mother why,
his friend had not come by.
Gently stroking his hair as she dried the tear from his eye,
"Son", was her reply, "maybe he has gone away perhaps he
will come another day".
The days passed, one by one the little boy's days were long.
He was fretting away, the little boy grew lonelier and quieter
with every passing day.
Then one day he heard a voice from beside him on the step.
His friend had come at last, but only to say I'm dead.
"I died", he said. The little boy grew brighter with each new day,
he smiled again and then ran off through the fields of long tall
grass, into the woods
To play with his imaginary friend.

Alice Margaret Burns

My Darling Boys

An egg, a seed, the passion and the love,
A foetus, an embryo, a baby, a gift from God above,
The tiny flutters then the kicks and ever expanding waist,
The swollen tingling breasts and increasing change in taste,
What a glorious feeling, I'm about to be a mum,
Safe inside my womb where no harm can ever come,
My darling boys grew and developed,
Until when born, in my arms they were enveloped.

My happiness is such, no words can ere explain,
Such perfect baby boys, and I recall no pain,
The joy, the happiness and love is deep within my being,
There is nothing in this world can take away this feeling,
But my darling boys have paid a huge price to be born,
The pain, the worry since their birth, just goes on and on,
Unlike when they inside my womb were safe and free from harm,
I can do nothing to protect them, just be there with open arms,
No matter what their size or age, or how feeble I become,
I hope they'll know I love them, and I'll always be their Mum.

Eileen Hutchison

My Mother

I've heard people say my mother is
my best friend.
But when I was a child my mother's
life was soon to end.
I missed out on a friendship I know
I would have treasured.
Just to see your face again would
bring me so much pleasure.
I'm still wearing your wedding ring
that I do dearly treasure.
It makes me feel closer to you
Because you wore it too.
And when my time is up and I'm
standing at the white pearl gates
I'll run into your arms and hold
you close to me.
And at last we'll be together.
And this time I'll be holding on forever.

Claire Morgan

The Power Of Anger

The cloud turned black with anger,
From white to a thick black, the colour of the night sky.
And as his anger built up inside him,
A power ran through him, a power strong and wild,
He tried to speak, but instead the roar of a thousand lions
    came out
And for a second the forth cracked open and the underworld
    was revealed.
And then fell a silence.
A silence so dreadfully long and empty,
The storm was over.

Sarah Anderson

The Sea Empress

The sea empress,
She made a terrible mess
Oil afloat, all over the sea
All that damage, and debris
Birds all covered, can't fly
Sticky wings, can't reach the sky
Every living sea creature is badly harmed.
Now everywhere is filled with alarm
Trying to get the coast, back to normal.
It's a trying task, for all the people.
Black and dirty are all the sands
But with hard work
    It soon will be
    Grand.

J. Moody

Sorrow

Your children are precious; they come from the your genes,
They're part of your family, part of your dreams.
You love and you care, you teach them what's right
And hope that through life they will learn how to fight

To live life to the full and develop their talents
Continue the cycle and meet every challenge
But then one goes wrong, they fall by the way
Their life becomes twisted and muddled all day.

They're always in trouble and start taking drugs
No longer the little boy whose joy was your hugs.
But a man you don't know a Jekyll and Hyde
Some days he is nice and some he is snide.

But we as his parents, are full of despair
Our job has gone wrong and it doesn't seem fair.
There's nought to be gained by weeping and crying
And nought to be gained by feeling ashamed.

His life is his own now, there's no good denying.
What can be gained by dwelling and sighing?
All we can do, and this is not cast,
Is pray that our son will recover at last.

Malvine Tieche

Love Your Neighbour

Keeping Holy the Sabbath Day,
Your spirit, while activating, so elevating,
Guiding all steps, each a different way,
Molecules of grandeur, floating silently by
Tinting grey on blue, a Palette hidden in the sky,
Dangling leaves, hanging contentedly many to a tree,
Gentle breezes tooting Mystic Choreography,
Dancing Ballerinas Pirouetting Puppets in a Jamboree,
An array of colour, beyond an artist's dream,
Petals having the delicacy of fairy wings,
Frankincense from Bethlehem, to heaven angels bring,
Honey bees and their floral dance, hum and sing,
Awaiting patiently alone in Gethsemane,
Calling, listen, hear as I say,
In the praetorian of life,
The question, whom do you want,
Is echoing, loudly today,
Is it Barrabus, or your saviour,
Your choice shall fashion your behaviour,
Either insurrection, or love your neighbour.

Christopher Noel Price

Our Spirit

Our spirit descends to transform
We leave our spiritual fathers to mourn
While we take up residence in this human form.

We spend so much time trying to conform
That we lose the essence of the birth, born.

Do our spirits journey, to find our soul?
Are life's pathways, leading us to a goal?

Or is this life a dream in time!
Are we living, or is this a mime?

Mooneen De-Burgh

Stone Trough's And Chimney Pots

The hills no more,
The people's gone.
Our home is down to dust.
The farm yard to has disappeared the
    animals are no more,
The hay stacks and the big oak trees the
    moonlight shone so brightly through.

The old church bell still marks the time
    as one listens and remembers.
The long hot days of childhood the laughter
    in the street of parent's love and brother, sweet.

As I now walk the cracked old stones,
    and think once more of all that's gone.
To feel the love, the warmth, the peace,
    and wish that I could live but one
    short day from long ago.

Faith Williamson

The Gallop

Anticipation burns inside me,
Simmering like the sun in a fiery African dawn.
Waiting quietly, inside I'm screaming,
Impatience to move.

Joy like a razor blade devouring my soul,
Thundering throughout my being.
Triumphant spring then hurtling forward,
Bolting on.

Exhilaration dances like a trickling stream,
The wind caresses my glowing cheeks,
Smooth motion, united together,
Gliding as one.

Soaring as a leaf rushing through a secluded alley,
Grace and power merged,
Flushed and elated the pace reluctantly slows,
Breathless, in a daze.

R. E. Smith

Senses

If you didn't have any senses what would you do?
If you couldn't read or write or even smell things, too.
It wouldn't be very nice if you couldn't see,
because if you had your face painted you wouldn't
know what to be.
Wouldn't it be nasty if you couldn't hear,
just because of the reason that there's something wrong
with your ear.
What about the people with their main use as touch?
Reading books by feeling for the rough and bumpy dots.
What happens to the people that can only use
taste, what if it's the disgusting taste of horrible
mint toothpaste!
So sometimes think how grateful you should be,
because of the way God made you and me.

Charlotte Newbury

My Valentine

I Love You, I Love You, Not Likely!
I'm glad your pyjamas aren't next to my nightie!
Just you snuggle down with your true beloved,
Don't worry about me I'll get back in the cupboard!
Don't be disheartened, don't be mislead,
I'm not bad at heart, just Thick In The Head!!

The Mistress!

Julie Marshall

Let's Ponder

Let's ponder on what Ireland needs,
It really blows one's mind.
The bombs, the guns, just evil breed,
And must be left behind.

    Religion, arms one's belief,
    But for this, must we kill?
    Spread hatred, anger and deepest grief
    For Him, crucified upon a hill.

Or is there love among the crowd,
That all so silent stand,
Why don't they shout and shout aloud,
Gunman leave our land!

    See evil power base with roots of hate,
    Thrive where love should dwell.
    Exterminate! Exterminate!
    We're on a road to hell.

So let all good men stand as one,
Seize friendships open hand.
Send the arms of death so far away,
Let peace come to our land

James T. Fairley

Evacuees

As I watched through the window on that September day,
The sun was shining brightly, yet everywhere looked grey.
Children stood there, row by row
Mothers stood there, tears began to flow.
Their little ones were off to unknown places.
Their sadness etched on all their faces.
When would they see their babes once more
Taken from them because of war.

Gas masks hanging round their necks,
Names on labels for all to check.
As I watched through the window on that September day
The children ready to be on their way.
Buses arrived in Convoy,
Children boarded clutching a toy.
Some with smiles, some with tears,
Just their eyes showing their fears
When would they see their mums once more
Taken from them because of war.

I stood at the window a child of four,
Losing her friends because of war.

Betty Brown

Darkness Before The Light

The dark days of winter fall around me
Like a cloak protecting me from the elements
It masks the pain I feel
Leaving me silent in this world so dark

I am hidden from the rest of the world
No-one wants to find me until the time is right
I keep on looking but the sea of darkness
Envelops me keeping me out of sight

The darkness comes in waves and I struggle to keep afloat
Distorted features in my mind's eye
I cry out for help and I feel a soothing touch
But I cannot see a soul

I toss and turn and then all is still
A calmness falls upon me and the darkness clears
Suddenly a light is shining and I see a face
She's helping me soothing me making the pain much less

The dark has turned to light and I feel blessed
My days of emptiness and loneliness are over
I feel better and able to walk slowly at first
Then gradually further until my goal is reached

Evelyn M. Schofield

The Land Of Dreams

As eyelids close, imagination opens up.
We are invited into a different world—the world within,
as the brain begins to tell the body stories.
Bringing to us a world of vivid colour,
of new acquaintances, and old friends—who never grow up.
These are pleasant picnics of the mind, outings to be enjoyed.
Meandering mind drifting across the meadows of sweet memories.
Teaching us, warning us, rehearsing our emotions.
Exciting new experiences, like falling through space
and how to run in treacle,
Fleeting images that float by uncontrolled.
Familiar objects in unfamiliar settings, size and substance.
Childhood fears that still remain.
Shocking events, that jerk you into wakefulness.
Elusive, transitory, . . . but disturbing just the same!
Is it a silent world—your world of dreams?

Ronald Bicknell

Old Photographs

Kept at the back of the bottom drawer,
Precious preservation of what has gone before.
Memories flood through the barriers of time,
Every emotion captured and conserved
In print, laid out for all the world to see.
A knife twists deep within my soul
The unhealed hurt starts to grow once more
As the briefest glimpse reminds me . . .

Anna Hoey

The Ballad Of A Blind Man

"The world is a strange but wonderful place",
I heard the blind man say.
"The world around us cries for peace,
but man gets in the way."
Then slowly the man closed his eyes,
and quietly slept with dreams.
He couldn't see the battle,
but he could hear the children's screams.
The blind man saw what man refused to see.
The world that man thought was perfect, that made everyone high,
was nothing like it was created to be,
because man had closed his eyes.
The blind man awoke and smiled,
he said that one day on earth angels would fly.
The war would cease, Heaven would be born,
if man would only open his eyes.
And once again the blind man could see,
what man today can only dream.

Emma Nyman

Editing The Times

Driving along Westminster corridors
Parking in a solo side-street
Ministers queue with honourable gentlemen
Chained to spare hospital beds
Waiting on nurses carrying whips
Who crush careers like cigarettes
Under white stiletto shoes
Made in Canterbury—
Where bishops come out of closets
To sermonize on moral decency
Impregnating lambs in mind and body
Upon sacrificial altars
And bastard offspring question beliefs
Answering to the greatest bidder
Blood, mud and semen
Smeared over tabloid sheets

Ikechi Anyalewechi

My Mother

A mother can be defined in many ways,
Like the golden sun with its beaming rays,
But words can't describe this mother of mine
You're one of a kind and completely divine.

Nineteen fifty six on July the second,
Was the day you were born and life you beckoned,
You were a cute little girl and turned into a fine lady
Then at the age of eighteen you had your own baby.

You gave me everything when you didn't have much,
Your loving affection had a golden touch.
I thank you mam for always being there,
And letting me know just how much you care.

But now is the time to start thinking of you.
They say like begins at forty and yours should too.
So have a great birthday with many more to come,
I love you mam, mother, and mum

Joanne Hamilton

A Life Of Bliss

The day has come, I'm feeling great.
No more worries of getting up late.
The alarm clock stays silent—I hated the thing.
No more rushed breakfasts and a quick cup of tea
Life from now on will be more leisurely.
I can do as I want, come and go as I please,
No rushing around, take life with more ease.
I've dreamt of this day for many a year,
My first day of retirement—it's finally here!

Joan Orth

Ode To Beverly . . . New Beginnings

You are one of many wonders
although no longer to be seen
a spirit of such great beauty
this to me, you will always mean

When you finally passed through
to a place no one an earth could know
I held my anger and sadness tightly
but I knew that you had to go.

You taught me that a spirit has to be free
there is nothing forever which I can hold
but I can treasure and enjoy life so short
even when my heart feels the cold.

A light shines in my heart now
you guide me along life's many highways
and slam on the brakes when I'm out of control
watching me as I live these uncertain days.

This one is for you Aunty Bev
with many people my feelings now are shared
this feels so good inside
because to share, this I am no longer scared

Marie Keddy

My Dream Man

I can't find Him, I wonder why,
This Hunky, kind hearted special guy.
He's in my dreams when I sleep at night,
So warm and loving, He makes it right.
When I shut my eyes he's always there,
So good looking with brushed back hair.
Will he hold my hand, I'll find out and see
He's standing there and he's waiting for me
I can make him love me, just when I want him to.
What I ask him I'm sure he will do.
I'd stroke his hair, his face I would touch,
He's so in love with me and I love him so much,
I love escaping with him just when I can
In paradise land maybe when I plan.
He's always there when I want him to be
No one can see him, but only me.
He doesn't exist, there's no one to care,
But in my dreams he will always be there!

Paula Wyatt

I Know

I don't need to call you,
I know what you're going to say,
I've thought of you all week,
And I can't make the thoughts go away,
I'm ready for you to tell me,
It will come as no surprise,
You've done it before after all,
Why was I so blind?
I heard about you and her,
Do you know that I know?
And when you tell me that it's over,
I won't put on a show.
I can feel it coming,
The heartache and the blue,
And even though you haven't done it yet,
I'm already missing you.

Zoë Ann Robinson

Who Knows Who Cares

No one knows the pain another person feels.
No one knows their suffering, or how to make them heal.
No one knows how much a person can endure.
No one knows the way to find a cure.
No one knows the confusion of thoughts inside.
No one knows how hard that they have tried.
No one knows the courage it takes to smile.
No one knows that life is such a trial.
No one knows the trauma of the family by their side.
No one knows the strength it takes to face the world, not hide.

Ruth Westhoff

Artificial God

Paint me a picture of your artificial God,
The one that you pray to each day.
Tell me the lies or the truth and the words
That the gospels and testaments say.
I cannot decide if it's fiction or fact
Tell me more of the stories you knew,
You can't just believe all the lies you've been fed
But it's entirely up to you . . .

Paint me a moon and some starts and a sky,
The ones that your saviour made,
Do you still wonder after all of the lies
If he gave you a tree to find shade?
Or was he just trying to improve all his toys,
Create a life better than you,
The tiger, the lion, the zebra, the ape,
The ones you keep locked in a zoo . . .
So paint me a picture of your artificial God,
Your God who lives up in the sky,
Then change it the day that you finally meet him
Up in heaven the day that you die . . .

Rhodri Thomas

One Day

There's something in your eyes which says you care
About the life I'll lead when you're not there
But do not worry I shall still be true
For all I have and ever want is you
My love is far more deep than any sea
And higher than the highest hills can be
One day I will return and you will know
The words I speak are true—"I love you so"
You are the sun, the moon, the stars to me
No matter where I go or what I see
When you're not there my world will be so blue
The pleasures that I have will be but few
So, when at last I come and find you there
Our love will be a thing most beautiful, most rare

Madeleine Jephcott

Friend Or Foe?

Someone who cares when one is sad,
Someone who cares when times are bad.
Someone who gives a helping hand,
Someone who try's to understand.
Someone who shares many happy years,
Someone who shares many falling tears.
Someone who to tell a secret so dear,
Someone who tells all whilst having a beer.
Someone who gives and not just takes,
Someone who leers at your mistakes.
Someone who congratulates when one's goal is within stride,
Someone who is really seething with jealously inside.
Someone who you could definitely trust with your man,
Someone who flirts with him every moment she can,
Someone who calls round for a girls night out,
Someone who's man has gone out with his friends no doubt.
Someone who's a friend . . .
Oh is that so?
Are you sure she's a friend or is she a foe?

Lindsay Alexandra McAlice

A Grain Of Life

I sit on the Sea Shore in a world of my own,
The sand and the water whirl round in my toes,
My mind, I feel, is that grain of sand,
I feel I can relate to the life it has had.
Each grain of sand tells a different story,
Loneliness, insecurity and all of its glory.
The rippling of the water crushes its way through,
Separating each grain like my life too.
The golden grain of sand, memories of before,
But a dark grain of sand now lies on the shore.
I feel it rushing towards me with a feeling of freshness,
My mind just like that grain, drifts back to happiness.
But then all of a sudden the water steals away,
That little grain which I longed would stay.

Gillian O'Keeffe

Untitled

You're the loveliest girl I've ever seen
Your eyes sparkle like a highland spring
Your lovely smile will always bring
That loving is a wonderful thing

Holding you is such delight
You send my heart into flight
Loving you is just so right
I'll be forever yours day or night.

One day I hope you'll be my bride
No more will I wander far and wide
I will always stay by your side
My love for you I could not hide.

I dream about you night and day
My thoughts of you will never stray
I'll keep on loving you e'er what may
And to be together, I'll always pray.

R. M. Hynds

Easter Is A Time In Spring

When the birds fly on the wing
Crocus, snowdrops, daffodils grow.
Farmers in the field doth sow.
Seeds of grain, wheat and corn.
Years ago a child was born.
Who at this time, grown into a man
Died on a cross, which was not his plan.
Three days later he did wake.
His Father's bidding for all our sakes.
Yes Easter is a time in spring
When the birds fly on the wing
A special time for remembering.

Norma Martin

An Old Friend

Between the church and railway, a long lost friend stands tall.
His arms reach to the heavens through the mists,
He's seen it all this once great tree—tots with bouncing ball,
When young we climbed about him with clenched fists.

His trunk's been used for shady rests, and shelter from the rain,
His friendly leaves dripped water down my neck,
His comforting bark I've cuddled when racked by heartbreak pain,
The tears we shared ran down into the beck.

But my giant old friend has now passed away,
And frozen as though carved out of stone,
His limbs hang scarred with death and decay,
As I stand here and look on alone,

Branches lie scattered like my broken dreams,
The mists now act as a shroud,
The dead wood groans with the suns warming beams,
Where once green leaves rustled so proud,

But next to the corpse young saplings grow,
A son or a daughter portend,
To bring comfort and joy in a few years or so,
As he did to me, my old friend.

Steve Blackman

Beauty

A quiet stroll along these rolling, spacious downs.
Each hillock revealing hues of greens, yellows and browns.
Confusions of colour in nature's floral tapestry.
Colonnades of evergreen pines, stand like the military.
Willow trees with branches forever cascading,
Hordes of dandelions in pretentious parading.
A multitude of butterflies flitting and fluttering by,
Majestic oaks reaching, seemingly touching the sky.
The flora and fauna, some timid, some bold.
This land, our heritage, a beauty to behold!

David Dorey

Tears Fall

Different religions and opinions make the warzone land
Violence can't be resolved by the shake of a hand
Up in the air or down on the ground
There's violence everywhere and it's always around
People killed, thousands each week
Peace locked away and too hard to seek
There's no prize to who will win
Blind countries can't see it's a sin
Hitting the headlines, peace talks failed
Innocent bodies, dead and unveiled
Countries destroyed by bullet and bomb
Hatred rules! Where will love come from?
People's possessions buried in the rubble and dirt
Tears fall as artilleries hurt
Effecting everyone all over the Earth
Why do they do it? What's it worth?
When will it stop? Where will it end?
It's come too far to come to a mend
Maybe one day, war will be never
Friendship rises, peace lasts forever.

Sarah Bache

The Holy Child

Born to us so meek and mild.
He was the Virgin Mary's child.
And in a manager there he lay.
With his blanket made of hay.

And in the sky that very night.
There was a great mysterious sight.
Which could be seen from here and far.
It was a beaming heavenly star.

Then angels came down from above.
To praise the child with showers of love,
The angels went to tell the world the joy.
That Jesus christ had been born, a lovely little boy.

They told the shepherds on the hills whom were caring for
their sheep.
They were sitting around the fire and had just been asleep.
The angles told them with a dance and a song.
That a boy had been born who was going to be a great king.

Then three strangers from afar.
Started to study that very star.
They followed the light from north, east and west.
Hoping that what they would find was better than best.

Lisa Anne Moy

Belief!

Life is what you make it, people often say,
But sometimes things occur, that cloud a sunny day,
Plans we make get broken, thoughts on Utopia subside,
Everyone has their problems, there's nowhere you can hide.

We question our existence, searching for a clue,
Answers don't come easy, when you're down and feeling blue,
Learning from mistakes, the process cause pain,
The will to start afresh, isn't always easy to regain.

Advice is not accepted, we struggle through alone,
Ignoring words of wisdom, "You'll Reap All That You've Sown",
Laying the fault on others, is easier to accept,
Refuting personal blame, no matter how inept.

"A Light At The End of A Tunnel", a phrase inspiring hope,
When all else fails to assist you, this will help you cope,
Time is a great healer, it's been said and it is true,
Be positive and strong my friend, this poem's just for you!

Carol Carey

Destiny

He was drawn to her side like a magnet,
the orchestra played destiny waltz oblivious to people they
danced until dawn, his angel in blue met her prince.
Sun shone fit to burst throughout summer,
as especially laid on from above, they laughed and they sang,
not a cloud in the sky. Fiery sunsets as never before.

Sunday walks up the Wrekin', glow worms peeping through grass.
Escaping from friends to their woods.
Stars sparkled above—one, brightest of all.
"That one's ours", he said "Star of the North".

Hand touching hand—like crossing of cables,
First kiss—Chemistry gone mad,
"Our love", he said "is too perfect to spoil"
Jealous gods. Did they hear—were they glad?

So proud of his wings off to Aden—the war.
Then a love–drenched letter he wrote,
"Your face ever lovely. Is always before me,
Yet more so—much closer tonight",

Cruel moon why so bright on that night of all nights why mar
perfection so rare?
Dreams of the future together—forever.
Turning to fear and despair.
Sweet precious memories remain crystal clear, happy laughter
with loving and living.
Their hopes—swept away—vanished with words,
one of our aircraft is missing.

Gwendoline Tallon Dunkley

The Night

Oh night majestic serene and calm
Your awesome stillness captivates the universe
You are the wonder of this earth plane
Your pact with the silver moon and shining stars is ideal

The moon cast her silvery rays upon you
While the stars shine out of the sky upon you
The hooting of the wise old owl penetrates your stillness
Oh mighty force of the universe
Keep me safe while I slumber in thy embrace

I. B. Hall

In Loving Memory

Why? Is the question we ask,
Why? Did it have to be there,
Why? Children all under seven,
Surely this question is fair.

How could anyone do this,
Those innocent lives he took,
There was no meaning, there was no cause,
But a whole community he shook,

The God above has all of them,
Wrapped tightly in His arms,
There is no more pain and no more tears,
They're tucked safely away from harm.

But what of the ones who are left behind,
For the pain they're still going through,
They will always remember for the rest of their lives,
That this horror was not dreamt it is true.

I did not know the "little Angels",
But my tears fall all the same,
My heart goes out and I pray for you all,
The tiny victims of Dunblane.

Lisa Marie McKell

Old Man

The old man was smiling but there was mist in his eyes
As he discovered a memory that he had tried to disguise
He looked down at this feet when he realized I knew
That he had been to his past and I had been with him too.

He walked to the window to let in some light
Then he flung open the curtains but the sun was too bright.
I understand every movement, what he was trying to say,
He was using the light to wash the memories away.

I tried forcing a smile but it just would not come
While the old man just stood there facing the sun
I moved my lips so to speak but the words come and went
The old man was crying because his pride had been spent

Leaving the old folks home I looked up to the room
Where the sun hit the window never touching the gloom
Then I felt guilty because I knew the truth
He had been locked away from his pride and his youth.

Richard Holmes

World's Apart

The distant past, a world away, I loved a spirit free.
In sparkling eyes I also saw, a love as deep for me.

It was too soon for me I think, haunted by the past.
As time went by, sad to see, a love that couldn't last.

It was the same for them you see, cruel memories from before.
To take a chance on fickle fate, unlock her guarded door.

I had no choice I had to stand, my battles still un-won.
In simple terms, I could have quit, but love I have un-done.

I tried my best to stem the flow, from trickle to a flood,
'til through my fingers, I let slip, the last of love's lifeblood.

The years now past, still pained inside, a love so bittersweet.
It grieves me now as it did then, let fate my love defeat.

M. J. MacDonald

Love And Life

Love, must be the hardest thing in life, to stand the test of time
A feeling indefinable, indescribable, oh so very fine
It happens in all walks of life, to all ages in different degrees
from mother love to puppy love then people love,
of the deepest kinds.

This unique experience, in its varying ways can overcome adversity
by mother natures way thus, love might be the hardest thing in life
to try to understand. These two things of love, and life go,
really hand in hand.
Mysterious and profound in each and every wondrous way.
They help to make the world go around,
as life begins each brand new day.
Love and life

Jean Richards

In Praise Of Younger Things

Now God be praised that He made all young things!
For moistly-muzzled calves; for leggy colts;
For puppies, kittens, birds with untried wings;
For day-old chicks; for downy turkey poults;
For little boys with tousled hair, whose shoes
Are scuffed and creased from some rough playground game;
For little girls in dresses of all hues
That put the very garden flowers to shame!
For lambs a-skipping round their bleating dams;
For piglets rending daylight with their squeals;
For proud young mothers pushing gleaming prams,
Strutting the streets on four or five-inch heels!
For young men, who, to prove that they are strong,
Performs the feats I did, when I was young!
For all such young things I am very glad.
They call to mind the good times I have had

R. H. Jordan

Lovely Melody

Black fingers quickly dancing on white piano keys.
Her music is made in heaven, her tunes escape from dreams.
Her hair like black velvet, her eyes dark blue sea,
She is beautiful and daydreaming, a real masterpiece!

Dark crimson roses adorning her hair,
Her eyes searching for him, so love is in the air.
Their sights are met full of love and peace and joy.
She is the night, he is the light and
each other's company how they enjoy!

The sol key opened his heart.
Love really is as simple as that.
Her skin is so dark his own so pale
but when souls are speaking for colours who cares?

Love and music walk together
with melodies out tunes and dreams.
It's the basic rule of life
hearts beat strongly under the skins.

Stella Kalogridis-Charalambous

The Hatching

As I sit upon my clutch of eggs and dream
each day away.
Till when the sound of piping's heard and I know
you're on your way.
The first sound I hear is very faint from deep
inside your egg, until a little hole appears
and your beak breaks through this vent.
The chirping's getting louder and then with all your might
you push against your protective shell, it gives,
and you break forth into the night
Exhausted! You lie there in the darkness,
your downy feathers wet, and then you struggle
under me and chirp you're quite content,
When morning comes your down is now all dry,
you venture into daylight, with me the proud hen by your side.

Margaret Grimes

Lost Love

Thinking about times gone by and how we use to be,
People say that it's a waste of time,
But it's not that way to me.
Our love is lost forever.
I know now what I've not wanted to before,
That you're gone now, that you're no more.
Our love is lost forever.
Trying to piece together a picture in my mind,
of you and me as we were, and how we could've been.
I'm missing you, missing you so much.
It's hard for me to live without your touch.
Thinking about times gone by and how we use to be,
People say it's a waste of time,
But it's not that way to me.

Abalene Odell

Goodbye Old Yew

The yew obliterates the skyline, he dances in the wind,
For the very last time, does he wait in trembling?
Dreading the chainsaw to arrive
I lie here and wonder is it right.
Can't quite decide on this last night.
Such a noble tree, with the power to kill.
I feel his darkness
From my windowsill.
It's taken hundreds of years to fill the sky.
He's sheltered the birds which land on high.
He drops thousands of berries, a bright crimson red.
I watch them falling, from my bed.
The tree surgeon is here, there's no turning back,
With rope and saw, gloves and hat
Now oozes out the poisonous sap
No more he stands to fill the gap.

Norma Planté

Dreaming Pastoral

Simple complexities,
The essence of a dream, and the flow of uncertain realities.
A flaming azure . . .
A shimmering silver light caresses a plush green pasture,
While melodies thicken into a hum of silence.
Movements, as if to music, culminate into a portrait of a trance,
    a still dance.
Darkness and light meet at the centre of the universe, in fricative
    conversation darkness and light harmonize,
All else, the vortex, drains colour from harmony, fantastic colours
    are dragged into existence calmly.
A unity of differences play wherever and however they will.
Some dance in the whirling winds of the tornado, others are the
    tornado.
Some visit the Sun or the Moon, leave by light and settle on a
    shifting dune.
These essences of a pure oneness are the universe, they are the
    differences,
They are the essence of a dream.
For only in our minds can we repose to an all inclusive
Pastoral scene

Michael Samuel

The Fisherman

Hear the ripple of the water
The whisper of the wind
The song of the bird
The beauty that captures all in awe
Then glance your head upward
To see the lonely figure of the fisherman
Standing still; engulfed by water and sky
Feeling proud and sure, like a child with a new toy
His look is pleasing
He casts his rod out again, waiting, watching, in silence
His thoughts his own
With no cares in the world
Sky blue turns to dusk
He wanders home, relaxed and ever hopeful!

C. Wild

The Guide Dog Puppy

I know you think I'm rather small
And that I'm not much use at all,
But I'll surprise you when I grow
I'll make a Guide Dog—that I know.

While I'm small I may be trouble
Biting things and digging in rubble
But when I'm grown I will calm down
I'll be the best Guide Dog in town.

While I'm small I may look cute
And I could grow up to be a brute
But in the sun or when it's raining
I'll look forward to Guide Dog training.

Other dogs may bark and growl
They may even make you scowl
But after training you will see
The perfect Guide dog is what I'll be.

Colin Bowden

"On Being Threatened By A Crow From A Dead Tree"

Passerine, who on carrion doth gormandize
What plumassier liveried thee
In thy sinister garb?

From your vertiginous citadel
Your dissonant cries resound
Intimidating Man.

I realize my mortality
Tellurian, that I am.
See, I have no fuliginous plumage.

No tapered fabric of the night
With which to flee your ominous onslaught,
Nor conquer your terroristic attitude.

Cease your raucous, cacophonous aria.
Let me, a mere mortal,
Pass unassailed.

Olive Cartwright

A Tortured Soul

Suffocated life form trapped in unwilful sin.
Down, black, dead, hollow like a rotted grave.
The emptiness goes on forever, will it never end?

Caught, trapped, nailed in the living past.
An eternity beckons, I reach out to touch it before it disappears.

Smash my still living head against a wall,
Hear it crack then spin.
It only thaws like ice,
I'm too strong.

Emotion, a source, an energy, alive,
A beat of a silent soul.
One that turned to stone.
One that's dead forever.

A glimmer of life that's now lost in darkness,
A gaping vortex of crucified souls,
Raw emotion, tortured blind.
Now dead, gone, least said.

Victoria Lawson

Christmas Cat

Fairy light eyes dancing aglow,
watching the tinsel waft to and fro:
Baubles reflect on a shimmering sea
of kittenish eyes full of playful glee.
Caught between Devil and Angel today
should she leave, or get on and play?
Mother comes in, and oh! What a mess,
little cat really puts patience to test!
Christmas decs were there for the taking,
and a playful cat saw fun in the making!

Alison M. Grimshaw

Tourists

Ever bent on catching the scene,
As though seeking to possess it forever,
They click their cameras,
Consuming roll upon roll of film
And forget to use their eyes.
The souvenir shopkeeper's wax fat
On those who must take home presents
For countless friends and relatives
And who will fill their homes
With mementos of the foreign parts
They think they have explored.
The coaches take the roads
Devouring the kilometres,
Lulling the hot and drowsy passengers to sleep,
So that they miss the very sights
They have come to see.

Margaret Dix

You And I

I could not make you see how, in my desolation,
My downcast heart was mourning in pain.
And you could never know that, in my mute isolation,
My fortitude I learned how to contain.

I could not tell you feelings of bitterness and shame,
Invisible to all who looked on me.
And you could never understand my incredulity.
My disbelief and blind despondency.

I could not be immune to life irrevocably shifting,
Imbalance and distress replacing rest.
And you could never feel my mind powerless and drifting
When comfort, strength, endurance were hard–pressed.

I could not show, I kept concealed, my rising fears and qualms
Which brought a new abandonment each hour.
And you could never rid me of those all imposing harms.
Thus, I am mindful now—I have no power.

Carole V. Brangham

The Moon

The moon is like a glittering thread,
That shines on me as I climb into bed,
A matchless wonderful silvery light,
Releasing moon beams, the queen of the night.

Her moonlight shines on my window pane,
And I see her there, silver but not plain,
Like a glowing lantern hooked in the sky,
Shaped as a sphere or one white eye.

She has no water no air no life,
But craters and mountains that climb quite high,
Also seas and valleys that form a face,
A flower in the heavens but a lonely place.

Sarah Morrison

Dreams

As moonlight weaves her magic spell,
Stardust dancing on her beams,
We search the annals of our minds for the Keeper of our
Dreams.
Drifting softly over thoughts in gentle waves of sleep,
Reality has no place here, in the images we keep.
Sinking slowing into clouds of gentle loving care,
A touch so soft, like a whispered wind carried on the air.
These feelings, real inside our mind, flutter like butterfly wings
Inside the loneliness we feel when a harsh reality brings us back
From this world of make believe,
Into sunlight, intense and so bright
We try to hold on to the dreams that we have,
Until we return to the night
Where we know we can leave all the sorrows we feel
we can smile as hard as it seems
Because we've returned to those magical spells held safe by
  the Keeper of Dreams.

Sue Moore

My Poem To You

And who would know that love is now,
When earth and wind do shake a steady bough,
And who would make for me my love in you,
As bright clear mornings make such sparkling dew.

And when my love is rested and at peace,
Like silken waters and the gentleness of fleece,
And when my love for you is life,
Would then my wish for you to be my wife.

And through life and love together we would go,
As pure and clean as all the driven snow,
And at the end of such a perfect love,
What more of life would there be need to prove.

G. J. Pearce

Oh Pretty Snowflake

Oh pretty snowflake from the sky,
you fall so softly from on high,
A cold white blanket on the ground,
Sometimes a little, sometimes a mound,
Squeals of delight as children play,
As snowmen are happily made each day,
Mum do you have a carrot, a piece of coal?
No more can you see the garden mole,
My wellies crunch through snow so deep,
Tree branches hang low as if to weep,
It's hard to believe next year they'll be green,
And flowers and grass will also be seen,
But Christmas has yet to come and go,
A festive season full of glow,
I love to see the land so bright,
My pretty snowflake oh so white,
I'll miss you when you melt away,
As everything looks so dark and grey,
But I know you'll come again quite soon,
A soft white blanket beneath the moon.

Andrea Evans

The Dancer

Three men running. Something's wrong.
Running. Steps. Alarm, alarm.
Someone shouts, "what's wrong, what's wrong,"
Men who are running shout alarm.
Men running, streets are dark,
Through the alleys by the docks.
Gun shots. Panic. One man drops,
Two men run, one heartbeat stops.
Dustbins tumble, breaking glass,
Men are trapped in the dark.
Two men trapped amongst the dirt bins
Filth and trash absolve their sins.
Ask no pity, expect no answer,
A gun, a smile. It's the Dancer!

Coral Rose Wyles

Wishes At A Wedding

For both of you we wish the best,
As you start upon your lifelong quest,
For love and laughter and joy together,
Being there for each other whatever the weather.
Both love the sea and therefore know,
the power of the storm when the
cold winds blow. But calm and
tranquil that same sea on a
sunny day on a week-end spree.
Life and love are like the ocean;
we are tossed and turned with our
emotion. But swim side by side in
the ebb and flow and sweet
contentment you will know
there is time for work
make time for leisure
then your voyage and marriage
will bring great pleasure.

Gloria Hollister

A Prayer On The Eve Of The Guillotine

Oh Lord, I do beseech Thee be thou fast
To rid me of this all—consuming dread.
For this tomorrow is to be my last.
When Madame Guillotine must claim my head.

Help me to hold myself erect and proud,
Ignoring cut—throat gesture, savage jeer
Deafen me Lord, to rantings of the crowd.
Though I be spared the final frenzied cheer.

Unflinching let me show no outward fear
Though inwardly I quiver like a leaf
Be with me, prove to me that thou art near.
Dispatch me with all haste Lord, make it brief.

For better were it, had I been a child
Unshod and ragged to a peasant born,
Than having been by dint of wealth beguiled
To holding those less fortunate to scorn.

Forgive them Lord—they know not what they do!
And oh that I'd shown pity—felt some sorrow.
But thou forgave as I do now forgive
Alas! Alas! T'would be too late tomorrow!

Celia White

Never Say Goodbye

The feeling that you're on the edge of a cliff.
You could fall so far or remain the same,
The edginess as he paces rapidly into danger.
Never say goodbye.

Hoping the dread you dream will never occur.
Minutes seem like hours, hours like days,
Your lingering phobia pumps in your mind . . .
Never say goodbye.

Kristina Mansi

Animal Transportation

Like deformed foetuses in laboratory jars,
the crammed cargo in wretched, moving display,
continues: legs and necks contorted, torsos
twisted, a tagged ear visible through a slat
at lower level. Bereft of dignity: foreleg side
by side with muzzle, blocked mucus nostrils
foraging for air; glimpse of unnameable part and one
trapped upside down and one without an eye
as if in dream filled, green field grazing.

Like branded Belsen victims, their numbers seared
red stained: marked for running in our bloody
cruel campaign; thirsty, crushed, standing
in their own filth, tired, thoroughly demeaned.
It is the stench of my belonging to the perpetrators
of such abominable suffering which sickens, not theirs.

Jill Adams

Memories

The days and years are rolling by
My oh my time seems to fly.
Days of childhood seemed never to end
I wonder if age is really a friend

Remember the feeling of joy everyday
Time blocks out things that were not okay
Oh to return to those wonderful years
Cannot even remember a few little tears

A mother and father always there
Such happy times we used to share
Now they are gone from my life for a time.
When together again the sun will shine.

It's nice to remember bygone days
Couldn't be done if I hadn't the age
Time to reflect with pleasure once more
How lovely I would feel if I was only four.

Janet Bladon

The Mysterious Night Walker

There is someone in the haunted house hiding, hiding,
There is someone looking, looking,
There is someone in there looking for someone to scare.
There is someone there moaning, moaning,
For there is someone as white as a sheet
Floating about the haunted house.

The door of the haunted house is open, open,
There inside the house is silence, silence,
Suddenly ghostly figures appear in front of me.
Then there is a sound of screaming, screaming,
Someone there is following me wherever
I go about the house.

There is someone coming closer, closer,
Someone is groaning, groaning.
There I suddenly see the thing in front of me with a loaded gun.
I feel more scared, scared,
Then the gun is fired at me.
Since I am gone there is no more of this story.

Roxi Khan

Hipp-Nosis?

Whilst wandering close to Barras Gate a while ago—don't
know the date—
I spied a gorgeous blonde female. Forlorn she seemed, and
rather pale!
As she approached so gingerly, she stepped straight–backed.
It seemed to me
A "model of department", she!

I realised, much to my dismay she wore a collar, stiff and grey;
Her neck erect. Stiffly came near. Was it Louise? Yes! "Oh,
my dear!"
I cried, "Alas, Louise, alas! Please tell me how it comes to pass
That I should see you in this state!" Louise grimaced, leaned
on a gate;
Related such a sorry tale I scarcely could forbear to wail!

At home, she said, the previous week she'd gone upstairs, her
book to seek
Up in her room. And, whilst she searched, unknown to her, a
hippo perched,
Pop-gun in "paw", below her, there, playing upon the bottom stair
At big–game hunters. Quite at home it waited for Eliz. to come
Back in the car. (She'd gone to town with Mum to buy a
dressing-gown).

Louise, descending, couldn't stop, o'er gun and hippo had to hop
And crash . . . This was the painful blow!
Was it, she sadly wished to know
What folk mean when they "jump the gun"?
At any rate, her tale was done,
So, giving a courageous grin, Louise left me, and went back "in".

Hugh Irving

Peace Wanted

There was a man as I heard tell
He was driven mad by an incessant bell.
It rang by day,
It rang all night
It was even ringing when he was unwell.

Important contact must be made.
With buttons and switches he played.
Crackles and squeaks,
Whistles and whirls
A list of names was displayed.

The sound it makes hurts his ear,
The man said it feels just like a spear.
So much to discover
So much delight
Bringing his friends so very near

This mad continuous annoying tone,
By Jove he no longer feels alone.
The persistent ringing
Peace wanted, quiet disturbed
He's lots of time for his mobile phone.

C. A. Hincliff

Our Dog Bob

I laughed and played with
Bob today he's full of fun
In every way.
He rolls and rolls and wags his tail
And when he bites it he
Doesn't half sqwail.
Full of mischief from head to toe
And every day he seems to grow.

Now he's started to climb the stairs
And when he's told off
Just sits and glares.
When he has played up
And just ripped up paper
He's told of good and
Proper for doing that caper.

But for a puppy life has just begun
And for us it means lots of fun.
Since he's been around
It's been a hustle and bustle
But who'd be without this little Jack Russell
Catharine Sherwood

"The Sea"

Oh!, mighty power of strength,
  Nothing is so strong,
I would go to any length,
  To be near to you so long.
Your powers draw me to you,
  They entrance and bewitch me,
There is nothing else, or no one who,
  Is as mighty as the sea.
Thundering, endless torrents of foam,
  Raging, surging, struggling to be free,
On your beaches I will roam,
  I hear you calling, calling to me.
Then the calm, clear cool waves come,
  Falling and tumbling as they rush to the land,
Shining and glistening under the sun,
  I reach towards you with my tiny hand.
    Janet Davies

Ghosts

Flying high
Flying low
Twisting, turning
Away they go.
As I study the swifts in flight,
Reminds me of another sight
I used to watch many years ago
When spitfires were weaving to and fro.
Young pilots and crew fighting the foe,
Oh! It was so long ago.
Now, watching the swifts flying so fast,
Like little black ghosts back from the past.
    J. Lyne

Flight

Flying high in the sky
A shadow cast as it goes by
Sure and swift, keen of eye
It sees all from on high
Not a rustle or a whisper
Comes from bushes in a cluster
Soaring high in the sky
With spreading wings and joyful cry
Her heart is proud, she's homeward bound
Food for her babies she has found
So, open your eyes and look on high
Perhaps you will see one pass by
The sky is full of things to see
So take the time, and look on high
Then you will see up in the sky
That wonderful sight as one goes by.
    Margaret Lily Dalling

My Aunt Lizzy

My Aunt Lizzy
She was busy
With her needle and thread
My Aunt Lizzy always deserved a pat on the head.

My Aunt Lizzy
She was dizzy
Spinning round and round I love my Aunt Lizzy
But she was always busy

My Aunt Lizzy
Her hair was frizzy
She didn't stop to fix it
Because the needle she was trying to thread it.

My Aunt Lizzy as a child
Always smiled
When people patted her head
While doing her needle and thread.

So that's the story of my Aunt Lizzy
Who was always busy
She died a few weeks ago
And she hadn't even taught of me how to sew.
    Sarah Jane Isabella Thompson

The Reason

The reason I must, the reason I believe,
The reason I'm joyful and no longer grieve,
The reason I'm planning and no longer review,
There's no more distrust, and the reason is you.

The reason I smile, the reason I glow,
The reason I'm high and no longer low
The reason I'm happy and no longer blue,
My life's worthwhile, and the reason is you.

The reason I cherish, the reason I yearn,
The reason to go forward and not to return,
The reason I'm contented and no longer pursue,
There's no more anguish, and the reason is you.

The reason I hope, the reason I need,
The reason I follow and no longer lead,
The reason I'm certain there's nothing to rue,
I know I can cope, and the reason is you.

The reason I care, the reason I drool,
The reason I'm eager and no longer cool,
The reason I express and no longer subdue,
There's no more despair, and the reason is you.
    Shirlee A. Yeates

Life

O massive spinning globe in space turning—
Entwining all our many thoughts and achievements.
Opening like a flower, by our seeking of knowledge.
Enriching the beauty of this globe.
But sadly, we also have our weaknesses, war, murder, raping
  of children.
An endless stream of destruction,
Which mankind, each in his denomination strives to eliminate.
This is life, a torture of time seeking perfection.
Like the stormy sea, the high waves of joy, the quick descent.
Overlapping each other, rippling on the sandy shore—
To return towards the horizon mingling with the sky into infinity.
And so is our life, as we come to our end,
Having caressed this earth, we mingle into the eternal blue of
  our ladies mantle in Christ.
Christ! Our only hope, as he on earth did pave a way of life
  for us.
He is our past, present, and future, and by recreating
  His birth each year.
We become a child again, immersed in mystery and joy,
Rekindling in our hearts—
Love—
The only light on this impressive globe—
That burns for ever, into eternal life.
    Laura Alzapiedi

Threatening Silence

Dark, sinister mountains covered with ominous black cloud
With a chink of blue showing through the shroud,
A ray of sunshine filtering through on a meadow yonder,
Time seemed to stand still and so I stood and had a little ponder.
Then dark grey and black clouds passed over the mountain range
No sound of wildlife or other human being
Just an atmosphere so eerie and strange,
Then a tumultuous crack and a brilliant flash,
And whilst for cover I made a dash
The thunder roared, the winds raged
And lightning streaked the blackened sky,
Thus the unusual but threatening peace had ended
Whilst the rain poured down and the winds howled on,
Until at last the dark, satanic clouds had gone.

Lesley Stevenson

Why!

Tonight once more I cried, how I wish my life to end!
Lost the main love of my life, my heart it just won't mend.
Down into the depth of my despair I start a lonely climb,
All the dreams, hopes and aspirations are gone for all time.

Divorced we may be now that's the choice you do make!
Me, I just feel it's a terrible mistake.
Nothing and no one could alter your course
Now all that is left is unending remorse!

Tears they stream downward, the same way as my soul
Alone for the future, no longer a whole!
Life has little meaning since we are apart
My body's a vacuum, it's broken my heart!

So many questions unanswered I can't contemplate
The reason just why, you walked out the gate.
I may never get the answer doubt anyone knows
What has gone wrong, when their love up and goes!

Perhaps after some time, friends say hearts they do heal
But can they really know the way that I feel
No, I don't think so, but that's not their fault
They are not the reason, my life came to a halt!

John S. Black

Joy Of Spring

Blossom is bursting forth, on every tree,
Almond and forsythia a beautiful sight to see,
Magnolia trees so full of blooms!
With flowers spread out like peacock plumes
The weeping willow a lovely shade of green,
Drooping; as if not wanting to be seen:
Daffodils, primroses; along the roadside there,
A blaze of colour, that makes you want to stare,
Bluebells in the woods are coming to life,
A picture indeed, in this world of strife,
But the birds are singing, the sun shines through
It's spring at last! So we can all sing too,
So lift up your voices and praise the Lord,
Maker of this earth, forever adored;
Beauty is there it's all around.
And the joy of spring knows no bounds.

Gladys Sharp

Victoria (Aged 14 Weeks)

God gave us for a little while, your sweetness as a loan,
Then missed you so he took you back, an Angel of his own,
Now mortal pain can't harm you, whilst you're in heaven above,
Our hearts and minds fill to the brim, with Vicky's purest love.
Selfishly we wanted to bind you to this life,
And keep you ever with us within this world of strife.
But now we know you're with us, in our heart and in our soul,
You bring us close to heaven, making us more whole,
And though our hearts may ache, may bleed, to hold you,
     kiss you, please,
We know God loving you loves us Victoria Louise.
May Holy Angels guard you, May our love ever grow,
In the one way that only we, loving parents, know.

Jim I. Croll

What Is Love

Love is passion
Love is pure
Love will be your sadness' cure
Love can't bring anger
Love can't bring hate
But, oh yes love can be your fate
Love is a feeling real and true
Love is a feeling I feel for you
Love can get you into a muddle
But love will always give you a cuddle
Love can sometimes be unfair
But in my heart it's always there
Oh the happiness love can bring
It can even get you a wedding ring
Love can bring you hugs and kisses
But love is a feeling my heart never misses

Charlene Russell

Time

Moments passing by me by the second,
precious seconds ticking far away.
Far away to other distant places,
distant and with no regard for day.

Priceless is this never ending concept,
We'd hold on to as much as we could make.
Limited for us with only life to live,
running out like water from a lake.

The element of time is far beyond me,
and way ahead when needed most of all.
It rushes by when I'd like to see it stop for a while,
but when I'm tired of life it hangs there on the wall.

Thinking of the time that's being wasted,
would I go crazy if I couldn't fight? . . .
The feeling that the world is passing by me,
the problem that this tunnel's got no light.

I'm trapped in a clone of yesterday,
waiting for a difference to occur.
But time is going at no miles per hour,
and the hands upon the clock don't even stir.

Anna Ashworth

Entangled—A Scurry In Wonderland

Figures on the darkening hillside, dance from bush to tree
Artificial light and shade, watch as shadows flee.
Most glide past in happiness, some in heartfelt fear
Yet the darkness holds a secret, a lonely lover's tear.

On hills filled with remembrances, her footsteps crush his doubt
An evening spectre dances on, the smile he shows without.
The trees will not dare whisper, the message the grass receives
Of a lonely, shattered figure, who dances through the leaves.

Yet falsehood soon is over, things are what they seem
And as for his fairy tale lover, it seems she was only a dream.

Stuart Donaldson

Energies

Gently and wildly the energies flow
     into the sun and moon I grow
Floating the clouds dreaming the dawn
     swinging the stars night until morn
Riding the winds drifting through trees
     caressing nature the birds and bees
Part of the whole and whole of the part
     where did I come from when did I start
Questions and answers do they need to be told
     All in the mind to be young or old
The balance is nearing now is together
     universal despair conquered forever
Shine spiritual light bright love wondrous friend
     Oneness eternal never to end
Gently and wildly the energies flow
     into the sun and moon I grow.

Jane Sherwood

Dreams Of Long Ago

Is that silver darting fish real,
Or is it a sinuous eel,
Clear waters clean and deep,
Is this a dream, am I asleep?

Fields of corn cockle and marigold,
Buttercups poppies and flowers untold,
Tall grasses butterflies of different hues,
Am I asleep, is this true?

Now awakened from a dream,
Of silver fishes in a stream,
Pastures bright and bold,
Left with memories of long ago.

B. A. Robinson

Untitled

Time is only fleeting as it passes by
and it's left a mark on my memory
of all the times that I used to laugh or cry,
And I've heard so many words
that I can always feel
but can never seem to say,
and there've been times I'll never forget
especially when you said goodbye to me
on that day,
And I'll always remember your long hair
as it fell across your lovely face
and as time passes by
this will be the memory that I'll always embrace.

Alan Dunn

Carpe Diem

Seize the day the dead poets said and we obeyed
leaving foolish friends behind in stagnant grey
shout to them were less deceived today
we made a fairy tale ending come what may.

Not toads and sprites and other such tripe
but leaving our mark although we may pay
some trivial smite so that we might
unquestionably capture it all today

Days in the clay will number many
those to live and love and grab chances few
trapped circles must break and steel intentions rule
knowing life's bitterness was not living it true

We would not let our epitaphs read such gloom
days spent in safety spell their opportunities doom
we show the path, no deception rules
The day and the challenge seized everyday by the few.

Caoimhin O'Hannrachtaigh

Night With You

I remember it, sharp as a broken dream, the night I spent with you
And watched the street lamps play upon the contours of your face
Across the shadows of the nodding tree
From outside your window, a turbulence of wind and leaves
    comes scuttering in
And voices in a quarrel, his and hers,
A jealous row about possession, briefly passing, quickly gone
Leaving the driven leaves to hiss and rattle with the next
    intruding gust
I wait and listen while your low sighs dwindle into the breath
    of sleep
Now dare I touch
And with shy fingers trace your shoulder's sensuous curve
Until they rest upon your cheek
An old man, captive to the sleeping young
So innocently taking prisoners from her pillow
A hand upon a cheek, so chaste
Yet closer than the act of lust
A trade in love's innuendoes
More indestructible than marriage.

Tom Owen

Ode To The Peach

The Peach is of velvet, a beautiful skin;
Compliments the Cream, but is nothing akin.
To the eye of the beholder a Lover's Seal
Cannot compare to The Peach's soft feel.
Her warm rosy colour with her spirit aglow;
She was Made in Heaven for The Cream to know.
If desires were dreams, then this would be mine;
That your love and my love would one day entwine.
But such as this is, it must remain just a dream;
For reality is Death for The Peach and The Cream.

Edwina Anne Stone

Countenance!

Daily, we look at this face;
Commencing at dawn, in the human race!
Our lives, likewise, in calibration;
Segmenting movement, station to station!
Eating, sleeping, working, everything we know;
Controlled by this, annoying foe!
Cause of tension, reason of stress;
Turning life, into a mess!
Has good use, apart from dismal;
Save people, heal wounds, emotional, physical!
Sometimes, the face, we'd like to sock;
The one that goes, by the name of clock!

Robert Denham

Love Complete

The love starts long before the birth,
No other feeling, so strong on earth,
A mother loves, right from the start
She gives her life, her soul, her heart.

So precious is this little child
Protected from the mad, the wild,
Mums there in times of pain and need
To clean, to clothe, and then to feed.

I watched you grow, so very proud
You stand out, when you're in a crowd,
We let you try, you make mistakes
I teach you how to give and take.

I watch you struggle, teenage years
You do not understand my fears.
The crime, the drugs, you spite my tears
A teenage child, never feels or hears.

No matter what you say or do
My love for you, forever true,
The words you use, they make me cry
But the love inside my heart wort die.

R. Seward

The Rose

I placed a red rose to tell you goodbye
And deep in my heart it started to cry.
The rose was so pure its petals so red
But placing it against you I started to dread.
I grasped the rose tightly trying not to let go
But petals started falling, why I don't know
When you hold a rose some people they mourn.
With its evergreen leaf and its prickly thorn.
When a rose is held against us it makes you feel happy or sad
It could be used for love, for sorrow, or for some to make glad
A rose tells tales about things it can do.
When it's handed to someone it can be like a dream come true.
It's sent to a loved one to give you their love
With goodwill and trust that is sent from above
But the story I tell comes straight from the heart.
Because when I placed a rose my heart fell apart
A rose was for sadness and for pain, and for cost,
To show all the love for two angels I lost.
So again I would just like to mention and say.
The memory of this rose just won't go away.

Pearl Miles

Poem After Someone Has Died

Last night I dreamt of you
Only a moment and you were gone
Someone asked who you were
And I could not remember
But as I woke
I spoke your name
And you stayed with me all day.

You are returning to me in my mind
Allowing a kind of frugal portion at a time
Because I can face no more
But slowly as you come
The cruelty of the day lessens
Until I am sure I can make you go whenever I want to.

Margaret Knight

Life's Lesson Of Love

Life can lead us to many feelings,
Some we just can't explain.
Others we are left with our tears to drain.
When you lose someone you love,
It's like you're losing your touch,
Especially when you miss them ever so much.
The pain inside shall never disappear,
But will get easier by each year.
Life must have a meaning,
Otherwise God would never have brought us here today,
So live you life in the best possible way.

Helen Ware

Fire Renaissance

A lone man standing and small fire dancing,
	Light the dead forest's twilight presence.
The fire fountain splashes his frozen mask,
	Igniting the troubled and meditating mind.

Eternally out into the star–scarred void
	Spreads the dazzling, fiery mist of self.
His flame no child of the broken earth,
	Unceasing, seeks the second and eternal dawn.

The fire sinks gently to darkening earth.
	Its tired embers form a fragile wheel,
Which, turning and returning, rolls into night.
	The last sparks dart away into silence.

The convulsible cosmos ages on towards its end,
	As clouds of light spin and fade in black.
The fields of flame implode to pale spots,
	And these melt into that first, flashing spark.

The spark stabs the chill, surrounding dark,
	And frees his mind from its brief pain.
Reborn, the fire burns smokeless and intensely.
	In distant heat new cosmic lights appear.

Nicholas M. Goddard

For Jesus Fight!

March forward! March forward! To liberate the world!
March forward! March forward! With Jesus flags unfurled!
The dawn of a new world is lighting up the sky!
"Our destiny is victory!" That is our battle cry!
We shout it out, and hold our battle cross of Jesus high!

March forward! March forward! His revolution's come!
March forward! March forward! Now Satan's day is done!
We'll overturn his crown, to set the whole world free!
For Jesus fight! Destroy the might of Satan's tyranny!
God's kingdom, here, on earth shall come! We fight till victory!

March forward! March forward! A new world for mankind!
March forward! March forward! To God's world, we'll be kind!
With battle drums beating, our battle trumpets sound!
Our Jesus flags are flying free! Now! Cross the battleground!
To God and Jesus, we shall be, forever duty-bound!

To battle! To battle! We fight till victory!

B. T. Lewis

True Love

Some folk band together, like the feathers of bird.
Many storms they weather, and never an angry word.
They never tired of talking, and miles they go a walking,
	If, they are side-by-side.
Their faces to each other, are lovelier than rain is to
The Indian folk, whose fields are bare of grain,
Whose parched earth is so barren, like the soul who
Has no friend, pride, so stiff and choking, and unable
to unbend.
	How lovely is the blossom tree! And though
Its petals fall, the memory of its beauty is
Treasured by us all.
So cultivate the lovely things in life, for all else
Fades away when tired eyes close, and body rests
for good one final day.
But like a butterfly—released from out its dry
Cocoon, the spirits soars—rejoicing.
	And all sweet thoughts will bloom.

Eileen R. Gibson

The Square Mile

Slowly the watchman treads the cobbled streets,
No need to cry out the hours now.
The houses, barred and shuttered,
Turn unfriendly faces to another dawn.

The cold, pathetic corpses of the dead,
Already lie unmourned in unknown pit.
Their limbs grotesquely twisted, bodies black.
Thank God that now they are in peace.

At last the city comes to life,
No markets, street cries or bustling throng.
Quick nervous noises of people in a hurry,
Heads down, faces covered, terrified of death.

One church alone in all that city
Opened its doors to troubled souls.
That too is empty, as if God
Had turned His back on young and old.

Slowly the cart winds down the twisting lane
And harvests now the sheaves of broken lives.
The watchword now, "bring out your dead" sounds clear
And people offer up their sacrifice.

Diane Brown

Sunrise

It was a still, calm, black darkness.
Until a big, red flower broke the ebony night that had
just passed.
With petals that opened to reveal dawn.

Then it got bigger to cover the whole world with light
and heat.
The birds began to cheap.
And everything awoke to bask in the sun.

Later the big flower began to close.
Taking in all of the light and heat.
To leave an empty, dark, dull place once more.

Kayleigh Rhodes

Dreams

It's dark and cold,
But the dream tonight is bright and bold,
Voices echo inside your head,
You cuddle down into your bed,
Memories stir,
Sounds whirr,
Pictures appear and fade to mist,
Things become visible, things that you've wished,
Something evil lurks beyond your sight,
Waiting to catch you before it gets light,
To look at it would make you weep,
But it disappears as you stir in your sleep.

Robyn Grant

Anything But Love You

I count the minutes when I am with you
For I do not know when I will see you again
You sit too close
Close enough for me to hear you breathe
To touch you
Kiss you if I dared.

And I want to scream, shout
Kick out at you and hit you
Anything
Anything but just sit here
Hopeless and helpless
And love you the way I do.

Karen Brayne

"There Is A Grave Where Daffodil And Lily Wave"

"Will there be daffodils and lilies now
Upon your grave, my love?"

"I think none will remain to mourn or bow
Their head in sorrowing above
My bed;
I had
No sorrow in myself, not I,
If only I would die . . .

But see! How seed of emptiness
Bears glorious fruit; I dwell in splendidness
Of light,
That sight
Restored allowed to enter in
And re-create in me a wonder-womb!"

"Wonder of wonders, then,
That daffodils and lilies lightly bloom
Within, beyond the tomb!"

Gordon West

The Forest Is Our Paradise On Earth

Beautiful flowers blowing in the wind,
Their scent is drifting on the summer breeze;
The air with soft music is o'er–brimmed,
As the leaves gently tremble on the trees.
A subtle symphony of sights and sounds,
As Nature tries to make my heart rejoice;
Little birds sing on branches all around,
A harmony of sweet, melodic voice.
Sunlight falls in golden shafts through the leaves,
Making patterns of lace upon the earth;
Creates a world of seeming make believe,
Where everything makes smiles and joy and mirth.
    This place on earth is where I want to be,
    To know beauty, for all eternity.

Colline Charles

Untitled

A letter for you,
C
Like the half–rounded moon
In a silent night sky
Surrounded by millions of tiny stars
Twinkling in a sea of sadness
Just like your eyes, when you smiled
Washing the waves of woe onto the shore.
But for how long will it last
Your happiness
Contained in a glass?
Fragile and thin, held up high
Above a hard, cold ground.
A thought of the consequences
Of your actions in this world
And slowly you would dip
Waiting for that final day
When the glass will smash, leaving you free
To forever
Fly away.

Anna Collishaw

The Fox

What is this before me there!
A fox comes out of this secret lair
I glance at my father, his excitement is catching.
I sense something wonderful is happening.

The fox slowly up to the barbed wire goes
Prodding a tuft of sheep wool with its nose
What he can do with that I haven't a clue
I must move a little keep him in view

Slowly to the nearby river he goes
Wool held firmly between his jaws
He went into the water head held high
I couldn't make out the reason why

Slowly under the water he swam
My father's face had no sense of alarm
The I saw the wool drift down stream
I asked my father what does this mean.

He said a wonder of nature had been seen this day.
If anyone asked I could always say
I have seen a fox if you please
Swim in the water to get rid of his fleas

E. Hemmings

An Easter Prayer

Thou camest Lord to bear my sin, hung on that tree by cruel pin
Thou suffered there to plead my pardon, died for me in
Satan's garden,
Even whilst thy body lay, within the grave in death's decay
Thou prayed "Oh Father hear my plea, have mercy on those
    that crucify me".

My heart was hard my will was weak, and worldly goods did
    only seek
Until one day it was fulfilled, a Saviour's blood for me was spilled.
Thank you for the pain you bore upon your worldly body sore,
Thank you that you rose to be, a light for all the World to see.

Thou art my shepherd, I thy sheep, please help me Lord thy
    laws to keep
To help my Brother, Sister too, to love my neighbour as did you.
Help me therefore gracious Lord, to have the strength to teach
    thy word,
To all around who know you not, and save their souls from
Hell to rot.

How sweet the name of thee Lord Jesus, how bounteous thy
    gifts to please us
How blessed are we to receive thy grace, here and now within
    this place.
Thank you Lord that you love me, enough to die upon that tree,
Help me Lord to sacrifice, my life to you to pay the price.

I beg thee Lord accept my praise, and that thou will my soul to raise,
To live with thee eternally, safe in the Heavenly Kingdom, Free.
And as I drop these earthly chains and leave behind my
    dead remains,
Please let it be that I have done, your will for others, Everyone.

Anthony R. Vellam

November

Barren boughs of bone
In the alabaster world,
Tremble at the sound of winter
Engulfing all in snow serenity.

Dangerously contagious cold,
Creeps up from the floor to caress your feet
Leaving them pleasantly numb.
An entire anatomy glowing blue, freezing
Perpetuum mobile of summer
Slowly dying out.

Home.
A renewal at a slower pace,
Down covers veil visions of heat
Of blue metamorphosing into promising pink.
Mine is a wonderfully scorching alabaster winter.

Yael Levin

England's Countryside

The fields of brown, the autumn hue.
The trees that weave a golden view,
Beauty as the harvest nears, that drives away all fears.
Then hearts of oak can swell with pride,
And love of England's countryside.

The leaves that tremble on the trees
Come rustling down on gentle breeze,
Carpeting the mottled ground with scarce a sound.
The silence of the men who died
For love of England's countryside.

Then winter, wearing softest white
Swathes the earth before our sight.
A robin on the window sill, a world so still.
So such sweet things in memory sighed
At love with England's countryside.

Now, as the springtime flowers bloom
Bursting to birth from earthly womb.
Calves and colts will caper past, a newborn world at last.
Life born from blood, yet death denied,
Is love of England's countryside.

Ray Blakemore

Autumn

Prune those roses before harvest,
Being as, when summer is over,
Early birds could have stolen the show.

Some of our relatives grew out,
From obscurity to be stars,
Give history its victory.

If you've found a fair way right here;
You could reshape old traditions,
While some search or swear to recall.

You've left a record on the wall,
Which makes good sense to passers-by,
They'll prune more flowers for harvest.

In our younger years we would gaze
At heroes with pride and feel dazed,
Little more than a moment long.

And got bunkered or just snookered;
We'd hit the green, not from pity.
Please, prune the bloom before harvest.

There's a spell of ardour amour on thorns,
Which schemers and dreamers will grasp.

Ryland A. Campbell

First Love

I loved you then, I love you still,
I guess in my heart I always will,
I only wish when time is right,
Our two hearts will reunite,

So until then, my head ways no,
And to others my head will go,
My heart know that what is true,
Is in the future I'm the one for you,

And until then I'll keep my heart,
Clean and fresh our new start,
'Till that time comes I'll keep my heart,
So that again, won't be torn apart.

Tore it apart, is what you did,
Went through a lot, I know we did,
In such a short time, I know that too,
But us together was like a foot and shoe,

And before I said, I love you still,
Be together one day, I know we will,
Destiny doesn't change, even if you try,
For what is for us, won't pass us by . . . ?

Gillian Larkin

Vinty's Eulogy

Bring back Vinty some people say,
Others say keep her away!
Since she's been gone
Prescriptions don 't take so long.
What did she do when she was here?
All her empty cans said larger or beer
Yvonne, Adam, Brian, Rudi all drink coffee or tea
and that includes me.
She said she was sad to go
For what reason we don't know
She was always on that phone
I'm sure she was ringing home!
Long words she may know and use
But they don't help to cut the queues.
Now the patients waiting for their drugs
Say the time doesn't seem to slug.
They don't have the time to sit down
They're in and out and shopping around!
There must be a moral to this rhyme
Get off your backside and you'll save time!

J. F. Nimmo

There Is No Focusing . . . Jrmk

There is no focusing when the shutter's closed
Yet in that camera lingers just a trace of you—
The handle of the clock stands soldier straight.

When the shutter blinks a seconds to encapsulate
'Before' is frozen—and ever after all will be composed
Around in image. In years to come this will be my cue.

I found a way to make speed over light dance—

By way of contrast to adjust the aperture—
Letting in light—to stream down the avenue.

So through the window we will see not me but you—
My focal vision in a frame so pure
Takes in all things lovely with one essential glance.

Deborah Jane Stuart

Time Will Tell

Tick tock tickety tock,
Hear the sound of your own body clock
Slowly ticking down life's track,
There is no way to turn life's clock back

Into this world we make our debut,
Young and innocent everything new,
From womb to cradle, and cradle to school
We learn from our elders to follow the rules

We grow with such speed time flies by so fast
Today, tomorrow, soon become the past
Energy throbs it vibrates through our veins
As we strive to achieve, to hold on to life's reins

To adulthood we all finally surrender,
to become the creators of our personal agenda
Mistakes are made, as we try to do well
The final outcome only time will tell.

Brenda Roberts

Granny's Lace

I must go down a country lane
To see my granny's lace again,
The hedgerows all in bridal white,
I think they look a splendid sight,
Intricate patterns of every kind,
My granny made table mats of those designs.
You have a look next time, you'll
See, the patterns that I mean.
Yes, I must go down a country lane,
To see my granny's lace again.

Dulcie B. Gillman

Burning Desire?

Down sterile corridors you wander,
To a place that Morpheus and
Hypnos will never bless.
Drugged dreams are thick and black as tar,
And pain hangs heavy in air, like smoke.
What suffering resides here, unwanted as cancer,
Bitter as self regret?
What burning desire was worth all this?
The flame of acceptance that stubbed your heart
Has now burnt out your life.

Lynnette Morris

Dawn To Dusk

I wake up in the light of the morn,
To the chorus of birds, who greet the dawn,
The day has begun for everyone,
Whether playing, or getting various tasks done.
The traffic is moving, a hive of activity,
Quite literally, the day is full of opportunity.

Children in their school array.
Hurrying past, chattering away,
Their standard behaviour is exceptionally fine,
The happiness around, is quite sublime.

Workmen seem cheerful and whistling along.
Hearing them, makes one break into song.
Noticing the flowers, decked with dew,
These are the things, that I like to view.
When the shadows of evening gather, and the sun glides away.
The time has come to retire, it's the end of a happy day.

Beatrice Davies

Ode To A Best Friend

Well to somebody I have said goodbye,
now I really need to cry.
Only this is very hard for me to do,
fortunately I have found a good friend in you.

Sadly, to allow my tears free reign,
evokes a lot of pain.
So thank you for being around,
a sympathetic ear to catch my sound.

You realize when I need a lift,
your friendship is a wonderful gift.
You understand when I need to be sad,
for this I shall be eternally glad.

So may I take this opportunity to say,
you are the nicest person in the nicest way.
Please remember, for you an ear I shall always lend,
just for being my best friend.

Deborah Anne Banks

"Memories Of Yesterday"

As restless waters flow along the shore
You're on my mind—and I think of you once more

People just don't understand
The way I feel inside
Knowing that I've lost you
and the pain I cannot hide

Back then I was happy
Walking on a cloud
Nothing seemed to matter
You made me feel so proud

All I've got is memories
Of how things used to be
My world was built around you
You were everything to me

Although it's more than twenty years
Since I saw you last
It seems like only yesterday
My future's in the past.

Tony Wilson

Dream Lover

Dream lover where are you now,
I seem to have lost you in the clouds somehow.
You came to me when I was fast asleep,
And gave me loving feelings so strong, so deep.

How I wish that you were real,
Then you'd be a man that I could feel,
So close, so warm holding me tight.
A real man to have, not a dream lover at night.

So please come to me where ever you are,
Don't hide yourself behind that star.
Come down to me on earth and stay,
To love each other forever and a day.

Lara

My Darling Child

My darling child
  For months I have carried you inside
Feeling kicks and turns
  So gentle and mild.

In weeks to come
  You will be born to me
Into this world
  Which you are soon to see

Someday you will kick hard
  Some days lightly and others slow
It's one of those wonderful signs
  How fast and big
You're beginning to grow

You are so protected and hidden away
  I can hardly wait for that special day.

Maureen Young

Colours Of Grief

The Colour of my grief is black, layer upon layer, it covers me whole; the weight and burden a heavy load, I cannot lift my head out of its depths no light at the end of my road.

The Colour of my pain is purple, bloods flowing purple, and I bleed, how I bleed. Hold me tight with the colour of compassion and love. So many tears do fall, crystal clear in their colourless light.

The Colour of my anger is red; stark bright blinding my sight my heart reeling in its excess, lay your hands upon to be still, whisper, let it go, let it go.

The Colour of my loneliness is grey, grey walls, grey skies, grey upon grey, no relief to the grey relentless void into which I fall.

The Colour of acceptance is blue, soft, soft, blue, like your skin, so smooth, so cool.
Wrap me in blue's lightness, wash away, blacks, purples, greys and blues, lift me to the sky, to bathe me in blue; it's time to say goodbye to you but I loved you, Oh, how I loved you.

Patricia Hayman

Another Day

Awake, awake, you sleepy head,
How come you still can lie abed.
The sun shines bright.
Birds sing with all their might.
Awake, awake old sleepy head.

Come see the lambs and rabbits at their play,
The busy bee buzzing on its way.
The trees stand high,
Flowers in profusion below.
Come, come and see the show.

All nature at its best for all to see,
No charge is made, just for free.
The blue sky above soft clouds drifting by.
The day so short, awake, come soon.
Night sleeps, here comes the moon.

M. Horwood

My Father's Garden

The scent of fresh rain
on the grass in my Father's garden.
The air now feels fresh, clear.
The magnolia tree has cast
a carpet of its petals upon the damp earth.
Each petal collecting droplets, like
small bowls filled with perfume.

Although I have been here before
it seems new to me, as if
the rain has washed away the old
and placed a new layer before me;
erased all tension, it had enveloped me
along with the room in which I stood
silently watching the steady downpour.
In that moment it brought,
like a midwife,
a new beginning
to my Father's garden.

Marco Farina

One Lovely Day

We walked together through the winters snow.
Walked where only lovers go.
We wrote of our love, in the snow on the ground.
And listened to the silence all around.
We walked hand in hand under a sky pure and white.
And knew in our hearts that the time was right.
To pledge a love that would never die.
To swear that our hearts would never lie
So we did together, what lovers do.
Always believing our love was true.
And we spoke of love, and burning desire
Felt our hearts were a raging fire.
Never dreaming that the melting snow
Would make the fire of desire burn low.
Never thinking at the end of the day.
Our love like the sun, would fade away.

Vincent Fitton

Leaving Me

Thinking back into my past
comes memories of our neighbours,
the kind old man would play with me,
the little old lady would give me sweets.

These special people have now past away,
but I know they have gone to a peaceful place
where we will be reunited one day,
where they won't be able to leave me again.

Sarah Holt

Fired Spiral

And the heart knew
That they would on the eve of the Summer solstice
Celebrate an event in Earth's journey.

That people and children would collect fir cones,
Dry sticks and straw and fill the trenched spiral.
Warm as people walked in and out
And the man maker of spirals, waved
And danced the energy of Earth
Into the setting sun and the rising new moon.

And the children and a woman naturally fired the spiral.

Stones from Dinas Emrys, Avebury and Stonehenge were
Placed in the blazing, smoking spiral. In the
Middle of Janes's field bursting with wild flowers.

And the drums drummed an event of inevitable spirit
Of the dragons's breath into the sweet brown earth.
Fire into Earth, Water, Wood and Sky.

And the people did this and they did that
And they did not wake up to the beautiful
Earth humming
In the heart of the great Awe . . .

Dei Hughes

Her Room

As I stand in the doorway,
I take a lingering look around.
At what was her favourite room.
The emptiness envelops me like a shroud.

The quietness is only invaded,
by the monotone ticking of the clock.
Passing away the hours,
as it had done through all her years.

The faded photographs on the walls,
show me her loved ones.
The wrinkled leather armchair
faces the television in the corner.
Like a sentry standing guard.

The scent of her perfume.
Lingers in the still air,
evoking memories of happier times.

The light is fading now,
with the setting of the sun.
Casting shadows around the room.

The shadows hide my tears.

John E. Shepherd

Charles' Silent Thoughts

And so the hour hath come,
That I am now free of this mortal pain
That I have endured with much
Aplomb and dignity, befitting of my
Station as this England's future king.

To be rid of this scourge of hate
And unmerciful tirade,
Levelled against me without pause of breath,
Saved but for the quietness and richness of
The night as she slept till dawn.

Methinks how good is fortune to have,
And me to pay, and yet still leave me a-plenty.
For such is my place, my right, ordained by
Some ancestral birth for which I and you my
Loyal subjects must be truly thankful.

For I, with sombre thoughts and guile, must now
Replenish lost gains of my forefathers past, but
Impoverished I am not, for just the smallest of
Fraction only she doth take, of what I have she
Knows not, and verily most truly in safekeeping got.

Freddie Jefferies

Lady Death

Oblivion is watching in the corner of your room,
tentative fingers reaching from the gloom.
Look around—you won't see them,
But when you shiver, you can feel them.

Compassion and love can't survive in her mind,
She takes friends and family and leaves you behind,
But one day you'll whisper your very last breath
And then she will take you, for she is Lady Death.

Sometimes she'll embrace, then reluctantly part,
Paralyse your mind, your soul and your heart.
There is no reason that is worth giving,
Except that she's jealous of those who are living.

She hides in the shadows that fall from our backs,
In a long flowing gown of silver and black.
Her eyes pierce the darkness with emerald green.
She is ready to pounce in a silent scream.

We drown in her aftermath—she lives on our fears, feeding
    from our grief for countless years.
But it is when we forget that life's as precious as gold that she
    reaches her strongest and then takes her hold . . .
Our mortality is balanced on the blade of a knife,
But the most evil thing about her is that she's part of life.

Sonia Haycock

The Big 'O'

A young man wrote, with itchy feet,
In life no luck, but his message so sweet.
He always wrote, from experience,
God, he had some resilience.

Beautiful lyrics, they teach his lesson,
You'd think he'd come, straight from Heaven.
'It's Over' and 'Blue Bayou',
Are fine examples, to name just two.

Was it his writing, his singing,
Or just his love, that sent hearts tingling?
Just to see him, on the stage,
Was a blessing, that become a crave.

Modest, gentle, and unassuming,
Yet his voice, could be booming.
Sat in amazement, you felt your heart within,
For then you'd know, that love will win.

Stand and applaud,
You would ovate,
Roy Orbison, to you
This poem, I dedicate.

Alan J. Williams

If

If only you'd been here, on my return
my life, would not have been so lonely.
My day's would have had the sunshine,
Keeping me warm, knowing you were near.

If only you'd been here,
my eyes would not have cried,
for each day, felt like one year.

If only now, I could have you,
it would be to myself,
for my heart could not share you,
with no one else now.

If only you'd called,
if only by reaching out, I could have touched you,
I would have been so happy.

Sherry Shirley

A Sonnet On War

Our skies are quiet now, the planes have gone
That dropped their fearsome, gruesome loads of bombs.
Our seas are clear, the battles all are done,
Our sailors rotted in their watery tombs.
We licked our wounds and counted up the cost,
Repaired the damage, built our towns again,
Still mourning for the ones we loved and lost,
And still remembering suffering and pain.
But since that time a hundred other wars
Have raged across the earth, the seas, the skies,
Men in the fight for Freedom and The Cause.
With horror's silent scream in children's eyes.
Can't someone, some day, solve the mystery
Why nations never learn from History?

Isabel Williams

The Man On The Corner

The poor old man on the corner,
he's there everyday.
Selling his fruit and vegetables,
always in the some old way.

Whenever I was passing by,
I'd stop and help him sell.
Then when he had packed everything away,
I'd listen to the tale he'd tell.

The tale about when he was young,
"I was just like you he'd say".
Then I would think to myself,
maybe I'll be selling ware
one day.

Stacylea Metcalfe

A Child's Innocence

One little child, all scared and frightened
didn't know what to do when persons unspoken of,
took advantage of one child's innocence and pride.
Robbed them of their lives and youthfulness.
Took everything without asking, without permission,
and expected no change, no reaction in that child's
behaviour, towards them.
No-one else noticed any change, not even the ones
who were supposed to care, to love.
No-one thinks for one second about that young person,
about what they could be going through.
The pain, the trauma, the hurt, the self-disgust or their shame.
May those people remember for the rest of their days,
and, may they never forget the damage they have
done to one small innocent child.
For that small child will never ever forget, until the day they die.

Cher Marie Anderson

Time

What is time? We cannot say
Though it rules our lives throughout each day.
From birth to death we live with it
And it costs us not one little bit.

There's a time to share and still have some spare
To take it easy as we stand and stare.
A time to give as well as to take
To waste or spend and also to make.

There's a time to smile and a time to cry
To keep it or lose it—we wonder why.
For school or work we cannot be late
Neither train or bus for us will wait.

When we grow old and cannot go on
Time leaves us quietly and we are gone.
Old Father Time takes us by the hand
And helps us into the Promised Land.

Morfydd Jerman

Life Is Like A Bubble

Life is like a bubble, floating in the sun,
Magic, rainbow colours, on its journey, just begun.
Then, the bubble burst and the magic goes,
As down the road of age, our life flows.

In a stream, we seem caught by the tide,
O'er which we must ride,
Of happiness, sorrow and pain

But the torrent leads to joy and peace
And a soul's freedom and release
Then, we see our bubble once again.
Through the darkest clouds and rain.

For age is just a journey we must take,
And if we smile, we'll see the colours once again,
Shining even brighter through the rain

Sunshine and shadow go hand in hand
The shadows cast, shed beauty or a sunny and
Life is a like a picture, depicting light and tone
When the finished painting is shown.

Betty Owen

Despair

Pity the folk who live on the street,
Hungry and weary, cold hands and cold feet.
Luck is not with them as they woefully beg,
Looking for crumbs where others have fed.
Their bed is a box in some rat–ridden hole,
Where they try to escape the rain and the cold.
How long will it last, this life of despair?
With no-one to love them and no-one to care.
But Spirit is watching and will hold out a hand,
To lead them above to a better land.
When they see they are weary and can struggle no more.
And they'll sleep in God's heaven with love evermore.

Joyce Marion Woods

For The Children

Good times
Of the best
Doing things like the rest
Being good
Like I should
Eating good things like I would
Solving problems for the rest
So sure of the best
You are the children of the years
Often sharing and releasing your fears
Unsure of all your plans
Always joining all the wrong gangs
Let's be safe, safe and sound
Let's be king and queen and wear the crown.

Sarah Jane Wilkinson

A Furtive Glance

At some distance I watch
The way those lips touch glass and stick for an instant
As tell tale traces of red smear.
I like the way her lips shine
Coated in gloss and alcohol;
I like her lips.
Her rigid digits trap a cigarette, squeezing its butt
With nails blood red or kinky black,
In this light, I can't decide.
I watch the expert manoeuvre
As her mouth of experience pulls
A sharp blast of tar,
Stinging her throat and peppering her lungs with
An inward and warm turmoil
From her favourite poisons.
She may lose her grip as chemicals hammer home
But she remains exterior calm
As she looks at me,
With lust, with pity or with scorn.
In this light, I just can't decide.

Tom Gardiner

Is There Something Wrong With Me?

The boy walked down the street
wondering why people were looking at him.
Was there something wrong with him?
Or was it the colour of his skin?

He felt alone.
Nobody was talking to him.
Everyone just stared and whispered.
Was there something wrong with him?
Or was it the colour of his skin?

What is wrong with me?
Why is everyone looking at me?
Why is nobody talking to me?
Why have I got no friends?

Maybe it is simply the colour of my skin!

Seeta Brahmbhatt

Dreamland

Kissed by the moon and stroked by a star
Shrouded by the down of a cloud
Embraced by the sensual cloak of the sun
Soft moonbeams all around

Floating free on a gentle colour
Lifted by a breath of silent breeze
Through eternal streams of shooting stars
And scented raindrop seas

Cradled by trembling thunder rolls
And laced with silver lightening threads
Melting though each carbon layer
On a star dust scattered bed.

Adele Meekins

The Sea

Sheer walls of water clear as glass
Jostle as they try to pass,
Curling over as they come crashing down
Droplets sparkling like diamonds in a crown,
white forth like lace comes into view
From the very waves it seems to spew,
Perfect droplets gleaming so clear
They appear to form from the very air,
An angry mistress in a storm
But a child's play thing when it's calm,
Ever changing from day to day
Tides come in, waves seem to play,
from aquamarine to deepest blue,
The sea can change to every hue,
An energy so vast it never ends
Not to be tamed its message sends,
Across the oceans deep and wide
Carried to all on every tide

B. M. Daubney

Untitled

I took your hand and climbed the hill
Closing my eyes against the bright sun
While the passing wind caressed my cheeks
And I felt the gentle peace around me.

I thought not of yesterday's stresses
Nor of tomorrow's conscience
I revelled in today's exquisite peace
And longed it would be unending.

I like to take and hold selfishly
These moments of delicate thistledown
Which soon will blow away and disappear
To be recaptured in some other hand.

I climbed to the summit of contentment
That afternoon that seems so long ago
Yet in time is only yesterday
Or today and all tomorrow.

L. McGeachy

My Darling Wife

"To,
  More than you, no one could I ever love
  Only you in my life, I pray to the Lord above
  Never to hurt you always to stay together indeed.
  In you, I have found everything I would ever need
  Certainly over the last ten years, you have made my life
  Above all, thanks very much for being such a lovely wife."

Bernard Ferns

Afternoon At The Tate

It rained outside, I think,
whilst we exchanged particles of this and that
and students with long hair and big boots
fervently whisked off reproductions
in tattered black books of all sizes.

Out of place, men in England shirts
with embarrassing bellies and white socks
pushed into plastic slip-ons, raced past
as if eager to escape the silence we felt obliged to keep,
but broke with the squeakings of our shoes.

College scarves and rucksacks, tweeds and pearls
stood before the gold–framed offerings,
ready to be devoured and spat out again
in an entirely new guise.
The artist was at our mercy.

And yet, I think we were also at his
because we could not see his face.
But we heard the rain, and we burst out into it and the world,
clutching picture postcards of Picasso
as if we somehow held the life of it in our hands.

Penny Insole

My One True Love

You are my reason for living this life,
With your beautiful face, hands hair and eyes,
In the night I dream of being your wife,
And gently floating through clear blue skies.
Your luscious red lips I wish I could kiss,
Your beautiful eyes are so warm and deep.
Cupid has shot my heart how could he miss,
Your love in a box I wish I could keep.
To me, you are gorgeous, loving and kind,
Yes, I would do anything to be yours,
Whenever I see you, you blow my mind,
My heart opens up and out it, love pours.
    Darling I love you I wish you could know
    And each time I see you, it starts to grow.

Alison Wilson

Mayfly Dawn

In this dungeon, dark and full, it's been my past for years,
Floating, skating, endlessly, waiting for the tears,
Still dreaming of another life when I shall drift away,
Open up my rainbow lace, on dew drenched stems I'll lay,

Underneath the surface glaze, I rest and wait for morning,
Dew drops circle up above, a brand new day is dawning,
Gentle movements soft and sweet are swirling all around,
Pressed firmly on the silky skin, a new world I have found,

Out into the moist drenched air, my lace now comes to rest,
Glistening, shining, delicately, the time I've looked my best,
Fleeting, dancing, joyfully now, as daylight dries my wings,
Music, gently, rhythmically, as the blackbird sings,

Among the reeds I dart and skip, searching for my mate,
Resting on this weary stem, is where I'll find my fate,
Waiting till dusk and then till morn, my time is ticking by,
Sinking, tangled, lace below the water I shall die . . .

Tina Dowell

Ricochet

Resounding force.
A blinding metallic collision
Sculpturing a concertina showpiece of
Splintered glass and shattered souls.
Reverently detached from emotive echoes
Of uniformed reassurance and mortal distress.

Smouldering carcass.
Harbouring the shells of speed junkies
Whose feckless bravado lies severed
Amongst helpless mobile technological perks.
A focal pivot of personal tragedy for
Public contemplation and judgmental reaction.

Inopportune waste.
A blockade of chaotic preclusion
Swept away on a tide of instruction to
Restore the visual flow of normality.
Reducing the bold statuesque illustration
To a statistical input in an annual report.

A. J. Tollington

Dreaming

The middle of the night and not a sound to be heard,
But then I heard the chirping of our little bird.
I came downstairs to look and was amazed with what I saw,
A dark haired, handsome prince charming standing at the door.
I stood there in amazement, couldn't speak but only blink.
He smiled so very sweetly, then gave me a little wink.
I felt like Cinderella, was I to go to the ball?
As this dark haired, handsome stranger stood there in the hall.
I stared at him and thought he's no-one from the past,
What do you want I asked, when I spoke to him at last.
I've come to take you away he said, to a land of milk and honey,
I just started laughing as I thought this very funny.
The alarm clock then was ringing, the time half past seven,
What a time to be woken up, I could have been in heaven.

Diana Emery

The Owl's Table

With gaze intent on brush and stubble field,
Black eyes take in the rapid failing light,
This land where future lies unseen,
For him and other creatures of the night.

Sharp claws grow restless on the roughened bark,
White feathers ripple in the breeze,
Slight movement in green grass below,
Alerts his sense to all he knows and sees.

On silent wing, he glides in powerful flight.
And pounces on his unsuspecting prey,
Gives screeching cry of triumph to the skies,
As dawn approaches with another day.

M. Heyworth

Why?

Please, somebody tell me why, it didn't work for me;
You were all I wanted, all I ever hoped you'd be?
Our wedding day was special, my parents were so glad
at last I'd found someone to love, but then it all went bad.

Was it just that we'd become so accustomed to each other
Or maybe it because I spent so much time being mother?
Maybe if we'd learned to talk about or hopes and fears,
I wouldn't be alone night now, fighting back the tears.

No matter what the reasons are, you're gone, I'm all alone,
and now I've got to realize that you're not coming home.
"I've met someone new", you said "I love her more than you".
It took some time before I'd let myself believe it's true
It was only when you packed your bags and gave me back your key.
Oh please, someday tell me why it didn't work for me?

Rosemary Armstrong

Ed

I saw a hero die today; a hero and a friend
I saw a hero die today, a hero to the end.
No headlong charge towards the foe, no scramble o'er the top
No tally-ho and away we go, with a swish of the riding crop
But bravery comes in many forms, and none as brave as he
As he looked his illness in the eye and braved the enemy.
Day by day, as strength decayed, he fixed us with a smile,
Death became a masquerade, as he fought off life's denial.
The enemy, it grew in strength; it grew and multiplied
His spirits rose, his spirits soared, he would not be denied.
Only his memory now lives on, but what a memory!
He gives us hope that we may live, and die as one like he.
I saw a hero die today, no medals will he wear
But as brave a man as ever lived lies safely in God's care.

D. McNulty

The Television

Tots T.V. is okay for tots but for teenagers and
    oldies it's not.
Emmerdale Farm's on twice a week if my olds don't
    watch it they totally freak.
Lottery show lasts 15 mins where you have to be
    lucky to get good wins.
Eastenders is the show from hell with Ricky, Grant
    and Ethel as well.
Vanessa is a girlie chat show.
If you're into music top of the pops is the place to
    be every Friday on BBC.
Sesame Street is another kiddies show with puppets
    and muppets and fun galore.
If you're interested in game shows there's plenty
    to choose from like Man O Man, Wheel Of Fortune or
    Play Your Cards Right With Bruce Forsyth.
Outer Limits is scary stuff but most people don't believe
    in it and call it duff.
News at ten's pretty boring, it makes me start
    snoring.

Sarah Louise Davidson

Mr. Turner Key

My name is Mr. Turner Key
And I live in a lock in a door.
It's a snug little place and I couldn't want more.
Fits like a glove and I'm often caught napping
When someone starts rot-at-at-apping!

I'm not always at home through no fault of my own
My mistress is p'haps a bit careless!
You'd never believe the places I've been
And the sights that I've seen
Would make even a key become hairless!

Sometimes, I ride in my Mistress's pocket—
And I like that except when it's dark.
(I wonder—who is that man she meets in the park?)
I sit and peep through the threads of the stuff
Quiet as a mouse—not making a muff.

At the end of the day when I've done all my turning
I feel quite worn out and for sleep I am yearning.
The moon is not shining and my house is all dark
Is there someone approaching?
Why! It's the man from the park.

Dorothy Quibell

Natural Revenge

I never saw Ilfracombe until now,
And I must rush home and paint,
Before the hasty-man comes with bulldozer
And ozonises the atmosphere—reference to
Scenic peace, capture the eye of yesterday.

The dread of daring commercial mind
Of independence and infantile behaviour.

Raise your glasses—another lath has been laid—
One more romantic village dressed in summer of century
Trembles at blemish–making finger of pick up
Bucket that snakes the air and rids the peace
of serenity—night-life of spiders and glow-worms
That fire the night with scintillates of gold and red.

You understand not the heart-searching
Of the intelligent mind—why this indiscriminate pillaging
of our heritage. But wait—an omen:
In the distance is sound-undertone—hurricane:
Soon the trees will fall like ghouls of laughter
And I smile—God has heard the prayer, within our hearts—
and I—
like millions, Rejoice in natural vengeance.

K. H. Round

A Tribute

As a youngster I remember the outings,
To pictures, museums and fairs.
I remember the stories you read me.
And the piggybacks all the way up the stairs.

I remember you helped me with homework,
You always drove me around.
You taught me to drive with no hassle,
You always kept my feet on the ground.

I miss all our deep conversations,
The glass of whisky we shared before bed.
I miss having someone to talk to,
Who doesn't talk at me instead.

There are so many memories of you with me,
I still drive around in your car,
And my bottle of 21-year old whisky,
Still sits, untouched, in the bar.

Very rarely did you ever judge me,
You were a help right to the end,
I feel I've not only lost a father,
But a dear and loving life-long friend.

Karen Lovatt

The Chip

A silicon chip, a fingernail sliver of insignificance,
Which dropped on a pavement, might well unnoticed lie,
Unless in sunlight's brief sparkle captured.
Yet on its surface lies the complexity of a great city,
Its parts communicating with beehive power.
Did man, who once crude pictures on rough rock did scrawl,
Really create this wonder, a delicate fragility of monstrous
        power possessed?
Great good does it promise, computing the design of life–saving
        drugs,
Like a modern philosophers' stone,
Yet also a darker side it presents, a chilling image mirrored
        in its cold surface,
A spectre of deserted factories, and jobless queues of
        frightening length.
For the mightiest machines leap at its command,
And human beings become an irrelevance.
Is the writing on its surface the writing on the wall, for those
        who work do seek?
The pen is mightier than the sword they say,
But perhaps not so mighty as the ghostly images etched on
        this fragile fragment,
Man's crowning work, which might yet all his other work end.

Stuart McEwen

The World Is Your Shadow

The world is your shadow.
It is the silence beating through an empty space,
That effects your life.

Life is but an illusion.
And the gift of love is to help break the barriers,
You must face.

An empty stare.
Shows nothing more than a confused face,
An eruption of the soul.

Pain.
Is the fine line between love and hate.
A senseless grey area encountered,
Through ignorance and selfishness.

Family.
Is there for guidance and support,
To teach of right and wrong,
And to supply the love to last an eternity.

The gift of love is a powerful thing

Please return the love you took,
For without it I am incomplete.

Paul Thornhill

Land Robbery

The green thieves crept into our world last night,
and stole the atmosphere from about our heads,
They planted nightmares for us to dream inside our
hollow grave-like beds.
They crept across our ancestors land reaping the harvest
in with one hand,
They stole crops which were feeding us
And filled our water sources with cement dust.
The green thieves destroyed our world last night
Whilst your nightmares cradled you tight.
They stole the moon and the stars,
Erected in every window horrible black, steel bars
They imprisoned us inside a tomb
And threw away our environment,
Polluted every possible room
And left our broken world with this testament;
They told us "we should have cared"
They told us "we should have shared"
If we had not been so greedy
Then maybe we would still be resting easy.

Nina-Ann Lewis

Wanderlust

Lying in the grass by the roadside
I spied a pair of tiny shoes
To fit perhaps a three year old
Scuffed toes but not worn through

Why had they been left there
Forgotten or just thrown away
Did the child prefer to run barefoot
On this warm and pleasant day

With the careless freedom of the very young
Did he kick them off his feet
And run with gay abandon
To the end of the cobbled street

Would he always seek that freedom
In his many future years
When danger crossed his paths through life
Or would good fortune banish fears

Where at this moment, is he?
Would he come back with Mum or Gran
To find his pair of shoes had gone
Amongst the garbage left by man.

Alexandria M. Keith

Jack, Denzel, And Me

'Twas a glorious night, a summer's delight,
the shire a hauntingly still.
And amidst the shade o' an evergreen glade,
be an inn call'd the 'Pig and Whistle.'
'Tis set 'in splendour'd trappings green,
O' woodland great and small.
Where weeps on high fair dewy leaf,
each tear on bloom to fall.
Blest rendezvous o' just repute,
this confidante for the meek.
Forsooth! therein be parlour'd friends,
hail kith and kin to greet.
Burrow'd 'n a garland vale, garnish'd with a stream.
There you have, my friend unearth'd, a loyal toper's dream.
With swish o' knee and toss o' tail, to a gait we daily stepp'd.
Nigh forty year have frequent'd here, Jack, Denzel, and
Myself.

Made merry did'st we, companions three,
with sonnet, song and good jest.
And 'pon my life, and the landlord's good wife,
no company has ever been best.

E. J. Elliott

Gateway To The Lakes

When heading north—along the M6
One of the memorable exit points—No. 36
The gateway to the lakes, as it is known
We do it so often, no need to be shown

The feeling of anticipation, you feel it grow
No matter how many times, it is always so
Memories of past visits, you drive and kindle
When on the dual carriage way, by passing Kendle

Soon our thoughts are of nearing Windermere
The large hotel on the right, we once stayed here
Sometimes we turn left, down into Bowness
No monsters here—they're in Loch Ness!

This time tho', it's straight on to Ambleside
Enjoying the views along Windermere lakeside
All is familiar, power boats and boats with sails
Reminiscing, we remember staying at the Prince of Wales

Through Ambleside, we approach Rydal Water and all the rage
Is Rydal Mount and Dove Cottage, homes of Wordsworth, sage
Hills, lakes, screes, beautiful scenery are all here
When thankfully, we arrive, this time, in Grassmere.

Harry Kevan

Utopia!

I have been asked to write a poem
So here I sit in the twilight
Pondering and musing with music
Wondering what to write . . .

Words nearest my heart are:
"Knowledge can last
Principles can last
Habits can last, but feelings come and go."

It sums up the philosophy of love,
and is a basis for marriage and humanity,
while turbulence and upset reigns,
it is the rock of reason and sense.

So, enjoy life, do not tarry,
Be prepared to love and marry!
Is it not better to have loved then lost,
Than not to have loved at all?

And when all is said and done,
There is always only One,
Who knows us leads us, guides us—
To the Elysian Fields!

Edeline South

For The Innocents (Dunblane)

In this cruel world,
no one every understands,
how one evil man,
takes lives with his own hands.

What did he have to gain
taking innocent lives,
causing suffering and pain
to all those husbands and wives.

May the sinner of this deed
rot in the darkest recess of hell,
and any evil person take heed,
for that is where you will go as well.

May those little angels who are above,
be united in heaven together,
and may God let them know,
they'll be carved in our hearts forever.

To all in Dunblane,
We cannot begin to comprehend
or measure the extent of your pain,
we can only pray that one day heart's will mend.

Gill Murdoch

Of Childhood . . .

Of happy days in tender years,
a future promise without fears.
Of river boats and babbling brooks,
late Sunday teas and comic books.

Of lazy mornings spent in bed,
With seagulls laughing overhead.
Of pink and white blossom and purple heather,
on summer days that last forever.

Of school, and friends with happy faces,
kids hiding in their secret places.
Of boiled sweets and favourite toys,
shared growing-up with girls and boys.

Of precious love in parents eyes,
Sweet innocence, youth's cherished prize.
Of birthday parties, gifts of things,
then Christmas and the joy it brings.

Of playing cards and stamp collections,
so little time for deep reflections.
Of hours that mark the time for men,
who dream to be a child again . . .

Trevor F. Woollacott

Treasures Of My Mind

We all keep a picture of those that we care for,
a photo kept locked away safe in a drawer.
Mine is a memory, a moment, a thought,
mine is a picture which cannot be bought.
It's not on display on shelf or in book,
it's here in my mind, so I can take a quick look.
My picture's of you and so you'll always be near me,
it's in my mind's album, marked those treasured dearly.

Roy M. Sparrow

Purpose Of Life

Life on the planet can be hell
Many people these days are not well
With the stress and purpose of living
Leaves some less in giving
As such are on the bread line
With nowhere to go and nowhere to dine
In the streets with no where to live
And the government unwilling to give
Although most try things for learning
There's no hope of finding or earning
What hope is left for future times
When there is so many problems with crimes
To help all those less able
Sitting down around a table
Putting people back on the straight and narrow
Giving purpose and being able
To contribute to society's life
Will hopefully prevent further strife

A. T. Higgins

My Dear Teddy Tom

My dear Teddy Tom his eyes big and brown
his ears all bent and worn, his face still has a smile
my Dear Teddy Tom

We have been together for many years
through times of happiness and times of tears
my Dear Teddy Tom

He's always been my friend, he's always been there
when no one else want's me, I can turn to my friend
my Dear Teddy Tom

Through many years we have travelled
and such happy one's they have been
and now you have passed away I shall miss my little friend
my Dear Teddy Tom

And up there in heaven where I know you will be
as you have been the best friend that anyone could be
for I shall miss you dearly
my Dear Teddy Tom

Lynda Jiggens

Museums Of Memories

Factories stand silent
Stark against the skyline cast
Factories stand silent, relics of the past
Like giant dinosaurs, extinct have become
Yet once a place of work
Where adult life begun
No more heard, the sound of machinery
Bursting into life,
Instead the sound of silence
Of poverty, of strife
A place of work, a way of life
Now silent now dead
No more work, no more choices
No more the sound of peoples voices
Just memories ghosts of the past
Are all that now remain
Housed in derelict factories
Relics of a long lost game.
Museums of memories.

James Molineaux Starr

Cuckoo

They say the cuckoo is a lazy bird, but is this true?
It flies for miles, over hedgerows and up in the sky so blue
Watch as it flies up high and then way down low
What is it searching for? I bet you'd love to know.

What is it searching for? You may well ask
It's searching to save itself from a very boring task
It's looking for a well–built nest, to claim as his own
Yes one ready made, which another bird worked hard
to build, but has now flown.

Though people say he's a lazy bird, I think he's very wise
Notice how the nest he picks, always fits his size
No flitting back and forth looking for pieces of twigs and vine
While other birds are working, the cuckoo settles down to dine.

Hilda Stewart

That's Life

Two ideas connect:
Like a jam doughnut and a red apron,
like a china cup and delicate hand,
like a predatory virus and a watching white blood corpuscle,
like a bed-time story and a sleepy child;
moments discernible, time nodes remarked.

Two ideas collide:
Like a new frock and a splash of ink,
like a ball of peony petals and a bouncing dog,
like a table corner, thigh high and an unwary leg,
like a taut temper and a final stretch of patience;
smudges and bruises hanging around for ages.

Why do collisions have more impact than connections?

Clare Farley

Devoted Lover

Mithali "I love you. I love you Mithali"
you are the first girl in my life that has woken up this heart of mine
and made me realise what love feels like.
Well, love to me feels like being hungry,
but when people are hungry they can easily eat something
and if they don't eat something they will eventually die,
but with love you don't die you just get hungrier and hungrier
and as you get hungrier and hungrier it hurts and hurts.
Until the day you are mine this feeling is going to go on and on.
Mithali I love you so much
that I can not take a second look at another girl,
because it feels like I am betraying you,
then I say to myself how can you betray someone
you haven't got but saying this
to myself still doesn't change my feelings for you.
These are just few of my feelings for you Mithali
I can not write or say how much more I truly love you
as it is undescribable unless you could feel my feelings
that is the only way you would know how much I truly love you.

Shahjahan Choudhury

Well And Forgotten

An innocent game, can often turn nasty
Someone gets hurt, deep down inside
Don't know what you're doing, don't have a clue
Then that someone you like, turns away from you.

Go and say sorry, is the answer you're given
Tongue and tonsils tied, this is what you do
Find her, explain, mumble an excuse
She'll forgive and forget, at least that's what you hope.

All's well and forgotten
She's over the pain
Friend's once more
The game starts again.

A new little lamb
Trapped by the hunter
She fights the battle
Breaks free and goes on.

Ilona Taft

The Little Tree

Little tree, you stand so still
Surely the breeze on the top of the hill
Can move your branches and flutter your leaves.
Please don't be dead—have you no will
to live and breathe and move like others?
See all those trees?—your sisters and brothers
They all have husbands and children and lovers
Oh why do you stand so still?

Crisp are their leaves and golden their faces
Remember your buds with their delicate graces?
Move little tree in the cool gentle breeze
For if you die, we'll only find traces
Of where you stood, so tall and so green
On top the hill, like a beautiful dream
Your trunk and your leaves with their infinite sheen
I beg you, don't stand so still.

Sandra Ellis

The Key Of The Door

This key is a special key,
Some would say a magic key,
All one has to do is find the right door,
If you're tired you will find a bed,
If you're hungry there will be food,
If you're lonely, upset or depressed there will
  be a cuddle,
But whatever else there will always be
Mum and Dad here for you.

Jennifer Allsop

The Phone Call

As I sit here all alone,
Staring painfully at the phone
He said he'd call some time around nine,
Maybe the weather's affected the line.
I flick the control to the T.V. set
My mind drifts back to when we first met
A passing glimpse, a quick hello
It quickened my pulse and made my temperature glow
He invited me back to his house for a drink
I really wasn't sure I'd have to think!
With lots of idle talk and chatter
We laughed and joked very little really, did matter
Then at last was that the phone?
I rushed to answer I was not alone
"Hello" I said, "Is that you?"
"Hello Gorgeous, it's you know who!"
"I miss you so", he went on to say
"I've done nothing but think of you all day"
We talked of weather, kids and life
Then he asked me, to be his wife!

Janet Carnell

The A1 From Alconbury To Norman Cross 1996

A changing landscape unfolds
Each day
another building crumbles.
Demolition at the mercy of a mechanical digger.
Relics of the past,
(The Great North Road)
make way for the motorized future.
The landscape, vast, barren, flattened, fen-like
Trees tied up like bundles of bracken
Houses, hotels, pubs, petrol stations
lonely, bare and abandoned
awaiting the inevitable destruction.
Traffic of the future
will soon forget the once familiar
landmarks of previous generations.
Juggernauts and cars speed their way
obliviously and mindlessly
into the high-tech future of the 21st Century.

Helen K. Reece

Time To Go Back Home

All confused all gone astray
Got to hide myself for another day
Live on the edge of a broken town
Where the nose of power finds its way around
Why make a promise that you cannot keep?
Lead a wild goose chase, never lose any sleep.

Sorry old world when dreams turn sour
As the cry of the sycophant echoes louder
Take from the minions who build your nest
No point in wondering "will I fail the test?"
Pity on the prisoner who lives to fall
Shame on the flatterer who stoops to crawl.

Don't break the barriers you'll lose the fight
Never win the war by doing what's right
The plans are drawn so the city will burn
Into the maelstrom of no return
The chief instigator has got no face
Cry requiem for a dying race.

It's time to go back home.

Wayne Weston

A June Death

You can die just as well on a summer's day
The contrast the greater, the flowers fresher
Anyway, tears dry more quickly on warm faces
Inside, desperate for familiar places
Perhaps they thought you would live forever
You didn't

Bob Drury

Sunset

From burning peaks in devil's robes
Our golden angel falls once more;
Raped by cold satanic probes,
Her cries are screams of midnight owls,
Her tears the mist of dusk.
As bloodied lips caress the skies
And darkness clouds those daylight eyes,
A veil of sadness surrounds her warmth,
The moonlit fields her barren womb.
The clutch of evil, its claws of ice
Tear her soft and fertile skin,
Her youth and beauty sucked dry with lust
Her silken mane to ashen dust,
Till all that's left for you and me
Are rings of frozen diamond,
Asleep in charcoal emptiness.

Simon Kelton

A Cry For Help

I can feel an earthquake erupting,
It's coming from inside of me.
My stomach's tightening in knots.
It's happening uncontrollably.

The cry for food still goes on,
but I pretend that I can't hear.
I'm living in a nightmare
as food as my only fear.

I stare into the mirror,
the tears roll down from my eyes,
I can hear them laughing loudly
"fatty", "thunder thighs"

I'm in a state of depression,
It's been going on for a while.
I used to be known as a clown;
but now it's hard to put on a smile.

I know this can't go on,
but soon I want to be able to see,
someone else looking at me in the mirror,
instead of the same fat ugly me.

Laura McDonald

'Neath The Willow

Tonight I heard my lover softly sigh
Beneath the willow where the black water stirs,
And witness to it only were the stars
Whose age eternal silence safe shall keep
That gentle breath that handed me the World
The moment when you whispered that you loved me.

I had not Earthly good nor fame.
No wealth was mine no beauty graced my face
Yet at that instant life became my friend
And slew that mocking demon solitude
And freed my heart to trust, and taste forevermore
The tender sweet perfection of your soul.

Hayley Elizabeth White

First Flowers On Shrove Tuesday

Hedges held fast the skeleton leaves.
Snowflakes swirled in the eddying breeze.
An east wind blew and tossed the pines,
Which squeaked and scratched in serried lines.

Winter pressed down on the muddy beds,
Where miniature irises raised their heads.
Colours splashed in blue, mauve and white
Green swords sheathed in the fading light.

By the gate, a clump of snowdrops grow,
With delicate buds unopened in the snow.
Their fragile stems turn to the fading sun
In faint remembrance of the Spring to come.

Pamela Taylor

All Is Not Well, In The Garden

There was Daisy and Rose, both dancing around, but where was
Violet? No were to be found!
That's not like Violet, to be late for our dance.
Not to worry said Daisy, with a last fleeting glance.
We will dance on our own, in the wind and the rain.
Maybe tomorrow, Violet will come, to dance once again.
The following day, was very sunny for spring, when up
Popped Violet with a sway and a swing.
You started without me! That just is not fair.
Daisy, and Rose, could not avoid Violet's icy blue glare!
Come on Violet said Daisy and Rose, here comes the
Human with his watering hose.
Oh! That feels good, that cool water, when seeping.
Let's wriggle together, before Ivy come creeping.
That Ivy takes over, and is green with envy said Rose;
She turns up everywhere, no invitation, just to pose!
Well, we all agree shouted Daisy, so let it be said,
We have less enough room, with three in a bed.
So we will all stay together, be firm and stand tall:
We will send that Ivy creeping, up the wall!!

Yvonne Graves

Betrayal

I gave you all I had to give,
You crushed my dreams, my will to live.
How could you leave those letters for me to find?
Didn't you know they'd destroy me, devour my mind?
The song you wrote for her tore me apart,
Each word is a dagger in my heart,
When you told her "If you want me, I'm yours",
You can never imagine the pain you caused.
How could you say that in front of my face?
Then walk off and leave me, back to her place?
All the nights I spent at home alone,
Were you with her? Should I have known?
I cannot believe that liar was you,
Was it fun, did it amuse you,
To see me cry, to hear my screams,
To see me losing all my dreams?
What you did to me, you just don't care,
But still when you need me, I'll be there,
When your life is empty, and your world seems black,
You can count on me, I won't turn my back.

Wendy Marshall

Dawn Of Gold

I'm glad we met when we were young, and shared our teenage years,
Despite our parent's disapproval and the taunting of our peers.

I'm glad we stayed the course, my love, and grew with one another.
That we faced all opposition, Love, determined to be together.

I'm glad our path was seldom smooth, that so much was
stacked against us,
For it challenged our love, and it told the world that nothing
would ever part us.

I'm glad that we can remember now, what we were like, when young,
You with your squeaky voice, Love, and me so highly strung!

I'm glad that, nowadays, together, as we sit and reminisce,
How thankful we still are, for all the years, and that first
youthful, tender kiss . . .

I'm glad you've given me all your love, as I've given mine to you,
With no regrets, and no "if onlys" just hearts ever faithful and true.

'Till death us do part'—please God, not yet, though I realize
we're growing old . . .
But when it comes, may we wake with each other, in the
endless Dawn of Gold.

Pearl Williams

"Cold Comfort"

They are gone now—the keepers of the South Stack Light
Reluctantly redundant; while the lamp shines bright,
Remotely automated by electronic wonders,
Impersonal controlling, free from human blunders,
It is progress taking over, where men for centuries,
From Wolf Rock to the Longships, Strumble Head to far Skerries,
have long employed their knowledge,
men's awareness day and night,
Perceptiveness that reaches, far beyond the tended light—
A fishing trip in trouble, children climbing dangerously,
Nesting sites that need protecting, baby seals far out to sea,
These good men have all gone now, no more summer visitors
Beside each fading notice, rusting gates and bolted doors,
For progress has brought emptiness, the soul is not in place.
No friendly word of greeting, no welcome in a face,
Now the light shines out from South-Stack,
far across dark Celtic sea,
And warning boom of foghorn echoes intermittently,
Unseeing lantern eye, that holds cold comfort in a storm,
Where now the helping hand, when seas run high and sails are torn
Who now will watch, who now will comfort bring
And tenderly restore to flight a seagull with a tattered wing?

Mary Purcell-Herbert

"Ben"

Beloved dog, so loyal and true,
For fifteen years I have cherished you,
From skinny pup, with paws so big,
And coat as black as night,
You grew in beauty and in strength,
Each day a pure delight.

You chased the rabbits, teased the cat,
The birds flew off alarmed,
It was all a game to you,
Not one of them was harmed.

I turned to you when in despair,
I needed help, and you were there
With wordless comfort tried to share,
A grief, I found so hard to bear.

Although now old and slowing down,
Your joy of life is still as strong,
Devotion in your eyes still shines,
When, as a pup, you first were mine.

I love you now, as I loved you then,
Please don't leave me yet, dear Ben.

E. R. Dudgeon

Panama Jack

Panama jack in his troubadour hat
Is dealing the deck from the back of the pack
In his riverboat suit he looks like a shark
His fins sticking out again

His holy old boat is staying afloat
Its wheel's spinning round, it's holding its ground
A dollar to share why don't you dare
Get his smoky old table in sight?

A tropical sun is thinking it's won
They sit in the shade watching it fade
They're playing their cards, what to discard?
Down by the green river tonight

Lazy old lil' is fiddlin' the till
She's dressing to kill, she'll give you a thrill
She'll dance to the sound of that hillbilly hound
Round the roulette tables alright

Sheriff redneck he arrives on the scene
With a gun in his hand he's looking quite mean
He's rolling around he's making it sound
Like he's on the attack for panama jack

David J. Hay

Count Your Blessings

It's easy enough to say we should count our blessings
Not so easy, perhaps
When you lose sight of what those blessings are
So perhaps these lines may help us to see how rich we really are

Riches are the sounds of life as each new day is born
Two ears hear and two eyes to see the morning dawn
Warm clothes to wear and two good feet to carry you along
Two perfect hands to do your will and two legs firm and strong
Riches are a loved one there to kiss you when you go
A friendly neighbour at the gate who waves and shouts 'hello'
A sure and steady job in life so you can pay your way
And pleasant folk to smile at you and work with every day
Riches are a free land, where you're not afraid to speak
People with a conscience where the strong will aid the weak
A land where justice is the right of all and not the few
Where children have a chance to grow up strong and straight
and true
Riches are the things we have, but never think about
The precious gifts other nations have to do without
Won for us in times gone past by men long dead and gone
They fought for us so we should count our riches one by one

Matilda P. Fishwick

Mother Nature

Writing this poem to the one I love
thinking of him as I look through my window
my mind strays and looks beyond life as it is
back to the beginning, back to Mother Nature.

I see the tall trees, swaying in the cool breeze
full of energy and life
I hear birds chirping merrily, nobody, just sound
and rabbits playing in the long luscious grass.

I see the flowers in bud, all pretty and peaceful
I see the sun, peeping through the clouds
Smiling down on the young buds, waiting for them to bloom
The colours so beautiful and mesmerizing.

I watch the spiders crawling along my desk,
I watch the winged insects flying past my eyes,
No fear in them, no fear to investigate new places,
Free and happy.

The shining stars appear against a black background
The full moon glows, king of the night
Life is resting, peaceful and calm
All this and more is Mother Nature at her very best.

Claire McAuliffe

Divorce

An ugly word—
So final and so harsh.
Telling of hatred,
And of friendship lost.
A word for the spaces;
Where the wedding picture, used to be
A white patch on the nicotine walls,
And the indentation on a bare ring finger.
We have to learn
The new vocabulary of
Alimony, access, custody.
Words for a world of shattered images,
And the protective walls of childhood
All
   Fall
      Down.

Fiona J. E. Mackenzie

Dreamy Feelings

Your warm embrace fills me with joy and affection.

Your charm and grace is always with me in
whatever direction.

Your smile is a dream come true and in blue times
I think of you.

May there be lots of happy events in our
endeavours that have been sent.

My admiration for you is great and your mind,
body and soul invigorate.

All the pleasures are mine and yours and your face
is one to adore.

I love what you bring to me, because of these I hope
our enjoyment and friendship never cease.

And if I had to give you a petal for all the
charming things I want to say, I'd have to give you
hundreds of flowers, perhaps one hundred a day.

Margaret Tokarski

No Answers

Shall I try to find an escape
or should I stay until I break?
Should I say no or should it be yes
Shall I find an answer or maybe just guess?
Will I act cautiously or just go insane
Shall I not care when they're calling my name?
Do I say how I feel or keep everything inside
Do I face how I feel or run away and hide?
Will I show courage when I need it most
Or will I turn away as danger gets close?
Will jealousy rear its ugly head
And naivete make me easily led?
Who knows the answers to guide us along
And who is to say that they won't be wrong?!

Karen Townsend

"The Highlands"

The beauty of the Highlands I never will forget,
Sheep grazing on the hills, and brilliant sunsets.
The purple shade of the heather, grass so
rich and green.
   Everywhere, around there was beauty to be seen
The majestic mountains with peaks so high that
hold you spellbound, as they kissed the sky.
The eagle—perched high on the mountainside
Surveyed his prey then swoops down.
Suddenly the sound of flapping wings
and the eagle soars with the wind.
The deer in the glen, look at peace as
darkness descends.
   All is quite,
      Another—day's at an end.

A. Butler

Hobbies

Most people have a hobby, fun things they like to do;
You may find the Golf Course beckons, to play a round or two;
For others a game of football, on a crisp October day,
Or perhaps watching your favourite team helps chase the
blues away.

Tennis, rugby or even bowls may suit the likes of you,
But those who'd rather stay in doors will find other things to do;
Perhaps it's snooker, perhaps it's darts, or even dominoes,
Whatever helps you to unwind, to beat those Autumn woes.

For us it's dogs, "Oh no, not again!", I thought I heard you say,
But we're entitled, to decide, how to spend our Saturday;
For just as you enjoy the day out, golfing with your mates,
We like to show our dogs, for us it liberates.

To see our little angel, winning first prize with style,
Makes all the hard work really seem worthwhile.
For to look after dogs takes toil, sweat and tears,
But it's worth it, in the end, when we hear the cheers.

Margaret Bell

The Joys Of Parenthood!

Time to get up
Hear the screams
Ending all those lovely dreams

Just eat your breakfast
Or I will tell your dad
You know what that means
So don't make me mad

Off to school, parents bliss
For the rest of the day, our darlings we miss!

Pick them up
And bring them home
Running and shouting
Endless moans
Not every couple
The chance to show
How they would love
Our children so
On the next occasion, before you shout as you would
Do remember it's an honour, parenthood.

Carol Jones

A Silent Wish

If I was granted just one wish, I know what it would be:
to have my Mum and Dad again, whom I miss so constantly
They leave an aching in one's heart, that just lives on in me
And so I often thank the Lord they both belong to me
We shared so many ups and downs, when life seem sad and blue
But there's no one in this whole wide world, quite like you two
And so my silent wish goes on forever that will be, there
might be an answer, I'll have to wait and see!

P. Holmes

Life's Like A Piece Of Cake

I feel so alone
like there's no one around,
to hear my tears
my life seems so pointless
I have nothing
yes I have more than some people
but I have no best bud
she left me for someone new
I don't have a life
fed-up,
washed out,
old news,
spring to mind my life has been cut up
like cake and too many pieces have been eaten.
I feel so used and unwanted.
I have to go
to find new and better things
to find myself.

Anna McColl

Untitled

Oh! What a busy world I see
With people rushing back and fro.
Houses, schools under lock and key
Crime–ridden cities where people aren't free.

This world runs along at frightening speeds
More cars, more people, more land.
Does anyone think of spiritual needs,
Nobody has the time to understand

That, if everyone had been of the kind
To curb their greed and be content.
To stop and think and calm their mind,
To look above and not behind

Then, the world would be more free
Like me, I'm anything I want to be.
I've papered my walls with the universe
And ride on comets with glee.

From my earth bound wheelchair
I have inner peace and harmony,
Beyond the realms of rainbow's hair
Beyond this world of money.

Sandra Peacock

The Alcoholic's Prayer

Alcohol (or drugs) why can't I see
What on earth you are doing to me?
I have no wife, no home to stay,
Only distant relations who'll put up with me.
Little child to another happens to say,
Why haven't you got a daddy today
Or come to think of it, any day?

The social lady to my wife arrives,
To check how, if at all, they survive,
What a way for a mother and child to live,
Depending on the state for what I should give.

Oh, alcohol, you'll be the death of me,
For no way clear to get help can I see,
Wish to the Lord, someone please, to pray for me,
That out of this state of despair,
The healing words of someone's prayer,
May lift me from this hell I'm in,
To self respect and to love again.

Ann Stevenson

Spring

The snowdrop with its head hung low
Seems to regret the passing of the snow
Frost at night and strong winds that blow
Embers of the once roaring fire still glow . . .

The daffodil blows its welcoming fanfare
From trumpet proud and a yellow so rare
Saying "Spring is coming, come see if you dare
But it's not warm yet, so have a care."

Hawthorn in the hedgerow with flowers so white
Looks like snow has returned for one last fight
But no, that white hedgerow, that magnificent sight
Means that for another year snow has taken flight.

The dawn chorus of birds is pleasing on the ear
Something we have wanted for a long half year
Apple blossom heralds warm days are near
Long hours of daylight, something we hold very dear.

The eggs of birds in well hidden nests
Kept warm by the feathers on the bird's breast
Caressed by soft warm winds from the West
Surely, Springtime is the season I love the best!

R. J. Chapman

The Last Wave

A different place I have fallen upon,
Where the nights are black and the future oblivion.
Days do not exist my soul says to persist.
I have experienced in my life setbacks and pain,
The demons that haunt me I thought once were slain.
They come in my sleep and my loneliest hour,
I try to speak but the words taste sour.
I am in a room all alone memories are my escape,
To unleash this power would mean to climb that tower of hate.
My words are not understood they do not know the meaning,
If you read and understand, it shows that you have feeling.
What will be said of me my work and life,
Can one person be allowed to handle all that strife.
I had it all now I walk this lonesome shore,
I see the sea I can take no more.
Then end is near I show no fear I walk and feel
the embrace of her arms.
Do not weep for me instead you should sleep easy,
in the thought, that my suffering is at an end and my heart it
shall have time to mend.
Dean Marc Brailsford

A Birds Eye View

Looking down upon the world, from high up in the sky,
Wondering what life's all about, and trying not to cry,
Knowing it's a journey, full of heartache and despair,
Giving us a reason for not wanting to be there.

Then we feel emotions swelling up inside,
Love, Joy and anger, and a few more besides,
Patiently waiting, to explode once more,
Into something beautiful, knocking at the door.

Everyday and every night, living in this world,
There's a lamp to guide us, deep within our soul,
Pursuing righteousness, Love and prosperity,
Being generous to the needy, and glowing within you and me.

What happened to self discipline and understanding? It flew
out the door,
A lot of cruelty and greed came in, asking for more and more,
Giving us a reason to try again to learn to live,
The way it was intended, and trying hard to forgive.

Will we ever fathom out the right road in life?
It's the quality of our journey, that's important to drive out strife,
We will smother evil with good, and hate with love,
But,......No where.....is secure,......as I see it from above.
Joan Yvonne Matthews

Pretty Penny

We have a lively six-year-old with lovely long dark hair
She is my husband's pride and joy, he takes her everywhere.
They stop and chat to all his friends, she just waits patiently,
No interruptions while he talks, she stay's close to his knee.

I buy her pretty ribbons, a bright red one suits her best,
And when we go into the town, the shoppers are impressed.
They always want to cuddle her an say "what is your name?"
My husband say's "it's Penny, and she love's to have a game".
When we go on our holidays she's first one in the car,
To Devon, Cornwall, Jersey, she never mind's how far.
Our family say we spoil her and give in too easily,
But it's hard to be firm with her when she smiles up at me!

She greets all visitors with a fuss, there's always lots of noise,
As she rushes round the bungalow searching for her toys,
She gets excited when she hears the children come to call,
They tear around the garden playing loudly with the ball.

Her favourite game is 'hide and seek', she knows just where you are,
Whatever cupboard there's no need to leave the door ajar!
And now it's time to settle down, with a rather grubby dolly,
Yes, 'Pretty Penny' is our lovely cross–bred Bearded Collie!
Janet Davey

The Last Journey

Sleep child sleep, on an angel's wing of down
Soon you will be in Paradise
your earthly life has flown

Wake child wake, hear the angels sing
You will live in happiness
With our Heavenly King

Rise child rise, the mist has rolled away
The Celestial Host is singing
That you have come this day

Laugh child laugh, you have no need to cry
All children go to heaven
The second that they die

Jump child jump, with every ounce of joy
Jesus will open up His arms
For every girl and boy
Norma Stilwell

The Apparition

Ghosts, ghosts everywhere,
Some believe and some don't care.
Whether they're different or lifelike,
either way they give you a fright.

Whispers, whispers in your dream,
Do you listen or do you scream?
Extraordinary voices in a mysterious way,
That's the life of today.

A floating figure across the floor,
Suddenly floats through the door.
Then a voice comes so near,
It's like a mass of total fear.

The time has come for us to say,
Leave us alone and go away.
The presence then leaves, with its smell,
It no longer feels that we're in hell.
Kara Vaughan Skillicorn

Nowhere

I turn to every open door and still I cannot find,
I want, I dream forever more the things I left behind.
I look in every single place for someone who I know,
But bow my head to a stranger's face, in fear that it may show.
I walk an endless, winding path searching for my dreams,
But everything reminds me that it's further than it seems.
I hope one day I will go back to places I recall,
And that some day I'll walk the track where I began to fall.
And so each day I hope for more and no one seems to care,
And thus each day is just a chore, for I am going nowhere.
Debbie Buttery

Untitled

Shaken numb I'm disillusioned,
Creator of visions and illusions.
Magician injured, maimed but fighting,
For a chance of compensation.

How to win this long standing battle
Against the fares of despair?
Where to look in desperation
To find solutions and salvations?

Is the answers with the spirits
are we surrounded in the darkness?
Is the light shining through the gloom
Will the wheel of destiny solve my doom?

What do good and evil mean
Is it a balanced equation?
Or is there no hope at all?
The Seal of Solomon may have the answer
let's rest now, sleep, I've made my computation.
Neil James Smart

I Don't Know

I'm not sure why, but something's not right
Things are too good, too rosy, too light.
It can't be this simple without a fight
But I don't know.

He says he cares and will for an age
But it can't be this easy to turn a page
For so many years I've been in a cage
And I don't know.

Something, a voice tells me not to trust
And somewhere, someone tells me I must
Not fear that tomorrow he'll just be dust
I still don't know.

It's been good and then worsened in the past
I know it's far too good to last
He'll be gone soon, and I know they go fast
I just don't know.

It could be heaven, complete paradise
We'll love each other and talk with our eyes
But it could just end with deceit and lies
I don't know.

Emily Jefferiss

Fragile Moment

Tick tick tick
Breaks the solitary silence,
The constant passage of time
Draws the end near,
So does each agonizing breath.

She recollects when
Her veins burst with the vigour of youth,
Her eyes alight with love, ambition,
Promise.
Time bore no significance then.

Tick tick tick
The mirage—no, fever of love
Swept all caution,
Only the sands of time
Revealed the virus she harboured.

Tick tick tick
Chimes the white tombstone,
The birds sing no more
And the splendour of spring is gone.
This fight is done.

Rosemary Alwoc

The Mary Rose

"Oh! Ancient wreck of the Mary Rose
Preserved in all your glory,
Oh! Phantom from your watery grave!
You tell a wondrous story!"
Rocked in the cradle of the deep,
Four centuries in time now past,
For 'rebirth' in another cradle,
Now gently raised from the sea so vast!
Caught in that strong net, you had no choice,
Trapped, like a monster from the deep,
But now your final voyage is over,
And once more you can fall asleep!
Swinging in your precious cradle,
Till you rested safely on the barge,
Your canopy soon to be removed,
To display your gleaming hull so large!
"So, Ancient wreck of the 'Mary Rose'
Enshrouded in mystery,
Henry VIII would be proud to know
You've 'come up' in history!"

Violet M. Malone

Dreams

I looked up and you were stood over me
Your eyes were shining so bright
Your skin so pure as you reached for my hand
And led me dancing off into the night

We bounced over mountains
And ran through the vales
Or we'd just lay for hours
Into moonlights we sailed

We conquered the world
In just over a day
A tear in my eye
As I begged you to stay

You were so handsome
So pure and so right
So strange, yet my lover
Who came in the night

And I'll always need you
My heart sings your song
And in the morning I'll wake up
And once again you'll be gone

K. M. Perry

London

On the embittered, emblazoned plane of past found glory
Where historical prestige has come and gone
Lie guns, banks, bombs, bullets.
And the lonely ones
Where upon dishevelled vagabonds challenge affluent
notions
Then comes reverberations and tense despair
Of muddled currency deals amidst innocent squeals
Beware like a thief comes daily grief
With the mind rattling around materialistic confusion
Where aristocracy's function is mere tourist fodder
Reminiscent of once fortunate times
When suddenly darkness descends
All is tranquil
Except for the forgotten ones befuddled under bridges
With associated squalor lies betrayal
Betwixt failed politicians and beleaguered bankers
There goeth capitalism creaking relentlessly towards chaos
The sparrow coughs at dawn
Facing fore square a polluted city
Meanwhile the rats multiply.

Finnan Boyle

Irish Eyes

When Irish eyes are smiling that's the words that are in the song.
But sad to say they have been filled with
    tears for so very very long.
A God given country of beauty of that there is no doubt.
But the people should look in rather than look out.
Many have died, many have cried
For a cause to them was justice and true
Some believing in the green, other's in the blue.
But what if it happened by some twist of fate
They believed in brotherly love, not of hate
No more killing of the innocents by either side
No need to cower but stand with pride
Live in peace, your destiny to be in control
No need for armed soldiers your streets to patrol
Children not knowing hate would be the order of the day
Catholics and Protestants together in the street would play
But sad to say, that even today the killing goes on just the same
For many it's heartache, others a sad game
It seems peace won't come for quite a while
Oh! When will we see those Irish eyes smile.

James C. Finnie

Out Of Darkness

If only we can keep forever the ones we love.
But it can never be and they leave us to grieve.
For all our years remaining, never gaining understanding,
Why it should be, that they were taken, so soon from me.
The only comfort to you now, you brought a glow
To their lives in the brief time they were here,
So dear were they, but surely they would say,
"We made the best of each day allowed us,
Don't fuss, there are some who take our place,
The love you see on their dear faces, will say it all.
We fill the gap for you, don't be sad all life through,
We bring joy again to that heart, so full of pain,
Please smile again for all our sakes,
All it takes is one fresh start to make life worth living,
So do not fear the days ahead, don't frown, but smile instead".
And we will soon be giving what you miss
A loving kiss from the heart,
Just one kiss,
It is very plain,
Will make you happy once again.
Freda G. Tester-Ellis

Untitled

A voice inside keeps telling me, 'Don't do it, for it's wrong'
Whilst many more keep coaxing, 'come on now, you be strong'
A constant battle in my head, I'm trying hard to win
So many people want to help, but I want to be thin.
When you look at me, what do you see?, you say 'you have no bust'
All I can see is flabby thighs that fill me with disgust.
People keep on asking, how did you get this way?
But I don't have any answers, I don't know what to say.
Why do people start to smoke? Or drink until they're ill?
Why do people dye their hair? Why do others kill?
I wish I could be happy with the weight I'm meant to be
I wish I'd never dieted, I wish I could be me
I wish we could all look the same, then I wouldn't have this fear
I wouldn't have to try and make the fatness disappear.
I wouldn't have to worry, if I weren't the ideal weight
I wouldn't look in a mirror, and see a body that I hate.
I know one day I'll beat it, you can be sure of that
The doctor says I'm dying, but I'm scared of getting fat
So from this day let the battle commence, I know I'll be just fine
For all the ones who love me, let the victory be mine.
Susan Cutler

Sweet You

The sky was blue, the day serene,
When you appeared upon the scene
The impact you made upon my heart
Meant you were mine, we'd never part.

Your eyes were blue, like the sky.
When I looked in, I thought I'd die
Lean and tanned, with arms so strong.
Tenderness and love also came along.

Our wedding day was two year on,
Your folk and mine bursting into song.
We made our promise, like all the rest,
Just a boy and girl, but we knew best.

The years have past since our wedding day.
We've had our troubles along life's way.
But with two fine son's we've been blest
Just like you, they always do their best.

Four lovely grandchildren, they're so sweet.
And their mums, that's life complete,
Now and forever pray we'll be,
A happy, caring, loving family.
E. J. Bishop

The World

The trees, like the wind is blowing
Harder than it has done before
The birds are all rocking and shaking
The leaves they all come to the floor.

Why is this earth so demanding
We haven't done anything to blame
If we have we don't know about it
And maybe we would hang down our heads in shame

But why does it go on hurting
Hurting, when we've done nothing at all?
So if anyone out there is listening
Please, please, hear my call.

Save us, and all of our children!
Without this life where would we be?
I dare not think of the consequences
I can't look that far ahead and see.

But life as we know it, is a mystery
There's no-one can ever explain
Why we all of us go on living
In this world and why? We must suffer such pain!
C. Stearn

Uppish But Safe

Beneath a mighty willow tree the tiny Morris stood
Impervious to what might be, when ball impacts on wood.
While Mary and her happy band prepared their glorious tea
of homemade scones and strawberry jam; at ninety-two for three.
In walked Arthur Blewitt, complete with floppy hat.
At eighteen stone, a giant, with a quite gigantic bat!
His partner, at the other end, a lad, who, still at school,
Was told, "Don't run out Arthur. That is the golden rule.
The Blewitts run the village pub, the only pub for miles.
We have a vested interest in keeping him all smiles!"
They trudge an easy single, so Arthur keeps the strike.
To Arthur Edgar Blewitt all bowling comes alike!
One pace, then crack, the ball departs through cover point for four.
The next ball is a 'Jaffa', so Arthur doesn't score!
To miss a ball is sacrilege . . . at least in Arthur's book,
So much so, that his next ball receives the Blewitt hook.
Up and ever onwards, the ball flies o'er square leg.
The scorer knows already it's six more runs to peg.
"'Twas probably the biggest hit yon park has ever seen,
But poor old Arthur's Morris now needs a new windscreen!"
John Eden

Taking Part

The trumpets sound, the flags unfurled
Above the best in all the world,
From every country they emerge,
Beneath the five rings they converge,
The will to win, to play the game,
Burns bright as the Olympic flame.

The years of training, sweat and tears,
The highs and lows, the hopes and fears
Encapsulated at this time
Of waiting at the starting line.
The crowd is hushed, the time has come,
The bodies tense, there goes the gun!

Muscles and tendons stretch and strain,
The goal's in sight! Ignore the pain.
Eyes sting and burn, each rasping breath
Sears the skin of throat and chest.
They pass the post to wild acclaim,
But win or lose, they've played the game.
F. Gerrard

Cardboard City

It really is such a pity.
For all those down on cardboard city,
It makes my old heart flutter,
Hearing them moan and mutter.
When I see them in the gutter,

Leaving home they take flight.
For a place they must fight,
we would have an awful fright.
While dreaming in our warm beds at night.
Of ending up there, "As we might".

With their heads low in shame,
I wonder if they have a name.
A lot of them are very young.
It really cannot be much fun.
To be forever called a "Bum"!

A fall from grace, do they deserve?
They really do have lots of nerve.
For some bread they do crave.
If we help them we could save.
Some ending up in an early grave.

Janet Allwright

Beauty

Beauty is a joy forever to me my mother told
Beauty is a thing of nature that my eyes behold
Beauty is all around us we see it everyday
Beauty is the things we do and the things we say

Beauty is the way we love all that's dear to us
It's in the hands that heal the sick and in the hands that fuss
Beauty is in the woodlands, see those mighty trees
How they spread their leafy arms and wave them in the breeze

Beauty is in the lush green grass we tread beneath our feet
Beauty is the newborn lamb as it utters its first bleat
Beauty is the flowers that grow from out the earth's brown sod
Beauty is a sweet green pea as it swells within its pod

Beauty is in the air above in birds that gracefully soar
Beauty is on the wild plains, in a lion's throaty roar
Beauty is deep below the sea that flows the earth so round
Fish that swims in shoals and in the seas abound

Beauty is the coral reef in seas so lustrous blue
For in the colours of them all there is a lovely hue
Beauty is all around us but if you think awhile
There is nothing quite so beautiful as a face that has a smile . . .

A. H. Wood

Mislaid Love

The nights are long, the days are cold,
The feeling is of growing old,
She doesn't want to carry on,
Her spirit is becoming wan.

He used to look at her and smile,
Their secret code when love was new,
Now love is lost, will it return
It's place taken by another emotion which has come too soon,
He doesn't bother to make her swoon.

She longs to hear romantic words,
That once he whispered on his breath,
All he thinks about is work,
She is lost somewhere in the depth of his vague memories of love.

What makes a man change so soon,
So quickly to forget to touch,
The person that he said he loved so much,
Can it be security, knowing that you are loved no matter what,
He will never know what he has missed,
He has simply—forgot.

Rosie Woodhurst

Seasons

What is this teasing softness in the air
That makes life tremble in anticipation?
Shyly, but with growing confidence
Spring's joyful delicacy and flare
For pristine loveliness is here.
No bashfulness as riotous summer throws
A Joseph's coat before our jaded eyes;
Colours urgently jockeying for position
And glorious perfumes, for who knows
How long this artistry will last
Till first a gradual and subtle shift
Begins within God's palette and the harvest
Like a ripe voluptuous woman
Flaunts herself, showing off her gift,
Before autumn fades, and creeps to hide
Beneath implacable winter cold.
Rain that chills the blood, and hail
Smarting, stinging, arrogant and bold,
Till teasing softness tempts again.

Ann Jackman

Reflections

Always ours to love, never to own,
It's a joy to share, when a child is born,
A new life so precious, a gift from God.
We have so much to learn, about life and love.
In sickness and health, we guard every step,
We watch them grew up, almost, every need is met.
Then suddenly we realize, it's time to let go,
Love gives till it hurts, yet we stay in the flow.
This wholesome love, is love at its best,
The true value was hidden, till we were put to the test.
As a child of God, we grow in faith too,
With many painful steps, for me, and for you,
Some fall by the wayside, and others turn back,
But we carry on looking, for something that lasts.
At the end of the day, when we look into our hearts,
We'll find Jesus was with us, right from the start.

Kathleen McBurney

Man's Best Friend

They say that a dog is a man's best friend,
That he's loyal and faithful, right up to the end;
Well, I really believe it, I know that it's true,
No matter what happens, he'll stick right by you.

When you are walking side by side,
Holding your head up, glowing with pride,
People admire this handsome pair,
They even openly stop and stare!

To see such a friendship between dog and me,
Makes them quite envious, and I'd be first to agree;
There is nothing quite like the bond we know,
It is special; a love that continues to grow.

Right through both our lives, 'til death us to part,
But the love still lives on—
In our memory and heart.

Barbara Arundel

The Dreamer

In the eye of the dream the beloved sleeps,
Images of life flicker and are gone,
Dream worlds arise then vanish,
In immensity the great wheel slowly turns,
Spinning out its trees of time bedecked with life,
Still the dreamer dreams, deep purple images of unreality,
The dream takes life, knows hate, fear, love, death,
Believes because of this that it exists,
In its distortion thinks itself as separate
A living dream within a dream,
Unheeding proud and arrogant
Unquestioning, it goes its way within the dream,
The dreamer and the dreamed, are they one?
And when the dream is ended, what then?

Robert F. Ward

Life And Lives

We are the belonging to the unknown, the places we cannot
reach at this moment in time, where people we love and care
for have gone. The place where the gates open and close with
every second that we breath, where time and people travel to
different dimensions and the belonging and destiny takes
them. We should not cry forever for the people we have lost
as their time is still but not with us.

We say our lives are complicated and full of pain, when
really we should be thankful for the time and life we have
and can give, for our moment is sacred in this world that
we live our life in.

Thank you for giving me this life
and for you both being my chosen mum and dad.

Suzanne Rees

Live Life For You

Do you feel all your responsibilities upon you
Insecurities, unsurities all around
Do you wish you had planned your life differently?
Do you feel there are no answers to be found?
The children, the partner, the mortgage, the bills
Commitment in the making of that choice
Do you feel everyone else must come first?
With the commitment did you also lose your voice?
Look at the life you live, question the dream
Face reality, it is not all that it seems
Shout out loud, for a life that is your own
Give yourself back to you, take time to be alone
If you don't, what then have you to look back on
Children grow, leave home, have their own fun
Then, will you sit there with a lifetime of regret?
Hating yourself for always saying "No, not yet."
Look around and take some life for you!
At the end of life "to one's self one must be true."
Remember, in this life, you only get 'one shot'
Go on, take it, secure it, enjoy the lot.

Denise Sweeney

The Little Fly

The silver pearl glistens
Like a single tear drop
A bubble of water as it sparkles with
Rainbow colours
It rests upon the spindled web
Flying happily along, unaware of the dangers ahead
The little fly gets tangled in the thread
Out of a dark tiny corner
The big spider appear
And the silver pearl splashes into a
Thousand tears.

Noosha Zabiela

Waking

I awoke one morning in a happy frame of mind
A new day was here, and I wondered 'what kind'
Would it be happy and free from stress
to keep me in my mood of happiness.
I peeped out the window with hope in my heart
as to whether the sun was shining, or not.
But saw once again the rain coming down
and the wind was blowing the leaves round and round.
But I cheered up again when I thought that today
I would spoil myself in every way.
A bath with my favourite bubbles and smell
the newest of lotions to my body as well.
So I indulged in spoiling myself in that Room
happily dreaming, with no sign of gloom.
I dreamed I was flying through the air
like a bird sailing onward, without a care.
Knowing that soon, I would land and see
the wonderful world, and I was free.
I awoke with a start when I heard a voice shout
"Are you ready yet Nanny, you're taking me out"

Alwynne Jones

On Moving Into Town

I listen and hear nothing—no beloved woods here,
No owl sits on these roofs, scolding the owlets for not
attending to
their hunting lessons.
No fox barks as he sniffs the air for rabbits.
No wild flowers hide behind old tree stumps, or big protective
clumps of grass as nature intended.
Here, the flowers are set out neatly in beds.
No longer can I stand near our pond, watching Mrs. Moorhen
and family, or the beautiful grey heron fishing hopefully.
There is no pond here.
Unable to sleep at times, what joy to wander the woods—
glimpsing
a deer and hearing rustles and squeaks.
In spring the nightingale sang—but not here.
So many little animals to see while I sat on a log,
The field mouse, the rabbit and ever hungry shrew.
Here the night sounds are, Voices, Radios, and Car doors.
here just a few wild birds. The rest are in cages,
As I am in a cage with invisible bars.
And on sleepless nights, my heart silently weeps.

Eileen J. Landon

Summer Love

Summer love and heated passion;
Obsession, possession and so much more.
The moon, the stars, the wind and sea.
More precious than those, most precious to me.
You were my world, my life, my heart
But then you ripped it all apart.

The tears I cried, that pain inside.
Those wicked dreams I dreamt each night,
Of me and you embraced so tight.
I'd wake, then break.
When reality dawned, you were not there and so I mourned
All over again.

Then winter came,
the birds are singing and people are living,
and so am I
I do not cry
For you
No-more.

R. Hargreaves

'No Better Friend'

You'll never find a better friend
She'll care and love you till the end
Her warmth and charm shines through each day
In a countless number of special ways

She's always there when times are tough
To help you through the smooth and rough
No-one could ever take her place
She's a credit to the human race

Her love grows and grows with each passing year
She'll guide you through your every fear
The person I am talking about
Loves you dearly without a doubt

So when you're feeling down and blue
And really don't know what to do
Just stop, and think, who's always there?
To comfort you when in despair

When you come to your conclusion
There really is no confusion
You will, then see, when in need of a chum
There is no better friend, than your Mum.

Nicola Laidlaw

Heartsong

There was no flash of lightning the day we met;
No thunder growled—the skies were silent.
The stars continued in their course,
Unportentous in their eternal harmony,
Unmoved by earthbound tragedy.

You took my hand and smiled;
And forever more my heart you'd hold,
Unknowing, in your own.

From whence did it spring,
This love; this love that you can never know?
Your life, your heart, are sealed elsewhere
And, bearing fruit, fulfil an eternal destiny.

And so I linger near, watching, loving, dying;
Yearning to speak the words
That would change the planets in their round
And bring celestial worlds crashing to the ground.

But silent I remain, and so will do
Until a new earth and heaven enable you
To know my heart and, maybe then, to take
My life to yours, eternally.

Angela Barratt

Simple Souls

Simple souls breath awhile in regular time,
Breath out your languid air,
Bellow the cool coals that cumbersome ill fit,
So warmed round a fuller figure,
Smooth, so in unison sit.

And they will not crack with unruly unrest and rigour,
For the heat will not sear or let smart,
But tame the hapless meddler
Who rues the day he denied his soul life's bread,
And denied the love in his heart.

Charlotte Homer

Untitled

As I sat in the park, to rest for awhile,
A cheery voice spoke, and gave me a smile,
Hello! I said, how are you today!
I'm very well thank you, my name is May.
Why are you sitting here, all alone,
Have you no family, and where is your home,
I live in a cottage, across the park,
You should go home, before it gets dark.
May I come with you, the cheery voice said,
I will be good, and was nodding her head,
Oh! Come on then, we'll have some tea
Goody! Goody! She said, and was dancing with glee.
So a pleasant day it was for all,
I really thought, I had been to a ball,
Then my little friend, was waving good bye,
As I looked up above, to the stars in the sky.

Elsie Keen

Inquisitive, Sacred Essence.

I'm safe, secure, in surroundings that are known.
The atmosphere is soft, calming, relaxing,
The beams of light, a delicate pale yellow.
The immortal psyche is at lay,
At lay around me breathing on my skin.
I feel aware, but at ease. Its aura smooths my being.
Gazing into the sky, drifting into deeper spirits' arms.
They pull me to them, but reality holds me down.
I want to let go—I need to let go.
Empty, dark space fills my eyes,
Silent air penetrates through me.
The moon; my God, whispers,
The stars; my prophets, wink.
Eternally searching for my inner self—my soul weeps for help.
My body is at present, my mind is echoed hence,
I call upon identity—I'm still dreaming.

Deborah Carol Hughes

Out Of Reach

Outside as the night nears
in my eyes so do my tears.
For you I cry my heart away
waiting for that special day.

In my mind I know it will never come.
This leaving my heart empty and numb.
I hear you call my name and I see your face.
But when I open my eyes you're gone without a trace.

Dreams are beginning to be my life
dreams of you and me, your loving wife.
No one could ever replace you.
Nor could they do to my life the things you do.

So how I here you say could I ever feel this way.
Well I do each and every day.
Try to picture in your mind my pain
and remember that I really am sane.

Maybe one day someone will see the light
which burns in my eyes so bright.
Maybe someday someone will notice me
but I know in my heart it will not be thee.

Ellen Miller

A Perfect Loss

Crushed velvet cover with satin so sheer
Set close to the skin to feel the fear
Sliding of silk with sinful shine
Shadows of near indulgence, a fragrance divine

Blending the breathing with delicious adornment
Savouring a delicacy with every moment
Sensing a cymbal crash after the snare
A slice of passionate perfection for the aching pair

One! Two! One! Two! Sees through the lies
Oops, sorry luv! Brought them down from the skies
Weeping and groaning to slaughter the aura
Back with the knitting, ignore the snorer.

Marie Joanne Levine

Sadness Of The World

Why do we fight,
When the world is in plight.
In need of great love and devotion,
People are dying from sickness and greed,
With only a few who can see their great need.

Why should our world be like this.
We could have freedom from want
and destruction.
If people could see, all that others
can see.
We would love all the world as
one family.

J. Chamberlain

Death's Release

Nurse entered the room so scented of lavender and forget-me-not,
In her hands the tray bearing the cup, the saucer and the pot.
Upon the bedside table it's now so gently placed,
Refreshing tea inside the pot Madame will never taste.
Her meagre few possessions scattered bout the room,
That now does serve the purpose of a temporary tomb.
Mementos of far better times earlier in her life,
When once a treasured mother and beloved wife.
But in more recent years life's not been so kind,
Her children gone, husband dead, dementia of the mind.
As she rests there icy cold, her life's last breath now gone,
There's no one left to mourn her, nor mark her passing on.
But it matters not now who is there,
She's not worried nor does she care.
Look down upon her as she lays in this last place,
She is no longer troubled held in deaths most cold embrace.
Her haggard, ashen, aged face no longer strained nor pained,
Instead a contented restful mask, through deaths release obtained.

M. Knight

Lie

When I look back, not long ago.
At things I've learnt and things I know
I wonder why I didn't do, the things
I've missed and never knew.
Or say the things I should of said
but I never learn or use my head
as life goes on and passes us by
one day older, one day less to die
it's the way it is, it's a fact of life
it's sharp and it's cruel and cuts like a knife.
'Life should be fun' I hear them sigh
but don't you believe it, it's just a lie.

Lynne Daniels

Great Grandmother

She's very old, yet reigns supreme
Straight backed, tight–lipped
Hands clasped before.

She cannot hear, so does not talk
Yet with her wishes so enforced
One trembles to agree.

Her hair is white and held in place
So not a strand may show
Beneath her hat when she goes out
To say her prayers each week.

Thank God I'm clean, white, pure in thought
Without the vices of this world.
How others live she dreads to think
Why can't they be like her?!

Eunice M. Birch

"Dreamy Little Number"

Into bed he hopped to slumber
wearing his dreamy little number
woolly socks to cover one's toes
preventing one's tootsies being bold
peeping out the duvet
to brave the cold.

Woolly hat to finish the attire
cutting a dash to relax and retire,
water bottle to keep him warm
to cuddle and help him greet the dawn.

Rise and shine the alarm is ringing
forget the cold the birds are singing,
Step into gear and make a brew
Come on man, what's up with you!
Take a shower and get yourself dressed oh,
and don't forget the woolly vest.

Dorothy Norman

The Maid Of Orléans

All in an afternoon they came, my voices, clear and still, from
the church tower at Domrémy pealed the bells that stirred my will.
Saints and angels at God's hand called me forth to save the land,
I thought awhile, my poor soul shook, to take upon me such a yoke,
a girl from farm and peasant stock; I could not turn the tide.

A vision blazed into my mind by some unearthly law,
the Saints all stood in glory, calling me to war,
The King he sat before me, a weak man it was true,
to trust upon a farm girl—was that the thing to do? I told him
God has sent me and how I heard each voice, from Domrémy
on horseback I'd come with little choice.

Priests and Generals helped me not my people to deliver, but
Orléans was in my grasp beyond the shining river. The King
was crowned, my task was done, then came the fateful hour;
captured, branded as a witch, endued with Satan's power!

Wild flames leapt about me and jeering filled the place, my saviour
I'll not doubt thee, I would behold thy face.
Bright golden realms of rapture were opened wide to me, I love you,
blessed Jesus, I have come home—to thee.

Richard Langford

Introspectiveness

Flying through your dreams as though you understand their meaning,
gliding past the stars, on a high, softly gleaming,
waiting for the one of whom your love will go,
dreaming past the hours, which light you aglow,
feeling through the sorrow, anger, pain, fear,
wishing that your loved one will soon reappear,
missing all the joy you had when you were young, carefree,
Sorrow feels the place where you will always end up lonely,
feeling happy, meaningful, bursting to get out,
anger grabs a hold on you, enslaving you throughout,
all you've worked for torn away by people who don't know,
by understanding other's feelings, their trust will flow,
Murmuring softly for the ocean to still,
Calmness is as clouds, the soft blue sky they fill,
Anxious for the day when all troubles will be gone,
I would carelessly sit this moment out thinking of the one,
She knows that one day this will all be a figment of mind,
Happiness is only what your inner-self can find.

Paula Franks

Love

What is love? I ask you!
To me, it's thought, and care,
Togetherness, by the fireside, with memories to share.

Good breakfasts, in the morning,
An umbrella for the rain
With tenderness at evening,
A kiss, to ease a pain.

Where does this feeling come from?
It must be from above,
That binds two people strongly,
In everlasting love.

Ethel McColl

Daniel—A Lament

So very dearly loved —
So warm, so vital, so alive,
So cruelly struck down—just only five.
So debonair, with so much zest for living,
Alas no more, bereft—no future giving.
So very greatly missed: Oh Cat Unseen,
You hold that very special place
Midst memories ever green.
Lie easy in your cottage garden bed—
Honeysuckle softly whispers o'er your head—
Whilst bird song mingles with the falling leaves—
And silver'd moonbeam its own magic weaves.
Here Matthew sleeps, the Academic One,
Some six years gone.
In these familiar ways,
You passed your 'playboy' days,
Requiescat in pace, Oh beloved pet,
We will not forget.

Maria Anna Hones

Across The Sea

You're miles away and I'm not there,
Don't think I've forgotten you, don't
think I don't care,
I play a song and you're by my side,
I can feel your presence and how I've cried.
Wanting to tell you how much I care,
Of how much I miss you wanting to be there.
I never realized how much love hurts when it's not to be,
When I'm so in love with you, but you're not
in love with me.
It's longing, wanting and emotions being thrown away,
But it would have been worth all that
just to hear you say.
You're missing me too and coming home tomorrow.
To mend all this heartache and take away the sorrow.

Vera Margaret Collins

Cry With Me

That unwelcomed parting, no help was near,
My love so blind, now only fear
Pangs or remorse, bring better tears to me,
Please pick up that phone,
And cry with me.

I look for you, yes for you, only you,
I think of you, yes of you, always you
Every night that goes by
My thoughts are of you,
A call from you, what ecstasy,
Please pick up that phone,
And cry with me

Yes there is hope, someone to care,
You were born, with the right to love,
Mem'ries we all share,
Stop close your eyes, open your heart,
Then pick up that phone,
And smile for me,
Yes pick up that phone,
And smile, with me.

V. C. Richards

Twelve Lines To Midnight

Like stars, they burn themselves out,
Saturating their souls with stimuli,
Alive only, in the noisy fast lane,
No reflecting, live for the moment.

Knowledge, puts paid to observation and reflection,
We've had our innings, image, image, image,
    Another civilization, bites the dust,
        come Islam, rule.

The south warm and strangely silent,
The north cool anticipating apathy,
And in between to summarize,
The west to dawn, the east to rise.

Liam Brennan

Summer

In summer the sun shines down on me like an enormous light bulb,
Black birds fly across the blue sky like a small paper aeroplane.
All kinds of birds twitter and sing in the morning sun.
Green grass covered in white daises like a green and white carpet,
Red and green apples grow and fall like winter snow.
Beautiful coloured flowers grow as tall as man in huge groups like a hedge,
Butterflies flitter and flap up and up like a piece of
paper floating in the blue sky.
Badgers hunting for food like man hunting deer.
In fields people having a picnic, crisps, cakes, jelly,
and sandwiches, an enormous party.
The blue sky, no clouds, like a sheet of blue paper up up and up,
A beautiful summer every where, sun and blue sky.

Victoria Baker

My Imagination

Figments of my imagination
opened to me through illumination
shed light on the shadow monster
who keeps you huddled in yesteryear

hiding only from your fears
imaginary feelings imaginary tears
who was it that made you hurt
pushed your face into the dirt

only you, you senseless fool
could find a way to be so cruel
can't you see the mess you've made
out of life you soon will fade

So figments of your troubled mind
have closed your eyes and made you blind
open up and you will see
life is so illusory.

Shaun Hopkins

"Barriers"

Contentment makes its way to the heart,
The warmth of this experience causes,
Icy emotions to thaw,
Drawing eternal love to call,
It breaks all barriers, burns all bridges,
And leads the last card to fall.

It undresses all experiences of life,
Not everything is ever perfect,
But when you loose something invaluable,
The price means so much more.

Carrying the message of each passing day,
And the ability to chase all those closed feelings away,
But the experience has profound meaning,
An intense purpose of sense.

To feel someone else's mercy,
Abandon all attempts to win,
In your mind's eye, and begin to take a long look inside.
Wild the power wisely, and you will create the answer,
To the deepest mystery, the purpose to meaning of life,
And to whatever it is that you truly treasure inside.

Nicola Robertson

Just One More

Walk one more road, say the king of the mind just
    one more day away
Just one more sword, to be pulled from the stone
Just one more dragon to slay
Just one more medal, to pin on my chest just
    one more girl on my arm
Maybe the battle that I win today
Will prove to the world I'm a man

Just one more quest, say the King of the mind
Just one more corner to turn just one more friend, to be on my side
Just one more lesson to learn
Just one more pearl of wisdom I need
Just one more piece in the plan
For I must learn what I don't know to prove to the world I'm a man

Stop right there say the love from my heart
That's just the play of your mind
He's well intentioned, he's brought you this far
But he's deaf and he's numb and he's blind
He loves you alright but he's programmed too well
He tries, but he just can't believe
He thinks that he's empty he's searching for love
And he's always living in need

Phillip Millichip

The Urban Tiger

He's haunched alongside the waterhole watching for the
Canine
Warthog:
Man's best friend.
When out of the bush, movement?
Again, and again, the metronome ticks.

Looking on he watches the rhino halt,
All occupants alight from within,
With this action suit armoured predator's begin to stalk the plain.

Held high and only shown briefly,
Cased rifles appear.

He, the mannequin adopts his role with pride
A sphinx guarding a small town in Texas,
Defending the ancestral rights of this primeval urban Tundra.

His feline spinal stones arch upwards toward the key stone,
Quietness, the predator strikes, a kill held within hands
    covered in silk.

A talon clad paw extends out to touch the metallic antelope,
The lid of the skin shines whilst hunger looks on.

Stephen Maughan

Rest

Within this scattered universe where mortals come and go,
the power of which there's no disperse took the dearest soul I know.
I saw what only others see to the bareness of the eye.
But the veil was lifted as it where, Ere I could fly.
Beneath, if only you could see as I, and share the joy of a
peaceful soul enshrined in a holy spiritual glow,
With a prayer of thanks to this unknown power, which most
of us term God.
I left only the carcass of the dear one that meant so much to me.
How wonderful said I to me, to have seen beyond the bones
and flesh and realize the soul's at rest.

Gladys Lyndon

A Sonnet For Emma Louise Gosden

It is hard to express my feelings,
With this paper and pen.
I wish I could see you again.
I have only seen you twice in my life,
But I wish I could take you for my wife.
I would give you love and devotion.
Whoops there goes my writing pad,
That was poetry in motion.
You probably think I am average,
To me you are the moon and stars.
I know you go for teenage boys,
That brag about the size of their cars.
    Just being your friend is good enough for me,
    Every time I see you I always feel happy.

Jason Foulkes

Forgotten Facts

In appearance, not very attractive,
Tattered, faded and sad,
Someone had been going on holiday,
And I had been packed in their bag.

Accidents are quite horrendous,
This crash was no exception.
I only survived by a 'whisker.'
Dumped in a Jeep, then hastened to garbage land.

I'm bulky with lots of adventure,
Romance, and murders not a few.
Beginning in space, following life's race,
Then finishing with a hopeful view.

Wisdom, conveyed by example.
Experienced, it thrills to the core.
Nobody pays attention.
In aeons past, I was adored.

I'm sad, but not dejected
Perhaps with an enquiring mind—hands will reach over
to leaf through my page? Have you guessed?
I'm the forgotten Bible, rich with 'new life.' Come and delve.

A. R. Harcus

Inner Combat

A barrier is created, we are
strangers on familiar land.
I long to reach out to touch
What was once mine, but can I reach?

I stretch and faintly feel life.
But the pulse is slower, not dead.
Just slower. I search inside
To cure this, but why? It's not my beat.

The beat picks up, a smile and
Kind words, which are soon destroyed.
A wall now between us, stronger.
I can make the climb because I want to.

Half-way, disheartened, is he making
The journey up the other side? I'm not sure.
I reach out to help him, our fingers
Do they touch? I long for something to forgive.

Natasha Low

Words Of The Imagination

We exist in a world of Words, overflowing to the brim,
Some, . . . are fresh Words that ventilate the air,
But, . . . words that sting, bring weeping eyes, so dim,
While other Words, are illogical and should not be there.

The farmer sows the seeds, and the poet speaks the Words,
Joined and separated Words, as in execution,
Words of dignity, like ancient swords,
And, the softly spoken Words, we hear through elocution.

Nagging relentless Words of mental cruelty,
Words of longing, Tender, Kind, Enraptured,
Ghostly Words that linger into eternity,
Hypnotic, dramatic, insensitive Words are then recaptured.

Sensuous Words of love whispered in suspense,
Kind or harsh Words and some aptly spoken,
Troublesome, criticising Words all so tense
Spinning 'Out of control' Words always being broken.

Words that distract, and some that disgrace,
Whatever the language, the Words mean the same,
Proclaiming the Words to the whole human race,
Words, forthright and true, they are all in the game.

Joan Y. Matthews

Beauty Of The Night

Stars lie silently in the moonlit sky of this land
like millions of eyes cast away from there souls
they watch over us.
The moon in all of its splendour beams out light
as pure as snow which is like a fountain of
silver decorating this imaginary land with
indelible flashes of colour and beauty.

A gentle breeze whispers its way through trees
and hedgerows caressing their leaves, softly
weaving its way from branch to branch.

Unprovoked the dawn chorus begins and soon
the night shall be over, all dreams locked
away until the final light of day has peacefully
slipped into the arms of the night once again . . .

Nigel Troy Mitchell

The Dress

I wore this dress the day you died,
And, as I animate the housewife our parents advised become,
I catch a reflection in the window glass
of the flowers in it.

I agree, it is very much the kind of dress
Mother wore,
You used to attribute mother for everything that didn't
happen in your life,
It was your life you know . . .

Marica Druskovich Clarke

Fate

I've watched the blossoms forming on the trees,
And flutter downward with the breeze;
Have seen the bluebells bloom,
And fade away so soon;
Nature gives, then takes away,
Regardless what we do or say.

Have noticed people praying on their knees,
Yet suffer awful tyrannies,
Seen children laugh and cry,
Suffer, shrivel and die;
Nature gives and takes away,
No matter what we think or say.

Most people search and strive for precious peace,
Others are restless with unease,
Wild wars proliferate,
Sending souls through Hell's gate;
Man can give or take away,
Regardless, oft, of what we say.

Elwyn Williams

Love's Needs

The need to love and be loved is born within us all,
not knowing why we seek it, or wait for it to call.

A bright light in the darkness, to follow when we're lost.
A pathway we must walk along, whatever be the cost.

This chain we forge together, the fetters we all bear,
a symbol of submission of which we proudly wear.

A silent bond between us, it could be just a glance,
a cry that we must answer, and never leave to chance.

The pain it brings, the hurt we feel, may seem a hopeless task,
but this we have to suffer, when we choose to wear love's mask.

What is this gift that we all seek, this precious thing called love?
yet often when we find it, place other needs above.

Don. Stone

To Say Good-Bye

The wind blows gently through the trees
The answers lay softly on the breeze
As you ask yourselves again and again why
while you hang your heads together and cry

The tears that fall, full of hurt and pain
As you look around at the memories that remain
A drop of rain falls from the sky
As you know you have to say good-bye

The sun will shine and warm your face
Knowing in your heart there is a place
A place of peace, a place of love
A place as peaceful as heaven above

Gayle Bruce

Loving You

"Love is blind," (or so they say)
But my love for you sees clear as the day.
It knows no bounds, is endless as time,
Finds no faults, (save for those which are mine).
My heart cries out when we have to part,
As empty as the night when it bears no stars.
The sound of your voice, mere mention of your name
Sets a pulse pounding, like a hammer, in my brain.
"Will we be together forever you and I?"
How the voice that speaks is like a devil inside.
Breathe deep your scent, lest I forget
The taste of your skin, should we ever be rent.
Two halves of the same cannot live alone,
My soul is content; it has at last found a home.
So tell me you love me; words of such bliss!
And then, oh so tender, offer me your sweet kiss.

H. Smith

Untitled

Lots of people say I'm a flirt,
But I never mean to hurt,
You're the only one I really love,
And I'd never give you the shove,
It's only a bit of fun,
It's not as if I've shot someone with a gun,
It doesn't mean anything to him or me,
So please just let me be,
Now we've finally got together,
I hope we'll stay that way together,
I love you with all my heart,
And I'd die if we fell apart,
I haven't seen you for a whole week,
And my life has been really bleak,
Only 10 more days to go through the pain,
then we shall be together again,
School is such a boring place,
But with you there's a smile on my face,
I can't survive without you
I love you, I promise, I really do.

Helen Vowles

My Beautiful Dream

"Finish your `A' levels, go to university, and get a good job",
Mum and Dad's dream was for me to be at the top,
They had good reasons but I had a dream of my own,
When I told them they would always moan,
I knew they would not understand,
So everything was in my own hands,
I had a beautiful dream to fulfil,
I really wanted to make it real.

While walking along a quiet street at night,
"Could you spare some change Lurve?"
Asked a homeless man sitting on the street's curb,
I felt down so giving him money made me feel better,
"Thank you" he said "You look glum what's the matter?"
Later he gave me some precious advice: "A dream comes to
life if you make it real,
Work hard to make it come true, the world's yours for taking, it's
no big deal",
So I did work hard, singing and singing, all day, all night,
Making sure I had my tone, my vocals, my lyrics just right,
Now I've made it as a pop star and my family are with me all
the way,
I filled their dream but especially mine,
And at the top is where I am hoping to stay!

Shaila Karim

A Musical Valentine

If Music be the food of love,
Then listen to me, how's this,
'Tis with pleasure I want to hold your hand,
And our love to be sealed with a kiss.

With a girl like you to think about,
It's not unusual to find,
That you really and simply are the best,
And you are always on my mind.

I'm head over heels in love, I know,
It may sound soppy, but it's true,
That you mean everything to me,
And I'm gonna keep on loving you.

There are little things I'd like to say,
But my Darling all I ask of you,
Is to say I believe, when you are told,
I love you, yes I do.

To you I want to say wonderful things,
Although I'm a poor man's son,
The perfect way of doing it,
Is to say them one by one.

Geoff Middleton

Durham's Dark Stones

The dark stones poked through the earth, new to light of day,
Peasants pondered on their worth, some threw the stones away.
Others tested, probed—and lo! Words flew from soul to soul:
The stones were now a fiery glow and proclaimed the birth of coal!

From meagre holes to shafts profound the coally diggings grew
Half–naked men strove underground, to shovel, pick and hew.
Headstocks against the skyline, seams well belong the sea,
Black wealth poured out from every mine to bring prosperity.

Hordes came along on eager feet to join the Durham clan
The march of pit boots down each street grew louder with each man.
The bounteous work and steady wage tempted the needy swarm
Rejoice my lads in this new age, but with it comes the storm:

A pit explosion blasted out, among so many others,
Sobbing women were without husbands, sons, and brothers.
Bitter strikes and hardships and a despoiled country scene
Fouled–up rivers and black tips where it was ever green.

Durham's collieries are now gone, the rail tracks quiet and still.
A coally age has all passed on, the landscape now tranquil.
Full circle has the wheel spun round, no more coal to be won,
Green shoots and blooms poke through the mounds, as the
dark stones once had done.

H. Knox

Autumn's Soliloquy

I never knew her beauty fair,
E'en whilst I saw her regal there.
My eyes were blind, I could not see
what now I miss whole-heartedly.

My mind with other thoughts was full,
and daily routine took the rule.
And in my heart, so full of care,
her fragrance failed to reach me there.

Until the winter slow crept in.
Until, so slowly, hushed the din
of thoughts and cares I thought were all
that mattered, until came the fall.

And only then I realized
the loss of one I should have prized,
but was no more, least for this year.
And only then—the silent tear.

Thank God for giving chances new.
For opening eyes to see what's true.
That in this world of cares and woes
He shows this love, in a single rose.

Wendy Berry

The Sentinel

A Panorama wide and clear
Perpetuates in crystal air,
(Across the seas of Puget Sound!)
An Olympian Grandeur to confound . . .

A back-drop cut by Nature's hand—
Gigantic! God's Eternity!—of sea and untouched land:
Of islands clothed in golden shades,
With trees a spectrum—reds and jades—and blues that only
    distance fades.

To dominate this peerless sight,
The Sentinel—Mount Baker—rises to majestic height,
Like a dazzling snow–capped cone, it's sheer above a range
Of lesser snows, unknown; set in Time, they're programmed
    not to change!

Far beneath the endless sky Mount Baker is at rest;
Clouds may cloak the lower peaks, but seldom reach its crest.
There is no date to mark its age, as rings inside a tree;
It cares not of the World's events that strive to set life free . . .

Mount Baker is a sign-post where mountain ranges meet;
The Cascades share this Beacon-head, like Sphinxes at its feet!
They flank the coastal shipping-lanes—they're near the
    planes above!
But it's that great old Sentinel—That's the one we love!

D. R. Payn Le Sueur

The Saviour Of Man

Learning, culture, social graces
Wisdom, wealth, man seeking status
Equal rights and education
But what of love?

Luxury homes, faster cars,
Man in orbit, sighting Mars
Party politics, progress, power
No time for love!

Divided nations, loss of life,
Passions, greed, religious strife.
Starving children, arms outstretched
In need of love

What to teach a new generation
Tolerance, justice, integration
Love thy neighbour, all creeds and colour
For that is love.

Man needs firm ground beneath his feet
A family home, a safe retreat.
And back to basics, his saving grace is
A woman's love!

Isobel Gunn

"My Quiet Friend"

He was my quiet friend, a gentle silent snail.
I let him slide along my arm and leave his shiny trail.

I kept him in a jar and cared for him quite well.
I used a sticking plaster strip to mend his damaged shell.

I liked to watch him stretch and knew just where he hid.
He liked to go to sleep curled up right underneath the lid.

When autumn turned the leaves from vivid green to brown,
I took him to a sheltered spot and gently placed him down.

Returning to my home, I closed the garden gate.
Despite my tears I knew he had the right to hibernate.

The speckled thrushes sang their greetings to the spring.
I thought about my quiet friend and his awakening.

The summer sun was warm, and on my path I found
A thrush's anvil with its proof, shell fragments on the ground.

Was this my quiet friend? My tears fell all the faster
For as I searched the silent shells, I found some sticking plaster.

Jean G. Pedelty

Flora

Under your hands, plants flourish, pansies turn
Twin-coloured faces to the sun; tendrils climb
Skyward on latticed wood. Roses gleam and fade,
shadowed by sun-fringed leaves. They're all your children.
You, to them mother and sister-soul, dark one,
Never happier than when with grimed, green fingers
You loosen soil about their lifted stems,
Giving their dry roots rain, to nourish them.

Under your shadow hands, rockeries glow,
Thrusting tumescent stems between ridged stones,
That speak a language of distracted love,
Foreign to sound, quite undecipherable.
Commune with it, close with it as Time's
Passing does, when the Beloved, walking at evening
Among awaken flowers, stars your glazed eyes.

Alan C. Brown

Since

Where have all those years gone,
How did time pass so swiftly by,
Since you were cradled in my arms,
Since I sang you lullabies?

How long since a tiny, trusting hand
Was held safely in my grasp,
When a kiss made everything better
And tears turned quickly to laughs?

Since that day of your dawning life,
Since I watched you learn and play,
Since trying to smooth life's rocky path
And guide you carefully on your way.

Since the beginning of time, to eternity,
Until that time all mothers know,
When I have to love you most of all
To set you free and let you go.

Gilly Lancaster

Sleep

Amber morning, subtle in approaching dawn,
glides across a misty, dark and outstretched form,
That in sweet slumber still succinctly lies.
In fingered light, until the darkness dies.

What strange and sombre night-time dreams remind,
Reverberating round a sleepy mind.
Inhaling passion in its drugged demise
That shutters all reality with ease.
Our foes lie still while lovers plan their scorn.
A sideshow for the past approaching morn
Whose symbols scattered on a coloured floor
Will make you shudder, then will be no more

Patricia J. Baldwin

Path To God

God, You are the light to my path
as I move forward in my life
to think of You is all I need
in Your wisdom You plant that seed
don't look back there is no need
all sins are forgiven if you but try
to do God's work you don't ask why
all you have to do is try
God is all goodness all else is groundless
God is meek and humble of heart
to love God you are not apart
you walk in His footsteps
as all prophets did
was not easy as God did say
go down on your knees and pray
God knows all we do
He was human just like you
in the midst of all that pain
He died on the cross He rose again
this world He made new again

Elizabeth Docherty

The Common Market

Now what is wrong with fish and chips wrapped in a newsy scene
Why should we use the camouflage that other countries seem
To thrive on; I don't care if I should lose the 'Frenchies' handshake
For I likes me drink in glasses, not soaking in me pancake.
So you can keep your crepe suzette and hope your soufflé rises
If I wants a steak, I cooks a steak, not warm meat in disguises.
I'll have cods roe not caviar and greens instead of sauerkraut
And me rice I'll have as pudding washed down by ale or stout,
At least I know it's not been made by help of people's feet
In shoes and socks they pick the hops me grapes I likes to eat.
So I'll have boiled beef and carrots and I'll thrive on mutton stew
No bolognaise nor pasta will I gorge
And I'll leave it to Antonio to toast with macaronio
I raise my glass to England and St. George.

Pam Owers

A Pet

Sharks would eat your
head off if they had
a chance,
so if you're really stupid
you'll try and make them
dance.
If you want a shark
for a pet
don't bring it to the vet.
If it wants something
to drink don't give it
beer, cause it'll go crazy
and laugh and sneer
So Beware
A shark is mad, it'll eat your mum
and dad, wouldn't you rather have
a cat or dog a monkey or maybe even a frog

But not a Shark

Stephanie Mahoney

Angelic Child

At night when you're in bed asleep,
I creep upstairs to take a peep.
You lie so still your eyes shut tight,
Your fair hair fanned like golden light.
I steal a kiss, and stroke a finger,
Then tiptoe to the door and linger.
The floorboard creaks, I turn around,
I'm sure you heard that lonely sound.
You gently stir and give a sigh,
But still don't wake, or even cry.
I leave your room and close the door,
And need not worry anymore.

Catherine Worthington

Untitled

Oh sweet child with the exquisite smile
Come to my side, bide with me for a while
Tell me the things which you most want to do
In your childhood years, of which I have only a few

I indulge in your laughter it's the best drug I know
As you shout and cavort while you play in the snow
Your radiance surrounds you as you smile at the door
While you stomp and you bash the frosted snow to the floor

I wonder if you realise how little time we own
Would it have been easier if we'd never known
We could have lived out our lives sadness never conceived
Instead we count each day as a bonus happiness, granted, achieved

I'm a weary old man and I have seen so much sadness
But you my sweet child have rendered me so much gladness
Now your illness has consumed your little body right through
I only wish that I could have died, and given my whole life to you

Janet Fry

The Gift Of Love

What have we achieved when the end of our day is near?
Our bodies are old and have no further use on this sphere
All you can do is lie there still, too much effort and pain
your energy is nil
But you opened your eyes and your hearing was good
You saw the children you cradled you adored and loved
They stood near by your side you saw the pain in their eyes
You heard their hearts breaking as they said their goodbyes.

Lynn Johnson

The Surf And Its Lover

I hear a sound like "Ah-ha-a-ash-shing-mm"
Of rushing currents bound for the shore 'n'
Bouncing upon it forevermore . . .
Coming still, rolling, thunderous,
Glorious, majestic and tall!

All drops dancing as one
Since the first dance was done;
Set into motion, each soaked in place,
Sunk into sponge of sand
Exciting the figure and shape of the land!

Receiving the wet again
Never a trace to remain of
The crest from which it came,
Followed by another
Receding teasing wave!

On down the shore's line,
Carefully to rest
Dressing the frame of the sea;
With a refreshing spray of white foam lace
To bless its virginity.

Mary Ann Marmont

The Garden

A sun–filled summer morning
in the garden
is a joy too good to miss.
The quiet hush as the day begins,
then bird-song,
swallows and swifts in flight
the cry of a lone gull overhead
is bliss.
Cloudless blue sky,
perfumed roses, foxgloves, delicate columbines, lavender,
bless the gardener.
The laburnum tree cascading yellow blossom
young blackbirds and sparrows
new to the world
looking round in innocent wonder.
These are the delights of the garden in summer
everyone's birthright.

Linda Matheson

Untitled

Here are all the pictures.
Linger if you will
over these spent days.

Over the brown river is the stone grey bridge
where the winter Sunday walkers
linger to hold time.
By the pregnant waters are the drowning trees
and the soaked black–leaf path
where the November robin sings.
Beyond, is the field that the midnight frost
makes silver.
Under this heavy steel sky
that lights the hills so hauntingly,
like the day-ghost of dead years,
are the earth's bones,
where memories sleep.

O my love, we have no tomorrow
for it is always today.
Linger if you will
over these spent times.

Katharine Ewart

Mañana

A lazy spring afternoon curls around eternity like the snoozing
of a cat,
Soft lace clouds gently sway to the sweet music of the breeze.
The blueness of the sky protects us from the evil unknown mat,
Let my eyes settle on what they know so my life can float like
a cloud at ease.

The faint smell of daffodils dances hypnotically around my
relaxed frame,
The trees move at ease as if teaching the birds they too can dance.
Children and mothers meander home, each singing voice
sounding the same,
None can shake my mind from this beautiful, willing trance.

I don't worry that these days may turn dark once more,
That the clouds might tumble to earth like a broken dream.
For today I sit on a sand laced Elysian shore,
And every sound and silence is adorned in a hazy purple beam.

Mañana, then I will move these weary but resting heels,
For today my mind doesn't wish to read my palm.
For this day I float with purple buses and sing with delinquent seals,
Today is not tomorrow, may my absorbed mind remain calm.
Mañana, sweet Mañana

Simon Jude Deacon

Happy Birthday, Mum

Words are such simple things, and don't seem quite enough,
To thank you for all the love you give, when things get really tough.
You kissed my cuts and bruises, and played your 'mother' part,
And now you kiss my pride and tears, when someone breaks
my heart.

Never one to accuse or judge, you let me live my life,
Although this means I seem to get into trouble and strife.
But you're always there to pick me up, and laugh me
through the pain,
And be the shoulder to cry on, again, again and again.

I thank you now as you've watched me grow, from a child
into a woman
For all your gentle guidance, that's helped me find out who I am.
Without the love or understanding, which you gave to me so free,
I wouldn't be who I am today, and I certainly wouldn't be me.

Grandma would be proud today, for all your beauty and grace,
Not only in your gentle heart, but in your loving face.
She spoilt you with many things, that money could not buy,
Which you gave to your tiny daughters, so that we
in turn could try.

And now it is your Birthday, a celebration of your life,
Where you in turn have butterflied, from girl, to woman, to wife.
You think of it as another year, but to me it's a little bit more;
More time to show I love and care—that's what Birthdays are for.

Louisa Baylee

Losing Myself

I feel I want to run away
but others I will lead astray,
My friendships are gone
my dreams and my fears,
Do I feel anymore
have I lost all my tears?
Can I be someone else?
I can't stand being me,
Can I be somewhere else?
Will you now set me free?
What is this pain and sorrow I feel?
Can anyone help me, am I lost, is this real?
Somebody help me, which way do I turn?
In the end I suppose, it is that I shall learn.

Adele Walker

An old distant cry

"The Turkish fleet makes for Cyprus"
an old distant cry of a Venetian sailor
ghostly echoed on the Kyrenian castle
and the rough rocky seashore,
reached the 20th century senator,
his English counterpart mediator,
his Christian allies of NATO,
but remained cool and idle.
Their Othello, the valiant noble Moor,
trapped by a Machiavellian whore,
deprived of his mighty roar,
could no longer stop an Ottomite invasion.
At 4:00 am on a misty Saturday morn,
the 20th of July 1974,
the Turks waged a bloody, vicious,
ruthless, easy, profitable war.

George Eugeniou

I Love You

Did I tell you today that I love you?
Did I speak of the way that I care?
Did I say all the things that my heart feels?
Did my words hold my love in the air?

Did I tell you today that I love you?
Did I say that I'm glad that you're there?
Did your soul hear my words like the rainfall,
Or more as the trumpet's blare?

I tell you each day that I love you,
Sometimes the message is clear,
Sometimes my words lose their value,
Sometimes through anger or fear.
Sometimes part of my meaning gets blurred and is lost,
But always and ever I love you, always I'm glad you are there
And when I tell you today that I love you,
You'll know that the thought isn't new.
It expresses my heart and my soul's thoughts, there since
beginning of time.
I'll tell you today that I love you,
I'll tell you I'm glad you are mine.

David John Brand

The May Blitz 1941

The night they bombed Coopers, I will never forget
The destruction was horrid, Park lane was a mess.
Churches and stores, houses as well
The place looked like hell
Paradise street existed no more
Almost every building lay piled on the floor
The road's impassable not one foot of space
Men digging for survivors' tears
Straining their face.
Blackened smoke choked by the fumes.
Searching the rubble that were
Yesterdays homes.

A. Connolly

Survival

A chill wind hustles through my being and I wonder
Why, without known reason,
The warm golden face of compassion changes to
Bleak winter in a flash.
Is this the rust of self doubt eating into our
Silence of understanding?
Is this the end of loving and the beginning
Of regret, the end of living and the onset of survival?
I am a survivor and so are you.

Eve Unwin

The Troubles

An empty street, too dangerous to walk through,
An empty pub, too silent and still,
An empty family who can only feel nothing,
An angry gunman, ordered to kill.

Everyday life has been brought to a standstill,
The idyllic landscape can only seem bleak,
It only rains bullets and only shines fire,
A once vibrant people can now barely speak.

Salvation was a peace conference,
An expensive piece of paper signed,
Hostilities were forgotten,
The old differences thought to be left behind.

Now once again the hush is shattered,
The paper blasted along with the streets,
The people and cities will carry on bleeding,
The politics lost in despair and deceit.

Kathy Burrell

Ode To A Turnip

Ah! Life giving fibrous tissue!
Revivifying root!
Easy to cook, nice to eat,
And cheaper to buy than fruit.

How then shall I praise thee,
O culinary king?
The food of Lords and Ladies,
No ordinary thing.

Behold the shape deific!
Behold the form divine!
A pointy bit, a straggly bit,
Best cooked in boiling brine.

Where does this wonder come from?
Where can it be found?
Where else but in the garden,
That sacred, hallowed ground!

Talked about with laughter, and for a pittance sold,
Yet in times of hunger, worth its weight in gold.
The turnip is the finest food, found beneath the sun,
But the best place for a turnip, is in my tummy tum-tum!

George Edward Pain

Untitled

What is a father?
Or should I say rather,
What is a dad?
A man I am glad to have by my side.

To talk to and share with the things
On my mind,
To laugh with, to cry with,
When the facts of life seem so unkind!

A man who I'm proud of and pleased to
have a near,
A man whose love to me is very dear.

A granddad for my precious son.
Who I know your heart, he has surely won.
A mate for my mother,
Like you there's no other!

Lynne Turner

T.V. Frenzy

Oh little box, box of dreams, box of joy,
See how you smile, and fool, and toy.
Counting out your every fee.
Fixated — hypnotized,
Staring softly—mesmerised.
I am escaping into thee.

Oh cunning box, box of fools, box so coy,
Your rolling sea, of grey, so sly.
Stealing my reality.
Addicted to your highs,
Attention now adrenalised.
Inducing every fantasy.

Screaming box, oh box of screens, do you lie?
My hopes beheld within your eye.
Media my remedy,
I hear your echoed sighs,
Singing louder than my cries.
Imagination rescue me . . .

Sarah Walker

Springtime

Now that spring is in the air
The birds and bees are everywhere
The blossom is blooming on the trees
And the snowdrops and daffodils are feeding the bees
The birds are making their nests in the trees
While the ladybirds are sleeping at ease
And the wind is blowing through the trees
The sun shines brightly in the breeze
When summer comes the sun will shine
And that will be the end of
  Springtime

Jamie Roe

Tramp

As I bent down towards you
You nicked a chocolate bar from my bag
You thought I didn't see but I did
I turned a blind eye
Your need was obviously greater than mine
You, with your scrawny dog
And the plaque around your neck.
And yet you stood up
On legs which you appeared not to have
And walked away.
Taking with you the hat
Which I had so generously filled
From my now depleted purse.
And where did you go to as you mocked those
Who you knew to be less fortunate than yourself.
And did it not occur to you beggar
That you are the unfortunate one.
The lemonade man with the champagne lifestyle.
Go home beggar
And see if your conscience will let you sleep.

Cath Townley

Someone Somewhere

There's a loneliness in my heart I'm feeling
There's a loneliness in my future
I'm afraid of seeing
A loneliness only one can feel
The emptiness, the frustration
The sheer desperation.
Nothing I do seems to change my fate
I've tried so hard
Please don't tell me I'm too late
If only someone, somewhere
Could listen and want to care
And show they'll always be there
I know then my loneliness would disappear
Because then I would have found someone at last,
To love me and be sincere.

Elvina Coombes

Into The Third Millennium

The hand that stirs the Millennium bowl is knurled and worn.
Those hopes that were so high are now forlorn.
That withered hand soon to be at rest
Stirs wearily. The aged soul distressed.

The hand now stirring the bowl is soft and smooth.
Her other reaches down and does the newborn soothe.
Potent her brew a drink for every human being.
People living in closest harmony: Agreeing.

What is this brew that fires the soul?
That thinking people seek—extol?

First, she saw people learning.
For understanding and truth yearning.
Then she saw co-operation and order.
Gone greed, hate, power hoarder.
She saw nations planning: Applying vision.
Applying wisdom and the fair decision.
Finally she saw in all things—effort,
And realized the rewards effort brought.

Learning, order, vision, effort
L.O.V.E. is the message she taught.

P. Churchman

Torn Apart

Please help me understand why many parents today,
Never together stand
They never seem to stay with the program
Then you're left with children like me,
where their heads all in a jam
Thinking who's side should I be on
When what I really wanted was for them to get along

I wish my parents could have stayed together
I wish our happy family could have lasted forever
I love both my parents so very dear
Now they've grown apart and I find it hard to bear

I wonder if they ever thought of me
Were they so blind that they could not see
How my heart bled, from not wanting this to be
With all this pain how can my heart be free.

I really need their help, but they cannot see
How much all this is affecting me
They said it was painful, that I'd agree
But deep down inside I wish they would see
That special love they ripped from inside of me.

Leomie Huggins

Serenity

There are goals towards which people strive which are
meaningless to me
Money and fame and a star-studded name are to some a priority
But as for me I'm a simple soul and not too hard to please
For I possess all my faculties and I'm thankful to God for these

For I am sound in life and limb; I can run and I can swim
I'm blessed with voice and ears and eyes and I can see the
starry skies
I can dance and I can sing and hear the birdsong in the spring
And watch as children laugh and play and wile the happy
hours away

I'm free to wander where I please through forest glade and
leafy trees
In meadows yonder I can dream, meander by a winding stream
And I have time to stop and stare at nature's beauty everywhere
And I'll express my gratitude in every way I know I should

Some folk give their wealth for pleasure
My freedom is a priceless treasure
I can watch the world go by
For I am rich beyond all measure

All the world can envy me
For I've achieved serenity!!

Mary G. Kane

The Lady Of Beauty

In this world of illusion,
Kindness and generosity are mixed
One person,
The lady of beauty,
Stands alone.

Her soft tender face,
Is turned towards the sunlight,
Her expression is unknown,
She lifts up her head.
With her floating garments surrounding her,
She is like a silk flower.
Her petals are the garments she wears.

The unicorn comes,
He walks steadily beside her,
Like the guardian of her soul,
He is devoted to her.
The lady of beauty.

On a sweet sunny day
never forget this pair, for they,
Are the dwellers of true love.

Natasha Grunberg

To Be A Butterfly

Oh to be a butterfly and flit from bloom to bloom
On resplendent wings of gossamer, casting shadows without gloom
To soar above the tallest stem and dwell in gentle breeze
Exposing to the warming Sun an image which must please

Is there memories still of days before your world became the air
When you crawled around on the earth below and could only
upward stare
When an expedition was required to access the nearest leaf
And when caught upon its verdant plain, to be regarded as a thief

Few friends you had in those days gone bye, you were but
vagabond or food
Avoiding powder, beak and claws was all you understood
But oh those days are best forgot now you have made it
through at last
To this carefree life of fluttering grace, though it will so soon
be past

The fleeting days you have are few in this heavenly estate
So savour all the blooms you can, before it is too late
Before the sparkle leaves your wings and your colours
become dull
And that gentle breeze deflects your course against your
strongest will

Then sigh your last with gratitude, this life was such a prize
Given to only the very few—who metamorphose.

Robert A. Walkert

Hampshire Rivers

Poplar and willow lined
they smoothly,
meandering,
ripple their way seawards.
Gentle and crystal clear,
weeds waving,
speckled trout filled
sleekly, fishily swimming.
Calm, placid and quiet,
smooth flowing
they gently move
south to their salty homelands.
Paddling place for children
their weirs;
picnic places
for families being happy.
Escape for men fishing, relaxing
at peace. Their world with nature communing.
Such beauty slow flowing, just curving,
quietly through meadows of gently sloping downlands.

Pat Rees

Market Day

How I yearn for the old market days,
When things were sold in the old fashion ways.
Hens in crates and eggs on plates,
Real pork in pies, pigs' heads with eyes,
All the goods on open stalls
Not from antiseptic halls.

Cheese and butter from the farmer's wife.
Not St. Ival or Country Life,
Fruit and veg. in wicker baskets.
Not in bags of see–through plastics,
Ducks and geese full of cackle,
Drovers coming with their cattle.

Villagers from off the hills,
Meet once a week to share their skills.
Now all that has passed, away,
We all live life the modern way.
It's take the car and quickly park it,
Whilst we all shop at the supermarket.

Gladys Rapson

The World About Us

When the moon is slowly rising o'er the mountains far away,
when the blazing sun has dipped beneath the sea.
You may stand and gaze in wonder at the flowers along the way,
and the many beauteous things that you can see,
at the many fields and meadows scattered round in different hue
on the gently rolling hills that you admire
when early evening stars show in a sky of palest blue
and cirrus clouds are blazing strips of fire.

Harold Guttridge

The Bronte Sisters

The smell of a book tells a story itself
The scent from the past gathers dust on the shelf
A timeless perfume of the pen fills each page
Giving life to ancestors from a forgotten age.

The faded yellow pages of a well worn book
Move closer to history with each loving look
The hard shiny cover is an open welcoming door
Unlock it, step back in time and explore.

A few short hours and the story is over
A well trodden journey from cover to cover
Back it goes on the shelf with extra care
Until another eager traveller finds it there.

But how can we ever in those few hours of pleasure
Begin the pain and care to measure
Of the hand and heart that worked the pen
And never knew their own worth then.

That picture would make the blindest eyes weep
But reader, theirs will not be an unquiet sleep.

Barbara Wilson

Blessed Are The Peace Makers

When countrymen stand against countrymen
Brother against brother.
When children's minds are warped with war
and we are made to know the score
A woman sits and mourns her loss
she weeps aloud as she counts the cost
No husband
And now her son she's lost.
What is land worth, when soaked in blood
and men lie dying in the mud.
Oh why, oh why must there be such pain
Why can't men be brothers again?
Is it not time at last
to awaken and learn from the past
and then once more hand in hand
people join from every land
and peace will reign throughout the land.

Josephine Holmes

On A Carpet I Ride

Whoosh!
Here I come I'm on a slide
Spiralling downward on a carpet I ride
The farther I go the faster I get,
Up and down like a sleek corvette,
When I get to the bottom I wave my hands,
As I fly right off into the sand,
I get straight up with carpet in flow,
It's off to the top for another go,
Whoosh!

Stefan Seddon

Time . . . Did, Can, Will . . . Change!

Who was I, am I, will I be
Where was I, am I, will I see,
The future in their minds, thoughts, looks,
The past is told in history books,
But the present is our time . . . to change.

We bring creature, children, into this world
Oh poisons, crime, vandalism, addictions, uncurled,
but development, recycling, good things as these
New life in ground, the air and seas,
Standards set today, for those tomorrow on their way . . .
change.

So let us care, do what we can
It's not too late to lend a hand
Cut out the bad, bring in the good,
Clear up our mess, as we always should,
Together we stand, to make time . . . change.

Rise up, dry out, stamp it, nurture,
Clean up, recycle, here comes the future,
It's not so hard to do today
"Help out" they asked from yesterday
We did, we can, we will make time . . . change.

Dawn Wright

The Four Seasons

Spring is here yet once again, I realize with glee;
When I look out of my window, the blossom trees I see.
Crocus, snowdrops, daffodils, stand covered with morning dew;
Signs of life are everywhere, all fresh and crisp and new.

Later come the summer months, with all the joy that brings;
Like roses, strawberries, butterflies, and hearing blackbirds sing.
The farmers busy in the fields, harvesting ripened corn;
While many gardeners everywhere, mow their fresh green lawn.

And as the nights start drawing in, autumn calls once more;
Children scurrying to the woods, gathering chestnuts off the floor.
Leaves are swirling at our feet, after falling without sound;
Red, brown, orange and gold, are the colours all around.

Gradually, the air turns chill, snowflakes start to fall;
Christmas trees put up again, with baubles, lights and all.
Snowmen standing in the garden, with pebbles for their eyes;
Christmas Day is here again, it's sure to bring surprise!

The Four Seasons have gone once more, another year has too;
We promise we'll do more next year, but it seems we never do.
And though the world keeps turning, and time goes ticking by;
With friendship, love and honesty, we can surely reach the sky.

Diane Kryger-Collins

Freedom

Freedom you're no angel you're the devil in disguise
You take my hand and lead me. With your silent lies.
You take me to the alter, of dishes, full of woe.
And what you really think I guess is, now you have a go.
The Lord is good they say—the devils not too bad.
But in the end you know yourself—it's really rather sad.
Oh freedom—so and find yourself and lead out sigh of good.
For in the end I think, you know, you really should.

John Henry Williams

Spring

The Spring of the year is a lovely time, it heralds in new life,
when young mens thoughts go out to love and the prospect
of a wife.
The daffodils have dropped their heads, the snowdrops gone, I fear,
the crocus too has disappeared, but other buds appear.
The cherry trees, in full array, put on their best pink dress,
but when it is discarded, we have, oh such a mess!
It makes a lovely carpet—our lawns take on new hue,
but underneath are daisies and dandelions too.
So many shades of green we see, in meadow and in field,
we eagerly await our gardens a spray of colour yield.

Our lives are so much like Springtime, we start from a seed,
you know,
some turn out like weeds and perish and some just flourish
and grow.
Some sting peoples lives in their passing, are colourless,
boring and sad,
but other give brightness and pleasure and make others
happy and glad.
And just as each flower is different, our lives are quite varied too,
God planted us all in His garden, so now it's all up to you.

Doreen Cragg

Blinded By Love

She was so sweet and kind
so I thought, that I must have seen blind

When we got wed, she gave us her bed
then suppose she must have been red

Then I thought she was changing her ways, from bad to good
'maybe'
after I discovered I was pregnant, with our first baby

As the years passed her moods went up and down
she seemed to take delight in making me look the clown

My husband went to my mothers, my sister was there of course
he told them a few home truths but they had no remorse

Days passed they never came, only sly comments and sneers
I said it didn't bother me but inside I was full of tears

Then finally they ignored my children so innocent and shy
I gained in strength as they walked passed watching my
children cry

'Though I'll never in my life understand
how a mother can make so many demands

Still I'm getting there slowly but surely
An epileptic who can't afford to get poorly

So I vow; not to be like her, I'll be a good mam
and I'll do for my children all that I can . . .

Ruth Smith

Memorial Evening Of Musical Fame

Outside Queens Hall I read, all seats sold,
Toscanini's first appearance.
Music lovers throng to wonder and behold,
at his genius and power.
From floor to roof the hall is packed,
Tense excitement fills the air.
The orchestra enters and starts to tune,
One hears the whisper he is there.
He appears amid great applause,
Raps sharply with his baton,
The performance has begun.
Material things fade and die away,
As a world of beauty holds sway.
The brass, woodwind percussion and string,
Are moulded together one living thing.
They quiver and sigh like wind in the trees,
The timps thunder their message like angry seas,
The concert is over, the people inspired,
Of continuous applause they never tired.

E. F. Ballard

Futuristic Vision

A lonely crossing by soul alone
Lord knows that I am flying home
Through misty waters in sound–filled waves
Back to the land of forgotten graves
Past ruins of an age gone past
Mountains, majestic, sinking fast
Yet, down deep, glistening waters flow
Fire red sun is sinking low
A troubled land that's born of man
Windows in my mind they slam
Yes, love was there but pushed aside
And lonely people won't confide
So generations dwindle down
A king no longer wears his crown
To a final look and shed dry tears
Thinking of those wasted years

Margaret McGiffen

Counting Our Blessings

When we all feel, depressed, and sad,
Life is dull and things look bad,
If we try to wear a little smile
life will feel a bit worth while,
don't worry about yesterday, it's over and done,
just try and enjoy every day as it comes,
have a laugh and try to have fun,
don't fill yourself with sadness and sorrow,
and try not to worry about,
what may happen tomorrow.

Lilian Seton

Valleys

Memories that float in and out from the reality of the past.
Visions that free-fall into the now.
Hopes that did not reach their full potential.

The place of the unfathomable myths and unpalatable truths.
The apartheid of tribe and place.
The inability to wander where I could wonder.
The people of the far city. The dark mysterious temples.
The mystery of bread and wine, the fearful mist of Mary's
holy incense.
The attraction of the other-sideness. The sound of the Riverdance.
The melody of souls and spirits held captive by those who
deny the holy place.
The green fields of the dark valley. The dark valley that could
not hold me.

Why could it not hold me?

Because the green valley of a dark place was growing inside me.
That precious green valley that had witnessed the spilling of
the blood of bloods.
It called me from the dark valley of the four–square temples
and theapartheid of body soul and spirit.

Colin Rudge

Just Like That

The old man laughed and said
"Who listens?"
I have become an expert in showing attention without paying it,
smiling without happiness,
giving an ear without listening at all.
"Who listens?"

Whether the other is listening or not no longer holds issue,
if he shows interest,
that's enough.
The patient feels good.
He goes on talking his rubbish and rot,
but even to his regurgitated mind
somebody is paying keen attention as if something very
precious is
being said.
Ego feels gratified.

Michelle Wilson

The Vale Of Espinhal

Here is a spot where beauty lies in breadth and depth,
And, before your eyes, the scene is changing constantly.
The morning mist which shrouds the view
gives way to skies so brilliant blue,
And sunshine drenches all around, and lifts the dew from
soggy ground.
Now we can relish nature's gift of colour gathered in the trees
bedecked with leaves and blossom.

The wooded slopes and mountains tall which hem the vale of
Espinhal,
Give rise to streams of water clear; and, hidden in their folds,
we find the villages of yesteryear.
The village church, the market square, just as in days of old;
The peasant with his ox and plough can still be seen in Soito now.

The meadows with their mantle green, where sheep and
suckling lambs are seen; their bleatings mix with other sounds
which fall upon the ear; the many varied songs of birds,
the croak of crow so drear;
The chirping of the crickets when the evening sun has set,
What beauty lies in all of this and how can we forget
The gifts which nature has in store
For those who ask for nothing more.

A. Holloway

They Call This Progress

Not only did fashion change the world of dress,
The wonders of the world have shown us progress.
Going to the moon seemed an impossible task,
But that impossible, has been conquered long past.

As oil comes gushing from the ground,
Such an abundance to be found.
Oil sheiks are unhappy, and wear a frown,
Now we are making a few million pounds.

Natural gas has proved to be quite cheap,
Divers are still working in the North Sea deep.
Nuclear power gives us all our electric,
But Oh, when there's a leak, they must quickly fix it.

The robot can work 24 hours in a day,
He's taken over from man without any pay.
Soon we shall hear the silicon chip,
Can perform yet another new trick.

Now we can journey from England to France direct,
Where the Euro Tunnel shows off its enormous project.
If no more wars we can guarantee,
The whole wide world will dance with glee.

Christine Moody

The Emmaus Road

I know that as I tread this road,
One walks, with me to share my load:
Along life's path he ever with me stays,
For I have his promise, "Lo, I am with you always."

So I do not fear what lies around each bend,
Knowing that he will be with me to the very end;
And when eventually I draw my final breath,
He will accompany me over the stile that we call death.

For the Emmaus road has no ending here;
It stretches on under skies that are sunny and clear,
With no dark clouds and blinding rain,
Into a land where there is neither sorrow nor pain.

There you and I will meet once more
Our loved ones who have gone on before;
For they have only travelled a few short steps ahead
Along the Emmaus road; they are not dead.

Joyfully together we will pursue our way
In that land where it is forever day;
There will be no darkness there to hide
Those dear companions who journey at our side.

Kenneth E. Jinks

What Is Life

Life is for living
Love is for giving
Bells are for ringing
Songs are for singing
Tears are for weeping
Beds are for sleeping
Food is for eating
Drums are for beating
So live your life well, for it has been said
Life has a meaning long after you're dead

P. Skinner

Patiently I'll Wait

I often call your name 'though you're not there;
I speak to you as often as I dare.
If there are such things as ghosts, I have no fear.
So long I've waited, in the hope that you'll appear.
Just me, alone in this large house that always seemed so full
When you were there, to share.
But now a year has passed without a word
Yet still I wait, in hope,
For just a fleeting glance to know that you still care.
Kind friends reach out, but do not understand
The desperate need I have, to touch your hand.
Some say that I should leave this place and start anew,
How could I go? For come the time that you might choose to show
And I'm not there, you would think that it was I, deserted you.
So patiently I'll wait, for however long it takes;
And if one night, that I should hear a creaking stair
I'll rush to look, in hope that you'll be there,
And if in disappointment I turn away,
Conflicting with my thoughts, I'll ask, as tears begin to flow,
Are there such things as ghosts? Perhaps, one day I'll know.

Valerie Braithwaite

Drive Past?

I may drive past
I'm not sure how I'll feel
I think I'll wait for the wounds to heal.

I shouldn't drive past
people will know me
I'd be forced to pop in, have coffee or tea.

I can't drive past
things won't be the same
it may even have a different name.

I won't drive past
when I felt there last, God how I cried
that was the house where my family died.

I could drive past
just to see what I find
No! Wait! Stop! I've changed my mind.

Catherine Virtue

Night's Fall

At the end of day, the sun completes its flight.
Burning crimson fire shoots stray clouds with light.

Darkness pools like smoke and creeps across the sky.
The flaming orb descends and smouldering embers die.

And by darkness chased, the glowing coals of light,
Dying, then give way; quenched by the winds of night.

The winds of night descend across a still domain;
Like voices in a crypt they howl away their pain.

A silent shroud of darkness covers all around
And dark, deep pools of shadows huddle on the ground.

The corpse - pale moon, she pierces the vault of shadows, and
Her lambent glow it leaches all colour from the land.

And when the dawn impeaches upon the black of night;
The darkened sky surrenders to the coming of the light.

Gibbs Hammond

Spoons

In silver spoons there are contortions,
smiling frowns all warped,
strangely inverted reflections.
The back and concave front, (breathed on, all buffed)
elongate, flip around, reflecting a child's laughing giggles.
In this joyous daze,
what lies ahead?
It's said that the future can be seen in spoons?
Can children see more than we do?
I looked in a spoon once,
I laughed, how silly I looked with a squished face that hid my flaws.
I stared.
Afterwards, I smashed all the mirrors in my house,
and hung spoons in place.

Gary Loke

That Day

We thought it was the end that day
we wanted to be together as much as we could
we wanted it to last forever that day
we really believed that it would.

We held hands really tight that day
both of us scared of losing each others' touch
we walked both quiet and thoughtful that day
I knew even then that I loved him so much.

We sat in the sunshine that day
watching the people in the crowded square
We both smiled and laughed that day
not really believing that it would end there.

When it came to an end, that day
we came home, said good-bye and parted
but the only thing that came to an end was that day
for us our days together had just started.

Katie Pottinger

The Greater Love

I love my England too dearly—too deeply
To wander away to some strange foreign shore.
Since that first day when my limbs stirred but weakly
Breathed then in old England and hungered for more.
I loved her antiquity teeming with history.
Revelled in relics, old castles, old moats.
Walked then in fancy with dear phantom people
White wigged and powdered in velveteen coats.
I breathed then in England and said "I am English,
No other country will hold me for long
Except under protest, imprisoned and fettered
For this is my country to which I belong."
It wouldn't work darling your heart's in the new world
While mine lies deep buried in graves of the past.
My loves are not your loves—nor my affectations
That first careless rapture how briefly 'twould last.
So let us part now still young and still loving
Knowing it hard yet knowing it best
To part while still strong, still free and still able
To heal with the years the dull ache in each breast.

E. M. Reece

Out Of My Window

The dark times are the coldest
But the air hangs heavy around me
A blanket I can almost see
A cold yet comfortable glow

The dark times are the scariest
But a certain thrill comes from ghosts and ghouls
Dismissed as thought for fools
Mysteries lie thick at night

The dark times are the loneliest
But in solemn silence, there's time to think
Into purple, blue life I sink
So brilliant world yet tragic

Gill Williams

Life After Life

Most of us know but one life,
and cannot envisage another!
But if we could travel to the end of a rainbow
or catch a dewdrop in the palm of our hand.
Or make a necklace, from, shimmering sunlight,
Sprinkled like Jewels across the sea,
If we could walk up the shaft, of a brilliant moon beam
Or glide in the slipstream of a butterfly's wings,
Then, precariously perched on the ledge of our newly found freedom.
We would then lift the veil of uncertainty.
We would feel such love and glimpse the life, that once
We knew so long ago,
And is forever ours to behold!
Alas! These things we cannot do,
Yet in our hearts we 'know' 'tis true
that we must 'hold fast' to our dreams,
For it's in our subconscious, that life exists,
The life Hereafter—True Reality!

Patricia Harris

The Faded Memory

If I should die,
I would know I had left a small piece of me
In this fair green land called England.
My laughter, my tears,
My loves and desires;
All that pleased me
And all my fears,
Have joined that faded memory
Of time and times gone by.
From years of longing
To be one with the past
Will spring that eternal youth
Of my memory, known to but few.
And I will reach my goal
To be with those of the forgotten land;
Meeting those from the rosy, forgotten times.
And I will be safe in the knowledge
That I have achieved all I have ever wanted.
And I will be at peace,
In your faded memory.

Sanchia Langdon

Rough And Still Waters

How God had outdone himself in the creation of these
miraculous waters which sparkled as the sky reached down to
engulf this huge emerald jewel. It glittered with pride as it held
on to the secret of what lay below. The underworld where
peace and tranquillity reigned, where time had no meaning.
Where storm and anger would bring more nourishment forth
to the dwellers of this abyss and fill the sea bed with treasures
that would not be discovered for generations. Here nobody
minded, here nobody judged, how wonderful a life governed by
serenity must be, where the word panic and fear are only known
on the border dividing this underworld with what lay above.

Eleni Mylonas

Sonnet On Bosnia

In spite of weather, wind or rain or sleet
Teams push and shove and scrum to make the line,
A spinning ball comes hurtling to their feet
Then shoulders crack and necks and heads entwine.
A player runs, completely on his own
Straight up the field to kick the ball on high,
A pause, then flags are waved and whistle blown
To tell us that our team has scored a try.

In Bosnia and Serbia a game
Is played with teams of humans—all so damned—
While planes and tanks and guns—it's all the same—
Scream and destroy the buildings and the land.
There are no rules—and fighters play, for what?
The final score for all involved
Adds up to nought.

Betty Finnie

Working Together

"I'll adjust my lens, for me to zoom,
Upon your beautiful pink rose bush in bloom"

"Please help! my lush petals many come to harm
If he zooms too close, I might lose my charm"

"Stand back! you creature I do warn
I'm her protector I'M THE THORN!"

In the garden, this is the usual row,
So I'll tell you something and I'll tell it now

The rose bush, the camera, the thorn,
in fact all three,

When working together make magnificent beauty.

Sally E. McBride

The Odd Old Boot

I was clearing the attic, me grannie's 'glory hole',
When I found an old boot, with a hole in the sole.
I thought to myself, there must be a pair,
But I cleared the place out, the other wasn't there.

So I started a search, through the family tree,
looking for an ancestor, with one leg, or three!
Then I heard how me granddad, stuck his leg through thatch,
and lost his boot through the hole, while mending the patch.

Now he daren't tell me grannie, what he'd done that day,
So he just threw the other one, half a mile away.
Now I'm thinking, maybe someone found that one too,
and wondered, like I did, surely this should be two!

Irene Simpson

Our Wedding Day

It was the loveliest day of my life
When we were made man and wife
All dressed up lovely and smart
Never again would we want to part
The smile on her face was a pleasure to see
It made me happy you must agree
Such a lot of thought went into this day
I will never forget it come what may
Joy and happiness we will share
Our ups and downs whatever comes there
Life won't always be a bed of roses
It sets its puzzles and its poses
But never let the sun go down
With a quarrel or a frown
Do all you can to please each other
Life's golden riches you'll both discover
And as the years pass away
I'll think back of my wedding day . . .

Percy Shakel

Gathering Pearls

If you can gaze up from the cradle and fix your destiny in the stars,
If you can rejoice in childhood yet see with ancient eyes;
If you can gather pearls and store them in faith's jars,
And keep humility's counsel with the wise;
If you can set your compass on far distant lands,
And being wrecked swim onwards to the shore,
To stretch a new sail with your own tired hands,
And seek their balm in the tears of the poor;
If you can drink in the desert, the nectar of the soul,
And crush the serpent with starvation's pangs,
And reap there a harvest from this heav'nly toll;
'Twill be the cord from which all mercy hangs.
If tears to you prove greater than the cross,
And fatherless you suffer all alone,
And more than human pain your agony you embrace,
Then I'll bow to Him who shares with me my throne,
And whisper at the last, "Thou art my son",
And stoop before thee, thy wounded knees to enfold,
And say to thee, "In my own name you won",
And melt with thee into the land of gold.

Paul Burke

Taking On The Storm

The late summer air is heavy and humid
With a storm that is soon to break,
Everything hushed and waiting, the parched earth anticipating
Its long awaited freshening from a shower it soon may take.

The dark evening sky is suddenly glittering,
A dagger of lightening is splitting the sky,
It is no use my pretending that this moment I'm intending
To be like other humans home safe and sound and dry.

The wet pale green grass is bathing my ankles,
The light green stemmed briony is cooling my head
Still the storm continues raging a losing bet with me it's waging
If it thinks it will be driving me skiving home to bed.

Nora Roden

"He Said He Loved Me"

He said he loved me, he told me so
He said he loved me and I'll always know

He said he loved me, he said he cared
He said he loved me and he'd always be there

He said he loved me, in his special way
He said he loved me, he said he'd stay

He said he loved me, when I saw him today
He said he loved me, as I watched him slip away

He said he loved me, when he said goodbye
He said he loved me, and forever closed his eyes

He said he loved me, I'll remember that always
The pain doesn't ease and it doesn't go away

He said he loved me and he said goodbye
If he loved me, then why did he die

Elaine Adair

The Homecoming

When I'm feeling low, as I sometimes do,
After things don't go just as I planned.
I look around and see what I have,
In my beautiful, Northumberland.

There are sandy beaches, rocky crags,
Rivers through valleys, and old battle grounds.
Castles, and gardens all on display
Walks and climbing for all to share.

Is it any wonder I love it so much?
The weather isn't perfect, but it's seldom extreme.
We don't have earthquakes, hurricanes or such.
It is my home scene, it's pleasant and oh, so green.

I sometimes go abroad, enjoy the sunshine,
visit my family and stay for a while.
When I return to these welcome shores,
It is then, to myself, I say: Why did I ever go away?

D. Gilholm

Four Seasons

Spring is the start of sunshine and flowers.
And just some sunny showers.
The children laugh and play away.
They can have fun nearly everyday.
But summer is better and much more fun.
You can sit in the garden and soak up the sun.
And do the things you want to do.
Without the rain in the way or you catching the flu.
But as autumn comes the fun starts to stop.
The leaves on the trees start to drop.
Then comes the wind and the rain
And out comes the coats and brollies again
But winter is worse as you've been told
In this season you're more likely to catch a cold.
So you wrap up and keep warm.
And hope there isn't a winter storm.

Noreen McHugh

Heartbeat Fast

Think that I nearly let you go,
How could I have ever thought that you
were not the one. Keep holding on.

I never stopped loving you, just think that
we nearly ruined one another's hearts.
Don't let them beat apart, just take me in your arms.

I saw your face in a quiet place,
where we used to dance at a very fast pace.
You would watch me strip down to lace.
While you just looked at me with your sweet, sweet face.

Climb this mountain, fight this love.
You're the one I'm always dreaming of.

I took your arms, you held me tight,
Make love to me for the rest of the night.

Climb inside your love, roses fall, I hear you call,
this is the time for our love.

When you touch me I scream, then when you
hold me I call your name. My love will
never feel the same. Keeping touching your
way into my heart. Telling me our hearts could
never part. At last, I hear your Heartbeat Fast.

Tracy Lee Smith

The Cycle Of Beginnings

Here it is, the not-so-happy ending.
I hear the sharp intake of breath
the silence
then, the apology
until, the finality of the good-bye.

Here it is, the sad and tearful ending.
I see the deep gaze of sorrow
undoing the love
destroying the trust
until, the familiarity of the good-bye.

Here it is, the cold untouching ending.
I feel no hands of comfort
but distance
of poles apart
until, the futility of the good-bye.

Here it comes, the pain of the new beginning.
I hear, and see, and feel
the cycle of inevitable partings
of loneliness
until, the next hello.

Eileen Duckworth

The Lord's Answer

"It is time", said the Lord, to his angels one day
"To go down to earth and find another".
They came to our house, I was only fifteen
But the Lord said it was time.
And I said goodbye, to my dear old grandmother

I was nearly thirty when the angels came again
It was a deep winter's night like many others
We knew they were coming this time and for who
Quietly and gracefully they entered the room on wings of love
The Lord gave us, and the Lord took, my mother.

I questioned His right to give me so much pain
I looked for the reasons for tears
I searched for the answers by day and by night
I explored my every word and every thought
I remember my anguish, the hurt and the fears.

Confusion has reigned in my head many times
But I hear his message as I grow older
There is a reason for living, laughing, crying and dying
The Lord has given me many things in this life
But most precious of all—an angel on each shoulder.

Colin Ivor Weale

Iron Lung

"The body is a vehicle for the soul,"
the boy thought as he lay there ill.
And his thoughts were like the depths of a well,
deep and so immensely still.
Then one day when all the changes were rung
he thought about how he would compose his song,
there in the throbbing depths of his iron lung,
deep and so immensely young.

J. D. Bailey

A Mother's Prayer

The sky was heavy with impending snow—
The silver moon hung in the heaven low,
In humble home on craggy hill afar—
A face looked up and wished upon a star.

My dearest son is fighting on the Somme,
No rest, no warmth, no niche to shelter from
The mass bombardment of this futile war—
My son, maybe, that I will see no more.

I hope, Dear Lord, that you will care for mine,
My heart and his with passion will entwine.
Remember them who give their lives for me—
As I entrust my own heart unto thee.

The sky was heavy with impending snow—
The silver moon hung in the heaven low—
'Midst death and dusk in foreign land afar—
Young eyes looked up and wished upon a star.

*My Uncle Owen Jones was killed at the Battle
of the Somme, aged 19 years.*

Bet Jones

"Land's End"

Gentle the breeze so blue the sky
No mist to mar the beauty
Rugged the coast hugged by the sea
Murmuring its tales of mystery
Oh England such beauty yours
Here at journey's end
So much I could understand
If I had time to spend
With you in all your loneliness
I'd love to be a part
Of you and all your beauty sane
Here today I leave my heart
A heart so full of gratitude
So in my 80th year,
At last I stand upon the rocks
Sensing history there
Sensing too your loneliness
Such mystery in the air
From the sound of the sea pounding below
Comes a glimpse of eternity there.

Annie Davies

Barriers

I was always hoping, praying, wishing I could find,
Someone who was capable to help sort out my mind.
Life becomes unbearable, I have no room to grow,
I have no direction, don't know which way to go.

I could not cope all on my own, demands made every day,
Night time brought the nightmares, and I cried the nights away,
For life I held no passion, somehow I braved the storm,
Vipers biting at my heels the moment I was born.

This life is spent in searching for the one thing I can't find,
That little piece of Heaven that will give some peace of mind.
I feel the isolation, hear the tolling of the bell,
Am I blindly marching on towards the flames of Hell?

We long for our lost innocence, the turn of a new page,
To give us hope, a future, the dawn of a new age.
Is a spark of optimism destined for a fall?
Like gazing in a crystal ball for answers to it all.

Alan Charles West

Surviving

He is the pain, the agony locked away deep within;
Never dared to unleash him, lest my soul might give in
For he, with all power, could quench me, could win
And I *know* he's not worth the heart of me dying.
He's the torture, the fever, the fear and the rage
Against whom I must draw my weapons, and battle engage—
'Til my enemy I bleed dry, his curse is my cage,
The dark, lonely chamber where, breathless, I'm lying.
He's the vulture that preyed on every breath I drew,
Took, devoured all I lived for, ripped open and slew.
I have nothing. Except I breathe on, gasp on, despite you—
You are he. I am she which you will not possess.
He is the blood that my battle wounds spill,
Staining my soul, running cold, running still.
But the anger that drives me won't allow him to kill.
Try to kill me, bastard! Ah! Drain me, restrain me!
Laughter's sweet as it echoes through his emptiness.
His daggers aren't sharp enough. *You* haven't slain me.

Sharron Burns

If

In this world, there are but few things to worry about.
If we are well, there is nothing to worry about.
If we are ill, there are two things to worry about.
If we get better, there is nothing to worry about.
If we die, there are two things to worry about.
If we go to heaven there is nothing to worry about.
If we go to hell, we shall be so busy, we shall have no time to worry!

Jean Webster

Torture

Hold a verbal gun to my head
While I'm in despair;
I'm in a hole, you're poking me
With blades of I don't care.
You sit around in silence
But your eyes tell me of scorn;
You make small comments, I feel smaller still
I wish I'd never been born.
I need your help to get me out
But you just give me grief;
You're my friends, but you're never there
When I need some relief.
Talk among yourselves, leave me out,
I know what words pass your lips;
You can't hide your amusement from me
So just tell me what you think.
Maybe you're trying to save my feelings.
But you're just hurting them even more;
Please stop torturing me
I can't take any more.

Tracey Carvill

The Little Flower

The little plant was left alone all day, no one had a word to say.
People glanced, they just passed on by.
They didn't hear or see it cry,
"Give me water! Please! I'm very hot, my roots
are cramped in this tiny pot."
Silence!!! No one heard or was it just that no one cared!
The leaves soon turned a rusty brown,
At last someone noticed, and showed
a frown, saying as they walked on by,
"I'm sure that plant is going to die!"
It was true, it came so fast,
That little plant seemed to die at last;
With little care and without a peep;
The owner threw it on the compost heap!
With crawling insects and buzzing flies,
The withered body on the compost lies,
Then nature comes to take a part,
A tiny seed falls from the broken heart,
And life begins again to bloom,
For the little flower from that stuffy room.

Tom Smith

The Windows Of The Soul

Look deep into her eyes my friend,
The eyes that the long lashes try to defend.
What do you see?
At first just reflections of you and me.
Look deeper. What do you find?
Those eyes portray the suffering of all mankind.

The eyes have seen wars that never should have been,
Have experienced hope followed by shattered dreams.
Have witnessed people dying for no reason at all,
And have watched the mighty ones fall.

These eyes are the windows of the soul,
But it's down the cheeks that the tears will roll.
Crying for the visions that are trapped within,
Crying for the pain of the people still living.
These sights are observed by us all
But we are used to them so we deny their call.
And that pain that fills our eyes
Is one that we ignore and try to disguise.

Vicki Lester

Betrayed

Her eyes like stars twinkled in the black night sky.
She turned her head slowly and with her green cat like eyes
stared at the flames dancing around the house. Like arms
trying to reach the stars overhead.
The colours contrasting dramatically with the midnight black sky.
Her long, silky, raven black hair blew with the wind as if wildly
trying to escape from the troubled young women.
But then who could blame it?
A stray strand of hair was whipping her tender chalky–white
face painfully.
A long slender finger retrieved it and tucked it behind a raw
weather–beaten ear.
She felt betrayed, betrayed and confused. Who was to blame?
She gazed accusingly at the silvery full moon outlined with
transparent clouds.
This made her feel even more determined, determined for revenge.
She slipped her long body hand into pocket in her beige coat
and felt the sharp metal blade of a carving knife stolen from
the house before it was engulfed by flames.
She smiled wickedly to herself revealing her wolf like teeth

Sara Cannon

Black White

Black is black and white is white
Black is dark, white is bright
Black like night, white like day
So much of a contrast
Different in so many ways
When we think of white, next we think of black
When we think of black, white is on the same track
Despite their differences
They are a pair
Without one, the issue is not there
Why must we be so deprived
Of friendship, relation and peace
Our lives would be so much better
If all our human pride would cease
Will there ever be a moment when we do not hear our world cry?
Unfortunately no, not ever, not unless you yourself try
Does it matter the colour of someone's skin
Or what culture or group they are in
Forget about black, forget about white
Try remembering the person who lives inside.

Marie Davis

Miss Divorce

The clouds unfurled, the storm has passed
My heart has feted with you gone at last.
As peace and I walked hand in hand
You reached out and severed her hand
Or so you thought, with your lies and deceit,
As she is always with me, from my head to my feet.

Daphne I. Talbot

Seasons

Seasons come and seasons go, it effects the way our feelings show.
Spring comes round so slowly, the buds they start to shoot.
Everywhere is bright and beams, fresh and new and sparkling clean.
The year ahead has just begun with a very watery sparkling sun.
This season makes us feel brand new, making plans of what to do.

Summer sun and hazy days, warm winds blow and drift away.
Brilliant flowers yellow grass, the sun so hot we hope it lasts.
This season makes us feel so good, fun and happy like childhood.

Then as autumn days approach the autumn leaves they blow.
Golden brown and crispy crunch as they're flattened on the ground.
Warm and inviting sunsets sets the scenes aglow.
With a chill in the air now this season is here
but enjoy finding places to go.

Now winter looms upon us, cold and damp, dark days.
Dashing here and dashing there, ice and frost is in the air.
Evening comes so quickly, lights are on in force.
Getting ready for Christmas lights our spirits which sets a course.
Of fires aglow for winter, snow and merriment in the air.
This is the season to be jolly enjoying the Christmas fare.

Linda Hilton

Thoughts Of Spring

Cherry blossom on the ground
Falling gently without a sound
Apple blossom clean and white
Like summer snow so fresh and bright
Oh! What a story our springtime tells
Of sights and sounds and flower smells
Oh! What a show our birds can see
No wonder they sing upon the tree
And when at last summer comes to stay
Spring has already had her say
And gives it up for summer's beauty
Knowing she has done her duty
For without spring where would summer be?
Still a bud upon the tree.

G. M. Shiels

On The Shore

What is it that you find here to take away the hours?
The waves of breath that beat upon the time of sand?
The dust of life been swept off by another's hand?
A seagull rises skywards, and I understand
That all of this is precious and it could be ours.
A moment is a lifetime when it's filled with thought
Of all the times we used to smile that can't be bought,
Of all the races won and all the battles fought.

When water falls on water, still I will not turn.
So how can I be smiling when there is no sun?
I sought so long for glory and I find there's none
But need no recognition here for what I've done.
The more I think of nothing here, the more I learn
Of life that was and will be when I am no more.
Of things that I have cherished and have suffered for.
I cry, but I know why I am here on the shore.

Linda J. Smith

Search

There is a hunger here that cannot be assuaged,
By beer or cars or cigarettes,
Or wealth or Ecstasy.

There is a crying voice that cannot be stilled,
By travel or music or copulation,
Or art or pornography,

There is a need that cannot be satisfied,
By belief or penance or devotion,
Or Mass or Rosary.

There is an answer that cannot be undiscovered,
By us, or crime or worldwide wars,
Or rape or cruelty,

Will prevail, and we will be lost.

June Cooke

My First Day At School

All the people staring at me,
And only then I began to see,
They were laughing and joking about me.

My first assembly was fun,
When I secretly chewed my chewing gum,
I sat down for so long I had a numb bum.

My form teacher is funny,
But I want my mummy,
I would like my daddy but he's in the Navy.

I went home that night,
To find a bright light,
To see my cat playing with a rat.

The next morning I went to school,
Then we went to the swimming pool,
And swimming was cool.

But I want my mummy,
But now she's in the Navy,
So now I have my daddy.

Lesley Richards

The Spoils Of Nature

The lion pounces on his prey,
Licking his lips, he eats today,
The wolf, prowls to the chicken run,
With a springy leap, he catches one.
The owl, with his beady eyes,
Spots a mouse, and down he flies,
Even the spider, in his web of thread,
Traps the flies, until they're dead.
It's a cruel world, but food they need,
They wouldn't survive, if they didn't succeed.
But man's the worst offender of all,
It's not for food, the birds do fall,
Shooting them down from out of their forts,
Just for fun, and a thing called sport.

D. Collins

The Moon

I look up at night to see the moon
I hope to go and visit it soon,
I wonder what it's like in a rocket
I wonder what I'll put in my pocket,
I wonder what I'll see when I'm there
I wonder whether I'll really care,
I'm tired so I'll go to bed
And I'll wonder the rest tomorrow instead.

Penny Turner

Our World

Now I stop and ask myself where has all the kindness gone?
I ask for nothing and do what I believe to be correct,
yet, no matter how hard I try it always seems to be wrong.
Like everyone else I was taught the rules of courtesy,
that to say "please" and "thank you" was correct.
The unwritten rules in our society,
that so many of us have chosen to reject.

It appears to me that only those who have learnt to respect,
a human being for being solely that,
ignoring all those class barriers that we erect,
and not judging others by the car they drive,
nor by the clothes upon their backs.
When we learn to respect the tramp
and understand that it is not necessarily his fault that he is there.
Okay, you may not wish to sit and talk with him,
but surely you have no permission either, to ridicule him.

I am no philosopher nor another Karl Marx,
I have no predictions of what the future holds.
But I do feel that with a lot less taking and a bit more giving,
this world, earth, we will be proud to call our home.

Charlotte Robins

Love's First Flavours

The winged boys of love's first flavours felt,
entreat the maidens eyes with wooing lust;
To place of soft and downied feathered nest,
a whistling softly love's sweet tryst.

With silken sweep on soft white flesh, and
eyes of burning soul;
She weaves and wrings a magical bonanza.
Towards heavenly mists they float, on honeyed
dew and sweetened light.

A dawning, what spell broken 'mid the rising hue;
What sweet mystical illusive wonder carried on
the breeze;
To sultry, sweeping and solitary shore.

Anne M. Davison

Please Save The World

There's pollution in Glasgow,
London and Japan,
That wasn't the case,
When a child, was my gran.

People must have destroyed the Earth,
The sky and countryside.
People have destroyed the world,
That you don't *need* to decide.

Very soon, the world will come to an end,
But I know something for certain,
The world is my friend!

Claire S. Taylor

I Know . . .

I know Algebra is important
and exercise improves your health.

I know exam results are crucial
and I can have any career I want.

I know marriage first, then children
and that some are poor and some are rich.

I know that fields can be turned into roads
and that some things can't be fixed.

I don't know why some illnesses have no cure
and some children are not loved.

I don't know why some are starving
and some just don't have a chance.

Maybe all we know is that we are born
and then we die,
what happens in between is unknown
By both you and I.

Sarah Payne

Quo Vadis, Homo Sapiens?

In former times a tale to tell
  Was taken to the village well
To learn which way the cat might jump
  One listened at the parish pump.
Men gathered at the local pub
  The social circle's age old hub
On favour'd seat they sat at ease
  A folded journal on their knees
They shared their hopes, their fears, their joys
  As they had done since they were boys.
Then Two L. O. from Savoy Hill
  Spread worldwide news both good and ill
And music came from many a 'show'
  With woodwind, brass and strings and bow.
John Logie Baird his scanner twirled
  And soon mankind saw all the world.
We sit alone from dawn or late
  With finger-tips investigate,
Midst other folk we've never met,
  The labyrinths of the Internet.

Eric G. Curling

The Stranger

I stood upon the lonely moor, the wind was cold and harsh, when,
all at once I saw a man, just walking then he stopped, and called,
To me? It couldn't be, for if he knew me, I didn't know him.

He called again so I did go to where the stranger stood
He spoke to me and I was dumb.
He said "About a mile away death is awaiting,
for it is the Army of the Maid.
"The Maid of Orleans," he said, quite fast and then I saw
ten thousand of his soldiers and yet ten thousand more.

To Orleans I fear we go to help our comrades there.
I saw the mud and also blood still matted in his hair
from the days before when he had fought to take this land so fair.

"The Maid claims the Lord's with her and all his angels too."
I thought well if he's helping her what will become of you?

His words to me were frightening, then in the sky was a
blinding flash and a silver bolt of lightening shot down and hit
his banner and burned it to a cinder

He knelt down on the floor full of sadness and remorse,
Yet I could not help him, for I'm only an old grey horse.

Mark Whitewood

Team Spirit

Margaret Jones was happy. Margaret Jones was sad.
She had just given birth to a big strapping lad.
Happy was she, labour was over at last. But sad.
Still no girl, the same cry from the past.
Why: she lamented, she was a mother of seven
Couldn't have girls, oh well leave it to heaven.

The years past bringing three more boys, then
At long last, oh joy of joys.
A beautiful girl born to Margaret Jones
Her life now complete. No more moans.
Looking back she smiles with pride, at her girl's
Picture, five boys either side.
The football she covets and dressed in her kit
Girls will be boys and, does she love it.

Dorothy Laverack

"Ode To The Stroke In The Wheelchair"

I cannot enter her world, she cannot enter mine,
I've tried so hard but still I'm on the edge of the line.
She stares as if a memory is running through her mind.
Oh Lord, oh God please tell me why, you're gentle and so kind.

She once was so full of energy but now sits and wait,
Motionless in a wheelchair, praying for a certain date.
Angel's in a world of silence, dependent on us all,
Her pride, her dignities been taken, now she's fragile and small.

Her world is cold and silent though I try to bring love in,
"I love her," but I'll let her go Lord, if you will take her in,
  "Your Arms."

Teresa C. Murphy-Hopkins

Autumn Poem

The tree is shaking off the leaves
tumble down on the ground.
The grass is green.
The leaves are brown and green sometimes
All the time it was windy, all the leaves were
down on the ground blowing quickly.
The flowers were yellow and pink and violet.
The tree is small but the birds fly in the sky
With the wind blowing. They go in the bird
both and come, down to find something
to eat like bread crusts
The clouds are grey and the falling dew becomes
a frost in the leaves.
The apples are good.
In the harvest is a gift of fruit like
apples and grapes and
plums are good for us.

Caroline L. Davis

Pirouette

She circled my life orbited my world
I looked upon with disbelief
Now gone from her that breath of life
suddenly snatched from me
Like a footprint in the snow
so clear then disappears
No time to say goodbye
only memories of the years
Backtracking on those last few hours
I grasp at moments shared
We walked through fields along the lanes
Oh, how we loved and cared.

Seven years she ruled
her domain with
precision, instilling
order through her
Kingdom at all times
Kaiser my Queen of Queens

Blanche Ali

New Toy

I have a new toy in my bedroom
it's big, yellow and black
and it sits in front of my window
because there is no other room than that.

It sits upon the floor
next to a lion, tiger and a bear
I think they are quite happy
to be sitting there.

My new toy is not a teddy
a doll or a car
it's something more unusual
the best I've got by far.

By now I guess you're wondering
what on earth my new toy can be
well let me tell you simply
it's a giant bumble bee.

Michelle Dickinson

Easter Time

Newborn lambs, chicks and spring flowers
Sun, snow, wind and April showers
Lots of eggs and hot cross buns,
Children having lots of fun.
Some people live alone and don't see anyone
It's just like any other day.
So why not take a posy and help to pass an hour away
Some people have to work while others have a holiday
Others go to church and also pray.
We all do something different when Easter time is here
But wherever you go, whatever you do
Have a happy Easter filled with love and cheer,
To last you through till this time next year

P. D. Dugdale

Untitled

Lost in my world, deep in a constant void,
My mind races to touch every corner of this inner space.
To examine the blackness that is surrounding me,
As I sit in bewilderment at life's hectic pace.
Until I am hit hard by reality,
As when a blind man first sees the sun.
Then I try to hide from these truths,
And I am frightened with nowhere to run.
The demons of truth do chase me,
From morning, through noon, till night,
Up until now I had closed my eyes to life's horrors,
For my life now has no clear sight.
Ignorance—I was happy when you had me,
To hide me from life's many faces,
Please take my hand once again,
Emerge me in a void where my mind races.

Angela Swarbrick

Just Heat

A grain of rice, small piece of bread
Sip of water to live ni dead,
See another day.

Sugar and water can save the life
What we wipe from the kitchen side.
A grain of rice, a crust of bread
The spill of sugar—someone's dead.

What we scrape from the plate after Sunday roast
Could feed a family; for father to host.

We get fat and thrive,
They're lucky to be alive.
We all have worries, bills and strains,
One crust of bread could stop their pain.

So think how lucky we really are:
We're thriving; we're surviving;
We're standing on our feet.
Our friends in the Third World
They're lying; they're dying
There's nothing to eat.

JUST HEAT.

Neil McIlveen

The Gifts Of Life

May the gifts of life flow through you, with sincerity by your side.
Let the spirit that's inside you, always be your guide.
For there are many things to learn, while we are here on earth.
And each one becomes more precious, as we begin to learn its worth.

Take the gift of tears my friends, for indeed they are a gift.
For when we're sad, and things go wrong, our tears can give a lift.
And then God gives us healing, that sweeps us clean like the tide.
Then we can face the world again, and feel all warm inside.

Take the gift of loneliness, when there's no one there to share.
We think of the days when we were young, with a loved one
and children there.
But then no longer are they there, for quickly they have grown.
Then suddenly your loved one's gone, and you are left alone.

But don't despair, for all's not lost, for God will be with you
And give you comfort in your loss, and lovingly bring you through.
Then slowly you'll begin to heal, and the sun will shine for you.
For with God there beside you, your life will start anew.

And most precious of all, the gift of love, that we must always share.
Never keep it for yourself, but give from the heart with care.
And in so doing, you will find, a greater peace of mind.
For God will give it beauty, for you, to give mankind.

June Margaret Avery

One Sunday Morning

"It took a great deal of anticipation,
Heart wrenching days and nights,
To tell you that me and your father,
Well, things aren't going quite right.

Come and sit down dear, I've something to say,
But it's something you're not going to like.
I've fallen in love with somebody new,
I think that I've met Mr. Right."

How embarrassed I was when my teachers were told,
My friends, they felt sorry for me.
But I soldiered on with my head in the clouds,
Ignoring the alleged tragedy.

Psychiatrist later, not to mention the pills,
Thought I'd sorted it all out at last.
Insecurity, jealousy. Trust was a thing
That somehow I couldn't quite grasp.

I know we can't foresee the future,
But women, please take heed.
When you're taking your vows, in your white wedding gown,
Be sure he's the man that you need!

Sarah Berry

Finbarr Harte

Finbarr Harte is his name,
I've never seen any one quite the same,
I've been to see him so many times,
All because he is so fire,
He's got the best voice I've ever heard,
And all he does is well deserved,
He has a great band as well,
And a lot of cassettes to sell,
He even has badges and key rings,
And a lot more other things,
One day he'll be on T.V.,
On T.V. for everyone to see.

Ashley Wells

Untitled

Lingering at the water's edge
Watching the sandpipers teasing, taunting a breaking wave
inviting disaster—it always happens at the right moment
The last exquisite moment: Triumph, as old as time.

An alarming clarity to my decision
All the reasons curved inward in my mind
Folding protectively around a central core
reason upon reason layered thinly—one atop the other
Forming patterns, curling, curving
crisping at the edges like yellowed newspapers.
One atop another, reason after reason: The final dried pages of
Someone's life.

One last walk on the beach
A sliver of the moon etches a sparkling path far out to sea.
One last walk—to bid a ritual farewell to
Summer
And the sea.

Zahra Homeira Laidler

The Albatross

Above the South's quick flowing tides
Straight through torrential rain she glides
When every other sea bird hides
The Albatross flies bravely

When mighty storms ceaselessly blow
Where the ships of men will hardly go
Their only fate the depths below
She wings her way so carefree

She's the mystic wanderer of the seas
The legend whispered on the breeze
Her airborne presence sailors please
The goddess of the ocean

So proud, so sleek, so born to fly
The majestic glider of the sky
If a million years or more pass by
She'll rule in lonely splendour

K. F. Hardy

The First Crocus Bloomed Today

It's Friday the seventh of March today.
It's sunny, the snow has gone away.
Listen all. . . . . now gather round,
Something is alive in that cold ground.
Through the kitchen window I saw . . .
only . . . one . . . there were no more . . .
One yellow flower, it's petals display.
The very first Crocus had bloomed today.

Just as if a magic wand
had made it appear beside our pond.
It proudly shows off its colour too,
I feel so delighted . . . wouldn't you . . .
Can't wait for the girls to come home from school.
But until then . . . . I . . . . must . . . keep . . . cool.
In our back garden . . . Hip, Hip, Hooray . . . . . .
The first little crocus bloomed today.

B. Godfrey

Standing By A Water's Edge

Coots, Moorhens and Grey Herons live through a tide of emotional seasons.
The sound of territorial swans break the silence with cracking wings.
Fishermen's lines and floats await that final moment of bite and strike
Environment conscious gentlemen clear litter from trodden
pathways and digest a total disregard by others.
Nature blends and adapts to all the elements which can be
offered in an ever–changing climate.
A distant church reflects in a pond reaching into its depths
and high to the eye to overlook.
Dragonflies glide with ability to hover and dance, departing
with speed over uncharted waters.
On a distant hill lies a windmill no movement but history past
is reflected by its stance.
Skies and clouds combine to paint each days change of style
and backdrop display.
Droughts bring thoughts of thirst and apprehension, can the
weather really be as punishing as this beyond man's invention.
Sit and smile awhile with outstretched hands feeling the wind
as it swirls and twists passing me by.
With lush surrounds and where nature abounds how easy and
relaxed a life I have found.
It's misty by now and the sounds take over of nature around
and my senses are at full test.
I pack up my things as the day draws on I reflect on what's
gone, I must remember from where it began.

A. E. Kirkland

Past By

If you should be unfortunate to loose your spouse
And feel at a lost, just you in the house
Just think of all those who have had no one
No memories to reflect on and certainly no fun
It's harsh getting old when the body starts to rust
Like an aging car, a service is a must
A trip to the doctor's for the annual check
With the years gone by, time to reflect
Put on the scrap heap, out of the way
Perhaps friends may call and see you one day
Families have the wrong perspective on life
Leaving the elderly parent cut, as with a knife
Getting old will happen to us all one day
So beware when it's your time be the first to say
Don't pass me off in a residential home
To be left by the way, completely alone
My brain still works, like an engine, it can function
But although being old, one does have enough gumption
That life will be slower when one gets to this stage
Or be it, so far, at an advanced age

A. T. Higgins

Forever My Love

In the not too distant past, your fear of love was strong
The fear of falling for the man who turned out to be wrong
So then you hid yourself away—retracting in your shell
Creating the illusion everything was going well

But deep inside the sorrow grew, pain eating you away
You had to find a happy life where you would always stay
One day there came the dawning fate holding out its hand
For you to hold and then be led into your promised land.

You found a greater peace of mind which you had never known
I know I am responsible, between us love has grown
I live to make you happy so that you can enjoy life
One day a fact I know for sure—I'll take you for my wife

I want to tell my only love, don't worry, it's alright
I swear I'll never leave you as our future is in sight
No girl on earth could take your place our love is far too strong
We two will be together, where forever we belong.

My darling please believe me, I need you—can't you see
To know you are my lady is so wonderful for me
I've never felt such happiness, you've given this to me
In years to come we'll still be here for everyone to see

Forever My Love

Andrew Halford

Inspiration

A sun filled sky,
A stormy cloud,
A gentle breeze,
Or biting wind.
A raging sea,
A golden sand,
Tall dark cliffs,
And rich green valleys.
A smile so warm,
A shoulder to cry on,
A comforting arm,
And eyes so loving.
Raindrops on a rose,
The sweet smell of lavender,
Thoughts so deep,
You could easily drown.
All of these things you have given to me,
Thank you,
My sweet inspiration.

Paul Roberts

Exams

Exams are coming and you're studying hard,
But always remember to be on your guard.
Questions will pop up where you don't expect
But if someone says copy, you must always reject.
So if your papers are not all finished,
Do not let your hopes diminish.
If you do, it will get you down and instead of a
smile you'll be wearing a frown!

Ricki-Lee Millward

Sad I Am

I am
The baby's dummy lying in the gutter
I am the tragic words the doctor has to utter
I am the empty bottle lying in the street
I am the pair of shoes that no longer fit the feet
I am the broken light upon the Christmas Tree
I am the boring film that no one wants to see

I am the teacher everyone loves to hate
I am the broken lock on the broken gate
I am the crooked pictures hanging on the walls
I am the rusty car that always stops and stalls
I am the empty house that family left behind
I am the lost boy that no one wants to find

I am the broken handle falling from the door
I am the starving child too scared to ask for more
I am the old clock that no longer ticks to tell the time
I am the sad I am the one that doesn't have a rhyme

Emily Ruth Tyrrell

Memories

The hills that rise above this land,
This good ole land of Wales,
Remind me of the valleys, pitheads, and the vales,
The miner with his davey lamp,
The baker with his dough,
The pithorse laden with coal dust,
The farmer with his hoe.

Ah where are all the good old days,
Past they're gone away,
Just scars and memories left behind,
to remind us of our ways.

When I was a lad, to the shop I'd go,
a penny in my hand,
For a bag of broken biscuits and
a day upon the sand,
Then home I'd go for supper, just
a piece of bread and jam.
Then up to bed to rest my head and
say goodnight to mam.

P. H. Rogers

Maxi

Oh sleepless night 'tis far too long,
No major worries, nothing wrong,
Husband sleeping like a log,
Between us Maxi our pet dog.

The kitchen warm, is his domain,
But door left open once again
Maxi's out and up the stairs,
And now our double bed he shares.

I try so hard not to concede,
One inch of space, he does not heed
My remonstrations whispered loud,
He looks pathetic, even cowed.

But will he budge, no bribe he'll take,
So there am I still wide awake,
Pushing, trying to squeeze him out,
Husband wakes up with a shout.

Expletives I could not repeat,
Must surely be heard in the street
With one expressive rolling eye,
Our Maxi says "What move? Not I."

Ellen G. Moody

From Where I Sit

From where I sit across white linen, neatly folded serviettes
fanned in shiny goblets, a friendly face beams across with
glowing cheeks and wind–caught nose, unspoken words need
no reply.
The loving smile and caring eyes show little of the tender
wounds and mending parts that prick and twinge as healing
works, making body whole to meet with mindful wants.
But so the love shows strong through talking eyes and
innocent words.
From within, without thought or contemplation for no re-
hearsal or appraisal to speak with love is needed.
From where I sit, eyes flicker as others enter and greeting pass
and smiles rebound.
Unseen guests pass time of day, each carefully scrutinizing
but carefully not seen.
The mirrored images of healthy glows and sun–lightened hair
reflects with pleasure of days enjoyed, and quiet words across
the linen are hushed again as heads incline to say hello.
Then once more hushed still yet again as busy girls bustle by
or hovering host with poised pen seeks to please and order
wine, but come the quiet, heads rise and close again to
private words.
From where I sit across white linen, years have past and
lightened brown is silver–grey. More smiles abound and
reassure of powerful
love, but with so few words all is very clear from where I sit.

David E. Wilson

The Grace Of God

He sits in the doorway, this once proud man
He's trying to survive the best way he can

His clothes are dirty, tattered and torn
His eyes are empty, his face forlorn

A cardboard box is a roof for his head
Newspaper and rags make us his bed

He has no future, he lives for the day
His past is forgotten, he prefers it that way

We forget that he also once had a life
A mother, a father and maybe a wife

We look away, we try not to stare
If we don't see, we don't have to care

We show him no mercy, our hearts are cold
He's just a vagrant, dirty, poor and old

We should realize, as we pass him by
That "there for the grace of God go I"

Patricia Chillingworth

Stop And Think Now

When troubles, trouble you, and life seems grim and grey.
Just look back and remember a day, when you were happy and gay.
When life looks as if you can't go on, look at the world
   around see what God has done.
See all the colour's to brighten our day, tree's and hedges and
   grass that's green.
Flowers all different colours all there to be seen,
Birds around stop and listen
Even the buzz of the bee.
Can bring peace you'll see.
Just take note of all you have against all you have not,
   then ask yourself do I really need all those have-nots.
Then you may find comfort in all you have got.
    Give a smile to all who pass you by to put that twinkle in your eye
It will lift you up as you see it return to you twice as bright.
Then your troubles will vanish out of sight.

   Vera Warnock

Seedless Dreams

Eternally Ethereal,
Breathlessly drifting,
Transported on Warm whispering feathers.
Intimately enfolding,
Homogeneous womb . . .
Rebirth.

Spiralling upwards,
Volatile delicate wings
of Gossamer brilliance.
Vaporize into irrecoverable
Threads of time.

Rainbows fill our eyes,
as heavy footfalls
of now
Echo the dark walls of devoir,
Where dreaming acorns are
indefinable and mysterious.

   Carolyn Marshall

Honey Suckle

Sweetly scented with trumpet shaped flower,
Lonicera periclymenum or familiar woodbine
A plant for the garden
Or wild in hedgerows, but
The small red berry,
You will find
Is poisonous, and therefore dangerous.

However, on a summer evening,
With its delicate perfume,
Through a open window,
Honeysuckle, will bring joy to a room

   Nita Ann Jones

Death At Christmas

Someone died today,
With few friends or memories,
From happy times long ago.
Today his friend is dressed in black,
Who leaves no shadow in the sun,
Or footprints in the snow.

No present underneath his tree,
No sounds of excited laughter,
Only his weary, lonely sigh.
And the shadows of his past,
Flit across his half blind eyes,
Whilst his friend watches him die.

Why should we worry about his fate?
We've all had our share of losing,
We try to forget tears we've cried.
But I was just thinking that whilst I laugh,
With my family, who are dear to me,
That someone, somewhere, died.

   Michael Price

Eulogy For A Friend

We all must live life to the full,
   And have our hopes and our fears
Until the day we receive God's call,
   And leave our friends to shed the tears.

But the death of one so young,
   The early loss of so much magic
Surely there must be something wrong,
   To feel the loss from a death so tragic.

Even as we suffer the pain,
   We each must realize we have our fate
But as our tears fall with the rain,
   We must not succumb to the hate.

For with each life must come a death,
   And for those of us who feel so sad
It's best to remember with death comes rest,
   And eternal sleep can't be that bad.

   Clare Shimell

Evocation

Gone is the Harper, gone from the hall
Where the wind now howls through crumbling wall.
Lost is the singer, lost is the song.
Sung by the Harper, sung to the throng.
Songs of youth and songs of age,
Songs of gentleness, songs of rage,
Songs of the days of noble deed
Done by the heroes born to the need
Songs that tell of the days long gone
That glow as the gold of the setting sun.
Songs to gladden the jaded heart
That as the Harper we may depart.
Gone is the Harper, gone from the hall.
Where the wind now howls through crumbling wall
Lost is the Harper, lost is the throng
Lost now the singer, lost now the song.

   Kenneth C. Mason

Man Of The Night

Watch out for the man of the night
The one who gives you such a fright
Under the bed, behind the curtain
Were he is no one is certain
When you're creeping up the stairs
You can feel his deadly stares
From the door, to your bed you jump
Was it the man of the night who made that bump
You look here, you look there
But the man of the night is everywhere
Under the blankets you feel at ease
Holding your breath and scared to sneeze
Next thing you know, you wake to daylight
"Phhew" who's afraid of the man of the night.

   Billy Cleator

From Darkness To Light

Where is the darkness
Where has the safeness gone
The light, is this the light
What beauty
But this is strange, this is frightening
Where is your hand, oh where is your hand
Hold me please, I need you
Yes, I love you, I have always loved you
But you would not hold me
You said I could only be strong on my own
I cannot be strong without you
You are gone now
I gave your ashes to the freedom of life
Do not leave me in the darkness
It does not feel good and I am frightened
My father, let my arms embrace you
Let me open my eyes, knowing you will hold me for always
And lead me to the light

   C. G. Mason

60

Lost In A Clockwork Crowd

Peering through the window bare
Silent as though there's no one there
Shadows fill the empty space
Mysterious, creeping upon the face
Of the clock

The hand searches carefully
Moving around nervously
Ticking with a steady pace
Over and over upon the face
Of the clock

As the numbers seem to merge together
Memories people share forever
My life dictated, moving along with the flock
I'm just another number upon the face of the clock

Sonia Inam

Romanian Babies

They are small human beings who lie on their beds,
with little strength left they rock their heads.

Nowhere to go
Nowhere to lie,
we are just left here to die.

They are alone with despair in their eyes
weak, so you won't hear their cries.
Left on their own
filth-ridden mattresses
are these babies' home.
We are the innocents, left to suffer so
no home, no warmth, or food
nowhere to go.
We just want to cuddle
someone to hold
care for us, and love us
and shut out the cold.
Please God, listen to our prayers,
and send someone who really cares.

Iris Tennent

Captured Thoughts

Inner fear and silent dread
Have captured thoughts inside my head
That creep into this empty shell,
These thoughts have found a place to dwell.

Thoughts, like a forgotten face
That disappeared without a trace,
Discover now this dormant mind,
A place that time once left behind.

Thoughts that utter not a word,
Nothing spoken, nothing heard.
But raging like a restless sea
Are thoughts that will not set me free.

Thoughts, though silent like a cloud,
Are sometimes spoken out aloud.
They often make me want to shout,
These thoughts that I can do without.

J. Y. Heath

The Rose

The rose stands in the garden
In solitude and silence
Forever waiting for the sun
With its warm, caring rays
To awake from its slumber
For its rays to caress
The delicate, gentle yet secretive petals
For the rays to gently whisper
"Now it's time for you to open."
"Now it's time to show your beauty"
"For the whole world to see"

Vena Dacent

War Child

Drowned in the blood of his neighbours and friends,
He floats.
Smothered by the bodies of those unknown,
He respires.
Stalked by the soldiers who killed all the rest,
He escapes.
Stabbed by the remorse for those passed on,
He dies alone.

Cara Taylor

The Chaffinch In Winter

Closeness of eve and morning lights
Is from the weak sun. And, in his course,
Ill-lights a flock from freezing nights:
Delivered scarce to free remorse.
Their chapter read; the question "out"—
Are these, this bounty, yours?
Arriving with his pretty shout
To take the fruits in "fours".

Know that the wild wind whistles;
In loneliness you know the wand, and "gone".
Wild winds over his Epistles.
The heath and He must blast alone.

So turns his way from Solitude.
"Much" is a timely flood.
Is a fire for the berries' adhering.
By those colours of His: "Autumn—nearing"
That we know have a visitor calling.
And the needy may be understood.
End.

Robin Sackett

A Memory

We sat, youngsters, in an Autumn night.
Our hefty Halloween bonfire before us,
Swaying grass around us, And a misty guiding light above us.

You said my name. You touched my cheek. You looked at me.
Eyes to lips to eyes. You held my hand,
Calming the tumult in my tiny mind,
The churning in my stomach. Nervous anticipation as you
moved closer.

Then closer. Your scent caught the breeze
And I saw your smile. A kiss.
Magic in a second, held for an eternity.
Another; a tingle became a sparkle;
A flurry of emotions concentrated in the warmth of your lips.

I remember you often.
You are worth a million words, commanding a
Million recollections.
I remember it often. My moment in heaven.

Jacqueline A. Maguire

Painful Seasons

New spring lovers enjoying
Each eve whisper dead
I alone under stars
Deep gloom under covers sob

Summer past in longful crying
I bear the pain of embarrassed face
Kneeling emotions pray for human kindness
God ignores my pretty desires

I look in autumn fog
No eyes look deep with second glance
Now longer nights enfold me
Lay silent no recallable loving memory

Winter children enjoying
No youth left for romance
No chance of happiness
Turns heart into sharp stone
Old maid left in bitter woe

Clare Heaney

Always

When I am gone please do not weep,
For I'll leave you memories forever to keep.
For wherever you go, I'll not be far
I'm in the sun and the moon and the first evening star.
I'm walking beside you wherever you tread
I'm there in your eyes, I'm every tear that you shed
I'm in all of the places we went together
Could I ever leave you, no my love never,
For I'm in all of the memories of the love we did share
Just close your eyes and you'll find me there.
Think how we walked hand in hand in the sun
How the sound of our laughter made us seem one
Then I'll be beside you the rest of your days
And the love that I gave you will be yours for always
And so when you think of me please do not cry
For while you still love me I'll never die.

A. L. Butler

Understanding

It begins like a grain of sand encased within a walnut shell;
Out of reach but ultimately attainable, imaginable.
The thoughts are tightly enmeshed,
No room for movement, or expansion, barely space to allow
    in a new one.
Then finally, something, someone callously breaks up the
    crust of fears,
Shatters the finiteness and solidity.
Then the mind unbounded and ephemeral quality, never to
    make laws or to be obeyed,
Never replicated.
It changes, moulding to the winds, dancing and laughing with life.
The nut shell has long since gone, broken like the other
    shackles of ignorance.
What takes its place?
Nothing, nothing and everything.
Knowing that we can never know,
Knowing that we can never grasp.
Just the realization of 'Eternal'.

Sarah Pascale Mettam

Just Me

Sailing around on life's dark lonely sea
I moored upon an island and thought I'd found my key
A key to end my life's sadness its loneliness and pain
Making me feel warm as the sun upon the summer's grain.
My feet on firm ground after sailing for so long
I heard a choir singing a joyful song
I heard the birds and felt warm wind upon my weathered face
After sailing for so long I thought I'd found my place.
I found someone to love and care for
Someone to share my heart
A love so strong we surely could not part.
But one dark stormy torrid night my boat set free
I felt myself drifting back into the sea
Slowly watched in agony as I was parted from my love
The girl I gave my heart, my angel from above
Now I sail alone again upon this lonesome sea
Thinking always of my lost love . . . alone again . . . just me.

Graham Mackenzie

The Song Of The Shore

I was away from my home
which is near to a beautiful shore;
the giggling waves, the silent sea,
the setting sun,
always poured a colourful dream in my mind.

The glorious scenery of the rising sun,
Gave freshness in my day
and the silent songs of the waves
brightened up my heart with hope.

A thousand stories, which I shared with you
will always be a sweet memory.
I miss you, I miss you and I am sorry
I have to leave you forever and ever.

Mrs. R. S. Anthony

People Tell Me

People tell me I'll get over him.
People tell me the pain will go.
People tell me I'll forget him.
But when? That's what I want to know.

People tell me there are more pebbles on the beach.
People tell me there are more fish in the sea.
People tell me there is more than him.
But where can I find someone as special to me?

People tell me I'm going crazy.
People tell me I must be mad.
People tell me I'm being a fool.
But why can't they see I'm just feeling sad?

People tell me it's all over.
People tell me it's the end.
People tell me, it's all finished.
But why doesn't that help my heart to mend?

People tell me it's a blessing.
People tell me not to moan.
People tell me I've been lucky.
But why can't these people just leave me alone?

Mary Bates

Looking For My Angel

I've been looking for my angel to come and rescue me,
Take me away from the harshness of reality,
All this madness and insanity,
I hope and I pray that my angel comes soon,
It's hard to make it through another day without you.

I've been looking for my angel on the cold dark city streets,
It's four o'clock in the morning I'm so lonely I can't sleep.
I'm sure I see the devil in all the people that I meet,
Heaven seems so far away hell's right underneath my feet

I've been looking for my angel through the bottom of my glass,
Another drink too many I swear the bar lights must be stars,
There's a sad girl in the corner sitting all alone,
Just waiting for her angel to come and take her home.

And angel you are my sanity in all this insanity,
You are my shelter from the wildest storm,
When I am cold you make me feel warm,
You are my sun in the pouring rain,
Give me strength and ease my pain
When you are my everything what can I do.
When it's hard to make it through another day without you

Steven Deary

The Glen

There used to be a magical place,
Down where the tram lines end
Across the road the entrance lay
It beckoned you to come this way

Like stepping into a brand new world
All your senses becoming unfurled
Everything seemed so quiet and still
Yet background noise happening at will

The sun flickering through the trees
Leaves rustling in the breeze
Insects making their presence known
Although themselves were never shown.

Birds singing their endless song
Nothing in this world was wrong
and yet through the silence being aware
Of water trickling down somewhere

Bees seemed to hum as they moved with grace
Flitting about from place to place
It seemed like time was standing still
No one could ever get their fill.

Marion Holt

Quarant Ore

Slowly the procession wended its way through the mighty throng,
While the little children, dressed in white strewed flowers as
they walked along,
Before the canopy all gold and white—before the priest who
held their God.
O glorious sight.

When at last they reached the altar, the priest resumed his place
To watch and pray another hour before the Throne of Grace.
For those who were watching with him for hearts that had
grown cold.
For those in their last agony, for those not yet of the fold.

While awaiting Benediction some people told their beads,
While others asked for faith and hope and help in all their needs.
When the little bell hand tinkled and the organ played a chord,
All looked with love on the Sacred Host: each murmuring—
"My Lord and God!"

As the candles were being extinguished, I knelt behind to pray
In thanksgiving to God for the blessings showered on me all
that day:
And my heart went out to the absent who knew not the joy
that was ours:
Of watching and praying with Jesus Alone for—"Forty Hours"

Margaret McCartan

The Dentist's Chair

I sit in the chair and start to shake,
    the tooth at the back, is a dull throbbing ache,
With mask, and gloves, and long white gown.
    The dentist approaches, his face in a frown.

"Open wide lad, and let's have a look"
    He says, as he grabs for his horrible hook,
A jab, a stab, a pull, and a poke.
    I've come to the conclusion, that this is no joke,

"It'll have to come out lad", he chuckles with glee,
    "Just a couple of tugs, and I'll soon have it free",
He picks up this needle that's full of novocaine,
    "Once you've had this lad, you'll not feel the pain."

With a tug, and a twist, a pull and a snap.
    Out flies the tooth, and it lands in my lap.
So with blood on my chin, and a hole in my gum.
    I'm starting to wish that I'd never come.

With my jaw all numb, I get to my feet,
    Dripping with sweat, and as white as a sheet,
My eyes suddenly open, I'm gasping for air
    My God, I've been dreaming, the damn tooth's still there!

J. S. Thomson

Winter In The City

Destitute and saturated with the dirt of the street
He shuffles along defying his swollen feet
Rummaging through bins for something edible
Never knowing what will be on his table

Chilled to the bone by the raw night air
He squats on a milk crate, he doesn't care
Outreached hands meet the warmth of the fire
Throw a log on, watch the flames go higher

His weather-beaten face flushed with meths
The sweet, sickening stench exhaled on his breath
Bottle held tightly, he'll not let it drop
His passport to oblivion, only death will bring a stop

Cardboard and newspaper, his bed for the night
Hiding from the yobbos, he doesn't want a fight
The drunken slumber provides an escape
The only way, the road he must take

There's little comfort on the streets in the city
Labelled unclean, there isn't any pity
Remember, if you see him he didn't plan it his way
He was dealt a bad hand and now he's got to pay

Helen Dew

The Man In The Moon

Carved within glittered silver,
Spying the winking,
Shattered fragments scattered in the black shrouded mirror.
From his sparkling face,
Tears of crystal fall in Night's echoing footsteps.
Polished by a cosmic cloth,
Of filtered navy was his face.
Amber crept across,
Straggling between the silver spiked wardens
Of the darkness.
He turned his flushed cheeks away.
Flames danced across his shadowed threshold.
Consumed by the burning golden ocean,
He was drowned in the dawn . . .

Rebecca Houghton

Love's A Gamble

To you love's one big gable,
I'd never know for sure.
You'd play with my emotions
You'd been in love before

You told me that you loved me,
And I gave you my heart
You took it away, never brought it back,
I'd been fooled from the start.

You came along when it suited you,
Just when you wanted more.
Well, now I just don't want to know
I've heard it all before.

I'm sick of all the stupid games,
In my heart games are over
Your love's not wanted anymore

Gemma Cunningham

Babe In Arms

The pulse beats slow along his neck,
    The eyes, unblinking, stare ahead
Drier than bone—and cold!
    The flesh is warm, the mind alert,
His heart beats steady—he appears well fed,
    But his face—it seems so old.

He stands alone, as still as stone,
    Feet on sand and hand on gun—
Defiant and cruel we're told.
    Lost is he to reasoned word—
Cornered! Like a hunted cat,
    His grip, so desperate now, on a life
Which other men have sold!

Alive, maybe, on a medic's chart,
    But love lies dead within his heart
Trained was he to shut it out,
    This seasoned twelve year old!

Cathryn Saveker

True Blue

Sometimes I feel so sad and low
Sometimes my feelings—I find hard to show
My heart cries out. For peace of mind
For truth—but not the hurting kind.
Emotions run wild—head's a mess
Nothing in perspective—in total distress
With shaking hands, I write this poem
To express the inner of the outer shown.
I know that actions speak louder than words
But what are actions, if they are not shared
What are words—if no-one hears
Emotional feelings—bring only fears;
Get yourself together, my voice tells my head
Anyone would think I was mourning the dead
But there go my feelings—so sad and low
If you've never been there—how would you know

Margaret E. Martin

The Jig-Saw

Round and round in circles,
This way, that way, all ways —
Is life really meant to be like this?
Something's missing,
The picture's not complete.
— A path is blocked; nothing to inspired us,
Something's missing.

One minute the puzzle seems near completion,
The next, it fades away.
Something's missing,
Searching and seeking and getting nowhere;
Forgetting, and clinging to what is there.

Something's missing.
And only when peace of mind is secured
The final piece will then be found.

Valerie A. Leach

A Mystic Moment

The fishing boat had gone long since . . .
Only a solitary gull,
grey and white, rode the sea-sway where
I swam in an ocean of Light—
Late late, rose set in a pearl sea,
In fiery radiance enfolding
The sky, the sea, the bay—and me . . .
And I—in spirit creaturely
and rare—did enter in . . .
   Not here . . .
      Nor there.

Christine S. Cornelius

Quiet Acceptance

Quiet acceptance and tolerance
When you know there's no way out.
No situation was ever helped when you raise your voice and shout,
Sometimes relief will come with tears
Like sun melts ice and snow
And with the passing of the years tranquillity you will know.
Our time allotted in this world
Is brief as in our dreams
So take what's offered with good grace
All is not what it seems.
Suffering is but part of life, as is joy and pleasure
Accept it all with gratitude
Enjoy your times of leisure.
Instead of weakness strength will come
To meet your needs each day
Who knows what lies in store for us?
Once we have passed this way.

Nora Pallett

God's Creatures

My sister has a cat called Lucy,
Gosh and she is very choosey,
My friend had a dog called Ted,
He would soon let you know when he had not been fed,
then there were two budgies Joey and Zoey they died,
now they will be singing in heaven, side by side,
then there is Tim the circus horse,
he loves the people and the applause,
then there are the lovely gold fish,
they swim so free in their bowl, by a pretty pink dish,
the sparrows keep on chirping happily,
even when the weather is cold,
the pigeons walk around, looking for food,
in all kinds of weather so bold.
Then there is the elephant so big and strong,
and the swan with its beautiful neck so white and long,
and the beautiful zebra looks like a striped horse that has
been painted by God,
these are all creatures of God, big and small, short and tall,
even you and I are all beautiful in God's eyes, no matter what our size.

Patricia Page

Life–Here–After

What a wonderful world this would be
if everyone lived in harmony,
with no pollution, or nuclear arms,
and all organic natural farms
where animals live happy and free
not caged, enforcing cruelty,
nor forests being torn apart
just love and friendship from the heart.
It's vital that we leave behind
a legacy that we were kind,
protecting future generations
then, we would deserve their salutations.

Dorothy B.

Dance With The Devil

Have you ever danced with the devil in the pale moonlight
Have you ever taken chances then turned in fright
What is it that makes us tempt the fates
Not lack of courage but the chance to fight.

Do we fight for glory or fight for peace
What is it that makes us seek
To change the world for better or worse
Come what may we are all cursed

So we fight with the devil in the afterlife
And for our children and the people who find
That their courage has gone and they live in strife.
They are not fighting the devil; they are dancing his life.

So let's dance in the moonlight and wake with the sun
Hoping that soon our deeds to become
Our lifeline and longer throughout the years
All fighting is over and wars overcome.

Sheila Storr

This Troubled World

The news on T.V. and in the papers too,
nothing but violence the whole world through.
Old people who ought to be safe and sound
are often found lying on the ground
murdered, bashed or disgustingly raped.
The world's in turmoil, the windows draped.
Parents and teachers not allowed to check
or even discipline, what the heck?

Drugs, bad language, drink and abuse,
we try our best but what's the use?
If only we could put things right
to make a perfect world without a fight
Little children could be safe and well fed,
old people safe in their bed.
What a happy world this could be
with peace on earth for you and me.

Hilda Coward

Do As I Say

'Why don't you smile', he said
   so I smiled
'Don't you feel better?'
   'I don't know that I do'
'Why don't you laugh', he said
   so I laughed
'Laughing' he said 'really suits you'
   'unburden yourself', my counsellor said,
   at fifty dollars an hour
You bet I will,
So I told him my fear at losing my job,
   And at forty six being over the hill,
I met him today, looking worried and worn,
   As though a sword was hanging over his head
'I hear that your college is closing,
Why don't you have a laugh' I said
'You'll feel much better after a while'
He looked at me—but he didn't laugh,
And I noticed he didn't even smile.

Tracy Hopkin

The Mind Of A Child

"Where do you go once you are dead?"
A wistful child to me once said.
And looking down to innocent eyes I thought, this child
deserves no lies. "To a place of love, a place of rest",
I explained to him.
I tried my best. He asked, "But if you leave your home, aren't
you sad and all alone"?
"Why no", said I "you do not mind, for there are people warm
and kind who love you dearly. For you see, they're members
of your family".
And for a moment, I saw a trace of understanding on his face,
And as he stood to walk away I said, "Why ask me this
today"?
He looked at me, eyes glazed and wide and said
"Because my dog has died. But it's okay, I will not cry, my
dog's with Grandad in the sky".
And off he ran, so free and wild and left me in awe of the mind
of a child.

Charlene Beswick

"Upon A Hill"

Upon a hill is a place I like to be,
upon a hill just to go there and be me.
Upon the hill and looking out to sea,
or down to the valley at cottages, and
trees, the church spire in the distance
pointing heavenly, or the sound of a far
of engine, to keep me company.
Alone upon a hill is good for me
you see, I take the time to ponder and ask
some questions that worry me.
The solitude and silence is a gift from God
you see, and where else could you find
that gift, among this worldly spree.
So take advantage of that gift,
and be like me you see and climb upon
a hill no matter where you be.

Janet Judge

Memory

Though much has gone, and death has taken much,
Still will the dream live on—to give to others
Such happiness as in the life that you passed on.

And though the memory fades of face and form
The woods we walked should vanish or give way before the storm,
Though words should lose their beauty,
    or Autumn leaves their gold.
Though laughter be forgotten and all the tales be told.
Yet still your dream will linger

Will never be forgot,
It will live within my memory,
When other dreams are not.

M. F. Dawson

The Passing Of Time

I wish we could halt the hands of time
Return to an age when life was sublime
When our greatest problem was what to wear
Or whether to alter the style of our hair

How carefree we were as each day passed
Thinking our age would forever last
Not knowing the changes that lay ahead
When the day would come and youth be dead

Like the relentless tide on the sandy shore
Destroying our footprints forever more
Or the leaves that are stripped by autumn's chill
Those symbols of nature will continue still

For we shall grow old as time marches on
And we must not long for the years that are gone
But be glad of the thoughts that we have of the past
Filled with memories that forever will last

Hilda Vass

The Death Of A Baby Seal

The baby seal with soft trusting eyes,
watched the approaching man—
The man had a club in his hand,
the baby seal did not understand.
When over the little seal the man stood,
and raised his club as high as he could,
the baby seal with soft trusting eyes,
mercifully (?) never understood.

B. Shaill

Romantic Nostalgia In Verse

Looking back we most of us can remember our first crush
But being inexperienced we felt we mustn't rush
Yet age does not come into it when you get down on one knee
My first love started early and her name was Barbara Lee
We would walk hand in hand enjoying every day
We'd be the envy of everyone but she had to move away
We spent all our spare time together until the parting came along
And when the fateful day arrived we both had to be strong
She was a policeman's daughter and the whole affair we
    found testing
For although we were both so young I always found her
    arresting
But it seemed somehow that to share our lives was never
    going to be
And I would have to wait for someone else till then I would be free
In any case I wasn't really ready for what husbands have to strive
It was going to be rather painful but you see we were both
only five

Reg Morris

Panic

Cars, photos and the ring,
Have I remembered everything?
Did I post all the invitations,
Have I missed anyone's relations?
Is his buttonhole on quite straight,
Will the vicar turn up late?
Has someone arranged all the flowers,
Will the food keep another two hours?
Did someone remember to collect the cake,
Will all the children stay awake?
I hope my mum won't start to cry,
And he remembers to wear a tie!
I can't stand much more waiting about,
But of one thing I have no doubt,
That even with all this stress,
All the work and all the mess,
Today will be the best of my life,
When he and I become man and wife.

Jenny Brown

Memories

As I lie upon my bed
Thoughts and dreams go through my head,
Thinking of all the times gone by
Lying there and thinking why,
Remembering the good and the bad
Making me happy and making me sad,
Then I turn my head to see
A photo — it's you and me.
Why Lord, why has he gone?
It hurts so much what's been done,
The love we had was so sincere
I wish that you could still be here.
I miss your smile, that look in your eye
Thinking of you I break down and cry,
I miss you son and love you so
Those precious memories will never go.
They will be with me until I die
Good night God bless and Son goodbye.

S. A. Dewey

2000 Years

The handle on the door had long since been betrayed
Not even light would pass that way again,
And the withered hands of a far superior world
Clutch tightly to the headboard of his bed, it would not be long,
Although he could wait a thousand years, he has waited twice
as long.
It would not be long, undisturbed, abandoned,
He has waited twice as long.

A stranger in his midst
A dropout in a world he could have once swallowed, but not now,
He no longer desired the need to reach
His thoughts were now for himself
And his mind strictly a private dwelling, he was smiling,
It would not be long.

So he turned his head and was gone,
But his eyes would tell the truth for that someone he once knew,
The burning tears were falling on a dying, coloured dew
For that someone he once knew.

A bird in the air had lost its place of rest
And the leaning tower was built . . .
For the stunt men of the universe.

Paul Coates

Childhood Memories

Oh, to be a child again; those happy carefree days,
To run through fields of daisies fair,
In sunshine or in rain, to pick the wild flowers growing there
In May time or in June, the bluebells, and the buttercups, the
fairy thimbles too. We pulled them to our heart's content, so
beautiful to see. The perfume and the scent,
you could not buy, were free,
My father's laces from his boots our flowers he would tie,
His pleasure; I will treasure, his love for us, and nature.
No gold or silver could replace; these memories are forever.
We had no need for modern toys, the kids depend on now,
There wasn't such a thing, as videos or telly,
No money had we to spend, we had good parents; love to
cherish the simple things that count
Mother nature's gifts were free, the trees and birds to sing
We knew them all by name; oh happy days of school, and
games, of skipping ropes, of rounders, and kick the can,

To mention just a few, I would not change these memories
For castles lined with treasures, for just and family shared
Tho' simple never grand, the pleasures, just happy days.
In God's own wonderland.

Patricia Ross

Sunk To The Depths

Hurricane winds increasing, wind jammer keeling
floors becoming ceilings, water takes on new meaning
ship turns turtle in a flash, all around galley bottles smash
lights black out with a crash, got to get out fast
day light streaming through an open door
struggle through what is now the floor
body oh so drained and sore
water surging in with a roar
drowning now a possibility, water rising above my knees
breath beginning to seize, why are they such cruel and callous seas
sea water now in my lungs, I can taste salt upon my tongue
feel so highly strung, my swan song is now sung
my life flashes before my very eyes
and I begin to cry
but I don't want to die
someone help, oh please try
water is now over my head, my prayers have now been said
I think, now I'm surely dead, float to the surface instead
after what seems an eternity a saviour gives my hand a squeeze
oh God thank you please, I am now so safe and free.

James Reid

The Attic—The Place That Time Forgot

The attic brings to me bygone days.
Those hazy, crazy days.
Lost amidst the dust and shadows,
such happiness.

I lose myself in memories of former bliss.
Entranced, my fingers wander as I reminisce.
Over leather bound classics, tarnished by age,
and toys long forgotten,
from my frolicsome days.

There stands the rocking horse,
after many a year.
Still grand and resplendent.
A toy greatly revered.

I cast my eyes about the place,
and a smile descends upon my face.
A knowing smile of knowledge gained,
That the child in me's still here today.

Ceasing to be in suspended time,
The place time forgot,
adheres to my time.

Amanda Nwanosike

River Of Life

Softly whispers soughing waters, words unspoken, dreams undreamt
eddies ripple, gently linger, then are gone,
their time all spent . . .

Lying deep in earthy slumber, settled far beneath the flow
surrounded by a stony silence,
thoughts of rock are all I know . . .

Now I drift, fragile, fleeting, faery boat upon a wave
memories of green life stir faintly,
to the tide I am a slave . . .

Clinging, desperate, to sodden safety, swirling with the surge I go
spinner of sweet widow's tears,
all the same, caught in the tow . . .

Embraced within my mother waters, caressed by her silken warmth
peace enfolding, waiting sleep of the unborn,
in this form yet to come forth . . .

Softly whispers soughing waters, words unspoken, dreams undreamt
eddies rippling, gently linger, then are gone,
their time, all spent . . .

Melanie Harvard

Lonely Or Alone

Alone, solitary, by myself. . . alone perhaps.
Each of us is essentially alone, but lonely?
In common with most people is this feeling,
the feeling of loneliness.

Sometimes it is but a fleeting, momentary thing,
just an occasional moment, persisting.
For some, it's a time of devastation,
to be alone with loneliness.

Sometimes we meet another soul . . . understanding,
feel close, at one with the other,
but part of us if always separate,
and still, we have loneliness.

Always there is a part we never share,
that is separate, only ours alone,
a private place, no strangers enter,
there, we breed our loneliness.

We are alone until we realize we are not.
The spirit, the force that is us
is within us and shares our life.
The animate existence, it dispels loneliness.

Ruth Daester-Garner

When?

When will this war ever end, Daddy?
When will you put down your gun?
When will Mum's tears turn to smiles Daddy?
When will we all be as one?

When can we walk in the streets Daddy?
When will the fear go away?
When will the soldiers go home Daddy?
When can we go out to play?

Years have gone by very fast Daddy.
How long since the troubles began?
Soon I'll be big just like you Daddy.
One day I'll be a brave man.

Now we are standing out here Daddy,
Father and son side by side.
Isn't it grand to belong, Daddy,
Walking together with pride?

Oh look, here the bastards come now Daddy,
Give me that gun in your hand.
I'll show them how it is done, Daddy.
Then we'll have peace in our land.

Eve N. Armstrong

My One And Only

You asked me one day to be your wife
To stay by your side the rest of your life
I answered yes right away
I will always remember that wonderful day

People said we didn't stand a chance
No good could come from a whirlwind romance
For better or worse was our wedding vow
Eighteen years later I'm still with you now

You're still my friend and lover true
And you still know that I love you
We have found peace and contentment
While friends look at us with jealous resentment

Our family came early we did not plan
They will leave us soon but I still have my man
In the heat of the summer, or in the very cold
I hope we will be together until we are old

We have had our spring and summer too
I still have an undying love for you
If you should go first I won't be lonely
For I will have memories of my one and only

Catherine Preuss

Dad

God's taken you away to a nicer place
But all I remember is your smiling face
The joy and laughter you used to bring
Especially when we heard you sing

The funny things you used to do
But that was just special you
We loved you so very much
But now you're not here for us to touch

I wanted you here to give me away
Because soon it will be my wedding day
I know you'll be there to share with us
And to give us your blessing we would love so much

We think of you every minute, everyday
And we're sorry that you had to go away
But now it's time for me to go
And please remember we love you so

And now I must say goodbye
As I look up into the sky
That was so very hard to do
But I will always remember lovely you

M. Dale

If Only

Five years ago you were so big and strong
I thought you would always be like that but I was proved so wrong
For last time I saw you I got a terrible fright
For standing before me was a stranger who weighed so light

You'd been taking drugs for a long, long time until you were
hooked and did not care a dime
You mixed alcohol with cannabis, LSD and some more
But you never took your insulin because you thought it such a bore

If only you had taken more interest in the prescribed drug
And left the illegal ones alone that were such a bug

The empty space created by you in the hearts of your family
and friends
Would be filled with joy and laughter and not loose ends
For you were so young, only twenty six years old
If only you could have withheld the urge and been more bold

But it's no good dwelling on what might have been
For you have now gone and will never again be seen
You'll always be remembered for how you were
You'll always be loved because we all care

We don't know where you are only that you're somewhere up there
So good-bye for now and do not despair
For in our hearts and minds you'll always be there.

Dianne Darville

Listen

As this world of mine awakens
It's dawn again once more
You can smell the dampness in the air
See the dew upon the lawn
Witness works of art in cobwebs
That have been spun from branch to branch
Set with pearls of crystal like chandeliers
with the breeze they almost dance

As the splendid arch of sunshine
Rises high above its globe
A whole new day is dawning
Its magic to unfold
You can see these clouds I gaze upon
White parcels full of hope
A whisper's breath on mornings breeze
A world that's full of scope

For everyone's allowed to dream
And some of them come true
This world that I'm describing
Look hard it's there for you.

David Robinson

Sun Sea And Sand

I have sat and watched a flooding tide
All alone on a sun kissed beach
Caress the cliffs on either side
Drown everything within its reach
Just lain and gazed up at the sky
And only heard a sea birds cry

I have sat upon a cliff top high
With a wild gale blowing in my face
Watched the grey clouds scudding by
All alone in that salt tanged place
Like troops great waves marched right past me
In serried ranks to crash upon the rocks
Little ships went hastily to the lee
Or stayed securely tied up in the docks

I have sat and watched a full tide ebb
Just me and miles of empty sand, like a spider in the web
Sea holds me with her watery hand
A man is a fool who is not afraid
Of something so capricious so sweetly enticing like a maid
With body warm lubricious.

E. J. Tucker

An Evil World

It scares me to think how the world used to be
There was safety and pleasure and security.
But now it's not safe to walk out of your door.
Nowhere is safe anymore.

So many lives have been taken away.
Children are found murdered each day.
Sexual violence on the tv.
Pain and hurt and brutality.
Drugs on the street, AIDS, HIV
We need to open our eyes and see.
Life's a roller coaster ride where everything's wrong.
So many twists and turns it's hard to hold on.

Now it's not safe to walk down the street.
You don't know what kind of person you'll meet.
Morality seems to have crumbled to dust;
For these days there's nobody that you can trust.

So many lunatics causing distress.
We've got to face it the world's in a mess.
The world is a hell hole where murderers thrive.
We've all got to change if we want to survive.

Samantha Jones

"Victors"

There they lay, on their last parade,
   Open order, in line, the grass neatly laid,
Unit, name, rank and number displayed,
   Killed in action, on active service, it said.
Line upon line, in ranks, in units,
   Armies, companies, platoons and brigades,
We salute them, mourning their lost youth,
   Recalling with joy their laughter; tears for the brave
We love them, we salute them, but now it seems
   They are the victors—they died with their dreams.

Norman Mitchell

My Lover

In all its glory, the wings unfurled,
the sun shone through, transformed into the phoenix,
fiery waters blinded my eyes . . .
From its sereneness had risen the devil,
Hissing . . . , spitting . . . I,
Frozen to the spot, not a single movement,
—Or eyes met; calmness.
The song began, it embraced my being,
its grace had captured my soul,
then it lay down beside the still waters
to sing one last song.
Its slender neck curled within its body,
caressing the beauty that I longed to touch,
I reached out my hand.
A salty droplet trickled down my cheek.
Together at last,
But still worlds apart,
A love song from my dying swan,
to which I had lost my heart.

Daren John Lee

Dragon World

Dragon world, a place be told, imagination is the subject of the day.
With crystal flowers and sapphire skies and when the ruby
sun ends of the day.
Dragons of colour, so rich bright, so many can be seen,
With the blues and the blees, bright reds and sparkling greens,
how plain can I really be?
A place of great beauty, so divine where loves fair.
And where dragons play all day.
So the shimmering scales and dancing tails,
Are they really actually there?
A dragon world is the place for me, deep down so hidden in
my mind.
A place to retreat to when I'm down in my life,
And will always be there, just behind.

Claire Barnes-Downer

Precious Gifts

If we had to pay for our freedom,
We would spend all we had to be free.
If we had to buy our sight and sound,
We would buy it willingly.

If we had to pay for a ticket,
To smell the beautiful flowers,
I am sure that for one scented second,
We would all queue up for hours.

If we had to pay to stand on the beach,
To breathe in the natural sea air,
Or look at inspiring coastal views,
We would go without food just to be there.

Yet none of these things we have to do.
They are given to us all old and young.
Let's enjoy and appreciate these precious gifts.
All free—yet priceless to everyone.

Devina Symes

A Little Child's Reflections

I look in the mirror and what do I see
Somebody there looking back at me
I put out my tongue though I know it's not right,
And they do it too and they do look a sight.
It doesn't matter how often I try
Or careful I am when I walk by.
I tiptoe so softly and turn oh so quick
But they still get there first and it just makes me sick
I look round the back but there's nobody there
Then I peer round the front and they give me a scare
For as fast as I put my face in the way
They pop up again for the tenth time today

Then I remember, I've heard Mummy say
Leave them alone and they'll go away
She meant measles spots but I think it will do
Just as well when referring to mirror men too
So it's no use them coming in there to play
I'll not look in the glass so they must go away.

Joy Morgan

Happiness

Happiness is a passing phase
It eludes one in many ways.
Sadness seems to be my lot,
Joy in anything these days I fear I cannot.
Circumstances beyond control leave me raw,
Life goes on, oh! What a bore.
One day my life will change and I shall be pleased,
For when that day comes I shall be released.

Maxine Gutteridge

My Best Friend

Loving you is easy, for you are my best friend,
For I know that I can turn to you until the very end.
You light the road adore me so that I can see my way,
Allowing me to follow your footsteps day by day.
Life wouldn't be he same somehow, without you being there,
To feel your warmth and comfort and tender loving care.
To know that I can turn to you at any time of day,
Knowing that you'll listen to the things I have to say.
There were many times in life dear Lord, when I had lost my way,
And heavy clouds above me had dulled the brightest day.
And I have turned to you dear friend in sadness and despair,
And you have shown to me dear Lord how very much you care.
For your light of love and wisdom, has shown me to the way,
The path that I should follow without fear that I would stray.
You've held my hand in darkness and shared with me my sorrow,
You've been my rock to lean on and helped me face tomorrow.
Your friendship has sustained me through many trying years,
And my faith has been rock on which I've laid my many fears.
And so dear Lord I understand and realize it's true,
When it comes to friend we can ask no more, for the best of
them is you.

Sandra D. Stockton

Demon Drink

Hustling, jostling, thronging crowd,
Making noise that seems so loud,
Each one waiting for their turn,
The demon drink, will they ever learn?

Don't they see what harm it does?
The states they get in, how it shows,
Staggering here and staggering there
Making out they have no care.

Lives are ruined just through drink,
Why don't they just sit down and think?
That loved ones at home just sit and wait
And cry with thoughts of all those states.

Drink makes you hurt the ones you love,
It also makes you want to rove,
The rows you have, the things you say,
My friend you'll regret it all one day

Why don't you think about your ways?
And try to start a brand new day,
Sit down and say and even think
No more I'll have of demon drink

R. Walker

Parental Anticipation!

As I pace and ponder my thoughts interact, with a reminiscing vale,
of myself as a teenager, junior infantile, a human being, a male.
Striding back-and-forth, along the corridor of a new life,
expectantly waiting for the news, of an arrival from my wife.
I remember being small, cosseted, cared for, adored and kind,
Looking back brings these thoughts to the forefront of ones mind.
A boy or girl? Tension saunters, as it gently proceeds,
its final goal, its destiny, is one that nature concedes.
Growing-up untainted, conceptions unimpaired, puerile traits
   accepted easily,
Adulthood brings forth apprehensions, that our fears teach readily.
Simultaneous reactions bear down forcefully, impelling the
   parturition imminently due,
Its passage from here to another level of life, as it travels, does
   it rue?
I've grown, expanded my body and soul, progression in my
   life is clear,
but to be in this position, where I am responsible, ultimately
   instills fear.
It's nearing the time, systems go into drive, commencement is near,
these months of growing, preparing to a born life, that it can
   now hear.
I'll never be the same again, I'm better, contented and proud,
I'm a dad, paternal protection my aim, I love my child out loud.
Its journey over, changes will occur, from today it'll give us
   plenty of scope.
It's future is bright in many ways, my child, my world, my hope.

David Ellis

Ode To The National Lottery

On Tuesday, when I bought my ticket, little did I think
I'd be back at my desk today, with paper, pen and ink,
'Cos I was going to win the lottery, the largest one of all
And get the twenty million pounds for the six numbers that I call.
But here I am again, at the computer and desk
Doing all the usual things, and trying to do my best
To make an honest living, as all good people should
With their hands, brains and muscle—not just a piece of wood.
No champagne for elevenses, just a mug of tea
Or coffee if you prefer it—the mug to make it is me.
No 10oz steak for lunch, just a cup of slim-line soup,
No witty conversation, just the usual dull group
To while away the lunch hour and get ready for the fray
That follows all the afternoon to the end of day.
Ah, well, what would I have done with twenty million pounds,
And all the begging letters the post would bring around.
Although, I'm very disappointed. I did give a little cry.
But blow to all the things above—I'll have another try.

W. Davies

Beautiful Teenager

Gaze beyond the futility of what reflects
Nature hates you for what you need,
When all before them were obscured
By motorbikes and blood shot doves

Graze not hastily on all fear
Merely that which fantasizes.
Soft, warm nurtured from seed, believe
The divine triumphs over the diseased.

Grass–stained out of earshot now
Let it rise, concave and vile
Released tension exhilarates, infiltrates . . . ecstasy!
Then . . . it all begins . . .

Dopey, smiling eyes of stolen fortune
Deepest red mask envelopes society's fears
Future? Not really an issue now; only peace,
Only 'aftermath' . . . only beauty.

David Hanson

Birdman

It's hot . . . but I'm cool,
I'm lying in a pool,
I'm accompanied . . . but alone,
Jack and Tom keep me prone,
My spirit is free . . . like a bird I soar
scooping up the bright–life memories to store.

I'm really alone, mobile and aware,
Fresh and alert in my wheelchair,
As I sit, breeze gentles my face,
I've shut the pain doors, the world is My Place,
I'm easy . . . I'm calm . . . I'm ready to explore,
My spirit is free, like a bird I can soar.

E. Mugford

Swoon

Happy and glee
I find her so positive and free,
An angelic angel to see,
Dark hair and fair of face
Soft to touch and tender to hear,

I like her voice and personality,
To kiss and caress I'd love so much,
Caught in a web of emotions, blush,
Eye contact making your faceted face flush.

Emotions say it all, no words can at all,
Chemicals upon the air enthused with feelings,
Open hearts and embarrassed faces,
Dry mouths struck dumb as jumbled thoughts form words,

Address exchanging conversantly
Things liked in common,
Shall I see you soon?
I longingly swoon.

K. M. Clemo

Love

Love is a feeling deep in the centre of the heart,
When you can't stand to be apart.
Just to see him makes my heart beat fast,
It's different to all those times in the past.
I gave him all my love,
Not a soul on earth or in heaven up above,
Could ever take his place.

Now he's said goodbye,
I just sit and cry.
I can't live without him, but he doesn't feel the same.
What can I do to show him that love's no game.
I need his love so much,
And dream each night of his tender touch,
Knowing I will never feel it again.

Tammy Barnes

As One

Take strength from me to guide you
Through your troubled path of life.

Take courage from me to discover
That you can leave the past behind.

Take the care that I can offer,
It will shield you from now on.

Take my hand and walk beside me,
We'll face the world as one.

Take the friendship that I'll give you,
And you'll never be alone.

Take my mind for it believes in you,
Let it harmonize with your own

Take my love from deep within me,
To embrace you when we're apart.

Take my heart and feel its peace within
And place it next to yours.

Take my life which you alone fulfil
It's waiting with an outstretched hand.

Take my soul and let it fill you,
Today, tomorrow, always . . .

Lynn Petty

Cries From The Heart

So cold, so empty, so alone, a pain like I've never known,
All the things done and said, all the memories in my head,
Wind please take them in passing blow, I have to let each one go,
Take the tears away too, cause there's nothing left for me to do,
And what will I do now,
I don't know what, I don't know how
I see a new look upon his face,
All feelings for me gone, without a trace
No matter what I do or say
This hurt inside won't go away,
I feel so scared, I feel so trapped,
I fear that I won't adapt,
He said he cared, I don't know why,
That too turned out to be a lie
All the trust I had is gone,
Now in my heart there is none
Inside the pain has caused a crack,
But will it ever mend back
I can't take it I've had enough,
I'm finished with this thing called love.

Rita Shalllcross

Daddy

As the summer sun melts the earth,
And the birds sing loud and clear.
I think of you, your voice, your smile
And shed a silent tear.

My summer days were filled with fun,
My winter nights were warm.
For you were there to comfort me
And now you've gone, I mourn.

You blessed me with your talk, your song,
You made me laugh and cry.
You touched the hearts of those you met,
And then you said goodbye.

The sky turned black and the rain it fell,
On that day you died.
I miss you more than you could know,
I want you by my side.

My days seem long and silent now,
My smile has faded away.
But the memory of the love I had,
Keeps me going day by day.

A. C. Lloyd

The Lord Is My Shepherd I Shall Not Want

Leaving Bethlehem, on route to the Dead Sea,
the bus weaves through barren terrain
clumped intermittently with Cedars of Lebanon,
whose lush greenness relieve the plain,
passing the spot recalled in Psalm twenty three,
the Valley of the Shadow of Death.

Accommodating hyena and snake,
here, the bedouin scrambles to slake his thirst,
carrying the priceless liquid almost until they burst.
The sun's warm searching rays cannot penetrate and bake
every niche in this seemingly bottomless valley,

The bedouins do not anguish over money;
Living simply in a tent;
Eating figs and date from the Palm
Finding their supply has been spent,
Self sufficient tribes in the land of milk and honey,
will sell a sheep or kid in Jerusalem or Jericho.

Mary Bennett

My Pretty Room

When morning comes and I awake!
My mind starts turning oh! For goodness sake
I wonder what! This new day will bring
Will it make my heart sing?
Then I focus on my room
As the sun streams in and am soon
Awake! I lie there taking in,
All the prettiness of my room.
My pretty room where roses dwell
The curtains, carpets, bed as well
A beautiful red rose standing near by
Brought from the garden for me to eye.
I must get up very soon
A few minutes more to enjoy my pretty room,
The birds are chattering just outside
In the garden as I lay here a while.
A voice calls out Mum
I'm starving says my dear son
It's time to start another day
Back in my pretty room I'd like to stay.

Maggie Coleby

Wishes

Make a wish and what do we get?
We get the things we want the best.
Girls want dolls and boy's want trains
and Dad wants things but never complains.
Mum is there to see them all through and
some day soon she' ll have one too.

Yvonne P. Dyson

Fear

The brown leaves crackle 'neath my feet
But I hear nothing
Save the panting of my breath
Gasping for air, my lungs at bursting point
Never in my wildest dreams has such a fear
Reached a crescendo
Like the final chords of a vast orchestra
And I run, away from the mounting fear
Which engulfs my thoughts, oh to end it all
But suddenly when once more
I fear that I shall fall
Something catches my bloodshot eye
A little flower, sweet and wild
Struggling for survival 'midst a patch of weeds
I run once more but gaze in wonder
And feel ashamed of my unknown fears
My feet retrace the woodland paths
And back once more in the haven of my home
Never more to roam in fear, but lasting peace
And happiness to end each year.

M. A. Auton

Spring

Spring, spring a lovely time of year
Flowers pop up here and there
The foals are all wobbly
The chicks fluffy and bright
They'll play in the farm yard day and night.

Cracked egg shells on the forest floor
More nests in the trees
The sun is in the sky today
And there's a lovely breeze.

Hana Lucy Gilbert

Your Room

I went into your room today and sat down on your bed,
caressed the big soft pillows, where you laid your weary head.
I gazed, about your room in pain, wishing you were here.
I sit up there for hours on end, it makes me feel you're near.
I see your shoes upon the floor, your records all around,
to hear your music blasting out, I'd love to hear that sound.
It's all still there as it was, your room is just the same:
the telly's in the corner, where you played your computer game,
your posters up there on the wall, your fishing rod as well,
tennis rackets by the door and one lies where it fell.
The desk is there with all your bits, your bike is in there too.
Your wardrobe's there still full of clothes, all cleaned and
    pressed for you.
Those certificates you won at school, they're on your
    windowsill,
your trophies that you won at sport, so many they over-spill,
I see all these with a broken heart. I can smell your aftershave,
and all these beautiful memories, son, I will carry to my grave.

Rod Leaper

The Farm

The farm is such a wonderful place
As it stands alone in all its grace
Not even a house to stand and stare
Only fields of barley wheat and mares
With trees all around so tall and stout
That reach up to the morning cloud
Until the cockerel crows at break
And then you know everything will wake
The cows will moo the horses neigh
And all the animals will come out to play
At evening time when the sun is high
And all the clouds go rolling by
The farm will begin to go to sleep
Ducks, pigs, goats and the sheep
As they rest their heads in the hay
There's been and gone another day.

Malcolm Sage

"The Driving Test"

The driving test should never be, it's the hardest
thing for you and me.
You try so hard you sweat and shake, but does
he care? No, he's just a snake.
With horns so large coming out of his head he
reminds you of the devil instead.
"Turn left, turn right", he shouts with glee.
The three point turn was next for me.
I stalled and jumped to no avail, you stupid
fool you know you will fail.
Parallel parking was the worst, I only bumped into a hearse.
When will this ever end, the test centre is
just around the bend.
A few questions now about the highway code.
I hope I'm not being too bold.
I close my eyes I grit my teeth, the devil
himself is tapping his feet.
"I'm pleased to say you have passed, my dear."
I can't believe what I hear. I open my eyes and what do I see?
The Devil. O! No!. Not he.

Wendy Ashmore

Honouring Nelson's Flagship

I looked upon Nelson's flagship
    And surveyed the scene around
The wooden deck, bell and ringing
    Those things with an ancient sound

Of glories past and battles fought
    Cannonball and Sword
These were the features of Victory
    With an Admiral of due accord

I looked upon Nelson's ship
    In admiration and delight
A part of English history
    A truly wonderful sight

I bowed my head to Nelson's ship
    To all who served her well
A Gallant Crew who made her great
    With a greatness they could not foretell.

James Turner

A Special Place

I love to stroll along the beach and feel
the sand between my toes
My thoughts so far away from the daily stress and woes
the tranquillity of it all is sheer bliss
I pass two boys playing with their kites
the seagulls squealing at such a plight
the boys laugh as they fly away
a young couple walking hand in hand
sealing their friendship with a loving kiss
the sand is now quite firm as I walk towards the sea
the water rippling around my feet
gentle and cool as I wiggle my toes
I notice a stranger standing close by
he smiles but does not speak.
I feel so content watching the waves upon the sea
There is a gentle breeze, a fine sea spray washes over me
While standing there I feel such peace
my heart gently beating the stranger smiles and walks away
I wonder who he could be as he left two footprints in the sand.

Jean Goliger

Life

I feel so tired as if I want to sleep
Hanging on to life that I want to keep
Time slows down, pain sets in
My life flashes bye including the sin
I remember mistakes and chances not taken
I remember the heartache and so much frustration
I try to hold on to that sparkle of life
As if I can cut through the darkness with a very sharp knife
I hear every breath, shallow and slow
I hope I will make it, I really don't know
I think of lost dreams and friendships gone
I think of regrets and things I got wrong
Remembering also the times that I smiled
And being so innocent, naive as a child
The moments I laughed, the great times I had
Remembering the days I never got sad
Listening to music, singing aloud
Promises to friends, the things that I vowed
I remember the agony along with the strife
But without these things there wouldn't be life

Victoria Fusedale

The Tides Of Life

The tides of my life are changing, as sure as the sea
comes to the shore, leaving behind its flaxen, in life it
leaves a scar, when life is full and bountiful,
you never want it to change, but life is very cruel,
it never stays the same, you try to find the reasons why,
and apportion blame, and wonder why like treats us this way,
is it really such a shame.

Denise Harrison

Vanessa

The angels of love play my heart like strings
As the saying echoes "It's just one of those things"
My heart is broken as if made of glass
My love-life reads like a comical farce
I'm afraid to say it but it has to be said
The place is vacant where you lay in my bed
One day this may change the place filled by another
At first just friends, maybe later, lovers
Is it all just a dream or could it be real
Highly unlikely the way that I feel
For now I'll live my life in this dream
Swimming in uncertainty, as if it were a stream
I struggle again to keep myself afloat
While all I feel passes by like a boat
My life was once orderly my aims were so clear
Chaos now roams with loneliness near
To love another so soon, would hurt me too deep
To sow the seeds of love I couldn't hope to reap
To tell you how I feel would be too unfair
Three words will suffice "Probably alone, solitaire"

Kevin Kelly

Thoughts

What are you thinking with that smile on your face,
Playmates at school or a three legged race
Running and jumping and having some fun
Paddling, splashing and days in the sun.

What are you thinking with your eyes shut tight,
Stars in the sky or the moon shining bright
The man in the moon or is it cheese
A tickle in your nose that makes you sneeze.

What are you thinking when you're standing there,
Eyes shut tight and head in the air.
Are you thinking of fairies with gossamer wings
Candy floss, chocolates, all wonderful things.

What are you thinking with your head on one side,
Fair ground attractions or a donkey ride
Sand castles with flags and pebbles all around.
Sea weed or shells that give off a sound.

What are you thinking with that a tear on your cheek,
Smile be happy and you'll find all that you seek
May your life run smoothly like boat on calm water
After all young lady you're our daughter's daughter.

Edward A. Parnell

Mother And Father

Mother and Father
you must be glad
to see that your baby
will grow to be a fine lad.

You will be both there for his cry
and you will be there for his first goodbye.

You must be pleased to watch him grow.
And also for the love you both show.

When times are hard for you or him
Find a place in your heart, just for him.

He will grow up to be a fine man
I know you will try to hold on, for as
long as you can.

He will marry one day
And make sure you know what to say.

He will also have Children of his own
He will also repeat the Love you have both shown.

Orla Byrne

Passing On

A cold, dry day . . . I thank God for this,
No rain to mingle with the tears.
But "Why is she dead?" I want to cry.
She was so happy . . . though old in years.
Oh God, why not take someone else . . .
Some lonely person, who wished to die?

Perhaps I should pray for my mother's soul?
But selfishly beg "Don't let me cry".

My children shall see me looking strong,
As if there is nothing really wrong.
They must not know the searing pain . . . the emptiness I feel again.
Yet when into the ground she goes, I stare down at my icy toes,
And feel . . . nothing.

Returning home in hired car, a little hand thrusts into mine.
My own small daughter comforts me, and I feel quite suddenly
A surge of love for her . . .perhaps what my mother felt for me?

I vow to be more like she had been . . .
The loveliest person ever seen
Goodness and kindness, all in one . . .
From mother to daughter . . . to daughter . . . passing on.

Joy Paton

The 1 2 5

That family will never be the same
Because their Tommy loved a train,
The long way home his pals would take,
But across the railway his way home he'd make.

A hole in the fence Tom made you see,
Where he'd climb through full of glee,
The trains going by Tommy loved to see,
But the 'one two five' was his specialty.

He'd sit and wave 'til out of sight,
Then over the lines as fast as you like,
One day, even though it was fine
A mist came down and covered the line.

Sitting and waiting, but all in vain
Tommy thought he'd missed his favourite train,
So across the lines, his heart full of hate
He didn't realise the train was late.

Tommy was only half–way over the track
When the 'one two five' hit him in the back,
He never knew, because he wasn't alive,
His trespassing was ended by the 125.

Jim Thompson

My Dream . . .

I would like to be something else, other than me
and this is what I would like to be.
I would like to be a mystical creature
a gold horn would be my main feature.
I would like to be a unicorn that could fly
with a horn that would sparkle as I am high.
My long horn would be made of gold
I would be exactly how I was told.
A shiny coat of white
that would shine, as I flew like a kite.
My eyes would glisten different shades of blue.
If it happened, it would be like a dream come true.
Everyone would stop and stare
wondering what is flying in the air.
Everyone would look at me
looking at how beautiful I could be.
All this would be my dream
only I know what this could mean.
This is my dream I wish to come true
the one thing left for me to do.

Amanda Fox

How It Used To Be

When I was very young, I lived
In a huge house, with lots of doors
And pretty painted ceilings,
Decorating each and every floor.

Gardens stretching far, at least as far as I could see,
Flower-beds of many colours, a pond, a pleasure
For one and all . . . and me.

As I grew, I began to notice
That what I took for granted wouldn't stay
As I recalled it. My mind saw what it wanted, but
My eyes could only picture the decay.

The gardens first, I saw, come and end
Abruptly.
Where the motorway so cruelly sliced them through.
The garden ponds have since turned rather murky,
"Strange," I thought, "they always seemed so blue."

Inside my house, my doors have halved in numbers
And very few will open up to me.
I should leave now and not return, remembering
The memory of how it used to be.

Edward Milner

Clowning

Be a clown, clown around
Fill the world with ups not downs
Make people happy, wear a smile
Everyday, not once in a while

Just keep on clowning
And stop that frowning
With idle chatter make them laugh
Hide your own fears, just act daft

A mask of smiles hides sad eyes
Conveying happiness and contented sighs
Shrug off life's doubts and fears
Who could laugh at a clown with tears

Laugh at the world, at yourself too
Soon others will be laughing with you
Life is a stage with much acting out there,
But how many notice, how many care

So when you are filled with cares and woe
Wear the mask and put on a show
No need for face paint, a smile will do
To everyone out there I've written this for you.

Carol Temple

Special

You're special
I'm special
Let's get together
And create something special
We'll be special to each other
We'll have a special life together
We'll have special children
And we'll live in a special place
Every day we spend together shall be special
When people see us together they'll see something special
I'll make you feel special
You'll make me feel so special
We'll do special things together
We'll have a special love for each other
We shall eat special meals
We shall sing special prayers
and give special thanks and praises
To the special creator
Who has blessed this union and made it special
All because we're so special.

Eric Johnson

Love Is She Is

All time frozen and yet running like the finest sands,
The universe, finite, sparkles in her eyes.
The strong man's heart I once knew falters,
Dissolving in warm hazy spasms under heaving chest.
She touches me softly, smiles with her whole body,
I sense my helplessness, so terrible, so perfect.
I close my hand over hers and drink deeply from her love,
Paranoia on hold, I unfold, pleasure too great to understand.
Caressing her words she murmurs her desire,
How can I ever give to her what I myself receive?
Searing beauty swells my soul with pride, her gift,
Growing around her, withering in the darkness of her absence.
Embracing, exhaling, a tear forms,
It contains a million emotions, few explored together.
I drift along with the meaning of life holding me tightly,
Paradise itself, bound in mortal form.
Happiness beyond prior comprehension is killing me,
The fall approaching would kill any man.
But if I should fall, and I should be broken,
Then let her take me high, as high as true love allows.

Andrew Bruton

The Link

We all walk hand in hand,
In unison we stand and fight,
Our link forms an incredibly strong barrier,
Which we hold up with our sheer might.

Our mirror reflection is our enemy,
They stand hand in hand to fight,
There is no difference between us,
The peace is broken and a war draws into sight.

The image begins to draw closer,
So we to draw nearer,
Weapons raised to each other,
The price of life grows dearer.

Conflict breaks out all around us,
Countries declare World War,
Death becomes a regular occurrence,
For every man that is killed, there are countless more.

My comrades killed in cold blood,
In months, weeks, days, I could be dead,
Our barrier is broken down,
Why them, and not me instead?

Lauren A. Daniel

The Glorious Arrival

Let's walk awhile, gaze at the trees.
The coming of Autumn came sailing the breeze.
The forest is changing her tattered green gown,
for radiant robes of orange and brown.
Draped in bright colours, crimson and gold.
These are the new shades, green is the old.
Stirred by the cool winds when sun kissed the trees
they dazzle my eyes with flickering leaves.
The chestnut the oak and beech all the same
vibrantly glowing as if all aflame.
The sycamore's boasting a fine scarlet sash
through which sprightly creatures busily dash,
disturbing the foliage that softly drifts down
to bare winding branches and carpet the ground.
Keep safe in your thoughts this picturesque scene.
For dark days await us, of this you'll but dream.
When stripped of their splendour as if all is dead
and many wise birds have gathered and fled.
Don't feel a sadness, as in winter creeps,
the trees are not dying, the forest just sleeps.

Debra Dowie

The Parcel

I knew when it came it was special,
Each fold of crisp paper, each strip of fine tape,
The weight in both hands balanced like scales
Mysterious contents, awaiting its rape.

Missing links held in the breath of this second,
Searching the mind for a hint of its content,
Delaying the unwrapping like rising from slumber,
Too eager to wait, too lazily wanton.

Soft–edged memories, delighted, disappointed
Too soon the promise, now steadfastly defended,
Distant recollections, a lifetime of waiting,
Moving the mind's debris, aromas remembered.

Savour the unveiling, strip off the wrapping,
Strewn on the floor, bereft, now exposed
Like life's carnage around me, there's no turning back
All is revealed, the mystery solved.

Gillian Drakeley

I Am Trying To Work It Out?

Trying to stop the cars, so he could go home,
Then there he was, lying in the road,
Those cars, knocked him over, flying in the air,
Ended in the road, Everyone was in despair.

Why anyone? Why him? Only a twenty year old lad,
I did not know him before, but it feels as if I had,
Last part of his life and I was there,
Why does life have to be so unfair.

Anger, Hate, Upset, What do I feel?
Cold, Alone, Afraid, Will this pain ever heal?
A few days on, and the pain is still there,
But, some people they just do not care.

It is like a cloud, hanging over my head,
Crying myself to sleep, in my own bed,
What is this all about?
I am still trying to work it out.

Samantha Jinks

A Homeless Plea

Where can you go when you're homeless and alone
Who can you ring and will they be home
How can you live out there on the street
With dirt as your roof and nails at your feet
How many times have you been cold
You're in your teens but feel so old
How many fools say serves them right
Not knowing the fears you have at night
You ask for help but there's none to be found
And again tonight you will sleep on the ground
You hope for a day you will laugh about this
In the warmth of your home won't that be bliss
And when that time comes and you walk past that door
Which has a child lying there on the floor
You'll stop and think that once was me.
Life is for fun but money's not free.

Donna Jean Smith

Freeman

Freeman, living in a free land
Governed by laws and rules
Freeman, with freedom of speech
Depending of course, what he wishes to teach
Freeman, nothing can keep him down
'Cept the nine to five that keeps him alive
A roof over his head, a comfy bed
Where all his dreams, where finally led
His need to be free, his need to be whole
Every passing day, sucked from his soul
Freeman, living in a free land
Being societies prisoner the best way he can
Until one day when he finds his release
For death is at hand to bring him his peace

Ian Morris

Observation

What happened to the smile? You do not see it much these days.
A blank expression on a face.
I walk into a public area, I am met with eyes that say 'do not invade my territory'.
People go out of their way, to avoid, to talk one to one, they prefer to use the phone.
Time goes on, we act more on our own, we build a bigger wall.
As we update our communication system we are quick to forget the most simple, it is natural in us all.
A smile on a face is rare to-day
Why has life become so serious where it has gotten to the stage you've got to pay for the privilege of a smile once in a while.
I know there is not much to smile at in the current climate.
Please, for me, smile, make it stick, it is worth it, to see a smile on a face.
It beats a blank expression on a face and eyes that say 'Do not invade my territory'.

Peter MacDougall

Sea View

As I stand on the shore and look out to sea
In come the waves, some bigger than me
In the dark I see a welcoming light
That means sailors beware, rocks are insight
The lighthouse stands so tall and white
It really is a beautiful sight
The ships go by I know not where
Laden with goods for everywhere
Out go the fisherman with nets held high
Hoping for a catch that customers will buy
It's a busy world on the sea
And underneath a mystery
Although a sailor I'd like to be
My thoughts I'll keep to myself
But we'll see . . .

Paul Deans

Sonnet For The Arms Of Winter

Oh winter is God's shrewdest test
of what is weak and what is fully strong
and winter brings creativeness to those who play in song
oh winter is life's biggest chapter, in many ways the best
and hibernation primal spirit embraces all depressed
mother universe, I feel her caring in the snow
to make that long step softer, where now I have to go
and forests by the misty morning dampened and caressed
but yet in evening's lonesome tones and sentimental gloom
And when the spring is bringing in nature's new born glee
overturning the endless spinning wheel
The quality of seriousness, the club that shares our doom
in vast transforming landscapes there for all to see
oh winter is the turning pike, in many ways most real.

Pius Meagher

My Life A Fairy Tale

You look at me with sorry eyes
Unable to see the truth
You glance in my past in your mind's own eye
Thinking you knew my youth.

To you my life was meaningless
As you see me seated here
No career to see me to my cob-webbed grave
No days at which to cheer.

My eyes to my forehead concave so deep
An oasis in the sun kissed earth
Dark wrinkles protrude from my weary skin
That have grown from my day of birth.

You look at me with sorry eyes
For my present state is frail
You will never know the life I led
Oh my life, a fairy tale.

Sandra Horton

Hope

I languish and lie, cat like stretching, and embark on a journey
through the peace of the air,
the occasional chatter of a bird as he begins the opening bar
of a sonata.
Then silence, where I am left to guess the following notes.
I sigh at the wind and struggle with my pain,
and in the shifting angle of the sun,
I hear the opening bars again.

M. Paine

The Thunderstorm

Crouched in terror and paralysed by my fear,
I squeeze the tear–filled mirrors of my soul shut,
And with trembling hands I cover my ears,
But it is to no avail, still the evil resounds around me,
Evoking and emboldening my heartfelt horror.

As my tears flow down my colourless cheeks,
I gaze into the pervading darkness before me,
I cannot discern anything I recognize,
Evil has turned all to ebony and divorced me from humanity,
Leaving me only with the frightened visions of my mind's eye.

I hear again the furious roar of the destroying demon,
And the torrents of rain lashing down on my shelter,
And the whipping wind as it lacerates the beautiful nature,
Causing devastation and detriment to the earth,
And brutal dishonour to all mankind.

The howling and screaming of the trees reverberate,
Revealing their anger and fear towards this savage violation,
An echo of my own poignant pain and feelings,
But we cannot escape from the wrath of this destroying demon,
And so with trepidation and yet hope we must wait for it to end.

Katharine Emily Bell

Too Young

Too young they said when I gave you my heart
Because I loved you from the start.
Too young they said when I walked you to school
Far too young to play the fool
Too young they said as the years slipped by
still together you and I.
Too young they said when I called you mine
And gave you diamonds on your finger to shine
To young they said when you walked down the aisle
I was happy with your lovely smile.
Knowing that always we would walk hand in hand
A symbol of true love that golden band
Now the years have flown away
Our love grows stronger every day
Old as we are friends proudly own
Too young they say to be 'Darby and Joan'.

J. A. Davies

To My Daughter

Dear Sandra

It was just before the dawn today I stood beside your bed,
You were sleeping very peacefully, as I gently stroked your head.
You seemed still, that little girl who not so long ago,
I held in my arms and rocked to and fro.

Such a gentle little girl, always someone's friend.
Such a caring little one, always a heart to mend.
As I look down on you lying there and the night time slipped away
In just a few short hours will be your wedding day.

Another road to travel, a new adventure to take part,
A brand new chapter in your life with the first love of your heart;
And if you have a daughter, happy hours you will spend
She won't be just a daughter, she'll be her mum's best friend.

With a smile to drive away the rain, a laughter that's her own,
The many happy hours you'll spend, will be yours and hers alone
And so I wrote his down to say, what you already know,
I'm so glad that you're my daughter and I love you so.

Sylvia Roberts

Death Of A Merman

Unmistakable is he
Who swims like a fish in the sea
With hair so blond and tail so blue
He is one of very few.

They all were killed by technology
Like the sirens of Greek mythology
Who no more can sing their songs of death.

It is sad that their last breath
Should be taken, not by pollution
But by our profound lack of imagination.

Jenny Morris

The Clown

Who could tell the clown was suffering from a broken heart
Funny face and funny clothes he makes the people laugh
Take away the greasepaint and the clowning clothes
Underneath you see a face the grief upon it shows

His sweetheart told him she was through, a new love she had found
Still he has to tumble and roll upon the ground
He has to wait until he's kicked by another clown
Only then dare he let the tears trickle down

Slowly he climbs up the rope that leads to the trapeze
The safety net is not in place his grief he can't appease
What a jester thought the crowd until he hurtled down
Then they saw him lying in the sawdust on the ground
And so we bid farewell to him who loved and laughed in vain
A clown he was to all he knew he had no other name

Joan M. Collier

Happy Days

How lovingly remembered that sunny August day,
Home from school and nearly twelve, my memories will stay.
Father asked if I would like to see some cricket played,
'Yes alright', was my reply, just a bit dismayed.

'Goodbye Mum' as off we went with sandwiches and tea,
To watch a game of 'bat and ball', so dull it seemed to me.
'Where are we going'? And 'How far'?, my gloom I could not hide,
Surely somewhere near to home, perhaps a short bus ride.

Anxious questions answered, my feelings were to change,
Because of all I saw that day, both wonderful and strange.
Another world within those walls, a land of magic stories,
The giant scoreboard, Father Time, museum of past glories.

Pavilion, grandstand, grass so green, the seats all painted white,
With lawns and flower beds, well cared for, it was a pretty sight.
I'm older now and many times, have tried, but never found,
To find the equal of the place that's called Lord's Cricket Ground.

James Adams

Poisonous Gas

"Jane's walked out on Frank."
"Oh, you're kidding!"
Why should she kid?
About such an interesting subject.
Leave people to their own lives
We all deserve privacy.
We all need protection from the vultures flying overhead,
Searching for some juicy morsels they can devour
And regurgitate later,
Deformed, mutated from their original shape
As hungry mouths attacked them.
Where do you gather all this garbage?
From the rubbish dumps?
Yes, that's it.
You find and examine your victims.
Carefully picked out from the pile of rotting debris.
You know someone always gets hurt.
You people with queer minds,
Spreading poison throughout the town
With tip of a sharp tongue.

Kate Chapman

How And Why

When young flower buds at night
tucking their precious petals in tight
As the sun sets in a lilac sky
Have you stopped to think how and why?

When cats slink out of front and back doors
and there is a silvery look to the moors
As the colour is darkened in the sky
Have you stopped to think how and why?

When light's go on, inside and out
it's time for nocturnal animals to get about
As blankets of midnight fall over the sky
Have you stopped to think how and why?

And as daylight is breaking upon a new day
it's time for creatures to quietly creep away
When the early morning starling is seen in the sea of blue sky
Have you stopped to think how and why?

Julie Knox

Spring And Summer

Not a cloud in the sky
Everything looking so bright
The trees are full of blossoms
Just making things look so right.

The sun is shining lovely
Just like a midsummer day
Everyone in the garden
Trying to make it pay

The flowers look so pretty
Glittering in the sun
The baby lambs are jumping around
And having lots of fun.

As we walk down the road
The hedgerows look so well
With all the leaves and berries
Not forgetting the smell.

The lawns are full of daisies
So out the mowers come
There is work in the garden for everyone
More for others than some others.

Irene Ring

Nan

Her body was once so vibrant and young She could do anything,
or be anyone, But all that she wanted was a family and home,

Look at her now just sitting alone—
For fifty years they were two halves of one.
The ups and the downs, the tears and the fun.

She has her children, who deeply care,
She loves them all dearly, they'll always be there.

But the person she wants is not around,
She wishes she could join him. She misses the sound. His
laughter, his smell, his just being there. She wants to be with
him, life's just not fair.

I look at her face, I see all the pain I want to give her sunshine,
and take the rain. I've a family myself, a husband, two boys.
Sometimes I could run, the craziness and noise, but I look at
my nan, and I know what I've got,

a wonderful family, it means such a lot. She's made me realize,
what means the most, and it's not the ironing, or cooking a
roast. It's being together, and showing you care. Always
listening, and trying to be fair. She looks up and smiles, tears
in her eyes, the photos of us
all, just how the times fly, she said she's been lucky, she's
had a good life.

She's had a great husband, she's been a good wife, she said
she'd change nothing, except for one thing, she wished she
had gone the same time as him.

Denise Lenihan

The Lesson In Life

In these days of war and pain, look to children watch their game,
They know not of adult confusion, petty crimes and dissolution!
Happy faces all around, no cross to bear to weigh them down;
Simple games and simple ways, sounds of laughter fill their days,
running here and running there, freedom time to spare.

Watch them closely, open your mind, learn from their simple ways,
learn to be kind, kind to men and women alike. Innocence,
innocence all around, hardly an agitator to be found, watch
them now, no!
Don't miss a trick children are clever at being quick; don't
close your eyes not for a second or you will miss something,
on which you had not reckoned.

There is a moral to this lot, rarely do children connive or plot;
Children are a happy lot, unlike adults who are not!
Learn from these children a lesson in life, no more trouble no
more strife; adapt some of their ways create a happy life
no more fighting the human race, let's see a smile on every face.

Alex Hayden

Simple Satisfaction

What a silly, lugubrious fool am I
To be so miserable, as time goes by
Why can't I be different and just like them
Those happy farm workers in the glen.

They till the soil, each long working day
And plough deep furrows, as though etched in clay
Their faces are weathered, from time spent outside
Those windswept, hard working men with deep pride.

They work hard and long, but still they all seem
To have the humour, of which I just dream
For they always smile, when you speak to them
Those cheerful farm workers in the glen.

"Good morning sir," some of them say
And others, "hello mate—it's a mighty fine day"
But no matter what, the greeting may be
Those farm workers, always seem cheerful to me.

To me they are spring, like a breath of fresh air
As they sow and they reap, what their efforts do bear
If I watch and I listen, with my feeling of woe
This lugubrious fool, might just smile then, somehow.

T. V. Woodcock

Strange Cardiff Weather

I long to see your smile as it warms up my heart,
Making it flutter among the bright open buttercups
Which soak in the last of the late evening sun's rays.
I look into your soft brown eyes clear as the reflection
Of a spring filled lake cast upon this cloudless sky.

Your intense gaze always musters up
The same strong feelings within me,
Sending a bolt of lightning straight to my heart,
Jerking my senses alive once again.
I love to listen to your smooth sensuous voice.
Your words always send me floating like the clouds
Rising in the summer heat
To drift carefreely over the open countryside,
Watching the immense trees
Swaying rhythmically in the soft summer breeze,
Oblivious to the world around them.

Your touch, tender but firm sends me crazy
Just like a wild late summer thunderstorm
As the lightning claps down in fits of frenzy,
Waking up the dormant earth
And the fast furious raindrops sizzle upon its sun–beaten face.

All this I feel for you.
You have stirred my emotions like no-one before you.
Given the chance I could have loved you if only I could have stayed.
Stupidly these feelings I admit only to myself.
If only I'd had the courage to admit them to you too,
Then I could have been in the eye of this torrential thunderstorm
Instead of being on the outside once again.

Angela Riley

The Ancient Stone

I stood in the moonlight, by the ancient stone,
What was this feeling of not being alone?
I turned and looked from left to right
No human could be seen that night.
I stood quite still, what was that I could see
Perhaps a reflection, perhaps only me.
I have this feeling of something near
Should I sense danger, should I feel fear?
I reached out my hand to touch that great stone.
What's that I hear, was that a groan?
Now I can see, no need to feel sad, that appearing is by no
means bad.
I can see through the mist that is swirling around.
A procession of people strewing flowers on the ground.
The way they are dressed is not of this day.
Am I caught in a time lapse in some strange way?
They came to the stone not seeing me there.
Should I make contact, should I dare?
Now they've all gone and I'm once more alone
With my hand still resting on that ancient of stone.
Was it a dream, was I really asleep?
Why then, are these petals all around my feet?

Anthea Mowling

Lost Love

They say you don't love me any more
To you I know now I was just a bore
But one day soon I hope you will see
Just how much you really mean to me.

I never thought our love would end
And my broken heart will never mend
For you and only you alone
Left me feeling as cold as a stone.

But my love for you will grow and grow
Yet time seems to pass more slower than slow
And if I had a wish I would wish for you back
But magic is something this world will always lack

I remember when you used to say that if our love should ever stray
We would find each other some very soon day
I'm waiting dear, were you really sincere
Or is it you memory that isn't so clear

They say that good times will come and bad times will go
But how much I want you no one will know
Oh please come back to me my love
God. Grant me one wish from heaven above.

Brenda Johnston

"Cherries"

England's sweet cherries
Culminate in a cul-de-sac.
Hungry men home from work
With a hunch on their back

Meals are ready
Awaiting the table
Coats on the floor
Although they are able

Wife makes remark
Not quite heard
Husband hits out
All so absurd

She reels back
Not quite sure
Hair out of place
No longer demure

He's sorry it's ok.
On with the meal and the chardonnay

Another day dawns back to work for the sack
England's sweet cherries in their cul-de-sac.

Lee Elmer

Tranquil River

To be by the dart in the early spring
To sit quietly and contemplate as the local birds sing
Trout swimming about in the current racing by
Whilst ambitious fishermen try with their fly
To pull a fish from the water trapped by the hook
But more often than not they just reel back and look
As the wily old fish continues to swim with a twist and a heave
Having sighted the bait they've decided wisely to leave.

To be by the dart in the early spring
One can realize tranquillity a wonderful thing
The birds by the river are really so tame
They'll hop so close to one as if playing a game
They'll eat sandwich remnants or seeds from ground
so close to one's feet
Not fussy what is on offer, cheese, bread, or cooked meat
Unlike the streetwise town bird they'll remain close all through
Just so long as they're respected to share the environment with you

So much is so fine when out by river and moor
One regret perhaps it's oft necessary to remain indoor
But holiday times give time to endure
So many extraordinary things that remind one of things pure.

T. B. Lattimore

The Secret Languages (Music And Song)

That mystical musical alphabet which is known throughout the world
Started its life many years ago, inside clouds that hovered and swirled
When the gods of good decided to share their love with all
Each opening up his big warm heart and whispering a unique call
These calls were then echoed in the clouds that were spaced nearby
And then these sweet calls erupted unto a listening sky
The clouds became abundant and blanketed the earth all around
And when these calls came together made a rhythm and an
alluring sound

For centuries that have long since passed alas man he had tried
To seek for roots of the knowledge that had been laid down
by his side
Trying to unravel the sounds that fell from the surrounding air
But all he could master in return was anguish and total despair
The gods they kept on looking at the determination upon his face
And in the end they all agreed to leave to man a trace.

The secret languages of the gods was thus bequeathed unto
the many lands
Allowing man to communicate through his eager and yearning hands
At last music could be written, in bars that could be measured
with time
Then these newfangled alphabets were twisted into a
meaningful rhyme
And wherever you may wander, and whatever is your illustrious goal
Music has an inspirational kindling which reflects the
passionate soul.

Sandra Morrison

The Cornish Fishermen

On the wings of the wind she has captured their hearts,
This land that they love has made them a part
Of its earth, its passions and spirits free,
Oh Cornwall!—Such is thy mystery.
The blues and greens of the Cornish seas, as they lash the rocks
and do as they please, bringing driftwood gnarled and twisted kelp;
Designs being made with nature's help.
Cornwall, their homeland, the land of their dreams,
Of Celtic cross and black and gold seams,
Hand-made nets on shoreline lay,
By waiting winch and pots of clay.
Treacherous blast of gales at sea, hurl ships against the coast,
Bringing fishermen to peril, as if haunted by past ghosts.
Lost fathers brave, replaced by sons—to keep the home-fire burning,
Wives and mothers wait at home—and pray the wheel keeps turning.
The murky depths its secrets keep, unyielding to the view,
Of broken hearts and wedding rings, mourned by just the few,
Stoics are the fishermen who never count the cost,
The graveyard signs their names in stone—
   the Loved Who Have Been Lost.

Shirley Knapman

The Windmill

On yonder mound, so tall and round
the Windmill stands up high;
The turning sails, the creaks and wails,
and clouds a-scuttling by.

Within my home I view the dome
that crowns the noble frame;
Again . . . a boy! I'm crowned with joy,
forgetting that . . . I'm lame!

The little hill that bears the mill
is carpeted—so green!
With sheer delight I claim the sight
the fairest ever seen.

The vigorous mind (who seeks shall find)
takes flight, provides the key
To realms unheard. Free as a bird,
my Windmill beckons me!

Edward Appleyard

Un-American Graffiti

In August, nineteen forty-four,
An American soldier knocked on our door.
Took my sister to a dance,
Next day the boy was sent to France.
Did the job for Uncle Sam
Then flew back home to Alabam.
To compensate us for the loss
Of chewing gum from Private Voss,
America dispatched Enola Gay
To melt the eastern threat away.
Having calmed the Japanese
Lifted Europe from its knees.
To demonstrate 'Good Neighbour' care
Saved one half from the Russian Bear.
I prefer a friend to a debt.
The account I believe is settled. Yet,
When that race decides to roam
People paint to urge it home.
Not me! My supercilious etymological frown
Reserved for the verb metamorphosed from the noun.

M. Batham

A Rose

The rose bud sleeps this early morn
Dew speckled—only yesterday it was born
Its colour peeps 'twixt bracts and waits the mid-day sun
Giving promise of the lovely bloom to come

Soon it will awake and in all its glory shine
A nature's gem, to thrill your heart and mine
A sight o'er which to linger thro' the coming hours
Surely the fairest queen of all the flowers

When, comes the evening shade 'twill fill the air
With fragrance—a perfume that's beyond compare
To give much added pleasure to they who chose
To grow with tender care, this lovely rose

H. H. Steventon

The Awakening

We talk of lovely scenery and comin' through the rye
But what of the towers of Babel
Reaching to the sky,
The flats that spread like rashes
On all sides meet the eye
And the mighty pylons, like mandarins on the march
Stride across the farmlands, midst beech and oak and larch.
Hush, did we hear a movement
An awakening to the danger
A message from an ecology group
'Til recently a stranger.
Do something now, we are all involved
Do not drag your feet,
Or someday you will likely wake
Faced by street, on street, on street.

Rosina Elsie Parkinson

Equality

All men are equal,
and should be treated like brothers
a few only know that,
but all of the others are weak and heartless
and think only of the best, of new cars and
mansions, not of the rest who are ill and
starving, homeless and poor,
grateful for what they have got
and not wanting more,
    But taking their lives and living it,
        doing the best they can
Treating everyone equal,
        cause equal's every man.

Belinda Jones

Spring Day

It is early in the morning the air is clear and it's bright
It is the dawning of a beautiful Spring Day
The shades have lifted from a black and fearful night
And the birds are singing in the trees so gay
There is a stirring in the grass a stirring in the trees
It is the sign of Spring with the bursting forth of leaves
A herd of cows are making their way
To give fresh milk for the day
A sly old fox makes his way home
To go to sleep after his nightly roam
A lamb bleats for his mother its mother with a baa replied
With a skip and bound he ends up by her side
So early in the morning as I make my way
I say a little prayer and hope these things will stay
It would be a pity if man's ambitions and his greed
Would overlook the future for his present need
To preserve what he can must be the first priority of man
So children can grow up and say
Oh isn't it a lovely Spring Day

W. D. Brind

When I Am Gone

Do not mourn for me when I am gone,
Instead rejoice, for I'll still live on.
Do not be upset and do not cry,
For I am still here, I will not die.
Do not wear clothes which are morbid or sad,
Instead praise the Lord for the life I have had.
Do not bring a wreath as a sign of your woe,
Instead leave the flowers and let them grow.
Do not forget that I'll always be,
Alive in you, in your memory.
But life will continue when I am gone,
So do not mourn, instead live on.

Delia Sale

Golf

Wandering aimlessly after the ball
Following a shot I do not wish to recall.
Distraction is so easily led
By a movement on the river's bed.
Young chub scatter at my approach
Dace, minnows, an occasional roach.
A pike!—That scatters more than me
Alerts a kingfisher in a far–side tree.
Eyes and ears are now tuned in
For any sound or movement to begin
Hovering, hovering, over there
A hawk, almost stationary in the air
Squabbling magpies, among the willows, flutter
Causing rabbits to jump and clutter.
A heron stalks, with its crafty grin,
The shallows, for startled minnows, to pin
Dip, dip, dip. The long tailed tit
Breaks the surface for bit, bit, bit.
"It's your shot", brings me back to my ball
Golf—It's not a bad game after all.

Ken Shurmer

Metamorphic Doubts

I catch a new face in reflection,
A steel gaze from the past,
New set, new props, new costume,
But old eyes give the game away.
I can't box you or contain you.
You're wandering the wings,
Ready to take the stage again
Repeating well rehearsed routines.

But the play has changed since your exit—
The audience witnessed your death
And cheered the conquering hero.
Yet, the drunken, out-of-work actor
Still haunts the cast backstage.
The show goes on.
Curtain rises on act two.
I, the one principle
Who cannot leave the stage
Until finale.

Still your presence is distracting
And your heckling may be heard.

Charles Frost

Graham And Nicolas' Day

This is Graham and Nicolas' day.
The start of their shared life, they're on their way.
Just five minutes ago they were both in their cots,
Gummy smiles and 'greeting', and we dimpled bots.
Now they sit here among us, gorgeous, sublime,
The future before them, no cares for time.
So, what advice do we give as they start on their road?
What do we say to ease the load?
Be lovers, that's easy, the attraction is plain,
But not the main clue in the great marriage game.
Trust is essential, a big part in the plot,
It ties you together, secures the knot.
Friendship is the main thing, liking each other.
Then when storms hit one, the other runs to give cover.
Put these clues together and the answer is clear,
You will have mutual respect, and hold each other dear.
Keep these things in mind as you go through your life,
And you always will be, loving husband and wife.

M. L. Welsh

Soul Comfort

Wound around you like a coiled up spring
Touching, tasting, breathing you in
Smell your hair, lick the salt from your skin
Reaching out to pull you inside
Hoping that with one glorious pop
You and I will become one
And the togetherness will be complete

This is time to treasure
To remember how once, there was no need for lies or games
A time to be cherished
To feel special and loved
A pit stop for the soul
Gently to be put back on track

And if one day I forget to tell you just what you have done
How your tender ministrations thawed my frosty heart
Remember this time and understand

Kate Morris

Pictures

A picture tells us how things used to be,
Pictures of people or a scenery.
They show us the sad times moments of glory.
You look at a picture and it tells a story.
We all have our pictures which we can see.
The good and bad times in our own memory.
There are many pictures in life today.
So don't be blind and just walk away.

T. Codd

Watching Love Go By

I am truly disciplined, I am still standing
Where you left me—Do you remember? It was
Where we watched love pass us by.

They said I didn't love them all, but
That isn't why I stopped. I stopped for the sake of
Breathing and caught love passing by.

I heard that they were arguing when love dashed
Out of sight. A reckless guy was speeding
When he had a rear-view fright.

They say she was milking them of money
When cruel love passed her by. He was
Looking in the mirror when it crept up from behind.

They were trading fur for leather–skinned when
Love came gruelling by. Boys were jumping
Over buildings, but they were never there on time.

When I was naming all my cravings love was
Gallant at my side, saying look at all the
Mountains and the people going by.

David Lambern

Housewife's Thoughts

Some wind today, will the washing dry?
I glance at a cloud, as it passes by
Children are playing, they giggle then shout!
Small baby wondering what life's all about
Always rushing, no time to stop
Too much to do, must go to the shop
Mustn't complain a home to run!
If you can't keep up, you're no more fun.
When husband comes home you greet him and smile
Day comes to an end, sit down but just for awhile.

Liz Hay

Columba

In the heart of an acorn, there's the promise of strength
As yet unfulfilled, but waiting to feel
The warmth of the sun, the touch of the rain,
The goodness of soil, combining to give
The fullness of life and beauty and power.

In the heart of a child, there's the promise of trust
Just waiting to grow and extend to the world
The message it needs so badly today,
But trust cannot grow unless nurtured with care,
Compassion and truth, discretion and hope.

In the heart of a man, there's the promise of power,
Power to invent for everyone's good,
But unless it is trained to foster a bond
Of nation with nation, its promise is vain,
And man will not learn of brotherly love.

In the heart of our Lord, there's the promise of love,
Love of creation of man or of beast
Of flower and forest, for the use of mankind
And that love is free for all to accept
Just waiting to bring all the world to unite.

F. A. Clegg

Mind Pool

Still water, a pool of memory, a thought in the deep green depth.
Some happening of long ago, or of love a secret kept.
And yet by the merest whisper, a familiar sight or sound.
Like a pebble thrown, with ripples grown, remembrance is found.

Such wondrous things this pool reveals from its translucent shade.
A treasure of memories held so dear.
Can rise to the surface, bright and clear.
A picture none can fade.

But a thought sometimes eludes us.
Though we probe, we never find.
Like a gem covered o'er by the sands of time.
Sunk deep in the pool of our mind.

Barbara Bradbury

New Beginning

Sunburst exploding inside me
Giving new dimensions to my life.
Streaking lights
Creating a halogen existence.
Emerging through the spectrum of feelings
Into freedom.
Metamorphosis complete
Obliteration of the past.
A bright new awakening
Anticipation and hope
Born again to greet a dynamic future.

Brenda Jennings

Reflection

On the dark damp streets of a city
A young stranger stands all alone
Assessing his new world before him
That he eagerly exchanged for his home

Still anaesthetized by his freedom
And the complacent shield of the young
He dreamed of his fame and fortune
The first day his new life had begun

But he was disturbed by a noise in the darkness
And from the shadows appeared a man
Covered in filth beyond recognition
So drunk he could hardly stand

But it's the face that arrests the young stranger
A face, he's sure that he knows
Now ravished by time and abuses
And eyes that seem very old.

The two men stood transfixed in the darkness
Then one hurried back to his home
For fate was harsh in her warning
The face that he knew, was his own.

John J. Cassidy

Portchester Castle

Should your eyes stray from my window
Outward, o'er the sea,
You would see Ruined Castle there,
Veiled in mystery

Where once in days, far distant now,
Knights and damsels made their vows of love
    To die for nought else,
    But the arms of their betrothed

The moonlight on the water glistens,
and, fairy shadows in the trees
    Doth give Romantic thoughts, and
Should you listen, you would hear enchantment
    on the breeze
As voices of forgotten days,
    float gently o'er the moonlit sea.

Kay P. Carter

Affray

Perhaps somewhere neath us who search,
Seventy five souls are now at prayer;
With words not heard in any church.
Of alternate hope and then despair;
Thoughts of sweethearts and of wives.
Who cry and know not restful sleep;
For thinking of those feared–lost lives,
that lie enclosed in waters deep,
Oh grant to them dear Lord I pray,
Swift rescue and the light of day;
Perhaps such is not your will at all.,
But on their sins please do not frown;
And when Your bosun sounds his call,
Please give Your blessings to their last "Pipe-Down"

M. J. Smith

The Roses Bloom (Or Echoes Of The Past)

The roses bloom where once we stood.
The house is gone, 'twas only wood;
And yet I feel we still are there,
The moonlight shining on your hair.

And sometimes those who pause awhile
May hear a laugh, or see you smile.

Though we are gone from that dear place,
And wander now in time and space,
Yet still our love must linger there;
Surviving death, so breathe a prayer.

And somehow we will surely know,
And join our prayers with those below.

Pat Walsh

The Circle Of Life

The circle of life completes itself
Always understanding that the end is near
We live, we die, we go through suffering and pain
Happiness, sadness, it's a never–ending game.

The circle of life will lead you
Options, paths and doorways
Always there for you to choose
Which ever one you will never lose.

The circle of life continues to hurt
Upsetting families with love for each other
We never know what each day brings
Maybe one day we will all live as kings.

Martyn Barsby

The Birth Of Baby Marcus 27 July 1995

Poor 'ole Debs, she was a Stayte
With baby Marcus, one week late
The Doctor said, 'Well Debbie dear
Don't think he's ready to appear.'

    Then on one summer Thursday morn
    Just as the rooster crowed for dawn
    Marcus thought, 'it must be time
    To show my face to mum of mine'.

Oh what a sight it was to see
There was Marcus at last—free!
He now had space to move, and boy
What a pair of lungs, oh joy!

    Mother and baby have a rest
    The morning light will bring you zest
    And time to know each other well
    Your future's now for you to dwell.

'Oh Debs, he's lovely, so are you'
He's Rachel's little boy in blue
And now it's time to celebrate
The birth of Baby Marcus Stayte.

C. Smedley

Yesterdays Valentine

Oh for the touch of your gentle hand,
A kiss to soften the hurt, a comforting
Word from your compassionate heart, a
Shoulder to shed an unashamed tear,
To enclose you in my arms at night and
Still find you there when I wake,
To turn my face and feel your breath
Sweet, upon my brow,
To watch your eyes quiver deep in sleep
Your lips, curved softly like a child's,
To run my finger lightly down your cheek,
Willing you to wake and hold me tight,
To see your eyes, dark with love,
Silently reflecting our hearts' desires.

Doreen Roys

You Were Mine . . .

My fingers trace the lines in your face
And roam shamelessly across the
Soft waves of your tawny hair.
Your warmth generates through my fingertips,
Reaching the depths of my aching heart.

My eyes search those of yours that are
Closed, but not empty, no, not yet.
My lips kiss your partly open mouth;
So still and so warm. My kiss
Searching for a meaningful response.

I caress your open hand tenderly and
Hold it tightly, pressing it close to my breast.
You lie there so calm, so quiet,
So beautiful—I cannot recall a
Beauty so rare, so strange.

A careless tear meanders down my cheek
To fall gently onto yours.
Mere minutes before, you were mine—
Now I realise God must have wanted
You far more than I . . .

M. M. Forshaw

Of Poets And Peasants

I come from a place called Newcassel, the home of broon ale and fried cod, where ootsiders feor aal of us Geordies, but us Geordies, we feors ounly God.

It's true what they say aboot Geordies, it's true that we like scoring goals. We're as soft as kid's claggy toffee, but hard as nails when digging up coals.

We liked to gan Co-operative shopping, miss the divi payed oot twice a year, if it wasn't that wor lass was working I'd have nee whippets, nee pigeons, nee beer.

They've shut doon aal of the shipyards, the coal mines received the same blow. Poor Parsons and Vickers, like a lass with nee knickers, are both feeling the draft down below.

It's aarful being short of the readies, for everything now seems so dear, but we Geordies are ever resourceful and use Plastic to ensure wor good cheer.

Man it's grand to have Kwiksave to shop at, they've got stotties, mushy peas and cheap fags, this helps to stretch oot me bit Giro, to have a wee bet on the nags.

Not divvint ye judge us too harshly, the balance of Fate often tilts, think on . . . for if it hadn't been for we Geordies . . . you'd aal be wearing plaid kilts.

John Moore

Car Shop

What's mine is yours
So please help yourself.
our radio, our CD player,
The speakers on the back shelf

They're all of excellent quality
And recently bought,
Don't worry about your access mode,
I know inside, they're the best methods taught

Don't concern yourself with
The hurt you may have caused,
The anguish and the violation,
Don't give it a moment's pause

Why go to the trouble
Of buying from the shop,
When cars are much nearer
You don't have to worry about the cops,

They give advice and questions asked,
Like have you been insured,
I give a smile but make no fuss
For what is mine, is yours.

R. A. Maynard

What If It Were Me?

Here I sit never alone
In the place I call my home
Someone who loves me
And knows where I'll be
Someone who cares all about me
A roof over my head
And a nice warm bed
I always know if I'll be fed
Unfortunately this can't always be said

Many a person sit all alone
With No place to call their home
No one to love them
Or know where they'll be
They can't say I have someone who cares about me
No roof over their heads
And no nice warm beds
They don't always know it they'll be fed
Some may even end up dead
Just think to yourself what if it were me?

Lorraine Gordon

In Tune With Nature

I watched a solitary swan glide slowly on the water
Putting its long neck and beak on its breast.
Passing through the park with its well–kept gardens
Noting the different flight of the birds as they left their nest.

Along side a footpath on my way to the village
Hoary plantain was growing, bryony and giant knapweed.
I could see the ivy–clad tower of the church in the distance
Quaint figures in stone all around the outer eaves.
Down the lane, the marshmallow, black horehound and hedge mustard
Were growing under hedgerows composed of privet and Wych elm.
Sometimes a multi-coloured butterfly or moth would flit round me
Several beetles crossed my path with their bright metallic shell
Glittering in sunlight and casting a spell.

All around me St. John's wort was growing in confusion
Wild marjoram and field mint were down in the dell
I saw overhanging crags where some jackdaws were breeding
And climbed cliffs where rhododendrons in profusion were gleaming
Years ago; in my minds eye—I remember it well!

Hilda May Corner

A Happy Anniversary

You've been together for twenty five years,
And in that time you'll shared love, laughter and tears.

You live for each other and that is true,
Something you did when you both said I do.

The future is your own and how you wish it to be,
Look after each other in the many years to come,
    as you both have looked after me!!

Hazel Bennett

Untitled

To crave beauty, to devour ugliness, to love hate.
To exist through the heart of the vitreous,
And to be unhappy still.

To ignore fact, to conjure opera, to live death.
To be under the spell of the cortex,
And to be dependent yet.

A sister but not a daughter, a lover but not a soul.
Counting the passage of borrowed time,
Flesh into stone, stone into dust.

I see only the circle of steel,
I know only the sparks,
I want only the silence in the woods.

And I'm so, so sorry, for what I do to you.

Ian M. Baldwin

Memories Cycle

Eternal memory, ephemeral quality,
Transcending human time and existence.
Unconscious memory, awaking once more,
Recreating life again, once more.
Growing unnoticed, unrefrained yet unfocused,
Whispers of strength take hold.

Eternal memory, innocent memory,
Never learns each human time.
And so memory, fallible memory,
Your existence is joined with kind.

Sheri Pilcher

Joey

Bright eyes had my Joey,
Shiny as the moon on a frosty night,
Then he went missing one day—
Had he got into a fight?
Well, why should I care? He was only a cat
And I've more problems than that.
Like a mortgage and bills to pay
And a world that grows more lawless by the day.

Black fur had my Joey, glossy and sleek.
Two toned from sitting half in sun and half shade.
He'd been a stray, we thought he 'had it made'
But he got sick one day and the vet said "No Joy"

So we made death easy for our boy,
Which is more than some people have;
or animals in laboratories in all their miseries.

Well, why should I care? He was only a cat,
And I've more problems than that.
Have I not my priorities right?
For the world is awash with blood and tears.
But—I do care, and I cry at night.

Patricia Phillips

Longing

When I'm in Winter,
I think of the things I miss about Summer.
The ripe juicy strawberries,
The hot summer days
The barbecues, Wimbledon and holidays
Oh!, how I long for it to be Summer again.

When I'm in Summer,
I think of the things I miss about Winter
The thick winter cardies,
The snowmen to make,
The bright lights at Christmas and staying up late
Oh!, how I long for it to be Winter again.

Charlotte Sivelle

A Nation Of Animal Love?

I search for peace, but it isn't to be, they're
out to kill, unfortunately me
To them it's sport, to me a nightmare, pointless
bloodshed, they don't care
on their big horses, jackets of red, they won't
Stop 'till they see me dead
They have their hounds, they have no bounds
Out for the kill they're after me still
It goes on for miles, and they're all smiles
They follow my scent here and there, I'm always
running, but going nowhere
My legs are heavy, my whole body aches, got
to keep morning, no time to waste
For if I do, death, appears, what it's like—I have my fears
The scent has diminished their day is now finished
So has mine, at least for a time
A little longer for me to live, until the day
my life I will give.

Karl Beese

Forgotten Promises

I catch your kisses as they float across the air,
Knowing it's the beginning of the end,
Wishing it didn't have to be this way,
Hoping for a new beginning.
You walk off into the distance like a hero from a movie,
I cry, willing you with all my heart to stay,
But, then, into the darkness of the night, you're gone.
I wonder, why me? Why like this?
I'd give anything to be with you one more time,
Feeling your arms around me,
To be lost in your embrace.
You promise me you'll keep in touch,
That our love will never end,
But, I know then our love will die.
I hope for friendship, but deep down know that even that,
is too much to ask.
I dream of summer and being in love.
I know that, one day, the hurt will be gone,
And you will be a distant, well loved, memory.

Felicity Curwen

"New York Puppy"

Up and down these strange streets I walk, I suffer kicks and people's harsh talk. I look up at the buildings where the humans go, like vast grey giants staring at me below. This concrete world in which I rome, will I ever find a home?
\A screech of brakes fills my ears. As a yellow taxi pulls up near, a large fat man bundles out, he shouts, "Hey Mutt!" and lashes out. I dodge his boot and give a sigh, why did he do it? I don't know why.
\Nightmare arrives, as black as coal, no one to fill my water bowl. No bone to chew, no meat to eat, no cosy fire to give me heat. I hope to find a cardboard box and an old bin with someone's thrown out chops. I stumble across two steel lines, there's a sound of thunder and a bright light shines. I retreat onto a grassy bank and feel the rush of the fire breathing tank. I close my eyes as it takes time to pass, then I make a tireful dash.
\I find a place and settle down. I find I still shudder and shake, in the monster's thunderous wake. I sniff the air for a friendly aroma, if I can only find an owner. Down a tunnel, up a stair, I'm still on edge I must beware.
\I don't know what to find in this hostile nation, a voice calls out, "New York Station!" I trot beside a four wheel crate into a room where people wait. There I sit beside a wooden bench, it is cold, my teeth are clenched. A scent as sweet as primrose fills the air, a kind old lady looks down so fair. Her glasses shine in the station's light. Should I run because of fright? She doesn't look stern but full of joy, as she picks me up and says, "Hey Boy." She gives me candy, I begin to lick it then she goes and buys my ticket. Two years pass without a care. Now here I am sat beside her chair.

Kelly Pearson

What Have I Ever Done To You?

You stare at me and wonder why I'm here,
Think I look really odd, I stand out, Why?
I'm no different to you.
Oh, I get it—I'm black! You hate me because I'm black.
Why do you think I'm so different? I'm no different from you.
My skin is different, but so is yours;
I'm black and you're white.
So?
Why do you criticise me? I could do it to you.
Why do you waste your time hurting me and embarrassing me?
I wouldn't dream of doing it to you.
According to you, you are the colour of day
And I am the colour of night.
Why can't you accept me the way I am? I do it for you.
Just remember,
the only difference between us
Is that we've got a different colour of skin,
Doesn't matter if you're black or white, if you're boy or girl
We're all the same,
We're all human.

Victoria Platt

Memoirs Of Morocco

To greet you at Asilah, many strange people
Women with veils to cover; just dark eyes to see
Donkeys laden heavily with crops and sheep
Being bullied by men and boys to climb the tracks, quite steep
Passing many palm trees with laden fruit of dates
Seeing eucalyptus trees in a bounteous state

Fez roads are dusty and cobbled, trodden by many feet
Tracks covered by market left-overs, hard set on the street
Small shops, dimly lit, full of leather and brass goods
Look very strange and different to us, form another world
Time has stood by for these different folks
Who honour their religion and tradition, to a 'fault'

What a beautiful country, offering us all something
The poor so without; the rich with everything
Beautiful sea, golden sands, palm trees and mountains
So noisy and busy in the towns and cities
So remote and quiet in the desert
Very many people . . . and then no one . . . perhaps a camel.

Ann Reeve

Healing Hands

Healing hands will forever be
A source of wonderment to me.
The surgeon's skill, new drugs the modern way.
And my father might be here with me today.
Instead, when I was only four.
He had to close the final door.
In those days TB had no respect for age,
He knew it meant an early grave.
Years went by, Christmas and Birthdays too
But the card that I missed most of all.
Was the one that would have said
Dear daughter, I love you
I am an older woman now,
And childhood days are gone,
But the love I had, for my dear dad,
Will forever linger on.

N. Butterfield

Untitled

Half eternity has passed by
And the spark that measured it must fly
While it flickers see the truth that's plain
You cannot live this life again
To walk by the sea or look at the sky
One morning after the day you die
And the dreams that we had yesterday
Are now ten million miles away
With nothing there to mark the place
Where once we thought we'd live in love and grace
Till time unending
Never wary of the fate that the gods were sending

George William Chalk

See This Amaryllis

See this amaryllis, it's from another land,
It blooms in this cold county, fed by a gentle hand,
It gives the home a lovely look,
Just like a picture in a book,
So if you have some time to spare
Do please come inside and stand and stare.
I guarantee you will not regret it.
In fact you never will forget it.
So if you have a friend in another part
Get them to send you one to warm your heart,
Although outside it's cold and snow
In my home there is this glorious glow
All in this house will be fuming
Once this lovely plant stops blooming.
Get one yourself so you can measure
This plants beauty and its pleasure.

Kathleen C. Jarvis

Eliza

Right to the end she remained the friend of
all her family.
Loving and loved like a hand in a glove,
    all so quite naturally,
No air's or grace's,
    or long sad faces.
though at time's plenty of reason to be,
    through two world war's
    and all the chore's,
Of six other children and thee,
We worked on the farm,
    which did us no harm,
At least from machinery,
    just basket's and scale's
    to tell us our sale's,
Would make enough for our tea.
With all her 99 year's,
    some pleasure's and tear's,
It was just not meant to be,
To make just one more,
    out of her front door.

Mary Heywood

The Night Sky

From my back room I watched the starry sky.
From my front door, I saw the climbing moon
drift over the College walls, like a balloon,
brilliant and round and radiant, sailing high.

Glorious it was, but that was long ago;
now mist and street lamps cloud the sky at night,
Veiling the constellations and the glow
of star-shine and of magical moonlight.

Once, and once only, I looked out, and lo!
There was the full moon, round and clear and bright,
and one attendant star shone, all aglow.
One magic, time–slipped, old style sky, at night.

Mary Stanley-Smith

The Search

When clouds of doubt obscure your mind
Just turn your back, put them behind,
The jibes of those who do not know
When unaccepted, will drift not grow,
We know one cannot sit on the fence
It gives no comfort, and makes no sense.
For each of us is here to seek,
For answers! Without which, we're weak
For Physical strength is alas not lasting
And without truth our spirit is fasting
So look ever onwards towards your goal
And it will grow—within your soul

L. G. Wyeth

"Homeless"

No one knows me, when they look elsewhere.
They don't know why I am there.
I am a nuisance, a disgrace.
Not fit to share their air
I am a bedraggled heap
A useless lump of unwanted matter
What does it matter if I am there?

They can escape from my familiar surroundings
They have no need to sleep under sidings
They can be where they want to be!
Not like me, alone, hungry and cold, left like mould.
To weather the storm all on my own.

I wonder why I am here today
Am I a monstrosity like they say?
I hold my hand out and ask for pity
But I receive looks that melt a city.

Denise M. Hall

Blessings

I thank you Lord, for the blessing of life ensuring my safety
thro' my recent strife.
My rapid recovery. I am feeling no fear, at times like these, we
feel you are near.
In these early morn hours all around are asleep.
As on Sunday's healing service, our communion we keep
Your presence is here, our faith much restored.
If your help is at hand, it's our one real reward.
Give grace then, please Lord, to those who are ill,
Granting within them a strengthening of will.

Grant please Lord, as I look over town with eyesight so good
that I clearly can see,
The twinkling of lights through the beautiful trees,
I pray to you now as we have always been taught,
You made the blind see!, and the lame man to walk.

Please graciously heal, as only you may, my dear wife's eyes,
I'd love her to see,
Things taken for granted, for certain by me! Beauty far
distant, as well as things near.
The birds and the flowers, . . . a glimpse of the sea!
The beauty of life we mostly enjoy, for which we are grateful,
and always will be.
Look kindly on Barbara! This, then I plea.

Eric Jeffrey Johnson

The Clan

Once upon a time, three mums, three dads—(a nice even
mixture of lasses and lads)
Set out one morning while skies were grey, to find new snow
and pistes—come what may.
There were also three husbands with their lady wives—in love
and so happy, enjoying their lives.
Eight charming daughters, lovely ones all, and four stalwart
sons who'd grown handsome and tall.
Four pretty sisters, a lively quartet, and a couple of brothers,
great pals, you can bet.
Four aunts and four uncles were there to be found, with two
nephews and six nieces somewhere around.
And then were the cousins—the last count was eight—could
there be more? . . . we'll just have to wait.
Relations by birth, relatives by wedlock, bringing in the in-
laws, creating a deadlock.
Then two mothers-in-law (as if one isn't enough!) a couple of
fathers-in-law, quite heady stuff!
Four grandmas, four granddads playing major parts to eight
super grandchildren, bless their hearts.

Oh surely that must complete this long, long list, 'cos to tell
you the truth . . . I'm now "totally piste". For that sure is some
party, seventy four there but when—you get down to basics,
there were still only 'ten'!

Dorothy Fieldsend

Adults

Adults say the strangest things,
they behave strangely too.
They say, "I must spend a penny"
when they really want the loo.
"That's the best thing since sliced bread"
means they like it a lot,
and my nan says that kissing boys
makes your teeth drop out or rot!
But when you can't get back to sleep,
and you really wish you could,
they tell stories about a big fanged wolf
trying to eat little Red Riding Hood!
Mum says spitting isn't nice,
(in fact, spitting is a disgrace),
but then she'll spit into her handkerchief
and wipe it all over my face!
"Not in front of the children"
is the silliest sentence by far,
that means they don't want us to see
just how childish they sometimes are!

Helen Long

A Lifeboat Crew

The explosive sound of the maroons, on a stormy night.
Then fast running feet, as the moon hides from sight.
As nine sleepy men, leave their families and their home
And put to sea, in mountainous waves topped with foam.
As a force ten gale, that blows from the west
On that storm swept sea, these nine men give it their best
For far out on that, wild cold cruel sea
Both boats and men in grave danger. There be.
As they battle the storm to save the lives of strangers
Back on shore families wait and pray, for all know the dangers
But there on the horizon with the coming of dawn
A boat full of thankful men, this time no reason to mourn
A rare breed of people are those unselfish few.
For these are the families and men of a lifeboat crew.

David W. Gilmore

I Shan't Lament For My Love

Are you mine or am I forever yours?
Is our love meant to be so great?
Or our meeting full of desperate fate?
Does love prevail without its horrid flaws?
Have we stumbled on a loathsome cause?
No we are not guilty of a lovers trait,
Instead lying here like a piece of bait,
Waiting to be tarnished with evil sores.
Banish these answerless inquisitions,
My love for you is bigger than God's wrath,
Our destiny is mapped out on a chart,
So we don't help fate make its decision.
But don't let our stars die in crossed paths,
For thine is surely mine till death do us part.

Lucinda Bowen

The Distance Of A Fragrant Rose

I waited for the rose to show her fragrant head,
And then one day a tiny bud began to slowly spread.
And somewhere in the distance I heard a new born baby cry,
A Fragrant rose, a little child both born to live and die.
I watched the fragrant rose sweetly blossom and grow,
A velvet red rose which won the Summer show.
And somewhere in the distance I saw a pretty young maiden,
A fragrant rose, a pretty youth both here to bloom and fade.
With each coming day her velvet petals faded slowly,
I saw time take away her dewy youthful glow,
And somewhere in the distance a pretty maiden reached the stage,
When youth had passed and she had gracefully
grown to middle age.
Alas the fragrant rose grows old and gently sways,
Her fragrant memories pass onto another new bud's day,
And somewhere in the distance life's message is quite plain,
A space of time is all each fragrant rose may claim,
A tiny bud, a glowing blossom, the fading petals, the dying rose,
New life, youth, middle age, and growing old, how quickly time goes,
And somewhere in the distance when life has passed on by,
There is an everlasting garden where fragrant roses never die.

Patricia M. Campbell

Without A Word

I walked away,
without a word.
Causing you distress,
I was confused.

My time, was not my own.
It was not right to spend minutes with you;
When we needed hours.

Seeing you again, has made me realize
there is something left to build upon.
Too precious to discard.

The flame still burns,
the second time around.
Let's try to get it right,
without a word.

Daniella J. Philbin

Two Weeks Of My Life

I had to go into hospital, for surgery on my brain,
I hoped that I was never going to have a fit again,
My head was cut open and a piece was taken away,
I've never looked back or been sorry since that dreaded day.

The surgeon performed a miracle, I owe him so very much,
For all his skill and technique and his steady touch,
The nurses were just brilliant, they looked after me so well,
They gave me pills and kept checking me and brought me
through that hell.

I'd drips in my arms, and in my hands, a bandage round my head,
I was also put on machines that restricted me to bed,
I couldn't walk, I couldn't eat, I couldn't even sit,
But after a week I started to move, albeit just a bit.

Two years on I feel so good, I'm glad I had it done,
About the fits I've had just six, I wish I could say none,
In my forehead I have dent, but it's covered by my hair,
Even if people see it, I don't particularly care.

For the long term future I'll have to wait and see,
I'm trying to finish most of my drugs very gradually,
I hope the fits will finish and the headaches will all stop,
But most of all I'm very pleased that it was not a flop.

Zoe Lambert

Goodnight Grandma

I can see you're slipping away from me
I'm told it's now the end
You're going to leave me on my own
On that I can depend

But, as I lay in my bed at night
I see your face before me
I feel your love and tender touch
And know in truth you'll never leave me

So when I close my eyes and think of you
And often that shall be
Those precious moments that we shared
Will bring you back to me

Then that warm old fashioned feeling
Will return to me once more
And all the fun and laughter
Will remain forever more

Thirteen years he's waited
He'll meet you at the light
Content you're now with granddad
It's time I said goodnight

Tracey V. Gill

Love

When you find a heart that loves you only,
You'll find my dear that you'll ne'er be lonely.
When you find love that's warm and tender
Then you've found a peace that will last forever.

When these things come your way
Have trust my friend, don't turn them away,
You'll find a warmth and be content,
You'll find that life is so well spent.

When you feel warmth in a summer breeze
Then you've found joy and a perfect ease,
When you find love in the words of a song
You'll be content just to sing along.

If you find love in a baby's smile
It will touch your heart for a long long while,
If you find someone who really cares
Then make sure darling you're always there.

And if I find love just for a while,
Then I'll be happy and always smile,
I'll treat it with kindness, I'll treat it with care,
And pray my darling it will always be there

Christine Gillin

The Spoilt Soil

Who took the trees from the fields
And covered the fields with grey
Who took the colour and green belts
And made all the birds fly away
  Who took the foxes' den
  And so slowly the foxes lives
  Who made the rabbits run
  And destroyed all the royal bee hives
Who took the blue from the sea
And who bloodstained the shore
Who to her love from her arms
And sent him to fight someone's war
  Who took the chastity from the sky
  And caused the sky spirits' pain
  Who took the source of our breath
  And soured the taste of the rain
It is we who have raped the earth
It is we who will bring it to boil
It is we who have poisoned the elements
It is we who have spoilt the soil

M. J. Smith

Dreams Do Come True

Even though we're miles apart
  fate will never let us part.
You're in my mind and in my heart
  since the day you broke my heart.

The first day I saw you was the beginning,
  and the end of something and nothing.
I dream of what one day will bring,
  joy and happiness only you can sing.

Time together would be so grand
  no where special just hand in hand.
God will hear my prayers today.
  and tomorrow will be another day.

Full of wishes and thoughts of you,
  precious time being spent by two.
Our hearts will be together,
  for we are meant to be forever.

Harinder Kaur

Little Snowflakes

Like little snowflakes sent from above,
They came into the world cocooned with love,
Adored and cherished they crawled then walked
Characters growing as they gurgled then talked.
Their laughter rang out as children's should do,
But, one day, darkness came as if on cue
When, with an evil mind, he walked our way
To take our little snowflakes all away.
Now all gone on that mad March day
Left with but a memory along life's way

Cathy Moncrieff

She's Retired You Know

While out shopping, I heard a friend say, she must be so
bored, with no work every day. Retired you know, be five
years or so, had to go early, her heart you know.
I think she goes to that W.I. she must have been desperate, to
give that a try. Then she does flower classes, and things for
the church, cooks meals, walks the dogs, and types a fair verse.
She sells eggs at the market, 'Botley W.I.' she doesn't get
paid so I can't think why. She makes card and things, (Her
daughter's a warden) so she helps there at open days,
just as a token.
I think nearer christmas, she starts making crackers, and does
things with paper, to make into wrappers.
Winchester flower festival, (I heard she went), with flowers
and props, some bought, some lent. Then she does wed-
dings, gone sometimes
all day, and all for love of course, or so I've heard say.
God knows when her housework, (If ever) gets done.
Now that I think of it, she's seldom at home.

Margaret Lewry

85

Peg's Box

Your box now sits upon my shelf
Still fine and strong, much like yourself
The gift you kept to always treasure,
like yourself gives endless pleasure.

A lovely face adorns the lid
which opens to more gems it hid;
unopened lace lies tucked inside,
Like wisdom you could never hide.

Your lovely face shone through my youth
you welcomed all and gave your truth
you laughed a lot, never did grow old,
you opened up a pot of gold.

Like the box throughout the years
always there, to quell my fears,
your agile mind remained the same
would comfort, spoil, but never blame.

And when I miss you, and I do
your box is there; and just like you
lovely, strong, and never defiled
so many hearts with love beguiled.

Barbara Peat

Tunics Of Scarlet And Blue

We stood on the Plains of Ab'rm in tunics of scarlet and blue.
We mounted dappled grey chargers on the field of Waterloo.
To the valley of death in Crimea, we galloped in glittering array.
And as with the floors o' the forest our young lives are a' gaed away.

When will the carnage be over, and men be finished with war.
When will the leaders of nations the battlefield abhor.
When we have the courage to ponder, and question the wisdom of strife.
When men see with eyes clear as crystal, the value and beauty of life.

How will this feat be accomplished, and peace be the object supreme.
When we as a people like Martin, share in his wonderful dream.
To live as much for each other, as we do for our own selfish ways.
To live in the light of the Master, and listen to what our heart says.

So when the drum rolls and the flags are unfurled, and the 'rousers they bellow and bray
Look through 'tween the flags are and the pageant towards a more glorious day.
When energy effort and wisdom are harnessed to feed the world's poor.
And we have a view of Creation that is peerless, untarnished and pure.

So enter the fight for our future, and live as men free from all guile.
Let us look to the widows and orphans, and change their tears to a smile.
Then we will find life worth living, new honours to win and enshrine.
And at the last sound of the trumpet, you'll have lived a life that was fine.

W. J. Bingham

A Resting Place

A desolate Church, gaping.
Dark sombre sentinel yews,
Brooding, ageless—absorbing
Autumn's child winds, while
Secret blood–shot eyes watch over
Lichen–covered limestone flags.

A spiny speckled ball, camouflaged,
Nestled in yellows—citrus, jaundiced,
Piled–up sepia browns, soggy beige.

A yawning hole captures a wayward gust.

A sensuous rolling motion to darkness.
A cold cadaverous cobwebbed womb—
Cradling.

For one, come spring, a Resurrection.

James Counihan

Inside My Head

Things seem so different as I lie awake
There are chances out there I need to take
Something strong inside grasps me back
My beliefs and confidence I do lack

I have high hopes and such high dreams
But none are prone to come true it seems
I have a world here inside my head
But instead I lay here alone, in my bed

I should be out there seeking all kinds of life
Getting myself into perpetual strife,
Effortless I ascend from my dwelling place
Out there I shall go in search for my own space

I must live my life, day by day
Learning to deal with whatever comes my way
Obvious to me, now I see
That I am not alone as one, but as we.

Joanne Cocks

Untitled

Last night I saw a lady weep,
It nearly made me cry,
She wept for the son she could not keep,
And then she asked me "Why?"
But when I said "I did not know",
She asked me "Was God friend or foe?",
She was not ready for spirits part,
In helping to mend her broken heart,
Spirit touched upon her, but she could not see or hear,
She could not feel their love, because of her own fear,
Her fear that her world was at an end.
How could she know, that all would transcend.
In my mind's eye, I still see that lady weeping,
But I am happy, for I know, that she's in spirits keeping,
They will guard, and guide her, and shower her with love,
And one day, when she's ready, she will turn to the power from above.

Jacqueline P. Howe

Sweet Bliss Confusion . . .

Legends of legacies, find me my unicorn,
Escape to Utopia, Velvet and black,
Shadows that never move, calmness that will not fade.
Moonbeams make laser beams, conscious, I dream,—
Bottles of better times, under silken sky
and with a sun made sea, trailing my veil.
Secret dark silhouettes, then the stone grows on stalks.
Pick me a golden lock, let your hair loose,
Leave me to wonder here, alone in Utopia
Don't stop for thoughts of me, let me go free.
Weakness that weirdly wild, gone to the shore again
Made from a mellow state, sail me away.
Breath me now sour words, tell me your story lies
Swim with me for the sky, gain as you dare . . .

Sally Spaticchia

Oh To Be Rich

A friend of mine the other day,
asked me what I wanted out of life,
Eight draws on Littlewoods I said, and of course, I'd change the wife,
A mansion in the country, a yacht for days of fun,
A butler at my beck and call, and a villa in the sun,
A Mercedes or a Roller, you can throw in a Chauffeur too,
And a few twenty year old leggy blondes, all with eyes of blue,
He walked away smiling, I then sat down and thought,
Would I really like to win a figure of so many noughts,
For that smiling face of my friend, I would see no more,
For I am more than content, to stay happy and be poor,
For rich I am in health and strength, and God I have to thank,
For happiness you cannot buy, with money in the bank,
What you never really had, for sure you'd never miss,
But if I ever won the pools, I'd blow it like a kisssssssssss

Joseph Walker

Willful Destruction

The echo of the lark's gentle chirp
Replaced by the workman's sarcastic quirk.
The oak's reaching branches, arching wide
Now a theme park's teeth–chattering ride.
The swaying grass, so straight and tall
Becomes a huge new shopping mall.
The gently flowing, glistening stream
Drained to make a house of dreams.
And when we're through, our work complete
The whole world paved like one long street.
As we've destroyed everything else
We'll turn around and kill ourselves.

Dawn-Marie Gibbons

Sea

Sea you are wonderful, wild and uncontained,
To be as free as you are a position to be obtained,
Whipped up by the wild wind, resting on the shore,
Cruel and yet caressing, who could ask for more?
A living for the mariners, a playground for us too,
Can sail and swim and look upon, grey green, black or blue
In all your moods you're beautiful; you fill me with emotion.
I love your mighty crashing waves or just the calm still ocean.

Sylvia Guiver

My Special Rose

Oh my lovely Rose my heart is saddened as I sit,
Here beside my window listening to the cold, cold winds
Cruelly lashing your beautiful pink head against the wall.

Oh what sadness to see your lovely petals fall to the ground.
There is nothing as beautiful as you to be found.
I should have saved you this suffering by taking from
Your long limbs some cuttings, but you were too beautiful
to be defaced, and you looked a picture through the lace.

So I pray cruel winds blow lightly and don't leave
My Rose unsightly, one cannot see beauty and
afterwards see it destroyed, without one's self being
destroyed, maybe because you are saying good bye.

I am so lonely tonight, I know you'll be back in a
different style, things won't be the same as they are tonight,
As I seem to love you as part of my life.

So my pretty Rose I'll wave you good bye,
And close the curtains as darkness is nigh,
I'll go to bed and try not to sigh,

When morning will come I'll pick your dead petals
And place them in a box in my bedroom
And keep them forever as my special heirloom.

Elizabeth Clancy

Pleading Love

Even if the time restricts us the space
Even if the men stop us the way,
I will love you.

Even if you doubt the greatness of this passion
Even if you refute this sublime love
Even if the hate takes possession of you,
I will love you.

Even if I have to carry with the weight of humiliation
Even if they ask me to forget you
Even if they force me to renounce you,
I will love.

Even if I have to love you in silence
Even if the distance separates me from you,
I will love you.

I will love you with the same brilliant of your eyes
I will love you with the same dimension of your smile
I will always love you.

Pedro D. Luis
(Ned-Lay) 20/02/90
Isla de la Juventud, Cuba

A Tribute To Liz

Flickering shadows by the fire, beside an empty chair,
Now I sit with memories and look with heartache there,
Memories of times gone by, days now in the past,
A dear one taken from me, but love will ever last.

A smiling face, a photograph, upon a table bare,
Precious things remind me of joy we once did share,
Of travels we had taken along the path of life,
Her journey now has ended, brave Liz, my darling wife.

What fortitude and courage she showed in the past years,
She smiled throughout the suffering and tried to hide the tears,
A mist now forms before my eyes and I quietly shed a tear,
I share my grief with others whose loved ones they held dear.

Her artistic skills and talents were varied and well known,
The garden glows with colour from flowers that she had grown,
The perfume of the roses seem stronger day by day,
As the sun's rays shine upon them their beauty seems to stay.

I give thanks for her good life, she always did her best,
I feel the void and emptiness as she has gone to rest,
I know that God in heaven now has her in his care,
And in his heavenly garden the flowers are blooming there.

A. H. Thomson

More Than Bridges

Life isn't just a merry go round
yet it seems we go round and round, like
the wheels on a bike covering old ground.
We are happier now than we've ever been,
but we've crossed more than bridges to
get to the place, before we'd set sail . . .
On the turbulent sea's, we've seen and dreamed . . .
that we'd soon get back to the calming breeze,
Where our lives combined as one.

Those bitter sweet moments where we laughed and cried,
I learnt more from you then, than throughout my whole life.
I shouted, you replied "No one gets out alive".
You were right, we don't, unless like past worlds we can
float around unknown, forever, together.
Over all those old bridges we'd travelled before,
through those we tried, we did come out alive.
Stronger than before but so much less than tomorrow
Wanting, holding, more and more.
It's basic, simple, yet so hard at times, to find
the right words but these three . . . "I love you".

Sharron L. Rushton

Summer Days

As spring warmth ever so gently intensifies and materializes
into the sweltering sticky heat of summer
We are once again turning our thoughts towards the delights
that come hand in hand with the season

Soft ice cream melts in the sun's searing rays of light
and sunbather's worship and marvel at its sight

Honey bee's take to the air and tender the pollen rich flowers
and we watch them while they busily see to our's

Whilst football fans throughout the land make ready
as a brand new season begins
Meantime girl friends and wives it seems turn up their chins

Gardener's amongst us gaze down upon the fruits of their
labour once again their taste I know we will savour

Children in the playground skip and play
why is this I hear you say

Because look say I pointing way up high
there is not a single cloud in the sky

So remember when times are bad and you're feeling rather sad
just smile and reflect it's so often the precious things
in life that makes us glad

Garry Veal

My Mum's Best Friend

Elegant Eleanor, dressed just so, always immaculate from head to toe.
Kind and mindful of what to say, whenever a stranger comes her way.
Sharing her life as a Missionary's wife, Eleanor can recall plenty of strife.
Her hours best spent serving the Lord, humbly and faithfully whether home or abroad.
Grace is said at her table before every meal, and back comes a 'blessing' no one can steal.
Well chosen china and napkins that match, all carefully placed when served from the hatch.
She has ridden a camel and slept in a tent, still looking 'the lady' whate'er the event.
From garden parties to bazaars in Church halls, Eleanor's quite willing to help at them all.
When sewing curtains and covers for chairs, she is often heard singing or saying her prayers.
Then having some fun with those near and dear, a time gladly reflected year after year.
My Mum's since passed on and I've taken her place, now Eleanor is my friend since I'm no longer chased.

Gillian M. Gemmell

Untitled

Listen to the crackling as the log fire burns,
Look at the flames as they twist and curl,
Feel the warmth that the log fire brings,
And embrace your loved one as the crisp wood sings.

Mandy Partridge

Justice

As the end of the world approaches all is silent.
Nothing moves.
Nobody speaks.
Waiting for it to happen. Just waiting.
Nobody can stop it.

There are silent screams and silent voices wanting to say stop.
Please stop!
But it is all too late.
Faces are looking horrified. Looking for a hero.
Someone to rescue them. Someone.

They're sorry. Oh look at their faces. The animals!
Nothing! Nothing could stop the inevitable.
Laughing laughing, silly animals! Oh the cries of pain.

Stop it, stop it, oh please stop.
Can't take the sound, the vibrations. Oh stop it please!
The end of the world has come, it has come.

The end of the world is forever and ever. Justice was done.
Don't stop it.
It had to come.
It had to come, didn't it?

Eru Umusu

The Uninvited Guest

Ruby Wallace came to stay,
upon one fine and sunny day.
She brought her bags, her hat, her coat,
and even brought her sailing boat.

She liked to have a snack for tea,
ten cakes or so she said to me.
She liked a little drink at supper,
It made her feel so much more upper.

She went to bed and snored all night,
While I sat up and saw my plight,
Ruby Wallace came to stay,
and now I wish she'd go away.

Fate took her sailing round the bay,
And in that boat she had to pay.
The boat just sank with all her weight,
Alas they took her in a crate.

Charlotte Stosh

Sleep

As nighttime draws and bed it calls, the night is closing now.
My bed it calls but still I pause, a little longer now.
Just five more minutes before I go becomes an hour before I know.
Just a wee nip afore I head to rest upon my nice warm bed.

After ablutions teeth and hair I reach the bed and slide in there.

Yet wide awake I cannot sleep, my mind it races, fast and deep.
Recalling all that I must do, jobs for tomorrow with the new.
At last sleep takes hold and off I head to far off places in my bed.

Maurice Keys

Sea Movements

The constant movements of the sea,
Repeated actions, not the same,
Compelling curiosity
These undulations to explain.

Describing sinusoidal waves,
Succession of recurring curves,
Produce a kind of stippling,
Like vibrations of one's nerves.

Reflected shimmering sun on sea,
Like many moving mirrors wink,
To dazzle folks bewilderingly,
Blind for a second till you blink.

The constant movements of the sea,
The repetitious drawn up peaks
Though breakers roll; This intrigues me,
Evades description that one seeks.

Elizabeth Foley

Whimsical Dreams

I sit with my back against the sea-wall,
The wall that supported me when, as a child
I threw my feet against it and stood on my hands.
The sun is dipping down into the sea
But the sand is still warm to the touch.
Darting fish now rhumba gently on the spot,
And little crabs are squatting beneath the rocks.
The sky is indeed a sailor's delight;
Its reflection turns the sea
Into a length of purple velvet.
I watch a child's sand-pie trickle slowly away;
And I am a child again.
I fancy my lovely mother crossing the beach
Her georgette gown fluttering gently in the breeze;
She holds out her arms
But before I can be gathered to her heart
The sun disappears into the sea—
And I am alone on the beach.

Pearl White Regan

The Secret Garden

She feels her way through the garden
undergrowth surrounding her vulnerable body
Emerald green lovelorn churches,
Statues stand decadent, white, covered in moss
galleries and staircases, overgrown, lily ponds—
calm.

A face from the past, she remembers it well
or does she?
It is deep in the back of her mind—
like a submerged dream.
The sunset shines—orange, he stands
between the archways, beyond belief
Her long dark hair sways in the breeze
—her scent carries across to him
Her dress trails the floor, her
frightened green eyes—flash—
she begins to walk—her heels
clicking the concrete
He approacher her . . .

Helen J. Smith

Perfectly Natural

There used to be someone I could turn to
When I was sad.
There used to be someone to laugh with
When I was glad.
But now that someone has gone
Now I turn to no-one.
I can't share my pain anymore,
I can't share my fun.
God decided to take you away
I say that isn't fair.
When I come home I can't believe,
You won't be there.
You used to run to greet me and
I'm sure you used to smile.
"Hello, you seemed to be saying,
"Haven't seen you in a while.
I know it's perfectly natural
For all living creatures to die,
But there's something I must ask,
Who's idea was it and why?

Melanie Gosling

December Rose

December rose rapped in foggy shroud,
Cold, but not so to lose your closed tight petals,
If sun breaks through your misty shroud,
A mid-day's thin sunbeam,
Show your heart to me,
And waft a promised fragrance to my pleas,
Soon erstwhile frost reaching for the eaves,
Will claim you so,
As it does the last brittle leaves off naked trees,
December rose linger still,
Cast your spell on me.
Before you die and lose your fragrance
To the vagaries of a winter breeze.

W. Albery

Leopard

Running gracefully through the
Dark black grassland
Dodging swiftly away from predators
Clear blue eyes glistening in the Moonlight
Fast as lightning
Motionless in the face of danger
Hunting its prey amongst the leaves
Quiet ready and still, going in for the kill
Its beautiful long legs pounce on its
Prey, its hunger finally subdued.

Nike Adeleye

Memories

A new-born baby softly cries,
Those all around have moistening eyes,
The air is filled with joyful wonder
As on this lovely child they ponder.
He walks, he talks, and brings great joy
To one and all—this lovely boy.
He's all grown up and married now,
Was oh so proud as he took his vow.
His children came, grew up, then went,
He felt his life was now content.
The time had come for other things,
The choir rejoices, a church bell rings.
Fluffy clouds go scudding by
They fill the lovely azure sky.
Soft whiffs of perfume from his wife
Reminds him of his happy life,
They laughed a lot, and talked some too,
Along life's way they aged and grew.
A secret smile, a lover's kiss
Memories are made of this!

Gwen Ives

A Day Dawns In The Mountains On Earth While Another Young World Ends

Dawn broke and we awoke, a bold group of summer adventure campers, feeling grateful for the cool morning breeze, E. T. Scifi explorers on another world; she, my friend, a morning greeting extended to me, so I handed her a daybreak dawn coke. Grasshoppers provided a morning orchestra. Our senses sought to comprehend the awesome magnificence of the mountain expanses that contemptuously challenged us to scale them, and which lay before us. The mountains stretched into the morning heavens full of exotic mystique. A silvery–grey mist obscured the brave peaks. Sparkling, star-like diamonds of morning dew adorned her lush hair, a neanderthal, beautiful, savage princess was she, as wild horses bolted down a slope in the distance, young, wild, free, and magnificent; beautiful, the way nature was meant to be until interfering horrible intelligent enslavers, Man, evolved. I snuggled back into my warm sleeping bag, minutes elapsed.
Then suddenly I saw it and there it was, a forlorn star, our star, our sun so pale, sunrise! The dawn occurred, the sun rose, a heathen god struggling for life like a weak kitten. Was it a macabre cruel god or a loving one, admiring its creation? Simultaneously and coincidentally, Betelgeuse exploded into a supernova. We lonely inhabitants of Earth are fond of the universe. We salute Man, infinity and eternity.

Julian Gaius Williams

My Endless Love

I think of you every minute of the day
I think of you with every word I say
When I see your face it makes my day
Your beauty no one else can portray

My love for you will never die
Though some would say I tell a lie
My love for you will last forever
I know that it will never sever

I am sorry if I have hurt you before
I now know I love you more and more
My love for you will last all eternity
It will not rub off like a novelty

I love you with all my heart
You, could say that I have loved you from the start
I believe, it was love at first sight
Since then I have known you are my guiding light

I wish you would love me as I love you
It is a dream I hope will soon come true
You may think this poem has come out of the blue
But for you there is nothing I would not do

Andrew G. Kane

Odyssey

Ours are children souls, human to be hope's harbingers,
light's joy, our life rolls.
Fertile spirit growing by love's tending and sowing.
Open with thirsty childlike heart, mind seeks, swims in a bounty
of mystery, for answers are its journey, in each quest a start.
Nature's globe of spirit, earth, brings as human our souls forth.
In a country of dreams, from life's river its waters, in
springs of light our source.
Gathers the voices of hearts and minds, spirits clear lens opens
to see forces of balance, spiritual battle unwinds.
Web harried by human pace in a made stranger's place.
Spirit lost in confusion misleads human, paths in forests of illusion.
Answers and truths are as real as we let be, for if in loving
return we make, then our spiritual nature, we will as
children souls see our lyrical odyssey.
From fear, rescinded light receded and dim, untended spirit
listen, love calls, from each atom loves hymn.
Every voice and laugh each life and dream, search with
your soul shine with its beam.
Born for empowering love's blessing, rejoice a life's colours,
feel more than the illusory dressing . . .

Paul Holland

The Poppy Fields Of Flanders

Tall slim poppies glowing red,
Sway back and forth, with the breeze overhead.
A multitude in great array,
Magnificent in the glory of the day.

Memories of years gone by,
Young men came to fight and die,
Their blood flowed red upon the earth
And lost the bright flower of youth.

Oh! How mothers cried,
When their precious sons died.
In a Flanders field far away,
Gone forever goodbye.

Joan Jasiek

Haven

At the edge of the wood, 'neath the brow of the hill,
Sheltered from the northern breeze.
Not a leaf stirred and all was still.
Amid the willow herb and trees.

The autumn sun smiled blandly down.
White clouds mutely sailed the sky.
Among dead bracken and tangled briar,
We met and embraced, Silence and I.

All was silent in that place—
But for the call of a distant rook—
The great tits chittering in the firs—
But for the talking of the brook.

That silence sweetly stole around
And wrapped me in its silken fleece.
Eternal tides ebbed without sound;
I smelled the fragrant scent of peace.

'No great event', you well may say—
But its balm will live with me again,
Surrounded by the city's day
And the warring words of men.

Robert Marsh

Homeless

While business people rush to waiting jobs,
And darkness lifts to light another day;
A homeless girl sits down and softly sobs,
And wonders why the world treats her this way.

Through streets and alleyways of power,
She idly drifts from door to door;
Searching for a niche in which to cower,
A friendly roof, a space upon some floor.

The cold that grips her bones is so intense,
For cardboard boxes do not make a home.
Onward drags this problem now immense,
Of those like her, thus forced to roam.

On lucky days a shelter is her goal,
A mug of steaming soup to call her own.
Maybe a bed of rest for each poor soul;
The need for care, when love has flown.

Tony Tipper

The Magnificence Of Science

Intelligent, joyful, that's Mr. Ward,
Batteries, bulbs and teaching is his sword,
For once he has taught,
The sword is let free
and goes to slice the memory.

Once sliced the data flows,
Like the sea it never glows
But all of a sudden it sparks and blows,
Away it went rocketing through
dimensions of science,
Then it is released to be known.

Dean King

Married Life

The years you spend together should be the best years of your lives
There shouldn't be a day that you wished you hadn't shared
Although you have your troubles and your strife
You should be glad you took those vows that joined you two as one
And as the years go sailing by and the children all leave home
Looking back at the years before should be one of joy and cheer
For the love that only you can share should be beyond compare
And as you sit and take a look at the time that's gone before
You can turn to each other and say
Ah! Yes these years together have been the best years of our lives.

Lynne Wheeler

The Yesterdays

In tranquil mood dare one reflect
  Upon one's life in retrospect?
    Idle? Fulfilled? Or circumspect?
Of unexpected happenings,
  Of pleasures and of gladsome things,
    Which to one's life contentment brings.
Of sadness, sorrow, of unrest,
  Of times of joy remembered best,
    A heart rejoiced, a hand caressed.
Of things perplexing, undefined,
  Of those solutions hard to find,
    And solving gained a peace of mind.
Of happy days, of shady bowers,
  Of rolling seas, of idle hours,
    Of strange compelling unseen powers.
Of April showers, of country walks,
  Of babbling tongues, of popping corks,
    Of family, friends, uplifting talks.
Oh, those reflective days of yore, compellingly relived once more.
Repeat the mixture as before!

Edward J. Moore

Heroes Tears

I walked along the Promenade, when suddenly without warning
A cloud of water came down like an iridescent shroud.
This was not ordinary rain, it was tears of pain.
And suddenly they were there, a row of heroes who had died
During the war. So handsome, so young, such splendour there.
They were local boys I had known. All on the threshold
Of a rich professional life. Families with such pride
And panache that now is not known.

Their cheeks still wet with heavenly tears
They told me of their tragic fears.
"We were so young to die, to give to others a better life.
We went through hell, horror and strife.
Yet all we see is filth and slime. Drugs and crime.
No one working, no one caring. Who is to blame?"
In two words I told the truth. "Do gooders are the reason
For this hell on earth.
They have taken away our decency and worth."

Mary Christian

What Happened To September

What happened to September
With its shades of gold and brown,
When all the leaves fall from the trees
And heap upon the ground.
As summer evenings early close
And heavy rain doth pour
Streams that wander through the dell
Become a deafening roar.
When skies at night are streaked with light
And thunder follows lightning
As Gods do with each other war
And everything is frightening.
Coloured birds from other worlds
Return to distant shores,
Autumn shades creep through the glades
Mid summer's dying embers,
It seems, I can't remember
What happened to September?

William S. Soper

A Talent

A talent is only a God given gift
Bestowed freely on each and all.
The bidding is—use it—do not just drift
With the tide; and go to the wall.

Start counting your talents, and to your surprise,
You will find you have more than you knew
Then put them to use, from early sunrise;
So helping God's plans to come true.

Once on the road, with a purposeful swing,
And a smile for the people you'll meet;
Amazed you will be at the change it will bring
To 'neighbours' you see in the street.

In my twenties I learned to give over to God
My life, to do with as he wilt
In service and love, my conscience I'd prod,
So a new kindlier country be built.

Now nearing the end of the road of life,
My thoughts turn to the One up above,
Giving thanks for receiving tranquillity—no fear—
And the joy of giving out love.

Enid Holmes

Autumn

The warm gentle autumn breeze
Sends an array of leaves coloured golden yellow
and light brown around me.

As I walk down the forest path I see the
wild roses wilting away in the ditches and the
birds eating the remainder of the blood red haw berries

I walk down to the bubbling brook where fish
swim down at great speeds. The warm autumn
heat is quickly fading. Dusk is approaching.

Walking back through the forest I see rabbits and
hares running to and fro, looking for food and shelter
to prepare for the long hard winter.

As I look around me I realize that nothing
can take away the beauty of this special place.

Sabrina McCartin

Lee House Garden

Grass of a soft and luscious verdant green.
And scented roses, maidens of the Queen,
The chirruping of birds, contentment reigns
And nothing more of nightmare fear remains
Soft as the turf, the soil on every bed,
On full fat worms, the birds forever fed
Whilst watching over all, in silence still
Church steeple makes one mindful of God's will.
Life is unsullied by the outside world
And time stops still. The future now unfurled.
Out one could go to conquer pastures new,
Surmount sharp pinnacles, cross chasms too.
Stay, for a moment, caution bids restraint
To risk high mountains soon might cause a faint
Endeavour, later in cool of even, drinking in
   beauty, then might be the time
When to Christ's purpose human soul could shine

Ann Cubitt

Lovers Lane

If our paths had not entangled
My mind meanders to what might have been.
Where I would be then
And you would be now.
Had your beauty not ensnared
"The victim of circumstance."
You had what I desired
I had what you despised
Time told terminally
Lovers Lane lay mangled.

Fred Hartman

Someone Just Like You

All my life I've waited
for someone just like you
who can love me to the end of time
and stay with me through and through.
When I think of you I feel like flying
Like a dream come true
You'll never see me crying.
I'll make you feel like you're up-above
Floating on the winds of heavens love
never wanting to return.
A love so strong
That nothing can ever go wrong
And as long as your in my arms
Life will always reveal your hidden charms.

Amanda Franklin

Together

Together, filling each other's needs,
Together, cultivating future seeds
Together, completing the pearl beads
And with each sacrifice desire leads.
Together, more powerful than any fate,
And faster than any speed, souls unite and no heart bleeds.
Satisfied, there'll be no more greed.
Fulfilled, it's a winners creed.
Together reaching heights, where vengeance disappears
And with fulfilment we'll wipe each other's tears,
And in those around us envy breeds.
Togetherness, is what the devil fears.
Loyalty and faith growing stronger with the years.
Together, lost blood is reborn. Mending all that has been torn.
Fears become an illusion, and masks unworn.
Together for the ride we'll move ahead and stride.
With nothing to prove nor hide. Hand in hand and side by side.
Together we stand, whatever the demands,
Stop pretending and take the upper hand,
Life's battles don't come easy, but together they certainly can!

Lidia Alghoul

The Four Seasons

See, here comes spring a gay young thing,
With wild flowers braided in her hair.
She runs and calls and laughs, for she
Hasn't a care.

Summers follows, her full beauty is regal to behold.
The days of golden sun drift slowly by.
And scented gardens full of blowing flowers
Are honoured with this crown of nature's gold.

Autumn more mature.
Takes days with shorter hours
She offers bowers of golden fruit, and with her wine,
Toasts the days still yet to come.

Lastly winter, silver haired.
Her hoary fingers stiffly freeze the morn,
And deck with beauty every bush and thorn
With wintry white apparel for the dying of the year.

Betty A. Stoner

The Prey

Darkness falls. A tiny mouse
Creeps from his little tree–stump house.
The golden, corn–strewn meadow sways
But an aerial movement meets his gaze.

A dark form silhouettes the sky,
Diving low, then darting high.
An owl! The frightened creature flees
As the bird descends, now, through the trees.

A darting movement, gliding on
Towards the scurrying mouse with scorn.
Long talons meet the soft, sad throat;
The mouse utters a melancholy note . . . No more.

Gary Bingley

Secret Dreams

I live in the town with my heart in the country;
It's been that way for a long time now.
As a child I dreamt of a hidden tree house—
A secret abode on a leafy bough.

My childhood home had the tiniest garden
With bare brick walls, not a tree in sight.
So imagination came to my rescue:
My pony? A wall on which I took flight.

I galloped along on my make believe journey,
The walls around disappeared from view.
With wind in my hair, all reality faded,
Fantasy took me to places anew—

A path through the wood to a flower strewn meadow
With sparkling streams and moss covered logs;
The quaintest old farmhouse with hay barn and stables—
Home for my pony and two lovely dogs.

I'm still in the town with my heart in the country.
The years have flown but it's not too late;
My children have grown, now I'll search for my farmhouse
And welcome you all through my five–barred gate.

Penny Osborne

Child Within

I don't wish to see those childhood years,
I don't want to remember those silent tears,
I don't want to feel the loneliness,
the anger, the pain, the constant stress.

I don't wish to see the life I so hated,
the people, the lies, to which I related,
I don't want to see the ugly child,
the boy, the girl, the meek, the mild.

I don't want to carry the child left behind,
I guess I'm just scared of the feelings I'll find.
I wish I could love you, and share your grief,
but the times we have, at the moment are brief.
As if something tells me to push you away,
then get in touch some other day.

I'm sorry!! It's hard, oh child within,
I know you feel punished without any sin,
I can't explain why I locked you away,
I guess I protected in my own little way.
Maybe someday we can talk again,
maybe next time I won't run from the pain.

Nikki Kingham

Aren't We Lucky!

As we lie and rest, our weary heads,
We forget about those, without any beds.
Their bed is a bench, a box in the street,
Whilst we have our beds, a LUXURIOUS TREAT.
We have rooms of our own, in a place we call home,
But theirs is the streets, where everyone roams.
We can wash and eat, in the warm and the dry,
But these only often have, the rain from the sky.
In all winds and weathers, they can be found,
In streets, in doorways, or lying on the ground.
Some are just sitting, whilst others they busk,
For just a few pennies, to give them a crust.
While we sit and groan, yet enjoy once more,
Some goodies, which to them, is a sumptuous store.
The days they seem longer, the shadows grow,
And off to our homes, we lucky ones go.
So when you go, to your bed tonight,
Just think and pray, for those in this plight.
We take our home for granted, so much each day,
But remember, to the Homeless, it's a DREAM that's FAR AWAY.

Ruth L. Atwick

Friend

A friend is somebody towards whom one wishes to express goodwill.
When you are with him that's how good you feel.

An encounter with a friend can happen at any time
And when you meet him,
The impression you have is fine
Just for you he was waiting.

You speak, cry, laugh, sing, ask, keep silent
The friend is there with you.
Hearing, crying, laughing,
Singing, answering, keeping silent too.

When the friend hears your good and bad news
You feel all the bad things fall down.
And there's no such thing
You feel like you're wearing a crown.

When the friend talks, the words seem made of light
It seems you are listening to the voice of your heart.
When you suffer he suffers with you,
Without saying a single a word,
He makes you understand the world.

Ana Maria De Souza Carter

Why The Hurry

We live in a scientific world,
where everything moves so fast
where everyone's in a hurry
and friendships do not last
because no one has the time
to sit down and have a talk
or go for a stroll in the garden
or have a leisurely walk
we might have all the latest electronics
such as computers and video games
but when it comes to your neighbours
you find you hardly remember their names.
Then one decides to have a baby
and when it is six months old
it is sent out all day to a nursery
while Mum goes back to work for more gold
can't we try to slow down and relax
and take stock of what we have every day
and give glory to God for His many blessings
and His love for us all day after day?

Irene Gilbert

Nothing New . . . But . . .

I'm in bed with the flu'—nothing special to do
But flick through Magazines and Papers,
Same People, Same names, same Stories and Games,
Nothing new in all of these capers.
Fashions going far back—main colour is black,
Designers try to keep work strictly secret,
Same Models, same Looks,—same ragbag 'Pukes'
Nothing new, to my ailing regret.
Every Paper to date says the world's in such state,
Enough to make EVERYONE ILL,
Same Murders, Same wars, same 'Fiddles' and bores,
Nothing new in their reporting skill.
what with famine and flood, mayhem and blood,
I just want to curl up and die,
Same Political lies, it's same on all sides,
Nothing new on which to rely.
Then YOU are standing there,—half of this loving pair,
Our two hearts beating as one,
Same tenderness, same smile, same caring guile,
Nothing new but LOVE, under the sun.

Joan M. Bridges

Marmalade Chat

Marmalade Chat was a wonderful cat.
He was charming, and sweet, and enormously fat.
A beatific bundle of striped orange fur;
a Cheshire cat smile, an outrageous purr.
As graceful as treacle, and three times as thick;
he'd eat twice his weight and would never be sick.

One Sunday, he snaffled the family roast,
and a whole sherry trifle—on top of the toast,
and the porridge and cream, and an omlettey dream,
and bruncheon of whiting and salmon supreme . . .
And Marmalade oozed to the terrace to preen,
and mellow in thoughts of an edible theme.

And nothing brought ire to this genial soul;
who'd obviously never been briefed in his role
for mice took baths in his watering bow;
and raided the larder right under his nose . . .
Dear Marmalade sunk in a fit of repose,
just sighed in contentment, and curled up his toes.

Marmalade Chat was a wonderful cat.
He was charming, and sweet, and enormously fat.

W. Helen Beard

"Remembrance"

I remember when my dad, told me all about the war.
They were not made up stories.
But of terror, blood and gore.
And as he told me all these things,
His face relived the past.
A nightmare that goes on and on.
That in his mind will last.
I sat and listened more and more,
relieved that I'd been spared
The noise of gunfire, fearing death
and living through that war.
I never have experienced the suffering he'd seen.
Imaginations not enough.
For I am young and green.
I'm glad my dad's alive right now.
To guide me on my way.
For if he'd died while in the war I'd not be here today.
Well, as they say, life does go on.
But memories—they last.
And they're what life is all about. Remembering the past.

Patricia Bryant

The Seagull

O'er mountains, rivers, lakes and trees,
Gliding, twitching, swooping merrily beneath—
Glistening blue waters of sea sparkle
The fishing boats like ink blobs
One a page of God's own creation
I soar on splendid wing freely.

The carpets of green seem pierced
By his symbolic writing of rock.
Towns and cities light up at night
Resembling groups of star–studded ploughs.
But highlight human limitations
I soar on splendid wing freely.

White snow and now carpets over green,
Fusion overseen by a ray of golden sunshine.
Droplets of rain then fall
Followed by a freshening breeze
To dry the finished picture
Of nature's own painting brush
I soar on splendid wing freely.

Patrick J. Foley

Down The Lane

Today I saw my children
Skipping down the lane,
Calling to the pony
Who tossed her coal–black mane.

Laughing at the greedy geese
Who hissed and gobbled bread,
Then turned away, with such disdain,
Though they had just been fed!

I watched them calling to the cows,
Their merry laughter sound.
The cows were busy chewing grass
And looked not from the ground.

The clucking hens ran down the lane.
The children scurried by.
Their faces sweet, with childhood dreams
As they gazed into they sky.

Oh happy days of childhood,
the moments fleeing fast
May the joy of youth's adventure
Be there whilst life shall last!

Susan Urmston

The Changing Year

I look in the mirror, and what do I see,
A trendy young teenager, that used to be me.
I look away, then look back again.
Now what do I see, grey hair and wrinkles.
Oh no, that can't be me.
My figure has changed, my eyes of grown dim
I can't tell whether it's a her or a him
But in my late years
I'm glad that I've got
So many dear friends
Who mean quite a lot
And when I am dancing
I go back to my teens
I think I'm still young
I can still have my dreams
But at the end of the day
When my curtains are drawn,
I just pray to the Lord
For another new dawn.

Ann Pearce

The Transplant

A black man dies, a white man lives.
The black man, life, to the white man gives.
The white man's heart, is dead, and gone
The black man's heart, still beats on
   An accident had caused the black man to die

The black man's injuries, were so vast,
That death, overtook him very fast.
Permission, to transplant, was not hard,
The black man, carried a donor card.
   The white man, was summoned and told to stand by.

And so, with infinite skill, and delicate care.
The surgeon, performed the transplant rare,
And through the darkness, comes a light.
As the heart of a black, beats in the body of a white.
   And so death gives life.

How? In this life or death situation.
Can there be any discrimination.
The mechanism, in all humans is the same
There is no excuse, it would be in vain
   The proof, was in the surgeon's knife.

Delphia Beer

Pomeroy

I was born in Pomeroy
A place as yet unknown
Where high up in the mountains
The wind is always blowin'
And deep down in the valleys
Where the land is ivy green
When I'm there all by myself
I alone am Queen

And over in the meadows
Where the cows are always grazing
The land here is so beautiful
It's really quite amazing
And when the wind blows through you
You feel like you're not there
Because the air you're breathing in
Is pure bred mountain air

And when I'm there, just standing there
Where the wind is always blowin'
I know that I am standing
In a place that is unknown
  Suzanne McCormack

The Talisman

When I was a child I used to play in a way I've since forgotten
As though the bones of the memory have long ago been broken
Fragmented; tossed into the air to disappear
The flash of their shape forever imprinted upon the eye
Their noise upon the ear

As I grew older I moved in a way that seemed in character
With a youth star-struck in the ways of this or that new actor
Self-conscious; lost among the rubble of my peers
Yet able, to scramble up way past their limping lives
Though it took some years

Now it seems as though it all happened in a way too fast to understand
In black and white instead of colour, and in a foreign, freakish land
And not even to me!; to another individual shaped just like me
And so it's hard to reconcile the stories that they tell with what I feel
And what I see

To put it all in context would only simplify the mystery
To codify and indemnify a slice of personal history
Make it ordinary; take the grandeur of its size
I prefer not to understand, to hold the past aloft as though a talisman
Seen through childish eyes
  Gordon S. Robertson

The Foul World

To see the world as it is today
Especially our own, in such a bad way

There's so much violence and drugs going on
It makes you think, what the hell's gone wrong?

With so much hate, and greed as well,
It's exactly like a nasty smell.

So, really who's the one to blame?
Or is the whole world going insane?

So what is the answer and I would say
Go back to the old days when things were okay.

When people were poor, but no violence then,
And the only weapon was a fountain pen

The world was much happier
  And people did care

But the best thing of all
  Was that smell wasn't there.
  Dennis O'Brien

Hurricane X

Out to sea the rage was breaking,
Faster, faster with each gust;
The ocean's waves grew grey and choppy
And the sea shore lined with dust.

Fish boats made towards the harbour,
Hurrying in their hard day's haul;
Out at sea great ships dropped anchors
And sea-men hid from the mighty squall.

Down she came like wings of fury,
Whistling, whining o'er the land;
Whipping boats against the harbour,
Crushing all 'neath her cruel hand.

Through the night she raved and ranted,
Tearing all to little shreds;
Trees in their majestic glory were
Severed from their stormy beds.

Then, at last the rage subsided,
With the early light of day;
Leaving behind her cruel mission,
Destruction, havoc, and decay.
  Ann Marie Page

Broken Man

Broken man sitting by the railway track
Down on his luck, nothing on his back.
How can a man make it so low
Drinking that whisky, drinking it slow.

Broken man sitting on the park bench
Down on his luck, nothing but his pet.
His friend is his dog, no place to go
Drinking that whisky, drinking it slow.

Broken man sitting by the garden wall
Down on his luck, will never walk tall,
Eyes bloodshot, weary, eyes to and fro
Drinking that whisky, drinking it slow

Broken man sitting on the church pew,
Down on his luck wishing life was brand new,
To ask for forgiveness scattered seeds to sow
Drinking that whisky, drinking it slow

Broken man sitting, has come to rest,
Down on his luck, when was life at its best,
Confused and so painful, life never glowed
That man drinking his whisky, drinking it slow.
  Kate Fretwell

Sharing

The pencil thin girl glides by
almost waif-like
in flimsy dress
that reveals the paleness
of her prominently blue veined skin beneath.
The gentle breeze welcomes
the new vase of yellow flowers
that she brings today
slowly approaching
she lays them (as she does)
side by side
and silently prays
before returning home to dream
some more

A sudden gust assembles
gathering
petal by petal
resting them on deserted grave sides
not so far away

The pencil thin girl sleeps
  Colin Worthington

Childhood Memories

Hazy days of long ago,
Past remembered things,
Ovactine in crunchy lumps
Jam butties by the stream.
Rainy days and wellingtons
Chapped lines around my calf.
The river overflowing
The roads are all awash.
Sit waiting, half way up the stairs
For bases to go past
Watching for the tidal as it laps the second step.
The piano mounted up on bricks
To stop in getting wet
The coke floats out the coal shed
To rest by the back door step.
My dad came home when I was five,
He went when I was one
My Mam said he'd gone to fight the war
I was glad when he came home.

Jean Moorhouse

That Midnight Walk

I love to take a midnight walk
Amidst the trees so tall,
The woods are dark and menacing,
I'm trying not to fall.
The twigs are crackling 'neath my feet,
The moon is shining bright,
It lights a way to guide me on,
But still I get a fright.
The owls they coo, the rabbits hop,
Mice run through the leaves,
The wood is dark with eerie sounds
And ghost-like shadows weave.
Suddenly a breeze gets up
I can feel the drops of rain,
The angels above are crying again
Feeling for all of our pain.
I think I'd better turn around and get back to my bed,
The eerie sounds are getting worse, have I disturbed the dead.
The moon goes in, the rain comes down, the thunder crashes
above me,
I wake up with a start, in bed, and my lover's lying beside me.

Pamela Cooper

Daily Life

The wild birds perch in the trees,
The branches sway in the breeze,
The church clock chimes ding dong,
As the birds greet the dawn with a song.

The rising sun is large and red,
Tinging clouds with pink over head,
Soon the workers will rise from their beds,
To face another day they dread.

Hustle and bustle as they rush to work,
Supervisors ensure they do not shirk,
They look forward to the end of the day,
And think of the amount they receive for their pay.

Among their worldly possessions they sit,
To being smug they will never admit,
Videos and camcorders are a must,
And a brand new car so it has no rust.

Worldly goods are not everything.
Happiness they do not bring.
A loving heart and peace of mind,
Is what is needed for all mankind.

Janet Boulton

My Troubles

Just a poor little thing when we found him
About three months old we thought
With one eye on his cheek, and his jaw bone smashed
We really didn't think that he would last.

To the vet's that same day we took him
An overnight stay it involved
He never regained the sight in his eye
But grew up to be healthy and strong.

The years they went by, but he never strayed
Always by our sides he stayed
Until that sad day when he wasn't so well
His end was near we could tell.

He died the very next day.

Seventeen years old was our lovely cat
A very good age they all say
But that did not help to ease the heartache and pain
When our precious Troubles was taken away.

Audrey Humberstone

Flight

The wind approaches
Rapidly in my direction.
Eager to thrust me backwards.
A circling tornado whirls around me,
Exerting its force right through my gut
And paralysing my motion.
I fight for the power to breathe.

I struggle to go forward.
Determined efforts to get free from this force.
Striding it out
With intense persistence.
My bliss getting blown to shreds.

I change direction
and the wind is my friend,
Moving through my aura
And causing me to fly.
I pass swiftly through the air
Controlling my flight.
Spreading my wings
I reach my sanctuary.

Caroline Gallagher

Dreamers Dream

My mind is on overdrive
Undercover, but so alive
Waiting for my love to fulfil my desire
But . . . will his love for me begin to backfire?
Why does he not answer back?
No voice beneath his crew
His crew of laughers that rocket the sky a million colours of blue.

But dreamers dream of dreams so blue
That one day the dream that they dream will come true
Seed me, believe in me
Do not pretend you're blind
You seduce my inner soul
And next you blow my mind . . .

My life is now in turmoil
I'm wrapped up in a minute coil
I cannot reach you
But my love for you is still so true
So I'll stand in line—wait for you
   In the numb contemporary queue.

Sarah Curran

Poets And Their Poems

You seek them here you seek them there you seek those poets
Everywhere. Where in the world are they? And do they
Know it? There must be one, two, three, plus thousands more I say
Their said poems they can be so proud although no such pay
Published they have a job to do just that although how clever they
Can be who the dickens are these poets to be or not to be
That is the question the answer will come we must agree

You are the International Society of Poets of that I am sure
You must get poems yes sir by the score
One, two, three and I guess a few hundreds and more
For instance I have sent three poems of my own, good
I would like to jolly well say I know I should
Am I a poet it could be so? Why well write them yes galore
It's the pleasure one gets as these poems are made up plus more
Pleasures and lots and of fun of that I am always so sure
The poems you can read are from none other than myself just Tom
Tom Sexton my real name these poems are from

Tom Sexton

Balcony Of Europe

Pounding surf drenching my emotions,
Restoring vision to normal,
Sucking my inner turmoil
Spraying calm on my soul
And wind spattering my brain;
Ever–changing is your mood,
Depths secret and immeasurable,
Unfold germs of riotous imagery gyrating
And spiralling forever;
You are the highway of the world,
A ghostly yacht shadowing a fishing boat,
Two lovers riding your waves testing stroke and distance
Take me on your highway—destination unknown,
Sculpture caress me envelop me,
That on arriving on horizon's shore
Black despair, that ever–pounding demon,
Will have been captured and chained in your caverns below.

Kay Anderson

Canny Cats

I know three cats, all canny.
With cocked ears, eyes afire, they plan, acquire.
One rat-tat-tats door knockers,
Makes important din to be let in,
This small tiger paddles,
Steals drinks from dripping taps with lazy laps.
And number two composes
Contemporary piano stuff with feet and fluff.
Cat three is still and wise
Seizing comfort's chances with sidelong glances.
Saucepan lids are lifted
Curtains flung awry for cats to spy
These canny cats are mine
Or, I should say, I'm theirs, bless their hairs.

Betty J. Bevan

The Ocean Of Life

A silver ship upon a silver sea,
Cleaves a white furrow to its destiny,
Though storm and tempest may destroy its wake,
From its destination it cannot shake,

Through perilous seas to its journeys end,
Life is an ocean that we all attend,
Our dreams, our hopes, our fears we will endure,
Try to do our best, we can do no more,

Oh precious gift of life which we are blessed,
It must not be wasted before we rest,
We must help all others along the way,
To fulfil their lives so they cannot say,

That their hopes and dreams were unfulfilled,
So our ships on their journeys have not failed.

Keith Tyler

Dusty

Picture a coat of fur that gleams in the sun,
Two ears alert to every sound,
A speed equal to a hare on the run,
Of love, energy and loyalty abound.

Two brown eyes that sparkle with life,
Four paws as white as snow,
A face that shows no pain nor strife,
A cheeky face, that's all aglow.

Picture a true and faithful friend,
who will stand by you through thick and thin.
All his life right to the end,
your love and care will satisfy him.

Whether you are rich or whether you are poor,
It doesn't matter to a four–footed friend,
a friend who is loyal and trusty.
When you can picture all these things,
you can picture a dog—my dog—"Dusty".

M. McCrossan

My Dog Smokey

As I sat watching my dog today,
I suddenly had a thought
What if he were human, what would he say?
He brought me his pulley ring,
He brought me his bone,
What would happen if he answered the phone?
I spoke to him softly "Do you want a walk?"
What would he say to me if he could only talk
Smoky, Smoky, Smoky, I called
As he lay down to sleep.
I think I'd better stop these thoughts.
Before they go too deep.

Melanie Wilcox

Death

I wonder what happens when we die,
do we leave our bodies and fly.
Is there really a heaven or a hell,
I wish there was someone who could tell.
Sometime in our lives we will die,
It seems no-one knows why.
There is poverty and war,
What really happens behind the door.
I'd rather be dead then go through the pain,
Of seeing others go through it again.
When we die there is heartache,
But soon forgot when we wake.
The sun it shines every day,
My turn soon what can I say.
People don't care if it happens to others,
They might start if it happens to them or their brothers.
Nothing left to say
But death is on its way.

Samantha Hicks

Swallows' Flight

Harken to the chirping swallows
As they line up across the E.S.B. wire
Preparing for the flight ahead,
Signalling the end of Summer's reign.
The approach of Winter's domain

For some, their first flight,
As they chatter noisily with excited pleasure,
Dive through the air like bungee jumpers
But others, more experienced, sit preening
Knowing it may be a one way ticket

Now one by one they take flight
Like a squadron of F-15's
On a special mission,
To seek out Summer, half a world away
So until next Spring, I say good-bye.

Denis Mahe

Revival and the Dawn

The experience of rising with the dawn.
Provides a feeling of being reborn
The wondrous sounds and that of sight
Proves the existence of a universal might
This might, this force, this resurging flow
Is nature's reveille that all creatures feel or know.
The varied echoes of many mixed and natural sounds
Of sea, wind and heaving ground
A contrast from a sleeping dark and earthly state.
To something that is mighty, obvious, light and great.
These massive forces that all embrace
Seem linked to a gigantic universal race
The supreme force or master of life and evolutionary control
Allows a mark, or point before the personal one and only goal.
This goal is possible by one and all
The prize a glittering everlasting cosmic shawl
If one should fail in life's first endeavours
They are reclaimed and return to material
and earthly tethers

Raymond King

Alone

Alone she sits
Memories pouring round her head
Ones of people, never alone
Ones of love, warmth, security
What's happened?
Children in the bedroom
Should remove the loneliness,
But not!
Needs for husband, comfort, love, happiness
Where did it go wrong?
Days alone
Nights alone
Togetherness never meeting
What does the future hold
For the woman who sits alone.

Sheila Dougall

Do You Hear?

Place the butter in the pan dear,
Yes. That's it love, keep it stirring.
Now turn the heat down, do you hear?
Now turn the heat down dear.

Chop the vegetables, careful now,
You don't want to hurt yourself.
Now turn the heat down do you hear?
Now turn the heat down dear.

There, it's all working well now,
Just keep your eye on the pan,
And turn the heat down do you hear?
And turn the heat down dear.

Don't cry now dear, you're not to blame.
But you really should listen next time,
And turn the heat down do you hear?
And turn the heat down dear.

A. Turner

You

You are my world, the one and only part
You are my life, that lives deep in my heart
You taught me to live, and showed me the way
You helped me get by, each passing day
You looked past the hate, and brought out the good
You gave me faith, and brought out my love
You gave me a chance, so I could get through
You gave me your love, and I gave you mine too
You gave me your time, that helped me a lot
You gave me advice, and said worry not
  "Without you I'd be nothing
  Your love to me is dear
  I never want you to leave me
  I always want you near"

Tracy-Ann Brooks

Wind

In the morning light and the summer breeze,
I can hear the wind whistling through the trees.

It sounds quite distressed, unhappy and sad.
Or maybe it's happy, joyful and glad.

Nobody knows neither you or me,
'Cos the wind is something we can't see.

It runs about like a trapped little child.
Skipping and prancing for miles and miles.

As if it is lost, wants to find its way,
But the wind will stay here from day to day.

Rebecca Whyte

Goddess

Silver orb
Caught in the lacy fingers
Of the old oak tree
Silhouetted against
The darkening sky.
She mocks me.
She, Isis, moon goddess.
She of the coiled snakes,
Mocks me,
Turning the blood in my veins
To ice.
No more shall I feel the warmth of the sun.
No more feel the gentle breath of Spring.
At my feet lies the darkling pool.
I gaze into its murky depths
And she is there
With her mocking smile,
Daring me to slip silently in
To those deep dark waters.

Christine Baker

White Light

White light glinting, glittering, gleaming,
Highlighting the ripples as a swan glides by,
Feathers ruffling, snowy, shining,
Stately beauty, proud and fine.

Clear white light, reflecting winter.
Snowflakes, snowdrifts, pure, untouched.
Sparkling ice in rainbow prisms,
White light breaking, sparking fire.

Drifts of snowdrops, cool, white wonder.
Blackthorn blossom in the sharp, east wind.
Gentler mayflowers' creamy perfume.
Perfection in the first white rose.

White horse cantering through the meadows.
Wings of white doves, flying free.
White light catching, keeping rainbows,
Dazzling colour, sweet purity.

Chrys Aitken

Bob The Collie (It's A Dog's Life)

O' please. Don't tie me up outside of a shop.
People go by. But some always stop.
They give me a hug a pat or a stroke
And say o' isn't he lovely. Well for me it's no joke.
I sit here alone all by myself.
Just watching my mistress get things from a shelf.
And I bet they're not for me.
No chocs nor a bone.
Then when she comes out.
She says Bob let's go home.
So off home we go. But it's the way that I like.
I can run. Roll over or do just what I like.
I've a home full of love.
Lots of good things to eat.
And she always comes in and brings me a treat.
Here's little Jake he's come to play ball.
I guess life's not so bad after all.

J. Chadwick

Forever Mine

There is a corner of this earth
that is forever mine,
away from life and evil birth,
it is paradise.
There is a place that love has found
through all the bracken paths
where only music throws its magic sound
on open space and light.
There is a garden once I knew
and felt the scent
of a rose, while in the wind it blew
but alas the petals bent.
There is a river too, I remember well
the dancing ripples
as against, the rocks, they fell
and bounced up again.
There are fields, there are trees
and skies too;
a golden rhapsody playing in the breeze;
all this, is forever mine.

Irene Elliot

Given Garden

A garden is truly a glorious sight
Displaying its beauty at Summer's height
Blossomed filled borders fashioned with flair
Taking your breath, demanding a stare,
An astounding effect of various blooms
Offering the gift of many perfumes.
The grass with its tincture of verdant green
Enhances the sight of this elegant scene.
I often gaze at this plot of land
Amazed how it all came so grand,
Is a garden created by seeds and a spade?
Surely it's God and his wondrous aid.

James Lightfoot

Entrancing World

You beautiful creatures of silver and gold
That I can admire but never hold.
You dart like moonbeams across the lake
Leaving silver bubbles in your wake.
How I wish that I could know
All the places that you go
And that my eyes could clearly see
Your beautiful world of tranquillity

Marjorie E. Parry

Earth's Womb

A warm gentle breeze fills the air, whispering softly, carrying
the sounds of earth's own voice.
A distant volcano speaks, calling, time to reveal her secret
inner body and rejoice.
For she is delivering new elements of life, from mother earths
own womb.
A silvery ash cloud, reflects from the last rays of disappearing
red sun, whilst new life erupts below, encasing the old in a
molten lava tomb.
As she moans and heaves, valleys of hot tears stream down
her face, as though crying with the pains and labour of her
new birth.
Constantly she pauses, puffing and hissing from her hot breath,
before finally bellowing out loudly for all that she is worth.
Her remaining tears of life, flooding out all her past yester-
days, beneath a flowing tide of emotion.
Exhausted her spent body sighs, whilst the tears slowly dry,
forming elongated arms, that cling to her sides, embracing her
warm body with insecure childlike devotion.
Her mouth open wide, she deeply breathes, inhaling new life
through the ashes of her womb, into mother earth's own
heart's core.
Peacefully, she sleeps, rebuilding her strength until nature
beckons her for a new beginning, to be reborn, once more.

A. Whittaker

The Dance

When I entered the woods with its gentle breeze
Blowing its kiss on sunbaked trees,
My eyes beheld in awe the scene before me.

A haze of yellow gold and red
A swaying dance of woodland bed,
This nature's royal banquet fed the hungry bumble bee

Heard were the birds in their song of romance
Giving note to the woodland dance
Puffed with joy on stately branch of greenest tree.

I watched the bees as they greedily ate
Each buttercup a golden plate
Each Campion Bell a royal goblet of sweetest nectar.

Soon the bees began to swell
From golden plate and goblet Bell
The birds sang high throughout the dell in sweet accord.

When I left the woods to its gentle breeze
Its joyful birds, its fattened bees
My eyes had beheld in each of these the dance of the Lord.

Veronica Bray

A Treasure

Of all the wealth this world could hold and broken hearts to mend.
No greater wealth will you unfold, than of a real "True Friend"
They help you through when times are tough and life is hard to bear.
Give you hope when things are rough, and always show they care.
Always hold out a helping hand they're worth their weight in gold.
I'm sure that in this troubled land their love brings wealth untold.
So be thankful for a "True Friend" whatever reason or the rhyme
A diamond! No need to pretend, a gem to treasure for all time.

Gloria Church

My Sister

She was pretty, not striking though.
Intelligent. Not an intellectual.
Good at school. An all-rounder
In English and Maths. And athletic . . .
She was good at that. Until the
Underdog, the underachiever,
Me,
Had a day. To bask in the completeness that only
Popularity brings.
The day that left 'dear sis'
(Her words not mine) crumpled in a wheelchair.
To see the glow that darts from unblemished cheeks fade on mine!
Yes, I flinched and my eyes did crackle at the tears.
Theirs not mine.
Then the determination speech, heavily punctuated,
Turned on me like a menacing tide.
So that admiration dripped from every pore
As readily as the tears.
And then I knew that she'd been touched by God.
Or at least healed by Jesus.

Sarah M. M. Bullock

Rosebud

A rosebud looking so fresh and new
and opening its petals to let the sunshine through.
Its fragrance so delicate and sweet
but it attracted someone she didn't wish to meet.

He abused the little rosebud leaving her petals tattered and torn
but the stigma he left within side her
made her wish she hadn't been born.

Now the little rosebud has grown into full bloom
but unlike other roses holding their heads up with pride
she bows her slightly over, knowing she has something to hide.

Is that a raindrop I see on your rosy cheek
or are they the silent tears you weep
and although to others you appear as a beautiful rose,
only I can really see,
that the thorns you wear beside you are also hurting inside me.

Lorraine Seymour

Untitled

Like a small and fragile springtime flower,
Wrapped tight to protect from nocturnal shower,
Held deep within that cool enchanting glow,
Lies the mystery that no man is allowed to know.

Cat-like in that silken feline way,
Hidden just below the surface that claw that keeps
the world at bay,
Not for you the milk white purity of the dove,
Instead the red hot tangle that is forever love.

James Baguley

The Wild Wind

The wild wind blows without temperate mercy
Steals the words from your lips before they're spoke
And when the wild wind blows with all its fury
It rips through your soul as well as your coat

The wild wind blows with the name of a lady
Her feminine anger none can withstand
Beware as Shelia, Sue, Sherly or Sadie
Sweep over the ocean then scar the land

The wild wind blows wherever it has chosen
Through sandstone canyons or down the Rio Grande
'Cross those Arctic wastelands, past ice caps frozen
This time maybe the Savanna grasslands

The wild wind blows around and inside of you
Sends blood rushing, from your heart to your head
Driving away the peace of mind you once knew
Fanning the flames of hot temper instead.

Stephen Jackson

Age, Time And Familiarity

Is it age, that causes passion to be spent,
or does time and familiarity do the deed?
Age, time, familiarity; they have not dimmed
my love for him, so why, please why
are not his thoughts the same for me?
Is it because I love him so that I
felt, but could not hold his tenderness, passion,
lust and love as it silently slipped from
my frightening panic of embrace. He seems
surprised that his heart feels cold, my fight
to keep the warmth within quite unheeded;
he sensed my misery but not the cause.
So many years of love and joy, it
hurts too much to think of lust and passion
spent—please God not tenderness too.
Never, never, so I thought, would age, time
and familiarity leave two hearts entwined,
one cold, whilst the other slowly bleeds
to death.

Margaret Fry

Drinking To Oblivion

I've just lost my job,
My love has gone away,
There'll be no prize for guessing,
What I'll do today,
Even the whisky deceives me,
Tells me my troubles are slain,
But in the morning when I awake,
I know there'll be twice as much pain,

So I get myself up, and reach for the hand,
Of my liquid companion, (to prove I'm a man).

I wasn't meant to live this way,
I don't want your sympathy,
All whispering and talking about,
"Poor alcoholic" me,
I don't need the poisoned juice,
I'm not dependent I've had my lot,
I'm off job hunting today,
So I'll have a good luck shot!

S. K. Gingell

Untitled

Spider, spider, spinning your web,
How clever you seem to be.
Round and round and in and out,
You go too fast for me.

Silent you run on your silvery thread,
Is there only me to see.
What a lesson we all could learn from you,
Of quiet industry.

I wonder where you came from.
I didn't see you go but there in
    shining splendour,
Your web was hanging low!

K. McGuinness

Gramp

Looking out of the window
with eyes that no longer see,
questions left unanswered, unasked.
The opportunity missed for eternity.

Tell me about your early days,
your brothers and friends, stories and dreams.
Tell me about Australia, the war,
the ups and downs, the plans the themes.

What were your feelings as a father—
kind, patient, loving I would guess.
Why only one child; health, choice, chance?
Can we start again, no more no less.

Yet you are still here—here
for me talk to, to ask for guidance;
to tell you I love and loved you,
to inspire and give me confidence.

Take care then Gramp and
please watch over me when you can.
I missed my chance when you were here
and won't now you are gone.

Andrew Lane

Welcome To June

The first red rose has broken bud
To welcome June—the fragrant month;
The month of meadows, perfumed breeze,
Laburnum groves and lilac trees;
Of honeysuckle sweet, which trails
on hedgerows freshly green, as yet
Untarnished by the searing summer sun.
The last few lilies nestle 'neath their leaves,
Demurely shy, yet loath to leave
Until their sweetness mingles
With the full, rich velvet essence
Of their love—the first June rose.

I. Broomfield

My Feeling

"I bet you cry when you get home"
The girls smirking,
I turned round and walked away,
I could hear them laughing,
I tried not to cry.

My joyful feelings are in the blue clouds
Floating in the sky.
My bad and irritable feelings are
Coloured black, grey and red with sharp teeth,
Which lives in stars and not on clouds,
And I have the bad feeling,
I am angry with them,
So what, I may have a different coloured skin,
Every night when I get home,
I have got the anger and I hide and go to sleep,
And started to cry.
I try to stop my self but I can't
It happens every day and never ends.

Angela Tsang

Inner Window

When the graphs and pictures
left no doubt about the damage done,
"I felt so sorry for myself," she said

—a strange and poignant thought, as though
an entity may split into two parts,
one observing the other with compassion
itself objective
towards the malaise that prompts the pity.

As in Maupassant's story
the fisherman follows the tiny coffin
containing his own severed arm.

Messages of corporeal hurt lodge
in the same mind that grieves
for the trauma, pities its other self—
valuing its own whole existence.

Sadness for another's pain is kind, but
this secret encouragement of ourselves
gives dignity and hope
to our only, lonely journey.

Bernard Baxter

Betrayal

Winter—beware!
When night's frost–bitten gaoler,
The snow—saturated, chapped Sun, eyes
Blood–dilated in the plated pool,
Casts his unforgiving shadow on the ground,
And slinks away, at the moon's challenge,
Secretly, subversively, to seek his surrender
At Summer's shrine.

Thus, this evening, despite
A land snow—draped and silver–shackled,
Through starved stems and frost–forged
Fetters, I saw Summer's spy, the Spring,
Seditious and seductive, mounting Nature
Swell–shaped; possessing with gentle tyranny
The captive branch; diffusing air–brush'd
Green over comatose brown, exploding iced bonds
And brash diamante tracings, facilitating escape.
Shivering, I open the gate, peer uneasily
Over my shoulder, aware that I witnessed
A treasoned conception.

Corinne Lawrence

Marriage

More and more the feelings grow inside of you, boiling to full
steam, waiting to burst free in an outbreak of emotion.

All of the time confusion and nerves mixing and tying knots in
the dark depths of your full hearts.

Ready to make a commitment, due to so much love and joy
from two so overflowing with happiness.

Realization that nobody, no matter whom, can brake that bond
in which your hearts are tightly clutched.

Inspiring so much beauty into the two of your lives, which
you shall lead together lovingly in good and in and moments.

Anywhere and everywhere you are, together or apart your spirits
will be guided as one, in an endless corridor of generosity and life.

Gratefully taking one another's hands, accepting each others
lives and loving the other for what they are.

Enchanting the freedom of life and freeing an eternity of love,
whilst becoming a single heart leading two separate souls.

Nikki Charters

Angels From Dunblane

I couldn't ever try to imagine, just how you all must feel,
That terrible dream, that awful nightmare, please say it wasn't real.
To lose so many babies, their innocence cannot be shown,
To take away their tiny bodies, his guilt will never be known.
to know you've held them and kissed them for the very last time,
And never hear them laugh again or say a funny rhyme.
My thoughts are with you all so heavy is my heart,
To know their lives have been taken before a chance to start.
Thankfully they're not alone, they're floating in clouds full of love,
And instead of just being babies, they're god's little angels above.
Hold onto your beautiful memories and live life through your
  child's eyes,
With your hand on your heart, keep on living and look
  forward to the sky.
I know for you things will never be the same, you never will forgive,
But hold up your head, remember their faces, you must carry
  on and live.
Your babies will be your guardian, so think on for awhile,
Think of your own precious angels, put on a brave face and
  for them, smile.

Alison Pearman

Collision

At one point in time though only fleetingly our souls did touch.
Drifting aimlessly, with no true course yet fixed,
I, the wind, caught you, the sails, and our paths entwined,
Two spirits joined and began to dance the waves.
Perhaps we had sailed together in a past life and remembered
the fear of drowning.
Because just as fast we were parted and the stars reset our course.
Had we sailed that course in lighter seas and with less baggage
We might have trusted one another and survived the storm.
Our charted courses never allowed us to sore the seas as one.
But in my heart and in my dreams, we did it a thousand times.
And we survived.
I the wind caught you the sails and we danced the waves.
We kissed the sky, the sun, the moon and the stars.
We were one for eternity
There are few people throughout our lives who touch deep
into our souls.
You, my friend, have a special place in mine, and always will.
In our separate journeys through life, if only in spirit—
remember this.
I sail with you and you with me—always.

Janice Deighan

Untitled

We pay for our health stamps so we may receive treatment
When I called upon my Doctor he refused me any treatment
I was force to seek the aid of a quack for my treatment
Who said that I had an abscess on my 'pendix
and gave me treatment which cured my appendix
She told me I was on a very dangerous path in life
and wanted me to change my path through life
Which I told her that was impossible on account of my life
which I had dedicated to my Lord Jesus Christ in nineteen forty
he had taken me down the corridor of life and gave me Life
which the Doctors were prepared to let me die not live
as I spoke to him in person that I would be of some life
to my fellow man in his fight against the vary hoarder
that were up against my country my Lord gave me life
he took me to William pit disaster Whitehaven where
my Lord Jesus Christ was there with me as a ghost
That unseen hand was there all the time when most
men were wanting to go out that hand punched my back
I said that I was the captain and recovered five bodies
from the disastrous wreck of human efforts.

Fred Scott

Parents Lament

Parents mourning till the end of time,
Never again to see the smile,
Or hear the laughter of the child they loved.
For they're now with God in heaven above.
No longer able to wipe away their tears,
Or put them to bed without any fears.
An emptiness, is now in that place,
That their child's love used to take.
Memories are all they have left,
They blame themselves and feel so inept.
What could we have done, where did we go wrong,
The guilt they feel is ever so strong.
Never again can things be the same,
All they can do, is try and block out the pain.
If they close their eyes and dream, maybe, they will see,
Their sweet loving child, as they used to be.
So as night time approaches and you prepare for sleep
Remember to ask God, for you, your child to keep.

Peter Redpath

Colours

Green is an emerald gleaming in the sun
The spiky cactus in the desert
The countryside in summer
And the stems of flowers in spring

Brown is the leaf floating down to the ground in autumn
The colour of hot gingerbread
The nuts on the trees
And the patches on a tortoiseshell cat

Black is a cat creeping through the night
And a cave creepy, cold and dark
Tar laid fresh on the road
A thundercloud in the air

Gold is treasure waiting to be found
The corn in the fields
The sun above the world
Coins jingling in your hands

Red is a ruby, red as blood, the sunset in the evening
The bricks in the houses, street lights warming up

Blue is the sea on a hot summer's day
The sky in summer, a blue school shirt

Michael J. Gunn

Takabuti

They anointed my body and wrapped it in cloth
Then laid me to rest in a coffin ornate
Supplying grains, and trinkets my new world to greet
And sealed me in a tomb airtight to sleep.

Some millenniums had passed until grave robbers came
They scattered my belongings and carried me off,
To an alien country where the language is strange
And placed me under glass for nations to scan.

My wizened old body is crumbling to bits
It will never withstand the long journey back
To my hamlet in the desert, sporting pyramids,
The land of the Pharaohs, my ancestral home.

Oft I wonder if my bereft mourners knew
That destiny would lead to my Celtic abode,
To rest for all time a shrivelled old mass
For spectators to ogle at while sauntering past.

My companion of old has turned into dust
His remains an attraction no longer marvelled at,
A relic authentic, a memento from the past,
I lie a in museum in Ulster's Belfast.

Marian Gillespie

Mum

Memories pass me by
One by one before my eyes.
Where do I begin? The list is endless
Days become years
Still you are there—the mum who cares.

You are the one who was watched me grow
Seen me through ill-health and good.
It's the best for me you want, I know.
There's been times I've made it hard for you
And still you've been all a mother should, my caring mum.

Now when so many miles lie between
Let the trust and respect still be seen.
And the distance will not be large.
Let's smile as we remember—but looking forward too.
Having hope in the God we put our trust

Today is for you—so don't forget
You're more than 'mum'—you're you.
Take care—I care for you too
Not just to-day but always.

Christianne Magee

Getting Nowhere

I travelled far but never arrived,
I reached out but nothing was there,
I talked but no one listened,
I looked for love in an affair.

I worked hard for no wage,
I sang sweet music to deaf ears,
I made a feast for anorexics,
I held out tissues when there were no tears.

I wore a dress for climbing rocks,
I offered love but was turned away,
I arrived on time to find no one there,
I was wronged but was made to pay.

I danced but there was no tune,
I listened for a sound that never came,
I waited in line though there was no end,
I threw the dice that lost the game.

I laughed though no joke had been said,
I ran towards no finishing line,
I slept despite not feeling tired,
I wrote a poem that didn't rhyme.

Joanne Pepper

Untitled

I can't help feeling something has been lost,
Not kicked away deliberately, or tossed aside,
But gradually forgotten, left behind,
An ancient song we no longer know.
Flowing, beating, running through our veins,
Down to the earth.

And still we search for comfort and success.
Happiness—intoxicating high.
We sigh for more, and once we have
attained our goal we start again.

And there are moments in the darkness of the night,
That we remember there is something more,
Or realize we have a soul, and cry.
Yes! Cry, laugh and let your body tremble,
For there is beauty still.

Remember the song of the stream, the
quiet of the rolling hills, and the
feint heartbeat of our Mother Earth.

Kryssy Hurley

The Gift Of Life

Everyone is special, we should be encouraged to think this way.
No two children are the same, one is chalk, while the other is cheese.
A child content to read a book, the other, always up to
mischief at play.
Equal amounts of love at home, children relate well to each
other, at ease.
Being there if they need your support, not always running to
their beck and call.
Encourage them to survive on their own, and offer support
now and then.
A child may develop talents that please, while others display
no talent at all.
Children loved, grow up to become well balanced, happy
women and men.
Encouragement, acceptance, is what the child craves most in life.
Whatever skills they master, they develop this at their own pace.
The mastermind, the absent mind, the high flying husband or wife.
Climbing great heights, or falling on hard times, a crisis that
most people face.
Using their own initiative, in a vital role they have to play.
Creating a home for their families whether in love or at war.
Choosing their friends, not their family, if they can survive life
that way.
They choose to be independent, with no one to answer for.
As they reach old age, they will think back over the years.
As they reflect upon their childhood.
With smiles as well as with tears.
The gift of life, for everyone, should be happy, successful,
and good.

Irene Littleford

Hunted

The shadow becomes flesh.
Moving as a bullet swift yet silent.
Was I seen,
Shall I die,
I slick my dry tongue over my drier lips,
And pray.

The chill of the night crawls up my back
And I shudder in fright.
Only knowing hate for this forest,
Only knowing hate for my morbid predator,
Only knowing I may never escape.

The night is growing colder as my twilight nears,
I feel a murdered soul of an icy heart nearing,
A shadow deep and dark
Is cast upon me,
Can you see the agony in my eyes.
Protruding aimless.

I think it's time to die.

Marie Boyle

Sorrow

Why oh why did the wee innocents die
How long will the victims feel for the loss to heal

The tears that I cried for the wee bairns that died
Our hearts ache with this coming daybreak

The feelings of grief is beyond belief
To lose someone close that you love the most

The sorrow you feel will be there again tomorrow
But as time goes on you will look back upon
The feelings of regret never to forget
But the good times you had the feelings so sad
For the wee bairns you had
Life must go on now just like the rain
Time will ease the pain
We know it will not be the same

But never the less we will do our best
And try in vain to ease the pain
for the families of Dunblane
for those that survived on the long road ahead
To remember with lament on this tragic event

Mary Bradford

Conventions—A Personal View

I wonder, on occasions, why we all should be such fools
as to bow to strict convention and abide by useless rules.
Until I try to bend 'em,—not as easy as it seems,
for they apply to daily life, and I'm concerned with dreams.
I suppose the major problem is that I'm persistent
in trying to mix the real thing with one that's non-existent.
I find myself regretting that we need such regulation
and the whole thing then becomes, to me, a source of irritation.
I fail to see the virtue of a system that's been based
on human fallibility—a fact that must be faced—
we all know we're not perfect, that, at least, we must accept,
but must we all resign ourselves to having to be kept
in a state of subjugation to stringent, petty laws
that, in any other context, would be thrown out clause by clause?
I am not advocating—as may be misconstrued—
A social revolution, but something more subdued,
just a gentle relaxation is what I'd like to see,
so that everyone could satisfy their craving to be free.
Free, that is, from guilt or self-recrimination
that nullifies the pleasure that one had in expectation.

Derek Parker

Whitby

When the tourists have tired and the sun has deserted,
When the harbour is silent and the salt–air chills,
This place becomes dark. Wind scours the cliffs
And drags at the moor, the seagulls cry—
And the black sea rolls under a cloud–choked sky.

On the hillside a skeleton, an abbey in ruin,
Stands guarding the graves eroded by wind
And centuries. Legends seep through the streets
Stories of pirates, of Wafts and White Wraiths
Gytrash, the Bargeist, and darker things—
Of Dracula, shipwrecked on a stormy coast,
Of bloodlust. The streets trap their dead
In the Yards and the corners and the salt–caked stones,
Ghost-sailors and whalers, their bodies long gone—
Yet their souls linger on.

And the wind is mournful and the houses are dark
And the pier and the lighthouse are lost in the mist.
This place keeps its secrets in the seagull's cry—
And the black sea rolls under a cloud–choked sky.

Gillian Lyne

The Understanding

I can't tell you how I'm feeling
While I walk this path alone
So I'll rehearse these thoughts of impression
And after this night
My faith will be renewed
And when I hear your voice
I find solace to enfold my heart
Once more your words have stayed true
This transmission will sculpture a new wisdom
Amongst open hearts
And while many doors will stay closed
The fire within these walls will burn for the eternal

Sally Boursnell

3:00 A.M.

Passing moments, fleeting thoughts, in quietness of mind
think of me,
Like chariots of fire they race, facing turmoil;
A feeling of warmth and tenderness is to pass, then,
Closeness of body but not in mind, soul searching the seek
the badness that reeks this impetuous flesh.
Lost, unsure, uncertainty roam this tiring space.
Sadness, failure, tears; time heals all,
A pause; a smile, a treasured caress, locked in a secret dream,
be calm mind, be still and warm your thoughts with ecstasy.
Sweet to taste.
Contentment.
My thoughts passed, I am better.

Lesley Dowse

A Wonderful World

Patchwork fields, hues yellow and green,
Blossoms pink and white to be seen,
In the woods the wild daffodils nod and sway,
As the winds have a message to say,
Among the trees a haze of beautiful blue bells,
The breeze softly caresses and tells,
We really have a wonderful world.

There's the shy deer, squirrels grey and red,
Wild horses roam, hoping to be fed,
Mountains, shades of purple with heathers,
Birds in the air, showing their feathers,
Swooping suddenly on their prey,
Singing their song seem to convey,
We really have a wonderful world.

Long shimmering sandy beaches,
With rolling waves, gulls screeches,
The lovable dolphins come to play,
With human friends, seem to say,
We really have a wonderful world
Please, please, humans, do not destroy it.

Myra Robinson

The Tyrant

He came toward her with a stick,
there was nowhere to hide.
He would never break her spirit,
he could only hurt her pride.
This cruel man was her father,
who never said what she had done.
But watching, silently in the doorway,
was her brother, this man's beloved son.

The years have past, the sun has shone,
her brother has long been dead.
The wounds have healed she's at peace,
he's sick and confined to bed.
He grieves about her brother,
his death too much to bare.
He talks about the good old days,
but forgets that she was there.

As she brushes away the old man's tears,
he talks of going to heaven.
But then her thoughts go drifting back
to when she was only seven.

Norma Davies

"A Spell To Make Your Teacher Disappear!!!"

I ask the pupils, Do you have a teacher that you can't stand
and you would like to throttle her with your own hand?
I have a solution at hand and quite near
you could always make your teacher Disappear

The smiles on their faces as broad as the sky
if it were up to them they would squash her like a fly.
They ask for the instructions and ask with no fear
for the joy of seeing their teacher Disappear

I tell them from the teacher the crumpled old hag
you will need to take her 10 ton weight bag
her wig and her falsers yes they will do
just pop them in and boil up the brew

But that's not the end you must approach her like a saint
her death breath is upon you, you feel you might faint
The last task in hand is to get her to drink the brew
watch her eyes pop out for it tastes like mouldy glue!

Stand back as you see a gap in her tum clearing
for now your teacher is surely disappearing
Now that she is gone thin air and no more
all that is left are her clothes on the floor.

Ashleigh Ovenstone

Headstones

Headstones:

Coverings for things buried and past;
A memory,
A name,
A pointer in the distance on the horizon,
like a ship's mast—

Something to be remembered,
Something to be found,
A message for the future;
Words without sound—

Symbols of life buried and past;
History overshadowed and cast
in forgotten tombs.
The future set in a mother's womb—
Their headstones yet to be laid.

C. P. Clarke

The Empty Chair

Your chair is empty now,
the clock ticks hollowly in the hall.
Yet time has no more meaning.
In eternity, none at all.
Were enough words said,
did we convey our feelings,
our thoughts, our intent and understanding
of each other?
Too late for our debate.
You cannot now complain,
the dead never do.
We thought there was time for everything
but your chair is empty now.

R. W. Kirby

My Goal

My goal.
What goal?
The goal to be immortal.
Keep going and the goal you seek,
You will find.
We all become immortal,
Remembered by family and friends.
What if I have no family or friends?
Who will remember me then?
You will have touched someone during your life.
Of that you can be sure.
Your name may not be spoken,
But the thought of you will linger.
The kindness you did,
Or was it some spite?
The punch up, a kick,
A kiss or was it a bite,
Someone on this earth will remember you,
Everybody sees you in a different way,
Thinks of you with a different thought.

L. E. Mileham

A Message To The Ones Left Behind

I read today of the young that have died
And the pain and suffering of the ones left behind
No words can comfort or wipe away tears cried
Only thing left is all the questioning in mind
Of why a tragedy such as this can be
And who can we blame for this poor injustice?
What's left in our lives we cannot for see
But the face of innocence we all shall miss
Why it happened we'll never comprehend
Life's so cruel to take a child so unaware
So I'll pray to God one day the evil will end
Maybe then the suffering will be easier to bear
So here's the message to the ones left behind
Your thoughts and feelings are not alone
It's your child and the world will not be blind
That sweet child could well just have been our own.

Karen Lee

Granny

I'm hurting inside but you're deaf,
I wish I'd known you before you left,
Come back to me and cure my pain,
I'm living here in vain,
I know you understand how I'm feeling.

If only you were here,
I might not drop a tear,
I miss you loads,
Let's communicate in codes,
I know you understand how I'm feeling.

Remember those summer days at the park,
As we sat against the trees bark,
Those were the good days,
Now come the greys,
I know you understand how I'm feeling.

We were close,
You remind me of a red rose,
And I suppose what I want to say is,
I love you loads.

Sobia Shafique

Our World

Mountain ranges span the earth pointing skywards their
snow–capped peaks.
Man endeavours with all his worth to reach the top,
vain glory to seek.
Far below in valleys green and in the forest clearing seen.
The mighty oak and ash lay prone, man's initiative to build is shown.

The rivers that flow down to the sea are dammed for the power
of electricity.
Causing all forms of pollution, man searches hard to find a
solution.
Ships of every kind and size haunted by the seagulls cries.
Ply their trade to countries far with goods of silk and lace and tar.

Crosses in fields with poppies seen and weathered monu-
ments on village greens,
Engraved with names of those who died in war, for peace and
freedom they never saw.
Jets roar where tiger moths once flew and the barrier of sound
is broken through.
Conquered outer space has been, earth from port holes can be seen.

Where proudly fly the flags of nations, governments voice
their recommendations.
Maps and boundaries and economy they scan, the future of
our globe they plan.
Solutions would not be hard to find if people cooperated in
one mind.
For all generations need to know a better world in which to grow.

Derek Tew

Old Haggard

Old Haggard is without a home,
He roams the streets with nowhere to go,
And, in some quiet park, in London,
A bench, where he lays his weary dome.
Old Haggard, wakes in the early morn,
Then sifts through dustbins, to eat.
An old crust will do him, till the night.
His curse is, he should never have been born.
Old Haggard quells his thirst with soup,
Received from the waggons, nightly round.
Then, cardboard boxes, he will prepare,
With others, to sleep within a group.
Old Haggard, is there, no matter what the day,
Never moving any further than Westminster
He will ask for money, for a cup of tea,
Thank you, then discreetly walk away.
Old Haggard, has to live a hard grind,
Though, he would never change it.
He blames society, for all of his plight,
And would be happier, if he wasn't blind.

T. G. Bicknell

I'll Dream Again

I'll dream again,
I don't know when
but some day when I come again,
when roads are straight,
and skies are blue
and flowers of a tender hue,
I'll dream again.

When fights are won,
and battles done,
and children play hop scotch in the street,
and lovers sit on kissing gate
and don't go home till it is late.

And you are waiting on the dance floor
and chandeliers throw lights of brilliant colours,
dazzling the room and all the others.
I'll dance, I'll sing again.

Sheila Yvonne Jones

The Child In The Snow

Oh to have the innocence of a child,
Running wild,
Like the animals in the snow,
No fears no cares,
Just raring to go,
The child having fun in the snow.

Laughing, squealing, shouting with glee,
Running away from daddy and me,
And then whoops!
Down the slide the feet go,
Scragging the knees.

The tears start flowing down the little red face,
And onto the snow,
Come!
Come little one,
Shall we go?
The child's answer was, No!
Running back into the snow.

Constance May Tolley

That's Life

When you sit and wonder when your luck will change
And something comes along that may sound strange
You wonder if this will be the day
When all the bad luck you've had goes away
But as it happens it was a false alarm
And you say to yourself will it do me any harm
So you keep on hoping that one day soon
The big one comes that will shoot you to the moon
Then you wonder why you're in such strife
Because at the end of the day that's life!

David Mackie

The Downcast's Riddle

A silly little woman asked a downcast, "What do you think
of the state of my life, how is it I sink.
With a school, a college, a university, to think,
how is it I don't seem to be on the brink.
I have diplomas, degrees, all the things one needs
to make me a person, oh don't you agree,
that with all this for me and all the money one needs,
I should be a person, not a person who grieves.
How is it, downcasts, how is it d'you think,
that with all this for me I'm not on the brink".
The downcast replied with a contented grin,
"You have all the qualities but not from within.
the diplomas, degrees and the rest that you bring,
means nothing to people and means one thing,
that you as "One" person which you are fond of to sing,
means nothing in life but to the one who brings.
So go now silly woman, ask what do you think,
at the state of your life and how is it you sink.

Tony Kemp

Compusense

Dumb terminal
my best friend,
stores all the secrets
that I send.

One way traffic
of random thoughts,
enabling
solutions to be sought.

Upgrades, speed-up
interaction,
providing greater
user satisfaction.

Software
for communication,
global network
of information.

Box-of-tricks
so reliable,
your contribution
undeniable.

W. Graham Price

The Grim Reaper

I heard the grim reaper
Felt his heavy tread
Strange voice calling me
As I lay in dread

It worried him not
My fear and my pain
As towards me he walked
Whispering my name

I saw the grim reaper
In my terror and fright
To collect me he came
In the dark of the night

But a light shone above me
So pure and so bright
And as I moved to it
The grim reaper took flight

As my eyes opened
My fear and pain gone
I felt a rare peace
Knew the battle was won.

P. A. Packman

War

A voice echoes from the dark,
the sniper aims and hits his mark.
The child's body slumps to the floor
he's just another in this war.

What wrongs had this child done
to be persecuted by the gun?
Did he know what this was for
this outrage of this bloody war?

This war like others, is a curse
for man's desire to own the purse of
land and wealth, its powers and greed
of which no man will ever heed.

So the poor and wretched sights of
death and torment with all its plight,
will never cease until the day,
the children have their rightful say.

Until that day we continue to die,
and many more in dirt will lie.
This bloody war without true cause
will devour all, without a pause.

Susan Marie Brown

Fragility

I hold this flower in my hand,
With gentleness I understand
The meaning of fragility,
We are alike, this flower and me.

Abandoned on the ground to die,
This flower grew to please the eye.
From all life's harsh reality,
God save this lovely flower and me.

Valerie Gamble

Eternal Spring

The mystery of Season Spring,
And why to it all things respond
—Growth brings happiness and hope
It is my wont to ponder on.
When sunshine taps the window panes,
It removes the shade from eyes
And entices one from slumber,
Dispelling haunting woes and sighs.
So be it with the heavenly warmth
When shared and thoughts incline,
As candle flame to dear Old Sol,
Is finite love to Love Divine.
So undefined yet understood
In part, by those who search doth make;
Time, the imposter, standeth still,
When timeless journey rebirth takes.
The lesson then of Seasons four,
Culminates in Season Spring,
Seen in that in which one sees a
Spring, with an everlasting ring.

Rhys Clement

The Little Jail Bird

Confined by my jail
I flap my wings
Searching for an escape.
The strong hold of their bars
designed to keep me in
the unbreakable,
I am trapped in my small cage
I know what I am
I am their source of happiness
My pain is their joy
'Sing little birdie' they chant,
but prisoners can't sing.
How I long for the open air,
how I long to taste the freedom
I've only ever dreamed off.
To spread my wings and fly high,
high above the clouds
That is my dream,
and a dream it must remain
For I am the little jail bird.

Rina Vyas

Light Of My Life

You were the sunshine of my heart
The happiness of my grief
The memories I keep are no longer nice
For I miss you
As you were the light of my life

I consoled in you
As I did no other
The memories I keep are so sad
For I love you
As you were the light of my life

You're a part of my life
That will never change
I hope to regain
The joy
As you were and are
The light of my life

Dawn Watts

Friendship

What is it like to be without
Warmth of friendship round your heart?
To feel the sharp and bitter pain
Of sadness when you part,
The need for someone near
To share your laughter and your fears,
To hold your hand in times of care and
Brush away your tears.

A Soul contented on its own,
With nothing to give or take,
Will surely live to rue the day,
When there is no hand to shake,
The joy of some great happening,
Is doubled up two fold,
When full of shining eagerness
To another it is told

Jenny McGarrol

Untitled

The icy rays of the cold moon,
no clouds to obstruct the blue beam.
Yet in her watery eyes reflected,
opposite, only warmth is seen.
Layer 'pon layer as hands catch sand,
The inner warmth slips away.
Entering the warmth, a brief respite
Born of pure gratification, to say,
adding more wood prolongs the fire,
soon like a mirror, her eyes no desire.

Gareth Williams

The Losses Of My Innocence

It's where I lost my innocence
But it's nothing special at all
It's dumpy in the wrong end of town
With pebble–dashed, mustard walls
The gate is always open
And the curtains are never straight
But every second that I spent there
Not one was spent with hate
The room that I grew up in
Is breezy and it's cold
And the covers that I lie in
are tattered and they're old
I'm not comfortable back there
but there's nowhere to move on
And a part of me remains there
even though that I am gone
Even when I'm older
I'll still be drawn to it
To try and find my innocence
and reclaim that missing bit

Toni Joanne Southern

The Travel Bug

The ties of life that bind you,
Are intertwined with love.
Without this bond,
You're free to go
Explore the world you love.

The mystic lands that beckon,
And sparkling eye blue seas,
Beam wildly and
Alluringly.
They only aim to please.

So don't bow to the hangman,
He'll never cut you free.
And if you try
To fight for life,
How tight the noose will be.

Sandra Beisser

Contrasts

A sunny washing day is here,
I put the sheets to dry,
They billowed out like galleon sails
Beneath the windy sky.

I scrubbed a small girl's muddy knees
And brushed her tangled hair.
The moonlight shone on her golden curls
A halo shining there.

While weeding in the cabbage patch
I saw the bryony spray,
Red beads for some wild sprite to wear,
I've lived a poem today—

E. Baldock

Special Moments Shared On Mother's Day

I came to you on Mother's Day,
Before your Soul was called away,
I wanted time to say goodbye,
Together we both felt and cried,
We didn't really talk as such,
It truly didn't matter much
What was to say was in our eyes,
We knew your Life was slipping by,.
I told you that I loved you so,
It wasn't easy letting go,
I held your hands, so frail and thin,
And feelings shared came from within,
I asked you if you were in pain,
You nodded no, we cried again,
I kissed you and I dried your eyes,
We understood our last goodbye,
You had your faith, and I did too,
Believing helped to get us through,
Those special moments that we shared,
Will stay with me no matter where.

M. Barber

Untitled

The world is going down and down
And something must be done
It started out as beautiful
But now is really glum
The sun above still shines on us
And gardens give us flowers
So surely man can change his ways
If benefits be ours
By tending to the "other man"
Instead of for "himself"
There then would be a lot less strife
And a better type of "wealth"

Louise Abel

The Thirst Inside

Before my body trembles with desire
    to make love, let me play.
Drowning in emotions, swimming with the
    tide, I follow your body moving
gently upon my skin, with teasing
    touch we search for pleasure that's
only found within.
    While caressing with your palms
we kiss, passion gentle but so deep,
    as down your spine my fingers run,
a feeling we long to keep.
    Naked in our youth we lay, tender
lips stroking each others, while
    tongue–tied in an orgy of feeling
which no words can describe, until
    our bodies flow with liquid
passion to quench the thirst inside.

S. Brown

Dawn

Watching
The calm full moon,
Sleeping, rising, then growing old.
A young dawn rises
And vast trees weep.

Silently through the glades,
Casting silver shadows on
Clusters of country flowers.
Awaking to the fresh dawn hours.

Raindrops bright, fall
Through the green baize leaves.
The golden world of buttercups laid
Under low branches seeking shade.

The mountain stream rushes
In passionate gushes,
Far into the forest, belay.
There, the wild birds sing
Still falls the rain.
I am morning.

John Joseph Browne

Winter Days

Warm fires
Icy snow
Frozen gutters
Hanging low

Freezing children
Firing snow
Hitting mummies
As they go

Snowmen standing
In a row
Children have made them
From the snow

Hats on heads
Scarfs round necks
Gloves and mittens
Fingers to protect.

Christina Wilson

"Life's Shattered Dreams"

Life!
How dare you
feed on her precious love.

Life!
How dare you
build her hopes and dreams.

Death!
How dare you
Interfere and destroy her Life!

Janette K. Simpson

James

I cannot watch you grow
I cannot watch you
    walk, run and play
I miss you as much
    now and today
As I did when you
    went away
The years seem to have
    just flown past
It's hard to believe how
    quickly it's gone
If you were here and
    with me now
A grown man you would be
    not the baby that went
    and left me.

Sharon Matthews

Oh England Please Help Me

The lonely cold night
was soon to pass.
Then morning came,
I was in England's last.

The ship was ready to
take us on board.
With its rusty cold body
on the cold misty shores.

The dock was filled
with sorrow and goodbyes.
The daunting decisions ahead
Would make people cry.

Oh England please help me
to keep my talent and wit,
for no dignity will ever be shown
down under, as it is slavery, and
hardships that we must submit.

Cassandra Dixon-Phillip

Feet Of Clay

My feet are of clay
Stuck fast–oozing mud.
Clomping through life
Not knowing which way
The horizon is far off.
My feet are of clay.

Clinton Dore

Heavenly Shrouds

The sky tonight was covered
in shrouds,
Of different colours and
different clouds.
Covering the stars with a
multicoloured cape,
like a quilted blanket with
odd sized shapes.
I envy their freedom to go
where they please.
They can blow where they want
and at their own ease.
Without any emotion they shed
all their tears.
They do not what they want to
without any fears.

Judy Webb

Untitled

Homeless, hungry, feeling ill and very
Cold from eating food,
That's been there for days, well
Come along and be very kind, and
I'm someone with a very nice mind.

Billie-Jean Brown

Holiday

The singing of the birds up high,
The trees, the breeze,
Their wings spread wide.
The distant hills,
The squeals, the yells,
The joys of spring and summertime.
The days grow long,
The years go on.
We seek, we hide,
Then paradise.
The ships in the ocean.
The far distant sounds.
The glory of love,
In this beautiful land.

Mary Campbell

Playmates

Two little girls went out to play
On a lovely summer day.
They laughed and sang as they ran away,
Happy and content that day.

They wandered down a leafy lane,
And sat down on a grassy plain.
The sun was hot and they fell asleep.
They did not hear the speeding Jeep.

The Jeep ran over them as they lay
And their life blood ran away
No more would they sport and play.
On a lovely summer day.

So all young mothers take heed I say.
Don't let your children stray away.
For into danger they may stray.
Even on a summer day.

Annie E. Campbell

Witch Curse

Stirring the cauldron witches brew,
Snails and frogs and puppy dogs too
For every witch is cursed with hell,
A fair young prince
Can't break the spell

Worship the devil the witch's cry
Come summon thee
Into the sky
No vale too deep
No hill too high
Worship the devil the witches cry

The full moon rise
The werewolf cries
Deep in the woods
The cauldron lies
Shrieking with laughter
The witches prey
Tonight will be their lucky day.

Michelle Akerman

Always You

When autumn leaves wither and fall
from the trees,
When cold winter winds change
the warm summer breeze,
When the dark silent night
covers the daylight . . .
THERE WILL ALWAYS BE YOU.
When things don't seem to be
going right in a troubled world so
full of strife,
When the roses in the garden,
their beauty have lost,
for heavy lies the silver frost.
When dreams are broken by reality
I shall not mind or care,
for you will always be there.
When I see the stars and morning dew
I count every blessing . . .
There will always be you.

V. Askey

Philosophy On Life

Let life take care of itself
Just be happy with yourself
Live life for today in the
Very best way and tomorrow
Will take care of itself.
Don't live to regret what you do.
Make sure you do good and it's
Bound to repeat upon you.

Tricia Kelly

Essence Of You

Your shape so
accurate.
A blessed figure lying there.
Precious curves and lines.
Your breathing very near.

Fingers running down my back.
Eyes so deep, you whisper to me
A head of burning hair
and an essence of security.

Lips that wander
over me.
My heart is beating fast.
You stir up my inner feelings.
This moment, will it last?

Your shape so accurate
Eyes so deep, so heavenly.
A head of burning hair.
You whisper that you love me.

Rebecca Collier

Love is Everything

In the quiet of my cottage
As I look across the fields
With, just below my window
Crowds of daffodils,
I think of all the years gone by,
Things done, and things in limbo,
Of everything that life has brought
And many things that come to naught,
But, year by year, as times go on,
I'm certain of one truth,
Those fields and flowers, say, as one,
That each year, after spring
The warm abundant summer comes
To show, that love is everything.

Kenneth Lewis

Apple

I sink in my knife
Piercing your skin
Breaking your body in two

Two green hearts
On my plate
Each half of a whole

Beneath that firm skin
You expose moist flesh
And your seed

The very core
Of yourself to me

In silent prayer
I bite and chew
And swallow down
A part of you

And I am nourished

Gwen Knowles

Our Children

Our children are scared
It shows on their face
They have lost their trust
In the human race
All the horrors that we
Bestow on this Earth
Our children inherit from
The day of their birth
The time has come for
Us to turn face
And make this World a
Much safer place

T. R. Moore

Life

You are born, and upon arrival
are a miracle,
You can move, cry, think, using a
mind all of your own.
You grow stronger, learn of the
ways of life,
You have your own style, voice
and attitude.
You go to school, move on to
College and maybe even
University,
You set personal goals, reach
these and thrive on your own
well being.
    You are alive.

Claire French

This Is For You

The pen is my voice
And the paper my orchestra
I am the composer
And you are the inspiration
This is a song of thanks.

Minty

The Cloud

A clear sky
With only one cloud
Soft and golden
Shaped like a stone.
It never changed
Or moved,
But sat for hours
Like a solemn statement

Next day I knelt down
Beside the sea
And found the cloud
And held it in my hand
A golden stone
Warm in my pocket.

This stone is a cloud
And a heart and a song
This stone is fire
And earth and water.

In my hand
I hold the world.

Stella Chapman

Time

Time will come and time will go
The pain I feel most never know
They say time heals, I'm not so sure
For this pain there is no cure

Time is given and time is taken
All without said rhyme or reason
Who's to say who gets what
Good or bad it's just your lot

You work and strive to build your nest
You scrimp and save you do your best
Then in the end it's all in vain
When all that's left is nought but pain

Pain will fade or so they say
Life goes on from day to day
Hopefully soon new dreams will come
Once again life may be fun

Life and memories hand in hand
Who but we could understand
Mums and dads they leave behind
When time is cruel and so unkind

Lorraine Driver

Moon Dreaming

Moonlight dreamin'
a heart's serenade
a silver stud gleamin'
a tree's grand parade
a star spangled curtain
the still of the night
the moonbeams a-dancin'
the swan's silver flight.

Moonlight dreamin'
a lover's romance
a night creature's screamin'
a little folk's dance
a mist shrouded dawning
the glow of the sun
the nightime's moon–dreamin'
the new days begun.

Michael Drury "Monolith"

Remembering

Those men, with loved ones all—
said they would go
    When country called,
and there did dare—and even quelled
    a stubborn foe,
They came not home
    When this was done—
But sleep they there!

The sun which heralds day—
    with every dawn
shines down long rows of marking
stones
    where those in silence lie,
Lights up the names of men—
    engraved thereon,
Touches at home—a soul—
    who yet may sigh!

Bill Rowan

"Friendship"

Friendship who cares
It's a thing of the past
Friendship they say
Never will last

An angry word
Said without care
Wrecks a good friendship
That's always been there

Too late to say sorry
Too late to forgive
It slipped through your fingers
Like flour through a sieve,

That's why I'll try
With all my might
To say only things good
And only things right

Please forgive me
For the things I have said,
Please forgive me
Or our friendship is dead.

Deirdre Coonan

Untitled

The landscape is like a jewel,
different colours all around,
were surrounded by a treasure,
nothing like it can be found.

I've been to many places
but nothing can compare
with the beautiful rolling countryside
that surrounds Herefordshire.

Elsie Homer

Country Lanes

We drive along the Country Lanes,
The lanes of Somerset and Dorset.
The spring sunshine enhances the scene,
The trees alive with budding leaves
Some entwining over head.

Now we see a male pheasant,
with colours gay and bright
his spouse is very drab, but she
is strutting by his side.

In the fields along the way
Sheep with little lambs at play.
Primroses growing in the hedges.
A black bird singing merrily,
Oh what a lovely land have we.
This lovely Land of England.

U. V. Davies

Ban Live Exports
A Thought From The Innocent

Lying down by my mother's side,
Watching the night go by.
Smelling all the flowers,
Seeing the bats fly.

Seeing all the horses,
Running wild and free.
Thinking to myself,
Why couldn't that be me?

Then in the morning,
My best friends have gone.
How much longer will this,
Evil trade go on?

Then it's night again,
And my mum sheds a tear.
She knows that in the morning.

I won't be here.

Louise Merrell

The Unwanted Visitor

Your dwelling is my hunting ground
No refusals on my entry
I move in corners, make no sound
Your tiny household sentry
I've learned to live with hatred
Putting horror in your eyes
My life filled with rejection
Though I cannot think why
I clear your house of insects
And in return I am repaid
By crushing me with paper
Or dust my traps away
I have no venom, cause no pain
My appearance has no beauty
My kingdom is in exile
Though I carry on my duties
And with some hope for times to come
Your hearts will open wider
For nothing changes the misery
Of the lonely household spider

Nicholas Ray

Pie In The Sky

Oh heavens above
I'm in love
There's a pie in the sky
And I'm falling from up high
Good grief
I've not worn my briefs

Emma Louise Ginn

Promise Broken

Half forgotten dreams
And promises broken
A wedding ring given
As a love token

What became of
Our dreams
Where did they all go
Into the mist of long ago

That wonderful day
When we became one
The church bells chimed
Blue skies and sun

Confetti and rice
Smiles and champagne
The heavens were smiling
Love never would wane

I wish time had stood
Still that wonderful day
For I still love you so
And it won't go away.

H. Brown

The Autumn Miracle

The trees outside my window
Are glorious to behold
For God has changed their colour
From green right through to gold

It's now the autumn of the year
And my September too
But I give thanks to God above
For all his love so true

The gifts I've known were many
The best my family dear
And when my time on earth is o'er
I know I'll have no fear.

My partner in his time on earth
Had faith enough for two
And in our times of trial and stress
'Twas faith that saw us through

He said I'll walk beside you
Through this life and the next
So he'll be waiting for me
Love divine must be my text.

Doris Hume

A Feeling

Tiny flying beings,
With wings as soft as silk,
With colours of the rainbow,
And some as white as milk.

They fly around in hundreds,
Not ones or twos or threes
They flutter up and down and round,
Like gently buzzing bees.

I feel them play, I hear them sing,
They're happy as can be,
A joyful note is in their throat,
All this, inside of me.

It doesn't happen all the time,
Just when you are near,
They sleep when I'm without you,
But wake when you are here.

These tiny flying beings
With wings as soft as silk,
With colours of the rainbow,
And some as white as milk.

Kathleen Moore

The Truth

I do know of it,
Although I don't know it,
It is spoken of,
Although it is not spoken,
It is listened to,
Although it is not heard,
It is felt,
Although it touches not,
I do think of it,
Although it isn't thought of,
It is needed,
Although it isn't told.

Laura O'Connell

Down Yonder Lane

Up the elm tree climbs the Ivy
close by a hawthorn bush
No berries proudly showing
But though dead, each twig
With grey-green lichen covered
Its crinkled petals like a fan,
Too beautiful to be made by man.
And further on around the bend
Two sturdy gate posts stand
Old, with moss and Ivy covered
And made of stone.
But alas, the gate
In pieces lies.
Too decayed to mend.
Did a horse get out of hand
and its rider thrown?

Mary Esslemont

Meditation

Just
Lie back,
Close your eyes
Relax for a while,
Put aside all
Thoughts of everyday living.
Just empty your mind
And there you will find
Strange pictures of faraway places,
You may travel afar—
Even go to a star,
See colours or light—even sound.
So, to feel the peace
And the sense of release,
Just,
Lie back,
Close your eyes,
Relax for a while
    And meditate.

Frances Adams

A Dorset Beach

Into the Dorset beach
I cried my tears for you,
Unformed, unborn child.

Digging deep into the sand
to bury my pain,
stopping my screams with
sandy sandwiches,
mingled with the roar of water
and the song of seagulls.

I quenched my sorrow
before it could take hold.
I am forever there, that moment
frozen in my mind, gazing at
the swollen belly of another woman
and knowing mine was empty, barren
cold in the summer sun.

Ann Margaret Pierce

Secret Feelings

I look forward to the phone calls,
And your voice at the other end.
The conversations that we hold,
And the love which we send.
I look forward to seeing you,
Whether alone with me or not.
For my sorrows seem to disappear
And temporarily forgot.
But most of all, my secret love
I look forward to the day,
When our home shall be one
And the love that we share,
Will be set free—
Without a care for anyone.

S. Bones

Toy Shop

At twelve inside the toy shop,
    The biggest I believe,
The toys were all excited
    For next was Christmas eve.
The fairy doll stood proudly
    As she tossed her golden hair
"I shall be bought I'm certain
    For a wealthy little girl"
A Teddy Bear said boldly
    As he shook his furry head
"I will be bought for someone
    Who will cuddle me in bed".
    But high up on a top shelf.
As high as one could reach.
    Were dolls four a penny,
Otherwise a farthing each
And when the shop was opened
And buying seemed so slow.
Those wee dolls, four a penny,
Were the very first to go.

Melda Larsen

Love Unrequited

You come to me from depths unknown
I have to let you in,
As though you are a part of me,
And I cannot begin to say
What feelings this brings in its wake,
No I cannot begin.

I struggle with your presence
Then give in,
For this I cannot fight,
And I cannot begin to know
To where my strength departed,
No I cannot begin.

Perhaps you'll come again today;
Perhaps this time I'll win,
I must wait and see,
But I cannot begin to know
How destroying you would leave me,
No I cannot begin.

M. J. Canning

Beautiful Love

The earth a-'fore my eyes
Matted in a blanket of green,
Darkened by the dying day.
A bare, stretched tree
Reaching to hold the magic air.
The sinking sun of an October eve
Rests within the boughs,
Embracing our love.
The sunset captured beauty
Freezes the world of time.
For time unmoved is like a spell,
Enchanting, enhancing human love.

Sarah Louise

Crazy Life

Do ya' hear it now, something small.
A clock ticking on the wall.
Blink, the seconds pass in time,
Sip it now taste the wine.

Hum drum life in the city,
pass the buck, say it's a pity.
Hundred stars in the sky.
Each represents a human lie.

Oh cover me now and let me sleep.
Close my eyes to quietly weep.
Needle comes to sing my brain.
Laughing now Ha! Feel no pain,
Say feel no pain,
I said I feel no pain.

Karen Cutts

Untitled

There's more to you
Than meets the eye,
I don't know what
I don't know why.
Perhaps the reason
Is really clear,
You are so far
And yet so near.
You give the attention
I've never had,
You can stop me
From feeling bad.
I love your eyes
Your voice, your touch,
I never knew it was possible
To love so much.

Tanya Stephens

War

Why does war happen
Innocent people dying
Just look at the world
Families and friends crying
Children are starving
Not a crumb for them in sight
Soldiers are fighting
They never see day for night

Guns firing loudly
Soldiers risking their lives
Bodies are falling
Where night live no longer thrives
Planes over head
Dropping bombs as they go by
People are sleeping
Dreaming that they will not die

Anita Garner

A Lifetime In The Fair

Lights that flash and fizz,
As the winter nights draw in,
Come gamble on this silly game,
Even if you cheat, you'll never win.

Roll up, roll up is the call,
Come ride on life's roller coaster.
Take a ride just for the fun,
Reads the tiresome, ageing poster.

Money dissolves in the air.
As the fair begins to swell,
I keep on riding round and round,
On this same old carousel.

For all the effort and the time,
Money and the care,
I'll keep on walking up and down,
This same old rip-off fair.

Rebecca Hogben

Castaway

I feel like I'm floating high,
Above these silky waves,
No time to catch my breath,
I know life's lost for days.
And if I start to fade away,
Before I reach the light,
The passing folds of time once lived
Will fade into the night.

The unkind and bitter taste,
The seas I've left behind,
Wind races through my face,
As though I have no eyes.
And if before I reach the shore,
I fall to unknown fate,
At least I know I've seen the light,
And life I've sought to chase.

Marcus Ian Duncan

Burning Pain

Like a candle burning bright
When there is no shinning light
I feel the sorrow
You caused the pain
I know my life won't feel the same.
I've lost it now
You took it then
Like being stabbed once again
You took all joy away to die
But I wont let you make me cry.

Jennifer S. Robbins

Just Couldn't Swim

A family of five are on holiday,
The kids are in the sea.
Mother and father are sunbathing,
The sun is beaming down.
It is too loud for them to hear,
A high pitched screaming sound.

It was their youngest child of three,
A funny little boy.
He was only five years old,
On that tragic sunny day.

He panicked too much,
And his lungs too tired,
To help him stay alive.
People tried to save him,
But that poor little boy died.

His family died that day too,
Their spirits just gave in.
And all because that little boy,
Just
 Couldn't Swim.

Amanda Malkin

In Praise Of Autumn

When summertime has had her stay
And Autumn comes along,
There is a change in atmosphere
And in the birds' sweet song.
There are berries on the rowan trees
And where the wild rose grew,
Fields, where earlier crops were grown,
Are ploughed for crops anew.
The many leaves upon the trees
Change colour day by day,
We watch their coloured glory
As we travel on our way.
Fruit trees are giving up their yields
To last the Winter long,
As Autumn's splendour we behold,
Praise God with joyful song.

Elsie M. Gowling

The Gift Of Art

Art and Convention
don't agree
Convention's the death of Art
felo de se
Therefore give expression
to your overtones
Not absolute—
unless it be the bones
of impulse

Convention is a barren myth
stillborn
in its own pitch
Alienated from the self
what's life
that we should be mindful
of its strife?

Choose death rather
in the creative struggle
Where Art remains
the everlasting puzzle

Angus Richmond

Retirement

We miss our own home
That's why we get cross
Not allowed to roam
Or be our own boss

Filling in crosswords
Dabbling in rhyme
Watching the birds
To help pass the time

Throughout the many years
The changes we've seen
Often bring forth tears
For what could have been

But we don't bask in sorrow
We just thank God everyday
We look forward to tomorrow
To yet another new day

P. Williams

Untitled

At the time of darkened moon
A sunny day we had
Upon its beam we went to sleep
To dream the dreams we have.

Martin Crossland

Childhood Memories

I am sitting here Grandma,
Your doll by my side.
Counting the tears
for you I have cried.

It is hard to be without you,
now that you are not here.
But each day my dear Grandma,
I am always very near.

The days that we spent,
together, just you and I.
The memories are all happy ones,
but still I sit and cry.

The last Christmas that we spent,
It was a happy day.
I wish there had been another
before Jesus took you away.

I will never forget you Grandma,
Or your kind, sweet smile.
And maybe I will see it again
When we meet in a little while.

Marie Hill

Take Me Now

I see the light, I hear the voice.
Take me now,

Hold my hand, take my prayers.
Feel my heart, hear my breath.

Take me now.
Live with me, love with me.
Take my life, take my hand.

Take me now.
Ask me to be yours.
Praise the spirit combing us.
Forever more I truly trust.
Take me now.

A. T. Elston

Past Memories

The days of youth forever past
In memories only will they last,
Happy days we all remember
Firework parties in November,
Christmas Eve at bed time
Hanging stockings on the line,
Father waiting to catch us all
Under the mistletoe in the hall,
A christmas tree a lovely sight
Presents we open with delight,
Mince pies and Christmas pudding
Just before we go first footing,
Sparkling wine to drink a toast
To absent friends and your host.

M. R. Warne

X-mas Joy

X-mas is here again you cry,
Stockings on the mantel hang.
Expectations running high.
Kids are yelling (screaming too)
It's just like a frigging zoo.
Put the turkey in at eight,
Dear God I've forgot the weight.
Open pressies, give a sigh,
More bloody hankies meet the eye.
Visitors come and drink your booze,
Leaves you feeling quite bemused.
Hoover round the carpet's stained,
Clear the vomit from the drains.
Put the empties in the bin,
All that money—it's a sin.
Twelve months—and do it all again!

Ron Stuart

Third Eye

Can it be, that eye can see,
A thought of what I feel is he,
Composition by projected me
Evolved into the wisdom we.

The past revolves within my head
A reason for it's being just
My dreams pursue a future dead
All life is now, the rest is dust.

As past creates the future cell
I've lived my "then" to be here now
Each mind must reach again and tell
All lies which passed this way and how.

But will they, care to know!
The hidden truth
Does wisdom curb this weary load
My friend the only proof is truth
I walk with my God,
This lonely road.

I. A. Gabb

All Seducing

Spells from heaven
descend unto us, teach
us the lessons of hell
and above. Embrace all
the glory, the glory
for us. Witness exchanges
from him unto us tell
me that we fall alone
unto dust. Willing and
able to bend all the rules;
forgetful and wanton
to be so bold, but then
being left with nothing
to hold. Battered and
bruised, you become old
take comfort with loved
ones as time evolves.
Remember renditions of winter
of cold. You already accept
the Earth revolves.

Munir A. Yoozooph

Together Forever

Through all the things
that we've gone through
with staying calm
and feeling blue.
We've always stayed together
It will be that way forever.

Those times now gone
you'll still be the one
to help me find a way
We've always stayed together
It will be that way forever
forever, together we'll stay.

Gemma L. Baines

My Guide For Safe Living

If you must go on the motor way,
Never do more than thirty.
When you're out doing the gardening,
Never get your hands dirty.

When you go blackberry picking,
Don't eat fruit from the bush.
If someone's talking in the cinema,
Never turn round and say 'Shush.'

When you're out enjoying the country,
Always shut the gate.
And if you must cross that road,
"Look out for that bus"
'Whoops' splat, too late.

Janette Salisbury

Invisible Thought

I can run with wild horses,
Or crash with the sea,
Rush all around the world
For one second with thee.

I can wrap myself around you,
Gently rub through your hair,
But if you turn around to find me,
You would find I'm not there.

We can dance through the meadow,
Like children at play.
I can be there just to greet you,
At the break of the day.

Fate brings us together,
So then surely destined.
For you're the wild horses,
And I am the wind.

J. Allen

Wondering

I wonder what you're thinking,
I wonder what you feel.
I know that one thing is for sure,
My feelings are for real.

I had these feelings once before,
I thought they went without a trace.
But now my heart skips a beat,
Every time I see your face.

Jealousy rears its ugly head,
When you kiss the one you love.
If that were my lips that you kissed,
I'd praise the Lord above.

I wonder what you're thinking,
And I'd really like to shout.
My feelings for you are very true,
And real without a doubt.

I really don't know what to do,
It's tearing me apart.
But one thing I'm sure I know,
I love you with all my heart.

Joanne Bolley

You Haven't Phoned

I feel low and sad.
I wish you would call.
You're out with the lads
Not thinking at all
How I am tonight,
If I feel okay.
Did you know I might
Leave you, run away?

'Though I'm loved by you
It's not worth your while
To say just a few
Words to make me smile.
You don't support me
So why should I stay.
I'm tired, don't you see,
Fighting you this way.

If only you'd made
The call, you knew
I would have stayed:
Like I wanted to.

Tamsin Holland

My Birthday

Alone on my birthday?
Well yes, in a way
But phone calls and cards
Helped to brighten my day.

I'll have a nice meal
Made ready at last
And think of the joys
Of birthdays long past.

Of a loved one now gone
Still in spirit with me
Just thankful to know
From all pain she is free.

Alone on my birthday?
Not really, you see
There are all these kind folks
Just thinking of me

So I'll drink my good health
With a glass of good wine
Then drink one more toast
To you good friends of mine—cheers!

C. T. P. Silver

Life

Some people are left on the pavement,
Some people drown in the well,
Some people claim to be content,
But then we are all hypocrites.

Equations, formulas,
Who wants solutions?
This world is just absurd,
Don't you think?

Role models are just an excuse,
For your hidden hurt,
Revolution in your head,
Will end in anarchy.

Monotonous time,
The snow drifts arrive early,
So call 999,
And worry about tomorrow.

Viki Galt

A Captive Audience

A captive audience waiting
for blood, a kind
of Anarchy for all
the world to see as
my throat gulps down
Another slice of
life while my brain
chews the fat of
yesterday's promises all
but one have been
broken and that one's
coming to an end.
A captive audience
waiting for blood
nothing changes.

Richard Kenneth Lyon

Revision

Paper flying,
Sweat dropping,
Forming lakes of blankness.
Blankness spreading,
Brain clogging,
Worry increasing,
Progress decreasing,
Muscles tightening,
Sickness creeping as time races.
Rain splashing and air tickling,
Calmness overtaking
as equations are working.

C. H. Oxley

Untitled

I can see a fly
Sitting on the ceiling
Upside down
And I can see a spider
He is crawling to the fly
Upside down
But the fly in unaware
That the spider's even there
And the spider doesn't care
In fact he's glad
If he doesn't turn his head
The fly will soon be dead
And the spider too well fed
To feel sad
Poor little fly he only needed rest
He surely did his best
To stay a winner
Poor little fly got caught up in a web
And the spider had his head
For his dinner

J. D. Baker

Tourist Attraction

Plenty of others have been before
So many, but they know the score,
And it's only May.

Keep off the lawn
This way please.
Tease.

If you enjoy looking at
Other people magnificent things
And strolling on lawns
You don't have to now.

Or watching a
Herd of graceful deer
In rolling acres.

I hope you will know
Where to find

Your nearest stately
Tourist attraction.

Penny Bicknell

Little Treasure

As I sit and watch her sleep within
Her cot at night.
I think of all the love she's bought
And all the joy she might.
She looks up at me and gives a great
Big yawn,
As if to say I know I will stay
Here until the dawn.
When mum will pick me up again
For change, cuddles and feed.
It's funny how mum seems to know
Exactly all my needs.
Love there is plenty of in this
Family of mine,
They argue, fight, and bicker
But there's love here all the time.

June Clear

Faith

Holding you in my love
United to you in pain
Encircled in the mystery
Of my lonely, lonely, heart
No protection from myself,
Faith, can I find you
Or, will you find me
Waiting, in silence,
For what,
My heart does not know,
Believe, being is my belief.

Brenda McAuley

Mother

You can tell
he always loved her
just look into
his eyes

You could see
she gave him comfort
when he chose
to be unwise

I know he won't
forget her
because his love
is always there

I know he will
always think
of her
because she
always cared.

Douglas Webster

Untitled

When you wake up in the morning,
And you see the bright sunshine,
Be grateful you are on this earth,
We all live on borrowed time.
Tomorrow never, ever comes,
Appreciate today,
Make the most of everything,
Before it goes away.
Never look behind you,
And dwell upon your sorrows,
Your yesterdays are over,
And today, becomes tomorrow.
You never know your destiny,
So don't hold on to your past,
Make the most of every day,
It could, just be, your last.

Karen Bernard

The Stepmother

The stepmother is an evil beast
It hisses and it spits
On your emotions it will feast
Its mouth, a bottomless pit

Its tongue dribbles lies
While its claws rip out your soul
Jealous emeralds for eyes
Loves destruction as its goal

The stepmother is a hideous sight
It chills you to the bone
So full of hatred and of spite
It will turn your heart to stone

It's foul, obese, a parasite
With poison in its pores
Its bulging skin is stretched so tight
Such heartache it can cause

The stepmother is a scheming misfit
But it doesn't make me scared
The loathing that I feel for it
Could never be compared.

J. Starkey

Is There A Heaven?

He always believed there was a light,
A light to guide you there.
He said it was a decent place,
A place up in the air.

I think he wanted to believe that,
Because he was so poor.
It was something he looked forward to,
That place behind the door.

They told him to be realistic,
They told him he was wrong.
They told him that his hopes were high,
But he still fought on strong.

When he died he still believed,
I wonder—was he right?
If only he could tell me,
But now he's lost the fight.

Jennifer Wallis

Lullaby For Dragons

Sing, sing, soft and low,
Songs you sing to children.
Low, low, soft and low,
Songs you sing to children;
While the nest shakes to and fro,
And the North lights flare and glow,
While the gale winds gust and blow,
Mother sings you soft and low,
Songs she sings to children!

B. E. Escott

Pass Away

I feel your footsteps as you pass
but I am hidden from your eyes,
I reach to touch your face by mine
but you pass through my hand inside
I long to touch your skin and smile
and taste your human tears awhile
to hold you in my arms again
and love you like the days back then,
I want to feel your every touch
but when I get there it's too much,
The power in your soul is mine
but when I get there I'm out of time,
We only have a little while
but when I see you I truth to fire,
I watch you every human hour
for you to stay within my power.

Katie Dixon

I Want To Be Like You

No family,
No friends,
No one to love or care for.

My heart is just sour,
My life doesn't exist.

No home!
Just me, yes me all alone.

No shadow, ghost or soul,
I feel as if I'm in a hole.

I want a home,
A family to love,
A friend to talk to when I'm sad.

I want a fire to curl up by,
I want a chair to sit upon
I want to be like you
And have all things that you do!

R. Ferguson

Mother's Day

Not so many years ago
A beauty walked upon the land
Her presence gave the world a glow
Her smile would melt snow's iron hand
She made her lover's life complete
Forsaking all her young girl's dreams
To help her babies to their feet
And loving, even through the screams
But though her sorrow sometimes showed
Her love was always there to give
Hope to the children, often cold
To all she gave that they might live,
That each fulfil their chosen goal
Mum, your children love you so.

T. Wainwright-Knowles

Undecided

A smile,
A chorus,
Be happy and gay.
But deep down inside,
Such sadness, dismay.

An act,
A performance,
For other to see.

Yet tears of confusion,
Leak out at the seam.

A scream,
A Yell,
Then a laugh,

No
A Cry.

Danielle Carroll

Lead The Way . . .

Lead the way to heaven, mum,
    Take me by the hand
Prepare a place there for me
    In that far, far better land.

This life is just a journey,
    With a beginning and an end
I'll need you there to comfort me,
    And to greet me like a friend.

The loved-ones that we gather,
    Make our troubles less to bear
Joined together by the love,
    That is there for us to share.

You've always been there for me,
    Through all my growing years
You gave me life, you gave me love,
    You soothed away my fears.

So lead the way to heaven, mum,
    Take me by the hand,
You didn't want to leave me now,
    I know, and understand.

Les Ogles

Poverty

No clothes to wear.
No shoes on their feet
No water to drink.
No food to eat.

They live in a
Most horrible way
Many hundreds die
Every single day.

They live in huts.
Made of sticks and mud
If only we could help
If only we could.

There is no rain.
The sun is hot
They all thank God
For the food they've got.

One big meal for us.
Can feed them for a week.
This is poverty
At its peak.

Lee Armstrong

Untitled

Wherever skies are blue
and sun and warmth abide
My love
Are you

And perfumed flowers
in fragrant soothing bowers
My love
Are you

Where soul–filled music
greets the air, there too
My love
Are you

In grass smells sweet
And life complete
My love
Are you

And when all is dark, and still,
there also will my love be—you for joy
enchantment, blissful ease all these
my life are you . . .

Carmen Gray

Lover's Lament

If I were you and you were me
then you would love me
don't you see, if you were me
then you would know
just how much I love you so,
you would know my very soul and
how I suffered from the start
to keep secret this burning love within
my heart. You would however,
be amazed from my very soul
how I am crazed. I'm not a "brave—
heart," I cannot sleep I often lay
awake and weep. I cry out to God
in vain, that perhaps one
day you will feel the same,
if only you would love me too, just
the way that I love you. But no
it's just a dream, it isn't true,
I am me and you are you.

Bernadette Francis

Ophelia At Rest

I lie here beneath the surface
Looking up, skyward,
Hiding here beneath Narcissus's image.
Camouflaged, secret and alone.
Blossoms float above,
Clinging to the film
That keeps our two worlds apart.
I shall neither eat nor utter
Beneath this my sapphire shroud.

I am cool and calm.
Water seeps in.
I feel its icy fingers caress my soul.
We become one.
I am absorbed utterly
Into this liquid iridescent world.
I am less than flesh.
I slip out of my staring eyes
To transcend this watery grave.

Helen Arnold

Eagle

I hear,
The whoosh of an eagle,
soaring to flight.

The flap of her wings,
as she weaves through the night.

Her screech of glee,
as she spots her prey.

Her moan of retreat,
at the break of day.

Joanna Grote

Flower Festival Thoughts

Sweetest flowers the church adorning
Fill my heart and soul with light,
Messages the Bible taught us
Clothed in blossoms for delight.

Rainbow colours blend in glory,
Orange, russet, mauve and blues,
Gold of sunset, pink of dawning
Nature's bright and fairest hues.

Round the altar, lilies shining,
Speak of hope and peace and love,
Roses, red for blood o'er flowing,
Lamb of God who died for us.

Thus the flowers tell The Story
Messengers from nature's hoard,
Surely all who come to see them
See, also, The Risen Lord.

E. M. Bowden

After The Bomb
The Beginning Of The End

We were huddled in our shelters
woman, child and man.
When suddenly there came the blast
it was then the pain began.

I whispered what do you think you are
ruining our lives like this?
It answered with screams outside
and a fire's crackling hiss.

Outside was a different world now
and as I walked down the street
I kicked ribs of leaves in the dust
and bodies dead at my feet.

The fire had replaced the sun
the dead replaced the living
the ash replaced the branches of a tree
from all the joy it was giving.

Evening dawned till the new day rose
under an orange sky
the hills had new places now
the homes had no one inside.

Samantha Tracy Mallard

My Father's House

Don't cry for me when I am gone,
I've gone to be with Jesus,
He's prepared a place for me
Within my Father's house.

He'll welcome me with open arms,
The arms he opened on the cross,
To give his life that I might live
Within my Father's house.

And there I'll stand in glory
Seeing Jesus face to face,
Serving at my Saviour's feet
Within my Father's house.

Audrey Coe

The Night

The Moon rose to her fullest
she lit up the darkened sky,
distant stars shone brightly
an odd cloud drifted by.

The night was drowned in silence
light breeze was soft and warm,
moths danced around street light
their ritual progressed without alarm.

Hours passed by in the stillness
darkness was turning into day,
dawn peaked over the horizon
while the Moon quietly slipped away.

Allan Reid

The Existence Of Life

Our existence reflects a sponge
A soft, absorbing plant.
The more water fed to the sponge
The fuller it becomes.
A young child is born a sponge,
Waiting to enter the sea of life.
When the sponge is full
No more is absorbed,
So is removed from the water.
This is turning old.
All the water flows away,
Back into the sea of wisdom.
Helping others to fill with joy
But leaves this sponge.
Empty.

Emma Rittmeyer

Christmas Time

Christmas again, who's been
In the garden and nicked
My hen, they had better not
Come back again
Let's put the presents under
The tree, then we'll have a
Tot of sherry, think I might
Just take a peak, better not
Be classed a sneak
Now I'm spending up all my cash
On the last minute dash
Rushing around here and there
Oh God the state of my hair
On top of that what will I wear
Just a few more hours to go
Gosh I wonder will it snow.

Jayne Lesley Holmes

Why?

Why do we bother?
Why do we care?
Why do we
Breathe in the air?

All of the time,
All of our lives,
Why do people
Keep telling us lies?

Why am I writing?
Why do I try?
All of my life I'm just asking,
Why?

Helen N. Farrell

Facing Death

It happened on a sunny day.
I don't think the scars shall heal,
It was my birthday happiness it shone,
To know moments later it was gone.

The doorbell rang to which I answered
To see a priest, my gran and Brendan
The silence broke, they did speak
Moments later it did dawn,
My aunt and uncle they were gone.

The road did claim two more lives
So take heed those who drive
Life is precious I can tell
'Cause my family went through hell

One year later
The rain does patter
In our hearts it does matter
Joe and Phill they are gone
But their memories carry on.

Leah McClenghan

Time For Us

Lets take a day to get away,
A day to be together,
Lets take the time to find a way,
No matter what the weather.

We are running here and running there,
Each in our separates ways,
With a nod to one another,
on those rare and calmer days.

What life is this with not a chance,
to share some time together.

So come with me, just find some time,
And make it last forever.

Eleanor Logan

My Lost Love

Tears rolling down by cheeks,
Days now seem like weeks,
Darling please hear my cries,
I cannot live with these lies.

My heart now is beating fast,
For our love could not last,
A young man came upon the scene,
To love him, she did not mean.

Now the hurt goes very deep,
As I cry myself to sleep,
No more will I hold you tight,
For now you have found your Mr. Right.

But I will always be your friend,
Right to the very end,
For my love for you will never die,
Letting out a lonely sigh.

F. H. Hounsell

See You Later

Find me quick if you can
I'm lost and alone
I can't reach out to people
Or call on the phone

Search till you find me
Please look everywhere
I'll go into a shell, or a corner
I feel safer there

Don't phone for a doctor
Cause my back's to the wall
I'm impersonating a human
In trouble, that's all

Have you come to the conclusion
It's a beast of a game
I'm hiding in the title
Slater's the name.

Brenda Savage

Jacobite Lament

Let him go, lay him down
He was a king, with no real crown,
Smash the worm, and touch him not,
He was a man don't tell me what,
Tattoo the drum and drone the pipes
Sing his song and right his right,
Let no finger close his eye
They showed beauty unlike the beast,
Sometimes he didn't not to please,
He was a man I knew him well
Into his shadow, can I tell?
Could goodness raise him to his light,
What man here, what foresight,
Let him go, lay him down,
He was a king, with no real crown.

Kenneth Bishop

Emotion

Come,
so strong,
my stimulus
of emotion,
more frequent,
more quickly
move in
and out
one subject
to another,
give me a feel
to be alive,
make me alive,
make me scream.

Monika Hutchinson-Traub

Racism

Racism is sad
Which often makes people bad.
I hope one day racism comes to end
and people become each other's friends

I hate to see mixed races fight
and people stand back with fright
I hope one day racism comes to an end
and people become each other's friends

I like to walk
and see mixed races talk
I hope one day racism comes to an end
and people become each other's friends

It's nice to sleep at night
and not listen to different races fight
I hope one day racism comes to an end
and people become each other's friends

Angelina R. Smith

For You

My dreams
My hopes
My aspirations
Are floating in the sky,

My thoughts
My wishes
My fantasies
Are freely flying high,

My regrets
My memories
My emotions
Are still strongly tied,

My heart
My soul
My passion
Holds a love that will never die.

Allison Cornell

Friends

You are there when I need
you most
you're my shoulder when I need
to cry
you make me laugh when I
am sad
you hold me close when I
feel bad
You shield me when things
go wrong
and you make me feel like I
belong

Claire Bridgeman

Look To God

When life becomes a strain for you
Pray that God will help you through,
Ask for faith and hope and love
And God will strengthen from above.

When the days seem far too long
And everything you do "does" wrong,
Remember there's a shining light
Helping to make the wrong things right.

Ask him for a merry soul
And for strength to reach your goal.
Ask for courage to pull you through
Believe in him and in yourself too.

Raise your head and hold it high,
Look way beyond the deep blue sky
And even when the strain's passed by,
God's love for you will never die.

Debra J. Laidlaw

A Fairy Tale

I fly over magic cities
To get to the place of my heart,
Beautiful creative mazes
From a tale that I'm a part.

A character in a story
Where other people lie,
Great glorious adventures
A very natural high.

And then when something blossoms
Among the feelings deep,
Leaving immense floatation
In mind, body, soul to keep.

Tucked in our little paradise
Away from where reality reels,
Gorged in the power of glory
An amazing hand God deals.

Suzanne Heath

Living

There are powers in the world
    that guide us.

I can only hope to grow
    where I am planted

And that whatever joyful,
    beauteous thing there be

Will smile and pass the time of day
    with me.

John Turner

Considerations

Dearest Jans.
When making plans
for domicile in foreign lands,
one doesn't want to look a fool
by absence of a swimming pool
with sheltered sides to keep it cool.

A tennis court
seems quite a thought.
Or maybe squash—more simply
bought?
A Turkish bath would be quite nice,
and then a porch well cooled with ice.
Or would that have to raise the price?

We'll need a gym
after our swim
to keep us all in proper trim.
So can you fix that little lot
before we come to "Jolly Spot"
and see exactly what we've got?
Or not?

James Blatch

Time Does Not Stand Still

Let us be happy
While we can,
For there is too
Much heartache,
In this world for man,
And time does not
Stand still.
Let us be happy
While we can.
Time does not wait
For man.
Life is short,
But goes on,
It always will,
But time does not stand still.

Shirley Lumb

"Snowflakes . . . "

I woke up one morning,
With a strange feeling inside,
I opened my curtains,
. . . Guess what I spied?

The expectation of green grass,
The sun or the rain,
Was all proven wrong
There was snow on the pane!

The snow looked like sugar,
All glistening and white,
Excitement was building,
I shan't sleep tonight!

From the corner of my eye,
I noticed something white.
Was it a bird?
Or even a kite?

Drifting down slowly,
Onto the lake,
It looked like a spider's web,
No, a snowflake!

Emma Pritchard

Contemplation

Alone,
I stare into the blue beyond
As I see the waves
in the shadow of darkness.
Crashing onto the
unresistant rocks below.
Crunching and eaten away,
What was once life,
But now no more,
and,
I wonder what will be.

Nichola Jagus

'Till Death Do Us Part'

'To love and to cherish
Until death do us part.'
The strong wedding promise
That is breaking her heart.

She looks at her bruises
They'll be easy to hide.
Glad nothing is broken
But her spirit and pride.

She stares through the window
At the free singing birds.
Her emotions are tied
In tight knots by his words.

She knows she could leave him
But he won't let her go.
"A marriage is for life"
So it's on with the show.

Lynsey Whitmore

Love Game

You tugged at my heart,
pulled the string and I followed
to the place where you tied us together
until there was no join.
Then you cut the string—
I stumbled and fell.
You only watched and played
like a cat with a mouse
until it can't fight anymore—
lies limp and helpless—
all messed up.
Tears washed away the experience
leaving a dull ache.
Tomorrow I will carry the memories
and grow a little.

Lindsey Bailey

Missing You

Life is somehow cruel,
When it leaves one all alone
But I feel you're always with me
No matter where I roam
I think of all the good times
The laughter and the songs
Why did you have to leave me,
Where did I go wrong?
My life is slowly passing by
Each day I shed a tear
I picture you as you used to be
And wonder, do you hear
The prayers that I pray for you
Before I go to sleep
I wonder do you see me dear
When all alone I weep.
I know we'll meet again some day
And when that day will come
I know you'll stand and wait for me
It's then I'll start to run.

Mary Devine

My Garden

My garden a delight to see.
God's gift to me.
The flowers, vegetables
Birds and bees.
Tree blooming brings delight.
Fruit for us to eat.
My garden is a joy and pleasure.
A place to be in to enjoy your leisure.

K. E. Sizer

Untitled

Below life I live feeling nothing
No pain no joy no love just anger
I am trapped in a body of pain
Trapped inside with nothing
Afraid to express emotion afraid
Trapped with just taunts
Trapped with my own thoughts
Like a bird unable to fly
Afraid to dance to sing to laugh
Trapped by their taunts
Trapped by my fears
Unable to know
Unable to show
    Trapped.

Gary Murray

Sailing Light

The anchor's weighed, the tide is right
The sky is clear, the moon is bright
The far horizon calls us now
And we will sail together

The future is our skyline clear
We live and love and know no fear
Without a qualm our course we steer
And we sail on together

Now we grow older, shadows come
We brush aside the doubts, yet some
Cloud a day, just now and then
Yet we sail on together

But comes a time when one is gone
To leave the other all alone
But memories stay of all the days
When we both sailed together

The tide for me is ebbing slow
The time must come when I too go
The sea is calm with quiet winds
Again we'll sail together

J. P. Armour

Icy Winds

Blow icy winds, blow
Shriek and howl with rage
Freeze tiny fingers
Play havoc with old age
Whip seas into mountains
Send ships scurrying for shelter
Uproot trees
Blow bucket lids helter skelter
Make chimney pots fly
Blow paper everywhere
Rattle windows and doors
But have a care
The hour is drawing nigh
You had your fling
Your energy is spent
But still you cling
Weaker now, fading fast
The wind has died
Peace at last

Alice K. Mackay

Ode To Mother

You nursed me when I was tiny,
Cradled me from harm.
Taught me what was right and wrong.
And gave me all my charm?

You then taught me to walk and talk.
Though, the latter you may regret,
You stood me in good stead for life,
For which I'm in your debt.

You gave me all your wisdom,
Although sometimes ignored.
I now know all you told me,
Was far my good, for sure.

The rest as they say is history,
Though one thing I know is true,
That I've been blessed for eternity.
With a mother as wonderful as you.

A. S. Watorski

Mother

The sky was very blue that day
The grass was very green
And amidst their beauty
There stood a lovely queen
No gold or silver crowned her head
No flowing robes of lace
No throne for her to sit upon
In soft replying grace
yet of all the queens in Kingdom Come
In this world, or the other
Not one could equal this fair love
The one that I call mother

Julie Monaghan

Untitled

I saw you today
You looked cold and unhappy
I thought I saw you today

You were riding your bike
The one that was broken
I thought I saw you today
You were wearing your coat
The one stained with your pain
I thought I saw you today
You were eating a cake
Fresh cream—your favourite
I saw you last night
You were smiling and warm
You were at peace

Jane Denny

To The Air!

To the air, to the air!
Through the clouds, so graceful.
To the air, to the air!
Ease the mind, so peaceful.

Soaring in the sea of blue,
Up and down and round and round,
There's nothing that I'd rather do,
High above the crowded ground.

To the air, to the air!
Seeking peace with Angels.
To the air, to the air!
Rejoicing in the danger.

To the air, to the air!
I never want to land.
To the air, to the air!
With this joystick in my hand.

To the air, to the air!
I'll never quit the sky.
To the air, to the air!
You'll always see me fly!

Andrew Bailey

Creator, Redeemer And Sovereign

The beauties of the earth and sky,
The brightness of the sun,
By night, the moon and stars on high
Proclaim the Holy One

The wonder of the human frame
And nature's bed of flowers
Show forth the glories of His Name
His creative power

But yet, the sinner in his sin
Forever would be lost
So God's own Son came down to win
Salvation at such cost

Upon the Cross of Calvary
He died my soul to win
He paid the price to set me free
from death and hell and sin

Come, let us join to praise His Name
Let's worship and adore
And spread abroad the Victor's fame
Both now and evermore

Peter Gavin McGregor

Childhood Memories

I remember my dad with a smile,
    for he was kind and good.
A man who worked hard for a living
    to provide me with my food.

But more than that—he gave me,
    a love for the fields and the wood.
To walk hand in hand with nature
    and feed my soul with good.

We shared a special bond,
    when youth was on his side,
We walked across the fields
    I tried to keep in stride.

We stood upon the Burnbank
    to watch the waters flow
And all the little animals
    that I had come to know.

Now he's gone forever
    and the pain within my heart,
Is eased for a while
    as I remember my dad with a smile.

Norma Grove

Bitterness

I sometimes wonder just how long,
    a lonely man can live.
Especially when that lonely man,
    has so much love to give.
He fell in love so long ago,
    and gave away his heart.
And then he found the girl he loved,
    was just a snobbish tart.
She left him flat cause he was poor,
    she wanted wealth's esteem.
She took her hook and went away,
    and broke a lover's dream.
So now this man lives all alone,
    there's no one there to care.
And he can't find another love,
    for she is always there.
He compares the girls he meets to her,
    and they just will not do.
And now he knows he'll spend his life,
    alone till it is through.

J. M. Thomas

Dear Friend

I have known you for many years,
more than I'd care to say.
I'm a lot older now, more weary.
But you still seem the same,
but somehow different.
Wiser perhaps, more secure.
Throughout the years,
you've been my strength,
always there in times of need.
Sometimes I wonder why,
why you bother with me.
A thing I'll never understand.
But I love you for it,
and I always will.
And this short verse,
was written to say,
thank you.

Keith Bainbridge

The Rain

The rain falls
Like glistening diamonds
From the black sky
The sun is coming
Through the clouds
with a rainbow
At the right it's
A delight to see
The sun once more
In the blue and pink sky

B. A. Linney

The Call Of My Native Land

Take me home to my land,
Where the salt water is the sea
And not my tears.
Where there is as much grass
As there is soil,
And as many flowers as there are buds.
And so the moisture of the morning dew
Glistens on the land.

From every pang of sorrow
Will evolve hope,
From every weakness,
Come strength.
Each dream will be reality
And from every life
Will come love,
And the angles wings will outstretch
Above us.

E. J. Lamb

116

A Lonely School Girl

I am a lonely school girl
'Rubbish' you might say
Been chucked out of all the
Games, that we used to play.
Nobody to talk to
Not a lot to say,
I hope that tomorrow
Will be a better day.
Life is like a predator
And I am like its prey.
I hope that God will
Save me and
Help me through the day.

Zoe Stevens

My Kitchen

My kitchen is a world apart,
and all my own design
the floor is red brick tiles,
and the ceiling of finest pine.

The dresser is the centrepiece,
full of treasures of great potentials,
and my shelves upon the walls
proudly hold the most essentials.

The window sill is interesting
full of bits of this and that,
but more important far
is the warmth and all the chat.

Great decisions here are made
on everything under the sun,
my kitchen is my castle
second best to none.

Winifred Forster

Just Curious

I wish I was a carrier bag,
Then I could see inside.
Why is that old man running?
What has he got to hide?
This lady is looking very smart,
Her bag is all green and gold.
Her clothes look very expensive too,
From Harrod's, so I'm told.
Is she really wealthy
Or is she just a swank?
A packet of ready salted crisps?
A letter from the bank?
This young girls bag
Is full, right to the brim
Three leaves, some sausages.
One pork chop for him.
Life from the outside
Not always what it seems
Life from the inside,
Often shattered dreams.

B. Limburn

Obsession

Thinking
Thoughts of you.

Luscious
Like your lips

Lionel,
All man, but never mine

Loving you
The way it makes me feel

Excitement, expectancy, elation
All because of you

You, you, you.
My ideal, my centre, my world

Roachford Dyer-Richie

Afternoon Tea

Kettle on the kitchen range,
How the fire light glows,
Water starts to bubble,
Then the whistle blows.

Warming up the sea leaves,
Careful of the steam,
Leaving pot to stand and brew,
While I fetch some cream.

Pretty cup and saucer,
Or perhaps a dainty mug,
All on a handy tray,
With sugar bowl and jug

Biscuits on a china plate,
Maybe a chocolate cake,
Fresh from the bakery,
The early morning bake.

Sitting in an Armchair,
With feet up on a stool.
Afternoon, the time of day,
I like the best of all.

R. Townsend

The Letter

Remembering the good times
Friends laughter and fun
On the day the letter came.

The hard fought battles
And the trials and tears
One the day the letter came

The sudden loss of
Confidence and pain
On the day the letter came.

A backward glance a little sigh
Anticipating saying goodbye
On the day the letter came

Must not allow my fears
To spoil the future years
On the day the letter came

It's over now one life ends
But a new one begins
On the day the letter came

Rosalind Whitney

Hues And Shadows

Translated from Malayalam by Thara Rajeev

Silent in the lone woods we sit,
The two of us

Blending into a rainbow
Like a hue, a shadow

Far away the lights of the inn
We went by fade and disappear

Like a lotus petal withered
You fall onto my breast

My fingers turn into a balm
Cool on your hot temples

My tears like pearls on your cheeks
Loosing their pallor

Your eyes reveal an ache
That's within my heart

The sweet joy that fills your heart
Overflows into my heart

Silent in the woods we sit
The two of us

Blending into a rainbow
Like a hue, a shadow

M. K. Bhasi

The Eighty Year Old

I have a rendezvous with death,
and like it not one bit.
I know it's coming very soon
this very scary trip.
I've loved life up till now
and really can't complain.

I'm not one of those people
that's tossed it down the drain
I was never a special person
whom God seems to select,
But I've always tried to be
honest, thoughtful and correct
I hope God likes me though
I've considered him a mate
and with a bit of luck and
good timing he might meet
me at the gate.

R. H. G. Francis

Loneliness

Loneliness is feelings,
Deep as the ocean.
Drowning by your own thoughts.
Gasping for air.
Like gasping for happiness.
Thinking of emotional thoughts.
Tears falling like a waterfalls
In a wild forest.

Josie Guy

To Remember His Visit

The face of wise pride
With a smile of wisdom
Which widens as his
Eyes scan the crowds
He speaks, and emotions
Echo round the gathering
Tears trickle as souls
Remember Suffering
Hardship, discrimination
Trying, fighting, crying
For a future
For us all.
The face of Vision
In conflict; sometimes alone
Losing friends
Making friends
Making Amends
One man . . .
Mandela

Penelope C. Price

Untitled

Perched upon the roof
Two little collar doves
Cooing to each other
Showing signs of love

Only an inch apart
Sitting side by side
Their feathers brush together
Their love they do not hide.

Singing songs to each other
In language only they know
Always being so close
In the love that they show

One little dove flies away
Its partner close behind
Nature's way of showing
True love to all mankind.

Paula Cranston

The Cork–Macroom Train

The Cork–Macroom train passed behind
   our little garden ditch,
with the gentle sound of engine puff
   and the rattling of the hitch.

We'd hear it coming down the line
   the rumble of its wheels,
and now and then a drifting sound
   though oft' times too a squeal.

So then we'd join together
   hustling for first place,
'till one of us would get in front
   to take the engine's place.

But now those days are ended
   the line is long closed down,
No more we'll see our puff, puff train
   pass by to Macroom town.

And oft' times when I think back
   through a passage now in grass,
I'd hear a sound and turn around
   then a ghostly train would pass.
   Martin Jolley

Memories

Look back in the past
And see what you can find,
Lots of memories of happiness and joy
All in your mind.

Some good, some bad
Things that you have done wrong,
You remember you being brave and strong
The future coming will be bright,
So you will enjoy it with delight.

Memories in your head
Remembered now,
I'm sure you'll look in the future
With no doubt.
   Louise Haughton

Untitled

From time to time, I really try
To work out where I am, and why,
And what it was I meant to do
And whether I am me or you.
But on reflection I decide
Not to be too dissatisfied
Since, after all, it's no disgrace
To fill an unknown bit of space.
   Ken Young

"His First Day At School"

There's such a dull ache
Across my breast,
My heart feels heavy,
I must do my best.
I feel I'm in mourning
Heavy tears could flow,
It's no good, I realize
I must let go.
I turn away and breathe deeply
I fix my grin,
Surely my feelings
Are not such a sin.
I feel a tug
His hand pulls free,
"Bye mummy, I love you,
See you at three"
His step is so carefree,
His smile so bright,
I can smile too,
Now I know he's alright.
   Denise Taylor

Echo Of The Fourth Dimension

Breathing the rainbows
of a thousand visions
I expand the frame
of the universe.
In a parallel second
echoes are reaching me
from the infinite.
Listening intensely
I hope to discern
the voice of Truth.
The pillars of the soul
erode in the foul air
of lost time
—the inner ruins visited only
by angelic tourists.
Black holes are reverberating
within the galaxy
making the balance shift
and new souls are born
into the fourth dimension.
   Anne Ogendahl

A Mother's Pride

Oh the hustle and bustle
The panic and the pomp
All the to and froing
It really brought a lump

The bridesmaids standing in a row
The mother in a flap
Who's doing all the shouting
He just wants to take a snap

Fix my dress, how's my hair
Oh my seams aren't straight
Oh my nail, watch my veil
I hope we won't be late

In the car, at the church
People stand and stare
Doesn't she look beautiful
It's the wedding of the year

Who stands there very proud
And holds her head up high
She just mingles with the crowd
And gives a satisfying sigh
   Irene Hughes

Reflections Of Time

The years have passed so quickly
It's hard to contemplate
so many things I'd yet to do
But now a year's too late

Was beautiful then, a little vain
with long and shining hair
My life was filled with compliments
I'd walk and all would stare

Now wrinkled, frail, so very weak
I have no strength to walk
I've nothing more to do but wait
Can even barely talk

A teardrop stains my pillow
with thoughts of past events
I long for lost adventures
That dreaded time prevents

Once warm and cosy corner
Is now so very cold
I must accept that I've become
So very, very old.
   S. Kyriacon

Don't You Know

Why can't you see,
I am hurting bad,
Why can't you talk to me,
When you know that I am sad,
My life is falling apart,
Right in front of my eyes.
But you don't notice,
I am breaking apart.

Why can't you see,
That I need some love
And it is really hurting me,
I wish I was up above,
But there is no way out,
I fall apart and cry,
But you don't seem to notice,
The tears in my eyes.
   Colleen Iseley

Reflections

Strange person in front of a mirror
trying to comb their hair.
Strange person in front of the mirror
trying to back comb their hair
Strange person in front of the mirror
scalding their roving hair
Strange person in front of the mirror
trying to create an image.
   A. Saini

Sundays

It's half past eight
Shall I get up
Or shall I be late
A tough decision on Sunday.

It's mass at ten
I must be on time
Must get up then
The right decision on Sunday.

When shall we dine
Oh when it's ready
Beef and red wine
A wise decision on Sunday.

A walk after food
Is a good idea
No, not in the mood
A good decision on Sunday.

Feeling full and lazy
Feet up is better
Heavy eyes and hazy
A great decision on Sunday.
   A. M. Green

War

Don't cry,
This war is going on,
But we don't know why,
Bombs going off,
Bullets through the air,
Shattered cities and houses,
Dead bodies everywhere,
'Tween pavement and stars,
This war rages on,
In this blood shattered city,
The sun once shone,
War is like murder,
And I hope it soon stops,
And the sun will shine again,
O'er the hilltops.
The birds will sing,
The flowers will bloom,
And no more will we hear,
A grenade go Boom!
   Derbhla Murphy

My Wish

There is different and
there is same but why
must it matter from
where we came

Why must we fight
for another
man's war

We need not to see
through stain glass eyes
the different but the
same inside

And then together we can
rebuild what we once
destroyed before.

Lyndsey Wing

Passing Years

It's hard to believe a tree
Once garlanded and gay
Could come to this—
A stump, but gnarled and grey.
To think the life that blossomed here
Has ended in decay
And all the dreams I once beheld
As quickly passed away.

Wendy P. Jones

Terminality

Forever
(A)
The
(Morbid)
Blackness
(Way)
Are
(Of)
Towards
(Looking)
Of
(At)
We
(The)
Cascading
(World)
Envelope

Andrew Sharpe

Craig And Clare, 20 July 1996

To wish you well this special day,
  A poem I shall write
A poem of your wedding day
  A bride all dressed in white

A groom stood waiting in the church
  Waiting for his bride
At last the music starts to march
  The bride has stepped inside

The flowers' perfume softly floats
  Carrying the bride
It takes her gently down the aisle
  And stops at her groom's side

The vows are said, the rings exchanged
  Soon everything is done
A promise made, the bride and groom
  Are now together—one

You're a very special couple
  Love like yours is rare
Treasure every moment
  A toast to Craig and Clare

Eileen Long

Untitled

There are so many things
that I should say to you
But there was no time
no right occasion
when I could put my hopes to you

There are so many things
that I should say
But I have found no words
to say I love you
I am an emotional coward

Perhaps tomorrow
Will help me find those words
that you are waiting to hear
There is no tomorrow
only today and yesterday

If there is no tomorrow
I have no hope
I am an emotional coward
who fears rejection.
I love you, and you are still here.

Angela Harper

Reflections

Water flowing, shining, bright,
Kissed by sun and pale moonlight
Or lying sullen in a pool,
Deep and dark and icy cool.
Each has its charm and magic spell
To catch the eye on moor or fell,
Or rippling softly through a glade
Reflecting sun and trees and shade.

O. M. Austwick

Courtesy

Whatever happened to courtesy,
That old-fashioned virtue supreme;
Did we really once have a happy world
Or was it only a dream?

Whatever happened to courtesy
When people were kind and sincere,
When everyone helped a loser
And the winner was always cheered.

Whatever happened to courtesy
Where envy and greed took no part;
When people were happy and fulfilled,
And everyone still had a heart.

Why must we all learn by sorrow,
It's not an impossible creed;
We could find peace of mind tomorrow
If to courtesy we would yield

You know, even now it's not too late,
Let's give it a try and make sure;
Perhaps it is just what is needed
To bring about a miraculous cure.

Margery Medlock

Mother

I had a wonderful friend
She meant everything to me
She was always around
When I needed a shoulder
But when she was in pain
All I could do was hold her
We'd wipe away our tears
And hope for another day
Then that day came
God released you from pain
Now she's in heaven
Peace at last
You was the best mother
A girl could ever have

D. Clay

What Matters Most

My hands caress your golden hair
that rests upon your neck,
I stop . . . and pause . . . a moment goes
lost within your stare,
In bed at night we lie as one
With darkness all around,
I hold you tight within my arms
My true love I have found.

Simon Ruddy

Cats . . .

Are just that.

No money, no bills.
No worries, no pills.
No pressure from bosses
No target weight losses
No taxes, no cars.
No cafes, no bars.
No teenager crazes
No mood swinging phases.
No mortgage,
No loans.
No faxes,
No phones.
No endless housekeeping
Just
Eating
And
Sleeping.

Cats . . .
Are just that.

Anna Rose Bailey

Intercom—Morning Call

On every day throughout the year
you say to us—"How are you dear?"
Our answers come in many styles
For some to us are full of smiles
Whilst others are just full of trials!

"My head is full of pain again!"
"I've gone and lost my teeth again!"
"Someone's knocking at my door!"
"I've dropped my specs upon the floor!"
"I can't remember—what's my name?"
"The kettles boiling once again!"

"I cannot find my woolly vest!"
"The window cleaners just outside—
I'm quite undressed, so where to hide?"
and some there are who cannot speak
their voices are like a mouse's squeak.
And near the end along the line
someone answers "Oh I'm fine!"
And some of course are still asleep,
the muffled sounds come from the deep."

Eva Smith

Silence (Holocaust)

Waves upon a silent shore
A world where sea birds cry no more
Where nightmare brings no silver moon
And flowers have forgotten to bloom
The summer breeze has lost its sigh
And trees stop waving to the sky
The sun has disappeared from view
Behind a cloud that once was blue
There's not tomorrow—nothing more
But waves upon a silent shore.

Brian Perry

Feelings

The nicest feeling in the world
 is laying next to you,
My wife,—and my lover
 and yes—my best friend too.

The nicest feeling in the world
 is knowing that you're there,
And even when you're fast asleep
 I know that you still care.

The worst feeling in the world
 is when we disagree,
Cause both of us can make a point
 the other cannot see.

We argue and we bicker
 but I know it's alright,
When I take you in my arms again
 and you kiss me good night.

I tell you that I love you
 and that will always be,
But the nicest feeling in the world
 is knowing you love me.

Anthony R. Healy

My Mum

I once had a dear old Mother,
Who was very kind to me,
And when I was in trouble,
She sat me on her knee,
One night as I was sleeping,
Upon my feathered bed,
An Angel came from Heaven,
And told me Mum was dead,
I woke up in the morning,
To see if this was true,
Yes, Mum had gone to Heaven,
Among the sky so blue,
So listen all you children,
And do as you are told,
For if you lose your Mother,
You lose a Heart of Gold.

Thomas Smith

Lost Love

When we wandered on the Moors,
You said, "There'll be no tomorrow,
On that night,
You were right,
For my heart is
Now filled with sorrow.

A. Bhambra

Sing! L.C.M.

Sweet charms are ever waiting
In the L.C.M. choir hall.
As we never know what's lurking
In the music teacher's roll.
Will he choose a rather jolly piece?
Which is enjoyed by one and all.
Or will he pick another script
Which makes all faces fall?
Will it be by a composer
Of whom we might have heard?
Or will it be another
Which sounds like some strange bird!
Are soprano parts all screeching?
Or may they actually, at last
Have a part that's smoothly flowing
With progressions free and fast?
Is this too much to ask for,
Or must we always yearn
For songs which have a tune to them,
And don't take so long to learn!

Julie Colleen Duffy

Asylum

Crazy feelings in my mind
I do believe I'm going blind
Facing things I'll never see
Flights of fancy carry me
Colours shimmer in my brain
Shades the line that keeps me sane
Sailing down the whitewashed hall
Voices crying from the wall
Yet smiling faces all around
Spinning round like rabid hounds
A masquerade of carousels
Feed the fire, this laughing hell
And so return the fife and drum
I can wait, my time will come.

I. S. Caddie

Eighteen

I hold on a memory.
A friend loved, but almost forgotten
I search for my calling.
Unaware what it is, I feel alone.
Only I think my thoughts
Strange and not clear
Confusion rules.
I once thought I knew
Now I realise I was wrong
Blinded by youth.
Influenced by people.
I don't understand myself.
As if I never really knew anyway
So much in the way
Yet still hope for a new
New what, I don't know
I want what I can't have
I don't understand the past
The future is unclear.

Tony Gallant

Untitled

As I put paper to pen.
I think of my little gem,
She is full of mischief,
Full of fun,
With a smile like the sun,
She is only little tot,
Her name is Charlotte.
I have not seen her yet this year
But her memories I hold dear.
On Wednesday of this week,
I will kiss her little cheek,
She will bubbly as we talk
When we go on a little walk
I am looking forward a lot
On seeing my little Charlotte.

Betty Onion

The Dreamer

I have always been a dreamer,
Building castles in the sky.
Gazing out into the future
Where my day dreams fade and die.
Words of wisdom wise ones tell me
Keep your feet upon the ground.
But my dreams do not allow me
To be rooted, I have found.
I can soar up to the heavens,
Like a bird with wings outspread.
Or I see the insects dancing
In the swaying grassy bed.
On the sea shore, sand grains singing
To the seas orchestral tune.
Where frothy curls on every wave
Make jubilant the spume.

Rosemary Booth

Rings Of Peace

Alone they'd be nothing.
Just five painted lifeboats, that
Would float aimlessly,
On a white waving sea.

Linked they become the world,
Five continents, making one
Human family,
In a race for glory.

The ring of blue becomes,
The seas around the Earth.
The sun in the sky;
A yellow hoop of hope.

The black soiled orb sustains,
A halo of fertile green.
Red circulation,
Carries the life of man.

Thus the symbol of peace,
Flies once more above the world.
Nations with nations,
Beneath the Olympic Flag.

Dave Rossington

Untitled

Guns are emptied and reloaded
And secret notes, are carefully coded.
Intercepted codes, decoded.
Outrageous modes and myth exploded
Land and time become eroded
Mother Earth is overheated
Lessons past it seems repeated.
Many things are overrated
And messages become belated
Some people by their blood related
And time run out becomes outdated
To this end my poem's fated.

Phillip D. Jude

Just Dreaming

In my dreams there is a prince
He whisks me off my feet
We walk all day together
And smile at all we meet

In my dreams we are at peace;
A world in harmony
Works together and improves
The lives of you and me

In my dreams there is no pain,
No-one suffers or dies
There's comfort and security,
The tears gone from our eyes.

In my dreams these things are real
But we're not as we seem.
Will you help me change the world
Or leave us all to dream?

Victoria M. Brown

The Black-Birds' Evening Call

Shredded clouds
Brush pass
The moon's
Full face.

The soft steel-grey
Of the sky
Shines like
Rain—washed glass.

And the blackbirds'
Evening call
Pierces my heart
With his dark arrow
Of desire.

Josephine Thomas

Smell

Why is it that the poets tell
So little of the sense of smell?
These are aromas I love well.

Fresh cut grass, Sunday Lunch.
Scented flowers, a lovely bunch.

Baby powder, Mothercare.
A brand new cotton dress to wear.

Autumnal fruits; Vanderbilt
Chrysanthemums, before they wilt.

Mandarin flowers that bloom in spring.
All the smells that Christmas brings.

Bakers shops with crusty bread.
Exotic odours that fill my head.

Of more aromas I could tell.
But these are the scents
That I love well.

Polly Fitzgerald

Hours

An hour asleep, an hour awake,
An hour for time to give and take,
An hour in which to go or stay
Are found within the hours of a day.

An hour to share, an hour for mirth,
An hour to think on an hour's worth,
An hour in which to hope and pray
All come within the hours of a day.

An hour to finish what's begun,
An hour for laughter, love and fun,
An hour to ponder better ways
To spend the hours of all the days.

S. E. Freathy

The Snowdrop

Nodding white head drooping
Bell-like, pale, transcending
Green droplets inside the petals,
Long stalk and painty leaves . . .
Graceful, demure beneath the hedge
On its own, proud and defiant
Against the frost.
Like an icicle standing straight.
The first flower of spring
Amongst the brown earth
By the mossy lawn
Rings its silent voice to life
Solitary, lonely, dignified.

Andrea M. Ashton

Time

Time is passing swiftly by
It waiteth not for one.
Can it be said of you and I
That some good deed we've done?
If not, we must, we cannot wait
Or miss a chance today.
Tomorrow, friend, may be too late
To show someone the way
So if there's someone here this day
Who has not made their choice
Do come to Christ, He'll put you right
If you obey His voice.
Give Him your life all
And say dear Lord, I will.
For I have heard thy loving call
May I this call fulfil.
I'll serve thee with a heart sincere,
A life that's full of love.
Show other ones the pathway clear
That leads to Heaven above.

Ken Morrish

For Mrs. Quammie

Today I'm not happy
Today I am sad
Today is the day
They buried my dad

How should I think
How should I feel
I really didn't know
He was that ill

He went too quick
within a week
That's the day
He fell to sleep

I wish he was here
With me today
Why did God
Have to take him away

As they lay him
Down to rest
I remembered
God only takes the best

LisaLouise Haidon

The Willow Tree

Standing still out in the cold
feeling sad and old
but when the children come out to play
I'm happy in every way
All the birds that come and sing
are lovely when they flap their wings
little insects that climb up me
know they're climbing The Willow Tree

Leanne Rees

Enterprise

A crippled mass of beggars
Each at the corner of every street.
Deformed by cruel and greedy hands
They perform their daily feat

Of scrounging from the passers by.
The people in their cars.
Their pathetic, doleful entreaties
Oh, how my heart it scars.

Yet who is the beneficiary
In this profit full career?
I'm sure it's not these limbless souls
Whose lives are not there nor here . . .
Whose plight we don't wish to hear.

Thomas J. Mansfield

Who Can It Be

There's something very strange
About the mirrors on my wall—
They leave me quite confused
I just can't make it out at all.
Through the one inside my bathroom
And another in the hall—
The person looking back at me
I simply don't recall.
She's elderly with wrinkles
And hair that's going grey—
No matter when I catch a glimpse
She always looks that way.
Yet come to think—I notice her
Looking back at me—
As I pass by the windows
Out on a shopping spree.
It's really quite confusing
If you knew me you would see—
I'm young, and blonde, my eyes are blue
That image isn't me.

Catherine A. Fincher

Love

Love manifests itself
in so many ways
It envelops us wholly
and brightens our days

Love is tender and giving
a joy to behold
With magical moments
for young and for old

Love has no counterpart
with which to compare
It is free, unabating,
each can have their share

Love is there for the taking
asks nothing in return
Its very existence
is something we can learn

Love can warm nations
cross boundaries far and wide
Create harmony and peace
across the great divide

Janice Honeybourne

Boys

I bumbledooby down the street,
Saggy down and mope.
Bumbledooby on do go,
Down the draggy slope.

Peter Charlie comes out of house,
"Lo", and join with me,
We draggy on, not say a word,
As doobdy as can be.

We to the sweet shop mopey go,
And gazy in at sweets.
Mouthy–watery—what can do—
With only ha-penny for "treets".

Then Old man Cronchy come creaky up,
And see us mopy stand.
He knows what we would likey eat
And puts money into hand.

We shrieky into sweet shop go,
And get handy-fuls of joy,
Then singey-dancey, no more woe,
Each happy chewy boy.

Andrew Purcell

Blue Stone Lane

Dedicated to the Young Survivors

Hold my hand
Show me the way,
Show me the door
To the black and white floor.

Show me the faces
Of coloured delight
Where songs are sung,
The dim crystal light.

The brisking of warmth
The silent dull pain
Where torture is calm
The silver touched palm
The blue stone lane.

Where soft fantasy lies
Stars of surprise
Sting wipe the eyes
Among strength and beauty
Red 'bread' of a king
Show me this place

No matter my sin.

Anna Driscoll

The Symbols Of Life Means

Trust and love
Friendship and understanding
Sympathy hope and caring
Patience and above all obedience
Life isn't always a bed I roses
It has its disappointment
But behind all this, there is
always tomorrow.

J. Campbell Jones

Betty Joy

We've laughed, we've cried
  The wife and I
Argued like any other
  She's my pal, my mate, my friend
And most of all my lover
The years roll by so quickly these days
  You don't realize how fast
We are getting older as time rolls by
  Hoping it will last
If there is a life afterwards
  I hope we are together
I can't imagine life or death
apart from each other
I love her dearly that wife of mine
  There can be no one other
When it's our time to go
  I hope we go together.

David Betty

Friends

In recent days,
that seem long past,
we cared,
we shared,
we fought,
we laughed,
my friends and I.

Through summer's silver,
and autumn's gold,
we talked,
we walked,
we lied,
we told.

In all the days,
of our lives,
we loved
we lived
we yearned,
we cried,
my friends and I.

Philip Radford

Condition

This plant is dying,
Its leaves once smooth
And healthy are wrinkled,
The ends turning yellow.

Fading where it was planted
It cannot say the reason why,
Yet once it drank the rain,
Still feels the sun
And knows the night from day.

Why then is it dying?
Are all its roots so withered?
Is the worm too strong
Who moves within the earth
That gave it birth?

This is the way of leaf and stem,
To die in silence, mute and dim,
As when we die in sleep,
Rooted in the earth deep.

Robert W. Lockett

Love's Purple Passage

You sent a silent messenger,
Lightly armed for love,
Who took my sentries by surprise,
To find the place where passion lies,
Waiting for the key.

And softly in his footsteps came,
Your sweetness like a rose,
That blooms forever in the heart,
Secure in soil composed in part,
Of pure undying love.

And with a smile you then disarmed,
My forces one by one,
And carried me enraptured round,
The pleasure-garden to be found,
Within you ivied keep.

So shield me with a lasting love,
Through all the years to come,
A fitting armour burnished bright,
Impervious to shock or fright,
And shining in the sun.

Alan D. Kerr

The Cycle

Before we met.
I was lost.
I was alone.
I believe I would be that way forever.
Than we met.
I was happy.
I was fulfilled.
I believed I would be that way forever.
Then you left.
I am lost.
I am alone.
I believe I will be that way forever.

J. E. Strange

"You Tear Apart My Heart"

The truth untold
As (the) beauty beholds
Our two lost souls
Coming together,
Together, forever.
Forever, together.

The lies untold
Begin to unfold
Like the seams
To my heart
As we grow apart

Just as my heart
Has fallen apart
As beauty grows cold
You suddenly grow bold.

(But) the beauty beholds
As beauty unfolds
The beauty untold
As beauty grows cold
'You tear apart my heart'.

Helen-Louise Gedge

No More Regrets

No longer am I slave
to sentimental dreams
when in the heart of night
hot tears I shed,
and restless waited
for the dawn to break
through yet another day
filled with regret.

Helen Weatherby

80 Plus

Who would begrudge him his place
in the sun,
or a seat by the fire, when life's
race has been run?
Who would deny him a chat
with a friend,
or stop him from having some
money to spend?
Who would prevent him from
drinking his beer,
or having his whisky, his
Christmastime cheer?
Spare him a moment or two for a chat,
your time is not wasted, be quite
sure of that.

Helen Margaret Hazlerigg

"To Want"

Isn't the world a funny place
Where nothing goes according to plan
But life wold be ever so boring
if it did, for every man

Everyone would get what they wanted
sometimes that would suit me just fine
but maybe the novelty would wear off
if everything I ever wanted was mine

But that doesn't mean I'll stop trying
to get what I've always had a want for
'cause if I at some time give up trying
I'd get nothing I ever wanted at all!

Ruth Childs

Emma

Granddaughter!
What joy
What fear
You came to us so unexpectedly
In winter
At home
What surprise and pleasure
Blond hair
Blue eyes
What tantrums and tears
A princess
you fly
But can you walk my darling
Not yet
But soon

Maria E. Dziecielewski

My Puppy

I have a little puppy,
Who's as black as black can be,
When I'm sitting by the fireside,
She jumps upon my knee,
Her name is Bess,
You'd never guess,
The things that she can do.
She pulls my stockings,
Bites my nose,
And other bad things too,
But most of all the thing she likes,
Is biting someone's shoe.

I have a little puppy,
And I'm very fond of her.
She's never in her kennel,
But always on my chair.
Each night when I come home from school
I take her for a run
I always try to keep this rule,
And puppy thinks it's fun.

Eveline A. Gilbert

The Fall Of A Summer Shower

Scattered translucent raindrops
Land on clean windowpanes.
Aliens from outer space.
Sprayed from cloud-holdings.
Bomb–shaped, but harmless.
They cling! Mosaic-like separates.
Bewildered, useless in their landings.
Tears, but not tears! Soul-cries!
There they dry, fade away.
Incinerated by summer's-burning-sun.
All that remains?
Just stains!

Anne Pauline Greeves

Normal And Abnormal

It is normal
To be abnormal
In an institution of abnormalities
It is abnormal
To be normal.
In an institution of abnormalities.
What is normal,
In our world, of abnormality?
What is abnormal, in our world
of normality?
If the psychiatrists
knew the answers.
To these questions.
Abnormalities
Would not persist and institutions
of abnormalities would not exist
on this side of Jordan.

Vivian Paulette Aston

The Dragon

The dragon sits with golden eye.
Her scales a-gleaming, all a rye.
The olden knight doth ride by
To battle his bold cry.

The dragon with tearful sigh,
Breathes fire by and by.
Of our hero there is no sign.

Now our story it is told.
To the moral, if I may be so bold:
He who risks the dragon's breath.
Had better wear a fireproof vest.

P. D. Higgins

Facts Of Life

It's a fact of life
Inside all of us there is one glow,
Which makes us all supreme
But not all of us know.

It's a fact of life
Anger and greed kill,
Which gives way to disaster
It wasn't God's will.
His teaching was that of love
Happiness and caring,
Above all was honesty
But humans became too daring.

It's a fact of life
Many never understand,
The importance of friendship
Upon this great land.

It's a fact of life
To live for today
Forget about tomorrow
You'll be safer that way.

Amandeep Dosanjh

Memories

How much shall I remember
When I am tired and old
What threads of recollection
Will gleam like threads of gold
Upon life's faded fabric
The fabric of the years
Time wears away the pattern
The colour disappears
The things that brought great sorrow
Grow faint and fade away
The hopes the disappointments
The dreams of yesterday
The trails that now I follow
May wither in the blue
But these will last forever
My memories of you

Hettie Vessey

Prejudice

You call me names
Do I react?
You try again
Still no reaction.
You laugh,
Making everyone laugh with you.
Why?

You're black, I'm white
Am I prejudiced against you?
Do I point out your differences?
Do I pick out your faults?

No.

You're thin, I'm fat
So why pick out mine?

Sally McKay

Alien Being

They invade our skies
    Invade our lives
Who are these beings
    Before our eyes
They take control
Immobilise us from our dreams
Transported through a lighted beam
Upon their space ship we are seen
    Beings from another life
Racing round our skies at night
Where do they come from
Where do they go
Are they sometimes in disguise
    Hand in hand with our daily lives
Cast your eyes upon the skies
Could those just be twinkling stars
    Or beings eyes around us spy?

Sandra Boosey

Mother Nature's Wish

A time has come for the world to rest,
Mother Nature, she always knew best.
Everywhere at peace,
Fighting no more,
For,
A time has come for everyone to love,
Make the grey skies blue above,
Bring colour back to our land,
Hand in hand let everyone stand.
Let us be joined as one,
Let this joining never be undone
Let black and white stand together
Always and forever.
This is Mother Nature's wish.

Vicky Birch

Time

Time is but an endless space
And man its idle toy
For no man will it ever wait,
To ease his sorrow or prolong his joy
To the lover fast the time does fly
To the weary oh! How slow,
But its pace is always just the same,
'tis but a fleeting glance and lo
The babe in arms now be a man
Who soon to dust returns
But time goes on unending
Heed not man's foolish yearns
So use well the time before you
Make better the path you tread
For unless man leaves it better behind
Far better that man be dead.

A. S. Roberts

Breaking Up The Love

At the moment we are alone
Not sharing or caring
nothing to do or say
You're not there when I turn to see
you're only in dreams
which drift away when it becomes day
No phone calls to each other
just silence
I miss you holding me close
and your lips kissing mine so tenderly
The embrace lovers have fades away
as so do we
We're drifting apart
Further and further apart we get
until each other images vanish
vanishing into the distance
just like the sun setting at night
but never to rise with each other
ever Again

Lynne Collins

Beyond The Extreme

When the horrors of the morning,
Are the nightmares of the night,
And the shadows of destruction,
Remain there out of sight,
Then it may be the only way of choosing
When death has looked you in the eye,
And then given back your breathing,
To scream back, "Let me die".
For when the bubble burst,
Yesterday remained there as a token,
bloodied in a space of time,
Shattered and unspoken.
And when all that's left is learning
At the loss of a beautiful dream,
Propped up by the pillars of yearning,
And left beyond the extreme!

Keith Harrison

Winter

In the freezing cold
weather the nights
grow darker.
The foxes get hungrier
and the mist and fog
start to swirl.
The golden leaves
swirl through the
air and the trees
are bare.
The ponds turn to
ice and bonfires
flames go every
where.

Omid Ghiassi-Farahani

123

I Wish . . .

I wish I was,
I wish I wasn't,
I wish I only knew.
I wish I was,
I wish I wasn't,
Still in love with you.
I wish I could,
I wish I couldn't,
Become something I'm not.
I wish I could,
I wish I couldn't,
Do something to change my lot.
I know I should,
I know I could
Make the effort, can't you see?
I wish I had,
I wish you could
Love me, just for being me!

Sarah Butler

Lands End

When you're standing on a cliff top
Looking downward to the sea
You can hear the water's anger,
It's the safest place to be!
The waves sweep in against the rocks
They pound onto the shore,
The noise makes me so nervous
As does the lion's roar.
What makes the sea so angry?
While its calm it cannot keep,
Could be the noisy traffic
That's disturbing it from sleep,
Maybe it's all the fishermen
In their yellow oily coats,
Or just the ocean liners
And the rusty bottomed boats.
I guess it's got its reasons
Never mind what they might be,
I'm safer on the cliff top
Looking downward to the sea.

S. Hinckley

The Presence

The night was rough, the air was warm,
As I sheltered from the thunderstorm.
The house was dark, the room was bare,
And yet I felt someone there.

I looked around, I looked about,
I had company, there's no doubt,
Yet I felt comfort not great fear,
That in itself seemed very queer.

I sat very still on the window seat,
My companion, rare, hoping to meet.
But no-one's there to be seen or smelt,
Just a presence. Oh, so keenly felt.

R. Champion

Honey Hill

I walk down the hill of honey
surrounded by spectacular buds
of gorse.
A pathway of golden splendour
nature taking its course.
Am I dreaming, A dream come true
To witness such sweet smelling beauty.
An experience, just for you.
Hush just listen, can you hear
This is pure music, to my ear.
Black and yellow stripes is her colour.
The stunning Queen.
The gorse's Lover.

Lois Sweetman

Eerie

Dark, cold, and eerie
As she started across the plain
Wishing she had shelter
To protect her from the rain
When suddenly she realized
That nobody was near
And if something were to happen
Well then, nobody would hear
And turning back towards the road
She broke into a run
And she ran as if, in terror
Like a rabbit from a gun
She did not look behind her
For she did not want to see
What was lurking in the darkness
But it was only me.

Audrey Costello

Life

Life is full of ups and downs
You can't escape my friend,
Every day of every year
From beginning to the end.

Life is full of joy and sorrow
Of fun and laughter and of pain,
Make the most of your tomorrows
After sunshine comes the rain.

Life is full of smiles and crying
After losing come the tears,
But there'll always be some winning
As we travel through the years.

Life is full of love and friendship
Music, singing in the air
Seek and you will always find it
All around you—everywhere.

Don't despair or be down–hearted,
Remember One upon the cross,
He rose again in glorious splendour
To share His life with all of us.

Evelyn O. Smith

Antiquity

As the years clip silently by
the ever shortening road ahead
inclines one to recall to capture
great moments of happiness, many
long since forgotten affairs,
the fulfilment of a long
awaited wish, or whatever.
    The pictures once so sharp and
clear slowly fade to join the
purest and make the effort the
more futile affair.
    The past is past its pleasures
spent its grief endured so
let it rest and for the present
the more thankful be.

Eric Trotman

Death/The Other Side

A psychedelic crescendo
A cosmic burst of light
Brighter than the sun itself
Softer than the night
Deep as an abyss
Shallower than a grave
Melodramatic melancholy
Gloomy as a cave
A fanfare of deliverance
Out of the shadows cast by fear
It's my turn to take the journey
Carried on a tear

Anthony Bailey

Thank You Lord

It makes no difference where we live
Here or in a foreign land
For we are always guided
By God's almighty hand.

When we go into the church
And are seated in our pew
When we bow our head in prayer
We give our thanks to you.

For you are always there
In everything we do
In times of stress and trouble
We always turn to you

We know not the path to travel
For the way may not be clear
But you will be beside us
And save us from all fear.

We give our thanks to you dear Lord
For the many things you've done
The sacrifice you made for us
Your own begotten son.

Margaret Stirton

Untitled

Let's not forget the way we met
Nor the way we said goodbye
Let's not forget we never kissed
Let's not forget the reason why
We were both committed
And kissing who's not permitted
Besides . . . we were both a little shy

Andrew Lewis

Big And Beautiful

It's big and beautiful
and lives in the sea
to be left alone to swim free

So please don't hurt
this creature large
for he was there much
before thee

The gentle whale is
near extinct
with man's harpoons
to see it sink

Just wait a moment
and reflect
and think of harpooning
will neglect.

M. Billington

For A Daughter's 18th Birthday

"You've got a baby girl," they said,
"a lovely baby girl."
I remember the excitement,
as round my thumb, your finger curled.

And since that day in August,
I've watched you slowly grow,
you're now a lovely lady,
as everybody knows.

I've got two lovely daughters,
Claire and Vicky too,
I might not show my feelings,
but I love you through and through.

And when eventually you leave,
to seek a life elsewhere,
part of my heart will go with you,
for you both I really care.

R. W. Sharman

Another Time, Another Place

Another time, another place
And whenever I see your face
You and I would be as one

Another time, another place
And you would always be by my side
My love for you no more denied

Another time, another place
And we might never have even met
These feelings for you I could forget

Another time, another place
And I wouldn't have all that I do
Only dreams of meeting someone like you

But in this time and in this place
And all the feelings are meaningless
My emotions must be put to rest

Another time, another place
Another time, another place
Another time, another place
David Lloyd

Heaven

Heaven's gained an angel
But Heaven's hurt my heart
Heaven you've gained a saint today
But Heaven's torn us apart

Heaven keep her safe for me
So someday we'll meet again
Heaven keep her love for me
So everything's still the same

Heaven you've taken her from us
But Heaven you've gained so much
In our dreams we'll remember
Her smile and her velvet touch

We've lost a special friend
And now she's in Heaven above
And wherever we may roam
We'll always remember her love

Heaven guard her well
Heaven's the place for her to be
Heaven is where we will meet
And Heaven's where we will be free.
Fay Pilbeam

Forgotten People

It's not the hell on earth I find,
They say it's in my mind,
Sometimes I feel I've walked away
And left my soul behind.

Some days are good and some are bad,
We face the rough and smooth.
I see a hundred worse of than me,
God help me face the truth.

I try to help the aged and sick,
I see them cry and curse.
I turn away and ask myself,
Have I the right to be a nurse.

There seems so little I can do,
To ease their troubled minds,
A laugh a cuddle one kind word,
And most of all my time.

So if at times I'm tired and slow,
And impatient I seem to be,
Please try to understand and care,
It could be you or me.
Audrey Greening

My Grandma

My Grandma was the sweetest
    person that you could ever know
She didn't like the ice and
    She didn't like the snow
But she loved her family
    each and every one.
And now we're going to miss her
    now that she has gone
So one last kiss I give to you
    before I say goodbye
You look so peaceful lying there
    I think I'm going to cry
So goodbye Grandma we love
    you very much
And everyone will miss you
    So very very much.
Aileen Hughes

Untitled

This isn't a poem,
    It's a piece of verse,
A doggerel rhyme,
    A poor one too,
I merely say in it
    I love Jesus and you,
If you feel that Anall
    it's a poem to you.
Paul Frame

Dumb Youth Breed

The dumb youth breed
like rabbits drunk on gin;

What becomes of your tomorrows?

I have journeyed far,
I know you like an old dream,
you are no more to me
than the glow of strangers
cigarettes

Once over you disgusted me
once over I disgusted myself

I await my tomorrows
like dancing moths before the moon.
And so I raise a glass
to a bibulous mouth,
jealous of no man

And concerned no more
with the fates of the foolish

I raise a glass
to a bibulous mouth
a toast to all tomorrows.
M. J. Sanderson

Despair

I cannot swim
Against the tide
The tide of life
    so strong

I cannot walk
That winding road
The road of life
    so long

I cannot see
Beyond the hill
The rock strewn way
    to climb

I cannot win
This race of life
For I've run out
    of time
Margaret Browning

The Lottery

Oh, to win the lottery
Now that summer is here,
To fly away on concord
To places far and near,
To see the seven wonders
Of the world,
And gaze in wonderment,
Looking at the pyramids
An wondering how they were built,
Without cranes or tractors
Not even sand or cement,
To live in a country cottage
With roses round the door,
And thank God for the lottery
I shall not have to work no more
Eileen Griffiths

Linda

No flashing, growling thunderstorm
Threw hailstone at the bowed and blind
With fiery, scorching thunder bolts
and searing lightening of its kind
No roaring gale uproots the oak
Throwing its carcass to the ground
With half the spirit of her rage
For Linda's temper is profound.

But soon her fury dies away
With tear–stained face upon my breast
And as the gentle wafting breeze
Abates the air with tenderness
So too, does love transgress the hate
Bringing affection fresh and pure
For this is what I treasure most
And always will forever more
Raymond Briggs

Autumn Morning

What was that
which brushed my face?
A spider's web that looks like lace
Bedecked with dew drops hanging there
Like jewels in a lady's hair
And in the border, daisies, white
Lift up their heads to morning's light
A crisp white frost covers the lawn
On this misty Autumn morn.
The berries on the hawthorn glow
Their beauty follows Summer's show
And robin for his breakfast calls
A "chip-chip" on the garden wall
The sun peeps through the misty shroud
And banishes the morning cloud
And all around the world is blessed
With autumn's warmth
and fruitfulness
L. Jean Smith

Think Of Me

When all around is howling,
And no one will share the pain,
Think of me of what we had,
And could have once again.

When nothing seems the effort,
When all is going wrong,
Then think of me a little while,
The pain of joy and song.

When life itself is heavy,
And people cause affray,
Please think of me a moment,
Don't let the memory slip away.
M. Turner

Second Coming

Lying dormant waiting for a call,
The crown prince of darkness,
wants to greet us all,
from a place beyond the human
imagination, a devil waits.

Discard useless follies like crosses,
holy water will not prevail,
not against the host or all
that is evil
his followers, wait silently, knowingly
both the living and the living dead.

Only one can save you and I,
it's been two thousand years,
the stories are no longer read,
still no sign of the second coming,
Yet!!!

W. M. Grayston

Soul Words

Teardrops rolling down my cheeks
And falling
Into a bottomless well
That never fills up.

My dreams now destroyed
And all I can see are images
Through the blurred visions
From my eyes.

Nobody seems to understand
Why every touch is like a dagger
Piercing through my heart
And I seem to have
No salvation.

My pillars of strength
Fell down years ago
And my confidence had
Crumbled through my fingers.

Darkness shadows over light
But still I imagine
Black silhouettes fighting my fear.

Ayesha Kanji

Beautiful Birds

We are flying high up in the sky
on beautiful big birds,
twisting and turning all night long,
through the shining stars,
and the big silvery moon.

Danielle Anderson

Fright

The dog howls
in the dark night,
I am all alone
but followed by fright.

As I turn the corner
he is still there,
I wish he would go
I must run; but where?

Through the jungle
I fight the trees,
as they march forward
I fall to my knees.

I ran from the park
onto the road,
and like a statue
I suddenly froze.

As standing before me;
was Fright!

Lukvinder Kaur

Have Faith

Have faith and you will move a mountain
Have faith and God will give
All that you do ask for and your life
to live
Have faith and He will answer every
little prayer
Have faith and He will keep you
In His loving care
Have faith and He will guard you
Every day and every night
Have faith and He will never leave you
He will keep you in His sight
He will hold you closely to Him
Your father and your friend
Have faith and He will love you always
His love will never end.

Sandra Birch

Today He's Alone

Love your enemies,
He did say,
And yet every day,
We fuss, we fight, we break his laws,
And still expect to see Heavens doors.

Who is my neighbour?
He was asked,
Shared his wisdom, yet never basked,
In all the glory and admiration,
And he had undying patience.

Even those who do believe,
Don't always manage to achieve,
To never break a single law,
They pray to him, but what for?
Only to get them out of trouble,
They thank him then on the double,
Leave him once again alone,
Forget about him and his home.

Caroline Allen

My Wish

If I could have a wish come true,
There's only one, I'd ask from you,
The one and only God above,
Could maybe grant, my wish of love.

This oh Lord, my wish would be,
To send my father back to me,
I miss him more as time goes by,
I'll love him till the day I die.

I know this wish could never be,
So if you could do something for me,
Tell him that I love him so,
Now, always, and forever more.

Martine Owen

Male Sensitivity

Cascading far down
In the far reaches
Of my stomach
There wells emotional lava
The pits of despair
Enrage the fires of unknowing
Caught off guard
Not one emotion is showing
We skip through endless thoughts
Turning the chapters around
Back to the beginning
And my beginning will begin
When the first tear has cascaded
From far below
In the far reaches
Of my stomach.

Kevin Hoyland

The Sands of Time

The sands of time
are slipping away . . .
and my life seems void of meaning.
What am I doing?
Where am I going?
I am torn between love, and life.
My heart is forever with the
man by my side.
My soul . . . Where is my soul?
My soul is with the birds
that fly on the ocean breeze,
My soul is with the flowers
that bloom in the mid-day sun,
Where is my soul?
My soul is free.

Lar Bennett

A Marriage 1987–1996
(I Do Divorce Thee)

I love you.

Don't ever leave me.
Onwards you and me against the world.

Damn you.
I want . . .
Voices raised.
Only a girls' night out . . .
Rules broken, rings tossed aside.
Children—see them at the weekend.
Energy all spent.

Take.
Hurt.
Empty.
End.

Catherine Holt

Forgotten Dreams

The wind blew her hair
'Cross her tear stained cheek,
Of vomit and booze
Her clothes they did reek.
Alone and forgotten
On that old cold park bench,
With nothing around her
But her own rancid stench.
It's hard to imagine
That a few years ago,
This wretch was "lady"
On "millionaire's Row".
But when misfortune befell her
And her life turned around,
She looked for her friends
But none could be found.
Alone now she wanders
In hunger and strife,
Her dreams long forgotten,
No aims left in life.

Gladys McFall

Dark Soul

Night's dark wing
Wraps itself coldly around me,
Covering the surroundings,
Taking my existence,
Swallowing my being,
My soul
My whole essence,
Smothering my world in darkness,
Does it always have to come to this?
Why such hatred,
Life is nothing more than death,
And slowly dying to get there.

Ruth Harmer

Identity Crisis

I am the "Sink"
I am the "Cleaner"
It is me
Submerged in "It"

The "Sink" looks through
The window
Is that a ghost?
It was once "Me"

The inanimate objects
Supersedes "Me" why?
I feel the hard surfaces
I feel the objects
I am "the Kitchen."

M. E. Christian

Hands

Your hands may be twisted
And bent with age;
But without them
You could not turn the page
Of your book.
Without your hands,
How could you carry your shopping home,
Or wash the dishes,
Or sweep the floor,
Or how perform each household chore?
Without your hands,
Your hair would be
A tangled mess.
How could you dress,
Or eat your food,
Or phone your friend?
There is no end
To the things you do
With those ten fingers
God gave to you!

Irene S. Igbinedion

Untitled

It seems a minute
Yet it feels a year
So don't be sad
Don't shed a tear
As a year is long
And I won't be gone
Never lost in time
As you are mine.

Paul Liam Mottley

The Roseate Cockatoo

You were such a friendly bird,
with feathers red and grey.
I would come to see you often,
you brought joy into my day.

One morning your cage was empty,
feathers on the ground.
The lock hanging broken,
you were nowhere to be found.

You were taken whilst sleeping,
away from the home that you knew.
My heart aches not knowing,
what is happening to you.

The last time that I came to see you,
you let me stroke your head.
Then to me you said 'hello',
oh please please don't be dead.

I have not given up hoping,
I don't want this to be the end.
Wherever you are I am thinking,
of you my little feathered friend.

Jean Lillie

Remember Me

Remember me please
From time to time,
Remember our love
And the way we cared,
The things we said
And the love we shared.

Remember our last kiss,
And the last time we met,
As I always will,
My heart won't forget

Remember each day please
For a minute or two,
Because I my darling
Will always remember you.

Joyce Collisson

The Sunset

I saw the sunset in the sky
It made me wonder why oh why
Do people need to rush around
When they could listen to the sound
Of sea gulls calling in the docks
Or water breaking on the rocks.

I saw the sunset in the sea
It made me think of you and me
Of times we walked upon the sand
And held each other hand in hand.

I saw the clouds turn back to grey
So ended yet another day
Of empty hours without you
Of wasted time when love was new
I saw the sunset in the sky
It made me wonder why oh why.

Brian Thorpe

Seasons

The skies are bright
The sun is white.
Winter days fall
To the night's blazing caul.

Silvery puddles dazzle sight
Badgers walk the lane by night.
Budding hawthorn, bright and gay
Daffodils pour sunshine on the day.

Strutting pheasants dance and croon
Corn fields wait the harvest moon.
Golden days, indigo nights
Gentle breezes caress your sight.

Autumn colours fill the fields
Leaf deep carpets ready to yield.
Summer melts in rainbow showers
Winter covers all the bowers.

V. R. Johnson

The Sea Side

I see the horses galloping in the
shallow water while the waves
splash against the rocks.
I hear the water swishing and
children having fun.
I touch the sand to make sand castles
I taste the salty water as I swim
in the sea.
I feel hot and very sleepy as I
sunbathe.
I think as the day ends and the
sun goes down and the birds fly
to their nests that it has been a
happy day.

Lisa Andrews

Dreaming Of You . . .

When I am alone,
I dream of you
As the moon strolls out,
From behind a cloudy cloak.
To cast beam of silver light,
Over many lands—now bright.
Creating shadows of the night—
You by me and I by you,
As we walk hand in hand
Upon a glistening path—
Whilst stars go by above,
Watched by eyes aglow with love.
Suddenly a quake,
And I'm wide awake.
My mind now dwelling—
On that dream . . .

. . . Alan Fowkes

Jenny

Plump Rosy Jenny
Plopped into my lap
With a swirl of pink skirts
   and black curls

Her dark eyes were sparkling
Her smile very wide
As she gently rocked backwards
   and forwards inside

With a thump of her heels
And a bend with her knees
She pushed herself straight
   and made for the trees

Her dimples were flashing
Her feet running fast
As she moved—Oh so joyfully
   over the grass

Julie W. Taylor

Taking The High Road

Bus snakes
car overtakes
throttle to floor
can do no more

Got it wrong
big bang
hospital bed
driver dead

Funeral dirge
vicar urge
take care
everywhere

Widow cries
congregation sighs
pray heed
don't speed

One life
one death
one amen

John Doyle

"Awaken To A Dream"

Words fly on wings of song:
With poem or verse;
In silence, to converse.
Given time,
This rhythm and rhyme;
With notes of music,
Will combine:
Together, to belong,
In the harmony of song.

D. H. E. Bradley

The Fertilization Of Life

Come forth,
Come forth oh noblemen,
Spur on your steed,
Do not retreat.

Which one will win,
Who shall it be,
To change the course of history,
Who dares to meet their destiny?

Oh kindly sir,
Can you not see,
The urgency with which I plead,
You grant my wish for humanity.

Leave not this damsel in distress,
Complete your quest,
So all can see,
The product in reality.

Ruth Goddard

The Churchyard

Flowers glimpsed across the path.
Questions of an unknown life.
Was I right? Was I wrong?
Did I try or just pretend?
Echo, echo
Memories flash—coming, going
—always dissolving out of reach.
Peace, the sureness of love?
Forgiveness and understanding?
Or just the silence of flower in a
    hazy light.

Pamela Tenniel Burgess

Self Portrait

Yesterday I met a man
with a rainbow in his hair,
he told me all his troubles
he didn't have a care,
he told me all about
the times he'd spend alone,
We had something in common
a certain lasting bond,
he told me of a person
of whom he'd once been fond

I listened for what seemed hours
to the rhythm of his voice
I couldn't tear myself away
I didn't have a choice
He told me more about his life
the periods of despair
We seemed so close together
Like two books on a shelf.
I then shook and realised
I was talking to myself.

S. M. Waite

Timber!

I'll tell you a tale,
Of a woodpecker—male,
That wanted to mate,
Though the season was late.
He was in such a hurry,
A rush and a flurry,
That he lost all control,
And pecked out a hole,
Which cut through the wood,
On which his mate stood.
And she flew away,
Not wishing to stay.
He's there to this day
Still pecking away.

S. R. Ramsden

Co-llab-oration (Dylan Revoiced)

You put a flower on my grave.
Full-heart could not know
A more beautiful elegy—
Elegy from heart of pure envy!
Envy of my prowess, my verse,
My Welsh pure lilting phrases,
My egg–white scrambled literature,
My pint–inspired ramblings
That some thought pretty.

How can you rewrite me?
How can death-to-life explode
Into the million syllables
Of sea-wind-force poetry
Hard won near bubbling ocean?

My dear child—try and catch me,
But you'll never match me!

Diana Lyons

Late Again

Late again,
That stupid train.
That's the seventeenth time,
On the Bakerloo Line,
That the train's been late . . .

British rail,
Worse than the mail,
The wrong kind of snow,
And the train won't go,
Late again, that stupid train!

Faizel Iqbal

Love And Hate

I could not wrench him from my mind
My every dream he haunted
I loved him so much it was torture
I'd do anything he wanted

I believed that he could love me
That I could make him mine
That my dreams could be reality
How could I be so blinded?

They tell me love and hate are close
How could I understand?
Until the day he hurt me
Turned my feelings upside down

I hear that he's in love now
A gorgeous girl stands in my place
I hate him so much that it's torture
As the tears run down my face

Rosamund Witcher

Pirates!

Where pirate ships are sailing
All though the moonlit path,
All round the deck the railing
Glitters in the dark.

Where pirates bury treasure
On the shores of Banga Nether,
It gives them glee and pleasure
To see their glittering treasure.

Aha! I've found the treasure!
I'm richer now than ever!
I think I'll keep the lot
Rather than let it rot.

And now I've found the treasure
I think I'll have a pleasure
And live my life at leisure
On the shores of Banga Nether.

Holly Manuel

My Spring Poem

Spring is in the air,
Blossoms everywhere.
The winter is gone,
The winter is gone,
The swallows sing their song.

The swallows sing their song,
Spring is very late,
The cuckoos got a mate.
Spring is here,
Spring is there,
Spring is everywhere.

The trees are bare,
Spring is in the air,
Hurry up spring.
Please, please, please.

Nikkita Ogden

The Affair

Their musical rehearsals
Are a façade.
Behind the mask
An affair is born;
An obsession of passion,
Their musical ambitions
Swept to one side.

They embrace,
They talk,
They play
The odd flirtatious tune.
Their talents wasted.

Their spouses are naive.
The master and the pupil,
The seduced and seducer.

Linda Morris

One Morning

One morning you awoke
felt the sun
sylphlike in wilderness
Nude silk and rare
Soft from the natural unconscious

Beauty of movement
Feline curves
Symmetrical hush
Not to waste the dawn

Never leave
Endless enrapture
I am soothed by the
nature of your feather

Jason Marsh

Precious Countryside

Golden sun that
crowns the trees,
Like diamonds
dew drops glisten,
Crystal waters
run from streams,
Where silver
fishes listen,
Ruby red the
poppies sway,
In grass of
emerald green,
Then a cloak
of sapphire sky,
This is Mother Nature's
living dream,
Our precious
countryside.

Dina Morgan-Thomas

Full Circle

Beneath the frost–encrusted ground
The awakening shoots still cling,
Gathering strength from all around
For their journey into Spring.

They greet us in their glory,
With faces all aglow,
The narcissi and daffodils,
Emerging from the snow.

The raindrops rest upon the rose,
A truly wondrous sight,
Like jewels upon a velvet cloth,
Sparkling in the light.

The wind can send a gentle breeze
Rustling through the trees,
Or gusts that send the saplings
Bowing to their knees.

The snowflakes flutter gently
From the grey sky up above,
To fall upon the barren earth,
Warming it, with love.

M. J. Courbet

The Imposer

This obstacle stuck in my path,
Is her evil, yet an angle,
Happiness is beyond the barrier
To get through will mean no more tears

He is there, tall
But she is there,
The obstacle which separates us,
From pure peace

Susanne Fleming

Facing The Truth

A pencil substitutes for pen
A razor substitutes for knife
To a husband in a house of love
Nothing substitutes for wife
A slipper substitutes for shoe
A pocket substitutes for purse
To the weak ones on a sick bed
Nothing substitutes for nurse.

A ladder substitute for height
A mitten substitute for glove
A candle substitutes for light
But nothing substitutes for love.

Idols cannot substitutes for God
Wigs rarely substitutes for hair
For those who really search for truth
Nothing substitutes for prayer

True Christian values based on faith
Are lasting to the end
Because in our God and Jesus
Nothing substitutes for friend.

B. R. Davies

The Sound Of Silence

Do you hear the silence
that sounds in an empty room?
I gaze out of the window
at the flowers in full bloom.

Lazy dust motes swirl around
Caught in the sun's bright ray;
I've no urge to move a muscle—
Could just sit still all day.

Do you hear the silence
that sounds in an empty room?
Do you ever feel regret
when they come home too soon?

Jacqueline Bell

Spirit Within

Across the sands of time
Through meadows flourishing
He follows the sun through day
The stars through night

Up mountains He climbs
Through deep waters He finds
His spirit is strong
His heart is full
And His mind is set

A voice speaks to Him
Guiding Him
He asks to be forgiven
Forgiveness is given
He asks for strength
He is strong

A promise in our wake
Harbouring each soul
His light shines within
Eternally beyond all

Caroline Gowers

Homeless

Living on the streets
No belongings or goods
Another day of begging
And grovelling on my feet

They sweep me aside
I should be gone
Dead in a grave
The best place for me

Alicks Fraser

Anaesthesia

Prick.
A tingle.
It spreads.
Up my arms,
Into my breast,
Marching upward
To invade my head.
This harbinger of sleep
Courses through my veins.
Cold comfort, warm release.
Consciousness surrenders,
Retreats quietly to sleep
In the dark grey realm
Of unconscious self.
Temporary death,
Peaceful breath.
Ceasing to be.
Ready to be
Cut.

Simon Thomas

To A Love

Close your pretty eyes
And dream sweet dreams of love,
And pleasant walks down by the stream.
In the shady grove
Where all the pretty flowers
The harbingers of spring,
Decorate the new born earth
While birds are on the wing.

Close your pretty eyes
And let the stars caress your dreams,
Let the moon with its bright rays
Bathe you in its beams.
And when the sun shall rise,
May it warm you with its rays
And may the God who made us all
Keep you safe always.

H. Jeanes

Thoughts

I don't want to forget
What I'm thinking
And feeling, now
In this life.
Good and bad,
I need to remember
So I can be
A perfect, understanding person.
Sometimes I think I remember,
But,
Before I can write it
I forget.
It comes like lightning flashes
But then disappears
Into the darkness.
I want to capture
Every moment and thought,
But I can't.
It scares me.

Amy Lumsden

A Sailor's Dream

Give me a boat and a setting sun
And a force six in my face
Give a me a coarse and a bottle of rum
And a star at which to race

Give me a bird to follow my boat
And a wind that will not cease
Give me a dream and a turn of pace
And give me a greater peace

Give me a wife and give me a son
And give me a daughter too
Give me a spray as white as snow
And give me a sky of blue

Give me a sunrise at my back
And a rainbow on my beam
Give a chance to sail in peace
And give me the chance to dream

Bernard Brady

We Are But Cogs . . .

We are but cogs
Brought together
Then moved away gently
To gain momentum
And to return

We turn
Through our work and our art
We turn
Through our families and friends

We turn
There's just us
Forceful and intertwined

You within me
I surrounding you
All that we can be
To replenish and renew

Essentially yours.

Mara L. Jones

Love Is Like A Raindrop

Love is like a raindrop
Much sweeter than wine,
It blossoms in the body
And also in the mind.
If this love of mine
Should ever die.
I will sit alone and weep,
Seeking solace only
In the thought of loving you,
And you for loving me.

J. M. Pollard

Sisters

Hear me my sisters
My blood runs through your veins
My heart feels your pain
Let the invisible cord
That binds us
Draw us in close
Even though the path we chose
Says no right of way
Let each parcel of pain
That lies deep inside
with so many labels
To set free first
We can never decide
Let this be a step to freedom
A new age
A feeling of being
Born again

P. M. Lightfoot

True Love

Scarce as bees on a winter's night
Whispering sounds of true love
howling like the wind in the sea
Silent like city life
It captures me
Throws me off balance
True love
Of a husband, a wife
Lasting forever
Till the day the sun sets its last
Stay together
Like rain in the desert
The warmth of another's heart
Always each other
Bound together
by
True love.

Kaylene Williams

Age

A lonely old lady looks out,
Watching strangers pass by.
She's alone with a book in her hand
Waving the world goodbye.

Who will notice when the lamp fades,
Among thousands that do everyday?
She's just one more in a hectic life,
Where the old get in the way.

Her eyes gently close shut,
An arm falls limp to her side.
The lines on her face are peaceful
Another old lady has died.

Jennifer Watson

Why?

Why do I feel like this?
Why do I feel so blue?
Why do I feel so all alone?
Is there nothing that I can do?

Why do I feel like this,
like there's nothing to live for?
Life has lost its meaning,
I really don't care anymore?

The birds flying in the sky,
don't mean a thing to me.
So chop down all the forests,
and pour away the sea.

Stop the sun from shining,
darkness would be bliss.
And please answer my question,
why do I feel like this?

Joanne Tillman

My Third Dachshund

My third little dachshund Fritz
has just been put to rest.
We had him for eleven years
That time he gave his best.
I saw him in the garden
I saw him all around
Alas! Today—nowhere to be found.
Eyes always bright and shining
Asking only for love
and a bit of dining.
Licking hand if we had pain,
Oh! I wish I had little Fritz again
He came with us on mountains
sands, and rides in car
just of late the little chap
could not go too far.
First on the bed at night
he knew he should not dare!
I hope if there's a doggy heaven
My little Fritz is there.

Helen J. Williams

The Strong Silence

I'm angry.
So angry that I want to scream.
I want to pick up the T.V.
and throw it out of the window,
I'd like to smash a few plates,
ornaments, and cups,
but where will that get me?
A few broken objects,
with no problems solved.
I could scream and shout
but my anger would prevail,
so I will not do or say a thing,
I'll just be angry in silence,
then the only thing I'll break is me.

Angela Harrison

Family Separation

Now they're apart,
I feel all alone.
I'm living with my mother,
It's hard not to moan.
  Dad's with another girl,
  I see them every week.
  I wish another family,
  for myself, I could seek.
A family that's happy,
like mine used to be.
A family that has holidays,
near the sand and the sea.
  A family that will love me,
  family that will care.
  I want a brother and sister,
  so my things I can share.
Now I'm at my new home,
I like it a lot.
I miss my real parents,
But my decision I have got.

Gurjeet Marway

Sea Poem

Down by the sea waves roll
As it breathes in and out
A never ending chat
As it calmly makes its way past us
On a journey
For how long no-one knows
The strong wind blows
The water rushes in
It hits the jagged rocks
They are ready for battle

Hollie Leandro-Edwards

Old Mr. Thomas

Old man, cold distressed man
No-love-to-caress man
Never-quite-expressed man
Died-an-ugly-death man

He said he saw my face
In his disillusioned dreams
He said I should be careful
For things aren't quite what they seem

He told me to never trust anyone
To never give my heart away
To never undo something done
To never lead myself astray

I know he was a hated man
People thought he was so cold
But I know how hurt he was
So withered, stained and old

That old man, cold distressed man
No-love-to-caress man
Never-quite-expressed man
My-better-than-the-rest man

Carrie Gledhill

Waste Disposal

He has thrown away his trousers,
Patched and baggy at the knees.
He no longer has to stand the smell
Of rotten fish and mouldy cheese.

We no longer call him dustman,
And if your tongue can make the twist,
He'll be pleased if you will call him
A receptacle receptionist.

I've thrown away my dustbin
Full of dents and made of tin.
For the council have replaced it
With what we call a Wheeley Bin.

It has wheels, a lid with hinges,
And one can wheel it like a barrow.
My only criticism is,
My paths are much too narrow.

So it stands there undetectable
Amongst the flowers in the garden,
A respectable receptacle.
No need to beg your pardon.

O. C. Jones

My Golden Hair Girl

With her beautiful smile
and long silk golden hair
she stood there playing,
with no fear.

In the sunshine she
danced and sang a song,
all through the morning
and all day long.

But one day the sun had gone,
leaving a dark rainy unhappy song.
I saw her laying there
sound asleep,
with blood dripping from
her head as I weep.
My beautiful girl is dead!
I cried.
In my head it was a lie.
In the wooden box which she lay I beat,
I left my golden hair
girl behind fast asleep.

Anika Murtza

Walls Have Ears Ya' Know

Walls have ears ya' know!
They know all we say,
they listen and they learn,
close attention they must pay.

Walls have ears ya' know!
Listening to what we say,
laughing and crying,
even when we walk.

Shhh! Walls have ears ya' know!

Bonnita Goulden

The Morbid Philosopher

From blissful sweet–grass hills
Amidst green seas of agony
A cancer of cold stone
Begins to creep through me
Flesh no longer flesh
And the seeds of death are sown
I watch the tangle grass enmesh
Me in a smoke filled throne,
I am a statue
And I am here alone.

Enchanted to this bitter place
A fairy castle inside me
Where fragments of my mind will lace
The brittle wings of fantasy,
An eagle who forever glides
The fickle breeze
Through which it guides
Me to its splendid majesty
In the cloud realm
Of insanity.

Kenneth Tofts

Crematorium

Yesterday:
   Garden of Rest
   Fresh flowers . . .
   Fountains spray
   droplets form and fade away.
   A New Day is born.

Today:
   Garden of Peace
   Fresh flowers . . .
   Fountains spray
   droplets shine
    in sun–kissed ray
    and fade away.
   A New Day is mine.

Tomorrow:
   Garden of Rest
   Fresh flowers . . .
   Fountains spray
   droplets form and fade away.
   A New Day is born.

Sidney R. Fisher

A Princess For A Day

You asked to be a princess
On a day just like today
To marry your prince charming
And dance the night away

You married your prince charming
Making promises for life
You're still a prince and princess
Better known as man and wife

So, love each other dearly
You've made us oh so glad
Go and find your dreams together
With love from Mum and Dad

G. S. Heywood

"Black"

The air black
like the clothes of those who lost.
Nothing to breathe
but pain that chokes,
tears that drown the soul in grief.
Hearts cannot beat
But freeze and ache and
cry at the dead
And the living dead.
Mouths cannot speak but scream
with anguish and plea for mercy.
The mother mourns the child she bore,
the life she gave that lives no more.
The sound of the dirt echoes on
and on throughout the hearts
of those who lost.
The heavens black
like the grave of him they chose.

Nectaria Hadjisergis

Try To Fall In Love

Each day as I see you go past
My heart starts beating fast,
You shall be the prince of my heart
For I shall never let you part.

I will never deny my love for you
For everyone knows how much it's true,
Every time I close my eyes at night
I see your face shining bright.

For you are the treasure of my life
Give me the chance to be your wife,
You don't really have a clue
What love can really do to you.

Just take a look and you can see
What falling in love has done to me,
I'll be here to share your pain
You'll never be here lonely again.

So take as much time
For I shall wait.

Rahanara Miah

While I Was Walking

Out in the open of the sun
grants a smile on everyone
listening to the glistening grass
as the dog and I walk past

As the corn sways here and there
in the distance we see a hare
looking at its twitching ears
waiting for another to appear

Ella Da'Silva

Thoughts

There is only one earth,
But there are thousands of places,
With millions of people,
And millions of faces,
There are hundreds of countries,
And thousands of stars,
But few planets,
Like Pluto and Mars,
There are lots of people,
Like you and me,
But we are the damage,
Can't you see?
Think of the animals,
Now there aren't lots,
I hope this made you think,
And that it's in your thoughts . . .

Fiona McIsaac

"Alone"

I stand alone and look around
I hear a noise, I hear a sound
One man laughs, another cries
A stranger walks away and sighs

People moving everywhere
Without a worry, without a care
I watch the people move around
Without a word, without a sound

I watch behind my silent wall,
My lonely tears begin to fall.
Tears of envy, tears of pride
I feel I want to run and hide.

I feel the people closing in
The noise before is now a din.
Yet still it all seems so remote
As I shrink down inside my coat.

I ask myself and cannot find
An answer that will calm my mind
To know with people all around
Am I so lonely in a crowd . . . ?

Suzanne P. Lynch

Scotland's Heroes

Scots wha hae wae Wallace bled
  Scots wha noble Bruce has led
Bannockburn won him fame tis said
  Knights o' chivalry

Bonnie Chairlie wis the same
  A noble Prince o' Stuart name
Culloden wis his dae o' shame
  Highlanders in chains

Rabbie burns he goat it richt
  He yaised his pen wae aw his micht
And gave the English verse a fricht
  Odes in Scottish tongue

Then Harry Lauder wae his stick
  His Glesca tongue it took a trick
Cracking Jokes sae can't an' quick
  Roars o' merriment

Thae ur some o' Scotland's greats
  In halls thur names neverberate
Each year whin Scots as celebrate
  Ne'er tae be forgotten.

Lachlan Taylor

Our Race

It's not fair
We're always getting picked on
Me and my brother Blair
We're always the school victims

It's because of our colour
It's because of our race
We're not so popular
Like every other face

We've been here two weeks now
And things couldn't get worse
If only there was someway, somehow
In which we could come first

Getting involved would be great
If they took us for who we are
If there was no debate
Then we wouldn't give a darn

The thing that hurts the most
Is the way they judge our race
The way they all boast
About the colour of their face

Rupinder Kaur Dhanjal

Life Is . . .

Life is nice
Life is fabulous
When you have friends
And people who love you

Life is luxury
Life is invincible
When you have money
And a home to live in

Life is pleasant
Life is powerful
When war is peace
And slavery is freedom

Life is fantastic
Life is nothing
When you ain't living it
To the ultimate maximum

Life is beautiful
Life is short
Don't miss a minute
Because they are sparse

Megteld Damming

1914

I gave my last prayer to Jesus
as I set off for war.
I should have given it to my mother
for she would have a son no more.
I had joined up with some local lads
we joined to give our all.
But none of them could save me
when it was my turn to fall.
I was fighting in the trenches
my uniform soaked in mud.
I died on the battlefield
amongst the foul stench of blood.

Justin Binks

Blindness

I hear your soft voice speaking.
But alas I cannot see.
Yet the words that you are saying,
Are like music played for me.

Although I do not see you,
I can feel your loving touch.
There is such a gentle tenderness,
The type that means so much.

And when I trace the outline.
Of the contours which are you.
I feel divinely happy,
I hope you feel so too.

However can I thank you.
For the eyes you share with me
But truly I am grateful
That your eyes help me to see.

Gordon Barnett

If Only

If only I had listened
To my head and not my heart
If only I had stayed away
We wouldn't have to part
If only I had told myself
We really shouldn't do it
If only I had told myself
I wouldn't be going through it
If only is an easy thing to say
If only I hadn't played away
If only.

Margaret D. McRitchie

Music's Enchantment

A ballad of sweet,
Or a verse of perfect,
A yawn as the lullaby
Takes affect.

Symphonic sounds
Softly fill our room,
Lifting the darkness
From cheerless gloom.

Love and passion
For days and after,
Seduced from the
Melody's chorus and
Laughter.

Sorcery of plenty
Spellbinding true,
Music is enchantment
Forever charms us new.

Lisa Joanne Stephenson

For Geoff

We never met
and yet
your smiling face
I knew so well,
followed by your cat
that sat
watching you grow
flowers, herbs and veg
or cut a hedge,
and dug a pond.
From beyond
no longer will you come—
gardening on my screen
farewell.

Marian Gledhill

The Tragedy Of Dunblane

Those children Lord at Dunblane school
Who had to face such fear and horror
Which ended all their tiny lives
For no reason we can offer.
So take them in thy home above
To live with thee in peace and love,
Safe away from earthly sin
And people who are warped within.
Then to those now left to mourn
Must try to picture them in Heaven
Just waiting for the day to come
To be again united in their love

G. M. Duxbury

Not Tomorrow

To get away from worldly things
Of man, machine and money,
To lie upon a sunny bank
And watch the bees suck honey,
To hear a crisp brown leaf
Drop to the mossy ground,
And watch a spider spinning its web
Without the slightest sound.

To see the sunbeams hanging
From a bright blue sky,
Is only something God can make
And money never buy.
To feel the peace within and out
Makes one feel without a doubt,
That God on high is always nigh
To soothe and caress a troubled breast.
Enjoy these things for Time has Wings
And today Never Returns.

Madeline Dora Kidman

My Best Friend

Forever faithful
Love abound
Oh! You mischievous hound
Warm heart
Wet nose
This poem for you I compose
Explosive with delight
On my return
Constantly at my side
Especially at dinner time!
Now you are gone
The joy we have shared
Brings me happiness
For the years ahead.

Antoinette Ghura

Drowning

Beneath the crashing, clawing sea
I heard a voice; you called to me;
You said my name and told a lie,
You said our love would never die.

It died a death; I'm left bereft
And I alone once more am left;
I know you tried, but time and tide
Kept us apart, so love has died.

I'd never felt like that before
And I will love you evermore,
But I just wish we'd never kissed
So I would not know what I missed.

Deborah Dereham

Thoughts Away From Home

I sit and glance across the bay,
My thoughts turn to a bygone day,
Was it the pleasure or was it the pain,
Or was it just simply all the gain.

Dreams may come and dreams may go,
Just like a ship going to and fro,
The winter the spring the summer sun,
We laughed and joked and had some fun.

The seasons come and the seasons go
I was once fast but now I'm slow,
A mirrored image comes across my face
And goes and vanishes without trace

The tide it turns and comes in again
The time is approaching half past ten
Time to pack my bags and go
As to where I just don't know.

Ian Massheder

I Fear

I fear
For I do not know
Causes me pain
I am afraid
Friends, never the best of
Kind words
I fear
It is to be goodbye
Pains me so
I will miss you
Grow apart, faint smiles
I fear
Time to leave
Pain will go
Though
Never quite got there
Gestures weak
I fear.

Phillip Chadwick

Organized Chaos

Any attempt for happiness,
Will destroy its ambition,
Until it's briefly distorted,
And twisted with-in its soul . . .

Made in an bid of normality,
But fails to serve any modesty,
Its hospitality flies away,
To a world of unopened hope.

Well in this way of what,
Is why we question how,
And an uncertainty of Yes,
Makes us fear and say no.

Then a thought that is lost,
Was probably never there,
Because life takes its toll,
And ultimately destroys dreams.

So diversity is timeless,
And suicide seems harmless,
But the time will come,
When the beyond . . . becomes the past!

Daniel Parsons

I Just Called

I just called to say I care
in the hope that you will share,
This moment of the day to be
in this world of mine with me,
To me such pleasure it does give
when in this world of mine you live,
That is why my dearest dear
I just called to say I care.

John Clarke

Time

Time here and now
Is like a vow,
Without a promise
Of tomorrow's paradise.

Time is infinity,
Maybe charming; maybe witty;
Time is days and nights,
Showing ways and showing lights.

Time will not wait,
Although it won't be late,
To an unknown destination
Made by man's own hesitation.

Time is in the past
But is never last,
To predict tomorrow's fate,
Which just cannot wait!

Pamela Soni-Tregaskis

Midnight Feeling

As I walk the streets of midnight
With out a girl on my arm.

I know what it like to be lonely
I know what it's like on my own
I some times wonder what happened
To all the loves I once knew
I feel that I have been rejected
and the rejection is make me blue

I think one day it will happen
a girl will come into my life
and be happy to be my wife

Then maybe I won't have to walk
feeling these midnight blues.

Trevor William Cable

Everyone Has A Dream

You can't describe a dream
No matter how hard you try,
A dream is something precious,
Something you will keep until you die

People dream of being famous,
Of one day being a star,
Or winning the lotto,
Or buying that wonderful car.

No dreams can be silly,
It is the dreamer's own,
No one can take it from you,
To borrow or to loan.

So if you have a dream,
Or something you'd like to do,
If you dream hard enough,
Someday it might come true.

Mairead McAteer

The Garden Of Tranquillity

Our garden is a pretty place
Tranquil, and full of grace
Frequently, when I feel blue
There, reminiscence of those I knew
Safe within this floral nest
Confident I've done my best
Tending flowers in every way
Feed, and nurture with each day
Looking upwards to the sky
Two dove–grey birds of peace fly by
Enticing them to flutter down
Garlands, to admire all round
Spectrum hues, vibrantly true
I wish, my loved ones, they were you.

Maureen M. Weitman

A Dark Night In The Wood

A dark night in the wood
Is not my idea of fun
With the leaves rustling
Bats screeching in the sky
The only light is a billion stars
And the moon in the sky
I think of my family
And all the fights we had
Oh! How I would love to be home
Now!

Christopher McMonagle

An Aspiration

I'd love to write a proper 'pome'
With lots of lovely words:
With rhymes and 'literation
'Bout bushes, bees and birds.

Perusing proper po'try books
whiles many an hour away
'Tis witty words that are the crux
They capture and they sway

I'm taken off on many tours
Imaginary—real,
from wild and windy mossy moors
to seas with sand and seal.

It is a world of make–believe
Of perfect, pure pretence.
Of threads that I would wish to weave
To make your thoughts fly hence.

But if my doggerel you've read
Perhaps you saw those moors?
Perhaps that seal swam swiftly, led
by words of mine—the image yours.

Patricia A. Wilcockson

Weather At A Seaside Town

Peaceful in summer
The summer comes and
wind is calm.
Flowers blossoming in
the sun children playing
in the sea making
sand castles for you and me
ice creams melting beneath
the sun you can't beat
summer in a seaside town
Noisy in winter as the
Sea starts to roar and
the rain starts to pour
People trying to shelter
huddled up cold and wet
waiting for the summer
to start again.

Rachael Weddup

Feelings

In order to find truthfulness
We must first know what it is to lie
In order to find happiness
We must first begin to cry
In order to find hope
We must first live in fear
In order to find the answers
In all we hold dear
In order to find honesty
We must first trust to fate
In order to find the reason
To what we now relate
In order to find our destiny
We must first open our eyes
In order to solve the problems
We must know the reason why

Kevin Mahan

Fading Lights

Where have all the stars gone?
What's happened to the sky?
What's happened to those velvet nights
I worshipped as a child

Those spangled lights
Those diamonds shining high
They were oh so brilliant then
Now they seem so shy.

I still look up at the night
I still gaze up on high
Perhaps they've lost their sparkle
or perhaps it's my old eyes.

G. Pratley

Untitled

Silver Birches, Maples, Yews,
overlook his resting place.
He lies cocooned in mahogany
against the sharp flints and chalk:
Downland earth and damaged turf
his only cover.
His spirit seems to hang upon the air.
It speaks to me,
stirring up old memories of long ago.
But it only seems like yesterday,
A single breath in time,
since he looked at me
and spoke to me
and said, "goodbye".
For ever.
So I sit and talk to him,
and feel him answer me.
And my soul cries out in anguish
and prays that his is free.

Gail Cheeseman

My Valentine

Devoted to my dear wife Sheila

It was February '42
When at a dance I first met you.
Your sparkling eyes.
Your cheeks so fresh.
Standing there in your lovely dress.
You looked so lovely so divine
You must become my Valentine.

Fifty four years have passed away.
Our love has grown more with each day.
Ages have passed, like sands of time
But you, are still my Valentine.

Frank Cressey

Your Name

I shall send it ringing
down the vaults of time,
woven in song,
joyous among
great pealing bells of rhyme,
echoing long
into Eternity.

As four golden arrows
I shall wing it forth,
cleave Heaven's breast,
Southward and West
Eastward and to the North,
finding not rest
but Immortality.

I shall sear it deep
upon the mind of God
so He will ask
no further task
of me lest 'neath its rod
aught else should mask
that one Identity.

John Terry

**This poem was previously published
incorrectly in The Other Side of the Mirror*

Untitled

And my heart shall not be still
And thought will rise,
   however feebly,
Unfettered by the weight
   of matter,
My eyes will look into the sun
   even if blinded,
And I shall not submit.

Elisa de Jager

Why Dad?

Please tell me Dad, I'd like to know,
why does it rain? Why does it snow?
Why do the birds sing in the trees?
Please tell me Dad, tell me please.
Please tell me Dad I'd like to know,
where's Mummy gone? I miss her so.
I miss her so it makes me sad.
Where has she gone? Where is she Dad?
Is it true what people say,
That Mum's with Jesus far away?
I'd like to know, I really would,
I promise Dad, I will be good.
Don't you cry Dad, please don't cry.
I'll wipe the teardrop from your eye.
I feel unhappy, when you weep,
so lay beside me, go to sleep
I don't think Mummy's far away,
I know that she'll be back someday.
But tell me Dad I'd like to know,
where's Mummy gone? I miss her so.

Michael Morris

Forgotten

Little rooms without any doors
Or light
All that can be heard is a weak
inaudible cry.

In one of those rooms,
On the bed
Is a child
Motionless
Almost dead.

Little bones showing through
blue tinged skin
Big brown eyes which would melt
the coldest of hearts
Left to die with no one to care
And no one to cry.

"Orphaned". "Why"?
"It's a solution" they say
"Overpopulation"
"Ha! Murderers".
But they don't see the tiny
coffins, laid
down into the ground 3 by 3 by 3
Countless lives thrown aside
Forgotten.

Alison Winston

Green Shoes

Green-as-emerald shoes, smooth—
subtle–outlined, curved and
lithe as seduction, you tempt me.

With your elegant posture
you would dignify any
woman's ankle, skimming smooth

as silk from heel to
slim calf, poised to reveal,
and up, up over hidden, inviting thigh.

If you were mine, what a great
change there might yet be;

no more sexual uncertainty,
no more flat–shoed woman, sane
and sensible, would I be.

No! In such shoes of jade and
rich attraction, I could grow
tall, sultry and sun–kissed

as velvet trees in cool
valley, breathing in the
heat and dust of the day.

Anne L. Brooke

Anointing Of The Sick

Outward and visible sign:
Oil and tears and sighs.
Don't heed what the rubric says.
Observe the pain in the eyes.

Outward and visible sign
For God knows what private hell.
Her breath is tainted with wine
And with lies which she has to tell.

Outward and visible sign.
Body, mind, soul receive
The healing grace of Him made flesh
The prisoner to relieve.

Outward and visible sign.
Strange it should be like this:
That a woman in tears is now set free
With oil, prayer, sighs and a kiss.

Christine Looseley

The Oak Tree

As I gaze upon its majesty
My heart is filled with pride
For its presence here has surely blest
This our countryside
For if I could have chosen
How to adorn this land
It would have been with the mighty oak
For nothing is so grand
To think that from an acorn
This mighty giant can grow
Man is filled with wonder
On how this can be so
Think about its power
Swaying in the breeze
Be in awe of its splendour
This giant among our trees
And when life is weary
And becomes too much to bear
Remember all this beauty
That we're allowed to share.

Val Harvey

Don't Despair

When you're feeling sad and lonely
Try not to despair
Remember there is always
Someone who will care
Just a little seed of love
In the hearts of friends
Will like a lovely flower bloom
With a warmth that never ends
So smile and try to see
The hope that's always there
Grasp the hand that's offered
And remember don't despair

Dorothy Slater

Four Walls

Four walls caving in
beating heart, beating in sin.
Hard bed, cold to the touch
any bright light is too much.
Darkness on the eyes a strain
here a few days, going insane.
Clock ticking, beating my mind
my feelings turning blind.
Silence is deafening to my ears
deafness will remain for years.
My ears will hear no sympathetic song
I'm being punished for my wrong.
All the things I wish I'd been—
Oh prison walls caving in.

Caroline Murphy

To Those We Love We Lend
Our Voice

To those we love we lend
our voice. Thus breathes
the sun her rays to sister
moon, thus the sky its
blue canopy to the air.

When thoughts of you
get entangled in my hair,
pauses of love blossom;
I share my passion with
rocks, earth's gentle locks.

When dares my brow
let slide my care
into my eyes, my lips
advance you rapidly
into my palpitating heart.

To those we love we lend
our voice.

Theresa Vella

Visit To Fraggle Rock

Though my visit was short and sweet,
I managed to see miles of peat.
Lots of rocks were also found
Scattered upon the barren ground.

The highlight of the week
Must have been the quiz night treat,
Although we didn't win
Does that mean we're really dim?

The company was really smashing
Pity it wasn't somewhere dashing,
Along 'Mine Alley' I trod tiptoe
Just in case I woke the S.W.O.

All the W.O.'s made me smile
I hope I didn't cramp their style.
So tie a ribbon round the old oak tree
The next time we meet I hope
It's you to me.

Sheila A. Brodie

Cricket Match

Clack of ball at flight from bat
Sharp cry pointing a "howzat!"
Daisies link the young at play,
Clatter of cups on plastic tray
Shuddering heat—haze, droning bee,
Boozing, snoozing, bored or dozing
Lazy game of summer's day
Play away, play away.

Vera Chidzey

Yours To Care For

Moon floating across the sky
Stars twinkling brightly on high
Mountain mists drifting on a breeze,
Deer lightly wandering through the trees
A brook, gurgling over bed of stone.
Giving life to flowers grown;
Trees of different shade and hue,
Waiting to meet the morning dew.
Birds sleeping, head under wing.
Wakening! A dawn chorus to sing.
Seas stocked with boundless treasure
Giving hours of endless pleasure.
For in this quiet of the night.
Before the flush of first light
Nature rests, and quietly slumbers
Taking to breast her many numbers.
This wonder world, one must not abuse,
It's a priceless gift; care how you use
So think! Before you cause her pain
This world of yours must so remain.

Norris Johnson

Pearls of Wisdom

Tear drops fall
On a cold white face,
Skin like pearls
Entwined with lace,
Unhappiness shows,
In mirrored eyes,
Shining with tears,
Old and wise,
Hands will grasp,
Onto round white pills
At remembrance of him,
Her eyes refill,
The pills go down,
Her smooth red throat,
To death she will sail
On her one–man boat.

Lynn T. Mann

Money Matters

You join the queue
to sign for the dole
a room with a view
a view for a mole.

In the lucky event
you land a job
pay the rent
become a snob.

Borrow some more
just fill in the form
they credit score
then fly off to the warm.

The wolf's at the door
but nobody hears
it's the interest rate
that inflates the arrears.

Makes the world go round
but can't buy me love
the theory was sound
but she gave me the shove.

Carl Roberts

Streets Of Tears

Streets grey as rain, dogs howling
    Can no-one hear the crying
Houses small and cramped like mice
    Can no-one feel the pain
Walls black as soot, cats calling
    Can no-one hear the crying
Floors bare, hard, cold as ice
    Can no-one feel the pain.

Smog from chimney billowing out
    Hail falling, feel the pain
Rain wet running down
    Wind pushing, hear the crying

Hunger breaks like the dawn each day
    Can no-one feel the pain,
Fear as the night, dark and still
    Can no-one hear the crying
Life they call it, death I say
    Can no-one feel the pain
Hell, rivers, streets of tears
    Can no-one hear the crying

June Diggory

Silent World

Oh what is the saying
What are they playing
I haven't a friend
They all play at the street end
Speak more clearly
Yours sincerely the deaf girl rose

You see I can't hear
The doctors say I've nothing to hear
I can lip read
And do brownie deeds
Although I'm in a silent world.

Suzanne Wilson

Soft Candle Glow

Soft candle glow.
Hot, wet kisses long.
Skin upon skin.
Sigh upon sigh.
Hand along thigh.
High upon high.
Cry, cry, cry.

Janet Norman

Labyrinth Of Darkness

Entangled mind
a web of fears,
pleading eyes
spill scalding tears.

Shattered dreams,
loss of hope—
a bleeding heart
that cannot cope.

Twisted thoughts
invade the soul,
evil spirits
take control.

Filled with horror,
crushing dread;
the will to live
a weakened thread.

Silently screaming,
death draws near;
as Angels weep
the Devil cheers.

Karen Bradley

Winds Of Change

The changes that come
With the passing of time
Are hard to imagine
Or even define.

How oft do we say
Could it happen to me?
Only to find
That is sweet reverie.

When things go awry
We are put to the test
And try to respond
It is all for the best.

With friends and companions
Our world takes the shape
Of a pattern of life
Which we cannot escape.

But to lose one of these
Causes pain and deep sorrow.
And makes the wind change
What will happen tomorrow.

Myrtle Regan

Father And Son

We never did see eye to eye
You left so suddenly I had to cry
You were my hero, my man of steel
I could not tell you how I did feel
We seldom talked or raised a glass
Lots of things were never asked
I came to you for just a while
You always used to like my smile
My wooden train you made for me
Now lies beside your rose bush tree
I left it there for you to keep
While you are on your long long sleep.

T. Ward

Why?

Across a thundering ocean,
Across a burning sky,
There dawns a mad devotion,
A will to be alive.

And through the early morning
We feel the bright Sun's cry,
And wonder at the calling
And ask the question, Why?

Grant Stapleton

The Rose

In the centre of my garden
There stands a jewel rare
Tended with such passion
and on such loving care,
Fed with costly blood food
The best in all the land
The Queen of all my garden
There in full splendour stands,
The face of this rare beauty
Blushing pink and red
By God's own hand was painted
As it gave birth there in its bed.
Like a newborn baby
Its head in sweet repose
I fill my heart with wonder
At the beauty of the rose

C. Robinson

Love

I see the colour of the ocean,
I hear the sound of the sea,
I can't seem to control my emotions,
'Cause you're not here with me.

I feel a cool gentle breeze,
pass before my face,
Please say that you love me,
And put my mind at ease.

A lonely boat sails before the sun
The big, bright orange one,
But I'd never leave you on your own.
'Cause you're mine, and mine alone!

Beyond the colour of love,
The moon, the sun and the stars,
I'll be there, wherever you are,
No matter how near or far.

In the dark a candle glows,
And lighten's up the room,
Like the way your feeling shows,
And brightens up my heart.

Farida Parvin

The Sea Trout

She shimmered through the water,
Like a shining piece of steel.
No hook or eye would court her
No tickler's hand would feel.

The silver dart rushed onward
To swim amongst the seal;
Past rocks and moor and homeland
No fisherman's easy meal.

Victoria Fletcher

Unseen Friends

Alone
Not Lonely Alone
I am in a world of
living creatures,
spiders, Woodworms,
Mites
How could I ever say
I am alone
When if I keep very still
and listen
To the Cricket's song
Nesting Birds in my chimney
The Spider overhead
finishing his web,
The woodworms gnawing away
my Chattels,
No I am never alone as
I lie here on a
Bed of Mites.

Lily Dempsey

The Photograph

The seaside memories that follow me,
Cannot forget, although I see,
The sand, the waves, the same blue sky,
You're not here my body sigh.

The velvet grass, we laid embraced,
I look now, can't see your face,
The green still here, but you are not,
Thirty years, have you forgot?

Steam Horses spin, our photo took,
That's all I've got in my red book,
Our arms around each others waist,
Your sparkling eyes, your loving face.

The seaside moon, full and round,
The beach, the kiss, true love I found,
Sadness came, the cruellest fate,
The parting of, our two years date.

Thirty years, have been and gone,
Where are you now, what of our song?
The memories hurt with thoughts anew,
The photographs, it is still you.

Stan Wakefield

A Terrible Life

I'm lying in bed
At this moment in time,
Reading a book,
And eating a dime.

I'm watching a programme,
Bored out of my brains.
The programme I'm watching,
Shows weird old planes.

Our house is in ruins,
The car is the same.
My nan can't walk,
And my parents are lame.

Our pillows are torn,
My sheet is in shreds.
I wish we were rich,
We could do with new beds.

Mum went this morning,
To withdraw her giro.
She couldn't afford to
Buy a new biro!

Simon Carpenter

Witness Of The World

Once more on the door my friend,
I mock thee no, not now,
You always knew of the future end,
Every detail why and how.

Before it came, I knew, I felt,
The world was about to give,
The God, the Lord had all but dealt,
The end. No more the will to live.

I see the praying people's lies,
Each one in vain is just too late,
The chosen few will always rise,
This always was the chosen fate.

All souls in turmoil and despair,
That is all except for them.
The only few who knew the truth
Like Japhet, cham and sem.

Help me please my soul is lost,
My heart and life is fell.
Mine ignorance was so great cost,
The story I thought I'd never tell.

Christopher Humphrey

Web Spinning

She left no shadows on this place
Silent voice, unseen face
Void of dreams that left no trace
Lost
To a passing breeze.

Wary of love that clipped her wings
And held her with restrictive strings
She knew its joys, but felt its stings
Torment
Like raging seas.

Her life became the shifting sand
A stranger in a foreign land
No comfort of a friendly hand
Disquiet
That knew no ease.

Her footmarks left along the lane
Are swept away by morning rain
Never to appear again
Gone
To a sweet release.

Mary-Catherine Holt

A Single Day

From dawn till dusk one single day.
A thousand agonies can portray.
So futile to worry not to live
Not to take but always give
Eternal strife tears one apart
Stifles all love that stops the heart
From "beating" in its natural way
Be natural, why should you fear.
A week, a month, a single year
For each is made of single days.
Down corridors of time we gaze
Then "rest" the day is ended now.
Let sleep renew each furrowed brow.

Grace Davis

My Homeland

Oh my wonderful country
How I love your changing scenes
From your hills awash with heather
To your silvery, rippling streams

Lochs so cool and beautiful
That take my breath away
Oh my beautiful Scotland
I'm blessed by you each day

To look upon your mountains
So tall and in command
What more could I wish for
Than a country that's so grand.

Mary Lowe

Friends

To have met someone like you
is a rare gift for me.
To have such a friend
never comes easy,
someone who cares,
someone sincere.
A friend that can make me smile,
A friend who's there all the time.

Friends may come,
Friends may go,
but there won't be anyone
like the you I know.

Forever, it'll be easy for me
to hold you in some part of my memory.
Forever, I hope you agree
you'll always have a friend in me.

Esosa

Baby I Love You . . .

Baby I love you,
I wish you would see,
We're perfect together,
Just you and me.
So come with me baby,
I'll show you the way,
To a place of love and romance,
If you would just give me a chance.
I'll be your baby,
As long as you're mine,
And I promise you baby,
We'll have a good time.
Baby I love you,
I hope now you can see,
We're perfect together,
Just you and me!

Shelly Summerhayes

Summer Night

Sweet scent of that summer night,
Taste of kisses pure delight.

Feel of arms so strong and sure,
Wanting it forever more —

Hold me close for I'm all thine,
Speak to me of love divine,
No more passion fierce confine —

Music from the surging sea
Makes it so it ought to be

Just a moment caught in time
Underneath the whispering pine,

While sea gulls' wild plaintive cry
Drifts away on breeze's sigh,

Through an azure moonlit sky.

Laura Edwards

Rich Man Poor Man

Love and peace divided
black and white at war.
Rich man undecided
what to use poor man for.

Injustice all around
protests fall on deaf ears.
Solutions not to be found
why? Corrupt why? Unclear.

No homes, no food, no TV
who cares for the nation.
Right and wrong won't agree
little chance of salvation.

Pressures mounting, people crying
self respect taken away.
Money, power, people dying
pollution wasting our world today.

Noreen McFadden

Where There Is Love

I often wish that I could fly
Fly high above, float in the sky
I would fly high high above
I would fly where there was love

Long time gone the love we knew
No one to trust to be true
Live and die, fight and cry
I'm going now so bye bye

Up in the sky my troubles go
No one to hate no one I know
Peace is here and so is love
Come fly with me high above

Barbara Green

Swallows

My love's bed lies empty,
soft and downy white.
He is gone, Dear Lord I must
not linger here and yearn.
The swallows home to eaves,
with their swift skimming lovely
flight,
Whilst I wait here, for him
who never will return.

B. E. Grange

Sleep

Hush-sh now, not a peep,
As I quietly creep
To my soft warm bed.
To lay down my weary head.

I am so tired,
Could really weep.

Just let me sleep,
A sleep deep, down deep.

Let there be silence in the night.
So that tomorrow
I will awaken with delight.
Amen.

Jess Cane

My Secret Garden

I have a secret garden.
It's all my very own.
It has a door and hidden key,
and a wall all round of stone.

Once inside my eyes behold,
the lovely things that grow,
border plants and roses
and veggies in a row.

As I walk the winding path
to sit beneath the trees
I hear the sound of calling birds
the buzz of busy bees.

And as I sit there silently
I say a little prayer
for all the beauty that I see
and all His loving care.

So when you see me dreaming
and my thoughts seem far away
I'm in my secret garden,
On a lovely summer's day.

Linda Catherall (neé Monk)

May Day

She slipped her small hand
into my roughened palm
"For fear I would run away",
I warned my golden–haired grandchild.
Her walk a dance, feather–light.
Baby shoes barely
tipped the meadow grass
Hers was joy in motion.
My hand cradled a fledgling
poised for flight.
Her bubbling life-sap
surged through my heart
easing out memories
of fragmented hopes, lost dreams
of my own childhood.

Ours a brief meeting of
spring and winter
bonded on our journey
in a flesh–love embrace.

Colette Cryan

The Old Banger

The engine is her heart
The plugs are her spark of life
Through her filter is the air she
Breathes, and the oil is her
Blood through her veins
The battery gives her life
But will never run down,
But occasionally may splutter,
The bodywork may be getting on
And slightly dented, but she
Keeps going, giving me
Pleasure and love to my life

Lancashire Lad

Voice Of The Average

So as we lumber on
Through a world, light on achievement
Heavy on defeat
Potential haemorrhaging from every pore
We reach out,
Steady ourselves in the sterilised
Chill of your shadow
We know you
We mourned when you died
We bathed when you shone
Your glory is our glory
It was us who whispered your name
In the theatres and bars
Till the whisper grew wings
Became a rallying cry
And you were a god for a day

Ian Morris

An Opposite Attraction

Summer's evening in July,
I remember thee,
He was tall and dark and lean
A dream come true

He was quiet, I was loud
Could this be an opposite attraction?
I couldn't tell if I liked him,
Half an hour isn't long,
Could this be an opposite attraction?

Are we different or the same?
Is he shy or is he my dream?
Could I tell if I met him once more?
Could this be an opposite attraction?

A lot of questions, nothing clear,
I'm confused, by him my dear
Is he shy or is he not?
He never seems to say a lot,
Could this be an opposite attraction?

Elizabeth Moffat

Untitled

It came,
lurking in the mist,
in darkness,
enveloping.
Searching,
scrutinizing,
questioning.
It had no soul,
no tangible existence.
Yet it was pondering,
studying,
absorbing its surroundings.
Trying to perceive,
to disclose why.
It retreated into the mist,
into darkness,
and then departed.

Sarah Nichols

"Flowers In Springtime"

I look out my window,
What do I see.
Yellow heads of daffodils,
Looking back at me.

There are crocuses,
Lilac, blue and white.
Primroses and bluebells,
Such a pretty sight.

There are birds singing,
On the grass so green.
Trees in pink blossom,
I have never seen.

I look out my window
What do I see,
Snowdrops glistening in the sunlight

They look so pure,
They look so bright.
The flowers in spring,
By the sunlight.

Annette Carver

Silence Is Nature

Silence is nature
Stillness all around
trees tower into the air,
clouds stuck in the sky,
silence is nature.

Insects tiptoeing
on the bare land,
corn field quiet,
rocks every shade of grey,
silence is nature.

Not a bird in sight,
nor a whimper of wind,

Silence is nature.

Melanie Man

The Rose

The sweetest smelling fragrance
Everybody knows
Is the beautiful scarlet flower
"The one they call the rose"

For couples who are sweethearts
So the legend goes
Always give their loved ones
"The beautiful scarlet rose"

It means I will always love you
As the years roll by
And I will always be there
Till one of us should die

The moral of this verse
So the legend goes
Is always treat your loved one like
"The one they call the rose"

T. G. Hawes

Freedom

What I'd only give to be like you
No care in the world, nothing to do
No more anger, no more hate
Always having time never be late
How I'd love to soar up high
Beside the wind I would fly
Looking down at the world around
Sheltering from life inside a cloud
Going afar, where I like
Faster than the speed of light
My life all filled with love and glee
How great it would feel if I were free

Lisa Daulby

Wishing Life Away

Why do we wish our lives away
Why can't we be content
With the day that we've been given
So that it is wisely spent.

Why did we want to be grown up
When we were very small
Why did we feel it was unfair
That we were not yet tall.

Why do we wish for the future
Next day, next week, next year
It could be worse not better
Than the day that we have here.

What age I've next to wonder
Do we start to be content
Feeling really satisfied
With the day that we've just spent.

I know its human nature
To want for something more
I only hope we find it
Before we close the final door.

Patricia E. Churchman

"The Coming Of Age!"

Don't be afraid to grow old,
It comes with every day,
Just learn to take what is to be,
and the games to play.

Take the rough and smooth together,
And climb the highest hill,
Then look back on your life's journey,
Have you had your fill?

We've all been young and foolish,
But you grow wise with age,
Don't put life's book down or close it,
Read every single page.

Have a go at everything,
You can do it if you try,
Don't say "I can't be bothered",
Don't let that chance go by.

Don't leave things until tomorrow
Or say "I haven't time",
all your life's for learning
it's too late when you die.

Janet W. Woolgar

I Never Said I Loved You

I never said I love you,
we never said goodbye,
once or twice I thought of it,
but felt silly when I tried.

I thought I'd tell you tomorrow,
or maybe a day next week,
I remember now I told you once,
but made sure you were asleep.

Time it beat us both,
it sneaked up way too fast,
the only time I see you now,
are in photos of the past.

I wish I could turn back the clock,
if only for a day,
I'd tell you then I know I would,
the things I wish to say.

You were always there when I stumbled,
helped cheer me when I cried,
but I never said I loved you
I never said goodbye.

Martin Moran

Breakdown

Dismal, dreary, dark and dank,
Akin to devil's lair,
Meandering and menacing,
Teasing thoughts that dare,
Silent stirring, shadows shoot,
Flighty as they flitter,
Breathless, breezy, icy touch,
Brain cells all a-jitter,
A soaring mass, a spacious void,
Brimmed with guilt unknown,
Concealed within the inner mind,
Where dread and fears are grown,
Latent, lurking, lingering,
Waiting for the kill,
Unsuspecting, then it hits,
Emotions thrown at will!

Shirley Mulder

Dad

Dear Dad, I love and miss you still.
I know you were so very ill,
And now you must be out of pain,
But how I wish you back again.
You left Mother on her own,
Like an autumn leaf she is blown.
She is so lost, that is true,
A little of my heart has gone with you.

We were so close in a quiet way,
Although not a lot you had to say.
The shrub you grew before you left,
I stand beside when I feel bereft.
While there, I talk to you and find
Solace, and a peace of mind.

I love you still and always will.
Life moves on, I've climbed the hill.
Several years now have passed
But the sense of loss will always last.

Gillian S. Roberts

First Love

Every day, I saw him,
Every day, I spoke to him,
I knew him so well.
But inside my head,
I wished he would never leave.

Every day I watched
His lips, tracing them,
My only way of hearing.
Silent world and silent love,
That only led to despair.

He never was and
Never will be mine.
I loved him, I hoped my
Voice wasn't strange to him.
If only I had heard his voice too.

Hannah R. Waugh

School Persecution

As I turn round she's staring.
I look—her eyes are glaring.
My name is called and I cringe;
"You are to blame", she does whinge.
"No", I shout, "It wasn't me!"
"Detention. Monday. Then we'll see!"
I am always getting blamed;
I wish teachers could be tamed.
She picks on me not on you;
Blames me for things I don't do!
It makes me extremely mad
And sometimes I get quite sad.
Life's bad enough already,
Without her making it more unsteady!

Elizabeth Cole

Sea Of Dreams

Green, green,
deep sea green,
waters flow
for all to see,
elegant quest,
elegant time,
mistress of the deep
sea of thine,
numerous enemies
none so proud
as the sea of dreams,
my invisible shroud.

Shelagh Ann McKeown

Trees In Bloom

I saw it when it burst in bloom
That leafy cherry tree,
As though a sweet red curtain hung
Between the sky and me.

Whilst growing near, adorned in white,
A taller tree rose higher,
As though its graceful waving boughs
Would challenge the church spire.

It brought me such deep happiness
The sight of those two trees,
I felt a sense of gratitude
And thanked God on my knees.

G. E. Chambers

Free Spirit

This pain I can take no more,
Please won't you let me die?
Undo these earthly shackles,
And let my spirit fly.

I could ride upon the raindrops,
or sit amongst the trees.
Drink the dew from flowers,
Or sip nectar with the bees.

Maybe paint a rainbow
across an April sky.
Or sit up there in heaven,
And watch the clouds drift by.

I could skip amongst the bluebells,
that carpet forest floor.
Go down to hear the seagull cry
and run along the shore.

But I'm locked here in this body,
racked and riddled with pain.
So please won't you release me,
that I may be free again?

Valerie Williams

Night To Day

Turn out the light
And close the curtain
For here comes the night
Where nothing is certain

As the night calls
And noise dies down
The darkness falls
To cover the town

Take down the moon
Let the stars fall
As dawn will come soon
And day will not stall

The world has woken
Out comes the sun
Morning has broken
A new day's begun

Rebecca J. Whittingham

Quo Vadis?

Who will blame Icarus
For ten double decker
Bus loads of travellers
Thrown at a mountain?

Or Einstein
For the people shadows
Burnt in an instant
On Nagasaki streets?

Or Nobel
For the milk churn
Nail bomb
In the rush hour?

Or the reclaimed toddler
For his torn trousers?

Graham Searle

En Route To The Algarve Spring 95

I never thought I'd miss you
I never wanted to.
I wanted to avoid that pain
But still inside it grew.

You cannot have the comfort,
The warmth, the love, that part
Without you sacrifice the space
And open up your heart

And yes we die as we are born,
Essentially alone.
But why feel forced to practise that
Which you could just postpone.

I guess it's fear of fettering,
The trap of such emotion,
So we could never bear to be
Apart, across some ocean.

It would be very limiting,
Would hurt to go away.
But as we age I wonder,
What's freedom's price today?

Angela M. Story

Awakening

Dawn strokes my eyes,
I rise,
First, with my cats,
To own the morning
Beneath far blue skies
Cain lies,
Somewhere, somewhere else,
Honing his hatred

Elizabeth Cobban

Your War

If only you hadn't bought that gun.
You thought it was a toy.
If only you stopped to think a while.
You never even listened.
If only you didn't pull that trigger.
You shouldn't have lost
your temper.
If only those people didn't copy.
You should have said,
"It is wrong"
If only people could have stopped
and seen what they have done.
Then they could see how others suffer.
If only you hadn't bought that gun.
You thought it would be
fun not knowing it
would cause a

"War."

Stacey Leanne Dickinson

O, My Love

O, my love thou long ago,
 Dark and lovely as thou art,
As dark art thou my bonnie lad,
 But dream through the day,

O, my love thou long ago,
 But I am urge—
By tender confession,
O, my love thou long ago,
Dark and lovely as thou art.

O, my love thou long ago
 O, let me shire,
No other love but thine,
O, my love thou long ago

O, my love thou long ago
I smell the sweet flowers and trees,
 And hear the wild birds singing,
 But my secret love,
Is no secret any more,
I even told the golden daffodils,
 Of our love thou long ago

June Bloomfield

Observation

Wisdom is so wonderful
it isn't for the young.
It comes from doing lots of things
and having lots of fun.

With age there is experience
of things you've done before.
But with mistakes already made
you'll always make some more.

You try to teach the young ones
the best rules to apply.
But do they ever listen? No!
They're the same as you and I.

When you're young you know it all,
you tell everybody else.
But later when you learn much more
you keep it to yourself.

Wisdom comes with age they say
according to the rule.
If you can't get old and wiser
then don't get old at all.

John E. Regan

"Bellamy's Wisdom"

Pwants and gweens are life to me
After all it's ecology
Twees chopped down I cannot stand
Why do we wuin our fair land

There is pweasure in a fwog
leaping over a sawn–off wog
But for better to behold
The twee untouched and standing bold

The powuting of our soil
It wealy wealy makes me boil
We even powute our air
But Government don't seem to care

It bweaks my heart to see man
Giving our pwanet a short span
If only he know pwofits
lay in the earth which he forfeits

It is the short–term pwanning
At the expense of long–term gain
That not only baffles me
It's dwiving me bweeding insane

John Sanderson

Sound Is Everywhere

Listen with your ear,
A sound you may hear,
A squeak of a mouse,
A creak of a house,
The tweet of a bird,
I'm sure I heard.

Listen with your ear,
A sound you may hear,
A twang of a guitar,
The chatter in a bar,
The roar of a car,
Outside and afar

Listen with your ear,
A sound you may hear,
The rain on a window,
And the tune on a piano,
Ticking of the clocks,
The sea against the rocks.
Sound is everywhere

Jenny Crampton

Life's Path

Gentle leaf swirling down,
Gently hovering to the ground.
Moving swiftly with the breeze,
Floating around completely at ease.
In one fell swoop everything's changed,
The wind has decided to rearrange.
Like a dagger in the heart,
This world has been torn apart.
Completely destroyed and taken away,
It has been left astray.
Terrified and all alone,
In a scary world unknown.

Clayre Waugh

Flowers

Flowers are so beautiful
all the colours I see
and watch the honey bee
busy as can be.
The colours on the flowers I see
are so beautiful and bright
they make the garden light,
a very pretty sight
The garden looks so beautiful
with all the flowers in it
they make me smile all the
while I like flowers.

Natalee Brehaut

Loneliness

Why do I sit alone,
Withdrawn, within my shell,
When there are people passing by
And some I know so well?
Why do I do nothing
When there are lots of things to do,
Like reading books that interest me
On subjects old and new?
What makes my life so empty
What is it bothering me,
Surely there's more to living
Than these four walls I see?
Why can't I make an effort
Just what is stopping me,
What must I do to help myself
To live, and to be free?
I know that I can do it,
The question is just when
Can I shake off this burden,
And start to live again?

D. E. Miller

A Man

A man's a man
No matter what
The colour of his skin maybe
Or the fact he doesn't fancy me
So why does he have to hide
Scared of what he feels inside
A man's a man
Even if he cannot see
Even if he cannot walk like you and me
A man still deserves to live
And give all he's got to give
A man's a man
No matter what the mirror shows
Or even what the future holds
This poem holds a simple message
A man's a man don't you forget it

J. M. Sheppard

The Lightship

Goodbye the lightship
Farewell the foam
Lower the lamp
That guided men home

Iron–grip anchor
Rock of the squall
Resting on, rusting on
Some harbour wall

Alas the light man
Pacing the strand
Driven ashore by
Technology's hand

Progress, ah Progress!
Insatiable mole
Dark road to nowhere
Behind, a dark hole

Light on the water
Friend you burned true
And it matters not saviour
We were glad to see you

Bob MacAlindin

Sub-Conscience

Frail fingers
of returning reason
grope the sodden web
of retarded sub-conscience
impeding mouth and eyes.

Through fog as cold and grey
as an eternity
of winter afternoons
I seek those
who strive to meet me

Sarah Barker

The Book Of Life

Another chapter has ended
yet another has just begun
The book that they call life
Is not always full of fun
But now the past is behind
Only the future lies ahead
I don't know what it will behold
Nothing for certain can be said
But the book remains unfinished
For it can never be complete
As we travel through the chapters
Page by page
No one knows what is ahead of them
They will meet

Faye Robinson

Our Dreamtime

Along a pathway dreamily
I wandered once with you
Along a winding riverbank
Through meadows that we knew.

The summers were so endless then
The happy days went by
But our chosen path soon ended
and we said a last goodbye.

We went along our separate ways
Not stopping once for rest
Now the dreams we dream of yesterday
Will always be the best.

Wendy Kay Brandon

Photo Album

Looking at the pictures
From present and past
Wondering why
The years went so fast

Memories caught in a moment
For all to see
Frozen in time
Are the things that used to be

A cheerful smiling face
From a while ago
In a place
I do not know

Some of the faces
Are no longer around
But in the photo album
They can always be found

Gail Timms

"Spring"

Leaves rustle along the ground,
    Summer's gone, trailing her gown.
    Blown, by the winds of Autumn.
But the wind is fickle, and on the hill
Turns, to beckon Winter on.
Who soon will come,
    In mantle white.
Shrouding, every thing in sight
Then with a mighty roar he'll go!
    And in the distant "echo"
You'll hear the "Voice of Spring"
With gentle fingers,
    she'll touch the earth.
Awakening Nature into birth.

Alice Walsh

Flowers Of Spring

First there is the snowdrop
Shyly peeping through
Even where the snow is thick
Still it surprises you
With its little cap of white
Huge banks are there to see
I will go and pick a bunch
And give them all to thee
Look! There is a crocus
And clumps of daffodils
Wild primroses in the hedges
And cowslips in the hills
I know where to find them
Each year I watch them grow
I'll fill your arms with bluebells
If you will with me go
We'll clamber over hill and vale
In the springtime of your years
For I will show you lovely things
And wipe away your tears.

Elsie Hollis

'Hello I'm Here'

Hello I'm here, I'm real,
Let me in, speak to me,
I want to join in.

Hello I'm here, I do exist,
I'm in the same room,
They talk to each other but
somehow I'm missed.

Hello I'm here, I'm going to speak,
They stop, they listen,
But they do not hear.

Hello I'm here, but do they
even know,
Would anyone notice if I got
up to go,
Sad to say but the truth is no.

J. Gatenby

The Fairy

Flirting with a Butterfly
Skipping in the breeze
Silly frothy dress she wears
Floating round her knees

Sunbathing on a lily leaf
Splashing with a frog
Playing kiss chase in the grass
Snoozing on a log

Sitting on a toadstool
Kicking at a stone
Looking down from treetops high
Watching the water foam

Batting lengthy eyelashes
Wiggling tiny fingers
Trying to look demure (but she can't)
She's mischievous Fairy Belinda

Gilian Kitching

The Sands Of Time

Through the valley of time
I have walked and ran with you my love
to find our hearts' desire

Through calm and troubled waters
we have wandered
but I will never tire till
we reach the end of our valley
and find the beautiful garden of Eden

And at the going down of the sun
we all return to dust and
again become lost
in the sands of time

Robert Bartch

Hot Air Balloons

Hot air balloons are
puffy, very fluffy
Huge pumpkins in the sky
2 of them is spy.
Floating, bloating
bursting through the air
my dogs and I
just stare,
Amazed and dazed,
As they move closer
in a pair.
Nearer and nearer
Now threatening
as they dare
Start landing were
we're standing,
wind rushing
through our hair!

Tina Moore

Untitled

Wouldn't it be wonderful
If all the wars could cease?
If everyone put down their guns
Declaring worldwide peace.
If Catholic and Protestant
Could just for once agree,
If the black folk and the white folk
Would shake hands amicably.
If we could work together
To end the trouble and strife
If each allowed the other one
Their own opinions in life
If everyone could only try
Giving instead of taking
If we could only realise
The mistakes we are all making
If we could be less selfish
And try a gentle way,
And listen to other points of view—
We might have peace one day.

Diana Newman

Ground Swell

Beneath the vastness of the sky,
Betwixt the twinkling of the eye,
The quartet in harmony dwell
Within the softly silent swell.

Transfixed by one discerning mark,
Dappled with the mossy bark
Of seas that calmly rage within,
Where all the elements begin.

Heavenly anchored by the mast,
Entreats them to the journey vast.
In sight of man made safety sure,
They venture onward softly pure.

A habitat for earthly bound,
Beyond that hindered silent sound.
Snow white the boat's cool heated deck,
Entices wanton cares for wreck.

With the elements cool caress,
I draw them with life giving breath,
To dwell in life upon my mind
With others of a precious kind.

Mark Young

The Sun

The sun glitters in the sea,
It shines right on me,
It's golden and like an egg,
It's burning and my head,
It's beautiful on yellow.
It's like a bouncing ball,
It's got a yellow golden crown,
The Summer-Summer Sun.

Abigail Powell

Untitled

"God grant me the serenity"
To be the things that I must be
To give my life to care for others
Then with time when I discover
I've lost my teeth
My hair is dyed
My figure's committed suicide
The family is gone
All flown the coup
No more nappies
No more croup
Then give me grace I pray to thee
That if my NHS specs still see
Let me fill each day with fun
Now that my work and toil are done

Diane McMillan

Into The Light

I was walking through the meadow
When I saw this wondrous light
It was pink, lilac, blue and gold
It transformed the gloomy night

I felt it pulling me closer
Right into its central core
It was then I heard the music
I yearned to see much more

Up ahead there were figures
They were hazy and not very plain
I wanted to be amongst them
I reached out, but then felt the pain

The pain was pulling me backwards
Out of the wondrous light
"Hold on" the voices told me
"Please don't give up the fight"

I'm back in the land of the living
They saved my life that day
No fears of death do I harbour
Now the light has shown me the way

Christine Hickling

Winter Days

When I retired the grass was green
    The stars were shinning bright
But while I slept the earth had changed
    To a glorious dazzling white.

The little shrubs had disappeared
    Beneath this snowy bed
And I saw a robin standing near
    In a little coat of red.

The sturdy oaks were laden
    With quantities of snow
And evergreens were smiling
    With a fascinating glow.

A fox had left some footprints
    As he travelled on his way
To reach a quiet woodland
    At the ending of the day.

Barn owls called from yonder glen
    To herald in the night
Thus winter days had filled me
    With a season of delight.

Margory Green

Tarmac And Green

The new roads spread across the land
And juggernauts abound,
While night and day are ears assailed
By noise that shakes the ground.

Yet here and there the country lanes
Still twist and turn and wind,
By fields and trees and tiny streams
The world has left behind.

And here and there, yes even now,
The wild flowers show their faces;
And those of us who loved the past
Are grateful for their graces.

The countryside that we once knew
Has changed beyond compare,
But yet, some quiet woodlands show
That beauty lingers there.

The new roads run where bluebells grew
And orchards once were seen;
But still the cottage gardens bloom,
And look, the hills are green.

Jean Shephard

Mountains Made Of Earth And Stone

Mountains made of earth and stone
so many exits to my home, no fear
have I of working hard, just keep
on plodding yard by yard.

Below the ground I live and stay
till darkness brings the end of
day; then up I pop my mountain
made, free to tunnel field or glade

A little devil, some might say,
when on their cared–for lawn I
stray, they'd like to gas and
wipe me out, but I'll live on
without a doubt, for God, He
made me to dig holes. He cares
a lot for little moles.

T. A. Gardner

A Request For Peace

Death
Oh sweet death
Hold out your hand
So I may take it
Show me your mercy
And take away this pain
Let me feel peace
I'm going insane
Let me be one
With those up above
Leave my body
To turn to dust
Give me a gift
That gift of death
Wrapped up in a coffin
Dressed in a black dress
Bunches of white roses
Lying on my breasts
Oh death, sweet friend
Let me rest.

Melissa Gardner

Imagination

There is a very special box
I wonder what's inside
Magic spells will undo the locks
What treasure does it hide

A sticky lolly red and bright
Or a fairy's dream
Winged horses ready for flight
Jewels fit for a queen

Golden strands so very fair
A crystal stream so near
A silken cloak for you to wear
Nothing you should fear

There is as well a genie's lamp
A wizard is there too
I can even see a gypsy camp
What you see is up to you.

Jill Maxine Harris

Beauty

She has the most beautiful body
With glorious raven hair
So as she passes by
You turn your head and stare
Her gorgeous eyes and pathos face
Will win your heart no end
When snuggling up her head to yours
Expectant of a friend
Her silhouette imprints your mind
There is no doubt of that
A most beautiful horse you've ever seen
An unashamed aristocrat.

J. Yates

Beauty So Simple

The dawn is now breaking,
Beauty it is making,
The birds are awaking
Above the hills they begin flying
Dew on the grass is glistening
While the breeze is softly whistling
Through the leaves
On the strong tree standing
Flowers are all opening
While animals are a-scurrying
The sun begins a shining
Wait! See the streams a-glistening
All the beauty of the countryside

Maureen Wilson

The Swan Of Avon

In river reflection
Like Prospero's crystal,
Did you see
Your crystalline plumes of Destiny
Gliding serenely on the
Waters of Time?
The music of your words
Soft as the murmuring of a brook
Cascading with the beauty of
A waterfall,
And mighty as a Tempest at sea,
Awash with mystic colours
of the First Rainbow after the Flood
Yet white and pure as the Swans
Of your native river,
Always elegant, full of grace,
Like your Spirit,
Flying free,
Reflected forever
In Waters of Time!

Victoria Verdi

Evening

An evening's torn fragments,
mesmerised forgetfulness
as a blue haze crept,
where shallows a river.
Drawn hues hover
cleansing drained thoughts
for a new day.

Douglas Scott

Good Fortune??

When fortune smiles on someone else
    And sunshine fades away
Trust in yourself and hopefulness
    There's always another day
Keep faith with all that you hold dear
    When everything seems lost
Look forward's to tomorrow
    Don't dwell on what it cost
Never look back in anger
    Give chance another say
For fortune smiles on everyone
    It may be, your turn today!

M. V. Worthington

Flamingos and Roses

We learnt one day (and this is true)
On our visit to the zoo
That if you take a flamingo
Plant it, daily weed and hoe
In the soil of a rose bed
That the two can be interbred
Pot the result and on your shelf
A rose bush that can prune itself

Stan Pastie

The Deer

The morning opened cold and white
No sun shone through the cloud
The birds were silent in the trees
The snow a dazzling shroud
I walked a path through virgin snow
And then I stopped to gaze
The memory of what I saw
Will haunt me all my days
A deer lay dying at my feet
Its blood spilled on the ground
His eyes beseeching looked my way
He uttered not a sound
I stooped and gently stroked his head
And saw his life's light dim
How cruel is this world of ours
To kill the likes of him

Joyce Craddock

Untitled

Was it time, was it time
  I held my breath
  I lay there so quietly
  Surrounded by warmth
Was it time was it time
I could feel the cool breeze
I looked up at last and
  Saw the trees
At last at last
  With the coming of dawn
The time had come
  A new rose was born

H. Lancaster

One Special Rose

The first rose of summer,
one special red rose,
from our own garden grown.
That was his way really,
showing me dearly.
how much he loved me,
now I see them with tears.
Thirteen years have gone by.
So many lonely days and nights
since he laid down and died,
without any warning.
But he is still near me,
with God's help he is at peace.
When I think of that,
I know the reason why.
So goodnight and God bless
you my dear,
with all my tears and
"Memories"
"Of one special red rose".

V. M. Moore

Disease

You!
You took a friend!
You take thousands of lives every year
Why?
What have they done?
So innocent!
Yet you take their lives!
Don't you care?
They deserve better!
The worry! The sorrow!
The anger! The pain!
Surely this is not right!
Some live,
With the fear that you may come back
Go!
Go away!
Can't you see you're not wanted?

Nikki-Ann Trow

Requiem For The Whale

Hear my cry, 'civilized man.'
Fathoms deep in oceans wild.
Why do you hunt me, maim and kill?
When I am as trusting as a child.

Roaming proud the seas forever,
Graceful it seems, to all but man.
Surely you can see despair
Please, I charge you, change your plan.

Realisation may come too late.
You will destroy a friend indeed.
Let me go my peaceful way.
Forget temptation, lustful greed.

Douglas Boughton

Nothing Left

Tomorrow never comes
Today remains a memory
Yesterday is in the past
The future never lasts.

My eyes weep with sorrow
My heart aches with pain
The love I had inside me
It was fighting in vain

Sitting in the shadows
With darkness all around
Should I repent my deadly sins
or be buried in the ground

I haven't much to offer
There isn't much to take
Someone has already done that job
Wiped me out for their own sake.

Louise Clarke

Daisies

Nodding in the summer light
Here and there are seen
The pretty little daisies white
So pure their petals are
And sometimes tipped with red
Each nods its little head
But when the daylight doth depart
And evening clouds there be
Why then we cannot see
Their golden hearts

C. A. Fletcher

My Grandson

Sweet darling, my grandson
what do I see
a beautiful baby
looking at me.

With eyes that are big
the colour of the sea
O beautiful baby
looking at me

Your face is a picture
so fair and petite
O beautiful baby
looking at me.

You'll grow up so fast
before my eyes will see
an impish young boy
looking at me.

Before very long
an adult you'll be
I'll see a handsome young man
looking at me.

Linda M. Stott

To My Husband

A gorgeous gift from God is he.
An angel sent to care for me.
And through the weeks when I am ill
He manages to love me still.
When I fall deep into despair
His loving arms surround me there.
When drugs replace my joy with fear
He says the words I need to hear.
He comforts me when I am sad.
He laughs with me when I am glad.
I trust in him. I know he'll stay.
I lean on him. I know he'll pray.
Oh thank you for this gift divine
A spirit filled man who is so fine.

Irene Green

Alone

Standing alone in the shadows,
a moment away from defeat.
People they wander right past me,
never looking at who I could be.

"Help me", I say to one passer,
"I'm lost without any home.
Tell me your secret to freedom,
my life, it wants to move on".

But still I stand here weeping.
It's lonely and cold in the night.
And I ask my soul for forgiveness,
to make it through alright.

Carol Bowers

The Castle

The castle looks down
on the higgldy piggldy roof tops
of the little town,
beyond lie meadows
where fat cattle graze,
and a few centuries earlier
battles did rage.
An army came led by a King
the castle was sacked,
now in its ruins
blackbirds sing,
within its walls
knights did eat and laugh,
today it is a sleeping giant
with a mysterious past.

Jean Williams

Reality

Marriage is not made in heaven
It's made right here on earth
Only what you both put in it
Makes it what it's worth
Get to know each other
Learn from your mistakes
Love and understanding
A little give and take
It's really just like making a cake
Corny, yes but true
You have all the finest ingredients
The rest is up to you.

Catherine Armstrong

Melanie At 16

She used to have a dirty face
But now she's very clean
But is very understanding
Because she's sweet sixteen

Ida Coe

Always

One moment in a lifetime
when eyes meet and lock
It seemed I'd known you always
This feeling that I got

Within a second
our souls embraced
It seemed I'd known you always
When I gazed upon your face

How can someone be this close
Someone I do not know
it seemed I'd known you always
And this feeling just won't go

Your life was far removed
And different from mine
It seemed I'd known you always
Somewhere, some place, sometime

A special friend you've now become
A friend indeed to me
It seems I've known you always
And you have known me.

Lesley Baker

Alone

Gone are the long days of summer
Chill is the autumn morn
Since you went and left me
Left me here alone

My heart went with you,
That morning, when through
No fault of your own
The angel of death came for
You, and left me here alone

If we had not gone out that
morning, and then if we never had met.
I would never had known what love was
But you might have been here yet
I thank God for the time I knew you.
And all the love you shown
But gone are the long days of summer
And still I am here all alone

Linda Scott

The Cat

The cat went out in the street
The cat went down the lane
I wonder what she'll find
Maybe she'll find a friend
I hope she finds her way back again

Sian Salmon

Parents

If we could go to yesteryear
And live our lives again
We'd keep with us our wisdom
But not take back the pain

Our lives would run just like a dream
With happiness not sad
And we would never make mistakes
The perfect mum and dad.

We'll listen to our children
A privilege not a chore
And follow their lives with interest
Then love them even more

We could not freeze this time we had
The years went skipping by
The children made their way in life
And sadly said goodbye

Linda Dance

Indecision

Whilst walking in the forest
the path came to a fork
I did not know which way was best
then I heard an old tree talk

"You do not know which way to take
but where do you want to be?
The choice won't be so hard to make
if you take a tip from me!"

"If right is wrong
then left is right . . .
Am I making sense to you?"

"But if left is wrong
then right is right . . .
and surely that is true"

"And what's right for me
may be wrong for you . . .
a fact you must agree"

"So all in all the final choice
must be down to you!"

Mike Kent

Woman

Woman,
Mother friend, lover
She fights a daily battle
to win the love, affection
understanding she deserves and
craves for
To find it is to behold truth.
Can you really grasp at the
gentle exterior and feel the strength
of the lion the protector in one?

Sarah Tappin

The Pebble

Another year has passed you by
you sit and sometimes wonder why
But like a pebble on the shore
Move to and through and gain no more
Until one day a tide so high
Lifts you up and makes you fly
The force of this you are not sure
But look in deeper there is more
God has thrown out His helping hand
'Cos on the beach you'd turn to sand
A pebble all alone you see
The strongest stone will always be
But on a beach with thousands more
Erosion will take its score
So alone you should stand
And you will never turn to sand
You think you've got the cruellest deal
But you will find it is not real
So eyes should open so should mind
And one true love you will find

G. Carter

Evening's Splendour

O give me time to stop and gaze
And see the wonders of Your hands;
The fiery sun beyond the trees,
The wheat a growing o'er the land.

The lark a soaring—O so high
I hear her, but I cannot see;
Let me God's handiwork admire,
And be alone at peace with thee.

The poppies a-dazzling in the sun
And honeysuckle's perfume rare;
The wild flowers each new day are born
And tell me of my Maker's care.

Olive Luetchford

Granddad

You are the best,
better than any of the rest.
I love you very dearly,
I hope you see that clearly.
I love you lots and lots,
I hope you know that really.

James Carrington-Howell

A Husband Is Just A Word

I lost my husband
A husband is just a word

I lost my best friend
My lover till the end

My security my feeling
My life's now full with grieving

I have an empty space
I need to fill its place

The pain it is so real
My heart will never heal

I lost all laughter and sense of fun
I lost my confidence to act as one

Any man can be a husband
A husband is just a word.

Sharon Dee Vanriel

The Silence Of School

The deafening bell rang.
350 clattering feet rush
through the halls.
There was silence
No bell
No clattering feet.
Not a child in sight
every class was full.

Lindsay Lewis

It's Cold

Twinkling dew scattered around,
twirling snowflakes fall
to the ground.

Run out in the morning
see the crystal snow,
it crumbles in your hand,
as the chilly winds blow.

Glinting, glistening,
glowing and glare
the ice stays frigid,
at Jack Frost's stare.

His bare, raw, dead, fingers
make me dread,
that on this chilly morning
I should have stayed in bed!

Kimberley Lilley

Don't

Don't let life pass you by
look—a silver lining in the sky
set a goal, work to a plan
don't become an also ran.

While you're living and in good health
don't just sit there on the shelf
life's experiences you can share
the opportunities are always there.

Whether you be woman or man
do the very best you can
don't live in sorrow, do not grieve
look at what you can achieve.

B. Harris

I Needed Him

I needed him, please forgive me,
I know you love him, but so do I.
I have put it right for myself and
for you please understand!

I love you too, that why I took him
I wanted part of you here with me.
I know you love me, and I you,
please forgive me!

Because you gave to me so freely
I will give to you.
Thank you for loving me that much
He is safe with me, so are you!
As you love him so much, yet trusted
me, I will watch over you!

Jacqueline Green

The Parting

The boat slipped from the Island shore,
I turned to watch the long dark land,
My eyes were wet, my heart was sore,
I'd hold no more my father's hand.

The moon shone in the starry dome,
I saw the Needles and the Downs,
I'd know no more the joys of home,
The villages and little towns,

No more high jinks at Compton Bay,
Or galloping along the sand,
Nor walking Downs at break of day
Or in the sunset, hand in hand.

I sat astern, and wept again,
And heard the water splash the side
As we sat waiting on the main,
In the slack water, for the tide.

And then the bell and half-ahead,
And on beside the ooze we ran
To that far shore without the dead,
Without my Dad, so fine a man.

Jenny Duckworth

Life's Dream

If life is but a dream,
Then one day I shall wake up,
To find I've slept away the years
I should have spent with you.
It's not too late to change the dream,
Fulfil it while you can.
Live each minute of each day,
Or life will pass you by.

Patricia Yates

To War

Have you been to war friend
Did you see men die
Have you seen their bloodshed
And listen to them cry
A broken man an empty shell
Returning from the fight
The ghost of a man you once knew well
Who fought for what seemed right
No gain to be had by oppressor
Who from greed the war began
To grasp and rule like dictator
No freedom for any man
Have you done with war friend
And the killing of mankind
Have enough lives come to a tragic end
Have you searched into your mind
Did you find an answer there
A reason why men fight
And when you laid your findings bare
Tell me—did it all seem right

Elizabeth Taylor

Shapes Of Life

Thank you, God, for creation,
In all its variety.
Thank you for human beings,
Thank you for shaping me.

The straightness of a sapling,
The shape of a gnarled old tree,
And people made in God's image,
Though it may be gnarled in me.

Few folk grow straight as saplings
Because of storm winds which blow.
The storms of sin, pain and sorrow
Distort us as we grow.

Yet in that tree is beauty,
That shape of a gnarled old tree,
And God, reshaping his image
Sees beauty even in me.

Thank you, God for creation
In all its variety.
Thank you for human beings,
Thanks for re-shaping me.

Mary Goulding

Homelessness

A man is sitting on the street
with hardly any food to eat.
"But why not just go home?", you say.
"Instead of sitting day by day
upon the rough and rigid road,
where people come and shop, then go."
Because he has no place to live,
and passers-by refuse to give
a spare one pound, or two, or three,
to help this poor man's desperate plea.
But why do people just not try
to answer this man's quiet cry
for someone to put their generous hand
into their pocket, and to understand?

Laura A. Cummings

Longing

As I walked through the park,
And looked up at the trees,
I could still hear your voice,
Amongst the cool breeze.

Soft grass at my feet,
The golden sun on my hair,
I could still feel your presence,
I knew you were there.

Why did you leave me?
Why did you go?
Perhaps it was fate,
Perhaps I will never know.

But I will long for the day,
When we will meet and be one,
You just wait for me there,
I won't be long.

Elizabeth Barton

Lost Love

I'll never forget the sadness I felt
when you left me all alone
and I'll always have memories of events
that happened before you were gone.
Tears pour when I remember
your face in the sunset's light
as we walked along the sandy beach,
hand in hand, until the dark of night.
You were my one and only love
and inside you always shall be
even though the angels have taken you
far beyond my reach.

Michelle Harper

Nature's Beauty

To walk along a river bank
On a lovely summer day
And see the graceful swans glide by
In all their fine array.
Or wander down a country lane
And breathe the pure fresh air
You might hear the cuckoo call
Just to let you know he's there
To see the stately tall pine trees
Reaching up so high
Their branches seem to touch the clouds
As they go drifting by
Yes! Natures full of beauty
Not always meek and mild
But even so, it can't compare
With the smile on the face of a child.

N. Donegan

Silent Witness

Once again, it's happened,
You've disappeared from sight,
Suddenly there is no noise,
Suddenly no light.

The crashing of the ocean,
As it slaps against the rocks,
Is it she who swallowed you,
Is it she who mocks.

The clock ticks, time goes by,
All is very still,
We wait but nothing happens,
I wonder if it will.

The flowers on the windowsill
Have begun to wilt,
She looks at him with tears in her eye,
His gaze is now so distant.

I look at him, I look at her,
And I begin to cry.

Zoe Whittington

The Tiger

Orange, black and white thou art
With eyes of fire that chill the heart
Nature's beauty at its best
Standing out from all the rest
Other cats of fawn or black
Snowy or spotted, something lack
For sheer strength and joy to see
No other creature matches thee
If from India, Siberia or Bengal
Thy majestic beauty outshines them all
Stealthily moving through the glade
Lost in the dapple of light and shade
In this world of senseless sin
Killed by man for thy skin
If they put and end to thee
What a sadder world this would be

D. Lee

Secret Words

Secret words by
    candlelight,
Take us softly through
    the night
To lie entwined like
    tangled hair,
To slowly brush away
    all care
Until the morn alights
    the sky
Our love deepens with
    a gentle sign.

Susan Orfila

A Hole In The Wall

'Tis a poor man's place of trade
Where he works to feed his family
A hole in which the clogs he's made
Hang loose from hooks cannily.
And he wonders
From a hole in the wall
Whose sins upon his head did befall?

From dawn to dusk the clogs he shaped
Iron nails for those with little cash;
Brass ones for those who aped
Their betters in an upper class
And he wonders
From a hole in the wall
Whose sins upon his head did befall?

For sixty years he sat at his bench
A craftsman with eyes so sharp
Shaping clogs for a bonny wench
And wished his wife did not so harp
And he wondered from a hole in the wall
Whose sins upon his head did befall?

Rene Cain

Remember

Remember only sunshine
Let the thunder pass you by
Think of all the smiles
Not the tears you used to cry

A bright mosaic can be made
From our broken yesterdays
Moments of love and happiness
You can throw the rest away

Say a kind goodbye
To the life we used to know
Treat the memory gently
Let the bitter regrets go

Keep the love I gave you
You will add to it tomorrow
Put the golden band away
But don't wrap it up in sorrow

Forget the shattered dream
It's gone, like all the flowers
Remember only sunshine
And that once we made it ours

J. M. Savage

A Student's Prayer

Dear Lord God Almighty,
My time of trial is here.
Examinations start today.
My mind is full of fear.

You know the many hours I've spent.
You know I've done my best
To study and to learn, and now
I face the final test.

In Galilee you stilled the storm,
Please do the same for me.
Calm my nerves, compose my mind,
Then set my knowledge free.

As I read each question,
Help me to understand;
And as I write each answer,
Please Lord, guide my hand.

Soon 'twill all be over,
Relief will flood my mind.
I thank you for your presence
And leave my fears behind.

T. McGeorge

The Gardener's Lament

Digging hoeing, weeding, mowing,
Don't know why we trouble.
Cats and dogs and acts of God
Reduce it all to rubble.
Perhaps we should have plastic plants
A lawn of Astro-Turf,
Some concrete gnomes and herons
And little painted smurfs.
Ten or more pomanders
To make the air smell sweet,
A rustic bale of nylon hay
On which to rest the feet.
Tall palm trees with silken leaves,
I think their shade will do,
We'll sit beneath the waving fronds
And sip a Malibu.
But would it really be much fun?
This world of sham and fakes?
Get out there with your wellies on
And dig for heaven's sake.

John Julietti

Birdsong

Little bird upon the tree
Do you warble just for me
'Cos no one else seems to be near
As you whistle loud and clear
I know I feed you every day
But for that I need no pay
Still I like to hear your song
I could listen all day long
It sounds so sweet upon the air
And lets me know that you are there
Where are you pals I'm wondering
Don't they also wish to sing
They seem to come when crumbs are there
Because they always want a share
So they should come and join with you
To serenade me like you do

N. Minett

Loves Rhymes

Life became a poem
And every minute rhymed,
I felt my heart was singing
And every beat was timed;
While you and I together,
In harmony complete
Loved each other freely
And found the giving sweet.

Wendy P. Frost

Broken Web

My heart pinned high upon the moon
too soon to glimpse the tepid truth
the web within your very own
sown upon your tailored sleeve
to beckon me believe no lie
and hold you nigh, yet far away
though ne'er to say, 'I love you'
and I, allured by vain intent
upon your letters, rarely sent
indeed, nor written, this I plea
beguile me not, for I may see
the truth behind your impish eyes
for no disguise will hide defeat
your own deceit shall fail you
so, ponder long the fading hope
trickling from your trembling hand
and understand the tears that fell
beneath your neatly woven spell
your broken web, now my cocoon
my heart pinned high upon the moon.

Elizabeth Wilson

Fantasy

Lover you are everywhere
I dream of you each day,
Your voice, grey hair and laughing eyes
Oh heck, you really have a way.
Those silly jokes, our fingers touch
My heart's just missed a beat
When you really hold me tight
I sigh and life's complete.
That certain way you look at me
Even though you are annoyed
It's now, just when I need you most
The telephone I avoid.
Your face I see in everything
Be kind and set me free
If a fantasy is what you are
Why can't you dream of me?

Derrick Williamson

The Good Day

Between the slender lofty trees,
whose boughs near touched overhead,
And sounds of busy humming bees,
My wandering feet are gently lead.
Down winding little narrow lane,
Across the rolling countryside,
To steeple church with weathered vane,
And darting squirrels quickly hide.
Patchwork of fields dappled green,
The waving stately heads of corn,
Then feathery sprays of barley seen,
And sound of bells softly borne.
The lark to heaven slowly wings.
With throbbing song that fills the sky.
And lovely peace of summer brings,
And scudding clouds riding high.

Oh God! The beauty I have seen!

Dorothy Ventris

Hanging Pictures

The picture on the wall
shows a girl;
Her head held in shame,
her eyes black.
I look into her eyes,
and they grow.
They grow so big,
They swallow me.
Until, through no fault of my own,
I become that girl
on the wall,
My head now held low and
Eyes dark black.
Looking out at the girl
with her head high.
Looking out beyond walls,
to the light;
The bright eyes of the girl before,
and the darkness that
surrounds us both.

Katrina McVeagh

Untitled

Colour is my world
How explain the days
Save as patterns built in praise
of some great plan?
A jewelled day gives evening
a merging Lif of troubled sea
With gentle opal cloud
Till night shuts all
in ebon night and gives us rest.

Norah E. M. Davies

My Grief

I can't believe you left me Dad
I can't believe you're gone
With pain like this inside me now
I wonder can I go on?

No-one knows the love I've held
From a child to this very day
When I used to cry at your picture
And hope you would never go away.

The regrets we shared were many
And we tried to sort them out
We achieved that to the very end
Of that please have no doubt

I hope you're happy where you are
And that you can see me from afar
Please don't be sad when you see me cry
It's just my way of saying goodbye.

Dianne Rees

Winter's Love

Did the frozen wonderland
Become enchanted too,
And did the brooding sky allow
Those peeping chinks of blue?
And in the everlasting dark
Of winter's night
Did you recall a spring time
That was filled with sheer delight?

Then wide–eyed near your window
Watch the jewelled stars a-gleaming,
From soothing meditation then
To deep, untroubled dreaming,
And did you find your paradise
Where life became so sweet,
Then wake to find the whole wide world
Was waiting at your feet.

E. Fuller

Memories

I know the Spring will come again,
Green buds break out anew,
And sunshine bright and gentle rain
Will nurture bells of blue,
But can they ever look the same
As in the days gone by
When, quietly wandering hand in hand,
There walked just you and I?
The sun will shine less bright I fear,
The blue bells be less blue,
Those drops may not be rain but tears
Which I shall shed for you,
My wood shall be of memories,
Of you and I and perfect peace.

Andree J. Saunders

Untitled

I sit and wait as time passes by
My heart lies heavy within
I smile a wan smile, oh how I try
I don't know where to begin.

I reminisce over things we have done
And those that won't be done now
The happy times we sat in the sun
Just lazing "tomorrow we vow."

We didn't believe it would be too late
Or that tomorrow doesn't come
We stepped back, and in stepped fate
And now the time has gone.

So if you have anything to do
Or any nice things to be said
Don't wait, and idly look at the view.
Do, and say those things instead.

Joyce Shipton

Morning Chorus Mid June

From inky hue
to powder blue,
surveyed are Heaven's skies.
So far a field
no bird songs yield
would wish to close my eyes!

Such time is now;
now hedge and bough
are greeted with their song.
June all survey;
soon, break of day.
sweet sounds; so loud, and long!

Sleep, close my eyes!
A sun shall rise,
tone deaf, become my ears!
Their serenade,
where it is played,
before bright sun appears.

Brian Michael Robert Stevens

"Old Father Time"

From estuary at Southend
To its source at seven springs
That's where I found a tranquil peace
When cruising on the Thames.

Old Father Thames in England fair
Goes on and on through time
It's tranquil waters ebb and flow
Like poetry in motion rhyme.

Where weeping willows bow in grace
A fisherman with trendy eye
Casts his line in tender haste
As cabin cruiser whispers by.

So now a flock of wild geese
A swan some mallard ducks
All swim in peaceful harmony
Towards the keeper's locks.

A. Sumner

Doorway

Today I walked through,
A new world appeared,
To my delight,
Demons and fears,
A glimpse at the future,
A glimpse at the past,
I carry these through,
Till these demons are ours.

Kathleen Bagley

Only A Dream

I carry your picture,
In my head and my heart.
I see eyes so blue,
And hear a cry so sharp.
I see ten tiny fingers,
And ten tiny toes.
Your body is warm,
As only a mother knows.
If I could give you life,
I would watch you grow.
With pride and joy,
Because you're my little boy.
Alexander is your name,
But it's only a game.
Yes . . . I carry the picture,
Of a baby that will never be,
For I, cannot . . .
Conceive.

Christine Foort

The Change

My life was surrounded by darkness,
The cloak of sin and shame.
But then I saw a light in the darkness;
That brightened up my way.

Enslaved in sin and torment;
By day and by night.
The Lord heard my cry,
And helped me out of my plight.

His hand stretched out towards me,
His love now in my heart.
I have nothing now to fear,
For my God is always near.

The love He's placed inside me;
Grows deeper, every day.
I just want to sing,
And praise him every day.

Sonia D. Yarnold

A Nurse

To be loving kind and gentle
To care and not be sad
To heal the sick and troubled
To make so much good from bad

To tend and mend the many wounds
To which we all fall prey
To our broken bodies they daily tend
To our spirits a strength give they

To be a nurse is all of this
To be all of this and more
To dedicate a life and soul
To be cherished to the core

To live by their example
To take a leaf from out of their book
To have a world of peace and love
To have nobody forsook

J. G. Brunnen

Thingummyjig

Come fly with me,
You creature of the unkambunkam.
The unknown.
You are an incredulous sight;
Item of my dreams.
You winged triosas.
I look into the sky
and see your eerie presence
Angel children stroke your wiry back,
as you nuzzle into gillyflowers.
Far away you go,
to your homeland,
of the Triosese.

Gillian Wade

Untitled

Why was I born
Why am I here
Why am I unhappy
Why can't I cheer

This world I'm in
Was not meant for me
Why can't I escape
Why can't I go free

Why do others seem happy
While I remain sad
Why are things that happen
To me always bad

Please give me the answers
So I can smile once again
And show me the sunshine
Please, no more rain.

Louise Rooney

Fragments Of Another Time

As I lingered in the ruins
Of an ancient Roman site,
A mirage of its former days
Suddenly came to light.

I viewed a large, square courtyard
Where flower beds were laid
And roses coiling pillars
Of surrounding colonnades.

Inside, where oil lamps flickered
Giving light to gathering gloom,
I saw furnishings and statues
Exalting every room.

Then, came the sound of footsteps
Treading mosaic floors,
And whispers voiced in Latin
Echoed through the corridors.

Too soon the images shifted
Into crumbled stone and pillar.
Just fragments of another time
Of this once, proud Roman villa.

Una J. M. Elkins-Green

Untitled

I want to be different,
the way that I am.
I want to change,
but I don't think I can.

Insecurity eats away.
it's taken over me.
Jealousy is the devil.
And the devil's in me.

I've met a guy I love,
And I don't know what to do.
I'm slowly ruining it,
but that's nothing new.

I want to be different,
the way that I am.
I want to change,
but I don't think I can.

Debbie Reader

The Bereaved

When we die, young and old,
God will send angels to help
us on our way.
They will take us to be
with our friends and loved
ones for all eternity.

James T. Bell

The Little Fox

A little fox went out to play
his mother Warned him not to stray
but did he heed her he did not
until he heard a frightful shot
he hid inside a great oak tree
his mother in anger he could see,
he trembled there till night did fall
and then he heard his mother call
he ran to her so full of joy
but she just said you naughty boy
I told you not to go away
to look for you I've spent the day
and now your father's tea is not done
I really have a naughty son
but even so she held him tight
and cuddled him all through the night
the little fox he strayed no more
he played outside his mother's door

S. Gray

Epitaph

The sun its radiance gone
The moon the stars, their brightness dimmed.
No light, no warmth for my cold heart
Drenched in the fountain of my grief.
Cold with the icy breath of loss
But ready to open as a flower
Blossoms in the summer sun.
Ready to take that warm and loving hand
That embraces and soothes my aching heart
Bids goodbye to grief and sorrow
And walks with you my love
Into the glory of the everlasting light.

Emma Hunt

Questions

Peering through the depths of my mind,
Into the darkness, into the clouds of grey walls,
into the wildness, the unknown, the future, the past.
Silence surrounds me like a cocoon
Entwining my thoughts, along the
distance waves of my mind

Will I live or die?
Can I support the seeds of fruitfulness
for my bosom yearns for life.

Somewhere hidden in the depths
of my mind the answer is there
but remains silent.

G. Stevenson

The Opportunist

The opportunist in Life,
Is the cause of so much strife.
They appear in many a guise,
All caring and wise,
With smiles to attract,
And caring words to match.

Tempting too often,
With promises soon forgotten;
Of friendship to flourish,
And love to cherish,
Of happiness and security,
Wealth and prosperity.

You may hold them dear,
But it's not you that makes them care!
It's your wealth, your fame,
Or some other gain!

If you are vulnerable and easily led,
Don't let your heart rule your head;
Then you will see it's all sham and trickery,
For their gain and your misery.

Kathleen B. Chamberlain

Songs

Songs stir the thoughts of days long gone
When we were young and life was new.
Songs then were light romantic airs,
Where moon and June would always rhyme.

Both happy memories and sad
Flood back as we remember them.
Old loves long since gone and faded,
Each with a tune that once we sang.

Bitter sweet and pleasant fancies,
The melodies of long ago,
The many dreams that might come true
If once upon a time could be.

Yet still we have such memories
That never knew the test of time.
What might have been can always live
In memory's rose tinted glow.

A. W. Flesch

Bangkok (Krungthep: City Of Angels)

Roaring motors fighting for space
Eager people running the race
Whistles blowing, tanois blaring
multitudes teeming, the chaos sharing

Haphazard buildings rising high
Cobbled together, devouring the sky
Frenetic mess of derelict and new
Urban jungle stops the sun shining through
Billboards bombarding
Colours colliding
As society keeps riding

Pink scabby dogs lie melting in the heat
Figures wandering directionless like sheep
Smooth smiling faces a mirage of peace
A fleeting moment for the madness to cease
The breath of the angels engulfed by the fumes
The devil pours his poison for he who consumes

Stella Bunnag

My Mum's Unspoken Words

When I kiss my Mother's face, and her hand I hold
and gaze into her large brown eyes, near sightless and so old
I speak to her, say who I am and hope she understood
Imagine then what she would say, if she only could

She'd say
"Unaided now I cannot walk and I cannot see
My words no longer freely flows, when you speak to me
I still can hear and know you're there, if you'll hold my hand
and I can manage 'Yes' or 'No' to show I understand

At times my track of thoughts I lose to take in what you say
I find my mind gets so confused and know no time of day"
and then my Mum would close her eyes, her hand still clasped
in mine
and I would leave her to her world, as both our hands intwine.

Mary Keeley

Thomas

Thomas my cat was tabby and black
His eyes were as green as grass
His face was daft
He slept in a draught
And oh, what a size he was
Both fat and chubby, tubby and round
His little tum near touched the ground
He followed me here, he followed me there
He simply followed me everywhere
He never did bite, nor did he scratch
He never did have a fighting match
And now my story is over
Alas my heart is sore
I left him back in Cyprus
Poor Thomas is no more

Denise Felstead

Found

I never knew you existed
I thought you were somebody else
All my life I called another man father
Unaware of the truth

A hidden secret
A lie told so long now forgotten
Uncovered by me in my innocence
Illusions shattered—relationships rocked

The photograph you sent has pride of place
I see no resemblance, but others say yes
We talk on the phone and we laugh and we joke
A thousand questions fill my head

I miss you stranger
I long to touch you, to hold you, to feel your embrace
To look in your eyes and find my place.

Susan Cox

The Old Woman

Slowly she rocks in her rocking chair,
An old lady, so small, and thin.
Her lean face brown, and furrowed with care
With a look so sweet, your heart she could win.
Sweet and gentle, her hair pure white
looks like a halo in the evening light.

She sits, rocking slowly, alone with her thoughts
Looking back to the past, where memories are caught.
She sees the man she loved, once more,
Enter slowly, through memories door.
He smiles, and beckons with lifted hand
Then vanishes, like grains of sand.

A host of forgotten friends she sees
Once more, in her dim memory.
Phantom callers are all who come,
To visit her, when day is done,
neglected, and lonely, she sits there,
No-one around to hear her prayer.
Alone, she waits for her call to come
When God will take her, the lonely one.

Evelyn M. Norris

Fire

The holocaust of forest fire, the twisted branch, the blackened briar,
The roar and crackle of the fire, twisting and leaping as it goes,
Destroying, burning, leaving waste, a green, lovely and
    pleasant place.
No birds remain, no life at all, when fire is gone.
A gust of wind to fan the flames, a rush of orange in exchange
    for green and pleasant land.
The thick and acrid billowing smoke rising, turning, twisting back,
A fog of life destroying gas.
No saviour even for the sacred ass, once grazing
On the green and luscious grass, growing in the glades 'twixt
Slender pine and spreading oak, until the hiss
And roar of flame, his life, and that of birds did claim.
The aftermath of holocaust is silence, where once was sound,
Instead of flowers, just blackened ground.
Tall sentinels of blackened pine, with branches on, but
    needles gone.
Outlined dark against the sky. From the branches where no
    birds do cry,
The mating calls, the love is gone, the forest remains silent
    and forlorn.
Oh rue the day that fire came, destroying life and leaving dust.
But nature in her wondrous way, when Autumn comes and
    in the fall,
Will shed her black mantle and her stole, and by the Spring
New life will come, and desolation will be gone.

Janet McKinney

The Old Promenade

There's a lovely walk not far from here
Well I think so to me it's dear.
Just an old promenade by the River Mersey
Stretching from Rock Ferry to New Ferry.

It speaks to me of long, long ago.
Of quiet happy days we used to know
When throngs of folk enjoyed this walk
in the summer on Sunday evenings.

It was a peaceful walk such a lovely view
Large ships sailing by a small yachts too
At night the lights appeared everywhere
on land on river and in the air!

Hymn singing—I hear either end of the prom.
Where meetings were held in memory lingers on
"Conway" and "Indefatigable" have gone from off shore,
The Ferry boats too are seen no more!

It's a different world now as one walks there,
Planes drone overhead, tankers rest by the pier.
It's a quiet walk too, just a 'memory lane'
The ones who still love it will walk it again.

Mabel Johnston Sperring

My Secret World

Every night as I close my eyes
My secret world comes to life

Somewhere I can be when I'm feeling down and low
There the future I can see
A place where I am at ease
And never ever afraid
Because when I'm in this place
All my troubles seem to fade

In my secret world there are equal human rights
Everyone lives together
There's no black or white

The days are sunny long and bright
In this secret world of mine
Where people can walk the streets safe at night
A place where no-one can bring sorrow to you
You can have lots of fun and laughter too
People can cast aside their fears
In this world of peace, harmony and no tears

Sarawat Azim

Remembrance

They tell me that my dad is dead
    But I know it to be lies.
He's everywhere I look around,
    In the flowers, land and skies.
He still keeps talking to me
    His voice is the singing of birds
There is so much comfort and guidance
    Said in language simpler than words.
He's a rainbow that brightens the world,
    He makes stormy skies clear again.
He's the light at the end of the tunnel,
    Welcome relief to life's bitter pain.
I refuse to believe he's no longer here,
    He's not dead to me and I'm sure,
He is making his way to a better place,
    He couldn't wait, but went on before.

S. J. Smith

'Gallon At The Bar'

An aftershave of smoke and strong whisky,
Odour Nicotine 70% vol.
Wearing clothes that had forgotten how to be worn!
Saying what I say
Never what I think,
Becoming a modern day missing link!
Not realizing I'd gone too far
There was always one for the road
and a gallon at the bar

Chris Murphy

The Wings Of Freedom

Above anguish and fear inflicted minds,
The cool breath takes her high.
Through the carnage of civilization and destruction of life,
Her divine dancing feathers fly.

Bombs of vengeful tyrants tear the sky,
Where the wind carries her wings of peace to
reach eternity.
The merciless slaughter of society reigns,
But still the dream-like bird breaks the discord
with her serenity.

Fiends of war, claw at the innocent and defenceless,
But the song of liberty flies with the bird of
freedom.
Shattering the malevolent barriers like water through a
fortified dam,
The dove of harmony rescues from callous
captors, her kingdom.

The murmur of her tranquil wish calms the
ferocious ocean.

Julia Datta

Empathy

Touch the hand gently, grasp not the gossamer
thread of the web that we weave.

Look, but don't linger on the reflection, the
delicate traces of sun and sorrow.

Feel, but don't say the words that we know,
when we cross the bridge together but alone.

Remember the moment, fleeting spirit of
our time, hold to the virtue of the spell.

Dry the tear that my heart feels, it
has fallen through the web—it has gone—
like the moment—to be remembered
in the hourglass of our emotion.

M. K. Mason

Never Love

I saw you and fell head over heels in love.
I've never spoken to you, but seeing you is enough.
You are so clever and handsome,
Whilst I am just ugly and dumb.
My love for you has to be held back by a dam,
Because you don't even know who I am!
You could have any girl, so why choose me?
I know our love will never be.
We will never be on the same team,
So why do I continue to dream?

Krishandeep K. Thind

Holiday Abroad

The drifting clouds in the sky above
The azure blue seas ebbing tide
The golden sands and signs of love
In bronzed, lithe bodies passing by

Long cool drinks at the beach bar
Pina colada and cocktails in coconut shells
Handsome guys, how tanned they are
Lazily watching the pretty beach belles

Evening draws nigh, the day has gone
Boys in their gear, girls' dresses too tight.
Everyone joins in the happy throng.
Clinging together in the heat of the night.

Day breaks, sun rise, the notice board
Oh no! The flight departs at ten A.M.
Safe journey, stewardess bids good day to all
Back home, England, holidays over again.

Sandra Bulmer

Abstract Feelings: Personification Of Despair

Despair is a feeling, a loss of hope
When people feel, that they can't cope.
When he is soaring up in bulk,
people always sit and sulk.

In our world, no-one has a care.
Despair is floating in the air.
When people feel there is nothing to say,
they deal with him in their own way.

Despair is here, there and everywhere,
when you don't want him in your hair.
They say that he will go away,
He's always back the very next day.

People say that it's not fair,
In other's lives he's very rare,
But I think he should be cast,
back where he belongs in the past

Where he shall have eternal rest,
and never to anyone be a pest.
Despair, despair, he's not there,
He's going, he's going, he's gone!

Amanda Alfred

Loneliness

It is very rare,
to be in solitaire,
but once trapped,
it is difficult to be unwrapped,
and throw away the feeling of loneliness.

Sometimes solitude can be bliss,
to be remembered like a first kiss,
the sun rests upon your eyes,
and the bird flies,
the trees sway in the breeze,
as you hear the humming of bees.
You dread the time of being woken,
but God has spoken,
the time has come to awake.

Once a certain time has passed,
of being cast,
on an island, far far away,
you no longer wish to stay,
but how can one break the spell
of being captive in a prison cell?

Sara Khan

War Time

There they are all waiting, line after line,
For the train to arrive that is always on time.
Solemn faces wondering where they will be going.
Some foreign country they were told.
Report at the station so they were told!.
The train's at the station they all start to board.
Saying goodbye to love ones is hardest of all!.
The train's slowly moving, out of the station
Women are crying, relatives waving.
The station is quiet! The trains have all gone!
It will be the same tomorrow, as this war goes on.

Florence Mary Wells

Seven Ages Of Man

I look at my daughter and what do I see,
A hungry little baby staring back at me,
Puking and crying all day long,
She falls asleep to a lullaby song.
Days go by, years too,
As she ties the lace of her new school shoes,
Every week she's with a new boy,
She uses them all as if they were toys,
She's now a young adult with a mind of her own,
With a stable job and a mobile phone,
She lives in a flat with a husband called Bob,
If you ask me he's a bit of a slob.
A middle–aged woman who worries about her age,
She stays at home like a bird in a cage.
70 years old in a nursing home,
No one to talk to no one to phone,
As months went by she became really ill,
She went to hospital and they gave her some pills,
A few days later she sadly died,
Nobody cared and nobody cried.

Martina Booth

Friends

First, there is wonderful Patty,
I have to admit she is a little bit natty
I really like her very much
And we will always keep in touch.

Second, there is lovely Tania,
Her favourite meal is meat lasagna
I helped her once when she cut her knee
We're very close, as you can see.

Finally there's exciting Laine,
Sometimes she can be quite a pain
She's really cool and has fabulous clothes
Hot pink leggings, I'd like to borrow those.

Ogo Okafor

Yesterday

Was it yesterday, when youth was king,
And flowers bloomed in early spring;
Was it yesterday, when the world it seems,
Was an oyster to fulfil our dreams;
Was it yesterday when we looked around,
And laughed at the treasures, we had found;
Was it yesterday, we looked on high,
And set our sights up to the sky;
Was it yesterday, we cast a sigh,
As our dreams broke up and passed us by;
And do we sit alone today,
Longing for one more yesterday.

Lade J. Henderson

The Senseless Age

Bewailing an era cast upon tragedy
Breathing in a fountain of unrealized dreams
Dejected spartan soul the reality we be
Weakened, we must face the day

Standing uncertain among the furore of life
Engulfed within a harsh terrain of hopelessness
Our aspirations carry us past despair so real
This dark image is with me now

I bear the weight of a lost generation
Rendered paralysed by the perpetual struggle
Misguided masses approach overwhelmed with expectation
Once motionless, now galvanized beyond constraint

Restless, they strive to negate their plight
Yet so forcefully obsessed are we all
Others then slowly sullen our prophetic sight
The gnawing at the spirit remains that deep

Forever ensconced in a nightmare truth
We stagnate, left scattered on the lying debris
Our fate discovered ensnared, animal–like, inside a cage
For all too real is the senseless age

G. M. Tremers

Should Have Listened To Mother

I tried my hand at making bread, easy so they say,
Love the taste and texture I'd eat it everyday.
Well full of good intentions the flour I bought was strong,
Let it rise and kneaded it, but somehow it went wrong.

My first was like a house brick, the shape was really good,
The next was like a baseball as heavy as a piece of wood.
The third was really soggy, like putty all the way through,
Cooked it a little longer, but knew it would never do.

Then I tried some bread rolls, and they just didn't rise,
So I put them in the microwave, they shrivelled half the size.
I really tried but have given up, guess I know the score,
My bread making days are over, won't make it anymore.

H. McCoy

Emotions In Quick Successions

On my bed, I lay, looking out the window
lo, a beautiful picture I behold
Such a wonderful peace encompassed
the village. Far up the sky was the moon
surrounded by millions of sparkling little stars
Peace reigned in the darkened village
Strangely, I felt at peace with it all
Contentedly, I snuggled into bed to sleep
Suddenly . . . there was a deafening roar
It was the thunder, I looked up in time
To see my beautiful picture distorted by
The flashes of lighting crossing the sky in quick successions
Suddenly the peace in me and the comfort
I felt disappeared. I was very scared
I could not sleep, I turned and tossed myself on the bed.
Dear Lord please help, I prayed.
Soon I was fast asleep, lost to the world.

Obiageri Nwanneka Okafor

Heal The World

A world of love is what we need
to heal the pain of all our deeds.
A touch of love we need inside
to help us cleanse our many lies.
Reach out your hands to the skies above
to build a new world of truth and love.

Look to the future with love in your heart,
the secrets you hide can make a new start.
Just open the door to express your faith
to overcome all the powers of hate.
Don't walk away from the fears of the past,
fight for your rights with the strength that you mask.

Children of the future need to protect our earth
from the spite and ignorance learnt since birth.
A better life will begin
when you express the feelings that lie within.
Reach out your hands to the skies above
to build a new world of truth and love.

Chantal Dickie

The Stairway To Paradise

Cold is the wind, blowing through the valleys of the mountains
As we ascend on our journey, to the summit we climb
The peak of the world is our one destination
The pinnacle of love with no bondage of time.

I fear not the cold nor the daunting horizon
My heart is ablaze with you by my side
The warmth of your smile brings sunshine and laughter
Together forever on a heavenly ride.

Paul Woodward

Needs

I do not want to live with the rich
Squandering money, throwing it in a pit

I do not want to live with the poor
Endless misery, with times of deplore

I do not want to live with demons
Gathering, inside the dark damp pits

I do not want to live with angels
Flying high, above all of it

I do not want to live with the politically insane
Where, needs of society are all the same

I do not want my children to grow up in this game
Material things, strike out so plain

But, I do want to live in a world
Where one day
Love, honour and respect will again reign.

Sandra Ford

Beyond The Horizon

When the tide comes rippling o'er the sand,
Frothy white, and twinkling silver in the sun.
I close my eyes, stretch out my hand,
And feel the presence of a friend long gone.
Upon the cliff top, on our favourite seat,
I think I hear her whisper
As the gentle waves retreat.
"Do not grieve dear friend—
Look out across the sea and know,
Beyond the blue horizon
Where earthbound spirits cannot go,
Souls await the ones they love,
Believe that this is so.
Life is a brief span before
We meet again for evermore.
When all is done and said—
Death is but a passing on ahead."
And restless in my bed at night,
I find it comforting to think
She could be right.

Florence Hindley

151

After The Game

Empty packets, tossed and turned,
Kicked around by the wind.
An empty ground full of debris,
And memories of what went before.

And now I feel like I'm like that.
Empty, tossed around,
With no real sense of purpose.
Memories of what went before
And perhaps what might be again.

Week in, week out, we stand,
Opening ourselves to pain and frustration.
Standing there alone and yet
In the midst of everybody.

And isn't life, and love, like that?
Opening up to pain and
Taking yet another chance,
We end up frustrated or made
To look a fool.

But still we come back for more
. . . same team, same love, same man.

S. Harrison

Bitter Sweet Truth

We meet daily and feed off each other, like butterflies living
for the moment.
Then dying to be reborn, starting again.
Each day becoming more and more confident, relaxing,
enjoying our new experiences.

Then it is gone, we look and see what we have done, so different
now, so involved, fearful of going further too late to go back.
We are left bereft, images of what we were, frightened of
taking that next step.

Others look at us and gloat, we had so much, too much, they
enjoy our discomfiture. They smile at our parting.

We should have stood together and turned our backs on
them, but apart we can't withstand their onslaught.

We cast one last glance at each other, knowing it's our last chance,
Neither willing to say "I love you" in case it draws us apart!

Vivienne Lansdown

Eternal Doors

When you lose someone you're close to,
Think of good times you both went through.
Even though you're feeling sad,
Happy thoughts can make you glad.
When someone you're close to dies,
Don't hold back tears from longing eyes.
For with each tear a memory drops,
With each thought the hurt stops.
Not completely, it never goes,
But gradually the pain slows.
Time doesn't heal but does assist,
To return your life to things you've missed.
Otherwise what is the cause,
Of entering eternal doors.

Claire Keighley-Bray

Sleeping Child

Little girl lies there, so sweet and serene
Shampooed and washed, smelling so clean
Eyelashes flicker, on ivory skin
Trapping the thoughts that linger within
Trying so hard the languor to beat
Though dreaming perhaps, of a special treat
Fingers all curled, round her favourite toy
The face of an innocent, gentle yet coy
Silken hair tumbled, all feathery light
A devil by day yet an angel at night
But when sleep overtakes her, all devils depart
This angelic child will creep into your heart

Sheila Kirby

Unity's Child

My little child, all golden brown;
I see all you represent.
In harmony, two made as one;
The island, the continent.

Your features a fascination.
So much written in your face.
No culture clash, just history smashed.
Perfection from mixing of race.

Not half–caste, but whole–caste;
You are doubly blessed.
Two tribes, not just one or the other.
Your heritage glows, like the tone of your skin.
Living proof, world of sisters and brothers.

From the cold, from the heat,
An ancestry complete.
So take pride in all that you are.
The English in you, lives there red, white and blue
And your African eyes shall see far.

Jill Senghore

Birthday Blues

Birthday blues are the pits at the bottom,
At the bottom is a heap of birthday dreams,
And wrapped around the presents are
Pretty bows of comfort, balloons of hope,
Twists of smiles and ribbons of kisses
And love that I misses.

Birthday blues and a single present,
A single card—a borrowed thought,
A thoughtless message.

Eighteen blues and many more to come.
As old as the last Christmas present,
As young as a fresh birthday cake.

It is not for me,
My mind is still in bed,
A thing tomorrow, soon a thing of yesterday.

Birthday blues,
And next year a deeper shade.
Party time.

It's my party
And I'll cry if I want to.

Amritpal Nijjar

Handicapped

Laura, Laura, little Laura, how it breaks my heart to see
You muted and retarded so that it seems unfair to me
That while we all must bear our burdens as well as we can cope
Yet for a child born with her problems, then these must telescope

She tries but cannot comprehend, well, lets leave such things aside
The angels only six years old and has a tongue that's tied.
We have a mutual feeling though that I know she understands
Because her little fingers creep into my wrinkled hands

All young lives are fraught with danger from stings and cuts
and burns
But when these strike the handicapped, ones stomach
overturns
Times, too, she fails to master many little daily things
But you love her and you bear with her, because your heart
has strings

And how we feel elated at the first time that we find
Some new understanding will light up her little mind
Stumbling over simple tasks is hard to entertain
Remember life has cheated her out of voice and brain

We shower her with affection but how can this be enough
She needs protection every day because the world gets rough
Every road spells danger if one lacks intelligence
For while we walk the paths of life, we all need traffic sense

J. W. Cash

Be Prepared To Leave Your Soul

Full of courage and adventure, you come in droves like
Lakeland Sheep,
With miles of brightly coloured ropes, to conquer out-crops
sharp and steep,
Our cold unforgiving mountains, will take no prisoners here,
Come only armed with fortitude, leave no room for doubt or fear,
Our crags will sap you of your strength, our rocks will take
their toll,
But the ultimate price for you my friend, be prepared to leave
your soul,
From Dropping Crag to Broken Rib, you come in tidal waves,
And walk the ridges, cairn to cairn, among the unseen graves,
You clamber to our highest heights, some never to return,
Year in year out, full circle, when will you ever learn?
We take your broken bodies, from where your humbled bones
once fell,
Dark silence holds your secrets now, with just the wind to tell,
So when you stand with upturned eyes, and see my beauty
has no bounds,
Listen hard beyond sweet natures noise, to the calm and eerie
sounds,
For those are spirits calling, of the climbers lost before,
Sometimes you'll hear them whisper, sometimes you'll hear
them roar,
With each call come a warning, for you my friend,—take care,
Look through majestic splendour, and see the Devils lair,
For he is here, believe me, and to him you'll pay the toll,
So come courageous mountain men, 'But be prepared to leave
your soul.'

J. A. Sherwen

Why?

They cup their hands for feeding,
And look with hungry eyes,
Why can't we help the people, why can't we save their lives?

They have no strength to wipe away,
The tears of fear and pain,
They've just enough within their arms to pray for drops of rain.

Their tiny stomachs bloated,
And legs so frail and thin,
The government says its been noted, but that's not feeding
the millions within.

Tiredly searching for scraps of food,
As the flies swarm around their heads,
An ear–piercing sound, a mother screams out, alas her only
child is dead.

A drop of water, a grain of rice,
That's all they ever ask,
Maybe we should hide our faces, behind a shameful mask.

We're not doing enough to help them,
They're dying every day,
So take a little time to think, when in a comfy bed you lay.

Joanne Wills

Gentleman Of The Road

Defiance glistened in his tired old eyes,
Seeing wistfully all he wanted before him,
His beloved cliffs against which the rolling sea drives,
Independence and the open road called him,
His snow white hair like the foaming sea hung
His memories of that seaside never fading
A seagull's cry like an alarm bell rung
Never again will the gentleman go wading
Enemies and friends along life's path he made,
Pride and solitude were his boon companions
To get back to his past was all he prayed
But he knew that it would never happen
He spoke of the sea with an air of pride
It was like he wished roving and free
With the elements raging and none at his side
Independence his shrine, his companion the sea.

M. Benstead

"Letting Go"

The only way to keep them is to let them go . . .
Though you feel they don't know what it's all about—don't say so.
Instead, quietly state your reservations
But don't make recriminations
For it will only serve to make things worse you know.
It's hard when you only have their welfare at heart
And it seems your world they're trying to tear apart
But you gave them life, you must let them live it as they will
It may not be to your liking, but they'll have to foot the bill
And though you can hardly look at them for unshed tears
Seeing only the child you've loved and cherished over the years
You must have known that they were only lent
That for you to be a trustee was what God really meant
So take comfort that you've tried to teach them right from wrong
And hope that if they're tempted, they'll be strong
Let them go now with your blessing and a prayer
And their knowledge that if they ever need you, you'll be there
And then the bonds of love will ever tightly grow
Because you've had the good sense to let go . . . !

Irene Bruns

Night Time

Quiet and still in the moonlit night.
Bats flit by with precision flight,
their meal awaits in the dark of night.
A mole's nose appears from out of his mound,
twitching and sniffing around without sound.
The dormouse awakes and scurries on by,
watched by the moon in the starry lit sky.
"Twit twoo", calls the owl as he swoops so low, watch out
little dormouse it's time to go.
All matter of creatures appear after dark,
keep your ears and eyes open, and silently walk.
All creatures are special, so treat
them with care, and remember that God
put us all here on earth!

S. A. Bock

The Drift

How many times have I walked here with Jamie running free?
Day in, day out, year after year, the air, a dog and me
How many moments have been spent in pondering the past
"If only . . . " and "I never meant . . . " creep up so very fast
And all the anxious contemplation of what the future holds
Great oak trees that have withstood duration look down and say
  "who knows?"
And what of changes coming soon? Can I adapt and must I learn?
The hawthorn laughs, the hedgerows croon
All nature dies and then returns
A lesson well and truly taught
This days philosophy
The peaceful mind that has been brought by higher things than me

Mary Denslow

Child Of The Ocean

Paper lies burn, all roses die,
And yet some never get a chance.
Flowers strewn across your silky heart,
The grave where my love lies buried.
Purple mist rises, whilst truth deserts,
Pale shadows fading to nothing.
Simple minds, with once simple hopes;
Potential was drowned in spirits.
Shattered whispers pour from my lips,
But do you still know who I am?
Such bitter, angry streams of pain
Flow from the sea green of my eyes,
Enveloping my soul, my all;
Reduced to this because I loved.
Ironic laughing echoing
From the sweet tree nymphs in the woods,
Laughing at me, with me, for me.
Can they not see I'm laughing back?
Purple mist rises, whilst hope descends,
Bury me in a mountain of tears.

Rachel Wagstaff

Daydreaming

In solitary moments we bid our minds remember
Those fires of passion that once so fiercely blazed
Now later on those fires are just an ember
The scars of life near have them all erased
For in our youth our desires are overpowering
With great restraint our feelings kept at bay
When suddenly there comes a magic towering
And the prize you seek is there upon display
With great joy and love you gather up your treasure
And keep it safe until the parting day.

J. Hampton

Feathered Friends

The heron awaits up the towpath with hope
for the fish to be stirred with the oncoming boat
A kestrel hovers overhead.
Some little creature will soon be dead.

The crow seems master of all he surveys
Swooping for chicks that have gone astray
A farmer with his gun fills me with sorrow
while a kingfisher darts like there's no tomorrow

As the woodpigeon hoots his lonely cry
A perky little robin comes bobbing by
your homing pigeon in his coat of grey.
Gets a little freedom when out for the day

The magpie looks proud and stands like a chief
Hiding the facts that he's just a thief
Seagulls appear like shifting sands
Not content with the sea they come inland

A sure sign now with the sight of the swallow
Springs on its way out summers to follow
They're far too numerous to put into words
This land of ours and its wonderful birds.

Ann Goodall

Today I Met God On The California Coastline

He appeared to come from the mission,
The figure dressed in white,
But when I reached the cove,
Below the headland,
He was waiting at the waters edge;
And forever it seemed, we talked
About the meaning of life, the
Inevitability of death, and the role
Humanity must play;
As he spoke, he showed me his hands,
And the scar where the spear went
Into his side; but when the sun
Began to set, he led me out into
The incoming tide
And beneath the waves he pushed by body,
Until it floated on the surface, but in
The distance, I saw the stranger disappear in
The evening mist.
At sunrise I re-entered the world
The eyes of my soul had been opened.

David Mobberley

Mother And Daughters

Wouldn't it be nice, if instructions were given
When the gift of a daughter arrived from heaven
Someone could have warned me, what lay ahead
As I stared at her asleep in her bed.

As the years slip by I am slowly aware
I do have something with which to compare
My problems, my worries, and genuine fears.
There the same as my mum had, for all of those years.

Now I've made it this far, and done not too bad.
Thanks to all the advice from my mum that I've had.
So I'll keep trundling on, just as I am,
Till someday, God help me, I'll be a gran.

Joy Adamson-Miller

Composing A Poem

Inspiration, taunting coquette, sneers,
Flirtatiously mocks the parched-for-thought brain,
Sonnets wield a bludgeon of mental pain,
Creativity cruelly jeers.
In the mind's desert, misgiving rears
For blank pages cannot conceal nor feign,
Hoping imagination once will deign
To put 14 lines end to my fears.

Yet soon flies open the mind's sauna door,
Visions and fancies are no longer sealed,
Russian boxes of ideas revealed.
Claustrophobic images now see light,
Escape mental prisons for ever-more,
Poem on "The Poem" here to write.

Caroline Cain

Our Eva

Many years ago, nearly two and ninety, in fact,
A baby girl was born—Entire intact,
Perfection. She lived and grew and laughed and cried
Embraced each day, spreading happiness world-wide.
She has shown vision and valour and vibrance each day
Vitality, and value, and vigour on display.
With affection for those she admired always
This accolade is for an angel. Attractive she stays.
What is her name, this Elegant lady?
An 'E', a 'V' and an 'A' spells EVA, (surname Bailey)
We're privileged to know our Eva. We're proud
And yet humble. We'll shout from rooftops aloud.
To extol all the virtues of this lady our friend
No words can do justice, or really extend
All our love and good wishes to this wonderful lady.
Enchanting, Victorious, Affable—Eva, we salute thee.

Kathleen Aldridge

Cold And Alone

I am cold and alone with no one to share
The long lonely nights that are waiting out there
The winter's chill it has set in
Have I committed some terrible sin
A knock on the door the ring of the phone
The sound of a voice to say are you're home
None of them come it just adds to my despair
The sound of the TV the hiss of the fire
These only add to this terrible mire
The sound of your own voice as you talk to yourself
The tick of the clock that's stood on the shelf
The room it is pretty with furniture in
But at the end of the night the walls are closing in
It is now time for bed you pull back the covers and
Snuggled in then it sinks in, does it pay to grow old
And alone.

P. Brady

A Working-Man's Hands

Weather–worn, calloused, gnarled,
A worker's hands, powerful, sure.
Used to the rigours and demands of life.
Dependable.

Nothing like the soft, well–manicured hands of princes,
Or the eager, greedy hands of the merchant,
Nor yet like the suppliant, incensed hands of the priest.
Different.

These are hands that construct, fashion, build,
That produce something tangible, real.
Hands that enhance God's world.
Creative.

In hands such as these,
Reliable, honest, strong,
Was the newborn son of God gently cradled.
Secure.

Louis Fielding

The Supporter—Euro 96

Fever grips our soccer world
Stadiums filled the flags are unfurled
Painted faces of the cheering crowds
A sea of colour as they sing out loud
Anthems are sung the games are on
The cheers the groans the chances gone
The trumpets blare the beat of the drums
As their heroes make their dazzling runs
Skilful passes from man to man
Spontaneous applause from every fan
The courage the skill of the ball control
Bring sheer delight on that vital goal
The winning team a championship side
Receive the trophy and so filled with pride
All fans and supporters those in the crowds
Their good behaviour they too should feel proud.

K. C. Burditt

Memories

Do you ever stop to think of all the years
that have gone past?
Do you ever stop to think of all the
loves that didn't last?
Maybe that's the way life is,
and love wasn't meant for me
Some people say it's just God's will,
and wasn't meant to be
But! Wouldn't it be nice if someone
special came along
To sweep me of my feet someday?
And sing a old love song
Of days gone by, when we were young
And of the love, that we once knew
Wouldn't it be nice to share that love again with you
So I hope some day that you will
come a knocking at my door
That special love that I once had
Then, I'll be alone no more.

Mary Devine

My True Love

He is my one and only true love,
For him I would fall from the sky up above.
I love him tons with all of my heart,
And I hope that we never will part.

If I don't feel well or I'm under the weather,
I think of he and I being together.
If he ever left me I'd break down in tears,
For when I'm with him I have no fears.

When he's in my arms I hold him so tight,
If anyone wants him I'll put up a fight.
When we are together we're so hard to part,
We've always been like that right from the start.

Sarah Millar

Mouse In A Rat Trap

Wee mouse, that trap was not for you,
—Although I've seen the harm you do.
The hosts of grubs and pests you ate
Made up in part your nibbling rate
At bulbs, and berries, peas, and fruits,
And winter stores of crops and roots.
A field vole you have always been,
Tho' oft in gardens you are seen,
You don't intrude inside our house
With fouling ways of common mouse.
Soft russet fur, round, tiny ears,
Teddy bear's face, eyes sharp with fears,
Creeping from weasels, owls, and cats,
You died because I hated rats.
My grief comes late—I wish you knew
I did not mean that trap for you.

Dorothy Keetley

Recall

When evening shadows fall,
Sit with me awhile and let us recall,
Days long ago that were happy and gay,
When passions ran high and youth held sway.
Hear children's laughter, the bark of a dog
As he chases a bunny around a log.
Smell the sweet heather, foxgloves too,
Arms full of bluebells picked for you.
See wriggling toes jump in and out,
As each rippling wave circles about.
Seashore walks when twilight draws near,
Your look of love; oh my dear.
Peeping at children asleep in their beds,
Footsteps as light as an angel's tread.
Now I am left; all are gone,
I walk the cliffs at early morn,
I am not lonely or alone
My loves I carry deep in my bone.
I thank my God for richly blessing
My life, with essence for true living.

Gwyniris Semmens

The Secret Promise

The map of a cliff, standing above the darkened sea.
The map of the island, swaying in the breeze,
The map of the dark, cloaking them both,
The map of the night, before the dawn broke.

The streak of sun's rays, between the bays
An exploration of difference amongst the same.
A boat which steers beside the waves
And lands slight upon the island's rocks.

Searching there, along the path and trees
before ending at the silver streams
The dawn kept up its secret promise
of returning after the dark grew upon us.

Natalie Russell

"Rescue"

You fly to me on diamond wings
Incandescent in the night
Touching me with your immortal breath
Caressing me with your loving eyes

Silky voice in my head
Enchanted vision filled with embracing light
Effortlessly carrying me in your strong arms
on your burdenless, soaring flight

Spiralling dreams fall into the space
Awaiting birth in the mind
Coiled around the traps of emotional storms
Kissing gently the furrowed brow, calming kind

The dream of love with you so true
Soothing my hurt with your tender caress
Fly forever our souls in heavenly blue
Sweet angel of light, drown me in your tenderness

Steve West

With Each Passing Day

Little lady with eyes of green,
There never will, nor ever has been
An earthly angel with a heavenly glow,
The purest being, as you slowly grow,
Into all that is good . . . with your innocent fun,
Your warmth equates to the summer sun

The level of laughter, of joy, and of pride,
Completes my life with you by my side.
When all else fails, and existence is tough
The power in your smile is more than enough.

My heart is dancing with a simple touch,
The tenderness in your fingers becomes a clutch,
The tone of your voice with all that you say
Makes life worthwhile with each passing day.

Carol Dobbins

Truth

Life's not a bed of roses, from the outset that's assured.
The dice are rolled the moment we descend upon this earth.
That first breath proved the miracle. That first breath sealed
our fate.
The future has begun for all. The dice? We watch and wait.

Unknown the path that lies ahead, most travellers pass us by
Tho' some will stop to hurt and wound us, intent to crucify.
Too soon we're plagued with thoughts of fear. Example
hunters kill.
Defenceless creatures, traumatised. The bait of iron will.

Then, man will fight his fellow men. What quality of mind
Excludes each moral thought and deed, to the detriment of mankind.
"Do as you would be done by" or "Love thy neighbours" theme
Is all we need to right the world! A thinker's favourite dream.

There's so much beauty in this world, it's there within our reach
Enhanced by love and kindness, forging harmony and peace.
By example may this message of direction be applied
To enrich the future wellbeing of each miracle alive.

Sylvia M. Linney

Suicide

Unearthly figures fill my throbbing mind,
Darkness moves in to secure its find.
I feel my life drain from my body,
As the dark crimson flow makes my
wrists all bloody.

I lie sprawled across my bed,
And I picture myself not alive, but dead.
My face so pale, a deathly white,
My eyes so dark and empty, used they to be bright?

I'm weaker now, and tired too,
My lips have turned an icy blue.
My body feels cold and lifeless,
Why don't I feel my life is priceless?

So death will have its way,
It will take my life by the light of day.
Some might say I was too hasty,
In taking my life so distastefully.

But you and I, we both know,
That because of the love you refused to show,
It was essential for me to end my life,
With such a wicked instrument as that cold, sharp knife.

Michelle Phelan

"It Touches Me"

People people everywhere.
Please listen to my every prayer.
Let us not fight.
Let us all unite.
Come on now hear my plea.
Let us all live in harmony.
Let us love one another.
Like brother with brother.
This world would be a better place,
If we all could be loving to everyone's race.
Where is humanity going today?
Let us all sit down think and pray.
Let us all be as bright as can be.
Let us all live in harmony.

Louisa Clare

"No More"

No more time to sit awhile,
To tell you tales to make you smile.
No more your loving face to kiss,
All your love I really miss.
Missing you more than words can say,
So till we meet once more, someday,
Sleep tight dear Granddad free from pain,
Until we are together again.

Wendy Miller

Springtime In The Meon Valley

The Meon Valley in springtime
Is a marvellous place to be
Trees and flowers with their perfume
Wild primrose with a fragrance
Are all around to see.
Bluebells in flower bud
With the long lanceolate leaves,
A meadow lark spirals to the heavens
In full song, a beautiful sound to hear
As in full flight, he trills as he weaves.

The song thrush from the oak tree,
The blackbird not to be subdued
Whistling loud and free.
The Meon flows quietly by
Fish jumping boldly out of the water,
In an effort to catch that evasive fly.
And as the dusk begins to fall across the sky
The birds fly off in search of roost
Night creatures begin their calls
And the Meon flows quietly on.

Roland Orridge

Important Things

There are two things important in life,
good health, and also wealth.
By that, I don't mean wealth in the hand
But a wealth of a different brand
Because anyone can have wealth from the start
By searching, what is in the heart,
When one understands, one's more aware
And learns and knows just how to care,
Knowing just how a kindness is shown
Realizing it's not meant for us alone,
Letting it travel down the years
Wiping away all the tears,
Till one day the deed in heaven appears.
Pass this on.

S. M. A. Crute

A Soldier's Lament

The battles are done,
and the war's been won,
but what about our comrades dead
lying among the poppies red?
They will never get the kiss
from mum and dad, girl-friend, or sis,
But did they give their lives in vain,
will the killing start again
now that the battles are done
and the war has been finally won?

But we are led by knaves and fools;
although they're stupid—they know the rules
and we are helpless, forced to follow
promises that are false and hollow.
And then My son will take his gun,
and go to war and fight the Hun;
the young will die once more again,
but oh! Dear God, please not in vain.
And are the battles then yet done,
and has the war been finally won?

R. L. Harris

Egypt

A land of
Fantastic Pharaohs mummified now dead,
A magical death mask to wear on their head,
The giant sphinx of lion and man,
Cartouches of people, woman and man.
Feluccas sailing down the Nile,
The Nile is 4000 mile.
Papyrus reed growing in the sun,
Adventures, discoveries not yet begun!

Jamie C-Warner, Aged 11

The Poet's Proposal

Feel the delight and the might of the poet's word
From the battles of glory to the humble flight of a bird.
Let the beauty melt your heart with words gracious and fair
For in the poet is a strength with which nothing can compare

Now let me enchant you and take a hold of your mind,
For these words offer beauty from which our hearts can all bind.
We should all be together our minds but a whole,
Then these words could be shared to enlighten the Soul.

The proposal is clear and I want you to know,
The poet's mind is alight with a heavenly glow,
We all have the power—this please conceive,
So have faith in yourself and in what you believe.

J. Drake

Gentle Creature Of The Night

It danced into the room so carefree,
A gentle creature of the night
Serenity giving way to anger,
Regardless of its plight.

Its wings e'er beating harder,
In its haste to kiss the light.
It embraced the flame so fiercely,
Its life fading like the night.

As its body grew e'er more weary,
Its spirit strove on the fight.
Until its final breath it drew,
That e'er so gentle, creature of the night.

J. R. Potts

A Storm In The Countryside

The birds had ceased their singing as the blue sky changed to grey,
The air was still, not a sound to be heard, a storm was on its way.
Even the leaves they ceased to stir as the clouds changed day
to night,
The calm was eerie, everything hushed, all the animals gone
from sight.
A distant rumble echoed forth a slight breeze moved the grass
Small drops of rain began to fall as a butterfly flitted past.
The wind gained strength and angrily whipped at gently
nodding flowers,
A blinding flash lit up the sky, silhouetting pylon towers.
The rain lashed down with so much force, large pools began to form,
The thunder cracked, the lightning flashed, this was a vicious storm.
But then the skies began to clear, the grey it turned to blue,
The rain it ceased, the leaves did shine with colours of every hue.
A rainbow arched its back across the newly–laundered sky
And once again a brightly coloured butterfly fluttered by.
The birds began to sing once more their plumage wet with rain,
And all the woodland came alive as wildlife stirred again.
The air was fresh, the sky was bright and the land had been
washed clean,
And then the sun began to shine, 'twas such a peaceful scene.

Kath Ward

Do They Really?

Fairy tale scenes of snow and frost
Seen through a curtain of freezing fog
Outstretched arms loom out of the mist
Like surrendering soldiers of forgotten wars
Each one alone in a silent crowd

Life is masked in a mantle of cold
Hiding the future, tomorrow unknown
The world awaits the melting of time
To waken the shivering quivering sleep
Of titanic forms with life–giving breath

Are they resting from their toil
And do they really feel the cold?
Stripped of glory yet still standing proud
Wrapped in a beautiful snow white shroud.

Christina Holmes

Granddad's Farewell

As I growl at the hands that feed me
There is no fight
Happy life, happy days
Happy night

To leave now and please God do it in one
Think of my past
It's been almost fun
From my corridor of fame, as I lie here,
I'm no coward, I'm not to blame

If life's a cigarette then, give me twenty
If life's a bottle, I'll drink plenty

No tears in my eyes, no hooded smiles
I'll drift away happy in my disguise

No more hiding behind a crooked smirk
Sons and daughters, grandchildren
I've done my work

No time for sorrow
No time to weep
I'm just a happy old man
Now it's my turn to sleep

Ged Murphy

Scottish Ballet

Rehearsal's o'er, and the washday performance is about to begin.
Already the crows in ragged, ebony rows, peer haughtily from
their Opera Boxes on the roof; Tickets free!—squawks a
loud–mouthed starling—nobody's darling but aye game!

That versatile conductor, the Wind—assuming the gusty
role of choreographer—coaxes a shy shirt to boldly flirt with a
flighty nightie . . . and we a' ken what that leads to! There
they go, fair set for the dance, holding hands in absurd
romance; Dainty frillies flutter their approval, while Milady's
tights sarabande deliciously in the breeze, to a weird string
accompaniment on telephone wires o'erhead, where wee birds
sit, like crotchets on a stave, waiting to be played. Caught in
mid-air on a prickly thorn, the long pants pause provocatively
in wicked, elegant style, fit to beguile—or even startle—some
tiny piece of wide–eyed femininity coyly dangling in the
wings! Later to be released, precocious things, by a mighty
puff from the Maestro himself!

The mixed audience chatters and cheers through a cre-
scendo that would do justice to the Theatre Royal, demanding
the usual curtain-calls . . . tho' many a like drama's been well
played out, unheralded, in your mother's wee back green!
Bravo!—roars a pie–faced Tom, derisively, from his catmint
seat in the stalls.
But Ballet's not his scene!

Doris Fairweather

A Last Farewell

I recall her last few precious days.
Silent and calm, yet with an intent gaze.
Her cold, frail fingers resting on the window ledge,
Eyes, pale and misty focus on a distant hedge.
Serene and still, held in a strange mysterious world.
What memories have her secret thoughts unfurled?
Does she relive the time when just a girl?
Her dainty features framed by dancing curl.
Or in the pictures in her mind can she discern
A handsome soldier gone to war? Her joy on his return.
I have no part in her sweet reverie,
No recognition on her face of me, I see.

She left me when the summer sun was high.
No loving word or smile or last "Goodbye".
The tears I shed don't wash away the pain,
Nor calm my soul, or make me whole again.

"But she was old", they say "and far outlived the span
Of seventy years, the Lord allotted man".

Oh! They must know, there cannot be another
To take her place. She loved me once! . . . She was my Mother.

Lilian M. Ball

Mr. Mugwump

He squats behind an ordered desk and ponders his PC
Bereft of wit or talent's muse, he covets every key
His dedication admirable has put the rest to shame
From eight to eight he's working late to stake his worldly claim

Though others went in search of fun and filled their lives with glee
And chattered on the why's of that and whether it might be
This man pursued his dogged course beneath the unseen stars
To sate his master's appetites and vaunt their selfish cause

And while summers vied with winters each bringing their domain
And children played and lovers kissed beneath his window pane
And dark hair grew to silver and eyes began to dim
With zest he tackled every task his marshals sought from him

But will the world remember when he finally expires
His brain exhausted by the heat of cruel ambition's fire?
And will they all appreciate a dedicated man
Who gave his life, his soul, his peace to further his command?

Or in the churchyard by the beech shall we find a tattered grave
The headstone ringed with ivy leaves to shadow out a name?
While in the choir the voices rise to sing "Cantabile"
Penned by a drunk one winter's night when poet for a day.

Peter Yorke Scarlett

Feelings

Fury is a blood red,
when eagerness is a sapphire blue,
and alarmed a shock white.
Unoccurring longing is like subtle peach,
a harming insult is an embarrassed pink.
But no one ever feels a neutral grey.
Sharing, like giving, is a golden yellow,
last, but not to say the least, is a sulking sea green.

Thomas Jackson

The Awakening Of Another Spring

In the grey of yet another dismal, chilly day.
I look out of the window in sad dismay.
At what really should enlightened be.
When the sly, old Sun creeps out for all to see.
"Will it change the sky, gorgeous azure blue.
And give everything else such a wonderful hue?"
Happy, darting birds will flirt and sing once again.
Bright flowers and blossoms emerge, a short while to remain.
For cheery Spring flows in, as another cold Winter bows out.
Making playful children stir, delighted to be active about.
Lighter evenings appear, from the once dark gloom.
And the world once more is in perfect, glorious bloom.
Huge, fluffy white clouds go sailing on by,
Forming ever changing patterns in the sky.
Shooting buds sprout on stark, bare branches.
While showering, light rain, glistens and enhances.
A solitary starling warbles merrily on roof-top high.
Day has slipped by, twilight evening is nigh.
Spring being the Earths awakening time.
Summer yet to follow, to be in its prime.

Sheila Graham

Prayer

The power of prayer is a wondrous thing
The clouds roll away and the birds start to sing
Hope is renewed, you're no longer afraid
And all because somebody prayed.

Flowers are in blossom, their scent fills the air
Life's road becomes pleasant when a carpet of prayer
The thorns and the thistles of misfortune all fade
And all because somebody prayed.

The bow of the rainbow comes into our view
Recalling God's promise to me and to you
For someone, somewhere, his voice obeyed
They got down on their knees
Yes! And somebody prayed.

Sheila M. Binks

Words Of Pleasure

Poems wanted so the advert said,
and having all the words in my head.
I picked up a pen and started to write,
the words came easy without a fight.
It was as if the words just had to come,
my mind alive for it was no longer numb.
In the words I found so much pleasure,
more valuable than a lone lost treasure.
As this my rendition leaves my pen,
I wonder if and maybe even when
Will I see my words in some book's pages,
if I do it will be worth more than wages.
Writing this poem has electrified my mind,
words are pictures I am no longer blind.
These words all came from me unbidden,
the mystery of words are no longer hidden.
I feel so alive far beyond all measure,
after writing these few words of pleasure.

T. A. Morgan

Dreaming

In dreams we live if we are clever
For dreams are the things that last forever
Reality is gone too soon
It only spans a change of moon.

But dreams oh dreams take you away
To any place on any day
They soften life's oft ugly scene
With things you dream that might have been.

So enough of life so often sad
I'll take my dreams in which I'm glad
I never cry if I am dreaming
In dreams the whole world's softly gleaming

So while you other folks are living
Through all the pain that you are giving
I'll stay apart in other spheres
And dream away my earthly years.

Molly Dack

'England Calling'

One lady and two cats you see,
Those magic words must hold the key
She feeds and grooms and strokes each day,
But they have nothing much to say.

An odd purr here, an odd purr there,
What do they know or feel or care,
They know she has her mind elsewhere
Kampala it seems, extremely rare.

That far away place unknown to her,
Is where her love has gone, her sir,
"Come back soon" I hear her say,
"I cannot wait another day".

Susan Payne

Water Beam

Darkness shudders, an aura arises,
Potential time, faces, no eyes,
Deepness, so shallow, thoughtfully untold,
No series of smiles, shimmeringly withhold,
Adjust, non-prepared, fulfilling flickering light,
Senses-sixth, shadows shiningly bright,
Arms pulling back, unspeakable power,
Decisive, unknown, eeriness over tower,
Correction so strong, deteriorating trust,
Moon subtle, so strong, deceiving lust,
Lurking beneath, stories unfold unknown,
Lifeless, though breathing, turning the throne.
Night seems to fade, dismissing the thought,
Memories disappear, once again brought,
Fear subsides, worryingly strives,
Un-influenced, tearing lovingly lives.

Narisse Hollington

Sands Of Time

How placid and quiet when the night draws near.
The sudden whisper of my dreams, shudders the earth,
holding no fear.
The soft haze of the clearing clouds, opens the gate to the
next life.
But the mind wanders aimlessly, with hints of confusion and
deceitful.
    Lies!
So delicately were dreams put, No change, Still life, No movement,
    My heart cries!
Why won't it stay the same? How it used to be,
When my precious memories used to be free.
But I can't handle the pace, so fast like life itself, in a mad craze.
Time is so unfair, just happy going forwards and nothing to spare.
But it has no feelings or conscious of how it's treating me!
The day are like seconds, months like minutes and years like hours.
My wishes are like fallen leaves decayed by age, how life was
    once sweet
My eyes had seen what I needed to see, but I move on hopelessly.
My guidance and love for life goes through a tunnel of No
Return,
    Just a dead end!
Fate has a lot in store for me good but mainly bad, how I
    hunger for the life I once had.
The dreams that seemed so real, there's no re-birth for I can
    never be bought
    Back to the Eternal Golden age and life I once had!

Bina Pawar

Getting There

Getting there was easy, it seemed the thing to do,
Getting there took no time, all your friends were new
Getting there, just happened, doors flew open wide,
The merry-go-round went higher and you never saw the slide

Getting there went your way, you travelled light and free,
Getting there needed no courage, there was no lock or key,
Getting there seemed one way, no other way to go,
The merry-go-round went faster and how were you to know.

So, ask the alcoholic, ask the down and out,
Getting there was easy, just try getting out.

Getting back is harder, it is the only thing to do,
Getting back takes a lot of time, friends are very few,
Getting back seems hopeless when many doors are shut,
The merry-go-round has stopped now, all the ties are cut

So, ask the agoraphobic who never dares go out,
Getting there was easy, just try getting out

Getting back will happen, but you alone will hold the key,
The key of life inside you that needs to be set free
Lock away and open up, your journey starts today,
This time please remember the price you may have to pay

Catherine Cloud

Alone

Across the land, and over the sea,
You'll always be in my heart with me,
No matter what you'll ever say,
I'm yours forever and here to stay,
I love you loads and that's for sure,
A love of which is virgin pure,
But no matter, what I'll ever say,
It comes back to you at the end of the day,
Do you mean what you say to me
and do you really want to be,
With me every single day,
But if you don't then please, just say,
And you could go and leave tomorrow,
and I would promise, I wouldn't follow,
but stay at home and start to pine,
Think your name, howl and whine,
I'd long for you more and more each day,
your face in my mind forever would stay,
And this will be the downfall of me,
I couldn't live without you, see!

Lee Hobson

Memories

I awoke this morning
to a cold and frosty morn.
Birds were singing in the trees,
and frost upon the lawn.
You see it's Xmas morning.
Children's laughter can be heard
as they open up their presents,
on this day our Lord was born.

I sit and watch their faces,
their names they come to mind,
of Bette, Doreen, Jack and Joan.
Of Xmas in another time.

Our mother's home was humble.
She did her best to make our Xmas great.
The apple, orange and the pear,
we did appreciate.
Now those days are over
a new era has begun,
but we won't forgot those times
when life to us was fun.

J. M. O. Rooke

Moment Of Truth

Sending off my poems, I'm high as a kite.
Hoping to be successful, and feeling just right
Trying to compete with poets by the score
Things you can write about are getting more and more.

Weeks go by, then one morning after toast
I'm looking and wondering what has arrived in the post
Hoping that I can shout and cheer
For another to be published, sometime this year.

You have to be prepared for the disappointment too
So many talented people are hoping it is true
To be the one selected, and lucky this time
So I must keep on trying with my rhythm and rhyme.

Evelyn M. Harding

Death

To look in the mirror,
is it me
looking at the blackness
looking over me?
He flows high up watching me.
The blackness and darkness
Never leaves me.

Death, what a peaceful word.
not knowing who, what or where you will be.
Smiling with happiness
or crying in misery,
is that the place you want to be?

Tamara Armitage

Winter

'Tis a time when all the snow's around
when all that's green is underground
not a speck of wildlife to be seen
only tell tale footprints where they've been
People attempting their daily chores
With snow reaching up and above car doors
The outlook is bleak and cold and grey
But seems as though it's here to stay
At least we think for several days
Before a thaw, with luck, on its way
The best solution in weathers like these
Is to stay indoors and turn the key
To keep the nasty freeze at bay
And know that you'll not go astray
With time, with hope, the dilemma will pass
So we can gaze once more upon green grass.

Sarah H. Meek

159

Untitled

If you could talk to me
I know what you would say
You'd plead for your life
You'd scream and you'd pray
But I'm in control
I've been given the right
Your life is in my hands
There's no point in your fight.

I've always dreamt of the moment we met,
The love between us should be the strongest you get
Will you ever forgive me if I take that away
If I deny all your rights, would that be O.K.?

I know how I'd feel if the tables were turned,
Is it worth the convenience to make you never return?
There's no point in me saying I'd love to love you
For I haven't the courage
I'm so far below you.

Clare Kelly

Dreamer With Ears

You dreamer with ears, widen your eyes and see
the wonders of divine creation.
The beauty of the earth, and all that runs,
in life drained out of the sea.
Order and detail, the bounty of time,
a record in fanfare of life;
reflected in patterns drawn high in the sky,
then far further out to eternity.
Look down or up, in a line of the mind,
bemused believer in all material.
The time has come to declare your faith,
and flower at the last account.

J. Vallance

La Casa De Los Muertos

Outside the world was filled with silence,
The bombs, the blood, the tears were done.
We only heard the door creak open;
Watched her come in from the sun.

A black scarf bound her head and ears,
Her white blouse bloomed a darkening red,
Her face was stained with dust and tears:
"Me debo descansar." She said.

She moved towards us, said "Favor?"
And leaned her rifle by my head.
She lay herself down on the floor:
"Me debo descansar." She said.

Outside the world was filled with silence
'Til with fury flew the door
On shattered hinges swinging open.
One crossed himself. Another swore:

"To Hell with whores and Nacionalistas,
The Devil take them if he will!"
"Enough, Alfredo!" Spoke the foremost,
"Against the dead we speak no ill."

Austin Murtagh

Dreamer With Ears

You dreamer with ears, widen your eyes and see
the wonders of divine creation.
The beauty of the earth, and all that runs,
in life drained out of the sea.
Order and detail, the bounty of time,
a record in fanfare of life;
reflected in patterns drawn high in the sky,
then far further out to eternity.
Look down or up, in a line of the mind,
bemused believer in all material.
The time has come to declare your faith,
and flower at the last account.

J. Vallance

Leave

And now I'm home again;
White linen and clean crockery for tea;
A chair, a pipe, a fire for me,
And space, and room to think and yawn.

And now I'm home again;
A crimson cheek, a friendly nod,
A sleep, a quiet talk with God,
And then to bed; fresh sheets and pillow there.

And now I'm home again;
And yet there's one who thinks
'He'll soon be going back—he'll soon be gone.'
Still on the music plays, and on.

Gordon Carter

Iris

My life was dull nobody to talk to
to tell my secrets my dreams or moan to
to walk with talk with or sit about
to have a drink, a meal or just go out.

A holiday in Greece is where I met you.
Just a chance meeting, for all we knew.
We talked and laughed and talked some more
who was to know how long for.

We liked the same things walking and eating
For us no more of just chanced meetings
always together day after day
was this going to last who could say.

Back home again a week then two
then the phone rang was it really you
could I come up for the weekend
is this were it all would end.

The weeks have turned now into years
I can now laugh at my early fears
I should have known it would never end
Who is it? You ask, it's my best friend.

Hazel Gardner

Why Oh Why

Why oh why do we have to cry,
Is someone sick, did someone die,
Why oh why do we have to cry.

So much evil, so much sadness,
Badness, madness,
Why oh why do we have to cry.

If all our tears were tears of joy
Like watching a child play with a toy,
The beauty we know and see in the spring,
Even the kittens playing with string,

Show goodness happiness and love each day,
Then nobody will need to say,
Why oh why we have to cry.

Venetta MacKenzie

Colour Collage

Blood—red Poppies,
Standing apart, from
Snow—white Daisies,
With big yellow hearts!
Tall, green, wild grasses,
Intertwined, edging the path—
In peaceful repose,
With no sign of wrath.
All gently swaying in tune with the breeze
Trembling with ecstasy
Through the trees.
Herald the dawn,
Of a brand new morn.

Freda Ringrose

Farewell To Glengarnock Steelworks

The fight was hard, we tried our best
Now all our hopes are laid to rest
'cause they're pullin' doon the work

The ingot bay, the soaker bay, bay "G", the mill and the store.
The noise the smells the workmen's
    yells, are stilled forever more, they're pullin' doon the work.

The mates you'll never see again,
    well scattered now are they.
It wisnae just a job we lost, on that
    sad and final day they're pullin' doon the work.
Some men a job will never see,
    some they still have hope.
Some have tried, the training course.
    others sit and mope. And they're pullin' doon the work.

I wish they'd never shut us doon, I loved that place you see,
The friends I made, the laughs we had,
    I'll remember till I dee, they're pullin' doon the work.

Some when reading this may scoff, and wonder where I've been,
But those who worked inside those walls
    Well, they'll know what I mean. Aye, they're pullin' doon the work

John Anthony Sloan

The Sunset

The clouds spread across the sky, like distant hills.
The sun tinged them with gold, one by one.

The whispery sprays of pink and purple waved across the sky,
Every so often a piece of light green mountain
was to be seen.

And as the sun was nearly down,
A pinky orange glow was glazed across a dying sky,
And then nothing, it was gone,
As slowly the Earth fell silently asleep.

Rachel M. Turner

Love Will Find A Way

If all the world was filled with love
And streets were paved with gold,
If only raindrops fell from above,
What a story would then unfold;
A story of love and kindness shown,
No hatred, wars, or people alone.
The earth would be warm with a gentle caress,
With people united in happiness.
If everyone believed in God
And in His footsteps gently trod,
The road would be wide with a welcome smile,
No-one would falter for mile after mile.
So pass the word to all your friends
That man to man should make amends
To drive the dark clouds far away,
And bring the sunshine down to stay.

Yvonne Bayliss

Night-Piece

The angel,
A child, will secure
This vault. Here he comes
Placing the motto,
Not charged with other mementoes.
What had been cast off
Wise dolphins have salvaged. A sea-breeze
Revives with moisture the land
Where dust and ashes fly.
If the stars streaming die,
Who shall illumine the night,
A flame that thinks? A gust
Fanning fire and sail.
The wind petrified,
Who shall stir
The air?

Alfred Behrmann

The Artist

He stands at his easel, so deep in thought
    Unaware of the world around
    Transfixed and quite spellbound
    Oblivious of every sound

Ah! His eyes light up—the subject he sought
    Has materialized in his mind's eye.
    Across the canvas his brushes fly
    And he breathes a contented sigh.
He works very fast, blending colours with skill
    Drawing a line here and there,
    Sometimes pausing to stare,
    Then leaving some canvas bare.
The daylight is fading—his hands at last still
    But now he no longer feels blue
    For his picture's complete and on view.
    He has captured the likeness so true

E. J. Sharman

A Giant Step For Small Dogs

I am only a little dog, quite small
Compared to others, only a foot tall
Walking along the road negotiating legs and feet
With prams, bikes and children is quite neat
Do people actually look where they go
The answer from our point of view, no
Mothers, children, workmen talking
Not looking where they are walking
Watching where we put our paws
There is no safeguard in the laws
That should a little one be trampled on
The offender does not walk away, and be gone
Forgetting the discomfort and the pain
Only our owners can help us regain
The strength needed to walk more
To get back home and repair the sore
That the large foot that caused the pain
Will not be repeated again

A. T. Higgins

The Marquis

It was dry that day there was no rain
That the marquis root went up in flames
In no time at all the whole building was burned
Now take heed my friends there's a lesson to be learned:
Don't play with matches, fire, or flame
Because it can only cause you anguish and pain
The trade that was there may have taken flight
But we'll work an oracle being here tonight
We will try and restore the good name
Now all of you drinkers come play the game
Now see the marquis, oh what a name
Rise like a phoenix out of the flames

Brendan Campbell

A Box Of Paints

There's a painter in the heavens.
Who loves many shades of blue
In his well loved box of colours
He has tints of every hue.

He chooses pale blue in the mornings
When he wants the sun to shine
And a darker blue at sunset
Which tells birds it's sleeping time.

He likes the many tints of green
That cover hills and fields
Our master paints a wondrous scene
And shows the power he wields

He is the one who colours the roses
Makes the jewels that fly in the air
His workshop in heaven never closes.
And his love, like his work we all share.

A. Brindle

I'm Alive

I am alive, you people out there
I hear you talk but do you care
My eyes are closed my body is still
One day I'll wake up, I know I will

It's not my fault that I'm lying here
I don't want to die, that's what I fear
Some fool in his car was driving too fast
Whilst crossing the road, I was the last

I'm glad my son just ran across
For if not his little life, he would have lost
My wife and son come and visit me now
My wife feels bad, we had just had a row

I want to talk but no words will come out
I wish I could get up and walk about
Dear God above please don't take me yet
I'm not ready to go, don't let me fret

Three weeks and I am feeling much better
I was able to tell my wife I love her
Thank you God for giving me my life
To be able to share it with my son and wife

Nora Smith

Silence

Silence echoes all around, where life stood still for you
Locked in time and space, outside of human view
Your presence still fills this place
I think I see your friendly face
I strain my ears to hear a sound
Yet there is only silence all around

The silence echoes through my brain
Yet somehow soothes the aching pain
The silence like a mantle over you and me
Binding us together for all eternity

M. J. Johnstone

Special Place

There is a special place I know,
Where I think all should go.
As you enter through this door,
You'll see more than you ever saw.
Words in rhyme, words in verse,
Through many worlds you will traverse
People's thoughts, most inner feelings
Words that have such deep meanings.
Such great works of the mind.
Within this special place you will find,
A place were expression is so free,
Somewhere you are privileged to see.
Love and hate, happiness and sadness,
Confusion, chaos, a world that seems like madness
An explanation of what you see or what you feel,
Sometimes none of it is real.
A place for your own explanation, a place for finding out,
A place for understanding what you think the world's about.

Lucy Round

An Empty Stage

The strands of my life are slowly dissipating
Like spaghetti sliding from a fork,
Spiralling down from whence they came
Falling in a mound.
The tenuous threads of my existence are no longer entwined,
No longer depict a scene or weave a pattern
Each one is gradually breaking loose.
Soon the canvas of my life will be as fragmented and tattered
As my being has now become.
A tapestry faded and worn as I too am fading and weary.
The backcloth is removed, the scenery stored,
The stage is empty and so am I.
No encore, my life has expired,
The curtain is drawn.

Barbara Woodyatt

Just A Dance

I never got to say goodbye
To hold your hand and tell you why
Why I just had to leave that way
I didn't have time to think or say
Say how much you mean to me
Or just how special you made me feel
You held me in your arms so tight
And winked at me all through the night
You told me I was beautiful
And that my smile was like the sun
You said my eyes were glowing bright
And that they would light the darkest night
You flattered me with compliments
And broke my heart with your pretence
I really thought I had a chance
But to you, all that was just a dance.

Emily Redmond

Reflections In St. Mary's Square

The pavement wide beneath his feet in broad expanse did lie;
No line of care showed in his face nor worry in his eye.
Hand deep in trouser pocket thrust against a chilling breeze
He strolled along with nonchalance bred from a mind at ease.

Hanging idly from his lips—a cigar long and brown
From which the smoke curled upwards when it wasn't taken down.
Admiring glances from his friends did make him swell with pride;
But nought could cause a falter or a stumble in his stride.

A business man or millionaire be he if truth be told?
Oh, Bless you, No! Not one of those; a mere sixteen year old.

H. Dennis Palmer

Yellow In A Sea Of Green

Florescent, opaque,
Interchanged with flocks of white,
Turning . . .
Red to bright plum.

Orange fades to cream.
Dulled but not senseless,
Death feeds a dream.
A host of colour
Inside crystals of light
Fading at night.

Spongy-like formations,
A heady scent of vibrant lime,
While . . .
Lilacs stretch out to meet blues.
Shadowy mixtures of wondrous hues.

A hint of pink,
A tinge of pine,
A complexion filled with reddened stains.
Pigmentation beyond your imagination.
Yellow in a sea of green.

Tracey Phillips

Winter Dusk

The secret lanterns begin to glimmer,
the deep snow on the ground and firs
shine back
lighter than the dusky sky.
Asparagus in the flower pots
    on the window sill
flatter against the pane.
The silhouettes of indigo coloured evergreens
wave against the sky
    becoming darker
all the time.
A sparrow hurries home,
the lanterns shine brighter,
the sky now dark.
    Night.

Rowena Strittmatter

The End Of The Season

The beach is silent, no ghosts, no people except me,
The shutters go up in the littered back streets
and on the piers and on the shop fronts,
the beach balls, arm bands dragged inside to gather dust,
then there is a silence, a sadness that can be felt,
the echoes of the last cheers have long vanished.
yet the sun returns to shine on an empty audience,
the tide is greeted from empty beaches,
the cruel autumn has made its presence felt,
stealing the joy, the heat, the sun, optimism.
They will both return tomorrow and again in vain hope,
The roar is one of grief.
I take one last look at the ravaged pier,
one last smell of the sea salt and pebbles
I glance at the abandonment.
I thought I heard gulls but was that a scream?
As I began to walk away I also hear the tide roar
its departure.
Stephen Prout

The Great Illusion

This is not that
But that is the way it is
Don't waste time on this
But live in that

At last the real from the unreal
And it's not the way round you think it is
The unreal is the real

The state is the way
The body is a means of play
Use the body to live in the state
That is there for all to know

I'll be there always.
G. C. Heath

Now They're Just Reminders

I hate that candle on the wall that we bought down by the sea
You insisted on buying it and giving it to me
And that romantic story that we used to read at night
Perched on the end of our bed
The moon the only light
And that Christmas card you gave me with the teddies in the snow
And that cheeky little message that I'd never let you show
And that painting from your mother I've always despised
But now I hate it even more
'cause it's the colour of your eyes
And that bobble hat you bought me in that lovely shade of blue
Was only meat to be a joke
But I grew to love that too
And your framed picture hung up on the wall
Your face laughing away
Says you'll catch me if I fall
They used to be mementos
That you really care
But now they're just reminders
That you're no longer there!
Alison Merry

Hurt

Many a times I thought to myself
To tell you my heart's desire
But the thought of losing you had stopped me
Again and again.

I told you my heart's feelings
That day—a day that had been so special to me
A day I had dreamt of
The day we had spent together.

But all I got was a cold look
A stare that stabbed me, piercing through my heart
Hurting me so much,
So much that you didn't realise
That my love for you is forever
Sadia Hussain

Sapped

Sap rose in his brain always around Patrick's Day
He took the plough sock to the smithy
To have it honed and pointed.

Horses well foddered through the winter harness and chains
clinking to go
My father got excited in Spring
Like a chicken emerging from a shell.

Out in the ten acre, he steered horses and plough
Turning black sods into furrows
Could March winds showed no mercy.

A rood he had done when I came with hot sweet tea
He savoured it out of the ponnie
And ate soda bread smothered in dripping.

Stretched out on the headland
Chuckled as he gazed down the field
Puffed a woodbine
Thrusted out his chest and away he went

Through all seasons
His booted feet plodded on the soil
Time reaped its toll
The sap rose last Spring without him.
Peggy Sims

The Smell Of The Sea

As I smelt the smell of the sea
Memories of childhood washed over me.
Of sand and shingle at the seaside
And breakwaters placed so evenly
Imposing the beach on the estuary.

Since then I've known shores with unbroken line
Stretching to infinity, with sand textured like flour
Without stones or shells, though you search by the hour.

Yet I long for the narrow shingled space
With the mud flats revealed as the water recedes at a pace.
Its return brings the scenes
Of breakwaters, slowly submerging like tired submarines.
Moored boats forlorn on their side
Then buoyantly bobbing in the thrusting tide.

The cry of the gulls and the splash of the waves
And the hurt of the shingle as you go down to bathe.
Memories of childhood lived by the sea
Forever, forever remain with me.
Peter Sowter

The Death Of Mining

Coal is black, coal is hard
　　coal is compressed death.

Mines are dirty, mines are damp
　　mines are mausoleums.

Pit folk are kind, pit folk are happy
　　pit folk are endangered.

Miners are tough, miners are hard
　　miners die young.

North East is industry, North East is mining
　　North East is finished.

It's all for money, it's all for gain
　　it's all for nothing.

Major decisions, major reforms
　　major disaster.

My grandfather was killed, my dad is dead
　　my son is a dead weight.

Pits are closing, pits have closed
　　pits are no more.

Coal is blood, coal is bones
　　coal is compressed death.
Ken Goodsir

Cobwebs

With hands thrust out to repel the advances of time
I brush away the cobwebs
And find a half century of memories to dust
The old mirror reflects only the wrinkles of age
And the greying hair
But the cheeks can still blush at the indiscretions of youth
Remembering tears, anger, frustrations, mistakes,
Lost loves, dashed hopes.
And the eyes can still smile and the heart beat faster
Remembering happy times, growing up, ambitions, love of a partner,
Children, life lived to the full.
This body that grows old is like a house
That creaks and groans
With care it will watch over all that lies within.
I put away my duster now
Secure in the knowledge that with the passing of time
The veil of cobwebs will protect the memories
Until I find the need of them again.

June Bennett

An Alcoholic's Lament

The old man sat by the whisky still
His eyes a-glaze with tears
He looked in the glass, that he held in his hand
    And pictured his wife's last years.
He pictured his children, long scattered and gone.
    Their laughs, their joys, and their tears.
He sighed as he took his last drink from that glass.
    I have wasted my happiest years.
Those days that were precious, how blind I have been
    For my selfishness, now I must pay.
For the girl I once loved is in heaven above.
    From me, God just took her away.
I must die as I lived in a world of my own
    Locked in alcohol, guilt, and pride.
To Thee Lord, I now pray, on this my dying day.
    Place my family once more by my side.

Pat Golden

Jimmy Lad

I know a builder called Jimmy
And a hearty man is he.
I haven't known him for long.
But there's something about him, you just can't miss.
The sparkle in his eyes,
and the kind smile that brightens your day.
He takes pride in all his work, while whistling along to a tune.
One day he fixed our pond, and said.
"Now then boys and girls, how's about that for a concrete wall?"
Then suddenly a frog jumped over his arm,
and gave Jimmy Lad, the fright of his life!
That was a right old laugh.
But I think the frog was more shocked than anything!

Nilmini Hattotuwagama

The Scales Of Justice

I used to feel proud to belong to this race
The one we call humankind
but the evil we've done since our race began
Weighs heavily on my mind
And talking of weighing, the scales certainly don't balance
They are very much down on one side
The side of injustice, dishonour and shame
No wonder we want to hide.
What happened to honour, good faith and fair play
It's an old-fashioned notion they say
But one day we shall find that all humankind falls short in
every way
And when it's too late to alter our fate
What will become of us then
So heed what I say and make sure you pray
For our race to be wholesome again.

Margaret A. Perkins

Sunset In Africa

Have you ever been to Africa where the elephants do roam
And Hippo's sing their songs as in the mud they loll
Lazy zebra's in the dust do roll in the mid-day heat
Hyena's laughing as they run by to seek
But most of all is sunset time when to one's eye does see,
the sun is like a golden ball with rays outstretched around it.
Soon it will be darkness as behind the clouds it falls
no rays of sunshine found.
The quiet of the night as the cricket's sing their song
and the mighty roar of a lion as he wanders on.
The monkeys in the tree-tops high in a forest glade
Swing and swing before a new born day
the hunter tracks away to find a tasty meal
But most of all its heartache as when the next rain will fall
For here among the hill tops no water to be found
The flies do buzz around and even when the thunder sounds
It doesn't rain at all, so come along to Africa
If only in a dream.

Elizabeth A. Wilkinson

My Mirror

I looked deep into the mirror the other day,
found someone familiar but in dismay;
Someone like me — shy and caring,
someone unlike me — strong and daring;
Someone with eyes full of happiness,
someone with words full of forgiveness;
Someone who's desperate about what the future holds,
someone who's anxious to hear secrets untold;
Someone who's keen to face the worst,
someone who's meant to always be the first;
I looked deeper into the mirror again,
but it was only me standing there in vain.

Inderjit Kaur

Joanne

I see her pain through misty eyes,
the shallow smile, the thin disguise.
Her love is deep, yet so well hidden,
the sullen face, racked and guilt-ridden.
Killing me softly with looks of mystique,
making me vulnerable, lost and weak.
How can I save this poor lost soul,
wandering aimlessly, never reaching her goal.
Never understood, wanted or loved,
yet always circling the clouds up above.
Will they ever realize this child's desire,
her endless pursuits that never tire?
Suspended in an empty sea of animation,
her solution, the glass care of 4th dimension.

Dene Lindley

Bleeding Me Dry

You're looking for a lonely face,
a twin soul of emptiness.
Nobody sees me . . .
but you notice my vacant stare.
I should see you like the ones before
but I still hold a faint hope.
That your company will bring a smile.
I care.
You know I understand.
It's supposed to provide a sense of worth,
but weak souls have used me before.
You just eat my insides.
Like all the rest.
I tend to your wounds. But you make me bleed.
I see myself drip onto the floor
with every word that drips from your mouth.
I wanted to help. But I wanted to be loved.
I only ever achieve one.
No one is ever there to mop up my blood,
but it's always washed away.

Kim Wade

Our Life

We're haunted by all those things we can't reach
We never get near them but can't forget either

We're caught by the thought of freedom
We are stuck at the beginning of the street of escape

We desire the feelings which destroy us
And try to love alone in a dark room

We want to reach our goals by thinking of the past
And we wonder why we are not happy

Andrea Moser

Seasons Of Life

Spring was lilies and roses and daffodils,
with outings and picnics and games,
Laughing, and dancing,
days full of thrills,
and oh! So sweet at time was this!

And then there was summer,
with long hot days to fill,
Swimming and boating
And moonlit nights so still,
And oh! So sweet a time was this!

And then there was autumn,
with courting and kissing,
and dreams to fulfil,
marriage, babies, child rearing years,
and oh! So sweet a time was this!

And now it is winter,
No flowers, or sunshine or thrills,
But long spells of darkness,
Cold and lonely and ill
and oh! How sad a time is this!

Jo Deguara Sammut

Reality

This world we live in, can it really be
A place of virtue and serenity,
Or is it vile, uncouth, unjust,
And filled brimful of sexual lust.

Is London really all they say it is,
A city paved with gold and tapestries,
Or is it just a nest of criminals
With greed and grabbing hands as their credentials.

Are honest men presiding at the country's helm,
And do they honestly protect the realm,
Or are they waiting like the vagrant hawk,
To help themselves, when nought is left but talk.

Douglas Arthur Watling

On The Westport Train

When the train pulled out of Dublin City,
It was around half past one,
The guard himself was rather witty,
After I had sprinted for the train,
Once settled in for the journey,
From East to West across the plain,
The jet lag began to overpower me,
As my body rocked in time to the sway,
All around me some people were chatting,
Whilst others took time to pray,
Occasionally I would stir with the rattling,
A young colleen so kind as could be,
Travelling back home to Westport,
Offered comfort and support to me,
Advising me to alight at Claremorris,
Alas no more of each other we both did see,
For I travelled on to Ballina,
And caught a bus for Port-A-Cloy by the sea.

Eamonn James McGrath

Talents

Use the talent, that God has bestowed on you—
    Appreciate, the precious gift, he has sent.
Within everyone, is the power to pursue,
    Improve, perfect, and thus achieve fulfilment.

How happy are those, who are to music, born—
    The singer, whose voice, an audience finds enthralling,
While graceful dancers, their complex steps, perform,
    Totally dedicated, to their calling.

The writer seeks the solitude of his room,
    And over the pristine page, his fast pen flows.
Adept, is the weaver, standing by the loom,
    Or, the specialist, nurturing the scented rose.

The greatest painter who has ever lived,
    How much he owes to God, is surely aware,
Or cathedral builders, whose work, has survived
    Time's grim ravage, wonders, all of us can share.

Worthy is the one, who can lend a listening ear,
    And bring comfort to another, in distress,
Whose unsung talent, is all around us here,
    In daily acts, of caring and kindliness!

Elizabeth Harris

Baby Josh

Oh Joshua, you smile so sweet,
As I walk in through the door.
Your face lights up, as our eyes meet,
Sweetheart, I love you so.

Before you came into this world,
I knew you'd be a boy,
I told your Mum, you were not a girl,
And to expect a baby boy.

Now here you are, our little man,
So wise and bright you are.
You are your Mummy's little son,
You're destined to go far.

You have eyes so blue, and lashes fair,
A tiny button nose,
With little wisps of pale blonde hair,
And the sweetest little toes.

With chubby fingers, reaching out,
And the cutest little tum.
Four pearl–white teeth, peep from your mouth,
And a wibble wobble bum.

Maxine White

Parenthood

Yes, babies are a big event,
Before them, you just came and went
Quite according to your mood.
Now—you think of baby food!

Babies, you just feed and change them,
Burp them and then rearrange them.
If you don't, they cry and cry,
They might be sick on Father's tie!

Rattles, ducks and baby's dummy,
Then the first word—it is "Mummy".
Your nights are not now undisturbed,
By this fact you are quite perturbed.

By toothless smiles you are quite smitten,
Grandma's bought the child a kitten!
Nappies, bottles, teddy bears
Are ever–present—but who cares?

Then, when parents' minds stop reeling,
Father gets that familiar feeling . . .
He turns around and looks at Mother
And thinks "I wonder—should we have another?"

Ursula Cutts

In Need Of Friends

I am a stranger, I am a hermit.
I wish I could come out of this dark room,
learn a language that people can understand.
Maybe someone might care for this garden:
Withered flowers will be watered back to life.
Maybe someone might help me get out of here.
Here I am, sitting thirsty, not being helped,
in this terrible night, in this lifeless desert.

Omar Seguna

Newmarket

It is roses, roses all the way
At high haven stables in Suffolk.
Spanish beauty and persian maid
Perfume the air with their fragrance.
Little white pet, Caroline testout.
Pink and white, red and gold, tumble over
Fifty-two stables festooned.
A glorious sight.

Just as lovely in comfort and care
Are the stallions and mares, fillies and foals
Housed in their boxes beneath.
'Much sought after' has winning ways.
'M.T.C.' is learning, much too fond of carrots—
and nuts.
'Darling Clover', one year old, certainly is
in clover.
Pampered, petted, cosseted.   More than any baby.

Trotting off to the Gallops in the merry month of May.
'Much Too Clever' is very pleased with himself
He is three years old today.   More Hay!

Irene Sylvia Brown

Howling Wind

Howling wind that whispers many secrets,
blow away this thankless task of living,
take me home on your gliding wings,
past the endless, winding streets of no forgiveness.

Past the barren dreams of hopelessness,
and the many tried for, failing conquests,
Over the streams of troubled visions,
to where the silver sea of life, still lingers.

Once there to mingle with the silent shapes,
that guard the crystal mountain,
and bathe again, in the healing waters,
of the longed for, youthful fountain.

My soul to wander evermore,
on the plains of pure creation,
until my soul is called upon,
to play its role, of incarnation.

Howling wind that whispers many secrets,
blow away this thankless task of living,
take me home on your gliding wings,
through these endless, winding streets of no forgiveness.

J. Greene

Happily

Happily the children skip to school;
Happily the kangaroos jump around in the pool;

Happily the birds sing on the wall;
Happily the cows lay in a hall;

Happily the teacher said to one child "Well done".
Happily the dog barked for a bone;

Happily the dolphins swim up and down the ocean;
Happily the waves rock the sea in slow motion;

Happily the whales roam around the great seas;
Happily the great strong winds blow the trees.

Martin Haverson

Too Late

You'll have to be careful and you'd better beware
or I'll shut down my feelings, till there's nothing else there
one by one, so you'd better take note
because only you fool, you'll be cutting your throat

There will come the day, when I'm empty inside
with no more emotion, there'll be nothing to hide
the face that you know, it has almost dissolved
and I won't have the time, to get so involved.

The monsters appear and take over your fate
you had a good chance, but now is the wait
to see if the name on the grave can be read.
Or if it's all over, and love must be dead.

The shadows creep up as the night starts to fall
when you're up the whole night as you're climbing the wall
to try and get back, the love that you lost
It's the ogre inside you, is what it must cost

It tears at your mind through the day and the night
all the pain and the sorrow because you lost the fight
for the rest of your life the torture awaits
and you meet with the devil, at his fiery gate.

David M. Took

Hidden Gold

Along a muddy woodland path we trudged
My friend and I—one windy day in March.
The greyness of the scene was faintly smudged
With that first tender green of budding larch.
And in a sheltered spot beneath the trees
Our disbelieving eyes beheld the sight
Of slender bluebells swaying in the breeze
Along with dainty windflowers—mauve and white.
Our footsteps led us down another Ride
Between the stalwart oaks, and ash, and beech,
Where thorny briars cascaded either side
And nodding there among them—out of reach—
Wild daffodils their hidden gold revealed
With yellow trumpets struggling to the light
No longer by the vicious thorns concealed
Their radiance swept winter out of sight.

Joyce Latham

My Prayer

Please—teach me the meaning of Life and lend me hope and loyalty;
Give me understanding that I may endeavour to see reality
And define what is merely illusion and imaginary.
Offer me strength that I may use it
And not abuse it.
Guide me through the blackness and pain
With faith that I shall see light again
When the darkness is travelled
And the problems unravelled.
Pour in my soul compassion and integrity,
Help me to avoid shallowness and infidelity;
Scatter on me, like confetti, a charitable approach to Humanity
And deliver me from apathy, hate and insanity.

Philippa Wilton-Pattison

Mam And Dad

Part of my heart is not with me
It rests so far away
It lies below where eyes can't see
It knows not night or day
Between my mam and dad it waits
Since they've passed through the pearly gates
And while my heart is pumping
With memories of joy it's jumping
Of the time we were together
The love they gave and whether
When it's me there in that grave apart
Will I find a piece of my children's hearts.

Austin Howells

Holy Willie's Prayer

I try tae gan tae Kirk every week, tae listen tae thy word,
Tae worship thee, mild an' meek, an' confess ma week's
transgressions.

Since I was a wee laddie, I've aye gane, tae Sunday school,
   though dreeping wi' rain,
Noo I'm an auld, wiser man, I still keep gaun, a' the same.

Thou art high in Heaven, worthy o' praise an' honour,
We worship thee, at eleven, an' banish auld nick in hell.

Oh Lord, remember me an' mine in ma prayer,
Lead us no' intae temptation,
I strive tae lead a life humble an' fair, tae be a guid disciple,
   father.

Mess John'll help me oot, wi' ony difficulties I may hae,
Whar that auld ain, the Devil is the root, we hae tae fight him
   till he's gane.

It's a fecht atween guid an' evil, lead us no' intae temptation,
Keep us safe fae the Deil, an' look owre ma weans.

I gie mair tae the Kirk than maist, a fittin' proportion o' ma wage,
At least I'm no twa–faced, like that ain O'Shanter, sheep–shank,
wha thinks himsel nae sheep–shank bane.

This nicht, keep thy watch upon us, close an' firm,
Gie us strength fur the niest day, an' ah'll no' mak a fuss.

In thy name I pray, Amen, amen!
   Dawn P. Allison

To Catch A Mouse!

Up a sloping mossy bank,
By a rill where rushes flank,
Came a weasel, cautious drank,
Then he turned and made his way.

To where the bush and tree grew tighter,
Roamed and weaved this furry fighter,
Then ear–weary, laid feet lighter,
As beady eye caught mice at play.

Balls of brown, soft and squeaking,
Unaware, the hunter sneaking
Round their pool of sunlight leaking
Through trees' leafy overlay.

Darting like an angry arrow
Startles linnet, perching sparrow,
Sinks white teeth in flesh and marrow,
Drags a luckless mouse away.

Up a sloping mossy bank
By a rill where rushes flank,
Runs a weasel teeth still sank
Disappears his homeward way.
   J. Brad Haigh

Dawn

I love this time of day,
Peaceful, yet so far from quiet,
The morning chorus rise and call
Birds and animals can vent at will
The noise of man is hushed and still
I hear and wonder at it all.

I love this time of day,
The brightening sky, the colours,
A breaking dawn above the trees
The light that satisfies some lost desire
Deep within the body's fire
And puts my soul at ease.

I love this time of day,
This lull before this rising morn
As the golden sun begins to peek
My head is filled with words and sights
But my lips are quiet,
It's a time to look, not to speak.
   R. F. Jones

Declan

For many years we waited, deliberated and anticipated.
Unsure and yet convinced that your arrival would be assured.

Almost eight years had passed, the time was now or else too late,
We planned your arrival with precision, calendar, jobs all to consider.

Then February 9th you appeared
with your fair hair and grey blue eyes,
you captured our hearts, to no one's surprise.

Now as I sit here and watch,
this bundle of dependence has become so independent,
with a twinkle and a smile and a determined streak so wide.

Our baby son so fair has stolen our hearts,
our lives now revolve around you,
with your own personality you, at two, are nobody's fool.

Our lives without you would be so desolate,
You light up each day with your smile,
your actions, your speech and your kisses.

What wonder is a child.
To watch and learn as he explores.
To love, cherish and adore.
   Edrina Briscoe-Conway

Faces

The world is full of different places
Different lives of different faces

Each one of those faces has a story to tell
Of lives that were good
Of lives that were hell

Each one of those faces has something of beauty
Something of honour
Something of duty

Each one of those faces has a life long dream
Where they live in happiness
As a King or a Queen

I know that I am one of those faces
With a story to tell from one of those places.
   Celine Kelly

My Birthday

Did I hear the postman knock
Surely it can't be a 7 o'clock
But there on the mat lie cards by the score
And in the day I got many more.

It's my birthday today you see
I will be 80, no surely not me
But I am, and I had a lovely day
With presents and cards along the way

Telephone calls, and knocks at the door
With flowers, and choc's and presents galore.
It's a day I will never forget,
I have only one regret.
I wish I was 80 once more.
   Edith M. Wicker

The Senses

What is an offer for the yearning eye?
The splendid colours of the evening sky
Blue, turning to palest green and apricot,
As down through soft grey mist, no longer hot
The slowly setting sun descends to earth.
As this to sight, so music for the ear;
Sweet melodies to conjure up a tear
Memories revived by lyrics soft and sweet,
And beautiful concertos with variable beat,
Philharmonic orchestras producing glorious sounds
From strings and winds and tympanist,
Joys that know no bounds.
Our senses bring such pleasures of touch and sound and sight.
The wonder of such treasures turns darkness into light.
   Dorothy E. Savill

It's Just Not Fair

My teacher says I could be great,
If only I would concentrate,
And learn my maths, my English too . . .
But there's so much work I have to do.
I do my sums, I write my name,
I know the rules, I play the game,
But somehow things don't work out right,
I have to take work home at night.
I can't have tea until it's done,
And there's no T.V., well that's no fun,
My friends can't call or mum will shout,
And if I moan, I get a clout.
It seems to me I just can't win; . . .
I do the work, . . . or I stay in!!

D. Gresty

Life Anew

Believe always life never ends,
Nature's life dies then new growth sends.
Watch trees as autumn comes,
Lifeless leaves the tree shuns,
Wintertime cold and drab,
Tree lays bare looks so sad.
Wait till spring a wonderful sight,
Tree bursts forth new leaves overnight,
Life has begun again life anew.
Trees live again, so can you.

D. Claringbold

"We Must Turn Back The Clock"

What can I say is happening today?
  In this great old world of ours
I don't really know how far things can go
  Ere we bring back the sunshine and flowers . . .

Everything seems to be on the decline
  It's around us wherever we look,
This country once shone but now it's all gone,
  And it seems, British pride we forsook . . .

Our ancestors would turn in their graves
  If they could see all the malice and greed,
All the anger and strife and the wasting of life,
  How on earth can we ever succeed?

Until, we wipe out at source this villainous course
  And just turn back the clock,
To throw out the canker and all of the rancour,
  And built not on sand, but on Rock.

Only then can we hope to put everything right
  We can't build on violence and drugs,
We must all make a stand and be proud of our land,
  And wipe out the villains and thugs . . .

Eileen Greenwood-Sadler

Magic

Live and let Lovers live,
Ever be mine,
But in these seasons of magic
The changes must come
The Unicorn of my fate,
Conjures the shifters to appear,
They fall from the sky,
To where we stand prepared for the flight,
Uncertain of our departure,
Or arrival in the times to come.
We don't so much as cry to heaven
As watch it weep.
The marking of the skin,
The Return of the Prodigal.
Enigma variations in our lives.
They stand with us and before us,
Willing us to survive.
Whispering that they're standing
The Watchmen to our hearts.

Lee Ryder

Alone And Afraid

Early evening, it's still light, everything's fine,
But not for long, as day turns to dusk, fear is mine.
Soon the curtains will be drawn, my vision confined to these
  four walls.
Who knows what's outside or even in the hall?
My head says 'be rational' but my heart thumps loudly in my chest;
Nearly time to sleep but I know I'll have no rest—
The journey upstairs to the bedroom I just can't make—
Another night spent cowering on the sofa, for heaven's sake.
Frustrated and angry, alone and afraid, noises all around,
Bravely I search the house but nothing is found.
Back to the sofa but the fear is still lurking in me;
I don't know why I get like this, no one's there, it's plain to see
Imagination runs riot, seconds seem like an hour,
I've made the house secure, I've done everything within my power,
I'll have to stay awake until it's light again.
Why do I have to go through this, am I going insane?
Five o'clock in the morning, sunrise, I've survived another night,
For a little while now, it's going to be all right.
The daylight hours go quickly, why is that always the case?
Early evening, it's still light, the strain shows on my face.

M. Hardy

My Bobby (A Tinge Of Sadness)

As I sit here in my armchair,
And stare across the floor,
My heart is tinged with sadness,
As I watch my dear beloved and wonder
How much more.

Kisses, kindness and affection
Abound your every move.
'Tis sad my darling Bobby
That age has taken its toll!

Yet a kind of understanding
From your big brown eyes alights
Brightening up my sadness on this
Cold and lonely night.

Your tail wags all the harder
As my tears they hit your face,
Your barking even louder as you
Try hard to say
"Cheer up, my own sweet Mary, there is no time to waste
We must treasure every moment and in our hearts retain
Only happy memories of our younger days."

Mary Wallace

Untitled

This I remember, I saw from a train.
A little brown pony that stood in the rain.
And all these years after, I come back again.
The little brown pony still stands in the rain.

Lesley Anderson

A Moment Of Silence

The tranquillity was absolute,
In a clearing in the wood,
The birds were hushed,
At that moment, still, the Earth stood.
The wind and rain ceased,
Not a blade of grass stirred,
The trees, majestic, were silent,
Not a thing could be heard.
Sun filtered through high branches,
Leaves, trembling they did not dare,
With weight of the heavy raindrops,
Though it was more than they could bear.
The sound of a falling raindrop
Would sound like a clap of thunder,
So still was that brief moment,
So gentle an act would rip silence asunder.

Mavis A. Goodwin

Parents

Some parents are always there
showing love and tender care
but what about those who do not show
where do all these parents go?
What do they do what do they think
do their hearts ever sink
remembering children so small and sweet
having needs they cannot meet,
could they help it why did they go
will the children ever know?
Were they ill or did not care
it happens to children everywhere,
will they understand when they are grown
and have children of their own?
Who can tell who can ever know
which way their life will go?
Who can place blame who can say
only the people who were there
but who are they to cast a stone
they may have secrets of their own

E. Matthews

Loneliness

Loneliness in my philosophy
Is not the feeling of emptiness "As they say"
It is the feeling of awareness
Opening your eyes and being conscious
Of this world which is so huge
Yet, so small
When captured all together
The sky and ground
Sea and mountains
In a wink of an eye
Loneliness is when you look up
Witness the sun and moon
Taking turns, so the sky in never alone
When you look down
And see how attached the grass is to the ground
That you have to pull their roots out before separating them
To be aware enough, to separate the differences
And state your existence
To look up at the mountains that are so high, standing so proud
Yet, not enough to reach the sky just like . . .

Marwa El-Ali

Sweet Release

From the moment that a man is born,
From the moment he leaves the womb,
He starts on the tortuous journey of life
To the goal of the beckoning tomb.
He lives in hope of a better life
As he marches on, tall and brave,
But the only assurance that life can give
Is a cold and silent grave.
He labours through life, day after day,
As his future he tries to secure,
with moments of joy and excitement
While hours of pain he endures.
How good it is at the end of the day
As he sleeps in blissful peace,
And how gracious is death, as she opens her arms
To give tortured man sweet release.

M. J. Moss

Granddad

I sometimes lie awake at night while others are asleep
Thinking of the love we shared
Thinking while I weep
You were someone every special
Someone set apart
You left me with those special memories
Engraved within my heart
Your smile will always be there
Even though you aren't

Laura Ellis

Granddad

I sometimes lie awake at night while others are asleep
Thinking of the love we shared
Thinking while I weep
You were someone every special
Someone set apart
You left me with those special memories
Engraved within my heart
Your smile will always be there
Even though you aren't

Laura Ellis

Coast

Electric blue lines speed through my memory
like the old asteroid Space invader in the Regal.
Sticky, singed carpet tugs at my sole
as I enter the den of inequity.
Eyes flash, grimace past the dancing puppet box,
limp corpses strung up, aching for the old 5p.
The seedy clown stares his paedophile smile
lusting for young laughter.
Cumbersome, aged machines lined up ready for metal,
round orange buttons, telling the tale
of a 1000 thumb prints.
Nudge, nudge, nudge . . . Jackpot,
is that all? Oh I forgot you're old,
ageing like the concrete underneath.
Though you're younger than the prom and sand,
Oh, if each grain could talk of what it saw,
the dog's cocked leg, dropped ice cream,
sweethearts heaving.
Do they remember the Victorian foot, the Viking stomp,
do they recall? Do they?

Andrea Fairweather

Old Big Ben

God bless old Big Ben
The unchanging friend;
Standing majestically in Westminster's Palace
Amid pomp and circumstance
World politics and upheavals

With amazing grace
She keeps timing and chiming along:
In all changing scenes of life,
Through all kinds of weather
Rock firm she stands as ever.

Worth her weight in gold and prestige
How we would miss her if she fell ill,
The loveliest clock ever
To grace the City of Westminster;
A national institution she is
Renowned the world over for her dignity,
Striking and chiming ability:
God bless Big Ben
She's a wonderful gem.

Katie Kent

The Garden (Remedy)

An enchanted garden, place to be
When tension and stress get into thee
A garden of peace and beauty you'll find
There to calm the turmoil in the mind
Fragrance of flowers now in bloom
Breathe away depression and gloom
Close your eyes sit back and dream
Listen to murmur of flowing stream
Squirrels leaping in the trees
Chirping birds, humming bees
Butterflies, fluttering in the breeze
Soothing music, soothing remedy
Relaxation, tranquillity, serenity
Near to our creator and eternity

Richard Lloyd

The Poet's Mad Business

The poet in truth is mad as a March hare,
Drunk with the fragrance of the vernal thyme
And the blackbird's song,
Or with the riot of colours in a sun–drenched clime.
Madder than a hatter is he, whose chief care,
In a fleeting period, is to build,
For ready sale, a thousand gears and one,
Now small, then large, as if to scare the sun;
Now plain, then prettified; into this and that will'd
By e'er–changing genteel tastes which make
New fashions old and old ones new, if fake.
He tends no luckier trade, aggrieved likewise
By silly fads; but here the difference lies:
His wares are words spun of the senses and uncommon
Thought that come in the wake of visions, prone
To stir his soul and set aglow his inmost being—
Such mad delight and trauma that scorn
All pains to bring it forth as felt, granting
The Muse's white–heat torch x-rays it all.

O. P. Kanu

Slow Rain

The year of a thousand rains began, slowly.
A cumulus of clouds, wispy white, slowly souring grey;
All symmetry lost, they coalesce, contort and ooze,
Slow rain.
And then in spate the rivers cry "No more!"
and the salt–leached sea brims with freshness.
Whether paling youth or bitterness an innocence betray;
Where sun–ripe dreams are flecked with grey,
Like rain–spent clouds.
And the smiling eyes of children darken,
Like a rain clogged sky.

Sean McHugh

Portrait Of My Love

She has eyes of deep brown under lashes long and dark.
Her dark brown hair falls around her face and shoulders.
Her willowy body entwines my soul
trapped in her love while her long cool fingers
rake my spine and her smooth white English
skin warm and soft
like her gentle pixie smile
excites the pulse of life that is my
life my love
so far removed in another clime
but her Yorkshire melody still comes to me
wafted over waves of space
or filtered through ocean depths
of submarine cables like the chords
that bind us and knit our souls
and harmonize lush green dales
with dry African heat
parched and denuded
with desire for her
cool refreshing spirit

Charles H. Muller

With It

Coca-cola pies and beans, produced the kids of whiz.
With tatty crisps, munchie bars, and lemonade with fizz.
Now what will natural foods bring out if anything at all?
Nuts and roots with greens and fruits, perhaps Neanderthal!

We know that he was healthy, but also lived in caves.
Our kids should all be wealthy, or in early graves.
Progress is rapid in this world, sperm counts are going down.
Some men have changed to women, has the age of man just flown?

In less than twenty years we'll know,
    a fingers count and toes.
If the span of human life, with all its cares and woes,
has now to end begetting, another evolved cycle.
Where microbes, viruses, and bugs become,
    the Trendy "with it" miracle!

James Pollock

'The'

Do not say 'The' French,
'The' Americans or 'The' Dutch,
'The' lumps them all together,
In a population bunch,

And 'they' are not a solid mass,
all the same, and all one class,
They are individuals too,
Who with their own uniqueness grew,

So if you want to criticize,
One of those awkward foreign guys,
You really ought to play the game,
And use the fellow's proper name,

Then we will know that all your spleen,
And exactly what you mean,
Is directed at the proper place,
Not 'The' Nation or 'The' Race.

Dave Edwards

A Jealous Misconception

Jealousy stricken, solitary and anon.
For once she loved and now be gone
Trembling touch with teary eyes
The one I trusted but now despise
Pawns in our game yet a different poise
My weakened heart afraid of noise
I miss her kiss our love like this
Forgone the strains and now amiss

Burrowed deep the hurt so low
Heavy hearted, my weary woe
She tries and cries and now to mind
A single manner for thee to find
For now I know her feelings true
Like sun and clouds, light shining through
At last I rest, her heart still thine
Sweet array, innocence so divine

Leigh Darren Brown

Resting Place

I sit here in my favourite spot,
Underneath the willow tree,
Where the thoughts I think,
And dreams I dream,
Become reality.

My secret little hiding place,
Where waters flow crystal clear,
And the sound of nature all around,
Is all that I can hear.

I lay down in the soft dew heath,
And let my fantasies wonder free,
While the gentle stirring of the breeze,
Makes the flowers dance for me.

And as the sun warms me through,
I close my eyes and dream away,
For here is where my heaven lies,
So here is where I'll stay.

Pauline Rudd

The Spirit Is . . .

A blazing fire to warm our hearts
A repairer of life if given all parts
A completely indescribable love
An inward peace that could only come from above
A light in the darkness to show us the way
The morning sunrise to start a new day
A quiet whisper, an answer to a prayer
A loyal friend when the world doesn't care
An outstretched hand that longs for a "yes"
Accepted as we are, nothing more, nothing less
Contact lenses when our eyes cannot see
A reason for joy, a chance to be free.

Helen Wylie

Motherhood

God's greatest gift to woman is the miracle of birth
For when you hold your baby, then you truly know its worth.
All those months of waiting, and in your arms they place
A tiny scrap of nothing with a little angel face
It's up to you to love him right through his baby days
And as he grows through childhood to teach him God's good ways
It's to you that he'll come running when he falls and hurts his knee
And you'll be there to comfort him and hold him tenderly
Then when he reaches five years old and school days come along
You hope you've taught him properly to know what's right
and wrong
Through infant school and senior school and so on through
the years
You'll know the joy of sharing his happiness and tears.
When he does his courting and he finds his true sweetheart
It hurts a little bit to know that soon you'll have to part
then wedding bells are ringing and you shed those silent tears
But you hope they'll both be happy all through the coming years
The love light shining in his eyes you see within him now
Rest happy in the knowledge that it's you that taught him how
to give his wife his true respect and always treat her good
And watch her with her loving ways as she goes through
motherhood.

V. Western

A Child's Day

It's a pleasure to wake each morning
Adventures new to find,
Before we've finished yawning
The night is out of mind.

Each mound of mud is a mountain
Each shrub a giant tree,
A grubby stream is our fountain,
And fills a child with glee.

A walk through the woods is our forest
With lions behind every bush,
Each gnarled old oak that looks oddest
Contains eagles that swoop with a shush.

Each brook runs alive with gigantic sharks
Just waiting there to kill,
A steam train's a dragon with showers of sparks
Doesn't life give you a thrill?

So off we go, way over the hills
To climbs the Pyrenees,
Then home we go with laughs and spills
To wash our dirty knees.

D. V. Barnes

The Other Half Of Me

My Love for him grows stronger
More each and every day
I know he feels the same for me
In his own very special way

When he pulls me close towards him
And hugs and squeezes me tight
I feel a warm sensation
And know everything is alright

As we walk along together
Looking at the sky so blue
He stops and looks into my eyes
And whispers 'I love you'

We share so many happy days
With memories which we treasure
They will remain in our hearts as long as we live
As our love will be around forever

I thank him for being a part of my life
And giving me all of his love
I know we'll be happy together as one
As he was sent down from heaven above

Joanne Denman

Life Is A Season

We are all born, when the season is Spring
We learn how to cry, we learn how to sing
We are all moulded, by the people we meet
Our life is then laid, like a dimly lit street
As we grow older, to teens and beyond
Our summer then starts, of which we are fond
Our adventures unfold, which govern our life
We may find a husband, we may find a wife
So now we move on, as Autumn draws near
Our life it does grow, year after year
Married, divorced, or happy and sad
It's time to reflect, of most we are glad
Some become frail, while others do fear
The passing of life, now Winter is here
As we breath our last breath, there is no doubt
The fire of life, has finally gone out.

Alan Gee

A Poem Of Days Gone By

The autumn of life can be good in its ways
When you turn back your memories to happier days
The trust in a child's sweet innocent smile
I hold on to these memories just for a while

The lark in the sky with its haunting refrain
Bring tears and sweet thoughts of my childhood again
The ramblings of boyhood through woods and through glens
I cling to those memories I still have that yen

But as we grow older and thoughts often fade
That yearning grows stronger of plans we once made
Alone in the dark of evening's fading light
I sit often pondering of things that I might

So here's to the young, may you all take heart
Live life as it comes right from the start
Go forward with courage no matter who dares
For true meaning in life is knowing someone cares

Walter Craig

The Shoot

Misty morning, beaters gather, dogs galore, what palaver.
Keeper comes upon the scene, shouting words almost obscene,
Out of chaos and confusion, order reined, 'twas but illusion.
In twos and fours and six and nine, onto the game cart they
did climb.
At last, at last, they're on their way, sitting on big bales of hay.
They reach the wood and all climb out then once again did mill about.
Come on lads get into line. The guns are here lets start on time.
The line moved forward at a steady pace,
One tripped over and fell on his face
The birds were hiding out of sight, then a beater shouted "right"
Bang, bang, bang bang, bang bang, missed
The gun stood there and shook his fist
Bang bang, bang bang, bang bang, bang.
The noise of the shots through the countryside rang.
The pheasants flew high and fast. Bang bang ah! A brace at last.
So it goes on drive after drive till not many pheasants are left alive
At the end of the day in twos and threes.
The beaters go home in the evening's breeze.
The bag has been sorted and hung up in braces
The keeper and boss have contented faces.

Michelle J. Ward

Wind, Water, Earth, And Sky

Wind, water, earth and sky is always all our lives,
No wind, no water no one living here,
No earth, no sky nothing growing here or there.
No light of day, no water flowing by, no earth
of flowers or wind to give us air.
No living things, no human beings nothing here at all.
The sun has disappeared into outer space, no light,
no sky, no wind or water flowing by.

Winnie Yung Man

Memories

Thinking of when we were younger
memories from years ago
Holding on to the precious times
never letting them go.

Pictures locked in my mind
of being together with you
Remembering all the different things
that we used to do.

You don't know until you lose someone
how much they really mean
You don't realize how much you loved them
until you have to grieve.

Now you've gone, I'm hurting
and I'm really missing you so
I wish that you were here right now
and you didn't have to go.

I suppose you had your calling
to the big house in the sky
but still I find I'm asking
the biggest question . . . why?

Donna Wigzell

A Tribute To My Mother

My mother is a gem, she is certainly the best
Nothing is any trouble and she never seems to rest.
She sleeps so little, she is up at dawn,
It really makes me want to yawn.
She walks so far, she puts me to shame,
Bright and breezy is the name of her game.
Don't think of sulking, even for a while
For when I'm with mother she makes me smile.
Her make-up is on, her lips are red
You would not think she had been to bed.
Her hair so blonde and clothes so smart
Watch out men she could break your heart!
If you could guess how old she is in view of what you have read
Give yourself a medal and a pat upon your head,
For although she sounds like a young queen bee
I'm afraid you'd be right with seventy-three.

Diane Carol Hlawka

River Festival

White orange blue glistening on the water
Streamers and bunting blowing in the breeze
People rippling in tides and waves
Noise gurgling
Laughter bubbling
Happiness and excitement surrounds you
As darkness falls boom whoosh explosion
Sparkles of Green White and Red
Flashes of falling stars lightens the
darkening canopy of sky
Then stillness and wonderment as the
final curtain falls
Contentment at the end of the evening

Katrina Dodgson

Sweeney

Now I'm sure you've heard of Sweeney Todd,
The murderous barber who enjoyed his job.
He enticed victims to his lair.
And sat them down in his special chair.
He pulled a lever, and down they shot.
Into the cellar, ready for the pot.
First he cut them nice and neat,
Then he shredded them into mince meat.
Alas, with lots of heaves and sighs
He made them into little meat pies
These he put in neat array
In his shop window everyday.
They sold at a price of sixpence per eat
Labelled under the name of 'Good English Meat'

Jean McCoombs

Untitled

A hard working woman right from her prime who fell for a
young man who worked down the mine
They married in secret against parents' will, hoping against
hope their dreams they'd fulfil

He worked down the mine and never did moan, she worked just
as hard setting up home
A family of three came on the scene, all well looked after
and kept nipping clean
All loved and taken care of until that day, they were
able to go along their own sweet way

Old age came along and maybe at last, a time to
enjoy and think of the past
But death came sudden on that day, hard work and
pit dust took him away

The woman took it hard but still she could fight, although she
thought of him day and night
She picked herself up to face every day and quietly went
along her
own lonely way

Surely now some reward would come for all the hard work and
the loving she'd done
But 'alas' no it's not to be, lying in that bedroom in agony
Praying to get better day after day but slowly, slowly drifting away

Clifford Aston

Aftermath

Charred images of merciless fates come to mind,
As the raven sings of recent finds.

Shadows crawl where they once did walk,
And ghosts cry out for they may no longer talk.

Tears run dry as the silence forges pain in steel,
And despair rejoices as she feasts on her empty meal.

The burden of reality sheds her heavy veil,
And in her face even jackals taste the pity in her tale.

Dawn comes slowly bringing a darkness worse then night,
The truth is revealed and watchers shudder in its light.

That is the reality that is hard to face,
That is the way hearts die.
Young dreams are shattered and life becomes a lie.

So remember the darkness of the dawn hour,
When the lies that were so sweet turn sour.

Remember the sleeping faces that lay so very still,
And forget that you know how to kill.

Linda Griffin

Trapped

A smile of innocence falling away,
You saw from her beauty as you stumbled her way,
With her eyes calling help in a soft silent plea,
You wanted to help her knowing not what would be.

Her blackness her aura, your reasons so right,
But you knew not her darkness and she not your pride,
Your love grew on stronger through tedious nights,
Of love and resentment and of holding too tight.

A love now so wasted yet too tired to die,
A product from both of you and neither know why,
That with love this desperate you still find the time,
To torture each other with truth you can't find.

A ring you thought would rid all your veils,
Would clear your view and set up your sails,
Yet metal does nothing but burden you down,
To a heart you can't promise to be always around.

Still the love there between you is strong as your hate,
Life long commitment, took just days to create,
Tied down so viciously whilst flying to free,
A hot summer sun ray in a cold autumn breeze.

Aleena Matthews

The Awaking Of The Monster

As he gives a big yawn,
In the morning of dawn.

He tries to get up with all his
mighty might.
Although instead trips up as he
has bad sight.

The birds are singing,
The church bells are dinging.

He gives a big roar,
Although it is against monster law.

He wished he was still in his bed of hay.
He did not care what people would say.

He woke up his brother Ned.
Then went straight back to bed.

Natalie Stanton

The Reconciliation

What can we say,
When years have passed,
What wasted time we both must feel,
Each day, each minute, to the last,
Must bring fulfilment and thus heal
Those doubts, those fears, we know so well,
Ephemeral though they be;
Replaced by warmth, contentment, love,
A bond 'twixt thee and me.
No time to dwell on what has been,
The future lies ahead,
To savour, drink, like vintage wine,
There's no more to be said.
Drink long, drink deep,
The wine will keep
No longer than we shall exist.

A. T. Pearce

The Storm

I savour each night and day
Each moment each second in every way
You cling to me like a limpet, with such fervent passion

Hush my darling there is nothing to fear
My darling! Said her gentle voice
Come close and rest upon my breast

Avariciously grasping her body to bring her near
His words a full of sigh
O' how quick our time will pass

Do not fret said she
For with—in this dungeon we do dwell
Has many locks to which there is no key.
Even though the lock be shielded we'll eternal be.

Darkness comes for but just a while.
Rest in peace now by my breast.
And shelter close from this stormy night.

Margaret McFall

The Fridge

Oh why is a fridge
Always full when it needs
  defrosting
    yet it's empty when it doesn't need doing.
      When the switch is off
    the butter melts the milk is sour
and the food is off
    the water runs the floor gets wet
    The only thing one can do is
    clean the fridge
    wipe it dry
      switch it on and fill it up.
I like it when the milk's cold
but not when the butter is hard.

Janet Poulsen

Sri Lanka's Lionhearts—The World Champions

The thud of leather on willow, the lines were drawn,
the battle was well and truly on.
A sea of lions in red and yellow fluttered by,
as the excitement and expectations rose to new heights.
The figures in blue were smiling on the field
eager, confident, brave lionhearts on centre stage.
The proud Australians were in a spin,
a hesitant mass in yellow trapped
in front of the uncompromising wickets.
The mighty Aravinda batted with eloquence and style,
slashing a century into the records books.
The cool, calm and collected Ranatunga
Lanka's captain scored the winning run.
The crowd went wild, the boys in blue ran amok
as Arjuna and Aravinda hugged each other,
a symbol of teamwork and the Captain's steady rudder.
The countrymen wept tears of joy,
numbed by the sudden realization—
the impossible had been achieved in Lahore.
The lion roared with delight—Sri Lanka had won the fight.

Ivan Corea

"Chris"

Why did he have to die so young
His whole life ahead of him, he did nothing wrong
Just a terrible accident that ended in death
Of an innocent boy who took his last breath

We will all miss his smiles, his games and his plans
For growing up and becoming a man
He was only a child, he did nothing wrong
Except doing a death he shouldn't have done

Why did you take him, where has he gone
Why did you make him die so young

If we found out he wouldn't live long
We could have told him we loved him
Before he was gone
We can only pray and hope that he hears
And we'll never forget those new special years

Claire Holsgrove

For Patrick

Too young to leave an imprint upon the face of Time
Yet your untimely death has etched deep lines on mine.
I can no longer hear your voice; its sound has left my mind,
The years erased the sweetness but lift the hurt behind.
A broken watch, a crooked pot, a card for Mother's Day
Are all that's left for comfort now you have gone away.
I have no need of special days, solemnly set aside,
Dedicated to remembering all those who have died
For though unceasingly I mourn your death,
I'll celebrate your life with every breath.

Christine M. Stickland

A Mother's Love

Little hands and tiny feet
Most perfect thing you'll ever meet
A new born babe needs love and care
And someone who is always there

Through school and college, work and play
Her mother's there from day to day
With love she'll watch her baby grow
And teach her things she needs to know

And she'll be there throughout the years
Crying sad and happy tears
Her child's a gift from God above
'Cos nothing compares to a mothers love

One day her babe will move away
She'll find a man who's there to stay
And she'll have children of her own
And give the love she's always known

Rebecca Murphy

Divine Inspiration

Sitting down on my own
Waiting for divine inspiration.
You know, that wonderful feeling,
That tingling sensation.

Where can you be?
You're taking your time,
You were here a minute ago,
Please hurry, I want you to be mine.

Without you I am stuck for words.
I cannot work, I cannot write.
I'm begging you please,
I need your rhythm and bite.

You are my reason to live;
The reason why I stay;
You are my source of life;
I long to be with you, if I may.

So let things be me way they used to be
And ease my frustration.
Because I need you, my love,
My divine inspiration.

Randolph Wilcox

Caress My Soul In The Rain

Catch all my tears with your lips,
   Drink my love only in tiny sips.
Eat my emotions, try not to swallow,
   Butterflies in my tummy, I'm so hollow.

Caress my soul in the rain,
   Hold me close to your heart again.

Trust my loyalty, not my pain,
   Not being with you is 'sunny rain'.
A warm breeze on a cold day,
   Is how I feel when your away.

Caress my soul in the rain,
   Hold me close to your heart again.

Never see me when your eyes are open.
   Always feel me, when distant happens.
Touch my heart without your arrow,
   I'll be here today, if you need me tomorrow.

Caress my soul in the rain,
   Hold me close to your heart again.

Lemanie Kelly

Old Age

I never thought I would reach this stage
Life is uneasy when you get to old age
Frequently frowned upon; through of with jest
No longer of use; life lacking in zest

An upstanding citizen, yes this was me
Never a break I worked constantly
Sixty years of life skill amassed
No longer wanted, my time has passed

My place in society is now filled by youth
Scrawny teenagers, spotty and uncouth
Imagine the knowledge I could share
If they would listen I would help them prepare

Open your eyes world and see the waste
Our aged persons disregarded at haste
Use our talents and life ability
And push aside the idea of senility

You too will reach this stage
Feeling uneasy as you enter old age
So carve out a niche for those still able
And make old age a time told fable.

D. J. Cordingley

'Dawn Dreaming'

Walk with me on the winds of the world
In that strange time above the dawn
Where the waterfalls are solid ice and never flow
And the trees are spiky antennae signalling other worlds of
complexity
"Help us" they say "They are killing us"

Drive with me in a land where headlights open canyons
And other realities vibrate with electric tension in the brake lights
Watch out! The raven rules the road
And silky smooth monsters with eyes of earth core devour the
fields we pass by

See the contrast crisp and clear—taste it
Breathe the tiny crystals, open your mind to the dawn
And watch the mountains rise up tall and strong
Dark against the light blue depthless sky

All this and more there is to see, open your "mind's eye" and
look above
And at the dawn, life's good—maybe!
Well, there's a lot to see no boredom in this world
The mind's world that is.

Steven Gray

Father's Day

They came in the grey
of that fractured dawn.
Those sombre men in mourning suits.

Platitudinous and
ruthlessly efficient
they took him away in an anonymous bag.

Our children Everest,
Methusla, shrunken now
To common size

Incomprehension muttered
behind our eyes,
minds lock, quarantined from the mundane

A lesser day dawned
haunted by sullen night,
gravid with realization
Birds sang, milk rattled, children played.

Fatherless, we watched
him leave us.

Archie Wilson

My Sitting Room

How does one describe a sitting-room?
Four creamy walls, a window wide,
With flowery curtains at the side,
The what-not there, the cosy chair,
Does this describe my sitting-room?

No, it's more to me than just a room,
It's home, it's a store of treasures galore,
Of gifts old and new, a picture or two,
My favourite chair, the brass candlestick there,
And a plant in bloom.

What tales the bric-a-brac could tell,
That Coalporte figure, the fairground boy,
Each given with love and joy,
The copper and brass to give me a smile,
As I sit for a while, and savour the memories well.

It's a room where friends are welcomed for tea,
And a place for a gossip, with folk who don't see
That the heartrug is shabby, and there's dust here and there,
But oh, it's so comfy, I really don't care,
It's all that I want, and it satisfies me.

L. Ancliff

A Mother's Interview

Fourteen years a mother, a domestic engineer
Doctor, nurse, nanny all rolled into one
Everyone cared for, household accounts well managed
What I wanted had to wait, everything was always gone

I struggled, went without, thought that was my worth
The years have past, no-one ever asked, what about you?
After all the unpaid work now I want something for me
For my interview I was well turned out, an outfit of navy blue

Confidently I sat before the young lady interviewer
My hair shining, fingernails spotless, a day work already done
"You don't have typing, word processing or computer skills
With your lack of skills, well you have none.

I really couldn't offer you a job as the office cleaner"
The words from her mouth were like bullets from a gun
Today's mothers raise tomorrow's adults, tomorrow's
interviewers
They forget all the sacrifices made, all the given up fun

The interview was my escape plan, I wanted my own life
But what is my worth? For so many years I have been
    JUST a wife
        Jane Carr

Emma

Her eyes are brown, her nose is wet,
I'm talking about a cuddly pet.

Doggy dinners, with things on top,
into her mouth goes a leftover chop.

She enjoys a bone, it's good to munch,
and later on, there's always lunch.

When she barks, it startles me,
I wonder what on earth it can be.

A visit to the vet is gross,
it always seems to make her cross.

I feel sure, she watches the clock,
and knows it's time to take a walk.

To catch a ball is such a joy,
or playing with a favourite toy.

The one down side to having a pet,
picking up poo' is a task you get.

Without her company, I would be blue,
a real good friend, who is loyal and true.
        M. Thomson

Thoughts Of My Childhood

Fingers awe gnarled, hair turning grey.
E'en, wearin' glasses, a bit slower the day,
Yet! As a Lassie, wee an petite,
Ah mind o' slim legs, magic winged feet.
Laughin' broon e'en, happy an gay,
Can I be fifty, 'twas jist yesterday.
Well I remember, nine Craigs in awe,
Oot in the street, kickin' a ba',
Or brither's playin' bools, that wis their domain.
Oot in the street, or up in the lane,
Sisters, as well we had our ploys,
Teasin' ither lassies, or winkin' at boys.
Saturday mornin' casino, tuppeny matinee,
Ma brither Matt, he always took me.
Sunday we sat rooned mam's knee, Helen, Alex, Mathew, an me,
Five ither young yins, perched oon her chair
Big e'en aw shining, the singin' wis rare.
These are my thoughts, as I sit here alane,
Happy my childhood, when a wis a wain.
        Nancy Craig Blaikie

Secret Of Life

When we are born we are innocent of all things
On reaching our teens we want all life brings
And reaching the age of twenty or more
We then discover that life is not a bore

With the beauty of nature music and song
And the love in our hearts as we travel along
On reaching our forties we are emotionally intense
We'd faced and overcome things by using common sense

Reaching sixty we look back on our past
The things we wanted and did could it ever last
Peace and contentment friendship and love
Is to be found if we all look hard enough

In our seventies we see ourselves as we really are
Thinking to ourselves could I have gone far
Did I help others as well as I could
And believe in the Lord as all of us should

Our love for each other overcomes hate war and strife
For the Lord up above gave us a life
When the time comes for us this life to depart
To a heaven above and a new spiritual start
        Barbara Webb

The Haunted House

All was still, no one was around,
    As I entered the empty house;
Then suddenly I heard a sound
    Was it a ghost or a small mouse?

In the corner where the moon shines
    Is a shadow of someone there,
If there's someone give me some signs
    As a big vase floats through the air.

As I go upstairs I now hear
    A sobbing coming from a room,
I go inside it and I fear
    What might happen in place of gloom.

I feel a presence, sobbing stops;
    As I go down, my legs feel cold,
Ghostly dog perhaps as it drops
    Beside me waiting for a scold.

As I leave the old house of woe
    And its ghostly wanderings there,
I think of them, as now I go
    Homewards, thoughts of which they would share.
        B. S. Mussellwhite

The Agony Of Losing

The room grows dark as the sun begins to fade
I sit here alone with the agony you have made
My eyes are dry, there's no emotion left inside me
No love, no hate, just emptiness surrounds me
"Time heals" they say, those that have never known
The agony of losing, of being left alone
Hushed whispers in the hallway, "It's shock, she'll come around"
But I know the pain that's waiting, I can hear the silent sound
Of my soul screaming questions that can never be answered
Now I stay in limbo, can't go back, won't go forward
I know others loved you, and others feel the pain
Of knowing you are gone and wondering who to blame
But you and I were soul mates, we were meant to be
And yet the cruel hand of fate took you away from me
Too scared to go living and yet to scared to die
Never seeing you again and never knowing why
There are no easy answers, no way to understand
The reasons behind the fate of every man
So now I walk a new path, an easy one to find
I'll stay here alone and quietly lose my mind.
        Tracy Hull

To Be An Astronomical Voyeuress
(Neighbourhood At 11:40)

The moonlight, lucid through tearful windowpanes,
rooftops glisten with the sorrow of the tempest,
smoke drifts away, unwanted and ashamed,
skies lie "Mezzo Rosso" with the coming of the morning sun
although the night is profoundest blue,
the celestial diamonds look down and smile,
and the pines reach out to heaven,
as Diana herself paves out her reflections,
the lights in the background,
purest butterscotch in colour,
so near, yet so far,
and the sky above us,
a world in itself,
beautiful, awesome world.

Sara P. Gallego

Paranoia

I was lazily walking along the road one day,
When I stopped and looked in a bargain shop window,
I then noticed that somebody,
Was looking at me through the window,
Oh my God I thought,
Who is he, what have I done,
I tried to run, tried to hide,
I couldn't even take a dive,
He continued to look and stare,
I tried to see who was looking at me,
I started to sweat, I started to cry,
'Cos I didn't know, who was staring back at me,
Then I did notice, oh silly me,
That it was my reflection,
That was looking back at me,
Oh well,
Tum te tum te tum.

A. Papakyriacou

The Last Word

Childhood memories stir black and white images
Of seven magnificent men.
Blazing away in noon–time glory.
Anne dancing in opulence amid Eastern treasures.
Nestling in the arms of a king.

From your long career imprinted on my brain
With clarity and pain.
How you tried to teach the likes of me.
In a hospital bed, ravished by cancer.
Anti-smoking campaign shown after you'd gone.
Looking straight through the camera to me
You refused to set me free
With everlasting immortality
You uttered:
'I used to smoke . . . I stopped.'

Mariella Cassar

Mother

A mother is the special person who is always there
She's the one you run to if you're hurt and things scare
The very special friend who always understands and cares
When you are young and life's simple and always such fun
Mum is always there for you, shining brightly like the sun
Then school you have started, and you suddenly feel grown
She is the one who waters the seed, the teachers have sown
In your teenage years when life seems to make you unsure
When the world around you is tainted and no longer pure
Mother is there waiting to help you, standing on life's shore
Then soon you are grown up, and married with true love
Your life is beginning again floating on the wings of a dove
Now is the time to give thanks to the mother who cared
The one person with whom your troubles you always shared
This is a special poem for all mothers living everywhere
Just to let you all know that your children really do care

E. M. Burrell

Holiday With Granddad

As we approached our holiday to Wales,
The first thing we saw were sheep and cows,
Wales is such a special place,
It reminds me of my granddad's happy face.

We visited farms when we were away,
And other brilliant places while we were on holiday,
Driving along mountains and countryside,
At Oakwood Theme Park there were lots of rides.

Our cabin was near the sea,
That's where we went swimming, my brother and me,
We played on the sand when the weather was fine,
If it rained granddad would drive and follow the signs.

Visiting Rembrook castle was a good day,
But it was time to be on our way
That was certainly a great holiday,
Wales makes me remember my granddad was
special in every way.

Joanna Humphries

Gran And Brassington's Mill

Head on Gran's shoulder,
We are as one in that dim little room.
The flames rise high around the bark.
The fire burnin'—blue, green and crimson, relieve the dark.
Joyce Kilmer's poem occurs to me,
"I think that I shall never see,
a poem lovely as a tree."
And thought, with a sigh,
Of that old mill nearby
Where those poems lie piled high, wailing for the steel jaws
of the whizzing saws.
Yet, their fate was already sealed
When, from the logs, the bark we peeled

V. Brady

Exams

It seems as if you've waited all your life for this to happen.
To leave school that is.
The day has come and everyone is so happy.
People who you've never spoken to say goodbye, and you
reply too.
Then the day is over and it's not so good.
You've got your exams the following week.
Panic!
Yes indeed that is what you do,
your stomach turns and you're not feeling so good.
Then there's that part of you, that wishes you either concentrated
more in lessons,
or that you wish it were next year you were leaving.
The exams are over, a sigh of relief.
If you do badly you can always take re-takes.
Now it's time to celebrate.

Marie-Claire Leonel

Nostalgia

Can we remember those bygone years
Those halcyon days of yore;
Will we ever forget those times in our lives
When our spirits did soar and soar.

Will you, dear friend, ever be as you were
Like I was, so carefree and bright;
Can we turn back the clock and be hopeful again,
Can we alter our darkness to light.

Have those happy years gone forever, my friend
To be lost in the depths of time;
Will they ever return to us just as before
And bring joy to your heart and to mine.

If we remember those far–off years
And think how we were in those days;
Then we'll find, my dear friend, that those years are still here,
It is us who have changed in our ways!

John Carr

176

The Old Church Clock

The old church clock sits high aloft, up in the old church steeple.
It tells the time to passers by, and warns the village people.
Through wind and rain and showers of snow, the clock ticks slowly on,
Quarter, half, three quarters one, the old clock chimes each one by one.
The time is there for all to see, when travelling on your way,
And there again on coming home, or setting out to play.
Now at the ending of the day, and you wander to your bed,
You hear the old clocks distant chimes, the time to lay your head.
Then whilst you're in the land of dreams, the clock still ticks away,
She sends her chimes at dawn again, to signal in the day.
Birthdays, weddings, funerals too, the church clock chimes for all,
Always looking out for you, from the steeple wall.
Now when you pass the church again, and wish to check the hour,
Think how graceful she does look, sitting in her bower.
Lets give a word of thanks today, from all the village people,
And always promise to respect, the old clock in the steeple.

Donald Futer

Oh Sinful Eden

In the light it is a place of captured beauty,
Where inhabitants are able to pace themselves in astounded silence.
But when night falls, the place is dark, deep, alone and slowly eroding.
Shredding the bare leaves with the deadly elements of acid rain,
Which is beyond what the mind's eye can perceive.

Soon there will be no more forests and no more beauty.
Leaving the world to be empty and open to the invasion of development.
The technological future.

What will be left of the world once machinery has overcome the powers of mankind?
A society that would enhance our standards of living?
No. A society which was desired and developed by man, but would later be rejected.

We, now find ourselves slowly drifting into boredom and guilt.
Constantly being reminded of what was once a world of natural beauty and peace.
Yet we do not learn and cannot put back what was right.
We can only expand.

We therefore, have denied the one thing that did no harm to humanity,
And have alienated ourselves from Gods Kingdom. For what we have done, we must be punished.
As we have added our country to the industrial life and destroyed what God had once created.

"You shall not eat of the fruit of the tree which is in the midst of the garden, neither shall you touch it, lest you die".
(Genesis 3 verse 3)

Emma Thomas

Broken Wings

Oh to be alive and free, and able to soar the sky,
Not to be trapped by anything, or one, passing it all by.
All that space, liberty—heavenly sanctuaries everywhere,
Being unattached, and not having a worldly care.
But I am attached by captivating bonds of love,
No peace—no representation of a white dove.
Destiny finds our worlds separated, as strangers we live apart,
For you hold no love for me in your concealed heart.
The emptiness within creates just a hollow shell,
Yet my love goes on, like a bottomless well.
My wings are becoming more withered and torn each day,
The essence of life fading, and slipping away.
I can only sit and watch this hasty world go by,
Surrendering all that I was—surely now I'll die?
Broken wings, no desire or inner strength to carry on,
Such thoughts, despair, I know are surely wrong.
But perhaps leaving this loneliness behind one dark night,
I shall again be free, I shall once again take flight.

C. L. Bowring

In Our World

In the beginning, as with the earth,
Our love was filled with heat, passion and light
There was turbulence and all was ready to erupt
There was freshness and newness, but all was corrupt

After a time, as with the earth,
Our love began to cool
The skies turned blue up above
And as the trees and plants grew,
So did our love

As people polluted the earth with gases, waste and fumes,
We polluted our love with jealousy, bitterness and doubt.
As with the earth, our love suffered drought

I missed the heat, excitement and passion
And set off to find planets that were new
That passion exists nowhere but with you

What I had overlooked was that the passion
Of the volcanoes, earthquakes and lava
Has been replaced with friendship and love of solid ground
And if our love were water, no deserts would be found

In our world.

Julie C. Doyle

All Alone Now

Johnny sat in his armchair with his arms quietly moulded and folded around his new home, the chair. He always made a big sound but yet his voice was now nowhere to be found. Johnny was dead but yet he still had to be fed. Every morning his mother would dress her little baby being polite, just like a lady. Johnny laid on his bed, where he could see all his ex-trophies in all different sports without a single nought.

It was only this time last year when we had to face our despair. 2 years he got, 2 years in the rot. Drinking and Driving they say but he still didn't have to pay.

My Johnny got life, life of trouble and strife. The doctors said he received brain damage. Oh God, how are we going to manage. Everyday Johnny could hear his old friends playing in the streets kicking the ball with their human feet. Everyday they would pass his house almost as quiet as a mouse, all just hoping not to be caught oh what a thought. Everyday he had to face the neighbours torments listening to their patronising compliments.

What is the future with this freak of nature maybe he may get a wife, Ha Ha? That's a joke, what a life.

I suppose poor old Johnny will have to stay alone using his ears like a headphone, unable to speak, unable to creep.
Poor old Johnny is so alone.

William Clarke

The Life Of Night

The mighty sun sinks in the western sky
and darkness takes his place
When Venus, star of even, rules on high
The Earth is filled with light from the bright face,
and Night is born!

Dark shadows lie among the murky dusk,
The Earth in silence lives.
And from the closing flowers fragrant musk
Comes forth and to the darkness beauty gives
For Night lives on!

The Queen of Night, the Moon comes in the east
To show her beauteous light,
And in that light all living, man and beast
Find that her advent clears all fear and fright.
And Night lives on!

A glow shines in the eastern sky; the dawn
Brings scarlet beauty forth.
Then heralding another lovely morn.
The sun appears, blazing with love not wrath
For Night is dead.

R. W. Hipkin

For Bumph Read Bunny

Every day, every now, through our letter-box comes 'Bumph'
    which I simply detest,
But one morning last week lay a little white note, which I
    nearly threw out with the rest
I read it, 'twas hand written by a child, 'twas a simple but
    genuine request
Lost—one small grey rabbit—if found please phone 638 . . .
    and the number was given
Thank you—and that was all that was said, but 'mongst the
    debris 'twas like a message from heaven,
In the first time for years I responded to 'Bumph' and
searched for
the little girl's rabbit
But, sad to say, before I could help, a fox came around, and
    the rabbit had 'had it.'
They say that in every barrel there's one rotten apple
But at the same time there could be a treasure
And that's what I found in the search for my 'Bumph'
And, believe me, it gave me great pleasure

Uisdean F. Murray

Under The Table

The needles clickin' to the purl and plain,
The washin' rescued frae the pourin' rain,
The mother smiled a weary smile
As she was knittin' a' the while.

The soup was shimmering on the stove
As under the table the brain strove
To the secret land that was his ain
Where he was king of his domain.

"Can I hae that stool?" He asked his Maw.
"What a guid wee castle, it's awfie braw!
You tak' that cushion for your heid
And drink this soup! It's royal mead."

Wide eyed with wonder, he gazed down
To see the circus and the clown
Appear like magic as he ate,
This hidden picture in his plate.

The king lay doon and fell asleep.
His mother's smile was full and deep.
She laid him in his tiny cot
And thanked the Lord for a' she'd got.

Margaret Rose Booth

Untitled

I viewed a world of a distant time,
Mellowed with age and yet sublime.
No burdened heart, but free of all
No cross to bear, no tears to fall
This world was mine and I was there
To muse a vision that ended where?
Bedecked with flowers, a winding stream
That patterned the path of a childhood dream
With head in hands and shoulders bent
A gaze that followed the brook's intent
The dancing ripples of a rainbow hue
Followed their course through a field of blue
Bluebells and marigolds in profusion there
Bowing their heads in acclaim or despair
With thoughts that followed the water's race
To its final goal, the sea's embrace
Where ships with sails as billowed cloud
Rode the seas with head unbowed
Alas, the dream as dreams decline
Faded and died on the seas of time.

R. G. Harrington

Dreaded Bliss

William the worm was a very smart chap, with a spotted
bow tie, and a straw boater hat, he was walking out Mary
his young lady friend, and he loved her from her head to her
wriggly end, he asked for permission from her Ma and Pa,
to take her out boating then onto the spa,
where they sat down to cakes and a nice cup of tea, and
soon he would say "will you please marry me",
she gave him consent and they were to be wed and
William went home with fine thoughts in his head,
soon Mary and he would wriggle together, and wriggle,
and wriggle forever and ever, how happy he was as he slid
under his gate, back to his hole in the garden so late,
he awoke the next day as if in a dream, and slid
past the spade and gave a loud scream!
He hadn't noticed before the spade was so sharp,
he hadn't even seen he was cut quite in half!
When Mary, found out what had happened she said,
"I think I'll stay home with my mother instead,
as for you William worm there's no need to tarry,
I can't make up my mind which end I should marry!"

Brenda Buckworth

Winter Dreams

The sun has lost its summer glow.
And the glare of winter is soon to show.
I stand at my window waiting
    for the first sign of snow.
I hope it comes and stays like a
    curtain on a lit up stage.
Like icing on a Christmas cake
    deep and white.
It must come for I shall take a
    sledge up to the highest point
and go rushing in the ice cold wind
    and in the soft white snow;
Lights and fires will be blazing.
Windows shutting out the cold;
    And we'll be raising a toast
    to winter and deep, deep snow.
Hand in hand, face to face
    we meet each other's stare.
With a whisper of lips and a push
    back of hair we're together, then and there.

Rebecca Hartup

Nature

Sitting out there, at the edge of the sea.
Serene, beautiful, ever free.
God's majesty.
No noise, peace of mind, fresh smell.
Trees swaying side by side,
Conveying messages,
Only nature understands.
Birds flying, one on its own or in a flock
Flowers so colourful,
Yellow, red, pink and white.
Flowers bloom as each petal opens.
The beauty of nature,
Is far beyond the human mind.
A volcano erupts,
It's explosive power.
The command from God.
Adam and Eve,
Took the apple from the tree.
Took their first bite, which was forbidden.
But their instincts were mutual.

Saberina Hussain

Charles—The Love I Lost

I heard his voice that day.
Then turned to see his face.
Our eyes met in that special way;
My heart began to race.

Is this what they call love? I thought!
How can he feel the same?
But then I wore the ring he bought
Before I took his name.

He had to leave me for a while
On business in Spokane
The accident made his car a pile,
He never smiled at me again.

Now in the Autumn of my life
Still there is this regret,
I never did become his wife
But would I still? You bet!

Audrey Margaret Brushett

Message

Because you left me
Don't expect me to lie down in the dust and weep
My swollen heart is still pumping
My heavy heart is still jumping
My soul has not left my body
  My persona is still intact
    I'll get over it,
    Fact.

Jan Phelps

Country Life

A green bush
Branches swings with a swish
Birds big and small
Colours black and white
Speckled and brown
Making a sweetly chirping sound
Badgers, foxes, hedgehogs, weasels and rabbits
All have their own habits
The wasps and bees there are lots to see.

Flowers beautiful colours
Variety of sizes
Like bright coloured dyes
Over the bridge the sound of water flow
Farmers with seed to sow
Country walk gives you a lot of thought
Nature all around
All making their own sound
Some animals are shy
Others are very sly
All hunters for food in and around the wood.

Marie Coyles

The Teenage Brain

Bright shiny colours all fill my head
Groovy impressions of a mind that's dead
Don't think for myself just follow a crowd
A member of an elite that just fool around

Confusion sets in where brain cells once were
Memories distorted of a past in a blur
A delusion of a life I thought was mine
Now I'm homesick and living a lie

I'm high in the clouds just mucking around
My friends come with me as I play the clown
By the time the night's over I'll be six foot underground
And for me the sun shell never again come around

It's over now, everything gone
I had my time, I had my fun
Only now I can see the wrong
In being one of them and following on

Ruth Blackmon

Mr. Policeman

Had a few in the pub
Had a laugh in the car
Had a sober driver
Had the soldiers of harassment on our trail
  Had to pull over

Had to get out of the motor
Had Mr. Policeman's trotters in my jeans
Had been stereotyped for the way I look
Had nothing better to do, did you?
Had you wanted me to give you a present?

Don't you have more serious crimes to solve?
Don't you understand I like to wear the clothes I do
Don't you remember, you thought our driver was under age?

I have had my privacy invaded
I had to tell you my address so you can monitor me
I will not change my identity for anyone
I still had the last laugh.

Malcolm Carelse

Friendship One Lost/Another Found

Dedicated to Jackie and Spike

On the wings of a morning she answered God's call
Slipped away unannounced from the midst of us all
There too was our friendship so recently found
Questioned unashamedly, then dashed to the ground.

Here stayed I, stunned disfigured and wanting
"Why, oh Why?" I kept asking without any prompting
No answer, no reason, nothing but discord
And a refusal, on my part, to accept with accord.

The years now number one score plus five
And here locked away I exist emotionally deprived
All those years I've refused to accept I had the need
To be close to anyone within the human breed.

But now there is sunlight streaming over the paper as I write
For a new found friendship has eased the long fight
It came quietly, hardly noticed, but then burst into light
And with it my appraisal of what is a human right.

How, when and where is there any use in wrangling
With things I cannot change
My lips say Amen now—but not so my heart
I'm grateful for tomorrow's friend and the chance to restart.

Frances E. Bradburn

Sea To Shore

The sea rolls quietly to shore
worries gone, and peace once more,
the suns colour is brilliant red
it slowly sinks into its bed.
Sounds of life's turmoil no longer heard,
no wind, no animal, no bird.
I am alone, awaiting you
the man I love if love is true.
I see my footprints in the sand
I feel secure, awaiting hand in hand,
the smell of the sea so clean and fresh
can relax your heart to start a fresh.
I stand alone, still waiting here
no one around to hear my prayer
how can you tell if love will come
and are you just the only one
the sun will rise from whence it came
life will continue just the same
the sea still rolls towards the shore
takes away the love I felt before.

Julie Airey

Life And Girls

We all live, we all die . . . most of us want to fly
When I go out I want to fly
But instead I try to die
Meet a girl, she's really cute
But she thinks I'm a brute
Down to the corner shop, pop an acid down I drop . . .
Can't go home . . . she'll hit the roof
Get stuffed, I won't tell the truth
Now she's knocking on the door
But we won't stop sh***ing on the floor

She loves to talk . . . can she sing?
Just for her I'd do anything
Like a drug, she makes me high
When I'm with her . . . I really fly
I want to be with her forever, will she love me?
No . . . not ever. She loves sport, equally I
But does she care if I live or die?
I dream of her, I think of her as my night and day
Could she possible be the same?
No . . . she's always looking the other way . . .

James Kitson

An Ode To The Big Five O

Now you are fifty sex can be fun
Just like a loaf really well done
You will either blossom or gradually fade
But like a good egg you have been well laid.

Marjorie Toon

Blood

It was a dark moonlit night; the woods they seemed so still,
little did she realize about the Madman's lust to kill,
he took his victims by surprise; they probably didn't feel very much,
his knife reflecting moonshine; until after that fatal killer touch.
There was blood dripping from his blade,
venom in every single word he said,
blood was a way of life for him,
he loves the blood fresh from any limb.

His evil eyes penetrate your mind they drive fear into your heart,
his knife so very long and tame until plunged to rip you apart,
the unexpected stroke of death no mercy shown for looks,
doesn't matter that you're a friend; an end not described in
books . . .
there was blood dripping from his blade,
venom in every single word he said,
blood was a way of life for him,
he loves the blood fresh from any limb.

William Bolton

Push Off Pushers

Scum of the earth that's what you are man
When you push that stuff called pot man
Your f***ing head is up in clouds
You screw up lives to make some pounds

Why don't you buy a f***ing gun
And shoot of heads and call it fun
That stuff you sell in plastic bags
Just like the body's on the mortuary slab

LSD is not for me
Won't walk around like a little zombie
So just in case you come and ask
Don't want no fix, shove it up your arse

So pusher get that buzz yourself
Just roll it up or snort it down
But don't go lying on the ground
Cause dirt like you just won't be found

Think before you take a life
That stuff you sell means only strife
Go out and get a proper job
Don't hang out with the crazy mob

C. S. Webb

Simple Lyric

If you were ever to die my friend,
would my heart ever mend?
I'm sure it would after some time
and the laughs we had would still be mine.

Death takes the innocent young.
The screamingly funny and those well hung.
Death is inevitable to all of us.
It could happen at home or even a bus.

What a sad loss to the human race,
the graveyard being your resting place.
So what's your gravestone, what will it say?
Here lies, RIP; who gives a s*** at the end of the day.

Each morn with skies of blue.
Birds would salute you in morning dew.
Free now from all your sorrows.
Alas, you will never see no more tomorrows.

Wherever you are now, a message you send.
That's if you were ever to die my friend.

Antony Leadbitter

Trickster-B*tch

Open up your mouth a little wider please,
I cannot get at your tongue.
I cannot tell whether what you are saying
Is truth or not.

Open up your eyelids. Larger.
If you keep the tell-tale stone
Behind that slit in your curtain
I cannot tell if you mean it.

Open up your hand.
What is it you're hiding,
In that cave there.
Come on. Open up your hand.

Open up your rib cage.
I've opened up her rib-cage.
There, I thought so,
There's a game inside.

Martin Hayes

Untitled

It will soon be far too dangerous to take a girl to bed:
She may have said she'd like to, but that's only what she said.
Even if she kisses you while stripped down to the buff,
There's still a chance she'll change her mind and play it rough.
So don't throw caution to the wind and take a foolish chance;
They'll soon be trying to get us gaoled for a penetrating glance.

F. V. Thomas

It's Only A Dream . . .

The way you undress me,
And caress my body,
As the touch of silk
Glides next to your body.
My soft tender breasts
Excite you so much,
And while we're still hot,
No-one can stop,
The fiery hot desire
And burning passion.
As I feel you quiver,
With excitement and pleasure,
As I willingly let you,
Release your special power.
My feelings seem real,
But they are just dreams,
Which I hope one day,
Will become reality.

Kanta Patel

Untitled

We've all been for an Indian meal
Now ask us how we feel
Running up stairs to the loo
Just to find that there's a queue
Banging on the door, be quick
There's your mother out here, about to be sick
All of a sudden there's a big loud fart
In comes Father, legs apart.
I can't take anymore
It's all over the bedroom floor
Well everything's been said and done
So next time you go for an Indian
Take a cork or some chewing gum.

S. Biggin

Life Is To Die For

Life is to die for
Burn the flesh but keep the box
And send it round again
and the preacher says
"everybody had a love of life"
Even the suicides?
He loved to f*** so let's f***
He loved to get out of his head
He got what he wants lets not pretend
Play at grieving for the family
a whispered lie about what he meant
to you and me.

D. A. Nelson

Pyramids Of Egypt

From pyramids of Gizah
pointing to Orion,
your star-struck pharaohs
winged to the sky.

Gold for final bodies,
mouth opened, phallus
erect, they steered towards Isis
to impregnate.

Sky intimate as earth,
on extended world
they built pyramids
in pattern of Orion.

Isis, Osiris, Horus,
trinity for long—ago Egyptians
fervent among stars.

Elsie Hamilton

Your Love My Dream

The start of night when daylight bends
To gather in her skirtly ends.
The start of night when it seems,
My daytime thoughts change to dreams.
For it is there we meet,
As I reach to gather silver teams
Of glittering stars from heavens bowers,
To adorn your hair like crystal flowers.
Neath your feet, spread soft white clouds,
Where hosts of fairies dance in crowds,
As the mellow moon in its mystic lure,
Profiles your beauty in contrast pure.
Your slender shoulders Milky Way draped,
Reveals the breasts which Cupid shaped
To such perfection, I kiss their tips,
With equal of love as I kiss your lips,
As the magic of nights enchanting skies,
Reflects the love in your pearl grey eyes,
And affection bright on your smiling face.
Loving me more than the distance of space.

Harry Walker

The Guttersnipe's Lesson

The guttersnipe, a world apart and sat upon the churchyard wall

Gazed down anxiously at the little toff kids, giggling amongst themselves, having a ball. Ere! Wot dyer fine sa'funny wid all these deaden's? He with a certain respect.

'Oh nothing' returned one of the children somewhat surprised. 'It's this epitaph' explained another but to little effect. ''Tis'n epic wot?' echoes the dirty child 'The Epitaph!' intruded the eldest child amid an eruption of laughter. 'This inscription', he pointed out snobbishly, these words upon this Tombstone. 'This epitaph. Don't you see?' 'Oh' squeaked the child who wished he had never asked, losing interest in it all as he munched through his half–rotten apple. 'I shall recite it to you', announced the cruelest child ' You obviously cannot read it at all'.

'Take Heed and Learneth this valuable lesson' began the verse 'Wherever you may be no matter who shall there be, always let your wind pass free, for not doing so was the cause of the death of me".

The cheeky young urchin sat a smurking as still as the graves before him and considered awhile. With the lesson truly learnt he stood up in readiness to flee 'Them's wise words them is!', he concluded revengefully for then followed the disgustingly loud noise of his own wind escaping free—and to wit—unashamedly.

Edward Reardon

It Takes Two

I always thought
People who placed ads were desperate.
And as I sit at my desk
I confirm, it's true!

But needs must.
My hormones have gone into overdrive
And no amount of chocolate
Will satisfy them.

So what will it be?
'Rampant red-head,
High sex drive
Get in touch with me
And your love life will thrive!'

Or 'Kind sensitive female
Into poetry
Seeks someone similar
To be intimate with me.'

Or why not
Just simply the truth:
'Desperate and in need of sex.'

Amanda Allbones

Dooms Day

I have travelled for an eternity,
Across a misty sea.
I have seen great pain brought upon the earth.
Decay and anger have fed upon my children.
I have come to pass judgment,
On the condemned souls, that walk the earth
for many a year.
Humanity is condemned to damnation.
I shall rain a thousand years.
For my word will tremble the earth.
For the heavens shall sing my praise.
I shall steal thy beating heart,
Keeping it for my own.
I shall feed upon your corpse, tearing your flesh.
Your blood flowing through my veins.
Scattering your bones across the earth.
Life will return.
Not a human will be seen.
Till this day, I shall not rest.
For I am the father of all living things.

Dermot Rgon

A Graduate's Dream Stalls

Intellect creates nothing, a deepening of the void.
Yet everyone wants a piece of stool.
Always already a piece of stool.
A piece of stool in this sweltering July heat.

One of my students has plagiarized from a key text.
Do you know of stool?
A radical Marxist, feminist deconstructionalist.
An author just like myself.

But a tribunal for academic offences now will prove
self-flagellationalist for us all.
Invent for him some mitigating circumstances.
For stool's sake get him off, and you'll be the new course
manager.

He admits he copied.
But he was too busy licking the sweat from his beautiful
brown baby's behind.
The Stoolians think he passed.
But in actual fact, he failed to give her a fifth child and
failed to hang onto her.

Richard Tyley

The Problem With Society

Violence doesn't solve a thing
People forget the trouble it brings
The scars and wounds they leave behind
All bear heavily on the mind

The police are powerless to stop the fight
It's not their fault we have this blight
They carry the buck, and the blame
But their excuses are always lame

The system doesn't back up their cause
The guilty parties always find a clause
The law's an ass, it favours the guilt
Around this system, no future is built

It will be sorted, it cannot last
The government will get off its ass
Peace and harmony will win the day
I hope it's not the innocent who pay

David Self

A Fart Poem!

A fart is a chemical substance it comes from a place
called bum, it penetrates through your trousers and lands
on the musical humm.
To fart to fart is no disgrace for it gives your body ease,
it warms your blankets on cold winter nights and
suffocates all the fleas.

Clare Pantling

Desolate

When I close my eyes, I feel the track my
    tear left as it fell,
If I push my mind back, I can feel where
    you had lain inside me,
But how long ago,
I can smell your warmth, feel your kiss, so
soft but wanting,
Feel your hand so gentle, but exploring,
Hear words spoken of love and forever,
Where are they now,
In you the want of me, in me the need of you,
Uniting as only two in love can, with a
    strength that would put stone or rock to the test,
But that life can tear apart like paper,
If I push my mind back, I see eyes full
    of passion and fulfilment,
Open, I see lonely and emptiness,
Where shall I let my mind live,
There will your memory, complete,
Here with me now,
Desolate.

Wendy Craddock

Untitled

His name I forget but his face I remember
The heat in his touch and the smile on his face.
His sweetness engulfed me as he moved to kiss me,
The touch of this hand to my breast lit a spark.
A fire was started deep down within me,
Warmed me completely, and opened my heart.
He had shown me that "Love" can mean more than sex,
That it's not just the meeting of two body parts.
In the warmth of his caress all doubts were forgotten
Being there was all that really made sense.
As the fire was cooling and the trembling subsided
We were brought together, my fear, at last, dispelled.

Cherron Leys

Benefit Blues No Hope

Not enough this, not enough that,
Need more money and that is that!
Don't want to work, there ain't none out there,
Society owes me,
So why should I care!
Bought a new car payments high,
Got the money from some benefit guy,
I owe my rent and things besides, debts I don't worry,
They can't throw me out
'Cos I've got a kid and that adds clout!
Yeh, the government stinks it treats me like sh**,
All I want is a home with everything in it,
But there's nothing out there,
'Cos the way I see it is you don't really care!

S. A. Birchenough

Desolate

When I close my eyes, I feel the track my
    tear left as it fell,
If I push my mind back, I can feel where
    you had lain inside me,
But how long ago,
I can smell your warmth, feel your kiss, so soft but wanting,
Feel your hand so gentle, but exploring,
Hear words spoken of love and forever,
Where are they now,
In you the want of me, in me the need of you,
Uniting as only two in love can, with a
    strength that would put stone or rock to the test,
But that life can tear apart like paper,
If I push my mind back, I see eyes full
    of passion and fulfilment,
Open, I see lonely and emptiness,
Where shall I let my mind live,
There will your memory, complete,
Here with me now,
Desolate.

Wendy Craddock

Colours

What colour am I, what colour are you?
What colour is that girl? Her eyes so blue.
What colour is that car, what colour is that dress,
It's the colour that always has to impress.

All white employees but the manager is black,
You say it's like one bad apple in a ripe sack,
But all black employees and the manager is white cold,
Then he is applauded for putting n*****s on hold.

You say it's freedom of speech, freedom of right,
F*** all that I say and it's time to fight.
The time is now to stand on your feet,
Right foot forward and don't retreat.

Brothers like Spike are fighting vigorously,
To stop this fatigue torment of coloured rivalry
Is it really significant what colour you are?
I'm a human aren't I. Not a dress or a car.

What colour am I, what colour are you?
We're identical in God's vision, so who are you???

Sam I. Diwan

You

The thrill of lust shivers down my veins
The sense of touch drives me insane
Your body so warm entwined with mine
Your lips so tender they feel divine
Sweet secrets that lies do tell
The sweet smell of you that love conceal
To insane lust as are lips do touch
As fantasies become are infinite love

Rhiannon Jones

Untitled

Easter's been and gone again,
When will I see you,
When oh when.

When will your body
be next to mine,
In a bath tub
Full of wine!

We could sip the wine
Through rose-coloured glasses,
then slowly lick each others
arses!

So think of me,
when your having
a bath,
then imagine me,
licking your

S. C. M. Swift

Predator

Cold moon, pearl white, gleaming illuminations fitfully, the
world beneath.
Dark and menacing the clouds, streaming shadows across
your face.
Gaunt, bare-branched trees, grope blind with gnarled fingers.
Spider-webbed bushes huddle, afraid of some hidden menace,
And small creatures scamper, frantic, for a darker place to hide.
Solitary, the owl hoots eerily through the night.
His shadow no longer soars, but his prey, unknowing, cowers still.
Tomorrow may be different but their "game" is over for tonight,
they are safe,
But, yet another hunter stalks, pounces, makes a kill.
Silenced screams, breath cut off, for her all living done.
Too late to run, for home, for safety, for warmth.
She lies, now, crumpled, bloody, on the virgin snow,
And he? He passes on, content, his hunger satisfied.
His sick mind knows no shame!

Jean Baines

Unknown Love

Nature's empty cradle, weeps
Crimson tears for what is lost.
A polluted river slowly seeps
Into a pool that doesn't know the cost
Of human life so precious
A child that never was.

The sheets that witnessed Life's creation
Now bear witness to its loss.
The blood stain of God's damnation
Grows heavy like a cross
To bear, forever to be remembered
A child's life I surrendered?

The monthly curse of fertility
Has claimed a life for its own.
Like a bride stabbed on her wedding day
All future hope is gone
But, I won't forget that easily
The child who lived and died in me.

Helen Batchelor

Ain't Romance A Waste Of Time

I'm so stupidly sentimental, sometimes I make my self sick,
I'm the sort that thinks birthdays and valentines should be
spent with the man that I pick. I've this old fashioned idea,
that Christmas is a time for loved ones and twosomes,
but the reaction I get from my fella is that love is all slushy,
and gruesome. I'm the sort of girl who likes flowers,
and sweet soppy cards, you can't beat em!
And a big box of fattening chocolates, who cares if I don't
even eat 'em! And I simply adore private dinners for two with
candles and wine, and all that. I don't give a damn if the wine
make me sick and I eat till I'm horribly fat. I'm incurably soft
about warm summer nights, walking hand in hand under the
moon, but he'd rather be sitting up on his own drinking vodka
and smoking till dawn. I've always had dreams about loving
being all gentle, kisses and such, with lots of soft teasing,
caresses and things you can't talk about much; but sadly he'd
rather a quickie, wam, bam, and where's my book. While I'm
laying awake with my sad shattered dreams,
he's snoring beside me, the fool! I suppose it's time to stop
dreaming, to face the fact that love is a farce. 'Cos every time
I start to dream of romance I seem to fall, flat on my arse.

Eve Stafford

The Way, The Truth . . .

Hello! Says Life. And then . . . goodbye.
A taste of joy . . . a long, long sigh.
Sorry! Can't give you another try.
Just time for a smile, and then a cry.
The sun comes up, the sun goes down.
First the laugh, and then the frown.

Maureen Buchanan

Emotions

A warm breath lights my life,
the fire of your eyes,
a fire that warms my soul.

A smile stole my innocence.
You first touch—feeling the power of love
experienced my forbidden dreams

The forbidden fruit tempted me,
floods of tears fell on my heart
the heart that beats for your touch
The touch I feel on my skin,
My blood a tempest in my veins
hot-flowing to my heart,
following a natural path
expressing those true emotions.
The power of our love.

Mark Fenech

Rejection

How dare you say death has no sting
Your passing meant the world to me
Why did you say 'No, please don't ring'
How could you die so secretly.

Why did you have to die alone
Why did you strive to keep at bay
Those who'd shared a lifetime with you
What is it with you anyway?

You shut the door on all my dreams
Remembering not those happy hours
But chose instead to plot and scheme
And finally said 'No cards, no flowers'

What happened to that Mother Love
That bound us close through years of pain
Or did you think we'd had enough
And couldn't go through it all again

So now we face a life without you
And grieving hearts put to the test
But the mystery will remain unanswered
Until we too are put to rest.

Marjorie Sutton

La Grange

The Building waits . . . its stone walls unyielding and stark
against the evening sky.

It waits for the artistic eye and sympathetic hand, waits
for the new breath of life in its hollow interior.

Waits for the re-awakening of laughter and tears, hopes
and ambitions, waits for the feeling of warmth in the still,
barren rooms.

Waits to envelope a new family into the security of its
walls . . .

What tales could it tell, this old building? What stories
were related by the peasant farmers?

How many generations lived within its frame? What sorrows
and joys were experienced in this block of granite?

Loves lost and won, marriages, births and deaths for so many
generations, so many lives intertwined . . . all now still and
forgotten.

The building keeps its secrets of years gone by, but is
waiting now.

Waiting to absorb the throb of new life into its very soul,
. . . waiting, . . . just quietly waiting.

Maria Harrington

Phantom

The trees are bare,
The leaves all gone,
No birds in song,
No sun in the sky.
Dark clouds drift by;
Just winter, and decay.

No one to hear your cries, in the night,
No one to stem the growing fears,
No one to brush away the tears,
No one to take away the sight,
You must remain, the Phantom of the night.

Who is this Phantom of the night?
The darkness, and no light,
No birds sing on the wing,
No trees in bud; don't despair;
Just thoughts in the stillness of the night.

Soft lights glinting on wet window panes,
Silence broken; birds singing again,
Voices greet each other; to begin another day.
The Phantom has gone away.

Jean Burbidge

Housebound

What can I see through my window
When I open the curtains each day?
Sheep, and their shepherds tending?
Or fields of new-mown hay?

No! There's houses and busy main highway,
Noisy traffic each hour of the day,
But that's only part of the picture,
So, listen to me, I pray.

Yes, listen to me, while I tell you
That when lifting my gaze high above,
A much different scene I encounter,
I see sky, the sun and God's love.

So if you're depressed, and you're feeling
The everyday things closing in,
Lift up your eyes to God's heaven,
Be still, and listen for Him.

The blessing will not be far distant,
If you trust His heavenly powers
And believe His Son came to redeem you,
Then happiness will surely be yours.

Bertram J. Mitchell

War Baby

1940 into this world came!
Blue eyes, blond hair, how mum did sigh,
Dad was glad, but also sad,
For in 1940 the world was at war.
A man called Hitler, most say was to blame,
Good men fought hard to rid this world of bad,
In the end good did prevail.
Hitler shot out his brains, punishment he would not take,
The Russians came with might and thunder,
USA dropped on Japan, a atom bomb,
And for three minutes, heat and thunder
Now in 1996 my hair grey, eyes faded,
Mum and dad of the past, 56 years now passed,
Greed by the few robs the poor, of which there are many,
Drugs now ten a penny.
Has man no clout, was Hitler cloned with so many.
As the millennium is in sight,
Oh let's hope God puts it right.

Graham Jones

Running Wild, Running Free

Your eyes burn into me like gems so bright,
I hear your soft breath as you prowl through the night,
running wild, running free . . .
Your grace and your power so swift as the wind,
Forever hunted as though you have sinned
running wild, running free . . .
Born unto the land as nature intended,
All that you are shall be defended,
Punished, mistreated for being what you are,
so magnificent and so proud,
Hear me, I am your voice, I will scream loud,
running wild, running free . . .
Pleasure and pain you know them both well,
so why does man damn you to hell,
A king of your domain to me you will always be, forever
Running wild, running free . . .
Running wild, running free . . .

Nadine Jones

Journey Of Life

With each day that passes a new life is born
Some come at night and some come at dawn,
But as we arrive and as we awake
We're already choosing what pathway to take.
And as we continue this journey of life
We come across joy, we come across strife
But we must appreciate these feelings we feel
Although sometimes we wish that life wasn't real.
At times we feel it's all going wrong,
Only these are the things that make us strong
So we can go on and progress in the light
Until the infinite spirit comes into sight.

Caron Greenwood

Looking For God

To look for God where would you start
Around the world or in your heart
Up and down you would search
Unless you started in a church

If you want God to be found
He's not up there nor in the ground
He's in your mind He's in your heart
So in a church is where you should start

He'll change your life from bad to good
Ask many people, He really could
If you don't believe it just give it a go
Learn about God and then you'll know

He's only thought of he's never seen
So get down to your local church if you are keen
Now don't be silly and don't feel odd
Give it a go and learn about God

Jennifer Knight

Life

I left my home when I was young, I cut the apron strings.
I spent my little money on drugs, and drink and things.
Somewhere along the line my life's gotten swallowed up
in this mad mad world we live,
I cannot think. I cannot hope. I'm acting quite insane.
When will this awful feeling go, how can I rid the pain.
Who can I put my trust in, how can I live again.

Shall I leave my cardboard box, shall I lose my freedom.
Is it worth my pride to go back to what I had.
Two people who adored me, their names are Mum and Dad.
To see the tears come in their eyes to feel their arms enfold me.
I'm home again, now I can live and put the past behind me.

Vivien Walker

Mr. Bee

Mr. Bee keeps buzzing, buzzing all day long,
Mr. Bee keeps buzzing, he just can't go wrong.

Mr. Bee keeps buzzing, buzzing all day long, he goes
flower, to flower, from daylight till it's dark,
He goes from flower, to flower, but he doesn't care a lot,

He goes from flower, to flower, and drinks nectar just
like wine, he goes from flower, to flower, but what
he does is no crime.

So when you see a bee, and he is busy buzzing along,
don't tell him to get lost, tell him to come along.
So when he leaves your garden, and his work he has
done, you will see the beautiful flowers and be glad
he came along.

Stewart Jenkins

Life

Is there a point to life?
To me it seems like trouble and strife.
Our world is polluted, animals are dying,
The world needs saving, but people aren't trying.
Think of the rivers, the oceans, and the sea,
They are so polluted, it seems terribly wrong to me.
We have such a good life, we should show our appreciation
Because people in the third world are dying of starvation.
If they are lucky they might get some meat, rice or grain to eat,
Things like chocolate sweets and ice cream never pass their
    lips even as a treat.
This world seems terribly unfair,
People with plenty to eat and drink should really learn to share.
And as for factories, car exhausts, C.F.C.'s . . .
They are damaging our ozone layer so stop and think, please.

Natalie Jane Goldsmith

Short Interlude

The sun feels good and warm upon my face.
The country air smells sweet and clean.
How beautiful it is, in this place.
So very different to others I have seen.

A friendly Nuthatch is singing on an old tree stump.
Not a single care in the world has he.
Many other birds are singing too.
And they are so happy, happy to be free.

The bushy tail of a squirrel passes by with haste.
And climbs yet another Oak tree.
But he is always careful and alert,
As he watches, with one eye on me!

Such a wonderful, perfectly, peaceful day,
With not a single cloud in sight.
All has been freshened with the morning dew,
And is beautiful, clean and bright.

Is this real? Or am I just dreaming,
It certainly feels that way.
But alas it is just for two short weeks.
Whilst I have my holiday.

Jean Mary Trentham

The Beauty Of Nature

In Memory of Renee

When the snowdrops and daffodils push
Skywards they appear,
Breaking out everywhere there is a hush
Showing no fear.

Like life they know is so short
They carpet the land,
The beauty for all to see is caught
So close to hand.

People are so much like the flowers
To see and love,
Open to all of natures powers
From up above.

As each year passes they all bloom
I think of you,
A reminder forever there in natures room
A picture so true.

Andrew Munro

Poem About Drugs

Drugs, Drugs why do we have drugs.
Is it because you loved it one day or was it because
you could not stay
but who needs drugs when you have each other
and your friends as well.
So don't get hooked to drugs or better yet . . .
Don't Touch Drugs Or You Might Get Killed . . .

Stuart Hart

Being Born

My eyes open
A sudden light
A shiver down my spine
I love this world
This lovely world
This pretty world of mine.

I learn to crawl
I take a fall
My hands and feet are sore.
I love this world this lovely world
This pretty world I saw.

I can walk
I can't yet talk.
It's too much for me yet
I love this world this lovely world
This pretty world I've met.

Now I'm eight I stay up late
Well later than before
I love this world
This lovely world this pretty world and more.

Laura Hare

'Discovery'

I went to visit deep down below,
I didn't intend to stay just needed to know,
I can't describe in words how I felt,
When I saw what was there I wanted to melt.
How can I have been so cruel.
Have I really been such a fool.

I saw a picture of misery,
A child, my child, part of me,
Huddled in a corner with no one to hold.
Have I made my heart grow cold.
So much confusion, fear and sadness,
What I've been afraid of isn't badness.

Will I ever be able to forgive,
What I had to do in order to live.
I've been so blind but now I can see,
The love I have to give is also for me.

Diane Simmonds

The Lovely Garden

As I look through my window, what a glorious sight I see,
A mass of lovely roses there, are smiling up at me,
They nod their heads in greeting, and sway gently in the breeze,
No matter what the weather's like, they never fail to please.

They're radiant when the sun shines, fragrant petals open wide,
And even when it rains their beauty cannot be denied,
The rain-drops seem to kiss the blooms, before they fall away,
This makes each pretty petal shine, in such a lovely way.

And they're in many colours, various shades of red and pink,
There's yellow ones and white ones, and orange shade I think,
They really are delightful, and a credit to the man,
Who made this Eden, just like God did, when the World began.

Fred Longbottom

True Love

True love, what is it.
    It turns your world upside down.
It makes you laugh and it makes you cry.
    that's what true love is.

It's all about sharing and caring
    that's what true love is.
To be able to talk about everything and anything,
    that's what true love is.

Be able to say sorry, to hurt when they hurt,
    to be there for each other.
That's what true love is.

Dorothy Thorpe

Park Band 1950

Here within this peaceful leafy glade,
Reflect on how the light and shade
Affect the moods of men who rest
Before their parts are played.

A band of music men perform
On yonder stand each Sunday afternoon.
One wonders if before they tune
They crave for calm clear weather, true to June.

For when strong winds blow on music sheets,
Strings and mouthpiece men do acrobatic feats
Contriving to control the flapped page turns,
With weather eyes for conductor's beats and signs.

Marches, waltzes overtures and suites,
Are "blazed away", with full repeats.
Until with well earned pay, they all depart.
Car parking is a weekly practised art,
and marchy, windy music fills the breezy air with fanfare!

Clive Robson

The Tea Party

When Jenny and her brothers, brought some little friends to tea,
I didn't know the difference,
that it would make to me.

There never was a party, quite like this before,
lemonade splashed the table cloth,
and tea spilt on the floor.

Derek hit his jelly with, a big resounding slap,
and little Mary's trifle,
slipped into her lap.

Fancy cakes were eaten, at a most alarming rate,
Betty tumbled off her chair,
and Michael broke a plate.

Sarah and Peter squabbled, over the chocolate cake,
but billy eating far too much,
complained of tummy ache.

I was a happy person, My nerves were very strong,
but wearily I'm wondering,
where did I go wrong?

Pamela Eckhardt

Grandma, Our Gift From Above

If ever there was a person who brought sunshine to all they met.
I'm sure anyone who knows you "Grandma" knows you're
the closest anyone could get!

If anyone could show God's love to those who are his children.
Just looking at your kind and gentle face, we know that
Christ has risen!

Knowing how hard you worked through life, one would think
that you would tire.
Instead you continue to work the very same way, our wishes
are your desire!

When I see your smile Grandma, it makes me feel warm and
safe inside.
We feel we must be perfect for this world, but from you we
have nothing to hide!

It's funny how we instinctively desire the world's riches when
setting our goals.
When the happiest moments ever in life are your wonderful
food in our bowls!!!

To know that you love us all, no matter of our faults and mistakes.
You give us a reason to go on in life, no matter what it takes!

Your heart is as precious as gold, your hands are simply the
definition of love.
If anyone could show us a piece of heaven, it's Grandma, our
gift from above!

Anita M. Huey

Illusions At Dusk

A bird is poised at the top of the pine tree
Is it a falcon, a vulture, a hawk?
Perhaps an eagle with feathers ruffled
Patiently waiting to pounce upon his prey.

Nearer, the figure of woman—so still and straight.
Is that a sceptre she holds in her hand?
Her gaze goes beyond the bird—far, far away—
Seeking and ever searching—for the unattainable?

Beyond the woman stands a man—motionless.
His head is bowed. Is it bowed in sorrow?
Does he contemplate a comrade fallen in battle?
Or is he simply resting and waiting?

Underneath that figure another man.
He rests upon his knees—in supplication?
His hands are raised—does he plead?
Or is this an attitude of prayer?

That watchful bird, the dreamy, queenly woman,
The man with lowered head and he upon his knees—
Each one poised and waiting—perhaps hoping
That soon a brave New World will arise—

Beyond the trees.

Ada M. Witheridge

Born Lucky

Only the fool swallows the bitter pill,
then begs for more,
the knife in the back,
the turned back,
or the cold shoulder to cool down those summer nights,
the antennas wave about picking up those missed signals,
courting disaster in time for the drunken wedding march of
tragedy,
Anima flies out of the window,
Animus gives up the ghost,
tears wash down another bitter pill,
whetting my appetite for destruction,
taking the tint off my rose coloured world,
and leaving only stones in my bowl of cherries.
I will sip the ambrosia nectar next I say,
I will get a break,
it's my turn,
I just hope it's not my leg this time.

Sharon Jane Ellis

. . . Love Theory . . .

True love is desperate, forbidden, needed, wanted.
If it was easy, would it be true, I wonder?
No chase, no fate, no destiny, no dream,
or does it just exist anyway?
I believe love develops in the want,
the challenge of true feelings, running deep into the heart,
Once there, never forgotten.
So hard to understand, uncontrollable.
No matter how desperate the denying.

To find it, is scary, the feeling so frightening,
because it is so beautifully right. Deep down you know.

Love exists in the true nakedness of one's soul.

Andrea Michelle

"Forever Falling"

My mind is engulfed by a blazing fire
Life—consuming, deadly, evil . . .
It cannot be defined by words
Only by carnal desire and uncontrollable passions;
Greed, hatred, death and even love.
Lusts as poisonous as they are sweet,
Souls as seemingly good as they are evil.
No water, whether from stream, river or ocean
Can quench the internal burning,
The burning of my mind, body and soul.
You tempted me with your pretty wares,
Your shining lights, your rules,
Your hideously controlled lives.
I saw not your lies, your poverty
And the blasphemous injustice of it all.
Only when I was brought down to your level,
Only then did my eyes open and look about.
Yet it is too late, and that I your charm,
I was tempted and now I have fallen,
All ablaze I continue to fall forever.

Anne Oakman

Black Is White

Together we're like day and night,
Because I'm black and you are white.
So why do I get all the flak,
And talked about behind my back??

My blood is red, my tears are salt,
My coloured skin is not my fault
And when I'm hurt, I cry like you.
But comforting friends are very few.

I only want to learn your ways,
To live in peace throughout each day,
And go home safely every night,
Without the jeers, the fears, the fights.

So let's be friendly, let's be mates,
Forget the self-destructing hates.
For without night there is no day,
And let our friendship rule, okay??

Lynne Tellier

Arnie

He's my little darling,
I love his little sharp eyes,
I love the way he walks on the mantelpiece,
And never knocks things down,
He's thin slender and grey,
He has a contented purr,
His ears prick up when he hears a sound
His tail falls low when he's hunting,
He walks with his head held high
He has a superior air,
He sleeps in a soft warm curl,
Good bye my little darling.

Rachel Whitehead

Love

For it's you I have to blame,
For the wind that whispers your name,
The stars in the sky, the moon so bright,
The heavenly silence of the night,
The birds singing through the dawn,
The flowers smiling around the lawn,
The laughing grass and laughing trees,
All the warmth through cold breeze,
My racing blood, my pure clear mind,
All the people that seem so kind,
I feel happy and I feel free,
When in my heart you're part of me.

Anthony John Ward

"Regrets"

My heart is full of unshed tears that threaten to overflow
There's nothing I can say or do, only to let you go
Something greater is calling, from another place and time
There was never time to know you in this world of yours and mine

Our paths just crossed and parted, joining sometimes a-while
We'd greet each other briefly sharing a word, a smile
But the ties of love and duty took us on different roads
And we never knew each other, as we bore our different loads

We always say "If only" as we think of things before
We always feel the pangs of guilt and wished we'd done some more
But life is as we make it, we can't retrace our steps
So I must say goodbye now and suffer no regrets

For tho' I didn't know you or share the life you had
I hoped one day as years went by you'd feel the words unsaid
And know how much I liked you the stranger, yet family and friend
I wish I said "I love you" before your life slipped to an end.

Sylvia McMaster

Untitled

Should roses carry thorns upon their stem,
Whilst other flowers wear an easier veil?
Should mountains cover Earth's most precious gem,
When sifting shallow streams will rarely fail?
Perhaps a sign, for those who roses mind,
That beauteous form will often danger shape?
Or warning dire, for those who diamonds find,
That trembling caves may threaten their escape?
Yet, know a meaning more than omens few,
And reason that the pain in love's desire
Contrives assurance for the suitor true:
The purest tune will need the dearest lyre.
Should roses carry thorns upon their stem?
For truest love, my soul, I would condemn.

David Pledge

All The Same

I can't do it, I just can't do it . . . you will never understand,
you give me the task, a pistol to my head.
I twist and turn in fevered sweating monologue,
you inspire my heart with a language now dead.

Eyes white and widened, hands shake in addiction's grasp,
profanities truth, spat with bladed tongue of poison.
Commemorative plaque, bowed silence, 80 years now slain,
tragic waste, trolleys and cars, and this battle rages on.

It's raining, a sadness that in its anger has no voice,
school railings coldly reflect, a neglected forgotten child.
Tears still warm, gestating the seed of insecurity,
buried deep, a memory held, a blue print to a suicide smile.

I still can't do it, I'm not a rebel just a concubine to the truth,
indignant adolescent outrage courses my post pubic veins.
Frustration, fertile and menstrual, the taboo of need,
anger bound are wounds when only sadness remains.

You made me do it, regressed infant biting at the breast,
furious power, I cried in hunger, still you never came.
Insensitive bastard, retaliation, empowering the illiterate mind,
equal feelings, to love is to hate, in my anger it's all the same.

Darrell Fox

Thoughts On Our Way

Cotton–wool clouds cavort 'neath the sky
Competing, contorting, then hurrying by,
People parading merge patterns below
Matching those shapes in a leisurely flow

Heaven and Earth we travel as one
Determined by Nature through the powerful Sun,
Suspended, sustained and kept in our place
Spread round the Planet all varied of race

Each has a time and a moment to pray
Thanking sincerely the gift of this day,
A mind full of thought for kindness and care
To offer to others who wish us to share

Days turn to weeks and the months into years
All of us living through hard times and fears,
But out of it all shines our goodness and love
In the deed of our sharing the good Lord above!!!

Sam Royce

T H E I R   W O R L D

How often does my brain transmit,
my thoughts toward the bowels of
the earth, to the abundance of life below.
Large, small and minute, they all inherit
their own planet.
In peace and in war they share man's own
destiny but unlike man, do nothing to destroy
their beautiful world.

Gerald L. Farrell

DRAGON DEGREE?

The dragon is an animal which I have never seen.
They say his tail is very long and coloured mostly green.
His spiky back is very large; his mouth is very wide
And if somebodies stand too close, they could end up inside.
When he becomes so angry he'll give a mighty roar!
And flames will leap through jagged teeth and scorch the forest floor.
The other creatures race away to find a tree or cave
And some will peep between the leaves if they are feeling brave.
But is he really quite as bad as everybody thinks
Or does his heavy armoured coat have many little chinks?
Would he really like to have some friends with whom to dance and play
Instead of causing everyone to scream and run away?
Perhaps we'll never know the truth which could be hard to find
As jagged teeth and fiery tongue do not seem very kind.
Maybe St.George could solve this task without his three–pronged fork,
And go to university to learn some dragon talk.

Sydney Frank Goodrich

Under The Sun

The leaves baking in the summer sun,
Radiate light and beauty,
I feel as though I am walking on a carpet of gold,
A cool refreshing wind, brushes past my face,
As I breath in the sun–drenched air,
It brings with it the taste of the ocean,
That lies on my lips,
I am surrounded by tranquillity and peace,
By orange and gold,
By azure and dark blues that seem almost black,
I am covered by whites so bright that they shine and
emanate a pale blue glow,
And greens and yellows and reds so profound,
That they seem as though they might melt with heat of the sun,
And fall to the ground in tiny droplets of colour,
Like the morning rain,
I feel as though I am in the middle of a dream set in paradise,
I am alone in my paradise,
There is nowhere more beautiful under the sun,
There is nowhere I would rather be.

Jasleen Sethi

Circles

The touches seemed so sure,
No doubt there would be more,
And once again he don't know why he's shown right to the door.
Where does he go from here?
No answers will appear,
Caught up inside a state of flux amid a certain fear.

It's all been said and done,
A trap springs from the fun,
Should he stay and wait round here or should he turn and run?
He's no control, he's told
This night he's feeling bold
But straight-talk just can't get around the echoes of the old.

He brings it on himself
He dreams like no-one else,
To chase unlikely rainbows in search of inner wealth
It seems he's got to learn
'Bout how to make life turn
Instead of honest foolish ways that words can always burn.

Craig Fox

Awakening

The Princely Porticos of Dawn unfurled before my eyes;
Impassive pipers publicized a new world in the skies,
And pictures of the futures tempted me to sing
Of my new conceptions on my awakening.

My eyes were bathed with images of previous lives since past;
My mind was filled with new found faith that I hoped would last,
And these heraldic tapestries I only hoped would mean
A brand new wonderful world on my awakening.

And as I saw my first sunrise on my awakening,
I wondered what new episodes my future life would bring:
I hoped the bonds of harmony would never be unbound,
And that the key to Pandora's Box would never e'er be found.

Robert D. Bovington

Famine Fever

The scorching sun beats down as I lie in the dust
On a plain that stretches brown on brown
Oh why is our land being burned by this heat?
What have the plants done to go without water?
The birds, the fish and the sky?
The emu, the ostrich, the tiger and lion?
All gone but for bones on a dry, cracked earth.
Can I walk till I reach the mission station?
Hope, water, hope, food, hope, despair
My lips are as dry as the desert sand
My skin is as red as cooking fire embers
What can I do to end this pain?
To spare me from this torturing place?
I dream, I die, I wake, I cry
Oh God, come quickly now
To end this agony

Gabriella Pugh-Smith

Time

I'm more aware of the ticking of the clock,
Tick tock, my spirit waits to hear the knock
To flee this body for an unknown trail
Which for a moment lifts the dividing veil.

Who knows the truth and fiction of my follies?
The evolution of eternities?
Where's plus and minus in my soul's swinging?
And how will the bell toll in its ringing?

What wisdom have I gained in this estate?
Have I redeemed the evils of past mistakes?
Or pierced the truth which weighs up all odds?
And brings me nearer to our Sovereign Lord?

Where rests my soul of eternal living?
To creep into a shell of further being?
Tick tock, my soul waits for the final knock
While listening to the ticking of the clock.

Stuart Plumley

Awakening

The Princely Porticos of Dawn unfurled before my eyes;
Impassive pipers publicized a new world in the skies,
And pictures of the futures tempted me to sing
Of my new conceptions on my awakening.

My eyes were bathed with images of previous lives since past;
My mind was filled with new found faith that I hoped would last,
And these heraldic tapestries I only hoped would mean
A brand new wonderful world on my awakening.

And as I saw my first sunrise on my awakening,
I wondered what new episodes my future life would bring:
I hoped the bonds of harmony would never be unbound,
And that the key to Pandora's Box would never e'er be found.

Robert D. Bovington

Sweet Embryo

Never for you a mother's womb
Your prison is an icy tomb.

No precious gift of life for you
Your brother humans say so.

Not for you those golden playdays
Not for you those happy schooldays.

Not for you the joys of birthdays
Your brother humans say so.

Humans talk outside your tomb
Some say live some say die.

Cannot humans see that once
They were dots like you and I?

For you no appeal. No earthly salvation.
Sentence is passed. Incineration.

But somewhere beyond there is a god
Who waits and who will say.

Come to me my little ones
To Heaven with me to stay.

Terry Coneys

My Friend

My friend lives on the other side of the street,
And a nicer person would be hard to meet,
For friendship, kindness, and humour too,
She helped me battle my illness through,
A knock on the door, a friendly call
With some flowers to brighten my day.
And a call at night asking are you alright?
Then I'll see you tomorrow she would say
And now I'm really on the mend,
She will always by my special friend.

Joan Mills

Lest We Forget

Amongst the cries and cheers sits a lonely old man,
He is no longer cheering but praying with his hands,
He is alone in his home hearing joy outside his door
But he won't cheer or join the crowd, he has seen this all before,
As they celebrate and party he sits alone in shame and horror,
Have they forgotten? Do they not care?
He holds a photograph and he stares,
He sees his brother, father, sister and mother,
All he did adore, all gone now for sure
This man is wise and he knows best, not blind like all the rest,
Who cheer a man with cold in his heart
A tyrant with a secret, burning lust for terror,
But they love him and they want him.
As they worship every word while he promises the world
They cannot see behind his cold, hating eyes.
He is insane, inhumane but with a powerful attraction
This old man has seen it all before the war,
How can the star of David shine again
When the people love to love such a man
And they want to give him fame.

Andrea Louise Lake

A Morning Thought

As I awoke this morning, and looked around my humble abode,
I can hear the morning breeze,
from the world outside.
I listen to the birds, in the trees so high;
their joyful morning chorus, is music to my ear,
the daffodils, and the crocus too, are opening their eyes,
As they stand together, full of pride; side by side.

I pause a moment; and send out thoughts of love, and of care,
to those many that live in fear.
"This: Sadly, brings a tear."
For those that are, on the brink,
of desperation, and despair,
There: World is in preparation for fending off their foes,
the separation, and their humiliation, treason and death.
It's very difficult, for those that are left, to digest: That the
world's in such distress all around.
"Where have they all gone wrong, Dear Lord?"
As I complete my dress,
I'm pleased to know, within my heart that we are not in such a mess,
but! This is England, by far the best.

F. Truscott

Crying Into The Wind

Scrape the surface
A fingernail slice below sedate serenity smiling
Churning scared and ragged
From his rasping spirit
Cruel steel eyes fed by her warmth
Stole away light
And proffered only despair

This once mild, captious keeper of her heart
Gave her a child
And her primal plumb line lifted her face
Into the sun
She revelled in those sweet hungry infant eyes
But the child swallowed her whole
Suckling drunk on her final maternal hue

Last night she walked alone
Resplendent in a glittering pain
This bright beautiful creature
Lost in a vast tangled prison
Deaf to her thousand sisters
Crying into the wind

Lynne Douglas

Tea Time

Sitting in front of the colour TV
With Mum in the kitchen shouting "it's tea"
It was bangers and mash and a spoon full of peas
So I sat in the chair with the plate on my knees
Mum shouted at me as my manners were bad
Then started to threaten she was going to tell Dad
So I picked up my plate and my apple for pud
And ran to the table as fast as I could.

S. Briggs

Danny My Brother

Danny, who's Danny, was he a memory
or my brother?
He played and laughed for hours on end,
I remember his smile, his lips,
They were the prettiest and smallest of all

I remember his wheelchair
full of stickers, full of memories
I wish he was still here,
laughing and playing
but now he's gone and all I think
about is his teddy he left for me
oh Danny my brother I miss you so
I think and cry for you,
why did you die Danny?

Sian Pow

Fox

Dark eyes peeping, ears pricked forward, nose up in the air.
Scents are shifting, swirling drifting, round him everywhere.
Carefully, a paw put forward testing muddy ground,
Senses tingling, body tense for any sudden sound.
Startled pheasants all a-flutter vanish through the trees
To hide away from teeth that chatter, dinner for his three.
Then suddenly it falls upon him, danger in the field.
Scents come drifting, floating downwind, hounds come running,
Baying, calling, kill him, kill him kill.
Red and white blur in a vision, don't wait, don't look, don't stare.
Lead them onward, outward wayward, through the copse
Across the common away from pups and lair.
Darting forward like an arrow, hounds upon his heels,
Heartbeat racing pulses throbbing lungs are bursting still he's
running
Hounds are baying huntsman calling, kill him, kill him kill.

Coral Rose Wyles

Cherry Tree In Autumn

Yesterday you stood there
Flaunting your scarlet and gold.
Came the brutish wind and stripped you bare,
Violated you, and left you cold,
Stark, naked and exposed to winter's air.

Bitter the wind and keen
'Winter's so long' you cried;
But grief gave way to calm and soothed you clean,
Purified you, washed away your pride.
And lo, the Spring returns a gentler green.

Joy Gadsby

Bullets And Bombs

Killings, maimings, bullets and bombs
In an age of computers, discs and roms
In the name of religion and politics too
Where the innocent die, for the ideals of the few.

Why is it we ask, is the killing a need
To make us believe in their cause or their greed
Why can't they just talk, in heated debate
Then cause such misery, with their pain and their hate.

They can only impose through sheer force, what they will
Their acts of atrocity, and their methods to kill
Blind to the tears, and the sadness they cause
With their flagrant abuse, of God's nature and laws

In the name of humanity, when will it all end
When they've taken away a man's right to defend
The things he believes in, through force or by fear
In the name of Religion, without even a tear.

G. R. Jones

The Green Sunlight

We will meet in the green sunlight
Before the world's awake
And the dew will splash on my ankles
To mark the path I take
We will talk awhile and be silent,
As only true friends may,
And my eyes will be wide with wonder
At the promise of the day.
We will pause, perhaps, by the churchyard,
Where moss and lichen creep
On the cool, cool face of the tombstone
Neath which you used to sleep.
You'll whisper of that far country,
Holding fast my hand,
Till time will jingle her gaoler's key
As morning sweeps the land.
So, over the hill of the Fairies
I'll watch you drift from sight,
And none will tell of our sad farewell
There in the Green Sunlight

E. M. Dickson

December 31st

Grey skies brooding over grey fields.
This scene a crop of grey thoughts yields.
Withered grass, the skeletons of trees.
The casual eye no future sees.
Even water, white with ice
Is stilled from rippling,
And all the dreary vista filled with silence.
No cheeky ducks, with bright-eyed looks
On ponds—nor placid cows chewing.
No lively ring of axe on timber hewing.
Not a shrivelled brown leaf stirs—
The earth is dead, but overhead
A flock of raucous crows
In perfect-patterned circle goes.
With joyful clamour wheeling.
And surely, God's eternal promise sealing.
Earth is not dead, but sleeping.

Mary Lee Haskey

Scared

Locked up feelings inside, my body ready to explode.
My heart beats faster, and a smile,
a faint, weary smile appears, knowing.
knowing that I can't carry on for much longer.
Knowing that one day it will happen.
The pain will break free.
But using all my inner strength, I will keep holding.
With all the power within me, I will keep what I have designed.
For what I have made, only I can destroy. Only I can know the hurt.
My pain.
No one else must know.
Only I can face the world, myself, Another body?
Brings with it fear, and life's expenses.
Alone I must gain faith in myself and in human life.
Only then will my emotions, my feelings slowly break free.

Jo McBain

Cry From The Heart

Isn't this a beautiful country of ours
The green scenery, the streams, the birds and the flowers
Then came the troubles in the year 69
The violence, the bombs the guns and the crime
The punishment shootings and another man dead
He died for the cause or so it was said
The jail terms began they put up a fight
Then came the martyrs from the hunger strike
But where has it got them we want the fighting to cease
Living in harmony contentment and peace
Bring back the cease fire and let's try again
So there's no more anguish suffering and pain

Doreen Craig

Until Then

Silent screams create an eerie hush,
    amid the chaos of disbelief.
Dry tears form a well, deep, deep within my aching heart.
Lifeless, his body lies heavy in my arms,
Crushing the very breath from me,
    that gave him life for so long.
Somewhere, a painful groan disturbs the peace,
And I realize it is mine.
Whispered words I can't quite hear,
Will never hear (have never heard),
Such beauty, I have never seen before,
And will doubtless, never see again.

My dehydrated body feels so weak, so sad.
I weep for all that might have been.
Somewhere, someday,
God knows my pain,
And may allow me to hold him again.
Until then,
Until when?
Until then . . .

P. Buff

Oliver

Oliver's eyes are a wonderful brown
His coat is so golden, like midsummer down
I take him for walks, through meadows and streams
He really must be, the dog of my dreams.
So constant and friendly, none can compare
Come take me a walk, get up from that chair
Let's find a new way, out in the sun
Into the fields, where rabbits still run.
No need to worry about bills anymore
Not when my Ollie waits at the door
Meeting new friends along the way
No need to feel lonely he fills my day.
Oh what did I do before Oliver came
Life was so busy, life was a game
But Oliver changed that once and for all
With Ollie beside me, at last I walk tall.

Elizabeth R. Dunbar

It's Cold Out There

Come inside little one, don't stay to stare.
Come inside little one, for it's cold out there.
Don't stay behind now, don't linger too long.
Come inside little one for I know you're not strong.
Don't look out the window, I fear what you'll see.
Come inside little one, come to me.
Don't wander, stay close now and don't look around.
Keep walking close near me with eyes to the ground.
Be wary of dark nights and witches with brooms.
Keep clear of dark caverns and holy men's tombs.
Come inside little one, come quick, run to me.
Don't dream of adventure, don't dare to be free.
Come quickly my baby, run fast now to me.
Don't turn around you won't like what you see.
Be hasty, don't dawdle, don't stay to stare.
Come quick little one for it's so cold out there.

T. E. Rowe

Speakers Dream

Have you ever dreamt of making the speech the triumph
that would far out reach anything you have ever done before;
Surely you have that's what dreams are for.
I am sure you have dreamt of being a star, with a speech
that will be your best so far, the acme of perfection
that will bring applause to make the welkin ring.
You are down on the programme, the speech to do,
Evaluators, critics, are waiting for you.
Introductions are over the time has come,
careful now, no err, err, or um, um.
Steady yourself be forceful and bold,
this is your dream, to knock 'em cold.

Dramatic and forceful, eyes are glistening—
fellow speakers, quietly listening.
Confident and assured—you knock 'em dead.
It not what you say it's the way it is said, the dramatic end
comes just in time, you stand silent, expectant, and feeling sublime.
A standing ovation, they applaud like mad, it's the greatest moment
you've ever had. Then—you awake—reality comes clearly—
It's just a dream.—Never happened really.

Ann Halliwell

Address Tae A Gowfie (Golf Ball)

Wee white–faced dimpled little ba'
ye maun be scunnered o' them a'
That hit then chase thee
Nae doubt ye'd like tae mak' a law
That would embrace thee and keep thee safe
Frae man and mace.

There's whiles ye maun be on yer hunkers
Wi'skippin' burns and dodgin' bunkers
But as round after round ye stand the pace
And hacks and slices ye can thole
Ye'd end up in that hallowed place
The nineteenth hole.

Donald G. McLean

The Stream Of Life

Gaily and swiftly the years come and go,
Like a bubbling spring, or a rippling stream,
That caresses, and turns, in the course of its flow,
To fade in the distance, forgotten, a dream.
Or, stolidly sluggish, it oozes its way,
Dull and depressing, exceedingly flat,
Devoid of expression or semblance of play,
A gigantic worm, yet as blind as a bat
To the beauty it passes, relentless and slow.
Or, rushing and turbulent, covered with foam,
Storm–tossed and wild when the hurricanes blow,
It rages, and sobs in its search for a home,
Blind to destruction, and heedless of rocks
That rear up their heads in the river of life,
Like the horrible teeth of a wolf, as he mocks
And snarls at a victim denuded by strife.

The years that have passed have left memories dear,
Or saddened by losses, or mangled by war,
But will those to come bring us laughter, or fear,
Or will they just bring what they brought us before?

Henry Caplin

My Sister

The love of my sister I'll always defend
cause I know in my heart she's my only best friend.
She's always there if ever I call
so I'd do anything for her anything at all.

When we were little we did fight all the time.
But now we are older I'd give her my last dime.
We've never been as close as we
are today and I hope in my heart
that we always will stay as two
can bear better the greatest of fall.

And so my dear sister this poem is for you.
I know it's not much but it's the least I can do.

L. Sandham

A Mother's Gift

My children, my children, you gave to me,
A most wonderful gift in humanity,
You gave me your life when you were born,
So that I would not have to mourn.

You gave me such wonderful pleasure,
Perhaps for me to leave you never,
As you grow older you might get bolder,
But do not forget you have still got my shoulder.

If you get married remember you have carried,
Me right to the end of my days,
You have a father, and you may rather,
To carry him more than me,
But never forget you are always free,
But not to humanity.

Allanna Lorraine Harper

Life

Life is like an open book,
You pause a while to have a look,
But as you look the time flies past
And you are quite grown up at last.
And as the years go flying by
You sigh, and then you wonder why
You haven't done so many things—
Your heart is aching—still you sing.
when others hurt you—tears suppressed,
When there would be such happiness,
If only we could understand
If we could touch, or hold a hand
If only we could give and take,
What a difference it would make.
So make the best of life my friend
For like a book it has to end.

R. Marshall

'Van Gogh'

Alone he walked in darkened path,
A talent bursting forth as wrath,
They never saw the man in he,
Caused not by you, nor me but we.

With heavy hand and heavy brush,
Master strokes in frenzied rush,
He slammed the colour bold in hue,
In maddening haste the picture grew.

They scorned because they couldn't see,
The visions that had come from he,
Perhaps 'twas them who in disdain,
Spurred the madman to his fame.

Cornfield, flower, face and chair,
He worked in manner no man dare,
No mirror image there would be,
He painted just as he could see.

In total solitude he grew,
Away from green and red and blue,
He lifted palette weighed in black,
They then named him maniac.

Rose Brigid Moynes

Untitled

Grey clouds drifting overhead,
a brand new day now dawns,
thoughts of what the future holds,
as my distant lover I mourn,
a relationship no more to be,
an emptiness fills the air,
a partnership we have no more,
no love for us left to share,
no comfort in knowing I'm alone again,
to do as my fancy takes,
when you lose the love that's held your heart,
only tears for tragic mistakes.

Sharon Brindley

Praying For Rain

Look outside it's raining, as the sun begins to rise,
But will it last for long enough falling from the skies.
It hasn't rained for seven years, the fields have all run dry,
The only sign of moisture is the tear that fills my eye.
The reservoir is full of dust, the river's full of sand,
What used to be a lovely lake is now merely dry land.
But rain has started falling, God must have heard me pray,
I hope we're going to have a storm, I hope it rains all day.
I feel my throat is very dry as I jump into the stream,
And as I feel the water I awaken from my dream.
I feel the sun burn into me and still the drought remains,
So I'll have to pray a little harder, for God to send the rains.

M. A. Germaine

A New Day

The silence hovers over the hills and the land.
Far into the distance there is nothing but peace.
The greying tones of night merge into the glowing embers of day.
The sun rises bringing a tender warmth to everything chilled
  by the coolness of dark.
The only sounds to be heard are the hidden birds.
Their songs need no words.
In their gaiety and calm they add the first hint of life to
  another new day.
Soon the people will rise and with them the noise and disquiet
  that are life in a world of time and nothing.
This minute, this hour they'll never see.
Such peace and such calm
drenching the world like the dew on a leaf.
It's a part of life man can never capture.
Yet if I had one wish I know what it would be.
That the essence of this morning hour were part of me.

Shirley Morgan

The Wonders Of Summer

The sunshine and flowers, tell us that Summer is here,
June through to September, 'tis a wonderful time of year,
We can sit out in the garden, for there is so much to see,
Right now I'm watching butterflies, and the busy honey bee.

Many birds have hatched their young, and about to fledge the nest,
Soon coming to the water garden, to feed, to bathe and rest,
Nature gives us all so much, which we tend to take for granted,
Like the wonderful coloured flowers, grown from the seeds we
planted.

The clematis and the honeysuckle, have now come into bloom,
And looking at the fish ponds, the water lilies will flower soon,
Around the pond in search for worms, Is see a blackbird and a thrush,
Disturbing the bull frog's slumber, who takes to the water in a rush.

New potatoes, carrots and peas, all growing in the vegetable plot,
With asparagus and marrow's, runner beans, leaks and shallot
The orchard with its apple trees, plum trees, pears and cherries,
A rhubarb patch in the corner, also brambles and strawberries.

When the sun beats down on us, we find some shade to put our seat,
We can watch the birds and smell the blooms, also pick the
crops to eat,
The beauty that we can behold, means nature's show has
been a stunner,
Thank you Lord for all these things; they are the wonders of Summer.

(R. A. Wenn) Wenn the Penn

Love

Love is like a sea of emotion, love is like a deep blue ocean
Ever changing, never still, giving you an inner thrill
Washing over each new person, will I find the inspiration?
Where is my own deep blue ocean? Can I give enough devotion?
Love has hurt me in the past, will I find a love to last?
For now my ocean's still and calm
It does not move or cause me harm
I do not know the depth of love, I see my ocean from above
Will waves of love appear for me?
For now I'll have to wait and see
The power of love is strong and deep
This power can be hard to keep
The sea of love moves constantly
With ups and downs surrounding me
I will not swim against the tide, I will not turn and run or hide
My ocean it will come to me "perhaps" I'll have to wait and see
The smallest ripple starts a wave, it grows to change and misbehave
It rolls like thunder to the shore and crashes with a mighty roar
This wave is washing over me
My ocean's here, my own blue sea.

Reena Myers

The Last Battle

On our land the battle had begun and today this war still
wages on and in force the enemies come, young lives they
take and many of these soldiers, have killed and raped.
I stood by and watched all the family die then escaped and ran
into the woods to hide.
I wander along a dusty road in this intensive heat with blisters
upon these feet and a cold wind blows then tears begin to
flow as I recall memories of the place, I once called home.
Sweat tricked down one's face and it became a constant
struggle to keep up the pace.

These bones protrude and this stomach yearns for food and
many days having had no water supply, one's throat has
become dry and much hunger inside then I wondered, am I
doomed to die and when tomorrow arrives, will I still be alive?
I could no longer stand and again I fell onto the ground and
this heart of mine began to pound and where I lay still this
immense pain in the body remains and then that rattle came
and I knew the last moment had come as I gasp for breath, the
battle death had won.
Beneath the moonlit skies, a body of a young girl lies and far
above the spirit travelled back home on the last journey all alone.

Valerie Barton

Goodbye

Our loved one has gone without goodbye
And all we really want to do is cry
For we are sad that she has gone
To our Father above The Enlightened One
To our family and friends who have gone before
She will be greeted with love for ever more
She will be with us but on a higher plain
Where she will be happy and feel no pain
She has gone through a door marked eternity
Where she will explore and discover with wonder
That life is not over
So cry and mourn until the dawn
Then let her go with all your love
But know that one day she will come and say
"Give me your hand and I will lead the way"

Julia Binks

House Upon The Rock

Strength is knowing who you are, and living your own life,
Believing in yourself, in hurt, in pain, in strife.
It's about setting your goals, and aiming for the sky,
No-one dares subvert them, no-one can reach so high.
You respect other people, and they respect you,
You have your own beliefs, opinions and points of view.
You've been through many traumas, trials and tribulation
But because you stand firm, it always ends in celebration.
People seek your advice, they know you know the score,
You've been through it all before, and never hit the floor.
Strength comes through perseverance, will power and determination,
It comes little bit, by little bit, and so you have a foundation.
Like building materials, you start with sand; the result is cement,
It is the main ingredient, for satisfaction and content
If you have the correct formula, then nothing can go wrong.
Your life won't fall to pieces, if your foundation is strong.
Strength dwells within you, and is a mighty force,
But what is the formula, and where is the source?

Rachel-Ann Bleakney

Anorectic

What is this illusion? I can't understand.
Why can't I hold tight her graspless hand?

I see it now in the loss of her smile,
Entangled within mazed webs of denial.

Her careless glow consumed by guilt,
Her gaunt eyes bleed—the blossoms wilt.

Cadaverous bones chew succulent curves;
That inner contentment gnawed at by nerves.

Those shapeless clothes reflect her mind—
An empty identity she hungers to find.

It feeds or her youth through spitting jaws
And clings to its prey with skeletal claws.

A mask of deceit, not a wavering tone.
Surrounded by people, she's always alone.

Katherine Harrold

Reflections

A cloud of sorrow hangs over my dreams,
As on a roller coaster ride through time it seems.
I Had Such Great Ambition,
Though not as a technician.
I could have been a train driver or firefighter;
An explorer, a racing driver, or moonlighter.
Instead, I am passing time,
In a place for the insane.
The mirror in the darkness brightens by the second
As a day for release is ever to be reckoned.
The thought of seeing my children again
Sends a vain flow of blood to the brain.

Malcolm C. Broughton

Seasons Of Life

My dear Lord as I close my eyes
Something stirs in my heart and begins to rise
A feeling of love and peace within
As my thoughts of what I have seen begin
The gentle smile of someone kind
Lingering on through the mists in my mind
Amidst wisps of colours entwined to be
At one with the Earth, Sky and Sea
Of the pure opening up of Spring
Like life itself it does surely sing
To catching the warmth of a summer's day
On a breeze we float along life's way
Through to Autumn and its powerful glow
As along its path we gently flow
Then to Winters so crisp and white
Giving frosty patterns through the light
So gentle all these things can be
As they touch our hearts and make us see
So my Lord I will close my eyes
And thank You for this wondrous prize

Catherine P. Nimmo

The Stair

Speckled grey marble so cold and austere
Beneath walls that speak silence and memory.
Smooth polished wood in a world of closed doors
A voice whispers, "Will you remember me?"

Sudden descent and flight from the past
The commotion dissolves into silence.
A plea not to go; a flight to the last
Left only with fleeting remembrance.

C. Carey

Men Oh Men

Men have ever so cushy a life,
First mum takes care of them—then a wife
Most commonly known as "Her Indoors"—
She has the pleasure of the cleaning, cooking and chores
He comes home from the office—His day's work is done,
While her day's work still carries on
Throughout the evening and into the next day,
But his week is finished when he gets his pay
He then decides without even a maybe,
The time is right to have a baby
If it's a boy then he'll prove his worth,
While she endures the agony of the birth
And when he's drunk and smokes his cigar,
His friends congratulate him—"How clever you are"
Now a family of three and ever-so-happy,
He sits and watches as she changes the nappy
Yes—He's so content to let life run its course—
He has the shock of his life when she asks for a divorce!

Ann Trainor

Barren Land

Raped and pillaged this barren land has been,
by time, the elements and war.
Its eyes now closed, what they have seen
on hills and valleys and shore.
On one side the people scattered within,
all are hardly and strong.
The other side, its neighbouring kin,
Falklands people have done little wrong.

Through ages past, the cause of dispute,
visitors flock here to see.
To take what they want, plunder and loot,
and satisfied they all flee.
I am here just a short time, in its history it's true,
to enjoy life the best that I can.
I can't change the past or affect the future too,
as, in the end I am only one man.

R. M. Smith

At The Fair

There's enchantment in a Summer fair,
colourful stalls, loud music everywhere;
Voices ring out with enticing cries,
coconut shines, bingo and nice hot pies,
Painted horses jog round and round,
and lively youngsters wrestle on the ground
fighting for coppers to give them some fun,
buying hats and dark glasses for the sun,
Some throw colourful rings, after many tries
come away, clutching their teddy bear prize.

There's a crack of rifles as men show their skill,
ghost trains in dark tunnels to give a thrill;
Balloons and lollipops, lost of ice cream,
high-up swing boats to make your loved one scream,
and then as she clings to your arms she'll sigh
for the time has rushed on to a sad goodbye.
Music is loud as the crowd go away,
but remains an echo of a tune they play;
"I'll have the last waltz with you?" Was the dance
when together we found our true romance.

Lavinia Brown

The Bicycle Song

A unicycle seems lots of fun
But with only one wheel you'll fall on your bum.

A bicycle is more in my line
A balancing act I can do just fine.

A tricycle makes a lot more sense
It's just as easy as sitting on a fence.

But whichever you choose it's got to suit you
No petrol, no fumes and ozone friendly too.

Karen Dodd

Thinking

I roam aimlessly through timeless space.
Used once; and discarded, by the human race.
I am one of a multitude, identical to each other.
Created by a human, for some reason or other.
I can only be used once, then I float aimlessly away.
But re-created many times, that very same day.
I can be wicked or vile, or gentle or kind.
It depends what the human has in mind.
I cannot control how I am used.
And my user cannot control me, when confused.
It is not my intention to cause anger or pain.
But human's cause me to do so, again and again.
Jealousy and envy, lust and greed.
These are a few of my hurtful seeds.
These seeds grow in the human mind.
And they grow more quickly than the gentler kind.
I am always ready for the human to use.
Sometimes in seriousness, sometimes to amuse.
It could be for progression, or it could be to thwart.
I have no choice. I am only a thought.

Leslie McKee

Mothers And Fathers—Who Are They?

Mothers and Fathers—Who are they?
I think each night as I pray.
As you've seen they always hurt me,
I suppose that's how it should always be.

They always manage to taunt and intimidate,
Which makes me repeatedly self-mutilate.
I look at them with pleading eyes,
But they choose to ignore my cries.

I used to be continuously abused,
Which was far worse than being used.
I managed again to recite my childhood,
Which has permanently left me scarred for good.

Mothers and Fathers—Who are they?

Catherine Baxter

Moving

All packed and full, the tea chests stand in line.
Cardboard boxes tied with string and labelled just in time.
"The van is here" somebody shouts now chaos reigns supreme.
With heaving, lifting, carrying out, and praying not another broken dream.

Now can be seen a dark patch on a wall where a picture used to hang.
There's still a loose floorboard out in the hall,
And the front door only shuts with a bang.
At last the rooms are empty the van is on its way
And in the stillness thoughts flood the mind of smiles and tears from yesterday.

One final look round and a whispered goodbye to what is now part of the past.

The future begins tomorrow.
But today you are moving—at last.

P. Hovery

Yesterday I Went To See You

The skin
(that one day unexperienced parents' hands caressed,
that one day unexperienced parents' lips kissed,
that one day unexperienced parents' eyes saw how it grew)
clings to your bones today.
The precious elixir is evaporating
drop
  by
    drop
towards a faraway place
—I wish I knew where!
Yesterday I went to see you
and I didn't recognize you.
You opened your eyes
and in that fleeting moment,
beyond drowsiness, pain and delirium,
you smiled at me
through your mask,
and I didn't know what to say.

Oscar Palazon

John Lennon

The wizard of rhythm buzzed with imagination,
Each word he wrote exploded into colour,
Twisting the meaning of fantasy,
Each word he sang created images of the impossible,
No one could describe the story behind his music,
For it was his escape,
He will be the Beatles,
He is the Beatles,
He was the Beatles.

Naomi Hands

Children Of Dunblane

The 16 children of Dunblane,
It really is a terrible shame,
A crazed gun man just walked in,
While they were running around in the gym,
Laughing and playing and having fun,
Next thing they know they'd been shot by a gun.

Children screaming, teacher dead,
Next the crazed man shot himself in the head,
The police arrive, ambulances too,
Parents run the few miles to school,
Parents screaming, children dead,
Waiting to find out if it's their child that's dead.

The wounded children shipped off to hospital,
The blue lights flashing but all is still.
The massacre that shocked the nation,
More worldly spread than the Coronation,
Money's still flooding into many funds,
But nothing will help to fill in the wounds.

Vicki Leanne Simms

A Friend

I wish I had a friend with a smile.
Who would say "I am taking you away for awhile."

Somewhere nice where people are kind.
Where you can leave the cares of the world behind
Where your broken tired heart can mend.
Where the pain you feel will come to an end.
Oh, for that friend.
Audrey Savage

Once

You made me feel wanted on top of the world
A beauty beholden, a new flag unfurled
My words so important, my voice like a song
Those feelings you gave me compelling and strong
Excitement; took my breath away
Like a rollercoaster truck
Fly up high, up above
Then thunder down out of luck
You told me you wanted me any which way
Then you left me, you dropped me just threw me away
For the feelings I drew in
The ups and the downs
Like ships in the night we passed did the rounds
As forever can go in the blink of an eye
Then for this forever, I thank you
Goodbye.
Kym Emsley

Troubled Times

What is wrong with the world today
We hear from everywhere
The news is bad in every way
Nobody seems to care.

There's fighting and strife all over the place
Cruelty and violence reign
There seems no love in the human race
Has the whole world gone insane

Will there ever be peace in the world again
Can values once more be found
We all must strive with might and main
To spread goodwill around

To open our lives to peace and love
To care for our fellow man
Embrace the words of God above
And do the best we can

As we travel on our road through life
In this world is which we dwell
To lift the load of pain and strife
Make a Heaven and not a Hell . . .
Thelma Bandy

The Apology Promise

He came into my room,
Apologized,
He looked at me now with different eyes,
"I love you" he said carefully,
I opened my mouth to reply,
but I couldn't repeat those words to him,
he dropped my hands and left me alone,
I sat crying and thought about his words,
and his evil ways,
bad memories,
due to my faults,
tears came . . . flowed . . . and stopped,
feelings of remorse came . . . and stopped,
I told myself what I needed to hear,
forget your fear,
and with my hand on my heart,
and my head to the floor,
I mouthed the words,
he'd spoken before.
Laura A. Wilson

Untitled

My heart used to stand straight throbbing with pride
It now lays on its back in the pit of my stomach
    trembling in shame
The shame is mine no others
It sits neatly on my shoulders like the weight of the others
For all to see how I failed my son,

    THE ADDICT

He needs it to make his life normal they say
What about me as I cry and I pray
As you sniff and snort whatever
One day this umbilical cord you'll truly sever
Always money you want for a good use
When I have none, you steal for your self abuse
You use family and friends without shame
There's always someone else to blame
Where did I go wrong I ask every day
To make you grow up this horrible way
They tell me it's not my fault, you do what you do
If it's not mine then someone please tell me who?
M. Bliss

Which Food?

Which succulent morsel can we partake
What indigestible crumb is the root of the ache
When in youth did our stomachs ever grumble
From mothers cooking hardly a hint of a rumble

Is ageing really a case of digestion
Do we eat wisely upon reflection
Should we roast boil or even fry it
Which is the healthiest way for my diet

Everything in moderation some may say
Until they discover their ulcers one day
Do we eat too often too much for too long
Should we let carbohydrates go for a song

So many foods they say cause great strife
A great many worries will come later in life
Now obesity is a very great problem
While anorexia nervosa's are scared when they wobble'm
Yet nobody knows what really is best
So we eat as we like and hope our minds rest.
Mike Reddington

For John

There once was a lad with an eye
For a lass in the W.I.
But she felt rather loth
When he plighted his troth
So she told him to lay down and die

My brothers live on Marmalade
My sisters live on Jam
But I'm the family Carnivore
And all I eat is Spam!

I offer no apologize for these masterpieces!!!
Terrence Roach

Spurned

Thine eyes are dark and brooding, so morose
They make my heart to wither and take flight.
You make my ways seem wicked and profane.
Instead my love is pure, vestal and alight.
Then take the moral high road and refrain
Your pure and chastened temperament maintain.
Let me the one to suffer venial sin,
I the one to expiate God's grace.
Could you not touch my heart with tenderness and care,
My pain and broken heart you could repair.
Instead you seek to say the last 'farewell'
With never sweet words to me ever tell.
So my existence held suspended by a thread
Your breaking of it I will always dread.
Ellen Hillary-Fawcett

195

Winter's Song

The leaves have left the boughs so bare,
And fallen to the earth to share
A brilliant carpet of gold and yellow,
And in a few weeks to wither and mellow,
And the north wind will blow.

Grey clouds quickly gathering speed
Darker ones now and then taking the lead.
Faster then slower, never the same.
And the north wind will blow.

The wind whistles strangely, a haunting song,
Moving the branches and grasses along,
It taps on the windows, the fences may fall,
Persistent in outcry, its voice warns us all.
And the north wind will blow.

The pond gleams like diamonds and pearls dipped in silk,
And whispering reeds are covered in milk.
Silent and quiet, the water is still
The song of the winter is here, until,
The north wind will go.

Pamela Jennings

Love's Message

Weep not for me for I am happy here,
The glory of God's kingdom is forever near.
Colours are so beautiful, fragrances so sweet,
No one would believe it—but will whene'er they meet.

Weep not for me—such warmth and peace abound,
Proving to all that glory does surround
Each soul that passes from the chains of earth
To enter in His kingdom with new birth.

So close to you am I, my love will always stay
To guide and help and cheer you on your way.
Be happy, know God's peace for all is free
And blessings will be yours—weep not for me.

Margaret H. Robertson

The Healing Of Myself

Thank you God for the creation that is me.
Thank you for the stillness that I am.

Thank you for the beauty that I know
The love that is me
The tears when I cry
And the joy when I laugh.

Thank you for the life I am.
Without this life how can I know
The world You have made
The family that love me
And all the blessings that I'm given.

Thank you God that I am me
And that I can say these things to You.

Jackie Draysey

Lonely Times

Sometimes I get so lonely,
often I feel so cold.
It seems that my dreams have
passed me, and the story just won't unfold.
There isn't a day that goes by
without me feeling so sad,
about the emptiness that now surrounds me,
and a friendship that I once did have.

Lonely times are here to stay
and I'm looking at you from a very long way,
do you remember the time when I first touched your hand?
We sang through my songs and we went through your grand.
And I say down with love
and up with sorrow,
no more luck for another tomorrow, lonely times
always shine through.

Andy Layte

'Love Is Suicide'

I search the crowds for my Dear Desire
But see only the corridors of everyday Monotony,
The one Love which has never breathed fatigue,
Yet a one–sided battle over Misery.

My eyes draw in on my Dear Desire
Just to savour for a second . . . Or two . . . Or three . . .
One daily glimpse of Beauty, so innocent,
Reveals a gentle personality, down deeply.

Really a kind heart, really a gem,
Though shrouded in Pretence for his peers, shallow.
For his soft complexion my fingers would adore
To touch; would make Infatuation grow.

Unobtainable means appealing, and Appeal
Means Desire, Obsession, Confusion so strong,
I'll never reach my dream as my dream is him
And he thinks I'm the definition of 'wrong'.

Optimism is just another blatant lie
Painted upon the pages of Hope,
We only agree with its beautiful speech
Because Beauty is the only acceptable joke.

Vicky Turner

The Power Of Love

Everlasting is the power of love
The power of love will never die
And when it seems all else is lost
Love shines through like the stars in the sky
Love existed before man and time
Love has made us what we are today
Everlasting is the power of love
It outshines sorrow and dismay
Maybe slowly with love's strength
War and poverty will retreat
Everlasting is the power of love
Without it life would be incomplete.

Rashpinder Kaur

My Valentine

It's thirty years since we said, 'I do'
But, like those folk that live on the hill,
That Crosby crooned and sang about,
This Jack still loves his Jill.

If pretty maids were all in a row
And, you were the end of that line,
I'd walk past them all, I'd take your hand
And say, 'Be my valentine'.

B. E. George

Loss Of A Loved One!

A flower so fair
a personality so rare
unselfish and giving
making life worth the living for others.

Need a helping hand?
She would always understand
she had so much love to give to others.

Hiding her own pain
her smile would never wane
she fought so hard to live
but always courage she would give
to others.

A last kiss we place
on her beloved face
now so pale and wan,
accepting she has gone
yet, knowing in my heart
that we will never really part
like all grieving mothers.

Margaret McHugh

Forever And Ever

We live in an age of violence and fear
Assault and road rage getting worse each year
Serial killers, genocide—next nuclear detonation
Leaving behind a state of death and devastation

Like in the jungle after a fire
Traces of life seek to aspire
Here one woman and here one man
Just like it was when the world first began

Just two people in a desolate place
Ready to be founders of the new human race
They vow no anger, just sweetness and love
Even offering prayers for guidance from above

The miracle of birth and another Cain and Abel
Growing up together in a family that's stable
Then suddenly one morning the younger boy
Is battered by his brother over possession of a toy

Alan Nicholls

The Dream

As I fall into this pit of darkness,
I see only horror in my dream.
Ghosts of past and present touch my skin
With their rotting flesh.
The dust of time sprays up under my feet.
Dark, black windows pass my gaze,
As hideous figures duck out of sight
To hide from my gaze.
But the light at the end of the road
Is all I can see in this darkened haze.
This pit of darkness,
Silent, and filled with fear.
From this darkened pit, faces leer,
Faces with eyes as ebon as the Styx,
Their mouths yawn in agonizing grins,
As rotting hands reach out and touch my skin,
As I pass through this pit of darkness
And come out of my dream
Without any fear.

Lee Hayward

Drug Takers

Behind the streets in the dark alleys and the dimly lit stairways
On a carpet of syringes, match sticks and silver paper
The young drug addicts, down-and-outs hang about

The bedding rolls and cardboard blankets
The lost sounds and wasted talents
Young boys and girls who fail to make it

From an age so young their unplanned destiny
To beg, to mug, rob and go into prostitution
Without a care money earned is owed, already spent

There is not cure of escape to freedom
The path is trodden, their destiny chosen
Only despair, doubt, sickness and death lies before them

S. J. Adkins

Will Winter Never End?

Out of the window—white is the ground
Depression and misery—all around
His coal is gone—his pension done
No warmth or comfort of summer sun
His faith is dead—no more this friends
Dear God, will winter never end?

The embers dying—his body's so cold
He never asked to grow so old
He prays each day will be his last
He closes his eyes—and thinks of the past
But as he sleeps he joins his friends
Dear God, For Him The Winter Ends

Patricia Dawson

Marriage Of Love

Side by side you stood with me
Into the future I could not see
The day that you became my wife
Happiness entered into my life

I speak of you with love and pride
My feelings I can never hide
When I say, your name out loud
Strangers know I feel quite proud

I've watched you laugh and sometimes cry
The years of happiness have rolled by
Happy times though some were sad
To be with you I'm always glad

I give you love, I give you care
My life I give for you to share
In your heart I'm sure you know
My love for you will never go

Trust, Understanding, And Loyalty too
These things I gladly give to you
Give to you so we can be
Married, In Love, For Eternity

Dennis N. Davies

Wonderful, We Should Have Had Them First

To hear one say, 'I'm not tired, I've just run out of imagination',
and another, 'Go away, you're annoying my sleeping',
Or later, disturbed when staring at the light,
'The colours have come out of the ceiling and are now in your
eyes' . . . makes for a transforming 'sunrise of wonder', a
grandparent's delight.

No moralizing, no talk of improving our mind;
just offering us acquisitive enquiry, inspired spontaneity,
crossing forbidding boundaries to open up
things forgotten, unseen or even undreamt . . .
the 'hard work', made simple, by these quintessential works of art.

'Fragility is a mark of value,
that which is not fragile is pretentious', so
these tender children, still immune to habits of adulthood,
come fresh to all the world: safeguard such fragile miracles.

'Sorry, I was day-dreaming', said grandfather, accused;
'I call that not listening', retorts the sharp four year old child.
Then 'Sophie's World' opens before us; we see, astounded,
the gradual build-up of private discoveries,
bringing fresh vision, new hope, and elders learning anew
from our young just how easy it is
'to unify the outer and inner worlds,
the ordinariness and yet the extraordinariness of everything.'

Peter Challen

The Tigeress

Beyond the rustling of the trees,
In the distance far away,
I hear the sound of panting breath,
The tigeress stalks her prey,

With head held high and the speed of light,
She quickly makes her kill,
With several hungry mouths to feed,
She'll see they get their fill,

She lies behind the blades of grass,
Her offspring having a feast,
There's usually nothing left for her,
But she doesn't mind in the least,

The weeks go by, it's time she left,
Her cubs are fully grown,
She's done her job, she's reared them well,
She sets out on her own.

The tigeress is a powerful beast,
Her beauty will provide,
No matter what she has to face,
She'll hold her head with pride.

Lilian Sedgwick

My Tree

Dedicated To My Mother

Oh Christmas Tree
You stand so tall,
You are wide at the bottom
But your top is quite small,
You fill my house with your piny scent
And prick with your needles but no harm is meant

You look so handsome with your pretty lights,
And you make me feel warm on these winter nights

I took so long making you look nice
With your shiny baubles and chocolate mice,
It's a shame you won't stay for very long,
As the new year arrives you will soon be gone

You'll look sad and bare when I throw you away,
Or I could plant you in my garden and then you can stay,
So this time next year, you will be taller, and this time next year,
To you I'll look smaller!

Goodbye for now,
For sometime you'll look plain,
See you next year, when . . .
I'll adorn you again!

Suzanne Bostle

Life

Life's a mystery . . . or so they say,
but to me it's tough
mercenary
depressing
vile.

I dream of another life.
A life so far gone, a life beyond me . . .
a perfect life — it does not exist.

I see a vision of a rebel,
an insensitive being,
one that is confident . . .
it's suppressed
deep inside a tower,
with no window, door
or gate . . . it's trapped.

I see it happening . . . an enemy
bomb blown up—there is pain, it hurts
the fragments of my life everywhere.
I am gone . . . gone where?
I am lost . . . lost to what?

Amreet Dhadialla

The Thrush

Slender flowered speckled
gentle charm,

Darting among the growing plants
towards my window.

Trusting—not too much—
Glancing with your soft eyes at my smile.
Your daily visit is my happiness.

Sylvia Westwood

Fate

As I lie here on the rich velvet grass,
the blue sky surrounds the atmosphere,

The smell of summer vaporizes the sphere of everlasting hope,

The breeze of dreams dances with fate, fate!
Will I ever be here again?

The romance of life and death teases my soul, it's great
emotion drinks out the fountain of my veins, do I live or do I die?

Only fate has the key to everlasting life.

J. E. Missir

Summer Is Over And Gone

The leaves are falling off the trees,
Swimmers have gone from off the seas,
Summer is over and gone.
Electric blankets are on again,
Days are shorter, nights are longer,
Summer is over and gone.

Christmas thoughts and Christmas songs,
For conker games the children long,
Summer is over and gone.
Buttercups are dying, creatures hibernating, breezes sighing,
Summer is over and gone.

The swallows to far off lands have flown,
Summer is over and gone.
No more sun bathing, much too cold,
Summer is over and gone.
No hot sun, no salads, no more picnics,
Summer is over and gone.

James McIlhatton Jr.

The Vets

"Well, we're here once again", I said patting his head
as I walked through the door passing others that fled
with their pooches, their moggies, rabbits and mice
after having some treatment that wasn't too nice!

I glanced down at Charlie, he looked up at me
we both knew what was coming—so just let it be
and just as I thought he was going to be brave
he ran under a table, his skin for to save

As his name was called out he quivered and shook
he seemed so defenceless, I just couldn't look
I didn't go in, I just sat wringing my hands
then, "that's it Mrs. Ashton, I've done Charlie's glands!"

Lyn Ashton

The Grey Cross

In the centre of my town
stands a statue tall and grey
weather beaten standing alone
reminds us of heroes from forgotten days.

Now we hold our heads in shame
for young rebels fighting for "the cause"
the claim,
but with masks to hide their shame it is not so.

The cross is silent peaceful and quiet
visited and it reminds us to be happy to be alive
and the sorrow of lives lost
in our world why can't it always be so?

James Kelly

Poem for Luciano Pavarotti on His 60th Birthday

60 glorious years of song;
Is it so?
Did the music
Ever flow,
From above
Into you;
Through the mind,
Into the heart,
So to impart
This sound,
So beautiful,
So round
From vocal chord
I do applaud,
I do applaud,
As thousands do;
and scatter notes
Of Birthday Joy
Around the head
Of you.

Netta P. Mills

Famine And War

A famine engulfs this country so poor already ravaged by
men at war.
A people wander for days on end starving and weak will
the suffering ever end.
A woman struggles past babe in arms, its limp and
lifeless body an outcome of famines harm.
Look into her eye's so full of despair searching for food
and human care.

A man cries out and then breaks down, his sons body a
bundle of rag's on the ground.
A tear runs downs his ravaged face, he dreams for a
moment of a better place.
The sight of his sons body again hits his heart like a speeding
train.
I look at his face once full of hope, drawn and haggard
like a piece of old rope.

Like so many other's full of despairing, look into his
eyes he's given up caring.
He slowly struggles onto his feet and joins the exodus of
a people beat.
So take heed those people who lead, you're killing your
own nation a people in need.

Craig Richard Harris

The Angel's Kiss

An angel kissed
last night my face
and set my heart
to ceaseless race
A touch so gentle
light and pure
left me in need
of so much more

So swift the touch
the merest breath
of warmth
against my face and yet
left night so long of restless sleep
and days of dark as blindness deep

How can I tell
someone so dear
that I would wish to hold her near
Then like my angel full of grace
return my kiss
upon her face.

Marcus Jones

The Death Of Love

Now, as I lay in the motionless sleep
I think not upon my wrong.
Instead I ponder over the good I did reap,
And a love that will forever be strong.

My love I left above the earth.
Whilst here I rest below.
Forever she will be filled with mirth,
And I an eternal sorrow.

For she did not harbour love for me.
Nay, 'twas for another man.
Whose heart was cloaked in jealousy,
And rid me of her he can.

Yet, it is not that he can, rather he did.
This loathsome thief of life.
The cup he took away from me,
And is sharing it with his wife.

However, it is of no matter to me.
No more do they make me sad.
For I know that this man's time is nigh,
And search will she for another lad.

Matthew James Smith

Roof Tops

As I gazed out of my window
Looking at all the houses,
I noticed all the roof tops
Had different colours and disguises.
Some were grey,
Some were black, and
Many looked like nutty-slack.
But more significant are the ochres and reds,
Though very few have green over their heads.
A striking ensemble of colour I see,
Not all the same as they used to be.
So I imagine I'm looking at hills,
Rolling downs, and ploughed up fields.
Not so boring, I say to myself,
As I close the window
And put flowers on the shelf.

Dinah Wolstenholme

Space Is Super

Going to see dark Uranus and
Neptune.
See the cold planet Pluto.
See dark Galaxies, bright stars and
dark and bright planets as well.
Round mighty Jupiter and see
Saturn's glistening rings.
Zoom to the grey moon and back
home to the blue Earth.

Samuel Simpson

Memories

Far off fancies plague me still,
Sunlight on a distant hill,
Rolling thunder passing by,
Raindrops falling from the sky

Memories of bygone days,
Sand and sea and summer haze,
Fill my failing mind and sight,
With endless visions of delight.

Youth, vitality—all is gone,
Pain and heartache linger on,
In my loneliness I see,
Visions of what used to be.

Friendship, laughter, family love,
Special blessings from above,
All of these worth more than gold,
To a woman, growing old.

Margaret Taylor

The Otter

She has no wings, yet flies with ease,
So graceful, skilful, with great expertise.
No restriction of movement to weigh herself down,
One minute a hunter, the next, a clown.
It is not the air she flies through this way,
But clear sparkling water frames her display.
Creating a ballet each time she swims,
With moods of the moment, fancies of whims.
Her large round eyes miss no opportunity
To play pranks on playmates within her community.
A social creature, so happy to be
An accepted member of her otter family.
With this assurance, she plays at her best,
Teasing and laughing along with the rest.
When a hard days hunting and play are done,
She cleans herself carefully, then rests in the sun.
In the sunlight, her well groomed coat glistens,
Her eyes are closed, but still she listens,
A humming bee and the sound of the stream
What a soothing lullaby to accompany her dream.

Pamela Harding

Untitled

Please hear me . . . !
I want to show you my poem,
It's just another poem full of tears and pain . . .
Pain . . . that took all my happiness away.
. . . Pain that is overtaking,
The spirit of my whole being.
Alone with my memories . . .
I try not to cry anymore.
. . . Those old moments . . . the pleasure . . . the happiness
. . . Memories mixed with the present
Are taking me with you
More and more each day!
And . . . you are the reason of my life . . .
Just because I can't stop loving you!!
When I look into the sky,
I feel my eyes shining . . .
But I never had anything mine.
Not even someone to love me . . .

When I hear love stories,
I feel my heart cry . . .
. . . All of this made me want to die

Ana Luisa Nobrega Gomes

Daffodils

Delicate, soft and fragile flowers.
A yellow that shames the sun.
From yellow petals to tall green stem.
From dawn to dusk they dance away.
On every occasion they swish about.
Dancing proud with their talent.
If I were a daffodil I'd be tallest of the others.
Like pieces of gold shimmering in the sun.
So when the winter comes they slumber up in bed till next spring.

Claire Kane

"Miranda"

She leaps and frolics on the sands
you can count her earth years on three hands
half girl-half woman–half woman-half girl
the moods of the world will have her in a whirl

Home sweet home is still her base
No worry lines sketched on her face
No ruined years as yet
she's still her mother little pet

Should we tell her of things to come
or should we let her experience some
We could tell of passions setting her on fire
We could tell of a lover who turns into a Liar
We could tell of depression that will cloud her brain
We could tell of sunny affairs that turn into rain

Half girl half woman half woman half girl
The moods of the world will have her in a whirl
The world (can be sweet) hers for the taking
but it can turn and attack leaving her bruised and shaking

M. A. Teece

Smitten Kitten

This little baby's one smitten kitten
The cat gets the cream
The hand gets the mitten
As long as there's a dream
The future is written
Australia France the U.S. and Great Britain
A thousand places in between
The poorest tramp
The richest queen
This little baby's one smitten kitten
The hand gets the cream
The cat gets the mitten
As long as there's a dream
The future is written
There's a dream so it's written

Gavin Wright-Hadley

The English Language

No wonder it's a problem to master the English tongue,
Absorbing words sponge-like from nations so far-flung.
Whether it's weather or whether it's whether or where or wear
or ware,
Is it hear, or maybe here, or is it their or there?

Add an 'S' to pear, it's spear but add an 'S' to pare it's spare.
Add a 'T' to ear, it's tear but then again it could be tear!
Join a 'G' to reed, it's greed, but join a 'B' to read, it's bread.
Add a 'P' to aid, it's paid, but add an 'S' and then it's said.

A witch can cast an evil spell but which witch should it be?
And which boy put the buoy at sea and which maid made the tea?
What heart beats in the noble hart and what son likes the sun?
And when a game is being played, what one's the one that won?

What father went much farther than he's ever been before
And which drawer holds the pencils and the crayons used to draw?
What raw's the meat the lion eats and what roar's the noise he
makes?
Teach a dog to shake your hand, which paw's the paw he
shakes?

With you, yew, ewe and ours and hours and time and thyme again,
With clues, and views and lose and news, I think it's pretty plain
That after wading through all this, there seems just one conclusion
To learn another language would cause far less confusion!

Casie Lianne Allan

Rain

Dedicated to Beatrice Wheeler

It is a world unto itself—many nations, many language, and
   many cultures.
When heat radiates, it is soft, soothing, trying, in vain to arouse.
consciousness.
If it is cold, it is a He, fierce, the final weapon to whip for sloth.
Morning rain, overcoat twisting, hat setting; hand in pocket, a
   glance,
the sun to seek, a tear drops down the creases, falls.
Puddle to pond, pond to sea, sea to the ocean; far out across
   the ripple silk.
Frozen—bleached of its populace;
rejuvenation, to water, water to drain
drain to stream, stream to river. River.
Dark at night it stones my pains.
Attention—you're missing something?
Awake and washed, the sun pauses.
Rain showers on a world of many nations,
languages and many cultures.

Nigel (Noog) Thomas Wheeler

Evening

Long, long ago I turned to you
As you came through the open door,
And my heart brushed off its cobwebs;
You were she I had waited for.

Dreams seldom live in the daylight
But at dusk when the sun's discreet,
Yet this time the moment was golden
And the afternoon air was sweet.

Many years have gone by since that meeting,
Many laughs, many hopes, many ties.
That day will remain unforgotten
Till the last of the two of us dies.

You were wonderful then. At that greeting
We knew it was always to be.
You are wonderful now—and the firelight
Glows warm as you smile up at me.

We are old and the spark of life flickers
But the magic of love still is there
When I kiss your soft lips in the morning
And smooth out the dreams in your hair.

John B. Sturgeon

The Somme

At first sight it's just a field no different from any other,
Then you see the trenches, the bomb holes,
The cemeteries with the soldiers graves, some with no name.
They are all heroes named or not,
They are heroes who died for a cause they'd began to doubt.
It makes me angry,
All those men dying for the greed of others.
The tears start to arrive,
But the wind blows, whisking them away.
It seems like it's the spirit of a dead soldier saying 'no, don't cry'
The peacefulness of the sight is shattered by my thoughts,
The sound of the chatter in the trenches,
the wails of pain and cries for help fill my head,
The guns . . . The guns, shooting the innocent, the ordinary people,
Not those whose war it is.
It's not the people's war,
They're not enemies,
But they are the ones,
The ones who had to die.
Why?

Elizabeth Fox

Soldier's Of The Forgotten War

I know that somewhere out there is a bullet,
that has my name engraved upon it in blood.
I've spent the years running, dodging,
and denying all that which has gone before.
But I know that the bullet is circling, circling,
and circling this world in its attempt to locate me,
and find me it will.

But I feel no regret only sadness that it has,
taken me long to be allowed to break,
these shackles of burden
to be rejoined with those I fought side-by-side with so long ago.

I know that this war that I remember has been long forgotten by now.
But I still feel the shame of it that no one,
wants to recall or hold up their hand to accept the blame!
But I remember everything,
and so do many others.
I only await peace from these tormenting memories,
memories that are forever etched upon my mind in both fire
and blood.

Fiona Barrowclough

"Winter Blues"

Snow that glitters on the ground.
People walk without a sound.
Their footprints lead to the park beyond.
Where they feed the ducks on the icy pond.
The trees with their branches stretched out wide.
With frost and icicles hang side by side.
The days are short and the nights are long.
We long to hear the birds sing their song.
Not much longer to wait for the spring.
With flowers that the mild air brings.
The smell of the blossoms will fill the air.
And all at once we know we care.

M. R. Cook

The Great War

Roses are red,
But instead of roses grow poppies instead,
They burst and bloom,
From in and out the dead men's tomb.

Hundreds of men did die,
As we watch their mothers cry,
While the mothers weep,
The fathers rest in a deep sleep.

The fathers dream about the war,
They dream and hear the plane's engines roar,
They hear young men's cries,
As nearly millions die.

Stacey Lynn Williams

Make The World A Better Place

The flowers, the trees and the clouds up high,
The world is beautiful, what a lie,
Yes look closely beneath the colourful veil,
It's a place filled with murder and betrayal,
With starving children and polluted air,
That's not the way to show we care,
Let's join together and each of us become a player,
And stop the destruction of the ozone layer,
How about the thousands that die each year from disease,
And the rainforests, help stop the cutting down off the tree's,
Can no-one else but me detect,
The lack of kindness and respect,
I mean, why do people steal instead of borrow,
Just think of all the sickness and the sorrow,
And there's no need for fighting or for lying,
Let's put our energy together and stop the world from dying,
Remember every little helps to play a part,
So stamp out the cruelness with a tender heart,
So let's make our stand as the whole human race,
After all, the world could be such a beautiful place.

Donna Flavell

Christmas Eve

A little Grey Donkey came galloping by,
"Pray where are you going, Grey Donkey?" Said I.
"I go to the stable," the Grey Donkey said,
"To soften the manger for Jesus' bed."

The Oxen plod solemnly home to their shed,
"This evening we pray to the Christ Child," they said,
"For this is the evening that comes once a year
When we beasts kneel to pray for our Saviour is near."

The Rings Doves coo softly their sweet too-ra-loo,
"A lullaby, Jesus, we're singing for you.
May the Lord bless all creatures at this Christmastide
And all who draw near to this Child's bedside."

J. A. Blakely

Crusade—Then And Now

Lord, as I kneel before thee I feel the pain of all mankind.
On my breast I wield the steel of destruction.
Lord, how can we achieve the peace of the world
    through the pillage and slaughter of its homes and people.
I speak of love to men whose sons have been put to the sword.
I burn the crops of the field and feed compassion to the hungry.
I give hope to the widows—offer life to the dying.
In your name I have suffered the degradation and committed
    the atrocities of war.
In your name I have brought despair and despondency when you
    asked for love and peace.
Through the darkness I heard your word.
In your name—I now lay down my sword.

Reginald H. Davies

The Words Of Self Belief

"Thank you," the word flowed easily from his lips,
So many reasons behind the words,
Without anyone knowing how much he meant it.
The reasons are so unique but hardly wondered,
"Thank you for my life," so capable to do many things and
one of a kind,
"Thank you for giving love," whatever direction it came from
and so precious,
These two things mixed together,
Make one whole, one soul, one mind.
"Thank you for possibilities which enable me to reach for the stars."
Whoever offers then, whenever they may lead,
Then he lastly said, "Thank you for self-belief,"
Which is put to great use,
It's a difficult but wondrous thing,
Once you gain it, you can never lose it.
"Thank you for everything, thank you for myself,
I have so much to give and so little time."
Let it be said, let it be heard,
Let it be remembered.

Christine Kirkby

Heritage

She giggles, they hold hands,
Arch, playful, passionate, in a
Conservatory under potted palms
One hundred years ago,
Damp seedbed of pricked out love and
Furtive kisses like the breath of unfurled buds.

Each generation strains towards the light till
Our twined branches, yours and mine,
With melding sap
Burst through the roof of heaven.

She didn't know she was my grandmother,
Her pulse would helix down the rope of time
To power the fusion of our lusts.
And in between? My mother, on a bench,
Loneliness drenching her November grief
As passion's claw emptied her soul of joy.

We are three women. Two dead,
One to go.
How long will the drum of heartbeats in my groin
Keep rangy death at bay?

Elizabeth Cairns

"Manna From Heaven"

Trembles the dewdrop on leafy stem
Greets the morn this Godly gem
Sparkles brief under morning sun
Then fades and dries. Its day's been won

Drink the earth its drying life
Manna from Heaven to ease its strife
Gone now the dew, its shimmering scene
Nourished the earth in vibrant green

Sparkles a life as does the dew
We, each a jewel, shining bright and new
Then each day the earth our life to sip
We shimmer then dry, back to Heaven we slip

We, each a jewel, from "Heaven's Bower"
We are a nectar the earth to flower
We nourish the earth as does the dew
Then fade and dry both me and you

Jack Hodges

Bliss

In the deep blue velvet skies, where the stars shine bright,
And the pale golden moon, sends a shadowed light.
Over the sparkling diamonds of a glistening sea.
Moving ever on, until it reaches;
The shoreline of the pebble decorated beaches.
Where shifting sands, left smooth and white.
Mysterious and beautiful in the quiet of the night.
It is at moments such as these,
The air sweetened by a gentle breeze.
That life itself seems full of bliss,
As nature bestows, an enchanted kiss.

Alicia Proctor

Transfigured Yet Reconciled

Transfigured? Definitely. Dramatically, utterly, exquisitely
Transfixed beyond belief and wildest dreams of being
Transfigured, transformed, resplendent in amaranthine raiment
Glowing iridescent, unrecognizable to many I know, I feel

Transfigured, lifted out of crepuscular half-light
Into bright rhapsodic sunshine which permeates, enfolds, yet
Reconciled? Indefinitely. To what? To pre-solstitial reality?
Certainly, willingly. Not to present vapidity, I was

Reconciled, restored to the aetherial duet
Transposing into the lyrical exposition in which I find myself
Reconciled, tranquil perhaps. With our tokens, our trysting
Resting in the apodeictic knowledge that the composition remains

Transfigured, transplanted. A great distance has been travelled.
Reconciled to absence? I've hardly begun.

Gillian Ania

"Anglo Saxon Poetry"

It was a sunny morn, and brill,
As Jen and Jim did twine and twirl,
Whocketh the stout thware him and hie,
Wen and shap and thruck and tie.

Through pleasance green did Ailsa wend,
Time with Bluff Hal of thwick to spend
Bird-sang and fox-bark did the noon-day rend,
As Ailsa and Hal thick covert did baud.

The huntsman thwock the started hind
Moll the cook oast and rye did grind,
The dallying priest forsook his flock
Feasting with maidens in far thurlock.

In times of war poor Dick and Will
Left sweethearts much against their will,
Against the foe they did whop and wham,
None were left to tend calf and lamb.

In St. Agnes-by-Water they continued their slaughter,
None were to take their wife or daughter,
With mace and stave they worsted the knave,
With thuck and thwock, to cheat me grave.

Bigham

My Dog Tikka

T hreats and scoldings do no good
   you seem alright you eat your food,
I t is an angry me when you chew things up
   someday I will forget you are just a pup,
K indness you look for when you are in disgrace
   you look at me with that cheeky face,
K id me on that it was not you
   you bring me trouble, what am I to do?
A way from you I would feel regret
   because I love you my own wee pet.

James A. Caldwell

Sold!

I'm laying in the darkness of this cold and lonely room,
The lingering smell of you in the air like a deadly sweet perfume.
This place used to be alive with love, we were hardly ever parted,
But we had everything and more too soon, it was over before it started.
I want to feel you touch me the way you used to do,
And feel the passion ignite in me as it only has with you.
You touched me deep inside, my friend, and scarred my battered heart,
You made me feel if I stopped loving you my world would fall apart.
So now you've left me here alone, my body is empty and cold,
You know I'll never get over you, my skin is marked as: Sold!

Carly Horton

Mother

Crescent shoulders
dark and porcelain skin
elephant–size thighs
face expanse
with two small holes
mahogany ebony cedar oak
with two trunk–size arms
elegant neck that ripples
two large fountains
before my right and left
your odour
strong like the he-goat's
back like the Chinese wall
palm the size of an elephant's ear caresses
my temple
my buttocks
my armpits
and lulls me to sleep

Mma still awake while
the neighbourhood sleeps

Dare Ogun

Retreat

Torment of love
Flinging form my desperate soul
Aspects which you never loved
And which I never knew.

Hostile moon
Bonding fast our souls with solitary intensity
Never to reflect upon the raging love
Ripping through my serenity.

Alone, I possess you still
Tearing from my body every grain of mortal sense
And forcing screaming fire within
Igniting with outrageous passion
Embers of my ever lonely soul.

Lucy Tibbits

Jezebel Junky

Candles lit beyond carcasses
die in liquid, but she fetched eyes
before I broke her oil.
I destroyed her pin fluffy;
I forced myself on Jezebel Junky
and now the pain drips fast inside of me. So my

fire crashes through the forest
where my pulse echoes in every tree and after, there are
blended ingredients for trouble and turmoil.
I cast a shadow for them to believe;
perhaps it will be hard to conceive,
but the lies are all they will retrieve. I'm

blazed with guilt and frightened to speak out,
the dirty kisses I've stole.
The bigger the hurt, the bigger the hole.
Too shy to look and too shy to show,
she fixes her dress and I
bleed to go.

Miss Sukhada Bumma

Drunkard

I looked at a tramp on the roadside one day,
And said to myself what a shame you have nowhere to stay,
I had my nice home and family too,
I didn't want an old drunk like you,
I couldn't stop wondering who would lend a hand,
And take you off the roadside when you were canned,
Whatever happened you ended up like this,
We're you once a young man with ladies to kiss?
As you sit in the long grass without a friend,
Remember God has prepared a home for you in the end.

Kathleen Killelea

Escape

They never thought that I would get away
The guard was watchful and the wall was high
The darkness closed and ended the third day

Once in a while they acted out a play
Saying, you're free, but that was just their lie
They never thought that I would get away

And they were old, even their cheeks were grey
Would I, so young, yet be the first to die?
The darkness closed and ended the third day

Sometimes I feared to see another day
Despaired, and even ceased to hope to fly
They never thought that I would get away

But then the wind blew north and came my way
There was a message in its wailing cry
The darkness closed and ended the third day

So while I walk the earth again today
They'll look for me in vain and wonder why—
They never thought that I would get away
The darkness closed and ended the third day

Elsie Karbacz

Music, At The Creation Of Life, Fades With Death

A child is born, his mother feels pain, then joy,
for his cries are music to her ears.

The child grows, his laughter, his tears bring
pleasure, serenading his mother through each passing day.

The boy became man, his voice not yet broken,
crystal clear, echoes through the church,
rippling past ears of young and old.

Man becomes maestro, upon a stage.
Tapping his baton lightly on a metal stand.
The music unfolds like a mighty roar
as an army into battle.

Imaginary notes, crotches, quavers
dance amongst the musicians, tormenting
all with their heads and tails.
Time passes, the man is old, his spirit leaves his body.
He sees a box, long and black, draped neatly
with a cross of flowers, sliding into the unknown.

The music that accompanied the creation of his life,
now accompanies him to death with voices sad and low.

It is here, the symphony ends.

Jennifer Polledri

At Rydal Mount

Oh April dawn in golden splendour! With Rydal Water
sparkling bright,
The morning mist and bird song render 'midst rising sun—a
wondrous sight.

This peaceful garden with pools and well, and pathway to the mound,
O'er shadowed by the Loughrigg Fell, and daffodils abound.

Ah! The summer-house with majestic view, yes, to write in solitude,
An atmosphere that can imbue such inspirational good.

Such dazzling beauty to revere in this spiritual retreat,
To gaze at distant Windermere, makes this tranquil shrine complete.

Under the wings of birds in flight,
to visit Rydal Mount now and then,
And fellow travellers like ships in the night, you never meet again.

Man is given to rend or mend
all nature's beauteous things,
In vain he strives to hasten the end,
but only his own he brings.

Prepare to surrender o' mortal fools
to whatever God may send,
Throw down your destructive tools
and with God's thoughts now blend.

Ian L. Fyfe

The Yellow Balloon

A sudden gust of wind, carrying with it the forlorn sound of a
child's cry,
And then the bright yellow balloon,
Escaping from its bondage,
And soaring high into the blue skies.
A second sun,
Gleaming in the light of its greater image,
Trailing behind it the broken string of its former slavery.

Free now to traverse the limitless space above and around it,
Yet not entirely free, as even now its journeyings are depen-
dent on the vagaries of the breeze,
Which lightly tosses it hither and thither on its breath.
Now dropping altogether, so that the balloon feels the call of
the green earth
Spread below it.
Then, catching it again, in merry sport, higher and higher,
Until it seems enmeshed in the cloudy islands.

At last it dwindles to a speck
And vanishes into the great infinity.

B. A. Page

A Day In The Life Of A Home Executive

6:30 time tae rise, in tae the loo an wash the sleep fae ma eyes
Pit on the kettle, prepare the breakfast, hiv a quiet cuppa first
Get the wears up an git them dressed, look at this place, whit a mess
Ur you no ready? Yer awfy slow. Is that the time? Ah better go
A couple eh hoors dustin away, it's a wee bit extra at the end
    eh the day
Roon tae the shops fir totties an sausage go home an make a
    pot a stovies
5 minutes peace tae pit up ma feet, hear them bawling in the street
In they come, that's them awe. Are ye makin' stovies maw?
Tak yer coats off, awe sit door, move along an make some room
On wi the kettle, time fir a cuppa, ah like a wee fag efter ma supper
Better git them in noo it's gettin' on, I'll hiv tae listen eh
    them mump on moan
Brush yer teeth on yer hair, wash yer face an git up the stair
Pit the kettle on again tae make a bottle an feed the wean
Good, they're settled, noo for me tae pit ma feet up an git ma tea
Then aff wi lights an doon wi the specs, aye, it's no easy bein
    a hame exec.

Avril MacKinnon

Candy Floss

As hazy summer sun warmly washes over me,
My memories soften to that day in June
When we awoke together and took off together
An exiting decision agreed by us both
To sit on the sand and eat candy floss

But clamorous traffic and people swarming
Irritated us like sunburn and salty air.
We complained, and frowned, and forgot
Why we went there.

But now I wish we could go back there
And recapture our innocent dream in June
To eat candy floss on the sand.

Linda Fuller

"Love"

You asked how much I loved you,
I stretched my arms out wide,
They nailed me to a wooden cross,
They even pierced my side,
They nailed me to that piece of wood
And left me hanging there,
They laughed, and jeered, and spat at me,
They didn't even care.
I watched and waited patiently,
For the final hour to come.
And I cried out to my Father,
Let my suffering here be done.
So I ask, how much do you love me.
Will you stretch your arms out wide.
And open up your heart to me,
So that I may live inside.

Jennifer Snowden

The Stare

She knows not that I watch her;
That as her eyes, pools of copper fire,
Fix, hard and lonely, on the stark wall,
My heart sinks while the stare grows colder,
For I can read the blank, unfriendly face,
Remember when it was the face I wore,
And love her as myself, alone, afraid;
Though she knows not that I watch her,
Nor that I follow her chilling gaze of stone.
Her body stiffens, forms a solid wall,
Protection from the taunting of the crowd,
Those that resent her gift and kill with words,
Destroying her, but they will never care.
I can do nothing now but watch and wait.
Yet the day she is too weak to hold the stare
She will turn to find a friend waits there.

Amira Tharani

These Are The Things I Have Loved

These are the things I have loved.
The gentle cooing of a turtle dove.
The scarlet red rose glistening with dew
The warm, friendly feeling of being with you.
Snow-capped mountains,
Giggling fountains,
A gurgling brook
And a good Christie book.
I love the coolness and freshness after a storm.
I even love my teddy although he's all tattered and torn.
There is the crashing sound of the raging sea
And a steaming hot cup of tea.
I love to watch the busy, buzzing bees
And smell the delicate pink blossoms from apple trees.
The yearning for summer on a cold winter's day,
The smell of freshly cut hay.
The patter of rain
And the whistle of an old steam train.
Of all the things that are mentioned above
It's my family and friends I most dearly love.

Deborah Wright

Last Flight

A free spirit flying to the invisible world above
Wandering cautiously awaiting God's Angels' greeting
No time for sad goodbyes or for tears to flow
For I am going to the paradise that has been
waiting for me for years
A paradise that will wait for you until your time comes
Your time to follow me into the arms of God.

Sue Gilkes

I Am The Running River

I am the running river you are standing by
to watch your face into the Crystal of the waters
my Eyes are bathing you in into the Heat of the Days
the Summer is filling up with the thirsty River—
with the water to give water to the thirsty—Soul—
you are Looking at me with into the mirror of the waves
the river is running through—the Shadow of your Face
into the Hold of my arms the Shadows are melting with
the Smile upon your Lips into the Asking of Sunshine
the Sun is burning with your Face filled up with
—Love—into the filling up—of Shadows—
the River is filling up with the running of the Time
you took me through upon a wave of a Crystal
your Eye sparkled in the Ray of the Sunshine
you saw into my Eyes into the melting of the waves
you stood by—to cool the thirsty Soul the River was Asking with
The water of your Eyes upon the brim of the lips you Let the River
with to run through the Summer the Hold of Love you
watched me with into the crystal of the water you stood by—
to give me water

Greatwood Gabriela

The Artist

Talent, they say, is a gift from the gods.
Not all gifts are welcomed of course:
some—unrecognized, abused, ignored—lie
rejected, out of tune, at last, decayed.
Some are not so user-friendly either:
Daedalus, that master-craftsman fashioning flight,
was not much blessed in what you'd call the end result.
But to create ens entium a work of art—
to forge or lazarate what lies yet concealed
on metal, paper, stone or clay and thence beget
o, a line, a jewelled cup, a word, a Parthenon,
music or a private star—
now there lies genius.
The Creator (it is said) took aery nothing
and breathed to give it life,
the simplest of artisans.
Lovers, more complicated, weave a silver cord
creating, like Arachne, a life-line from
a thread of their own spinning.

Piffa Schroder

The Rotting Relationship

Things left unsaid,
Needed gestures, fast asleep,
Not there, left in bed . . .
Past promises, no care,
Just forgotten, couldn't take,
The time to remember . . .

Little effort, has no conscience,
Life is busy, it's so easy,
To forget, who you are,
Why you're there!
Life is fast, no room to share,
And no flowers to send her . . .

Mind dragging days,
Wonder will he change?
Will mind join a kiss,
To know why and when to?
Simple answers, but untold,
Bad habits left to tender,
January, February . . . coldly blow on . . .
To December!

Heiderose Wong

Reflections At Bladon

Rest on old man under your glistening tomb,
    The years of trial and sweat now strewn.

Sleep on old man with Clementine your wife,
    No more blood, toil, tears and strife.

Relax old man under these sunny skies,
    Bombs do not fall, only the bird cries.

Dormez-vous old man, all Free France remembers still
    By placing flowers at this grave on the hill.

Stay still old man, who travelled over land and seas
    To meet war leaders and plan for peace.

Rejoice old man in the victory you gained,
    By sovereign and people always acclaimed.

Honourable old man, once Minister so Prime,
    Parliament still reveres your leadership sublime.

Now here old man, with loved ones you surround,
    You've earned this peace deep underground.

I'm so glad to visit Bladen here
    And recall how once together we conquered fear.

In Britain old man, Winston Churchill, that name
    Stands for all time in memorial fame.

Eileen H. Weston

On My Own

On my own I close my eyes and I pretend he's near,
I feel his warm and gentle touch, his arousing voice I hear.
All alone we walk for hours holding each other's hand,
The sun slowly sets beyond the horizon as we kick the golden sand.
Eyes are fixed in motion, bodies locked in a loving embrace,
Tentatively caressing each other whilst standing face to face.
Then when at last his lips meet mine our hearts both miss a beat,
Silence fills the darkening sky, waves gently tease our feet.
I wish I could stay here forever in his arms entwined,
But sadly this enchanting, intoxicating place is only in my mind.
The private walks, holding hands, none of it exists,
And the chance of an affectionate, passionate embrace has
    sadly gone amiss.
In the cold light of day all this is but a dream,
Reality takes over me and nothing is what it seems.
When I open up my eyes everything becomes clear to see,
That he is madly in love with another and doesn't even notice me.
I'd give anything for a kind word from him, one kiss or a
    caring touch,
But I know he doesn't even realize that to me he means that much.
So even though he doesn't want me my love for him has still grown,
I'll keep my dreams and keep on loving him but only on my own.

Jill Watson

Brave Man

This was a brave man brave till the end
As a young soldier he fought for his country
and fought till the end, returning home
triumphantly to family and friends.

This man was a husband, a father and friend so
loving and caring right till the end.
Forty years and more of struggle and strife,
this loving man cared for his family and wife.

This man worked hard each day of his life to
put food on the table for him and his wife.
Struggle came easy as so did his smile, for
this man was no angel but he did have style.

Struck down by an cancer in the autumn of life
He fought once again this time for life.
The memories are strong for his family and wife
for this was a brave man for all of his life.

Michael James

Silent Words

What silent thoughts we tend to keep,
Within our minds—and do not speak.
And time goes rushing by each day,
With words we should, but do not say,
To those we love and hold so dear,
And live beside, year after year.
Our lips seal words within our reach,
Beneath the commonplace of speech.
The full sweet words that mean so much,
When love is gone and out of touch.
And in the silence that is left,
We sit alone and feel bereft,
And think too late of some kind word,
We might have said—and they have heard.

Helen Gibbs

Nature

The birds, the flowers and the trees
Oh, so wonderful are these
With rivers flowing in between
Perfecting every view and scene

Birds so friendly yet so shy
And dainty clouds among blue sky
The flowers with their petals so adorning
And trees to shade as sun shines through in morning

Friendly ripples in the stream
As rocks and stones so intervene
Whilst wild and gushing waters surge
Down waterfall to rivers merge

This beauteous world complete with many guises
A place so full of wondrous surprises
Concealed and yet revealed so as to render
A glorious mirage of fashioned splendour

Nicholas Bryans

'The Rainbow'

I was walking along in a world of my own,
Troubled inside, and I felt quite alone,
Though people were passing me all the while,
Oblivious was I, to even a smile.
Then, I became aware of the colours so bright,
They drew my attention away from my plight,
I had tried for so long to shake myself free,
Long since giving up, what choice could there be?
Now I stood in awe of a beautiful sight,
That came down from the sky, a miracle of light,
It seemed to show me the way ahead,
Calm and clear, I was feeling uplifted instead.
The rainbow appeared to show me the way,
To a new kind of peace and happiness that day,
I'll always remember in moments of thought,
That to my life, a new meaning it brought.

Rosemary E. Nightingale

Would You Want To Be A Soldier?

Will I live tomorrow
Will I still be here
As a soldier I must ask "when will I disappear"
Will I live to watch my children growing strong
Will my friends know me
Will I still belong
My home is not my home now
My life is not my own
Every day I battle
To save my land and home
Every day I work till night
Every day my mind takes flight
Oh who would want to lead my life

You may think I speak selfishly
After all I'm still alive
But every day as morning breaks I say
"I can't survive"
Although my body seems to live
My soul is already dead
There is no life inside me indeed it must be said.

Samantha German

T.K.H.R.

Help me, I'm drowning.
There's no more to say but that.
The waters are flooding in.
I've had to throw out the spoon and use the bucket.
More clumsy I know, but it moves more.
The delicate spoon was only good for when it dribbled in.
But now it's gushing.
Please stop the waters.

It's just too much.
I know one day it'll take me,
I'll disappear.
If it gets beyond my ear I'll go under, I know.
And I can't float; the weights on my feet are too huge.
Every so often the sun comes out,
But then the storm comes over,
And the rains come down.
Please stop the waters.

Christine Morris

Untitled

In times of war, as a soldier he stood,
For King for Country and for family,
For all that is right and all that is just.

In times of peace, a fair man was he,
Never too quick to judge on what
He was not there to see,
Yet still he would rather give than receive,
For a gentleman was he.
A husband, father, grandfather, a man of family.
He will live in the memories of us all, for our eternity.

But for now at God's right hand he sits,
Husband, father, granddad, we will always remember thee.

Shaun Holland

Pleasure Beach Fair

The men from the clouds, with candy floss hair,
Are selling their toupees, at the Pleasure Beach Fair.
And all of the girls, with peach melba frocks,
Selling their perfumes, as novelty rock.

Big ape-like men, with embarrassed eyes,
Are selling their knees, to a coconut shy.
And all of the rich girls, with magical ponds,
Selling their goldfish, till the gold is all gone.

Immature boys, with looking-glass eyes,
Inspect the girls, expecting a prize.
And all of the girls, with curls in their hair,
Ride the helter skelter, at the Pleasure Beach Fair.

Robert Sampson

Painful Serenity

Friends should always be there
But they're not.
Promises should always be kept
But they aren't.
Just blips in the eternal cosmos of everything.
And the paralleling paradoxes of emotions
Love and Hate,
Wisdom and Stupidity,
Tears flowing like poison, yet
Laughter understood as belittling.
The hand outstretched in friendship
Also forms a fist.
Conversations ignored
Silences wounding.
Forgiveness begged for,
But still the grudge is borne.
And the cyclic patterns continue
Endangering peace of mind.

Alison Black

The Losing Battle

I can't take anymore. I want to scream,
About something that was once my dream,
I'm trapped, I feel there's no way out
My voice is lost, no-one hears me shout.
I'd let myself go but I can't stand the pain
Stay where I am and it hurts just the same.

It's a vicious circle, I can't escape,
I've well and truly swallowed the bait.
Help me, save me, my cries are lost
Love was the game, now this is the cost
I'd try to run but it makes me stay
I'm not strong enough to keep away

Watching the bars of my cage close in
I know this battle I'll never win
If only I could set myself free,
Try to kill it, before it kills me.

Lindsey Wright

Reminiscence

While turning back the pages to the days that are gone,
I remember it well the tears that fell the day I was forlorn.
While strolling down to Middle Abbey St. to the newspapers,
He said to me, "My name is Liam Shine. What can the matter be?"
"You don't understand I've no electricity—
No cook no heat no light no bottle can I make.
For my little mentally handicapped girls life is at stake."
"You say you have three ones three ones two
Ones one hush now we will see what can be done"
It was Mr. Shine alright when I arrived home that night
To see my home shining bright
Six years have passed today it is but long
The newscaster has just announced
Mr. Liam Shine was killed in road traffic accident today
This cannot be I cried farewell my friend at last
For you were the miracle that was in my past

Bernadette MacDonald

The Wanderer

On the road again the past behind
with heavy load again, I seek to
find another truth for a wandering
man, who's misspent youth still in the van.
I travel on not knowing why, for
another truth is another lie.
Yet still I journey to and fro
akin to tidal ebb and flow, for
that I seek I can never find, as
truth is only in the mind.
But I continue on my way, looking
forwards day by day.
And as I labour with life's load,
I always find the alternate road.

Ben Herbert Brumel

A Rum Do

Freshly pressed people,
Their elbows rest on the bar,
Trying to pretend,
That they are not what they are.

The quiet morning chatter,
That rises to a shout,
Is this what Sunday pub drinking
Is all about?

Their best friend, for now, is the barmaid,
She's here to help pay her bills
And her smile will keep them all drinking
So their money keeps ringing the tills.

Microwave lunches are ordered and eaten
By diners declaring their value unbeaten,
And the clatter of plates, and spoons, knives and forks
Rises and joins with the popping of corks.

So, if you're planning to go for a drink
Down at your quiet local pub,
Just remember that on a Sunday
It's a race for the bar and the grub!

Margaret Burgess

Missing You

Dawn breaks and finds me tired and weary.
After another sleepless night.
My eyes sore from the tears that fell and stung my cheeks.
My heart aching, yearning, my stomach churning.
The light filters through a gap in the curtains and lies
On the pillow beside me, where you should be,
and illuminates my sad face.
My body aches from restless slumber, fully alert I take
inspiration from the fairies
"You are a laughing pebble tumbling in the stream", they say.
I think not, I am far from happy, but tumbling and reeling I am.
I ask them of you, and they reply, "you are the coloured
glass rubbed smooth by ocean waves"—are you?
You are far from my reach, I have to leave you in the safe
hands of nature.
Elements more beautiful than I.
You sail upon crashing waves. Beneath clear blue skies,
shadowed only by snow capped mountains and breathing
crisp fresh air.
Love their beauty as you love me and they will beckon me to
your side.
We both live beneath the same blanket of stars,
Look up to the one that shines brightest, it will hold my
thoughts, messages, and love.

Fay Harby

Night Killer

Night killer's out there without a doubt,
night killer's out there lurking about.
No time for the victim to prepare,
no time to shout and cry in despair.

The knife comes down again, again,
the victim shouts and cries in pain.
The stain on the floor is thick and red,
she goes to the hospital it's too late she's dead.

The police are on his tail so fast,
they've locked him up they've done the task.
They sentence him to ten long years,
the man the murderer can't believe his ears.

"I'm innocent, I'm innocent" the murderer cries,
"found guilty, found guilty" comes the replies.
Thrown into a cold, cold dark cell,
he whimpers and says "this place is hell!"

He's out, he's out, out for revenge,
wouldn't you like to know what happens in . . .

. . . The End.

Jenine Kendall

This Rebellious Heart

Her glossy ring-u-lets were made
Suspended in a bright cascade,
To be the garland and the frame
For Beauty's wild and restless flame.

And were I a wind, what storms I would blow;
Or a thunderous river in full–throated flow,
All Hell could not roar with such furious force
Nor dam up my waters and poison their source.

And were I a rock which would bury its head,
Under soft fragrant moss on a balmy earth bed,
I would rest and be glad to have banished regret,
When I chose to remember or chose to forget.

And were I a man no doubt I would start,
To take by the heels this rebellious heart.
But I am a fool; a monkey at play,
Who damned all his treasure away.

Brett John

The Care Assistant

Lucy is frail and elderly, she does not see
the forty-six year old Mother of three
I am the nice little girl, when she opens the door
who has come to help with the every day chore.
While she does the dusting, I Hoover the floor
Together the bed change we manage to do,
then off I go to clean down the loo.
She will make a pot for her and for me
Then we will sit and enjoy a nice cup of tea.
Time for a chat of things that are past,
How everything changes, nothing seems to last.
It is time for me to leave, but she would like me to stay
She says that I have brightened up the whole of her day
but alas my next client awaits
So I turn as I reach the front gate.
And in my mind's eye the years have flown by
And it's me I see standing at the door, waving goodbye
to the nice little girl

Kathleen Snaith

My Restless Spirit

As I'm standing at the door
My restless spirit calls for more
Why the end has come this way
No one knows the way love works
All its twists and funny quirks

Finally the time has come
Our last hour the clock has won
As he walks away dejectedly—
Was it me?

Stolen moments all repaid
Hurtful words have all been said
I close the door my past behind
Was our shared love true or blind?

I wish that I could find the words
To tell him how my heart still yearns
How it hurts me to the core
And still my restless spirit calls for more.

Joanne Russell

My Mistake

Then he said it, just like that
From the horses mouth, straight off the bat.
He turned around and said it,
I thought my heart would burst.
He looked at me and uttered those immortal words.
He said "I love you my darling, I'll always be true."
My mistake was saying "I love you too."

Vicky Manton

Castles Of Sand

Silently I stand and watch you sleep whilst passing your room
I just had to peep.
Your day has been heavy and needless to say you look like an
angel now
the dirt's washed away.
A tanned face against a pillow so white contentment and
God's blessing
will guide you this night.
The day has been glorious and you have been so strong you
were the king and we played along.
Our make believe so stealthy so grand to defend our castle
that we built with sand.
The battlements to ward off the attacking throng they could
not beat us for we were to strong.
No one could take our victory away no one but the waves
could beat us this day.
But tomorrow we will build a stronger domain and when the
tide comes in we'll drive it back again.
So sleep on little king as I stand by your bed plan your
tomorrow in your sleepy little head.
Together we will show them what we can achieve in that
wonderful land of make believe.
So sleep sweet dream, dream away, dream of a tomorrow even
better than today.

R. C. Craddock

Prelude To Dawn

The scent of blossoms fills the air,
A sense of peace is everywhere;
And natures creations in composure lie,
Beneath a moonlit starry sky.

In the porch hangs a lantern bright,
Silver moths swarm round its light;
And apple tree so still and tall,
Casts its shadow on the garden wall.

Slumbering are the deep red roses,
In their fragrant darkling closes;
And the laburnum heavy in full bloom,
Bows in homage to the moon.

The lilac like a maiden fair,
Dreams with blossoms in her hair;
And clusters of forget-me-nots,
Sleep beside the scented stocks.

But soon this lovely night divine,
Will fade into the mists of time;
And the dawn will break to prepare the way,
For the birth of another day.

Edith Garcia

Love?

You walked from my life one cold winter's day,
I knew that things shouldn't happen this way,
The light went out in my eyes as you left,
And darkness descended alone and bereft.

The bright lights of London beckoned you there,
You hardened your heart, what did you care,
She lured you and took you, no beauty is she,
She knew all along you were married to me.

Alone now I sit, thinking of you,
I hope that one day you think of me too,
My life has not ended as once I thought,
happiness now is all that is sought.

So while the two of you cuddle and kiss,
I know that one day it'll be me that you miss,
I wasn't the one who cheated and lied.
I stayed honest and true, alone how I've cried.

I gave you all that I possibly could,
A love that was true and honest and good,
No part of my life do you want anymore,
But one day I'll get what I'm looking for . . . True Love.

Gail Wilson

Double Trouble

'Hello, and how are you today?'
I heard a lively lady say.
As I mingled here and there,
It was a charity affair,
'I'm very well, and how are you?'
I replied, as one is apt to do.
The face before me I seemed to recall,
It belonged to the days when I was small,
'Have you ever been told you have a double?'
She chortled—I thought, look out here comes trouble,
'Her maiden name was so-and-so
Then she married and became a Lloyd you know,'
You're the spitting image of her I do declare!
Same nose, same eyes, same teeth, same hair!
And I, munching my cake, my mouth full of jam!
Said—'That's probably because that's who I am!!'

Jean Lloyd

Modern Cargoes

Forty toner juggernauts with carbon black exhaust pipe
Humming to the ferry ports on wide motorways
With cargoes of fruit juice, teapots, cabbages,
furniture, motorcars or sweet summer hay.

Sleek silver subway train speeding to the station
Swishing through the tunnel on bright metal rail
With a cargo of typists, secretaries, managers and
young city slickers reading their mail.

Fat bellied jumbo jet resting on the tarmac
Destination florida or some sunny shore
With a cargo of tourists, first class executives
M P's and millionaires what a frightful bore.

Top heavy ferry boat steaming out of Dover
Rolling in the channel swell as seagulls doze
With a cargo of motorcars and families of day
trippers thinking of duty free and cheap french booze.

Barry Edmunds

Wolf Prints

Another foot disfigures the freshly laden snow.
Treading carefully with every deliberate step,
until a distant cry penetrates the cold night
air. Stopping instantly, he scans the dark empty
woods, searching with those haunting eyes.
Standing so very still, he picks up every sound,
even the snow softly landing in the thick fur
of his back. A northerly breeze stirs the snow
and turns his warm breath in to a watery mist.
It's cold tonight, very cold, but the faint smell
of death is on the wind, bringing all senses
up to full alertness. His body tingles to the
atmosphere of his surroundings, then moves off
in to the darkness. Somewhere there's a kill
and he's going to claim it.

Andrew Morgan

Personify—An Individual Person

I married young, these things are done.
Left my career for a family.
Housewife, mother, that's me.

Days of joy and days of despair
Days of hurt with no one to care.

I am the person that cares for the family.
Housewife, mother, that's me.
Who is the person that lives underneath
The mother, the housewife? Still can't you see!

I am that person vibrant, alive
The person with hope, with dreams and ambitions
Who do you contrive,
That person to be
The mother, the housewife, me.

Yvonne Edwards

Suicide's Child

No one understands how deep the pain lies
Outside there is nothing, just tearful eyes
But inside is great trauma, new confusion everyday
It hits you so hard, bruises won't fade away.

Your mother tries to take her life once, and you can forgive
When she keeps on doing it, you don't want her to live
The pain just gets deeper each time she does it
It all becomes too much for you to rise up above it.

She might as well be dead, survival isn't worth the cost
It eats away at you, thinking about what you've lost
You feel unloved, and left with no one to trust
You have no security, your compassion turns to rust.

To stop getting hurt again, you ignore both family and friend
But then who's there for you to help your heart mend
You are left on your own, increasingly bitter and cold
Longing for someone to be there for you to hold.

Emma Lawley

The Price Of Beauty

The old dark mills overshadowed our town
As did mine shafts, up and down
Slag heaps, chimneys, smoke and grime
Played their part in this chapter of time

Industries grew and so did wealth
Without much thought about our health
War was over and all seemed well
Days of youth, I've lived to tell

A thing called progress joined the race
And ever so slowly, changed the place

The scene has changed—it's all anew
No pits or heaps to spoil the view
Beauty's absence so long ago
Is now in splendour on full show
All this alas, has come at a cost
Can't blame Mother Nature for jobs now lost.

Eric Nurdin

A Child Of Mine

Joy she danced within his eyes,
while excitement danced upon his cries.
Upon his lips laughter danced.
About his bare white feet sparkling water pranced.
Sunbeams danced upon his face,
adding to the magic of the place.
Contentment, she danced without sound,
her sweetness filling the air all around.
On that wonderful day in the sunshine, with happiness he played.
In an enchanted place, where dreams are made.

Sheila V. Baldwin

The Captain Prayed

The froth of the waves, so fresh and ferocious,
that the Captain prayed.
He prayed to heaven and hell, to calm the fury from that sea if only
for a moment so as to force Death to put away the scythe from
his hands. But the waves kept on coming, slapping the ship hard.
Curving their palms in crushing grasps.
Tossing the ship violently as if it were but a feather in the wind.
Engulfing the world. And the wind did blow.
As if it were hell-bent on blowing the ship off the face of the Earth
and into the deepest, darkest, coldest crevasses of its abyss.
O how the Captain was afraid! O how he shuddered.
O how his lips mumbled such a prayer of promise and pity,
that the wind and water lashed his face and smothered his words
to keep it from Heaven's ears.

With one faint breath the Captain let out a grey lament,
which was answered with claps of thunder so loud,
that the waves shrank away and the sea retreated.
Then the lightning shot through the clouds and stabbed at the sea.
The sea defeated lay obedient. And the captain and his ship,
haggard but saved, limply resumed their way.

Claudine Galloway-Williams

To My Granddaughter

At last you have a Christmas break
from your first term at school

It must be rather wonderful
to put away pen and rule

No early arising,
the start of every day

No bus to miss, no work to do
but spend the day in play

The tree to be dressed, the parcels unwrapped
there's quite a lot to do

I hope that Santa's lined up
something special just for you

On Christmas day we must thank
God for all of his creations

Of Night and Day, Rain and Sun
and flowers for every Nation.

Spare a thought for needy children far across the land
and hope they will be provided for and given a helping hand

Have a Happy Christmas and plenty of good cheer
and look forward to the challenge of the next new year.

Leonard H. Pease

The Thoughts Of Michael Jackson

Fame, has left me standing alone,
if you're so innocent,
you cast the first stone,
I know I'm not Jesus,
but I know that I'm pure,
as pure as a child, right down to the core.

I'd love to get married,
but I'm so scared I'll be used,
Who can I trust?
I'm so confused.
I'm still a child at heart, when will they learn?
See, my father was so strict, so very stern.

It's 'cause I have children around that they say that I'm 'gay',
but I lost my childhood and I love to play.

I hug children with innocence,
I dance with emotion,
Healing the World is my life long devotion.

They think that I'm guilty, and say that I'm bad
but I'm not, I'm Innocent,
it all makes me so sad.

Valley Michaels

Thinking Of You

Thinking of you all the time when I'm alone,
forever missing you

I want to hold you, to love you again, but
what can I do . . .?

You've left me now, gone away to some other
place, forever to stay

There's a sadness I feel that I can't express,
a feeling of emptiness

Thinking of you, hurting because of needing you,
being without you . . . what can I do . . .?

My heart burns, my head hurts, my tears fall all
because you're here no more

I want the memories to stay, but slowly they're
fading away

I only hope that when my life ends all the memories
come back and stay

That we meet again in a special place, together,
forever again.

A. M. Donegan

Life's Rich Up

Taste the wine of life's rich cup
peace and serenity rises up.
These arms unfold and reach out to embrace,
beyond the clouds without a trace.
Then when the richness is no more,
dig deep within the earth's great core.
Find buried within this mighty land,
a source of richness close at hand.
Look across the still waters deep,
locked in the heart forever to keep.
To trace life's rich cup once more,
lift one's spirits as never before.
Drink in the wine that lies within
this rock of granite, pure and free from sin.
Take hold this cup of richness, divine,
in paradise, the wine of life's just fine.

Dawn E. Noonan

"Peace In Our Time"

Some talk of peace, they speak of hope and mention freedom too,
yet some of those who say these things, then stir the devil's brew.
They plant their bombs and shoot their guns, they kill or hurt
  and maim.
This isn't talk of peaceful ways, it's just old Satan's game.

One day we all could have our peace, our hopes, our future too,
but not while evil forces creep to terrorize the true.
Till that day comes, we shan't forget, we sane ones will remember.
While devil's strike, with all their might, we good folk won't
  surrender.

Patricia Lynch

Why Do We Do This?

Unnoticeable actions through the unknown lives,
Different feelings,different actions, different thoughts that are made,
Artistically perfect, exuberant imaginations that are brought,
So quickly, even without any actions.

The days go by as fast as the wind,
When one thinks of death and sin,
Why we live in this insubstantial fashion,
As we think night and day of what will happen.

People die every day,
Without getting a chance of something to say.
Why do we take things for granted?
Is it because our minds are slanted?

Some people are frightened even to tell,
As they are afraid of going to hell,
Why do we treat aristocratic people so kindly?
As we don't even know what we will find.

Unnoticeable actions through the unknown lives,
As the world gets hidden more every day,
Why do we live in this strange fashion,
As we don't even know what will happen?

Reem Kadry

Time Apart

Without a gentle presence
malevolence attacks the prone through any foil.
A rumble from the street churns
in the dishwasher's belly. A shallow breath gives
voice to new pressures within
a room. Bearing down upon you. Bending the spine,
once strong, into a question.

Reeling from the undertow
once can only strain to glimpse the calm. Resting, high
as the Portuguese sun she
lazily reclines beneath. Without confusion.

Across these tired British streets
there is horror apparent in all things; crippled
lilies by a sickness bed.
Crumpled letters by a lovers bed as we sleep.

Brian Anderson

Gratefulness

A family we need,
To love, understand, oh yes indeed,
Is it that simple or that perfect?
No! But then what do you expect?
Six years of tension, panic and stress,
No more money, holidays and less.

We are so keen to mutter "Life's so unfair"
Then there are the dying, the imprisoned, the homeless
they're all there,
Upon reflection your family is your wealth,
Think of the others not just yourself.

So then be grateful, a loving family you've got,
Perhaps not as much as some but more than a lot!

Deborah Mann

Baby Hannah

My beautiful darling baby girl,
So sweet and cuddly to me,
I love your eyes, your baby soft curl,
You fill me with great joy and endless glee.

And when I put you to my breast,
I love to nibble your little toes,
To see your eyes upon me rest.
Your lips curl up in laughter pose.

You love to play those funny games,
Of farmer's horse and peek a boo,
Try clapping hands or saying names,
I'm coming . . . I'm coming . . . Boo!

We all love you, family, friends alike,
Your brother and sister dote on you so,
And when you cry we all rush to make it right,
Don't grow up too quickly my darling . . . go slow.

Deborah Baker

School

There is a place I cannot stand
The place is dull
  drivel
  cruel
It's no fun at all
It's a place of grey
And total misery.
It's like a mission setting off each day
Wondering if we would ever make it back safe.
The sergeant ordering out like happy hour in a pub
Being put in a dark miserable room
Like the world's going to end
All for blasting at the sergeant
The misery increases
The dreadful torture
As the day goes on.

Ben Dales

The Season Of Summer Time Comes Again

It's the season of summer time which has come again
Weather so hot, the gleaming sun burns down on you
Cheerful people feeling the heat but nowhere to cool down
A relaxing time all around for others to enjoy.

The sky was blue and peaceful with a slight breeze
The sun was shining making a wave of heat flow
People everywhere surrounded with a sense of happiness
A ray of sun shining giving a scene of summer time.

The delicate wind sways the growing grass in fields
The wonderful scenes of brightly coloured flowers
The sound of buzzing bees surrounds the sky above
A beautiful combination of creatures to be seen.

Melting ice cream and sticky young hands come around this time
Happy children having lots of fund in many places
Families and loved ones are together, talking and laughing
What a joyful season to enjoy this time of the year.

Denise Wright

I Walked In Dreams

I walked in dreams along a winding path
An endless path, for I could see no end.
On either side, woods of hostile trees
No light on which I could depend.
Branches on trees appeared as arms
Reaching out to touch me as I passed.
Fear wrapped around me as a cloak
Then I saw the light and home at last.

I ran, stumbling along this path without an end
Snap of dried leaves beneath my feet.
Heard the sombre hooting of an owl
In this nightmare of terror and defeat.
I saw you then, tried to reach you
Held out my hand, but you were no longer there
I woke in horror from this fantasy
To reality . . . you had left, no longer cared!

Betty M. Varley

To Feel At One With Nature In The Garden At Dawn

I feel at one with nature, in the garden at dawn,
The birds are sweetly singing, heard by ears of corn,
Flowers are gently stretching, I can smell their sweet perfume,
And the trees and grass awakened by the gently falling dew.

The calmness of the morning, I stand and think awhile.
As the sun does rise and glow, with its ever present smile,
To start the day my own way, means so much to me,
In the garden with mother nature, where it is so peaceful and serene.

Michael J. O'Rourke

Poetry For Beginners

I've been asked to write a poem
It's really quite a task,
There's so much I could write about,
   Where does a poet start?

My life has been quite varied
I can't remember some,
I'll cross that off my list of if's.
   Now I'm back to start!

Perhaps I'll gaze into the future
At my age there's not much left!
But I've always said be positive.
   Now I'm back to start!

No doubt, whoever reads this
Will say, she's off her trolley.
I've tried so hard to make my mark,
   No good I'm back to start!

Writing poetry is quite difficult
Still I will persevere, and if—
I achieve success with this, three cheers,
   I'm past the start!

Freda Symonds

The Woodland Intruder

The sapphire sky is bright.
Diamonds glisten from high above.
The moon shines down on the forest;
his twin in the stream.
Wind calls for the sky to open,
his tears fall down a pone the trees.

Thunder breaks out, and the wind hears him calling.
A silent gallop is heard
It is familiar to them.
Louder and harder it becomes.
Twigs are broken, underneath the hooves.

The winds call out the pain to the stranger.
Stones fight and crush each other,
From the heavy animal and rider.
Winds howl, louder and louder.
Thunder yells and lightning strikes
trees fall and wind cries for peace!

Sara Harman

The Old Man

The withered hand now lies still
The face now furrowed
Through the passing of time
Upon the mantel, pictures stand
Reminiscent of a childhood past
Now long gone.
The clock ticks on
Now he sleeps
Within the everlasting darkness of death
His lifeblood drained from within
The haggard face now gaunt lies still
Time has passed away for him
Unnoticed people pass on by
As the clock upon the mantel ticks on
Within four walls
An old man lies
Forgotten within his home.

A. Harvey

Arachnid

The pollen–laden meadows ripple,
The seas of grass on hedgerows lap;
While clouds and swarms of insects wing,
Arachnid waits within her trap.

She'll hang so still and patiently,
This summer's day her time will come;
When tired and lazy meadow fly
Will blindly find the orb she's spun.

And so to dark, as insects roost,
To hide away from cooler air;
Arachnid labours half the night,
To spin and weave, and make repairs.

And with the dawn, and early dew,
Arachnid's orb of silk will shine;
But soon returns invisible,
To trap the lazy meadow fly

Andrew D. Hunt

Time Waster

Your mortality is dripping away.
Right now it might seem funny.
But what consumes your existence?
Job, clothes, bills or money.

Moaning, wrapped in self.
What's engraved on your epitaph?
Boring, miserable, no-one, or,
Was liked, was loved, could laugh.

Confined in a world, big as your street.
Discontented, at the end of the day.
Struggling forward, no way back.
Breathe your last and waste away.

Dawn Clayton

Fragments

Sitting in quiet contemplation I look upon the
world with grief, and as an overwhelming sadness
fills the theatre of consciousness; crying out
for me to free myself from the bonds of moral
twilight; where I have dwelt for years and years,
too afraid to look because I didn't want to see
the pain, the voice of truth struggles out from
within me; and through a dark night of my very soul
I see the fragments I have stored now as a picture
of the whole. Human rights, human wrongs. Genocide,
murder, rape; mayhem of every kind. Paranoia, rage,
hunger; man's inhumanity to man. Drugs, death,
injustices, lost causes, indifference; nothing
works anymore, and as I kick out against the
world I feel nothing. No past, no future, just the
long moment of experience, for I am acclimatized
and too far gone to stop the rot that sweeps
the world. But then I am a voice alone.

Marian Keech

All Alone

All alone day and night,
memories of days gone by.
Feeling lost without a soul,
all alone.

Remembering the hands that once caressed,
caress no more.
Shadows appear where light once shone,
still, all alone.

Hours, days, weeks go by,
loving words just past me by.
Tears for days that are no more,
silence falls, when all alone.

Reasons to live, reasons to die,
questions unanswered,
will I be,
all alone?

Peter Williams

Bobby

He came in to my life in the middle years
bringing joy and laughter to dry the tears
A precious little one so loving, filling days
with dreams and make belief

Blowing bubbles feeding ducks skipping jumping
and playing with trucks
Off to the park to swing on the swings running
playing and sometimes he sings

Down to the station to see the trains
books and crayons on the days that it rains
If we are lucky and soon the rain stops
on go our coats and we go down to the shops

All too soon this innocence to disappear
school days beckoning to fill his year
I pray good fortune shines upon him as he
treads life's way—I will remember Bobby
as he is to-day

Jennifer A. Phillips

Precious World

We thank You Lord for life and prayer,
We look around and we know You are here,
The calming waves, a beaming sun,
A newborn child, a life begun.
The Bible tells of how You died,
And how You Lord are by our side.
Day and night, night and day,
The Bible tells of what You say.
You teach us Lord to get along,
By book, by prayers, by word and song.
To You I give my endless love,
I get it in return,
I listen Lord of what You say,
Forever I will learn.

Rachel Rees

The Tryst

I hesitate to speak my heart dear love,
Pearl of so great a price.
Perhaps were you not all in all to me
The pain of words unsaid
Would not then end in doubt so pitiless;
And yet suffice, suffice to see,
That you, yourself, are wondering.

And so I keep my counsel—you love's gift
(The pearl is pledged not bought)
And in my wayward blundering
Adrift in life's contrariness,
I cling to hope that may I yet succeed
In gaining what I sought,
And seal the solemn moment with a kiss.

John M. Davis

Masquerade

Masquerade people in masquerade balls
Living a life without living at all
Blank faces behind the mask.
All the grey auras in dazzling shades
Wearing false personas to masquerade
as someone, when there's no one at all.
Crafted expressions on emotionless faces
Speaking of visits to imaginary places
Laughing and cheering, but at empty words.
Staging their actions, to set the scene
Never ad libbing or they'll shatter the dream,
of existence, that they once read.
Acting their parts as time carries on
Having experiences, yet not feeling one
All the substance, without the soul.
Alas the bell chimes, and it's time to go
Everyone bows, it's the end of the show
No tears as, the lights start to fade;
Can I join the masquerade?

Paul Harvison

Experience

Birth is not a beautiful thing,
It is full of pain, anxiety and confusion.
It wrenches us out of our shelter,
Separating us from our protection,
Throwing us out into the world of uncertainty
With no resources.

Death is no different.
We come to the inescapable hour
Struggling hopelessly against the inevitable,
Afraid we shall be called upon
to act in a situation
of which we know not.

The space between Birth and Death
is called the Living.

Loveday Harmer

Hey Mum

Hey Mum what makes the birds all sing
And what makes our doorbell ring
Why does Dad smoke and I'm not allowed
Hey Mum what's the difference in the clouds

Hey Mum why is it be quiet wait and see
Can I have jam and cakes for tea
Hey Mum why is it you say go ask your dad
Why are you sometimes happy and sometimes sad

Hey Mum why am I so small
And you and Dad seem so tall
When I get tall I'll be so glad
Then you won't keep saying go ask your dad

John Spratt

For The Love Of . . . Whomever

Should I desire thee
As if a sparkling white wine,
A mysterious elegance
To which one might dine,
A desired contentment
In a bleeding heart,
The whisper of the willow,
A most gratifying start.

The gleaming dove of sincerity glides
Way beyond that silver tide,
Entrapping my conscience, my soul, my mind
It rids me of bitterness aside,
Of my dreams and my wishes,
A desire to have hold,
Of that mysterious elegance,
To which my love is untold.

Mallissa Morgan

Let Them Rest In Peace

So who are we, to judge the lives
Of those we've mourned with tears,
When we ourselves will be so judged,
By those of later years?

Biographers may delve and search
The archives of the famed,
To seek out some derisive fact
Of which they can be blamed.

But is it right they should malign
These souls in holy rest,
Who cannot speak in their defence,
But gave the world their best?

They earned, in life, the world's acclaim,
Whatever sphere it be,
The appreciation of their peers,
Their hopes and destiny.

So let them rest in peace benign,
Seek not to blight their name,
Lest you, in time, Biographers,
Will so be judged in shame.

Oliver R. Hounsell

The Longed For Days

How I long for the days when the countryside was innocent
a place of serenity and charm.
Where you could stroll unhurried and at ease
and unlikely to come to harm.

When a solitary walk down the woodland paths
was a pleasure and a joy to be there
where the wind in the trees and the russell of the leaves
were never a cause for fear.

How I long for the days when the churchyards were sacred
a haven for thoughts of the dead
where gravestones were free from graffiti
and feet would respectively tread.

When you could lazily bathe in the sunshine
without worry from the U.V.A.
the grass and the rivers were free from pollution
and fall out of chemical spray.

When you look at the sky on a clear moonlight night
it's easy to think that the world is alright
and hard to imagine there's evil and corruption
in a human race that's bent on destruction.

Norma Jones

Roar

When I died and went to heaven
Don't ask me how I fared
Just pat me on the shoulder
I did my best I cared

I'm weary from the life I led
But that's all in the past
Now I sit at heaven's gate
Overwhelmed by peace at last

Remember how we walked and talked
We yearned for strength, vulnerability we purged
We turned our heads and watched in awe
A splash of crimson when sunset emerged

I am ushered by a friendly voice
A face that's full of wisdom
Such pleasurable euphoria
is found only in God's kingdom

I've been told I must go back
And roar and roar and roar
And if that don't make one cower
Then I must roar and roar some more.

Hilary Feldman

Sandcastles

I don't build castles in the sky,
because, my hopes and dreams of yesterday,
like sandcastles, have been washed away.

A girl, with laughing eyes, now old and frail,
whose marriage, also disappeared,
dissolved upon the sands of time,
embittered by the years.

Our children too, have come and gone,
occasional phone calls, from distant towns,
just say, "Hello, how are you mum"

The storms of life, have washed away,
those castles once so treasured.
Old age, full of fear, and decay.
In empty days is measured.

Hours spent gazing into space,
I watch death's spectre, at my gate,
waiting for me, to embark
upon the silent sea

As finally the tides of time,
erase, the remnants of my dignity.

Sheila A. Green

The Way Things Were

As a child things were great, fields to play in, rivers and streams,
dens in hedgerows, climbing of trees,
Bike rides and skateboards were a must, space hopper fights
get covered in dust,
Presents at Christmas under the tree, look at the tags, which
one's for me.
Snow on the ground, cheeks rosy red, extra thick blanket
thrown on the bed
Daffodils blooming in spring fresh sun—loads of housework,
get your chores done, learn how to iron really great fun!
Packed off to school satchel on back, stand at the gate want
to turn back, grabbed by the hand led away
Soon be home time—can go out and play
In at eight—bath and bed, pleasant dreams oh sleepy head.
Wake in the morning, porridge and toast,
Uniform on—green and white—giant spring onion in a certain light.
Teenage spots appear on face, start filling out from the waist!
Playing with makeup—styling your hair, smiling at boys that
don't really care.
Holding hands, a clumsy kiss, no one ever said it happened like this
A first love, a crying eye, a never again passes you by
Stood at the alter—shaking inside, feel the love from your
partner close by
Expanding stomach, patter of feet, don't read on it's another repeat!!

J. Johns

Beth's Baby

A baby fell from heaven—he didn't have a name
He was playing with a spirit and thought it just a game.

He landed very gently in a warm and cosy space
The spirit who was searching couldn't find this place.

The baby then fell fast asleep, was nurtured and well fed
He forgot about the spirit searching overhead.

The baby stirred and called, the spirit to play a game
I promise I won't fall again, for I now have a name.

The spirit found the mummy and blessed her with a kiss
A kiss that was so whisper light would be possible to miss.

The baby and the spirit soared to play in heaven again
The baby asked the spirit to ease his mummy's pain.

The baby said, why is she sad, why won't she stop crying
The spirit said she won't stop yet, she thinks that you are dying.

The baby said how can I die, I know she hasn't forgot
She said that she did love me and that my name is Scott.

A teardrop fell from heaven and fell right down through space
And the mummy then knew he'd gone when it gently wet her face.

Carol Didlock

Tuesday, 9th July 1996

Vanilla scooped/Chocolate ladled;
(Sultry August's passions are
far too fierce for ice cream)
The stainless steel scoop
can be seen to disappear from view
below the ledge—
beyond the desperate gaze
of imploring young eyes;
into the stomach of the old yellow freezer.

Then—Reloaded,
(Refuelled) with a dripping mass
of dark delight
it rises again.
A sudden pantomimic gasp escapes the child,
('It's gonna be big, Mum—look, two scoops!')
The second, deposited upon the crown of the first, begins to sink.
A tell-tale dribble escapes,
from between the aproned man's fingers.
Greedy hands, outstretched, receive their prize,
and wolfishly consume the pound–paid mass.

Martin E. Edmonds

Magic Moments

It was only a silly childish prank
They all do in their time,
But being tired and thoughtless
And, treating it like crime,
I lashed out with a stern voice
That stopped him in his track,
Yet he faced me like a good'un
Fighting bravely to keep back
Those tears, which filming round his eyes
Gave off a sparkling light,
His face becoming crimson
As he strove with all his might
Against a losing battle
To prove he wasn't weak,
Then a great big wondrous tear drop
Fell splashing to his cheek,
I took his hand in mine then
And said, don't look so sad,
Then he made the moment magic
When he murmured, "Sorry, Dad".

A. E. Amery

Peace In Our Time

It's fifty years on from the war dad
And what did you get for your pains
Did they give you a medal and say oh well done
And that's it for the rest of your days

Perhaps they gave you a pension
If you picked up a wound that was bad
'Twas a weary old man that came back to us
Yet when you enrolled just a lad

And what was it all about dad
Just what did it prove in the end
That our country is great its men are the best
We're a nation that will not bend

They wouldn't do it today dad
Die for their country and Queen
They'd say you get lost you've made all this mess
I'm not part of your killing machine

But it's fifty years without war dad
So perhaps it's not all been in vain
Maybe we've learned from our past mistakes
That the glory's not worth all the pain.

Sheila M. McArdle

But Why?

You smiled like the sun,
You shone like a star,
You were always there when I needed you,
And close by my heart,
you will not be forgotten,
I'll never forget the happy times we had,
And all the tears we shed
So now it's time to go,
The last question I will ask is,
Where are you going to go?
I'm going to heaven high up in the sky,
Higher than the clouds,
And higher than the birds can fly,
The golden gates are shutting now,
Good bye,
But why?
A rose will die,
And maybe the sun won't shine,
But why?
Good bye.

Amy Stanley

Colour Blind

The colour of one's skin
Is such a trivial thing.
Be it yellow, be it white,
Be it blacker than the night,
It matters not a jot.

Some people of a paler hue
Can't wait until the sky turns blue,
With summer sunshine beating down
Hoping for their skins to brown,
What shade it matters not.

But some who bask from early dawn
Think nothing of unleashing scorn
On those whose skins don't match their own,
Though, perhaps, it's just of a different tone.
What a lot of rot.

It is sad to reflect, it boggles the mind,
If misfortune strikes, and that person goes blind,
Then those that were mocked become people, that's all,
They were all the time, it is sad to recall.
What a shame.

Irene Calvert

Body Mind And Soul

There is a feeling that I cannot hide
A feeling that is so very deep inside
It is there with me every day
When she looks at me in her special way
When I am with her I follow my bliss
Her presence is something I cannot miss
To be separated from her would tear me apart
As she holds in her hands all of my heart
Her voice is so silken to my sensual touch
I love her, I love her far too much
By my side she will always be
As she tells me she loves me infinitely
Her blaze of red and her torrent of green
Fill my heart with fire whenever we are seen
I can feel a force taking over me
It releases emotions to set me free
I try to take hold but I lose control
Of my body mind and soul body mind and soul
When I am with her I follow my bliss
Her presence is something I will not miss.

Paul A. Davies

Intrusion

Breaking and entering is a crime
But it's the victims who do the time
Your home is invaded by persons unknown
And your place no longer seems your own

You lock all your windows
And bolt your door
You're a prisoner in a home
That once was yours

Feelings of anger and depression set in
Not knowing quite where they've been
Cleaning everything in sight
And wondering if they'll return tonight

Feeling insecure and all alone
Not even wanting to answer the phone
Not knowing who to trust
Was it a neighbour or a local thug

A prisoner locked away with your thoughts
With no consolation there to be sought
A life sentence in a home you love
But they don't care because they're only thugs

Christine Dand

Holy Waters

I-could-climb, the-highest-mountain, with-you, right by my side.
I-have-dreamt, I'm-drowning, in-the-sea, and-with-you-, I
have, survived.
I feel, as though, the "Pearly-Gates", have-opened-up, for me.
I feel, as though, I-have, been-blind, and-now, my eyes, can see.
This-beautiful-world, we-live-in, is more-beautiful, than-before.
Since-you, came-in, to-my-life, and knocked upon, my door.
I think, of-what-the-blind-man, is-missing, with-no, sight.
The gift, of-seeing-the-midnight-sky, and-the-stars, go-out, at night.
His-mind, has-no-image, of anything, on this earth.
Having-been-born, a-blind-man, since-the-first-day, of his birth.
We-must-not-take-for-granted, the-gifts-we-are-given, free.
The-beautiful, shades, in roses, and-the-colour, of the, sea.
You-don't-need-any-money, to-buy-these-precious, things.
You-just-give-your-soul, to-Jesus-Christ, and-then, your-
heart, just sings.
The-sinner, will-go-home-crying, when-he-tries, to-make, you-fall.
For-his-jealous-eyes, will-be-amazed, when-you-walk, away, so-tall.
You-won't-know, where-it-came-from, this-faith, within, your-heart.
But-you'll-walk, through-life-together, and-you-will-never, be apart.
I-am-baptized, with-holy-waters, since-you-opened-up,
heaven's door.
And-I-have, a beautiful-radiance-now, I have-never, felt before.

Linda George

Love Re-Incarnated?

It seems so long ago, yet it was only yesterday
Since you came into my life and I found that in a day
My whole being has changed and I am in love once more
But it feels like we're old friends, knew each other once before!
So have we ever met? In another life maybe?
And did our paths cross, as it seems our destiny
Is for us to be together until the end will come
For to me, you are no stranger, with you I feel at home.
Yet I am so very sure! I have never seen your face
If I had I would remember, the time, the day, the place
And I would have been so foolish to look around for love
'Cause no one has ever made my pulse race the way you have!
And now I find that this new (or is it an old?) romance
Has brought the memory back of another love, by chance
And I am sure that your past will not leave me surprised
Yes, your eyes show recognition, their meaning can't be denied.
So if we loved before, who were you? And who was I?
And did our love blossom or did it founder and die!
Maybe we'll find the answer as the years shall pass away
By living our past life again in this modern, present day.

M. J. Ellerton

A Dear One Missed

Two lines of poetry to start,
  Two lines coming from my heart
Are all I need, a seed to sow,
  From which eventually will grow
Others lines to fitly show,
  How I missed your presence so,
While waiting for that deadly foe,
  Time, which ofttimes keeps us far apart,
To loose its grip, and then depart.
  For I have longed to hear your voice
Not others that were not my choice,
  To gaze upon you as you smile,
And be in heaven for a while,
  Seeing all that I desire,
All that sets my heart on fire,
  Encapsulated in your being.
Which I can never tire of seeing
  And in loveliness must be,
Greater than all else I see.

K. S. H. Blanchard

A Vision In White

In the distance the daylight's dawning
Drawing her blindly towards the sea
In the wind she hears him calling
Before she ends life tragically

She cannot see beyond tomorrow
Waves a-crashing at her feet
Hypnotized to drown her sorrow
Life for her is never sweet

A vision in white her dress a-flowing
Barefoot she floats across the sand
In the breeze her long hair blowing
As he reaches to take her hand

For in her face he saw a haunting
'Twas her aura he feared the most
Yet what was even more than daunting
Was in her eyes he saw a ghost

Whilst standing close beside her there
'Twas then it became apparent
For all that remained was a chilling air
But for her spirit she was transparent

Paula Marozzi

One Day

One day the Lord, he took from me
My brother John, so I couldn't see

Now at the side of God he'll stay
Watching me, both night and day

All the angels, there up above
Are caring for, the one I love

At the break of day, or the dead of night
You'll always see, that special light

He's happy now, and that I know
Because the Lord, has told me so

One day when, my time has come
And my life, is nearly done

I won't be scared, of what's to be
My brother John, will care for me

At heaven's gate's, is where he'll be
Sitting waiting, so I may see

That day I know, will come to pass
We'll walk together, on heaven's grass.

A. Fidler

Peace In The Glen

The glory of the mountains, soaring high above,
The pine trees and the fern clad hills,
fills one's heart with love.

You've never known what peace is,
Till the sun is way up high,
And you're half-way up Ben Nevis,
So you just sit there and sigh.

At the beauty and the wonder—
Of the mountains all around,
Till the cooling wind and whispering breeze,
Are the only lovely sounds.

For the main thing in this world today,
Is appreciating things,
Like sheep high on a mountainside,
And birds upon the wing.

So if you take heed of little things,
And practice them each day,
There'd be no need for greed and hate,
If man could go his way.

Lucy Piercy

To Abide A Cruel Memory

Abusive to my mind,
My brain Aborted the recollection,
The memory being Abhorrent and unkind.

Absorbed into the care of my intellects engine,
the disagreeable memory sticks,
like a growth, or an Abscess.

If only, like an Abscess,
The memory could be cut out,
or an Ablation be promptly performed,
in its similarity to an unwanted, dysfunctional organ.

Kindly received would be my brain's Ability,
to pass on the memory to my bowels,
Where nature could rid me of the undesirable,
and the sewer could match the unpleasantness of the memory.

No one will ever know or understand,
Memories exist only in the mind,
this one,
Absolute.

Sarah Lawson

As Still My Heart Continues Bleeding . . .

I just can't get him off my mind,
I've had other offers but to them
My eyes are blind,
he was always there for me
tender and kind,
but now the farewell letter to
me he has signed.

I just see his face when I close my eyes,
And for all others around me my love dies,
The tears are falling from my lonely eyes,
The tears that are formed as my heart cries,

My love has never been stronger than this,
I realize now the things I will miss,
the fun we shared and the meaning of bliss,
and when for the last time he contrived to kiss . . .

My tender lips that always will be,
his forever, eternally.

I know that him I'll never
stop needing, as still my heart continues bleeding.

Kelly Street

A Rural Dream

A new abode, a tranquil haven, in the countryside.
My dream of rural life had at last come true.
Such expanse of the sky, and the land so wide.
Desired moments to stare where scant, wintertime was due.

As nights became longer, bleak days stretched ahead.
Soon the earth was white, and the wind so strong.
It howled as in torment, I cowered in my bed.
Fearful my vision of life had gone wrong.

Snow melted away, the fields turned to green.
New shoots soon appeared and trees no longer bare.
Wildlife abundant a delight to be seen.
Birds distinct warbling filling the air.

As days grew longer my qualms grew less.
Spring always heralds new life, fresh hope.
Then a tiny miracle my doubts did suppress.
With my chosen way of living, I knew I could cope.

He or she alighted at my feet, and gazed into my face.
Dark eyes so trusting my Robin red beast friend.
Together in the garden my hopes fell into place.
A little bird has told me, dreams will never end.

Enid Davies

Friendships

Friendships are fickle.
Are we not like the waves of the sea,
Tossing and turning with regret and deepest sympathy.

Love maybe golden,
Like the warmth of highest summer.
Or like the road with no turning or ending,
That goes on and on without her.

Love maybe a struggle,
To keep to the right truth
Love maybe the word
That's never said enough.

Love maybe quenching,
Like the life of a given spring.
Love maybe something she said,
When we let our heart pull the string.

Love has its ways, like reading a borrowed line.
Love has its bays, that we go into to cry.

Friendships are fickle.
Are we not like a great ship on the sea,
Sailing to a distant horizon, half hidden, that's pure majesty!

Andrew Gridley

Growing Pains

I'm hard me, hard as nails
Not deep down, not inside
I joined the gang, stole and lied
Not deep down, not inside
fell off trees but never cried
Not deep down, not inside
Got to show off in front of my mates
Pulling up flowers and jumping high gates
But not deep down, not inside
Parents just say it's boisterous play
The little rascal, he's a tear away.
Not deep down, not inside.
Hidden secrets and silent tears
Pressure from our childhood peers
A decent man I'm hoping to be
Look inside at me, At Me!!!
But not to worry mums and dads
You know deep down we're all good lads
We blossom forth with individuality
At a certain age we enter reality

Gary Bradley

Tragedy At Dunblane

The thirteen of March was a terrible day
Sixteen of their children were taken away
When a crazed killer came to town
And shot their little children down
Death came in the early morn
When from the community the heart was torn,
Eleven other children were shot in the affray
But they lived to play another day.
Pain and heartache and disbelief
Mingle with shock and inconsolable grief
Life will never be the same again in the community called Dunblane
To save the children a teacher tried
But in spite of her efforts she also died
All her efforts were in vain as the killer shot again and again.
Nothing we can do or anything we can say
Can bring consolation for the tragedy on that day.
As for their young ones the people cry,
The question they all ask is Why?
Sixteen children and one teacher now are gone
From the class that once was primary one.

Leonard R. Walton

Ode To The Man I Love

You're all that I am and more than I am,
You're all that I feel and see,
You're all of my life and are my life
Now and eternally.
You're the love in my heart and are my heart
Whether near me or far away.
You're the light in my eyes, you are my eyes
Forever—come what may.
You're the tears I've cried and the smile on my face,
You mean the whole world to me.
You're the pain in my heart, the joy in my heart,
It goes on endlessly.
You're all that I dream, you are my dream,
You're heaven on earth to me.
You're the love in my world, you are my world
Wanting you constantly.
You're the strength in my life and all of my life,
You're the blush that takes over my face
Because you're all that I am and more than I am
And no one can take your place.

Maureen Stradling

Heart Of Stone

Love is like a diamond, and just as hard to find,
The edges they cut deeply into your soul and mind,
it can break you or elate you,
make you smile and make you frown,
but my love for you for ever true,
shines like a jewel in a crown.

Come, fly upon the wings of love into another world,
Where passion is the fashion, and ecstasy unfurls,
To a land that's full of wonder,
Where love is no surprise,
like the sparkle of a diamond,
or the twinkle in your eyes.

Let us float upon the clouds of love,
dally there together,
love and laugh,
make promises and I will leave you never.

For I could never leave you love,
lost and all alone.
My life would fill with sadness,
and my heart, would turn to stone.

V. M. Di Franco

Myalgic Encephalomyelitis

Woeful is M.E. please hear my plea,
For all who suffer this disability,
Which unrecognized goes, I suppose,
Too difficult for some, to diagnose,
The dreadful feeling of weariness,
Causing concern and much distress,
When just to stretch out under a duvet,
And to the Lord, for help to pray,
M.E. affects those who have been too athletic,
Burned themselves out, much too energetic,
Treated not with compassion, but surly contempt,
My heart for them is truly rent, existing on a ghastly diet,
To disbelievers, I just say, "try it,"
When feeling depressed that you're living in vain,
The Coxsackie virus entrance does gain,
Which appears to be of the strain,
Affecting the muscles and brain,
Yet, regarded by some as work shy layabouts,
Always looking for hand outs, one day they may get what is overdue,
Remember, it could happen to you!

Helen Maxwell

The Power The Strength

The power you have was very strong
You chose to use it oh so wrong
The power I have is also strong,
But never will I use it wrong.

For what is strength.
It is, to me, to go down on a bended knee,
To help someone,
To understand,
To lend someone a big strong hand,
To hold someone so very tight
To tell them it is all right,

To chase away the fear of night,
To help them grow in daylight.

For who is strong, For who is weak,
Are there any meek.

Who has the power, Who has the strength,
Who will be strong,
Who will be weak,
Maybe one day you will see,
The strength that I have within me.

Johnney McGuirck

Weep? Not Quite

Weep?, not quite, but nearly
when love lifts me to heights beyond
all vision.

Higher still on wings of joy and bliss.
Weep?, not quite, but nearly
as upon soft feathered wings—
gently down I drift—
Then dear heart, know this,
I am lost just for a moment
in an embrace so divine,
enfolded in such splendour
that only lovers can define.

Sleep, be still my dearest love
and upon awakening find
within that precious moment
our very souls entwined.

To see, to touch—to hear—know you are near,
dare I love thee so much!

Go, yet leaving me, stay and love me.
Weep?, not quite but nearly.

Gwendoline Morgan

My Lost Love

I loved a soldier long ago
When all the world was new
But he had to go to fight the foe
What else was there to do?

I loved a soldier long ago
When the sky was always blue
But he heard the rat-tat of the drum
The far off roarin's of the gun
And he had to go—to fight the foe
What else was there to do?

I wrote to him most everyday
And told him of my love
We said our goodbyes at the train
He never came my way again.

The years have passed and I am old
There's silver where there once was gold.
But I still love my soldier brave—
He's lying in a lonely grave.

Ann Leigh

The Pilgrimage

I look back now in thought and prayer about our merry little band,
Was it a dream—were we really there as pilgrims to the Holy land?
As travellers we became more aware of how it was so long ago
From that first communion we did share our Fellowship began
to grow.

Those early rises and restless nights, the hectic days and wondrous
sights no mortal words can ever describe the emotions and feelings
deep inside. We saw some old and twisted trees in the Garden of
Gethsemane and sometimes had to shed a tear when the Spirit
felt so very near.

My Bible to me now is more complete as I remember the dust
and the heat, transporting myself way back when to that little
town of Bethlehem. We found a quiet spot here and there for
meditation and personal prayer. Each one of us has a special
thought to have been in the place where Jesus taught.

The life of Jesus soon came and went because he was especially sent
But the teachings of Jesus are never done, My ministry has
only just begun. Some went in the Dead Sea to float and
across Galilee we took a boat; We stood on that shore almost
in a trance looking out into the distance.

The holiday now is nearly over as we go homeward to recover
Remembering always when we had a look and followed the
path that Jesus took. So take a candle but before you light,
think of just one of those wondrous sights Let the Spirit
within you refresh anew, like a drop of glistening morning dew.

Jennifer M. Wright

Mother And Child

Doubt the trees are green,
Doubt the sky is blue,
But never, my darling doubt my love for you.

For it was not so long ago,
You were my precious embryo,
And now here you are, my bright star,
My pride and joy,
My loving little boy.

It was worth the anguish, the wait and pain
For you my sweetheart,
I would do it again and again.
I treasure every moment,
From the time I first knew,
Right through to the day,
I first set eyes on you.

You were perfect then, just as you are now,
I could never possibly be without you
I wouldn't know how.

Life before birth may be peaceful and mild,
But nothing could be better then bring, mother and child.

Samantha Beardman

Untitled

The yellow corn fields sway gently in the
Summer breeze, and like a sea of sunlight
they waver to the fallow edge.

The sweet smelling flowers fill the air
and the fields come alive with dormice,
whose havens lie among the tall stems.

Like royalty they live in this golden
land, till summer's depart and
harvest's dawn.

Helen Hillier

Ode To Food

Oh food, food, oh manna so great
You taste so good I hate to waste
Those Quiche Lorraines and custard creams
that I nibble while reading magazines.

Oh Horlicks drink that nourishes me,
I want the world, the whole world, to see
That I cannot live without my Sugar Puffs
And no dessert means I'm in a huff,

All-Bran, Cornflakes, and Weetabix
Come out to play at half past six,
While lunch involves a fillet of fish,
a portion of chips and an ice creams dish.

I know it's bad to have too much food,
but every bite really feels so good.
There is but one thing I would like to say
—food inflates my waist day by day,

Pravin Jeyaraj

Waiting

Inside my heart is a memory
Straining against my soul to break out.
Time stands rock still suspended in stone.

In a distant life I once knew who you were.

Loving everything natural I see, my gaze seeks
Lands far away—from which your soul speaks.
With a passion beyond that which I understand,
A feeling you are out there continues to grow;
In a dark whirl of dreams; a life long dead;
Torn apart easily as two halves of a thread.

Fear echoes through my heart, that we will fail to re-meet.
Opening, again, our hearts to a love sharp yet sweet.
Return to reality becomes harder each time:
Your vision grows quickly, flashing through my mind.
Out from a world which I am no longer a part:
Uttering your love your soul pierces my heart.

E. Parfitt

Untitled

Feeling sorry for oneself,
Is it really a crime?
You recap all the bad things,
The bad things that have happened to you.
What life has shot at you,
Has it all been your fault?
No, you really don't believe that.
How could so many things go wrong,
At the fault of your own hands.
No, it's not all your fault.
You have had it tough,
But believe it all not,
It makes you stronger,
It makes you wiser,
You're a fighter, a winner,
You can make it.
Now smile,
Laugh, make all those bad things,
An exam life gives you,
That you will pass!

Jeannie Sheridan

The Garden

One day I felt sad and lonely, so I got in my car and went
To visit a beautiful garden—a charity event.
The flowers bloomed in profusion, the birds were singing above,
The scent of the grass and the flowers breathed an aura of
    peace and love.
I looked for a quiet corner away from the busy throng,
And saw on a seat near the fountain a listener to the song.
Her eyes were blind, but she smiled at me as she gently
    fondled a flower;
She could not see its beauty, but could feel its fragrant power.
Not far away was a deaf and dumb man enjoying the vivid display—
He couldn't hear the singing birds, nor say what he wanted to say.
And then I saw spastic child in a wheelchair in the sun—
She couldn't control her twitching limbs, she would never
    walk or run.

I went on my way feeling thankful that I was healthy and whole;
That I had all my senses, could enjoy my life to the full.
But each of these damaged people could feel the spell of the place
At one with the glories of nature—part of the human race.

Joyce D. M. Reeve

The Pole

Stuck in the ground at the edge of
Rabbit wood it stands
Its purpose warning, years prevailed, sign has gone,
Alone it now stands grey rusting,
Surrounded by trees quadruple its age,
Meaningless its existence, a scar on the landscape,
No need it has the grey pole.

Darren Jim Turnbull

Would I Ever Know That Joy Of Youth

Would I ever know that joy, of the wonderment of youth,
Rejection had been my companion, for a time I hid that truth,
For I had to race at time, mocking stretching forth,
But sorrow always beckoned, pain, confusion took its course,
It gripped me as I tried so hard to find me in that pain,
That silent screaming, even in my dreams it never waned,
That inner peace obscured, just beyond my reach,
Trials of life consuming me, like swirling waves on beach,
But then I came to end of self, wounded to my Lord I burned,
His love reached out, of his tenderness I very quickly learned,
Would turn sorrow rejection, into countless endless praise,
No longer time stretching forth, in dreaded dreaded haze,
For his heart of love would teach my wounded soul,
To find healing there, hopeful now is my certain goal,
Yes I did find that joy, of the wonderment of youth,
In my heavenly father was hidden, knowledge of everlasting truth,
For I can once again be a child, happy in my father's care,
I know everything I do, my joy with me he will share,
A father loving tender, all caring for my need,
My youthful folly gone, his child now will her father heed.

Nancy Moon

The Damage Is Done

It was just between you, me and the stars
Our secrets to be kept behind bars
For a lifetime long
But with a single slip of the tongue
And our secret has been told
I have to be bold
Face the sniggers, laughs and lies
The whole world ignores my cries
I am alone now
The only question I ask is how
Did the stars speak and tell
Did they hell
I have to pull together and be strong
Hope and pray it will not be long
Before rumours die
And I can take a deep breath and sigh
Then I must be brave and thank you very much
For your evil touch.

Gillian-Clair Eckersley

At Christmas

Twisting and turning, silently glides on shimmering snow, 'neath
    bright starry skies.
Resplendent, emerges by silvery light, dispelling the awe from
    a shadowy night.
In magnificence, splendour, the sleigh bells do ring, invitingly
    joining in whom all do sing
Of the birth of the child, born in a manger, laid in a crib,
    unaware of the danger
Awaiting a young man, gentle and true, sent to earth to
    spread knowledge, to you and to you.
The travel o'er lands, far distant and near, in faith to live long
    and never in fear.
Red berries of Holly and ripe Mistletoe,
Songs of sweet Jesus, melodic and low.
A letter to Santa tells it's Christmas, at last,
Where's the map, there's a chimney, please don't hurry past.
Gifts not of gold, of frankincense or myrrh,
But a teddy for him, and a dolly, for her.
Fir trees and crackers and lots of plum pud,
Chestnuts a-roasting look scrumptious, and good.
Whence replenished and rested, the reindeer turn tail
And Santa and reindeer bid a hearty farewell,
Wish good health, good luck and happiness to all of mankind,
For one year more they will leave all behind,
With them they take many stories untold
And return to their home, the North Pole and The Cold.

B. K. Burnell

The Old Railway Line

The distant melody of shunting trains
rang down the old track.
The whistle of the guardsmen's signal
notifying that "all aboard".

And so the train chugged into speed
and gathered momentum.
The smell of fumes mixing with the
essence of countryside, taking with it
people to their destination.

And so I shall wait for them,
these people of long ago.
I shall hear the train shunting,
once more, down the line.
I shall see a shadowy figure wave from the
ruined signal box.
And again the phantom voice announcing the next
arrival.
And the skeleton crew will go about their
daily routine, down by the old railway line.

Wendy Ann Kirkham

Inner Journey Of Life

Life is complicated, well it is to me.
And what have I got to show for it?
A few moments good, many a moment bad, but still haunting
Still hurting and twisting this mental torture inside.

It starts as a baby, well it did for me,
This complication of confusion.
Memories of death, memories of life, not understanding
but knowing the pain of missing and wanting.

It grows stronger, well for me it did.
The hurt is now fear: fearing memories, fearing life to come.
Not knowing hurts and confuses me.
It's too complicated to know, so I fear it all.

Life is too complicated, well to me it is.
And why do I have to show anything?
I know my memories; I know my fears; I know these painful journeys.
Yet the wanting, the needing is still painful and confusing.

The inner journey of life they should call this, well I would anyway.
And what does it mean? Do we know? Does anyone really know—
What's in store, the way we really feel? I doubt it.
They're too stuck in their outer journeys to realize.

Samantha Jones

219

Hunter Or Hunted

Silently stalking, his prey in his sight.
Mirroring its movements so as not to cause flight.
An image of beauty, captured for life.
One shot in a thousand, his head bows as he sighs.
A trophy to treasure, to be admired by all,
To view from a distance in a great hallowed hall.
But what of the man who fired the shot,
Is he proud of his work?, many say not.
Night after night all alone he stays,
Perfecting the art that he practices by day.
A lonely existence, made of his own choice,
Few would refuse a man of his poise.
Many have said they would incur Gods wrath,
Just to be immortalized in his next photograph.

Vicky Gorman

Fingers Tall

Fingers tall and tapering of weather beaten brick,
Abandoned now, like rotting sentinels do stand.
Yet they mark not decaying walls of factories now dead
They quietly mourn an industry that died within this land.
No longer do they funnel black smoke to mouths built high
But silently stand, defiant, stark against the sky.

Oh tall and tapering fingers, once warm and belching soot
From fires that roared through night and day to hold a head of steam
Then breathed with vibrations from the engine down below
That watched the flywheel slowly turn, the polished conrod gleam
And rang to people's voices, the morning whistles call
Heard the clip of steel tipped clogs, saw women dressed in shawl.

Oh fingers tall and silent, now like rotting trees do stand
Your broken mill-shed windows display each a neglected frown.
And so you wait, forgotten, lost, your usefulness outdone
Till man with tractor, spade and crane will bring you crashing down.
No sentiment has progress, bricks and mortar mean naught at all
To man or state that did once depend on factory chimneys tall.

Frank Ravenscroft

Her Sons

They stand like winter trees
Who bear no grudge against
The ground which bears them,
And yet are silent in the twilight's dwindling glare.
Who stand together and yet, are each alone within
A captive thought or falling tear.

Conceived by nature, and by the same,
Ruined to a memory.
Her sons,
Their death
To keep,
Soft as shadow, slight as sleep.

Michael O'Connell

The Four Seasons

The ground is covered with rusty leaves
Leaf upon leaf, blown down in the breeze
Crunch under foot, trees creek all around
Life's disappearing, hiding away, underground

Cold biting wind, ice in the air
Grips the land and strips it bare
Nakedness covered, by snowflakes falling
Tiny buds appear, Spring is calling

Snowdrops and Crocus cover the earth
New life is beginning, new song, new birth
Trees and their branches heavy in bud
Leaves are uncurling, redressing the wood

Summer is hear now, the warmth of the sun
The birds dance, and call out "the battle is won"
Bright colours abound from the flowers in the heat
What a shame, what a wonder, it has to repeat.

Tracey Muscroft

Another Summer's Day

Hanging baskets plants in tubs,
Beautiful borders, pretty shrubs,
These are the delights that summer will bring,
Everyone is happy, even the birds sing,

Horrible loud music, mini cabs tooting their horn.
Dogs barking, cats fighting, dustmen waking you at dawn,
People having barb'cues, filling your garden with smoke,
Enjoy the summer? You are having a joke.

Hanging baskets, plants in tubs,
Beautiful borders pretty shrubs,
So put the radio on kid, light the barby, and fetch the beer,
Isn't it smashing, now that summer is here.

Maureen Arnold

My Fleeting Thoughts

While I walked in the timid moonlight
You were far from my fleeting thoughts,
You were just the crunch of the frosting ice
beneath my unclad feet,
Twinkling blades of once sweet succulent grass caught my eyes,
Which opened wide and kept a steady gaze
on what I thought was once crystal,
but which soon dwindled down,
to still, watery mirrors,
freezing my toes in a secret alliance to help them escape
from my much restrictive feet.
I cannot feel their prickling presence now.
They are numb,
perhaps they have eloped and joined their lovers,
Far away in a place where it is glorious daybreak.
Like when you left me in the inky night,
With no weapon to fight off these devil demons,
who have come to claim me.
And as their clammy claws took me,
You were still banished, far from my fleeting thoughts.

L. E. Marshall

Midnight

Midnight
A whispering howl
A black ocean like a coma to me now
The unscented mist
In the darkest hour
Of the twilight zone
Of the devil's power

The absence of colour with the unexplained myth
From the truth and the lies
To the graveyard shift
The dark half of the day
With a bitter smell of fear
With the pain of a heartache
Of the one single tear

The light of the stars
Mixed with a street lamps shine
Will soon fade away
With the early morning light
The light of day and the birds' first song
Wakes up the world and wakes up the dawn . . .

Mark J. Adams

The Colour White

Steep chalk cliffs leaning over the ocean,
Fluffy white clouds drifting across the sky,
A ghostly figure standing in the doorway.
Snowdrops standing in the long grass,
Angels from heaven in a shining white light,
Swans swimming around the lake.
A polar bear in the Arctic Circle,
Footprints in the fallen snow,
A piece of paper on which I write,
A poem called "The Colour White".

Lisa Kennard

Untitled

When the fear of your own mortality plays trombones down
your ear
And the yearnings for an earlier life make the future seem too near,
When the truth of an old adventure makes you only want to sneer,
Then you have reached that time in existence when nothing
will be clear.

Do you walk through the woods with your old closest friend?
Do you fret on the smallest mistake?
Do you work like a dog for a mountain of Gold?
Do you search for that 'thing' in the lake?

It's so easy to sit and do nothing
Let the wind take you further away
To rant and to rave at what might have been
If no one had gotten in your way.

Oh I think I would like to be noted
For things that I'm going to do,
Or some kindness or marked achievement
That is humane, artistic or new.

But I know in my heart I'm a dreamer
And my fate's all planned out for me,
So I'll muddle my way on life's highway
And just hope that you think well of me.

Charles Bramley

"Autumn Love"

My heart stood still, as you came through the door
still so handsome, so tall, still the man I adore
we idly chatted through the evening chores
then with dishes washed up, locking windows and doors
we settle together for an evening at home
the clock ticking softly, and distant traffic drone
slowly as body and mind relax in peace
our eyes meet, and our pulse race
the clock can't be heard above the beat of my heart
you're holding me close, we're no longer apart
our kisses are gentle, undemanding and warm
safe with each other, like calm after storm
then as we sit, in the dim glow of the fire
our fingers reaching each other with desire
in the dim light, I'm totally yours
lost in the ecstasy of love, behind locked doors
slowly as our arms untwine
contented in the knowledge that you're still mine
your fingers touch my hair, now going grey
who said its only the young who have their day.

D. R. Bond

It's Draining

The curtain wags its tail
to welcome in the sun.

Surreptitiously it creeps between the sheets
to wake us

Leaving its thumb prints all over your body.
I rise and dress.

Skating over the mirror's surface,
I look shaky

On my toes after last night's shin-dig—
the prodigal son

Who returns not to find a propitious feast
but a shanty-town sink

Gaping with grime–throated cups,
the floor scattered

With debris now that the tide has
gone out

And an abandoned umbrella bound like an irreconcilable
promise of fulfilment.

The radio rain, criss-crossing out the day's expectations
scratching the vision of hills in the distance.

Martin J. Ball

Soldiers For Christ

When I was young I used to dream of great exploits for God
and Queen;
Of battles fought, and always won! And great heroic feats unsung.
But as I grew, so faded those daydreams of youth and
yesteryear . . .
.
I saw that life was often dull and drear: gone were the times of
make-believe;
For I in no way could retrieve those youthful days of yesteryear.
And life seemed just an empty dream until I met my Lord and King.
He came to be my Saviour first, and show that He could
quench my thirst;
And take away the emptiness that pleasures here could not express.
He taught me how to trust and stand upon His Word, with
sword in hand.
He gave me breast-plate, helmet, shield; before which Satan
has to yield.
A belt of Truth He gave to me, which, He said, would keep me free!
Upon my feet my Saviour placed shoes of His Gospel, firmly laced.
He stood before me, my Captain . . . strong; and bid me stand
against all wrong
. . . a soldier of the King's Army; soldiers for Christ . . . you
know Him too!
I see His likeness—clear–in you . . . and as I look, I see a band
of countless souls on every hand . . . a mighty awesome
Army, made up
of folk like you and me.
Called to stand within the ranks, to praise and raise our songs
of thanks;
To listen to our Lord's command . . . trust Him, as He leads us on—
TO VICTORY . . . soldiers for Christ.

John Whiddett

Town And Country

It's winter, in the country
Everything barren and bare
The trees have long since shed their leaves
The fox has gone to his lair

Soon all will be alive again
For spring is round the corner
Bringing the leaves back on the trees
Making everything just that bit warmer

In town it is a different scene
Although streets seem deserted
They are all lit up, folk are about
Visiting pubs, going in, coming out
Seeing friends, living life to the full,
Playing squash, table tennis and even pool.

Oh yes! There are many places to go
Before spring comes along and melts all of the snow.

J. E. Madlin

World Of Dreams

The soft gentle seas
flow with the wind
the scent in the breeze
makes me stop and think . . .

Swimming around the deep depths below,
I am fulfilled inside so deep
moving away along with the flow,
sending my soul to sleep
looking around to see my surrounding,
so heavenly it seems
the whales far away are sounding,
within this world of dreams
this is an everlasting vision,
now I can live in blessedness
finally I am being given,
a peaceful sense of happiness . . .

A fantasy beyond any dream that's mine
people don't picture this everyday . . . never
even all the way till the end of time
I would want to stay . . . forever.

P. K. Sandhu

221

Tales From March

Scattered rain on fragments of glass
Windblown shale scratching at the water's edge
Sunshine riding the waves eluding the lion's mouth.

Racing clouds skim the horizon
Windblown fields shudder in the cold
Gnarled black bones stretch and grasp the sun
Soon the leaves will grow.

Wind tumbles the seeds of life
Cast them far I prey.
Over mountains and coast lands, throw your dice
Send them on their way

Tales from March you bring to me
Whispers in the budding tree
Hope for all that want to see
The spirit that is eternity.

D. J. Thomas

Tranquillity, Serenity And Peace

To feel cool fingers upon my brow
Gentle. Soothing, restful
I feel at peace with the rest of the world
As in your arms I'm gently curled.

Softly talking, embracing, sweet names,
Cuddling closer, contented, remains
Drifting along on a cloud with a dream
Sweet face shines above, eyes gentle, serene

Your kisses so tender, amazing, divine
Your lips to me honey, taste just like wine
In your eyes, I can read your love so deep
In your face is desire, so intense, so steep
My darling, my love, you're all my own
My heart, my love seeds so gently are sown
You've soothed away my aches and pains
And in their place tranquillity reigns
At rest my head lies on your breast
So sweet and soft and gently caressed.

Adoration my sweet, stands out a mile
In your face, especially your smile.

Joan Vincent

Fox Hunt

The race is on, the horn does sound,
Competing are the fox and hound,
The huntsman sit like Kings up high,
The objective is the fox must die.

With hounds up front the huntsman chase,
To catch the fox they must gain pace,
Over the ditches and across the land,
They chase the fox, the kill is planned.

Now minutes pass, the fox is done,
His legs are weak, no more shall run,
Alone he waits, the hounds appear,
His eyes they widen and show his fear,

You call this sport, or is it fun,
The fox is dead, the deed is done,
Man has killed for his own pleasure,
The fox destroyed at man's own leisure.

Paul Hughes

The Meaning of Life

Standing here, I wonder why,
As I look at the earth, and gaze at the sky.
The birds that sing, the flowers that grow,
Why am I here, I would like to know,
But as I wander down memory lane asking myself yet once again,
Why am I here, I now know why,
As I look at the earth and gaze at the sky,
This great gift of life was given with love,
So no time will I waste in wondering why.

Constance E. Newland

If I Could Go Back In Time

In my weakness I did frighten you, in my anger I did hurt you,
In my despair I drove you away.

If I could go back in time I'd go back eleven years,
Begin our life together again, without all the tears.

If I could go back in time I'd go back twenty years,
I'd live my life again without all the fears.

If I could go back in time I'd go back to where my life began,
I'd change all my ways for you my love,
To be a better man.

If I could go back in time and do all that I say,
I wonder if you would have me back my love . . . Today

Every morning I wake and breathe in the air,
I cry out with the deepest regret, take me, Lord
This life without love I cannot bear.

I hate living, always have and probably always will.
Until my heart, with love and truth
Someone can fulfil.

Nick Hartland

One Last Drink?

"Mum, there's a party, please can I go?
    everyone will be there, everyone I know?"

"I suppose you can dear, but if you take the car,
    be in by twelve and don't go far."

She's young and impressionable, a vulnerable thing
Her friends have her suspended, like a puppet on a string.

The drinks they'll buy, the drinks they'll down
Seemingly a normal night out on the town.

Have a laugh, have a half, a vodka, whisky, gin,
They use her, they abuse her, they snigger and they grin.

The next day they call, on the way to the fair
Giggling and joking with the stories they share.

They stand at the gate and look from afar
At all the closed curtains and the wreck of her car.

All standing in silence, all numbed they stare
Wreaths in the garden for the friend they had shared.

The vision of flowers makes all her friends think
'Was it that one for the road, that one last drink?'

The light has now gone, yet the days still remain,
With flowers the reminder of the stupid game.

Julie Ann Chandler

'Ode To A Working Man'

Millwrights, welders, artisans
Pipe fitters, turners skilled of hand.
Brassware, chromium plated parts
Ghosts of men with whicker carts.

Bustle, hustle, rush hour noise
Shops all busy—coloured toys
Buckets, buttons, bracelets too
Winged chariots, to arm 'The Few'
Spitfire, boffers, churchill tank
Armour plate from 'Quarry Bank'
Shells from kynochs, I.M.I.
Lights to open up the sky
Holts brewery, ansell (Aston Cross)
Priestly, Matthew Boulton, Whatt.

You want it made, we'll do it right
The lads I'll graft all through the night
You've had your profits (and much more)
So please don't kick us out of door
To join the dole Queues once again
Cold and hungry in the rain.

William Kendrick

Please Make It Through

Hello to you, my niece or nephew
the baby inside, who is struggling to see it through.

Everybody out here is so wishing for you to make it through.
We all want to see your eyes to see your smile
as a matter of fact we're all hoping to see you.

Your mummy really wants to see you, to hold you, to kiss you
and to love you too.

Your mummy has seen you on TV
But that was because you were bleeding. You're only eleven
weeks old and yet you are already feeling pain.
Please make it through.

We all know it's very lonely in there surrounded by water and
feeding tube but please stay in there baby and come on and
make it through.

People are loving you even now so when you make it through
there be people here already loving you. You have three
brothers, who want you to make it through.
Their names are, Nicky, Daryl and Jaydon.

So please my darling baby you have to make it through. You
can see the sunshine, feel the rain, smell the flowers and hear
the music there's lots to leave behind if you go and there lots
to live for too
So please baby make it on through.

With love and lots of luck on your survival

Z. A. Martin

"Silence"

The silence fills the house,
grief stricken,
what! What?
She asks,
the worst has happened,
a child has flown to heaven,
an angel now,
death is a painful thing.

The dripping of a tap echoes the silence of the house,
throat gulping,
wanting to cry,
numbness and disillusionment,
sighing,
What a life, what a life.

The silence of one's thoughts,
remember her,
Precious Angel,
always remembered by us on Earth.

Samantha McCarthy

Till Death Do Us Part

Till death do us part why should this be
We love enough for eternity
It terrifies me that when we go
How two souls could meet I need to know

Before we die we must make a pledge
To meet again down at the village
If I die first I'll wait for you
If not I pray you'll wait there too

Just promise me with all your heart
No matter what we'll never part
I could not live to see a day
That finds my love has gone away

I need to know we'll be together
Even after death for ever and ever
They say if your good you'll be happy above
In Heaven we join with the one's that we love

But how could it be heaven for a soul's lonely heart
If we never shall meet for at death we must part
I shall wonder the earth till I see you again
Like a ghost that's in limbo, in love, but insane.

Paul Jones

Childhood Memories

Thinking of my childhood, it seems so long ago.
The days seemed so much longer, those days of long ago.
The summers filled with sunshine, the winters with so much snow.
Those days of childhood memories, those days of long ago.

Thinking of the memories, where everything seemed so big.
The penny lollies and black jacks, those sweets that made me sick.
The happy days and laughter, those friends of yesteryears.
Those days of childhood memories, those days of fun and tears.

The Saturday morning cinema, watching batman and cartoons.
Going to school and Sunday church, learning all the rules.
Where everything was simple, where everything was bright.
Those days of childhood memories, those days of pure delight.

Looking back at those years, sometimes sunshine, sometimes tears,
Dreams and wishes, hopes and fears, for times ahead and
future years.
Childhood days of fun and laughter, free of worry, stress and fear.
Looking back at the freedom of those carefree happy years.

Janet Davidson

Untitled

Dedicated to F/Lt. Jeffares, RNZAF. 37 SQDN.

Oh Jeff he was a sheepman from down Invercargill way,
Tall and lean with nerves of steel and eyes so quiet and grey.
He joined us in the desert—it was in August forty two.
He'd carried out many a battle stooge—Jeff and his Empire crew.

The 8th has called for a maximum show, when things were
getting tight.
They'd done it many a time before, on many a still dark night.
But we'd changed a wheel at take-off, for those desert flints
were sharp,
And Jeff in his true New Zealand style, helped us to get it apart.

"We'll catch them Jock" he called to me, with his eyes so calm
and grey,
"What with extra boost and throttles wide, we'll make that E.T.A"
So with flaps half down they roared away and soon they were
lost in view
Far to the West where the battle raged, Jeff and his Empire Crew.

The target appeared, they dropped their load, the sun was
beginning to rise,
Jeff pulled away, set course for base—pressed on in lightening skies.
Nobody saw that menacing shape of the Junkers eighty eight,
He came in fast at the blind spot, for Jeff and his crew were late . . .

There was gloom that night in our desert camp and although it
was long ago
Just spare a thought for Jeff and his boys, they died for me and you.

I. A. Neilson

This World . . .

This world is not a perfect one,
although it could have been.
Before this race called humans came along.

As before it was just nature,
peace and harmony.
But once we came, all of that went wrong.

We tore down precious forests,
leaving creatures without homes.
We dug up all the land, and just for greed.

We took the creatures' freedom,
polluted sunny skies.
And now we've even gone and wrecked the seas.

We've taken all the minerals,
and metals from the ground.
We've wiped out certain creatures just for spite.

We've even killed ourselves,
by having many wars.
But how can we solve problems with a fight?

Richard Oriel

Somebody's Son

He lay in a doorway the place he could bed.
A dirty old jacket pillowed his head.
Such a young man still in his teens.
Not a man not a boy somewhere in between.
He looked so unhappy his face spoke of pain.
he's arms bore the scars were needle met vein.
I thought as I saw him he's somebody's son.
Whose life will be over before its begun.
So if at a party maybe just for a joke.
Someone offers a tablet or maybe a smoke.
Think what your doing is death worth the thrill.
Its the price you might pay for taking a pill.
Don't lose your life for what may seem like pleasure.
Say no to drugs and each moment treasure.
Think of the young man somebody's son.
Whose life's nearly over before its begun.

Cora C. Mann

Remorse

The years which fly so swiftly by with such increasing speed,
Have left us all with broken dreams and unattempted deed.
The things we meant to do and say, the love we never showed,
The debts that never can be paid, the promises still owed.
Oh! Could some oracle of fate which oversees the plan,
Return me to those times in life were all my faults began.
What pleasure then would fill my heart, what happiness unfold,
If recompense could be made, and feelings truly told.
How heavy falls the hand of time upon a dream unfilled.
What pain the aching heart must bear, what sorrow now instilled.
So count the blessings in your youth, and cherish everyone
With thanks to those who shaped your life and now are sadly gone.

Leonard Muscroft

Scent Of A Woman

All her sweetness and charm,
Wrapped up in a parcel of skin,
The smile in her eyes, the touch of her lips,
The smell of her hair, the curve of her hips,

He followed in her wake,
Buried his face in hair,
Inhaled her fragrance,
Laid her soul bare.

Bottled and shelved it,
Market it with ink,
Let his love for her grow high,
Then left it to sink.

He followed another scent,
A scent that was new,
Pursued it,
Memorized it,
Then shelved that one too.

Nina Giani

My Memory

Oh dear what shall I do
Since I've got old I'm forgetful too
Where have I put this
Where have I put that
Oh deary me where is my hat.

I've lost a belt, a jumper too
Goodness me I've lost a shoe
Have I paid all the bills today
Really have I paid my way.

When up to bed at night I go
My mind goes wandering to and fro
Is everything safely locked up at night
Oh goodness did I put out that light.

I really must take myself in hand
Just like a musician with a band
Dear Lord up above please make my memory good
Then I will love you every day
Bless you God you have made my day.

Mavis Hall

Aberfan

When the earth moved in Wales, it wasn't
the same, as the reason we give it,
when love is to blame.
In a country where coal, is said to be
king, we found to our cost, there can be no such thing.
For the value of life, and of love in those
hills, is more precious than the sound of underground drills.

Not just for you, the heartache and tears,
the whole world has shared with you over the years.
Not just a village, whose children have died;
towns, and cities, even continents cried.
And miners, whose courage was never in
doubt, gave a new meaning to "Hearts that are stout."

In the face of adversity, so painfully
cruel, we asked the same question,
"Dear God, why a school?" Your faith,
and your dignity, courage and pride,
Remind us of our faith, you have been our guide.
Who better to teach us God's wonderful plan?
You can. You can, Aberfan.

Dave Allen

What A Poet Is (Not)

A poet is not, but that which is poetry is,
How can a river or words exist, with no conforming matching bliss
Does any cloud have substance? Without its own shaped form!
Therefore ask not of me, please, I beg, am I a poet, "Born"
Likewise then, see not the poet, but the existing magic craft, where
bye as does each dawn, its own intrinsic beauty hold, for you
Then reader of this poem see, how each word, like "Angel
dust, ensues
Cascading from the mind, and each has its place, and each its "Hues",
Tell me, what does a rainbow convey to you, if not its reds, its
greens, and blues
Leaving one in wonder that it's arc of light, so splendorous to behold,
'twas not made by us, but nature for us, to see, to be observed,
from ages old So it is with more humble effort, that "poetic
man", perhaps?
Deems it "His duty", to postulate, elucidate, even to pontificate
and when reading poetic verse as this, how you should even
"Imaginate!"
Where—as, ordinary saner mortals (Not of the poetic ilk)
Worry not if words are harsh and dull, unlike cool water, or
flowing silk not so
"The poet", who weaves the words for them to show his
"trade mark",
Yes! Never sure his words have stirred your soul, to know
both, of the utter joy of "Heaven", or the cold dark "hell" below.

Thomas M. Maher

Solitude

The glade was draped in a
blanket of golden crispness,

The woodland bird blinked not
conscious, that he was her only witness;

The girl wondered aimlessly on kicking at the fallen foliage,
Deep within the fathoms of her mind.

Why? Had it happened,
Yesterday, they were so ecstatically happy;
Too many words she had let slip from her tongue, She knew

Would he ever see it in his heart to forgive her?
Or was this the death of a perfect union,

A tear fell upon her icy cheek,
She sobbed a sigh which was carried off by the whistling wind.

Through her sorrow she saw the bird,
Perched on the limb, alone like her;

As she advanced, he turned and soared above,
Not caring why this girl wept.

She brushed the droplets from her face,
And headed for the road, deep in thought once more; not knowing
What lay ahead, in the path of her destiny.

Christine Child

Untitled

Put my love under a microscope, what do I see,
The cancerous cells of jealousy,
If caught early enough there would be some scope,
But caught at this stage there is not much hope.

From an innocent start it's taken its hold,
A small piece of gossip on which I've been sold.
It started the mind on a journey of thought,
Suspicion and hurt are the feelings I've bought.

What do I do, should I say what I feel?
And chance being told my suspicions are real?
Perhaps I keep quiet and hope for the best,
Let the cancer take hold and let God do the rest.

Patricia M. Dainton

The Voice Within

There are many sounds around us, for us to hear.
The words we use, in the sounds of time, are for all of us to hear.
These sounds we here, which meditate within our minds.
Like the chorus of song, in the sleepless nights.

As we ponder through our daily works and wonder upon the plane.
And seek the help from all who speak and whisper in my ear.
For the sound of music plays this day, as I climb within my mind.
The whisper of this sound within, has open'd up my mind.

The secret that we are looking for, is closer than we can imagine.
For only if we open up, and knock upon the door.
For the "I", I have within my mind is waiting at the door.
The voice will call, within my mind to bring me joy and
wondrous things.

For life upon the plane we seek, is far from all this care and strain.
The time will come, to find this voice within.
You all will think the silence of your mind, for the voice
whispers in your mind.
"I" have been here all the time.

Roger Shepherd

Peace

Peace did make the sun, seem brighter than before,
It took a lot of work, but happiness it bore,
But then the troubles started, what did it all gain?
Nothing but unhappiness, and peace went down the drain.

Next there was the ceasefire, we thought we'd peace again,
But after a year it was shattered, like glass in a windowpane,
I remember that night very clearly, everyone was miserable and sad,
The idea of peace ending, being replaced by something so bad.

After lots of talks and discussions, the ceasefire again has come,
But life will never be the same, as before for some,
For these many people, the suffering will not mend,
I think the peace is wonderful, but how long 'till it ends?

Lyndsey Anderson

The Old Man

The lines of time on his aged old face
Sunken eye's his skull embraced
Skin so pale, where once cheeks shone
Bravely fighting, to coax life on.

Body frail, arms so thin
Slowly beats a heart within
Those hands so thin, so frail to touch
Cared for others, Oh' so much.

What thoughts passed through his sleepy mind
Glorious days so far behind?
Or days of youth, does he dream!
When he was part of life's young team.

In his sleep, his face does smile
Remembering life as a brave young child
Now he is alone, it seems
With happy memories, In his Dreams.

Henry Irving

Faerie Tale

When night's dark cloak drapes o'er the sky,
And people wrapped in slumber lie,
In depths of yonder forest old,
There lies a wonder to behold.

Eyes of blue do shyly peep,
Then from their hiding place they creep,
The tiny people men persist,
In faerie tales alone exist.

Hand in hand to form a ring,
Their clear sweet voices gaily sing,
In language of another time,
Enchanted words of ancient rhyme.

Shafts of light on gossamer wings,
Clothes with rainbow colours tinged,
Waist length locks of golden hair,
Cascade down skin so creamy fair.

But once the moon begins to fade,
And daylight wakes to take her place,
The faeries disappear from view,
To form the drops of morning dew.

Allison M. Hudson

Rwanda And Burundi

Deep within those war torn, blood soaked, God forsaken lands,
Where no sane man would choose to coexist,
Live the gentlest of creatures in their concomitant bands,
The mountain bred gorillas in the mist.

If only man could learn from them their tolerance and calm,
And shrink from confrontation at all costs,
Then future generations would be safe and free from harm,
And dignity and pride would not be lost.

No matter what our colour, creed, or origins of birth,
We'd do well to emulate this gentle beast,
We must learn to live together to secure our place on earth,
Or humankind will ultimately cease.

Jill Layden

"The Ghost Ship"

'Tis a strange tale I tells thee sire,
    Of days now long ago,
'Twas on a clipper ship in 'Kidwercy Sire'
    We were loaded and lying low.

'Twas a raw cold night in the lantern's light,
    Cold fear gripped my threat!
There to me right, 'twas a fearsome sight
    A ghost pirate crossed the deck to port!

I cried 'lour he here, hold fast 'n' draw near!!!'
    I'd me cutlass held tight in he hand!
There's now that I fear, do I make myself clear?
    Our sort water, or damye on dry land!!

He laughed, mocking me, for he could plainly see,
    There was nothing a mortal could do?!
        'Your anger you see, (he cried out to me)
        Will make a dead man out of you!'

For I've crewed, this ship and sailed on each trip,
    The devil won't leave me behind!
With a rye smile on his lip, at his blasphemous quip,
    He said him and me, are two of a kind!

Mike Carte

Families

Families cannot be plucked from a fruitful tree,
Brothers, sisters, mothers, and fathers will be what they will be,
It's sometimes hard to tell them how you truly feel,
But they are all the Lord's cards that He chose to deal,
So make the most of the times that together you may share,
Because one thing is for certain—they won't always be there.

Clare Dawson

Where The Heather Hills Adorn

Where the heather hills adorn,
Yearning for you, lost, forlorn.
Sweeping down from sky to sea,
Purple haze you beckon me.
Brushed by clouds borne on my sighs,
Exile's dreams light dimming eyes.
Reaching out could I but touch
Tartan snagged in bracken's clutch.
Wrenched from out the sodden soil,
Your roots, my heart, how you omit toil!
When the torrent's run its course,
Lay me down in bed of gorse.
Softer still than distant dune.
Breathless piper; timeless tune,
Swirling o'er dank, wooded glen,
Reeling wild with folk I ken.
Skerry bleak adrift no more,
Sound embraced by kindred shore.
Love betrothed when I was born
Where the heather hills adorn.

Brian J. Davison

What Have We Done

What have we done? How can we mend it?
Why are we killing birds, animals, plants, trees and rivers?
Look into the future, what do you see?
Look into the past, how many differences can you find?
When you listen to the past, what do you hear?
When you listen in the future, what will you hear?
Will you notice any differences? If yes, how many?
I cannot count, I think there are too many?

Katrina Maclean
Inverness

The Dream

I had a dream that felt so real
I was walking in a poppy field
The sun was shinning all around
A singing bird made the only sound
In the distance I saw a familiar form
With arms open wide to welcome me home
I felt I could fly as I ran through the field
To be with you was my only need

The vision went hazy when morning arrived
I felt uneasy when I opened my eyes
The dream was so real I was sure I'd find
You would be lying by my side

With a heavy heart reality dawned
I was lying in bed all alone
I longed for sleep to come again
To reach my love in the poppy field dream.

Thelma M. Robinson

Without You

Like the closing of an autumn door
another one reopens

The emptiness and the pain is breaking
my heart

I never thought that we would have
to part

Not in a lifetime!

Our love was like a bird just flying
softly and gently and now I need
time, precious time to repair the broken
wings

But you won't be with me that makes
me want to give up hope, give up life but
I can't keep flying with broken wings

Yet I can't keep flying without you!

Lindsay Robinson

Our Spite Of The Traitor

As they gathered on the bus,
They sat and took their seats,
They quietly chatted, but didn't realize,
It'd be the last time they would ever meet.

Slowly travelling down the London roads,
A traitor before their faces,
Now they existed, but by tomorrow,
They would have gone without a trace.

At half past ten it happened,
And many lives were gone,
Remains, blood and crisis,
This caused by only one.

But the people got their justice,
And he was then gone too,
Only his remains were found,
With the rise of the morning dew.

Many believed he deserved it,
Others looked at him in spite,
For the people he killed, didn't deserve,
To die on that February night.

Jemma Williamson

It's The Children

Soldiers spill their blood on a foreign land
But they are army men, and they understand!! But do the
children?

What is war? What is its need?
Man against man, for power and greed!! And it kills the
children.

They are our future! The new human race
The seed that we sow, in a warm loving place, they are our
children!

Seed will not prosper, sown under battle sod!
It dies in the ground, covered in blood! The blood of our
children!

Jesus said "suffer the children to come unto me"
Well! Heaven's full, and there's a queue down to purgatory!
A
queue
of children!

Dammed is the man, who harms a child.
Who causes innocence to be defiled, he will answer, to the
children!!

Let each day be filled with peace
Let all strife and warfare cease, for God's sake!! And the
children.

Olga Margaret Moorhouse

Spotted Leopard

You know how it feels to be hunted,
Spotted Leopard.
From the first moment you open your dangerous black eye
you have a sense of fear.
Am I right, clever one?
Were you not gifted with speed so you could escape
the dreaded blast of a bullet?
Is it anger that causes you to be so fierce?
Or do your enemies drive you out of your mind?
I cannot help but admire you,
Spotted Leopard.
How can you stalk some harmless creature and
calmly prowl away guiltless?
Am I right when I say you like to torture and kill small animals?
I can see that evil side to you,
fast one.
Just the thought of a knife even touching your precious
coat is enough to set you off, isn't it?
I can see now you want to taste my blood,
sink your fangs into my arm, Am I right, Spotted Leopard?

Kate Shakesby

A Sense Of You

In bed with you at night,
Even when back to back,
There is a jig-saw sense of contours,
Fitting to a perfect whole,
And the uncertainties which crowd my day,
Fade with the touch and taste of you.

There is a magic spell,
Cast on your body by an unknown hand,
Which make those similarities to other men,
Dissimilar, un-uniform,
When you are in my bed with me at night
And I have all the touch and taste of you.

But nights alone are hard,
And beds, however pliable and soft,
Consistently refuse my shape, except in dreams,
When memories of you are clear.
Then space becomes familiar shape
And I recall the touch and taste of you.

Valentina Dunmow

Four Wall Syndrome

These walls are closing in, it's a claustrophobic sensation,
A consequence of life in this domestic reservation.
Impounded by pure fate, manacled by invisible chains,
My mind is screaming "Let me out!", but my body just remains.

I don't dislike this place, how could I? It's my home,
It's just I can't stand to fester here, I need more space to roam.
Suffocating in this jaded atmosphere, stark partitions all I see,
Stagnating as each day passes, and yet wishing to be free . . .

A slave to my own environment is what I've now become,
Waiting for something to happen, but knowing it shan't ever come.
Waiting for a messenger, holding some miracle key,
Waiting for my wings to grow, so I may vacate this tree.

A life of wishing, a life of hoping, a life of solitude,
I need to study my dilemma with a different attitude.
Dreams are a form of escapism, or so I've heard some say,
And yet I've escaped a thousand times, but never been away.

Kevin Langwith

Thoughts Of Mine, Deep Spiralling

Deep spiralling into the cavernous abyss of my soul
Darkness threatens to engulf my very being
Oppressive heaviness seems to drag my physical shell.
Into the oblivion created by my own tortured mind.

Problems created, although to others they hold no substance,
Better to keep my own counsel and ultimately become even
    more alone,
Subservience to a society which pays no heed to the emotions of
    it sufferers
But laughs raucously because it does not wish to try to
    understand

The void of my emptiness knows no bounds, and leaves no
    room for hope or sunshine,
The blackness descends once more, to obliterate all feeling
A feeling of despair the only allowed to be experienced
All emotion buried, beneath an exterior which contracts the
    inner self

Acquaintances have tried to glimpse inside my true presence
But none have gained access to the raw essence of my very soul,
No-one can invade the security of my deepest, darkest self,
Which is my solitude, my sanctuary, sometimes even my
    salvation.

But 'life goes on' a blanket of despondency seeming to
    surround all I do
Darkness overhead and all around, still appearing to be my destiny,
Yet they say 'everyone has the power to change' and hope
    for happier times
But the darkness is overwhelming, and threatens to undermine
    my very being.

Lynne Murray

John Masefield, Poet Laureate: A Sonnet

Masefield's John was a great innovator,
He thought that the time had come for a change,
That ev'ryone from the Pole to the Equator
Was entitled to read his "Salt Water" range.
His language was sometimes rough and disgusting,
The ordinary citizen would know it well,
Saul Kane in "The Mercy" was wild and untrusting,
A first-rate candidate heading for hell.
John was made O.M. and Poet Laureate, too,
But this job, to him, was no sinecure,
Poetry was not just for the favoured few,
His mind was so clear and his heart so pure.
    He fought very well and now he is gone,
    My favourite poet; "I salute you, John".

George Barron

A Walk With Nature

My love and I went for a walk
A route we didn't plan,
The sun sifted gently through the clouds
Its rays shaped like a fan.

We strolled along the riverbank.
What creatures would we see,
But all we saw was a tiny vole
Scurrying back home for tea.

A weeping willow bowed her head
And almost kissed the grass,
While a couple of ducks quacked noisily
As a barge chugged slowly past.

A hump back bridge and down the lane
With a soft and gentle breeze,
Which causes the leaves to dance about
On the tall majestic trees.

Seeing all these lovely things
And hearing birds in tune,
When you're with the one you love
Even winter months are June.

Judith Clements

Grandma

No longer as active as she was,
No longer as funny as she was,
Unable to cope with reality any longer
She hides from it all in her sleep.

The familiar things she knows so well
Erase themselves from her memory.
She has no control over it,
She doesn't know me.

Her body aches from the strain,
Of bending to put on her slippers.
The frustration shows in her eyes,
As she is unable to walk alone.

Her body struggles to keep up with her mind,
Even though it too goes slow.
The walking stick is a common feature,
Soon to be a chair.

I like to think of her as she was,
Before the disease, old age, set in.
When her eyes were bright and carefree,
And she recognized and loved me.

Gillian Lycett

The Way, The Truth . . .

Hello! Says Life. And then . . . goodbye.
A taste of joy . . . a long, long sigh.
Sorry! Can't give you another try.
Just time for a smile, and then a cry.
The sun comes up, the sun goes down.
First the laugh, and then the frown.

Maureen Buchanan

Lost Love

Our love was meant to be for life:
  but did it die?
For now the chain that held us fast
  seems loose and we have drifted now
    Apart.
The friendship that was close
  more near than breath
  more dear than life
  and more important than eternity itself
that friendship now is lustreless,
  for something warm has gone.

And so I'll never fall in love again —
  I'd never risk that much.
    Once only could a man risk Destiny,
    and I gave all to what we shared —
    willing to risk what's dear on earth
    and all my hopes beyond.

That was a very special love . . .
  Where did it go?
  I'd like to know . . .
    Eric V. Hudson

A Perfect World

Why do people argue, what makes them want to fight?
There has to be a reason why the world's in such a plight
Little children starving, people being killed
Wars in foreign countries, young men's blood being spilled
If everyone would understand, we have to talk of peace
Learn from words of wisdom, all wars must now cease
Put the past behind us, start our lives anew
Fill our days with useful things, there's so much we can do
Love and help our neighbours, do good when we can
We can build a better world if we just think and plan.
    Connie Fortune

The Oceans Beauty

The ocean is a world of thought,
With its type of love involved in its waves,
No one has experienced what we've been taught,
The beauty of the tide, the rocks and the caves.

We dream to visit the deepest of the deep,
Passing by the life and soul of the fish,
But instead we kill them every week,
And the beauty sits in front of us on a dish.

No one really has a clue of what they are doing,
And say they do, but they don't,
Whilst the dish is half empty, we're sitting there chewing,
They say they'll stop, but you know they won't.

The cycle of destruction will never mend.
You can start the circle but it can not end.
    Rachel McGrath

Amnesia

I can't remember what it was like
To be tiny, pink and smelling of talc
Everyone wanting to hold me and cuddle
This sweet innocent little person
So very vulnerable but cared for
All of the time without any cares.

I can't remember how it started;
To feel passion, desire and give love
Without reservation and receive the same
With the same overwhelming energy.
To feel no inhibitions and free to give
Everything I could to please and be loved.

I can remember how it feels
To have my love rejected and thrown away
Like an empty shell of no further use.
To feel pain as intense as any fire
When realizing there was no return.
I wish I didn't have to remember that feeling.
    Coleen E. Lothe

Christmas Morn

Hasn't seen the ice to glitter so?
Hasn't seen such pureness of the snow?
Hasn't seen such holly berries grow?
But Lo, 'tis Christmas morn.

Each child awakes to wondrous sight,
Has slept excited through the night
Impatient for the new daylight.
To herald Christmas dawn.

With laughter, songs, and gifts to share,
And hearts so light, without a care.
But remember in a manger bare
Where the Holy Child was born.

They bought him gifts of frankincense
And gold and myrrh, and with tenderness
The shepherds knew the Lord to bless.
Them all for evermore.

So now two thousand years from then,
Pray—peace be in the hearts of men
And children know joy in the world again
For Lo, 'tis Christmas morn.
    Rebecca Joel

"Blackfriars By The Thames"

Bathed in August sunshine Blackfriars so transformed
The Thames with silver ripples a rising tide performed

Old HM Ships at anchor still "dressed up" over all
They Royal occasion, a banker when a million people were
"London's Wall"

The river walk, London's river is a treat
behind the traffic's roaring down a London street

Southwark Bridge gleams blue and white in the summer sun
Majestic Tower Bridge, down farther a little to the right

The River Thames gives pleasure
and quite a lot of fun
Passenger boats plough at leisure
in the noon–day sun

A tug is pulling barges busily on its way
Scene—Blackfriars by the river
on such a glorious day

The Thames today is simmering
with a silver crown
Blue skies and sunlight
and people smile, and turn brown
    John D. Ainsley

Mavis' Song

Oh that I had cherished you more
When your sweet presence was still felt,
When love was here for each hour
And time stretched without limit.

You have left such an empty space
Since death has taken you in cold embrace.
Your pain and suffering still lie within me
If I could but see you as you once were.

I try to remember your beauty and serenity
But I have been cheated even of these,
The camera in my head shows only your face
When ravaged by death's wasting disease.

You were so very young to die,
I always believed I would be first
How could you leave me all alone?
To function through each endless hour.

We had something so very special.
Perhaps when time has dimmed the pain
I can think of you more often
With only love in my heart again.
    S. E. Johnson

Untitled

Break me free from these thoughts of mine
and say I'm only dreaming
and promise me each time I wake
I have another day.
Tell me that these fears of mine
have long to be assembled
and leaving all I've come to know
will never reach the brink.
Grant me that though time will pass
we have another life time,
that though the clock must tick away
each minute will not pass.
Our friendships here will never age—
as each day will bring a new,
for is the future not a word
we say in years to come?
Wipe away your sorrows now
for tears shan't be remember—
and although our time has ended here;
your seat is saved by me.

Favil Virr

Silent Friend

Death! I'm not afraid of you, I see you as a friend,
For when you come to call on me my agonies will end.
Don't dally on the threshold, we both know your intent,
To the darkness of your bosom my soul I will relent.

So quit this hesitation! It's so undignified,
I'm begging you, oh silent friend, come lie here by my side,
Squeeze the last breath from me with your dark and fatal power,
The pain is such I can't endure, not even one more hour.

Oh thank you friend, relief is such I really can't explain,
Like shackles being severed, freeing my tortured brain,
Like drifting on a cloud of mist, descending round and round,
I've left my weary body, and tranquillity I've found!

M. J. Attridge

Just A Little

Show a little kindness
As you go along your way;
You never know when you may need
A little kindness back someday.

Share a little laughter
With folk who walk your mile;
For one day the echoes of their laughter
Will reflect within your smile.

Offer a little friendship
When you meet somebody new;
You just may find that friendship
Is what he's brought for you.

Give a little love
To the special one you meet;
And you will find that when you do
Your world will be complete.

Gail A. Allman

Yesterday's Man Today

The year was nineteen hundred and five.
The sky was continuously grey.
He worked in a coal mine, dejected, exposed, vaporous, numb.
His face bold, prematurely looking old, drenched by a lung
devouring black dust. He smiled proudly as he walked down
the street weak and unsteady on his feet.

In the nineteen nineties his son is a modern computer man,
face clear of dust, collar and tie, light yellow suit to match,
clean shaven and tidy. His face looking younger everyday of
every month, of every year. The sky continuously blue. He
smiles proudly as he walks down
the street, strong healthy, and steady on his feet.

Allen Green

Case Under Review

Bouncing bitch with barking bite
Fox, dirt roller of the howl moon rite
Mad dog demon of the scenting hare
Command deaf circler with a knowing sneer
You've chewed our shoes and torn our chairs
Filled house and car with penetrating hairs
I discussed you with the vet last night
Your beastly futures far from bright
We joked of spicy southern dishes
You featured main course in my wishes
It's not good cuddling on my lap
or snuggling to me whilst I nap
Such lack of meat upon the bone!

It would disturb us both to use the phone.

Martin Kelsey

The Lonely Heart

Black as night were my thoughts as I wandered on alone.
Bleak as the wild north wind, my heart was cold as stone.
Wrenched and broken like heavy boughs laden with the snow,
Tramping, plodding on and on for I had far to go.

Which road to take, which stile to climb, which star to guide me there
Oh God of love please pity me and take me in Thy care,
But no-one spoke to comfort me, no guiding hand I felt
And in my anguish, arms outstretched, I stumbled as I knelt.

With clasping hands and trembling voice and bleeding heart I prayed
To trees and stars and sleeping birds, to all things God had made.
But no-one answered, no-one cared, and in my misery
I slumped upon a mossy bank and sleep brought dreams to me

And in my dreams my heart was light, 'twas floating on a wave
The sea was all I thirsted for; it was my lover's grave.
With happy heart and peaceful mind, my eyes the depths could see
And then I heard his gentle voice—"dear love, come down to me".

And slipping quietly from the wave my heart sped far below
Into the dark mysterious depths where plants and flowers grow.
And lying on an emerald bed, I saw my love asleep.
My heart I laid upon his breast forever in his keep.

G. M. Stokes

"Sea To It"

Oh! Sea you can be rough
mariners then have to be tough
Gales with winds force nine
Sailors waiting for it to be fine.
You are greater than the land
Reaching our shores by the sand
Smashing waves against the rocks
Calmly entering bays and lochs
We sail on you in a boat
As a swimmers we swim and float
Miles and miles of sea form an ocean
But still this vastness is all in motion
Then below the surface of the waves
Swims the marine life, some in caves
In the arctic regions you turn to ice
And floating it may look quite nice
But for mariners it spells disaster
Dreaded for every ship's master
So with many waves "Good Bye"
I'll be on the crest of one high!

Denis S. Hudson

I Am Me

Everyone staring from the corner of the room,
There Camera eyes at full zoom,
Inadequate fat and ugly I feel
Absorbing my faults and making a meal.

Are you the beautiful slim and sleek
Or am I the clown so fat and meek
Don't laugh at me I'm not what you see
No matter what covering I am just me.

Susan Vinnicombe

229

The Eyes Of A Child

Two tiny mirrors, like fathomless pools
Slightly glazed, in those first early weeks,
Then they gradually clear, and an innocent stare
May be framed by soft skin and pink cheeks.

They gradually change to a colour,
Perhaps grey, brown, green or blue,
Or perhaps even flecked, and they look so direct,
With a question, which says "who are you?"

They show every kind of emotion,
Of laughter and sadness and fear,
Of hurt, and of joy and of wonder,
But never anger in innocent years.

They can make the hardest heart turn to jelly,
As they look at you, wide, moist and clear,
They can turn unhappiness to sunshine,
Or your world upside down with their tears.

They can smile on their own showing mischief,
And in later years perhaps drive you wild,
But you'll never find love so pure and so sweet,
Than you'll find in the eyes of a child.

Marcia Phillips

Appreciation

To look at the stars on a frosty night,
  To walk in the light of the moon,
To see an owl in silent flight
  As the small mouse ventures too soon.

To awake one morn to a world of white
  With a silence that one can feel,
The snow falling silently during the night
  Makes a magical world unreal.

To see the sun on this world of white
  Shine with a beauty rare,
Surpassing the tranquil beauty of night
  With a breathtaking brightness so fair.

These pleasures cost nothing, but the use of our eyes
  And other senses to feel the pure joy of living
In a world of delight . . .
  Where it's nature that does all things well.

L. F. Verran

Mother

The mother sat in the chair showing no emotions
As she held the burden of the world
On her weak, thin shoulders

One breakage, one sign of weakness
Would mean ruin and failure.
If she was to beat the poverty and worthlessness
Her life was destined for, she had to be strong
Not only in the world, but also the home.

Did she have matter? Was her life meaningful?
Did the unanswered questions running through
Her fragile mind have answers?
Was it all too much for her dictated life to take?

Of course there is no multiple answer
She had to be strong and fight the many prejudices
Society had to offer, after all she sat
Cradling the future in her arms

Kelly Gallagher

Sunset From A Beach

The sun is a semi-circle in orange and gold,
Sitting there on the ocean looking quite bold,
It moves in rhythm with sharp silver waves,
It touches the darkness of creepy beach caves,
It goes down in minutes, every ten by an inch,
When night falls closer it makes your eyes flinch,
It's finally gone—not sure where to,
But if you go there tomorrow it will be there for you.

Victoria Bennett

Changed

So shy, so quiet, is the way I use to be,
Never known to speak and never know to see,
Until one day I changed, I saw the light;
The world became known to me, my life
was now bright.

The very first moment I saw you in my sight,
I knew it was time to speak my mind
and to feel my inside,
So now I tell you what's happened to me,
No longer the person I use to be,
So happy, so glad that I met you,
You bring me happiness and lots
of joy too,
So, what else is left to say,
Well, that I love you!

Bahar Cemal

A Little Spark Of Progress

You're a little boy of four years old
yet so much younger in mind
you can't walk, talk, nor even see
why was nature so unkind?

"I couldn't do the work you do"
has been expressed many a time to me
It's what the child can, not cannot do
that holds the precious key

It opens up new ways of thinking
this is a good place to start
build on what he's already got
in body, in soul, in heart

You like being tickled, you smile and laugh
babbling sounds, you hear so well
then one day you heard my voice
what followed, made my heart swell

A wave of emotion came flooding over me
as you lifted your head, saying my name
a little spark of progress
but to me, a burning flame!

Lynn Begley

Memories

Let us remember the good times,
  The laughter and fun that we've had—
We know that in life things are not always good,
  Sometimes we're unhappy and sad.
But let us remember the good times,
  Not dwell on the sadness and tears . . .
Remember those things that bring smiles to our lips,
  Happy memories down through the years.

Sue Deft

Sounds

Have you ever laid in the sun,
Soaking up its rays?
And listened to the different sounds
That mark a Summer's day?
The lazy splash of a waterfall,
As it gently tumbles the rocks,
And the quiet humming of the bees,
As they seek out different stock,
The chirp of an insect just by your ear,
That makes you shift about,
And the distant lowing of the herd,
Mingled with stockman's shout,
The gentle rustle of the grass,
As a field vole scuttles by,
And the quick blue flash against the clouds,
As a Swallow cuts the sky,
The Ringneck doves gently break your sleep,
With their soft and gentle call,
And you realize then that the day is past,
Enclosed in Nature's Hall.

Richard G. West

Dad

Oh my father you wonderful man,
You were good from evil you ran,
I love you still though death us do part,
You went from me with love in your heart.

Oh how I suffered when you had to go,
Feigning joy so you would not know,
I have no regrets for things that have passed,
You're now at peace, the pain did not last.

There's no beginning there is no end,
Life's a circle, death is a friend,
In the circle you're old and then you die,
In that circle you're born and a baby will cry.

You're now in Eden with family you share,
Though you are far you will still care,
I love you still though death us do part,
Please wait for me with love in your hearts.

Joan Guignard

War

War is horrible, war is bad.
When I hear about war it makes me sad.
To see refugees homeless, like souls lost.
It's not the money, it's the lives that cost.

Not many have the will to live.
What will the children inherit?
There is nothing to give.
Sadness and hate is what most possess.
War has made their lives a mess.

They have no homes, in camps they stay.
How much longer will it be this way?
I wish the war would end tomorrow.
It would be an end to all this sorrow.

Martine Swaep

Sunset

The sun burns like a ball of fire in the sky,
You sit so small, in awe of what you see as
blood red, melts to cherry then to pink.
Drawn into this world show piece, thought has no place,
Silence rules. All senses are awakened but have no voice.

The melt down marks the end of one more day,
In celebration of life, it provides its great display.
As the colour fades the spell is broken.
The chill sets in and your mind once more begins to function,
Your soul is released and life is once more a burden.

Such a scene is stored within for times of sadness,
Its power never fades. It revives your spirit when all else is dark.
As you savour its beauty, your mind is slowly healing.
Although each day comes to an end, rebirth shortly follows,
With such vigour and delight, it drowns all of man's sorrows.

Sara Burns

Fear Is . . .

Fear is a baby taking his first step
Students sitting for exams
A first drive out in the car
or a phobia of spiders.
Sleeping in the dark
With thunder all through the night.
Or waves crashing against the shore
As the stormy seas rock the boats alive.

Fear is being threatened by a bully
Graduating but not employed.
Having no place to live
Alone in a strange place.
Possessed by evil forces
knowing when danger is near.

Fear is being afraid,
A feeling of dread, alarm and anxiety.

JeeMei Yau

Pottery

An appreciation of the oil painting by Paul Caulfield (1969)

Red announces itself like a storm.
Yellow follows closely, a snake.
And green, blue, purple make their mark.
But white, pink, orange hide,
So all to see
Is only timid edges.

Carefully cut in half by dimensions,
Two and three.

Up is two,
With clear–cut black.
Ascending . . . fading,
To tiny curves and circles.

Down is Three,
With empty eyes.
Descending . . . booming
To mind–filling solids.

Thin sharp black and space.
Obvious contrast.
Bright . . . alive
And rotation performs.

Joanna Cock, aged 16 yrs.

The Unknown

It was cold in that dark, dark alley,
and rats ran here and there.
Nobody ever came to the place
There was no one there to care.

No sunlight could ever get in there,
on the other hand—nor could the moon,
It was always sad and dark there,
No morning, night or noon.

'Unhealthy' was how they described it
for of course, none of them dared
to admit to anyone else there,
That deep down inside, they were scared.

It was said that once, a man had been seen,
with a wizened face, and a beard,
He was, I expect a ghost of the past
The unknown that everyone feared.

One day, perhaps, the sun will shine though
and children play there with their toys
and instead of the rats and the white bearded ghost,
We'll hear laughter of young girls and boys.

Mary Jones

Saturdays

Saturday is here again, my heart is torn in two,
For Daddy's come to take us out, but Mummy can't come too.
We go out to the seaside, sometimes a special trip,
Just pretending to be happy, but I bite my bottom lip.

For nothing seems to be the same, unless we all can go,
The days are gone of family fun, they won't come back I know.
Back home again, full up with treats, we're told to say 'Goodbyes',
We kiss our Dad and hug him tight, there's tears in Daddy's eyes.

We run indoors as he drives off, to show our Mum new toys,
She hugs us tight and draws us close and says, 'I love you boys'.
My Mum and Dad have 'split' they say, I don't really understand
My little brother starts to cry, I gently take his hand.

I try to comfort him and say, 'Our Dad will soon be back'.
He thinks that's fine, but I just know, a Dad is what we lack!
I wish they'd kiss and make up, stop making all this fuss,
Be happy like we were before, why don't they think of us?

The emptiness won't go away, the house seems really lonely,
I long to have my Dad around, if only, Oh if only!
So Saturdays I learn to dread, that's when I feel most sad,
The moment when we say 'Goodbye', Dad says, 'Til next week lad'.

Sonia Mills

Thoughts

What can I do to ease the pain that lies so deep within
And tell you all my secret thoughts, but how do I begin
I need the key to open up my heart so you can hear
These feelings that are locked away and yet so very near
The sorrow that it causes the heartache and the tears
Have built up inside of me over all these years
I am holding on and won't let go it's cutting me in two
I've never asked for help before please tell me what to do
People say just let it go and then your heart is free
I pray that this will happen Lord because you hold the key

T. Markbride

Lament For The Rain Forest

Fertile once but barren now
Stripped of all she once held dear
Cowering naked—downcast eyes
The joy of youth replaced by fear
Memories of what had been
Soaring high and home to all
Grasping, greedy chain saws march
And Oh! The mighty how they fall
Worshipped in those distant days
Her gifts gave pleasure—but no respect
Men took their share—demanded more
Rape and pillage-burn-dissect
Fertile once but barren now
The gifts are gone—no life around
Vanished is the Shangri-La
Just a stretch of ashy–blackened ground

Eve Salmon

Untitled

In a world with no meaning how can
one person mean so much to another
How can one small thing mean so
much that it takes over a life, if this
one small thing take over such a
massive thing as an entire life How
can this one thing take a normal
thing like hurt and turn into such a
massive aching pain that trashes a
person How can this small thing
take happiness and turn it into such
immense joy How can such a small
thing dictate so much

Maybe it's not such a small thing if it
can do so much, change so many
things, hurt so many people
How come it's such a small word

Philip A. Bennett

Angel Of The Twilight Zone

Have you seen a little white haired girl
Barefoot, running down the lane.
Don't know where she's going, poor child,
Did you hear her call my name?
An angel of the twilight zone.
Don't know who or where you are
Lost down the path of life
Poor daffodil so fair.

Wants to take large airplanes home
Big ships from out the bay.
Collect all the world's iron
To keep it all for play.

I see you just standing there,
Seeking, searching what's not there.
Trying to catch a rainbows end
And bright stars everywhere.
Time has just stood still for you.
Somehow it's just not there.
Oh angel of the Twilight Zone
Pure daffodil so fair

John McDonnell

City Night

Walking through the city night,
engulfed in the darkness exposed by the light.
Watch your shadows stretch then condense,
anxiety of the day seems less intense.
Getting the night in the city,
street corner sirens, seems a pity.
Attention dressers are ignored, too vain.
Strangers incognito, seem arcane.
Shop dummies seem to have minds
The zombies on the streets have left theirs behind.
The dummies have moving eyes.
They are having a game, we just don't realize.
Spin round one called your name.
Don't be embarrassed you know you're sane?
They dress and follow to the club you are in.
Then return unnoticed as day breaks again.

Frank Hall

A Chocoholic Moment . . .

Chocoholics crave chocolate in any state or form.
Hot chocolate, solid chocolate and even chocolate cakes.
On Mondays, Tuesdays, Wednesdays, Thursdays . . .
Chocolate every day and night.
One bar perhaps or maybe two or three.
Luscious, yummy chocolate, yes that's the stuff for me!
And it has to be made by Cadbury, Nestle or Rowntree.
Time outs, Yorkies, Boosts and Mars Bars . . . (Oh the list goes on
forever I don't know where to stop).
Eat chocolate when you're happy, sad or just feeling bored,
but one thing is for sure that chocolate is the cure!

Sara Chadwick

"An Ode To My Friend" "Breath of Life"

"Thirty three" years from today: I met my life long friend.
The ward, was named "St. Hillier",
where babies first stated their claim
With babies' cries echoing through the rooms:
It was the "Happiest" year of the baby boom.
"Sheila's" my name! How are you? I am feeling, pretty
"Groggy" and "Blue"—The "Labour Ward"—filled with "Mums,"
carrying around, their heavy tums—whilst Sheila
"Slim still! Walking around! Leaving me! "Round" and Plump"
Holding on—to some "whale" of a "bump"
We saw each hour of the night—until the early morn/radiant
and bright.
"A beautiful" bouncing baby boy "Born to me"
"This was Russell my son you see.
To "Sheila" my friend
"The precious gift of a girl."
Linda was her name.
Some "Thirty-three" years on! We both chat, and smile.
Agreeing it was all!—Well and Truly worthwhile!

Rachel Baker

Untitled

"Send me to springtime in childhood, innocence, truth!
My harvest the wind flower, withering fast.
I seek the woodlands' secret bower
To find the primrose and coltsfoot flower.

Bring me to summer full, sensuous, sweet.
Red roses pick'd for passion's flight.
Body with earth tuned to the bright sun's
Zenith, on the noonday race.

Give me grace in my autumn years, dear Lord!
With harvest of all my life has been.
Memories of roses, endless days of sun
Now but shadows on the moon's soft run.

Winter comes unbidden. Now beckons my mortality.
The sky weeps frozen tears for all mankind.
Upon the gale until a quietness steals and lo!
Sweet snow falls softly over all the earth
      And all earth's griefs are gone."

Susan C. Jones

Whose Fault?

She sits silently, clutching her babe to her breast,
She knows that only time will tell
That death is for the best.

The scorching heat dries the already barren ground,
Her eyes cry out in agony,
But she never makes a sound.
The tiny child's distended stomach heaves a last farewell,
His sufferings are over now,
At last he's free from hell.

You say that God loves everyone; so how can He stand by
And watch this awful suffering, and hear the children cry?
Why does He stop the rainfall and parch the barren land?
How can He let this happen and never raise His hand?

My friend, why must we pass the blame when the fault lies
    with you and me?
Are we too blind to notice, or don't we want to see?
There's food enough for everyone, if we only had a care,
God's given to us in plenty, it's up to us to share.

Susan Hall

Breakfast In February

Jenny Wren came looking for her breakfast
To the rockery to see what hides
Beneath the plants and in the sides
What has she seen? Something bright green.

Deftly she pulls it out
A caterpillar so big and stout
Just when she is about to eat
A Goldcrest lands at her feet.

He might be the smallest British bird
But on tiptoe he stands so tall
And makes Jenny Wren feel so small
Defeated, she leaves him to eat her meat.

However come September, Goldcrest lost his tree
His conifer was cut down due to a mistake
He had the biggest loss and paid dearly for his greed
Jenny Wren is still here to have her feed.

Myrtle E. Holmes

My Fall

I've fallen down the class ladder to the bottom rung,
I don't know how it happened or indeed when it was done—
I just know I had money once and now I'm very poor,
And some so-called friends went with my wealth—
Of that I can be sure.
So from upper class to lower I slid gently to the floor,
I did not feel it happen until I could fall no more—
But the strangest thing in all of this in spite of lack of "dosh"—
My life is so much richer than at the time when I was "posh".
I've got a wealth of love in my life that money couldn't buy—
A stash of friends and happiness I couldn't price-tag if I tried,
So all's not lost—I've learned so much and don't regret at all
The upper class I grasped—then lost
When I had my fall.

Gillie Bishop

True Friends

You're warm, cuddly and caring too
Yes my friend I do mean you
When I come home you're always there
With always a wag of the tail to share
Watching your antics makes me happy
Because we're such good friends you're never snappy
To make you happy is all I wish
That's quite easy just fill up your dish
If I give you a ball or a toy
Your eyes they sparkle and light up with joy
A chewy treat wouldn't go amiss
You'd shake a paw or roll over for this
To have a dog is to have a friend
The love you share will never end.

L. Mawdsley

View From A Window

I look from my window on a view so serene,
Hills topped with snow, no green to be seen.
The birch trees, covered in frost, shine bright,
Truly, as silver, a wondrous sight.
The loch so still, as a sheet of glass,
Colour uncertain, I wait for clouds to pass.
A faint ray of sunshine, hits the top of a tree,
Ice blue sky, in the distance I see.
A heron, so regal, goes gliding by,
To join the seagulls, high in the sky.
Their calls loud and clear, in the cold morning air,
Sharp eyes on the water, as they congregate there.
The gulls swoop and dive and downward they go,
Silent now, settling in the water below.
The heron continues to fly back and fore,
Then suddenly turns and heads for the shore,
To slowly glide down to the bank of the stream
There is stands, tall, still, all quiet, let it dream.

Margaret Jean Thomson

Every Day And Night

Every single night, I say that same old prayer,
Hoping that someday he will really care.
I want him to hear me.
I want him here with me.

But in his world, I am not included,
Yet anything he does, I am not deluded.
He'll never see
The feelings inside me.

Every single day, I get that same old feeling,
As though something about him is going to be revealing.
My hopes begin to rise
When he looks into my eyes.

But the feelings I've got will never come true.
He will never say, "I love you."
Dreams will not deceive me.
So why can't I believe me?

Laura McAulay

Drifting

Sitting alone with only the silence which surrounds me,
I have nothing but the little air I breath and the
memories which are slowly disappearing like my soul,
I hear the wind whispering softly,
The sound comforts me and I feel myself drifting further
from my body.
I don't feel alone or lost anymore, but somehow I feel free,
Free from this world's destruction,
I am dying like the world around us all,
Nobody cares,
And as I start to see the brightness of a light ahead I
wonder if finally I will be free.

Sonya L. Davison

My Pet

Oh I thought he loved me,
Till me flew out the door,
Up into the tree stops.
That stood so still and tall.

His cage stands empty now.
The room so silent and calm,
Upon that bright and sunny day
My little bird flew away.

I've looked everywhere for him.
Asking people I don't even know,
Now it looks like rain,
No I think it could be snow.

My feet ache, my head in a spin,
I wonder what will become of him,
Home once more, oh what can I see,
Yes it's my little friend waiting for me.

E. A. Bennett

I Am The Sea

I am the sea
I am as big as the earth
I reach up high and touch the sky
I go on forever, never stopping
When I am mad, very mad I twirl and wave and blow
   and knock big ships from side to side
When I am happy, very happy
I am as smooth as butter, I shine like velvet blue
I carry big ships from port to port loaded with socks and shoes
And food to keep people going
I keep creatures under my coat some are big, some are small
I feed them all
But sometimes humans cannot see I can be as cruel as cruel can be
I swallow big ships and treasures and all devour fishermen
   catching my fish
I stay still for artists to draw my beautiful coat of blue
For poets, I show myself so they can write about me
I let them draw me even when I'm as mad as a wild horse
I am a jewellery store, giving my jewels to those earth people
   to show them off

Stephen Quinn

Agoraphobia

I view the world through patterned net,
a sombre, insubstantial place
of muted hues; my neighbours race
to and fro like clockwork toys,
aliens, unreal, remote from me.
I turn to look into my room,
a womb-like cell where I can be
safe, secure, unworried, free
from fear, the all–pervading fear
that keeps me prisoner. I'll stay here!

I'll lift the corner of the net.
A moment's gaze. I'm safe inside!
Out there is grief and pain—I'll hide.
I'll stay cocooned. There's the door,
a step or two alone? But no,
I might be ill—one day I'll go.
But then I drew aside the net,
I dared to enter through the door
that leads to life, and even more
to victory. And yet—I'll not forget!

Margaret Walker

Untitled

I once had a dream that I was king
And I had the power to do everything,
I'd raise my hand, and famine was gone,
And even the blackbirds burst into song

Disease and illness was a thing of the past,
And loving one person, was made to last
There was no dole-queue, no one was poor.
And no one was made to go to war.

There were no muggers or killers of men.
Children were safe, and played with their friends
There was no rape of women, all were safe
At last, this world was a better place

Louis Fraser Forsyth

Impossibilities And Miracles

Impossibilities, the mind must equate,
Cannot be performed in the natural state,
Miracles are performed by one adept,
Before your eye if you just accept,
The evidence you see is truly real,
Unless of course you just don't feel,
That what you saw didn't take place,
Impossible, but it's something that you must face,
Impossibilities, the mind must equate,
Cannot be performed in the natural state.

Robert Dodds

Forever

How hearts must yearn to see them now
Dismiss the years that have gone and know
It was just a dream, and all is good
Oh if only we could, if only we could

Our only comfort, small though it be
To visit afar—to travel and see
Some piece of stone, all gleaming white
His name upon it, shining bright

Oh my darling boy, so here you are
I've searched the world, I've travelled far
Worried and wondered about your fate
To find you here at this late date

For years and years as time has flown
I only wish that I had known
How it happened you came to be here
My need so great to hold you near.

Can I rest now that I know all this?
Do I have peace—to live in bliss?
Oh no, it's not like that at all
Forever, forever you'll hear my call.

Hunt

Patience

Why does my heart trouble me so, why can't I let my feelings for
him go? I love him and yet deep down inside—
My happiness drains through me like the last midnight tide . . .

I want him and still I know he's not mine, but the very thought
Of him makes me smile—he's special to me in a strange sort of
Way and sometimes I wonder—not knowing time or day

Is this love? So fickle, so false? Or the prison in which my
Heart beats on barbed walls which torture and strain my poor,
Weary brain into wondering if he'll ever love me the same—

My feelings are those that only a female can feel
When that man that she finds takes her heart to steal
I'll wait for a day: No! I'll wait for a year, I'll wait for this
Man who I think is so dear . . .

But after all this I know deep inside that unless it is mutual
My feelings will subside—for there is only so much that one
Person can take and I've only one heart that this man can break

So what will I do, dear reader, please say—should I give up or
Continue this way? One thing is clear and this much I know,
It'll take quite some time for these feelings to go . . .

Rowena Rumbelow

Springtime

The winter chills have left us and the sun is shining through
The skylark wings his way across the sky
The garden is a mass of bloom and underneath the bower
The speedwell looks around with starry eyes

The delicate white snowdrops and the cheerful aconite
Are the first to show their flowers in the Spring
The pure white narcissus and the golden daffodils
Stand tall as they sway gently in the wind

Nestling in the hedgerows with their faces to the light
Are the primroses and violets, full of charm
The clusters of muscari, bluer than the bluest skies
Shelter, with the polyanthus, by the palm

The tulips in their majesty, so sturdy to behold
Display their glorious colours, pink or purple, white or gold
Forget-me-nots protect them as they bloom around their feet
And the bluebells spread their carpet in the woodlands—
   what a treat!

Sleeping through the winter in the ground so cold and bare
It's hard to realize that they can come to life from there
But the good Lord in his wisdom breaks the hardened soil asunder
And sends to us the beauty that fills all our hearts with wonder

G. M. Neary

The 7th Candle

The 7th candle glows,
A spine chilling wind blows.
The mantelpiece changes a darker shade,
My silhouette began to fade.

I see my life flash before my eyes,
The bad things I did my conscious denies.
The 7th candle lights again,
My body fills with unbearable pain.

An angel came down unto me,
Bearing a light so bright I could not see.
She held out her hand to lead me away,
The 7th candle went astray.

Simon Houlders

To My Daughter

Today is your silver anniversary,
It's time to celebrate,
The world is your oyster,
Out there for you to take,
you are two special people,
That God made man and wife,
He knew, that you would be together,
Through all your natural life,
One day when you both grow old,
you will look back in time,
and remember all those years you shared,
and treasure for all time
Right now its not important,
The world is at your feet
you have a life to live,
and pastures you've not seen,
Then one day, you will look around,
Then know, those memories,
were the only seeds you've sown.

C. Glendining

Communication Skills

I can speak. I know how to communicate.
I can shout. I know how to communicate.
I can write. I know how to communicate.
I can protest peacefully. I know how to communicate.
I can protest violently. I know how to communicate.
If you noticed my peaceful protest, I wouldn't need to protest
    violently.
If you noticed my report, I wouldn't need to protest.
If you noticed me shouting, I wouldn't need to write a report.
If you noticed me speaking, I wouldn't need to shout.
I know how to communicate.

Alvan J. Lewis

The Snow

Snow, a great white show
a blanket of ivory shining bright
sunshine revealing diamonds glimmering, glitter shimmering
snow so cold to touch and hold,
turns to water so fresh and pure.

Clouds all grey, bleak on this day
Cushions enfolding more feathery flakes
they fall lightly gliding drifting
whether breeze or not.

Trees all white clasping cotton wool on branches
One small breeze the disperse of shreds
to carpet the floor of the outdoor beds.
Bright is our light no bulb to bare, enlightening,
to see it feels you're in a stare.

People pink faced and full of glare
footprints leaving their place on the ground
animal or human, whatever found, signs of life.
Another day fades away, darkness falls
on white sceneries, instead of black

Diana Neill

My Baby

Sleep well my baby
Sleep softly and sweetly in the arms of Jesus.
Do not feel the pain of an anguished world
wrought with murder and destruction.
I borrowed you for such a short while
dried your tears, saw you smile.
Now you are free to live your dreams.
Your soul can dance with the angels.
Sleep well my baby
I know you will not wake—you are gone forever
Yet forever you are in my heart.

Elsie Francis

Revelation One

Once again, I loudly complain
Of the troubles dropped on me today.
There was rain, that blocked up the brain
So the kids couldn't go out to play.

I made an appeal, for my troubles reveal
Someone must have shown a black ball.
Truth is real, and nought can conceal
That my troubles were nothing at all.

I began to pray, and that took all day
In seeking a sign from our Lord.
A star seemed to say, go out of your way
To visit some people abroad.

Troubles you'll find, to boggle your mind
That is borne with acceptance and grace.
To those of that kind, are usually blind
But look for the smile on His face.

Frank Williams

Moonstruck

Moon arises, life begins, an owl hoots and bats its wings.
With a shuttle of legs and a scurry of feet,
The mice weave in throughout the wheat.
The owl calls out into the night,
Its young need food before it's light.
She picks up sound and rises up,
Tonight, maybe she is just in luck.
The young so weak they need their fill,
Their mother knows and tries to kill,
Swooping down with outstretched claws
She hears a noise, it makes her pause.
A man and gun appear at gate,
The owl is doomed into her fate.
The shot is pulled without a stutter,
"Good hunt tonight!" I heard one mutter.
No babies get fed and they too will die,
Sit back and think, all this, but why?
Because man is mean and nothing's considered,
But nature will hit back when poor man has withered.

Deborah Kenton

War!

As we advanced like a walk in the park,
The enemy troops aimed for the mark,
The cannons fired as the doomed marched on,
Till the last man dead and gone,
I fail to see the point of war,
With its dead and dying on the floor,
Pointless, painful, blood and gore,
Help feed insanity's ravenous maw.
As we advanced like a walk in the park
Heaven and hell did grow quite dark,
Across the death field bleak and stark,
Did man's insanity leave its mark.
I demand the point of war,
With our hate and evil at its core,
How many are to feed its maw,
Man's bitter nemesis,
Bloody war!

John Robert Hill

On Watching Testament Of Youth

How talk of war when that's a world away,
Yet moves more closely still with each new breath of day,
The flickering screen portrays a generation's call,
When splendid youth gave gloriously its all.
Now we know the squalor of that bitter field,
And when at bugles blast how barren was its yield.

And now more dangerously we blithely move towards our doom,
And talk of how, how not, and sometime maybe soon,
Oh God! On whom we rest our merry strength and meagre promises,
Guide us and turn us from our wilful wantonness,
And help us in the world's dark night of soul,
To love our bickering freedom more than war's most
    terrible irrevocable toll.

Haidee Turner

Strangers In The Night

I couldn't go to sleep till quarter to three
Everybody was awake, including you and me
The whole world came alive, from midnight till dawn
I felt like a deer or was it a fawn
Maybe it was you, maybe it was me
Whatever it was, I couldn't get free
And couldn't close my eyes
Because this whole town came alive
Then out of the night came a satellite or two
Whatever it was I suddenly fell asleep
Then I woke it was quarter to five
At last it was dawn, not a cloud was in sight
The world was fast asleep, except the birds that sang so sweet
Black night had turned to aqua blue
That quickly changed to powder blue
With just few stars to show the way and half a moon to light the way.

Joan Ester Maryan

April

Temperatures rising, land of gold, April's here, I'm sold
April, April, April, it's nice now you are here
To see so many colours brings me so much cheer.

Oh, daffodils in abundance and tulips holding tight
With pretty, pretty primroses for sheer delight.
The magnolia is magnificent sure you would agree
Pink blossom in profusion sways gently on breeze

April, April, April yes thank the Lord I see
A technicolour of azaleas sheltered from cold winds
I just love April and everything she brings

Birds are building, quickly, yet another work of art
They're so happy singing, even when showers start.
The scent from the osmanthus that so openly transmits
Is just another part of April, of April's bliss.

Trees are looking beautiful, so beautiful lush green
With their tinted colours that make up April's scene
And bluebells in woodlands just waiting for you
Millions upon millions that stand still to view

I only wish April that you could stay this way
April, April, April, you must give way to May.

David Black

Autumn

Autumn is the best time of the year.
The leaves change colour from green to gold,
Such a lovely sight after summer has passed,
The air is fresh, we hope it will last.

When autumn comes the sounds are rare,
The birds do twitter and the trees are bare.
Once more we whisper as time passes us by,
Autumn don't leave us, or we shall die.
The weather just changes from warm to the cold,
Sometimes we suffer, the young and the old.
But as we walk along life's way, hoping to see another day,
The seasons come and change the air, but I think,
"Autumn is just the best time of the Year".

Annette Brotherton

St. Paul—His Mission In Greece

St. Paul, great Apostle to the Gentiles
Jewish Sanhedrin of persecution,
Received an apocalyptic vision
On Damascus road he made his conversion.

St. Paul, God's mouthpiece his writings to the Greeks.
The Acts of the Apostles proclaim his mission in Misia.
A second vision, beseeching was a Man of Macedonia.
He travelled through Phrygia, finally reached Galatia.

St. Paul, denouncer, postulator against idolatry.
Left Veria for Athens from the foot of Mount Olympus,
Came before the Council of the Areopagus,
Debated matters religious; converted Dionysius.

St. Paul, criticised, molested, feared by the Jews.
"This man contrary to law preaches the Gospel."
They reported him to Gallia, the Roman proconsul,
Jewish demands of execution he refused to fulfil.

St. Paul, inspired minister, narrator, author.
Returned to Jerusalem, faced arrest, the governor.
Appeared before Roman tribunals—was charged a traitor,
Appealed to Caesar—failed, was beheaded, became a martyr.

Mary Pelidis

The White Horse Of Dartmoor

He gallops free across the moor
This beautiful white horse
With mane a-flow and head tossed high
He travels through the gorse

The sun shines bright
The skies are blue
The blends in with
This moorland hue

But when the snow comes on the tors
And winter's here again
The grass has gone no food to eat
He shivers in the rain

Down to Widecome he'll roam to shelter through the day
And kindly villagers will see he gets a feed of hay

For Dartmoor can be very bleak and beautiful as well
But if this horse could only speak of this I'm sure he tell

So if you go to Dartmoor and see its tors and streams
Look out for this pure white horse for he is not a dream

For he is wild and he is free to wander as he will
In the woods near the stream or just standing on the hill

N. Gill

Restless Ecstasy

The sun–filled sky of the spring
The unknown face behind the clouds
Drifting through the ashes of my memory.
Now, the out of focus shadow
You shall wither away.

Riding on a road to a place
A place called paradise, a place of spirit,
A dimension of light and love,
The only place of justice,
Where rivulets are of pure honey.

Dawn and twilight,
The earth's everlasting companies,
Just like a tender flower,
Without the admiration of the rain
To nourish faith in you.

Weeping for the life your wishes never led.
No longer a destiny to fulfil. Lying shadowless at last,
In restless ecstasy, in eternal rest.
All the serenity you gained
With the departure of your soul. Escaped.

Bahareh Javid

One Day In The Life . . .

The rustle of leaves, a shaft of light,
the first sounds of life it's the end of the night,
the morning explodes, the quietness gone,
another busy day, let's join in the throng.

The sound, the smell, the polluted street,
we are closed in our cars, our souls never meet,
the stifled rage of emotional turmoil,
the distinctive stench of fumes to de-spoil.

One day in the life of a human being,
what chance have we of openly seeing,
what damage there is and will be forever,
unless we strive and try to endeavour

Lets draw in a breath and take a look
at a brand new page, a glossy new book
lets all break free like a fountain of birds,
and hold in our hands a poem of words

Words can be changed with the swiftness of hand,
our futures, our lives can this be re-planned
Lets build a world full of brightness and cheer,
one day in the life of that we hold dear!!

Vanessa Ball

Crystal II

A great yellow moon hangs in the sky
The black earth below is slim and bleak
A door comes to light, etched sharply in both.

So you can walk to the moon . . . ?
A lamp shows the way.
The moon takes on the shades.
A ceiling and door coolly welcome, sub-lining the way.
A clinical workshop spans the globe, holding it firm.

A delicious pink Dorad sits aloft;
A firm black mussel waits below;
Two lights show the way . . .
All this in the moon.

Two roving eyes watch through the moon . . .
Or are they men with torches coming for me?

The tension's too great, a divider in the brain.
A great hand steals from the moon,
The pink, black, to grey.

Yellow rises again, against the black earth.
Peace in each hand, stroking the brain . . .
Peace and near sleep.

Mike Watts

Poem Of The Honest Truth By Two Ex-Visionaries

What is the answer to a question?
Make it as easy as you would like it to be.
Why is the earth not flat?
There would be no hills to climb.
Where has it all come from?
Some say there is a God.
Who do people think he is?
I think he is the solution to all our dilemmas.
When will he come back again? Ask a stupid question . . .
How do you define love? Look in the Bible.
Which is the best book to find it in?

It is all full of knowledge, but in riddles. Love, I think,
is pain and pleasure mixed into an imaginary ball
and thrown at the unsuspecting offenders of being innocent.
This is my theory: my own Bible.
Love is the question to all answers. It is a mystery of
everything we do, whether it is for pleasure or for our own gain.

So, when does this "ball" come and strike you?

It happens when freedom turns to obligation.
It is the same as your heart being threatened with a gun
and thrown into the prison for gullible believers of the word "love".

R. A. Goslitski

Searching for the Stars

Set before me, around me, surrounding me,
Some might call it night
But look again through a stranger's eye
A stranger not to sight, but to soul.

Only then might you see,
Not a darkness but a light
Which suddenly shines forth from this once black prison,
A star with such might, and your eyes engulfed stare.

From these eyes a glory can be seen,
The darkness is overridden,
And the speck of light gleams gloriously calling of a
beauty within once hidden, now shining so bright.

Set before me, around me, surrounding me,
some might say it's fearful
But only if you haven't seen the light,
Of Hope, of Strength, Of Happiness
No more tearful.
This strangered soul no longer,
But tinged with glory gleaming, united as one.

Clare Kelly

A Woman's Lament

He says he really loves me
So how could he forget our anniversary
He says he really loves me
So why can't he remember I don't like peas
He says he really loves me
So why doesn't he listen when I tell him of my day
He says he really loves me
So why can't he help in the house sometimes
He says he really loves me
So why can't he find time to talk to me
He says he really loves me
So why do I feel so alone
He says he loves me.
Really?

M. Marshall

Fund-Raising

I was asked to help and fund-raise for the local
    handicapped unit
I hadn't done anything like this before and
    wasn't sure I could do it.
At first I was quite nervous and didn't think it
    was my style
Approaching people for donations took me quite a while
It then became much easier and my confidence increased
People were very generous and put me at my ease
We arranged discos, jumble sales, raffles and fairs
Bingo, spot the ball, fancy dress and games
Everything we could think of was turned into an event
And very much to our surprise
People thought their money well spent.
The money now was regularly coming in and I
    had caught the bug.
Fund-raising can be very hard work
But also lots of fun.

Mollie Crawshaw

Laughter

The next time you meet a friend of yours
Why not say something daft
Because I'll guarantee you this much
That your friend will start to laugh.

Now laughter's like the sunshine
It brightens everything around
And cheers the hearts of those who hear
Its very happy sound.

So take some time for laughter
and make it part of every day
Then just like the warm sunshine
It will chase all your clouds away.

Michael Rielly

Quiet Moments

Take a quiet moment out of your busy life
Let your mind meander away from stress and strife
Reflect upon God's blessings, be they great or small
That at one time, or another, are bestowed upon us all.

Take a quiet moment sometime in the day
Dream awhile, and ponder, let your thoughts stray
Not to what you cannot do, but to what you can
Always be that person who will lend a helping hand.

Take a quiet moment, time to understand
All the imperfections in your fellow man
Each of the failings in ourselves which we don't see
For nobody is perfect, none of us fault free.

Take a quiet moment to pause, to realize
All the wonders of creation right before our eyes
So beautiful, so bountiful, everything given free
To us, from God with love, unreservedly.

Mary Holder

Changes

It used to be peaceful here, calm and serene
Now it presents quite a different scene.
The views of gentle hills, green fields and trees,
Are now of machines, rushing around like bees.
First came the bypass, bisecting the land,
Then a housing estate, much too close at hand,
A refinery is viewed from the kitchen sink,
Now a sewerage work, oh dear what a stink.
The noise and the dust and the smell jar the mind,
Progress it's called but I don't find it kind.
Gradually industry is fencing us in
The rape of the countryside is surely a sin.
How nice it would be to have you own space,
To be one with nature forget the rat race.
But those days are gone and will be no more,
Oh! To turn back the clock and be like before.

L. E. Oakley

Lost Loved One

Deep in my eyes you see the hurt
But you cannot feel the pain
Of the day my sunshine stole away
And tears fell down like rain

A thousand thoughts won't bring you back
I know—because I've tried
A million tears won't bring you back
I know—because I've cried.

Fate breaks a very fragile heart
But love is not in vain
God slowly puts the pieces back
And wipes away the pain

S. Cox

Summer's Retreat

Summer is over, she's played her part well,
it's time to depart, to bid us farewell.
Autumn approaches, brings chill to the air,
trees that were green, shed their leaves, now stand bare.

Hedgerows once so colourful, bright
Now stand empty, void of all life.
Migrating birds take off on cue,
Leaving our shores, for pastures a new.

Fields that did flourish with fine golden corn,
cut down for the harvest, lay barren forlorn,
the roses of summer, hang on till the last,
but even they soon, will fade and pass.

Temperature's dropping, frost on the ground,
soon we'll be greeted, with snow all around.
As the hours of darkness lengthen and grow,
My heart feels much sadness, to see summer go.

Colin W. Howard

Olive Trees

The blazing hot sun shining down,
On the dry crisp ground,
The Olive Trees swaying in the cool breeze,
Jagged lilac mountains,
Gnarled Olive Trees,

Wavy leaves,
Dark knobbly branches,
Crooked tree trunks,
The hot sweltering air,
The scorching hot floor.

Nicola Schofield

Teenagers

Stress and tension from school and home
"Finish your homework, don't dare moan"
Struggling with course work, is it right?
You can't afford to sleep tonight

Rushing out on the perfect date
Get a move on don't be late!
Couldn't Mum just take the hint?
You need some money, you're totally skint

Struck with acne and seaweed hair
Your earring's broken, nothing to wear
You're meant to be going to the club in town
Your skirt's too small and your top gapes down

The average problems were mentioned above
Spots, homework or falling in love
Adults think we're all the same
But try letting them play the teenage game.

Sally Phelps

Wind Of Change

The wind will fry you if you let it.
Doves fly high to escape winds of change.
Old men cry, and reminisce about a year gone by,
and still the wind blows.

The trees don't change,
they just get thicker, and older,
Cut them down—, they only took three hundred
years to grow.
Best protect from the winters eve and driving snow,
cover the evidence of the year gone by.

Ghouls haunt these pastures now, where once
great forests grew, now great cities grow,
boom—, and die.
Counter existence after pre-existence—, Why?

The wind will fry you if you let it!

Stefan Harris

Father

The man who picks you up when you cry
    answers your questions when you ask why.
The man who helps you to crawl
    with whom you first kick a ball.
The man in your life for every sector
    who stands over you as your Lord protector.
The man still standing in the aftermath
    who races you to the end of the path.
The man who's there when all done and said
    when you sleep on the couch he'll carry you to bed
The man who whether you're sixteen, six or zero
    he will still be you're biggest hero.
The man who's there when you bring your first love home
    when he is near you're never alone
The man who offers comfort and support
    free's you when you're caught.
The man whose a friend whether young or old
    who warms you up when you're cold
The man whose presence makes you feel glad
    a friend, a helper, an authority . . . dad.

Alan Bradburne

But Forgotten

The excitement of the birth of a child, into the world
The calm of the aftermath is a great feeling, 9 months of hell
in some eyes

"But Forgotten"

The reach of 5 yrs old is the storm of my father leaving and
Evaporates from life. Mother has found a boyfriend, by the
time you're 15 yrs. old sexually abused, and not a person to
talk too. Scared, now for life. No confidence in yourself, can't
really say or rely on anyone around you.

"But Forgotten"

19 yrs. old, now in the army, you try to harden yourself up, it
backfired, no blood, no fighting, just had no confidence in
yourself, next step prison, drugs, crime, all for what, just a
waste, Mother has forgotten, Father forgotten too. This may
sound short and sweet a lifetime of Hell

"But is never forgotten by me".

P. B. Falloon

To Jo

A child of God you were born to be,
His love was in you for all to see.
The gifts of His Spirit you had in plenty,
No wonder we feel just a little bit empty.

Your joy in living and loving and giving
Flowed over us all whilst you were living.
Yet, in your absence, your spirit's still here,
And we'll try to live up to all you held dear.

As a wife and a mother you gave comfort and love,
And this will continue now you're up above.
As daughter and sister your love will be treasured,
With memories so precious they cannot be measured.

Your friends and relations will all miss you so,
But your joy and your laughter
Should help them to know
That your spirit stays with them wherever they go.

As the Lord is now holding you close to His breast
And with His love to guide us, we know you're at rest.
We'll love you and miss you and do what we can
To spread joy and laughter and follow God's plan.

Romilly Fenlon

The Long Dark Road

It was 10:30 pm on a long lonely road, dark was the night, I
was alone. Fear was my companion all the way. Cattle grazed
in the dark over the fence, along the long dark road, the
snorting of bulls as they cropped the long grass, cheered my
spirit up, I travelled on.

No more sound of grazing cattle, everything was black before
me. I wished for a bottle torch filled with kerosene oil, corked
with old newspaper to light my way along the long dark road.
Still I hastened.
Faster, faster, my heart beat till I came to a house along the way.

I knocked, then the door opened unto me, "What can I do for
you?" she asked.
"Could you please trim me a bottle torch to light my way along
this long dark road?" "Come inside why not stay for the
night", she insisted. "It is too late for you to go alone along
this dark and lonely road. There is a spare room."

"Thank you, you are very kind, even though I would like to
stay and sleep for the night, I cannot, I must go on."

"Then refresh yourself, eat and drink, then be on your way."
She made it so quickly. I hastened to the table to tuck in, "this
sure is lovely."
She smiled sweetly, "Your torch is ready when you are." "I
thank you very much for everything." "You are welcome, but
remember to return the bottle." I laughed. "I will see you
then." I was half mile along when the torch went out.

Samuel Freckleton

My Life And Family

My life is full of useless things,
Boring days and happenings,
These days of mine just pass away,
With all my family who like to play,
My Mum I find acrid at times,
Her reason being she's in her primes,
My dad he lives quiet far from me,
But there's still a good affinity,
My sister Vicky and I are close,
To poison our love you'd need a strong dose,
My brother Jack I find quite fond,
Loves collecting frogs from any old pond.
My feelings are there to see me through,
Whenever I'm feeling blue,
So there you have it for all to see,
An idea of my life and family.

Danielle Gallagher

How Dare They?

The modest moon shines chastely through the night;
Her sister stars support her, as they spread their Heavenly light.
What dire deeds does man commit, beneath the earth's dark shroud,
Undiscovered, unseen by the otherwise sleeping crowd
Of innocents, amongst the seeming peace of night,
Where those awake see only artificial light?
Few raise their eyes to the beauteous Heavenly moon
And stars, which fade in morning's sun too soon.
The world awakes and the noise and bustle of day
Brings the discovery of night's dark horrors and disarray
Left by intruders—thieves and worse human refuse.
How can they, how dare they confuse
God's work on the earth, His masterpiece of creation?
How dare man spoil it with his work of degradation?
Shine on, modest, silent moon and twinkling stars;
Maybe man will see your radiance—and wars
And other crimes will cease
And God's world will know His everlasting peace.

Pamela Flavin

Hope

Hope is a lamp that lights our wishful thoughts,
Those images that float in the mind's eye,
Pictures that we would make reality
And set beneath a clear and cloudless sky.

Hope is our refuge in the tragic hours
Of waiting for we know not what reply,
A verdict that will shape the lives of those
We love, for good or ill, we know not why.

If hope in disillusionment should fade
And like a precious bloom wither and die,
The happiness we dreamed will drift away,
Silent save for the echo of a sigh.

Jean Crawford Green

La Petite Grande Bouche

Lovely little Lucy her voice through laryngitis lost,
Lovely little Lucy stay that way at any cost.
Your friends don't find your loud voice endearing,
All except one, and that poor sod's already lost his hearing.

These cruel poetic words that I express
Are apportioned with a great amount of jest,
For I was told by your mother and if true
Not all the fault belongs to you.
The truth it would seem at that very moment you were conceived
That is, if your mother is to be believed
Your father, a newspaper vendor of some note,
Whilst making love cleared his throat,
And at the final climax he bellowed
Evening Herald, Evening Herald
Because of his eccentricity it would seem
You inherited an over-compensating decibelic gene.

Mel Wilkins

Us

I think of when we were together and all the
good times we shared,
and then I get to thinking about if you
really cared.
Sometimes I forget you know, that we're not
going out anymore,
then I suddenly remember and lower my
eyes to the floor.
I sometimes think to myself 'what's the point
in living?'
Then I remember an important lesson of
forgetting and forgiving.
When I see you standing there looking so good,
I have to shake and remind myself that now
you're only my bud.
I really miss the feel of your touch and
all your boyish charms,
I'll never kiss your lips again or hold you in
my arms.

Lucy Harrison

The Shelf

A tiny string of blue beads encircles a candle in its glass holder.
Those beads were your anklet of identity when you were born.
Next to the candlestick stands a simple wooden giraffe.
You made it when you were at school.
Beside the giraffe, a prayer plant.
No Photographs.

I want to listen to your music, look at your photographs;
But not yet, not now. Maybe tomorrow.

I began to write about your life, so filled with achievement,
Disappointment and sorrow.
I started to paint a picture to capture the expression of
overwhelming freedom and joy I saw on your face
At the mortuary.

I have not finished these things.
Not yet, not now. Maybe tomorrow.

Anita Meloche

My Beautiful Place

I live where to me is a beautiful place.
Where time does not stand still but moves at a much slower pace.
Surrounded by fields of all colour and shapes.
Corn, potatoes, flaxseed, and rape.
Animals there are many, domestic, tame and wild,
Nature's bounty is endless, in the eye of a child.
I wake every morning, when the birds start to sing,
A new day beginning for all living things.
There is much to see and do, but there's no haste,
For time goes more slowly in my beautiful place.

Mary Deacon

Loving Hands

Hands so delicate in shape
That are capable of giving but rarely take,
Whether they are bejewelled or bare,
They are equally beautiful and very rare,
Look at them thoughtfully, a story will unfold,
You know what is there, you do not need to be told.
They are smooth hands that have loved and lost,
Often clenched together counting the cost.
The touch of a child's soft skin
Is a blessing they hold within,
On bended knees they come together in prayer
For a person whose life you no longer share,
Unclench your hands, he knows you can still use them here,
He is aware of the kindness they can spill around
And God alone knows what happiness can be found.
If you look to the future with hands open wide,
Someone will grasp them and stay by your side,
Your hands so pretty, your heart so true
Will doubtless bring happiness reserved only for you.

Selinda Routledge

Tears Of A Rose

Do you see the tears of a rose?
Can you feel the empty heart of a leafless elm?
Feel the loneliness of a single drop of water
and the warmth of a snowflake?
Capture loving tenderness from a cactus who laughs at the clouds?

Do you feel the tears of a rose
falling into the softness of a rock?
The leaves listening for love,
yet blood drips off the thorns.
Can you hear it when a flower speaks your name?

Richmond Haddow

Escape Into The Crimson Sea

Fire in the sky burns bright and pure,
It looks so beautiful, for all to enjoy.
Looking up at the open space,
Swimming with elegance and crimson grace.
I want to be in the air, to fly amongst the colours.
Red, yellow, orange and gold,
Beauty burning bright and bold.
Its violent outburst of passion and fury,
Only then can you see nature's true glory.
But sitting here on the surface of the earth
I feel like we have fallen victim to a curse.
Here lies death, suffering and starvation,
These are the tragedies resulting from the greed,
    power and politics of our nation.
My hatred for being earthbound and restrained
I want to rise up and feel the heat again.
Then the fire vanishes from our sight,
We're now embraced by the beauty of the night.
These are the entities we can see but not hold,
All we can wish is for it to stay gold.

Bhav-Neeta Parekh

Spirit Of Youth

It was my birthday, your present sent,
a beautiful rose, with such a scent.
And planted in the garden bed.
The glory of the row it can be said,
and year, after year, its flowers arrive.
Growing taller, mightier, and fighting to survive,
and as each rose bud starts to appear,
its head held high, it has nothing to fear.
The redness of the flower, starts to show,
into the warm air, more it starts to grow.
Blood red is the flower itself;
as if a finger pricked upon a thorn.
Has dripped blood, upon each tiny petal, as it came to form.
So now it shows off in all its glory;
the beginning and end to the roses' story.

Shirley Alison McGlade

That Little Big Word

If is such a little word and seems as if
it should be heard a lot, and is as I recall,
even if it is so small
If can mean so many things like if she
can or cannot sing if she does or if she's
not, if she smokes a little pot
If's a word I rather like, if I only had a bike
If's used so much it is obscene but do not
let it change your dreams
If only is a common phrase and puts you
well into a daze and if they fall into
a sleep they may be wakened with a beep
and if that beep's a false alarm, I'm sure
it's never done no harm
So if, again it must be said, is not
a word to lie down dead, it keeps on
rearing its ugly head if only if were
when instead.

Martin Hall

Treacle Covered Roses

There's a gap around this small world,
There's a void too vast to fill,
And a path that's lined with ancient thoughts,
A hungry hunter's kill.

Then came gold from depths of darkness,
Like a star that lights the land.
There were treacle covered roses,
(But with thorns that bit my hand.)

Outside there's a storm that's raging,
There's a wind that cannot cease.
But my treacle covered roses,
Though not perfect, bring me peace.

I feel that time is standing still,
I see my every thought collide.
I watch my treacle covered roses,
In the winter, bloom outside.

And I run to find a new world,
As it slips before my eyes.
Only treacle covered roses,
Knew this life was such a lie.

Kirstine Y. M. Manson

Being A Winner

When you rise still weary, after a sleepless night,
Dawn breaks triumphant in royal colours bright.
Prayers softly spoken, borne swiftly on wings of light,
To the Throne of Grace, far beyond human sight.

The mid-day passes, and weariness remains.
Little joy for this sad heart, still playing yesterday's games.
Petals falling gently, like words from your prayer returned,
It doesn't really matter, when all your bridges have been burned.

Off to bed and still wondering, too much time to think.
The evening sun still blazes, waiting upon the brink.
Speak to Him about your troubles, tell Him it's so unfair,
Your world empty as a desert, and no one wants a share.

Don't long for a tomorrow you may never know,
Why expect only good times, they can melt like the snow.
Come rest unhappy soul, deep in heaven's night hours,
Be of good heart, if you want the sun, try to beat the showers.

The brave also get weary, and have been heard to say,
"I've run the race done my best, there must be another way".
Should the going get tougher, and the ice decidedly thinner,
Keep at it like the tortoise, and know the thrill of being a winner.

David Hall

I've Avoided All Of That

My girlfriend has gone and left me.
She said for her I will yearn.
I'm not too worried about her leaving,
But I'm scared she might return.

I've never been married once,
And not even been married twice.
So I've avoided a marriage break-up,
And the disputes over the children's rights.

I've avoided going into pubs,
And so avoided all the fights,
All I've done is stayed at home,
And listened to music all night.

I enjoy smoking my roll-ups,
And drinking my cups of tea,
And when my boat comes in I'll board it,
When everyone else is at sea.

The problems I've had I now look on,
As blessings in disguise.
It's a similar thing to flying saucers,
As they are angels in the skies.

Peter Marcus Fleming

Revenge

Wrapped up in silence, alone in my bed
Thoughts of the nightmare arise in my head
Feet on the staircase fill me with dread
Here comes the nightmare, I wish I were dead

Tears start flowing, there's still some to shed
The fear of knowing what lies ahead
Feet on the landing it's closing tread
Again it's the nightmare, I wish I were dead

Pretend to be sleeping, my body's like lead
I long for a safe place to hide me instead
Feet in my bedroom, I should have fled
Face up to the nightmare, I wish I were dead

Hands 'round the weapon, the adrenalin sped
Strike in anger as the room turns red
Feet up ended, the wounded bled
There goes the nightmare, now it's dead

David Newton

Curiosity

A tiny arm extended, finger upward pointing
A furrowed brow intent on what she sees.
A question in her mind already forming,
Excitedly and beaming broadly, turns to me.

Her world was hitherto small and secure,
But now she perceives how large it really is.
What wondrous sights and smells await her pleasure
If she can only get to where the action is.

Her walking is, as yet, somewhat unsteady.
She has a language that is known to her alone.
But limitations such as these do not restrict her,
It's exciting to explore outside her home.

Trees in the park wave back to her in greeting,
The flowers by the stream and birds all fascinate.
The children playing on the swings call to her
And she hugs me tight while for her turn she waits.

A granddaughter whom I very much adore is she.
I'm her willing slave, her wish is my command.
"Nanny—want home". I understand her meaning
And when we arrive she runs to her mother's arms.

Joy Harman

Peace In Ireland

The killing went on for 25 years
My parents didn't tell me but I have ears.
There were people killed every night,
And I knew it was wrong not right.

It has finally stopped
And I hope it will last
So we can all forget what happened in the past.
No more bombs nor guns nor tears
And we'll all forget our awful fears
Though they can't be forgiven for the harm they have done,
From now on we should all join as one.

Emma Morgan

The Storm

Misty mornings, scorching hot days.
Distant rumblings far, far away.
Thunder clouds gathering.
Rain bouncing high.
Scudding clouds in a darkening sky.
Flashes and flashes of zig zagging light.
So swift, so frightening, so bright.
Rumble, crack, rumble, crack, crack.
Thunder following or preceding light.
People scurrying across the night.
The storm brings a chilliness.
Although stiflingly warm.
A prelude to the thunder.
The lightning, the storm.

D. Rodgers

Snowflakes

Softly floating down from the sky,
Nothing stops it until it hits the ground,
On a snow covered path with footprints everywhere.
Where I walk in winter,
Flakes fall all around.
Lakes are iced over when the flakes fall,
Ankle deep in snow.
Know Christmas is near when the snowflakes are here,
Enveloped in white during the night.
Snowflakes.

Gordon Millar

Don't Make Me Go To School, Mum

Don't make me go to school, Mum,
   I have a pain up here in my head.
I really don't feel very well, Mum,
   Please let me stay in bed.

Don't make me go to school, Mum,
   I feel all sickly and ick.
With a pain down here in my tum, Mum,
   And I think I'm gonna be sick.

Don't make me go to school, Mum,
   I sprained my leg yesterday.
It's all swollen and painful now,
   Please let me stay away.

Don't make me go to school, Mum,
   My blood pressure's really high,
My temperature's gone through the roof, Mum,
   And I think I'm going to cry.

So that's why I can't go to school, Mum,
   With a pain up here in my head.
And a pain down there in my tum, Mum,
   I really should stay in bed.

Nichola Webster

Untitled

Even if the sun was allowed to set
for a million more years,
you would not see me.
And should we pass on a country lane,
alone, but for nature's own,
you would not spare me a glance.
This I know.
But with the stars as my witness
as they shine in the night-time sky,
I shall lie awake for the rest of my days
thinking of you.

Stephen Clarke

Deafening Silence

I look, I listen, what do I hear?
A deafening silence, no one is here.
The world is full of people just like me,
Anxious to hear, eager to see.

A crowded place, lots of people there,
I scream out loud, but, no one will hear.
A million people all around,
but, they and I don't hear a single sound.

I'd like to think there's someone to care,
then who will know? When no one can hear,
My plea to break this loneliness,
to give one single heart that I can caress.

I guess no one will ever know,
I hide my feelings, they never show.
Maybe someday I'll find my mate,
I just hope and pray it's not too late.

I'm sure everyone's experienced being alone in a crowd,
and wanted to holler and shout out aloud,
Look, I'm here why can't you see?
They're all too busy being alone like me.

G. Losty

Shattered Heart

Oh my darling I wish you knew
All the pain I'm going through
I'll probably never see you again
In my heart there is lots of pain.
It seems you were there only yesterday
Without you my world seems grey.
When you were with me, I had no tears
You were the one who would calm my fears.
Everyone else has someone to care
You're not with me so I despair.
You and me were joined as one
Now we're ripped apart, the damage is done.
You are the only person I truly love
We fit together like a hand in a glove
You're the silver lining in my cloud,
Not just another face in the crowd
I know there's a heaven when I think of you and me
To my heart you have the key.
Why do we have to be so far apart?
I'm alone to pick up the pieces of my shattered heart.

Maria Dudley

Dreaming Seems Simple

Against the backdrop of the sea,
   I saw your face for the first time,
      The whispering wind cooling my skin,
         Starlight reflecting from your eyes.
Reality seems unreal sometimes,
   A poem filled with images,
      Of you and I stood hand in hand,
         Watching the waves lolling to shore.
I'm half asleep, half of the time,
   And dreaming seems simple to me,
      Your warmth smelled sweet against the cold,
         And seemed to fit the scene so well.

Karl Grafton

To Autumn

Summer's almost past and done
the sun with watery rays breaks down
on sullen shores, who've had their fun.

'Too soon, too soon,' the sad waves chant
for tiny feet, their prints implant
to wander homeward, sad, forlorn,
hand with Autumn soon reborn.

Thin breezes swirl now, through the grasses
eddying sand through dune-like passes.
Trees with changing leaves a-tremble
wait their call—fall, then dismember.

Skies once azure—now uncertain
await the Autumn's paler curtain
and misty moon's unwinking eye
wistfully clouds,
time's passing by.

Phyliss Littlewood

An Ode To The Small Business

From dawn to dusk from the rising sun.
The small business man and wife are never done.
Butcher, Baker, Greengrocer too
Fishmongers, newsagent, working the whole day through.

They work and toil until the job is done.
No overtime paid if the hours become.
A friend and confidant as people pass through their door.
Accountant, adviser and much, much more.
A friendly smile, a cheery hello.
Taken for granted from many they know.
But now they are becoming a dying bread.
Growing in one big plot from supermarket seed.
As they gradually disappear and the high street is bare.
Jo Public is the loser, not this business pair.

Barbara Mitchard

A Doggie's Memories

"Would you give someone like me a home",
I asked you, with yearning eyes.
And yes you choose me from all the rest.
When you bought me from that dogs' home.

You named me Bruno, I was brown you see,
Couldn't have been bought by a better family,
Lovely walks with master over the hills
Playing around with two lovely girls

Then God took me away from you all
After only two years that were wonderful
Memories I will treasure forever
Of my family, who couldn't have treated me better

Please do not worry or fret for me
My pain has gone I am really happy
So smile for me, please do not cry
I'm watching over you all, from God's house in the sky.

Hilda Cook

Painless (Once Smitten)

Moronic shifting I look up what do I see?
Do I care anyway? No not really, doesn't really matter anyway
Nothing really matters, I don't get it now
Guess I never will.
If I don't know by now I accept I never will.
I eat drink but it's just to stay alive,
So I'm not really tasting, I'm never enjoying
It's just life, guess I never will
If I don't know by now, I know I never will.
Painless once smitten by you now I can't look you in the eyes
I can't, my eyes are clogged with hardened salt, tears of old.
I can't see but it doesn't really matter.
The whole world's horror
Incomplete prayers: pray for me, pray for me my friends
Oh it doesn't really matter never mind don't worry anyway
It's my fault I don't really matter
I guess I never will
If I don't know by now I guess I never will.

Giles Lewis

Courage To Reflect

A heart fragment by love long ago.
A fragility and vulnerability within her very soul.

A strength that comes from a depth within.
An empathy for her fellow men.
An envious streak controlled and conquered.
Sadness felt with unbearable pain.
Unrequited love still shadows remain.
A temper quelled by nature's ageing.
Old woman speak wise words to me.
Nurture the good parts, toil against the worst.
We are all many facetted as a diamond,
with all its wonder the light dances and
emanates from the very core, but turn it
slightly and it dulls but turn it again and
it comes to life once more.

Jane Robson

Lonely Traveler

As the day breaks on a misty morning,
A stranger walks a lonely road,
The sun is cradled by snow capped mountains,
Smoke rises like ghosts from wooden chimneys,
He hears the sound of children crying,
And mirthless laughter all around,

A blind man asks him for a cane,
And as the stranger passes,
The mist clears and the blind man sees,
The sun breaks free of its icy bed,
A smell of cooking reaches out,
Once again the children laugh,
And the lonely traveller disappears.

Chris Williams

Untitled

Love at first sight, it happened to me,
You walked in the room, you were all I could see.
My heart was pounding, I thought my head would burst,
Nothing like this had happened before, this was the ultimate first.
The feelings were mutual, I'm happy to say,
We loved each other darling, more and more each day.
We married three months later, we didn't want to linger,
And oh! How proud I was, to see your ring upon my finger.
Forty years together, we've had such a wonderful time,
I'll be forever grateful, that you were meant to be mine.
Now my heart is broken, my life's in little pieces,
The crying and the heartache just never never ceases,
You've gone to live in God's domain,
But I know one day, we shall meet again.

Audrey Ousby

Concrete Trees

Walking along where children play
On not much grass and dust bins high
Tall grey pillars with weeping eyes
Or houses they may seem to be
They stand aloft above the trees
Cast their shadows to hide the sun
Brings forth smell that never frees
Man and beast from pigeon holes
To see the green grass here below
That's all they have among the throes
Of what been planned for friends and foes
To escape the smell of human waste
Say hello and you waste your time
For fear you grab what is not thine
Old folks plead come down to me
For I fear the steps and those not seen
When night comes down and hide the worst
The creeps come out and often boast

Ron Carby

Cynthia

A host of brilliant stars ablaze at night
Surround the Queen of heavenly light
The illustrious moon goddess abides
Within her court of princely guides

Like a jewel suspended in the sky
The silvery moon of love rides high
Adoration from lovers serenading
When a-courting, when a-courting

Cynthia silver-footed Queen of my delight
Proudly sails through the bejewelled night
And the diamond glint of a falling star
Cascades through moonbeams from afar

Star-studded princes of the night all gleam
And the goddess of the night rules supreme

Anne Cooper

Creation Of A Bloom

Have you ever wondered about a true English Rose,
I hope to give you insight, or at least here goes,
I wanted a flower of elegance and scent,
So off to a Garden Centre I expectantly went,
I met an old man who looked rather rough,
But he was no fool for he knew his stuff,
He explained about Flori bunders, then went on to Hybrid Teas,
They were interesting, special, as you will see,
He took me to a spot far away from the rest,
Then exclaimed, "Young Man, these are my Best",
I gazed in amazement at the beauty I saw,
No other flower could possibly present more,
Crisp green leaves on every stem,
Holding a bloom, the plant held about ten,
The petals were of satin their shape unique,
My quest was over, I no longer had to seek,
So I bought my first rose with pride and joy,
With a grin, walked away like a little boy.

David Osborn

Dawn Song

The long night passes—
The sleepless watch of stars fades
With the unfolding azalea streaks of light;
The first notes of hope infiltrate—
In the dawn—the blackbird's song.

The sweat of night, the restless fears
Give way to the smell of moss and rain,
Flower of elder set by fronded path,
While mist wreathes about the sequestered lake,
In the dawn—the wood dove wakes.

The striding edge of hills does battle
With the crumpled breath of night,
Call of pleasant rapiers the larch wood,
Screech of joy and wing and swan,
In the dawn—the lark's flute.

Dawn lifts the compliant curtains of night
And over the white–fringed bay gulls cry,
The feathered hands of seaweed swung by tidal melody,
(Even night's captive behind the shadowed bars hears)
In the dawn—the full symphony

Rosalind Taylor

Peace

It isn't the sound of the roaring waves
    As they crash on the cliffs in the storm.
Nor is it the creak of the old oak tree
    When the wind blows and alters its form.
It isn't the lightening that flashes and flares
    Through my window when I'm in my bed,
These things are alarming, but all that I see
    Is my baby asleep near my head

Margaret Whiteside

The Creepy Old Churchyard

There was a big, dark and lonely churchyard,
No one dare enter at dark or early dawn;
It's creepy and quiet and said to be haunted;
So people have said it's true anyway:
Yet no one has really proved it is;
There are shadows and howling noises!
In a churchyard that's not unusual;
Then one night I could not sleep;
So I took a walk in the churchyard;

Noises of owls and foxes I heard;
But yet I did not see anything spooky.
Then I saw something by the church;
Just shadows or someone in black.
Overheard an owl hooted then swooped.
Making me crouch behind a grave;
Then I felt something rub my leg;
I did cry out but it was the church cat.
Then I decided to turn back home.
When I heard footsteps creep up on me;
But to my relief they went the other way.

T. A. Shires

Silent Words, Broken Thoughts

Simple words are hard to explain, once they are told
there's no looking back from this day to that.
The way you feel can't be described, the situation is
unsteady and deprived.
Silent words the unthinkable act, would definitely
destroy future plans and acts.
The once bed of roses is now a layer of tears.
You saw him today for the first time in a long while.
Your mind was made up to forget all about it, but
you feel that the look that was passed was the
feelings of happiness that you never had until you last met.
As you walk into the distance, the corridor of the
future, one quick glance causes the tremors to extreme.
You'll see him again with your silent words and
hope the silence will be broken and you will return.

Kelly Rudge

God

God to us is an invisible spirit indeed
He is our best friend when in dire need
With his kind and soothing words
He caresses us and guards us with his birds
When all is lost and helpless I stand
I call upon God and once more I feel grand

God himself governs nature too
And God makes sure we have plenty to do

Hands and feet we use the most
God, in these helps us to the final post

Without the good Lord
We would feel unassured
About our world that we do traverse
And Satan would us surely curse
For without his power and dominions
Satan would win in my opinion,
Gods Kingdom is coming, of that I'm convinced
We must stop all this sinning
Or we all will be jinxed.
Amen

S. V. Simons

Laughter

The happiest sound that I can hear,
Is laughter singing in my ear,
It cheers me feel up when I feel sad
It makes me feel so very glad,
We're often told don't do this don't do that,
Your to young forms and to old for that,
But laughter is for the young and the old
So lets get together and let us be bold.
We will laugh together the young and the old,
Where ever we come from the best thing to hear
Is laughter so happily dancing from ear to ear.

Alison Wolstenhulme

Departing Feelings

I am positive you know
how sad we are to see you go.
Still very proud of your achievement
we must be in complete agreement,
for you to start a brand new life
in Australia with your wife.
A special son who's like no other
how glad we are for your dear brother
to help us bear this parting pain,
'til years fly by and we meet again.
May all your wildest dreams come true.
Our love will always be with you
I expect it helps to know we care
When we are here and you are there,
Good luck in all you choose to do
Good health and wealth we hope for too
Now the time has come, it can't be wrong,
Heads held high, confident and strong.
As on your great adventure you both go.
'A Great Success' Some future date will show.

Mary Trott

Dad

In my baby's eyes I can see,
all the things you meant to me.
And all the things I meant to you,
the love, the joy and the worry, too.
The love and joy were always there,
the laughter, the smiles, the times we shared.
A friend, a father, a son, a mate,
To find it better? I hesitate.
Now you have gone
but still I can see
you there,
in a baby, looking up at me.

David John Dale

Sea Mist Depression

As I sit at my window
I can see the sea mist, carried by the breeze,
it envelopes the trees, the hills are shrouded
like deathly spectres under its wake,
it's day break.

During the day, the mist may stay and go,
the spectre may lift, the sun may shine,
it depends on the weather whether or not
the spectre remains.

The day draws to a close, the spectre has gone,
the sea mist has lifted, perhaps the dawn
will see it again, will the spectre return,
or will there be a bright shining day,
who can say.

M. H. Young

We All Take Death Differently . . .

When you lose that special friend,
people say your heart will mend.
But the way you take death is not necessarily the same for me,
as everybody takes it differently.
As some people can carry on with their lives,
with others, they find it so hard to survive.
You walk around in a daze, not really with it,
with your nerves and patience stretched to the limit.
The pain in your head keeps you awake at night,
and keeping thoughts of suicide from your mind is one hell of a fight.
You're frightened to talk to people in case all they think you can do
is moan, and the constant thoughts of being alone.
The most hated sentence in the world, and you know I'm not wrong,
is the one that goes: well life must go on.
When I hear this being said I want to be sick,
so I just turn my head and walk away quick.
When all I really want to do is shout out loud,
It's not wrong to be different, not one of the crowd . . .

Philip Wilkinson

Friendship

To be able to cope with this world of ours
It is tolerance and patience we need.
Wherever we're going there's no need to rush
For surely we'll get there without any fuss.
With friends who stand by us when troubles befall
How grateful to them we should be.
It's no way to live if life is a fight.
This shouldn't happen, it just can't be right.
There's such an abundance of pleasure in life
That makes it worth living and seemingly right.
So often we want more than nature intends
But what could we want more than our closest friends.
Let us live and enjoy life whatever it be
We can only do that if there's real harmony.
So it's up to us all, the young and the old,
As this thing we call friendship is worth more than gold.

Margaret Yale

The Coal Man

Oh! You coal man at my door
With your back worn down and your eyes to the floor.
How your bowed body tells the story of labour,
And how, the ground beneath your boots has moulded your nature,
As you raise your head you see the light,
Your sacks, you lift with all your might,
Your cap is flat, your gloves so black,
In the frostiness of the day, you are here not to stay,
You're a darkened square on the chequered board,
Where you're no king or Noble Lord
Your hands are cold as blackened leather,
And in your face we tell the weather,
As you walk, as coalmen do,
To and fro until you're through,
And when the flames warm our hearts and our feet,
We'll remember the coalman in the street.

Anna Szeremeta

The Meaning Of Poems

To be a poet, what does one have to do to make a poem ring true?
Do you have to be young or old and write down what you think?
What does one have to write about to make the poem come alive
Would it be the sea or countryside which we admire with pride?

I have been to many poets' meetings and listened to their words and verse
Reading many books from well-known authors
which came from poets in the past.
The poets live on and last, poetry a part of life
of joy and sadness and gives us a meaning
and understanding in this world of madness.

I think I know what makes a poet
and the thoughts come to life in their head
they take the rough with the smooth and write what they think.
Writing in pencil, pen or type or ink
Even when one's dressed or in the nude,
but to be a good poet one must be in the mood.

Douglas Williams

Friends

We all need friends if but to say
Hello and how are you today
A cheerful grin a flashing smile
And life is suddenly worthwhile

When life seems grey and rather glum
Just confide it to a chum
The clouds will lift and in its place
You trust again the human race

As each new day—begins to dawn
There is no need to feel forlorn
Just place your trust in Him above
The one and only source of love

So even though the skies are grey
Your friends will pull you through the day
And joyous gladness fills your soul
With hope eternal for your goal

M. Tickle

My Wish

Your deep dark eyes, lovely lashed and lusty,
stare into the depths of my very being,
holding me defenceless and exposed,
my heart pounds and there . . . I find stillness
and my soul flies with yours to the heavens . . .
Never before this.
Never imagined this.
Never let these feelings be taken from me.

Set them in chiselled stone,
locked inside a maddening labyrinth of caved passageways,
in the furthest, far-stretched mountain,
hidden behind the bellowing crash of the most thunderous waterfall,
in the most devilish, deepest darkest lagoon.
And never shall anyone or anything tamper with this,
for this love is sacred
and my wish is togetherness, forever, eternally.

Susan Jenkins

O Pellucid Mist I Bow To Thee

I stare change in the eye
And desire such a fear,
Abhor its touch; smile at its shadow,
Possession of mind; eviction of logic,
O pellucid mist I bow to thee.

A hiding place; none.
Crawling, through each vein, a dark companion.
To pierce the eye; to close the ear.
O pellucid mist I bow to thee.

There can be no comparison:
Spiritual; physical,
The Autumn pasture beckons
And trails into forever . . .

Ross Markham

The Crucifying

They drove in the nails with powerful blow.
He cried, "Father Father. Don't let go
Don't forsake me I am your son"
Jesus Christ the chosen one
    Please stay with me.
With tear–filled eyes
He cast one last glance
Over the crowd who were by now in a trance
His head bowed low
And his limbs became loose
Pilate said, "It is no use at all
He's dead, he's dead.
And without crime
The only blame is yours and mine."
Just with that the sky turned black
The soil shook and the earth did crack
    Mercilessly
He cured the blind
He helped the lame
And yet we treated him the same as any criminal

Roslyn McLeish

Love

Love is dangerous, love is stupid
Even made up a man called Cupid,
With a bow and arrow by his side,
Love is a dangerous ride.

People get hurt and end up crying,
Love is stupid, Love is trying.
People fall in and out of love,
Who needs all the trouble, Who needs love.

Love is something which two people have,
Love is special, Special to have.
Mixed emotions and confused feelings,
Nobody knows how one another's feeling.

Love is stupid, Love is blind,
love can be hard to find,
But when you find that special one,
Hold onto them and keep that one.

Michael Pickles

The Somme July 1996

A golden crop approaching yield
Awaits the blade on that battlefield
And poppies push their scarlet head
From factored ruts where mortals bled

From the dwindling mist of a summer morn
They were bid to walk through a firestorm
A harvest of courage ripe to the sickle
Pouring forth blood in profusion and trickle

In cordite, metal, flesh, earth and blood
They were brought to stubble by the thrust of that flood
Division, battalion, platoon and brigade
Exposed by the thousands to that enfilade

Now in peace and silence this harvest is laid
Wrapped and secure in death's welcome plaid
Under tombstone, poppy, or wherever perchance
In the fragrance and shelter of the fair fields of France

P. MacClory

A Poem

A poem is mostly meant to rhyme,
Sometimes it's about monsters with lots of slime,
Or sometimes it's about watches that tell the time,
Sometimes it's about fairies that would fly,
Or sometimes it's about a butterfly that flutters by,
If I read my book today,
I wonder what the poem will be,
maybe it's about ghosts, spiders or ghouls,
maybe it's about sport, games with basket balls,
nobody knows.

Sarah Louisa Gosling

Untitled

As I walked along the beach,
The sun beaming down on my face,
I watched a baby seal,
And thought with a lot of grace.

As I closed my eyes with the soft breeze on my skin,
I felt as though I was floating with my freedom within.

Then I opened my eyes and saw the deep blue sea,
A beautiful wave came crashing down,
And there I saw before me,
The sun setting over the horizon.

Then I sat on the yellow sparkling sand,
That felt like the crumbling of
Salt through my fingers,
And watching the sun go down,
With the smell of the salty sea and sand.

I watched the last bit of the sun go down,
The tide was drifting in, the sand was disappearing,
I felt like the world was ending,
I felt the last of my breath come,
And there I felt I had died with the sun.

Lyndsey Hobbs

Never Forget

It was that day I saw him walk in,
I guess I didn't expect it at first.
he walked right up to the bar and ordered.
It was then he turned and saw me.

I was sitting with my latest boyfriend.
drinking and laughing with him happily.
It was then our eyes met with a spark.
And I knew straight away that it was love.
That moment when I first saw him,
I knew that I would never forget him.

Rachel Dance

It's Time To Be Happy

It's time to be happy, let life's spirit run free.
It's time to be happy for you and me.
Let the past be buried.
Let the future wait.
Each hour of the day, is on what we should concentrate.
If you can't, then sew a new stitch.
Or be brave and scratch that itch.
For life will not wait for us to decide.
It will continue its journey to the other side.
And a waste it would be not to have tried each flavoured cake.
For those of us who have this life handed to us on a plate.
Don't seek grandeur.
But peace of mind.
And remember.
It's time to be happy, in this life of yours and mine.

Bernadette Fortuna

A Closer Look At Nature

Have you ever looked at wild flowers growing free for all to share,
Not a penny do they charge us, as they show their petals bare,
Wild Iris standing tall, and cloaked in royal blue,
With all the pomp and ceremony, of a king and crown that's new,
Looking down on his peers as he casts a regal eye,
To his regiment of Blue-bells, marching time to the sky,
Intoxicating perfumes with all her petals spread,
Dithering and trembling as the smell goes to her head,
Scattering the footpaths and gardens all around,
The Apple Blossoms laughing, without making a sound,
Timidly awaiting, is the shy Buttercup,
For the warmth of the sun to encourage her face up,
As she needs reassurance, she clings onto a friend,
And reaches for the strength of the Dandelions hand,
He likes the comfort of a gentle touch,
For no-one looks at him, or praises him much,
Who cares about his vibrant yellow head,
One-o-clock, two-o-clock, and puff, the seeds have spread.

Sandra Hemingway

A Fragile Little Seedling

A fragile little seedling was given life one day,
she saw a beckoning light beyond her
and I prayed that she would stay.

My prayers I know where answered but not as I had planned,
her stems of life were fleeting just as drifting sand.
The petals of this new born were tainted from that day,
but she brings joy and happiness to me every day.

The layout of her garden is unknown to mortal man
    God alone knows this he holds the master plan.
    Though thorns and weeds surround her,
    her beauty will outshine,
        I'll nurture her with loving care until the end of time.

Each new day she'll know my love,
until God's Almighty Hand
picks my treasured little blossom
    for his heavenly promised land.

Gillian Davey

Gunpowder, Treason And Plot

I did not see it as treason.
Rather loyalty as a reason.
The government called it betrayal.
Even though the plot did fail.

It was an all so perfect plan.
A plan for which I did hang.
Drawn, quartered, and thrown in a fire.
All because I was branded a liar.

It was because of my gunpowder plot,
That my name in history is never forgot.
But I do not wish to be remembered each year,
For hatred, cunning, evil and fear.

Natasha Peters

Time Warps

Men come and go racing through lifetime's clock
Striding forward and sometimes walking backward
In order to satisfy modernization
To be the first . . . for what?
Mistakes, punishments, new discoveries
That turn stale with age.
All documented into History Books, yet
The lessons never seem to reach into man's heart.
Still he destroys
For the next generation to build up
And knock down again.
What is man achieving in order to make his ideal world?
Stop, think,
What if man were to listen
To watch and to learn from his mistakes
Could he ever lie harmoniously with nature?

Tricia Hawcroft

Away From It All

Silver flashes shining bright
Where small fish dart and catch the light.
It looks so cool and peaceful.
Good air to help unwind you.
Time to relax and calm you.
Take your time—enjoy it!

Rushes moving with the flow.
Dragonflies hover, settle then go.
It is so cool and peaceful.
Good air does unwind you.
Time to relax and calm you.
Take your time—enjoy it.

Smell the sweet scent of flowers
Wafting in from woodland bowers.
If only I could spend all day here
But work calls and I must go.
I will find more time to relax and calm me.
I'll make my time—I so enjoyed it!

Barbara A. Wallace

A Lonely Lad

Ted wanted to leave home.
To travel the country lanes,
He always wanted to roam,
So he took his tools and planes,
His money was all in notes.
So it meant he needed change,
He had to take with him coats.
Also under-clothes so to change,
He had worked for a farmers team,
Looking after cattle and sheep,
He would not come to harm,
It was easy to work for his keep,
He met a lonely farmer, who took to him,
So Ted stayed and work for awhile.
After weeks living there with him,
He was made a partner, it was special,
After two years he met the farmer's niece,
Then they courted for sometime,
When Ted asked her to marry, it was nice,
They wed and lived happily a long time.

J. E. Storton

Pleased To Meet You!

Her teeth were clenched, her eyes, tight shut, her breath was
    soft and shallow.
The life within her coiled and paused, as if to make her wallow
In a moment of ecstasy and pain—before pushing hard with
    all her strength again
She bore this child of hers ever near the moment of his birth.

Oh! The sharp relief, the wonder of it all, no pain now but a
    feeling of euphoric bliss.
Another pause, then "Here we go again." A forward thrust,
    much stronger now
Insisting that all of this should be completed swiftly as a team
Towards a reuniting on the outside from the warmth and
    security of within.

For all these months she'd gotten to know him, speaking to
    him every day.
Sharing dreams and asking questions, revelling in the way
He responded as he wriggled and moved inside as if to say
"It will be good to meet you and to let you hold me close"
"It's warm and safe inside you, but as I hear your voice and
    feel your touch
I cannot wait to be there too."

The time had arrived—this time of meeting
With fear in her heart and a lump in her throat
She pushed with all her strength and was rewarded with a
    lusty cry.
"He's here" she whispered to herself and as she held out her
    arms, her mouth was dry.

Hazel Pavitt

Precious Moments

The leaves slowly change from green to brown
Hedgerows become sparse, all the apples are down
Days become shorter, nights become long
Time to recall know, all things that have gone

Gone far from sight but in memories stay
Precious moments that happened in some long gone days
I cast back my mind to reach long ago
Recalling times that were special that made love grow

Everywhere all around the wheels of change are turning
As I gaze into life's fire I see the logs that are burning
Bringing back thoughts of warmth and cheer
All the happiness of many a year

Now in quiet solitude
I think of times long ago
Of people and places that I used to know
Where are they now in their golden years
Are they remembering with just a few tears
With so much to recall and so much to share.
I feel safe and contented in the love that's still there

Patricia Pope

247

The Passage

Inexplicable is this sadness I feel
Inside I cry tears, but why?, no reason my heart whispers.
But my mind will not listen.
The shadows it throws hold tight.
I struggle to emerge from the darkness.
Like a butterfly from its cocoon.
Outside is sunlight and laughter.
The grass is still green.
Roses heavy with their perfume.
Life still vibrant around me.
My spirit tries hard to break free.
To soar into the black velvet night.
Amid stars that twinkle a welcome.
The darkness of infinity wraps loving arms around me
At last, at last, my spirit is free
Sheila Radestock

A Momentary Scene

Proceeding, moving within the track
Nearing to the railroad signal and crossing sign
Telegraph poles and connecting lines
Holding hands, linked under early evening shadows
Reflected solitude, frozen within, still frame
Echoed images of a yesterdays landscape

Suspended angle, moving eye
Time takes hold then releases, past perspective
A moving passenger, passing, disappeared
From darkness into bright light
Rising white to the pictures vertical edge
The arrival and the farewell
A momentary scene
Tina De Jong

Sun Of Dawn

Another 4 AM,
The lingering sickness
Of Anticipation and Lust,
Ever flowing blood
And whirling uneasiness
That we may never again endure
The warmth-filled caress,
Unforgettable to the brain
And fated to remember the passionate glimmer of sun
Within those eyes

Mine, alive with unsurfaced emotion,
Now—Emptiness
As a Rock shatters the glass,
A small child's smile turns to tears
She Screams
And salty morning dew falls downward into the darkness.
Sadie Rosanna Humble

Lovers From The Past

Some instinct seemed to lead me,
down this quiet country lane.
I saw a young girl standing
by a field of golden grain.
Although I was a long way
from my home across the sea,
it seemed as if I knew this spot
and young girl close to me.
As I walked towards her, and gently
took her hand.
The waving corn around us seemed
to understand.
The leafy trees above us, as if a spell
they cast were whispering to each
other they're two lovers from the past.
The songbirds they were singing,
their love songs to the morn.
As two young lovers gently kissed
to love again reborn.
Cyril Purvis

Poverty—And The Unwanted Cheque

It lay, unwanted, in her hand,
His cheque despised and never sought.
From him resolved all gifts are banned.
Her favours never to be bought.

But, as her fingers flexed to tear,
In thousand pieces such a slight,
A childish voice in deep despair,
Gave doleful notice of its plight.

"Please feed me with this cheque despised,
"And grant my days a longer stay.
"To me, such gifts are highly prized,
"And bring tomorrow's brighter day."

She banked the cheque, and wrote her own.
She listened to this child's sad plea,
Imploring her by deed condone,
His pseudo-generosity.

So, when at times, she feels the cold,
And wonders, "Was my cheque too late?"
She hears two voices, young and old.
A child's, a man's say, "Thank you, Kate."
Emanuel Herwald

St. Ives

Just thinking about it could make you cry.
you'd wake up in an unfamiliar bed.
It was bright, so bright cream
And loud; seagulls screaming and circling.

You got up.
You felt that the morning was not waiting for you.

To the beach, down the windy roads.
Yesterday's sand in your sandals.
Bucket and spade, reading book and doll.
And the sun playing hide and seek in the clouds.

The sea greeted you
Gush! Surprise! Then retreated and repeated.

The smell of salt and washing powder.
Staring at the sky and other children screaming.
Building sand castles, that always collapsed.
Finding sea sanded blue and green glass.

Using the sandwich packets to shape a mountain of sand;
No flag on the top, but a doll.
There; conquered, discovered, recorded.
St. Ives.

Sarah Mitchell

"When The Sky Is Looking Grey . . . "

When the sky is looking grey
Call on me for a place to stay
Don't be shy, don't be afraid
Don't look back, your life is made.

All the things you think are you
They'll only hurt you if you let them rule
Open your eyes and come outside
Spread your wings and learn to fly.

Out of sight and out of view
They are not really hidden from you.
Look in deeper and you will find
All those thoughts are in your mind.

Come inside out of the rain
Come and play a bigger game
Look around, don't be too proud
Change your mind and shout out loud.

All the things you feel inside
Let it out, it won't hurt your pride
Tell me what there is to tell
Break out of that hollow shell.
Alexander John Thomson

Land Of Despair

In the shadows, far removed, from any light of day
the epitaph of loneliness, where all around is grey
there are no walls to cloister in the echoes of the past
that haunt this desolated land, where light is never cast

Ghosts of wasted chances, traverse this vile land
sunk in their abject misery, oblivious to all around
chances of what could have been, what will and never be
flit through this filthy landscape, for as far as I can see

Night and day are meaningless, this land remains unchanged
devoid of any goodness, this is where evil reigns
the devastated wilderness, from where our nightmares come
this is the place you'll find me, this is where I call home

Inside us, each and everyone, this place, always exists
to brutalize our tortured souls, with clubs and whips and fists
when reality gets too much to bear, we retreat into this world
and analyze what could have been, as our past life is unfurled

I spend my time examining the choices that I've made
my memories of happier times, have all begun to fade
and all that I am left with, is all I will ever be
a resident of the strangest land, created just for me

Dave Skeaping

Inside Tears

First her parents left for Cyprus,
her mother, cried to stay.
She blamed her husband,
for losing her children.
That miserable weeping day.

Time does not heal, and doesn't forget,
I've watched her over the years.
She's a daddy's girl,
this she would not admit.
But she cries those inside tears.

It took many years to come to terms,
with the emptiness she cradles inside
Her daddy's not here, to love, and be near,
Or to comfort, whenever she cried.

And now, yet again, she suffers the pain.
For her brother, has left her as well.
Now they've all gone, and her tears flow free,
She fell in my arms and softly sobbed,
"How can they do this to me?"

R. B. Allbeury

No Laughing Matter

The fears they cannot face, too hurtful to think of cause
Frightened to sleep, afraid of day, of sudden light and
opening doors.

The choking terror, being held down
The wish they could just die
Longing for love and affection, trust in someone's eye.

The torment that someone they trusted
Looked up to, for truth and care
Has betrayed them, soiled them
Hurt them and spoiled them when tempted into their lair.

Sudden blinding light shatters safety of night
Harsh voice, terror again comes to smother
The longing to run and hide away from the hurt and deceit of
another.

Now that they're older
They still have bad scars
Things make them angry or too mild
Visions flash them back, people's harsh words
Again they're the tortured child.

They cannot enjoy life as others, join in the fun other have
They can smile and smirk
But it doesn't really work, these quiet ones have no real laugh.

T. P. Bradley

The Stream

Far up the hills where the air is fresh and clear
amidst the heather and gorse and occasional deer.

It starts its journey descending not knowing where it's going
Spring, Summer, Autumn and Winter even when it's snowing.

Gently it winds its crooked path over the rocks so bare
quenching the plants and animals showing that God does care.

Moorhen with her chicks do swim and flowers that feeds the bee
The enchanting wonders you encounter on your journey to the sea.

Under the weeping willows you create a shady nook
Where the insects mystically dance, you have to stop and look.

Through the meadows you meander where the primrose and
daisy grow
The farmer tills his soil so fine for the seeds he has to sow.

Under the bridge you do rush where the ivy spreads and clings
cascading down the rocks a wagtail stands and sings.

Wider and deeper, a branch aloft a kingfisher takes a dive
Children laugh and play, sail their boats, it's good to be alive.

Oh little stream, that grows and grows on its journey to the sea
The pleasure of life you give to us all I truly give thanks to thee

G. Dunster

Chasing Rainbows

Your sadness is like a puddle.
It doesn't reflect clearly
It disfigures you, making you confused.
I wish I could ease your pain
But if I gave you a star to shine with
You would shed the light on someone else.
If I sent you the clouds, you would only hide behind them.
When you stood under the waterfall of your desire
Did it leave you refreshed and content?
I thought it would but I was wrong.
It tormented you in your sleep, and it laughed at your dreams.
You walked a strange road, trying to find your pot of Gold,
But the rainbow was always just out of reach.
I know.
I saw you wandering after it, hypnotized.
The heavens opened and rays of sunlight came down upon you.
They warmed your skin.
You smiled and opened your eyes, awake at last.
You were like a flower, only mortal.
I hope you find what you're looking for.

Natalie Fernandez

A Lonely Marriage

Homeward bound from a laborious day's work,
United with a sea of crumpled, fatigued and anxious faces,
Envious of those with loved ones, sharing free flowing words,
. . . no matter how trivial.

In comparison to the reception of a split personality,
Surfacing its ugly interior from the depths within,
Fluctuating at inopportune moments like an overused elevator.

No one to share, care, understand or show an interest,
Such yearning to love from the core, cautiously withheld,
For each day is like treading on fallen snow.

Loved from a distance it's often been described,
Similar to a river flowing downstream, only to reach a waterfall,
Falling into a destiny of emptiness.

The mind wanders aimlessly down different avenues,
Pensive thoughts of the purpose of existence,
Trapped in a relationship like the chick covered in its eggshell,
Afraid to break out.

Nights are filled with dreams of elation, as the cock crows the
break of day,
Reality ensconces once again, and spirits cloud yet another day,
In the life of a lonely marriage.

Manuela Christina Wallace

God's Sea

God's sea plays many parts
it's made or broken many hearts,
so serene and peaceful when the waves are lapping
so strong and angry when the waves are crashing.

Liners, yachts, or even a barge
the sea is there for the people at large
to use for the pleasure
of the sunshine and leisure.

Lazing on a yacht as you sail round the bay
nothing to do but to lounge all day
watching the sunset o'er a calm blue sea
life seems worth living when it's all so carefree.

But what lies beneath the sea so cruel
collecting ships and bodies as if they were fuel
to feed its avaricious, insatiable hunger
helped along by the storms, lightning and thunder.

And once in the clutches of the sea
it doesn't give back so easily
so enjoy God's sea but don't treat it with contempt
whichever way you use it, none from accident are exempt.

Eileen Neal

Nothing

As I walk, each step sinks me further into nothing
An abyss of sun and sand is before me.
The hill I once climbed is ahead of me again,
Nothing changes: all remains the same.

How scantly can the mind think on nothing?
An oasis looms before me as I gaze.
Onto this plane of yellow earth of flakened salts
And reach for that penetrating deep sky.

Yet can I still find your footprint
That now quickly vanishes in the wind.
No-one comes to this place, I am alone
With memories of you still haunting me.

Circumstances change me, they come to my life freely
Then they leave.
As the wind to the desert they muddle me
And leave me empty yet full of pain.

As the sun they burn me
And like the wind they chill me to the bone.
They want nothing but to chain me
And use me as their own.

Rachel Rainey

When The Penny Drops!

What happened to the penny sweet? Once a joy in my life,
Made my mouth curl, and my eyes shine bright.
And what happened to the days, when a treat was ten pence,
It seemed like a fortune and the reaction was tense.

I'd grip the coin so tight in the centre of my palm,
I thought that the print would do permanent harm.

Suddenly ten pence has no real meaning.
Children look disappointed and end up screaming.
Now it's gold that makes eyes shine.
The rising cost of sweets is becoming a crime.

Then the paper rounds start for a measly pay.
But feel like thousands by the end of the day,
When the job becomes steady and money's no worry,
We look for the things of real value in a hurry.

But coppers are still disregarded in the gutter as dull,
By those who don't realise and think their lives are full.
Money soon becomes just a souvenir of your life,
Sentimental value for all the joys and the strife.

When you have it, you believe you have everything.
But without it, it seems you can't have anything.
That is when the penny drops!

Faye Louise Barker

Just Paddling

You sit, blue watered eyes a-staring
Out the window at the world
What have they seen since your beginning?
Tell me what I may know

A smile, you say you've had your moments . . .
You have them still, when you can remember your name
And all that you once were.
But they are fleeting now
So swiftly washed away.

A tear spills over, then many flow down aged cheeks

The waters broke. Without consent
You were thrown into the river of life
To float, swim, fight currents or drown.
Now you sit, just paddling,
Safe, they think.

Hands wet with wiping my own tears
Helpless I watch as you slip from my grasp,
Sliding down the muddy banks of memory
Into the river of oblivion

Moira Espin

Autumn

Life drifts by, like ripples on a lake,
leaves rustle on the trees, soft as a flake,
leaves of amber, red and gold,
The swish of the grass, as it blows in the cold.

The leaves fall, gently, soft as thistle down
Here them swirling round the woods, like a ladies gown,
Up a tree a squirrel sits, getting ready to sleep,
Busy scrambling up and down, for to earn its keep.

Birds await in the branches,
Waiting for food, taking their chances
The squirrels gather, their winter store,
They sit around, hoping for more.

A woodpecker, pecks away at the bark,
up above there's, the sound of a hark
The farmer nearby, fetches in the cows,
In the next field, there's a pig with her sow,

Up above, there's the sound of a thrush,
There's a rustling sound, in the heart of a bush,
Soon the winter snows, will cover the earth,
Then the whole county, will start its rebirth.

Margaret Ellison

"Chechnyan Torment"

An uncanny silence, rats scurry out of sight,
As if an incredible happening was about to take place.
Clouds open up to reveal the "Russian" might,
Who had a complete disregard for the "human race".

Seeking out their targets like "Birds of Prey",
Dropping "bombs" everywhere, destroying all in sight.
"Devastation", "Mutilation", where bodies lay,
Mortally wounded victims, crawl on their "bellies" and into
the night.

Gentle folk can be seen running the "gauntlet" every day,
Their "shattered" lives put at risk for a "loaf of bread"
Dodging "sniper's" bullets along the way,
Some not so lucky, another "hit", as the "blood runs red".

Packs of hungry dogs scavenge, are kept at bay,
The stench so bad, too much for one to bear.
Feeding off the "Corpses", to survive in their own way,
"Expressionless" faces, transfixed, can only but stare.

In the ruins of a tiny chapel, a melancholy chant,
Safe, an "unborn" child in the mother's womb.
Lighting a candle for "Peace", brave yet so gallant,
Knowingly, another "direct" hit, could become her "tomb".

P. B. Howells

Peace

Sensational sounds of the early songbirds,
Disturb the tranquillity when they are heard.
With the eastward rise of the scorching sun,
Another day has just begun.

Through the transparent pane I see;
Thawing frost causing the grass to glitter green.
I lay in bed and to my dismay,
Shattered is the peace portrayed.

Above the tender twittering; adored by me,
Like thunder, the rumble and roar comes repeatedly.
Reoccurring, the shotgun fire,
Depicts that the soldiers have yet to retire.

This fearless firing is a portent of doom,
Bringing nothing but a wealth of gloom.
Our conflict continues like a routine,
The atmosphere no longer serene.

Our lives are led by hope and prayer,
The mental torture seems so unfair.
If only a compromise could be reached,
We may then to witness Peace.

Claire Harris

Ozone

She walked hardened pebbles
Feeling sand between her toes,
She walked darkened streets
To places no one goes.

Her heart sat heavy in sadness
Her eyes all puffy and sore,
Faces torn and ugly
Smell's not sweet any more.

Rose's in December, snow in the spring,
Coat's worn in summer, what destruction they bring.
Land under water, starvation in tow,
All beauty left dying, as nothing will grow.

Wildlife a struggle, silent in song,
Rivers and lakes, oh pray what goes on,
Devil's a waiting, people disguised,
Caring and sharing, what sinful lies.

Slimy greens, food without taste,
Aerosol cans, and toxic waste,
Do we live, survive and try,
To save this planet, before we die.

Susan Byrne

'The Zone'

The breeze runs past this worn down eye,
circles flow from those endless panes.
The birds fall down from that moistened sky,
as the truth of the grave surely reigns.

Oh time, time, it's here again.
Slowly, slowly, here it crawl.
Head falls back, count one to ten;
watch that leaf simply fall.

Everything obeys, nothing rebels,
enclosed in our cages, tight as stone.
In the distance those endless bells,
surely beckoning to this mindless zone.

We just breathe, that's all we do.
Speak from our mouths, sit in our chairs.
The tightened autonomy as a man-made zoo,
laughing in groups, crying in pairs.

Oh my friend, why do we wait?
Just what is expected to conclude this tale?
Our hardened moves leave thankless check mate,
for from this case there is no bail.

Andy Cowan

"Spring"

Spring is coming, you'll be glad to know,
You can see the changes as they grow,
The lambs being born in open fields,
Their mothers watch, from harm they shield.

The cry of the robin building its nest,
Flitting about with bright coloured breast.
The pure white snowdrop pushing its head,
Out from the dark brown earth of its bed.

Leaves on trees will soon be showing,
Branches reaching, to the sun, and growing.
But most of all, people are brighter,
The winter is over, steps are lighter.

It's still a miracle, in days of space travel,
How nature does her seasons unravel!

Barbara Taylor

Enchantment

We stood to watch the unicorns play in the
    dappled light of dawn,
As the sun rose slowly skyward through the
    misty breath of morn.
We could not count their numbers as they
    pranced before our gaze,
They came and went mysteriously through the
    soft pink–purple haze.
The trees were gently sighing in the singing,
    whispering breeze.
And shafts of light came tumbling down through
    the myriad of leaves.
We can only wonder at their majestic,
    mystical form,
And recall this treasured moment each time
    we need it born.

Ann G. Lowden

The Prince Of Peace

This world is passing fast away
To make way for a world that's going to stay
A world of beauty and delight
Portraying the majesty and might
Of God who has promised to restore
The ravaged earth to peace forevermore

Where nations of the earth rejoice and sing
Their praises to the one proclaimed as king
Jesus Christ the saviour of mankind
Will rule in justice
Righteousness and peace
Where love will rule and never cease

No more the sounds of cannon roar
To shatter, maim, destroy the destitute, the poor
This wonderful planet earth will yield its increase
And all people of the earth will reap the feast
Of the eternal promised rule
By Jesus Christ the prince of peace

E. G. W.

Tug Of War

Slave to the demon,
Slave to the devil.
Bringing me down to your tiny level.

Deception, deceit is always on your mind
Never a thought of what you're doing
to other people's lives.

You thrive on hurt
You thrive on pain
It's the only way you know you'll gain

There's no point in fighting this battle
you win every time
I'll just go on hurting till the
day I die.

Michelle Lingard

Turn Off The Light

Turn over the table chairs
  smash pots and pans
Take away beds, beddings, drawers, clothings
  Fridge, the washing machine, cooker, the microwave
Damage all the central heating my personal belongings
Destroy all documents, passport and such make me a total non-entity
Take down the curtains—mash and smash the windows
Throw out the TV, the video, the stereo records and tapes
Give away the food, the cigs and drinks
  Tell the whole world she won't
  I can't and when you go turn off the light
  Z. Ali

Changes

Took a walk through village on a bright winter's morning
The people my old friends I wanted to see
I strolled down the Boreen by the hawthorn hedges
Could this be the Boreen that was once home to me?

It was the same Boreen where I played as a youngster
Where I once called home; a haven for me
I walked on the road by the old Moy river
But the lustre had vanished from this place by the sea.

The barren's the same as is the old Moy river
The wild rugged landscape is as it used to be
With its mountains its mists yellow gorse and green bushes
But the old friends had gone those I longed to see.

On a spot by the river I paused for a moment
And gazed at a cottage now empty and bare
A cottage once filled with much love and laughter
And I thought of my old friends and the times we spent there.

The mountains still stand tall in the distance
The mists and the rain still swirl in from the sea
And the old Moy river will flow on forever
New friends replace old ones that's how things must be.
  Mary C. Soden

What Shall I Do?

I look at the clock
it says ten past two
everyone's asleep but me
what shall I do?
Perhaps I'll watch TV
No, wait, there's nothing on
I could always read a book
but that would take too long
I know, I'll tidy my room
it could do with a clean
No, I can't do that
the noise would wake folk and that would be mean
I'll get my Walkman and listen to some pop
but wait, the last time I did the batteries went flat
Did I buy new ones?
No, I forgot
Maybe I'll just go to sleep like everyone else
or perhaps remain awake
pondering what to do next.
  Rachel Cripps

Evolution To Pollution

As I walk through this field so green
Sometimes I gaze upon the scene
I see blue beauty in the sky, as I watch
swallows winging by, I think about man's
foolish ways, and how the Earth's seen
better days. Everything is poisoned so,
pollution everywhere I go; it's in the rain,
it's in the air, it's in the rivers. Does
Man care? I exist as well you know, I have
to live as best I can. I'm just a rabbit
in a field who lives on earth with thoughtless
man. If I could only speak today, these are
the words that I would say.
  Margaret Irvine

Waiting

The hours pass by so slowly,
As I sit here all alone.
Waiting, waiting, waiting, for the ringing of the phone.
Is that your footstep upon the stair?
Calling to say that you really care.
Was that your key turning in the lock?
But no, it's not you, just the ticking of the clock.
How I long for your sweet touch—
Your smile that lightens my life so much.
I live in hope from day to day,
Tremulously longing for you to say—
That you will join me, and share my life,
Filling it with joy, and free from strife.
Or will you dash my hopes and dreams,
For you are the pinnacle of all my schemes.
I think of you from dawn to dusk,
So please do not destroy my trust.
My dear love, I need you so, I cannot bear to let you go,
Do say that we can look forward to—
A loving future, just me, and you.
  Sylvia Smith

Dumblane Remembered

Like a dove of peace
Their laugh has drifted
Their little smiles vanished
Where are their tiny breaths
Their little heartbeats gone
They appeared as fresh as morning dew
But now they lie asleep
Their little bodies still fresh and new
Not make a move nor murmur
Gone forever are they now, but in our hearts still here
Remember them as playful pals
Remember forever dear
  Melissa Dowlen

'Pearly Eyes, Dawn Surprise'

Sunrise, early skies, peachy dawn, pearly eyes,
Morning mist she came and kissed the Spring and Autumn flower,
She drifted gently over land and came into my bower,
Pearly eyes, a dawn surprise curtain of the day
Is lifted by the breeze of morn to lift the mist so early born,
Those pearly eyes did drift away,
The curtain of the dawn.
As mellow sun got up, and played with pearly eyes.
I stood beneath my scented bower
For me my crystal ivory tower
To watch the morning rise,
To lift my heart and feed my eyes
To see the magic change of skies
The curtain of the dawn,
And realize that pearly eyes when now drawn back
showed blue and misty skies,
So when the mellow sun got up and played with pearly eyes
I knew for certain that new day
Had come with dawn surprise
  Trisha Collins

What A Dear Friend

You were my shelter from the rain, just as the sun came out.
My light amid the darkness after it turned bright.
You came to help me through my pain when I'd suffered it myself.
My knight in shining armour, but I had to save myself.
What A Dear Friend.
You said you'd help me heal my wounds as long as they
weren't too sore
Or that I could not get by without you, no not anymore.
When times were tough and things were hard,
you were not there.
It's times like that I needed you there.
I've come to learn the kind of you and we'll never see eye to eye.
I guess it's true, what they say,
Good friends are hard to find.
What A Dear Friend.
  Donal Kearney

Untitled

Where do I go to when I sleep?
That peaceful death from which I can return.
That land of rest, yet not eternal.
The land where silent rears I weep.
Where do I go to when I sleep?

Sleep may be like the sea when calm.
Or like a raging tempest deep.
Those visions that can do no harm
And those were silent tears I weep.
Where do I go to when I sleep?

Will death come so gently, eternal and deep.
So peaceful and forever free.
Is sleep the cloak that death may bring me.
Where life exists as memory.
Where will I go to when I sleep?

Where we gather at the eternal door
Now cloaked in knowledge may I enter in.
My journey over the answer complete
Locked safely with me my journey done.
I know where I go to when I sleep.

Carol Lesle Lane Cilmeri

Good Housewife That I Am!

Rise at six thirty, breakfast at seven
Chores to get done or I won't go to heaven
Baby's flask and husband's bottle
Feed the cat and try not to throttle
the kids with jammy, sticky hands—good housewife that I am!

Here's milkman Fred to collect his money
"Morning Mrs. Twitty—nothing in the kitty?"
Never mind, payment in kind
Same smile, same wink, same negligee pink
A "thank you ma'am"—good housewife that I am!

Debt repaid and good deed done
Carpets sprinkled and swept the lawn
Time for a break and a cup of coffee
Drat that confounded moggy—piddled all over my 'Woman's Own'
Kick the cat to kingdom come—good housewife that I am!

Decisions more to tax the brain
Must feed the tribe on tribe's return
Endless planning, endless chores
Had enough, fed up and bored
Suitcase packed and slammed the door—
    good housewife that I am . . .
No more!

Patricia A. Maubec

Maggie's Place

It's a little bit of Heaven down at Maggie's place
with the roses, the lilacs, and sweet pea
where the squirrel, stoat and pheasant
do roam about so free:

Just down beyond the meadow,
the fox's 'call' so shrill—
as if to mourn the corncrake,
once so common, now 'tis still.

The primrose and the foxglove,
and other plants beside,
do tempt cross-pollinators
as they hover, perch and glide:

The Fuchsias and 'bride's blossom'
of contrasting, differing hues,
enhancing one's dream in perspective
from different points-of-views;

Now Maggie's place is a treasure-trove,
not to be found in London's town—
So, when next you're passing by,
please peep in and gaze around.

Kevin McCann

Bear Thoughts

I sit all day,
propped up in the corner of a room.
Not moving,
but watching.

People parade their humanity before me,
not thinking,
but acting.

All a meaningless charade.

I sit all night,
propped up in the corner of another room.
Not moving,
but wondering.

Into what
    the sleeping child will grow?

How fortunate,
    I'm just
    a simple
        Teddy Bear.

Colin Maxwell-Charters

Memories Of Paul

Restless nights when sleep won't come,
I tune my mind to sweet silent memories.
And relive once again times past,
When we were young, in love,
and life looked bright,
Before death turned his
face and looked at you.

A. Marlow

Angel's Tears

The Angels look down and weep
As over the world their watch do keep
Their tears falling softly on the world below
Is it any wonder that they weep so?
Have you seen the refugees?
Fleeing from the horrors of war they are seeing.
Tired, hungry, footsore and lame
Who then, for this is to blame?
Greedy men who have no heart,
They are tearing our lovely world apart.
Children from their parents torn
Wandering about lost and forlorn.
When your Children kneel to say a prayer
Would they say a special one for those less fortunate over there.
Why, oh why, can't men live in peace
Then these senseless wars would cease
Our world would be lovely again
A world that is happy, peaceful and sane
Then the Angels could look down and smile
On a world that is good and worthwhile

E. M. Geldhart

Baby Sarah

Dear Sarah, child with angel face
Wearing your bonnet trimmed with lace,
Sitting, laughing in the sun,
Amusing, charming everyone!

The clouds of dawn that April morn
Sailed through the sky when you were born,
And bird choirs cheerily did sing
To herald in the new day-spring!

Your infant days will fly away
And my sweet cherub this I pray
That life to you will always bring
Happiness, loved child of Spring!

So enjoy your tender years
Little Sarah, with no tears,
Sitting, laughing in the sun,
Amusing, charming everyone!

D. Townshend

"Growing Up"

I can't explain it, don't know why,
I'm empty inside,
Don't know how to cry!

It's sad, it's lonely,
It's desperately wrong,
changing forever,
do I belong?

Hold me, love me,
Show me I'm true,
bless me, touch me
make me feel strong and new.

I love you, I need you,
I want you to know,
please don't leave me,
help me go on and grow.

Losing, rejection,
Lost in a crowd,
I want to be noticed,
jump up and shout loud

I am truly alive!

Laura Bishop

Summer Love

Long hot days of summer
Are a joy to behold
Sets the mood for lovers
Or as I am told

Walking in the garden
Holding hands, alone
Looking into each other's eyes
All their worries gone

The sultry nights of feelings
Lying side by side
Sends the senses reeling
Love cannot be denied

Summer love is different
Like a whisper in stream
Who would want to change it
summer's such a dream.

Jean Fitzpatrick

Untitled

Conflagration is at hand
The signs are there in every land
We avoided war for fifty years
Now inward chaos are our fears
The science men produce new
   wonders
The working man trips and founders
Automation takes its hand
So out of work in every land

Phyllis F. Straker

Night's Goddess

Winter moon,
Shining pool of light,
White and cold,
Floats in a navy sky.
Shrill cries
Echo in an empty night.
Shining white orb
Casts long shadows.
Frozen night,
Chills leaf tips
With a white glaze.
Nights cloak,
Covering naked trees,
Floats peacefully on its way.

Amanda Weeks

Unspoken

I cannot talk
I see no way
To say the things I want to say.
My tongue is still
Yet beats my heart
For words and voice are two apart.
My silence holds
A thousand tears
A life of hidden hopes and fears.
My mind, it hears
A thousand voices;
Spoken out—the heart rejoices.
Yet never past
The lips they reach
This actress here forgot her speech.
For every word
I kissed goodbye
A fragment of my heart did die.
And now, alas, my heart is dead
For every word I left unsaid.

Julia Simpson

When The Night Weeps

Mist white and soft
from the Kamogawa River
enfolds the willows,
but the weeping branches
are in my dreams.

Why, even in sleep,
the fragrance of cherry blossom
gathers beneath my futon pillow
these warm Kyoto nights.

How I envy
youthful lovers passing
their interrupted hours
not alone
not needing
to write a poem on love.

Bernard Durrant

A Prayer

Oh Father of all living things
Of You eternal praise we sing,
and trust in Thou who conceived all
to righteousness the sinner's call,
and bless all nations one this earth
with lasting peace in land of birth,
and teach us all in love to live
and each our failings to forgive.

Matthew Kamsler

Untitled

Recumbent, on a playground bench,
I watch my child at play,
And think of all the things I did
in my first yesterday
Everything looks simpler than it did
When in her place
complex is the adult world she'll
One day have to face
She seems to do so little
Yet clearly, I recall
The things that pleasured me at two
When ten, weren't much at all
and when, in time, she takes my place,
And sits upon a seat
And watches on, as her child plays
in the local park, or street
I wonder if she'll recollect
The times when she did play
The games, this very moment,
I am looking on, today.

B. Kitt

"Dear Old Sid"

In a room full of old folk,
   One man is so alone,
Slumped in his chair,
   His thoughts are unknown.

His face shows no expression,
   His aging eyes are so dull,
A man imprisoned in time,
   With a dying soul.

On a table beside him,
   A cup of tea, no longer hot,
He's given a bib and a straw,
   Whether he wants it or not,

No one has respect,
   For him who has fought a war,
All bravery forgotten,
   He deserves so much more.

All dignity is gone.
   Talked to like a kid,
Please spare a thought,
   For "Dear Old Sid".

Kerry Martin

Children Of Now

I want to sing to the music
Haunting my soul
Life Forever
And not grow old.

I want to dance to the rhythm
In the beat of my heart
Change the world
Make a better start.

I want my every encounter
To be wholesome and sweet
To have a direction
And strong beliefs.

I want the new generation
To have an open mind
Consider others
Be humane and kind.

We are the hope of the future
We must learn how
To save our planet
We are the children of now.

Rebekka Collins

Lost Days Of Innocent

Oh how fond the days,
When we were so innocent.
We ate jam and sugared bread
On dew wet grass,
And played the childhood games
So simple with no sense.

We ran with the wind
Sweeping our tails of hair behind,
And made short but frequent trips
To see our granny so dear.
The days and things,
Just flowed by without a thought.

Now the bread is gone
And with it are the games,
Also granny's left.
With her, the house we spent much time
And loved as part of her.

Now all that's left,
Is us, our friendship strong;
And memories most fond.

Nuala C. McGroary

Luminary

Beautiful, awesome, argent, round
In silken, woven midnight gowned
With often misty halo crowned
Inspiring thoughts profound.

Focus in the sky's black gyre
Gath'ring light reflecting fire
With myriad speck adorned attire
Insisting my desire.

Glist'ring always pearly white
Far above the skylark's flight
soothing through nocturnal fright
Emoting deep delight.

Casting off untainted hue
Which fragments in the forming dew
Thus enriching dawns still view
Provoking poets new.

Mark J. Hollywood

"Moments To Share"

I strolled along a leafy lane,
Sweet scented after gentle rain,
And paused to watch the world around,
And little puddles on the ground.
I leaned against a wooden stile
To watch the lambs at play awhile.
I saw a blackbird in the sky
And heard a streamlet tinkling by.
A squirrel scampered up a tree
And then gazed shyly down at me.
The sun came out to warm the air
And shone around this vista fair,
I smelled the flowers in the hedge
And watched a butterfly on a ledge.
So far and wide the views expand
To show the beauty of the land.
I carried on along the way,
Enjoyment in a perfect day.
　　Just one thing more before I go:
　　Have *you* seen God today?

Diane Grindley

Ocean

Ocean of sound,
In back–street lanes.
And underground
In hollow trains.

Thrusting out
In loud flight paths.
On motorways,
On hazy days.
Where muted din
Is held within,
Our fragile stratosphere.

Ocean of sound,
In meadow deep.
In nature's ways
We gladly weep,
And laugh like
Carefree children.

Ocean of sound,
So soundly sweet.

Michael Corcoran

Untitled

Cats are mean, nasty things,
That kill the bird that sweetly sings,
Oh, cats of all things!
Their teeth are like razors
Their claws are like knives,
I don't know why God
Invented their lives.

Kate Dixon

Who's To Say . . .

There are no birds
There are no bees
Just a few black charred trees
All that's left of nuclear war
Those that did have
have no more.
The sun will never shine again
In its place acid rain.
Our lives are over
condemned to doom
So much death
Condensed with gloom.
Who's to say
Our knowledge has grown
It's all down to man
We should have known.

Lauren Carter

Autumn Leaves

Standing stately branches high
The leaves gently sway
As the breeze hurries by
The colour of green to red and gold
As autumn gently begins to unfold
Soon not a leaf is to be seen
Instead of shades of red and green
The branches bare and white
With snow
Little birds no place to go
So off they fly on hastened wing
Till they return one day in Spring

Ada Jones

The Smile

I listened as you spoke.
I smiled with happiness,
proud of your trust,
confiding thus in me.

I did not speak,
and there I was at fault.
My silence and my smile
were hurtful, I could see.

You thought me mocking,
doubtful of your acts.
Indeed it was not so.

I understood your hurt
but could not speak;
could not explain.

I failed you then, I knew,
but could not speak!

A coldness grew.
I only felt despair,
Oh, still I could not speak!

And now it is too late.

Geraldine Squires

The Poppies Of Our Land

They lived happily ever after,
For the country they had saved
Was now free from the laughter
Of the warfare they had braved.
Millions of men so noble
In their fight for our cause
Which, although on a scale was global,
Is now remembered with muted applause.
Did I say remember?
Oh how can we forget,
The men of war in November,
The men we never met?
　　One day we shall understand
　　The poppies of our land.

Anthony Williams

Wondrous Land

Please come with me
And take my hand,
Do not be wary
Come to my land

Hear the harmony
The birds do sing,
Release my hand
Go under their wing

See the flowers
They sway to the tune,
Drunk in the rhapsody
And so be you soon

My wondrous land
In soul and in mind,
Can be yours also
Have faith and you'll find

Bridget Docking

Zoggits

Zoggits live in queer places,
and they're very very small,
but they can do anything,
anything at all.

It's hard to see a zoggit,
it's hard to catch one too,
but there's nothing,
no there's nothing,
that a zoggit cannot do.

If you're lucky,
a zoggit might find you,
then,
abracadabra, whack dee doo,
they'll be nothing, that you cannot do.

Chris M. Murphy

Snookered?

My hobbies playing snooker,
Trophies and cups, I'd win,
My young son showed such interest,
I taught the game to him.

Day by day, he practised,
I was so proud of him,
And so, to encourage,
I'd often let him win.

As years went by, his play improved,
He won so many games,
I really had to play hard,
To keep up with his fame.

I've retired, and older now,
My potting's getting slack,
I take aim at a red ball,
Miss, and pot the black.

I play my son, but I know,
It's very kind of him,
Before a crowd of onlookers,
He often lets me win.

Pauline Markham

Justification

His nearness shakes her,
as the wind
a leaf upon a tree,
silently she prays to thee.
Bread of life
he places in her hand,
amen.
Her voice deliberately cross.
Once outside,
the fear to the ground
she can toss.

Bernadette O'Reilly

The Face Party

Angry faces scream and shout,
Secret faces creep and tiptoe about,
Frightened faces run and hide,
Fat faces are all big and wide,
Sad faces cry and scream,
Greedy faces scoff ice cream,
Boring faces sit and stare,
Ugly faces have bright pink hair,
Cold faces shake and shiver,
Snotty faces slime and slither,
Happy faces jump and play,
Pretty faces smile all day,
Naughty faces pinch and bite,
Tired faces say goodnight,
Helpful faces carry your books,
Grumpy faces give you black looks,
Loving faces laugh and giggle,
Baby faces like to dribble.

Stephanie Littlechild

Love

Love is all over,
Love, love, love
You can't touch it
Love what is it?

Is it in a rainbow?
Is it in the rain?
Is it in the sunshine?
Is it in the snow?

I can't touch it,
But, I can feel it.

Victoria Measor

These Things

The season of autumn will soon be here
  Pick the hops to make the beer,
Jack Frost's nip will be here to stay
  and so they've gathered in the hay.
The berries on branches to abound
  Birds can eat them from the ground
  The rains they came the other day
  and tried to wash it all away
My friend my dog, in rest, asleep.
No longer lying at my feet.
So while I wonder, what will be
A rainbow appeared from sky to sea.
In brilliant colours as if to say
God had promised another day.

Eileen Haynes

Our Tom

Tom is very naughty.
He's really in a fix,
He chases little dicky birds,
And spits at all the kids.

He's always rather dirty
As he climbs up all the trees,
He's never round at bath times,
Like me he's dirty knees.

Mum asked why we had him,
We must have won a bet.
But Dad said no we didn't.
We got him from the vet.

One day I'll go to London.
A pack upon my back.
And with me on my journey,
Will be my friend the cat.

So it doesn't really matter,
If his name is Tom or Mick.
As one day he'll be famous,
He's the cat that went with Dick.

Edith Cavell

Easter Paean

That day at Calvary
Jesus died on the tree
Blood and mud mix'd down
As biting thorns made a crown
The world's fate was decided
Sweet Lord, in heaven above
Receive me in Thy caring love.

J. A. Shaw

The Wonderer

Give me one last song
For your memory to wash away
Where did I go wrong?
Why I couldn't make you stay?

The warning fear I recognized
Nothing had been running so smooth
You're leaving me; I realized
Why life have to be so crude?

But if I find the will
There could be a life
Goodbye winter chill!
Spring comes to live!

There's a thrill in me running
To get back in control
I can feel the sun coming
To take me to it all

Without you; I will survive
To music; myself I sway.
I never want you back in my life
But maybe; for just one day!!

Maria Agius

A Kid's Dream World

Ice lolly mountains
Cherry-go-arounds,
Sherbet dip fountains
Dancing clowns

Curly wurly climbing frames
Candy floss hills,
Icy–cream waterfalls
Toffee–sponge daffodils

Sugar coated fairy cakes
Slides made out of jelly snakes.
Watermelon see-saws
Marzipan swings,
This is a kid's dream world
Made of all sorts of yummy things!

Kelly Ede

The Dolphin

Azure, mystical crystal blue sea
Warmed by a chameleon sun
Colours changing constantly
before its course is run
Under its warming protection,
Silver dolphins watch and play
Giving love and magic
asking nothing on the way
Their gentleness and wisdom,
a legend of the sea
Where did they come from?
It's a mystery to me
Did they have their origins
on Venus or Mars,
I wonder if they know
the secrets of the stars?
Are they man's guardians
to prevent some damning crime
Care takers of the planet
through an ageless endless time.

Elizabeth Allen

Can You See It?

Is it big or is it small?
Is it fat or is it tall?
No it's way above us all

Is it round or in disguise?
Can you see it with your eyes?
What are the colours that you can see?
Can you eat it for your tea?

It glisten high up in the sky
Slowly it fades I don't know why
The sun comes out, the rain will fall
Then it shines above us all.

Kathryn Bocking

Our Sundays

I clearly can remember
The way it used to be
Together every Sunday
We used to watch the sea

Sometimes when it was windy
The waves were high and rough
In the warmth of one another
You joked and made me laugh

Sometimes when it was rainy
The weather damp and cold
Heard love songs on the radio
And tightly we did hold

Sometimes when it was sunny
On the grass we used to lie
So close to one another
And watched the sky so high

Time flies and passes quickly
Nice memories left behind
I wish that I would keep them
Computered in my mind.

Rita Gauci Davison

Billy

A torn and twisted body
A tortured soul and mind
Billy a victim of cruel jeers
One of Billy
One of a kind
Crippled by a car
Screams heard near and far
Spirits lift
High as a kite
Broken body flew in the night
An innocent boy was Billy
Hit by a drunken fool
A drunken fool's living nightmare
Billy's wheelchair
Being the proof

Jennifer Grocott

When I'm Five

When I'm five I'll go to school
I'll do my sums and write and read;
dolls and prams I'll not need
When I'm five.

When I'm five I'll learn to swim
and rocks and shellfish I'll explore;
I'll run along the sandy shore
When I'm five.

When I'm five I'm sure I'll be
so good at games and climbing trees;
no more falls and grazing knees
when I'm five—

But Alas I'm Only Three

Audrey M. Jones

Drugs

Drugs is an addiction
You just can't seem to kick
If you've got any sense
You'll drop the habit quick

Drugs can kill
There's not just the one kind
Don't take the pill
Strangers sure won't mind

You're just another life
Thrown in the gutter
You're not in any strife
You're just another nutter

And even if you live
There's other diseases
Your life could be ruined
Because of these sleazes

So just be careful
When the dealers come along
Just say no,
Try to be strong

Niamh Burke

Untitled

As the world slips past the window
And technology takes you away,
Staring beyond the view
the landscape filled by you.
That day, that night,
I should have clung to it tight,
The rhythm, the rocking
The motion and mocking
of the train that drags me away.

Ruth Fuller

Blemishes

To wander in these lonely valleys,
I will spend my time.
As to suspend
From a ring of embarkment,
Here is where we draw the line
Sleek metal hastens its life.
It hastens to reach somewhere between
Value, and a simple nothing.
Images flow through
creeping between life's lines of sun,
As this glow enters the heart
Burning its pulse,
Reaching for the soul
Here our cotton hearts lie
And with this, the soul of the dead
draw pictures in our minds,
As we try to imagine
someone else's suspended time.

Rukhsana Malik

Untitled

Your pale blue eyes, that said so much,
That shone with your love and devotion,
Seem oh so cold, and distant now,
Void of any emotion,
I try to look into their depths,
To read the words they say,
But there is no love left within them,
No message to portray.
No longer do they shine for me,
Shine with your desire,
That showed how much you loved me,
That set my heart on fire,
For now the fire has gone out,
The 'Loving Flame' is dead and cold,
There is no need for words between us,
For your eyes, the story told.

Pat M. Johnson

Life

Life is like the ocean,
It's deep and full of dismay.
It never gets any easier
But gets harder day by day.

The experiences of growing up,
Are something quite extreme,
Love, alcohol, sex and drugs,
They aren't like how I dreamed.

No one understands these things,
Or what they put you through,
But these things can affect anyone,
Even me and you.

You only live life once,
Or so that's what they say,
Live life to the maximum,
This may be your last day.

Vicky Wood

Untitled

Just put your arms around me,
    And show me that you care,
Leave aside the bitterness,
    Our love is so unfair!

Forgive the hurtful words we say,
    Erase the pain within,
Just for moment in your arms,
    Free form harm and sin!

Look into my eyes and smile,
    And tell me you are true,
Although we fight and fall apart,
    I never will hate you!

Forever in my heart you'll stay,
    Through heartache and through pain,
Whatever differences we have,
    Our love is what we gain!!

Helen Elia

People Without Seed

Thin legs
Swollen tummies
Sad. sad eyes
People crying
People dying
While we eat their food

Switching off our telly
Getting on with our lives
Forgetting the moment of sadness
We had for the people in strife

How can we help them
Do we really care
Is giving a little money enough
Do we really want to share

Who gave us the right of greed
Are we any different
From these people without seed

Laura Dickson

Pathways

All my pathways lead to you,
And when I would diverge
From the destined track
The wind tells the rain
to turn me back
The willow will not cease
to plead its directions
With leaves continually turning,
Whilst the eager pointing poplars
Shake their kind impulsive arms,
And even the high gull
Cries his disapproval.

R. W. Hebbs

The Lost Pet

He lit up my life
Like a bolt of lightning
With his cute little furry face

I'd always stop
To give him some fuss
I could never give him enough

He had a good life
They say to me now
But did he really, I wonder?

Locked in a cage
From dawn until dusk
What crime had he done to get life?

But still he always
Seemed to smile
Did he put on a brave face?

I'll never forget him wherever he is
My pet, my friend
Good luck, God bless and goodbye

Louise Priest

Good Times

Here lies as dust,
The last goodbyes,
Of Thomas "Good Times" Miller,
His life was spent in search of drink,
Which proved to be his killer.

Good times were had by all who knew,
This man of many sides,
It's true to say that this includes,
His twenty seven brides.

He's gone it's true,
But still he'll live,
In memory and rhyme,
For after all is said and done,
His life was one good time.

A. Sainsbury

Memories Of Youth

A fading picture, dirty street,
    broken stones beneath my feet,
shoes with holes and socks I'd none,
    times that now are long past gone,
bows and arrows, guns and toys,
    go away don't make a noise,
fields and streams, ponds and fish,
    take me back, oh' God I wish,
games we played and secrets kept,
    the fear inside, the nights I wept,
no time to waste it must be done,
    sleep my body, the battle's won,
the only thing not in my plan
    I slept a boy and woke a man.
now I think I'm getting old,
    my body's weak, I'm feeling cold,
I'm only glad I have the key.
    a fading picture comforts me.

Ian Lauder

My Need

My need of thee is greater
Than anything I've known

My need of thee is frightening,
With a presence all its own

My need of thee is vital:
Without thee I cannot live

My need of thee is all I need
And all to thee I give.

E. Wheeler

Dreams Of You

I dreamed of you before we met,
   Although I didn't know,
That it was you I dreamed about,
   Those many years ago.

I dreamed of you and saw your face,
   And wondered was it you,
Who was the one I dreamed about,
   How will I know it's true?

I dreamed of you the day we wed,
   Our love can't fade away,
I want this one I dreamed about,
   With me to always stay.

I dreamed of you when you were mum,
   Your love I learned to share,
With children we had dreamed about,
   You gave your loving care.

I dream of you my darling wife,
   And know I always will,
For you are now my everything,
   The 'you' I dream of still.

D. M. Wood

The Day I Fell Off The Earth

The day I fell off the earth
I had been lying on my bed,
When I suddenly became aware
That the ceiling was touching my head.

I floated out the window
And up in to the sky,
People stared as I ascended,
The more polite ones waved goodbye.

"Goodbye, dear world!" I cried.
"Goodbye! Goodbye! Goodbye!"
But I didn't feel any sorrow,
I could even cry.

Now I'm drifting past the stars
And the world seems very small,
It's blue and white and beautiful,
No bigger than a ball.

And now it's gone forever,
Something I cannot touch,
I wish that I was there again
And I miss it very much.

Jason Creed

Poise

Kat looks at me with emerald eyes
Dares me to make a noise;
His tail-tip twitches gently as
He crouches there, with poise.

He springs, and as he does so.
I shout a warning cry.
He's got it! No, he hasn't!
The sparrow flashes by!

He glares at me with angry eyes
Why did I make that noise?
Then turns his back, disdainfully,
And walks away, with poise.

D. M. L. Wilks

This Forlorn Lady . . .

This forlorn lady
With eyes so pale,
Wears a heavy heart now . . .

For this forlorn lady
With a soul so bruised,
Is crying silently . . . . .

Rosalind M. Miller-Bastian

Early Friday Evening

The offices have closed the door
The building sites have stopped
Another week has stilled its roar
And silence cloaks the shops
In emptiness that fills the street
Because the places close
Before the laughter and the beat
Arrives in startling clothes

The traffic moves its homeward way
Beyond the litter bin
The pub is open all the day
But few are stood within
The doors to open and embrace
As some return to town
The evening wears a smiling face
Where once there was a frown

Mark Sampson

Dreams

Drifting through a sphere of mind trips
In a world personal to one's self
Imagine a world of goodness, happiness
Sunshine and good health

Living a life of complete perfection
No homelessness, pollution
Not a world of neglect

Soaring above a purple jelly mould
Hearing children's laughter
A good joke to be told

Dreams are our wishes
Our imagination's door
Unlock it and enter
To see what life has in store.

L. Hardman

The Hostile City

Walking through the City streets
Beneath the man-made Mountains.
Where plastic trees and plastic flowers
surround the concrete Fountains.

Dirty walls of factories past
are painted with our dreams.
And faceless people looking on
Whilst the City screams.

As darkness falls and I'm once again
inside my High—Rise Tower,
I gaze below as shadows flow,
before the midnight hour.

Letitia Smith

The Stars In The Sky

I tried to count the stars in the sky
And the grains of sand on the beach,
But that's just so high a number
That I really could not reach.
I tried to explain what you mean to me,
And how strong my love is for you.
But that was also so hard
As the number was much too great too.
Imagine a fish without water.
That's how I'd be without you.
Think of a lonely lost dog,
That would look like me too.
I love to have you a part of me.
You make me feel just right.
Feeling you inside of me,
We could be as one all night.
I always lust after your body,
I want to know what's in your mind
I'd like to understand what makes you
The best I will ever find.

Heather Gooderham

The Black Cat

Watch out
Watch out for the black cat
'Cause it stalks
And once it finds you that's that.

There's a trembling little girl
Hiding in the corner
But the black cat finds her
Now she's no longer their daughter.

It scratched her
Scars cut deep into her chest
And now, no matter what,
She'll always think she's second best

Her clothes cover the scars
And she pulls a mask over her face
Then she crawls into her eggshell mind
She's got to get out of this place.

She weakens
She's dying
Instead of laughing,
She's crying.

Theaopden Brouw

And I Love Him

I'm crying silently
The pain is unbearable
I've been attacked again
He's driving me insane.

Best years of my life
Thrown back in my face
A loving family I wanted
He made sure it was not to be.

His women friends
Think he's all I could need
He's young, he's fun
The fault—you know lies with me.

Oh where can I go
Just how do I leave
This continual beating and bruising
That no one can see.

Lonely and sad I'm sent out to work
It's never enough, only one job
I just want to die
Oh God teach me to fly.

Donna Lorraine Montegriffo

When I Was Six

I'm picking my nose
I'm standing in Church.
I'm up on my toes
Trying not to lurch.

They're singing a song
Called Moody and Sankey
I don't know this song
And I've lost my hankie.

I wish I was out
In the nice fresh air.
I could run and shout
Or meet a friend there.

Oh! Moody and Sankey—
will you never stop?
Oh! Where is my hankie?
Oh! Where did it drop.

The end must be near,
how slow the time goes.
That's why I stand here—
still picking my nose.

Sophie Tetlow

Impression

Who are they?
Who is he or she?
A victim of oneself of parenting,
teaching, poverty, wealth, or is it
society?
Is it to escape reality hardships
and difficulties of life or lack of
knowledge, self worth, boredom or
even a game?
But if it's a game,
what a high price to pay,
Who is there for them?
Who is there for he or she.
At the end of the day?
Are we as people, friends, family
Do we stay or walk away or
fail them?
Is it fear or lack of understanding.

Jan Johnson

My Feathered Friends

As I sit here in my garden.
Enjoying the peace on my own.
hoping no one comes to the door
or calls me on the phone.
I love to watch the birds in flight.
So much freedom
What a beautiful sight.
Then as they land, quite near to me.
I put down some food for their tea.
There's a lovely blackbird
a chirpy robin too.
They look at me, as if to say.
"Good morning" how are you?
Yes, I do love my garden
and the birds that visit me.
A lovely blackbird, a chirpy robin
and sitting near by—there's me.

Christina Russell

Worth

There is a worth so great
It uses up all words
And still is left unsaid

There is a beauty so immense
It swallows up all dreams
And still is left undreamt

A pain that cuts so deep
It suffocates all thought
But still is incomplete

There is a pleasure so divine
It devours all truth
And still remains a lie

Dan Connor

Universe Tall

So small, chasm tall,
A ball floating in space,
Innovation born, in the thoughts,
Of a mere mortal man.
Dreams of future/past deeds,
Wait for happy seeds.
Friends few, yet sort not,
Love's fool, and cries too.
Years, tears, fears, careers,
All mean nothing, all mean everything,
All seem interesting, all seem boring.
For on universal highways
Where light years and saint tears,
Are like the blinking of an eyelid,
Or the passing of a millisecond,
All our problems, seem to mean,
Very little indeed.

I. P. Martin

Thoughts On Leaving School

Laughter, smiles, activity,
Hum, buzz, things happening,
Learning, knowing, discovering,
Purpose, aim, ambition,
Caring for others, rewards,
Friends, talking, sharing,
Security, protection, continuity.
Being someone. Being wanted.
Doing something.
Into a void.
Nothing.

D. W. Pattullo

Togetherness

We sat together on the wall
And heard the plaintive seagull call.
We saw it fly upon the wing
And heard another seagull sing.

The girl, she played upon the sand,
As mum and dad walked hand in hand.
Above us all the birds did wing.
Again we heard the seagull sing.

We kissed and sat with joy of heart
And hoped we ne'er would have to part,
And as we saw the seagull wing,
We heard our playing daughter sing.

The sun went down, the day is o'er,
We heard the sea break on the shore.
We hope the morrow more joy will bring,
When again we hear the seagull sing.

Ryan J. Hodgetts

Mud-Flats

Time and the tide running out
ages–old, man–sculpted flints,
uncovered, still slice the flesh
for the painter standing staring there
the long beaches with their wild beauty
all run, bald, pitiless and bare
to a glare at the heart of the sun.

Last night's moon had lit the rain
pearled on the cool grass;
the warm rock cannot comfort this hand.

The tide turns again, in time,
gulls and sea and sky;
vast galaxies past sights turn free,
finite in alien infinities.

The watcher, pained holograms of time,
stands cold like stone,
the canvas blank and bare.

Chris Terry

Absence

I miss you friend,
As once I missed my mother's breast
Before I grew
To solid things.
I miss you,
As I miss that piece of me
I freely lost
In finding harmony.
I miss you,
As I miss that rare simplicity
That coloured life
With beauty.
I miss you,
With each eager backward glance
Around the winding corners
Of my ways,
Wondering where the warmth went
That filled the empty space.

Barbara Harvey Jones

My Angry Mind

Earth shakes beneath my feet
houses fall around,
the longest second slowly creeps,
burying my town.

Tall buildings rise above
caging my escape,
they slowly bend towards my way
and crumble in my wake.

I hear a crack, a shaft of pain
falling to the ground,
pushed and shoved and kicked again
buried, never found?

Deep inside I hear myself
a child who knows the way,
shouting out, "follow me,"
"up and over," "play."

But it is too late I find myself
captured, tortured, slain,
paralysed and staring out
as dust floats down like rain.

Nicholas Stephen Aldridge

A Friend

A friend is one who fills your heart
With a warmth you can't explain
A friend is one who stays with you
When you are feeling pain
A friend is one who is always there
When dreams do not come true
A friend is one you care about
And need your whole life through

Daphne Dodd

The Dance

We whirl and whorl
Circling, spiralling,
Round and round.
Feet slide, glide,
Point toe and heel,
Heel and toe.
A Yemenite here
A Grapevine there,
Step back, step forward,
Step forward, step back.
Welcome the sun,
Welcome the moon.
Dance to the elements,
To left and to right.
We are not witches,
Nor Druids,
But the Wednesday afternoon
Circle Dancers!

Margaret Wallis

Winter Memories

A winter's day spent by the sea,
The taste of spray upon my face.
Bitter winds that blow the sands,
It fills most every empty space.
A lonely gull, a plaintiff cry.
Is echoed on the greying sky,
and ships that sailed the winter tide,
lay safe in harbour, side by side.
I watch the waves they crash and fall
As they embrace the old sea wall.
Visions of a summer gone,
And sounds of children at their play.
Fill my head as I wander on
and warm this cold, cold, winter's day.

Moran Newrick

Lights

Flashing amber.
Urgent red.
Squealing brakes.
Spinning head.

Flashing blue.
Thumping heart.
Bloody vomit.
Car, torn apart.

Constant green.
Endless fight.
Medics too late . . .
Turn off the light.

Tina Prior

The Raindrop

Precariously trembling on a leaf
Gold in sun and crystal clear,
Emanating colour of autumnal bronze
Green cushioned, a rain cloud's tear.

Sparkling like some precious jewel
Fools the inquisitive jackdaw clown,
Cocks his head and in peculiar gait
Surveys the leaf with raindrop crown.

Petals of roses in cascades falling
On the breeze with scented air,
About the ball of mirrored water
Faceting rose–hued magic there.

A mysterious dance of preservation
The spider spins her silver thread,
She, though supped the lovely bubble,
Did not disturb it from its bed.

In all its splendour nestling there
Effect unnoticed in nature's course,
Did suddenly spill to soft brown earth
The very essence of all life's source.

Jo Rosson Gaskin

Feeling

From the dark to light,
Lighting all of life,
Living because of nature,
Nature being the creator,
Creating the universe.

The world forever spinning,
Like a piece of coal in the galaxy,
As a speck of dust in the universe,
The mother letting us be,
But forever changing us.

Time passing in a blink of an eye,
Becoming past, present and future,
Only one who really knows,
Being creator but also tormentor,
she is one, one in all.

Christine Gair

"Daffodils"

From the "Coldness" of the "Winter",
Comes an "Ever–Welcome Sign",
it's something "Rather Beautiful",
Once again it's, "Daffodil" time,
With those "Lovely Rays" of "Sunshine",
Moving "Gently" in the "Breeze",
So "Lovely" and so "Graceful",
Nestling "Down" amongst the "Trees"
With their "Golden Crowns" of "Glory",
Giving "Us" their "Hopeful Cheer"
To make our spirits "Brighter" and
"Guide Us" through the "Coming Year"

Sheila Salter Phillips

Antseiling

From a hole at the top,
I take a peep,
"Oh goodness me
This one is steep!"

This daring descent,
A challenge to all
Adventure before us
We shall not fall.

No need for helmet,
Harness or rope,
We are sure footed
Whatever the slope.

I call to my friends,
"Come follow me!"
Down to the ground
At breakneck speed.

We pass dozens of cousins
Retracing the track
Bottom to top . . . "Oh no
We have to go back!"

Hilary Veits

In A Spider's Web

In a spider's web,
We are born and bred
Weaving a thin thread.
Travelling along
As fast as we can go,
life is one big show.

Dreams and wishes,
Some score, some have near misses.
As we spend our time
Wonderin' why we're here.
Life is an art,
Dicing with death
'Til death do us part.

In a spider's web,
We are born and bred
Dreading life without love.
For love is a must helping us
To avoid hate that vegetates.
But if love's gate is open,
Love can win if chosen.

Lindsay Jupp

Synonymous Beings

Deep deep down
As deep as the bluest sea
I see you
Then I see me

I see my reflection
A reflection of me
Which reminds me of you
Which sees me as I do you.

I see you as a mirror
But I cannot see me
What I can do is hear me
And see how I would feel

Although I cannot find the words
To express the way I feel
Just look into my mirror
And everything is real

So show me what I can be
And I can imitate what I see
The most of you inside me
And the most of me in you.

Gayle C. R. Harte

The End

It looms around every minute and hour,
Waiting to strike and cause despair.
It ends the gift of mortal life,
Causing destruction in its path.
Always waiting impatiently,
Never resting—always alert.
Never willing to stop,
Never daring to show its face.
When darkness approaches,
It's always there—waiting.

Lucia Oshinaike

"Mother Of The Bride"

My outfits hanging on the rail
It's a delicate shade of green
My hat, shoes, gloves and bag
Will all complete the scene

My daughter's getting married
She looks lovely in her dress
For 6 long years they've tarried
but now the date is set

Then one day came the bombshell
She telephoned to say
She'd had a change of heart
and there would be no wedding day

We talked and talked to no avail
The magic died she said to me
I've fallen in love with someone new
So I cannot marry now you see

Until these clouds have rolled away
and happier times have come
I can only wait and pray
That she will find her special one

Sheila D. Bryant

My Mother's Passing

The light was fading
A lamp was by the side of her bed
There was a clock in the room
Outside the room there was life
I held my life by the hand
And I wept
And I waited
My mother has passed

Phyllis Cannon

Don't Dis Me

What do you see, come tell
me, could it be a disability?

I see you, you are able?
You see me, disable

I seem to have a disadvantage,
This is not of my own language,

Who can say, I have no ability,
but label me of disability

I look different, I may not talk,
I may lack vision or not even walk

I feel disowned, I feel discarded,
I feel uncomfortable, I feel retarded

To disavow, dispose of me too
To look upon and to disapprove

To dislike me, on your first sight
We are all human you have the right

So now take notice and take heed,
I have blood and like you bleed

You see me different, well I disagree

Listen up, just don't dis me!

Prudence D. Petrez

Angelo

Your touch sends shivers through me
Your kiss drives me wild
Lingering
Caressing me, reaching my soul.
Penetrating my being with
Intense words
Words that mean so much
Treasured for a lifetime,
Never to be forgotten.
You mean the world to me
I couldn't breathe without you
You're all I'll ever need.
Protecting me from a
Cruel, harsh world in a loving embrace.
Wrapped in love.
Nothing else exists except
You and me. Us.

Melanie Cox

England, Sweet England

Oh my country, oh my love
as summer dies and fades away
wilt thou not keep for me
one single faded day?

A silver moon on a velvet sky
a sprinkle of stars over the night
the breeze dancing through the woods
the rising sun spreading its light

and yet still the morn o' dew
the hope that a sunset brings
the scent of roses in the air
the mystery when the first bird sings

As I said one faded day
is all I ask of you
oh my country, on my own
whatever would I do?

Emily Eastwood

The Green Spirit Of Summer

Give to me your loneliness,
And share your tears and pain
That I may give you happiness
And make you live again.

Give to me your aching heart
And I'll give you a true love
Forget the emptiness that's past,
And start again with new love.

Tell me the words you dare not say,
Give to me your sorrow,
Give to me your yesterday
And I'll give you tomorrow.

Give to me your sadness
And I will bring you laughter,
Let me have your ache-filled past,
For I am the Hereafter.

Mary C. Thomas

If!

If I was something other than I am
I know in a flock I would not be a lamb
If my dreams reality beckoned
To saunter towards it every second
If there were peace on this earth
A great and rousing ambitious mirth
If wonders of the past
Happened at last
If visions of love
Seem like gifts from above
If the world gives you strife
Remember if is the middle of life

Kristian Davies

The Real Red Rose

How can ye bloom sae fairly?
Ye rugged plant o' love.
There to convey such beauty
Tenderness to share and to give!
While underneath it lies . . . a thorn,
To gash and to cut,
Deep into the flesh of any man:
To hurt and pierce the heart,
Rip it open . . .
Tear it apart!
And all the while it's laughing at you
With deepest irony;
Showing off its blood–red prowess.
All for the sake of . . .
Love!

James C. Lyon

Images Of War

Shattered, crumbled,
Mangled, tumbled.
Broken, dead.
Battle, bloodshed.

Ragged children,
War like a cauldron.
Conflict, death,
Take your last breath.

House destruction,
Orphans depend.
Shelters, starvation,
War does not mend.

Lois Perrin

Why Oh Why?

She sits around thinking
Why oh why,
Why did she weep
Why did she cry

Why did she wander
Far and wide
To try to let out
Her hurt inside

Why did she hide
Her grief so long
Why was she playing
A game all along

Why did she let
The years slip by
Hiding her grief
Hiding her cry

Now she looks back
Saying why oh why?
Why did she weep
Why did she cry?

Stephanie Lowry

The Atrocity

The innocent victim a child
Unwanted, unloved, rejected
Delivered amidst war it cried
Result of rape, disrespected
Who will care
Who will be there
Mother violated
Father hated
A creation in fear
Who will shed a tear
The product of violence and lust
Through the fighting in the dust
Born and discarded.

Olwyn Fairless

Friendship

I feel it's very wrong of me
and yet I must admit,
When someone offers friendship
I want the whole of it.
I don't want anybody else
to share my friends with me?
At least I want one special one
who indisputably

Likes me much more than all the rest,
who is always on my side,
who never cares what others say
who lets me come and hide.

Within his shadow, in his house,
it doesn't matter where,
who lets me simply be myself
Who is always, always there.

Anna Neocleous

Betrayal

Sleep safe my darling gently lie
You know not yet that you must die.
With early sunlight namely dawn
For you my darling I will mourn.

Sleep well my love do not wake,
Soon your last breath you will take.
When sunrays end eternal night
Your soul to heaven in its flight.

Sleep; sleep sound my pet
Morning has not come as yet.
Safe in my arms, you'll never know
I betrayed you, though I loved you so.

G. Whiteford

Feathered Friends

I looked out of the window today,
and saw the little birds at play,
and there upon this merry morn,
I spied a blackbird on the lawn,
a-chasing off the starlings there,
who picked their tidbits up with care,
when stern commander blackbird came,
they flew away to treetop home,
but little sparrows stood their ground,
and carried on with what they'd found,
a lonely thrust stood watching by
till Mr. Blackbird caught his eyes,
he and the sparrows flew away,
and blackbird knew he'd won the day.

J. Haslam

A Poem For Paul

My tiny sweet child, now sleeping,
How I miss you, so very much,
Your perfect little fingers,
with your gentle, tender touch,
One day angels came and took to you,
Way above the clear blue sky,
I wonder where you are right now,
While I sit here asking, why?
I'm thankful for the time we had,
Every moment that you smiled,
You gave me love and happiness,
My sweet darling little child,
As I sit and think about you now,
My eyes fill up with tears,
I miss you more and more each day,
Throughout the growing years,
My love for you will never fade,
Or ever go away,
For, I know we'll meet again my child,
Somewhere, some other day.

D. K. Sharp

My Boys

Your hearts are full of good
and love you will always have
good fun you fill the house with
so much laughter you fill my heart
with love and peace.

I love you more than words
can say my love for you will
never fade you fill my life
with pride and joy I love
you both for ever more.

You shine like stars up in the
sky my love for you will never
die you shine so bright so
big and bold my heart sings
out forever more.

The time has came to say goodnight
love you both with all my might
wake up wise happy and bright
then we will start a brand new day.

Susan Fennell

The Iron Mountains
(The Forth Railway Bridge)

From Fife's bold Kingdom in the North
To Queensferry's harbour mouth
Spanning the ship–lined River Forth
A steel sky-way travels south.

Iron mountains, massive and sublime,
Built on the blood and sweat of men,
Soar through a century of time
Like Highland ranges o'er the glen.

No purple heather clads their line,
No deer roam near their form.
Bright majesty and beauty shine
When golden sunsets follow storm.

Deep, deep beneath dark tide and wave
The mighty columns thrust their piers;
But deeper into hearts once brave,
Cold steel disturbed the widows' tears.

The toy trains trundle on their way
Dwarfed by titanic mastery.
Do tiny travellers pause to pray?
Or thank great men beneath the sea?

Frank Parker

Oh List

"Oh list", to a gentle voice
  Calling you and me,
Hear it call from shore to shore
  Across the mighty sea.

"Oh list", to a sweet voice calling
  Across the desert sand,
From mountain peaks from valleys low
  "Oh list", in every land.

"Oh list", to the universal voice
  Calling round the world,
Awaken to its fluted notes
  Let the inner ear unfurl.

It calls to the soul of every man
  Where nests a captive bird,
With radiant plumage never seen
  His rapturous song unheard.

Open up his jewelled cage
  Let him spread joyful wing,
In answer to that gentle voice
  His throbbing throat will sing.

Marjorie E. Dawson

The Plane Crash

The plane crashes
People dying
Blood curdling screams
People dying, scared and crying
As the plane crashes.

Mountain echoes everywhere
Scared silence fills the lonely air
Holding, wishing, praying and thinking
People are hungry yet care
As the plane crashes.

Help us they cry
As the snow drops high from the sky
As they cry they wish they would die
As the plane crashes up
above the mountains high.

Sheralyn Bryce

Typical Evening

Often there is trouble,
When you have a nagging wife,
Problems there are many.
And they often start at night
Like "Have you put the bottle out?
And then locked our front door
Have you turned the lights off?
'Cause you left them on before,
Did you turn the gas off dear?
Then check the cooker too,
Did you put the cat out?
Then lock the back door too,
Have you put the blanket on?
Then made a cup of tea,
Then we will sit and drink it,
then retire you and me."
We then forget the nagging,
We cuddle up real tight,
Our bed is nice and warm,
We sleep away the night.

Christine Lamb

I Could Only Stand And Stare

The sun shone down from heaven
Upon your golden hair,
A mighty ray of light it wove,
And I could only stand and stare.

The moon shone down from heaven,
As you were lying there,
It spread its beams upon the earth,
And I could only stand and stare.

The stars shone down from heaven
Upon your cheek so fair,
I knew that you had breathed your last,
And I could only stand and stare.

Then darkness came upon the earth,
And hid your face so rare,
I saw your body laid to rest,
And I could only stand and stare.

Mary Baird-Hammond

Are You Searching For A World

Where all your dreams come true.
A world of peace and love and hope.
No reasons to be blue.
Compassion felt for fellow man.
True friendship that is real.
To be in charge of your own life,
To know it's safe to feel.
Where you can put your faith in others.
And be trusting with oneself.
You need to search no further.
Just look inside yourself.

June Gregory

Quoth The Raven

"Tiger Heaven", tiger haven,
Here they have a peaceful time.
Nevermore, though, quoth the Raven,
Visiting their native clime.

What is more, too quoth the Raven,
With the constant cars in streams
It's a noisy so–called haven,
Not a place of quiet dreams.

They are safe, though, in their haven,
No-one kills them for their bones.
Would you like it? Asked the Raven;
Grass and boring pile of stones.

Aren't they happy in their haven?
Cats, no doubt, will hate the snow.
Never, never quoth the Raven,
Never shall you really know.

Muriel Smith

Morning

With the first kiss of morning,
I will bring unto you,
A velvet red rose.
Glistening in dew.

To the valley I'll go,
And bring you from there,
A vessel of sunlight,
And pure morning air.

I will run through the meadows,
Of grass, sweet and strong.
To bring to you music,
Of the blackbird's first song.

Blossoms I'll gather,
Heavy with mist.
To lay by the face,
That the morning has kissed.

Valerie Goodwin

Utopia

The splendour of the Scottish lochs,
the rugged heathered tree clad rocks,
such awesome beauty to behold,
so many wonders do unfold.
The clear cool water in the burns,
meandering on in twists and turns,
where naked tree roots can be seen,
no longer safe, begin to lean.
The crashing waterfalls resound,
no sweeter music could be found,
Utopia is here on earth,
mine eyes have seen it here in Perth.

Carole Glenda Nutt

The Forest Tree Of Life

The forest in the tree,
the host in every mortal.
This life is one identity,
embracing every morsel.
Each part a little of the whole,
each separately free.
Creature, plant and human soul
embracing you and me.

Ever ending, ever reborn,
aware of existence
Life journey's alone.
All parts in a sixth sense
perceiving the others,
as members of family
as sisters and brothers.
Love is the root of the tree.

Matthew Tulip

Remind Me

I do love tiny babies,
    thy are so small and sweet,
but don't forget the mess they make,
    when it's time to eat.

Remind me of the washing,
    the pile a mountain high,
when am I going to get it done,
    and where's it going to dry?

Remind me of the sleepless nights,
    the to-ing and fro-ing,
I must get my head down,
    the night is swiftly going!

Remind me of the trips to school,
    the loading and unpacking,
what are we going to eat tonight?
    I really must stop snacking.

So when anybody hears me say
    that I might like another,
would someone please remind me,
    three boys are enough for any mother!

Karen Richardson

To My Carer

This verse bring my love and gratitude
for your tender loving care.
I really don't know what I'd do,
if some day you were not there.
I hope that you do not regret,
the day you took me for your wife.
Little did we realize then
how my health would cause such strife.
Thanks for standing by me through
good times and through bad.
You have proved to be the best
of pals that I have ever had.

Marie Leeming

The Open

Now everything is silent
Now everything is black
The sky the dark deep ocean
The wind at our back
The stars a twisted tangled map
That only few can follow
The moon my torch and companion
For tonight and for tomorrow
The grassy bed where I rest my head
Wrapped up like a cocoon
The crickets chirp and sing the songs
Beneath the candle moon

David Chittem

The Birth Of Death

Angry taunts and curses,
Alarms stridently ringing
A cacophony of noise
without the silencer on.

Blazing cars as barricades,
Faces ghoulish by the fire,
Sparks leaping skywards
In a pyrotechnic display.

Men in anoxatin, balaclavas
Festooned with orange sashes,
Munching greasy hamburgers,
Swilling down cans of lager,

Traffic disorganized, diverted
shops looted, housed burned,
Ethnic cleansing, Belfast style
while peace lies dying.

Gerald Johnston

A Piece Of Quiet

The peace of a room,
Without light or sound,
To relax your mind,
Let it wander around.
   Buy a ticket.
For your train of thought.
Explore far off lands,
of which you were taught.
Travel through endless caves of ideas.
Where answers to questions,
just may appear.
Imagination takes you for a ride,
Fantasies need, no longer hide.
Imagine a room without sound or light,
And give the world a rest,
just for the night.

Gillian Dobb

The Weather

Well, I'm English, aren't I?
So I've got to mention the weather
It crops up very frequently
When we get together.
Every time we meet
We talk of this and that
Then we're back to weather
As we sit and chat.
Maybe one of these fine days
Did I say fine? There's rain ahead
We'll sit and talk of other things
And reminisce instead.
All about the old days
The roads we trod together
Then we'll go and spoil it all
And talk about the weather.

J. Bradshaw

Listen

Listen to this and
bear in mind a loving
friend is hard to find.
When you find one
sincere and true never
forget the old for the new.
I met you as a
stranger I met you as
a friend. I hope our
friendship will never
come to an end.

W. J. Cummings

Beauty Dying

Beauty lay a-dying
In the litter strewn street
Human's like little robots
Trailed their weakened feet.
Oh, man! What have you done?

Beauty lay a-dying
In the forested terrain.
Mighty giants stood dejected
Drenched by the acid rain.
Oh man! What have you done?

Beauty lay a-dying
In the once green countryside.
Now the grass had withered.
Ruined crops spread far and wide.
Oh man! What have you done?

Beauty lay a-dying
Thro' the world her death cries rang.
Followed by an eerie silence
For no birds sang.
Oh man! What have you done?

Mary Rennie

Time

Time is such a precious thing
And time can mean so much
It's time that rules our
Daily lives
Time keeps us all in touch
Time heals our grief
And eases pain
But time won't go away
We go to bed at nighttime
And wake up on time next day
Without time we could not
Survive
It's time that keeps us
All alive
Time a broken heart
can mend
And time stays with us
To the very end

Jean Worsfold

Marry Me

Take my hand and lead me
Into the rest of my life.
Make the promises of love
And talk about Eternity.
Hold me forever in your arms,
Unite with me in adoration,
Take me to the depths of love
And marry me.

Pauline Strange

Sabotage

She looked into the mirror
To realize one day
That Time's relentless fingers
Had torn her youth away

Had sabotaged her beauty
Stolen all her grace
Destroyed her precious sparkle
And ruined her pretty face.

She thought her heart was broken
Her vanity was great
But ruthless Time informed her
She must accept her fate.

She had to change her values
Realize her age
Enjoy each fleeting moment
And turn another page

To find her ageless spirit
Imprisoned in the clay
Cruel Time can never sabotage
Nor even take away.

Joan Brook

Spring's First Daffodil

I turned the bend and topped the rise
And there she stood before my eyes.
A silhouette against the green,
More radiant than any Queen.
No oriental colour gay
Could beautify her neat inlay.
No Paris chemist could prepare
The fragrance of her perfume rare.
No man–made satin, silk or lace
Could dignify this lady's grace.
No party frock or pinafore
Could match the yellow dress she wore
Not artfulness in new design
Creation of a hand divine
No poet described or ever will
The charm of Spring's first daffodil.

John Cowley

Timeless Note

The faded postcard
pinned to the billboard read,
"May wandering in these gardens,
bring that which you seek."

I wandered through
the coloured perfumed seas,
I wandered through
the shades of green
by pebbled streams,
I wandered over soft warm grass,
Lingered under trees,
and knew the postcard wrote, content.

D. Elizabeth Smith

Untitled

A year's gone by without you there
it sometimes seems so hard to bear.
Your smiling face
your loving touch.
Dear Mum you're missed so very much
we know you sit at God's right hand
he'll keep you in the promised land
where pain and suffering are no more
I hope one day we'll find that door.

E. Lewington

When The Evening Comes

It's quiet at last,
The children are in bed,
No more tears or tantrums
It's got to be said,
Thank goodness it's evening
a time to reflect,
on all the days events.
From breakfast to play group,
Shopping and lunch,
amusements and pastimes,
Crisps and biscuits to munch.
The fights over tea time,
I'm not having that
can we watch the T.V.
can we have postman pat?
When the evening comes,
I get a chance to sit down,
do a crossword, read a book
and just potter around.

Mandy Hilton

Cover

When you look, who do you see
The real me or the moulded me
Moulded by others careless minds
Minds of opinion, criticism and doubt

I was at one time my own person
Able to think with my own mind
Make decisions with my own thoughts
And live life as an individual

One individual turned into a world
A world so ready to mould
I no longer am my own person
But a person moulded by people

I now share thoughts and decisions
No longer living as an individual
Now I live as a group of minds
Sharing opinions criticism and doubt

One day I may be free to think
Free, one day to make decisions
Free to live as an individual
For now I'll live as the moulded me.

S. A. Clay

Creeping Mist

See the grey mist creeping
As it passes o'er
Blocking out the beauty
Of the heather–clad moor,
Silently it hovers
As it swirls around,
Sheltering little creatures
That scurry on the ground.

See the grey mist creeping
As it passes o'er,
Making ghostly images
Of dead trees on the moor,
Silently it travels
When it starts to roam,
But the hills and fells,
And Moorland
Is the grey mists home.

Nora Kathleen Cooper

Trust

Should I give you, my heart to keep.
Could I rest, and go to sleep.
If I gave you, my very soul.
Your eyes see, all my hopes unroll.

Would you find, feelings there.
Sorry, sad, and laying bare.
What if, you tell another man.
My every thought, every plan.

Uncover them, for all to see.
So they could, stand and stare at me.
Or would you, try to understand.
Wipe my eyes, and hold my hand.

Keep the secrets, all untold.
Help deepest fears, to unfold.
Be my friend, no matter what.
Even when, you know the lot.

Jane Brooks

Dad

Though my heart is heavy
And my eyes still full of tears
Deep down I feel the comfort
Of your love through all the years

Though now I cannot see you
Nor hear you nor touch you
Your presence lingers on and on
Beside me and in my thoughts

Our love for one another
Was so pure as only can
A love between a Daughter
And her one and only Dad

Di Bishop

Thoughts Of An 80-Year Old On The Millennium

Two thousand?
Two thousand and one?
What fun!
For living so long—
A song.
For still being here—
A cheer.
Whichever year,
No fear.
Let's celebrate,
Early or late,
Whatever the date.

Doreen Bryden

Love And Hate

Love is a bouquet
Hate is thorns

Love is an aroma
Hate is a stench

Love is tender
Hate is morose

Love is facile
Hate is dense

Love is solace
Hate is a struggle

Love is belief
Hate is anguish

Love is splendour
Hate is bleak

Love is elation
Hate is vexation

Love is ailing
Love is celestial
Love wins over
Hate loses all!

Fatima Khan

Our Rose Garden

Roses Roses Roses
How we both loved roses
Which one you would say
This will be in our garden
For your Wedding Day

Roses Roses Roses
Red pink orange yellow
All the colours of the rainbow
But we always knew
Only superstar would ever do

Roses Roses Roses
Beautiful scented flowers
They will always remind me
Of the happy times I had
Dad with you.

Roses Roses Roses
Is now heavens Roses scent
As long has the skies are blue
I your only daughter
Will always miss you.

Jeannette Christine Downing

Teenage Love

My eyes bled water
as he turned and walked out of the room
I felt a sense of loneliness
and inner sense of doom

Did I hurt you so much
explanations can't be told
but I'm not some kind of possession
that can be bought and sold

I wanted a life of my own
but you couldn't even trust me
and then I asked myself
what kind of relationship can this be?

The love we share is strange
I'm not sure if its real
but I need some time alone
to work out how I feel

One day you will realise
that I'm a person too
not an amusing object
that was created just for you

Jacqueline Halvey

Time

With most things in life
The question is time?
One hears quite often
Of its loss or its lack.
It measures our lives
A most definite line.
Running short, running out
But not ever back.

John Winterburn

Who?

Who needs us, feeds us cares for us
   when into this world we scream?
Who teaches us the wrongs and rights
   and loves us when we're mean?
Who bathes our knees and mends the hurt
   when others do us down?
Who cheers us up and makes us laugh
   when all we do is frown?
Who protects us from the world
   and often from ourselves?
Who excuses our mistakes
   and shoulders them themselves?
Who slackens off the apron strings
   to set us free to live?
Who never holds their love from us
   but only ever gives?
Who is this angel in disguise?
   not sister, father, brother:
Who hasn't guessed the answer yet?
Who hasn't had a mother?

Sarah Brown

The Final Day

The night will come,
nowhere to run,
the sky will dim,
there will be no one in,
their homes.
Away,
people will stay,
their hearts filled with fright,
running from the night.
Only the good and holy,
will see the light,
fly like a kite,
at great height,
but then again the Lord might,
spare me and my child,
'cause I'm not wild, anymore.
But still in a ball,
I will stay curled,
awaiting the last day of the world.

Sallie-Anne Betts

Just Good Friends

You wanted to stay friends
So we tried
You enjoyed all the attention
While I cried
You wanted all your freedom
Me here waiting
For your call, your voice
Anticipating
Can't be "Just Good Friends"
'Cos I still love you
Hurts too much
Rather be without you
So please don't come around
Please don't phone
I don't want to be just friends
I'd rather be
alone.

Adele Hyndman

The Speed

The speed, adrenalin, pumping rush
Of life; flashing in the gleam
Of eyes once alive; with the
Same fervour as the ones before.

How little life must mean
To those with such speed and
Adrenalin, such pumping rush
As he had that night

The sharp, shooting,
Tingling sensation
He endured, with such firmness of
Jaw; is envied as much as he
Envies those without.

To know so minute details of
Such pain, is pain in itself
As it is to those who shared
It; the speed, adrenalin and
Pumping rush of life.

Emma Mumby

Today The Island Children Win

Island kissed with summer sun,
Children playing having fun.
Bouncy ball thrown to the beach,
Missed the crab just out of reach.

Bucket and spade litter the sand,
Dainty footprints bare as your hand.
Castles beneath sandy feet,
Only the waves do clean sweep.

Run, jump, make a splash,
Water skier cutting a dash.
Boat, float, paddle or swim,
Today the Island children win.

Robin Pearcey

Untitled

Love is like a cold
We catch it through the years
And just as you can cope with it
It suddenly disappears
Have you ever noticed
We do things to ease the pain
And as you're getting over it
We catch it once again

K. B. Smith

Child's Play

The children's playground used to be
So full of fun and joy.
The laughter that we often heard
From every girl and boy.

The cheeky grin upon the face
Of one so very young.
From twisting up a puckered nose
To sticking out a tongue.

These were the days when children were
Allowed to roam out free.
When good old Gran and Grandpa
Would sit them on their knee.

But sadly times are changing now
And for the worse I fear.
The innocence of children lost
With each and every year.

And through it all we live with hope
The future will be brighter.
For children all around the world
Their burdens will be lighter.

Helen Kilpatrick

Little Blackie

Little black cat,
Playing with
my pen,
you don't care,
who won the
battle of Hastings
or who is,
popular how,
you don't mind
if I'm a beggar,
or a king,
you only live,
for the moment,
and surround us
with your
feline love.

George Pluckwell

A Mother's Sense Of Loss

I stood and watched
My precious darling child.
It seemed just so incredible
that she was now a bride.

The pains of her childbirth
seemed but yesteryear
and yet a young woman
was calmly standing here.

Kissing, and cuddling her
and wiping her tears,
I had been oblivious
to the passing years.

How then could a stranger
just stealthily appear
and take away from me
what was so very dear.

Then God, quite miraculously,
whispered in my ear,
He is specially chosen
for when you disappear.

Theresa Whelan

Love Is In The Air

I smell the beauty, in the blossoms
of the trees.
All the aromas, gliding, and mingling
in the breeze.
I feel the sounds, like music,
Tingling vibrations.
I feel all life, and loves,
palpitations.
I know the footsteps, on the floor,
I know so much,
I could tell you more.
So happy, so healthy my life,
no axe to grind.
You learn so much,
When you are deaf, and blind.

Andrew Darroch

Sam

Sam the dog we loved so much
To us he was a real soft touch,
A loving dog with feelings true
No wonder why we loved him too,
The holidays with us his been,
Hills and sands and grasses green
No one can ever take away,
Part of our life our dog did play,
Sam a loyal & faithful friend,
We loved him tell the bitter end,
In our hearts he'll forever stay
A treasured memory locked away.

Barbara Ann Sayers

Untitled

The cut was deep
Slicing his sleep
And reality mixed
With the dream in his head
Dark droplets impure
Scattered and stained
Like paint from a brush
The canvas, his bed.

The next cut was deeper
His dreams ran like rivers
To join his soaked sheets
Not secret anymore
She found out
And the knife
Held it to her heart
Then embraced her lover
And his whore.

Lynsey Russell

Cat

She had a name among the children
she was owned though no one cared
locked out at bedtime
had her kittens duly drowned

She sometimes slept in the undergrowth
or in the darkened woods of beech
she never slept in warmth
the windows were all bolted

The feline shadow getting old,
just disappeared one night
Then they found her cold
a litter of kittens beside her
They were alive and healthy
but she . . . was dead.

Natalie Ingle

Untitled

To dreams in the night
It just a candle in the night giving
a friendly glow, a chair to sit
by the fire bringing memories
so sweet, visions of dreams
in the night.

The candle flickers and glows
so bright, outside the sky so
dark, a moon red glow, a million
stars shine like a thousand
jewels of dreams in the Night.

A candle to show us to our beds,
where two arms hold me close, a
heart that beats like a drummer
beats is drum, and a mass of
honey gold hair, sleep's like
an innocent child dreaming in
the night.

Jean Gill

Kings Pond

Alone with my thoughts
Surrounded by nature
The odd snap of a twig
There's so much to capture

Swans gracefully passing
Like silk tickling velvet
A breeze playfully kissing
Enriched all is kept

Sunlight caressing my every move
Wishing and wanting dreams on the run
Leaves peek-a-boo with my shadow
Tomorrow's memories have just begun.

Lorraine Lane

Carpet Love

You plug it in, you switch it on,
Then run it round the room.
It picks up fluff, all the dirt,
Plus bits of cotton too.
You may run it up the curtains,
It does upholstery too.
That modern vacuum cleaner,
Is literally part of you.
You're glad when you have finished,
Then tuck it out the way.
Knowing you will see it,
At least, every other day.

J. Brame

The Frog

There's a frog in our garden
And a witch lives next door.
I said, "I wonder
Who that was before?"
No I ain't kissing it
Like it says in the tale,
Besides I'm not even sure
That it's male.

There's an old black bucket
Where he's made his home,
Near a wishing well
And a garden gnome.
To us he is special,
Big eyes and large smile,
He's a prince among frogs,
Hope he'll stay for a while.

Linda M. Yaxley

Obscuriosity

Here, there, everywhere,
Anywhere is,
Constantly turning, twisting,
Messing up
And down and around,
Here about
Are many things,
Utterances of
Dissatisfaction, imagination, action,
Factions,
Warring, conflicting, arguing,
Never will agree,
Today's tomorrows will soon be,
Lost in the realms of obscuriosity

Owen Hurrell

Such Is Life

Such is life that we must feel
Saddened by what we know is real,
Find release in fantasy,
Comfort in that which cannot be.

Looking round at what is done,
Looking back at what is gone,
Do we truly wish to stay
On an Earth so stark and grey?

Gone is green and life so free,
Cast away by you and me.
Trees as old as Time itself
Take their place upon the shelf.

What is it that we've sacrificed?
A piece of Earth so lowly priced.
A home to lives as great as ours,
Misused, abused by man's rude powers.

Cry "stop" and "no", we must atone
For all the harm already done.
Progress must not take hope away.
Man does, alas, have feet of clay.

Les Watkins

Evaporating Tears

If I could paint a picture
to portray my love
I'd draw a rainbow from the sky
and build a bridge between our hearts,
that I could always walk across to you.

If I could play a song
to kindle laughter in your soul
I'd let the sound of Summer rain
pour it's music gently over you.

If I could dance the way I feel
I'd spin the stars into a cloak
and wrap you in it's folds
to keep you warm and close to me.

If I could write the story
of a moment in your arms,
I'd drench the empty pages of my heart
in merry sunshine to make you smile,
and evaporate your tears.

Yasmine Cajee

A Memory

A mourner in a cemetery
Filled with thoughts of fond memories
Of joys from the past
Of a love now gone
Like the wind she was swept away
to a place far beyond the sky,
a teardrop slips from his eye
as he looks towards the sky
With memories of her warm embraces
and the softness of her voice
of a love that has now gone
of a love always to be treasured
by one man in a cemetery.

Caroline Agirbas

The Rabbit

Coat like coal with silver whiskers,
Shiny and silky.
Small round face, long floppy ears,
Squint nose always twitching.
Eyes, dark, brown, mysterious,
Round and full of secrets.
Wondering if she was free what a
life it would be.
Hopping, running, jumping around,
In long green grass with sky of blue.
Happily in the grass she sits,
lots of things to eat.

Yvonne McEwan

For You

Like a flash past the bird window
grasping minds slip solid word reality
missing the velvet touch of being
and feeling life too hard like a hammer
hitting a nail.
Blowing the wind way bending with
and staying for nothing
we move on
but slowly . . . so as to share.
No pleasing explanations only toying
with the endless
and content never to get there.
I found me here.
Still to let go but go on
and see how you fly . . .
beat your wings
only to realize you could be a fish.
No don't hold your breath! Breathe!

Michael Kryzaniwsky

"Weeping Willows"

Feathery frond's dancing,
Soft green enhancing.
A back-cloth of pine trees
Quiet in the gentle breeze.

Turned to a frenzies whirl
The yellow flowers all unfurl
And pollen on the wind is thrown
And sufferers begin to groan.

It seems to me an awful shame
That so much beauty is to blame
For so many of man's ills
To make him take those extra pills.

Slanting sunlight turns green to gold
And gentle peace takes its hold
On aching body and tired mind
And quiet rest is there to find.

Yet, when everything is still
One can sense the divine will,
And with a simple faith will see
A vision of eternity.
Anne Toley

My First Easter

It was my first Easter,
It was really very fun,
I got a chocolate Easter egg,
A Mr. Blobby one.

Upon this merry holiday,
I found it really fun,
That everything I got that day,
Was chocolate for my tum.

Everyone I saw that day,
Was full of chocolate too,
Sitting on thc toilet,
Me on my potty too.

They all sang jolly songs that day,
But I just googaad plenty,
Until it got to six o'clock,
And everybody wenty.

It was late that night,
As I awoke in plight,
With my stomach up tight,
I just puked all night.
Michael Simmonite

The Feeling Inside

I'll never forget the feeling I had
The day I heard the news
Your brother's died and gone to heaven
To us we couldn't choose

The pain I felt deep inside
When getting up each day

Knowing I couldn't see you again
This pain wouldn't go away

You were not there to fight with
Or to hold or touch

I felt the pain I had inside
Just seemed to be too much

I'd sit down on my own sometimes
Anywhere, I didn't care

Because no matter where I went to sit
I knew you were not there
I know I'll never see you again
Until I'll join heaven in the sky

But I know I have to live my life
So I sadly say goodbye . . .
Annmarie Liddle

"To The Moon"

The moon above in the sky so high
doth shine so clear and bright
I watch the clouds go passing by
that hide its glorious light.

And isn't the moon just wonderful
that small majestic ball?
It is a sight most beautiful
the purest gem of all.

It is light to lead me
through storms and shades of night
I always gaze where'er I
at this celestial light.

I love to see it peeping
out from the clouds so vast
as evening shades come creeping
o'er the weary world at last.

And when I'm tired and sink to sleep
that dear, old friend, the moon
doth hover round me and doth peep
into the darkness of my room.
Marjorie Tochrane

The Blind Boy

O say what is that thing called light
Which I never enjoy
What are the blessing of the sight
O tell your poor blind boy?
You talk of wonders things to see
You say the sun shines bright;
I feel him warm, but how can he
Or make it day or night.
My day or night myself I make
whenever I sleep or play
And could I ever keep awake
With me it were always day.
With heavy sighs I often hear
You mourn my hopeless woe;
But sure with patience I can bear
A loss I never can know.
Then let now what I cannot have
My cheer of mind destroy
Whilst thus I sing I am a king
Although a poor blind boy
Peggie Molloy Flaherty

Continuation

You are born
You are clothed
You are fed

You are schooled
You are taught
You are read

You are woman
You are loved
You are wed

You are mother
You are old
You are dead
Alison Michele Roberts

Desert Dreaming

I danced across the desert
As I reached for the moon,
Then a mind it had infected
Said we'd get there pretty soon.
I thought that he was lying,
As I stretched into the sky,
And now I sit and wonder
Why the future passed me by.
Hayley Nicholson

Horrible Weather

When the weather is bad,
It always makes me sad.
When the weather is rainy,
It never makes me brainy.
When there is thunder and lightning,
I can never go out and do some cycling.
Every time we have some sun,
Soon the rain and hail would come.
When there was a hurricane,
We had to flee before it came.
I hate bad weather,
But I wish it made me clever.
Trevor Pipe

Bonfires

Windows slam and neighbours glare
  Washing lines are suddenly bare
Shouts of anger fill the air
  But I don't care—

I've raked up all the fallen leaves
  And gathered up the garden weeds
With household rubbish piled on top
  I never know just when to stop

Now it's burning, well alright
  It really thrills me such a sight
Spiralling clouds of thick black smoke
  I'll just give it all another poke!!

Now there's nothing left but embers
  Smut still linger in the air
I wish these folks enjoyed bonfires
  Then all this pleasure I could share
Ann Elizabeth Rabbage

Two

Two loving arms to hold you,
To keep you safe from harm,
To keep away the fear,
To keep you nice and warm.

Two loving eyes to watch you,
To enjoy your every move.
To sparkle with desire,
To shine with total love.

Two lips to kiss you better,
To whisper special things,
To linger on your body,
And smile at what that brings.

Two hands to hold your future,
Your furrowed brow to smooth,
To rub away the tension,
To caress and ease and soothe.

Two hearts that beat together,
Someone to adore you,
Harmony in each subtle beat,
A lifetime of love before you.
P. Vance

Stroke

I wish I was not here dear
I would rather be home with my friends.
I wish I could talk and walk freely.
But on you my comfort depends.
I try to make you understand.
That my needs are different to yours
My body is trapped in a shell case
And there is no-one to open the doors
Someday I hope a cure is found
To release the prisoner within
From a cell that is twisted and silent
And here I must stay as if duty bound.
Patricia Ann Biggs

A Loved One Never Dies

When summer's shadows fade away
And flowers fall asleep,
to wake again another day,
like memories to keep.

When winter breathes her chilly air,
and all the trees are cold and bare
and we no longer seem to care.
With hearts too sore to weep.

I look upon the snow–capped hills
where winter's heartless icy chills
create a giant frozen bed
were sleeps our cold and silent dead.

No loving arms to hold them now
no loving kiss upon their brow.
No words of hope to calm their fears
asleep within a veil of tears.

Now bitter hearts are left to grieve
If only we could still believe,
the teachings of the Master's plan,
to house the soul within the man.

Margaret R. McPhee

I Think Of You

I think of you my darling
Though you're not far away.
My love for you grows stronger
As winter comes our way
My mind drifts back to nights of love,
A picture in a frame,
A windy hill.
A swirl of cloud
I see your face again.
Your face is gentle as a child's,
Your body soft and warm,
Please stay with me, my darling
Till night becomes as dawn.

P. J. Carpenter

Anguish

Oh, the anguish of a mothers heart.
To, have a babe and then to part.
To see its sweet and gentle smile.
To hold it for a little while.
And then to see the cot so bare,
To know the little child's not there.
    Only God alone can know the cost.
To have had and held.
And loved and lost.

Louise Poulson

He'll Help You Through

I felt just like a broken reed
    when I lost the one I love,
For me there wasn't anything left
    except the One above,
He helped me realize, I had
    a family who,
Relied on me and needed me and
    I needed all them too.

I looked around this beautiful world
    and saw the Lord God's work,
How could I feel so sorry for me
    and my responsibilities shirk,
Get up and go, I told myself,
    my loved one I have lost,
Would want me to build my life again,
    no matter what the cost.

I know that God is helping me,
    in everything I do,
So, if you feel as I have felt,
    I know He'll help you too.

Olivia Alwyn Outhwaite

My Garden

My garden is a place
Of wonder and tranquillity
Beauty fills the smallest space

Flowers nod their heads in greeting
Paths winding under foot
Curving turning a place for meeting

Trees standing tall and stately
Their fruits on grand display
Twisting swaying in the wind
Leaves dropping on the ground they lay

Roses with a heady scent
Clematis climbing high
Upward onward heaven sent

Tiny daisies grouped together
Colour mingled in each bed
Marigolds like royalty
Lift their swaying head

Forget-me-nots as blue as skies
Where else but in a garden
So much beauty lies

Jean Hosker

Now You've Gone

Now you've gone I feel distraught,
All alone though I know I'm not.
I didn't get to see you,
Before you went away.
You left without a word,
Goodbye you did not say.
You leave me here with a broken heart,
Pleading for you back.
I cry for you day and night,
But now you've gone for good.
You're not coming back,
I know that now.

All I want to say is . . . "Goodbye."

Donna Jones

The Human Fire

So you're gone . . .

I'm remembering a day gone by
When our every function had one desire
Before the blinding crash
That sent burning embers
Into a thickening plot
The two sides met, headlong
And did encompass
Framework falling, lingering
Lying there to rot.
You introduced a brilliant flame
Into our special game
Molten, fragments blown in by the wind
Ignited by a breath of air
I could barely hear them sing
Their strange song
I thought so then
But I know that now
A human fire needs oxygen
To keep a kindle burning
    . . . So you went

Eileen Sanders

Dream World

I rather live in a dream world
full of life with fantasy.
Lost in a cloud of dreams,
full of joy without pain and
not awaking to reality,
hich turns my dream world
into a nightmare.

Alice Field

Alone

When you were here my life was full
of laughter, joy and sunshine,
Now you have gone my life is full
of sorrow, love of mine.

You were my love, my life, my being
You were here to wipe my tears,
I look around at things, not seeing.
Where are you now to hush my fears?

Now I walk around our secret places
I turn to look, but you're not there,
I see the old familiar faces
I feel my heart, it's cold and bare.

Why did you die and leave me here
Why couldn't I come too?
To be left alone year after year
When all I want is you.

J. P. Smith

To A Snowdrop

White sentinel of Spring
Guardian of frost
Winged–petalled butterfly
Green–edged and frilled,
Who sent you?
Have you come too soon?

Winter is late, but you are early.

Who tells you when to come?

Do blackbirds tap their feet
To invite you up
To Earth's cold soil
To view the grey sky
And frozen trees?

Dainty Lady of the Spring,

Welcome!

Gwyneth M. Bere

Pause For Thought

Sharing we find the unity
To break down the pain
It's the way we stay whole
In accepting we gain.

When my road is very rocky
And my balance simply gone
Life isn't that much fun
When I struggle to hold on.

Could you bring me a present
The greatest of all
In my moments of sadness
Be there if I call.

How simple it reads
Hard when reality calls
Learning to be there
Makes our priorities fall.

Elizabeth Hunter

Untitled

I feel like hell tonight
tears are rolling down my face,
I turn on the light
and feel the empty place,
space that used to be yours
and mine,
it felt so fine,
Now all I can do
is wipe my tears away,
and get through the day,
how could I ask you to stay,
when all you do is run away?

Willems Sandra

Morning

When the sun comes to light,
The grass sparkles with dew,
It's the magic of morning
That is always like new.

When the sun comes to light,
Then the fields do awake,
All the trees are alive
But not a breath do they take.

When the sun comes to light,
All the birds sing and fly,
Everything is golden
Till the moon claims the sky.

Debbie Collis

Autumn And After

Autumn colours touch the trees
Blends of rust, red and gold
Leaves go fluttering to the ground
A sign of winter's cold!

Where once a tree was full of leaves
There is no skeletal wood
With but a berry here and there
Providing birds with food.

All along for the spring again
With trees and bushes green
And life made new for all of us
Who appreciate the scene.

Presently a bud shows forth
Trees stir with gentle sound
Leaves appear one by one
New life shoots through the ground.

Then summer suns with warmth aglow
Bring forth the budding tree
Flowers and bushes live again
God Beauty—Given Free.

John Moss

Untitled

Peaceful forest where the ashes
Of my dearly departed were laid.
Nature heaven returned to
Silence marks the place.

Cold water, I think of as silver
Why is silence gold?
Death is nature's great silence
And I think the grave will be cold.

A. Northfield

The Other Woman

He looks at her lovingly
Wanting to touch
her sleek form
While gazing at her
longingly.

He needs her, loves her
Wants to be with her
His wife could never
Know
what he feels.

He snatches one last
glimpse of her
from the bedroom
window.

He must wait
till tomorrow
to be with her
how can anyone
say
she is JUST a car.

Anne Riley

Representatives Of The People

Before an election?
    "They'll serve you quite well."
And when it's all over?
    "Time only will tell."

        And where do you find them?
            "In restaurants and bars,
        Or driving around
            In big, fancy cars."

And when things go wrong
    Do they share the blame?
What are their answers?
    "They're few and the same."

        "That is an area
            Quite beyond my control"
        Or "It's World Economics,"
            Or "It's some other's role."

Yes! They can be in power
    For nigh twenty years,
But they're never the cause
    Of your Vale of Tears.

Robert L. Cooper

Quiet Moments

Times are a-changing
nothing's the same,
Life's moving
but we are to blame,
moaning and squawking
When things don't go right
Just look at the pleasing
things of life,
the beauty which can be
found in the woodlands and glades
flowers and ferns on parade
Carpeted with bluebells all around.
The animals footprints on the soft
leafy ground. Through the woods
we walk on by, just watching
Where you step and then you'll see
the secrets to be found just you
look around. Open your eyes, the
Windows of your mind

Eileen Annette Jasmin Jones

Whatever The Weather!

On a hot summer's day
The sun beams again
The land gets so dry
We all wish for rain

On a cold winter's day
Our fingers go numb
We're all freezing cold
We all wish for sun

With darkness around us
And cold winds that bite
We all need some warmth
We all wish for light

With snow on the ground
As white as a feather
We wish it all gone
Whatever the weather!

Steven Tanner

My Window View

The blossom is upon the tree,
And in the wind it waves to me,
It always looks happy never sad,
For that I am glad,
That the blossom is upon the tree,
And in the wind it waves to me.

Frank Clatworthy

Dreaming

Dreaming all night
never opening your eyes
a dream is a dream
to let you sleep.

Opening your eyes
to your dream life
still dreaming,
still dreaming.

Dreaming can be better
than real life
dreaming up your
own life to be.

Wishing things that
can never be
dreaming for yourself
a life to live
just for you.

Nikki-Marie Hinton

A Blue Mood

The sun has gone, the skies are grey,
In the house I have to stay.

I'm all alone and feeling blue,
Don't know what I want to do.

Round and round my thoughts do go
While sitting here, full of woe.

Sewing, knitting, all must wait,
Until my mind will concentrate.

I want to move, but here I sit,
Does it matter? Not a bit.

I'll rest a while, I've time to spare,
The work will wait while I'm not there.

But through the window I can see
A shaft of light, to cheer me.

Clouds of white, no sign of rain,
Now I think I'll smile again.

Doris Green

Memories

Pale images reflected in a window pane,
Through leaves awash with summer rain
Bring back to me, my very dear love
Aching memories of another afternoon
When we could meet and be alone
In that forbidden London room.

Ruth Street

Buried Pain

A chance meeting in the street
Knocks my balance
Makes me weep
Forces back images
So desperately buried.
But there was no funeral
Only a hasty shallow grave
So easy for her to uncover
The corpse . . .
To make me look into its face
To strip away my layers of control
For the corpse is not dead.
Although hacked and mutilated
It clings to life
To push its way through the ground
To taunt and torment
To inflict tiny stabbing wounds
And a sinister whisper
Don't ever think you can forget.

Hazel Christie

Memories

The family ties that I described
come quickly back to bond
a specialty and closeness
that I thought would be long gone.

It was an age ago
that such a bond was set
and yet I feel it back again
just like when we first met.

The tenderness you've shown
brings such warmth it makes me glow
so that the pride I felt before
has returned to haunt once more.

The love I have for you and yours
is difficult to control
that it sometimes has a tendency
to bubble and overflow.

Christine Mountney

Sibyl

In the soft translucent dawn
That heralds an autumn day
When the world is wrapped in mist
And the earth is shadowless,
I wake to a strange enchantment
That has in it the voice of doom,
And grey cowled monks
Do tread their cloistered ways.
A wandering spirit restless, seeking
Seems to fill the air around
And all is devastation and decay.
Silently, I weep, for those gone before
For the utter desolation
And the weariness of fear.

L. Usher

Remembering A Friend

Remember when
in days gone by
Beneath a dark and war–torn sky
you held my hand
while others cried
remember when?

Remember when the sirens wailed
we'd start upon that weary trail
singing "The sweet nightingale"
remember when?

Although those days
are at an end
I'll not forget the special friend
who held my hand,
while others cried
remember when?

Jill Axworthy

A Summer's Day Upon The Shore

I sit and watch
the rolling waves,
the seagulls
s-c-a-t-t-e-r
the cliffs,
the cargo ship
in the distance
destined for another shore.
I listen close to
those waves,
that roll upon the shore.
They tell the story,
of the fishermen of before,
the bathers that did not beware . . .
and, the sailors that used to be,
the waves whisper
their legacy to me.

Kallie Catitia Nolan

Hartshead Pike

Pointing to a summer sky,
Kindled beacons years gone by,
O'er hills beyond its shadow cast
Mossley's shield through winters past.

Aching limbs, gasping breath,
Pounding heart and beading sweat—
Phoenix like we have stood the test,
Of harsher times upon this crest.

Farms below in fields of grain,
Ashton town, meandering Tame;
Oldham's mills with eyes aflame
And Rochdale's Gracie grew to fame

Saddleworth Moor a glance away
A shredded heart kneels to pray
Searches for the son she lost
Who lies beneath forsaken moss.

Bathed in sun this aged Head
Brings to mind when I am dead.
'Scatter my ashes' as you like!
One windswept day, on Hartshead Pike.

Robert Clayton

Black And White Delphiniums

Delphiniums so tall and proud
Not standing just where they're allowed
But in glorious shades of blue
Standing where they want to do

Not as man is not allowed
To stand tall and be proud
If his colour is not right
In a glorious shade of white

You will not be bent and bowed
You will be able to stand proud
But if you were of the human kind
Things are different you would find

You could not stand as man should
As man of any colours would
No matter if he's black or white
It's only just, he has the right

To stand tall and be a man
Live with family and with clan
That is what the world should be
That any man should be free

B. P. Wymark

"Who Will Wipe Our Tears"

Children of the world cry out.
Lost, forgotten, silent shout
Hope and love, unknown to them
Their playground is the devil's den.

When feelings lonely, lost in despair.
Destitution so hard to bare,
Keep them safe and free from harm,
Fold them in your loving arm.

Hear their cries in dark of night,
Guide tiny steps into the light.
Send your grace upon each child,
Mercy, mercy Jesus mild.

Lift all hearts and eyes to you
Let them know your words are true
Grant to all the peace of love,
To be ever prized by him above.

Make us watchful in our prayers,
For all your children everywhere.
Saviour of all souls in need,
Save the children, Lord we plead.

J. A. Du-Feu

Bitter Love

I hate you, bitter love
with all your secrets and your lies
I hate your hypocrisy
and your talent for disguise

I hate the smile you give
that has no honest truth
I despise the promises in you
for a sweet and lovely youth

I hate the feelings you awake
that are never meant to be
I still fight against this hole
and the blackness you put in me

My dreams are still in grey
and my days are still too long
I hate you, bitter love
for you have done me wrong

I hate you, bitter love
for a heart that will never mend
for the promises I made myself
that I will never love again.

Katrine Lembcke

Untitled

As the sun goes down,
It calms my soul;
Its warmth,
It stills my spirit;
And I can just sit,
And enjoy the thought,
Of purely being in it.

Louise Sharp

The Blindman

They tell me of a sun
that shines in the sky,
And the story of birds
I hear sing.
They tell me too of an
opening flower
When it is what they say
is Spring.
They tell me of the smile
of love,
And the hurt of deceit
and lies,
With my hand I did
once touch,
Tears in a woman's eyes.

Penny Macassey

Unity

Sometimes I feel at one
with the timeless incandescence
of low fenland skies,
touching down on the black soil
of this ancient land,
invincibly reclaimed from the sea.
The piercing cry of the curlew
sharpens my senses;
with outstretched wings
he circles in flight,
ne'er questioning his existence,
so why should I?
Too many philosophers
have challenged simplicity,
but I need look no further
than this land,
this sky,
the eternity of nature,
to know that I belong.
Sometimes I am content—just to be.

Sally Karpe

Leaving

Ever thought what it would
Be like just to leave
Everyone you loved
Your family, friends your lovers
People say it's easy
Jumping over sticks is easy
To some—others who have
Disabilities would find it hard
It must take so much
Just to get up and leave
leave everything you've worked for
leave the people who have
Been there for you when times
Were good and bad
I would like to know what
It would feel like
  Start a new life
  be someone new
  or would you
  would you feel alone or lost
    Carly Hopkinson

My Damsel

Way up on yonder
Down by the quay
A damsel sits both night and day
Birds whistle and bees buzz
I long to go to the one I love
I wander and wander around each day
But I can't get to my damsel
She's too far away
One day I'll get up on yonder
And when I do I'll say
I love you dear damsel
Let me take you away
Then me and my damsel we'll wander away
Way up past yonder
And far, far away
    Susan Bebington

Dreamer's Dream

The moon is like a big glass ball,
Full of wishes from us all,
And each and every night,
We all jump in to our delight,

The moon is a search light,
Scanning the starry night,
In search of a dreamer's dream,
Because he hates to be mean.
    Victoria Ann Greensmith

Dad

He ruled us with an iron hand
his way was always right
to him there was no in-between
all things were black or white.
Those early days, I have to say,
were not the best I've had
for we never did see eye to eye
me and my old Dad.
The years passed by, we all grew up
then left the family home
till the day, sad to say
Dad was left there all alone.
He was getting old and feeble now
his health was failing fast
and I knew I had to see him
and forget about the past.
I nursed him with such loving care
which I was pleased to do
for I got that rare second chance
to say "Dad, I love you".
    I. Hodgson

Bramble

Once in a while our lives are touched
  By a woman and loving heart
Whether it be human or animal
  In our lives they become a part

It seems not very long ago
  When friendships were quite new
That a little yappy, happy pup
  Chose to be with Dave and Sue.

As years went by she turned into
  A loving and faithful friend
We knew that she would love us
  Right until her days would end.

So very sad, our dear Pet passed
  So peacefully away
She's with her mother 'Bracken'
  Now running through the hay.

Now down the lanes and parks,
  Amongst the fields we'll amble
With loving thoughts of a dear Pet
  Our most cherished bramble
    Sue M. Aldrich

"Galahad" A Sad Welsh Tomb

We watched them sail to far off war
Their future so uncertain now
The pain we felt that awesome day
So proud but deeply hurt somehow

As we searched the faces there
Frantic—worried we should miss
Our soldier son amongst the crowd
No chance to hug, no goodbye kiss

There was no thought of fire and bomb
Of friends we knew so well to die
Pilots—swooping low to kill
Make "Galahad" a sad welsh tomb,

They gave us reasons, told us why
We found it hard to understand
Why all that time—they lingered there
Close to safety near to land

Those who watched that troopship sail
For them time does not ease the pain
They are left to mourn and grieve
Remembering prayers that were in vain
    Jack Ricketts

Desolation, On A Wet Winter's Day

Grey,
skies today.
Wild winds, hold sway.
Sweet Summer, seems so far away!

Fleet winds, make moan.
Mild, alone,
beside a phone:
amid things we own.

Outside,
whose vision, WIDE
COUNTRYSIDE
wears wet—weeping, does abide.

How drab a scene;
where feet have been
along wide valley; in between!
Now,—lacks lush green.

Still shrill winds stay
throughout today.
Shows no respect, for work or play.
Still weeps grim grey.
    Brian Michael Robert Stevens

If

If eyes be the window of the soul
Then I choose not to see
To deny myself the possibility
Of what could and might be

A self imposed cage
When all I long is to be free
To battle with the conflict
And retain mental stability

Bound by invisible chains
In the confines of my prison
Not to dream, not to wish
To deny myself vision

But my eyes are wide open
And the soul cries out in pain
At the sight of twisted fate
And destiny mislain
    Tracy Everett

Night

Dark, precious dark
Creeping over countryside
Filling pools of shadows
With a sea of blackness
Clinging to the bark
Of trees, turning on the tide
Of time.

Peace, contended peace
Moving through the amber wood
Turning every leaf
From green to dusky grey
Making daylight cease
From the place where once had stood
Our lives.

Cold, numbing cold
Flowing over rock and stone
Covering as with sheets
The earth and silent day
Once so young, now old
When at last we are alone
at night.
    Robin T. Kiel

My Little Friend

I have a small friend.
He is very dear to me,
I awake to hear his song so clear,
As he sings so cheerfully,
He waits so patiently,
For all the crumbs we share,
He fills my heart with joy and love,
And makes my life so dear,
If all the people in this world,
Could be like my little friend,
What a wonderful world
  it would be.
    Catherine Cosgrove

World War Zero

Each combat a beat,
A dagger twists,
A round heart,
Inside, a red bath.

The revolving dagger rusts,
The copper poisons cells of brain,
Obsession runs riot in blood,
Stranded in a battlefield of rejection,

Gasping for breath
It curls like a cat,
Shivering in scarlet ice,
This must be the ninth!
    Lyn Byrne

Betrayal

The door to my heart is open wide,
The lock has been broken,
You've been inside.
All my secrets are known to you now
I hope my heart will mend somehow.
Have I been a fool to allow you access?
I thought my heart knew best,
But all I possessed has been stolen
By a thief who's left my heart broken,
And the pieces are too large to hide.

Jewel Patricia Maynard

The Way

Each moment of every day you gave
was precious in your sight
and I have blindly stumbled on
as if in darkest night.

The lights you gave I have not seen
I did not know your way
but you so gently lead me on
I cannot be afraid.

You love me Lord I know not why
I'm such a wayward child
but all I really want is you
to live within your smile.

Forgive me Lord in all my ways
I do not understand.
Just take me, lead me, keep me Lord
ever in your mind.

B. J. Bramwell

Christian Science, As I See It

Pure white shining light
It came to me from a great height.
In the beginning
When all was made
God is love, there is no shade.

Made by God, good to behold,
It's the truth
Can now be told.
Made in His image,
And likeness too
Spiritual man is really true.

Thomas it was who asked the way
Jesus answered, I am the way,
The truth and the life.

It was Phillip who did say
Show us the Father, this very day.
Jesus answered, the Father dwells
With Me, His are the words
You hear Me say.

Kenneth Roy Munns

Secrets of Nature

I'm sitting down, all on my own
late one summer's night.
Watching the stars coming and go
between clouds drifting so slight.
A gentle breeze moving
the leaves in the old willow tree,
rustling so lightly as a message
from someone much greater than me.
So peaceful so quite
with no one in sight.
How I enjoy this late moment
with no electric light.
The darkness is soft, is close
like a magical feeling—
when all of a sudden my life
is given a purpose, a reason, a meaning.

Marianne Clarke

Greenwich Park

Have you been there, have you seen,
Greenwich Park? Oh! It's so green.
So many paths, so many trees,
and always there, that gentle breeze.
Winter and summer, it's the same,
take a ball for that quick game.
Look! A squirrel near that tree,
Oh! Really such a lot to see.
People sitting, people walking.
People laughing, people talking.
Children's voices, boats and swings.
Cricket, football—happy things.
Greenwich Park, stay as you are
Don't ever change your ways.
The generations yet to come,
Will need those happy days.
Have you been there, have you seen.
Greenwich Park? Oh! It's so green.

Sidney Smith

Discovery

I heard the music
But never knew that I could dance
Until I moved my feet.
If I could feel my freedom
I'm sure I could fly!

W. Campbell

When Love Dies

A sad lonely place
My tears hide in the rain
Is this world crying with me?
Can it feel my pain?
The sun's gone into hiding
It has no reason to shine
The sky sheds its tears
Is its heart breaking with mine?

The flowers have lost their perfume
They've nothing left to give
The roses lie dying
They've lost the will to live
There's no warmth in this life
It's all faded away
The stars in the night
No longer come out to play
The man in the moon
Hangs his head and cries
It's a sad lonely world
When all you live for just dies

Samantha Jayne Lee

My Everything

You're my life, my strength
The dawn of each new day
My everlasting light
That burns so far away

You're the early morning dew
The briskness of the breeze
Which winds its way down the hills
And gently rocks the trees

You're my brightness of day
My stillness of night
Where the moon and stars
Sit patient and bright

You're my river that runs
The birds that fly
You're the mist that rises
And touches the sky

You're a choir of voices
For in my heart you sing
Without you I'm nothing
You're my everything.

Sally Chatfield

Up And Up

Let's get up and let's get going.
Be it rain or be it snowing
Put your best foot forward fast
Or you will surely be there last.

The wind may howl the gale may blow
Over hillocks high and low
Whichever way the dice we throw
It comes up trumps
So smile again
No need for tears
The sun will shine so banish fears

Summer comes and fresh and green
Grass and flowers will be seen.

B. D. Young

As I Go Along Each Day

As I go along each day
Hoping not to lose my way.
I always have to pray
That God will have his way.
For this I cannot alter
And I know I must not falter.
These things I cannot change are
so very strange.
They are hard to understand and
To think that they are planned
Is beyond my comprehension and
Hardly worth a mention.

T. J. Wilkins

Summit

It was just within my reach,
So near that I could taste it,
I knew that if I pushed myself,
I would be the one to take it.

I imagined what it would be like,
To be the victorious one,
To be the one on top of the hill,
To be the best, second-to-none.

My memory never lets me down,
The feelings come back so well,
How my vulnerability crept in,
And my expectations fell.

I don't feel bad, at least I know
I gave it my best shot,
I tried my best, it was all I had,
And this is what I got!

Lesley P. Rainey

The Great Potato Famine 1845–1851

The blight arrived—
    Consternation!

        The crops decayed—
        Ruination!

The people searched—
    Desperation!

        The people hungered—
        Starvation!

The million died—
    Devastation!

        The families scattered—
        Emigration!

The some survived—
    Integration!

        The dead remembered—
        United Nation!

Paul G. Murphy

Who Am I?

Who do I see
What do I feel
I feel unsure.

What do I think
What do I read
I feel lonely.

How do I know
How do I speak
You'll never know.

What is my world
What is my song
An unopen book.

What is my future
I am my future
I have to be strong.

Who is this girl
I am this girl
You never asked.

Michelle Jones

Untitled

You left us at dawn,
that day in March.
The frost on the ground,
the cold, the quiet.

We were there through the night,
saw the undeserved pain,
of life's last night.

The heat from your body,
as the last breath came.
Your spirit left,
and rose to Gods light.

"We Never Again Will Be The Same"
S. Wharnsby

Mid-Summer Storm

Fast gathering skies
Racing to dawn.
Clouds jostle their way
In the grey misted 'morn.
Leaping and spilling,
Cascading below.
Windblown and wretched,
Large droplets now flow.

Quenching the treetops.
Pulsating on leaves.
Tremulous rooftops
Now spilling their eaves.
Turbulent galleys,
Wet streets shining grey.
Pounding on windows;
Sweeps in the new day.

S. J. Woodcock

Daffodils

Once more they come
The slender yellow ladies
A hundred smiling faces
Advancing to their places.

Clustered in the borders
Fragrant proud and golden
Dew kissed and ever beaming
Their heads all crowned and gleaming.

Oh how those precious ladies
Do charm me with their dancing
On breezes gently swaying
I find them so enchanting.

Angela Melvin

Another Lonely Night

Moonlight and imagination
Through open curtains stream
I lay there sleepless in the night
Yet still begin to dream
Fears and fantasies collide
I'm caught in their embrace
Solitary in my room
Midnight is a lonely place

K. Willers

A Moment Of Time

We all need a moment of time
To come to our senses
We all need a moment of time
To search for our defences

'Cause sometimes we don't know
Right from wrong
Sometimes we don't know
What is going on

We all need a moment of time
To think of one another
We all need a moment of time
To see what bothers

'Cause sometimes we lose
The road to our dreams
Sometimes we lose
And cannot follow the stream

We all need a moment of time
If that's what we have to do
We all need a moment of time
Just for me and you

Tonia Deliens

Rain

Raindrops fall
out of the sky
I wish I could reach
to the sky
and take it away
I love you
to stop the sound
and live in peace
while the sun comes out
I'm crying
the clouds fade away
and the wind stops blowing
I'm alone

Tiina Overmark

Frozen Embryo

Time up!
'Use before this date'
'Best before 5 years'
Time to expire
30,000 plus!?

only a number—
among millions.

Permission requested?
depends if manufacturers
can be found.
Permission requested?
waste material not consulted,
easily replaced.

Will they be missed?
No!
Will they be missed?
Not sure . . .
Will they be missed?

SUBJECT CLOSED!!!

Reopen 5 years from now.

Maureen Bates

Holidays

Sun, sea and sand
With a music band.
Is my type of holiday.
Dancing–prancing just mucking about.
Is my type of holiday.
Beers, cheers then people saying dear.
Is my type of holiday.
Everyone is happy
Let alone chatty
Fish and chips
With chocolate dips
Is my type of holiday
And best of all
Totally cool.
Holiday romances.

Sabrina Moore

Autumn

Sun–kissed leaves strewn all around,
Carpet-like upon the ground,
Trees stand bare; bonfires abound,
Autumn is here!

Harvest fields now idle lay,
Crops all safely stored away,
Farmers tired, but glad to say
Autumn is here.

Amber and brown, erased by white
Snow and fog, and fires each night,
With an alarming bite
Autumn Has Gone!

Anne Harrison

Love Never Dies

A lady that I loved,
had to go away,
but I know she's with me,
every single day.

All my life she watches me,
pointing out the way,
showing the right direction,
every single day.

Beside my heart she stands,
that is where she'll stay.
helping me on my way,
every single day.

Karen Bigwood

Football

Grown men shouting, fighting. Crying
Wives with children waiting
Men with helmets rushing in to
Stop the blood

Doctors working, stitching. Yawning
Angels tending injured
Scarves of many different colours
In the mud

Judges frowning, listening. Tiring
Lawyers asking questions
Many bruised and battered, saying,
"Yes, M'Lud"

Media writing, telling. Showing
Pictures with their stories
Cameras caught up in the fight
Crash with a thud

More men shouting, fighting. Crying
Wives once more are seen
This can't go on—it must be time to
Stop the blood

Chris Jones

Unwanted Touch

The fingerprints
you left behind
with your first touch
on my body
I loved.

The fingerprints
left behind
by a total stranger
disgust me.

Just that one
unwanted touch
left a scar
on my body
Forever.

Thomas Van Schaik

Just Leave Me!

You've ambushed me with questions
You've cornered me with your fears
And half of the questions you asked
Well, they reduced me to tears

Why can't you just leave me?
Act as if I don't exist
'Cause if you ask more questions
I'll answer them with my fist

This pain has now taken me over
Along with sadness and confusion
I'd like to think there are no problems
But that's just an illusion

Maybe if I wait a bit longer
This problem will just fade away
Or maybe it will go unnoticed
Like empty glasses on a tray

So please, no more questions
I'll struggle through this on my own
Your concern was much appreciated
But I think better when I'm alone.

Anisa G. Llewellyn

She's Gone Away

A mountain of emotions
A massive heart of pain
Is building up in side of me
And driving me insane

I do not know the where-abouts
My life is heading for
A helping hand and guidance
I desperately implore

Infested with hysteria
My life I cannot face
Intolerably my heart aches
I need her to embrace

Where is she now I'm needing her
Please don't take her away
I need to feel her near me
Lord send her back I pray
I know that death takes every one
But not my girl not yet
Please just a little longer
I'll be forever in your debt.

Paul Jones

Maybe

And for a moment
They cast off their shells
of other lives
And entwined
Getting scratchy grains of sand
On their consciences.

Bernie Jackson

An Ideal Man

Dark and handsome, rich and strong,
I've waited for this man so long.
Designer suits and flashy cars,
Fancy restaurants, clubs and bars.
Important friends or so I heard,
That hung upon his every word.
Foreign trips and business meetings,
Endless handshakes, fickle greetings.
This business had a shady side,
But what I could not quite decide.
Whispered phone calls day and night,
The truth, I knew, was soon in sight.
One careless word and all was clear,
It was as I had often feared.
For love and fear I could not leave,
For me there would be no reprieve.
Escape for me would be my loss,
You see, I married a mafia boss.

Kim Goulding

The Affair

The agony of waiting
Footsteps that are not yours
The fierce anticipating
Through the endless lonely hours
Seconds ticking
Minutes dragging
Ash trays filling
Patience flagging
Then the meeting wild and thrilling
All my longings now fulfilling
Such a love to only borrow
What the future
What tomorrow?

Marie Curzon

Who Am I?

I dig on down.
What do I find?
Intrinsically a desire to discover,
To root out, to feel, to emotionalize,
To expand, to grow, to create,
To take off into infinity.

On Pegasus' wings I continue on,
Here is knowledge at last.
I'm fulfilled, I exist, I am.
I will be for ever and ever,
Not coming, not going,
But being still in my own soul.
Peace, calm, tranquillity.

Sara Teek

The River

It's rushing along,
It's fast and it's strong,
The river is fierce and wild,

It tumbles over rocks with a roar
And a rush,
Breaking the gentle hush

The river runs strong,
Its life is long,
But the river dies,
With a heave and a sigh,
It dies where golden sand lies,

It slows its pace,
It's not in a race,
Not in a hurry, not in a rush,
It will just flow,
Onward it goes,
Towards the open arms of the sea.

Sarah Scott

Scars Of War

So stale the air, with echoes of cries
Twisted melodies to question and whys
Life but destruction has come to be
Now in limbo, where once so free

To taste but bitterness all around
A blanket of corpses engulf the ground
false insecurities, shivers and fears
Exhaustion, anger, blood stained tears

Weakened limbs and hollows eyes
No longer trusting for fearing lies
Horrid stories one day to tell
Of days once spent on living hell

Tormented souls of innocence passed
Never for ever does happiness last
Knowing no longer how to smile
Except to exist someway—somehow

Tortured flesh, scars so deep
Longing miracles for quantum leap
for times beyond when all would heal
And life no more would other steal

S. Kyriacou

Heart Broken

Lord please take me,
And make it quick,
For the one I love,
Has given up and quit.

I feel me fadin'
And gone away,
For my heart been broken
Lord what can I say.

I hope there's room,
For a burnt out sole,
Goodbye too everyone,
Who had rock 'n roll,

My heart's been broken,
Oh there goes my sole,
Please Lord take me,
For I've nowhere else to go.

Kenneth Cahill

Untitled

Poetry can rhyme,
Or should rhythm win,
Each boring line,
Two lines or three,
Rhyming can be hard,
You and me can succeed.

Elena J. Partridge

The Wind

A breeze is gently caressing
The straw on the eaves,
The wind is slowly undressing
The tress of their leaves.

The sheep on the green hills
Stand in the lee of the land,
Whilst the large stately windmill's
Arms go round and round.

The rose trees blood red flowers
Lives area nearly done,
And the Earth's many powers
Are seemingly reduced to one.

The winds breath is a murmur;
A sign for change to begin,
And heralds the end of the Summer
By singing the Autumn in.

Rachel McLaughlin

November

No birds fluttering all over the sky,
   The nights get longer,
   The days get shorter.
The old oak tree is fully bare,
   No coloured leaves,
   No little breeze.

Laughing children slipping on slush,
   Throwing snowballs making mush,
   No birds singing,
   No squirrels to be seen,
   But I don't care because
Christmas is near.

Saoirse Barrett

Sweet Baby

Sweet baby let me wipe your tears,
   whisper in your tiny ears
   and wipe away those fears

Tiny toddler all kisses and cuddles
   you really do get into some
   real fine muddles

Little child be bold and brave
   and somewhere along the line
   try to behave

Those adolescent years brings
   another flood of tears,
   but now, you, must learn
   to face your fears

An adult you've become but guess what?
   I'm still your mum and to me
   you'll always be my sweet baby

Doreen Hutchison

In a Poet's Eye

The soaring eagle's lonesome flight
High in a clear blue sky
The sweet and swallow's summer dance
Caught in a poets eye

The leaping fish return upstream
The fox that passes by unseen
The owl caught in a bright moonbeam
Seen in a poets eye

A wave cascading on a shore
The calm before the thunder's roar
A dawn that herald's peace once more
All in a poets eye

Edward B. Bagnall

On That Heavenly Night

The wind blew gently upon my face.
   I found true love,
   in this heavenly place.

The air was cool,
The breeze was warm,
   We lay entwined
   Until early dawn.

The ocean waves
   Splashed where we lay,
My love for him will always stay.

We walked hand in hand along the sand,
   Listening to the heavenly music
   of the Angels' band.

My moistened eyes had seen the light,
   my love for him was clearly bright.
   Where we met and lay,
   on that heavenly night.

Julie Ann Sadler

Poem Of Feelings

The way I'm feeling now
Is hard to understand
I don't know why
And I don't know how
It's easy to say "I love you"
But only if it's true
The bond between us has grown
But I'm standing here alone
I'm thinking of things to write
If only you were in sight

I miss your gentle touch
I miss you oh so much
The time we spent together
We said we'd be here forever
Last thing at night
We held each other tight

The time we spent went fast
The love we had has past

Helen Whitehouse

As I Go Down The River

As I go down the mine,
I shiver and shout,
As if the wind,
Would blow my light out.

As the light goes out
I simply cry,
As I feel as though,
I'm going to die.

Down the mine,
It's scary and cold,
But it doesn't stop me,
from doing as I'm told.

I can't read,
I can't write,
And I can't see,
Without a light.

Louise Giles

My Love

You were my love in springtime
When all our world was new.
We loved each other dearly
With a love so sweet and true
Endless years we had together
Envied by not a few
Through fair and stormy weather
We stayed forever true.
Now you have gone my darling
And I am left so blue
I still remember yesteryear
And our love so sweet and true

E. Hollis

Bag Lady

How do you cope?
When she screams out in the night;
A name that doesn't belong to you.
Don't worry,
Don't be aghast,
She's not having an affair right now;
Just an affair with the past.
That's a bag lady.

Did she tell you?
The hows, the whens, the whys!
That the body succumbed and betrayed;
Sanity fleeing,
Yet, still she clings
It's uncontrolled nights that conspire,
To return to these things.
That's a bag lady.

Paula-Anne Hawkins

Untitled

Meg my pony,
she's a dream,
her velvet coat,
as smooth as cream,
her eyes that glisten,
like a beam,
make her movement,
a joy to be seen

S. Chapman

Furniture And Friends

Mr. Carpet down there
Looking worn and threadbare
It's to you that I'm talking
Do you tire from feet walking
Up and down on your sinews
With their oddly–shaped shoes?

And to you Mr. Chair
Do you bother or care
As you admire and contemplate
Each bottom you accommodate?

Not like old Mr. Table
Boldly upright and stable
Having numerous uses
Like the well–worn excuses
About resting tired feet?
This poem ends incomplete

Sara Moffat

As I Sit Here Alone

As I sit here alone
By the fireside, I gaze
Out my window to see
The mist coming over
The mountains and I know.
There's hope of
A good day tomorrow
When a new day dawns
For me. Yet there may
Not be a tomorrow God
Only knows what will
Be. I will cherish the
Beauty around me. 'Tis
A beautiful sight to see
I watch for the moon
And the stars shine
As the sun sets fading
Glow. Roll on swift night
In silence blow and blow
Thy breeze of sunshine blow.

Kathleen Keogh

Death At War

I looked and glared
Sudden fear
It troubled me so
Reminding, I must go
Those weapons of war
With all there might
Blasting, blasting
In the dead of night
I stumbled I tripped
The mud it was red
Bodies lay dead
Guns still firing lead
And then it came
Deafening my brain
Oh why so slow
The pain, the pain.
Now I am a number
What a blunder
Needless to say
I am dead.

Ray Wales

275

Untitled

The sun shone on me lately
and warmed my weary flesh,
It kissed my newly troubled eyes
that they might see afresh.
With kisses, that though gentle
insisted I succumb
and give up my inheritance
to play a broken drum.
It would not beat to keep time
with the song that I best knew
but forced me to sing loud
words that felt untrue.
So now that clouds have drifted in
I'll learn to love my song again.

Laura Doherty

Thalidomide Baby

A child born into a society,
governed by scientific and
medical superiority
Little did they know or
realize the devastation,
caused by thalidomide.

With eyes so bright,
and mind alert,
a malformed child
with limbs deformed.
Another innocent victim
of Thalidomide is born.

A mother's tears,
a mother's pain,
The father's utter
sense of shame.
The genetic price
their child will have to pay.
Thalidomide baby will have to
Face life in a very cruel way.

Georgina Brennan nee Conroy

My Isolated Planet

My world is weird,
    Reasons why,
I wear my front to keep me in,
Yet it's there to let me surface.

I sit, I look yet hide away.
Feelings run from toes to hair,
    I'm in despair.
I want to tell you what I feel,
But unfortunately shy.

Please let it out,
But no He's there,
Chained me to my insides deep.
I'm in despair.
Hot, red I feel.
Unfortunately shy.

Michelle Larkin

"The Sea"

As I stand here on the shore,
listening to the ocean's roar.
I wonder what lies over yonder,
beyond the horizon and the sun
another day has just begun.
In other lands so far and wide,
do they too, look towards the tide,
getting a feeling of awe inside.
As I stand here it seems to say,
respect my natural strength and
power in every way.
Then as the evening comes along,
once more our day has gone
now to join other lands nearer the sun.

S. E. Cook

For Mum

Kind of heart
And fair of face
A lovely lady
With such grace
Simple, humble, ever true
Always there for me and you
Loving life, always caring
Every moment was for sharing
Her life not easy
But her special way
Made every day a happy day
Those left behind will miss her so
But in their hearts will always know
She is watching, so have reason
To celebrate her life's new season.

Sally Carter

The Golden Heart

I walked alone in the park,
I walked alone in the dark
Until one day, there came my way
The dog with a golden heart,
So now she walks with me,
For she's my eyes you see
This wonderful dog with a golden heart.
Donna is her name
In her I do confide,
For she is there to guide
The dog with the golden heart.

Marjorie Edwina Ashley

Could I But Dream

Could I but dream,
That dream again,
Your loving smile to see,

Could I but feel,
Those sweet caresses,
Your arms wrapped around me,

Could I but see,
The love light shine,
In your sweet eyes of blue,

Could I but hear,
Thy beating heart,
That echoes with vigorous passion,

Could I but dream,
That dream again,
And awake to find it true?

Carl Blair

The Tramp

There he sits
A lonely man
Getting by
The best he can.

In tattered rags
Where was once a suit
Old tattered shoes
Replace a shiny boot.

Holds a bottle tight
Alcohol its content
Talks to his friends
The one's he invents.

He gets cold at night
Stays cold all day
Been offered a hostel
But its charity, won't stay.

He once was a proud man
But what can you do
Don't kick him when he's down
For one day it could be you.

Colin Wells

My Lady

My lady is so true and proud,
Receiving compliments nice and loud,
Her shape is sleek and very flash,
And doesn't loosely spend my cash,
I gladly buy all that she needs,
So there are no doubting seeds,
She is ready all year long,
To boost me up and keep me strong,
My lady you see I more than like,
Because my friend she is my bike.

Steve Thorne

"My Son"

One day a little boy, was sent
    Me from above
A boy for me to cherish, a son
    For me to love.
A proper little devil, full of mischief
    Full of fun
And such a cheeky little face
    But loved by everyone.
Many years have passed since
    Then,
My son is now a man
And he was sent a little boy
    Someone to call me nan
Life isn't any easier, sometimes I
    Feel forlorn
But I never will forget the day
    My little son was born.

E. Harrison

Searching

I crossed
the lines of innocence
looking into
the deep darkness
I hid
my heart
to
maybe
find my true self
I lost my soul
trying
to
find
my sun

The reason
was
you

Josipa Supan

At The Dentist

'Open wide'
The dentist cried,
'Just you wait and see,
When I'm done you won't come
back to bother me.'

It wasn't my fault,
I was only young,
I didn't know the difference,
Between right or wrong.

He shoved his fingers,
In my mouth,
Then he started,
To poke about.

I needed to swallow,
What else could I do,
So I shut my mouth,
And crack,
His fingers broke in two!

Sarah Barber

The Blind Man

The green fields
The blue sky
The golden corn
In the early morn
Dogs barking
People larking
Men walking
Girls talking
Did I see them?
No

Did I see the grass flowing
The wind blowing?
No

Did I see the tree shaking
The branch breaking?
No

The shining glitter of the dew
If only I knew

Noel Hegarty

Seas Of Fate

A wave,
Strong and smooth,
Rushing, rolling, rocking my world,
White crests on fire,

Your face
Lingers in my mind,
Eyes . . . Deep pools of silent waters,
Immovable?
Untouched by it all,
And yet,
Strangely sad,
Overflowing with what could have been,
I think,
And tears rise in my eyes,
Of how fate and time,
Have cut our ties.
If I called you,
Would you come?
Or have the tides of time,
Washed our love away.

Val Bishop

"To Mum—With Love"

Even though you are not here,
We hold our thoughts
Oy you so dear.

Your strength was there
For all to see,
You will always be so special to me.

The simple life that meant so much
Will never really fade away,
Your joy of living was there to see,
Now, will be, in pure harmony!

Trish Phillips

Untitled

Humming birds,
    swarming bees,
        woodland's green,
            marshy streams.

Amber browns,
    reds and golds,
        scarlet petals,
            fall from a rose.

The gift of life
    the human soul
        mother nature
            she knows.

B. Spencer

High

Cruising through the gates of reality
Into the realms of fantasy
I saw you waiting
On the corner of my dreams

We caught magenta clouds
As a world in shrouds
Orbited through rainbows
About our restless minds

But now I'm falling frantically
As I hit the lawn of reality
I lie alone in painless pain
Watching the destruction of times reign

My heart still echoing with screams
From the chasm of lost dreams
And my spirits only hope lies
In another ticket to paradise

Katherine Ann-Marie Ward

Diamond King

He moves quickly, tongue flicking
Body glides across the floor
Lovely shade of chocolate brown
Cream smudges, underneath many more.
Smooth, silent, without hesitation
It takes great boldness to be feared
For his intentions are hard to read
A sudden movement would be taken
To be this reptile's very next feed.
He stops dead. But alert of danger
Forked tongue moves faster than before
Round lidless eyes cold and black
He moves toward me a little more
I step near him, softly speaking
My words oblivious for he cannot hear
I bend down and gather him up
Showing no alarm or sudden fear
He is harmless. It is all fake
For he is Diamond, my pet King Snake.

Sandra Horobin

I Behold Love

I behold Love:
Love stands
    Before me;
What can I possibly desire?
I Embrace the Darkness
    With open arms.
Today I fear not fear.
I fear not unknown
    Of mankind:
Let love embrace me:
I want only you.
Tonight let Love
    Entwine fear;
Let the world embrace
    The world.
I want to embrace
    My love.

Shamshad Akhtar

My Wish

My tender heart
This pulsing flesh
Still bares the life long scars
Of childhood love
Of wasted dreams
Of bargains with the stars
So take my heart
This pulsing flesh
So I may lay and slumber
And dream of times
When I loved you
And life was still a wonder.

Michael William Kirkman

Peace

I look into the clouds
And I can see,
Peace and harmony
for you and me,
An end to fighting
An end to war,
finally we get
What we've been fighting for.

I stare into space
And I feel free,
with sanctuary and silence
That may cease to be,
It's peaceful now but
How long will it last?
There is always the threat
of a nuclear blast

We must lay down arms
And show heaven above
It's not the only place
With peace and love

Paul McDermott

If There's A God

If there's a God,
Would we have war?
If there's a God,
Would we have hate?
If there's a God,
Would we have illness?
If there's a God,
Would we have rape?
If there's a God,
Would we have pain?
If there's a God,
Would we have child abuse?
If there's a God,
Would we have death?
If there's a God,
Does he have a heart?

Heidi Barber

Dreaming

Have you ever longed
To be alone,
To lie and dream
In some place unknown,
In some beautiful place
Where there isn't a sound.
But for leaves of a tree
As they float to the ground.
Where there isn't a sound
But a gentle breeze.
The call of a bird
Or a murmuring stream.
To lie and dream
In soft grass.
The scent of wild flowers
Drifting past
The rays of a warm sun
Upon your face?
Oh, just to be
In this beautiful place.

Alma Quant

A Lament

A Goldcrest dead,
Half a halo on its head;
I mourn its absence in the conifer
And buried its tiny body
Beneath the sunflowers
To ignite their glory;
And with its mate lament.

Hazel Weight

Rich Man

Take me to your place of hell
The place you want me to be
Ridicule me for where I came
And tell me what I should be

Taunt me for being who I am
And never let me be free
Yours is the perfect knowing
For you all carry the key

Tell me I'm full of wrongness
Right I know you must be
Brought up in a world of sameness
You tell me what I have to be

The journey to your evil place
It does not worry me
I know I am a richer man
Than you can hope to be

Lynn Rennie Muir

My Pets

There he is on his swing,
Sitting up like he's the king,
Pecking at a bowl of seed,
Then sings and has another feed.

The "Walkies" word is all needs,
To find his bag and various leads,
"Let's get your ball for you to play,
Now go and chase it—that's the way".

They float around in a watery trance,
In a peaceful way they seem to dance,
At feeding time there is a riot,
Would you want this creature's diet?

My bobtailed pets have different ways,
Of greeting you on diverse days,
Some are friendly, some get cross,
And some just tell you who is boss.

So have a go and guess my pets,
Get them wrong you'll owe no debts,
I have written about four kinds,
All with totally different minds.

Clare Bayliss

Feelin' Fine

I am a feline figure,
There's no doubt about that,
My name's a household word,
Quite simply. I'm a cat,

I don't get amongst pigeons,
I'm too discreet for that,
I'm never let out of bags,
I'm a super clever cat,

It seems to me, that's why
My nine lives are still intact
You see I'm only fiction.
And that's a definite fact.

Jose Herron

The Point

The point that we mention
In all of our ways
Is a mystical point that's covered
in haze. What is this point and
where does it get to, is it the
point that gets out to get you?
The point is, the point that I
mention and the point of this
is my contention. What is the point
is the point just an invention
or is it the point and that
is my dimension!

Brian Walters

Loneliness

Loneliness is a privilege
That comes to those who ask.
It gives us time to think and wonder,
And time to understand.

The mellowness of Time-out,
The wonder of Peace,
As time trickles slowly by
The fine white grains of sand.

Sitting sat a-lonely
All things can come to mind,
Float around head and heart,
While Quiet holds your hand.

Thoughts of love come seeping,
And friendships come and gone,
Friends of now remembered,
And quietly you stand.

Loneliness is a privilege
That comes to those who ask,
But that time spent with others
Is the all life–giving land.

Julee Sanderson

Did You Ever Have That Feeling?

Did you ever have that feeling
that you were going down?;
the world was falling with you
and you couldn't hear a sound.

Did you ever have that feeling
that your sun had gone away?;
all the world was happy
but they wouldn't let you play.

Did you ever have that feeling
that you weren't really there?;
you watched the world on a TV
and it made you scared.

Did you ever have that feeling
you had just closed your eyes?;
you see everything clearly,
when you open them, you're blind.

Linzi Kemp

Untitled

Oh Great Gran dear I'm one year old
You helped me on my way
Without your love and kindness,
I might not be here today.
Then when I was well and doing fine
The Good Lord struck you down
I know we'll meet again one day
In heaven underground

Margaret Prouse

You're all around in

  every way
I feel your love Lord
  every day
You are my shepherd
  I am Your flock
My life with You Lord
  is solid rock
For Your guard of me
  even only one
You paid the price
  with Your only son
Now life I have with
  You oh King
All praise and worship
  to You I'll bring
"My Lord my righteous
  Saviour"

Leone Calderbank

A Soldier's Lament

Death, sadness and all the pain,
Bodies lay in the pouring rain,
The loud noise of a firing gun,
Whatever happened to that word fun,
Seeing another bright day,
Seems to be far away,
Think about the people that died,
All the families that must have cried,
We must stop these horrific wars,
That start without a real cause,
Looking around there's so much hatred,
Even though human life is so scared.

Louise Garner

Hurting

When you called him to heaven.
Our little one was only two
So much love we gave him.
Why did you need him too.

Can't you see our heartbreak
You left us so much pain
Why did you fail to listen
We prayed so hard in vain.

Our faith is truly shattered
Our trust is way down low
When you didn't listen
There was nowhere else to go

One day we may trust again
And build a life a new
Just now we have no anchor
Our grief is much to new.

Joan Walker

School Days

In class 6 I had a good time,
Until Mrs. Goodwin had her accident
And then I didn't feel fine.
I've made loads of friends,
Who I won't forget,
In all my pastimes
They were the best yet.
This school has been
The one I've liked best,
The boys were naughty sometimes
Which I couldn't stand
Mrs. Goodwin then had the football band.

I've got to leave you all behind
Some new friends I have to find
What the future holds I do not know
I only know I'm sad to go.

Christopher Grant Watts

Decision

I wondered, as if to say
Should I go? Or should I stay!
By chance, a thought that came to me
Decided what that answer be!
Surely go, was loud and clear,
But then if so? Could lead to fear,
So, stay was obviously, the choice,
Be satisfied with what you have,
I'd recognized my own voice,
In determining the reason why!
Was not a difficult thing to try,
After all for us to learn.
We toe the line, and wait our turn
Should we push ourselves too far
We may not find out, who we are?
As my mind went into pray,
The decision?
Should I go! Or should I stay?

Peter G. Marriott

Beach Memories

As I gazed into your eyes
And the water lapped over our feet
We promised each other no lies
No heartache—no deceit
Under the blanket of stars
We proclaimed our love
This beach was ours
Our love was from Above

The years have passed
I sit on this beach alone
Good times go fast.
How could I have known
I sit at the silvery edge of the sea
Beside me our daughter plays happily
On the same beach where we loved to be
And you my love are just a memory

Joanne Murray

Memories Of The Past

There's a bridge of golden memories
From here to heaven above
It keeps me very close to you
It's called the bridge of love
As time slips by, but memories stay
As near and dear as yesterday
Beautiful thoughts of one so dear
Treasured forever love sincere
Deep in my heart your memories kept
To love and treasure and never forget
Beautiful thoughts of one so dear
Treasured forever love sincere.

Margaret Taws

Frozen Beauty

Petrified
Ghouls stare grotesquely
In awesome wonder
Across the Ages.
Waterless falls
Hang motionless
Suspended midstream
Their soundless roar
Echoing in unseen caverns
Lost to all
But the creatures of darkness.
Silent stone–bound forests
Climb captured cliffs
Stretching their frozen branches
Towards a skyless heaven
Deep in the bowels
Of the humid earth.

Penelope D. Crowe

The Whisper

In the silence came a whisper
from the far side of the moon,
And sailed around the cosmos
like ripples in a lagoon.
On the wings of a dragon
flying through the mists of old,
Breathed the voice of the wise one
so soft yet so bold.
The Zephyr it embraced me
from the west it wanders free,
It whispered, "I have a message"
and said, "It is for thee".
"Dream the dream of castles
floating in the sky,
For one day I will show you
that is where they fly.
Dream the dream of rainbows
with colours Oh so bright,
And my love will caress you
forever and a night."

Ron Cormack

Moving On

Hello remember me?
I used to be your friend
But then I got sick and couldn't walk
And all of that came to an end.

Just 'cos I'm not perfect
Like you like to think you are
I can still get served a drink
Although I can't walk to the bar.

You think I am embarrassing
Because of my wheelchair
Well it may surprise you all to know
That I don't really care.

I trusted you all
Thought you were good friends
But all you were,
Were fair weather friends.

But when I get better
And rejoin the human race
For you my 'friends'
There will be no place

Gillian Morphy

'Abuse'

In your eyes I see sadness
Because of all this bloody madness
In your heart I seek forgiveness
for the people in this business
In your body I feel weak
I have no power to condemn or speak
In your presence, near or far
I have the need to reach out
and comfort
In your face, I see sadness
   If only I could bring your gladness
   In your heart, I seek forgiveness
   for all those people who are
   abusive.
In my heart, you'll see sadness
Because of all this bloody madness.

Rosie Simuyandi

Friendship

How sweet the touch of friendship is
When life is tinged with sorrow
How comforting the knowledge is
That someone cares tomorrow
What Life will bring no one can tell
But we can rest assured
If friendship shares our path with us
We'll always smile through sorrow.

F. C. Robinson

Self-Murder

As the razor cuts into the skin,
Pouring blood from within,
Letting out all my sin,
Let me be forgiven.

The razor cuts deep inside,
Freeing all my stupid lies,
Free at last I hear them say,
Whilst I sit here ending the day.

The pain I feel as I do it,
I would never put you through it,
It releases all my anger and tears,
One long stroke for all those years.

I'm fine now slowly going.
I hope no-one sees me going,
For I don't want to say good-bye,
Or even let them hear me cry.

Tracey Laws

The Darkest Hour

My sunshine has gone,
The rain clouds are here,
I wait by the window,
As the end draws near.

I sit and gaze
At the people below,
And remember the good times
That I used to know.

She was the warmth,
But now she is gone,
I can't live in the cold,
I cannot go on.

I no longer smile,
I no longer sigh,
I'm unable to laugh,
And my tears have run dry.

Soon it'll be dark,
I'll lie on my bed,
This cruel world will end,
And I will be dead.

Neil Carpenter

Who Knows

Had I done this,
Instead of that.
If I'd been thin,
Instead of fat.
Had been a mouse
Instead of a cat.
Who knows?

Gerald Bruce

You

You are the brightest of the stars,
You are the shine of the constellations

Without you the zodiac patterns would
not show

You are the Universe that I live in,
You are the sun and moon that show
me light

Without you the biggest star would be
small

Will you be the light of the world
for me?

James Carr

The Waking Of The Sun

I sit in silence,
Of the tranquil waters,
I can see moonlight,
Shimmering, upon the lake.

Through the forests of darkness,
The shadows of the night,
Can be seen, wandering
From tree to tree.

Now the Autumn leaves,
Whistle on gently by,
As a rare mild breeze,
Drifts on into the night.

Quietness befalls,
The moment in time again,
As I sit, I take in the sounds,
That cannot be heard.

And, I wonder why,
So much peace,
Can be broken,
By the waking of the sun.

Darren Stenning

Already

Already, my child
lives in this house.
His uncreated presence in each room,
and clattering, unsteady feet
just round the corner of each door,
sprawling on the floor
waving fat arms at me
to pick him up.
I would.
Sitting at our silent table
I would spoon his food
and laugh.
Splashing in the bath,
a warm–washed infant smell,
and in the little room
I'd snuggle him to sleep.
I would.
Already, my uncreated child
lives in this house.

Wendy Jean Berry

Lament

Hail the humble singer's song of grief.
The words tell a sorry story.
Don't let them change your belief.
The power and the glory.

Instead let us sing songs of joy.
Walk through fragrant meadows.
Even if we go through life being coy.
Let us all be brave fellows.

Sorrow! Sorrow's everywhere.
On mother's green earth no one cares
The besetting sight of delicate people
The tired, the hurt, the feeble

Stephen Gambles

Dunblane

As tears ran down those parent's faces
Ambulances driving away,
No one in this world will forget
That sad and hurtful day,
Children of but four and five
hoped that day would never arrive
But the world is left sad and lonely
All because of that one and only.

Susan Finnigan

Non Stop John

He milks the goats
He feeds the duck
He collects the eggs
He spreads the muck
He saws the trees
He chops the wood
He sweeps the path
He clears the mud
He's up at dawn
He collects the mail
He cuts the grass
He makes a bale
He gets the baby
He goes for a walk
He passes me
No time to talk
He goes to work
Nine to five
When he gets home
He kisses the wife
He goes to bed
At half past ten
When he gets up
He starts again
"Phew" it's non stop John.

Derek

A Cardboard Horse

A cardboard horse
That was of course
With horsy thoughts
And coughing snorts
This horse is a jumper
A cardboard thumper
Only in the reign
Would he get vein
Never broken
Never tamed
Only in the rain
He'd become lame
Surely unique
With cardboard feet
A very flat racer
This horse of paper

Craig Shuttleworth

Anita

Tears curve a long profile.
He's etched out what's
scratched back.
Angry tendrils smack
across the wet-look,
no regrets.
Fists throw a long kiss.
Love's sly look
slides from
a lengthy smile
of hideous distortion.
Contortion.
No regrets.

Elizabeth Rose Richards

"Our Daughter"

Today I became a mother
A milestone in my life
What will the future hold for me
A mother and a wife
A little scrap of nothing
With eyes of gentle blue
My darling Teresa
We think the world of you.

Your hair is like the sunshine
Your smile is heaven to
We waited such a long time
For some-one just like you
All our love is with you
Our lives we hope you'll share
For darling daughter
We want you to know
we care

P. M. Barltrop

The Sun Sets High

I'd stand to watch the sunrise again
To hear the dawn chorus song
As long as you were by my side
Waiting through night, though long.

The most beautiful sight I ever saw
Was the sunrise upon that day
When you were there beside me
Watching nature's way.

Upon the swaying summer trees
The sun remained to rest
Lighting the sky in glory rays
Creeping in from the west.

While as the night was chased away
You left without saying goodbye
Until this day I'll never know
Why you leave as the sun sets high.

Sarah Marquis

Time

Time alone does not stand still
Like a country lane it winds at will.
It goes along the country lane
Which has no end to close it in.

Time has no beginning, has no end,
But repeats itself again and again.
Nature uses it as a clock,
To breathe life, to take stock.

If only we could find the time
It's so elusive and never still.
It races on and never waits.
Unabashed, tho' brave, we never will.

Time is fast for man and mate
For human beings it will not wait,
Whilst they map out their lives
Time will never let man survive.

E. M. Bruce

The Coming

On the rugged highway
Twelve priests concealed twelve men
And a lusty bachelor
Crawls to maturity,
Angel of infancy
Robes loosely flowing
Two paradises in one
A sacred well
The lake of fire
Breaking the horrid silence
The people we abhor
Nature's bonfire burns on
The mountains of desolation
Sick with desire
Crumbling palace of growth
Wakes from its golden slumber
And troubled pleasure
We stand in quivering isolation
A terrible beauty is born
Held captive by years.

Jon Keoghan

Prisoner's Lament

They took away our socks
They took away our boots
They took away our shirts
They took away our suits
They left us in our bare skins
They exposed our naked bellies.
When the rain came pouring down.
They gave us back our wellies.

C. Groves

Nostalgia

I love to sit and ponder
Now that I am growing old,
In the comfort of my armchair,
I can let my mind unfold.
Soon I am transported, back to
Those Halcyon days of my youth.
When you and I walked hand
In–hand, happy and content.
Oblivious to the dangerous times we
Lived in, especially from the skies.
So we made our plans for our future
Not knowing what was to come, for
Soon you were sent overseas,
Never to return,
Only in my heart and mind,
Now I am growing old
I can close my eyes and soon
We are back together,
In those wonderful Halcyon
Days of our youth.

Joan E. Davies

By The Pond

Light froze the first movements
Darkness gently subsided
The sun recreated the illumination
Through shadow
When only the moon betrayed

A tree prepared a forest to hide
Seedling peeked befriending sky
Willow turned down
To nature's sound
Why by a pond it weeps

The bulrush coaxed a little duck
To nest inside
Its shady mass
Gentler still a wren weaved by
Mimicking the dragonfly

Trout splashed about the rippling,
Muddled through an opening
Frogs retreated to the muddy bank
Toads looked on
Newts just danced
        Simon Kelsey

Re-born

A speck of dawn
is our being born
to plunge in earthly
ways.

Where life is a school
of lessons to learn
hate, anger and greed
to overcome.

Unknown journeys
down the path
meeting old friends
and loved ones anew.

Memories are not so good
of past lives lived
and loved ones lost
in days of long ago.

As we are led again
to Heavens Golden Gate
welcoming the peace and quietness
for our spirit and our soul.
        Margaret C. Kerr

The Dreamcrusher

The tiny heart of a nightingale
beats quietly for her
and under the stairs wrapped up in silk
her love with eyes of pearls

He crushed all her dreams
he died very young
his skin could not hold the beauty
of a young man in love.
        Fredrik Christie Rodsaether

I Walk

Across the meadow and yonder
To a field of golden corn.
The birds are singing as to
Herald the coming dawn
I walk as countless who have
Done before, to see that field of
Glowing corn.
To see it harvested
To see it stored.
But my thoughts are on the
Coming morn, then once again
I will tread that meadow,
To a field of golden corn.
        E. F. Smith

Poem Of Love

It is felt from the heart,
It goes straight to your head,
It can strike whilst awake,
It can strike whilst in bed.

Songs are sung about this,
Without it we'd miss,
All the comfort it does give,
To the lives we all live.

It's sign is a dove,
Everyone needs love,
From inside love glows,
No boundary it knows,
It's a wonderful thing,
It can make people sing.

When life is tough,
When life is rough,
Nothing comes above,
When someone shows love.
        Judith Donaghey

The Angel's Promise

Did you know that when I die,
I'll be an angel in the sky,
And watch the whole world down below,
The mountains hiding rivers flow,
I'll greet the angels coming here,
And comfort them—their every fear.

Did you know that when I die,
I'll be an angel in the sky,
And see the flowers in their glory,
Each flower telling its very own story.
I'll see the beauty from up above,
And fill the world with undying love.
        Claire Edwards

Peer Pressure

'Go on do it' they chant,
It won't do you no harm,
'Go on take it' they yell
Trying to turn on the charm.

What people say, what people do,
It doesn't have to matter to you.
You are one, they are another,
They're not your dad, sister or mother.

It's up to you if you do it,
It's up to you if you care,
'To be in a gang'
I wouldn't dare!

What would your friends say?
What would they do?
What about Mum, Dad and Gran too?

Would they say 'great, let me try'
Would they help you to die?
Will they say 'stop it'
Will they care?

Don't try and find out don't you dare!
        Carrie-Ann Nicola Weston

"Cockroaches"

Yesterday: Love's oaths
        sweet words
        and promises

Today: Injected poems
        projected music
        and love affairs

Tomorrow: Cockroaches nest
        over the dried roses
        the dilapidated bodies
        Lana Mandila

Life Is A Mystery

I want to be me
but who am I?
I can touch the sea
but not the sky.

Life is a mystery
everyone must stand alone,
people will call your name
but where do you feel is home?

Life can be easy
or life can be hard,
life isn't written
or determined by a card.

Life is what it is
and life is what we'll be,
so you can be you
and I will be Me.
        Heather Pegrum

Tribute To The Racehorse

Thoroughbred animals bred for speed
Highly tuned instruments of speed
Highly strung designed to run
Like light from the sun
Like the wind through a cove
Onward they go
Their skin gleaming with sweat
Pulse beating faster ever faster
Blood pumping faster ever faster
Through veins ready to burst
        David Boath

Modern Life

Today is another long day
Like yesterday,
Young people growing up
No money, no work
Babies being born
Countries at war
Killing, killing, killing
People starving,
People dying,
People crying,
Refugees fleeing from land to land
Homeless people begging
Young people mugging
It's just another long day
Like yesterday.
        Rebekah Cassell

Life

Fate oft' time casts our plans astray
And treats us most unkind
But take good heed of what I say
And just bear this in mind.

The grass would never grow so green
Without the rain and snow,
The air would never smell so clean
Without the wind to blow,
If no dark clouds bedecked the sky
There'd be no silver lining,
If no misfortune came our way
We'd have no joys worth minding.

Life's road with hazards is beset
We strive to reach our goal,
But fate decrees how far we get
Before time takes its toll,
And when from striving we are freed
And earn our last long rest.
We'll not be asked "Did you succeed?"
But "Did you do your best?"
        W. B. Champion

The Up And Coming Death Of Martin Spay

The room was bright,
The room was light,
As Martin Spay sat upright

One more day,
And one more night,
No longer existed
For Martin Spay.

Faces staring at his eyes,
Martin felt strange inside,
How he wanted to let them go,
But he couldn't while on Death row.

In the chair,
The clock Tick-Ticking,
Tasting his final meal,
His dry mouth he was licking,
Two more ticks he was sure,
Then Martin Spay would be no more.

Christopher Wright

Bimbo!

He sits alert by a babbling brook.
With a little red worm upon his hook.
A sudden splish
A sudden splash
Followed by a silvery flash.
The little red worm makes the dash,
down the brook on the hook
The one the fish has gone and took.
A flip, a flap and a mighty slap
as the silvery fish lands upon his lap.

J. G. Marriott

Soliloquy Of An Oxygen Molecule

I and billions like me
We are of life its breath,
And every breathing living thing
Without our help is Death.

Blood's haemoglobin picks us up
With every breath you take,
And even when you're fast asleep
We're working for your sake.

We burn your calorific food
To carbon dioxide,
Using up some oxygen,
Which needs be re-supplied.

But nature's alchemy decrees,
Providently there's no doubt,
Green leaves breathe carbon dioxide in,
And oxygen then breathe out!

Leonard Furnival

Untitled

If I had never met you
A million tears or more
And would never know the joys
Of loving you before.
    Oh! Alone am I for you
    Oh! Alone I cry for you.
But now that we have departed
May I bid you well
Until you meet your own dear—
Hearted, you can never tell
How life and love has changed
You dearly, that's for us to dwell
And may we both say
Life has taught us and well
    Oh! Alone am I for you.
    Oh! Alone I cry for you.

Mavis Gorman

Gently

If you're going to hurt me
Let me down gently
I think the world of you
You'd say
As my heart misses a beat
Thought I had found my hero
My knight in shining armour
Everything I ever wanted
I saw in you
So I gave you my heart
And now you're gonna
Tear my world apart
Shatter all my dreams in two
So I won't beg you to stay
Cry or make a fuss
Just let me down gently
For I never asked
To fall in love.

J. McEwan

Strength

I opened my hand
and cupped inside.

Was my little section of life
trying to hide.

I looked at it there so desperate
and faint,
and thought of all the things
in my complaint.

Life was so hard,
it wore me quite thin.

From the tips of my toes
To the point of my chin.

I must abate it and push
it back.

Close my hand and keep it intact.

Janet Niklaus

Echoes

The moment was ours
The memory still
Of love that we shared
And all that passed
Between two entangled hearts
Night becomes dawn
Shadows still linger
Of warmth and your song
The serenade sweet
The harmony true
A heart sings its love song
And echoes of you.

Jan Poole

Boys In Green

Boys in green boys in blue
Would your country do for you
What you have done for your country
Will it ever set you free

You fight her wars
You bear her scars
You conquer countries
You reach for the stars

You bring her home the spoils of war
The Golden Trinkets you've killed for
The foreign lands that you have seen
Its Lords and Ladies, kings and queens.

And when your time at last is done
In combat jackets you no longer run
How will you fill your day long hours
Mowing the lawn or pruning the flowers

Russell David Gill

Don't Cry

Do you believe in love,
then believe in me.
I'll make you feel,
sweet as can be.

I hope I don't scene you,
and hope I never hurt you,
but if I ever did,
please believe, I never meant to.

I feel I need your love,
and need it so bad,
I truly feel for you
and never wish to make you sad.

Every tear you cry,
hurts so much.
I need to hold you,
feeling your special touch.

We can slow it down,
feeling the love grow.
As our love gets stronger
I pray, we never let go.

Yasar Razaq

The Quest

Deep in my mind my thoughts unite
Up through the dark beyond the night
Beyond the stars that shine so bright
Into the void to seek the light.

Why can't I see what lies ahead?
I must have hope, if faith has fled
Or face the future filled with dread
When this earthly shape I shed

This my quest like all mankind
Thus I seek but never find
The answer, back in time enshrined
Eludes me still, for I am blind.

James Waller

Henry VIII

Henry reigned from 1509,
most people thought he was a swine,
he had six wives and, killed two.
He flushed Anne and Kate,
down the Lou,
he is famous for his six wives,
but three of them died.

Nichola Reece

The Earthquake

The earth does tremor
The ground does shake
The walls do tumble
The windows break

The light has gone out
It's all gone dark
The children, they cry
The dogs, they bark

We sit and wait
For morning to come
We then can see
The damage it's done

Silence at last
The sun breaks through
People are rising
So much to do

We clear up the mess
And start a new day
Things back to normal
I like it that way

Sue Bowering

From The War

Here in the silence of people waiting,
My mind drifts to a place
Where I once was. And will be
Again. To where happiness is
And always will be.

The waiting goes on, and on.
The silence continues. Until,
Later, a shout is heard. A
Cry of hope, of love. Of waiting
For too little for too long.

But there is still hope, always hope.
I think of that place, and it
Pulls me through. The people,
The love everlasting. Trenches
Cold, wet, vanish into the
Past. Where I no longer go.

Where soon I will go no more.

Suzanne Cotton

March On

I await the spring and weather fair
For country walks in clean fresh air
The primrose and the daffodil
Smiling after winter's chill

The trees take on green velvet cloaks
And dust off days that winters choked
Once more I walk in pastures green
A mass of blue-bells can be seen

A stoop and pick a bunch of gold
As life enriched this flower holds
These bells of life ring out to say
The earth has been renewed today

Edna Duncan

The Expectations Of Life

If I should die
Think it not a loss,
For I have gone to a better place,
To a place of beauty.
And think it not as death
But as an everlasting sleep of dreams,
For only in dreams am I truly free,
In dreams can I fulfil my destiny,
In destiny fulfil all expectations.
The expectations of life.

Paul Sherman

A Thought Inside My Head

Something creeping forward,
Something in my head,
A thought that's long forgotten,
A thought that I was dead.

In a graveyard late at night,
As the clock strikes one,
Something shining in the darkness,
Something called a gun.

Noises by the gravestones,
Noises coming close, and fast,
I am breathing in a breath,
A breath that is my last.

As the finger pulled the trigger,
The noise went all around,
The bullet got me in the chest,
I screamed and hit the ground.

It was all a nightmare, so I was told,
As I climbed into my bed,
It was just a dream, a thought,
A thought inside my head.

Karen Davidson

Untitled Pleasures

Bodies together
By a kiss
And a touch
Legs entangled
Air hot,
Lip caressing.
Sweet juices mixed,
Then it came
Oh, beautiful pain,
Laying in a mixture
Of pain and pleasure
In erotic love.

Loreen Lowans

Impatience

Power to the schoolboy
impatiently waiting for his bus
scuffing his shoes on the hard ground
looking around menacingly at us.

Transistor radio at his ear
peering down the lane
he doesn't want to go to school
he doesn't want to use his brain.

He wants his own bus
a red one if you don't mind
to be filled with teachers and parents
and anyone else so inclined.

A suicide driver would be hired
who could laugh as the speed flowed
someone who is brave enough would do
to drive the bus off the road.

So on this sunny morning
He takes his seat on the bus
directly behind the driver he sits
and stares around at all of us.

Tony Jackson

'Looking For Answers'

Will I still be here tomorrow,
to see the green grass grow again?
Will I be here stood on this spot,
underneath the sun or the rain?
Will I see the leaves on the trees?
Will I feel the touch of the breeze?
Will I laugh or cry again?
Will I feel happy or will I feel pain?
Or will tomorrow ever come?
Perhaps for me, but not for some.

Alison J. Hughes

The Mirror

Look in the mirror,
what do you see?
Look at the face
staring at me.
Look at the eyes
and watch for the sorrows.
Is it happiness
this person wallows?

Look in the mirror,
what do you see?
Do you see tears
flowing and free?
Do you see joy
locked in a heart?
Or do you see happiness
without a spark?

Look in the mirror,
what do you see?
Because I can't believe
this person is me.

Rhianon Evans

Colours

Red, white and blue,
struggle and resurgence.
Unity and peace.
A green cloud, emanating from
the east.
Blind genocide as the mother implodes.
Helpless poultry clawed and ravaged
by the vengeful eagle.
Saved from the jaws of black death.
Red, white and black,
not content with grey.

James Mears

Dark House

A dark house,
A deserted hill
All strange,
All still.

Running footsteps,
Piano playing
Cold winds blowing,
Trees swaying.

An icy touch,
Owls screeching
Dark outside,
Rats creeping.

Nothing found,
The house is still
Then gravel crunching,
Nothing seen until . . .

A ghostly figure,
A light flickers on
Softly crying,
And then she's gone

Rachael Kania

Floridian Fluffballs

Clouds, clouds floating by,
Floridian fluffballs in a piercing sky,
Such shapes and sizes, colours too,
From white to pink and greyish blue.
Floating along in fine formation,
Battalions of nothing, no destination.

Oh! How I wish that I could fly,
I'd catch those fluffballs in the sky.
Some are thick and some are thin.
And I'm sure that some have thunder in.
Some changing shape and configuration.
Some fly along in desperation.
Oh! How I wish that I could fly,
I'd catch those fluffballs in the sky.

Jacqui Harland

Boy And Beast

A fair hair boy came riding
across the meadows green—
Taking the horse to water
was his daily routine—
Bare-back, he galloped, gripping the
horse's mane,
They rode as one together, flattening
grass with pleasure—
Nostrils wide, ears pressed back,
the horse a chestnut mare
Knew her way, for everyday using
the same old track,
To the water's edge they went,
never wanting to go back,
Boy and beast, finding peace
on a river bank.

Barbara Deutsch

Nature's Song

Whisperings of the wands of time
stir gently in my ear,
moving, soothing, quiet voices
beckoning me near.

Listen now, they seem to say,
listen to our song
and gently, like a puff of wind
they carry me along.

Soft and warm and comforting
they whisk my thoughts away
to a land of time forgotten now,
to dreams of yesterday.

Velvet grass and scented air
of flowers in full bloom,
blending in with all around
as if in nature's womb.

I give you this, and more, she sighs,
just look, and smell, and touch.
Look after me, she quietly cries.
Do I really ask too much.

Sandra Lockley

The Child

Euphoria, desire,
A flower opens,
A butterfly spreads its wings
Higher and higher,
The mood and the music
A lonely child sings

Hungry and needing
the child cries,
Impossible to satisfy
wounded and bleeding
Alone in the dark
Hurry, or the child will die.

There's horror, there's hate,
The world is a cage,
But there'll always be prayer and hope
So we procreate,
pass on our despair,
And expect our children to cope

For love, our only consolation,
We torment and abuse
The weak ones starve,
The strong indulge;
But the can only lose

Annabelle Charbit

Regrets

How can I find release
When remembrance sadly begets
Sorrow that gives me no peace
I harbour so many regrets.

It's painful to think of my youth
So boastful and knowing it all
It's hard to face the truth
Of my anger, my pomp and gall.

And then when I went to work
I was not always loyal and true
Always ambitions would lurk
With many a sharp word too

As a mother I know I failed
Impatient and not always kind
With children who constantly wailed
Inner strength was hard to find

So now as I sit in my chair
How can I ever forget
My faults and actions unfair
I bow my head with regret.

Sheila Beatrice King

Drowning In The Baths

Below the surface of consciousness,
A child, playing at dead,
Hung suspended,
A pool of silence enclosing him.

He might have been floating
On the Sea of tranquillity
So peacefully he lay
He might have been asleep
So relaxed was his grip on life.
He might have been
But for the tell–tale blue.

Seconds sweep by.
Time keeping track
Of the back-stroker
Sweeping past the boy
Unconscious of his passing.

Jean-Noelle Lyttle

God's Gifts

Great beauty in the world abounds,
In each different nation.
God above thought it out,
And planned the whole creation.

He made the birds and animals,
Bright butterflies and bees.
Spiders weaving silken webs,
Squirrels in the trees.

He formed the thick rain forests,
He made the desert sands.
And pools, lakes and rivers,
In many distant lands.

The greatest gift He gave the world,
Was when His son was born.
For that was a miracle,
On that first Christmas morn.

Eugenie Barker

Ben

Your eyes so big your face so round,
You listen to every single sound,
You follow James around the room,
Don't worry you can play with him soon.

You make me laugh,
You make me cry,
I'll love you until the day I die,
I'll help you grow into a man,
And help you in any way I can.

But you are my youngest and very last,
Please don't grow up so very fast,
For you are my baby my bundle of fun,
The light of my life my beautiful son.

Corrinne Mathews

The Civil Servant

Hello Sir, good morning, Sir,
the rain did shine,
the sun did fall,
did it, it did, good Sir.

Hello Sir, good evening, Sir,
I'm off to see
the shining rain,
the falling sun,
will I, I will, good, Sir.

Hello Sir, good night, Sir,
no rain, no shine,
no sun, no fun,
just blinking stars
that make you sleep,
will they, they will, good, Sir.

Charles Flores

Pony

My friend has a pony
If him to me she would lend,
His show name would be steel wind
For he is a dappled grey
If him to me she would lend
To the local show we would go

The pony's name is Jody.
And what a lovely name it is
If him to me she would lend
She would be my best friend
And if he lived with me
I would ride him everyday.
At night I would watch him,
Galloping in the field
His glittering grey coat catching
The moonlight, racing like a
Steel-wind.

Helen Falvey

Never Say Goodbye

All alone in a tiny room
beneath the trees you lie,
I want to be there to hold you
I want to be there to cry.

I want to lay beside you
to wake you from your bed.
I want to tell you something
I wish I had already said.

I want to tell you I love you
and that memories will never die.
I want to hold you in my arms
and never say goodbye.

Tammy Ruth Fudgell

The Funeral

Marie struggled to be gay,
Hoping love would win one day.
No one ever heard her cry,
No one ever thought she'd die.

All were gathered at the church,
Round the coffin on its perch.
Then they gathered all around,
For the burial in the ground.

Then they gathered for their drinks,
Chatting, sobbing in their minks.
Then they kissed and said "Good-bye".
Who had thought of Marie's cry?

Just one figure no one knew,
Lingered from the leaving queue,
Wondering what was to be done,
Who would see to Marie's son?

Overcome by sheer dismay,
Quietly she began to pray,
For those most pathetic souls,
Who'd just played their major roles.

Amelia Hill

Little Town Sparrow

Little town sparrow high
above the shops
nobody seems to care
whether you're there or not
I care, I care a lot.

Sometimes I hear your cheeping
Echoing down between the shops,
Yet you seem so happy
amongst the din,
I'm glad I heard you;
you make me feel so warm
within.

Isabel Wild

Every Time I Go

As I go and as we part,
I feel you clutching at my heart,
And as the train rolls down the track,
I vow that I will hurry back.

The countryside, it flashes past,
And on my heart a shadow's cast,
For every mile and every view,
Is one more mile away from you.

And as your form grows dark and small,
I place my suitcase in the hall,
I settle down and breathe a sigh,
And hope this week will hurry by.

If life affords me just one chance,
To catch and hold that true romance,
Then I shall do what I must do,
To ensure that one sweet chance is you.

Andrew J. Barnes

'The Blind Mountaineer'

He feels his way with confidence,
And paces measured stride,
The wind and rain his compass,
The curlews call, his guide.

From whither does he wander
Across the snow–capped hill,
Where eagles nest and buzzard dip,
And the morning air strikes chill.

For if his thought be pondered
In the context of a smile,
This man has found true happiness,
Increased with every mile.

In his face, the true contentment
Of a man who sees the light,
For his soul finds consolation,
In the darkness of his night.

Constance M. Cattell

Cardboard City

What should I do
When I'm blue
You know me
Please don't say
I'll be yours
When I'm down
On the rent
Every day
I'll come home
Racking my brains
Thinking of a way
To get myself out
Of this cardboard city state.

J. Paton

Night

I walk at night,
Saddened by the day
Through shattered hopes
And broken dreams,
No loving hand
To guide me on my way.
I walk at night
Searching for a door
To flee somewhere
And be someone,
The one I should have been.
Or better still,
To fade away,
Unborn, unfound—unseen.

Laszlo K. Clements

Suttee Or Sunbathing

This is for you my love
that I burn my body
to a golden–brown
inside the lotus garden

Suttee

Heat lures a gardener
he smiles lazily
rhythmically cutting flowers
still living

I observe them
falling down slowly
quiet by now
like my thoughts

In the sun's fire
we glow self-sacrificingly
purifyingly smouldering
dozing off with devotion
stupefied by the scent
of eternal nirvana

Dorota Motykiewicz

The Hurt Will Stay Forever!

I walked along the sandy shore,
My love for you will grow no more,
You cheated on me with my best friend,
My broken heart will never mend!

Sharon Finlayson

Life's Highway

As I walk along life's highway,
I ponder for awhile
and stand in great amazement
at that which before me lies.

The birds, the bees,
The flowers, the trees,
The rivers, the ponds,
The mountains, the valleys,
The browns, the greens,
The rusts, the reds,
The earth, the sky.

What more can be said.

God's gift to man
is great indeed,
Let's cherish his gifts
for future needs.

Our Sons and Daughters
can be blessed the same,
so long as we play
at the cherishing game.

P. Little

The Forest

Have you ever walked the forest
Listening to the trees,
The message that they give you
They whisper in the breeze.

The sunlight glistens through them
It catches all their hues
The patchwork of its colours
Show the autumn season true.

The shadows of the branches
Spread across the ground,
Light and dark together
Like mysteries spread around.

The crowded overgrown forest
With each individual tree,
The solitude of growing
Is it not like you and me.

Liz Joy

Buzz-Words At The Barb

Square–eyed intelligentsia,
Bip! Bop! Burp!
Vacant looks.

Wysiwyg, Viglens and genies,
Mouse and Microsoft,
Hypertext and logic paths,
Rams and Roms,
And, Arc Pipfdreams!

Ahhh! . . . Miverva soft.

Sensitive sensors,
Chunky controls,
Cross–curricular Petcoders!
Inter activity!
Pic 'n mix!

Mad about Cad . . .
Wild visions and hawk V9?
Share it?

My left brain hurts

Joy Jones

Walking The Fields

I was shy and frightened
of you because I was
so small and to me
you were like a giant.

But yet the joy that
filled my little heart
when I walked the
never-to-be-forgotten
fields with you.

You were always happy
and full of life and
jokes, to see you that
day lying on a bed
surrounded by candles
lighting the way.
Knowing that I would
never walk the fields
with you again.

Margaret Haberlin

A Poet

To Write Bad Poetry, What Is Worse
Or write bad prose in form of verse?
I would that all these awful folk,
Could on their daily muesli choke.

Pretentious and conceited tripe,
Enough to give true poets gripe!

Alasdair Seton-Winton

Man

Sadly this century ends,
So far from early man.
And with myriad regrets
Time unwinds his sacred span.
O! Folly is man's wanting
Of this you must agree,
For with one foot, one step,
Destroyed a living mystery.
For swiftly the seraphim
Astronauts ascended.
The man craving, rockets to
The firmament above.
Then with lust descended,
Defiling the moon we love.
Taking away our secret trust.
By forever spoiling
Our gentle moon's dust.
For he was very much a part
Of man's pathetic lonely heart.

Sonia Ruckley

Only Me

Put the image from your mind,
Forget the photos left behind,
Don't look back lest you go blind,
Only look to me.

To propaganda, close your ears,
Don't tell him 'bout the wasted years,
You know 'twill only end in tears.
Only speak to me.

Shrug off responsibilities,
Save yourself and not the trees,
Don't worry 'bout the wanna be's,
Only think of me.

I can fulfil all your dreams,
Rely on me to still your screams,
You can't deny what kismet deems,
Trust yourself to me.

I know that this is gonna last,
And though you think we're movin' fast,
Your only reference is your past,
Don't panic, you're with me.

Nicole Fewtrell

Light And Shadows

In Memory of Dunblane

A slaughter of the innocent
Brings out
First fruits of suffering.
And from the horror
Of that time of grief
Arise
Such things
As man himself
Could not devise.

We think of Stephen,
Martyred, first,
And of Apostle Paul
Who shared the sight
And later helped to form
A world
Of tenderness and light.

Jean-Maria Lach

Untitled

New Zealand
Ez a new land
New and zeal
Wel and zane
N z need a law
z, elan waned
Eze and lawn
Nz: A wee land

Jason C. Lofts

Walk Freely

I walked the streets of heaven,
And I saw such beautiful fields,
Along side were the daisies,
Their beauty was heavenly,
But, as I looked around me,
My Jesus I did see,
His, beauty, I could not tell thee,
It, was more than heavenly,
He did not speak,
Just looked at me,
His eyes of love spoke
Volumes,
His love for me, was there
To see,
And they told me too walk
Freely.

Joan Sheldon

The Slade

Do you remember the cool shade
Along the Slade
On summer afternoons so long ago?
I remember, I remember
And at my back I sometimes hear
The purposeful tread of Uncle Fred
As he ran for the number one tram.

Do you recall the parade
Along the Slade so long ago,
Past George Mason and Bon Marche
To the school below?
Frisky Freda in the doorway,
Tossing her curls at me,
Stockings quite lascivious,
Gym slip above the knee,
Insidiously libidinal
And full of daunting snares;
I hurried through the school gate
Into the hall for prayers.

J. M. Farmer

Holidays In Bielefeld

This year we went to Germany
Which is miles and miles away
By bus and boat and motor car
Three weeks we were to stay

We loved the German houses
Their verandas hung with flowers
The variety left us gaping
At the Inns and covered bowers

The German cakes were lovely
Full of fruit and juice and cream
Each day I tried a couple
Quite fat now I could scream

Germany is lovely
So fresh and clean it shines
No dogs' dirt on the pavements
'Cos they face such awful fines

But come the day we get too old
To do the things we planned
We'll sit at home remembering
Our holiday in the Father land

Elizabeth Robertson

No One Said . . .

No one said that life would be easy
Or that you have any right

No one said that you're owed a living
Or it is yours to take

Everyone will try to wear you down
If you let them

Someone will be there for you
When you're low down

Someone is there with a helping hand
To share the burden

One must be strong
And play to win

One has to beware
Has to take care

You can do it
But you must try

Don't give in or say
"When I die"

No one said

Glynn A. Bonner

Wordsworth Heaven

This afternoon I've decided
to go meditating at Tintern Abbey,
but now, walking through my garden,
I wonder, will it make me happy?
I could wander lonely as a cloud,
I could just read,
but what is more secluded
than to sow and weed?
Daffodil watching beside the lake,
is that what I'm seeking, though,
the rambling rose at my gate
is absolutely radiant?
It's all there, right in front of me
poetic beauty, lyrical scenes,
but it took me years to see
that all I had to do, was
to open up, and reach out
—for my own Wordsworth heaven.

Hanne Secher

A Bird, A Flower and A Tree

When there's no place to look and see
a bird, a flower or a tree
and nothing meets the seeing eye
but monolithic monsters high.
When babbling brooks no longer flow
with fishes darting to and fro
then all humanity will cry
in the fear this world may die.

But in this universe of ours
man must learn to cope with power
ere he finally destroys
the lovely things that bring most joy
and once again he longs to see
a bird, a flower and a tree.

Sybil Parkin

Consummation

This is the season when I come to you
Across deep fields
And all unhindered by October dew
see cattle sleeping.

There is no reason why I should not come
Into soft fields
Ne'er so completely sea and air were one
While cattle sleep.

And thus with trees on fire I come to find
you gently weeping
The union of glad eyes is on my mind
and cattle sleeping.

Robert Lindsay

Why Are We Here?

A world full of hatred
And not enough love
A world full of violence
That can never be understood
A world full of laughter and also tears
Why has the Lord brought us here,
To a place that we all fear
Locking our doors and windows shut tight
Even frightened to walk alone at night.
I'll never understand why we are here
Until I see the Lord near
He will hold out His hand
And give me a key
And whisper, "It's the key of love
Come on fly with me."
I will then have the answers
But won't be able to share
Until the people I love dearly
Can meet me there.

N. Isherwood

Three Kinds Of Love

My mother's face so fair
always smiling always there.
The day I met my boyfriend
To him I always did attend
on the day we wed I was his only.
Me and my husband never lonely.
Four years passed ever loving
having my first child we were doving
love the day my little girl was born
a lovely face not forlorn
four years later not adorn
my little son was born.

E. Whiting

FLIGHT

EARTHBOUND I SOAR—
MY SPIRIT SHEDS
ITS HEAVY HUMAN GARB
AND WINGS ITS RADIANT WAY
LIKE SOME BRIGHT STAR
THAT DARTS OUT FROM THE
CLOUDS
AND SHOOTS INTO THE NIGHT,
STORM–TOSSED NO MORE,
UNTRAMMELLED, FREE,
SHIMMERING WITH LIGHT AND
ECSTASY.
DO NOT GO
THIS MOMENT WHEN I FLEE
SO JOYOUSLY FROM EARTH
AND ALL ITS STRIFE,
TO STRAY IN FIELDS ELYSIAN,
DISSOLVED IN RAPTUROUS HAR-
MONY,
WHERE PAIN AND JOY ARE BOUND
IN A SHIMMERING RAINBOW
OF SWEET SOUND.

Nalini Wickremesinghe

Millennium

Goodbye to the 1900's
Welcome millennium . . .
Let our country prosper,
Let us all stand proud
If only, we could stop violence
Stop bickering amongst ourselves
Stop all the bloody wars,
Stop! . . . for a single moment . . .
Think! . . . what are we striving for?
Our children are the future
We hear this everyday . . .
They have to grow up faster
Do not take their childhood away . . .
They need time to experiment
To be happy, know how to play
If only . . . life was so simple . . .
In our world today . . .
Goodbye to the 1900's
Welcome Millennium! . . . year 2000! . . .

Cynthia Lesley Rayers

The End Is Nigh

The clouds are gathering up so high,
Atomic waste drifts on by,
Winds howling as if they scream,
The ground is blue not brown or green,
Seconds to wait and it will go,
Rain hail sleet or snow,
Houses and cars they are no more,
Billowing noises rip to the core,
Animals humans run to hide,
Yes the end is nigh.

Sarah Ann Marshall

Untitled

Orkney—land beyond dreams
Cool grey skies
White–crested waves
Boats on the horizon
Rising and falling
Life as it is

Old men and peat banks
Women willing
Fire for the winter
Keeping out chilling
What do you want?
Life as it is.

Children are playing
Noise and fighting
Normal behaviour
The world is a-righting
Politics what's that?
Life as it is.

J. K. Stevenson

That's Life

As I look back over my life,
Times of troubles, and of strife,
As a child, busy at play.
This is how I filled my day.
Never a care or thought, of tomorrow,
Never thinking of times, of sorrow.
Those times come as they must.
Now I am grown, time goes so fast,
How quickly a year becomes the past.
One year, two years soon it's ten,
New Year's Eve, here we go again.
What will it bring, what will it be,
As the months go by we will see.
Spring, summer, winter, and the fall,
Seasons change for one and all.
So live your life, live it well,
How long, we will live no one can tell.
So live each day, as if your last,
Very soon, the future will be the past.

V. Carter

'Our Baby'

Mummy and Daddy, that's me and you,
Nothing in pink, but loads in blue.
For now we share a special joy,
All things good,—our little boy.
The love we share, made us our son.
Now as a family we have begun.
No longer two, we now are three.
I send you my love, for giving me Harry.

Cay Tabor

A Matter Of Survival

Father I have sinned.
And I am so ashamed.
I am the fool who never learns.
And my heart is breaking.

Father I have sinned.
And I am so tired.
I am the shadow in the dark.
And my fears are waking.

Father I have sinned.
And I am so alone.
I am the wolf amongst the sheep.
And my soul is dying.

Father I have sinned.
And I am so afraid.
I am a man who walks alone.
And I am tired of crying.

Margaret Elizabeth Moss

Religion

Strangers on the Moor Land,
Shadows through the night.
Pilgrims on a walk about,
To fight the good fight.

Soldiers in their thousands,
Countries far away.
Wars to win this century,
Peace on Earth today.

Starvers in the poor lands,
Victims all year round.
Bombers in the sky light,
This Lord he must be found.

Populations have served him,
And died in screaming pain.
Will the next generation,
Serve the God with no name.

Will our children of the future,
Sing praise to this God
And died like their fathers did,
Playing soldiers in the mud.

C. B. Schofield

A Thought Spared

I got this plea come through the door
To help the old folk now,
And deprived children all around
I want to help somehow.
It touched me very deeply
That a child could never have known,
What Christmas was, or presents
In all the years that they have grown.
The things we take for granted
Roast turkey and Christmas pud
Tree lights tinsel and crackers
Would be magic from where they stood.
But then this got me thinking,
That's ok for the small
But for the old and lonely
It's the saddest day of all.

Julie A. Jordan

Cloud Power

Some see in dark clouds
grim wonders
frightening with lightning
and thunders.
Some say bright clouds
like banners unfurled
bring life, beauty and fun
to the world.

Douglas Carter

The Hop-Pickers

The families went to kent
to hop-pick for farmer bent.
The arrived with horse and cart
they had to have an early start
mums and girls had spare red knickers,
essential items for busy hop-pickers.
The lads swanked about in new boots,
and had the farm girls in hoots,
they were told to sleep in an old barn,
and wash themselves in the torn.
Cooking meals was a bore,
as they'd have liked a lot more.
Jinny wrote the their Dad.
"Things here are very bad",
He came and fetched them in the van,
They did a flit, plus friend Stan.
who'd slashed away some hens,
and little porkers, from their pens.

Ursula Meldon

St. David

St. David's day, the 1st March,
Is special to the Welsh,
He slew the fiery dragon,
And made Wales safe at last.

We're very good at singing,
Or so the saying goes,
But most of us are miming,
We can't reach all the notes.

Our national sport is rugby,
As a nation, we are proud,
We love "Land of my Fathers"
And sing it very loud.

A Welshman is a friend for life,
They love their beer too,
Their love for "Hymns and Arias"
Is known the whole world through.

"Our David" as the patron saint,
Has served us long and true,
I'm proud to be a "taffy"
And hope that you are too.

David Ackerman

Daydream

Veil of time rose bright
Floating through my sight
    Old horizons dream;
Keep—in spectral light
Tall battlements that might
    Awesome to me seem.

Moat with misty stream,
Golden rainbow gleam,
    Pennant flying high
On the tower's stone seam,
May-be for a Queen?
    Yes, she's riding by.

In my dream I cry
For she's fair and shy,
    Loves her truest knight;
Awake! For years they fly,
Now I'm grey. Death's nigh.
    And my dream! 'Twas right!

Teresa J. Smith

Within Me

I look deep down inside,
I see a black emptiness.
I see no trust.
I feel no love.

If I cannot see trust,
How can I trust?
If I cannot feel love,
How can I give and accept love?

Lisa Seeney

Summer Daze

Remember how the pastel shades,
Emitted through a summer daze;
Had danced across a surface calm,
To settle in this palm.
Remember how the morning new,
Was resurrected from the dew;
Heartened by bird song at dawn,
Fanfare for that morn.
Remember how the day was spent,
Laughing through fields, backs bent,
And then as one to fall and fire.
Rest beneath some leafy spire.
Remember now that winter nears
Its cloak of long night's tears;
And we do cover up but find,
Solace in the mind.

Keven Smith

epistle from ephesus 1996

Under the winter–blue dome
our laughter soared to the sky
like minarets of sound
rising in the amphitheatre,
reverberating with
the ancient repetitions
great great is diana
not paul in ephesus;
great graven image
many–breasted goddess
eternal potency and lust,
the joy of heathen whoredoms
in the wide silence of stone eyes.

Hilary Semple

T.V. Heaven

Rain and pain and gallowed grief,
Hold that shot in disbelief
Hypnotise with gruesome lies,
Uncover something underneath.

The need, the need to see the bleed,
To plant a thought like evil seed,
The fight and fright but it's alright,
For in the mind is out of deed.

The war's and gores and broken laws,
Taking lives in scores and scores,
Just for fun we watch the gun,
and see the hero get what's yours.

Only play from day to day.
As long as that's what mummy's say,
You'll never guess as we progress,
From Freddy's dreams to dear O. J.

To turn a cheek with world so bleak,
But angry acts are what we seek.
We say lets pray and gentle stay.
Despising those whom choose the meek.

Brett Moore

In Our Quiet Evening

Thoughts are like memories
That drift from the past.
Little reminders
Of what we did last.

If you open your heart
And sit back in your chair
I'll creep up and whisper
Softly, can you hear?

Our footsteps are silent
Hand in hand through our past.
Flying high over our future
And at one in our hearts.

Graham John Faulkner

Season's Moons

A fiery moon is taking away summer,
On the autumn road towards winter;
On this many closing-dusk of nights.

Trees and redundant chimney roof-
tops—
Carrying pigeon of ochre globe;
Transporting seasons—
Continuing clock of Earth.
Ticking the nights away:
Houring the days.

Is that a face on the taxi-moon,
Is he taking
And telling us the weather?
A clairvoyant:
That the snow is coming:
Crystal ball moon.

Stephen Castree

Transience

Happiness is transient.
Feel it in the movement of the dance
before the pain of the stretched muscle
hear it the silence between
the notes of the symphony;

In the dark of a star–lit
sky, when I hear you breathing—
happiness when I touch you
my lover, beloved;
In the green leaves of changing
seasons

Hold me beloved, lover.
Imagine you
near . . . Happiness as intangible
transient, light as
sting of the guitar, to dream in
your eyes,

This stillness touching my soul.
I weep. To reach for you,
lover, beloved, and never know.

L. A. Churchill

Untitled

Cover me with fields
    Enfold me in streams
Wrap me in clouds
    Surround me with trees

No-one gets close to me
    No-one can touch me
No-one can hurt me
    No-one can reach me
No-one can love me
    I am alone—Untouchable.

P. A. Twelves

Sleeping Town

The night was filled with coldness
A chill was in the air
The hustle of the daytime
Began to disappear
The rain fell with the darkness
The wind outside was strong
A distant car was pulling away
And the night ahead was long
The close knit of our household
Began to settle down
I focused through our window
To see a sleeping town
All the gates were shut now
All the curtains drawn
The world seemed to be sleeping
The world began to yawn

Zita Stockbridge

Alone

Feeling lonely,
Out of place.
In the way,
Too much space
Surrounding me,
There's no one there,
My only comfort
Is this chair
In which I sit,
All day and night,
Telling myself
I feel alright,
When really
For so long I've known,
That I'm unhappy
When alone.

Catherine Page

Full Circle

A laughing child with golden hair,
A loving hug to show they care,
Tears that are quieted with a caress,
When a mother holds them to her breast.

Mingled feelings watching them grow,
Knowing that someday they will go
and also feel the joy and the pain,
Watching their children doing the same.

The laughing child is there once more,
Silently peeping around the door,
Gazing with longing at the frail figure
lying on the bed, asleep now forever.

Katrina M. Anderson

The Stream Of Life

How cold is the breeze
That blows the whistling trees
Clouds smother the sky
Birds fly on high
Singing in rhyme
To the beat of time
So free without a care
Just like the breath of air
Wherever you go
The stream of life will flow.

Nicholas Fletcher

Why?

With no eyes to see it,
Why does the sun set?
With no tears to dry,
Why does it rise?
With no war to win,
Why does light bless the battlefields?

With no mother to embrace,
Why does the child cry?
With no people left,
Why do church bells ring?
With no-one alive,
Why does pain still hurt?

With no dreams left,
Why do we still sleep?
With no future ahead,
Why does a heart beat?
With no destiny to keep alive,
Why does the imagination still work?

Emma Chase

The Guru

He said he had the answers,
He said he knew it all,
As he stood tall, erect and handsome,
In the middle of the hall.

The rules were really quite simple,
Be kind and loving and true,
If you could be good to others,
Then they would be good to you.

So we paid the annual subscription,
And followed him about,
And watched as he counted the money,
That we had all paid out.

Trust was very important,
Be celibate now he said,
So we all took a vow of chastity
As he took his friend's wife to bed.

So month by month we listened,
And learned just what to do,
If you want to enjoy the Good Life
Then become a simple Guru!

Stella Jones

Weather?

Standing start from windswept cliff
So afraid of falling over
Tumbling into tormented seas
Instead of four–leaf clover
Gripping tightly with numbed fingers
As well as numbness in my head
Feeling that I'm not in Kansas
Or at home in bed
Thoughts race past in much confusion
A decision can't be made
Longing for the friendly sun
Let me come out from the shade
I feel the storm around me
I feel the stinging rain
I feel the creaking branch above me
Protests from the grain
I'm so cold and blank minded
If I go on then I'll be bland
Standing start from windswept cliff
Falling with my heart in hand.

Lynne Nicholson

Starshine

Starshine, in skies darkly clearing
Galaxies glinting
Eternally bright
Starshine a million years nearing
Others worlds hinting
Belonging to night.

Starshine—different from moonlight
Clear and like crystal
When the stars sing.
Starshine—lighting a June night.
Haunting and wistful
Soft magic to bring.

Molly Rodgers

Frenzy

Rush and tear
No time to spare.
Hither, thither
Nerves a-quiver.

Rush and tear
No time to care
For human beings
And all wild things.

Rush and speed
A frenzied need.
A greed for wealth
In spite of health.

Rush and strain.
What is to gain?
Nothing, save
An early grave.

Joan Robson

The Birds Outside

The birds outside
My window today
Have taken my darkest
Sadness away.

When the door was closing
And the light disappeared
As the pain was overtaking
And the black hole came near.

I heard a comforting voice
She had begun to sing
I heard the delicate sound
Of her small china wing.

Laura Brown

Together

Step up,
Step down,
Together we see the same view,
Separately.

Go out,
Come in,
Separately we live the same life,
Together.

Working,
Resting,
Being the life with each other,
Forever.

Dorrie Stock

My Fine Old Horse

My fine old horse please pull away
Tug on your bridal, heave your way
Along the towpath drag your line
And you will get there in time.

A heavy barge to pull along
Some seventy ton of coal to drag
So heave my horse and pull away
And butty boat behind does sway.

So barge and butty move along
Through bridge and lock, do carry on
So heave my horse and pull away
The day is long for everyone.

Bargee and wife take turns to stand
Guiding the tiller with their hand
So heave my horse and pull away
Tomorrow begins another day.

My fine old horse please take a rest
Your job is done you've done your best
And plodded on through wind and snow
So take a rest before we go.

B. Smedley

Tainted Blue

I picture you there's shades of blue
A tainted glimpse of light
I've often learned that broken hearts
Give up without a fight
And for those who know of tearshed
To give up that's just not right
So close your eyes a mystic dream
Such wonders go untold
The echoes of your laughter
A million dreams unfold
I'm woken so sincerely
First light to greet my face
Dry soft each tear from morning sun
This heart I have a space
There's memories and there's laughter
To dream and never end
As then, first kiss of morning sun
Soft tears again to roll
With innocence, a birds at song
Some things I've no control.

Alexander MacLean

Falling in Love

Roses are colourful, strong,
Fragile, and true,
But there is no one on this
Earth, as wonderful as you.
You are the sunshine, the stars, and
The flowers, but when I think of
You sometimes, you are a storm,
Around a bolt of lightning, in a
Tower.

Joy Helen Kettlety

The Corn Field

Lovers lie in the long corn,
Whispering sweet
Words of love,
Fragrant red poppies
Perfume the air,
A hot august sun shines
High above.
Unleashed passion takes over,
She groans
Entwined in his arms,
The cornfield quivers,
The poppies dance,
And the lovers are
Lost in loves
Magic charms.

Margaret Maher

Dear Jayne And Paul

We thank you both for what you've done,
By giving us our first Grandson.
Although he came a little late,
We really didn't mind the wait.
To see him now so cute and small,
Makes waiting for him worth it all.
We think he's precious as a pearl,
Now, how about a baby girl!!

With lots of love,
from Nanny and Grandad Pickford

P. Pickford

Man United

Everyone's waiting,
Shouting and screaming
Wanting the game to start.
The ball is kicked
Everyone's apart
Hoping to score a goal.

"Man United" have got the ball
Ready to score but had a fall.
The "Saints" come forward
And take the ball,
The crowd starts screaming even more.

"Man United" have taken it.
Giggs has kicked it.
The goalie has missed it.
And falls forward.

There stands Giggs
watching the goal being scored.
The crowd is shouting Giggs
Make "Man United" Big.

Sukawant Bhatti

From The Heart

Eleven years yesterday
Seven years today
Words can not express the years
Which we have spent building
Our dreams and hopes.
We have achieved so much
throughout the years with
determination, love and faith
in each other.
We strive to achieve and gain
the very best of our abilities
and hope that one day we
will find true happiness, for
life is not easy there will
always be obstacles in our way
but, with our strength together
we will make our lives better
and continue to love one another
more than seven years ago.

T. L. Hammond

I Loved You Once

I loved you once, last year.
But my love for you has changed to
Loathing and hate.
All the time you were with me,
You kept thinking of the girl
You really loved back home.
You pretended and you pretended
That you loved me.
But you were only after my money.
I have trouble, every day
Thinking 'how could you?'
I could never look at another man
And trust him with my heart
Like I did with you.
And it'd be all down to you.

I'll never forget
How you've changed
My normal life.
I'll be scarred forever.

Sokina Khanom

An Ode To My Love

He's tall dark and handsome
And he's mine
His spoken word is truly divine
His smile is like a treasure trove
No treasure I can behold
His eyes are a sapphire blue
Like the blue sky rushing by
His sense of humour leads us
To our fate.
One day we shall mate.

Denise Thomson

'The Old House'

Cold, stark, it stands there,
Forsaken, desolate, none to care,
Once, a shelter of joy and mirth,
Now, decayed of little worth,

Just as the seasons came and went,
It stands alone in bleakness,
Quiet, silent, quite content,
Or, does it yearn for a re-birth,
As mortals upon an aging earth,
Has its builder given it a thought,
Or was it created, just to be bought,
Is it still a friendly host,
Or, as the end of mankind
Become a ghost.

James Lewis

Who Cares?

The wind howls so loud,
In the dead of the night,
and I long for some arms
to hold me so tight.
I'm scared and alone,
in danger, in need,
and I yearn for a heart,
so strong it would bleed.
The rain beats down harshly
against my walls that are cold
and to survive through the night
I have to be bold.
With no food in my body,
Just an empty sad feeling,
I sit by the wall
where the paper is peeling.
No carpeted floors,
the cupboard's all bare
I just need to know
is there someone who cares?

Mandy Cox

Is 50 Old?

Is it too late to love
To have one last fling?
Is it too late to start again
To try one last new thing?

Is it too late to rock 'n' roll
Or dance the night away?
Too late perhaps for nightclubbing
To return at the break of day?

Is it too late to change a job
Or go for pastures new?
To go on long, long treks
Or dance barefoot in the dew?

Is it too late to have short skirts
Or ride a motorbike?
Too late to dye your hair?
Perhaps we'll take a trike!

We'd rather have a lively life,
But prepare for hearth, so cosy!
We've got to get the knitting out,
But still enjoy Bon Jovi!

Eunice Doyle

Hail Messiah

See the Wise Men searching far
Guided by a wondrous star
Light from heaven transcending all
Shines upon a lowly stall.

In the manger meek and lowly
Lies the babe begotten holy
Centre of the Godhead three
Born in all humility.

Bowing down in reverence sweet
Placing at the infant's feet
All their gifts so precious rare
Gold and frankincense and myrrh.

Shepherds in their awesome fear
Watch the heavenly host appear
Peace on earth good-will to me
Christ is born in Bethlehem.

Unite mankind in one accord
Praise your Saviour, King and Lord
In triumphant songs of joy accord
Praising Saviour, King and Lord.

Charles Leverton

The Boatman

My love is on a fishing boat
Riding the Ocean's waves
He was due home before now
It's dark and very late

The witching hour has come and gone
And still there's no sign
Where is my fisherman love
At this black and lonesome time

There were no gates this evening
Or rough stirring waters
Perhaps neptune's called him.
To his bed beneath the sea

It's hard to know what may happen
No one can ever tell
The depths of the ocean
Or what its strength may cause

Hurry home my love
I'm waiting there for you
Why didn't you learn to swim
When it would be of help?

Emma Louise Devane

A Kitchen Prayer

Take two cups of happiness
a cup of laughter do,
season well with love and hope
a pinch of goodness too.
Add a cup of faithfulness
Then mix with patience long.
Sprinkle now with joy and peace
a ray of sunshine strong.
Share this food with warmth and grace
in kind and gentle ways.
Tenderness and hands that care
such blessings all our days.

Margaret Jackson

Time And Space

Time and space are one in grace
Finding both important in this race
Called life, if life is what we live
yet many live without a life
And time is long and grinds away
The emptiness with each awakening day
If only space was made for all
Space to give and answer life's call
To find the time the greatest gift
Time to listen let spirits lift
Time and space are always there
So give a little and try to share.

June Martin

Nature's Walk

In a world ever changing
Full of poverty and despair,
It's so hard to see the good in life.
The beauty hidden there.

It's not so hard to notice
But we're blinded by our pain,
Injustice, in our daily lives,
Routine, so called mundane.

So come with me my trusted friend
But only if you dare
We can walk this road together
seeking out the beauty there.

We'll cast away our troubles
See nature at its best
Look beyond all man made things.
Put nature to the test.

It's there we'll see real beauty
Amongst the greenery and the trees
to watch the birds, the rabbits
feel the calm in nature's breeze

Gail Phee

To See, To Feel, To Hear

To stand atop a mountain high
The path was steep, so hard a climb,
To view a scene you cannot buy
And feel the chill, and see the rime,
To hear the silent dormant power
So humble on your lofty tower.

To stand upon a grassy plain
With walks so easy underfoot
To see the golden dancing grain
And feel it's gift from man's output,
To hear bees buzzing loud and clear
A fertile land for future year.

To stand in glade of forest near,
The path so twisted like the tree,
To view the ever timid deer
And feel the peace envelope me,
To hear the wind go whispering by
A wondrous world for you and I.

Kathleen Thornton

Lottie

Lottie with your midnight hair
cascading down on shoulders bare.
Eyes that sparkle bright as star
I wonder Lady who you are?

Skin as fresh as morning dew
velvet soft with rosy hue.
Spin your web of silken fire
Lottie, Lady of desire.

Take my heart and bury deep
the wonders of a dream like sleep.
Hold my love in warm array
Lottie of my yesterday.

Your gypsy soul with spirit free
cast a spell of mystery.
Dance barefoot with arms unfurled
my Lady of the underworld.

L. M. Jones

Forgetful

Just a live to say I am living
that I am not among the dead.
Though I'm getting more forgetful
and more mixed up in the head.
There are times when it's dark outside
and in my dressing gown
I don't know if I am retiring
or just getting out of bed.
So if it is my turn to write to you
there's no need getting sure
I may think I have written.
And don't want to be a bore.
There I am beside the post box
with my face very red
instead of posting you my letter
I have opened it instead.

Frances Rhodes

Quest

Enter the long dark tunnel of night.
There are clamours, fearful things
that grab and grasp.

False bright moon calms,
Dazzling images, luscious ephemera.

Plunge again into stifling
inky unknown.
Moving on and moving on;
Cold clammy fear sweat.
Where will we be when it ends?

Will we survive these suffocations
of razzle dazzle; of glittering
blighted earth, potent lethal rubbish?

Can there be a sunrise, unhampered
by damaged isotherm;
Released from this muck-matter?

Then may we be extra-mundane.

Jenny Hunt

A Soothing Dawn Mist

I drift into another day
Morning releases me of night
Threats of bad dreams gone
Light a comfort for now
A soothing dawn mist
Dark shadows now past
Silver raindrops dancing
Smooth sunlit breezes
Evening slips easily back
Brightness not to last.

Sheila Duru

Lost Homes Of Wales

Beyond those lonely, distant hills
Where rivers of the Tiefi flows
Where often mist, the valley fills
And purple heather grows
Today I walked the rugged path
That twisted, to and fro.
Amongst those very ancient stones
Set there so long ago.

Gone are the happy, joyful sounds
Of children at their play
And in the garden at the back
No flowers grow today
Some of their names I knew
To name but just a few

Down beside the Tiefi river
As it winds, towards the sea
No more we see the distant lights
That from their windows shone
And the darkness now pervades the night
For all the lights are gone

E. L. Lewis

The One To Care

My sadness is a sad thing,
   My love he asks me why?
The only answer I can give,
   Is "hush—don't make me cry:"

My loneliness is a tragic thing,
   Like the old, weak and frail.
My love he tries to comfort me,
   And does it wrong and fails.

My dearest Lord, O' help me;
   Because I know you really care,
I cannot make him understand,
   It's him, I want to care.

Denise King

Tribute To L. S. Lowry

All is purple
Why purple?
Has the painter
Run out of colour
And the piper
out of tune.
Are the grey skies
of Salford
under a never–changing
gloom.
No more time for
match stick people
under a match stick
sky.
Just a loving tribute
to Mr. Lowry
from you and I

Maurice John Conboy

Untitled

Your lips are like cherries,
Your face all aglow,
Your body so curvy,
I'm dying to hold.

The sweet smell of Spring
reminds me of you.
Mind you,
I think of you
all the year through.

Caroline, my sweet,
I'm in love once again,
so be my Valentine,
and dream girl, God sent.

W. M. Paterson

Love Hurts

"Love Hurts", a saying I have heard
It strikes my very core
I think this saying is absurd
If it hurts, is it love anymore?

When love is lost, and feelings gone
My tears will start to flow
When love's full course is all but done
Where is there I can go?

When love is all that's strivin' for
Yet just cannot be found
Can lovers strive again, once more
To turn their lives around?

And so when love cannot hold on
When souls are torn apart
It surely will not be too long
Before it breaks my heart.

Rebecca Thomas

Falling In Love Today

I fell in love when I was young
and I thought the world was mine
to be in love is something
that we remember by and by
He speaks to me with words of love
for his love is true and kind
we know love is something that
in the world we live by day
when taking a stroll just through
the park when the sun is shining there
the trees they are so beautiful
with their blossom hanging over there
would make you feel so happy
when I sit with my true love there
so now to all young leaves
who fall in love today
remember to be happy
when you fall in love today

George Cunningham

Remembrance

Memories of your kindness,
Your warm and gentle cheer,
Infiltrate our minds,
Now you're no longer here.

But we know that you are watching,
And smiling from above,
Your much loved face is smiling,
Basking in our love,

Life goes on when bodies die,
Your soul has not expired,
Just gone to a peaceful world above,
No wars, no pain, no fires
We'll reunite one happy day,
The family all as one,
And 'til that time can come to pass,
We'll recall the ones who've gone.

Rachell Robinson

The Universe

The sun and moon and stars come out
Part of our galaxy no doubt
They are part of our universe
From the beginning when God made earth
God the greatest living being of all
Made them before the fall
Of Adam and Eve and his family
Who wronged God it's plain to see
But Jesus will put right all the wrong
And it will come out in poem and song
Never more to wrong again
His living has not been in vain

Alma Hindson

Faith, Hope and Charity

To have kept the lonely vigil
through the darkest hours of night,
not a solitary betrayal of the faith
before the sunrise brought daylight.

Through the gnawing of the subterfuge
held all doubts at bay in mind,
by listening well to that inner-voice
for all hopes in heart to bind.

Where so blinded by the light of faith
to see all such hopes were vain,
then why by all true honesty
should charity I ne'er profane.

Robert R. Smith

A Prairie Spring

The winter snow has left the plain
As quickly and silently as it came.
The budding aspens and cottonwood
Spread vapour sweet, to all who would
Stop to view the carpeted glade
In crocus colour all arrayed.

The wily coyote lopes along
His head held closely to the ground.
Rabbits scatter and gophers flee
In fear his dinner they may be.
Duck and geese their sermon scorn
The silence of the breaking morn.
A shimmering heat will soon arise
To claim a day in Paradise.

Max A. Perkins

Autumn Of Life

Here's to life
Not strife
The gales sway in the trees
And the leaves fall in the breeze
There is no escape
But to await your fate.
So to the tiller dear friend
Pursue the bittersweet to the end!
Take courage in your hands,
It is a passport to all lands.
You come into the world alone
All considered you will atone
But life is Heart's ease
So every opportunity do seize
Compassion gives life to all.
But do select lest you fall
And give the lie to all, no tall
One does not wish to die small!

Betty Celia Kimbell

Painted Faces

War paint on red Indians
Geisha's with white faces
Grease painted thespians
Going through their paces.
On corners ladies of the night
Ply their trade, on a cash only basis
Clients would never pay their price
If they hadn't well made up faces.
Tourists back from vacation
Each lugging large cases
All tanned from sitting in the sun
from oil applied to their faces.
Circus clowns in the big top
tripping over shoelaces
Make us all laugh, as they fall about
red noses on their faces.
What do they all have in common
none of them from the same place
each with a different profession
you guessed it. A painted face.

Eileen Waldron

The Days Are Long . . .

The days are long
The nights are longer still
But with every passing hour
The pain grows less.

Now that the fog has cleared
The future is way open, clear
And very bright.

The happiness grows stronger
With every passing day
And now the time goes by
In leaps and bounds

Now there is no looking back.
No regrets and no remorse,
Only relief at finding a new happiness

Friendship.

Jenny Whitaker

Living Souls

A child is born, a new life starts
A little creature wins our hearts
A little child who knows no wrong
Who enters in life's busy throng

A child who's born by God's good grace
With chubby hands and small round face
Who looks into his mother's eyes
As cradled in her arms he lies

Each moment as a new life starts
Each moment too some souls depart
But if they have along life's way
Trusted God and learned to pray

Then just reward will lie ahead
In paradise just as he said
Where pain and sorrows as will cease
And they'll live on in perfect peace.

R. A. Murray

Carol

She's grown up now to womanhood,
How quickly time does fly,
It seems but only yesterday
Her brown curls scurried by
Those curls are shorn,
She walks sedate
And looks all starry eyed
For tomorrow is a special day,
Our baby becomes a bride.

Beryl Clark

Guardian

With your unlettered charities
A magic disclose.
God the vision, has heart
The pull and the tulips
Takes a tongue that speaks to day
In form me what is started.
By those men in a turnip field
Whose bread is hard and crusty
For everything will work out
The arousal of your passion
Works labour in a farm field.
And yet each one says no word.
The bread is old and flat.
What makes our homo sapien bread
Others gaze at an untaken job
The man kneads his knees
What answers to be found
In dark bowels as these
Underneath the sailor's punches
Is anything left to pay or state

James McCambridge

Galilee

The water she ripples
Gently in the breeze
Casting to catch you
Like a fisherman's net
Such a vision of beauty
With the hills and trees
Such an image your mind
Could not possibly forget
What gives these sea shores
Such tranquil peace?
That the whole world
Struggles to find
Are we captured in bonds
That we cannot release?
Or my friend
Is it all in our minds?

Martin McKenzie Edward

Life And The Open Seas

I'm drifting on a raft
Upon the open seas,
The winds have torn the sails down
The ropes are hanging free.

The winds are all the lies I'm told,
The tides are all the wise,
How can you guide this driftwood
With thunder in the skies?

Who is steering this old wreck,
Who is leading it astray?
And how will I repair it
When the winds have gone away?

Danny Diggins

Lucy Dreaming

Soft black fur, contented purr
Green eyes dreaming
Of tigers bold with stripes of gold
In the sunlight gleaming.
Through the grass black panthers pass,
Do they eat fish and cream?
And play on stairs and lay on chairs
Or someone's knee to dream.

Oh! Tiger-cat and Panther-cat
I am a cat like you,
With padded paws and long sharp claws,
A tail and whiskers too.
So my dream wends to my jungle friends
Oh! Do you dream of me?
Come stay with me and play with me
And we'll have fish for tea.

Marjorie Williams

Christy At Seven Days

The phonic thunder
    Of one
Who made you;

Unerring to musk,
    Flexuous;
Tit–gummed.

Ghosts swim
    In the half tones
Of morning.

Lawless; you lie
    Like the day,
Unformed; crumpled.

Arms searching
    For clues
To wordless questions,

Your useless vulnerability
    Unmentioned; I, too, have known
Your hybrid impersonal faith.

Michael Brown

Setting Her Free

She lies in bed,
A tear in her eye,
The pain gets worse,
She's hoping to die.

The agony's prolonged,
Pain shows through her face,
Though her heart still beats,
It's a slow, unsteady pace.

To the people who visit,
And sit by her bed,
She says she's in pain,
And longs to be dead.

Then one day her son,
Cuts her suffering short,
As he turns off the switch,
To her life support.

Before permanent night,
Covers the light of day,
She holds his hand, smiles,
Then passes away.

Philip Smith

Speak Softly

When sacred dreams are wrenched apart
And sorrow fills the inner heart,
A seed of beauty doth replace
The anguish there with gentle grace,
In silent tears the mind doth soar
So near yet far from perfect lore,
To see the path the saints do tread
That sight of glory still unread,
To live each day for daily bread
Yet, dwell in part in heaven's stead,
How then in life's short measured span
Can mortal being fulfil God's plan.

Carol E. MacKneson

The Good Wine

No one could see
How good the wine was for me
It made me mellow
And a good fellow
The world was green
Goodness could be seen
Wherever I went
Things were serene
But alas we know it was only a dream.

One wakes and sees around us.
A world permanently asleep
To the thoughts of others
And no thoughts of one's destiny.

Gemma Louise Woodall

Train Journey North

Purple rain rolling forward
press-gangs fresh ploughed furrows
Into close-up perspective

Rape seed breaks patchwork monotony
Criss-cross hedged
Forever

Poplars stark gainst dove–grey skies
Empty happening
Conjuring worlds away

Vacant faces
Mutate animated conversations
To instant memory

The view will work its will
Another train again
Nowhere to somewhere

Patricia Thompson

The Weight Of The Wind

The weight of the wind,
Is bringing me down.
I can't face my troubles,
Where's the hole in the ground?

I'm longing to hear,
A friendly voice.
To say don't be scared,
That I do have a choice.

All I have suffered,
All those terrible blows.
What's my purpose in life?
I wished I could know.

Voices and bright lights,
Penetrate through my mind.
Clearing my sad thoughts,
They're so gentle and kind.

"Stay on these roads."
The voices do say,
"We'll guide and protect you,
We'll see you don't stray."

Melanie Shaw

Heartbeat

My heart had been my own
    for 'oh so very long'
I felt that things would stay
    that way,
Believe me I was strong.
You had a tiny key, which
I didn't know was there.
Surprisingly a 'spark'
    became a mighty flare.
If it hadn't been for you, this
    heart would be quiet still
Now it beats like a thousand drums,
And I hope it always will.

Doreen Hartley

Metamorphosis

Arid and bare
Thought devoid
Ideas unclear
No work performed

Pleasantly bright
Fertile ground
Concepts abound
Work performed

To-day all—clear
But will the drought appear.

David J. Bennett

Sudden Grace

The angels were up to their old tricks
I should have known
But to dance in pure delight again
Isn't easy to resist
The message seems to be
There is so little time
When honoured by the angels' grace
Do not decline

From precious moments held
Captive in eternity
Higher understanding comes
Through one beloved's eyes
Shock! A recognition
You are me, and I am you
Hold onto this
Don't let it sleep away
It is the great secret.

Sara Boyle

The Vagrant

He tramps o'er vale and countryside,
He may be poor but has his pride.
His worldly goods upon his back.
Carried in an old worn sack.

Nuts and berries form his banquet,
The stars at night act as a blanket.
No alarm to wake him in the morn,
cockerel does the job at dawn.

He doesn't have a grand position,
He's broken faith with all tradition.
He'll beg and steal from where he can,
And wonder how it all began.

He looks back on his early life.
His home was full of hate and strife,
And on reflection he can see,
That at long last, he now is free.

Audrey Donoghue

Dews

Dew drops from everywhere
From the eyes, there are tears
So precious, so beautiful

I'm crying, it's raining
The sky is crying with me

Even a drop of water
is a life-saver in a desert

With so many colours
from a crystal
so clear
you could gaze mystically into a sphere

Bubbles full of air yet so light,
dancing merrily
until it disappears
Frozen icicles, so solid
sparkling together
with the soft snow

So many mysteries, so much passion
store within these dew drops

Jenny Cheung

A Milestone

I am a milestone on the road
I weigh a great big heavy load
I've been around for donkeys years
and no one seems to bother me.
  A Milestone
As I sit here day after day
My work is never done.
A person came a painted me.
And I'm as proud as I can be.
  A milestone.
They put up signs above me
It made me sad you see
But then it cheered me up again
When people noticed me.
  A milestone.

Lena Stapleton

To Sasha—My Granddaughter

Your flaxen hair so beautiful, so
Beautiful on one so fair!
It falls about your pillow there,
Its loveliness beyond compare.
I think about it oft a day the
way it falls in disarray—about
your lonely face.
You see! It doesn't matter
How it falls on one so young
as thee, for your beauty is
your youthful and that is what I see

Yvonne Barron

Death On A Corner

It stands there in the darkness
  A shrine with lighted candles
Dreams are over
  Someone died here by this roadside
Who were they? A son, a daughter
  Father, mother?
How old, how young
  How long ago?

Shrines with candles
  Reminding the living of the dead
Now just memories
  Death on a corner
A car too fast
  A curve too sharp
Lives were lost
  How long ago?

Margaret A. Rice

Untitled

Now I know the real you,
I just want to be with you,
All of my life you were the one
the one for me,

  I can't believe you're here with me,
  It all seems just like a dream
  Oh how I hope it will always be
  now and forever always together.

Sarajane Metcalf

"This" Man Of Straw

I often stand, and stop and stare
Time flies by to I know not where
Birds pass by on their endless flight
The majestic sun gives of its light
I feel a breeze gently brush my hair
But I stand still, and stop and stare

I often stand, and stop and stare
Fragrance fills the sweet night air
The sun lays down to have its rest
Baby fledglings sleep in their nest
Peace enfolds me in its evening wear
As I stand still, and stop and stare

A quiet has descended upon the ground
Lulled to sleep without a sound
The moon bows to let darkness fall
Around me there's no sound at all
No ones concerned that I'm still there
So I stand still and stop and stare

Vera Hutchinson

The Secret

I must be the luckiest person alive
To have found my heaven on earth
I don't go round all sad and blue
My life is full of mirth
I only need enough to live
Of the paper thing called money
But I do need laughter, love and joy
And a little taste of honey
I have the sweeter things of life
And they cost me not a penny
I found the secret long ago
And my reasons are so many
I thank the Lord for each new day
I look at it with love
It helps me cope with what may come
The strength I get from him above
Is always free, no strings attached
Is just there for the asking
What other gift is there for all
And is always everlasting?

Valerie Linstead Smith

This Boy

When a boy kneels down
And clasps his hands,
And prays to the good Lord above,
His greed turns to need
As your heart is a part
Of his prayers for your undying love.

What this boy desires most
Is a lifetime of loving,
Harmonious, passionate, wild but mild,
His prayers speak of you,
And I know this is true,
Because I am that God praying child.

Trevor P. Reader

Grandad

He died a few years ago
Although memories of him live on
His music cheered us up no end
And still does even though he has gone.

I loved him then and I love him now
My love for him will continue forever
Tears still swell when I think of him
As I wish we could still be together.

I was very close to my Grandfather
Who was a jolly family man
I remember the summers in his garden
And the fun we had with my nan.

But he has gone forever
And this truth I must finally face
Some say he is watching over me
And I am happy if this is the case.

Melanie Rayner

Help

I feel like I'm old,
but I'm only ten.
I feel like I've lived my life,
but I'm still a child.
Sometimes I want to curl up and hide,
shut my curtains,
shut my eyes.
Pretend the world is full of peace,
then I face the reality of greed.
I wish I could fly.
Why do people pry.
Ask yourself why.
I can't escape my fame.
I feel I know who is to blame.
I'm as angry as a flame.
I'd like to change places with a dove,
only for a day,
then I could fly,
up, up and away.

Hayley Dodwell

A Starry Night

Have you ever stopped to gaze,
  Upon the beauty of the night
When a silver moon is beaming,
  Skies so clear, and stars so bright
To see so much perfection,
  In endless worldly space
Makes you feel that all around you,
  Silence reigns in heavenly grace.

Just to stand and stare in wonder,
  Breathing pure embracing air
And felt that God was near to you,
  Gave thanks to Him in prayer.
For surrounded by the stillness,
  Of such loveliness profound.
You'll surely know a perfect peace,
  And your life is lived abound.

E. Wills

The Stream

Ever going round and round
down and down, past trees
and bushes, ferns, and rocks
fish dancing, ants beetles
scurrying by silent waters
rushing down.

A man dressed in white stirring
butterflies at his command
light shining through the forest
Jesus stirs a little more
birds singing.

Leaves blowing, falling down
at the stream's edge, forever
floating down and down
round and round
down at the stream.

Paul Latham

Window Of Life

In the light of the evening
the night approaches the dark.
Their stands an oak tree full of musk,
As it stands strong and able
the bark it's crusty and old.
But the strength of its
bough gives shelter to young and old.
Many years have passed by and the
leaves have left their shine.
But Autumn is approaching
to give that glowing shine.
The warmth of orange colours
make us glow inside.
Giving it further splendour
that winter is thine.

J. M. Veitch

My Mother's Prayer

This night I lay me down to sleep
The prayer my mother said
Then tenderly she fondled me
And tucked me down in bed

I pray the lord my soul to keep
In her most reverend way
Her special care throughout the night
To await the coming day

If I should die before I wake
Yet I get the joy of living
My shining star high in the sky
Will guide my road to heaven

I pray thee Lord my soul to take
Her prayer seems to end
The sleepily heard her final word
Which was of course amen

Robert Angus

Contact

Wood
and the soft
contact—
the child.

On the fungal
dense bracken
on which patinated
moss grew.

I saw her
and laughed.
Then scolded
about the stained
white frock.

Patricia Lewis

No Sod Unturned

Someone did my garden.
He 'didn't move a thing'.
Wonder how flower seeds
got into my biscuit tin.

Two crocus came in sight
the daffodils have all gone.
And so has the little path
I used to walk upon.

The garden gnome's not fishing
in his little goldfish pond.
He's perched upon a tree stump
clutching a pipe in his hand.

The bluebells are non-smokers
and having a protest march.
Whoever my gardener was
he's upset the apple cart.

The moral of this story is:
If you have precious plants
don't let any old gardener in
leave the work to the ants.

Rosemary Stanford

Versus (Life)

Wallow in your colourfulness,
Prolong your yellow'd youth.
A year for every shade.
One day,
The rain will dust away the ugly truth,
Mother nature cradled you,
Until you were old enough to die.

Annemarie Curran

I Need You

Boy I need you,
I really do.
I know in your heart,
you need me to.
All you said was goodbye,
I laid in bed,
I just had to cry.
It was like you died,
I just wanted to hide.
You took part of my life away,
left me torn and broken.
I just wanted you to stay.
but no you had to go away.

Diane Sanders

How Many Times

How many times must I count the hours,
Sleep just a whisper away.
How many thoughts crowd my weary head,
Passing the time until day.

How many birds will fly over,
Migrating to warmer climes.
How many bees buzzing nearby,
Delighting in heather and thyme.

How many clouds in the blue sky,
Too high to bring any rain.
How many trees in the forest,
Shelter creatures too many to name.

How many songs to hear singing,
Filling the air with sweet sound.
Music the language of love,
Highlighting the joy that I've found.

How many prayers left to say,
Until that last curtain comes down.
Rejoicing in each day I've lived,
Preparing to face the unknown.

June Hilliar

The Saleswoman

Here I am, on the M25
Not for me the nine to five.
Wind in my hair, the open road
Mind that lorry; watch that load.
First appointment, here we are
Find a place to park the car.
Confidence rising, pitch that sale
Flatter the client, it never fails.
Second appointment—another sale
My luck is in; I can not fail.
Third and fourth are not so good
It starts to rain, I raise the hood.
Last call now, I'm dripping wet
Smile has gone; my face is set.
Back in the car, on my way home
I'm feeling down and all alone.
On to the M25—Oh damn
I'm caught up in a traffic jam!

Honor Knowles

DYSLEXIA

I CANNOT READ,
I CANNOT SPELL,
BUT THIS DOESN'T GIVE YOU THE RIGHT,
TO MAKE MY LIFE HELL!!!.

MY I'S LOOK LIKE U'S,
AND MY B'S RESEMBLE Q'S,
BUT THIS IS NO REASON TO BE AMUSED!

I HAVE 8 O-LEVELS,
AND 2 A-LEVELS TOO!,
BUT THIS STILL DOESN'T,
SEEM TO MATTER TO YOU.

I WAS RIDICULED AND TAUNTED,
LAUGHED AT AND TEASED,
ALL BECAUSE IT MADE YOU PLEASED!

I MAY BE DYSLEXIC,
BUT IT'S NOTHING TO ME,
I JUST SEE WHAT YOU CAN'T SEE.

CHRISTINA L. MAYLOR

Vision

Vision like the truth
Pure and undiseased
Poisoned by the lies and sounds
Rolled from our tongues with ease.

Wayne Reid

Ode To Stephen Gately

I lie awake and think of you
I only wish my fantasies were true.
I love your smile,
and I love your ways
and always will through all of my days.

You say "Love me for a reason",
I'll love you for loads more,
from me to you my love I implore.

"If you were mine"
I know I would find time,
for my love to grow ever more
You are the "key to my life"
You guide me through all my strife
You have that magical cure.

But as you are far away
our love will have to wait
till another day,
But until then my darling, my sweet
I give to you my heart and soul to keep.

Catherine Davies

Catching Time

Reach out and touch,
does anyone care?
Look through the stars,
is anyone there?
Time waits for no man,
suitcase in hand.
Travelling through time—
do we understand?
Blink and it's gone—
time passes by.
Past in the future,
look to the sky.
Advanced in years,
life is so short.
Man is the future.
Time is not caught.

Jean Reeve

Who Cares?

As I sit huddled in this doorway,
Staring out at passers-by,
My worldly goods in a plastic bag,
A cardboard box in which I lie,
For I am homeless,
Hungry and homeless,
Can anyone spare me 50p
To buy a cup of tea?
But everyone is too busy,
To stop and spare some cash,
They're laden down with goodies,
And don't want to be bothered with trash,
Santa's face is twinkling,
Above the high street stores,
Beckoning the shoppers,
To buy their gifts galore.
But what do I get?
Does anyone really care
Sat here cold and freezing,
How life is so unfair

Jennifer Peers

Jagged

Inside my head
oceans of words
crash and whip on jagged cliff
every crevice is salt and sea
flecks of frothy silver
leap the blue–black
diamond studded sky
seagulls shriek distress
an albatross in sight

One salty drop
escapes
trickles down

Above me
you smile
wordless and safe

We do not share
the storm
nor the calm anymore.

Lakshmi Kern

A Time To Sleep

The night has come now
The light has gone
My life is over
My mind is numb
But do not sorrow
I had my day
My moving moments
My time to play

The music's stopped now
But do not cry
I raised my family
This is not good-bye
When I am thought of
Please laugh, don't cry
I will hear you
And heaven sigh
Please don't forget
I'll still be with you
And love you yet

Reta A. Cleary

Untitled

See you in green
my hopes are easily seen—
see you in blue
all is true.
See you in yellow
what a funny fellow—
see you in red
with love and hate you thread.
See you in black
all my hopes put in a sack!

See you in pink
still with hope is a link.
See you in grey
please, don't with my heart you play.
See you in white
lift my hopes and love in kite
see you in brown
do tell me love is not a clown.
See you in clear—
so say—I am yours my dear!

Dorte Otterstrom

Does God Really Care?

Does God really care,
about how this world might fare?,
With brutal deaths day by day,
no one really has a say,
how upon this world is run,
Everyone just out for fun,
politicians have no clue,
they just want money from you,
they get richer every day,
we get poorer in every way,
Does the crime really pay,
or should the law people obey?,
what are we really here for?,
to see blood hate and gore,
World Wars one and two,
a sight no one wanted to view,
old people living lives forgotten,
young people making them feel downtrodden,
So the question most people share,
is does God really care?.

Lynsey Watkins

Street Tramps

They wander on our highways
the street tramps of our welfare state
those on whom fortune never smiles
life's casualties of fate . . .
Some shuffling by or shaking
as far as they can go
within the limits of the day
into the evening glow . . .
Or peering in shop windows
the expensive gifts inside
but only with unseeing eyes
for them long since hope died . . .
For most are lifeless robots
with vacant faces drawn and white
and only God knows how or where
they make their way at night.
Or why they should not be so loved
or cherished or allowed to be,
the third world shadows of our time
drifting aimlessly . . .

Jo Lehan

Memories Or Dreams

My memories are like pictures
on a cinema screen
I see, I feel, I re-enact
so many of the scenes.

I see silvery clouds in a clear blue sky
different greens on the leaves of the trees
then I feel the warm caress
of a gentle summer breeze.

I see pastel colours of roses in bloom
smell the aroma of their subtle perfume
oh such beauty I see
akin to designs on a tapestry.

I watch as a summer shower
waters fertile land
I feel one with nature
life feels truly grand.

Why do I not see myself
in any of the scenes
is it because my memories
are merely my dreams?

Mary O'Brien

Football

The teams are ready,
And off they go.
The crowd stands up,
And begin to roar,
They stand together,
With the excitement.
And thrill.
Waving their banners
Of their home teams.
A goal is scored,
And some fans scream,
The adrenalin flows.
As another goal is scored
They reach fever pitch,
Singing their songs.

J. Barr

A Shadow—In "E" Minus

A shadow.
A twinkling blink across my visual orb,
that distracts now, from that upon which I look.

Casting skyward.
Struggling against focal disjunction.
Squinting through a myriad of
blinding blood clots cavorting within my optic cavity,
to spy upon this cloak of my confusion

A circling spot in an indigo sky of fading light.
I look upon you without a marching clock in sight.
I watch you tickling cotton candy
clouds and dancing with a sulphur sun.

A shadow.
A symbol of tranquil cunning.
Of striking fluidity. I wait!

A twitch now within a grassy knoll.
Hopping cautiously towards a land of diamond frosting.

A shadow.
Plunging downwards.
Joins a shadow. And I watch it fly away.

Fiona Jane Churchill

A Friend . . .

A friend was a little ball of fluff, our daughter brought home
one night.
'It followed me all the way here, she said, her eyes all misty
and bright.
You just haven't the heart to turn it away, so you make it a
bed for the night.
A small dresser drawer is just the right size, we tucked it in
snuggly and tight.
Rising next morning no kittens in sight, we look in her bed-
room finding both breathing light.
Years passing quickly find our daughter's of age, she's soon
to be married were all a bit dazed.
But the cat's a great comfort he's one of a mould, wherever
Mum is you don't have to be told
We're all of his family, we're all of his fold, but the years
moving fast are taking their hold.
Well he tries very gamely to quicken his step, the days that
are warmer he gets a bit of help.
The vet's of no comfort, he just shakes his head, saying he's
really in pain and would be better off dead . . .
He's given a needle while we've not long to wait, so I stroke
the frail body and pat the weak head.
We put him to rest in his garden at home, the place he loved
dearly to wander and roam . . .
But he's still in our thoughts though he's now out of sight,
and wego out at dusk to bid him goodnight . . .

Robert W. Lee

Old Man

On a cold winter's night in the old wool shed,
Lying on the floor was a man named Fred
He had felt the cold and the hot burning sun,
But Fred was no quitter, he didn't want to run
He didn't have many friends and only true one he had
Was an old sheep dog and for that he was glad
For Fred knew what loneliness was in every shape and form
Fred had his memories and his heart and been torn
So on this cold and miserable night
Fred knew he'd seen his last look at light
The only regret he had at this time,
Was that his only friend would be alone
Fred knew he would pine.
As the dog huddled up to his master's chest
Through the brown eyes of sorrow, he's done his best
He had given Fred all the love he'd had
And as his head came down on his paw
For the very last time, he took one last look at the old man
And closing his eyes, he joined Fred in the land
Of make-believe, where togetherness is forever.

Amanda Taunton

May Morning

First gentle rays of sunrise sweep across the sky
In pale anticipation of a bright spring morn
Ascending lark, a sentinel, sounds the clarion call
Herald of a glorious day, harbinger of dawn

Lace spun webs of gossamer hidden in the mist
Their fine silken threads now shimmer with pearls of dew
Adorning beauty—so silently revealed
On flowers grass and hedgerow, ephemeral and new

Towering beech trees dapple the sunlight
Lofty cathedral of peace and tranquillity
Bluebell painted woods resound to the cuckoo's call
Fragrant drifts of colour flow on to infinity

Jeani Mary Bearne

The Black Dog

When I awake from fitful sleep
And feel him standing there
When I first open up my eyes
And see his empty stare
I know the day is grey and dull
The sun all cloaked in cloud
I feel the weight of winter's pull
And feel the lonely shroud.

As selfish thoughts pass through my mind
I cry out to my shame
Go growl around some other soul
And ease the mental strain.

Whose fiendish master is this cur's
Not sent by God's permission?
I fear his name is Satan
And the black dog's name . . . Depression.

Christopher J. Whelan

Wanderer

Oh Nomad, in your humble tent,
what dreams your mind when day is spent?
Oh Nomad next where will you go
on well–trod trails your people know?
Oh Nomad, out in the desert still
what silent joy your ears may fill.
Oh Nomad, on your camel high,
what wondrous sights may please your eye.
Oh Nomad, wandering without care
and breathing unpolluted air;
Oh Nomad, would you swap with us
who daily commute on a diesel bus?

Denis Leonard

Dearest Nearest To My Heart!

Into my life you came,
And I delight in what I see,
I thank the Lord up above,
For the happiness you have bought to me.

To ramble through the garden of life,
With you and the fleeting moments we share,
Would be all to short for me,
To show how much I care.

I thank the warm summer breeze,
That blew you gently my way,
And the loveliness you bring to me,
When I see you each and every day.

Like a lighthouse a tower of strength,
That shines through out the dark night,
I know in my heart I will never get lost,
Because of my love for your radiant light.

All of my body and all of my love,
Will always belong to only you,
Now always and forever,
In your arms I will always be true.

Eric John Stevenson

Rose Petal Wishes On Silver Strings

Overstepping boundaries to ease the burden.
Distant pleasantries only fade into nothing;
Somehow sleep appeals to me more.
Eyes that elude my gaze into dreams.
Hands that wrap around mine in fantastic
Sojourns into new realities.
Static minds twist civil diplomacy
Into my way of thinking, my reality.
Fate conquers the fool, submitting to
An all too unrealistic sensibility.
Taking risks and risking chances on an honest heart.
The world becomes nothing; and we become nothing.
The eyes and hands are only too real,
Knowing that in all their pathetic reality,
There is no room to dream.
Rose petal wishes on silver strings,
All our hopes and our dreams,
Build the reality that bridges the
Great distance between you and I,
Between today and tomorrow.

John Brierly-Voss

Christmas Day

Christmas Day is almost here, your favourite time of year, but this year just won't be the same without you my dear.

There will still be lots of presents, the turkey and the tree, but Christmas won't mean anything 'cause you're not here with me.

The family will be coming to help me celebrate and baby Tom will love it, he'll think it's simply great.

Behind the smiles we're wearing there'll be a silent tear, a fervent wish, a heartfelt prayer, I know that you'll be near.

Although we cannot see you, you'll be close at hand, and though we laugh and socialise I know you'll understand, that deep within our hearts it just won't be the same, we'd abandon Christmas just to have you back again.

Sylvia Pearce

A Childhood Memory

Shimmering burn born of the mountain,
Crystal clear, thirst quenching fountain;
Swiftly down the hillside flowing,
Greetings from the heather growing,
Singing to the rocks in passing,
Sunbeams on your surface dancing,
Onward, onward, ever prancing,
Till at last you reach the Dee,
There to join the torrents racing,
Ever faster to the sea.
You may think this your destination
But the winds that blow across the ocean
Will lift you back to mother mountain,
There to replenish that crystal fountain.

Len M. Cross

Until Tonight . . .

Until tonight,
no sign of death had spoken.

Her body breaking on the shore;
black waves sucking and spitting.
Seema's hair from the sea, catching.
Letting go . . .

Seema:
the girl of my daydreams—
fast was the news over Anglia;
how slow to mould and realize.

Reviewing our last dance,
that girl once more,
for black hair, hers and mine.

A shallow stone with a moss of memories.

Julian Allard

Fear Of Being Alone

I do not know what it is,
Just fear I suppose,
That some day I'll wake,
The air still,
With an empty, aching silence all around,
A coldness that no one can explain;
I would be a fool to think it couldn't,
It could happen anytime of any day,
My only wish is,
It will be a long time away,
If at all . . .

Elaine Olphert-Obudo

My Little Girl

My daughter is growing so strong and so tall,
It hardly seems she's been a baby at all,
With a face like an angel and long flowing hair,
And a slender young body, it just isn't fair,
She would look really stunning in beautiful clothes,
But my daughter lacks interest in any of those,
She throws on her shorts and an Arsenal shirt,
A pair of old trainers all covered in dirt,
With her favourite football and new goalie gloves,
She goes out to play the game she really loves,
In these days of equality they do what they like,
For Hayley that's football and an old motorbike,
She's not quite the sweet little girl I had planned,
But if you're a parent then you'll understand,
Our children can't be what we want them to be,
We just have to love them and let them be free,
To me she is always the best in the world,
And whatever she does she's still my little girl.

Diane Huckin

A Fairy Tale

The big cat preens itself
whilst the bird circles
chirping excitedly like comic stars.
The man watches from a short distance,
he recognizes his lover's display
and begins to silently undress,
keen to join the play.
He hides, and sings a few tweet-tweets
but when he looks again
she has disappeared.
She wolf-whistles him
from a branch just above
and a beautiful woman gracefully slides
into his outstretched arms.
He pulls her down and they kiss and make love,
the big cat turns its head and the bird returns.
The wood is quiet!

Simon Flood

My Kids

Two fine children, growing each day,
I worked very hard, I had bills to pay,
I missed them growing, I was never there,
But to say I don't love them is very unfair.

If I told them off I was never right,
So should I stand back and watch them fight,
For children to learn they have to be told,
For time flies by and they'll soon be old.

Now they're at home with just their mum,
All seems okay and they're having fun,
When I visit each week, we sit down and natter,
About everyday things that don't really matter,

Time soon flies and I say goodbye,
No crying this time, my eyes are dry,
Do they miss me? I don't know,
No emotions do children show,
So goodnight my loves, please take care,
And if you need me I'll be there

A. Best

Free Spirit

We've been together for many a year, this old body and me,
So long in fact that sometimes my spirit would like to break free,
And fly off to the heavens and have a look around,
And really see what's going on, no longer 'body bound'.

And when I got to the gateway, would they let me go on in?
Oh that I could wander round and meet my kith and kin,
and we'd walk along together, through fields of poppies red,
And laugh and talk and wonder, if I were really dead . . .

But after a while I'd have to say, I think it's time to go,
Cos' I really feel I'm being missed . . . Somewhere down below,
But I know with all my heart, I'll come back again one day,
And we'll take the poppy walk again, only this time I will stay.

And then we embraced together and said our sad goodbyes,
And I turned from the gate and waved . . . then off into the skies,
Well who do you think was waiting, when I finally got back below?
My old body sat in a chair "welcome back I missed you so!"

Judy McEvoy

The Music Of The Soul

A yawning sun draws mists of solitude
Over heavy eyes.
With reluctant sighs she returns to her
Trenches of thought.
In a swamp of scattered memories
One can hear their echoes reject a premature rebirth.
Dreams are swallowed by murky shadows;
Smothered hearts starve for love.
When a fresh song tastes the joyous herb
Withered melodies slumber
In the dust of sight.
In the soul's core dissonance laments.
Twisted chords forever sound sombre symphonies
In Man's endless search for serenity.

Triona Hourigan

The Final Thought

My body it is sleeping but my soul is wide awake
I'm alone in my bed rest not a stir nor a shake
I am blinded by the darkness and moving shadows, on the wall
I feel a presence watching over me distant voices I recall.
My eyes are like lead and my body I know is blessed
I'm no longer alone for I've now lain down to rest
I leave behind no tears but I'll always be there
in thought and in mind my love for all to share
remember happy times, all the things we shared together
to remember my true feelings and keep memories with you
forever
I must go to sleep now but my dreams I share with you
think not of heartache but good times old and new.

Kaylie Weir

"An Old Flame"

Tree top shadows, like figures past;
September nights gone by,
The song and dance of sweet Romance;
When young were you and I.
Autumn leaves, travelling light,
Some in a hurry, some in flight.
Romantic notions, many do.
Never forget, remember you,
Rustling leaves and scented eves,
Where insects sip the dew,
September nights, those starry nights
Were heaven sent with you;
Her golden hair, a colour rare
and his, a silvery light,
They sit in the shade, and can be seen
Holding hands, and what it means;
Her golden tresses he caresses, scent whispers in her ear,
Will you be true to me, My Love, and marry me, my dear;

Yet, every fall, I do recall those starry nights we met,
That one Propose, I don't suppose I ever will forget:

Sarah Hall

Disguise

I am your spirit softened,
I am your soul who wishes to be free.
I am the one who hides in your shadows,
Who makes the moves you make.
I am the happiness in your smile,
And the glistening in your eyes.
I am the hurt in your heart,
I am the depression in your cries.
I am the chill that runs down your spine,
Which makes your hairs arise.
I am the words you shout out.
I am you in disguise.

Sam White

My Love And I

All my life I've searched,
Everywhere I think,
To find someone like you,
With quality, like mink,

And when I met you my love,
I know I'd struck gold this time,
Now the problems righted,
Everything is fine.

We seemed to be as one,
In everything we did, it's true,
It was nice to think on,
As we drank our brew,

Life has not at all been bad,
Indeed it's often made us glad,
And now we've reached the final page,
The tears fill my eyes,

As it's time to say goodbye,
I thank you for your love so true,
My mind keeps asking, "Why"?
And I thank my God above for the day I met you.

D. Lloyd

Toaster

Just last week I bought a toaster for twenty pounds
It really makes my toast nice and crispy brown
It's better than my grill, and it gives me a thrill.

Popped up a thousand times, it's the best thing in my home
It toasts bread thick or thin, and it is all my own
It is gleaming white, I use it every night.

I don't eat cereal, so I don't need a spoon
I'll make some toast again, really really soon
Yes I'm really pleased, but it's not good for cheese.

Nathan Luker

Why 1996

This young man is thinking why should it be
As I question reflections of society

Why don't we care anymore for our old
Why tear up country for another road
Why do we let our children run wild
Why is our greed never satisfied
Why is it right to always want more
Why haven't we any respect for the law
Why do we have to strive to compete
Why tread on others to avoid defeat

Answers below and I'm ashamed to say
How awful we're brainwashed to live life today

The old are pathetic
This country's not aesthetic
The young should be free
We're slaves to jealousy
Judged by our wealth
Only care for ourselves
We're rats in this race
And all that counts is first place.

Martin Rich

Night Whispers

While others are sleeping in the dead of the night,
I know you're passing over in full–bloodied flight.
A prolonged pain as I hear you start screaming—
Screaming like some unstoppable demon.
But where will it end and where did it start?
The man with the coldest stone for a heart . . .

As I hear a faint screaming in the dead of the night,
I know someone's dying in the whispering light.
You beckon the lost soul, you beckon, you call;
The people gather, you gather them all.
But how do you live with yourself as a new day dawns?
Sleeping in a coffin . . . the devil's own spawn.

Caroline August Reed

A Stroke

I sit beside her bed, this woman, kin,
She who has been so many things,
Friend, Mother, Dictator, my love, my bane.
Dying before my eyes.
Not the gentle death of prose,
But the harsh reality of paralysis,
Slow starvation, her ordained end.
The once plump face a skin draped skeleton,
Living eyes staring from dead sockets,
Eyes that cry without tears,
Eyes that beg for God knows what,
Eyes that have no voice,
Eyes that plead with me.
But I am helpless.
Her mouth hangs slackly, drooping silent,
She once was the champion talker,
Often have I wished her silent,
Stop her chatter, yearned for peace,
Now I long to hear her voice,
Speak the unspoken horror in her eyes.

Jill Mack

"Inspired By A Basket Of Shells"

I take from this basket a number of shells.
Their beauty I handle with awe,
I imagine the sea, and the creatures they held.
The waves, as they tossed them ashore.

I wander the sands, in hope that I find,
A shell that is special to me,
Some that are large, and some that are small,
And some with the sound of the sea.

And so in natures bounteous gifts,
In the sea and on the land,
I look for mine upon the shore,
And find them in the sand.

Mary Lammas

My Shining Star

Looking up one still, dark night
There it was, a shining light
Although for years it had been there
It was the first time I felt aware
My eyes were drawn to where it shone
A cloud appeared and it had gone.

Yet for me it meant one thing
My heart grew light, faint bells did ring
The largest star up in the sky
It called to me—I wonder why?
Life's problems seemed to shrink and go
Drawing strength, somehow, from its glow.

When burdens weigh heavy and sadness reigns
It beckons me through window panes
Beyond the clouds, shedding its light
Not seen by day—only at night
It's there for me, so very far
Shining still, my own bright star.

Doreen Brooks

Life Has No Barrier!

Lovely young thing lying in the cradle
Were you born with a silver spoon or a rusty old ladle
Life's long road has just begun
Sometimes it's misery other times it's fun
Breaking the ornaments and best crockery
Isn't it just one big mockery
Living our lives from one day to the next
Learning the ins and outs like something from a text

Will we be poor or will we be rich
Or end up looking like a wizard or witch
Will we wear diamonds will we wear rags
Or will we be telling all the latest gags
Grow up to be an actor or a teacher
Perhaps become a lawyer or a preacher
A doctor maybe or where does life end
For a lonely heart that just won't mend

Sometimes life will take its toll
What will be will be so let it roll
Money won't buy the best in life
All it creates is trouble and strife

Ann Copland

'Life's Illusions'

Preconception guides my life
An artist paints my dream
And with his brush adds soft blue clouds
For my small head to lean

Then strokes of grey, strokes of black
Brush against my view
This is how the artist's hand
Says life should seem to you

Now it's complete and I can see
A now 'distorted' me
I then step back and dare to watch
The framed 'Discovery'.

Carla Piccin

Life Goes On

Love is blind, but so is life.
Enjoy yourself, whatever the price.
Only one chance is what you get,
So if things go wrong, don't feel upset.
You always learn by your mistakes.
If it's hard, just give and take,
In good time, you'll be alright.
Love and caring will make things right.
Friends and family are what we need.
Money and power results to greed.
All your troubles money can't help.
Even greed you will be by yourself.
You always need someone there for you,
Loving, caring, and also true.
So just don't worry if things go wrong,
always remember, Life Goes On.

BE HAPPY

Barry Taylor

A Scene From My Window

I sit at my window, and what do I see,
the little birds flitting, from tree to tree,
Some on the ground picking up bits,
there is a box, next door
with a nest of blue tits

Some times I see a magpie or two
all the little birds away they shoo
there is a jay that sits in the tree
I seem to think he is mocking me,
at night there comes an owl
who, sits in the tree and says
twittwoo

Muriel Tester

A Reason For Living My Life

Life had no meaning, no love, no reason
my world revolved around tablets to make me stay
in a life with no sun, no moon, no season.

My family wanted to help but found their efforts were in vain
I was on a self destruct and all I felt was pain.

Then one day you smiled at me and filled my heart with joy
and suddenly my life changed because of this precious little boy.

They put you in my arms and I loved you from the start.

We announced it in the paper, we were so very proud
At last we were parents and we wanted to shout it so very loud.

You saved my life and made me smile
You made me stop and think a while.

There were music and trees, flowers and birds
No tablets were needed to hear your first words.

I saw the sky and found the sea
and even realized there was a better me.

I became alive because with your many charms
My dreams came true the day you put my grandchild in my arms.
I couldn't live without you as your life is entwined with mine
Pray God you may be so close till the end of time.

Joan Croad

Healing From The Heart

We read Lord, of the wondrous healing, and we believe.
What we would like to ask you Lord, is
Grant us the healing of our hearts, for
That is where the danger of anger lurks.
Because what is within will either lighten or darken
The lives of the people around us.
We take offence over such little things,
Instead of forgiving in a way that is complete,
We go through the motions to forgive.
But so often, the angered flame never dies
It may be snuffed out, but it is still left to smoulder.
Then Lord, how often does the smouldering
Erupt! Into a far greater strength of anger.
Grant us thy healing Lord, healing from within.
That we may radiate our christian love,
That we may stand firm in your name;
That we may show to others,
However much our feelings may be hurt,
We can forgive completely. Because Lord
You have given us healing from the Heart.

Mavis Helen Blakeney

The Four Seasons

Spring, when bulbs and buds are peeping out for us to show
    that once again
God has awakened the earth from sleeping, and it's good to
    see the April rain.
Daffodils like shafts of sunlight, waving gently in the breeze
Crocus, purple, gold and white, growing underneath the trees.

Summer, such joy to see the sun, brightening the beauty of
    the world,
Holidays and all good times begun, flowers and trees are all unfurled.
Birds a-twittering in the branches, in and out the shady hedgerows
Sweetest songs in all the world, mingling with the breeze that blows.

Autumn with its rusts and browns, trees now shedding falling leaves
Bringing with it smiles and frowns, swallows in and out the eaves.
How sad to hear the merry notes of birds beginning to wane,
O how we dearly long to hear those cheerful lovely songs again.
A little sad, perhaps we weep, but know that we must pause to think
That even flowers and trees must sleep, but they again will
    surely wake.

Winter with its icy blasts, crispy white a carpet lies,
Summer sun and warmth is past, sounds of weak unhappy cries.
Frost and snow and bleak winds blowing, down on bended
    knees we pray,
And as we wonder and ponder time is going,
And soon the spring will once again be on its way.

Doris Vellam

Fears Of War

The fears of war came yesterday,
With no respite, it's here to stay,
Shooting, killing and maiming too,
War is here for me and you.

It started with a stupid thing,
No thought to what it all may bring,
We fought each day until 'twas done,
And then we knew which side had won.

The ships that sunk, the men that died,
Surely we know that each man tried,
When it's over we count the cost,
Of all the men that each side lost.

We grieve, we weep, we mourn the dead,
The untold tears that we have shed,
And in the years that duly come,
It's part of history, for all but some . . .

George Hunter

Fly Angel Fly

Fly my angel fly
Far beyond the sky
I may be crying, because I'm trying
Trying to say goodbye

Fly fly like a dove
Taking all your love
Where you are going I can't be knowing
It must be high high above

We had a love that meant so much
Now I must live without your tender touch

So fly my lover fly
No use to wonder why
When you were leaving, you said no grieving
So fly angel fly

I know it's time to say goodbye
So fly angel fly

John L. Howson

The Eyes Of A Child

In the eyes of a child, what do we find?
Needing, and longing spring to mind,
Dancing, when a smile appears,
Melting when they turn to tears,
Trusting all they recognize
To comfort them, and soothe their cries
Lighting up to show their pleasure,
Laughing, happy, both together,
Pain will feature, when they are hurt,
Clinging to a mother's skirt,
Until such time, for them to doze,
That is when their eyes, just close.

L. J. Thomas

The Silent Knock

The tick of the clock, the silent knock,
four drab walls as darkness falls.
An old armchair, a dying fire
a lack of love and burning desire.

She remembers the good times,
children, grandchildren, the reading of nursery rhymes,
Friends who have all long since gone.
leaving just memories to dwell upon
a son who went off to war in a far distant land,
and did not return the way he had planned.

Sad and lonely, she sits with a book
turning the pages with a worn distant look.
That is how it is when one gets old
to go to bed early, because one is cold.
If only she thinks, I could turn back the clock
and banish once again the silent knock.

G. T. Bulpitt

Such Harm

My passion burns once more because you called
My lust with dragon's scales and claws is built;
I shall possess you in this winter's night
Defile and wound and feel no shred of guilt.

For in past times you injured me enough
You stole my hopes and robbed me of esteem;
You said you were a dreamer. What of me?
You never listened once to know my dream.

My honour was impugned by all your lies
But still refused me license to condemn.
Tonight you will repay in blood–red coin,
I will have now what you denied me then.

My claws will mark your flesh from neck to thigh
My scales will rasp upon your fragrant skin;
There's no appeal and no defence to save,
No door to close to stop me getting in.

I will be paid, I will exact revenge
Though you may cry and plead and curse my name,
But mine will be the victory at last,
You shall not do such harm to me again.

A. Oxford

Spring

Spring, sweet spring arrived this day,
on view of all to see,
The flowers began their fashion show,
and the lambs gambolled over the lea.

'Tis a wonderful sight, as the days come and go,
And the buds on the hedgerows appear,
In their new shades of green, which are many it's true,
And the fashion for this time of year.

The flowers burst forth like beauty Queens,
With skins both dark and fair,
But their waxen gowns of every hue,
Make them beauties beyond compare.

Their faces you see are perfection,
Their gowns need no human aid,
God's hand is extended to all of these,
As they're born and as they fade.

The coming of Spring is so wondrous,
One feels a new world has begun,
As each new year brings the same sweet signs,
And proves that God's will has been done.

Beatrice E. Edwards

Thoughts

As I sit here looking out at the calm breezy afternoon
my heart is content with joyous thoughts of you.
I miss you words cannot say.

My heart is content but yet sad as I cannot hold you,
touch your peach soft skin or run my fingers through your
silky hair.

As the birds soar gracefully through the cloudy grey sky,
their beauty is amazing, but your beauty is astounding,
it would make the Greek Goddess of Love,
Aphrodite hold her head down in shame.

Your name and the words you speak are engraved not only
upon my heart,
but, also in the book of legends for all mankind to see, from
now to the end, whenever the end will be.

Take my heart and hold it gently, don't let it fall or you will break it.
Never again will anybody be able to mend it.
Take my heart and treasure it for I am rich in love but poor in money.

Many men will want to worship you,
many men will want to hold you.
Many men will want to kiss you
but there will only be one man who will love you
and that man is me.

Davinder Reehal

Muffin's Ball

"I'm SURE I left it somewhere in the hall, my lovely, pink and
squeaky, rubber ball!
I've searched high and I've searched low; where they've put it,
I don't know!
It's not under the table, nor under the chair, I've even looked
under the cat, with long hair!

I managed to sniff in the airing cupboard; for a minute or two
my hopes really soared.
A closer inspection found an old rubber glove and it
WASN'T my
toy: the ball that I love!
It's not in the wardrobe or under the bed—might be in the
garden, beneath the old shed.

I tried in the toy-box and in the bin. Oh! Who, I wonder,
committed this sin?
I MUST have my ball—without it I'm sad, whoever has hid it,
is making me mad!
I'm feeling real faint. Oh! What can I do? I've looked in the
bath and behind our loo!

It's wicked! It's cruel! It shouldn't be done—to stop a poor
dog, from having her fun!
I've nothing to chase and nothing to worry, I'll find out who
did it and then they'll be sorry!
But wait! Just caught a whiff of pink rubber ball, it's high
up above me and I'm not very tall.

I spy it at LAST! It's on the T.V. How cruel life can be, to a
wee dog like me!
I SEE IT! IT'S THERE! High up on the top, me, being a Cairn,
I'll beg till I drop!
I WANT IT! It's MINE! My lovely pink ball, NEXT time I won't
leave it, out in the hall!"

Joyce Dobson

Early Retirement

Early retirement, this is the life.
No more dashing, struggle and strife.
My D.I.Y. Can be done at leisure.
I'm told it will give me lots of pleasure.
First, I'll pop out to the shops.
What a price for two pork chops.
Then I'll go home and get my duster
and polish with all the strength I can muster.
When I've finished with "elbow grease shine"
the house should look completely divine.
Shall I wash the dishes or Hoover the suite
Or lay on the couch and watch Coronation Street
After that, there's a good football match
(But I really should mend that window catch).
Goodness me, how the time flies
It's almost time for beddy-byes.
After a whole day of being so busy
I feel really exhausted and even quite dizzy.
When I retired, they said I looked fine
But now I feel one hundred and nine.

Katharyn Grant

Love

Do you know what love is
do you dare to be seen anywhere
showing that you care?

Would you visit any place:
look at any face
and without surprise
look into and read, someone's eyes
finding within perhaps a heart that cries?

Could you help them to abate, and
get rid of their self hate
and above all have the patience
to wait until with strength of purpose
they no longer feel worthless
and can walk through the gate of fate
with, and to love.

Ann L. Harrison-Webb

The Bone Crunching Porcupus

Whenever you're on the 30 bus
Beware of the Bone Crunching Porcupus
He lives under the seats, where he giggles and neaps
(and is thoroughly dangerous)

He might leap from mid-air and tear at your hair
And pull it right out by the clawful
He then might miggle and mawg and squiggle
(he can be thoroughly awful)

His favourite treat is a mouthful of feet
He could crunch them all up by the plateful
He'll lick his lips and slibber and glips
(he can be thoroughly hateful)

The worst thing of all is his blood–curdling call
As he gnaws at your toes he's so gleeful
And when he's done he'll shiffle and blum
(he can be thoroughly lethal)

The lesson is thus, if you travel by bus
Beware of the Bone Crunching Porcupus
He lives under the seats where he giggles and neaps
(and is thoroughly dangerous)

Gabriella Braun

Summer

The flowers are blooming
The grasses are greener
The busy bees are buzzing
What a change to winter.

Excitement fills the air
Aroma of summer is here,
The sun is bright and fair
Thanks to the glowing sphere.

The mating season for the four–legged beasts,
Suitable time for ever–ready feasts.
The thankful birds are begging for more,
Flying around like agents of war.

The time for love and kindness
My loved one's care and sweetness
Of the beckoning beck of purity
Of the flowing streams of eternity.

Philharmonic season of joy
As tempting as a decoy
Come and play with my musical toy
To soothe away the mischief and ploy.

Daniel Ayodele

Sad Facts

When God made this world, His wonderful creation,
He meant that we should live in peace, each and every nation.
It wasn't His intention when he placed us on the earth
That we should lose His values nor misplace His worth.

Now this world has many troubles leaders come and leaders go.
Animosity surrounds us, what next we do not know,
The crime rate rises higher with every passing day,
Blamed on unemployment, or so the wise men say.

We live midst stress and poverty.
Famine, wars and strife,
Useless killing,
Useless waste of life.

Guns are ever ready, nuclear stockpile high.
Finger on the button, tell the world goodbye!
We wonder what it's all about, we ask the reason why?
But will we ever understand no matter how we try?

And yet in man we find much good, great humanity.
Kindliness and courage, compassion and charity.
Often given with no thoughts of self gain.

This gives us hope in faith we pray, maybe all's not in vain.

Doreen Wilkinson

Waiting

How quiet it is, how peaceful it's become.
The snow falls silently, the air feels warm.
Trees turn white, grass no longer green.
Birds are silent, no animals seen.
Oh blessed earth, it's become just a dream.
The snow is fall out, the bomb brought that.
Houses have fallen, streets made flat.
All became rubble, this was no dream.
No one had a chance, not even to scream.
A cry in the darkness, can be heard now and then.
The bomb has not yet brought, that life to an end.
My end is coming, I feel it draw near.
I know that now, I have no more to fear.
Bring me peace, and my soul to rest.
I no longer wish, to exist like this.
I pray to God, please take my soul.
I'll never have the chance to even grow old.
Peace is coming, as my life ends.
I damn those who did this.
Who brought earth to its end.

R. M. Willis

First Grandson

I wonder what you're thinking as you lie there in your cot,
Brain cells growing rapidly, now you've got a lot,
Each brand new experience you'll commit to memory,
To be recalled in "Flashbacks" when you're "93"
What is it that makes you smile when you're half asleep?
That turns quickly to a frown and it looks as if you'll weep,
Are you aware, I wonder, of all the love for you?
Lying there so innocent, with eyes so big and blue,
Gradually developing your character and traits,
It won't be very long until you're out with girls on dates,
We'll watch you grow up baby from an infant to a man,
Enjoy the life ahead of you, give it all you can,
Respect the folks who love you and love them in return,
Appreciate the good things, right from wrong you'll learn,
Keep your head held high and follow the true road,
Remember that no harm will come if you keep life's honour code,
So with these few short guidelines to help you on your way,
I'm sure you'll be a happy chap—and your life will be o.k!

P. Kirkham

Mixed Emotions

Anger, Hurt, Jealousy
Lust, Envy or Hate,
Very seldom do we love or do we love to hate?
All these mixed emotions are put in one large bowl
When we need one we take it out and give it a go.
We don't care who we hurt
And usually it's someone close
All we care about is the hate that's eating us the most.

Claire Owens

Flickering Thoughts

Flickering thoughts are starting to fade,
If only I could return to those delicate dreams.
But he awakens me bluntly
As he shouts and shrills with senseless schemes.
I try to ignore, though constantly fail
To defend my senses from such rough means.

Distant images of life as it was,
Seem as a broken dream in this strange head,
Which always prefers to stay on the edge
Though far away from this boring bed.
My thoughts may often turn and churn an ugly image
And then all I shall feel is this thickening of dread.

As my mind creates come sort of sense,
Harsh voices disturb my short spell,
Whilst my lover below creates his sordid vision
His fantasy with a paper used as a shovel
Thus confining the evidence to a bin.
Flickering thoughts are beginning to dwell.

Jessika Jones

Being Mum

One day you dream of having a baby, soon you grow older
and your dreams become maybe.

Eventually, your baby is made, asleep in the womb for nine
months is stayed.

Labour starts, excitement hits the air, but worry not because
nursery is there.

Watching and waiting until "it's time", a babe is born and all is fine.

Your child is born you're overwhelmed, their first cries. Oh
what a wonderful sound.

All is well and you leave for home, taking care of your infant
now alone.

Watching them grow gives you endless pleasure, but being
mum is far from leisure.

Helping them strive from day to day, watching them thrive
whilst at play.

Toni Alouane

Eternal Shine

Each lost in the other's eyes, hands entwined,
Bright smiles and eyes that sparkle,
Together they shine; becoming one whole,
Thriving on the unity of their hearts.
A short time has passed, but eternally smitten,
Complementary personality, physical closeness.
Yet apart-insecurity.
Missing the safety of the other's arms, doubting,
Longing for confirmation from three little words,
Alone is dull and lacks love's eternal shine.
Time drags on painfully until they are together again,
Then it slips by unnoticed,
Doubt a distant memory now as they regain their special glow.
Both used to flirt and live for mindless fun,
Now they live only for each other,
And for the radiance the other's presence gives them.
Their souls glitter in content harmony,
As the world goes on without them.
A shared smile, knowing they have each other,
For life. For love. Forever.

Lisa Presley-Caygill

Eternal Rain

Please don't for long leave me alone,
Always be there when I come home,
For without you there to comfort and cheer,
My life would mean so little my dear,
You are my strength, my guidance too,
Without you there I just couldn't do,
You build up my character when I don't feel strong,
You help me to discover if I've gone wrong,
You are my sunshine it must be plain,
Without you I'd have eternal rain.

L. P. Smith-Warren

Untitled

She lies cosy in her warm bed
listening to the rain on the roof.
There'll be no washing done today.
She wonders 'will it stop?'

She thinks of the children under her feet.
Fighting and bickering with pent up energy.
She wonders 'will it stop?'

She looks over to her husband snoring
and sees the deep lines of worry on his face.
she wonders 'will it stop?'

She rises as the postman closes the gate.
She picks up the wet brown window envelopes from behind the door
she wonders 'will it stop?'

Janet Westcott

Only Lent

If we recall the morning dew, fading evening clouds of blue
The sunbeam gleaming at its best we watch the birds come
home to rest
This wondrous world where we were sent but remember it is only lent
All animals on earth must roam large elephants to smallest fawn
It's their world as well as ours we should on animals have no powers
Make no mistake you have one chance, make good your life,
it's gone at a glance
Spread your love it's heaven sent but remember this earth is only lent
The forest tree must be left alone these wonderful forests are
the animals' home
Just like the seas with the magnificent whale they will all be
gone if the killings prevail
We all must take care of this wonderful earth and tutor our
children from the time of birth
But it's got to be now, no more time can be spent, as this
wonderful earth has only been lent.

Moira Callan

Ignorance Is Bliss?

Placid are the cows bedappled black and white,
The long tawny meadow grass grazing,
As I come by at silvery twilight,
Wondering again at love amazing.

Now clouds of satin cows drift by,
Or graze, air patches of rhythmic rasping,
The sea beyond silvered as the sky
While love lies in wait ever grasping

At an eternity of love divine.
But you, cows, in ignorance chew the cud,
Know nothing of that open door's golden shine,
The flower unfolding from passion's bud.

Your bodies roll-ripple, no B.S.E.
While love's beneath my hands silken flows:
Body heat upsurges, envelopes darkly,
Eyelids smile dreamily, as she goes.

Richard Burdon

Untitled

There cannot be a deeper pain than this,
So dear to me the precious life she nearly took,
And so deep her sorrows concealed within her heart,
That she could tell them not.

How well she hid the torments of her brittle mind,
Behind that painted face so calm, so strong,
The outward mask we knew and loved so well,
The inward mind we could not dream to know.

She fought with strength to win the battle almost lost,
It drove at her, but she could ask no help,
Then finally, from her almost suffocated soul,
She cried out, for torment she could bear no more.

Only then could people come to aid her,
Only then could people know the truth,
But now it's still not too late to save her,
For she can finally come from within herself.

Margo Rees

Midsummer

The earth is caressed by the spirits of summer,
the life pulse swarms—a golden, joyous murmur.
Nature celebrates with overflowing zest,
the sun nourishes the divine Mother's bequest.

In loving fusion the Summer Queen and King embrace,
their devotion shines through on nature's face.
In the cool evenings breezes, life whispers and sighs,
a contented lullaby echoing in the summer skies.

The Sun King evolves into shinning splendour,
bringing light and truth to this realm of thunder.
His sacred quest will begin soon—a hero's flight,
and He will swallow the dark to become Lord of Night.

Helen M. Howell

A Trip To The Cotswolds

I went on a day trip recently with a group of ladies I know
I had never been on any of these trips before
And hope there will be some more
Our destination was Stow-on-the-Wold which was also new to me
The country scenes as we travelled were a lovely sight to see
I really did enjoy myself exploring the tiny shops
with their many gifts so rare
But there was no time to linger with so little time to spare
I joined the ladies for a hasty snack
Before it was time for our journey back
But oh! How the time did fly
On a lovely day that kept quite dry

Ethel Brooks

The Tune

My tune was taught by tinkers, it was old as it was new,
A tune to play on dulcimers, a tune for Xanadu;
A tune that teased the heart of man and tickled it with flame,
But not a tune for seven knaves whom I refuse to name.

Who sat in sequined trousers on illuminated cubes,
And played my tune on trombones which were framed by
  neon tubes,
Who plucked at flashing banjos with their phosphorescent thumbs,
And beat with lighted drumsticks upon diamante drums.

The pianist had "Maxie" flashing huge upon his back.
The black notes were the white notes and the white notes
  were the black.
The mirror-fronted keyboard showed infinity of hands
And everybody gibbered in this most debased of bands.

They put my tune to torture in a crime beyond the law,
They played it on a stirrup pump, they played it on a saw.
A young man stood and simpered it, a woman sang it "hot"
This tune a tinker taught me—and I wish that he had not!

Denis Cronin

Peace

At last peace has arrived, it's what we all wished for,
But will it work or last? Or will we just want more?

No more massacres of the innocent, just peace all around,
No more living in fear, no more bombing sounds.
No more fighting for power, just peace that joins us together.
No more wars and discrimination, we hope the peace will last
forever.
A larger population we live in, this gets incredibly cramped,
This leads to things like famine, and large unemployment.
People get jealous and sad, and have little money to spare.
Some have more than others, it just isn't fair!
Then greed and destruction starts, people get hurt.
Wars start all over again, peace just does not work!

Meera Khosla

The Four Seasons

Your warm breath caresses my skin like a gentle summer breeze,
Your smile is as bright as the mid-day sun,
When we are together, we move as one,
How I love those long, hot, summer nights.

When autumn falls, the leaves float gently in the air,
Making contact with the ground, as softly as your fingers
touch my face,
When you are with me, in body, thought or dream,
My heart flutters like the wings of the migrating birds.

As the snowflakes settle onto the cold winter ground,
In my heart I feel warm as we lie together,
Like two logs nestling in the basket beside the roaring fire,
We make our own heat with the intensity of our passion.

When spring finally arrives, with warm rain and bulbs peeping
through the soil,
You make me feel like a new bud beginning to unfold,
I open up to you, I love you,
You are my summer, autumn, winter, spring,
You are my four seasons.

Beverly Teague

Transplant Poem

Transplant, transplant, my doctor cries,
I pack my bag between the sighs,
I rush to the ward in my mum's car,
It doesn't take long, it's not very far,
Emma, Julie, Rebecca, Kristie.
Those are the nurses waiting for me,
It may be my nerves, I feel a bit lousy
I am given a drip to make me feel drowsy,
I don't know about sleep as I lie on the bed,
I have many different thoughts going through my head.
"It's time, it's time, it's time to go,"
The nurses words hit me with a blow,
The porter arrives, for once on time,
I'm wheeled to the lift away from floor nine,
We arrive on floor one, to theatre we rush,
The anaesthetist arrives, gives my line a flush,
I lie on the bed not a murmur or peep,
The injection is given and I drift off to sleep.

James Wilkes

If I Could

If I could take you to a place,
I would choose to have the beach in front of my face
To lay down on the sand and fly in our dreams
Just like the bird when they fly on their trees
If I could touch you somewhere
I would touch your hand to hold it tight and take you on a flight
A flight to heaven to be together now and forever
If I could do what I want I would stay close till I die
But my love will never end
Even when I am buried under ground
If I could send a message to your brain
I would send a paper with my heart inside
No wonder I will never die as long as I keep on the try
I do this because I love you so do not regret
If you deny my love that will be it
I will simply vanish one way to heaven
They say you forget what's in your past
But I will never forget you because you are my past
So I will stay love you for now and forever
Because you are the only love in my entire life

Ahmed Afifi

Sometimes

Sometimes when things will not shine bright,
When round they rumble through the night,
When nowhere does an answer gleam,
Not a chink of light or narrowest beam,
It sometimes serves to stand away and
view the subject from afar.
Perhaps as though impersonally without
constraint through a door ajar.
And suddenly like crystal, clear, akin
to the sharpest focus appears.
The simplest easiest and most obvious cure;
so blatant as to be obscure.

Jean Brown

The Love I Lost

Once upon a time I had your heart,
I imagined us together never being apart.
I loved the way your eyes always look at me,
Entranced by your gaze, your soul is what I see.
You walked away alone leaving me to cry,
Why did it end? You have to tell me why.
My appearance is deceiving for you don't know how I feel,
Believe in what I say, I promise that it's real.
I wonder if you've replaced the love that I gave,
You threw away my dreams, my hopes that I saved.
Time is standing still, and my emotions are the same,
My love is everlasting, but I can never love again.
I can't escape the hurt, the memories which you hold,
My sealed note of anger is starting to unfold.
Exposing raw wounds, it's deep in my tear,
It's unconditional love; I'm always right here.

Ann Baxter

Forever With You

A love so strong yet he has gone,
I know not where, but how I care
Please tell me now I need to know,
is he with you? Why did he go?

His face I see both day and night,
I long for him to talk and shout,
our love so deep, it can't be right,
the days go by, so much for fight!

One day I thought his voice I heard,
a distant sound but it was him,
my love I called, but no one came,
what is this mess, who can I blame?

And then the love we always knew ran through
my veins and then through you,
what joy I felt beyond belief,
to feel you there, oh such relief.

Love never dies, goes on and on,
of course it's there, how can it leave?
No, no my love. It must be true.
I know with love, I'm forever with you.

Annette Line

I'll Go Tomorrow

She was five years old and very bright
And could be very haughty,
If things weren't just going right
She was also very naughty.

I remember once when things looked black
She suddenly announced,
I'm going away forever today
And I'm not never coming back.

So off she went to pack her bag
Complete with doll and teddy,
Down the stairs she let them drag
Then bellowed loud—I'm ready!

Little feet trudged toward the door,
Tears brimmed in sheer defiance,
I wonder, when she gazed at me,
Did she loose her self reliance

Did she feel the yearn for my embrace
Or was it just a touch of sorrow
For as the cold rain touched her face
She said "I think I'll go tomorrow"

Vera Croft

Dreams

How fascinating dreams can be, when youth sits at old one's knee.
When age and youth in thoughts combined — forget the passages of time.
Sweet youth with poignancy so rare—the memories of the old one share,
who recalls the time when youth so sweet—the world, his route, beneath his feet.
Of this the child can only dream—and view it with a dreamer's eye the old one's adventures long gone by.

Betwixt the two—both youth and age—there comes a time of test—
when strength is weakened—the soul needs rest—when hardship and sorrow
take their toll—and dreams once so great, now seem small—
As man goes on in years, he boasts to youth—and forgets his tears—and speaks of victories untold . . .

The child listens to all these things—and wishes time had fleeting wings—
and a world to own as his dominion—and to descendants leave an opinion—
of how success was brought to all his schemes—
and to his descendants bring the same sweet dreams!
Ah, age and youth in reverie——
are very much like you and me!

Melsa Dowdell

The Flame

Shout! I then yearned my genius to caress the flame.
Moody, magnificent as thoughts simmer with time.
Shatter me, break me, fragile me.
An unspoken rebel with fuels that burn,
creation is only me.

Spin, spin, anger corrodes, spin,
nothing but colours to run down silent words.
Spill the waters like we do?

Do you like the mad inside me?
It won't disappear!
It strays from mile to mile, sparkling, spitting.
It will undress gentleness and taunt loving.
Spin! Like the wheel,
The noise is the monster that wavers with obsessions.

Is this the disguise, the dying wish of a greater man
that dances with she who cries?
It flies like the burden it is
and hatred is the fool it seeks.

Kris Barker

Untitled

The feeling got stronger each day
I felt as if two people were pulling me apart
one way then the other
the feeling was heavy and sad
For it was not light and happy
it was ugly
not beautiful
for this feeling is stabbing me.

Nilda Peeling

The Sea . . .

I endeavoured to seek the soul of the sea,
Like I, solitary, secretive, and adjacent to no where,
She divulged nothing to me,
Only that! She cried and sighed,
The pulse of her heart, erratic with the ebb.

Eroded as the rocks she smites,
The solace, I so yearned, was lost in her roaring breath,
To be left! Only with, slaked lips of bitter sweet tang,
Foaming virginal white, as deceitful adulteress might,
Tempting, luring. Obsessing the soul of man.

As coarse as the shale beneath my feet,
Reality! As sharp! As quick as the grave,
loom's mourning as the wake,
No escape! From the pursuer I hoped to forsake,
No loving warmth from her caress.

No friendship, only sadness,
Distress!
Still lonely and distant, like me, as she!

Terence F. Berwick

A Chatty Murder

I choked and ran home as fast as I could,
Not daring to remember what I had seen in the wood
A fountain of endless chatter, a cry of pain
An unknown hand carving the murderer's name.
A chatty murder, they called it, a terrible death,
They dared to name the victim, her name was Beth
The thunder snapped and growled, causing a frightful scream
The killer smirked happily, his mission had been a dream.

I got home and jumped on my bed with a groan,
I felt so miserable, I was home alone
I thought of the killer; strong and swift
The killer that thought of death as a gift.
Then I got into bed and tried to sleep,
But I felt so scared, I wanted to weep
Then I heard a key turn and I froze in fear
I knew it was the killer, death was near.

Ama Okafor

That Still Small Voice

We walked on the shore by the rippling waves,
As the sun broke through the morning haze,
Sending a pathway of twinkling lights,
From far over the water,
To land at our feet.
How good it is to stroll this way,
Along the beach on a summer's day,
Shall we forget those chores we left?
and lay in the sun to dream and rest.
But "Still Small Voice" is telling us,
Just go on home and get things done,
And when you see the setting sun,
You then can say "Well done! Well done!"
For tomorrow is another day,
To walk again on the shore this way.
This stolen hour is sheer delight,
Because we do, what we know is right.

Eva Whiting

Only In My Dreams

She comes to me in the still of the night, but only in my dreams.
She talks to me about my love for her, but nothing is as it seems.
I'm hypnotized by the sound of her voice and the smell of her hair.
I make love to her in the darkest depths of my mind,
but is she really there.

I look in her eyes and see the thoughts in her mind,
she tells me she loves me and love is what I find.
I kiss her lips and feel their warmth as she breathes,
I don't want to wake from my dreams
because that's when she leaves.

But as I wake in the morning and find she's not there,
I remember the sound of her voice and the smell of her hair.
She's left a message in my heart and I know what it means,
It says she will always love me, but only in my dreams.

Philip Quinn

'Transient Days'

Winter vanished, without trace,
The crocus bloomed and died.
Then daffodils, their golden glow,
Lit up the world, with pride,
Their leaves, tied up in bundles then,
To wither 'till next spring.
The spotted tiger lilies, pansies, poppies,
So short lived, each thing.
Showing daily from the window,
How time, keeps moving on.
Three more months, full circle then,
Since that fateful day.
When I was told and all 'hell' let loose,
My man was, "going away"
Even my love for him is dying,
No admiration left.
He killed me too and tied my broken limbs
in bundles
I hope I bloom again, next spring.

Olive H. Henderson

Paradise Relost?

Man first dreamed of Mars and then of the stars
And abused the blue planet of Earth.
His contempt was repaid by the horror he made
Only now he has learned of its worth.

Its balance destroyed as he dreamed of the void
And plundered the oil and the coal,
With no thought for the trees or the whispering breeze
That were part of his God–given soul!

Is it now far too late and must man meet his fate
Without even time to relent?
Or can he repair the soil and the air
Of the Earth that was once Heaven sent?

Ken Horsfall

'Choice'

It's never too early,
and it's never too late.
Enjoy the fun
It's yours to take.
Time is short,
So make it count.
Be the first with that forgiving word,
Or an offered smile of peace.
Mistakes can happen, it's not the end
with help from you the rift can mend.
If you bear no grudge
Then you'll suffer no ill.
Let the others continue the fight until
exhaustion takes its toll.
Take in good part the mistakes you make,
when things go wrong
Don't count the cost.
Remember that when humour's found
Then it's never truly lost.

J. J. Houston

Church-Makers

They climbed on sketchy ladders towards God
with wire they hewn grey rock into heaven
invaded the sky with hammers, defied gravity
took up God's house to meet him.

And came down to their lean soup and bred
They slept with their wear, stinking wives
—Quarrelled and cuffed the children, was
drinking—and died without happiness

And every day they took to the ladders again
Yearn for another summers a wallows,
grew greyer, shakier, became less inclined
to help a neighbour on a fine evening.

To leave the tower to others, stood in the crows
well back from the vestments at the consecrations
envied the fat bishop his fat smile and warm boots
looked up, and said: "We bloody did that!"

Michael Rutz

To Breda

You live your life, taking so much care,
You're one so innocent, so easy to scare.
To me you give so much comfort and love,
with you're around I'm as light as a dove.

If I just want to sit and chat
I know you'll allow me to do that.
And with your baby sister, you'll laugh or
share a cone,
or maybe dance and sing a long to "Boyzone".
There's a lot of ways I could end the poem.
But I'll just say, without you B, it wouldn't be home.

Amanda D. Wallace

Tell Me Your Secret Moon

Oh tell me! Please tell me—
You great big moon,
What are your secrets—
What makes you shine?
Will you remain in that gigantic sky
To lend us your light till the end of time?

Please tell me! Yes tell me,
You dear old moon—
We earthlings would like to know—
What you in your bosom hide,
Is there a single strand of life on your breast—
Too superior to be seen by eyes such as ours.

Or is it that thou art only placed there, magnificent moon
To lighten our path when the sun goes down
You've lent us your moonshine since time began
What have we earthlings to bring to your aid?

Victorine Z. McAllister

I Am I

Peer group pressure!
Is this how we measure the way
We live our lives?
Do I want to be accepted by
Others, at the price of my own
Individuality?
No! No! No! This I do not.
For why should I alter myself to
Fit into others' ways?
I am I, and of this I am proud.
Like others I will be, when in my shroud.
I am a being, unique, with a soul.
Ought this I to sell, to be
Part of the whole?
Never, I say.
I am I, and this way I'll stay.

T. Matthews

Telling the Beads

I am untouchable, I'm lonely, language has failed me!
I need words—I have words
but, I can't make connection.
The tapping and the clicking of the beaded rosary,
makes more sense to me as it slips through ancient hands.
Their voice speaks at some primal level of my being.
And in the silence, filled with hushed sound,
where language as I know it falls apart.
The beads, beat out an ancient rhythm on the other
archaic words are wrenched out of the heart,
futility, horror, pain and pointlessness.
Like smoke, the language stutters in the dark
but, it makes such sense and the grammar
that constrains it
is simply, the rapid pulsing of the heart, broken
by now in so many different places.
The alphabet used by man is no use to me
paradoxically, the language I've been seeking
is in silence, that alone has made me free.

S. M. Kelly

Love Hurts

His big strong masculine hands tenderly touch
The heart pulsates with yearning for his feel
Love between them hurts so much
It's an emotion which is so real
Entwined around each others bodies so bare
Tis a natural thing indeed
To look at them you see how much they care
Off each other they do feed.

When they kiss electricity passes through each artery and vein
An intense and pleasurable sensation
An orgasmic intensity makes you feel insane
Love is a revelation
Need each other, think of each other, be selfless in thoughts
and be rewarded by constant devotion, which can not be bought.

D. Loague

A Mother's Child

What would she do without her?
She's only two years old.
She gives her life a meaning,
her future—she feels bold.
They loved him . . . but he's gone.
He wanted more from life, he didn't want commitment,
nor did he want a wife.
So, she faces life without him.
She is not so sad to-day, as she stands at the kitchen sink
and watches her child at play.
Life is not so bad.
No . . . she will not be sad.
To grieve? Do not be silly.
She loves her life.
She has it all.
Her darling daughter . . . Billie!!

C. Hallam

E.C.T.

It keeps raining in my mind.
The puddles surround me.
My head is a sponge.
Needing just a little longer.
I feel the bitterness, I should be free.
Feel the guilt and dismiss me.
The silver plates refuse me an exit.
Inactive from society.
Nowhere to take cover.
They seek you out.
A life of intention, stolen.
To fly like an eagle.
Then caught like his prey.
Floating like a cloud.
Inclusion to inclusion.
Red lights to blackness.
Silence.

Emma Cooper

Courage

One night I had a dream that I was sailing on a boat
Suddenly it began to sink and there was nothing to keep me afloat

The waves of the water were crashing and slapping against the sides
The lower the boat began to sink the higher became the tides

The night was getting darker and my mind was full of fear
And then I heard a whisper, a voice came in my ear

I know how you are feeling and the fears going through your head
But keep your wits about you, otherwise you could be dead

The voice sounded so stern and I could tell that it was true
The message was loud and clear and telling me exactly what to do

Then suddenly out of nowhere there came a flash of light
Then all ever so quickly I seemed to lose my sight

I know that I came through and something gave me strength,
When I woke up in the morning I felt like I'd swum lengths

Who knows what gave me the courage
I needed to save myself, it's something I'll never know
But I'd like to think it will be with me
Wherever I should go.

K. Kilsby

Missing The Comfort

I have shed my last tear, I have cried too long,
Now I know it's time to change, to a happier song.
After all those long dark days, and what seems like endless nights,
now out from the blackest tunnel, shines a ray of light.

Drifting from the shadows, a newer brighter day,
No longer shall I wish that white, was a moody dull grey.
But the shadows soon reappear, and as the lithium will fade,
happiness I once did long for, was just a dream too late.

Rodney McConnell

Earth Mother

Your heart beats to the same rhythm
As the earths drum.
You pulsate with her
Your heart is full to overflowing
With a oneness that is rare.
Your serenity and sincerity attracts people
Your knowledge astounds them
Your determination frightens them
You are apart of the landscape.
To walk out into the landscape with you
In early morning or as the sun slips into the sea
To see with your eyes
To feel the earth vibrate under our feet
As they squelch into the wet mossy earth.
As you lie arms outstretched facing heaven
Your whole being vibrates in time with the earth's beat
As you and the landscapes are one.

Andy McCarthy

Just Us

Let our touches be naked,
Of other no trace.
Be open and sensual.
See only the other's face.

Let's be lost in the depth of our bodies,
We fall into every pore.
We act as though we are starving
Tasting as if there's no more.

The passion, the love, the warmth,
Our bodies feel adrift.
Don't sever the connection.
Just experience the celestial lift.

Let paradise open her gates.
Our need is understood,
The love is flowing freely
Shoots the magic of our love.

Eileen Jones

Lake Of Dreams

Looking outwards, I take a look within,
at a lake full of my dreams.
I want to take a dip within my lake,
but maybe it's just too deep;
or maybe it's just too late.

If I try hard enough, treasures I may find,
and secrets I may unlock.
The key is within my grasp,
but my grasp can't hold the key;
unless, perhaps, I know what I want to see.

A shimmer of hope flickers across my lake,
across my lake of dreams.

Jason Lewis Trehearn

The Temp's Lament

I have no claim on you—no no!—not one.
I may not change a single word or deed,
But follow the same course, proceed alone,
And if I hear your name must take no heed.
The four walls of an office marked the stage
For our first meeting and, too soon, our last.
Two weeks ago? To me it seems an age.
Already you're a memory. You're in my past.
But I recall your wit and piercing eyes
And through dull hours breathe a farewell prayer.
O stranger! Do not mock me, or despise
A silent message in the City air.
Distracting laughter echoes lingeringly,
Your face is wrought into my memory.

Penelope Maclachlan

Tears Of Love

You said you would be there forever more,
You said it would be just like before,
You told me we'd always be together,
You told me you'd be there forever,
But why did you go and leave me crying?
Were you crying like me?
Were there tears on your face?
Tears that I didn't see.
Did you feel the same way as me?
Angry and lonely, yet free.
No more fighting, no more fears,
No more anger, no more tears.
As I sit here alone at night in the dark,
I feel my world is falling apart.
I start to think about you,
Are you feeling lonely too?
Please don't go and leave me all alone,
In this big lonely house that once was home.
Please don't leave, Daddy, please don't go,
Don't you know that I love you Daddy, I love you so.

Paula Mealey

My Daughters

This tidy house is standing still
Perfect bliss one could say
Oh how I wish I could turn back the clock
And see my daughters play.

Many games, books and toys
Were scattered across these floors
And sticky little fingerprints were all around the doors.

Two pairs of tiny red wellie boots sitting in the hall
Raincoats, panda brollies all these I can recall.

There were two hamsters
Willie the mouse, tropical fish and kittens too
Children I'd never seen before were asking to see our zoo.

Then there were the Ballet dancing years with
Lovely music of days gone by
The Ballet shoes now hang on the wall
Please excuse me while I cry.

I never thought the day would come so soon
When my Fiona and Avril would grow up and leave the nest
I guess they took the largest part of me
With them but I'm so glad it was the best.

Eileen MacDonald

Prejudice—A Question Of Colour

A rose is a rose whatever its colour
And that surely goes for snapdragons too.
Petunias come in various colours
From whitest white to darkest hue.

The list of flowers is too large to catalogue.
In a little homily like this.
And their colours are so many ad varied
There's not one that you could dismiss
Because its colour failed to please you
You'll be sorry if you did.

Why, then, should people be so different?
And why take it out on the innocent kind?
Who can't help its colour any more than the flowers can
What's in the genes will surely grow
Like blonde locks or brown locks or black locks or ginger
Whatever's there is bound to show.

And skin colour too—oh! Yes we're all coloured
Be it black, brown, yellow or pink shall we say
If it were not for this genetic arrangement
We might all be a sad shade of Grey.

Eileen Collins

It's Spring Again

How lovely to awaken to a bird song, as if from a dream,
Or nightmare, after a winter so dreary and long
'Tis time to be out and about in sunshine to shout,
Amid showers and sunshine and insects all floating about.

What a great feeling; refreshing and glowing the sun,
To allow for romping and racing, having and allowing for great fun,
A longer time for reflection on things well done, and to do,
Especially with valued loved ones and lots more friends to woo.

So here we are again, with flowers to spur us into life,
Another year of joy and wonder, with hopefully less strife,
The wearying woes and pain have gone, but still not forgotten,
Because we have still not thrown out lot in.

What joy would be a longed for repeat,
Of childhood aspirations and dreams so sweet,
Carefree as we grow wise, mature and robust,
Not to think of times, so long, low and full of lust.

Let spring revive and restore our dream flow,
To life more rewarding as onward we go,
To more happiness fulfilment and laughter; with less sorrow and woe,
Reminding us that through all that, it's spring again with its miracle glow.

Mercia H. Farrah

Missing

It's been so long since I saw your face, since you vanished
without a trace. But even though we're far apart, you live
forever in my heart. For you are my son and you'll always be,
deep within, a part of me.

I remember well that happy morn, my tears of joy as you were
born. Now missing from my life, my boy and missing from my
heart that joy. But you're still my son and you'll always be,
deep in my heart, a part of me.

It's sad to think you'll never know that as a baby I watched
you grow. I woke each night to give your feed and tended to
your every need. For you are my son and you'll always be,
deep in my heart, a part of me.

Such sorrow and such pain I feel. My broken heart will never
heal. For your mother stole you from my side just to save her
foolish pride. But you're still my son and you'll always be,
deep in my heart, a part of me.

And now I sit here all alone. You do not write, you never
phone. But each and every night I pray that we will be
reunited, one day. For you are my son and you'll always be,
deep in my soul, a part of me

Now, I just hope that you will know, although I'm not there to
watch you grow. I am so close while we're apart because
you're in my thoughts and in my heart. For I am your dad and
I guess it's true, deep in your heart, I'm a part of you.

Timothy Gorman

The Snowflake

As I fall down from the sky, mountains, rivers, fields nearby.
Gushing, blowing, pure and white,
Slowly falling around and loosing height.
My friends are around me, close at bay,
Above me, below me, slowly they drift away . . .

I'm promised I'll land on a good bit of turf,
Way down yonder on a planet called Earth.
There I may stay for a day or two, being admired as part of a view.
Then I am told I shall slowly melt,
A process that thankfully can't be felt.

Made in Heaven, I know I'm unique,
But now I'm feeling weary and weak.
Dark, windy, lonely and very cold, not long now, or so I'm told.
I know I have now almost reached the ground,
Everything's quiet—I can't hear a sound.

But something's wrong—the Earth looks grey,
I wish I could see better, I wish it was day.
This is not quite what I expected, this is not what I recollected,
For as I land, I know it's the end of me,
For me and my friends have drifted into the sea . . .

Elaine Copeland

The Thunderstorm

I saw the thunderstorm approach
And I was safe within my house
As with a mighty pow'r of doom
He sent His winds all through my room
And through the streets and shepherd's browse.

I saw the thunderstorm approach
A rain like that I'd never seen!
The flood ran through the toxic way
Washing the evil dirt away
Leaving a trace of red, so clean!

I saw the thunderstorm approach
And the heavens seemed to burst
As He spoke with rumbling might
To be heard all through the night
And gratify our secret thirst.

I'd seen the thunderstorm approach
And having seen it I was wise
For all we are and all we seem and all that we pretend to be
Despite our knowledge, pow'r and pride
We Are But Toys In His Dark Eyes.

Jenny Birkenfeld

In My Wildest Dreams

Each night when I lay down to sleep,
It's the same dream over and over.
He appears, my knight in shining armour,
my wild romantic lover.
He holds his hand towards me,
He pulls me into his arms,
Here am I with this stranger,
But cannot resist his charms.
I feel as if I am on a danger trip,
Yet I cannot refuse his touch,
He makes love like I never
Imagined, oh I want this man so much.
Then as soon as it's all over,
He'll quickly disappear
Leaving a kiss upon my lips
Until the next time he does appear.

Lynsey Morgan

The Panther

Whilst at the zoo, I chanced to see
A beast that gave me ecstasy.
It was the panther, so sleek and decisive
He was gliding back and forth.
Baring, his teeth looking so aggressive
Showing me all his worth.
I did not hear a sound from him.
Making such a fine display
With his looks so hauntingly grim
And yet so charmingly gay.

Colin Jennings Wallace

Plato: Light Relief

"A little thing is a little thing, but faithfulness in
a little thing becomes a great thing."

If you are blessed with but a little thing
Do not be sorrowed:
If your little thing is faithful
(and never borrowed)
It will become a great big thing
—So promised Plato

I tried this out with my little thing
And stayed with my woman
And my little thing stayed a little thing

I'm only human
I went unfaithfully to bed
With my next-door neighbour
And we had a great big thing together
And she's in labour.

—Poor old Plato.

Angela Kirby

Through The Window

With cautious stance and slow advance,
To take a chance and have a glance;
Through the window.

To look and see, what lies beneath.
To find the key to what might be;
Through the window.

What pleasure? What pain? What loss? What gain?
What power may reign? Whether mad or sane;
Through the window.

A bottle, a bong, a poem, a song.
Weak, wise or strong, a right, a wrong;
Through the window.

A cheery light, a cold dark night,
A friend, a fight. It's all in sight;
Through the window.

A passage, a road, an urge to stroll,
Along the channel to the soul;
Through the window.

Anthony Oldroyd

Too Late

I never really knew just how much I loved him.
Until it was too late.
I would give anything to have one last hour, one more minute
with him.
But it is too late.
To tell him that I loved him, miss him, need him.
But it is too late.
At night I talk to him in my head and ask him to appear in my dreams,
so I can tell him everything.
But there is just darkness, emptiness.
It is too late.
My only brother has gone from this world.
How could he leave us all behind.
I just want him to know that I love him.
It is too late.
I hope he can hear me on the other side.
I know in my heart he is with me all of the time.
It is definitely too late.

Victoria Williams

To A Soldier From A Mother

Congratulations on your passing out son.
You've proved what you can do.
I'm so very proud of you.
I hope that you are too.

When times are bad, and things get tough,
And when you think you've had enough,
You just sit down to have a rest,
It's off that butt, and do your best.

When all your cash is running out,
And when your corporal starts to shout,
It's keep on going up that hill,
Then on that square to do your drill.

As you go along, in your new career,
I will be thinking of you, to me you're very dear.
May you always be happy, whatever you choose to do,
But don't forget that I am here, and will be missing you.

Annette E. Walker

Understanding

How long will it take for us,
not to be afraid?
Afraid of life afraid of anything
that's new or different.
Fright gives way to hate!
When we overcome our fears
of things we don't understand,
we will cry tears of remorse for our actions.
Let the tears flow, for in each tear
there is an ocean of knowledge.
The tears will fall upon the soil and
give life to the flower of understanding,
which will blossom into peace.

John Wawman

Mist Upon The Water

See it swirling 'cross the water, dancing, drifting softly moving
Where it came from none can answer,
Where it goes a mystery also, see the mist upon the water
Prancing lightly, not a ripple as it passes by—no whisper
Not a sound but silence follows, eerie mist upon the water.

At the sunrise then it exits till the next night it re-enters
Lightly touching and caressing as it dances on the water
Clothing everything with mystery
As all night life watches spellbound,
Sees the mist upon the water
Playing on its flimsy surface, moving smoothly as it passes
By the banks along the river where each night it comes caressing
Every leaf on tree or bushes overhanging as they will do
Meeting mist upon the water
Till again the sun comes driving
Gentle mist back into hiding from its light.

Valmai McLaren

Youth

Years of my youth
Where have you gone,
Why did you pass so swiftly
I had only just learnt,
The lessons you taught.
When you went away and left me.
The heady sweetness of first glance love
The exquisite pain of parting
The chance to put the whole world right
I had my soul and heart in.
Adolescent shyness
Emotions now controlled.
I learnt your lesson too well youth
You taught me to grow old.

L. B. Dunn

Sunlight: Light Of Life

Sunlight bathing blossoms evokes a baby's smile.
Sunlight silvers ocean waves, mile after lilting mile.
The first is pure but fleeting, ravaged by age and rain;
The latter for millennia has soothed the soul in pain.

Sunlight warms the stubbled cheek of a tired vagrant,
Sunlight coaxes the snug cat from fireside to a fragrant
Bed of herbs. Both bask there in the golden warmth,
   rich as a millionaire;
Luxurious in his glossy coat the feline grooms his hair.

Sunlight brushes wheat fields with blood–red poppy highlights.
Sunlight gilds the hay rolls, when summer yields to autumn nights.
The fields sway rhythmic to the welcome cooling breeze.
Then squirrels dream of copper carpets shed from bronzed trees.

Sunlight midnight–mirrored casts shadows on the snow.
Sunlit moonbeam-traitors show night-flight bombers where to go.
The moon, a cold relation, stares back from wintry sky.
Yet, when Sun's last explosion bursts, both good and bad shall die.

Janet Lancaster

'Dunblane'

Dunblane, Dunblane, Dunblane,
The town that dare not speak its name,
Sixteen children murdered in Dunblane,
Whose to blame, whose to blame?

Dunblane, Dunblane, Dunblane,
The narrow–minded bigots in the Frame,
The Boy Scouts certainly did not play the Game,
Were they blame? To blame, to blame,

Dunblane, Dunblane, Dunblane,
Where are the Trick-cyclists, hiding, it's their Game,
Hiding in the woodwork, while others take the Blame,
Prescribing drugs such as Vallium, Prozac, Priadel and
Mogadon,
   all great Names,

Dunblane, Dunblane, Dunblane,
Do they bear the Blame,
Where sixteen children died in vain,
Were they Mothers to blame? To blame, to blame. (Amen)

R. Paterson-Howe

War

Against them, with them, fighting for our lives,
see through them, renew them,
the truth hitting us like knives.

The danger crept up behind us, causing
our instincts to jump into power, victory
so near we could smell it, but fear
is so audible that in our hearts it was louder.

Looks between friend and foe were
exchanged as we joined together in sweet
harmony, a day to be remembered, a
moment in time, a fight to be forgotten,
as friends combined.

Louise Olsthoorn

The Boy And The Picture

A young boy stood, at a big store window.
His face was pressed to the glass.
Nobody looked or took any notice.
As the busy crowds went past.
He was gazing at a picture. In a gold painted wooden frame.
At the bottom of that picture.
Jesus Christ was signed the name.
The boy didn't have any money. That picture for to buy.
And yet from that little picture. The boy couldn't take his eye.
Then suddenly a stranger came. He was an old man.
Bent and lame.
He said, if you cannot buy that picture son,
I will give you one the same. Then reaching deep into his pocket.
The picture that he took out.
Was same picture as in the window.
Of that there was no doubt.
He gave the boy the picture. And said, do not, thank me son.
Then, without further conversation, he vanished into passing throng.
The boy looked at the picture
His gaze he couldn't take from
That face in that little picture was the face of the man, just gone

John Joe Finn

The Promise

Melancholy moments of seclusion untold
Clandestine lover, exciting and bold,
Feelings fluctuate—ecstatic then low
Emotional exhaustion much worse than physical blows.

Love should be easy but not just a game
To play with a heart only leads to pain.
The promise of devotion and the touch of a breast
Makes this fleeting happiness much worse—so you've guessed

I'll offer my heart, my life and my all,
To give your life meaning, fulfilment and joy. Yet so tall

Is the order, but I promise it true.
Only in return I need all of you!

Friend am I, friend indeed
A transitional phase which creates a need,
A need in me which you fulfil
Yet keep my distance—I have to still.
To be too close restores my belief
In you and I—our sweet release.

Cathy Pownall

Red

Will Scarlet deep in the forest, locked in Robin's embrace.
Red–breasted Robin, glaring from the wintered holly bough.

Crimson berries joined in a jewelled wreath, pierced by the
    eyes of Christmas.
The ears of the fox, like flags, in a field of growing corn.

Scarlet fingered autumn burning fox-brush leaves in mist–filled
    silence.
Poppies, dancing in their millions, remembering no wars.

Mahogany eyes of the Oak King, hair aflame, running across
    the heathered hill tops.
Rosebuds garnered in the rusted morning, no modesty
    amongst them.

Ruby mouth of the Beast, blood on his lips, covering you with kisses;
Rage in his eyes, like flickering firelight, he breaks you open in
    the wine–dark shadows.

Cranberry dawn stains the cheeks of the young girl
Blushing at midnight's remembered heat and the hand of her
    lover on her naked breast.

Vines, drunk with power, hold the rosy grapes to ransom.
In the orchard, russet fruit dreams on the branch and the wild
    strawberry trembles in the ground.

Brazen copper sun, painted limbs away, sleeps abandoned on
    a coral ocean.
Fiery comet dragon lifts his garnet and whispers, "I wait for
    the King".

Agnes Meadows

Life's Road

Looking back down life's long road,
With crossroads, twists and turns,
Reaching back to distant times,
Where a faded memory burns.

When young we skip along that road,
We live on hopes and dreams,
Our walks direct, so smooth and straight,
Edged by laughing streams.

We age, we trip, the road can narrow,
We're slowed by troubles and woe,
Just as suddenly it will widen,
And we're happy as we go.

We will fall down, we will get hurt,
The road will twist with sorrow,
But as we walk over life's next hill,
We see a new tomorrow.

If we're lucky the road will be really long,
And as we reach the final bend,
Maybe we'll see a welcome light,
To mark our journey's end.

Gail Guest

Ripples

Bobbing about, floating along
Listening to many birds in full song
The crackle of a twig, the bob of a bait
The ripples that surround us, happy us make

Time is enduring, time can stand still
Look for time in the ripples that water surface fill,
But underneath the ripples, deep water flows along
The same way for centuries—there nothing can be wrong.

The main things go on, deep and unperturbed
The same as forever, nothing new nor disturbed
The ripples in our life may seem like deep water flowing
But underneath the ripples, it's the same way we're going

Ripples seem like torrents in a turbulent life
Weaving in and out like currents, creating wear and strife
But it's all on the surface in the Grand Plan of things
Can we stop and study ripples—there's nothing new that it brings.

Cecily Mellon

Special Gifts

A petal on a rose.
The sun in the sky.
Water flowing, a sweet apple pie.

The wing of a rainbow.
The bleat of a lamb.
A spider that's spinning whenever she can.

The sound of laughter.
Friends making plans.
A kind word spoken, and to open hands.

Gemma Ierston

A Evening Stroll

Sweet fluted bird song drifts to my ears
Angry rain–filled clouds ready to shed their tears
Age–old trees sway in the warm breeze
While the fragrance of nature tickles my nostrils to tease
Shades of green all around
Rolling hills and meadows I've found
Ears of wheat gracefully move to and fro
Striving for the light so they can grow
Hedgerows of hawthorn cropped short and stout
The day is almost over, there's no doubt
Rich golden colours of the dying light
Reds and yellows, it's a beautiful sight
Soft mother earth beneath my feet
Countryside and nature,
    Oh what a treat!

Michael J. Abbiss

If Tears Could Talk

If we could store away,
Each tear that fell,
In years to come,
What tales they'd tell.

Tales of pain, loneliness, hardship, anger, loss,
Tales of joy, happiness, delight,
Let's not forget,
Laughter day or night.

Oh!—if we only could store away,
Each tear that fell,
In years to come,
What tales they'd tell!

No pieces put together,
Of happenings that might have been,
Tales of misery of exuberance,
People truly felt within.

If tears could enlighten posterity,
Of what brave faces have hidden,
You and me,
Will go down in history.

Linda Jolly

A Country Lane . . . 1916

I sat upon a public bench
Eroding time of day
Observing of a lad and maid
That happened along that way

Their happiness it seemed serene
Alone, 'twas theirs to share
In two short years that soon would pass
The war their hearts would tear

Like all the youth who faced the truth
His country's pride to save
This proud and honest cornish lad
Now sleeps in unmarked grave

When news arrived one August morn
Those left behind were gathering corn
The village mourned for weeks to pass
None more than that poor broken lass

And so at last the years have passed but memories long remain
Of that fine lad and his fair maid who walked that fragrant lane

Yet sometimes when in wintertime, whilst walking through the rain
The maid still blinded by her love stands waiting in the lane

Julian Nicholls

Sunrise Sacrifice

Standing at the edge
The sun rising
Spreading warm rays of fire on the horizon.

What has gone before
The moon
Will hold secret and never tell.

A reassuring touch,
Knowledge withheld.

A curse
A cry
A sacrifice,

Or a dream.

The dawning of a new day.
New hopes, a new life

One more thing for the
World to put behind it
One more thing to forget ever happened

As if in answer, the sun
Floats nearly full on the horizon

Warming the land, last hold cold by the night.

Cat Hogan

Greeks (Ancient And Older)

The Olympian gods were a restless crew,
Drinking Nectar with nothing to do.
Zeus flung his bolts to the barren ground
'Mid thunderous applause from all around.

What was he doing? The Great God Pan;
Tootling his pipes and scattering ban.
His eerie music would addle the brain,
Causing panic now and again.

Narcissus, a lad of fair complexion,
Fell in love with his own reflection!
Confused he moped, hour after hour.
He ended his life; as a pretty flower.

The Argonauts with Jason in front,
Sailed through the fateful Hellespont.
He took by stealth, the Golden Fleece
Then set off home to his native Greece.

Where have all the Trojans gone?
Sent to Hades one by one, by a wooden horse on little wheels.
All for Helen! And Achilles' heel.

. . . Beware of Greeks bringing gifts!

V. R. Fisher

Phantom Horse

Galloping along the moonlit shore,
With the wind the phantom tore.
As the stars glittered in the sky,
Beauty shone in the horses eye.
As for the rider the wind in her hair,
When she rode him, she had no cares.
For only the girl rode this Phantom Horse,
Only she could ride with such a mighty force.
They were joined as one in the moonlit night,
As the magic of the moon shone down so bright.
And as the dawn came, the girl felt fear,
As the Phantom, beauty disappeared.

Suzanne Louise Wyatt

Life's Joys And Fears

Life, a coil of joy and fear inextricably bound,
What is there in its seething womb to be found,
To enlighten God's meaning to the world?
Why is it in this coil we are hurled
In unending, stretching forever space,
That men make their goal, their race,
To pinpoint their purpose, man's reason for life,
Yet within the mind, the heart, there is strife?
We are stretched and drawn, while the soul curls
Inwards, strung like a string of pearls
Life is the attraction of joys and fears,
Swinging, like pendulum, between laughter and tears.
It is the struggling seed bursting its shell,
It is man's escape to heaven from hell,
An endless vortex of healing,
A whirlpool of feeling.
Christ knew, as nailed to the Cross,
He could see the good within the dross,
That we might know in the final extremity,
That in the circle there is eternity.

Sylvia Robinson

Destination Unknown

You? Just spawned by chance
     at some bleak darkened point of what-will-be.
Or? Is there yet without,
     perhaps, a somewhere-God who gently smiled;
     and at your birth, turned fragile time aside,
     caught at your hand to ease the each-day pain,
     held out his arms for shelter, sorrow—warmed.
     (Or—saddened—knew your need to turn away?)
Who yet, at last, may gift
     some silvered sleep, and hushed eternity.

Margot Collingbourn-Beevers

The Bridge O'er The Humber

On surmounting the bridge o'er the Humber
My amazement and not just surprise,
The kaleidoscope view of the north bank,
The wonder, the new titled "North Humberside".

On entry from the western approaches
The crocus that first caught my eye,
Such wonders the gardener produced there,
And grandeur, I'm sure that no-one would deny.

On entry from the north and east likewise,
The colourful array's just the same,
With the hue of the red and white roses.
Such beautiful scenes there called "North Humberside".

But sweeter than all the roses,
A shopping spree there's just the same,
With humour and excellent service,
I'm sure you'd appreciate "North Humberside".

Arthur Cattle

Struggle

Mean dreams of tomorrow keep me alive,
I will buy new fasteners for the gates to stop
them rattling in the wind.

A new shed will cover the gardening tools
Another corner will be neat,
On and on these small additions push life—
to the next pay day.

And the dreams, the real dreams die
before they become reality.

Elaine Booth

The Legacy Of Love

I close my eyes and see again
The reverie of youth's sweet summer:
The mist of dreams, the warmth of hopes
Innocent and not yet faded;
When the past was so full
Of love and life and laughter
How can the present excel, or even compare?

When the source of inner strength lies in the long-ago,
Of what does "Now" consist?
How to field life's vicissitudes
When its inspiration lies in love, long lost,
But truly cherished?
Its eternal flame radiates an all–embalming power:
The strength to bestow that love on those around me,
Who, while no less deserving,
Do not speak the language of my soul.

A clarity of vision,
Comprehension of silent emotions fighting for expression—
Such are love's legacy.

Madeleine Lewis

Lady Nature

The wondrous sights that we can see
When we look with open eyes
The grass that when in spring is green
The clouds that race the skies
Boats that on the rivers float
Trees that are green and shady
Feathered friends with song in throat
Oh! Nature what a lady.
When winter snow is gently falling
Robins with breasts all aglow
Little fir trees from the woods are calling
Green branches tipped white, what a show
Then darkness comes over the earth too soon
There are only the stars and a silvery moon
Still we can see the sights though shady
Oh! nature what a lady

W. Taberham

Alzheimer's

I see I'm told with saddened eyes
An alien world around me
I have been set from the
Stresses and strains of life
I see no evil
And feel no pain
A touching hand comforts me
My hands reach out
But I know not who's there
I live only for this moment
As the last I have forgotten
My butterfly existence is with me constantly
Forever flitting from one dream to another
Never ever to settle again
Until the time has come
To be at peace with thee
And my being is restored.

Pearl Simmons

The Calm Before A Storm

A cool crisp breeze rustles through the trees,
Like a fall of rain rippling water.
Dancing among the hidden branches,
Tossing and tumbling between the leaves.

A savage cloud lurks in the distance,
Darkly threatening the calm of day.
Pushing away the lighthearted clouds,
Sinister and evil in its stance.

A roll of thunder trembles the sky,
Like a knelling drum before a war.
Twisting the clouds to figures of stone,
Spiralling quickly to the storm's eye.

Anna Packham

The Shark

The shark,
Dynamic yet cold–hearted, dominant yet callous,
The unpredictable beast of the deep,
Unmoved by the attention, people from the world above.
It surges through the water, as its superiority overwhelms you,
A smuggest grin wipes over his face,
As the elegant master's greeted by a bound of silence.
But the shadowed side still being concealed,
The frenzied invasion still to come, yes, the psychopath of the deep.
The arrogance makes your nose twitch,
As your sense of protection is distorted.
Silence, quiet.
Its eyes glimmer like a camera flash,
As they drop into line. With the unsuspecting prey
It waits,
Now, making its move under a blanket of tranquillity,
The prey is neutralized.
Its body swings like a tree branch, in a force 9 gale
The stomach is satisfied, as it swims its way back
To the unknown.

Jamie Lowry

Shipping With Time

I am here alone with my pen
Letting it take over the page
It seems a good idea to write
Silently, I'm expressing my rage
The world around me busily works
While I'm just writing away.
Everyone's busy doing something exciting,
While on this page my thoughts do stray.
I hate when I'm stuck with nothing to write
While all the world does bloom
But now of course, I would be stuck
Right in the centre of all the gloom
Well, how maybe I'll stop and think of
Something quietly happening.
The kettle singing on the rage of the fire
Lit like a light with little desire

Olive Kelly

Summer Seasons

Summer is here once again
brighter I thought it would be
As I sit in the garden each day
I look around what do I see
You're not there anymore
A picture in my mind I adore

Oh my darling the flowers are bright
The grass is greener and in sight
Yet in my heart the garden is bare
For you're not sitting in your chair
My thoughts for you will never die
As I sit in the garden I look at the sky.

Oh my darling I wish you were here.
To sit in the garden beside me dear
We use to sit in the bask of the sun
The two of us had laughs and fun
No longer are we together
You've gone at peace forever.

Mary Gilfillan

"Her Fate"

You looked at me with your yellow, bright eyes
And purred aloud from your content. Your fur
so long, your pretty face, the old facade.
Past years have battered your frame, so unfair.
You never asked for him to come and so
You hissed and snarled and spat at him; beware
The poor new other cat. He felt so low
Because he lacked a mother's love from you.
Had done nothing to deserve this strong hate.
So now the other cat does not feel blue.
And now you see you crafted your own fate.
No solace for you in your latter years,
And all because you loved to box his ears.

S. E. Williams

Memories of a Country Lad

Memories can be sweet when as a child,
You'd run and play in meadows wild.
Through long grass you'd run.
Everything then was so much fun.
Time to watch the kingfisher on riverside.
From my home made hide.
Or lay on riverbank to tickle trout.
When rested, on do go to something new.
Worries in those days were so few.
Scrumping, running, playing fox and hounds
Scampering through thickets, jumping streams,
Were all part of childish dreams.
As a boy I had many plans in mind.
A shepherd I thought I'd be 'cause they're so kind.
A fireman was to be my next desire.
To race the roads to douse a savage raging fire.
Many miles I've measured.
So many things and thoughts I've treasured.
None more so than those I gained when I was just a boy.

L. Smith

Falling . . .

Fall from the sky like the drop of rain,
Fall to the ground from an aeroplane,
Fall from flight like the wounded dove,
But never ever fall in love.

Fall from a tree to the ground below,
Fall to the grass like the flake of snow,
Fall from the hand like a childhood toy,
But never fall in love with a boy.

Fall from a boat into the sea,
Fall like a seed from the sycamore tree,
Fall to the earth from the clouds up above,
But never, ever, fall in love.

Sarah-Jayne Maylin

Pain At War

We are recognized by our filthy clothing and worn-out
expressions,
As we stagger back from the front line a tremor shoots the
ground as bombshells hit the floor,
many of us cannot walk,
Our feet leave a trail of blood as we stumble and try to move,
We cannot hear or think as the gas-shells blast behind us,
The gas is pouring around me . . . help!
As we force the gas mask on we hear a cry,
A man tries to seize a gas mask . . . but he is too late,
The gas is thickening now and my comrades have disappeared,
You could not imagine what it was like to carry a friend in your
arms as he was withering and dying in agony,
His face seemed torn apart and blood dropped from his injured leg,
Listen to me my friends,
What I have experienced is that it is not glorious to die for
your country,
But pain and agony,
For when a friend is to die in your arms . . . you lose all hope.

Matilda De Santis

A Focolarino

Only a ripple I on the time stream,
While ages roll,
Drifting on in the space scheme,
Yet with a goal.

Only a unit I of the man-team
From pole to pole,
Toiling on with but one theme—
To play my role.

Less than the glow-worm, I to the sunbeam
That lights God's scroll,
Praying on that my love gleam
May light the whole.

Pamela Baker

The Wreckers

The Polly May, she danced away upon a stormy
sea. Pitching and tossing her decks awash as
She made her way heading for Cornwall a
cargo of china clay. Upon the coast there
shone a light like a guiding star it must
be the port of par yelled the skipper who
later looked bewildered and not amused
when he heard the news for it was the
wreckers that lit the guiding star that
led them to the rocks instead of par.

C. J. Browne

Two True

A Gemini I, beware, I may not be what I seem.
Here, there, everywhere, playing the fool, feeling
the fool. No one laughs.

My clothes are fine I think, and different.
Different is the word, echoes the retort. Put on
something that matches.

I am never understood or appreciated it seems.
Perhaps my twin personality is too much for
mere single minded mortals.

I fear for the future, yet live for today. Jack
of all trades, master of none. A pessimistic
optimist.

So much love, locked within, beware the twin
who holds the key. I am day and night, past
and present. I am what I am.

Like the moon, I am within reach. I can and
have been walked upon, yet no one is my master.

Look up to me my loved ones, as you would
the moon. That is all I ask, and in return as
one, I will watch over you.

John H. Hancock

315

Love's Torment

It all seemed so true,
Not a care in the world except for each other.
The time went by and no longer could we be.
Separated from the heart, your words meant so much.
Vanished from sight but not in mind.

In our eyes we would always be one.
Thoughts faded to just dreams,
Wishes that could never be, even in love.
Pulled away from reality.
Fooling only ourselves that there could be anything.

Now we are far apart,
But somehow deep inside I can't let go,
My days are filled with shadows of love,
My dreams are only of you.
Feelings inside I can't explain.

The things you said, the way you said them.
My heart will always be there.
In another time, another place,
Maybe things would be different.
But you're too far away to know.

Andrea Spragg

The Invisible Dark

Sunbeams stream through riven clouds
And kiss the leaves of bright–tinged trees,
And scatter pools of dappled light
Upon the grateful, grassy ground;
But Darkness still remains.

For what bright beam of sun or lamp
Could e'er remove the Dark of bitter, selfish hearts,
Which, unrelenting in their strife,
Stride arrogant on earth's fair fields
And cast their shadows like a blot
O'er every human throng?

Though every inch of earth should floodlit be,
And every natural shadow chased away
'Til all things should be naked to the eye;
Still this Darkness, this dripping, foetal
Darkness of the human heart would still remain.
And still the crawling slime of subtle stealth
Which oozes in the dark of selfish minds
Would leave its bitter trail
Of emptiness and hollow death.

Martin Clacker

Lady Of The Marshlands

The sylph she rises from her watery rest,
Her silver hair floats like a cobweb veil.
Her gown hung heavy on the dank, still, marsh.
Is she of this world or was she sent?
Hypnotic, she glides and weaves,
Drawing me close into her lair.
With her mystic charm,
I am rendered spell-bound and silent.
Though I yearn to flee, still I remain.
The wind is her consort,
And they unite in their power;
Stealthily they dance a heady spell,
Enticing, seducing, they are one!
She stops and beckons me in—
Such dangerous beauty
No mortal could resist.
Intoxicated and weak of will,
The 'mystic' is victorious.
I fall into the ether,
Down, down, ever deeper . . .

Julie-Ann Hall

The Lost Years

This is for you Tina, and also for you Wayne
To help ease your heartaches, and some of your pain
I want you to know, that over all those "lost" years,
I have loved you both always, and I have cried many tears

Can't tell you how I felt, Tina, when you opened your door,
I thought you would say "Sod off, we don't need you anymore",
But when you both gave me a big hug, and a kiss,
I felt, deep inside, it's been worth waiting, for, has all this,

All those years of searching, not knowing where to look,
It was like starting to read, but never finishing a book,
But now we're back together, I couldn't be more glad,
and I'm so very happy, that you still love your old dad,

I know over the years, you have both lived your own life
and our Wayne, has got Kerry, a cracking good wife,
with a beautiful daughter, Rebecca, and Karl their son
But I know that your lives haven't always been such fun

But now I have found you both, I want you to know,
I won't lose you again, I won't ever let you go.
I want us all to be happy, and never again sad,
As I'm just coming to terms, of being called granddad!

Barry L. Ravey

Mother

You made my childhood so safe and secure
Fond memories of you, will long endure . . .
Photo albums do help recall and renew
The wonderful bond I shared with you

Your example was like a shining light . . .
Even though you were no longer in sight
Everything about you was so good and true
One of the treasured and special few . . .

I learnt about caring, courage and tolerance
The wisdom you taught me was common sense
In this tribute to you, it must really be said . . .
I learnt to cope with the difficult years ahead.

To your very devoted, family and friends
The thoughts of your goodness never ends . . .
How we all miss your love, ever sweet smiling face
Your qualities were so rare, and you had such grace . . .

You died too soon, far too young and yet
We could not possibly ever really forget . . .
For there is not anywhere else another . . .
You were the best and most perfect mother.

Sylvia Davis

Joys Of A Pianist

The piano is my instrument
It is the best by far,
I love to touch the ivory keys
From the "A's" right up to the "G's"
Back down the scale to the end of the bar.

The piano gives me pleasure
With feeling you cannot measure,
An uplifting untold as countless melodies unfold
That I most certainly treasure
In every hour or fleeting moment of my leisure.

Piano concertos of by-gone composers
Have us rooted to our seat
Which gives our souls an uplift
So very hard to beat
In this world is welcomed as a truly splendid treat.

I really enjoy a Sonata, by Beethoven one of the best,
A Noctune by Chopin, an Etude by Liszt
Some of which rather tricky, not a note must be missed
For when a piece is complete the reward is so sweet
The repertoire is ready a special guest to greet.

Betty Dora Tye

For My Dad

The darkness is my enemy,
Whilst daylight is my friend.
The pain that grows inside me
I know will never end.

In dreams my father comes to me
And then he disappears
The need I have to speak to him
Just brings out all the tears.

I think of all he taught me,
The examples that he set.
He cared and loved me deeply,
Made sure all my needs were met.

I'd love to see him once again
He'd never have believed,
The support my family have given me
In all that I've achieved.

Just to seek advice from him and open up my heart,
There is so much that I have to say, after all these years apart.

So, Dad, if you can hear me, although you've long been gone.
I love and miss you deeply, from your very lonely son.

Derek Homer

Dunblane Children

God, take the children of Dunblane,
and keep them in your care,
we know they'll be alright,
as long as you are there.

Innocent little people with charm,
cheekiness and sunshine smiles,
just memory for the parents,
the families who ask why? And cry . . .

The families will never forget,
the hearts that always ache,
the children's lives that could have been
of the lives that he did break.

So rest in peace our children,
we prey and think of you,
in heaven you'll always have each other,
in everything you do.

Mummy's here and Daddy to,
Oh, the tears they have cried,
be brave little ones and think of them,
and they will be by your side.

Suzanne Hellawell

And They Say There Is No God!

I'm lying here on my bed,
Thinking of the words that someone said,
There is no God was what they told me,
How can they say that, I just cannot see.

As I lie here completely at peace
The sun is shining like a golden fleece,
The world is full of beautiful things, too many to list,
Please tell me how can God not exist?

The birds are singing so sweetly outside,
Through the air the butterflies glide,
The air smells fresh, the sky is clear
It's easy to tell that summer is here.

Some people say an explosion created all this,
I'm sorry to disappoint you but that's just a myth,
The true creator of all things is our Lord above,
All glory and admiration must go to him along with our love.

Andrea Armstrong

(The Blighted Nuptial) Valediction

Now nature's yearly secrets are shrouded over,
Pregnant mother, unfolding still
Her never ending mysteries.
Holding mature dreams still dear,
Dark Adonis romp his Eastern Star.
She was here in mine arms,
Yea, in this affectionate grove . . .
Giving life—thus receiving in return . . .
The busy bee and the red rose.
Now she must out of clay return . . .
Like a babe plucked
From its mother's womb
Prematurely, severing
The knotted bond ingrained.
She is wither my soul
Is well–nourished, feeding
Mine brain, my life!
Consolation reposes in a swift
Reunion of the sprites and souls
Wherein my heart is gone.

Babatunde Olumide Ibitoye

Valentine's Day

When a young man's fancy turns to love,
His heart is beating loudly,
He pens a message to his love,
And hopes he's done it proudly.

Such feelings strongly overtake,
Whiles common sense and pride,
The heart has powers we cannot fake,
A power we cannot hide.

Love conquers more than that they say,
The air is full of joy,
Special modes fulfil that day,
For every girl and boy.

Even in nature, there's no holds barred,
Wee birds begin to sing,
They choose a mate, and then are paired,
To herald a new made spring.

February the fourteenth, we play our part,
To win the ultimate prize,
To win and woo that loving heart,
For the lady we optimize.

George A. Gunn

Untitled

Are country ways so pleasing as some folk like to say?
Are song birds singing sweetly to greet the dawn of day?
And do the tiny animals live lives of peace and quite?
Or are they just a dinner for the predators of night?

When birds sing out their morning song it is to stake a claim
And warn all and sundry off their territorial domain
From the largest to the smallest, all display their rights
But still end up a tasty morsel for animals of plight.

The sun is stopped its right to shine on earth's responsive clay
By concrete, Tarmac and housing plots of man's industrious play
Sure nature will repair itself if left to natures ways
And balance justice hope and love will reign without dismay.

Leaves and fruit and branches of stately trees so rare,
Are working daily to repair the wastes, and oxygenating the air,
Which helps the life of all in need, preserving the living strain
For so to start territorial posturing all over again.

These are the country ways my friend with no regard for life
Of trees or birds or animals subjected to life's daily strife,
And if you think this daunting listen to the history of man.
And think of life's meaning instead of an awesome country plan.

Ann Griffiths

Fallen Beauties

Branches swaying too and fro
As seedlings thrive on the floor below
Sun seeps through springs new leaves
As dew drops fall upon young trees.

The seedlings grow up tall and strong
with thick trunks and branches long
As they reach an amazing height
They come to the end of their treacherous fight

As strangers come, they fell the trees
The trees that once blew in the breeze
It takes no time to chop them down
And then were left with open ground.

This once most beautiful sight
Is now a sad and serious plight.

J. Tointon

Baton Of Life

Man and his image
Mirrored runners, mirrored race
Beyond shining childhood days
Take contrary pace

Till the Reapers eternal harvest

The heir apparent inherits
Title to the deeds
Till he invests his issue
His own immortal seed

Why thy cruel wisdom
Oh universal sage
That a man should learn his depth of love
Only at his father's grave

Jerf Roberwitz

Magpies

Magpies, leave my garden—Please!
Black and white robbers, vagabonds and thieves.

Your loud raucous screams are really quite scary,
It leaves my garden birds timid and wary.

You dive-bomb and harass my ring necked Dove
This gentle bird is my 'special' love

You chase Sparrows, Robins and Blackbirds too,
Only Squirrels and Wood Pigeons will stand up to You

Oh, you have brought me your babies,
Squeaking and beguiling

Their quaint, playful antics
Really just keep me smiling.

And, you've dipped bread in the water to soften
I have to forgive you,

But Please, don't come so Often!

Pam Bowyer

Decree Nisi For Daddy

Little Girl
You hold his fears in your eyes.
A simple smile shreds his heart
still hesitant with decisions taken
over many long yesterdays.

Laughter that delights him when you're there,
he uses blade-like when alone
to slice a guilt ridden soul
Lost in an embryonic stillness.

Forgive his trespasses Little Girl.
He seeks a self
that yearning has taught him exists
when the whispering grew so loud
it hurt his ears.

Sarah Jane Ford

A Botanical Wonderland

There is Lily Of The Valley, and Forget-Me-Nots to see,
There are daffodils by Wordsworth, and orchids for brides to be,
Lobelias, dahlias, tulips, and gladioli on the ground,
Carnations always seem to spread, their beauty all around.
Children making daisy chains, it fills your heart with glee,
Petunias, violets, and buttercups, what a sight to see,
The crocus shows its lovely head even as the cold wind blows,
But the one which means the world to me is a beautiful
lustrous rose.
Love was more than a word to me, it became a way of life,
Upon the day, my dearest Rose, that you became my wife,
In every year that's passed since then, you've blossomed,
bloomed, and grew,
Your love and strength and fortitude, have always seen us through.
The six small seedlings that we bred, are growing day by day,
Susan, Edward, Margaret, maturing in every way,
Matthew, Marc and Katie, have still to bloom and shine,
But with patience, love, and tender care, they will, to the end of time
There are two other flowers growing, and in a not too distant day,

They'll have the joy of their offspring, for such is nature's way.

Edward Allan

The Debatable Land

Come freend, let's ower this cranky stile,
And make our way tae windygyle,
Where man an' beast sae often met,
Tae hae their spiel on matters prest,
But, wheesht, ah see the peewit fly,
Disturbed by reivers curdlin' cry,
An' could that be the gathering bent,
On some cauld mission hardly kent?
Look, freend! Ahint the mist and moor,
That's surely Willie and a' his crew,
Thundering ower the heather braes,
Intent on mendin Percy's ways,
Look! See the twa hae made tae speak,
It chills the blood, the pact they keep,
Fur sleekit foes are headin nigh,
The Scots are doomed an' sure tae die,
Let's haste and fire the beacon set,
Forewarned, they may yet flee the nest,
The walls of Cessford Keep will hauld,
Tae shelter them that wad be bold.

Elizabeth A. Shillinglaw

War

When you hear a gunshot and you are used to it
When you fear to go out,
When children play inside games
Instead of football and hopscotch,
When you see men in camouflage
Instead of casual or suits
When foreign items are rationed
And exist no more on the corner shop.
That my friend is war.

Thérèse Maxwell

Still Life ' . . . *Talking Of Michelangelo* . . . '

Shall these stones live, and preach their sermons still?
    Stern–browed Moses proclaims the rule of Law
And Justice, vision of a promised state.
    David-Apollo, motionless, vibrate
With sensuality, human and raw,
    Reflected aspect of the divine will.

Meanwhile, souls flocking to St. Peter's, pass
    The *Pieta* protected behind glass,
Lest any should defile the Christ in stone
    As cruelly as broken flesh and bone.

Trumpets of Law and Justice vainly blow,
    And human passions urgently cry out.
Grief, tenderness and pity whisper low,
    Of Hope, glimpsed dimly through the screen of doubt.

Terence A. Neal

Friend Or Foe?

Ruffled feathers seeking solace under the railway bridge,
Sad, squinty eyes, a look of hunger, perching on a ridge,
A coat of well worn feathers with a missing middle claw,
This pigeon is a sorry sight and looks so very poor.

His shelter may be dry but biting draughts can climb such heights,
Disturbed sleep is the norm due to sporadic bright car lights,
And often when he slips into his first dream of the night,
A train thunders up above and his stance is rocked by fright.

Tomorrow as you eat your lunch time sandwich in the park,
He'll flutter down, then sidle up, and beg or leave his mark,
He may not have the grace or the elegance of a swan,
But one thing is for certain, on this earth he does belong.

It's unfair to call them vermin, some pigeons carry post,
And others are kept for racing, in lofts as warm as toast,
Many guard Nelson's column in Trafalgar Square each day,
They're a part of our institution, preserve them I say!

Paul Andrew Younger

Uncle Jackson

Uncle Jackson my dear friend,
His house all tidy and neat.
Street–wise, clever and quick on his feet,
Yet quickly advancing in age.

Struggling with life, but understanding at heart,
His life's not suitable for him.
With acceptable qualifications but jobless still,
underneath I feel sorry for him.

But Jackson, reliable and strong with a brave face on,
Battles on through life's mysterious path,
With high standards and ambitions already set.
I wish him the best of luck.

To be a poet someday still,
His first publication just so near,
But yet not so clear.
He'll achieve it someday,
But meanwhile I still love him so.

Jayne Parkinson

A Moonlit Night

A tranquil peace swept o'er me
As I watched the changing scene.
The clouds that danced o'er a moonlit sky
Seemed reckless, yet serene.

The wind blew fresh against my skin
And I stood as on a stage,
And watched the sea toss up its foam
Upon the rocks beneath.

The beauty overwhelms me
As I gaze upon it all,
And the stars that flicker yonder
Hold a promise for us all.

Helen B. Lyon

Ode To A Sweet Old Lady

She's a sweet dear old lady who is now 84,
There's always a welcome at her front, or back door,
Contented and happy so loving and giving
She envies no others, that's her way of living,
She's a smile and good morning for all that she meets,
As she does her own shopping in her village street
She visits her neighbours to see they're alright
And prays for her loved ones at bed time each night
She's known heartache too, when her young son he died,
But bravely trod on as her teardrops she dried,
It's now 17 years since her husband passed on
But he's with her in spirit although he is gone
To Australia 2 daughters and son they did go,
Without fail, she writes them, each week I do know,
I'm really so proud, I'll not find another
Perhaps you have guessed, that she's my dear sweet mother.

Elizabeth Clark

Drivers

There are cars of every size and colour.
Jags, Volvos, and little Minis too
Lorries with their heavy loads travelling to and fro.
Or maybe to the nearest port for Calais
Or another European port.
Motorbikes that roar past them
At breakneck speed you could not catch them.

The drivers they are all different ages
Young ones who take corners on two wheels
Learner drivers with their instructors hoping their test not to fail
There are as many ladies driving as men now
But the men still think they are the bee's knees
There are coach drivers who take us to the seaside
And everyday the children to and fro from school
Some take us to town for shopping
Others the elderly on a mystery tour.

There are A.A. and R.A.C. drivers to help with breakdowns anywhere.
Police cars and their drivers when accidents occur
Ambulance men and ladies to move the injured
While fireman wait with engines ready, what would we do
without all these?

Ada Lilian Sidney

The Laughter In The Downstairs Room

I lay in the darkness at bedtime
and I talk to the Lord in my prayers
I forget all my childhood sufferings
and hear only laughter downstairs.

The wind angrily tugs at the window
the rain pushes hard on the pane
and I pray there will always be laughter
to stop it from happening again.

I think back to my loveless beginnings
to the mother I knew I once had.
Why did they take me away from her?
What was it I did that was bad?

I admitted to smashing that saucer
I was honest about kicking our John
I even said sorry to Sally
so please tell me what I did wrong?

Suddenly the laughter gets louder
and I know they will come for me soon.
God, please let me stay here forever
I love the laughter downstairs in that room.

Paul Saunders

"That First Peep"

There I sat in Grandma's room,
With a new sister on my knee.
I was alone in the afternoon
willing her to look at me.

Grown-ups were in the other room,
Sipping cups of tea.
I knew that it would end real soon,
And I did so want to see.

Then she quietly stirred a mite
And there for me to see—
Tiny hand clutching mine so tight,
She slowly gazed at me.

Those eyes they were a sapphire blue,
Two gems beyond belief,
She didn't cry, she didn't coo—
To my intense relief.

Her downy head craned back to see, she mouthed a rose-bud ooh . . .
I wondered "Does she want her tea?" 'Cos I was hungry too.

But no, we found it was her way, of waking up from sleep,
From then until this very day—my memories of that first peep.

Lynne Taylor

Imagine

Washed over with the waters of wonder,
Engulfed with the tide of feelings.
The nature of the land and sky forever changes,
With that of your heart and mind.
Drift with the magic of miles of space,
High and low, low and high.
Slide down the rainbow waterfall,
Cascading its pure colours down to the fields.
Fields of whispering, whispering grass,
Yellow, golden but swaying with the wind.
Clouded over with cotton wool clouds,
Casting a shadow the angry clouds.
Used to cleanse the make-up of the sky.
But a ray of hope, peace, it will blow over and
Again the sun will dance on the golden grass
Feeling free, a flying free, you're free
To wander beyond the huge mountains
And beyond, who knows what you might find.

Farzana Hakim

A Typical Tramp

In doorways and alley ways you'll find a tramp,
Sleeping in all the dirt, cold and damp.
Begging all day until there's no light,
Sometimes giving passer-bys a fright.

A homeless stranger begging off other strangers,
Thieves and kids adding to their dangers.
They steal from the tramps and run off in the dark,
Knocking over dustbins, making dogs bark.

The tramp will wake up quickly, his tin has disappeared,
Something has just happened that he's always feared.
All of his money has been taken away,
He'll move on now, there's no reason to stay.

He'll move on further to another place,
Looking along the streets for an empty space.
There he will start his begging again,
Until one day he'll die in bitter pain.

Gillian Kathleen Bell

A Pauper's Grave

The old man sat on cobblestone
with a tear in every eye.
A world that had no place for him
his only roof was the opened sky.

No one to care where he went to
he knocked on doors, for him no room.
Some misfortune took all from him
at night he slept beneath the pale moon.

In the rain, wind or sunshine
he sat there, his clothes all tore.
And in snow and frosty weather
upon his feet no shoes he wore.

He grew weary and weak from hunger
his face all wrinkled, old and grey.
Everyone ignored his begging
his home is now a pauper's grave.

Elizabeth Dunican

To A Grandson

Dedicated to Adam and Sam

One precious life enwrapped in mother's womb.
Awaits the call from nature to be born.
And in that fleeting time from dark to light.
Creates the joy of love and sheer delight.

So let the gods deal out with gentle hands.
A child who knows and understands
each crooked path that passes by,
and reflects its life without
a jaundice eye.

W. P. White

Untitled

Faraway land, calls to me
It's over mountain and over sea,
Will I drive or fly a plane,
To reach this land; with the burning flame
The fire burns, and all but consumes me,
And soon its resplendent powers turn me,
Over time and space its calls are answered.
As once again its halls and temples
Light the imagination, and filled with samples
Of Gods—Kings—Queens and Nobles
Tell of their doings, as in fables,
Unfold before me as is my right
As once again on some star bright night
Shall flights of fancy, return me too;
Like moonlight across the water flew
As thoughts return to those ancient times
When Pharaoh ruled, and that land was mine.

Ruth Littlecoh

Memories

Gardens looking pretty, as the summer sun does shine
As I see the children, who I wish were mine
Laughing as they play, in the summer sun
Again I wish that I, could have that much fun.

But I am too old, as I am getting on
And soon I think that I may well have gone
As my youthful days, have passed me by
And as I die, I will cry
Unless I end my life, in the summer sun
Watching the children of today, having so much fun.

Amanda Davison

The Storm

I watch the sunset.
Beauty climbs over me.
I watch the stars coming into our world.
They bring the moon.
He is their King, I watch the sunset.
Day meets night.
And colours wash together like a sea of happiness.
I watch the birds skimming the water suddenly a wave breaks
The sea of colours disappears and a grey colour comes over me.
The waves are great white horses running over the dark sea.
The wind is the horses' master. He and his power run wild.
Takes down all boats to the deep.
The whales and mermen are peaceful. So happy and fun.
But the storm is coming they run away from the wind into the deep.
They are away from him there.
Suddenly the sun gets out of her bed in the clouds.
She is the Queen of this world.
The wind said, "forgive me". But the sun said, "no".
So he is locked up in the sky.
The sun is his master.

Gemma L. MacKenzie

Tidiness

For the life that I have I thank the Almighty
But why dearest God could you not make me tidy?
I'd love to be tidy that you I can tell
But looking around at my bedroom, oh well
The table beside me is pretty you see
But the twenty things on it are needed by me
There's my phone and my lamp they're usual but then
Three perfumes, two face creams, two combs and three pens
The clothes that I've worn only once are not soiled
But I can't hang them back with the clean that they'd spoil
So they lie on the dresser heaped up on a pile
Till there are so many worn once I just have to smile
So many clothes that are just in between
None of them dirty, but none of them clean
On my dressing table the chaos runs wild
I wonder was I like this as a child
And so once again I ask the Almighty
Why dearest God did you not make me tidy?

Anne Btash

Letting Go

I think of you when autumn leaves are tumbling down,
I think of you when snow and ice lies all around.
And when the birds above begin to sing, calling out it's spring,
  it's spring.
I think of you.

I pray for you each night of every day,
Wishing you God's speed upon your way.
I pray your strength will face adversity, that he will bring you
  back to me.
I pray for you.

I need you more than words can ever show,
I have your love this much I know.
Although we are so far apart, you are forever in my heart.
I need you so.

I gave you life, so many years ago.
From a tiny child I watched you grow,
Tried to ease your every pain, till your sunny smile came back again.
I gave you life.

Came the day I let you go.
For I knew it had to be.
You were searching for your destiny, searching high and
searching low.
I let you go.

Doris E. Brown

Jelly Cupcakes . . .

Jelly cupcakes for breakfast
I can see from the wideness of your eyes
Your doubtfulness and surprise
You enjoy every bite

Up at 4:30 this morning
To make cupcakes for you,
This man,
To make sure you go
To work with an intimately warm tummy

Tonight the house will be empty again
A hungry plant you left on my window sill
Will breathe for you in your stead
A venus fly trap
Will protect me tonight
How welcoming!

I close the toothpaste tube
You left open this morning
"Old habits die hard"
Mum's words
She's right again, dammit

Amena Raghei

Adieu My Little One

I watch your little brave face,
With the happy smile that shall never wear off.
All my dreams have been shattered;
By the unfairness of Nature.

"Why?" I ask myself.
Why does it have to be you and not me?
Never shall I see you again
Until my frail body lies in my solemn grave.

How can life be so unfair?
All the joy and happiness you brought me.
Never had I been so happy in my entire life
As on the day you entered the world.

You were too beautiful to be described.
Once I held you in my arms,
I thought I had it all.
You lit my heart with joy.

All my pride and joy to be taken away
Leaving me with nothing but hurt and misery.
And though the power of death has severed us,
Know that my love for you shall always be greater.

Haddijatou Jack

A Dirge

Who will build homes for the homeless poor
For shelter is gone when the night is over
Where can they go? Even bread is do dear
And so dear are boots for the children's feet;
The path is perilous that they will meet
Ills will beset them on their weary way,
A warm luxury bath, wait "make their day"
Whilst hotels rise for the visitor's head
They will await a 'scarce' hospital bed;
Despair fermenting as an iron cage
Staring rise to thoughts of an inward rage,
Motorists so thoughtless, double and wild
Killing and maiming both adult and child,
Drug barons trap the wealth turn away young
Why wonder at the cause of millions lost
On the bottomless pit of the N.H.S. care!!

Ameliana Gee

Tranquillity

Linger awhile, unchain your mind and let your thoughts roam free.
Cast off the binding, cumbersome tensions
Which this complex society weaves unconsciously into our minds.
Unwind, like a gently flowing stream
Meandering its way downstream to unite with the tranquil lake
And is accepted as a mother retrieves her lost young.
And is enfolded into a loving secure embrace.
Yes! Tarry a while, hark to the sound of the dove
To the wood pigeon's wings beating then air
In a slow powerful thrust.
Wait! Did you not see the leaf fall from the tree!
Plucked by the fairy hand of mother nature's
Aide-de-camp, the breeze!
Think of its dainty descent to the emerald carpet awaiting below
Swirling, twirling, gliding, drifting freely,
Unchained, unfettered like the thoughts in your mind now.
Relax, and so find sanctuary in the all cleansing,
All healing remedy of—sleep.

Elizabeth Boultwood

Under Tow

Under tow
The rig groans with the to and fro
The TV is out and the phones are down
12 hour shifts, so there's till 9 to go
Smell of kerosene, rattle of chains
Is it any wonder big John is insane
And every day feels like Monday
The hum of the diesels, won't let you sleep
Not long till breakfast, at least you can eat
And everyday feels like Thursday
Try to count days, till you loose track of time
I'm only doing 3 weeks
Feels like a lifetime
My baby's got teeth now, so I've been told
Next time I see him, he's going to seem old
Eventually the day arrives, it's time to leave
Kerosene down draft like a summer breeze
And there's plenty smiling faces
As the rotor's twirl towards the beach

Kevin Cordiner

Tears

Tears like memories are hard to let go,
When they meander down the aspect of your face they grow.
They reflect and glisten with such magnificence and grace,
It's hard to cry in this beautiful place.

Tears are juices of the soul,
They link our hopes and fears,
for tomorrow and yesteryear.
As they play with time,
Peace withers away.
Now the tears flow passionately strong,
Who is right?
Who is wrong?

Olivia Briody

321

The Storm

How I long to reach the top of the hill before the storm breaks,
Bees plundering honey from the heather leave a humming in
    their wake,
The squelch of my feet on the springing turf, as upwards I go,
To watch this thunderous sky, which hangs so low.

The sudden startled cry of the Grouse, as they raise their
    powerfu wings,
Soaring upwards, calling to the curlew, make for safety, before
    the storm begins,
In the pervading stillness of the fell side is the eerie call of the
    'Kite',
Plovers and blackcock winging their way across a sky dark as night.

Forked lighting shoots across the sky, like applause when a
    Fencer Strikes,
The thunder roared like a rock, splitting with dynamite,
I stood watching the falling mist, knowing it to be rain,
Pelting down with needle like precision, making the countryside
    smell sweet again,

Across the valley the sky was peeping blue,
Starting the coloured Rainbow in all its glorious hue,
On the hillside the spicy smell of flowers and plants so rare,
Filled my nostrils with an invigorating air.

Pink flowers of the Heather close against the storm,
Cloaking in the secrets, where the Grouse eggs are born,
The scent of these with bracken across the fells and hills,
All go to make a stormy Fellside, the most beauteous of things.

Gwineth Brown Willis

Song Of The Wind

Coasting, tight–tillered, full speed, brimming sail,
Harnessing, channelling, fanning the flame.
Thinking, uncovering opening . . . then;
Nothing. Change tack.
Again;
Laterally, subliminally, subtly, when,
Passion and focus, full–hearted and fine.
Loosing . . . no holding, caressing so tight;
Night:
Still keep,
Hoping to find the treasure,
From the love inside.
Taking the measure of the shell,
Finding the keys,
Changing the locks.
Reaching the crypt,
In the cavernous depths.
Gently unfolding,
The secrets inside.

Elizabeth McFarlane Abdulla

Did She Ever Love Me?

Did she ever love me, this woman prostate on a bed,
sweating, panting to give life, first a body not a head.
Her first born, her only born, conceived in love or hate?
determined to stamp the date, in words that would berate.
No kisses soft, no loving arms, alone, but part of them
always punished and admonished, confidence to stem,
My escape was to marry, so early and so driven,
but help in times of desperation was never to be given
She was right and I was wrong, opinions not to parry
subservience, I found, would always make her happy
So never wanted, never loved, back from where I came,
to care, to wash, to feed, to dress, alzheimer's makes its claim
No longer steel, but grey and smiling, happy and content
to let me take control, her energy all spent
I watch her sleep, secure and safe, kiss her and wonder why
she loves me now in the way I wanted, all the years passed by
And as I hold her tenderly and tears fill my eyes
the wasted years, the bitter words, why could we not be wise
We sit together in the garden, bathed in evening sun,
I hold her tightly in my arms, I love her, my Mum.

Sandra Cartwright

December

The cloak of night has flicked the face
Of dawning day and left it blinded,
So cold it dawns in misty blue.
In curling whirls of foggy frost
The earth has disappeared, and lost
That lovely glow of Autumn's gold.
Fields that once were green are white,
Each blade of grass is scabbarded in ice,
Each leaf left on its branch is surely solid.
Each exhaled breath takes form and stays
To haunt the next. Each hair a mix of greys
Beaded with pearls of solid dew; white diamonds
That catch the light and, sparkling softly,
Caress the eyes of winter's shorter days.

Teresa Snow

Untitled

Alike some large window . . . Gaping.
Ah, the farcical behaviour of adults!

    Three-piece-suit-business-men
    leave the toilet with an itchy nose,
    Clandestine lovers wine and dine
    blissfully unaware of a crowd of eyes that stare.
    Loners display a large collection of bloodshot eyes.
    Silence is out . . . Solitude at its peak.
    You drown your sorrows, you look a fool,
    you pretend you're having a "quiet drink" . . .
    Executives sign hurriedly drunken contracts,
    couples foment deceitful plans,
    office girls shake off some of the boredom in alcoholic stupor . . .

Some of the babble lands in my ear . . . I dispense the sweet juice.

Marc Gourdon

Satori

Sometimes when you're out on a limb,
it can seem like a sin to wave at the passers-by, who've superglued
their lips so they would never have to say " it's good coming
up or going down", but it's okay to wear the crown if the
crown fits even
though your insides are ripped to pits and God has left you by
the wayside with nowhere to hide.

Even your thoughts travel at light speed and eat the energy of
your mind with a carnivorous greed and you don't know if
you can scream when you're left on the edge of a silent screen
with nowhere to go except inside your head.

Sometimes you realize you're alive in a world where someone
cares but finds it hard to bare the only soul we have from
above, but hey it's okay, just keep walking the dust path of
life and forget your troubles
and strife and luck will lend a hand to you, you lucky man, and
we blow like the sands of time each light grows brighter as
days turn to night and night rages into day, mean a life
somewhere on the other side winter sits defiantly waiting for
spring to step on stage and she does for all of her glory and
life begins again, whoa what a story.

Steven White

Utopia

Take heed you little children of what your elders say,
Play your games and have your fun, cherish every day.
No worry or anxiety can touch your days of good,
Of chocolate drops and candy-sticks, a fairy tale childhood.

You think you're so hard done by, to school you have to go,
Don't waste your time with idle play, learn all there is to know.
Plentiful are holidays to frolic time away,
Carefree days to laze about, enjoy them while you may.

Never strive to be grow up, time passes all too soon,
Let childhood be a melody and finish out its tune.
Youth is our own Utopia, we know not at the time,
If only it could flow on still, forever like a wine.

Joyce Gibson

Jamie

A fairer child you could not fine, his eyes, his nose were part of mine,
His smile would sooth the day away, sending your spirits
soaring and brightening the day.

Then night would come and gloom descend with broken
dreams you cannot mend.
Your heart is aching, and tears fall, as happy memories you
recall.   The dawn is here, the day awaits, have I the strength
and courage to struggle through another day, trying so hard
to be carefree and gay,
but hardly hearing what people say.   The idle chat, the
wasted voice, comments made with no genuine feelings.
I cannot be bothered to try to understand or even be a part of it.
As life's pattern evolves it is hard to understand my heavy
load.   "What have I done? what have I said?" goes round and
round inside my head.
Oh, for the night, its dark cloak enfolding, hiding me from
life's stark glare, where I can rest in solitude and my soul I
lay before you bare.   Please guide my path and show the way, give
me the courage to face another day.
For seven months we felt your love, that gentle innocent love
that goes deep into your heart.   I see your smile, and feel you
in my arms,
So, why did we have to part?

Ann Osborne

Special Friendships

You were always there when I was in need
And from all my problems I was freed
My life has never been too dull
As you've always been reliable

In every way you have been great
You are my friends from fate
It seems like I've known you forever
This friendship will always stay together

I will stay for you every day
And help you in any possible way
Ahead, there are many years
So come to me if you have any fears

My loyal friends, I can now see
Too good, you have been to me
You're both seen as a special friend
To you, a helping hand I shall lend

This friendship is more than precious
And will always be special to us
As we've helped each other to get a grip
We all know we have a lasting friendship.

Charanjit Sandhu

Ode To Jim Morrison

Have you gone Jim
   Did you really die,
Leaving us to face the music.

Could the lizard king
   still be alive,
Chameleon changing or simply disguised.

Do you walk amongst us
   we innocent slaves,
observing in silence we were once your domain.

Through acting the fool
   you were able to hide,
your sensitive soul to the world.

Did you retreat Jim
   did you give up on life,
To follow a path of solitude let no one else inside.

Still the rumours have grown
   and now they insist,
the truth we've always known.

   At Père Lachaise lies an empty place
   Is it yours Jim? Is it yours?

David Kinsman

Love

Love is beauty personified,
It touches deep in everyone—
Nobody can hide from its vice-like grips.
Love is all empowering and it strips
The fragile outward image
That makes us feel secured to our own bed of rock.
But we are lured by this blinding, star-like intent,
Which many seek but do not find;
They arise bitter and lament.
Love is like life's beacon—a torch from up above.
In this world of violence and deceit
We must be cautious not to quench the light of love.
Love isn't a word or sound;
We feel it in our heart.
Earthly existence we are bound
But with love we cannot part.

Lisa Fox

Not Today!

Can't think
Can't write
My minds a blank
Don't know what to do
Don't know what to say
I think I'll give it a rest for today

But my brain is worrying
I need to express
Got to get it all of my chest
Nothing is coming
My pen has no ink
Come on girl—think

I guess it just means there's nothing inside
No feelings that I'm trying to hide
Just wait until I'm really depressed
I've found that's when I write my best

Lindsey Wright

Disillusioned

I was so sure of you once.   You had shape and form,
imbued me with strength and kept me from harm.
We were walking in step, hearts beating as one.
Could face any rival and never succumb.
Some things won't change whatever betide
for such were the absolutes learned at your side.

But now, now things are changing it's harder to tell
who stands for the values I once knew so well.
The subtle destruction of things I hold dear
so tugs at my heart-strings it's tempting to fear.
Loyalty's costly when fashion dictates
and the press of the world is strong at the gates.

I'm less sure of you now as the vision's obscure
with things that were certain appearing less sure.
Those well-defined features so etched on my mind
are fighting a battle 'gainst much of mankind.
I was taught well!   Though you crumble to dust
eternity's values are still worth my trust.

Maureen Anne Browne

Pardon

Deafness is my only crime
Not occasionally, but all the time.
Words seem jumbled, and hard to follow.
Your mind seems, empty sad, and hollow.
If I say "I didn't hear", people sigh, and often sneer
They raise their eyes, as if to say,
"I wish this man would go away".
But deafness does not go away.
Sadly in fact, it's there to stay.
So when you say, "You don't listen".
My eyes may begin to glisten.
So please, try to understand.
Being deaf is far from grand.

T. C. Martin

323

The Red Balloon

Warm, sunny day—not winter
For then there's nothing special
About balloons.   And this was special.
She blew it up herself
With great pauses, full of fearful joy,
Before each hollow, whispering expand.
And as she blew
That shining globe in front
Was all her world.

Buoyant, proud, she carried it outside.
Wind whisked it from small hands
Into the road. A car was coming.
She saw 'twas Tom, her friend: he wouldn't hurt it.
But Tom, eighteen, in that split second saw
Only the red temptation to destroy:
He grinned at her, and swerved—
But over it.

The sun was gone; her world disintegrated.
And people, busy with important things,
Said, "What a fuss! It's only a balloon."

Evelyn Watts

"I Need"

I need a life that I am happy with.
A life full of joy and laughter.
And when I get sad and upset,
I know that someone loves me.
Someone is there to comfort and hold me,
Someone who can tolerate all my strange ways.

I need to get out of this rut.
The rut I have dug myself into.
Here at the bottom,
It is deep dark and muddy.
But no one will throw me a rope,
To try to pull me out.
At least not a rope that is long enough,
Or one that can take the strain.

Maybe someday I will get out of this rut.
I could build my own rope from hair.
Or maybe I'll let myself wither away,
Just like an autumn leaf.

Karen Hill

War Is Power

What is it that makes men destroy one another
Don't they know that our time will soon be over
So many men die and it's all in vain
Tomorrow it starts all over again

What happens then you almighty planners
Who sit at the top and wave your banners
When you take the toll and count the cost
Do you ever realize just what we've lost

What has been gained at the cost of these lives
Do you ever spare a thought for their wives
We're all the same, yellow, white and black
Why do you tell us we have to fight back

Does it matter which flag blows from the stand
Is it so important to hold on to that land
Not for the people who plough the field
Is it all for you, more profit to yield

We're brainwashed into fighting your wars
Fight for your country, fight for the cause!
You start wars, you stop wars, life is cheap
and we follow on like a herd of sheep

Karen Henriksen

"If Only I Could Touch You Once"

If only I could touch you once,
I'd know my feelings were real,
Then, even if you didn't return my feelings,
My heart could start to heal.

And just to feel you in my arms,
Would make me feel alive,
But not being able to be near to you,
I really couldn't survive.

I stare into your photograph,
And wish that you were here,
Then I could tell you how I feel,
And losing you would be my biggest fear.

Seeing you rarely like I do,
Is not enough for me,
To be close to you is important to me,
This I hope you'll, one day, see.

If only I could touch you once,
It would be a dream come true,
If only I could touch you once,
You'd see how much I care for you.

Maria Cracknell

Dragon, Dragon

Dragon, dragon, your fiery call,
Makes you the fiercest of them all,
Scaly skin and copper flecked eyes,
Shine with a light that never dies.
Just how I wish I could know,
Where you come from and where you go.

Dragon, dragon, your smoky flame,
Makes you impossible to ever tame.
Large barbed tail and long sharp claws,
Shine with ice that never thaws,
Just how I wish that I could have known,
Where you came from, how far you have flown.

Dragon, dragon, your dark green snout,
Makes the smoke waft in and out,
Powerful feet and a leathery wing,
Mean you are the ruler of everything.
Just how I wish to feel your breath,
Now that you have been and left.

Hannah L. Colby

Dream Garden

A lush green carpet, is spread all around,
Brightly coloured flowers cover the ground.
Yellow, blue, some pink and some white,
All pushing and swaying to catch the light.

There's life all around us, but we do not see
The early morning silence, broken, by a buzzing bee.
Worms slither, spiders and ants rush to and fro.
Here comes a butterfly, what a wonderful show.

Nestled in the corner there's a trickling stream,
Cascading with a sparkle, what a pretty scene.
A pond with lilies and frogs, fish by the score,
But everything stops as you open the door.

The bright morning sun dries out the night dew,
As night disappears, a fresh day starts anew.
What a beautiful sight, the birds flying by,
With billowing clouds soaring across the blue sky.

Is it all a dream? Such a wondrous sight,
Now Tamil doves and wild pigeons burst into flight.
All round are sounds of life, begging no one's pardon,
Oh, how I wish I had a real garden!

R. F. Hooper

Baby's Journey . . . Out!

I can see, wow!! Where am I who am I.
Look I can move.
Listen, who's that talking,
it must be my Mammy.
Oh, Mammy look I can move,
Mam, why won't you answer me.
Can't you hear me. Don't you love me.

I'm getting big now,
I've got fingers and toes.
And even my hair is growing but Mammy don't seem to care
she won't talk to me, but she knows
I need her, she won't hurt me.
Wait a minute, what's going on, no, stop, don't take me.
I am not ready, leave me alone. Mammy tell them stop, tell
them Mammy
I am too small, I can't live.
I need you Mammy, please . . . but it was
too late. Mammy didn't really care
she let them take me. I really wanted to see you Mammy,
but now I never will; you took that chance when you took my life
thanks Mammy . . .

Jackie Foley
Knockanore, Co. Waterford

Surfing The Storm Clouds

Suddenly the memories come crashing back
And there I am twenty years ago, on the threshold of youth and life
Standing inside the courtyard of my school, my spirit nurtured
    and nourished
By its medieval stone, with its William Tyndale stained glass,
    the cracked sundial
Mysterious stories of priests escaping through the
    underground tunnels
Esoteric delight in everything I saw

I remember adolescent stirrings of desire
Sexual power exploding passionately through my body
Rebirth like the sap of trees in spring
Engulfing changing everything
I breathed the pure air, and danced under the sky
Dazzled by life in its joy and darkness
I accepted all judged nothing
Became one with the eternal ocean
Looking deeply into the sky
Sometimes seeing storm clouds
I became an adept
At surfing the storm clouds

Alexander Buchan

Tranquil Thoughts

I appreciate my adopted county,
Rugged cliffs and heavy sky;
Trees bending as wind howls by,
The wilderness and freedom,
Heavy breakers foaming on the rocks,
Bringing smell of foreign land,
The mighty Atlantic Ocean.

There is beauty: Winter with its bitterness,
Spring lifting birds high in the sky,
Summer with warm sunshine,
Noise and heat, as traffic goes by.
But appreciated retreat
Is the beauty of the moor,
Where many walks are in store.
Autumn has its colour glory,
Harvest with its bounty,
And peaceful, quiet evening,
Is the contentment of receding year.

Soon be winter, time for rest,
To recuperate, and start new year afresh.

L. Milly Saunders

Dunblane

Minds filled with sorrow, hearts filled with pain
Eyes filled with tears, when we think of Dunblane
Those innocent babies, so senselessly killed
With hatred, his soul, must have been filled.

So much heartache, and so much grief
That a man could do this is beyond belief
To walk into that school, and shoot them down
Those innocent babies of Dunblane Town.

Those innocent babies, to Jesus have gone
But those who loved them, have to go on
Robbed of their child and watching it grow
Each parent must have loved their child so.

Those little children will never grow old
They've gone to a better life, we are told
They're safe in God's keeping, out of harm's way
Waiting for parents to join them one day.

We must pray for them, when we say our prayers
Not just today, but throughout the years
We may not know that Town called Dunblane
But we know, no more, will it be the same.

Charlotte Evans

The Robin

Robin, robin speak to me it seems you try,
I call your name, do you hear me cry,?
I would dearly like to know,
Are you cold out there in the snow,
Would you not come to live with me,
Without your feathered friends I plea,
Come within my kitchen warm,
And dry yourself, on this cold morn.

Can you tell me what it's like to be,
A little bird, and all you see,
So many things you must have seen,
For now, two winters, you have been,
Outside my window cold or gale,
And yet you never do look pale,
Your breast it looks so rosy red,
Don't you ever go to bed.

I look out, when dawn awakes,
You are always early never late,
I feel your presence each new day, and wonder if, you will ever say,
What it is that brings you here, but please my robin come next year.

Ivy Barton

A Single Prayer

I once could hear I once could touch
I had a life but now it's not much

Is there a question I can ask out there
and will I find the answer to my prayer

People here, are they laughing at me
I just don't know I just can't see

Is there a question I can ask out there
and will I find the answer to my prayer

Smashing into objects falling on the floor
my life is becoming such a bore.

Is there a question I can ask out there
and will I find the answer to my prayer

What's left for me now I just don't know
is my life at an end or is there hope.

Why? There's a question. Why me?
I know, don't tell me it was meant to be.

Angela Simmons

"Yuletide"

Surely it can't be Christmas again, it only seems six months ago,
That we stripped off the tree, and down on one knee,
Swept up the make–believe snow.

I stirred up the puddings in August and added a cup full of brandy,
The cake is a mess, I hate to confess,
So will keep the icing-bag handy.

It is Christmas Eve and thank God no snow, though the sky is
    a dangerous blue, we must listen to forecasts, and look at the sky,
And pray for fine weather, and clouds passing by.

At last it has dawned, our Lord's Natal Day,
And hark, I hear car wheels on gravel,
And there is our John, and Janet and Kate,
And that six year old rascal, who swings on the gate.

I am much too weary to go to the panto, Humpty Dumpty must
    topple without me,
And dear John must cope with the ice cream and coke,
And the six-year old sick in the foyer.

And now they're all gone, and the house is a tomb,
So hurry up Christmas, come back very soon,
For family life is a God–given boon.

Mary McDonough

The Fox

Breathless with heart in mouth pounding on
The body weak the spirit almost gone
The sound of bugle blast and merry men
With hearty laugh and spirit broken horse
That tramples foliage in its path
The baying hounds that follow on its torturous trail
Consistently they plunder on to lead to his betrayal
And on and on he moves his weary frame
While panic and confusion fill his worried brain
The breath he draws grows weaker by each movement
Yet onward goes the Fox
Followed by men, hounds bugles horse
All intellect and civilized of course
As dusk and cold begin to fill the fragrant woodland scene
The fox numbed by the chase bedraggled fur and mud
splashed face
Has run so long and hard to keep his brush like tail
Alas to reach his lair and hungry cubs has failed
As crowd on horse back watch the hounds rewarded by their plan
I wonder which is animal, is it the fox or man

David Bonner

My Broken Radio

The radio is on its head,
with a supernatural prodigy announced,
The Mazzy star of distraction,
confirms the definition of sound.
Blue-tonic, northern uproar in Geneva,
4th dimension rebellion in Peckham,
the chemical skyline is disrupted,
Why on earth do we let them?
Lush fields uplifted with voices,
A heavy stereo blasts out vibes,
Crazy God's of endless noises,
of music they will be deprived.
A cast of thousands gather,
to see the pulp of the black grape,
The manic of streets and preachers,
the deafening silence keeps us awake,
The drugstore is attractive and open,
the drinks are clearly flowing.
When will this afterlife of depressing isolation end?
My mind is a blur, an oasis and most of all not knowing.

Phil Viles

Human Nature

Lonely man, crouched on a shore,
Silhouetted against the dying sun.
Motionless,
Lost in dreams of timeless eternity.
Eyes staring,
Seeing images of fantasy and stretched reality
Moving through his vision.
A lonely tear falls.
Is it a lost love for which you grieve,
Or some inner self pity?

He sits,
Unaware of the audience he commands.
Shoulders hunched against the weight of many burdens.
Does he carry my troubles
Or can I just relate to his feelings?

Lonely man why do you sit alone
And stare across vast oceans?
Why do you cry and hurt in silence?
And why do we all stand watching you suffer? . . .
Or is it that you cry for us too?

Michael Cox

Green Was Our Land

The trees, the fields and hedgerows disappeared from view,
A supermarket in its place, a petrol station too,
Noisy diggers widening roads, mud is everywhere,
All bringing extra traffic to pollute our country air.

What is happening to our beauty, the lovely countryside,
It's being churned and gobbled up, taking country pride,
Nowhere for the birds to nest or space for children's play,
Just a mass of bricks and roads where fields and hedges lay.

There will be no striking landscape for children of today,
Only concrete jungles, cold and dark and grey,
No touch of dew upon the grass, no daisy chains to make,
Surely this has got to be a terrible mistake.

When will common sense prevail, leave beauty well alone,
Keep the building in the towns, maintain the green belt zone,
Give us back our wildlife, hedgerows and the fields,
Together with the harvest and all the fruit it yields.

We know that progress must be made, in this day and age,
But not from land where food is grown and cows and sheep do graze,
Leave alone our beauty, our little country pleasures,
Guard against life's one free gift, our natural treasure.

Joyce Whitney

Alien

Expect you've come across them when walking down the street,
You know—these market research gals with statistics to complete,
They approach you with such eagerness 'twould be
    churlish to resist,
But I bet my kind of answers get their knickers in a twist!

"Do you use any of these washing powders in your automatic?"
This is only the beginning and I fear she's gonna panic,
I wait for her reaction, first the gulp and then the blink,
"No; I still use elbow grease. I do my washing in the sink!"

"Do you do any eating out or take holidays abroad?"
When I answer in the negative she starts to look quite bored

"How about these packs of frozen foods?"
"No; I don't have a freezer"
She thinks, "I've picked a right one 'ere, what a miserable old geezer!"
"Did you come to town by car today or use the park and ride?"
I really musn't giggle, 'twould be most undignified

"I'll have to rush, here comes my bus"
(I've missed it now, Oh! Damn it!)
"Yes that's right, you've guessed it dear, I'm from another planet!"

Nancy J. Owen

Sea Faces

Sea the foam–backed waves as they wave to the elements,
Sea me, sea me before I die, yet! Not to die
Merely to surrender and lie,
In the lull and the calm.
Sea energy, movement as the great cupped hand of the sea,
Once more spews up its message on gravelled shore,
Sea hands caressing, flowing, seeping into cracks and crevices,
Before being drawn back to the great expanse of sea.
Sea face strewn with foam and seaweed, rising up menacing!
Then curling down in a great sea muscle of strength, pounding
Ever onwards to the shore of infinity, another sea face.
Perpetual motion, undulating tides within the sea.
Sea face calm, sighing to tranquillity with the blue–faced sky,
Infinite infinity as sea and sky become one, sea gull fly!
Sea face freckled, speckled with molten gold,
Solar fingers lightly brush and mingle from the shore to infinity!
Sea face stirs, the restless fingers of the wind, sail in
Rocking the ebb and flow into motion, life begin.
Sea the foam–backed waves as they wave to the elements,
Then brush on water again to merge within.

Pat Morand

Saved

God only knows I've had enough,
there's nothing left to fight for,
living this life is far too tough
and my heart and emotions are raw.

I'm at my very lowest ebb,
nothing left in me to be strong,
then a whisper inside tells me that
how I'm feeling now is wrong.

I'm sinking in a deep dark pool of despair,
my will ready to give up the fight,
then I feel myself drawn up to fresh air
and a tiny dot of light.

I break the surface, I gasp and shake,
I feel strangely weak with relief,
the blackness lifts and my soul awakes
to the only true belief.

How many times have you rescued me
with outstretched hands of love,
you have my heart for eternity
beloved Father of heaven above.

Valerie Kay Copley

The Good Husband

The promises you make,
so real, but yet so fake.
I often try to leave,
but nobody can believe.
You buy me flowers every week,
for forgiveness you do seek.

I wear long sleeves,
oh long dresses.
Even in the midst July,
under the hot burning sky.
Only my husband and I,
know the reason why.

You hurt me, you beat me,
at the time you smile with glee.
Then after your savage rage,
you want to start a clean page.

The blue bruising appears,
and we both are in tears.
You say I am your one and only wife,
as I feel the final stabbing, the final knife.

Lara Williams

The Watcher

Its silver blade bathes my face,
Yet we are parted by numerous space.
Its shadow may wane and be no more.
But its crystal shade will return we're sure.

Welcomes are seldom upon its face,
Yet to all are offered peace and grace,
Its beauty is radiant and high above any,
Yet visitors are few, but admirers are many.

A traveller's guide and yet friend to none,
Unknown neighbour is the secret one,
Wanderer of paths untrod by any,
Passing alone and yet seen by many.

Cloaked in a gown of silver and black,
With face ever forward, not showing the back,
Holding an attraction in mystical ways,
Gaze those luminous eyes from a shimmering haze.

A heavenly pilgrim yet with a heart of stone,
Rules all and sees many from a celestial throne,
A puzzling identity now revealed none to soon,
Will produce, The Watcher many know as the moon.

S. N. Gerrard

This World

Dear World, One World,
One Moon by night and Sun by day,
A multitude of Stars to light our way.

Our World, One World,
The feel of Sun, Rain and Wind,
Soft Snow falling, Seasons passing.

Fine World, One World,
Earth and Ocean, Sunlight and Shadow,
Moonlight and Rainbow, beautiful colour.

Lone World, One World,
Global life in infinite Space,
Held in trust by the Human Race.

Great World, One World,
In trust to us, that trust betrayed,
Too many times, our World may end.

If through the World Pure Knowledge reigns,
Pure Air, Good Earth, have pride of place,
With Natural Life, this World remains.

Dear World, One World and ours to tend,
World without End.

Peggy Leaver

Death is Not the End

Death is in the air, it's all around us everywhere,
It happens to us all whether short, thin, fat or tall,
The only thing in life that is fair,
We have to live for today, not tomorrow,
Live life to the full and hope to be remembered forever,
Not to be forgotten, oh no! not ever,
Like a flower we bloom and grow,
Not like the weeds that choke us as a foe,
We need the earth, wind, rain and sun,
To flourish and survive when our journey has begun,
We shouldn't despair and worry about our fears,
Save our tears, live long and be happy throughout our years,
So when the time comes for us to say goodbye,
With our last breath we'll heave a sigh,
Peace is now upon us and life hasn't really come to an end,
We're now up high, looking down, having travelled the road
      and turned the bend,
Death is then not the end, just another step in time
We have nothing to fear,
When the appropriate time comes near.

Trudy Lapinskis

Untitled

I want more money than I could ever want,
I want more money than I could ever need.
This is most definitely, the first sign of greed.

I want to live in luxury,
I want to live in a mansion.
That would be ideal, but I don't want the attention.

I am poor and I am hungry,
I am cold and very alone.
It's not much fun, on the streets, on your own.

"Can you spare some change?"
"Can you spare a meal?"
Do I really deserve this awful and raw deal?

I might be alone and hungry
I might be tired and cold
But I'm not a liar . . . The streets aren't paved with gold.

N. Ward

Charlie's Woe! (Or A Jacobean-Farewell)

I stand on the deck of the ship,
Thinking of all the mistakes;
of the flight through the heather,
and all the other sad dates!

Of Derby and what might have been
are not just some distant dream.
But what if I'd listened instead,
Of running away from those redcoat fiends!

I let my men down at Culloden,
and now I've paid the cost.
Of ruling Great Britain and Ireland —
My Jacobean dynasty is lost!

I am going back to face my father,
Who held all his dreams through me!
How am I going to face him —
I'll just have to wait and see!

I wonder what will happen
In two hundred years or more!
Will a Stuart be on the throne,
Or will I be a figure of folklore!

Prue McCullough

The Water Meadows

Leaning on sun—warmed gate as I walk the water meadows,
the river's note changes as it passes over shallows
of bleached stone from deep, quiet reaches.
Whilst folds of gentle pasture
Stretch from crested hill of wood and copse,
the oak stands in sentinel grandeur
Over all, guardian of land, water and rock.

Pat A. Seagroatt

Cloudburst Of Material Possessions

Cloudburst of material possessions
Luxuries raining down
Washed away in a flood of things
Possessions falling all around.

You're running away from the crushing weight
Of the falling possessions
As a stereo crashes down
More follow in vile precession

Then just as suddenly as it first came
Nothing will ever be the same
Because the things have gone again
But for disasters they're to blame

Cars they have crushed and lives they have ruined
So much suffering they've caused
After seeing such fine riches
Our minds are filled with greedy thoughts.

Amy-Claire Todd

Tragedies Of War

The war is over
The enemy has gone
And all that's left behind
Are the tragedies of war.
War has no feelings,
No justice, no law.
Brings devastation and disaster—
Leaves homeless and fear.
  A young mother searches for her little child
Among the dead and dying.
A baby, barely a few, weeks old,
Clings to his dead mother; crying.
Many are victims,
Few are spared,
And those that survive
Will always be scared,
Haunted by the horrors they saw;
The dead,
The dying,
The victims of war.

Rosemary Fletcher

Blackie

He was hatched in a nest near my back door,
Leaves and twigs made up his floor;
He cracked open his shell one bright sunny day
I could hardly take my eyes away

This miracle of life, so fragile and small
His brother and sisters made up four in all,
Making their debut before my eyes
All too soon they'd be flying in the skies

He chirruped and fluttered and grew every day
I didn't really want him to fly away
But he had to grow up and learn to catch food,
If he watched his Mum closely, he would soon be good

He was growing too big for his nest, and so
With a final flutter he was ready to go:
I watched his attempt as he learned to fly
Saw his darkening coat and black beady eye

He flew to his Mum, high up on a tree
Then turned, and seemed to nod to me;
Goodbye little bird, be brave and strong
And I'll listen for your warbling song

Joyce Smith

The Lost Fight

The church bells echoed in the dark room full of life
Mocking the tired soul alone in her melancholy mood.
"Not just yet! She still has time! But not much!" they seemed
to laugh.
Pointing and staring, the invisible demons crushed the tender
silence
Which had veiled the woman like the hand of a mother
But like the mother was no match for what lay ahead; the
inevitable.

They followed her down the hall as she looked for her only weapon
Which could combat this hungry, indestructible enemy.
"Not just yet! She still has time! But not much!"
Perhaps they were wrong, perhaps the doctors were wrong,
Perhaps this is all a dream, a nightmare; a terrible nightmare!
She could only hope that they were wrong; that everybody
was wrong.

Her heart seemed to slow down as she reached for the small
bottle on the shelf.
The room began to fade as she struggled for her weapon but
alas it was too high.
"Not just yet! She still has time! But not much!"
"Why is life so cruel! Why is God so cruel! I'm still
young!" she screamed in anger.
She fell to the cold ground clasping onto the last signs of life but
She did not have time, it was over, her life was over, she was dead.

Ram Sachdev

Wanderlust

A restlessness lurks beneath my skin

Yet roses bloom full–blown outside my door
where honeysuckle spills its flowers for the bees
and foxgloves blow pale trumpets to the breeze
that moves the summer evening's scented air
fledgling buds press against my windowpane
a nightingale pipes its sweet refrain
swallows dart high against the emerging moon

Yet I would leave this place
its mellow walls
its rolling park land and hallowed halls
and take an unseen path into the wild night
to wander the world

Until the trail full–circle turns and brings me back again

Sarah Randall

The Page

I turned the page.
The words lifted themselves up and grinned at me wickedly.
They knew what was hidden in those lines,
they knew the feelings of their writer,
they knew I didn't know.
They were making a fool out of me.
Just like the pictures, which also stared back at me.
Meaning something, but at the same time, nothing.
They sat, waiting for a reaction,
waiting to see if I knew what they knew.
I didn't, I couldn't.
I tried to see the message behind what was written.
Why did he write this?
He must have had a reason at the time.
He must have had a goal, a thought, an idea.
Only he knew what it was, what it all meant.
He was guided by the light I couldn't find.
The glimmer in his eye as he wrote turned into
the glimmer of hope I felt.
Hoping I would understand, if not now, sometime.

Joanne Jackaman

The Greatest Love Of All

March 17, 1994
There you were in all your glory
our beautiful twin girls Emma and Sophie
full of pride, in total "awe"
nobody would love you more

Over the months we watched you grow
the different characters we came to know
Emma so quiet so subdued
Sophie the entertainer, any audience would do.

Jan 9, 1995
This is the day our world fell apart
For you had been with us for less than a year
This is the day all parents fear
This is the day our Sophie died

We have no reason no explanation
just total and utter devastation
now Emma no longer has her twin
it is indeed a cruel world we live in.

Nina Cabrelli

Farewell

When will the pain go away?
When will the hurt ease?
When there are no longer memories of you
That day will never come
You are always in my thoughts
There was no time to say goodbye
You slipped away in the silence of the night
Your pain has gone
Your hurt was eased away
Mine will stay as long as there are memories of you

K. Taylor

You My Wife

The days, the weeks, the months pass by.
White clouds and grey cross over the sky.
The earth, the moon, the stars, the sun,
a roll of thunder like a distant gun.
These things take a place in life.
Yet in mine there was only you my wife.

The sorrows the sadness the gladness and mirth
The cry of a baby slapped at birth
Heartaches and longings, suffering and pain
Trees and flowers, sunshine and rain
These things take a place in life
Yet in mine there was only you my wife

The parting, your leaving, has left me alone
The great love I had will never be known
You tender caress your loving kiss
For the rest of my life are things I will miss
These things took a place in life
Now they are no more my wife.

A. G. Burnard

Birthday Surprise

Looking down upon the world, sailing across the sky
Was something that I hoped to do one day before I died.
A trip was then arranged for me by my family dear.
They knew of my ambition and it was my sixtieth year.
So I was there and helping fill this big flat plastic bag
First with cold air and then with hot, until it was made to drag
The basket quite upright and ready for to fly.
We clambered in the basket shell, stood waiting for the cry
"Let go the ropes!" It came at last we floated gently away.
Above, the burning gas made sure we didn't stay.
My heart leapt, my breath was still my head was in a spin
I looked up at the great balloon, then the basket I was in
Took a deep breath, then gazed out upon a wondrous view.
We were two thousand feet in the air and it all looked strange
   and new.
I looked down from the basket's edge two thousand feet below
Saw tiny cows and houses and a ribbon of river flow
Down to the sea. Everyone was quiet, there wasn't any fuss
A great big shadow floated below. That shadow was us!
The evening sun was setting now and it was time to land,
The orange flame roared once more. We're down, it had been grand.

Priscilla Angela Kirk

Essence Of Summer

The trees on the skyline of cool leafy green,
The shimmer of hues, as a swallow's wing it preens,
A shaft of sunlight that warms all it sees,
The familiar sound of the buzzing of the bees,
The peace and pure beauty all fill one with awe,
The inheritance of all whether rich or poor.

Beryl H. Kew

Autumn Glory

With summer at an end
It takes the slightest breath of wind to send
Those painted leaves of red and brown
Tumbling to the waiting ground.
The trees, soon bare,
Get ready to prepare
For winter's sleep,
Though we would like to keep
The glory that is autumn.
Those quiet languid days
Have magic in the air,
As through the drifting autumn haze
Which spells the waning of the year,
We pause, and hear
The echo of some distant song
Which rang in far–off summer days.
But now a peace descends;
With summer at an end
We have the glory that is autumn.

Sheila Blundun

The Crossroad

A crossroad is reached, yet which way to turn.
Your dreams hang in balance,
A future unknown.
So complex a decision,
Fraught with worry and fear,
Your life lays uncharted so which way to steer?

A crossroad is reached, it looms up ahead.
Your traffic influx,
Neither green or yet red.
Each path bares altar, with sacrifice in tow.
Laid sleepless with chaos,
In amber bathed glow.

A crossroad is reached, your choice all alone,
A wilderness of thought,
Betwixt you and your key,
So bid enter, cry open, the doors of ye fate.
Head high, walk proud, and let thee walk straight,
Into unknown's bittersweet gate.

Paul Robinson

Insomnia

How long is the night, so lonely for me
How long is the night, why all eternity
Those ebony hours, how I wish they would go
So bleak is the darkness, hours passing so slow
I lie hear and listen, I hear not a sound
For nothing is moving, there's no-one around
At last it is over, my tortuous night
The sun is now changing, the darkness to light
Birds singing in chorus, as they greet the dawn
The world now awakens, a new day is born

Lucy Tripp

Janglim

Love's never been so earthly close
to shout from hilltops, an earnest boast
slow sweet awakening to realize
alone never again at sunrise

On your breast, deep desired relief
comforted by touch, sense belief
strange to think our choice was made
fate doubtless woven by fairy braid

To speak by yearning of an eye
the scented drawing flower to fly
and hearing beauty to listening soul
is drinking pleasure from heart's bowl

I can't think of a thing more sought
for money spent can't buy this thought
never able to trade feelings this way
of growing love for you every day

Geoff Goddard

Sisters Forever

Since time of birth I could not see what was to be my destiny.
My thoughts and learning were not bright and of my future
there was no sight.
To help me through my troubled years and time to come unseen
God gave to help me through fears a sister called Kathleen.
Through every family in the land the families are the same.
The bond between the young and old whom God gave all
same name.
The bond the love the heartache shared stands solid firm and true.
The time of loss cry for time to start anew.
Through times of stress and times of fear that comes through-
out the land.
Cling on to everything that's dear united we all stand.
God gave us all the right to live, to all he granted peace
God gave us all the right to love so that future wars may cease.
The reason why I voice my words so strongly and so clearly.
Is to put my feelings into verse of a sister I loved dearly.
For of all the things throughout the land that are never heard or seen
I'll know when every thing's unfurled, I've a sister called Kathleen.

Joyce Simpkins

Circle Of Friends

A circle of friends in a corner.
Talking about you.
They point and stare picking out faults.
They like to gossip.
One like another.

They lie to get their own way.
They don't care who they hurt.
The Gang of parents.
No better than their children.

Such a tight circle.
You try hard, but it can't be broken.
They lie, saying, even swearing,
they are doing good

Moaning and grumbling,
till they get their way.
Voicing their opinions.
They listen to none.
But listen, you must.

Gareth Owen

Solitude

I think I may be going blind,
my soul let me leave so much behind,
My guilt is not there, I do not
have a care, just fears and sadness from everywhere.
I choose my solitude inside my home
where I can be still but the feelings will roam.
I have no answers no reason to live
nothing I think I have that is good enough to give.
The darkness inside the bad memories still come and
go whenever they please.
Where will it take me, where will we go,
Let the dreams lead me where I have been but do not know.
The end is my reward the peace I will feel
and the hope inside that what I am is not real.

Katy Lynaugh

Don't Dump Anymore

I wandered down the lane today
And strolled by the river on my way
I did not see any fish that swam
Just a hypermarket trolley and an old pram
Empty coke tins and that plastic bottle.
Like weeds of the river, the flow they throttle
The hedgerows too suffer much the same
Is it modern packaging that is to blame
Or is it the people who in their haste
Don't behave so well and just dump all of their waste
The countryside should be a pleasure for all
Not a huge tip for man's rubbish to fall
So please dear people as you walk down the lane
Stop dumping your rubbish, for it is a great shame
Then we could have a nice stroll, near the river so clean
With fish swimming in there, a fisherman's dream
The hedgerows would blossom, the flowers would bloom
And all the small creatures would have living room
So I ask you again, and in fact I implore
Please keep our countryside tidy, don't dump anymore.

Frederick Jolly

Freedom Of The Press

Words, words, words, bandied all about.
Sometimes kept in context, yet often used without.
How damaging this often is, so hard on families too,
Of victims in these onslaughts, with redress alone to sue
And bring to heel transgressors who beyond the lines have trod,
To win a headline story, and promotion in a job
That trades in human misery, but is it ever thought
How individual freedoms are thus sacrificed or bought,
As opium for the masses, to have their fix and fill.
Uncaring that their fellow men are going through the mill.

Eileen Ramsey

Land Of Dreams

I dreamed of a land free from sorrows,
No yesterdays and no tomorrows.
No one cared for worldly wealth,
And all enjoyed the best of health.

There was no fire, flood or drought,
A wonderful place there is no doubt.
There was food aplenty for everyone,
And how nice to see children have such fun.

Flowers bloomed in every hue,
And the green, green grass shone with dew.
Birds sang sweetly in the trees above,
There was no hatred, only love.

Oh how I wished that I could stay,
Just sitting dreaming time away.
But life goes on here on earth below,
And we must work, as you should know.

M. Muirhead

A Chinese Painting In My Soul (1971)

I rush again and rush again
To olden days, so full, so gay,
And the sweetness of living dreams
Flows through my mind, takes me away . . .

The silver yarn of moonlight flows,
A stone fountain, so grey, so old,
The yearning trees on Margit Isle
Memories fill me thousandfold . . .

This island was me, the branches my arms,
The river dark like my turgid soul,
The moon danced one more waltz with me,
The gayness gone, the night grew cold . . .

But I will weave and weave again
A prodigious stream of silver yarn
Of moonlight memories so gay
And like a brushstroke: splash and gone . . .

Ian S. Shaw

Friendship

Forever, together, through smooth and rough ride
Right or wrong, stand proud by their side
In times when they're lost, show them the way
Everyone needs someone, whatever they say
Never lose touch, if life draws you apart
Despite years of distance, keep them in your heart
So don't be shy, tell them you care
Half of a problem is easy to bare
Inspirations are lost, dreams won't last long
Prayers unanswered but friendship still strong

Nicola Demaine

Eastenders

Eastenders is on every week,
It gives me such a lovely treat,
Cindy and David are having an affair,
They do not make a perfect pair,
Pauline has lost Arthur we are all sad
We knew all along that Willy was bad,
Peggy Mitchell is the landlady in the bar,
She has a reputation of going too far,
Lorraine and Joe have joined the cast,
Poor old Joe cannot forget the past,
Carol and Alan are finally wed,
Let's hope there are no more tears to shed,
Baby Ben for Cath and Phil,
He had meningitis he was very ill,
Grant has eyes for Lorraine we all say,
But will it work out at the end of the day,
Ricky has sent Bianca a birthday gift,
Let's hope this will heal the rift,
Now my story has been told,
Continue Eastenders you're made of gold

Claire-Louise Jones, age 14

Inishmaan, 1996

Took a giant step
Into the tiny aircraft,
All weighed and set,
Both luggage and self.

Over the broad Atlantic
Slabs of the flat rock beckon,
Guarded by Dún Conor
And 6000 miles of stone
Walls built by islander's hands
To protect their tiny fields;
Wrested from rock, reclaimed by seaweed,
Torn from the sea on their backs,
Now cattle, sheep and donkeys graze.

Electricity, gas, and telephone ease
The lot of hardy Gaelic people.
In outboard–engined currachs they fish;
By plane and boat the guests arrive
A summer bumper crop.
Till winter seals in and
Returns the island to its people.

Bernie Doyle

Reasons

Dedicated to Jessica Bethan Absalom

Reasons to be glad to be alive and to be me
Sometimes escape my mind and my eyes don't see
The real beauty of things around and about
It's sometimes easier to wallow in misery and self doubt.

So I'm taking a few minutes to reflect, put the world to right
As my being sad and miserable is not a pretty sight
Although it's something I'm used to, I'm sorry to say
Perhaps a long overdue shake up would be an idea for today

Just think of the flowers in all shapes and sizes
Their beautiful colours, each deserving prizes
All the animals with the great pleasures they bring
The birds in the trees, the amazing songs that they sing

A rainbow, a butterfly just a few to remember
The changes in the seasons from January to December
Hearing a newborn baby's cry, seeing her first smile
The feeling of love, of being loved, these are no trial

Each new day holds something to discover
With this knowledge I know I will recover
From the 'woe is me' syndrome that tries to take a hold
Yes, I am pleased to be me you'll be glad to be told.

Dawn Lesley Absalom

The Unknown Soldier

When you fell, and you were dying
Could you hear your loved ones crying?
Or do they know, even now
Where you died, or when, or how?

What was it for, your shortened life?
Was there a lover, friend or wife?
Do they wonder, or even care
If you still live a life somewhere?

You came to war, young fit and strong,
It makes no difference, you still have gone
When you died in some forsaken place
And no-one could recognise your face.

Were you blown apart or burnt to soot?
Did you fly a plane or fight on foot?
Was there a letter that simply read:
Missing in action—presumed dead?

Now you lie in this peaceful field
With so many others, who too were killed
Where flowers bloom and grass is mown
And you remain as just—Unknown.

Martin Forge

The Meaning

The Meaning of life is a puzzle to us all,
We do to please others facing tasks we might fall.
We may go through life trying our best,
Not knowing the reason we live one long test,
We wake up each morning ready to face the whole world,
For the next generation their future we build.
But what is the importance of living these days,
When people in life choose to follow bad ways.
What is the meaning of the life that we each live,
We are taught to be nice and the bad things forgive.
We live with the violence, the anger and pain,
But nothing can prevent it from happening again.
Nobody knows the real meaning of life,
But to know the real meaning is a gift without price.

Gail Janet Thornton

'A Quiet Mind'

Lord! Grant me the gift of a quiet mind.
Time for friendship far and wide.
Neglected friendships to our dismay
Remembered in passing, fade away.
Family problems bind us too,
Time consuming we soldier through.
Tears; blur the vision of the faces we knew
A quiet mind will clear the view.
Precious years lost forever.
Waste not time value measure
A quiet mind a gift to treasure.

Doris M. Peel

Mind Squad On Patrol

Send them in, it's going mad,
Find the thoughts behind it.
Lock them up and throw away the key
They're nothing but trouble, them mad thoughts.
They wind and grind, they spill and bubble,
They lie resigned to a life of trouble.
So send them in to hunt them down,
The mind hasn't yet flipped.
It's not too late to salvage sanity,
But if we leave it too long they'll rip it to bits
With blades
With guns
With bats
With bombs;
Anything they can lay their hands on.
Destructive things, their mad thoughts.
So go after them, mind squad
And don't come back till the victim's sane
The mind is precious and so it should stay
We want it working normal again!

Simon J. Moore

Westbury White Horse

Carved on a hillside for all the world to see,
Is an ancient monument, of local history,
The White Horse at Westbury, etched out in chalk,
Is just outside the town, where I love to walk,
The hills are rolling barrows, the air is pure and clear,
Walking on this wilderness brings a special tear,
There's light, love and laughter ringing around the Hills,
As hang gliders in multi-colours—test their every skill,
Children slide down freely, upon the lush green grass,
Family cricket and football abound, picnics where you pass,
Kites flying majestically,—in the cool breeze,
Tangled hair and glowing cheeks, are just some of these,
The experience that it offers, is there for everyday,
To give you a lift, clear your mind, and blow cob-webs away,
The magic of the greenery, and of the valley below,
As you look north, south, east and west, gives a radiant glow,
As you walk with God, and see things naturally,
This is like heaven and everything is free,
Its beauty I've tried to capture, is just one small part,
The White Horse is on my doorstep, and always in my heart.

C. H. Cruse

Missing

As the light filters across the sky,
Dawn has almost come.
The birds arise, and start to fly,
But, as yet there's no sign of the sun.
Different shades of blue,
With a slight tinge of pink.
As another day starts anew,
. . . But where is the missing link?

There are no voices,
No sounds of sadness, none of joy.
Our rivers untouched, no-one's made any choices,
To ruin the sky.
But the era of darkness is coming so near,
Filled with plight and of suffering.
With dread and with fear,
Until finally one morning the birds will cease to sing.

And it all will begin, once more.

Christy Whatley

The Homecoming—C 980 AD

Weary, weary his watch over the whale's way;
Long lonely the night—long lonely the day,
Benumbed by the cold, bereft of his sleep.
The dreaded sea serpent astir in the deep.
The Great Star in the sky still guiding him home
Through the wild waters white edged with foam.
The sea wall is reached, now steps he ashore
'Midst ruins of homestead where 4 months before
The pitiless pirates with plunder and pillage
Had ransacked and raped and razed the whole village.
Some found fate in the flames, some food for the fox
And some thrown far below to the foam covered rocks.
Right past the ruins he rapidly strides
To reach the dark wood where the deer herd still hides.
'Midst the tree trunks and shadows he trudges on without stop
And glad is his heart as he gains the hill top,
Where safe from the Northmen and secure from all harm
Are his cattle and crops and his folk on the farm,
And he hurries ahead as he hastens to greet
His own darling wife—his dear Meadow-sweet.

W. G. Waller

The Manor House

The manor house stood on a hill
Amongst green foliage and trees
Forgotten and still,
The cobwebs of time looked like a blanket
Shrouding windows that seemed forbidding
Enmeshed in nature's web,
No key to open the door that was hidden
Telling of bygone events and past years
Of horse drawn carriages
And nights of melody and laughter
Under the glass chandeliers,
That become mirrors of reflection
Of bygone days
To make way for changing times
Overgrown are forgotten pathways,
Forgotten was the door without chimes
Pity the Manor House that knows no restoration.

Jeannette Simpson

Who Are We?

You've never seen me,
I've never seen you.
I could be green,
You could be blue.
I could have three heads and sixty toes.
You could be ten foot tall with an even bigger nose.
I might be from Venus.
You could be from Mars.
We aliens are all the same,
Wondering who we are.

Eleanor Gurney

The Lifeboat

I'm a lifeboat on the Titanic,
When it started to sink I began to panic.
The shouts and the screams from the people below,
Said, "It's an iceberg not a big lump of snow".
I went into the water with a mighty crash,
The Titanic went down without a sound or a splash.
It was said that this ship was unsinkable,
But what happened was really unthinkable.

Elaine Cartmail

The Suffering Children Of The 19th Century

Children gloomy,
Work to be done,
Children bent,
Children crippled,
Children deformed,
Children injured,
These are the children that work like this.

No sympathy,
No help,
No rest,
No play,
Just work, sleep, work that's done every day

Happy children once,
Gloomy children present,
What's to be done,
Help is needed,
Rest is needed,
Shorter hours needed,
"But do they get these things?"
The answer is . . . No!!

Gemma Milden

Untitled

Simple moments were dispersed like leaves in autumn
In the last whispers of the wind, in vain aqueous flutters
We seek for remnants of innocence
Then we decided unanimously to find the angel.
Now we close our eyes, frightened
How are we supposed to become stone—we, that we were
created by dough, built on the sand, beside the sea
Now we close our ears, tired
How can you search for the meaning of every lapping
Who are we, and in which side of the world should we stand
And if we don't belong here, where do we belong
Which May of those who passed and those who'll come
Will plait for us a wreath of poppies to adorn our foreheads
And let us laugh, like before, unsuspecting in unconcerned plains
When are we going to stand under the threshold of that house
With the walls having something from the sun inside them?
And the open windows leaving the sky float free without destiny
So that we can behold the angel who won't wither our eyes
But only in a moment of an unutterable bliss,
Will let us scatter in the eight corners of the winds.

Maria Giabouri

I'll Always Remember

Every passing day has its pain and tears, now that you're
gone I only have souvenirs,
No-one can replace the Nan that I've loved and lost,
I'd gladly exchange anything to see you, whatever the cost.
I long to say the words, I never got to say,
I want to hold you close and love you, forever and a day,
If I could turn back the clock to change any heartache I've caused,
I'd do it all today and show all my remorse,
I know I stole the gold from your hair, and I put all the silver
threads there,
But you never gave up loving me, and I knew you always cared.
You always showed me strength and courage when I needed it most,
But I never knew what I had until your battle for life was lost.
I'll always remember you and I will keep you close to my heart.
But most of all never forget that I've loved you from the start.

C. E. Haynes

Snowflakes

The swirling flakes of frozen rain
Fast falling from a grey dismal winter's sky.
On touching the ground quickly melt and disappear
Still endlessly they fall to earth
Twisting and twirling in the chill of the January air.
Soft moist petals of our atmosphere's making
A wondrous sight for all to see
If only I could be as free to drift along
In time and space without nature's need to erase.

Pauline Briers

Think Of A Colour

He stared across the room,
Smiling to himself,
Knowing what would happen later,
Hatred tearing away at his heart,
As he prepared for the fight ahead.
And so giving the signal to his friends,
They stalked their prey,
Circling around him,
Pleased at the sight of fear in his eyes.
And then they struck.
Hitting hard and fast,
Again and again,
Until they had no anger left.
And once again they walked away,
Thinking that they were heroes.
But the real hero sat alone,
Bruised and battered,
Tired of feeling pain.
In their eyes he was a colour.
In his eyes he was a person.

Emma Stent

Tell It As It Is

How can I justify what I have done?
Why am I unsatisfied with the attention of one?
How do I live with the guilt and the fear?
Why am I hurting those who are dear?

What happened in my life to make me this way?
How can I fulfil my potential and do as I may?
What was it, I wonder, that put thoughts in my head?
How was it done, what was it they said?

Was I called names or bullied at school?
Was I under pressure to succeed and not to be cool?
How did I compare to glossy magazines that I read?
Why did I so often wish I was dead?

Why am I still not happy with my life?
What holds me back and leads me to strife?
Is it that I lack confidence, or is it that—
I cannot stop feeling that I am fat.

Yvonne Cator

Night

Ghostly shadows, catch my eye,
what is that? . . . a bat flies by,
The screech of a cat
The bang of a door,
The hoot of an owl,
and so much more.
These eerie noises reach my ears,
and bring with them so many fears.
The full moon shines in the sky
    so bright
The glittering stars . . . what a Pretty
    sight.
These come to say the day is done,
and now I sit here all alone.
I flick the switch and turn on
    the light,
and close the door on that thing
    called Night

Aimi Glossop

333

The Highland's Daughter

The lush, green grass beneath her feet
And the sun slowly setting behind the mountains.
Everything was perfect,
Majestic, peaceful in her final hour.
She watched the dipping sun, the silver of the loch
And the one thought returned to her,
This is the place to die.
The sun had gone and the clouds descended
To meet the rising mist.
Her mane of coppery fire blew gently in the breeze
And the music of the lone piper drifted on the air.
She lay her head upon the grass and listened to the song,
It filled her every fibre as the sleep came sweetly to
    her tired limbs.
He looked across at her and smiled,
The cycle had been done.
Never again would the Highland's daughter leave the glen.

Carrie Mansfield

The Psychology Of Spaghetti

I've just come up with a theory,
But my name is not Freud or Darwin,
I didn't bring about evolution,
But my theory is really quite charming!

The psychology of spaghetti,
But a psychologist, no sir, I am not,
I could be though, I have what it takes,
Don't you agree that it takes what I've got!

This discovery could change my life,
I'll be famous in a hundred years from now,
I'll probably be dead by this time of course,
But it would take that long to figure out!

So, what is my psychology of spaghetti,
I think I've kept you waiting long enough,
All right, I'll explain but first be warned,
Understanding might really be tough!

There are many psychological theories
And like spaghetti, you can get in a tizz,
So my psychology of spaghetti,
Is that spaghetti, is what psychology is!

Joanne Smith

'The Bright Morning Star'

My gaze, with gladness, alights upon her;
    Her lustrousness and unadorned
beauty glows with a vibrancy as she
    lies in the velvet darkness of the night.

The 'Bright Morning Star' far outshines
    all others, who in her presence
become mere sparkling points of light.

I glimpse sight of her through the windows
    as I go about my nightly tasks,
valuing her presence as the long hours pass.

Then as the dawn rises and the sun's
    rays, in fierce domination, overcomes the night,
I watch my lovely companion, gently
    fade from sight.

Maureen Sawyer

Confusion

Sole searching, treading the path of time.
Seeking a meaning lost for all time.
Here now night and day, time brings on decay.
Past and present, fighting for honour and our behaviour.
Fate and love, truth and justice all to no avail.
Romance and mystery pay honour to the Druid Kings.
Run to the hills the new age God has awoke.
Dawn brakes and the fool plays his passage of life.
Mine or yours it has a price.

P. Sutton

Memories Of The Alps

On Alpine meadow as one walks by,
the views of mountains catch the eye
the snow and ice on peaks above
they shine so bright in the morning sun
the sound of water rippling by it starts
from glaciers way up high,
the air is fresh and clean it is a tonic
for all to breath.
The marmots bobbing up and down
as they leave their homes beneath the ground
the mountain paths get very steep so take
a rest and even sleep, just take care
for safety's sake let one walker stay awake.
When one is resting up so high one may not
notice changes in the sky, as the sun
begins to set the mists is rising as you feel wet
this is a sign to head on home before
the walkers start to roam
to lose one's way at such great heights,
it's not the place to spend the night

Dennis Dewberry

All My Dreams

I long to stroke your silken hair
And realize my dream is real
To touch your face and know you're there
How strong this love for you I feel

To lay my hand upon your breast
And hear your beating heart within
To feel your body with my caress
And give to you my everything

All those things I long to do
For you are my life my dreams
Every thought I have is you
I never lived before it seems.

Roy Perrott

Lonely Man

I love you so
Bitterness is inside me
I feel so confused
Do you want me
I am not sure
I don't know anymore
Fear of what is coming
Thoughts I try and wash away
But they rewind and play again.
I can't care, love, give anymore than I do
Please show you love me
Give a little back
Patch up my broken heart
Let me be with you.

Neil Johnson

Natures Way

How the stream trickles on a hot summer's day
Going so gently through stone and through clay
It seems to go nowhere it just trickles by
Until the first drops seem to fall from the sky

In no time a torrent angry and white
Is rolling along at a terrible pace
And as I look downward I see where it goes
Meeting with others upon the hillside

The lake it is waiting I see far below
Waiting to receive this great angry flow
And then the rain stops and after a while
It's back to a trickle through clay and through stone
So I do not wonder why any more
That this little trickle can turn to a roar
For it is just nature restoring the balance
Of keeping the lake to a suitable level

Joan M. Morris

The River Taf

Meandering forward through the crags and swelling onward
to the sea
The little stream that was a spring has now to realize its
precious dreams
It now becomes a river great with rapids, falls and mighty lakes
Forward it goes in endless praise talking and gurgling on its ways

It deepens twists and turns and roars o'er waterfalls and
mighty moors
It's met by many smaller streams anxious to realise their
precious dreams
The fish enjoy its depth and girth as it tumbles and gurgles
across the earth
It has now become the pride and joy of fishermen and little boys

Its hunted secrets now reveal fine salmon sewin, trout and eels
As the willow grows along the banks lapping its flow in merry dance
The moor hen speeds to call her brood with a tasty dish of
fish, their food
Forward and onward rolls the Taf with a roar and a swirl to the
sea at Laugharne
O'er many miles it's travelled with glee, at last to realise its
precious dream.

Raymond Phillips

Dream Traveller

Dreams are forever, they're not just for today,
Dreams are our own, they can't be taken away,
Just close your eyes, put your body at ease,
You're off on your journey, to wherever you please.

You may go in to the future, to a time you've not seen,
To some far off planet, where nobody's been,
To a fairy tale castle, it's a wonder it stands,
With little green people, who use their four hands.

Your journey may take you, to a time long ago,
Where dinosaurs roamed, and man should not go,
You'll get quite a fright, when you come face to face,
With a big brontosaurus, and your heart starts to race.

Dreams may be pleasant, you may feel a warm glow,
When you think of love, that you had long ago,
This love that you had, may now be your wife,
And you dream this warm glow, will last all your life.

Your dreams are now over, it is time to awake,
And the times that we had, it's now time to forsake,
With a shake of the head, real life starts again,
But we know it's so easy, to dream travel, any when.

Alan Winston Curtis

The Queen Mother

It happened for me during the war, when I was a little boy, I
found a love, a loyalty, that ere has given me joy, amid the
bombing, trouble and strife, my king was there, and his royal
wife, visiting victims of that ugly war, caring and sharing, and
trying to take more of the grief being felt, and the hardship
endured, showing the nation how much they care and letting
us know that the problems were shared.

I truly loved my king, and on the day that he died, along with
my schoolmates I broke down and cried, I was about fourteen,
but I didn't care, I let my tears flow, let my heart hang out bare.

when the shock of this faded I carried on with life, and
gradually realized I still had his wife, my queen was still there,
with her serenity an charm, giving and caring, gentle and warm.

My love and admiration has grown over the years, no scan-
dals, or upsets, no tantrums or tears, this precious lady has
gone quietly on, brave as a lion, honest and strong, even in
twilight she still soldiers on though retirement age has long
since gone.

What a wonderful service she's done for this land, the effort,
the dedication, it really is grand, and I knew that eventually
the time would come, when I could say from the heart.

I LOVE YOU QUEEN MUM.

T. M. P. Tomsett

I'm Here, Where Are You?

You should be here to see the mountains
To hold my hand and walk the paths
To feel the heat of summer burning
Turning fields to golden brown

You should be here to see the flowers
Patch–worked colours in the valley
To hear the whispers through the olives
Stirring leaves to shimmering sea

You should be here to share the sunsets
Glowing golden on the hills
To lie with me in gentle dusks
To feel the warmth of day retreating

You should be here to touch my body
To hold me close beneath the stars
As we submerge in passion
Beneath a Spanish sky

Sue Jenkinson

Shirley Valerie

Forty years ago today as a sweet little babe
in my arms you lay.
Your first breath of life with ne'er a cry
Not one of your family had a dry eye
when meeting you for the very first time
this pink mottled girl—blue eyes, auburn curls,
features fine—was your father's and mine.
You have grown and grown and worked very well
through childhood, teen years, adulthood—to tell
a few years ago with a lilt in your voice
you had finally met the man of your choice.
Your wedding day came as you walked up the aisle
on the arm of your step-dad you gave me a smile.
You stood by your groom a radiant bride—
no-one could take away my pride.
Today you are forty I'm still very proud;
you are one of those people who stand out in a crowd.

J. Morten

Vicious Circle

To delve into the past would hide tomorrow,
With tomorrow bringing hope, taking sorrow;
Sorrowful memories dissolve in relief:
Relieved to find love, displaced in grief.
But when love takes a turn it's sad
    to know it's real
For reality brings conflict within the
    hearts we feel.
But when the feelings aren't mutual,
    the love can't last
And if the love can't linger then we
    delve into the past.

T. Hawkins

The Loss Of A Loved One

When you lose somebody you love
And you know they have gone to the land up above
You hurt, you cry, your heart does ache
A smile you find it hard to make
But please don't spend too long feeling this way
What does it achieve keeping happiness at bay?
Instead talk about them, laugh about them,
Just like you used to do
Remember what they mean to the likes of me and you
We have our special memories of our loved ones' years
Their hobbies, their lives, even their careers
Maybe in your mind you're thinking of a particular day
Or you're thinking of something they always used to say
Maybe there is something else that is special just to you
Something that with them you always used to do
As for the family to help them in their sorrow
Please keep their lost one's name alive
And talk of them tomorrow

Julie Mawer

Victims

Poor bloody little mangled mouse!
Your spirit's left its velvet house
Destroyed in merest game.
Our well–loved cat
Committed that.
Is Cat or God to blame?

Jemima doesn't need to kill.
Three times a day she's fed her fill,
She only hunts for fun.
But can we say
She should not prey
While fox and hounds still run?

O Lord! That still in Man and Cat
There's something that loves hurting, that
Must make the weak afraid,
Till Kingdom come
Millennium
Sees Cat and Man re-made.

H. O. Aldhous

The Night Sky

When I was a child the heavens were bright.
Hundreds of thousands of jewels in the night.
Gone are the days when we saw all those stars.
Or gazed at Jupiter, Saturn and Mars.

Numerous galaxies light years away.
The morning star at the breaking of day.
Now with the street lamps and floodlights around.
Brightness pollution does really abound.

Comets and meteors come quite close to earth.
But even these things rarely show their true worth.
Most stars are hidden we see but a few.
The bright shining moon is all that's on view.

Pauline R. Jones

Flowers

The delicate anemone white
pink and blue, enjoy the sunlight,
parrot tulip with ragged petals
and on which the butterfly settles.

The arum lily rich glossy leaves
has so many fans arranging, weaves
iceland poppy is very well known
if a strong wind the petals are blown.

Grow profusely the forget me not
clusters very nice in flower pot,
luscious scent has familiar sweet pea
and much loved by a wandering bee.

With its pale glaucous leaves, Marguerite
their flowery mop heads look a treat.
Amassed around the gardens, the rose
everywhere it seems that flower grows.

Peony with its showy flower looms
with its voluminous silken blooms.

Gwendoline Albon

The Soldier's Dream

The moon is my candle
The sky is my roof
The grass in the meadow my bed
There I gaze at the stars in the heavens above
For I know they shine down on someone I love
Your love and your kisses I miss most of all
Those past nights of bliss are now memories all
My eyes are so tired asleep soon I'll be
Perhaps when I wake the world shall be free
Then back to our loved ones we go once again
To walk in he sunshine and laugh at the rain.

Edward Graves

Dawn Death

In the cold light of dawn
A young man's life withers away
For what, the passion
That drove him, that, which was forbidden.

Take away from him
His life, his love, his future
Take away his passion
And youth no longer has reason for that life.

A dream in the throes
Of converging with reality
A dream now fading
Along with the life, now without reason.

In the cold light of dawn
A young man's life ebbs away
With the tide that will take him
To a place where reality is, what was once his dream

Hannah M. McCormack

Wish

From this world, you took a holiday,
Left us here with words still to say,
Through your life, to God you wanted to be near,
But now you've gotten there, I wish you were here.

I looked around but all I saw,
Were all the things that left me blind before,
I didn't want to see them through my tears,
But now that you're gone, I wish you were here.

Matthew Fallows

When Love Dies

How can I forget you, we had a lifetime of love ahead,
Somehow you lost love for me! And found someone else instead.
I am so sad now you are gone, something inside my heart had died,
The great times we had together, alone now my misery I hide,
How two people can share so much of themselves, we lived as one,
Solving our problems together, turning problems into fun.
I know, I know, Life must go on! But mine will end today.
No strength to carry on without you, what more can I say.
Somehow I failed you, no one can take your place,
Remembering how you told me, no remorse upon your face.
I loved you so, You were my life, to you it was a game!
To show how much I love you, I will take the blame.
We lived and loved together, but for you the love ran out,
I should have seen the signs, when for no reason at me you'd shout.
They say it's better to have loved, than to have never have
   loved at all.
They say nothing of the lover left alone, no one hears them call.
The pain of being on my own again, to be alone in our bed,
I trusted you, I loved you, I believed every word you said.
My eyes are sore from crying my heart is full of pain.
One last request before I die! Don't break anyone's heart again . . .

Peter Dunning

New Life

A tiny babe with eyes of blue;
That's how we like to think of you,
Lying in your mother's arms,
Protected, shielded, from all harms.

A young child playing in the sun
With other friends, just having fun,
Not knowing yet what would befall
This little child—yet Lord of all!

And so you grew into a man
For this was part of God's own plan.
A wooden cross made from a tree;
Then you were killed—aged 33.

But though your years on earth were few
'Tis by your death we are made new.
Ready to serve in any way;
Ready to serve you every day.

Jean Dean

Life

Life seems to be so low all the time
it doesn't have to be like that
life could be the best in the world,
with no killing or wars.
But no there has to be killing and wars
I don't see why
life is the best thing your folks can give you,
But when five year olds get killed
what are you doing to them
they haven't lived
They've not seen anything
they didn't do us any harm
They only wanted to live their lives happily,
But they didn't, because their lives
were taken.

Eve Lara Walter

The River Of Life

We all sail down, this river of life,
each searching for our own personal goals,
but the river is full, of trouble and strife,
and the boats we ride, are full of holes,
we fight for every breath of air,
so we can carry on, our merry little way,
but in the river of life, only hope lies there,
onwards till the light of day,
so swim to the nearest, distant shore,
it's not as far as it seems,
there is so much, a heart can endure,
just don't give up your dreams,
don't let life, slip you by,
and regrets, what could have been,
because in the end, you'll only cry,
the past is over, time to wipe the slate clear,
no matter how long in the water, you tread,
just don't give up your dreams,
keep your goals tight, in your head,
because your destiny, is closer than it seems.

Share Hancocks

If Only

If only I'd met you when you were twenty two and I was
Seventeen.
Would it have been the same, or is it better now, this
dream?
If only, we could have lost our innocence together, and
be as we are now, as one.
If only I'd carried your seed of love, what a gift it would
have been!
If only seems a wasteful game.
But if only, for the rest of time, you love me, like you
did last night.
Then nothing's been in vain.

Janet Jeffery

Des-Res

We've tried to sell our house in the daily news.
Lots of "voyeurs" came around to criticise our mews,
"Don't think much of the kitchen, more cupboards are needed there
And we'd have to knock the wall down between the lobby
and the stairs
Are you leaving the cooker? The carpets you are of course
The guest room's a bit pokey and we'd have to replace the doors.
I don't like the shape of the garden but I'm sure I'd get used to that
The bathroom's really small though, you couldn't swing a cat.
All curtains and fittings are included, so the agent said,
It's not as smart as our holiday home in the southern Med.
I'll knock you down 5,000 you're asking way over the top!!
"Thanks, but no thank you. This house for sale is not"
Now we're taken our house off the market,
Pokey bathroom and guest room and all.
We didn't know how much we loved it
Until the purchasers came to call.

Josephine Burnett

The Train

The acrid smell of steam, oil and soot
Embrace the walker of the trodden way,
Hustle, bustle, push and shove prevails,
But soon, a seat—await departure . . . slow
The jolt—you move and quickly gather speed.
Through hazy windows watch the flashing view,
Like an old-time movie the scene is taken in.
Blurred close-up—but distant ever clear.
The rumble and the shake bizarrely harmonize
With metallic clickerty-click . . . a dying sound.
Pipes, cigars, the many cigarettes
Imbue the oxygen–denied atmosphere.
Nausea . . . choking . . . smarting eyes.
Exit brings relief in breeze–purged corridors
Soon to return to silent partners
Dumb, as though conversationally useless,
Each struck with an unknown tongue.
Arrival at the destination brings
Calm . . . but no desire to relive
The inevitable return.

Clive Cookson

The Mind Of A Poet

Tortuous mind! There is no sleep!
So many twists and turns and authors yet to speak
Wild imaginings of thoughts, sights and sounds
searching for that which is yet more profound!

Relentless mind! There is no remorse!
As you charter your heavily laden course
Sensations and emotions to scrutiny exposed
As onward and forward, in haste, you propose!

Cruel mind! There is no peace!
Quiet, not the mind, for the images never cease
Passion feeds this furnace driven by desire, by despair!
There is no asylum, no sanctuary from this castle in the air

Prolific mind! There is no defence!
You sup from my spirit, my soul, your thirst still unquenched!
Hunger for that elusive inspiration, born of blood, tears and
perspiration
no pain too great a price to pay which may result in your
exaltation!

Oh! Ecstatic mind! There is just no denying!
Smitten by this awesome flow of passion, so unerring
Scolded and rewarded by this ethereal temptress
This mind! No longer a curse, but beautiful, gifted and
blessed!

Laura St. John-Byles

Summer Love

The crisp of the grass
the sound of the sky,
everything's gone
'cause the summer's gone by.

Now that time's passed
I remember those days,
when nothing seemed to matter
all life was in a daze.

But one summer my life changed
I'd been to a place which once frightened me,
Going to that place with one friend
and coming back with a million.

My love for a place had never been so strong,
I looked in the mirror and saw
nothing wrong
I had lacked in myself confidence and
had cried in shame,
But now after that wonderful place
I would never be the same.

Lorna Hamill

Forks Of Life

Routine Street . . .
All too familiar—
Wears out my feet.

Hope Lane . . .
Is where I'll go—
It reduces my pain.

Heartache Road . . .
Is racked with despair—
It can be an avoidable abode.

Deception Way . . .
Is so dishonest—
I'll not face the dismay.

Future Close . . .
Is somewhat unknown—
If only I could get a dose.

The Final Road/Death Avenue . . .
I hope is not too soon
For there is so much in my life I must do.

Stephen Clark

Untitled

You turned my life around in Minnesota
who cares how to get free of horrible memories
the past behind
too hurt to tell anyone

In June yellow flowers from the garden
to show how much I cared

I didn't know
what you felt or thought
confined to be house
endlessly turning over in the dirty rooms

Not excepted to be a saint
but endless silence made me sick

One empty Saturday evening
cold wind noises
from my lonely heart

In September a clear decision
I had to leave
rid of that deceitful man of mine

I felt intoning my mantra words

Pine bunk bed for sale

Marjut Karsisto

The Presence

I enter the old haunted house, creaking floorboards at every step,
A blast of cold air caresses my face;
The upper stories beckon, I'm drawn to them like a moth to light;
Curiosity, excitement mounting, breath becomes laboured,
Pearls of moisture appear on my forehead and course down my back,
With a pounding heart I nervously take hold of the banisters
And begin my ascent upwards, slowly mounting one stair at a time;
I stand before a closed door, feel the pulsating energy within,
Its tentacles reach out towards me, but don't touch, just feel
    the aura around me;
The door slowly opens, It awaits, It has been awaiting my
    arrival for aeons.
I enter reticently, eyes darting from side to side, nothing to be seen
And then a bang, I jump, body shuddering, the door is closed,
    I can't open it,
I turn and feel It, we're alone, just the two of us, the Spirit and me;
As we merge, become one, I know that there is nothing to fear,
A calm overcomes me, an increasing warmth cloaks me;
The Presence called out telepathically and I came, now it
    separates from me
And hangs there, suspended, permeating the atmosphere
    with pure love,
It lifts, a whisper in my ear, a gentle kiss and I feel It no more,
Happiness overwhelms me, elation fills my soul,
I stand alone in the middle of the room, alone and at peace
    with myself.

Susan E. Cooper

Valentine

I've long thought of you as charm and grace
the spirit that could light my day
if I could but hold you to my breast
these words I'd gladly say.

If you knew how long I'd cared for you
and longed for you each day
if you knew how much I loved you
you would not one hour delay.

Who is it then that loves you so?
Who worships from afar?
How sad that you may never know
and stay just as you are.

How sad that all my caring
all my love should come to naught,
yet you will stay within my mind
and be its sweetest thought.

Brian McQuinn

Utopia Or Be Damned

Terrible world we live in where overall violence rules
Where has the gentleness gone from life, folk don't have
    any scruples?
For what reason do people not love each other greatly anymore?
Soldiers, airmen and sailors too, went to war—to save us all—
    for what?

Today our youngsters are open to all diversions,
A growing generation for tomorrow's conversion,
Their minds and bodies poisoned by temptation,
Drugs, porn, lack of love, simply no emotion.
Too much, too soon, bombs, guns, knives, boots and fists—

Maiming one another, but where there's life, there's hope,
Just a little purification needed here and there—
They must spare more thought for each other and the future,
Let them endeavour to survive, may love be the cure,
Then they will grow in charity and thoughtfulness to each
    and everyone
We must pray and beseech God's help for the return of values
    long since gone.

Marie-Christine Hornby

The Countryside

The steep rolling hillsides,
The valleys of green
The dirt tracks and pathways,
Were many have been.

Away from the hustle and bustle of life.
An escape from your worries,
The trouble and strife.

In the land of your ancestors,
A place where you're free,
To blend in with nature,
And enjoy what you see.

John Horncastle The Autumn Of Life

New Friendship

We haven't known each other long
But we have a bond that's good and strong
We met by chance and right away
We seemed to have so much to say.
We explored our common ground
And were amazed by what we found.
Things that we had both been through
People we both found we knew
Places where we both had been
Although we each remained unseen.
We communicate across the miles
Imagining each other's smiles
Sharing joy and sharing pain
Making sunshine out of rain.
Having found each other, we know
Our friendship will just grow and grow.

Ruth J. Davison

Lavender Days

Lavender her memories, fresh as youth her tears.
Not marred by ages cobwebs, or dimmed by passing years.
In truth, she is as young within, as on that fateful day.
All happiness was swept aside, when Edward went away.

It was, he said, his duty, to fight this evil war.
Love's smiling eyes, swore to return, and leave her never more.
A love that was eternal, she was to be his bride.
Unfulfilled her hopes and dreams; for darling Edward died.

The path of life then coldly bleak; such endless days now incomplete.
Alone midst tears, that flawed her cheek, retired to memories
safe retreat.
No fragment of reality could breach that barricade.
So time flew by and gradually, the rose began to fade.

Serene, the aged maiden, awaits with fragile grace.
A secret smile upon her lips, that welcome death's embrace.
Restored, her youth and beauty, at last she is set free.
Safe within her Edward's arms, for all eternity.

Paula-Jane Barnett

She sits by her window
Watching children at play
Remembering times
When her hair wasn't grey.
When her dreams were all new
And her life was just starting
Her body more supple then.
And her hair held a parting
But sadly you see
Time has taken its toll.
And loneliness has a big grip on her soul.
When all that is left to sparkle her eye
Is a memory of her life that is passing by.
Her home is her prison
Her time she has served
Her imagination's her transport
Isn't this so absurd?
This lonely old lady
Was once somebody's wife
Now she sits at her window in the autumn of her life

Donna Giblen

The Garden Pond

Dear friend, please pause, do not go far.
See how happy we frogs are
In this garden pond you made for us,
As we mingle here midst reed and rush.

Stay, friend, and see a blackbird drink.
The waterlily blossom pink.
A dragonfly dart through the air.
You'll be so pleased you lingered there.

And while you rest beneath clear blue skies.
And watch the many butterflies.
Hear the serenade of the mistle thrush,
As he visits the pond you made for us.

Veronica Jewell

Songs In The Night

The earth is sleeping and the night seems
like eternity:
Filled to abundance with riches so precious
that God Himself was left a little breathless
when he made them.
'Tis a false presumption—but oh! Tonight is
different—there is no separation.
God and Earth are one!
The Heart that once broke is whole again,
and like the Sun, shines upon the world and
warmeth all in its intensity.
They sky like velvet set with diamonds, glorifies
His presence.
The shrouded hills pay homage to His sight—
and the trees in rapturous whisper sing—
Songs in the night.

Ruth Wharf

"For A Lost Cause"

I have gazed at the ship leaving time, dignified,
Taking you, so unkind, far away from my sight
And I have seen the hands that will touch you tonight,
Lulled by thousands of waves born from the tears I cried.

My love has gone astray on the shore of your life,
It has died in your shadow, has faded away
And my soul crucified on the clouds of the day
Has watched over your steps and played a gentle fife.

I have dried out the tears that had wrinkled my face
And thrown away my pain to the vultures of gold
But the wounds of my mind that I hate, that I hold,
Are eating me within, leaving an empty space.

For the seasons will pass, alone, without your love
That backfires on me like the bullets of war,
Where my senses are dying to the sun ajar,
Where I stand, where I stare at the moon high above.

For the call of my heart is without a reply,
For my hands that reach out have touched an empty space.
I am nothing for you, but a forgotten face,
But a "was", never been, an ineffective ply . . .

Marc Edmond Malfait

Missing Love

Deep in my heart your memories I keep,
Nobody, knows how often I weep.
No one knows the pain I bore,
Beneath the smile I always wore.

A loving memory clearer than gold.
Silent the voice I love to hear,
Far away from me, is the face I love so dear.

I knew there never could be another,
Gentle, lovable, sweet and kind.
These are the thoughts that come to me,
When the thought of you enters my mind

Nurzan Ahmed

Life In The Midlands

I stand by my window and look down the field,
Once it was cultivated, gave a good yield,
Now it's a motorway, rushing along
Lorries, cars, busses never a moment
to hear the bird's song.
Last week the snow stopped the road up.
Nothing could get along, they trudged on foot,
Leaving their cars after waiting for hours
Have to come back again when it all thaws.
I went outside and could hear not one sound,
Nothing was moving—all gone to ground.
After a few days snow is all cleared,
Vehicles rush on again never a pause,
Life in the Midlands—I love it of course.

Eileen Woodfield

Journey Through Pain

As I watch the sunrise,
Tears fill my eyes.
Another day dawns,
My heart's full of cries.

I look around me, and
Emptiness greets me.
Without you my love,
There is no meaning to life.

I have searched many an escape,
But I'm back to where I've started.
I seem to be a person standing,
With no direction, hope or future.

Therefore I must die a thousand deaths,
Before my eyes can fully open,
To the sunrise of my soul,
And to the sunshine of a new beginning.

Olga Mistry

To-Day's News

Great excitement of life on Mars
Earthly 'Rail' Strikes and Motors Cars
Grinding towards 'Internet'.
'Outer space' Distortions,
The inner life, confusion and abortions,
Destroying the right of way.
Shrieking cautions
Without the light of day.
Into the night of the satellite
And Heavenly Decay.

Arnold Wright

Dream Time

Upon the scorched earth wastelands
Of the antipodean sands
A group of musicians of untold mirth
Played tunes that rocked the earth

No stimulants could revive the times
Of oscillating sweet–natured tunes
Even rumours spread of heretical wealth
Did not deter from their expert stealth

A dream that does not seem to be
Or would ever, ever see,
But by seeing and believing with the naked eye
They still would not reason why.

The jazz with these phantasms
cannot seize the day's good ways,
Still, the land's God–given goods
Is the proof that delays the day.

Patrick Brett

Kingdom Of The Sea

Diamonds of reflected sunlight on the sea,
Shrill cries of sea gulls as they soar free,
Shoals of iridescent fish dance with the tide,
Dolphins play, and enchant us as they glide
Past our vessel as we journey on
Towards the horizon, where the sun has gone.

Night descends, wearing a cloak of blue,
The water darkens to a greener hue,
Stars adorn the sky like a bridal veil,
St. Elmo's fire dances off the starboard rail,
The boat rocks gently on a cradle of foam,
We chart our course towards land, and home

We sail past rocks where seals bask in the sun,
Past fishing boats, busy where great shoals run,
We round the headlands, and we are home,
Back from the places where seafarers roam,
But it's for Neptune's Kingdom we always yearn,
The sea's in our blood, and we shall return.

Yvonne Butler

An Ode To Freddie

Freddie Mercury, what a performer, what a star!
When he took the stage, people knew he'd go far.
To me he was fantastic, to me he was the best.
What energy, what power, he sang with such zest.
Millions loved Freddie, from simply "all around."
Everyone listened to that, "Oh amazing sound."
When Freddie was in concert the crowds went wild.
The fans varied greatly from adult down to child.
He led the greatest band, "That is for sure."
His fans were always thrilled when they heard or a tour.
As talent goes he was at the top of the tree.
His songs, ballads, and videos brought joy to me.
But alas Freddie died, and now he is gone!
People try to copy him but we know there was only one.
He's being missed by many, as each day goes by.
They flocked to see him off, just to say "Goodbye."
But legends live on, many say forever.
Who could forget him, me? That answers "Never."

Peter Hanson

Love Grows . . . Love Hides . . .
Love Is Blind . . . So Blind

There was a mum from begotten,
Whose cousin's cousin fancied her rotten,
He thought he was a dove,
He came flying from above,
Only for her to know, that he was in love.

So when green eyes are smiling
(Smiling just for you) it's
To show how much this dream of mine
Can so very much come through
So put away those dark brown eyes
And let the sight shine true (Blue)
Not black, nor brown, nor red, nor grey
Nor pink, nor yellow, nor white, not pale
Just green, just green, just like this Queen
'Cos this light of mine shine true (Blue)

Yvette Avonda Wiggins

The Crystal

There it was, the crystal, the superbly cut reflection
of our own souls, an art creation, a natural source
of human existence, it is.

To look at it, to touch it, to feel it, enchantment
beyond comprehension. An abyss will intrigue.
The crystal is enchanting, enlightening, within the
feeling portrays; mystery, darkness, so alike fear.

Are you frightened to question human existence
and the battle of thoughts through one's mind?
Can you perceive the reality above normal reality?

Calm as solemn seas I see, yes, I see a light,
though bright. It creeps, slowly, slowly.
Aaargh! A shine divine. I feel a warm soul,
though it is mine, an experience to transcend so fine,
so divine. It is exerted, emotional.
Combination—rare as rare, the power, the knowledge,
the ecstasy, the relief, the release of my very own soul.

A shimmer, intriguing, mesmerizing, dulling

    I am strengthened.

Dean Michaels

Dribbles

When early morning cold damp mist lends itself to rain.
We watch its tortured journey, dribble down our window pane.
Should noonday sun poke out his face to warm this
patterned pane.
It will turn it all to steam and drive away the rain.

The sun moves on to evening breeze, drawing moisture from
land and seas.
Starts its journey once again and brings us mist for
tomorrow's rain.

R. A. Nye

Just Remember

A lifetime of memories lie beneath
This solitary rose
As a loved one rests forever more
Last days of life are gone.

Those who are left will remember
With tearful eye and aching heart
The one who has gone knows only peace
Anguish, with death, does depart.

A time of grief, to recollect
Happier times gone by
Wondering were there things left unsaid
As to reconcile thoughts you will try.

Gone is the pain, take strength from that
In heaven there's no good or bad
Just joy everlasting, so fight back your tears
Only mortals like us, can be sad.

Ken Helm

Wonders

They say there are Seven Wonders of the World, but surely
  I've seen more.
The sun that shines, the wind that blows and the rain that
  soaks you to the core,
The laughter of an innocent child whose face lights up this world,
Prince Monolulu whose hand I held, while walking down the Lane.
A starry night, a comet bright, an eclipse of the moon, the
  mention but a few,
The sights I've seen again.

The Post Office Tower, I've had dinner there, I've stood and gazed at
The Empire State and couldn't see where, the top could be.
I've been caught by a Hurricane at sea,
The boat that rocked, the waves that roared, was another
  wonder to me.

And in May on a lovely day, I've seen the bluebells in the wood,
I've watched a hot air balloon go floating by, up, up in a blue
  sky,
And I knew a mere mortal could, if only I could, one day do
  the same,
But lack of money is the name of the game.

There are so many wondrous things to see, so many yet to do
  as I stand and gaze
At the Moons new phase, and feel at one with the world and
  all its wonders.

Marie-Louise Sceats

Untitled

Politics is part of everyone's life
Whether father, mother, husband or wife.
Conservative, Labour or Liberal, which one to choose?
What would you gain, and what would you lose?

We vote in a system of first past the post
To give one party the chance to boast
The chance to put their plane in gear
Whether or not these plans are dear.

The Tories have been here for a very long time
And saying they've been tough on crime.
But people are tired of all the "sleaze"
As such affairs put one ill at ease.

New Labour, the say is a cunning plot.
Ten pence in the pound, but at the expense of what?
So many U-turns, you don't know their plans
Been in opposition so long, they've become also-rans

The Liberals are the party in the centre,
The one that fewer people enter.
With all the ups, there have to be downs—
Whichever you vote, there'll always be frowns.

S. A. Smyth

Untitled

Who are the lonely among us
Fellow travellers on a train
A bus or in a crowded street
Using time as a drug.

Look at the passing faces
Presenting a facade
Of defence against all
Who dare to pry.

Who are the selfish among us
Treading on others and using
The weakness and insecurity
Born to some and bred in others.

Who are the compassionate among us
Sharing and caring for those in need
Easing a burden relieving a tortured mind
A therapy for even themselves.

Who are those among us
Prepared to stop and ponder
Along this race of life
Alas too few.

Lilian McGeachy

First Love

You are my everything,
the sun, the moon and the stars.
When we are close it's heaven,
I would die if we were to part.
For forty long years we've been together,
and I believe that you still care.
Because you were my first love,
and I know you will always be there.

Christine Barton

It Was Fairies Wasn't It?

Walking through the woods
on a hot summer's day
the sun shining through the tree tops
was glistening on the stream nearby.
Then I couldn't believe my eyes
no surely it was just the sun
playing tricks on my eyes
wasn't it?
Or, oh yes that must be it
dragonflies darting about here and there,
the glint was the sun reflecting off their wings
wasn't it?

Low I stooped in the undergrowth
edging nearer to the stream,
these little creatures that I saw
had long golden hair, wings, that sparkled
and although not much bigger than a dragonfly,
I know it was fairies I saw that day,
wasn't it?

Susan Smale

Beloved (River Of Dreams)

Here amongst this war–torn land, I sink my head in my hands.
I think of home miles away, I start to cry and start to pray.
I see a puddle with a face. It takes my mind to a different
time and different place.
Back to England in 1910, to the time I met her and life began.
We sailed along the river of dreams, with nothing to fear or
so it seemed.
Just then I hear a sound, it takes me back to this battleground.
But what of my beloved across the sea, oh what has become of she.
I hope she's happy, I hope she's proud and if I die on
this bloodied ground
I'll wait for her in the mud and sand to lay together hand in hand.
But if I survive this terrible war but our paths don't cross anymore
I'll light a candle every night, and dream of the day our souls
reunite.

Gary Chard

The Cat

Tail erect, head held high
Proudly aloof, alone walk I
Revered, reviled, rebuffed in turn
None my secret heart shall learn

Far–off, ancient days remembered
Egypt's Pharaohs, many splendoured
Worshipping, their homage pay
At my feet their tributes lay

Savage, medieval days
Familiar in the magic ways
Of witchcraft, I fearful, dread yet scorn
The awesome cry, Heretic! Burn!

Jewelled eyes of emerald, topaz, gold
Reflecting agonies untold
I, victim of their mindless hate
Endure the Sorceress' fate

In torment, tortuous darkness prowl
Haunted, as the screeching owl
Rends the night with eerie cry
Sphinx-like in my silence, I

Joy Goodenough Taylor

A Garland For Tyler, Aged Three Years

Tyler came one November Eve
With his parents from Los Angeles
To the house next door where he climbed the stairs
A feat for him, never done before.
On summer days into my garden he came
To hunt for bees and butterflies and other game.
Quick—here now—there now—in a world of bliss
And to find flowers for his vases—
"Oh! What shall I pick."
Happy, happy Tyler of merry eyes and burnished hair.
The year has passed, and Tyler, with life ahead
Must go and leave us to our long lost dusty dreams.
My wish for him is that the Fates be kind
And protect him from the War Gods' Cries.

Kathleen M. Phillips
-1995-

Transmutation

The mountain quarry at Carrara gleamed
as sunlight steeped the valley's marble rock.
The sculptor pointed to an awkward block . . .
'This may have been rejected, but I dreamed
last night of such a piece and size. It seemed
to me I even had the power to mock
the intransigence of stone, somehow to shock
this slab of nothing into what I schemed.'

The art of sculpture is to take away,
attack the marble and release the form
from lifeless cold to breathing pulsing warm.
And sure enough, here is a child at play,
and here his mother, summoned from the stone,
absorbed in thought, proud, sorrowful, alone.

Clive Craigmile

Death-Tombstones-And-Artificial-Flowers

No point of going to a sacred place of rest,
And letting your tears fall
Onto a spray of artificial flowers,
Which show no emotion
As it withstands the elements
Of rain-snow-wind, and frost, and of human nature.
But nestles in the pot, as rigid, cold, and indifferent
As the corpse that lies beneath,
And will remain there even until your day is done.
No fragrant perfume fills the air, to draw the bumble-bee
As it gathers its daily crop of pollen,
Or colourful butterfly to lay their eggs.
No meaning to sense of smell
It's only to say—I've done my duty
I won't be calling so often, or if ever again.
The day is over, life is done.
What should have been said or not have been said,
It's too late now it's all in the Master's hand.
Death-tombstones, and artificial flowers
Were made for each other. Just a means to an end.

J. W. Hendra

Deep Inside

To believe in yourself, having inner strength,
Is a worthy cause yet long in length.
What do you do when everyone disagrees,
Do it for you, or don't to please?

Promises, promises can always break,
Leaning on one person is a mistake.
Never trust anyone is the safest way,
Trusting yourself means you'll never pay.

If you are lonely, and need to talk,
The one who was there may take a walk,
Depending on one person is a dangerous path,
Love 'em and leave 'em—do you wish you had?

Do you wish there were no decisions to make?
Do you wish there is no such thing as fate?
Can believing in yourself be so wrong?
Life is tough, yet we live to be strong.

Carolyn McCarthy

Because

When I cried
she thought
there was something in my eye.
When I hurt
she asked
if I had indigestion.
When I bled
she would not see.
And when I said
I need
she walked away.
And now,
I no longer cry or hurt or bleed,
no longer need,
I am emotionally anaemic,
All systems shut down,
And she says,
"Please love me, why don't you love me?"
And I say
"Because".

Yvette Edson

Untitled

Like a new life beginning the lily slowly unfurled
Showing its golden beauty to the world.
I watched, mesmerized, as one by one the petals broke free
And then I thought of you, who had given the flower to me
And smiled.

Shelley Woodroffe

My Rose Is Gone

Gone is my sweet, sweet rose,
plucked with a cruel might,
from the tender bed of our love,
and so I am lost in night.

With my love did I nurture,
I cared with a lover's feel,
gave breath with a lover's kiss,
and guarded with a lover's seal.

Yet now, lost, I stand alone,
listening softly to sounds anew,
for your singing voice were my ears but made,
its melody gone with your adieu.

As I taste the new–fouled air,
I accept your flower's depart,
but the soil of any is fertile,
and forever your roots rest in my heart.

Gregg Morgan

For You My Brother

Deep down in my mind I cannot stop but think
that there is a ray of hope for you my brother,
I have tried in my despair in my daily life, my island
to find the reasons that wander in your fragile lonely mind.

What is it that you are longing? What is making you give up?
don't you see hope for tomorrow and you are destroying your life?

I have heard hundreds of people drowning with drugs and
alcohol not caring for their surroundings, ignoring the ones
they love planting seeds of pain and sadness, each of them
trying to die.

How can I help you my brother
How can I reach to your heart,
how can I show you I worry
and I do cherish your life.

If only my voice and prayers were to reach to you my brother
I would get rid of your mind all the darkness and the sorrows,
I would allow you to find a future in your tomorrows
and the reason to be alive.

If you could . . . if you only could . . .

M. Rojas-Mitre

Fratercula Arctica

Sailing back to the states, the "Sea Parrot's" huge white flags
Wave for the wind, to take them home.
A white bellied bird flies by, its triangular beak, blue yellow red
Looks for a marine life meal for it to be fed

Another flies lower, its black top absorbs the sun
Looking for food for its burrow–living daughter or son
A sailor shouts out "old bottlenose is back, and he's brought his friends"
The sailor guesses that land is near and in his eyes forms a long journey tear

Just the last bird to stay, and not to fly
Uplifting feeling in the crew it makes
Standing on a small rock near by
Triangular eyes observes the well named ship
It then flies off to follow its friends
Now the sailor calls to the bird
"Ever thanks my Puffin friend. I wish well your family too, and see you soon"

So the sailor overjoyed, nearly back to his wife he loves
The puffin back to his nest now
Maybe, the sailor thinks, these are the seas' doves

Ian P. Fairey

Upon Reflection

Aren't we all of common bait
when we bite the words that fill with hate
We the prophets can't deny
or fail to see within the eye
The envy of the heavy sigh
for these rich adorned that passed by
Critic makers are we all
when with the ear that we befall
The voice so trained to patronize
that starts resentment so to rise
One is cause, and one, effect
both together they reflect
Our differences are so relate
it is obviously our fate, that we are all
of common bait.

Agnes Burns Lawson

A Troubled Mind

Do not grieve, or anger fill thy heart.
'Tis love you seek and to give thy love you need.
You can put your trust and love in one so near,
Do not look far or long for what is dear.
These precious needs bring beauty of a kind,
And calm the waters of the troubled mind.

A flower cannot raise its beautiful head,
We all need love to bloom, the lest be said.
Your sorrow and despair will soon begone,
And happiness surround you like a song.

Joyce Rose Phillips

Time Will Heal

"Time will heal" is all I hear
From friends and family and everyone I know
But whether you are far or near
I've tried and tried but can't let go

It doesn't matter how long ago
Where I am or who I'm with
For in my heart I'm sure I know
"Time will heal" it's all a myth

No matter how hard I seem to try
To forget the past and get on with my life
To everyone else I'd be telling a lie
To say I don't want you as part of my life

Why is it I always feel that way
When they only need to mention your name
So this is the price I'll have to pay
Forever feeling heartache and pain

Elaine Murdoch

A Star Is Born

Within each night a star is born
To light the night from dusk till dawn.
Though what's to gain from this true sight,
Is up to man to choose its height.

For some it means a happy sign.
For some it means that life is fine.
Though some may say that love's not true,
For me it shows my love for you.

So see a star and think of me,
And wish me well where'er I'll be.
For there I'll be calling your name.
With every star my eyes could claim.

Ahmad Faisal Aljunied

Emptiness

Sunlight flickers on empty trees
With empty people shading under.
Dull greyness is all around,
What happened to the brightness?

A young woman calls for her love
But deaf ears turn to deaf mouths.
Unutterable silence is all around,
What happened to the laughter?

People shuffling, mindless of direction
Herding together for mutual comfort.
Bleakness is all around
What happened to the hope?

A deserted city mourns for itself,
Dust lies with nothing to disturb,
Emptiness is all around
What happened to the soul?

S. Frame

Idyll (Elizabethan Love Song)

My love was true, and how he did love me
In lilac time when trees were dressed with flowers.
If ever two were one, then surely we
Sitting amongst the full and scented bowers.

In lilac time, when trees were dressed with flowers,
We sat and gazed, quite silent, lost for words
Sitting amongst the full and scented bowers
The only sound—sweet trilling of the birds.

We sat and gazed, quite silent, lost for words
The spell of love and passion wrapped around.
The only sound, sweet trilling of the birds
As petals blown from blooms lay on the ground.

The spell of love and passion wrapped around
The night grew cold, we had to kiss and part
As petals blown from blooms lay on the ground
And trembling clasped each to the other's heart.

The night grew cold, we had to kiss and part,
If ever two were one then surely we,
And trembling clasped each to the other's heart.
My love was true, and how he did love me.

Kathleen D. Spencer

The Photograph

The glow from this face a light in the room
brightens each day when the morning's in bloom.
Changing each day as I clearly compare
a life like resemblance as I am looking at her.
An unforgotten past that changes with time
as I look on with pleasure at this beautiful smile.
A glow that keeps glowing brighter each day
maturing not ageing, changing with grace.
Floating through life like a butterfly, new
sheer pleasure your presence adds life to the room.
A caption of time, irreplaceable past
as I look at your face
through a photograph.

Adele Parkes

My Baby

A cry of pain and then at last, I have my baby in my arms,
Oh how tiny and fragile he is, I just want to give him a kiss.

Down my cheeks I feel tears roll,
Yet it is hard to describe the feeling though,
It is like a warmth enveloping you,
Like walking in the morning dew,
Like champagne bubbles on your tongue,
Like laughing and playing and having fun,
Like all these things rolled into one.
Yet even this is not enough to describe,
The feeling of how much you love this child,
This little bundle lying in your arms,
That you would protect from all harm.

Little feet and little hands, all wrinkled like an old man,
Beautiful eyes twinkling and blue,
That look expectantly up at you,
For one journey has finished and another begun,
and he knows I am his mum,
The one who will give him everything he needs,
Who will love him more with every breath he breathes.

Sarah Jane Ruvolo

Modern Painting

Ill–tempered blues and greens snarl at each other,
Crisscrossed with streaks of incandescent red.
It says here, 'Portrait of the Artist's Mother.'
Oh what a life his daddy must have led!

Gordon P. Wallace

The Speedy Route Of An Arterial Road

The motorways of madness, that run throughout my shell,
have had some drugs along them and I don't feel very well.

Cul-de-sacs of memories that I thought long were dead,
have now been re-diverted, straight into my head.

Two years ago that happened . . . it seems like yesterday,
I'm quite enjoying this now, in a funny sort of way.

Why George . . . hello . . . long time no see . . . really November '73,
well, who'd of thought that, still, must fly, catch you again
George, when I'm high!

It's really not bad this powdered stuff, now that I'm over the
rough, oh, high . . . ahhh . . . I know that face . . . oh yes, of
course, you're my dead aunt Grace!

Mind you, your memory never dies, funny,
I could have sworn you had blue eyes,
still, I don't get here very much, bye now Grace, keep in touch.

Oh I have such wonderful times, sniffing, talking, writing rhymes,
can't wait to see who else I'll find, down the back-streets of
my mind . . .

Paul R. Seymour

World Service From Bush House

The chimes of Big Ben not only tells the listener
  The Gmt Time but that the service is accurate, reliable and fast
When the announcer says. This is the news, you instantly associate
  It with the best news service in the world
Why kill and split the world's best radio station
  When it is more educational move informative than the rest
Whether it is audio or video
  Nothing can beat the good old BBC world service radio from Bush
House Boy oh Boy
  Please do not be a kill joy by getting rid of a British Institution
The truth and aspect is that
  BBC world service is one of Britain's greater assets
It is about time for the public to call on the Governors of the BBC
  To protect the integrity of the world service and stop it
being broken up if John Birt
  Wishes to get rid of dirt he should clean his home and leave
  the BBC world service alone
It is about time for each and everyone to unite
  And preserve the BBC world service and chimes of Big Ben

Harish Shah

That Day Will Come

I realize now just why it was
That God took you away,
He knew the pain was just too much
And that you couldn't stay.

It's something that I've got to face,
The sadness since we parted,
I know I've cried a million tears,
It's left me broken-hearted.

I sit alone in silence now
And think of you so much,
The laughter's gone that we once shared,
Also your smile, your touch.

Flowers die, but will live again,
To me it seems unkind,
They will bloom for me to see,
But you'll be there in mind.

The minutes go so quickly,
And each hour passes by,
I know one day we'll meet again,
A reunion in the sky.

F. Chambers

Paradise Found

I turned the lane and climbed the path that lead upon the hill
And there it stood, alone, tumbledown peaceful and still
Who would have thought not far from a busy road, could
  dwell this sweet abode.
I caught my breath gazing at the view, and at once I knew
This will be mine I will spend my autumn days to make it live again
With windows wide to gaze across the lovely countryside
I turned again towards the tumbledown old place, brambles crept
  around the door through the cracks beneath the floor
Dear house your worries are no more for I will give you quite
  a different face.
Time as time will do moved fast I was back again at last,
The shed where once a tractor stood, a bright new kitchen of
  oaken wood
Once where stood the old prune shed lilac pillows and covers
  draped my bed
Through my windows I saw quite clear, on the hillside, three
  small deer,
Roses and daffodils in bloom, looking back again to my lovely
  bedroom
Lilac and gold in the morning light, mirrors around to make it bright
Bringing me happiness all day long, sleeping contentedly
  every night,
What more could one ask from our dear Lord above
To awaken each day and be filled with such love.

Iris Gulliver

Decisions Made . . .

The harsh reality and blinding truth,
conflicting images—too much to boot!
Decisions made; rejected, regretted;
the judgements of Nemesis expertly perfected.

A synopsis of life, not known but made,
the path chosen not easily laid.
The flawless beauty of the night,
does not pale by adventurers of might.

Birth is life and life is death,
the rites of passage is serious yet . . .
the time of now will be the time to come;
for what will be, has already been done.

Not all is black and white today,
for colours are muted and turn to grey.
The sands of time turn for everyone;
decisions made are effected by all and none.

The harsh reality and blinding truth,
are made such, but only by you!
Decisions made; regretted, rejected,
the judgements of Nemesis thoroughly implemented.

Anastasia Karasinski

"Dear Bill . . . "

No words of wisdom, pith or wit
Are penned herein.
No clues, no revelations here, to bare my soul,
Disclose my sin.
No sentences concealing
Hidden depths of fire,
How blank this mask, my face,
How bland these words, revealing
Nothing I desire.
Pauline Pullan

If You Dare Turn Out The Light

Let those with fear repose the night,
In slumber safe turn out the light,
Exalt the gloom with plays profane,
In wretched hours the dead shall reign.

Come walk with me who seem so brave,
Come be my shadow view your grave,
Join in our plays that grace the morn,
The line where life from death is torn.

Come show you're brave as fearful sleep,
Come walk that line let evil reap,
Behold! Your grave dare lay your head,
Be brave or fear choose your bed.

Some lives run short no time to waste,
You choose to fear be gone in haste,
We'll part this once take heed I say,
You shall return I cheer that day.

The hands of time will strike you down,
And wrap in my darkest gown,
Safe slumber deep repose the night,
And if you dare turn out the light.
Ian Deal

Warning To All

That drink was your contract to die,
    You're very stupid my oh my;

I am the loaded gun against your head,
    Soon I'll go off and you'll be dead;

Your life is so near to its end,
    You used to think I was your friend;

You're not the only one going to die,
    Let's find someone else let's play eye-spy;

This is going to be so very inhumane,
    You're going to cause so much pain;

I am the one, you won't get far,
    I am the one, I am your Car!
Justin Barnard

Each New Day

Dawn brings to each a brand new day
Will we use it wisely or squander it away
As light sweeps darkness from the sky
What does it bring to you and I
A rush to cope as life will demand
Shall we brush aside what we don't understand
No time to listen, to seek, to find
No time to let our thoughts unwind

So many blessings we take as our due
Yet without our sight what would we do
How many times do we see and smile
Stop to think on that for a while
To hear, to walk, to love, to play
Do we ever linger to wonder and say
Thank you Lord for the blessings we have
Though our heart may be heavy, eyes sad
We still have much we could lose today
Time is so quick to slip away
K. W. M. Heasman

To "Love Divine"

When flowers are gay, and skies are blue.
They bring to me, sweet thoughts of you.
When birds are singing, in the trees.
They sing of "Loves" sweet melodies

I lift mine eyes, to see the stars."
And find the heart, within me—stirs
To heavenly lights, shining above
Wrapping me soul within their "Love"
When earth is dark, and clouds appear
I choose a "thought", to draw you near!
I choose a dream, or memory.
Deep in that constant heart of me.
That gentle voice of "Love Divine"
weaving your thoughts so close to mine.
That movement beautiful to see
Embracing all "Eternity"
Come closer now, and closer still
Entwine your heart and mine.
Until there is not one but two to bless
That everlasting consciousness.
F. M. Edmonds

Our World

Speak not to me of the world today, a world of change, of
    greed and gain
Where man no longer cares for man, a selfish world—I own to shame.

Speak not to me of countries far where women starve and
    children die,
And men are so intent on wars they're deaf to a people's
    suffering cry.

Where man no longer honours man and kicks a fellow when
    he's down
Where scandal fills the tabloid news and nowhere morals to be found.

Could I look back to a world of old, where children, loved,
    however poor
Were safe and happy in the fold in innocents unspoken law.

To-day the world has gone a rye, no longer we protect the young,
Families split, and children cry, and wars still carry on and on.

Speak not to me of our damaged world, through ignorance we
    wrought our shame
Crime, destruction, loves defiled, murder in frustrations name.

Polluted seas, rain forests torn, beasts extinct, all down to greed
The legacy we leave behind, a broken world, just left to bleed.

Speak not to me of chosen men who make our many hideous laws
What of the Ten Commandments, did God not give these for a
    cause?

If man could live again by faith, in loyalty and honour stand
And each one hold unto his own, we might just save our
    broken land.

So speak to me of a future world, where fellows care to share
    their worth
And wars shall end and sense, shall reign, to break this bitter
    hell on earth.
Anne Scott

Our Uncle Famous

Our Arthritic, knuckle-twister sits:
Shadowed.
Fibrous—clamped and muscle—mute:
Our Uncle.
The two gold medal winner, smoulders,
His twin, deep-blues twinkle a memory,
Rejoicing, as he spasms to a full stop:
The giggly thinker.
With that split—melon smile, gurgling a gleam,
His relish and hope is infectious:
Our Healer.
Our two gold medal winner of life.
Our Uncle Famous.
Chris Garner

Hell On A G String

My friend was bought a violin,
And oh! The noise she made.
She scraped and sawed and squealed and screeched
Through every piece she played.

Her teacher used to block his ears,
Her neighbours moved away;
But my friend loved the row so much
She would not stop all day.

She ate her meals up in her room
Between a scrape and squeal.
Music, you could never call it
'Cos the sound was quite unreal.

Her mother tried to hide it once,
But that was doomed to fail;
My friend soon found it—what a shame!
And loudly sawed a scale.

I stayed her friend through thick and thin
And no-one heard me curse
The reason was that I too played
But I was even worse!

Juliet Corbett-Jones

What Do You Do?

Love is something you can't ignore,
It's something that builds up more and more,
But when there's love, there's always hate,
So why do we think love is great?

When your love has broken your heart,
Do you stay, or do you part,
If only you could forgive and forget,
Maybe you wouldn't be so upset.

You're so fed up of all the lies,
And now you can't stop the tears from your eyes,
Maybe if you leave for a while,
This disaster will end with a smile.

You're not so sure about what to do,
When your love has just hurt you,
Do you listen and believe,
Or do you think he just deceives?

Tammi Gordon

What's The Point

What's the point, the pain never ending.
Day in day out.
Night time you lie there thinking what's the point.
The point is people love you for yourself
They don't see the pain.
Only you know,
But if you are not there they feel the pain.
Because there is no you anymore,
So that's the point.

S. Waters

The Magnolia Tree

The snow lies white on the upland slopes
And frost still prisons the earth.
But a blackbird sings on the top–most branch
Of the tree that means rebirth.
Over the flowers that lie asleep
Its branches spread like wings,
Each flower held up like a chalice of love
To where the blackbird sings.
Soon will the violets wake to the sun
And the daffodils flaunt their gold
But the cups of ivory flushed with pink
Spring's blessing will cherish and hold.
Their petals will fall on the greening grass
As the days grow warm and bright.
Yet the love we shared as the tree grew tall
Will live like the flowers in the Lord's clear light.

Muriel Leech

Fond Memories Of My Dad . . .

There the brightest shining star
Shines down on all to see
and from the glow from which it brings
it tells me it is he
He had died, I thought and dropped a tear
But inside there was no fear
from human sights his soul had gone
But now I would never stand alone
through all the pain and tears and strife
all he lacked was fateful life
and every night I watch and I am glad
that the bright shining star is my dear Dad
and the reason it grows
only me and himself really knows . . .

Irene Divine

Your Angered Crows

Repeated blows rain down on my chest,
Shattering my solar plexus, shredding my heart.
Kicks begin to rupture my kidneys.
The butterflies you set free in my stomach,
Turn to angered Crows ripping at tender flesh.
Your eyes irradiate my face, hot flushes flay my skin.
Bones break under no apparent pressure.
I would alert authorities to your assault on my willing body.
But no bruises grace my skin, no visible blood seeps from
endless veins.
No evidence for jilted jurors to consider.
Your innocent smile turns way.
I drop to aching knees waiting for the final beheading.
You walk away, hopefully grappling with your wicked sense
of humour,
Leaving me to live my dying days in a world of grey.
A colourless shadow of my former self.
A broken man.
I enter the winter of my life forty six years before qualification.
I'm sure you meant me no harm,
I apologize for bleeding on your self-esteem
I will leave as I entered, in pain.

Steven Watkins

Where Are You

Falling up the station steps
Drunk with happiness and kisses
Where are you now
And all the other long nights in between
How I hunger for the sight, sound and scent of you

Standing with you at midday
Underneath a brolly, running wet with rain
Leafy trees and sodden wooden steps
The memories remain

Days run into weeks and empty pointless nights
Such aching in the depths of me
Sad ponderings invite
The trysting hour no meeting brings
And a telephone that never rings

Enid Gardner

Perfect Love

Oh wondrous God's look down on me I feel you are with me
to help me see the secrets of your mystery, open my
eyes so that I may see. I feel all around your presence
so sweet bringing love and peace with all I meet, I feel
my life changing more complete, a love so strong a love so
sweet, never leave my side never let me wonder away from
the love you are sending me, for I am just a soul once
lost, but stronger now full of love and lust. For wisdom
And knowledge all I will find with you my sweet God's here
by my side.
  A time to heal,
  A time to rest, time to remember all of life's best.
  A time for giving, for sharing and caring
  A time for love
    Oh wondrous God's.

Deirdre French

Sunset In Dyserth

We stood by a stile near a hedge of green,
In rapture we gazed on a wondrous scene;
A masterpiece of beauty; blue and gold,
Crimson and lilac; colours untold,
Enchanted isles of dazzling hue
Set in lakes of azure blue,
An Eldorado in the heaven's above;
A veritable paradise; the home of love,
Celestial world where joy and peace reign supreme.
The mystic fairy land of a lovers dream.

'Twas a sunset we watched, in thought we were there,
In that Eden of Beauty beyond compare.
Entranced we gazed at that wondrous sight
Till slowly it fled before oncoming night.
That dreamland of ours slowly sank in the sea
Until the last glorious gleams we could faintly see.
Then the purple curtain of dusky night
Softly shrouded it all from our sight.

J. P. Keenan

Fireside Dreams

Oft'n I sit and stare.
  By the fireside there.
  Long hours it seems.
Through eyes veiled by dreams
Watch flames twist and dance,
  Soft glowing amber light enhance.
  Shapes that be in constant change.
Unveiled from repertoire much that's strange.
  Pale blue spires capped with snow,
  Emit from white heart there aglow.
Shafts of flickering fire flight pierce the gloom.
  In this now darkening room.
  Shadows writhe as if in pain
Locked in battle with light again.

R. F. Ware

Broken Threads

Oh to enjoy conversation again,
Alas, the thread breaks—I lose the drift
Since a blood clot set concentration adrift.
There is pain—frustration at being slow
To regain the contact I used to know,
But, there's no romance in misery's dance
So, I'll change the record—sing a new song,
The feelings inside me are very strong.
With faith, my hopes I'll realize
Have charitable thoughts from me arise,
Float them into verse—refreshing—new,
They'll give readers insight to my point of view.
Book covers opened are doors to their contents,
Revelations in verse shall be my monument.

Audrey Luckhurst

New Year Resolutions

New Year Resolutions are made upon this day,
The mind is willing but temptation's on the way.
It intervenes and blocks the path
Of good intent, with the aftermath
Of recrimination and sad regret
That those good intentions have not been met.

But for those of you who kept your word,
You can be proud, you have not swerved,
And when you've seen the whole year through
The praise received will be your due.
The uplift felt must surely thrill
And make amends for force of will
Used on those days of apprehension,
When succumbing would have eased the tension.

You're now entitled to some praise
For standing firm throughout those days.
May you look back and have no fear,
You can continue another year.

L. R. Burdon

A Need For Help

A cry for help I'm sure it was,
Endless pictures of regret,
A tiny baby cries in vain,
It stands no chance I'm sad to say,

A camp it was of refugees,
A picture it was that saddened me,
They stand in vain and plead for help,
Their legs no more can hold them up,
They lay slumped upon the broken floor,
A sorry sight for all to see,

Their eyes show the need for help,
A need so plain it's misunderstood,
Their cries are heard all over the world,
So now someone must surely go,
And give the help they're waiting for.

Diane Ralph

Gone But Not Forgotten

While chubby angels slumber on billowy white clouds,
While peaceful music fills the air with its haunting sounds.

Proud white horses carry you wherever you wish to go,
And everyone has the time of day to stop and say "Hello".

While we cry our silent tears over what has passed,
You sit in blissful harmony free from your pain at last.

Where cherub's endless giggles are heard all day long,
Where peaceful white Doves serenade you with their song.

Gardens full of every flower swaying softly in the breeze,
And a warm and gentle wind rustling quietly through the trees.

The beautiful scent of Roses lingers always in the air,
While you remain at perfect peace looking down without a care.

And so we want to tell you that although we had to part,
You remain forever in our lives and always in our hearts.

Tracey Branscombe

Love

Love is a weird thing,
Pain and torture is all it can bring.
Your heart gets taken away,
Without you even having a say.
Guys come in and out of your life like a breeze,
But you can't forget them with such ease.
You think they're ideal,
But later you find out they're not real.
Heart broken yet once again,
Having to go through all that pain.
It's time to stop,
Or you'll get hurt even more
And that'll mean, a heart, that's very sore.

Sonia Ahmed

Sweet Bird Of Youth

Sweet bird of youth, so swift and free
As you fly o'er the hills and mountains and trees
Never a care for the troubles of the world
From which your angel wings carry you
small innocent herald
For yours is the unshadowed moon-shaped valleys
Where free-flowing rivers meander along grass-green plains
And lily boats drift carelessly on the shore
Gently pushed by lazy currents
Where crickets dance and rejoice all day long
While the labouring bees strive so earnest and keen
To please their unsatisfied Majestic Queen
There you will stay small fragile friend
While we must endure the morbid months
Bombarded by rain and hailstones from above
And frost like a blanket spreads o'er the sloping streets
Until Spring and the morning of your awaited call
When you will thence return
Bringing your charm and happiness to all

Nasreen Shaikh

The Rose

Is that a little rose I see
Are you crying, why are there tears
You look full of the world's fears
Tattered clothes, messy hair
Doesn't anybody care, it doesn't seem fair
You look around you, all you see is another bomb
Now your home is almost gone
Look at that man, he's holding a gun
You have to go, you have to run
With this fighting, shouting and gun shots
Everything around you disappears and rots
You cannot find your family the ones you once knew
Your brother, your sister, your Mum and your Dad
Now you're alone, hungry and sad
Just now everything seems quite
You can still hear the echoes of last nights riot
Remember when you were found and taken away
On that quiet, deserted and smoky day
You should be a rose that grows calm, bright eyed and mild
But now you are just a little Bosnian child

Lesley Kane

Untitled

Within the heart there is many a dream
Only the beholder can know what they mean
Love and hate, pleasure and pain
Held within, with nothing to gain.

In the future we see old age
Like reading a book and turning the page
So many wishes that never come true
Wanting so much but what can we do.

Life is too short and so full of fear
I want someone to love, someone who's dear
All of my dreams have now floated away
Because I have you to love everyday

J. Harrison

Fledgling

Go my child! The world awaits you
taste of every sweetness, revel in
riotous living; know ecstasy, live! Who
knows what need of memories there'll be;
pin your hope not on safety, don't you remain
cocooned, bound and shackled by convention.
shun suburbia child, lest your disdain
to laugh or cry, and dare I mention
love? Quite freely give of it even be
it unrequited; not only to a lover.
to a child, woman, friend, any human, see
how many different loves are there, discover
this, and never will you be bereft
of hope. In this world or the next
When you've lost the taste for, left
all riotous living, have known ecstasy,
lived true unto yourself and found
these many loves; in quiet moments see
how true it is. That hope remains, abounds
and memories are an absolute necessity.

Gwyneth Sealey

Snow

The leafless trees stand stark against the sky,
The warmth of summer seems so long ago,
The barren branches claw their hands on high,
The northern wind sends forth a whirl of snow.

Ere long the snow will gather strength and fall,
Each silent flake a patterned wisp of white,
Covering fields and ditches one and all,
Quietly falling steady through the night.

Perhaps when morning comes the sun will shine,
A brilliant spotlight on that scene below,
The bright reflection dazzling to the eyes.
Like some great echo from the world of snow.

Robert Lynn

My Special Friend

You were such a comfort to each one
You brightened up their day.
Their hearts somehow felt lighter
Each time you came their way.

There was something in the words you spoke
That always held great thought.
You had a quality of life
That was divinely taught.

Your faith was a sure anchor
That held you in life's storm
And out of all confusion
Your presence brought a calm.

Your life a living sermon
By your actions you were known.
Your hand placed firmly in the hands
That sit on Heaven's Throne.

And though you left the earthly shore
Your race of life well run.
You've entered into your reward
With the Eternal One.

George B. Walker

A Letter To My Darling Billy

Darling Billy, Today I was so happy on my shopping spree
heavy bags, new price tags, I went into the Cosy cafe for tea
I looked forward to my tea with scones and cream and jam
then I glanced towards a quiet corner and saw this lady with
this man.

So much love it was obvious to see
no eyes for other people, and certainly not me
I got up and ran leaving my tea, and bags on the floor
stumbling across the room heading for the door

My eyes were misty and stung in the sun that shone
for in that fleeting moment my happiness was gone
I wish, how I wish I'd not seen those two
my darling Billy I want so much to come home to you

I want everything to be as before
Before I decided on tea and walked through that Cafe door
now I'll be left with our letters written when you were away
but I've always loved you, my darling Billy, more than words
can say

I wonder if you'll keep my letters written in the past
but my darling Billy this must be the last
perhaps you think I'm being romantic, stupid or even silly
but the man I saw today was YOU DARLING BILLY.

Pamela M. James

The Magnifying Glass Life

The boy in a bubble
No one sees his trouble
All offering a piece of advice
But they all know he's paid the price

Male version of a lab rat
He never wanted any of that
He gave them an inch, they wanted a mile
If only he got paid to smile

He should have gone
When he had the chance
But curiosity caged him
He waited for a second glance

He needed her love
And someone around
But he screwed everything up
And just dragged her down

Time used up thinking
With none left to spend
But where in the world
Will it all end?

Michael Linford

Song

I am a woman who lives on the edge of the land.
I gaze out, out, over the free sea.
From where I stand,
the sands holding onto my feet,
the huge water invites me into itself.
I am the woman who will plunge in naked.

I am a woman who lives in a small town.
I gaze out, out, to the wild moors.
From where I stand,
the small houses compacted around me,
the big winds draw me up onto the raw land.
I am the woman who will fly a yellow kite.

I am a woman who lives on a planet
   (the size of the soles of my feet).
I gaze out, out, out, through the ultimate night.
I will stand,
despite the gravity of fear;
infinite space beckons me.
I am the woman who will bear a little light.

   Elizabeth Quarterman

V. E. Day: Observing Silence

Poor grandfather bequeaths a half smile today;
The family rallies to the cause of lunch.
He says nothing—his half smile has much to say.
Stooped in warm new sun, he remembers the burn.
Far off, his eyes rifle through valleys that stay
Dug out in his face by Time's stealthy advance.

Daughter, nephew, grandson, shall each take a seat
Having kissed his head, now the Great Feast is served.
Such respectful beauties shall know how to treat
Forefathers, heroes, killers of tyranny.
They'll learn their freedom, know the bastard he beat
And thank him by living, breathing, speaking joy.

Eating and sharp talk of politics begin
But I'm still watching him, entreating prayer
To appease my new monsters that rage within.
He sees in my eyes that torment lives on
But his wisdom is muted behind that grin—
They stop, see our eyes locked across Time, screaming.

   Andrew Ford

Thirty Little Children

Thirty little children playing in the gym
A mad man comes in with a gun, and commits the ultimate sin
He shoots their sunny faces and sixteen of them die
He turns the gun upon himself and a community so stunned cries

Sixteen little children so tragically taken away
We'll no more hear their laughter, we'll no more see them play
Sixteen little children so innocent and kind
When obscenities like this happen, I think that God is blind

   Steven McDonald

Love—What Is It

I have heard the word love everyday of my life.
People say I love you, they say you're my true love.
But what is this word love
To me it is just a big con.
Form what I can see, love is hurt, pain and tears.
It is just a waste of years.
Love is nothing to no one,
Everyone cares for themselves.
Love is just a word said for people that have nothing better to do.
Some believe in love, some don't
It depends on what you have been through I suppose.
The letters 'l''o''v''e' spell love.
What is it, tell me please.
Love turns out to be hate, it turns out you get used.
What is that love thing?
I don't believe in love, it is nothing to me.
It breaks your heart into bits and bits,
"Fall in Love" listen to me and don't do it!

   Satveer Sandhu

Perfection

Multitudes of colours are everywhere.
One blink of an eye, a cloudless sky.
Trees and flowers in their prime.
Such beauty and grace, lights up my face.
Birds chirping their special tunes,
as if knowing, the month of June.
Sense the warmth all around.
Bees buzzing amongst the flowers,
I could gaze for hours and hours.
Treasured moments of pure delight.
Every morning, noon and night.

   Ellen Jean Jones

Grandad

Gentle Jesus up above
Please send Grandad all our love
Tell him just how much we care
And how we wish he was still here.
Since he's been gone our lives have changed
And nothing left here feels the same
The days are long, the nights are cold
Everything seems grey and old.
Everything, that is, but him
Whose memories are never dim
The pictures and the photographs
Remembering the way he laughed,
The fun we had, the games we played
Oh Grandad, how we wish you'd stayed

But even though you're far away
Your memories are here to stay
There will not be, there's not been yet
A day in which we will forget
The happy times we shared together
We love you Grandad; now and forever.

   Claire Hill

Two Worlds Apart

My family, I know very well, my son and daughters (two).
Their in's and out's, their up's and down's.
Their joys and sorrows too.

I cared for them in many ways. They did not want for much.
Then thro' the passing years they went their different ways.
I myself found life anew in an unexpected way.

My family. Know me NOT AT ALL! We haven't even met.
They cannot, or they will not come to terms and do not understand.
That Dad as was, is now called Lynne and will be forevermore.

That they cannot comprehend, I well can understand.
But time and our creator will heal their troubled minds.
And in the end all will be well. That's the way of ALL mankind.

   Lynne J. Braithwaite

To My Little One

When you left me on that dreadful day,
I thought you had gone away to stay.
Your heart so small and yet so big,
You are on every flower, tree and every twig.
You are the gentle breeze that blows through the meadow,
The trees bend like the weeping willow,
I do no more weep upon my pillow.
When I picture your heavenly smile, I remember our walks
In the fields within that heavenly band,
Together in love, hand in hand.
You guide me through this earthly maze,
You are like the morning dew that the sun do gaze.
During times when I feel sad,
It is you I remember and all that we had.
You appear to me in heaven so bright,
Just like that wonderful spiritual light.
I do not look upon that day and cry my dear,
For I know that you are always near.
I look upon every day so bright,
For I know that someday we will reunite.

   Sharon Adams

Khan

Khan—mighty chieftain Khan,
why raise your rifle so?
A bullet has sped—another spirit is dead,
And its killing must stand at your door.

O Khan! Forgive—I see now why
You raise yourself with battle cry.
They're coming Khan—they're coming this way;
Oh, a mighty fight you're fighting today.
You won't take cover as the bullets hum;
Though ten of them, and you but one.
You've settled with five, but five are alive,
And they're nearer now—oh! You cannot survive.

Khan—mighty chieftain Khan,
What is that patch on your chest?
Its colour is red, and it spreads and it spreads,
But you don't even glance at your breast.
Khan—warrior of Hindustan,
Why do you smile at the sound?
You smile and you fall as the trumpets call,
And you ride to the great hunting ground.

J. Castel-Nuovo

Natural Serenade

A collage of brightly coloured birds stand on snow white
sand at the interface between land and ocean.
The radiant sunlight shines everywhere but focuses on this
iridescent mosaic.
The only sounds that are heard are a perfect blend of under-
tones and natural resonances.
A multitude of soothing waterfalls present themselves.
The sky is cloudless and has been painted crystal blue just for
the occasion.
The horizon is merely a distant mirage.
A light breeze caresses and cajoles every tangible entity. It
leaves no plant, flower or animal untouched.
The very static calmness that is being witnessed is so moving.
Human presence can only be felt through distant eyes.
It is only unspoilt beauty that prevails.
It is only nature that has a voice here.
As the hours pass, the scene subtly changes.
By nightfall, the same setting takes a different guise.
Sunlight has turned into moonlight; the sky has darkened and
the birds temporarily hibernate to give way to nocturnal life.
More hours pass and the cycle is complete.
It happens all over again but when I awake it will be under a
different light.

Parul Amlani

Recollections

Malt whisky and brown boots an old rocking chair, a place on
the back porch a chill in the air.
A crackling old log fire a dog by my side, and the beautiful
woman I took for my bride.
My mind flickers back and I love to recall, the beautiful woman
I met in the fall.

Corn fields and ripe barley long days in the sun, the stream
with clear water where we used to run.
Star–studded heavens blue sky all day long, fresh trout that
keep jumping and a humming bird song.
Each day I remember when I used to stand tall, for the beautiful
woman I loved in the fall.

Now I'm old and I'm lonely pray God give me rest, and take me
to heaven with those of the best.
But one day I'm going I'll go to his care, with brown boots
and dog and an old rocking chair.
It's not to be yet and each new day crawls, towards the
beautiful woman I lost in the falls.

I just can't help thinking my time is quite near, I'll go to my
maker without any fear.
Then when my time's up I'll say my goodbyes, to sweet
stream and ripe barley and star–studded skies.
And I'll wait on the back porch and I'll hear the sweet call, of
the beautiful woman I loved most of all.

Christine Ormrod

'The Gulls'

To be woken by the seagulls wheeling in the sky,
Is fulfilment of a dream of all the years gone by.
Today the sea is calm and blue—glinting in the sun,
The feeling is of happiness for old and very young.

A wind begins to whisper around the dunes and trees,
The sun has lost its brilliance with the onset of the breeze,
The sea becomes uneasy, the waves are edged with a white,
The seagulls scream and fly around, nervous of the night.

And now the storm clouds gather, the sea is wild and grey
The gusts of wind get stronger, a ship makes for the bay.
The thunder roared as the lightning flashed
The waves rose high before they crashed.

With the dawn a rosy hue lightens up the sky,
The sea is calm and boats appear—the gulls are flying high.
Another day—another chance, a backward look—a second glance,
Who knows what nature has in store while the gulls play gently
   by the shore.

Peggy Tyndall

Dunblane

As I heard the unwanted news,
My heart sank to the ground.
The school was silent and still
also with no sound.

I started to cry because I couldn't
keep it inside.
The minute silence hurt everywhere
the poor parents were full of despair.

How could a person be so cruel
to the innocent 5 year olds at the school.
I feel sorry for the parents who are in pain.
I give my prayers to the people of Dunblane.

Louise Duffy

All Seasons Fight

When sharp and sceptre frosted night with crystal shield,
faces Summer siege, her armour studded with sky's glittering jewels
Wind blow hot, wind blow cold, at whatever cost.
The wind that sang of our love is lost.

For now, no breeze plumps the sails.
No gust removes Autumnal trails.
No thrashing of great green tops.
No whisper twists the ears of crops.

If seasons grieve when they should sing
If Summer shivers and barren Spring
her cue forgets, leaving all unclothed.
I, alone shall stand unmoved.

For not long since, was I struck down
Unclothed from love's embracing gown.
'Twas I who saw my own life's clock
stick at the darkest hour and stop.

Dawn Evans

A Lost Friend

Many times upon this earth
We ask the question: why?
Is there a God in heaven above
who lets our loved ones die?
Why is there cruelty, suffering and wars
When peace is all we ask,
Who do we put our trust in
Is this not a simple task?
We hope our souls are everlasting
We sometimes pray that this will be
A happy life for those we love
Surely this is plain to see.
Heartache is a sorrowful thing
Grief is never ending,
To all of those who have lost a friend,
Faith, peace and love I'm sending.

Joan French

Here's Hopin'

Ah'd like tae turn th' clock back, tae fin ah wiz twenty three,
So if ah cood hae three wishes, 'at's fit th' first wid be,
'Cos things wint at a slower pace, 'n' ah cood cope nae bad,
Bit ah hinna a hope o' keepin' up noo, 'n' 'at's a bittie sad.

Mi second wish is fer a wee hoose, wi roses up th' wa',
A wee bit gairden 'n' an aiplle tree, 'n' a Scottie dog 'n' aa',
Ess is things ah've bin wishin' fer, fer as lang as ah kin myn,
So if ony ane o' 'em comes true, 'at wid be afa' fine.

Bit th' thing 'at's foremost in mi heid, is worldwide peace 'n' quiet,
Ah dinna like tae hear o' it at a', fin somebody cazzes a riot,
It's an afa' world wi bide in, bit it's fowk 'at's made it 'at wye,
So mi third wish wid come in 'ere, 'n' fer perfect peace ah'd try.

If ere's onybody higher up listenin', dae ye hear mi earnest plea?
It disnae maitter aboot one 'n' two, bit cood ye grant wish
　　number three?
So's wi cood live a peacefu' life, er is aat too much tae ask?
Ah leave it in yer powerfu' han's, ess gigantic, mammoth task.
　　Irene A. R. Smith

Hope

Paradise, but short–lived
Our joy like the bright fire,
Our sorrow like a thunder in blue–clear sky
That strikes our hope
like a lightning
But cannot burn it up.
Like a mythical bird emerges from the ashes
A new hope.
　　Iliana Metallinou

Just For Love

If I could have anything
My wish would be for you
To be with me through these nights
Kill this loneliness when I'm blue

If I could rid my thoughts of doubt
And of thinking you don't care
I would feel a whole lot better
And each lonely day I'd bear

But these feelings they remain,
And the heartache will soon start,
If I could just spend some more time with you
I know it would heal my heart.

So there you have my feelings
My thoughts so plain and true
We may be apart for quite sometime
But I'm still so in love with you
　　William A. Mavers

The Circle

Dark afternoon in winter and all the trees are bare
The landscape looks deserted as if nobody cares
If we thought this was forever how grey our lives would be
Without faith in God's renewal and hearts empty like the trees

Young daffodils stand coyly bedecked in bright green leaves
Yellow heads are nodding gaily caught up in sun and breeze
Resplendent and yet innocent to the joy that this sight brings
As we gaze in adoration at these bridesmaids of the spring

Long lazy days of summer blue panoramic sky
Trees bow their laden heads to all the people passing by
The earth's ablaze colours as flowers curtsey to the sun
That heals our minds and bodies as each glorious day is done

Now autumn is upon us and leaves turn gold and brown
Then fall like graceful dancers gently to the ground
Night's curtain draws in earlier as nature clears her stage
And this cycle is repeated as we move from age to age

God promised never to leave us and if ever we're in doubt
We just need to watch the seasons it's what life is all about
　　Jean K. Burton

Juvenile Recollection

Naivete's fraudulence uttered to me, false diagnosis of love,
thought by he. Lies all the time in infatuate greed, a
descendant of choice, hardly of need.
Tears of imposture of emotions scarce, simply
mistaken for the clothes that love wears.
Transitory blindness by fabricate pledge, reluctant
commitment nearing the edge.
Disparity comes as the juvenile part, he with his negligence,
my empty heart. Passing of time and maturing reflection, a saviour
had come with a chance of protection.
Truthfully spoken in all he expressed, like all
saviours, healing, and sent to redress.
Each word flowed like water from virtuous tongue,
no point left unmade, no song left unsung.
A vigilant novice at what I now knew, no model to
follow, for experts are few.
And intense in confusion, the child finally knows
that the water will calm with the wind's final blows.
And amidst her reluctance the child finally falls,
for the forces of love push more strongly than all.
　　Katie Boyle

Gone

According to Einstein, in theory he states
Space, time and motion, inter-relate
To travel at speeds, comparable with light
The observed would soon disappear from sight
Back into time, as only they can
And see it all happen before it began.
　　N. V. Richardson

A Housewife's Pleasure

Another product's just come out, they say we ought to try it.
It cleans and smells quite nice they say, I think I'll go and buy it.
So I go into the drug store, and I know I'll feel just fine
Smelling all those household things, my nose does overtime.
First there's disinfectant, it smells so fresh and clean
And then there is the polish, and good old Mr. Sheen.
I walk along the aisle a bit, there's just so much to choose
Window cleaner, oven pads, and bleach to clean the loos.
There's a spray to clean the microwave, a tub of shake 'n' vac.
There's Domesto's multi-cleaner, so the germs, they don't
come back.
There are also bathroom fresheners, to camouflage a stink.
I wonder if they work at all? It makes me stop and think!
But before I go and buy one, I have a little dare
I wait till no-one's looking, and spray it in the air.
But the trouble is they change things. It isn't fair on me.
Do I choose original, bouquet, or potpourri?
I fill my basket to the top, can't think of anything else.
I just can't wait to get them home. And try them on the house.
Then I scrub and spray and polish, until I ache with pain.
And I stick them in the cupboard, and they're never seen again.
　　Christine Whibley

Silence

It is so quiet it hurts
But peace is here.
People look at me strangely,
Like I am something to fear.
Why do people not understand,
That frustration gets the upper hand,
When I try to speak
But there's no help around?

However, for all the failings in my head,
I have other attributes instead.
I see more than anyone else can see,
I can see the love, the hate, and what's going to be.

But hark at that silence,
It is so deep.
It hurts so much
I could weep.
　　Doreen Benham

351

Ova

Gallantly, she battles her way,
through the soft interior.
She roams awkwardly through the tissued walls,
and waits desperately for her partner to arrive.
Her hollowness aches to be filled.
For hours she has travelled,
down narrow, twisted tubes.
She is certain, something has yet to come.
Then she hears first sound of movement,
from the surface of her shell.
She freezes into a comfortable position,
and feels a sudden touch from within.
She freezes into a frenzy.
She now has valuable luggage to carry.
She has become fertilized.
Her journey has been completed.
Another life has been created.

Joanne Craze

Last Days

The old man sat, hunched up in his chair
Contentedly sitting grooming his hair
His face is now so wrinkled and pale
Looking exceptionally old and frail
The years have passed him by so very fast
Memories are all which remain from his past
Now he is old his legs are all weak
His bones so brittle and you can hear them creak

Now he has no interest in life at all
People who care come to him when they hear his call
Shaking his cushions which are propping him up
He sits and slurps his tea out of a cup
The nurse comes and gives his face a wipe

Then he sits and puffs away on his favourite pipe
Watching the smoke swirling like clouds in the sky
He's just watching and waiting to die.

Jill Smyth

A Beautiful Creature

Thundering down on firm hard around,
Dirt and dust flying around.
Graceful movements both fast and slow,
Wind through his fur in a gentle flow.
Eyes sparking excited and bright,
Dark in colour just like the night.
This creature is beautiful, full of life
Gentle and kind in his strife.
Gliding smoothly and free,
How wonderful a horse can be.

Kim Smith

Mr Nobody!

I know a funny little man,
Who is living in our house.
'Tis he who pops up whenever he can,
Yet he's as quiet as a mouse.
Of course we've never seen his face,
And yet we all agree.
The mess was made all over the place
By Mr. Nobody!

It wasn't me with the dirty feet,
Who left footprints on the floor.
Although I was the one who had a sweet,
I didn't put finger marks on the door.
This may all seem like a great big fuss,
But why—can you not see?
The shoes on the floor don't belong to us,
But Mr. Nobody!

I wish I knew the reason behind,
The mischief that is caused by he.
But I know one day I will be able to find
Mr. Nobody!

Tracey-Jane Marchant

The Silence

If I am no more a life of yours
If light, your smile my final breath
If I may never your truth behold
Let no dark place dare hinder nor deceive
Nor rage to taint—this our last embrace
For I cannot forget—my life was ever thee
In all that was ever real, ever felt
Never forget, for I take your smile
It tells of innocent purpose
Such emotions
And in the silence ahead—such memories
For a while I have breathed the sometimes dream
Touched the never
and I will take your image, our last embrace
To shake the very emptiness, the dark face
and all its savage intent
For I cannot forget
What I have always known within.

Leslie Downton

I Am What I Am

You can say what you want about the clothes that I wear,
You can say what you want about the length of my hair,
You can say what you want about my unshaven chin,
You can say what you want because I'm not listening.
I don't know you people so don't pass judgement on me,
One thing's for sure, I'm as smart as you'll be.
I ain't no hooligan, I ain't no yob,
I've got my own place and a good steady job.
If you people don't like me it ain't no loss,
'Cos all of you people just ain't worth a toss.
One thing's for certain, we'll all end up the same,
Six feet under with a stone with our name,
Or maybe cremated and our ashes they'll scatter,
With no mention whose best, because it just doesn't matter.

David Jones

Bear Tale

Sorry I'm not Paddington nor am I Pooh
I am a great big cuddly teddy bear who will always be there for you

I know there are times when you are feeling so unwell
Remember I will listen but I will never tell

I will share your dreams, sorrows or even joys
as I sit here day by day among your other toys

Just give me lots of hugs and kisses
then we will never be blue

Because I am your special teddy bear
sent here to comfort you

Mary Shaw

My Beautiful African Sunset

Surely as the sun sets and travels low below
    I think of you
As my beautiful African sunset
    Bright and multicoloured
You are all those colours that I see in an African sunset
    Bright and warm you fill my heart and soul
I glow like a light flickering in a gentle breeze
    You are never gloomy
With your smile the heavens want to burst open
    And smile along with you
Your bright eyes twinkle and dance around your face
    Like flames of fire leaping around
Gently warming everything in sight
    Your energy for life is truly amazing
When I look at you
    I just want to scream, shout, dance, sing, be silly
Is it then a wonder
    That I think of you
As my beautiful African sunset
    Bright and multicoloured.

Mwansa Curtis

Mountain So Majestic

Mountain so majestic, tall and free
What a challenge you bring to me
As I look up to you, your beauty I see
Oh this is the place I love to be
Mountain of mystery so much you have seen
So many hikers setting off keen
They struggle higher to reach the top
Till with aching feet they finally stop
To see the beauty all around
The lakes and mountains so free and not bound
Mountain you're a challenge to me each day
As I walk on life highway

Sandra Marsh

The Writer

To sit in the lushness of this grass
And feel the wind blow
I am at peace, alone, but at peace
Almost like the birds swinging back and forth
Amongst the tall grass blades in the afternoon sun
But deep down lies the turbulence
Of an unleashed writer
I would like to reach out to you
Bring you right inside my soul
I would like to look into your eyes
And see, acknowledge your understanding
To lie simply in the enclosure of your arms
Feel a warmth and a strength
Woven from love and security
Your silent acknowledgement . . .
You do not have to understand
The world of the writer
When I sink low, hold me, silently acknowledge
But you do not and therefore you do not read me
And you will never see me as I truly am.

Jacqui Rukuba-Mpawulo

Dreams

What are dreams, if not the furtive imaginings of ones mind,
Aspirations of a kind.
Reality, sometimes, though not altogether right,
Aren't those the dreams that haunt our night?

What of the dreams that besiege us by day?
Aspirations you might say.
Aren't dreams mostly based on hope?
Without them would we really cope?

What are dreams by night or day?
Aspirations, what are they?
Unfulfilled yearnings, hopes and fears,
We need them don't we, through the years?

What are dreams, if not the means by which we grow,
Aspirations, I don't know.
Surely we need them to help us see,
And to sit and dream of what might be.

Aleida Eaton

Who Cares?

They sleep in the street, on the tube, in the park,
Dreading the winter when nights are so dark.
The struggling goes on year by year.
Is there really no one out there who can hear
Of the plight of the homeless living in the street,
No roof above, no food, no heat.

So they lie in a doorway, or railway yard,
Until evicted by an irate guard.
they have to beg just to survived,
Wondering if tomorrow they'll still be alive.

We have a home, a car, food and money.
For us there is plenty of milk and honey.
Open your eyes, look around and see,
There but for the grace of God, GO YOU and ME.

Margaret Chanan

Life

How is life? I hear you say,
It gets better everyday,
But for some it can be bad,
It can make you completely mad,
It can be short,
It can be long,
It can sometimes make you strong
Other times it makes you sad,
It makes you thankful for what you have,
So along life's weary path
Enjoy yourself and you will laugh,
Life is precious, can't you see,
Life is a gift for you and me.

Joyce M. Blanchard

Bluebells

Tread upon a pulsating velvet carpet
A blanket of quiet stillness in lilac hue
Gathering together a richly created perfume
Along in the morning dew

Favoured trees with sprinkled azure flowers at their feet
Weave grottos of silken blue
In natural beauty state
Swirling flowers winking bright
In perfect silence, they simply wait
Through the rays of the morning light

Serene and jovial is the gathering mood
To admire and love
Pretty little things bluebells
Swaying provocatively; as if waiting to be picked

Oh, how beautiful and divine!
A celestial sea of cerulean bluebells
Standing so unique
In a huge vase at home
On the window sill or by the phone

Frank G. Romano

My Clouds

Look!! Saturn whirling around the Sun
A big black bunny on the run.
Ah!! A dragon fierce as fierce as he can be
Breathing fire, just missing me.
A whirlpool sucks the clouds away
Turns to a tree, the buds of May.
As black as black, it frightens me
All is dark, so very dark
The dogs are cross, they start to bark.
Come the dawn, as grey as ever
The clouds are low and close together,
Just like a giant stamping round
Sounds like thunder, a crashing sound.
The wind blows stronger, breaks up the sky
Imagination gone, but I am proud
To have seen my awesome clouds.

A. E. Allnutt

The Forgotten

As life retreats before their eyes,
Like little children, but more wise,
They sit around the old folks home
And hope today someone will come,
A relative or friend perhaps,
To fill the long and lonely gaps
That form the basis of their years,
Which once were filled by laughter, tears.
They do not know the time of day,
Bewilderment has come to stay;
New inmates come, and others go,
Too frequently to get to know;
A light shines through their failing eyes
And warms the visitor, who tries
To see the soul, which still is there
Behind the sadness and the stare.

Patricia Corrigan

Friends

Friends can be jealous, possessive
  and even a little obsessive.
They make promises they cannot keep,
  preventing you from precious sleep.
They may not listen when you need them most,
After all don't they have problems of their own
    to boast!
But a real friend will lift you up when you are down
  and take you out on the town.
They'll comfort you when you are sad
  even if they think you are a little mad!

But most of all a true friend will love
  you deeply from the heart
and thus from you, will never part.

Pauline Conway

February

It's February, it's winter, it's cold,
Everything living is put on hold,
Nature is holding her breath and waiting,
Bulbs start peeping, anticipating
Spring that's creeping near.

It's February, it's bleak, it's bare,
Winter's frost fills the air,
But life comes forth to burst anew,
amid the snow and icy dew,
Thank God, for spring to cheer.

Denise Cameron

Built On The Clyde

Quiet empty barren dockyards
Scarce of boys and men
Long gone are the ships
And the dreams
Never to return again

The town is like a graveyard
Silent sombre and so sad
No hope for the men on the corner
Thinking of what they once had

Heads were held high
Hearts bursting with pride
To see those famous words
"Built on the clyde"

No longer for fathers to teach their sons
No longer for families to stay as one
No longer will anyone put up a fight
To built those ships that now pass in the night.

Anne Bush

The Body

The body lay still
On the soft feathered bed
The body lay still
Not a twitch in its head
The eyes they glared up
And the brows they hung down
The body lay still
And as cold as the ground

The body was thin, it was fading away,
The hair once so soft, felt now more like hay,
The skin once so smooth, was now wrinkled and grey,
The body that live yesterday
Is now dead today.

For deep in the ground, covered in dirt
There is no more pain, no more hurt
The body is buried deep in a hole
Soon no body, only a soul
Only a soul and a spirit to fly
The body is dead
But the spirit won't die!

Theresa Stirling

Sunset

I see the painted sky as it swirls up overhead
The blue blue sea, the crescents white
The sun on the horizon, shining, giving light
Everywhere I look I can see the painter's stroke
in the white curly wisps of smoke
That rise above the sea.
Showing the artist's talent for all who look and see

The shapes in the clouds like waves upon the shore
Every time the sun sets above the ebbing flow
The clouds, their movements now are slow.
The waves no longer blue are golden
As the clouds and sun together are rolled in,
Into one continuous shore,
The sight is one strange beauty I have never seen before

But now imprinted on my mind.
Never again such beauty will I find.

Julie Anne French

Potato

Secretly growing, buried in deep earth;
Dreaming of green Heaven in the Sun.

Deep, rich, carpet of soft, broad leaves
Shading the earth, feeding the fruit below.

With age comes wither, mould, decay;
Brave stems collapse,
Brown leaves prostrate upon parched earth.

Autumn rains descend, anoint the desolate grave.
Dark, damp earth,
Pregnant with pause, alive with expectation.

Fork sinks deep with careful reverence,
Releasing sweet fragrance as golden treasure tumbles,
amazing,
Upon the tousled surface.

Tim Watson

Goodnight, Godbless

Close your eyes now, it's time go.
People you loved and lost are waiting to say hello.
I can see you're tired, this has got to be.
Your journey now, will be pain free.
The sun is shining, the sky is so blue.
It's as if heaven is opening just for you.

Your journey's begun now, I can tell by your face.
Gone is the pain
There's a smile in its place
As I kiss your cheek, and stroke your hair
Wondering why life's so unfair
But realizing I'm not the only one
To lose a very special mum
And when it's time for me to go
I know you'll be there to say hello.

Gina Holzherr

Funeral

I saw the coffin lying there, I knew there was a still
born baby inside.
Soon to be turned into ashes, why? What had he done?
Mother and Father upset for their new baby died and they
don't know why!
Didn't get to say we are your parents, welcome to life in
the real world.
All they got to do was say goodbye and have a good cry.
I cried as I know what it's like to have someone you love die.
I've been there, seen the coffin.
Wondered why? What it would be like to be there inside a
tightly closed box.
I believe in "Life after death." I know the little baby
is up there being born again, living wondering where his
family are for they are down here grieving.
Why does it happen this way?
Isn't there something else that could happen instead?

Helen Osborn

354

Born To Defend

The streets were wet and windy
As lamplight fell on pools
Of rubbish–laden waters
That the ghostly moonlight cools

The weary, beaten soldiers
Their faces damp and cold
Their feet so sore from marching
Their looks so stern and bold

The lone rebellious Irish man
With whisky–sodden brain
Sings his staunch rebellious songs
And takes to arms again

The glint of Thompson in his hands
Gives off an eerie light
As it spews its message of death
Into the war–torn night

And back at home in England a mother waits in vain
Just a medal and a pension for a bullet–shattered brain

And so the fight for Ireland goes on without an end
And men they keep on dying for a land born to defend

Michael Harris

"Ciarán"

Ciarán is just a little boy, who has not yet turned two,
His sturdy limbs are brown and smooth, his eyes a greyish–blue.
He toddles through the dew–filled grass and stops dead
    now and then
To stoop and pick up something strange and bring it to his den.

It may be just a bit if coal or little piece of stick
He tests each one and gets such fun from giving it a lick,
And if the rain has made a pool on some indented ground
His eyes they gleam and what would seem a devilish light
    abound.

He tiptoes in and wets his feet, then mucks his hands and face
Till of the skin, God gave to him, there's not the slightest trace
The common things we see each day are new and strange to him;
To little boys 'tis a world of toys and their joy grows never dim.

And so he goes from day to day and never stops to rest,
It balks my mind where he can find such energy and zest;
And when sleep, comes he just succumbs and lies down
    where he stands
You'd think the world was standing still to watch his
    outstretched hands.

I place a pillow 'neath his head, a blanket round him fold
And know within that small still frame, there beats a heart of gold . . .

Nellie Cronin

Untitled

Roses in full bloom
June.
Bush, shrub, floribunda, climbing,
Patio, miniature, rambling.

What a diversity,
What a harmony of colour and outline to see.
A pretty sight
To delight.

Roses as a sign of love—Valentine's day,
May enhance birthday, wedding, funeral, any day
With posy, painting, garden—glorious array,
In their very special way.

Sweet fragrance too,
From a few.
Cosmetic,
Exotic.
Medicinal can be,
Aroma therapy.

May we enjoy with thankful happiness,
One of the loveliest flowers on earth.

H. J. Stanton

Rebirth

We start from a seed inside the womb
We grow with the speed of now
We acquire Spirit from time that's passed.
Into the world we come
Youth, adult; young and old
To take what we must learn.
Child, friend, lover, parent
Then time comes for us to fade.
When our bodies touch mother earth
We rest our weary spirit
Dispose of our worn body.
We lay in wait
For the rebirth.

Angela Preston

Reflections Of Time

Where is the time
The time to reflect
The good things—the bad things
The things to forget.

We go about our daily tasks—
Without stopping for a moment to quietly ask—
Where did they all go—
The hopes and the dreams
As you reminisce sadly
All is not as it seems.

Look to the future—
Don't dwell in the past
Make each day a memory
Then you know it will last.

Judi Wick

My Confession To You

The love I feel for you is: Trusting, Blessed, Faithful,
Magical, Wonderful, Strong, Personal, Special, Sincere, Heaven,
Heart Rending, Deep.

I cannot run from my feelings no matter how hard I try . . . this
love I feel for you is real. The truth is I cannot imagine life
without you, I know I want to spend my whole life with you . . .
and hope you feel the same too.

I want you to know I love you and will always be there for you . . .
I Love You a thousand times over and over again . . .
This love is heaven–sent.

You cannot imagine how I feel about you . . . I know,
whatever I cannot give up on you, I love you too much.

Angela Gordon

Times And Seasons

What sort of life would we endure
If it were not well measured out
In spans of days, weeks, months and years
Changes of season never in doubt?

Without our nights how could we cope
Bereft of sleep at close of day?
We would not wake refreshed anew
To meet our problems without dismay.

What if we had no week-end break
From weary toil without a rest?
God ordained rest one day in seven
So we could survive six days hard pressed.

The year itself is marked by seasons
And most of us would despair
If we had perpetual sunshine
Or continual frost to bear.

So in the span ordained for us
Let us live one day at a time;
By using this simple method
Our lives could become sublime.

C. M. Smith

"The Observer"

I watch
I am on the perimeter
I am unnoticed, I am not involved
They are involved they are noticed.

I watched I am unnoticed
Each states a point
There is the occasional interruption.
I do not speak.
I am not involved.

I watch I do not speak.
They shout. They shout loudly
I am noticed
I am not involved.

I watch I am involved
They strike out to hurt I speak out
I am involved they watch.

I watch, I am the perimeter
I am present I am noticed, but I am not involved.
They are involved
They are noticed.

Carol Lesle Lane

Untitled

You hold my heart in your hands
And then you simply threw it away just like an old empty box

We drifted apart and I won't feel the same feelings again

What am I doing in here? This is not my place
This world of mine is now so dark and scary
I'm crying my heart out because I can hear
someone else calls your name
And your voice is coming through my window, tonight
I wish I could dream your dreams
So all your dreams will come true
While, miles away from you, my dream is dying fading away
I won't own up
How long can this go on?
I had it all and now it's gone
I didn't know I had so much to loose
All my hopes are shattered on the floor
I keep on searching for someone to be mine
But in the room there is just my shadow

And I wish I could drag myself into your memories
And burn my heart into your soul.

Elena Sartore

Death

The lingering odour of death's disease
Masking the devil nobody sees
A wave of darkness slowly stifles
Deadlier than a thousand rifles

Closing in to snare its prey
Leaving the body in a state of decay
Living off its victim's blood
A life is lost to satan's flood

Nowhere to run, no where to hide
I found that out that night I died
The thirst for blood I cannot quell
For I am damned to rot in hell

Scaring, screaming and snatching souls
Sleeping soundly on scorching coals
Wishing to God I was in paradise
With no more brains and hearts to dice

Destined to remain in tormented anguish
Praying for one last wish
Just one kind word softly said
With release me from the living dead

Steve Williams

Hope

Have you ever felt left alone,
Like you'd never make it till dawn.

Have you ever found some patience,
To calm your angry voice.

Have you ever won the race,
And saw the loser's face.

Have you ever watched the rain,
Falling down in pain.
Have you ever realized those are your tears,
But you never cry . . .

Have you ever thought you could die,
Before you even make your move.

And you could never find the right direction,
Looking for your own perfection.

But still, you hope for a perfect place,
Standing along in grace.

People say: "Nothing is perfect".
So your hope slowly fades away . . .

Margareta Ferek

From Our Deepest Roots

The measure of man, through the essence of time,
Should grow and flourish like a developing tree
Feeding from the roots of memory's past prime
To stretch higher the mind, into eternity.

Oh, wind be kind, dear sun be woken,
May our branches be refreshed by the purest rain;
Should our bough be bent or even broken,
May a hand reach forth to heal it again.

Each good thought is as a budding flower
Which, when nourished, thrives and changes
Our memory, to a colourful, fragrant bower
Of gentlest blossoms that time arranges.

The fruits of our endeavours will sustain each other
When tenderly prised from our willing clasp
To ensure every man may be as a our brother
Protected from the chaos of a greedy grasp.

Many are the trees in the orchard of life
Bearing their fruit for us all to enjoy,
Then casting each seed which can combat the strife
Of every day cares which could cause us to destroy.

Jean Taylor

Untitled

And who shall say our love will fail,
Fade away or slowly pall?
They talk in vain who say these things,
Our love will last surmounting all.

It is not like a lovely flower
That grows and blossoms in the sun,
But fades and droops when blows the wind
Till all its strength and beauty's gone.

No liken it unto a tree
Whose branches grow and spread with grace,
Who stands the gales and braves the storms,
And still can show so fair a face.

And though it may not show to all
The flowers of love the whole year round,
The roots of love grow deeper down,
Making foundations sure and sound.

So who dare say our love will fail,
Fade away or slowly pall?
They talk in vain who say these things,
Our love last, surmounting all.

Vera Wochner

356

My Sister

It's nice to hear your voice
At the other end of the line,
Someone else to share with
Someone special to call at any time.

To share all my thoughts with,
To tell my deepest fears,
To share all my laughter,
To comfort when there are tears.

Someone I can be myself
Without fear of rejection.
Someone I can mirror with
Just like my own reflection.

A special chat, a special hug,
A tear, a joke, a smile,
A time to just say nothing,
A time to go that extra mile.

But most of all
A time to be there,
A time for us together,
No matter what, we will be always and forever.

Sheila Williams

Artist's Impression

People are like colours, both young and old,
Some are subtle, some are bold,
While others are green, there envy shows,
Greys are serene with graceful repose.

Some are happy with pink faces glowing,
They are the ones we all like knowing,
Some are fat while others are lean,
Then there are the generous and the mean.

Some radiate warmth while others are cold,
There are those who like their story told,
Others are retiring and very shy,
Some are inquisitive and like to know 'why'.

If the artist could take a mixture of all,
He would mix and blend the warm with the cool,
The fat with the lean, the generous with mean,
The inquisitive with shy, the graceful and serene.

He'd take his canvas and his brush,
And daub and stroke in no great rush,
Until his imagination all fired,
Produced the work of art desired.

Sylvia Baldwin

Mandy

As the sun rose, it carried Mandy out of our world
Even as we slept, her body uncurled
The sunbeams shone down to warm the cold land
God, in his kingdom had grasped Mandy's hand.

With his strength, yet with gentleness he lifted her high
Past dewdrops and the dawn chorus they did fly,
To a world of peace and tranquillity, free of pain
To begin a new life—to start over again.

But those left behind, begin a new day,
Life goes on, but such a lot still to say
Words left unspoken, actions never done
Mandy is oblivious—her new life has begun

No 'goodbyes' to be uttered, was Mandy's rule
No tears to be shed to collect in a pool
Just keep memories deep within your head
Awake in the daytime, or asleep in bed.

Mandy is at peace now, safe with white doves
Surrounded by thoughts of the people she loves
With each passing cloud, or newly formed rainbow
Our thoughts and love for Mandy will never cease to flow.

D. Jones

Dear Mr. Sainsbury

The Tropical Fruit Squash you sell is really very nice
Especially in the summer when I top it up with ice.
It's lovely in the winter too, when warming it at night
However, there is something else which prompted me to write.

The bottle which contains the squash is rather big and heavy
And when I go to pick it up it is not very steady.
Carrying it around the store before I homeward go
Then walking up two flights of steps, it nearly lays me low.

I like to have a tipple when I'm working at the sink
And on one such occasion there, I began to think
Would it not be possible in your factory to use
A lighter plastic container when bottling this juice.

I'm getting on in years now and as my grip is weaker,
When I pick the bottle up to put the liquid in the beaker
I'm worried I might drop it, with consequences dire
And so Mr. Sainsbury I am writing to inquire

If you could harken to my plea for a lighter drink to carry
When you would have my gratitude and maybe that of many.
I look forward now to hearing if you're able to comply
And sign off, Yours most hopefully of a positive reply.

J. R. Parsons

Samson And Tyson

"Samson and Tyson", the strongest men of their day
struck down by the women they chose
Enticed by their beauty—conscience out of the way,
And their trail of glory, forever they froze

"Delilah and Desiree", Beauty Queens in their day
made helpless these strongest of men
Hand–cuffed and imprisoned the price they had to pay
And the women were richer than they had ever been

Samson is recorded among the Hero's of Faith
And Delilah was the woman he loved.
Tyson is known as Hero in the ring.
And Desiree just a woman he heard of.

Samson in prison prayed to his God
To forgive and once more renew his strength.
"And the pillars came down", So The Bible records
Killing Samson and thousands with him.

Tyson was sentenced to 6 years for his crime
(And the woman to a lifetime of shame.)
Now that it's over will Tyson be champ once again?
Or will the heavyweight bow under the strain.

Gwen Desmier

A Memory From When I Was A Child

As she laid there dying
On the pavement in the rain
Her coat was all blooded and
her face so full of pain

The car didn't stop, it never even
Slowed down
It just kept on going
as it knocked, her to the ground

"Help me, please" I screamed but
the people just walked by
"Help me, please, I beg you just
don't let her die".

I took her up in my arms and
she cried with all the pain
But the tears she cried were washed away
with the droplets of the rain

One woman did stop and she looked
down at us, and said its just a
dead dog why make such a fuss.

Dennis Delgado

'Leanne'

When Leanne says she's not pretty
Not stylish, bright or witty
You know she lies

Yet, in her eyes
In every pale reflection she might pass
In every stolen glance into the glass
Its 'truth' cries out
And thoughts of beauty put to rout

What shame it is that one flat mirrored pane
One snap shot from a thousand frames
Should represent the whole to you

When beauty's lived in all the world
And all the world's a kinder judge of you.
Simon Chell

The Golfabet

A is for Andrews, the course of the Kings.
B is for bunkers, and forty eight swings.
C is for caddies, with knowledge and brawn.
D is for divot, or holes in the lawn.
E is for exercise, walking around.
F is for finding lost balls on the ground. G is for golf, "a funny
old game". H is for hookshot, that buggers your aim. I is for
iron from putter to wedge. J is for joy, when putts hole from
the edge. K is for kitbag, full of your clubs. L is for last hole,
and off to the pubs. M is for mashie, to get your balls high. N
is for near, as your ball trickles by. O is for open, the big
match of the year. P is for putting, after saying a prayer.
Q is for quiver, when your nerves reach your knees. R is for
rough, when you land in the trees. S is for swing, with
smoothness and ease. T is for terror, at the cost of club fees.
U is for umbrella, when caught as rain pours. V is for veteran,
flat cap and plus-fours. W is for woods, you tee off with
these. X is for x-ray, when you're deep in the trees. Y is for
yell, when someone shouts "four!"
Z is for zap, when you choose to ignore.
Stephen Marshall

My Poetic Devices

Try to explain feelings with only words
Creating happiness, perhaps rhyming verse.
Transform a couplet into emotion,
Trap tiresome tears using alliteration.
Symbolic imagery to steal a picture for your mind,
Or the sound I hear through onomatopoeia;
Fumble, crash, grind!
An overworked cliche of 'I love you',
Describe my life in a metaphor or two.
Sarcastic irony: it's true, poetry always makes sense,
Diction enabling tone,
You can't write the effect of feeling tense.
Inanimate objects breaking the heart,
Assonance, enjambment all perfect the art.
Just like my life, maybe I fear,
"Poetic Devices"
Rhymes the falling tear.
Marina Athina Fryett

Not Again

In the morning fears of going downstairs
In late and drunk last night nobody dares
All of us are now awake
the roaring starts and we shake
This goes on throughout the week
none of us barely even speak
Parents sometimes just overreact
The discipline they had we lacked
Parents call us a disaster
and say that drink is our master
in many houses drink is trouble
so are fags, but drink is double
Anna McMahon

Her Only Romance

She stands in the shadows,
withdrawing a needle from her arm,
discoloured veins grin as they fill,
with the bitter sedative charm.

Her young eyes are glazed,
blistered skin a powder white,
thoughts are lost among pretty rainbows,
satin and silks dress her night.

Crawls into a damp doorway,
lays her curly blonde head down,
her sad teenage reflection,
watches the dying girl drown.

This trip is her last one,
there is no second chance,
syringe falls from a pocket,
which became her only romance.
Allan Reid

The Sting

A warm golden day, a cloudless blue sky,
The fresh greenness of springtime delighting the eye.
Around me bright flowers abundantly grew
Gaily flaunting their beauty, in every rich hue.
The loveliest beckoned, drawing me nigh,
I breathed in the fragrance and murmured a sigh.
Closer, I knelt, and to touch — my arm flung,
When suddenly, shockingly, an angry wasp stung.

I cried out in pain, tears ran down my face,
As bewildered I stood and considered the case.
This insect, so handsome in glossy striped coat,
With venom, despoiled a moment remote,

A moment of wonder, of rare happiness.
I turned to my mother to explain my distress.
"I wouldn't have harmed it at all", was my cry.
"So why did it have to hurt me? Tell me why".
J. Harding

White Coated Sadists

From behind these high and white–washed walls,
Drift cries of pain, they are animal calls,
For this is the home of Sadistic games,
And this is the place where Satan reigns,
Where the white–coated Sadists practice their 'art',
With skilful hand and cold, cold heart,
So patiently they work with such dedication,
Is it really a science?
Or just mutilation?
But the truth is well hidden by the Government's lies,
Whilst the scientists drip acids into animals eyes,
And watch them squirm and writhe in pain,
They have seen what will happen,
But they will do it again,
And again they will torture, and cripple, and mar,
Until the people all shout,
'Stop You Have Gone Too Far!'
R. S. Strong

"Life"

Down in the deep woods, where sun and shadows play.
Down by the babbling stream I used to spend my days, and dream,
Dream of another life somewhere far away
Wander in strange places, meet new people see new faces.
One day my dreams came true
I travelled to far countries
Made friends with strangers
Had my adventures, and also saw danger
Years pass by quickly, and far did I roam
But as I grew older I longed for my home.
With my own kind once more, and no longer alone,
I came back today, my deep woods had gone
And traffic not shadows moved in the sun
There were houses and shops where my wood had been
And under the roadway ran my little stream
Olga Clay Forbes

Reality?

I'm lying horizontal in a vertical world,
not understood, just another screwed up girl.
Yes, I'm lying in the back streets of the everyday mind.
In the village of my thoughts and people of my kind.
It's not me that's twisted, just the nearest conclusion
Your everyday's a lie, a complicated illusion
The truth is hard to live, care and thought are hard to give.
I'm lying horizontal in a vertical world
My thoughts are different, my thoughts are, mine.
I'm lying horizontal, but I'm doing just fine.
I pick dreams from my head, like daisies from a field.
Plastic sheets upon my head want help the way I feel.
You can tie me up, you can twist what I say,
but one day soon my time will come, and I'll just float away.
I'm lying horizontal in a vertical world
My thoughts are different, my thoughts are mine
I'm lying horizontal, but I'm doing just . . .

Sarah Starkey

Sample

You first notice the pungent sweet aroma,
See the murky red lip and hug the sides,
Bobbling bubbles burst and
Around the perimeter, the raucous, swollen liquid
Fades to pink, where at the heart
It appeared burgundy.

Long delicious fingers
Clasp the body warm smooth sides,
Raised to stained crimson mouth
Slowly, deliberately, violently, it glides down . . .

A fertile sweet musk peppers the humid air,
She, with lithe back pressed to the wall
Adorned in a snug, screaming, scarlet dress,
Smiles to her near lover.
He gazes furtively into the goblet and down the tinsled hall
For another.

Linda Parkinson

Panther

Eyes like emeralds follow its prey.
Each movement noted, each muscle responding to that
movement,
A coat of inky black blending with the night.
White teeth glistening with anticipation,
The chase is on with speed and muscle power.
A deer, powerless against the black shadow is brought down,
pain seers through the deer.
The panther tearing at its flesh,
teeth turning from white to crimson red.
Blood flowing like red wine.
Satisfied the panther surveys the carnage,
he turns and melts into the night.

Fiona McNab

Her Great Wall

Carve a place for myself
I make my flesh my own
Make a name and write it in red
Let it trickle away and let Jordan wash my sin
into red wine forgiveness—little shimmering vines, deep satin
crimson
They curve, writhing, snake-like
    with their anger and cleansing alcoholic venom
draining the medieval poison:
    Imbalance.
Today, yesterday's bad blood;
This steady alteration finds constancy.
Little stonehenges all over my body of my own creation
There's no body, quite like me now
Nobody who, quite likes me now
I am an enigma
And the mystery is concealed
with the Great Wall of myself.

Hayley Pounder

Hi-Tech-Trauma

I thought technology was to help me,
With my everyday criteria,
Yet, instead, it causes me hysteria,
The cooker has seen better days,
The knobs fall off and it sways,
The fridge is no better,
It freezes everything in sight,
Icicles form on the butter overnight,
The telly it hisses and whines
And the video likes tapes that it can unwind,
Now the washer is the last straw,
There seems to be more water on the floor,
And there's such a draught from the front door,
Oh, how I dream of having things new,
Things that work and don't need glue,
I dream of the day when I can sit back and say,
Technology has worked for me today,
One day my wishes will come true,
But until then I'll keep making do.

Karen Pye

'Is It Thursday Already?'

I'm lonely, like that naked blade of grass
who survived the lawn cutter.
I wish I was surrounded like the raindrop,
falling among friends, cascading freely into the gutter.
I'm sad, like the final picture of a refugee
removed from peril and horror.
I wish I could experience their relieve and joy,
instead of this desire for there being no tomorrow.
I need help! but do people really care?
I wish they did, surely they'd help me from my despair.
Love. Compassion. We've all receive a ration from God.
Most of us disguise it somehow, somewhere, hidden in some
profound fog.
Yet I've seen the writing on the wall. It tell's the
truth about us all, and when I've read it once or twice,
after all, it is advice. It tell's me over and over again,
John, John, don't give up, say your prayers . . . and start your
life again.

J. Golightly

My Love

She came into my life like a snowflake from above
She melted my heart with all her passionate love
She danced and played with my mind like a single, caged
white dove

Should I trust this angel that came from above
Is she a worthy person to give my undying love
Shall we coo and fly around like two mating doves

I shall give my love, to the snowflake that fell from above
I will give my heart, and all my passionate love.
I will ask this one question to the fair lady from above
Please, please don't discard my beautiful honest love.

Stephen Mullen

Dialogue

Everyday I speak words to everyone I meet,
Everyday I share part of myself with life.
Why then can't I share the part of me that
means the most to me with those I love?
Why can't I show them 'Me'?

My mother and my father knew me well, they thought,
My wife and my children know me well, they think,
Yet again, can it be that they are right and I am wrong?
That my image of my inner self is imagination not reality.
Why can't I know, or do I want to?

I have seen respect flower into a bloom called love,
With this love comes mental and vocal communication,
I must guard against the gradual onslaught of silence,
Long days of talk only of mundane matters,
The bloom of love withers without the nourishment of dialogue.

Ian Comrie

A Last Goodbye

I recall when we were lovers, that was in the good old days,
People change like the seasons do, now we go in different ways,
I never meant to put you down, I can't find the words to say,
It's plain to see you are restless, I am glad I moved out of the way,
Had you never loved me so kindly,
Had I never loved you so blindly,
If we had never met, or if we had never parted,
Perhaps now we would not be so brokenhearted,
My heart—wrung tears are deep, I promise thee,
My sighs and groans of pain I hide, so that you'll be free,
Freedom for your heart, freedom for your soul.
Freedom to search for life, freedom to reach your goal,
A loving kiss, A caring smile and then we sever,
A loving touch, A last farewell, Goodbye for ever.

Michael D. Curran

Anonymous Friend

She sits, she smiles and gazes intently.
The black thing is smiling back at her.
A gap appears in her face, teeth are showing,
A giggle escapes.

It runs towards her, now slows, now stops.
It caresses her soul with its innocence.
It has knowledge of nothing, yet it knows everything.
It shines with a glory she may never know.
This tiny creature is her new found friend.

It has run past her, is heading for the door.
Eight legs moving faster than attentive eyes can see.
The gap lessens, closes and creases appear,
A tiny frown, on a flawless face,
A face that does not understand.

So short a stay, so precious the memory
Of her tiny anonymous friend.

Rachel Kendall

If Only

Mournful sadness, darkest deep,
    Born these eyes only to weep,
Cast aside the salty water,
    Lies someone's son, or someone's daughter,
For one who stands where none compare,
    There lies only a deep despair,
Endless sadness makes its home,
    The host on earth, eternal roam,
A look that holds a thousand sighs,
    Is caught in only lonely eyes,
Spiralling chasms to glimpse the soul,
    A body lies broken, when once was whole,
To look into the eyes of lonely,
    Beseeching, whispering, they breathe,
    "If only . . . "

Joanne E. Payne

Abiding Love

Caring, it's reaching out beyond one's self
This time span of dependency and trust
Two waves of emotion on a never ending merry-go-round
The highs, the lows, wanting it to end
    yet not wanting an ending
Somewhere in all this is a closer
    union with body and soul
In the weaknesses comes forth strength

The menial tasks overtake the mind
It cannot take on board the enormity of it all
Love must win through and finish what it has begun
This parting from each other is only for a short time
For I, being the care, am now wanting
    and dependent and trusting
Looking into the light
I am sheltered from the storm
    And now I will take my rest

Thelma Brooks

"Spring"

I've gazed in awe, at northern lights,
and beauty of the southern Cross, I've seen,
roamed Tropic Isles, with golden sands,
blue lagoons, and verdant greens.
By contrast, observed the awesome sight,
of huge icebergs, ablaze with light.
Sought grateful shade, oasis give.
In deserts cruel, so vast, so huge.
One wonders, that there's life, to live.
To many foreign lands, I've been.
So many wondrous sights I've seen,
but none compare to English spring,
with bluebells,—Hawthorn blossoming.
The joy of such emerging life,
obliterates all thoughts of strife.

Francis W. T. Cooper

Remember Me

Fear embraces him slowly
On the rocks he walks along
The little child inside of me
Tries so hard to belong

The eagle's eyes grasp him slowly
As the rocks embrace his smile
The sky was all so dark
As the eagle fluttered its heavenly wings
And left me with a memory
Of all those loving stings

The waters flow more softly
As the sun starts to rise
Reflections calm me slowly
And I hear his soft reply
Please please please
Just let me cry

John Mason

Shadows Of The Sun

Spirit Divine, mystery of the mind,
Moving unhindered through space and time,
Give to thought and feeling a form
With ageless nature from first dawn—
Let teeming images fashion
Perfection in parade and pattern.
And when the wheel begins to spin
Make it stir the parts within
To show how much you care
Despite the pain man has to bear,
That while alive he must die to see:
Life is the eye of eternity.
For out of decay, new life springs—
Out of silence, some sparrow sings—
In the midst these snare twins smile,
Man walks immortal, lost but awhile.

Robert Louis Dummett

A Perfect Dinner

Warm and snug,
At home on a rug.
People watching telly.
Waiting to fill, their bellies.
Barney's already fat
and white and black.
Purr purr, quick put him down by the fire.
He's worm out just like an old tyre!
Dinner's brought in, the smell's wafted through.
Barney's woken up oh dear! Here goes the stew!
Barney jumps up and down trying to get at the stew.
People shout "Oi you!!"
"Beastly beast."
"Get off that, its our feast."
He runs away and hides behind a chair.
He doesn't take his eyes off, he sits
there and stares.

Katie Biss

Thank Him

It is good to say thank you to God,
Thank him for all that you have,
For your eye sight,
That you may see the beauty of his trees,
And how blue the heavenly sky,
The white clouds, as they go sailing by.
The blue sea, filled with all kinds of creatures,
And the Bible, with God's word to teach us.
Lovely colours of the rainbow, after the rain,
God's promise, never to flood the earth again,
Thank God for all these things,
For your family,
Your fathers and mothers, sisters and brothers,
Daughters, sons, and all relations,
For the place where we live, whether large or small,
Some unfortunate people have nowhere at all
There are so many things to thank God for,
To forget his existence is a bad thing to do,
Every minute—every second—he is thinking of you.

Barbara Jean Waterfield

Tranquillity

Faint tendrils of light creep languidly across the sky
as the sun awakens from its slumber.
And climbs slowly over the horizon.
Gently waves ripple rhythmically onto the beach
which will soon welcome the arrival
of Apollo's worshippers.

But now,
at this moment,
time holds its breath,
as it awaits the rebirth of the dawn
and bids farewell to the shadows of the night.

Janine Kelly

For My Friends

What will I do without you?
How will I cope with you gone?
The future is calling to all of us.
Its tempting force is too strong.

The bonds between us shall not break.
They will just stretch around the world.
To the farthest places that we may reach,
Growing stronger in us all.

And now I call on the sun,
To burn through my skin,
Straight to my heart,
So you can look in.
There's something inside,
For each one of you.
It's buried down deep,
But it's shining through.

Lee Delaney

Facing Reality

War, conflict, hatred and agony,
Among those who kill.
Unobtainable happiness, lost among the years.

Anguish, confusion, possessions and gifts,
Forgotten by the dying, left by the living.
A pathetic argument.

Thousands disappeared, one by one,
Going away alone.
Disheartened by armies, killing for no reason.

Thinking of nothing but a future,
A life not worth living.
Care is needed, none is given.

The end is coming, trouble passes.
Regaining normality.
Evidently gone.

Emily Mower

First Love

I recall, went spirits soaring, the pain of love,
'twas joy enduring.
When, once somewhere, time had no will,
its opium lingers still.
Hearts and hands and minds entwining,
a parting kiss to leave one pining,
Thoughts that meet
and eyes that speak
across some crowded room.
A fire that burned so bright within,
and smoulders still,
loves sweet caress to light again.

R. Evans

The Butterfly Of Yesteryear

For Jillo

We walk together, my childhood friend and I
Down memory lane for just a little while,
And share again those golden sunlit days of yore
Of laughter, love and joy on some happy bygone shore.
There are no words, words that other people need,
For each of us knows how the other feels.
We have travelled back through the years
Across a moonlit river of time
Back to the ghosts of children past
Meeting again on remembrance path
The folks we have loved and left behind
And share again for just a little while
Their loving funny tender ways and smiles.
But time moves on, and the world is calling us back
And yesteryear is fading quickly into the mists of time.
We stop, looking lingeringly back, my childhood friend and I
Across a moonlit river of time—and Smile
For we knew we had heard beloved voices whispering in the wind
And we had captured the butterfly of yesteryear
Briefly in our hands.

Ilona M. L. Fisher

Mother Earth

Please excuse us for our misdemeanours
For once born we are overshadowed with ignorance
On our quest for contentment
You do not deserve the injustices we bring upon you
By our greedy journey through life
On which we ride upon your precious skin
Fools we are to shame you
As we dare have the audacity to create our own paradise
So sad to see you bludgeoned by this apathetic race
For it was you that gave us our earthly heaven
In all your best faith.

Raymond E. Fullstone

New Age Man

The modern man,
No longer hunter-gatherer,
Computers, cars and science,
Now in men's hearts,
Where once were only ploughs and bows.
We go now where birds and fish once ruled,
Feeding millions,
Healing many more than before.
Musicians now kept in little black boxes,
Played at a whim.
Metal minions to do our tasks,
The stars only a dream and a few tears away.
Miracle-men of past could only say.
It would never happen. But we pay,
For each blessing comes a curse:
Black trees, poisoned water,
Millions more to feed.
We are at a crossroad,
So we climb for the stars,
Or leave the Eden of Science?

Elvis Vaughn

Memories Of You

My life is like a pathway
Made up of fond memories of you.
I remember with pride the day you were born.
I remember the day you came running to me
Crying, knees grazed trousers torn.
I remember the day you rode your first motorbike.
I remember fondly the friends you used to like . . .
I remember that day you drove me to France.
I remember that one time you asked me to dance.
I remember the pride on your face when your H.G.V. you got . . .
.
I remember that special girl Debbie, the love of your life.
You really loved her a lot.
All these memories of you, Paul, Son and friend
Fill my every day.
Only one sad memory fills my mind,
That's the sad day God took you away.
Thank you Son for giving me these memories.
Love always, Mum.

Lavinia Sharp

Inner City Wasteland

Slanted sun strikes sleazy, on
crumbled, crumpled, long ancient crusted brick.
Guttered, cluttered, easy gone
discarded package, wrappings piled thick.
For wearied, forgotten street,
condemned.   Coagulated, corroded
City Heart with rotten beat.
Sold, sealed, peeled, so eroded
Myth. Infirmity in finite.
Boarded, marauded, morose eye sockets,
paneless, without pain in sight.
Propheted unprofitable.   Pockets
of vermin. Vile Decadence.
Saturated, dissipated, sterile
remnant. Our Inheritance.
History, once revered. Revoke . . . Revile.

Jem Baker

The Harvest Moon

Your blood–red hunger fills the sky,
Displaying its rage, its wrath.
Swiftly you rise and we
Cower before this vision of a thwarted soul
Wretched, agonizing, you seek
Revenge on those who betrayed
You, with a face of fire and ice
Your spirit lies far within.

Anne-Marie Mongan

A New Dawn

Promises made for better or worse
Now disperse;
Misplaced loyalty meets its demise.

Trying to be what was required,
To be desired;
Betrayal ends the disguise.

Broken trust, broken faith, broken dreams,
How ill life seems
When viewed through unveiled eyes.

Perspectives change, confound the senses,
A new dawn commences;
Success or failure within it lies.

Emerging facets of self unfurl,
Delicate pearl
To nurture as old refuge dies.

Determination and self-reliance
Breed defiance;
Doubts abate, the spirit flies.

Yasmin Elizabeth Freeman

Fire Lily Duet

In sudden wonder, wild flowers are noted,
Sweet, playful nobles, caught in mid-dew's departure,
whetting the lush taste, it falls away,
vain in itself, becomes its end;
pure and nothing more.

Displayed intentions, thatched thick in wedlock to our audience,
hold no place in this moment,
all those that left us for another bride
breathe wholly in heart; whisper our thoughts raw in truth.

The essence of our vermilion light, relates to this,
our innate hunger for spoilage and deceit,
In both seed and flesh a mutual fate binds our division,
A righteous pain; fire burnt to the last,
is best remembered for shattered embers.

Gayle Fitzpatrick

A Wonderful Rainforest

A day in the life of a tribesgirl,
Would be a real adventure.
To live in a wilderness of trees, plants and animals
And with barely any light from the sun.
Doing tribal dances round a blazing fire,
And singing tribal songs.
Listening to wild animals calling high up in the trees,
I wonder what they are saying?
As I bathe in the warm river
I relax and look around.
Smelling the sweet fragrance of mysterious plants.
Then as the afternoon draws on,
And the sun dips behind the trees.
I fall asleep in my hut.
When the moon and stars shine bright,
The night's animals hunt their prey.

Kirsty Reilly

Passing Time

I saw a man the other day, with heavy feet he made his way,
Head bowed low and eyes so old, with heavy coat, he still was cold.

His face was thin, his features drawn, closed to the world,
    he stumbled on.
He brushed my arm, as he passed by, I heard him mutter,
    "Why, Oh Why".

I didn't understand, what those words meant,
    coming from the man, with body bent,
I stood and watched, the old man go,
    'Where did he come from? Where will he go?'

I felt so sad, for the man, yet I knew not why,
as something within, placed a tear in my eye.

It was more than sympathy, though what, I don't know,
I felt so helpless, as I watched him go

End . . .

R. Taylor

On The Death Of A Loved One

For nearly fifty happy years we lived as man and wife.
I know not now which way to turn, what's left for me in life.
Why can't I count my blessings? So many I have had.
Why do I weep so often? Why am I always sad?

I'm told to let the tears flow and they will ease the pain.
Perhaps they help a little, but nought can be the same.
I thought I had more courage and now I find I've none.
For nothing means the same to me now that he has gone.

My family, friends and neighbours have all been very good
And I try to show I'm grateful, as a real true Christian should,
I look around and see how many share a grief like mine.
I'm not the only one who is left alone to pine.

Perhaps, as time goes by, the hurting will be gone.
I know that, with God's help, the victory can be won.
I must be strong, for your sake, my dearest Bill
And know, where'er you are, you love me still.

Irene Cross

Treasure Beneath

Slivers of grey amongst shining blue
Gliding below wooden carrying crew
Above abated dawn silent and true
Below cool solace quarried too few
Armoured steel focused aligned if a cue
Soft flesh targets ascending into view
Encircling shrieks as of gulls high the sky
Flashing cold steel drawing crimson and cry
Larders ahoy, secreted joy
Neath purity ebbs to exist
Pathos draws inevitable mist
Them victorious edged with blue
Those below quarried too few.

Andrew Smith

"Spinning Web"

Like a spider his web spinning reeling me into him.
Caught fighting to escape the burning venom, on the
tip of is inviting tongue.
But secretly wanting to feel,the "cold taste of death"
As he gently caresses the life from my still body.
Lying in wait, I feel his presence, his power, to
take me into another dimension—a world of—
pure sweet indulgence.
Wanting, needing, to feel eternal life—skin ice cold
to touch, eyes burn so invitingly bright.
To be caught by him and kept—waiting for him
to feed me love with his newly found life.
Never wanting to be cut free from his "spinning web",
As I'm to used to this new and different realm,
To deeply caught by his soul, in his ever
reeling, "spinning web."

Dawn Walker

Beauty

She dwells where mountains, lofty, proud,
Catch sunbeams on their snowy crests;
Where roaring torrents churn and foam,
And where the wanderer makes his home,
In solitudes so blest.

But when the dawn breaks o'er the sky,
And rosy light fades into blue,
She wanders in the vales below,
Where violets and bluebells grow—
Kiss'd by the morning dew.

When glittering moonbeams glance and dart,
On glistening waves, unruly, free—
When twinkling lights, so far below,
To home–bound ships, the harbour show—
She walks the cliffs with me.

She is mysterious, gentle, shy—
Who spreads enchantment all around—
Who, unassuming, roams the earth,
And adds to Joy, and Peace, and Mirth—
Where Happiness is found.

Isabel Grimshaw

The Loch Ness Monster

Fae the water it appeared,
Three big humps an'wan green ear,
Gliding alang, wae its heid in the air,
Fear'in naeb'dy, stauning there.

They a' staun an' stare wae fricht,
At see'in sic an aufy sicht,
The folk couldn'y bare tae stay,
An so they a'ran up the brae.

As it made its monstris turn,
It gar'd the water, foam an' churn,
He hud the loch, for his very ane,
As if he wis king on a thrane.

Robert J. Gormley

Home Thoughts

Silence—
So real you can touch it
Until the clatter of the cat flap
As she—
Tired of tracking wary birds
Bursts in
Demanding food, love, attention
In that order

Noise—
Children spreading chaos, biscuit crumbs
Laughing, shouting, arguing.
Bringing life to the silent house
Until they leave.
Peace.
Silence reigns again.

Valerie Dwight

Moonlight Shore

Walking the shores on a moonlight night
With nought betwixt my soul and heaven
The music of the crystal sea, like pearls
of ancient mystery.
Threatening shadows of the rocks loom against the velvet sky.
How many barques that sailed the heavy seas
Did end their days in misery?
When mermaids heard the dying calls
and prayers
Plucked brave mariners by the score
Through the frothy heaving waves and led them,
gently, to their watery graves,
Where Neptune rules and is the King
amidst the wrecks and masts of old.
And still the mystery of the sea
will linger far and wide.
When walking the shores on a moonlight night
We must stop and listen and
lend an ear
To the music of the sea.

Anne Christable Davey-Young

Too Late To Turn Back?

I'll go tonight, I just have to go.
Only five hours left, it's going too slow.
Pressure from Mum, pressure from school,
Wherever I am, I feel like a fool.

Nobody loves me. Nobody cares.
I hear them all laughing or else they all stare.
I do my best, I always have done,
They go in their groups, can't I have some fun?

Now it's time, there's a letter on my bed.
It tells them no fear, I won't be dead.
I will survive, I will get by,
No longer will I have to live this lie.

There's no turning back, it's cold out here!
My bag full of food, my head full of fear.
I really don't like this, I'm out on my own.
I don't think I can do this. I'm going home!

Kelly Sales

Untitled

If thy feelings are stronger than thy mind,
And thy heart is filled with genuine love.
Await with desire for a love, so kind,
Flowing down from the deep blue sky above.
If thou should'st wait, longer than thou live,
Because a red rose awaits to bloom still.
Leaving all that thou hath yet still to give.
For eternity return in good will.
And upon the grave, that thy name is wrote,
Weeping my folds in pain and affliction.
Eternally covered with soil to rot,
As my feelings engross with deception,
As I think of what is to come along,
To kill oneself was indeed very wrong.

Rachael Montgomery

"Angels Of Dunblane"

Sleep little angels sleep
Sweet dreams are yours to keep.
Your innocent young lives
Savagely cut short.
Whilst loved one's doth weep.
    So much anger, questions
As to why? This animal,
Slipped society by
    Sleep little angels sleep
Hush now, don't you cry
    your faces of Angel's
your wings will fly
your memory's cherished,
By these Hearts you touched
    Their hurt is unbearable, their pain too much.
In such a tragedy
There is always a lesson we can learn
No place is safe
We are all victims of evil

N. M. Burton

Why?

I often ask myself why,
why did my Papa choose to die,
the answer is I do not know,
for I still love him so much so,
I often write my emotion in poem,
He would be proud if only I could show him,
once my Papa was dead he got cremated,
at this point a part of me got amputated,
the way he battled fought and fought,
chasing all the dreams he often sought.

Angie Gordon

Street Life It's Me

In this world I weave a spell and pray to
God to let me die and go to hell but
What little does he know of me for I can't
even see the real me as I sit there in
my chair and try to laugh and grin and
Swear with a needle in my arm and I start
to take my poison to keep me calm 'you
ask me why but I don't know I'm not the
same person I used to know all around me
people laugh but the sorrows and depression
in side me will always last. Seven
o'clock it's early morning the new day has
just started dawning yet inside I am morning
for I know the day shall be boring. So if you
see me sitting there spare a penny and try to
care there's lots of us out there who've been
cast aside and never to be known and
that's why we all live in this strange little
world all of our own.

Shereen Hemsworth

Fragrant Memories

Honeysuckle and wild roses, awake in me fond memories
Of long ago when I was young,
Of happy days beneath the sun.
Flower–filled meadows, waist–high grasses
Dancing in the breeze.
Purple clover, golden daisies, scarlet poppies,
all of these,
Dainty, heady meadow–sweet,
Buttercups and marguerites
Small feet dabbling in the stream
So long ago, seems but a dream.

Those days were real, so very real,
Treasured memories thrill me still.
Precious days of childhood
Long since left behind,
Honeysuckle and wild roses
Are in my heart entwined.

Helen Hughes

On Shakespeare

Biographers of Shakespeare are at odds
when dealing with that strange phenomenon:
How he, who was no idol of the gods,
seemed also, like a fish, inclined to spawn
those five-act plays in blank iambic verse
on characters from ancient history
who come to life and speak as they rehearse
the lines that lure the ear for tragedy.
How come that one, that mediocre player,
writes comedies that touch the human heart
on themes that show he could command a flair
for theatre and stage–performing art?

Or, was he but the vendor of a name
that offered pseudonymity for fame?

Struan Yule

The Story Of The Other Cross

There's an episode oft forgotten from that story of the cross.
Which can show us there's still hope for us, instead of total loss,
For crucified with Christ that day were sinners, one on either side
Does it need me to remind you what they said before they died.
The one cast doubts upon him, saying if all you say is true
And you are the true Messiah, save us both as well as you!
But the other one feared God and said, "Remember me, I pray",
And Christ did answer, "You will be in paradise with me today!"
This simple story tells us all, there's hope to the very end,
Because in that eleventh hour, he's still our Saviour and our friend,
Even though a sinner, he'll forgive, if only we but ask,
"Remember me, for I believe", that prayer is but a simple task,
You do not have to suffer and think that life down here's the end,
It's so simple to be saved and to live for ever with that friend
That friend, the dear Lord Jesus and his Father, in all glory,
Repentance never comes too late, as you'll remember by this story.

Harold L. White

My Super "M-A-A"

My dear "M-A-A,"
You're the golden wealth in our life.
You're so precious "M-A-A!"
We felt secure in your affection,
Although we were so little.
So far as I can remember,
We played outside and if anything happened to us,
We would run—run and go to you for comfort.
Before I came of age
God, you took away my "M-A-A!"
I can't find the "M-A-A," I love.
She left us so suddenly
And her smile has gone forever.
I pray for you "M-A-A."
God bless, we love you always.
You're everything to me
My super "M-A-A."

M. Shafiullah

Another Day

As I awoke this morning
And heard the blackbird singing
A lovely fragrance filled my room
As all the flowers came into bloom
It's such a glorious sound and sight
As we come into morning light

Throughout the day we rush around
And don't have time for sights and sounds
If only we'd more time to spare
To tender things with loving care
As mother nature works away
And magic's yet another day
Of beautiful things for us to see
All around in the scenery

Soon night time comes around again
We pray for sunshine then for rain
Our beautiful carpet of plants and flowers
Are back asleep for the next few hours

Maureen A. Horne

16 Little Angels Of Dunblane

Even the angels in heaven cried today.
Wednesday 13th they were taken away.
16 little blooms growing into flowers
Their little lives snuffed out in the cold early hours.
On the morning their lives were full of fun.
Then came the horrible man with the gun.
He ended their precious lives in 3 minutes of madness.
And left the whole world in a numb sadness.
How could that killer do that and why.
That day he made the strongest men cry.
The Lords now taken the cherubs to heaven above.
To wrap his arms around them and give them all his love.
Now they are happy they can't be hurt no more.
Please help those mothers and fathers whose hearts are sore.
Give them strength to carry on and heal.
Please Lord let them know how sorry we feel.
Lord give them all the love you can.
Because of the tragedy of inhumanity from man to man
One day the dark shadows of evil will close the door.
And peace and happiness will be here forever more

> *Maria Woods*

Midnight Knock

Oh why, oh why humanity can man not ever learn
of all the wars the world has fought
that all men could walk free.
They said I put some posters up
when four men called for me.
We drove a long long way away
my head was in a sack.
Is it just one week or maybe it is four
that I've laid here in the dark, upon this cold wet floor.
My body racked with awful pain and fear flows on the floor.
There's twenty other souls in here but none of us dare speak
when we feel a rush of air we know they're coming in
and if you hear them call your name it's no good playing dead
for they will simply kick you hard or stamp down on head.
On body parts already crushed they crush them just once more
and copper wires they then attach to all my body parts.
Now at last I'm looking down and there's no going back
around the world there are free men and if they should be told
will close their eye and shoulder shrug
and say that it's not true.

> *William Oliver Corney*

A New Day

First stirrings of a new day, a breeze sends messages across the trees,
The grass glistens with dew and invites bare feet to tread on it,
Cobwebs take on different shapes as they glisten in the first sun's rays,
Birds sing noisily, unaware of me as I quietly on my patio sit.

Cool? Yes, but it's such a fresh coolness it brings a feeling of peace
No one is awake except me, I am the only person in the world,
Today could be the day when excitement knocks on my door,
giving me news of an adventure to come I had not dreamed could be unfurled.

An invitation to visit strange and unexplored lands, maybe across the sea,
A letter, asking me to visit friends or family closer to home
Tickets to see a show that I have been waiting to see for a long time
Or news of family to visit me, here, so I need no further roam

Each to his own excitement, I can find enchantment in everything I see
I can marvel at the brilliance of nature, the earth, the sky,
I can imagine all the places I need to see, visit them in my mind
In my mind I can swim, walk, run and even fly

I try to live in peace, loving and caring for those in my company each day
If I succeed I feel satisfied that life has meaning, is not in vain
When someone tries to lighten my life and make it happier still
I know there is a reason for life's strife and pain.

> *Janet Keogh*

To Alexander

You lie there sleeping,
  what do you dream of?
The day's events, a battle, a feud or a
  crusade high in the skies.
You are at rest—at peace with yourself,
Lying naked, kept warm with your love.
(I'd like to touch, to reach out would be cruel.)
Innocently displaying your form to
  anyone who may enter,
The door is closed, the room still
Only my restlessness stirs . . .
  and upsets the calm.
You are both far and near
Your breath reminds me of your closeness,
  we are together again.

> *Lee-Anne MacMillan*

Jones

Jones is a cat with an angelic smile.
Cherubic. Seraphic. A smile to beguile,
That says we are friends, and I'm your true mate,
As he craftily pinches the food from your plate

Jones is a tabby, with white nose, vest, and feet.
Similar in looks to others you meet.
But there is a difference, and some say he's odd,
For he is a cat who's an awkward great puss.

Jones is a cat who weighs half a stone.
Perhaps not the heaviest cat I have known.
But when he has settled himself for a nap,
He feels like a ton weight asleep on your lap.

Jones is a cat who thinks he's a dog.
Somewhat a cut above any old mog.
When walking the dogs, or giving out bones,
Turn around, and you'll find, along comes Jones.

> *V. Osborne*

Miner's Holiday

The Sunlit beach alive with colour. Bodies brown, red, white,
stretched out in honour of the Sun, and freedom dearly
bought, with toil and sweat and tearful thought.
In the bowels of the Earth for many a month, away from light
and pure air, we strive to win mineral to the Nation's good,
and many a limb and sinew tear.
All year saving up the cash, for an extravagant jaunt and a salt
sea wash.
To pretend to the World we haven't a care, with shining wet
bodies and tousled hair.
Whilst we wait we do other things, like football, tombola, and
the 'Sport of Kings'.
TV watching, hobbies galore, until we reach that sandy shore.
All too soon our wondrous time is well consumed like tasty wine
Awareness grows as we return to a rat-race world of work and
earn, and where we know we have to go. Back to the dust and
darkness . . . BELOW!

> *Graham Littlewood*

Peace

Where is peace? I wish I knew,
For some days, I feel so blue,
I'm tired and weary, just can't go on,
But self-pity I know is wrong.
My words just uttered fly back in my face,
The whole wide world seems it's running a race,
Just let me rest and have some peace,
New life my body will then release.
Yesterday's gone, tomorrow's near,
With rest at length I have no fear,
It will get better and then refreshed.
Peace perfect peace I will recollect.
Was time well spent, all on my own,
Sorting out both body and bone,
Thoughts of mind too deep to see,
And only known by me.

> *Elaine Miles*

Society

Live in harmony, strive to love,
In this desperate world of hate and greed,
No morals, no peace, kill or be killed,
What about the children, the mouths to feed?

To what end, and when will our conscience see,
That such pleasurable darkness and mental pain,
Is so wrong in this oppressed time,
Where is our hope? The world is insane.

When all is lost and death knocks your door,
When you conform to your God of this land,
Mankind inventions and road you will strive,
Surely you will be die and add to earths sand.

No-one seems to laugh anymore,
As hurting is much more fun,
Evil is our very best friend,
From this we have nowhere to run.

There is a hope from a very special friend,
Who can give joy in the spirit to all men,
He gives life beyond the life of mankind,
From our birth until the very end.

Darren Riches

Loves Valley Of Dreams

Music my soul let it sing to your heart,
From our outer minds together we'll part,
Escape with me this reality,
For a dream is where you belong with me,
Look within joint imaginations here we see,

I the unicorn beholds your soul,
Within the valley of dreams,
Beholding all fantasies,
Within the purest means,

Each step upon the virgin ground,
Upon the unicorn's heart does pound,
Releasing the ecstasy,
Of love within this fantasy,
For this love is greater than all belief,
For the flow of streams as is love only relief,

Now all emotions broken through,
You must see all that is true,
As you belong to me as I to you,
Release the unicorn from the fields,
Set free your soul and all it yields.

Teresa Wooster

The Standard's

Introducing the Spearheads! Fingers of Flame!
The rallying point led them to fame,
Generally depicted like spires from our church,
As if from the Bible, put into verse.
Replaced by a lion, recaptures the day,
The rest point to heaven, but the lion leads the way.
Three crosses placed left on the Union Flag,
St. George! St. Patrick! Great epics achieved,
St. Andrew! A disciple of Christ we believe,
Add to these crosses blue and gold,
Unseen changes for history enfolds.

Blue to remind us no less, of gallant souls passing
In deep waters, in the air—ere we forget
Gold represents those shining warrior's face,
Sanctified by service into the Throne of Grace.
The tussles remind us, as life begins so it must end,
A golden fringe in a frame of love understood,
Binds them together into one great brotherhood.

Hylda Eversfield

Housewife

Here comes the female Walter Mitty,
Plying her Hoover in a dream.
Did you not know I'm clever, pretty?
Things are not always what they seem!

These are not trousers, apron, head-scarf —
This is my gorgeous Dior gown.
Singing you hear, now please don't all laugh,
That is a voice of great renown,

You see the cook with dough for kneading;
But deftly in the sculptor's hands
This 'clay', imagination feeding.
Soon as a noble statue stands.

Rhythm and warmth of ironing sends me
Floating off to some distant shore,
Glamour and luxury surround me —
I am no housewife anymore.

Key in the lock! See my lover come,
Tall, dark and handsome as can be,
Only a husband he seems to some,
But he makes dreams come true for me.

Ruth Barclay

Just Fred

Fred is just a common name,
When spoken short and sharp,
Not like the warmth of a summer's day,
Or the warbling of a lark.

Yet when he came into my life,
It was like a breath of spring,
With strength and love and laughter there,
To cope with everything.

Days lengthening into years,
So glorious were the days,
Of work and love and happiness,
A miracle in many ways.

We thought that God was with us,
But He must have been elsewhere,
When Fred was lying oh so ill,
He didn't listen to our prayer.

But when the sunlight hits the water,
And everything is bright,
I'll know that Fred is with me,
In every lovely sight.

D. E. Crawley

Jeannie

I watch her smiling as she sits in her chair,
Watching the television, with a blank stare.
Ask what she's watching, says she doesn't know,
Her eyes say it all, but her smile makes her glow.
She's had a few strokes which have left her this way,
The curse of the cigarette has had its day.
The feeling has gone in her right arm
But doctor says 'no need for alarm.'
As I look at her now, she fills me with pride,
This disaster has left her, nowhere to hide.
But through it all, she never complains,
The sound of her laughter will always remain.
Not even a shadow of what she used to be,
Can only be remembered by the ones who can see.
A hard working woman, a mother and wife,
A granny and great granny who's been cheated of life.
A shoulder to cry on, a rock for us all,
She will always in my mind, be ten feet tall.
This woman I talk about, is not without flaw,
She happens to have me as a son-in-law.

Charles Trail

Forget Them Not

They flew by day, but mostly night
These heroes we must never lose sight
Some came from countries far and wide
To fly shoulder to shoulder by our side.

They flew through flak, night fighters too
When they returned they'd lost a few
The danger they faced was so immense
They flew there under no pretence.

The chances they had to remain alive,
The odds they came to about "two in five"
The chances of completing a full tour (30 op's)
The odds you see were rather poor.

Mid air collisions did occur
Bad weather was often present there.

These brave young men of long ago
Pressed on regardless to fight the foe
They carried on without a lull
Many paid the price, in full.

They did this all for you and me
Fifty-five thousand died to keep us free.

G. W. Lea

Work Is Black And White

A lot of friction and a lot of burn
Silent thunderstorms of anger rage through my mind
Unacceptable human behaviour countless times
I want to play
I don't want to work
My feelings are sinking beneath the level of pleasure
Sinking into the depths of hard times
There's no easy solution when there's nothing to learn
Boredom produces itself to me
I'm waiting for my turn to cross that borderline

Tension in the air speaks its own language
Sometimes my feelings are bent
All I want is some colourful beauty
Surrounding my environment
I want to play
I don't want to work
I'd like to regain my sleep at night
You should be made a crime
Work you are so black and white

Anthony G. Chapman

Restoration

The house stood isolated bare and still,
nobody lived there in the house on the hill.
O! They did so many years gone by,
when its chimney towered tall to the sky.
So proud and noble was its structural form,
its red bricks shining, its well kept lawn.
Then, flowers grew in beds amassed,
now unkempt, under glass all smashed.
There's no laughter peeling around the walls,
only coldness, stark emitting from its halls.
No warmth of heat, of love of passion abounding,
just blackness, enveloping the drab surrounding.
The lane leading from it narrows and twists,
two lovers are seen in young married bliss.
They took the wrong turning and entered this way,
looking up they behold the house in all its array,
for they can see its beauty as it was in the past,
the potential it possesses as it hides behind its mask.
They tenderly nurture with love and with taste,
the birth of restoration in this beautiful place.

Joan C. Ashby

Night Shift

It's 8 p.m., the start of my shift
My eyes towards the clock I lift
Twelve hours to go, an awesome plight
Through dusk and dawn, I'll work all night

It's 10 p.m., the light is fading
Night draws in, the blackness cascading
I press a switch and bright lights flare
I draw the blinds to ease their glare

It's 1 a.m., a baby is born
A bundle of joy, all pink and warm
I think of my children tucked in their beds
I hope sweet dreams are filling their heads

It's 5 a.m. and dawn is breaking
Birds are singing as day is waking
I think to myself 'three hours to go'
I yawn and stretch from head to toe

It's 8 a.m., my shift is finished
I grab my keys, my woe diminished
I head for home, weary but glad
And think 'perhaps that wasn't so bad.'

Kerry A. Hemsworth

My Dreams

In my dreams I'm famous
Red carpets line the corridors of high class hotels for me
All because I'm passing through
Maids, Butlers, Chauffeurs,
All kowtow to me
And I nod here and there in appreciation

In my dreams I have lots of money
Bank Managers jump with glee for me
All because I have large sums to set free
Clerks, Typists, Messengers
All kowtow to me
And I wave here and there in appreciation

Alas I wake,
And there are no riches no fame
Nobody around kowtows to me
I fetch, I carry, I clean . . . . . .
I yawn and ask my boss
'May I retire early, I need to get back to my dreams?'

Anne Etuk

The River

Beautiful river, born on a mountain side,
Twisting and turning your way to the sea.
Flowing on gently, rippling soothingly.
Serving man, beast and meadow with water so free.

Man tries to tame you, diverting your pathway.
Through town and village sedately you flow.
But sometimes rebellious, you burst from your harness,
Mindlessly flooding as forward you go.

Then come the 'morrow, left far behind you
All that is blemished, ruined or dead.
With loss of momentum, your wrath now subsided,
Shameless and innocent you slink back to bed.

Life's like the river born on the mountainside,
Each finding our level as pathways we make.
Taking the easy way when faced with obstacles,
Oft times ignoring the hurt in our wake.

Impatient and selfish we rush on unthinking,
With sights firmly set on the challenge ahead.
We should be mindful that just as the river,
Our footsteps, where'er, we can never retread.

Mary Jones

367

The Seal

Under the thick crisp ice,
Swims around, the little fellow,
He's not green, blue, red or yellow,
His beautiful fur and little nose,
His little tail, no feet or no toes.

Camouflaged against the ice,
One minute you see him,
Then you don't,
If you're 14, 15 and a boy,
You'll see him as nothing but a target toy.

If you're one of these hunters,
See him you will,
'Cause there's nothing on your mind but to kill,
When the hunters are finished,
Blood, guts, and white fur just lie there.

You're used to the ice being white,
But when they've finished stabbing it dead,
The ice is a bloody colour red,
The fur lying there like a parsnip peel.
This beautiful animal is the seal.

Tanya Seaman

Watershed

Whilst I in balmy groves did lie
And love did shield all hurt from me,
I knew that soon reality
Would come with his stern fist for me,
And take from me my comfort bed.

I knew that this my watershed
Had come. The other half of me
Must join and make me whole again.
The fusion burnt my soul, trod on my pain.
I looked upon the place where I had lain

And there it was, so beautiful.

Phyllis Silvester

'The Real Me'

Look through the keyhole, under my skin,
You'll see someone different, someone special deep within,
Please do not judge me by the way that I look,
It's just my outer shell, like the cover of a boring book.
I have feelings, they run so deep and true,
I'm so scared of rejection, if only someone knew.
I look into your eyes, it's the three words I want to say,
Like a candle being blown out, every time you walk away,
Can you not love me for who I am, now who I wish I could be?
There's such a loving person inside waiting to be set free.
I feel I'll never have you, but loving you carries on,
When I see you with someone else, I cry but must be strong,
I know you'll never want me, it really breaks my heart,
But I can't blame you, I've known right from the start.
Why do looks matter? If you just stopped to see,
When you look through the key hole, you'll see the real me.

Caroline Varndell

Mother Earth

We plough its flesh,
we pollute its blood,
we do this earth or ourselves no good,
we have taken away its right to survive,
we grow fat off its belly, it has nowhere to hide.
I hear it grown in dismay,
for all its resources dwindle away,
soon this earth will give up on us all,
for we only ever take, never give at all.
We are the rust and lice on the land,
we are the vermin which is getting out of hand.
The earth is our heartbeat
so we had all better pray
for once it stops . . .
JUDGEMENT DAY . . .

D. Beese

The Prince Of Rationality

All the days of my life
I will fight
to stay the ruler of my own mind
In the land of consciousness
I will be the prince of rationality
Sarcasm will be my sword
Honesty my shield in battle
May I ever taste the bitterness of loosing
I will fight
to try swallow the pain
Drink it
as if it was nectar of the Gods

Peter Van Eck

Why?

You were boy,
You were woman,
You were mother,
You were child.
You were father and you were daughter,
All so easily beguiled.

You were sister,
You were lover,
You were husband and sweetheart.
You were baby and you were brother,
All insanely torn apart.

Oh dear God . . . they were infants,
Was there nothing you could do,
They were man, wife, son . . . and beautiful
They were abandoned,
They were Jew . . .

Beryl Wilkinson

She's Got The Bottle

An empty bottle, like her empty life
Drunken with desperation, she's paying the price.
A hang on feeling, she's shut the world out.
Like a new born baby, what is life about?
Lost her battle, but nobody's won.
Dying to hide, but where can she run?
So, she reaches out, and all she can find,
The first thing there, which will submerge her mind.
Make her forget, to prolong the pain,
When she is sober she's mad, but when drunk, she is sane.
No other option, like a dead end street.
Forced by the power of the bottle she can't beat.
Days merge together, weeks pass her by.
Soon even her soul, doesn't hear her cry.
Time becomes drowned, as more of her sinks.
Into the depth of the bottle, the bottle, which she drinks.

Eleanor Pontin

Jigsaw Pieces

There is a secret part of me that you don't know,
You may know me, but you don't know.
You think my emotions are naked and unfurled,
You think my emotions are revealed to all the world.
I keep my special feelings,
I keep them in my heart,
I might show you some,
But I always keep a special part.
It's not a place of sorrow, it's not a place of joy,
It's little bits of everything,
That know one can destroy.
I have held them since my childhood,
And I am adding to them still,
The sum of my mental possessions,
My passions and my will.
My emotions have different masks of happiness and fears,
And one sad face, that's always full of tears.
So I will show you Jigsaw Pieces,
But not the puzzle made complete,
Your mind can paint my picture, but not the me, replete.

Martin Coles

The Peterloo Massacre

'Twas early nineteenth century one hot and cloudless day,
When throngs of citizens did amass their feelings to convey
To folks in high authority, just what they thought their rights
should be.

O Peterloo, O Peterloo, what dreadful price you had to pay,
O Peterloo, O Peterloo, on that sad and disastrous day.

The weavers, spinners, Irish too, did all march down to Petersfield,
The children, men and women too, who were determined not to yield,
They surely must have been hell-bent, to get a man in Parliament.

They wanted one to fight their cause and make a better way of life,
They shouted, screamed, fought without pause, with stick and
stone and sharpened knife,
The Hussars and the Yeomanry tried to suppress what had to be.

In ten short minutes all was o'er, the flag staves gashed, the
banners torn,
Caps, bonnets, shawls all strewed the floor, the scene was
bloody and forlorn,
The trampled wounded bodies lay, the sabres surely had their way.

O Peterloo, O Peterloo,
What a dreadful price you had to pay,
O Peterloo, O Peterloo, on that sad and disastrous day.

Alice Hilton

Masquerade

Who understands me?
I am but a character in a play.
The play of life.
The world is my stage.
My thoughts, feelings, ideas, are superficial.
My life is a farce;
Determined solely by my script:
Written by my peers.

You don't know me.
For you take my personality at surface value,
Where appearances are deceptive.
You see but half my face; half my character.
The day-to-day me.

For no one can reach out to me;
Save me when I fall;
Explore the extremities of my soul.
How can I permit anyone to penetrate my core?
When there's no one to trust;
No one in whom I can confide.

I am ice. I do not feel.

Natasha Brereton

Last Week

I sit at my desk and remember
The house at the top of the hill.
It was my mother's home; the one she left
Last week, for the last time.

My desk is covered in papers, my heart hurts,
While my eyes ache, dry and tired.
I'd like to go away and rest
In a dark place for a while.

But my mother loved brightness
And gallant flowers in primary colours!
In the sunshine her ashes, light as air,
Will carry far across the moors.

So I will not go and hide in the dark.
She would rather I stayed in the light,
Unafraid, sorrowing, but not too sad
To let her go.

Joan Bovell-Eberhardt

Joy In Love

There are many pleasant moments in the course of busy life.
These are often termed as heavenly when not concerned with strife.
Yet the ultimate euphoria, I think you will agree;
Is when couples join together and can live compatibly.
Only fools seek endless paradise, just dreams that fade and die.
But to grow in love brings confidence on which each can rely.

In the secret sensuality of sharing in delight
With love's embers glowing warmly in the middle of the night.
For the giving and the taking ecstasy you share as one,
Heaven makes its brief appearance giving life before it's gone.
In the rapture of the intimate enabling you to feel,
The greatest gift from God to man is pure in love and real.

P. M. Burdock

The World

Hunger, sickness, crime and frustration
One, maybe all, in every nation.
Depression, unemployment also prevail.
Corruption worldwide on a massive scale.

Tampering with nature by means of pollution,
Governments scramble to find a solution.
Innocent children being abused.
Mr. Average so confused.

Politicians talk of peace not war,
The stored away bombs are hard to ignore.
Memorial at Austwitz for six million Jews
Ethnic cleansing still makes the news.

Millions live in poor sanitation,
Fighting disease without medication.
Animals killed for profit and pleasure,
Elephants tusk a sought after treasure.

Deep in our oceans is nuclear waste
Tomorrow's generation can deal with our haste
From human behaviour to diseases like cancer
Through genetics and D.N.A. we look for an answer.

Brent Riley

Nature

The sun blazes in the purple sky
The burnished gold blaze of fire that will never die,
The meadow is shining silver like a silky silver gown
Dew on each spiky blade of grass slowly dropping down.
Clouds drift weightlessly light, fluffy cotton clouds,
   brilliant white.
Over mountains and calm seas, over hills and tall oak trees.
Bees buzz around the brightly coloured flowers,
I'm overwhelmed by nature's magical powers.
Birds singing loud but sweet, searching the ground for
   morsels to eat.
The first signs of rain now appear, the sun behind the
   clouds starts to disappear.
Animals run into their holes as the rain thrashes down and
   the hard wind blows.
The clouds are deep grey and there's just a touch of light,
The sun goes down, it is now night.
The moon rises in the black sky, an owl hoots "Towit towoo,
   towit towi".

Lynsey Ann Cropper

My Sunset For You

Words will not come easy, as I watch this sunset,
Matching the sunset in my heart,
During the sunset of my life
And yet, through this timeless scene I am reborn!
Rising and shining–bright to my fullest form.
Bursting and beaming, filled to my fullest capacity
Rays, hot and burning, stretching beyond limits,
Reaching the deep wants of my soul,
Waiting there in sweet, dark, contentment.
The power of this love will not dim as in the setting sun.
Not pass under the horizons misty pink haze
The light in this love will burn eternal
leaving others breathless at its beauty!

Maureen Murray

Parcel

The parcel came with the late post.
Stiff brown paper without wrinkle.
Tied, not taped. Symmetric
With two loops round and one across.
Correctly addressed with full post code.
Closely bound and binding.

She knew it held the effects of
A sister, lately dead
And their long dead parents.
Books, a notepad with her father's handwriting,
Photos, black and white, with some sepia toned,
Of her and her sister as children.
Their parents when young and their parents too.
A Great War medal for an uncle
With the Widow's Penny.
A new slim prayer book.

"Better unpack it now"
Her grandson was coming.
He might think it was a present.
She knew it was a past.
Michael Lee

A Meeting

A smile splashed into a grey sky,
It's a navigated silence,
That breathlessly colours the sky red.
The wind steps in,
Begins chanting the echo of a past storm.
Time leans forward to her and holds out its hands,
Steely black hooks clasp hers.
For a moment they talk in honesty,
Of the road she has travelled, and the future,
Like a beautiful glove she will wear.
The gloves hold surprises, and as she slides her hands in
Each fingertip will enfold—
A new dream.
Margaret Matheson

Paradise Of Peace

My mind wanders at a paradise of peace,
No more shouting will deafen my ears,
No more tears shall be shed from mine eyes.
No more heartache shall be caused,
No more peace therefore destroyed
For I see a world of peace and harmony.
A world of love and devotion.
Our races will all unite in spirit and soul,
Bound to be together and present in all.
This is the world I hope to see.
Thought I know in my heart it will never be!
Sonia Varzgar

Purple Velvet Eyes

Every living being shall someday die,
But all shall not truly live.
I wish to live, before I can live no more
I wish to give, all I can give,
From heart to soul, from love to hate
I wish to give it all!
Never indifferent shall I be,
For indifference is not reality.
To love, to hate, to truly feel.
That is living, that is real!
I wish to open up my eyes, see beauty all around,
In every sight, every single sound.

Wish no more now shall I,
For I need to live before I die,
I need to seek the truth of being
A truth I may not find, a truth impossible of seeing,
Now that I shall do, as I leave pen, paper and go
To live, to love, be free, and know
The truth that lies in every soul,
The truth that lies deep within, the eyes of purity,
   and the eyes of sin.
Stephanie Shankland

Magic Lunation

The end of a moon: Walking slowly through the branches,
Dodging all those stolen glances,
Judgement made on the basis of name,
The simplicity borders on fame

The forest is filled with the smell of damp bark,
Pungent as it is, it is pleasant,
Peace and piece of mind, long since borrowed,
Easier understood, now walking through the wood.

Without a flashlight, the dew sets in, pine cones sting,
The birds cease to sing, throw away the cellular as it starts to ring,
The cave is cold with no mod cons, the ingenious notion,
With panegyric songs, without the prize, though, content to gaze.

Loss of interest, incapable of care,
The mind is still working behind the barren stare,
Smelling oleander, adapted to instruct
Authority the evil, not wanting to suck.

Open spaces the sacred places, leave the present, practise
   retrogression,
No interest in the measure of duration,
Slower sinking deeper to neolithic insanity, sick of appearance,
Glad of vanity: The new moon has come.
John Bermingham

Teamwork

Grey clouds gather in to take their seats
Hushed, expectant
Beneath them lies their only chance the show to see
With calloused hand he takes a wrap of leather
Looking skyward
We might just make it, you and me

No clatter of angry pistons
Nor frantic charge of a nameless wonder slashing, munching
His tongue clicks twice, asking quietly
An honest power answers strong
A living, massive, muscled engine
Rips the sod in furrows long.

Cutting on for he sniffs the rain
The toil intense if the earth is wet
The ploughman marvels, feeling humbled
He's upped the pace, though bathed in sweat
The last row done now, blinkers off
With yoke undone and lighter tread
They turn for home as the crowd's applause
Cools both brow and noble head.
C. T. Postans

Summer Days

It was an awful May my dear
With winds so bitterly cold
I had so many aches and pains
They made me feel quite old.

The flowers didn't want to bloom
They were in a sorry way
Until the sun could tempt them out
In the greenhouse they did stay.

But then came June and pretty soon
The countryside turned green
We had the morning chorus
And flowers could be seen.

In July the days were long and warm
The sky a vivid blue
One day we had a nasty storm
That frightened me and you.

August, the farmers are busy out in the fields all day
The combiners steadily drive up and down harvesting wheat
and hay.

Soon morning mist and shorter days will mean September's here
So we will both look forward to the summer days next year.
Mary Moulton

Turning Back The Time

I wish that I could turn back time
To start all over again
To share the love that we once had
Instead of being so lonely as I am

I miss your smile, the touch of your hand
The scent of your perfume
The kiss of your lips
God, how I miss all this

Just to reach out and touch you
To embrace you in my arms
To pull you closer to me
To smell your heavenly charms
To run my fingers through your hair
And touch your tender skin
Oh God, how I miss all this
If only I could turn back time, Ann
My love
I would throw away the key.

Harry Hartland Leach

Cornwall

Zennor, Penzance, St. Ives and Pendeen,
Grassy fields are blooming,
in yellow and green.

Little granite houses all made of rock,
stand on their own,
or together in a flock.

Tin mines lie empty,
silent and mean,
Zennor, Penzance, St. Ives and Pendeen.

Joanne Louise McCulloch

Snow Flakes

Snow flakes falling from the sky,
They fall upon the hill tops high,
Descending on green fields and hedges,
And icicles form high on ledges.

The snow falls softly to the ground,
Its falling never makes a sound,
From whence it came one shall not know,
A winter wonderland of snow.

The air is warm, the snow flakes cold,
Such mystery of ages old,
All is quiet and all is white,
Such beauty on a winter's night.

Magic moments fill the air,
As faces through the windows stare,
They look upon old fir trees tall,
A snow white mantle covers all.

A path is trodden with footprints deep,
The lane ahead being slippery steep,
A snow plough toils from early morn,
Snow drifts gathered with rising dawn.

Philippa C. Benacs

A Thank You Prayer

Thank you God for a voice to sing,
For legs that walk and arms that swing.
To push a pram or lift a load,
To twist and turn as we are told.

But spare a thought for those who can't,
Who cannot hear and cannot chant.
Who lay on beds distraught with pain,
For those who'll never walk again.

We rarely think that what we have
Would make another very glad.
So thank you God for gifts you've sent,
And please forgive our discontent.

C. E. Nicholson

To Those I Leave Behind

Come you who loved me, in whatever way
even if we ne'er shared a word
These words are for you, to take heart anew
rom now on, my love is assured

Accept what you feel, don't hold it back
If tears arise, then please let them fall
As you weep, allow sorrow, all in your time
To turn into tears of great joy

Could we have been closer and shown our love more
Maybe, but all's not lost now I've died
Trust in the mercy of that which is love
We've eternity for loving in new lives

So adios for now, we'll meet again
Think logically if you'll feel better
If you'd rather scream and shout, let it all come out
Letting cheeks become wetter and wetter

Vincent Smith

A Birthday Wish

Hi Trish, you've reached the big five-O
Who would have thought all those years ago
That any of us would still be pals
Out of all those guys and gals

In Blandford Forum during sixty-two
A town that appeared to have a lot to do
To look back now we must have been barmy
But that could be something to do with the army

For thirty three years we have been around
To share in memories that abound
However there has to be one regret at least
We cannot join you at this sumptuous feast

We hope that the hangover doesn't cause much pain
But we shall be thinking of you from sunny Spain
So enjoy the evening and get up and go
All out love as always Shirley and Mo

Maurice Snook

The Tree Of Life

Oh beautiful tree, bend your branches low
and let your leaves caress my face.
Soothe away the tension that I wear like a mask
thereupon.
Shade me from the fires of heaven
Shelter me from the wind and the rain.
Hide me from this humdrum world that is filled
with so much pain.
Wrap your branches around me.
Comfort me should I cry.
Let your roots be my roots
If I should lay me down and die.

Joan Lunt

"Silence"

The flickering rays from the setting sun, cast
deepening shadows.
Listen now, to the sounds hidden within the
silence of the night.
Creatures stir, large and small, some will cry
their plight. Often hidden by the day
they stealthily come, seeking what they might.
Whispering leaves dance to the breeze,
moonlight filtering through the trees,
Carefully tread, so as not to warn,
the creatures of the night.
No fire, no broken twig to disturb them,
Whilst we slumber, the wood breathe's life
to these creatures, which, if seen by us
give such delight.
Now we must creep away to prepare our day.
Leaving creatures large and small, to enjoy
their own silence of the night.

Helen Phillips

Sometimes

Sometimes O' Lord I find it hard
To comprehend your love
And understand what the Bible says
About you, the Great Man above

Sometimes O' Lord I'm frightened
Frightened of who I am
Frightened to commit my life to you
Frightened to be your lamb

Sometimes O' Lord I sit and think
Just not knowing where to begin
To tell you all the wrongs I've done
And ask you to forgive my sins

Sometimes O' Lord when things are good
And everything's going my way
It's easy Lord to just forget
To thank you for today

Sometimes O' Lord is a word you don't use
When preaching your love for me
But true, undying, unconditional love
You died to set me free

Joanne Bailey

Please

Twinkling stars up in the sky
Will Christmas come by and by,
Will there be lots of toys
For all the little girls and boys?

A train for me, and a tunnel and a track
A doll for her, with lace and satin on her back
Can we keep them for all time?
Tell me stars will the clock strike midnight at the chime . . .

Will there be food on the table, on that day of the week,
For the little Bosnian children who are getting so weak?
Will there be a tear in their eyes,
As Santa goes sailing by?

Tell me stars, so shiny and bright,
Will Santa stop here or there to-night?
Will he give a thought to those in need?
I hope so, I hope so, I do indeed.

The little ones fighting for their life
Can do without this War and strife,
In Bosnia, life is cheap or so they say,
How cheap then is your life on Christmas Day?

B. P. Thornhill

Treasured Love

Miles apart we both are,
But my thoughts of you don't wander far,
For this today is your special day
And always in my mind you do stay.

Grandmother and grand-daughter to
each other we are,
A very special relationship no one can mar.
My love for you travels a very long way
And it will always be with you day after day
So this is my gift to you that money can't buy,
And no one can take it away no matter how hard they try.
Treasure this love and keep it safe,
For with you it will always stay.
A special love that we both share
And in your heart I'm with you today.
So grandma lift a glass with me today
For you mean so much in a very special way
Which is something I'll treasure until my dying day
For I'll always know you'll never be far away.
Love you always and forever.

A. J. Cowx

The Great War

The call to serve—your king needs you!
Oh! How we marched, so staunch and true
It didn't say that we might die
Beneath a foreign blackened sky.

Bullets are flying overhead
I turn to my comrade, he is dead
Just another mother's son
Blown to ribbons by the hun

The face before me I don't know
But I must kill him he's the foe
Forgive me Lord that I must kill
A man who has done me no ill

The smell of death is all around
And rats are slithering in the ground
I pray if there's a God above
Keep me safe for those I love

So long ago—or so it seems
I had so many young man's dreams
When oh when will this war end
When can I call the foe, my friend?

Mildred Brown

The Old Rocking Chair

So I take my pen to write a few lines
To solace your mind in such trying times;
To sit so cosy without any care,
Your haven of bliss: the old rocking chair.

Remember the rhymes on grandmother's knee
The ditties you learned when you were just three;
You cannot forget from your mother tongue
The poems you learned when you were so young.

For how can you learn if you are not told
Words from your teachers, the poets of old?
The funny people who write funny lines
To limp you along in your most hard times.

Our thoughts grow many in the roll of time,
Recurring memoirs, never–ending line;
When your ninety three with thoughts in the air,
Cosy; carefree; in the old rocking chair.

Ponder my words, just a few, could be rare;
Cosy; carefree; in the old rocking chair.

Dennis Parkes

Her Face

I was holding my daughter
while she was still hours old.
And I stared down into her face,
I got lost in her face.
So young but old, perfect.
Sleeping eyes that would soon wake
and see the world in an unknown way.
Tiny mouth that would speak words never heard.
Soft skull above the thoughts
that would carry her and shape her life.

History unlived, centuries to come,
this face would live long into the future,
live past my death.
And that thought seemed so right,
for until hours ago I was alone.
Now half of me goes abroad within her body
and the loneliness is gone.
My life is accepted, my initiation complete.
All my life I've carried a child inside me,
but now it's set free and I am left as a man.

Stephen Zimmer

"Life's Little Room"

In my head, life's little room
Time of change, pressure of doom.
Thoughts of failure are in my head,
all in my hand, in my time of change

Happy events of this year, unsure,
What's my position within this room
Can life get worst, can it be better.
These my thoughts in life's little room.

My head worry's my body can't sleep
Wandering eye's deep in my mind
In to silent decay, in to silent ways
Death is always a worry, we have not much time

Plenty to learn plenty to tell
Years go by. They soon pass by the soon mount up
I am on this earth. As God's little child
But what's to say. He'll come one day. One day

Hills and mountains, ferries and cars
I climb them, I ride them, in my little room.
It's all an escape route, it's all in my room
My head it now sleeps, never again to be cruel.

Gary Cain

Feelings Of Love

How can anyone else understand her feelings
If she can't even understand them herself
She's just mixed up, she doesn't feel loved
She's looking for someone to go out with her
To have all the love she gives returned with more
She wants to find someone now
Before it's too late
She gets offers she refuses
Because she wants a full relationship
Not a fools relationship
She wants a true loving affair
Not with just anyone
But with someone that will give her all
The love and support she needs
She knows what she's doing
She's looking for a man she can love
And a man that will love her back
A man she'll love in the future
Like the man she still loves from the past.

Laura Kay Rayment-Bunnett

The Healer

Time heals they said, when you were taken from me,
I felt the pain of loss engulf my heart.
Mysteriously and without warning you went from life,
As God's rainbow vanishes from sight.
You died as Autumn dies, mature and richly beautiful.
Shall I now walk alone with no strong hand to hold?
My tears fell; and nature also wept, to join in my mourning
Till our own forest wept with cleansing healing rain.
Sparkling and fragrant when the sun appeared.
Comforting me then, as did a thought and memory of you.

As winter's snow entombed my silent grief, I felt and knew
your presence as before.
Waiting with contentment for the eager spring,
When Mother Nature bears her early babes,
She will share our secret and rejoice.
Gladly bringing forth the fragrant blooms.
Befriended by the faithful sun and rain.
And now I feel the power of Nature's hand.
Knowing God's wonders with all my senses;
What sorrow I had known, but now the gift of joy;
Our son is born—another life—another hand to hold.

Betty Hutton

Trapped

I feel nothing, see nothing, hear nothing.
No! There is a voice.
It sounds very distant, it is very faint,
but yes, I can hear it.
It sounds like crying, weeping, yes, it is weeping.
It wants to be free, cannot get out.
I can see it, but it is blurred.
There is a cage, bars,
its hands gripping the bars.
There is so much hurt, so much pain,
so much emotion.
It wants to . . .
it wants so desperately to give.
It is trapped somewhere,
pleading with me to help,
to help find the key.
But it is so deeply buried,
so distant, fading now.
The voice is gone.
I hear nothing, see nothing, feel nothing.

Debbie Jean Brazier

Baby Crying In The Night

Baby crying in the night,
Calling out for touch and sight
Of mother's milk, of mother's breast,
For arms enfolding, warmly pressed.

Fragile bundle, needing love,
Eyes searching hers above;
Finding in another's face
That you also have place
Within the human family:
You also are a member of the human race.

Are you so needy, so dependent on another,
Are you indeed the Son of God—Holy, Divine?
Are you, sweet Son of Mary,
Are you her Lord—and mine?

What Power is this that is so weak?
What Majesty, to lie so still at another's feet?
What Love, that needs another's love?
What God is here? But He who from above
Has come to be with us, to share our pain,
To share our joys, our sorrows—and our shame.

Nigel Coatsworth

Monday

This morning, owned by no one
wind rocked the wading cattle
stirring a surge of egrets
then rippled to an altered calm.
One yellow poui shed its reflection,
soft splinters on the slow green shimmering
sun was a great flower, spindling pollen:
buzzing white light that trembled
till it hummed a fine heat
unconditioned,
this morning came, vivid as sliced oranges
and the unmanned, unmanoeuvred world scape
broken open suddenly . . . Living.
Inhaling a.m.. . . Exhaling p.m.
workers waiting at the terminus.
The engines of the clock in Moffat's office
power their lives
power the slow machination of the bus uphill
waiting at the terminus hired hands of the clock
reach out to strangle me for profit.

Anderson Peter Stanley Desir

Progressive Mobility

I arrive at the home with my music and balls.
Set up my equipment, to some rooms
Make some calls.
Arrange all the residents, we're about
to begin—switch on, here we go, if you
want to—join in
arms to the left—knees up and down.
Remember your breathing—work up a sweat.
Come on, keep on going there's more
to do yet.
Now have a soft ball, follow me, roll it round
In your hand—how are you all feeling,
You're working just grand.
Now slowing down, circle feet, stir the pot.
You've all done so well.
'Till next week. That's your lot.

Heather Hingerty

That Drunken Feeling

Stumbling around in darkness, trying to find the door key,
A few too many beers tonight, blurred shapes is all I see.
I wish I'd stuck to orange juice, I'm feeling awfully sick,
My head is really pounding, like someone's bashed it with a brick.

I have the door key in my hand, but now I can't find the lock,
My legs are feeling weak now, I think I'll have to knock.
But waking the parents would be a bad move,
    they'd see what state I'm in,
Next would come the lectures, like I've committed a terrible sin.

Eventually I have success, I'm now inside the house,
I fumble around for the light switch, as I tiptoe like a mouse.
At last I'm in my room, and collapse on to my bed,
I try to ignore the pain, and the throbbing in my head.

The sickly feeling's back again, my head spins round and round,
I can't be bothered to stand anymore,
    as I fall with a thud to the ground,
I don't remember anything, where I was, what I did, and with who,
But I don't have time to think about that,
    too busy being sick down the loo!!

Marie Hinsley

Shy

How shy can you get,
How stupid can you feel,
Some can talk all they like,
But others feel they are never right,
Talking to strangers is not so easy,
I don't understand what happens to me,
Words are lost at the back of my mind,
My tongue has gone, gone too far for me to find,
I swallow hard again and again,
How long before they leave, how long, then,
Suddenly my heart goes boom,
I look and see, eyes glaring at me from each corner of the room,
I wonder who they are,
To find out all I need is ask,
My mouth opened and closed quickly,
In my throat I felt something tickly,
Had anyone heard?
No because I spoke no words,
To this day I do not know,
Where people there or was I alone?

Sagdha Ahmed

An Orphan's Wish

I wish I had a mummy to cuddle at night.
To make me feel safe when I turn out the light.
But being an orphan — this isn't to be,
When the light goes out there's no-one but me.

I wish I had a daddy to play 'ball' with me.
To take me to the park where I could run free,
But being an orphan — this I can't do,
For I have no parents to say, "I love you."

Joyce Stokes

The Forgotten

His pride is broken, he seems to know no shame,
His ears seem oblivious when people call him names,
He's been kicked and spat on and worse it seems,
His life is a nightmare, a never–ending bad dream.
He gropes in the litter-bin looking for some treat,
Anything will do, as long as it's something to eat.
He finds a half–eaten sandwich, you look away in disgust
As he picks off the rubbish, the dirt, and the dust,
He returns to "his" doorway and the blanket lying there,

Settles down with his find, like a fox in its lair;
Put's the notice round his neck, and the medals by his side,
"Spare A Coin For An Old Soldier" and slowly sits and cries.

Roberta Holmes

Time

A time in our life
I'm sure everyone reaches,
When one sits down and wonders
and asks thyself,
What is life all about?
Are we all sent on a mission
to stand the test of time?
Or maybe sent by superior intelligence from up above.

I'm sure we all sit down and wonder
What life is all about,
We search for an answer
to why each life finds a beginning,
As each life comes to on end.

So as I sit here and wonder,
What is life all about?
I smile to myself contently,
For life, is a miracle in itself.

Amanda Crisp

Dear God

I've a heart full of love
But it's feeling so low,
I can feel it pound in my chest.
Please help me keep smiling
Because as we all know
It's the solution that always works best.

I know in this life
There'll be more sent to test me,
And I know I'll get through, come what may.
But at times I can't swallow the lump in my throat
And the tears I just can't blink away.

Some pray for things impossible
All I ask for from above,
Help the things within me pull me through
Strength, laughter, courage and love.

Dawn Clayton

My Dad

I think my dad is really nice,
Especially when he smells of Old Spice.
I love to sit upon his knee,
I especially like the way he squeezes me.

All day long he sits in his car,
When I know he'd rather be in the bar.
He often sings in the bath,
You should hear him, what a laugh.

He loves to watch sport on T.V.
In his favourite armchair, with a cup of tea.
When I try to talk he tells me not to whine,
He's off to his computer that's his favourite pastime.

My Dad often has his nose in a book,
He'll take no notice, when I shout "Look."
He blinks his eyes and start to doze,
Good, I can change the programme before he knows.

Helen Stoneham

A Taste Of My Tears

Our love was like a budding rose,
Our petals were entwined,
A birth of love on kindred souls,
With a destiny to find.

Togetherness that was untold,
Our love outshone the sun,
Foreverness, we vowed our loves,
To always be as one.

But the rain fell down upon our love,
Our love began to die,
The thorns were sharp that made us bleed,
The tears that we cry.

Then that day came, the petals fell,
Our hearts became entwined,
But the roots are strong and firmly planted,
Deep inside my mind.

My love for you will never die,
My empty heart still shows,
As time goes on I am sure there will be,
Another budding rose

Giles Abraham

Untitled

Surrounded by the misty darkness
She prays for the seek of light
That shines through dimness itself
And battles to grasp her

The blaze gave her warmth and excitement
It touched her cheek and moved upwards to stare her in the eye

A commotion and tingle raised in her body
Starting from the tip of her toe to the edge of her mind
There it stayed!
She felt the heat of passion rise from the depth of her heart

She had become an explosion.
And longed to explore the core of that mystifying light

She followed the ray of heat
That lead her to its owner
She was going insane
From wanting to touch that power that was making her so passionate

As she came closer to the mystery
She attempted to stretch her hands and . . .

Suddenly the light vanished!

Nour Gowharji

A Silent Room

A silent room, blue smoked haze.
Heavy green curtains, red arm chairs.
Brown lifeless carpet, woven, worn thread bare.

A clock, a pendulum, that does not swing.
Time stands still. No key for the spring.

Green plastic plants, a lifeless lie. Green fly die.
Black marble fire, tinder bone dry.
Ashes piled high.

Piano in the corner, out of tune.
Boredom waltzes to a song, time goes by.

Light washed windows, years of passing rain.
Sashes nailed closed for the darkening of the sky.
No entry for the tame.

Cobwebs on the corner of a flaky window pane.
Spiders on a sill, playing along the grain.

Table to one end, papers on a tray.
Cold spilled tea, decades marked in stain.
Scones, rock cakes, in the bin again.

A silent room. Heavy green curtains, from sill to sill.
Empty red arm chairs. No one's in. Again.

Gerard K. Sweeney

The Spirit Versus Science

I don't want to know the 'ifs' and 'buts'
The 'whats' the 'wheres' the 'whys'
I just want to see, the beautiful bee,
And the glorious butterflies.

Don't ask me to look as I gaze
at a brook, for the answer to it all,
Just let my glance, see the sunlight
dance on the splash of a waterfall.

As I gaze in the depth of a reedy pool
where tiny creatures play, down there
are things that the microscope brings
into larger than life they say,
I don't want to know, I just want
to go where the dragonfly flies away.

G. Hill

The Onward Journey

Pushing darkness through the night's haze
I put down my bowl and gather the light
Rare and delicious I feed my gaze
An orange, spicy, festive bite.

Marching the harvest underground
I put down my bowl and gather the seed,
Full and contented I make no sound
I have taken my fill to succeed.

Rising up to be the heavens
I put down my bowl and gather my life
Wiser now I have used all I was given,
Lifting the bowl I now am the light.

William Gardiner Rose

House—weary

I'm going out!
I'm tired of tables and chairs,
I'm tired of walls that hedge me all about,
I'm tired of ceilings, carpets, stairs,
And so—I'm going out!

Somehow or other, what I need today,
Are skies that are blue,
Birds that twitter,
Winds that shout!
I want Mother Nature's friendship,
Thus I say,
"Good-bye, I'm going out!"
It's just house-tiredness.
Trivial humdrum strain!
    Monotony!
But when I've climbed the hill,
My heart refreshed will laugh and sigh again,
Dear Home—I'll love it still!

Nora Walsh

A Story About Alman And Pureeya

Alman is
working out into the Sunny Brown and Green
periodically trying
to stray from his survival machine
his eyes are all curious, he has problems
in his attempt to sort out his dreams —
spends all his earnings on friends
says he's in love with an English girl
he wants to be her complement ——
now this visionary really does suppose
she's a star without her clothes
and infatuated by the don't knows ——
Alman's met his match, made his catch
a bourgeois who desperately years to be detached
and this Pureeya has an independent type of mind
feels 'what's not mine cannot be defined
yet in this world we should share all' ——
as always this pair will rise and fall.

D. W. De Piro

The Miracle Of Corn

I walk in the quiet evening breathing fresh air into my lungs
Looking at the green corn and believing,
I shall see it beautifully golden before the winter comes.
It sways so gracefully in the breeze like ripples on the sea,
Whispering naughtily to the trees
"Come down, come dance with me".
The tree being master of all plants waves back happily
I am over one hundred years old and you new born still be,
So stay green for as long as you can, for when your hair has
turned blond
You will be slain by machine or man,
And helpless I'll watch from my home by the pond.
The green fields are empty now, I remember you waving goodbye.
You are so wise to hibernate before snow clouds gather in the sky.
I'll keep a lookout while you are away,
And let you know when summer is here.
Then I'll watch for you by night and day, I know you will
soon appear
Then we can whisper and dance again, like we do every year
Till then these fields for you I'll reserve,
Because sweet corn the earth you deserve.

Gwendoline Rosemary Stewart

The Locket

When I awoke one Christmas morn, so many years ago,
My gifts were spread before me, my eyes took on a glow,
Which package should I open first, it was not hard to see,
My eyes alighted on the one from my true love to me.

A lovely golden locket, etched flowers on the case,
Containing on the inside a likeness of his face,
Around my neck I hung it, delighted at the gift,
I'd never take it off again, it gave my heart a lift.

We basked in our good feelings, we shared a marvellous love,
The world it was a lovely place, as if blessed from above,
The days and years began to pass, wherever did they go,
We wallowed in our happiness, and it was rightly so.

The locket was forgotten, placed somewhere in a drawer,
I never thought about it, life never was a bore,
We had matured and altered, life completely rearranged,
Our love however stayed the same, it never really changed.

On looking in the drawer one day my locket I espied,
My heart it danced, began to sing, as if I were a child,
Around my neck I hung it, transcending time anon,
I wear my true love's gift to me, though he be dead and gone.

Anne Williamson

Fire On Malvern Hills

Malvern hills are very high
And in the summer very dry.
People go up there to see
And have a picnic for their tea.
Then when it's dusk they leave at last
And leave behind some broken glass.
Our hills are what we all admire
Until that glass sets it on fire.
It burnt the ferns and gorse and trees
And now there's nothing left of these.
The firemen worked with all their might
To fight that fire right through the night.
Last year, the fire was very strong
It burnt those hills a mile long.
And then on, a very muggy day
A thunder storm it had its way.
This cloud it burst with all its might
Moved rocks and earth from left and right.
The story of this poem is true
So take your rubbish home with you.

Ada Lane

New-Found Freedom

It has to be more than a whispering shadow
Out there calling your name.
For you can hear that unlikely sound
On misty mornings for miles across the plains.
It travels slower through wedded-true but choking weeds.
It waits for you it waits for me it knows our needs.
So I'll get up one morning while it is early.
Though I've kept watch day in yearly.
For all my efforts would come to smile
If Jesus were to talk a while.
But to the peoples pleasure and dismay
He'd only ask the time of day.
But would he forgive me if I were to say
New-Found Freedom that's not me that's not you.
That's not anything you do.
For down every, avenue lies a theme
Where Devils dream and Angel's scheme.
And at the gate the tiger waits unchained.
But there's something in affection gonna still him where he stands

David Ashley Reddish

"Davy's Testimony"

Is it nothing to you—all who pass by
That the earth is my mattress—and my blankets the sky
My only one life is severely restricted
To alcohol—I'm really addicted.

Most pass me by—I seem a bother
Yet in God's eyes, I am their brother
Some laugh at me—indeed some do jeer
All because of that first pint of beer

You'll find me often—on poverty's seat
Hoping and praying for something to eat
Even a morsel—to keep hunger away
As I ofttimes had nothing—since yesterday.

I call you young folks and I want you to hear
Please, don't ever take—a first pint of beer
For the earth's still my mattress and God knows on high
That during the harsh winter—my blanket's the sky.

For there's folk like me in every land
So please do try and understand
And tell your own heart—when you hear my cry
There, but for the grace of God—go I.

Walter Jarvie

A Brief History Of Flight

Balloon: Joyful in freedom as mist on the mountains,
   Drifting in sunlight on an unseen wave.

Glider: Striving for flight with fabric outstretched,
   Captive of earth—seeking liberty.

Wright Bros: Newly fledged wings and pulsating sound,
   Seeks footholds—where none before had been.

Lindbergh: Dauntless moth in the night braving seas
   On unknown flight—that we may follow.

DC3: Egg whisk of the sky beating clouds,
   Frothing war and peace.

Jet: A new concept ushering in tomorrow,
   Shrinking the world—closing gaps to friends

747: Lumbering leviathan—ark of the air,
   Bears floods of humanity on a sea of wheels.

Concorde: Lightning spans the oceans above the clouds,
   Thunder marks it passage to the New World.

Spaceship: Defying the gods on Mount Olympus,
   Streaking for tomorrow—into eternity.

Michael E. Berger

"China Blue"

A prayer for China, was said last week,
He was taken, from us in his peak,
A nicer rarer cat, you'll not find,
A talkative Siamese, only one of its kind,
A faultless character, so quite unique,
It's a shame, about his scrawny physique,
He was the runt of the litter, a slip of a thing,
But to his loved ones, he was "the king",
A more, much loved cat, you'll never find,
But, it's sad, we were all left behind,
Your "China Blue" eyes, were your best feature,
You were such, a lovely perfect creature,
With cherished memories, of your eight years
We try to stem, the flow of tears
God, has called you to His side,
Any negative feelings, we now must hide,
The grieving times, must be in the past,
Now that you're resting peacefully, at last.

Joyce Susan Harvey

Sunshine At Midnight

She came in the dead of night;
she held her hand out to me . . .

Blinking rapidly,
    the question was on the tip of my tongue:
    But . . . Shh . . . She smiled.
I was dazzled.

In a trance, I gave my hand to her but . . .
the purse; my life companion,
it fell to the ground; spilling . . .

Gasping, I tried to gather my paraphernalia.
    Shush . . .
she tucked at my hand gently, firmly.
    But . . . , the sharks! I cried out.

Smiling, tucking, guiding,
head held high,
she stepped out; me in tow
sighing sweetly, she whispered to me:
    'The still waters are what you need . . . '

In that dark, star–bespeckled night, she took my hand firmly.
And together we knifed the water, plunging into the deep end . . .

Pinkie Mekgwe-Magocha

Firelighter

Burning, burning long–suffered ills within
Coal–dust hands ash black
As the sins of ages upon their souls.

Tired and bitter eyes in steady watch
Sulphur draws ignited match
Through smoke–filled eyes the flame appears.

Remembering battles won, heroes unsung
Wheezing through the miner's lung
Wond'ring who got through Heaven's Gate.

Cold blue knuckles leant upon the grate
Praying exemption from eternal doom
Amber glow dissolves the heavy gloom.

Memory calling pleasant days since birth
Dustpan, shovel sweep across the hearth
Reclining slowly from the task complete.

Enjoying labour's fruit amidst the heat
Sinking into cosy armchair deep
Weary eyes and mind fend off sleep.

Tightly gripping life's fraying rope
Thoughts of courage, faith and hope.

Bernard Duffy

A Summer's Day Near Lincoln

The prospect lay ahead, bright verdant gold;
The brilliant hue of waving wheat
And golden green with interwoven
Hawthorn hedges, rectangularly clipped;
And here and there,
A solitary copse of jet-fir, burl–birch dimity,
Incalescent basks.
Conjunctive fields of dun–jade earth,
A human foil to Nature's
Emerald, lie
As well placed patches on a velvet–green.
And indolently grazing cattle roam—
A dazzle-blaze of black and white.
Strategically set an isolated
Collage, greystone–thatched, suspended
Empyreal on a smoke-silk-skein:
The silent evidence of habitation.
Beyond the minster shimmers, mirage-like,
Against a cloudless, azure sky.
All is silence, but for the Sun.

Neville L. A. Tidwell

Floundering

Be still and listen, but we don't;
Divine plan to learn and we won't
Think it's all an emotional jail
Parents, teachers, seem to prevail

Being young can be hard and lonely
I guess at heart I'm rather homely
Silence a privilege of the strong
Self pity may beckon that it is wrong

Silence divides, so mother says
Perhaps I'll understand her one of these day's
Some things she says are just an illusion
That only adds to my confusion

All of us have gifts and talents
You guessed it was said by parents
Without discipline there's no life at all
I just want to have a ball

One cannot have wisdom unless you learn
That much I know and do yearn
Give rapt attention to one another
Again a lesson I learned from mother . . .

Jean Tennent Mitchell

Reincarnation

Then through my eyes and memory,
I picture things that used to be
And wish that I was still a child
That never knew the grief of dying.

So unaware that from its birth
The safest place to be on earth
Was to stay suspended in the womb,
To sleep, to dream, forever still.

Where slender strands of tenderness
Held back the urge to re-emerge,
A seed of joy and pure delight
Into this harsh cruel world of light.

Then force the child, completely bare
To wear the mantle of despair,
And falsely girdle it with pride
So that its conscience it could hide.

Where fear would stalk us to our death,
The reincarnation and rebirth,
To be recycled in the womb,
The seeds of life, that spell our doom.

Edward Robinson

Deserted Street

I was walking home in a rainy night
along a deserted street,
the street lamp had a flicking light,
puddles around my feet,
houses boarded up with plastic glass,
echo sounds of children playing,
these days nothing last,
everything is always changing.
There's tales of ghost coming out at night
to walk the street,
then disappear when the dark turns to light.
I was worried one of these ghost I might meet,
I kept looking around
watching for moving shadows,
listening for anything that glows.
I came to the end of the street,
my walk came to an end,
no ghost did I see or meet.

Michael Dymond

The Countryside

The countryside is full of surprises,
With plants and trees of different sizes,

Colourful patches here and there,
Framed in green for us to share,

Birds and animals always busy,
Butterflies and bees make me dizzy,

Trickling streams and flowing rivers,
Please look after it for others.

Lily Homer

The "Jewel"

If you have it in your grasp, don't lose it.
Be always on your guard and hold it safe.
Don't let it dim, or fade or even bruise it,
It's the one life's Jewel hard to replace.
As children we are given it to treasure
Though we don't know of its value at the time;
It is only when we grow and see the beauty
of its glow from the tender-loving-care that
made it shine.
There is only one, so special, Jewel, more
precious that untold wealth,
It's the one we live and pray for
May we thank the Lord each day for,
Yes! You've guessed it, it's the Jewel
called "Health."

Barbara Woodley

Homecomings

Oh what bliss it is to know
There is a home to which we go
When we have been on holiday

Although sometimes we would rather stay in the place that's given us
A chance to recuperate from the daily grind
But we can always find

A variety of things to do which much pleasure brings
In serving those who find life hard although they're blind
To the benefits God's given them to enjoy
Their hands He could employ

In ways which they've not known
And they wouldn't be alone
But with a company of believers
Who love the Lord with all their hearts

There are certainly many parts for them to play here on life's stage
It's written down on every page of the Gospel message
In love which they can receive
When at last they all believe
In the Son of God!

H. I. Jones

Untitled

My gift is my poem and this one's for you
You are the sweetest girl I ever knew
My love for you is pure and natural
Your tender kiss, no longer fictional.

I write to you in despair
Your loving care and shiny hair
I could search this world all over till my life was nearly through
But deep down in my heart, my heart knows I couldn't find
    another girl as beautiful as you.

You're the girl that's stolen my heart
Your eyes are like emeralds, they shine in the dark
When tomorrow comes may be you will see
You are such a special girl, the sort that's meant for me.

How lucky you are to have a name like this
To confuse and compete against your sis
So nevermind, my dreams may come true
For you are the sweetest girl I ever knew.

Andrew James Marchington

A Mother's Plea

Six months have passed since that cold grey day
The judge found you guilty. You were going away.
I looked at you with sadness my eyes wet with tears
The judge looked at you sternly. He gave you three years
As your mother I felt helpless, full of anger and pain
I remembered you as a baby with your first toy train
Where did I go wrong son was I to blame
I ask myself this question again and again.
You have hurt me so badly I will never be the same.
Can you start again son or will you continue to steal
I will always be here son you're my flesh and blood
I hope these years change you to the son I knew and loved.

Sonia Gaston

Earth

Man's creating dreams this world has never seen
Flashing thoughts of inspiration
It's no illusion all this confusion
It's too late for a revolution
The world is surrounded by pollution

Recreation of our nations
See if we can change our destination
Survivors of atomic fear
And it's to late to shed a tear

Recreation of a perfect nation
Never changing our die hard creations

Oho what a long hard slog
When all anybody does
Is dog eat dog
This ain't the way this world is meant to be
Oho no
This ain't the way this world should be
Can't you see no one's free

D. J. Sweetman

Who Heals The Pain?

How will this tale, in future days be told,
As holes appear within the stratosphere,
And rays of high intoxication, hold
Mankind in self—inflicted bouts of fear?
Where poisoned tears, cascade from open skies,
Contaminating ev'ry living cell
That venture out, and innocently die
In ignorance, beneath the Passing-Bell:
Where lands lie barren, desolate and waste,
As evil's root, the root of life cuts down,
And lines the coffers of the unabated
As fortunes of the innocent fall down:
    Yet, as we ponder on whom we should blame,
    Mother Nature, Forever heals the pain!

Graeme Leslie Jennens

Bloody Hell

The sun is out, but not within.
That time has come of doubt again,
Hormones coursing through my veins,
Beats fast my heart and aches my brains.

No longer thinking straight or clear,
Attempt to calm the rising fear,
Alone once more to face the beast
So dark the Lord, my mind his feast.

Farewell sane psyche, I'll soon succumb,
The flesh is weak, receptors numb.
Twenty days plus one I need,
For strength to face the week I bleed.

No open wound or severed limb,
But cursed woman's womb within,
'Tis not the loss of haem which tires,
But turmoil fuelling mental fires.

D. A. Cobbett

"On Love And Hope"

Why do I wander through this garden of tears
Plucking at the petals of long–forgotten years?
Searching in vain for the freedom of youth,
Rejecting the horrors of absolute truth.

I turn my back on the safe and the wide,
Preferring instead to choose the harder ride.
They call me back "Life is secure!"
Another day there I could not endure.

I want to marvel at sunsets in far flung places,
To mingle with crowds whose names have no faces.
To travel the night with courage as my guide,
Chasing rainbows and feelings free inside.

I crave escape from this prison of modern living
With its class–ridden culture of taking not giving.
I need open seas, azure skies and a mystical view
I have to take the journey, but only with you.

C. J. McCairns

A Grandson's Grief

A grandson's grief,
No one wants to listen,
A grandson's grief,
I'm sorry too,
A grandson's grief,
Told to stay away,
A grandson's grief,
They don't want me there,
I only want to know if she is happy,
I only want to know if she's with someone somewhere,
A grandson's grief,
Only she really cares.

Jason Smith

Through The Order Of Choice

Choices swirl through and distort thoughts
Erecting a barrier, prohibiting any logic.
Logic choice as to a suitable return,
Pertaining to a simple gift of warm, friendly affection.
A mere gesture coupled by an appreciative return,
Is the notorious, sought after choice.
A soft cotton smile breeching confusion
Warm, welcoming and appealing, non expectant,
Yet obligation touches me from behind
It speaks words of truth urging me to surpass anxiety.
It perseveres and drives all doubts to the background,
Sending it home, like an exorcised demon.
Finally the swirling begins to cease and the distortion clears
My mind rests as a choice has been made.
It slowly descends, fluttering in the soft breeze
And lies softly on my conscience,
Snuggling down to my warm, cosy pillow of thought.

Gerard Harrington

"Goodnight Baby David"

It's hard to let you go now,
And tell you sweet "Goodnight".
As I never knew your features,
Or held you close and tight.

We never shared a moment,
In which we laughed or cried.
We didn't have a chance for anything,
As time was not on our side.

I can only imagine your beauty,
That a Baby Child creates,
And I can only imagine your smile,
As you enter the Heavenly Gates.

For I know you will be happy,
In the Heaven that's full of Peace,
And to know you're being cared for,
Can help my lonely tears to cease.

For you're surrounded by the love of the Lord,
As you are laid down to rest.
And of course our love is forever with you,
So David, "Goodnight and God Bless".

Especially for you
Amanda Rose Leighton

Untitled

Lying still on a silent ward, unmoving, unseeing, unspeaking;
but not unthinking not unfeeling . . . not dead (. . . yet).
If I could no longer reason or remember or think.
Memories could not hurt me; memories of whom I used to be.
Now it requires such effort to even blink.
I dream of shouting "Hey, wait don't ignore me—I'm still there"!
But only in my mind.
I speak in a new voice now but it is interpreted as meaningless rage.
"P.V.S." the doctors wail, for I have no awareness they can gauge.
I'm not retarded not senile, neither demented and no vegetable.
But an ordinary person trapped in a lifeless cage, a useless diseased
shell, a burnt out engine, a broken crutch.
A body that is burden onto itself, too weak to survive
unaided, but powerful enough to prolong my anguish.
A body riddled with lines and hooks, pipes and tubes; tubes
to nourish, tubes to breathe plus two more at either end to empty.
Only one tube missing yet providing that alone is their human duty.
One final thing I crave — that being freedom, a drip administering
mercy, peace, eternal sleep.
They can do more for me, no more treatment have they to give.
My right to die means more to me now than it ever did to live.
Still I wait needlessly on, every second a million years, each
moment's price a million prayers I cannot say, a thousand
tears I cannot weep.
The remembrance of pain and isolation of the night just passed.
A new dawn, another day, fresh start fresh hope against hope
that this will be my last.

Yasmin Pasha

A Day At The Beach

Dawn on the horizon,
Pale yellow fingers reach out to the world.
The sand stretches restlessly,
Under waves of silken sheets.
Your footprints and mine.
The water is cool.

Bright noon sky,
Creates a cavorting, cobalt sea.
Waves playful and brisk,
Tumble happily on the beach.
Children's footprints.
The water is warm.

The sinking sun,
Closes the curtains on another day.
Sand snuggling wearily,
Under a red rippling blanket.
My footprints alone.
The water is cold.

Katrina Thomson

Love

Not for one night, not for one year,
For all time.
No limits, no rules, no constraints,
Crosses all barriers.
Race, beliefs, generations,
Even death.
No respecter of station in society,
Brings great men to their knees,
The leveller.
Inspires poetry, art, invention,
Induces contentment, satisfaction,
Creates life.
But it also destroys.
Suicide, murder, war,
It can claim them all as its children.
How many sins are committed for its cause?
It's love.

Alison Walker

My Love

I want to tell you something but I'm not sure how to say
I hope this little poem will help me find a way
It's all about my love for you and what you mean to me
Your thoughtfulness, your kindness your love and honesty

The love we share is beautiful, one I cannot comprehend
But one thing I am sure of is our love will never end
I compare it to the sunshine on a bright and glorious day
But then I realise no because the sunshine fades away

So maybe it is like the stars as diamonds shining bright
But once again in time they're gone there only for the night
Perhaps it's that it's like the rain that makes all things anew
But when the rain has stopped I find it's just the morning dew

I thought it was the howling wind so powerful and strong
But I turned around to hear it and found that it had gone
My love cannot compare to these my love is pure and true
My love lasts for eternity my love always for you.

Lesley Preston

Kill

One by one they walk in line
Eyes wide open and composed with order,
Imagined truth from recognized deceit
Their comrades lie on a violated border.
The gruesome evidence that shows the cruel
And blends the bad in with the good,
And turns the victory into defeat.
Of death and life which is the tool
That turns wise men into a fool?
And when the kill intoxicates
And turns our kindness into hate,
Where are our minds to elevate
The red sharp blade we lubricate?
For death will hear no crying voice
And sweeps away a man's pretence.
The kill will take our liberty
And imitate our influence.

Leslie Edwards

Memories

Terror flooded through me as I walked the dreadful path.
Echoes of yesterday, of hardship in my past.
The streets, once familiar, now looked all the same.
The burnt-out shells of houses held tales of pain and shame.

The noises, wailing, filled the air, sirens, the hum of
aircrafts, that came from the devil's lair.
The ground, littered with bodies, brothers, sisters, dads.
The downcast eyes of mothers, eyes misty, faces sad.

I escaped the slaughter, but still I paid the price.
For dreams like this, haunted me, throughout my later life.
Wounds and bruises heal, but not the memories, scars.
They're always there, enclosing me, just like iron bars.

Regina O'Mahony

Untitled

Think of me with love, when I'm no longer here.
Think of me with compassion for I am but flesh
and blood like you. Think of me with joy, of
days of laughter, filled with fun, when our two
lives were just as one. Think not of anger, tears,
and strife, for these are just a part of life, to
strengthen love, and make us strong and teach
the way from right and wrong. For you my love
will always be a very special part of me, just
call my name and I'll be there, to share your
days of dark despair. For love like ours can never
die. For we are one you and I. I have not
gone away from you. I only have a different view.

Shirley DeRoo

Untitled

Forever in my heart an idol is here
His name is Michael. He's a dear
I play his C.D. I kiss his picture
Up on the wall it's a permanent fixture.
When you were down so was I,
To hear your bad news I broke down and cried
For you so lovely, I love you so much
Who I felt and kissed you, when we touched.

But I heard the good news the other day
I was so happy, hip hip hooray!
So now I look forward to see you again
But I know I can't wait until then.
You bring so much pleasure to all your fans
Including me, with your lovely tan.

Goodbye, I'll close now with one last kiss
And I know I'll make that it won't miss
Till I see you again the month of November
It'll be a night to remember.

I love you always Michael.

Christine Guntripp

Time To Move On

I listen for your key in the door
Yet, I know, it will be no more
I look at your chair that's empty now
I see you smile and your wrinkled brow

Yesterday has gone with moments of bliss
How I long for your warm kiss
Memories strong, though in the past
Are still within and will always last

Time moves on yet lingers still
All through life there's a bitter pill
There's good, and bad, in life's race
We climb the hills with God's grace

We must smile and contented be
Though heavy our cross we are free
Free to break through the chrysalis skin
The butterfly flies and a new life begin.

V. O. Phillips

Fate To Be Met

Belief in a theory, belief in a dream,
Defended in fury beneath the moonbeam,
Fight to the death, overcome opposition,
A fate to be met, hold fast your position.

Enemy rises, chill to the bone,
Noise filled emotions, deafened, alone,
Blood flows along channels, trickles away,
Life stamped out, decay more decay.

Belief in a theory, belief in a dream,
Romantic suggestion, beneath the moonbeam,
Reality triumph's war leads to death,
Reality echoes a fate to be met.

Celine Nolan

The Day's End

The air was cold with a misty fog,
On a bleak winter's morn of saddened loss.

Not a single flower blooming, or leaf on a tree,
Not a bird in the sky, so lifeless and free.

The cars are arriving, they pull up outside,
The people are gathered awaiting the ride.

Black clothes and pale faces, silence and tears,
No talking or chatter, no laughter do they feel.

People pass by, they look but don't speak,
They continue with their lives, their own worries and grief.

The journey to the church, so painful and slow,
Anxious to arrive, but can't wait to go.

A single bell chimes all through the grounds,
Breaking the silence that surrounds.

Inside lies the box of a life passed by,
No reason, no answer, just a question of why?

What once was a coffin made of wood and brass,
Now remains a pile of smouldering ash.

Marie Arnold

My Nanny

Oh Nanny you are so very dear
I am so glad you are still here

Though your memory it fades
You still have some of your old ways

Things we did still play on my mind
But in your head these things you can't find
Oh how I wish you had your mind

Memories you have no more
So people might ask what you've got to live for

But I know while you're still here I'll treasure each and every year.

Lorraine Marie Linfield

My Beautiful Daughter

I remember the first stirrings in my womb
And loving the tiny being that would become you.
I remember you emerging, as fragile and precious
as beautiful butterfly
And feeling the love that only a Mother can know.
I have loved you for all of your life—maybe longer,
Your hurt is my pain
And your tears are tiny knives in my heart.
If I could hurt instead of you I would,
If I could shelter you and hide you away
From all the things in life that would
If I could heal the scars with tiny kisses
And stitch the cuts with threads of love—I wound.
Always remember, my precious baby
That when the rainbow appears at last
And all grey skies become golden clouds
And the stormy rain becomes butterfly kisses
We are here, now and always, not just through teenage years,
Together we'll break down the walls of black and grey
'Til you stand once more tall and proud ready to face the world.

K. Smith

Freedom

As fast as the wind, you gallop away.
Towards the east at the break of day.
The moors are aglow, with a golden light.
You are gone away now, out of sight.
Down the combe that leads to the stream.
Where you can graze, and roam and dream
Up with your hooves! A swish of your tail,
Gallop away till the end of the day
Free as the wind, may you always be
Gallop, gallop, gallop away.

Mary Griffiths

Basics

Stepping out, walking tall, a lady pure and simple
Six inch heels, tights so sheer, even has a dimple
Wardrobe from Emmanuel, the cost astronomical
The dates she keeps, the company, is hardly economical
The Rolls is there, the chauffeur tall, with uniform immaculate
Arrival times, and taking home, just could not be inaccurate
With trips to town so commonplace, the country not outrageous
The manor house, the shooting lodge, are truly advantageous
A blissful cruise in summer seas, of course the captain's table
The water calm reflecting sun, it dare not prove unstable
I rest my case, it has to be a style beyond luxurious
I would not wish in any way to be a mite censorious
Why is it when she patronizes life so rich and swanky
If tears should fall her escort has to offer her a hanky?!

Doris Holland

Break Away

On this day, I break away.
One last chance to grab my dream.
To throw this stone down the stream.
Freedom from all of this pain.
Calls out in a whispered tone.
No more suffering ever again
Grab my children, we're on our own.

I'm over the moon, years of hell.
Couldn't come too soon.
On this day, I break away,
Break out of my shell.

No more days and nights
Of painful, violent wars
for no one knows what goes on behind closed doors.

Did I get it right?
Can lone birds fly?
For I no longer want to live a lie.
For on this day, I break away.

T. J. Ashley

The Easter Visitor

As the vicar gave the Easter News,
Some ladies jumped upon their pews
An extra worshipper had wandered in upon this happy day
And it looked for all the world as if he had come to stay.

You could follow his progress without a doubt
As around the pews he ran—in and out,
Up the aisle and round the nave;
The faithful did a Mexican wave.

The vicar stopped the service and said, "Is everyone alright?"
"Yes", the reply; but I must admit it gave quite a few a fright.

All at once he spotted his chance
And down the aisle, with a sort of a dance
Out of the open door he ran,
And once again the service began.

The sidesman came with collecting place to place your money upon.
He whispered in a low soft voice, "don't worry, ferrets gone!"

Mavis Scharnhorst

Mania

I awoke with a start and my soul took wing.
I left behind all dreary things.
With gay abandon I shook my feathers
Like a bird that's been in chains and tethers.
I spread my wings and took to the sky
And soared above life as I learned to fly.
Far removed from captivity,
Attaining far reaches of creativity;
Euphoria embracing my every feeling;
Elation setting my head a-reeling;
Mania invading my every pore;
Madness overtaking me right to the core.

Eileen Lawlor

"Granddad"

I see a child laughing, I see that it is me.
Running through vast green fields, being chased by you.
Now I see me smiling, as you pick me up from the ground,
I scream with delight as you spin me round and round.

I see a child playing, I see that it is me.
I'm playing in a little house, that you built with love and care.
Pretending it is real, imagining it is all mine,
Wishing I could stay there until the end of time.

I see a child crying, I see that it is me.
You help to console me with your words of sympathy.
Starting to feel better I give a little smile,
Knowing that I'm safe and sound as long as you are near.

I see a woman crying, I wish it wasn't me.
You had to go and leave me, I wish you could have stayed.
I have never felt so alone as I did on that day.
So if there is a heaven I know that you are there,
I hope one day to thank the Lord for all the times we shared.

Elaine McInally

Friend?

There goes the smile,
Here come's the pretence.
The knife in my back turns inch, by inch.
You were my friend or so I thought,
but your mouth betrayed your deepest thoughts.

You froth at the mouth, like a rabid dog
Unreasoning, unbending,
you spew your vile contemptuous heart.

But I'm wise to you now.
I know your game.
What was once in the dark has come forth into the light.

I shall no longer be at your beck and call.
I have discovered your deceit and your hypocrisy.

I'm a survivor, I guess I was born that way
and I can subsist the end of a friendship
which way nothing more than an illusion,
a fraud, a fallacy.

A. Holness

A Country Lost

War torn, sadness, loss of love and life.
Debris, destruction, homelessness and strife.
From beauty, peace and culture.
From friendships, smiles and care.
To genocide, rape and murder.
Mass graves hidden everywhere.
Families gone forever, their fates remain unknown.
Neighbours hating neighbours, no forgiveness can be shown.
For a country once united with a single flag and name.
For Yugoslavia and its people, life can never be the same.

Linda Scott

Gentle Evening Of Evenings

Gentle evening of evenings be kind to me,
Summer evening breeze, gently cool this lonely soul.
On the wings of silver birds bring me solace.
Send me scented fragrance from your sweet blossom,
    That in ecstasy I may lye for a while.
I will cherish this night of nights,
This deep purple night.
To the clear mountainous regions in the sky will I fly,
On the wings of a golden Eagle.
And there, I will find a kingdom,
Far greater, far more supreme,
And my dream of dreams will be answered,
For there I will be welcomed with open arms,
Yes I will reside there,
Then, in one moment of time, I will remember,
And look back for a while, and I will smile,
On this gentle evening of evenings.

K. Vasilis

Valleys Of Morn

A golden sun shines, upon the valleys of morn.
A wisp of wind, blows over fields of corn.
The bluest of skies, over this jewel of the sea.
This country I love, means so much to me.

Cows are grazing, in fields so green.
A beauty of places, I've ever seen.
A place so lovely, on this golden dawn.
I love them all, the peaceful valleys of morn.

The friendliest of people, you'd wish to meet.
A nod, a handshake, as you meet in the street.
The black of porter, the sweetest of ale.
Happiness and laughter, is not for sale.

Walking the roads, the freshness of streams.
No-one could visualize, these wondrous dreams.
A place of peace, in a land so green.
The best of places, that you have ever seen.

In the distance, a chapel bell rings.
Sweetness of the voices, as the church choir sings
The bluest of skies, on this golden dawn.
The air is sweet, in the valleys of morn.

Kevin P. Collins

My Dream Cottage

Oh, how I long for a cottage,
And garden all my own,
Where I could sit, and reminisce
Among the flowers I'd grown.

I see a rolling lawn
With a apple tree, for a shade,
There's sweet scented, stocks and holly hocks,
And a rockery I'd made.

I sometimes think of travel

And of far off foreign places
Then I see my garden
With its peace and pansy faces.

I'd never want to wonder
From my cottage, and garden small,
With the blackbirds, song in the morning,
And friends who sometimes call.

So if you ever pass along the road
My way, please stay awhile
And have a chat,
Or pass the time of day.

Alice M. Reynolds

Untitled

Each day slips by but I still haven't done anything
I go to work, come home from work then I sit down and think
I think about what I can do to change
I wonder what a caterpillar thinks about
just before the pupae stage of his life
does he think about the transformation
does he know he's going to be a butterfly
does he sit in the cocoon just knowing
that when it's all over he's going to be beautiful
a thing of such delicate beauty that one day
he could be captured and mounted in a frame
I don't think so who knows, who cares I think, I do.
An angel once told me to keep moving, boy was she right
her eyes were full of such love that if it wasn't for life
I think I might have stayed with her forever
a subtle smile crossed her mouth, she looked in my eyes and
said 'keep moving, don't worry we will meet again'
that's my fate! In dream form I'll always remember how pretty
she was and until I find her I'll be alone
I hope she's out there or I'll be one lonely old man
Perhaps she's waiting for her butterfly,
she could be waiting some time

Anthony Hartley

"My Life"

My life of four score years and ten
Is nearing its final scene.
I have so many memories
Of how wonderful it has been.

The century was only young
When my life on earth began,
And so many changes have I seen
Of achievements wrought by man.

Drama and dance have played their part
To illuminate my road
A devoted family, friends and pets
Have shared life's heavy load.

I've travelled a bit and taught a lot.
And striven with might and main,
To leave the world great memories
Where I'll never be seen again.

And as I continue along my way
My heart sings out this code,
God bless you all, my treasured friends,
As you journey along life's road.

Kathleen M. McKee

Ten Minutes In The Life
Of A London Commuter Statistic

Empty, yet full; as the carriage arrives,
In a Newspaper city, that never meet eyes,
Heads bowed in thought with their carrier bags,
As they're slowly perusing their standards, and 'Mags'

Nine thirty five, it's B.R. Waterloo,
As the masses converge on this "carriage-like zoo",
It's a total congestion of humourless suits,
Therefore habit's dictate is there are never disputes.

An orange is peeled, and aromas abound,
Still eyes to your paper, don't dare make a sound,
New faces alight as to waken these sheep,
Whilst the newspaper-suitmen impassively sleep?

Baggages, briefcase, bifocals for coats,
Bright lairy jackets like Notting-hill floats,
Briefcases open, while fag packets shut.
In this sea of F.I.S., Irvine Welsh, Pizza Hut!!

'Vauxhall it's Vauxhall", announcer informs,
As "rough guide to Sri Lanka", rubs eyes and then yawns,
No murders, no muggings no outrage thus far.
Means it's business as usual on planet B.R.

Adam Roberts

Peace What Price?

O Wanton Spirit, flee now this tortured shell
Take with you the pain and the dreaded fear that binds this
soul to hell. Rise high above this bedlam, this very core of
death. Free this body that felt the wrath from upon the
monster's breath.

Leave this arena of mad'ness, that wallows in a quagmire of
mud. Where the forces of evil sustain their lust on a feast of
gore and blood. Where the hand of human suff'rance reaches
heavenwards from beneath the mire. And the bodies of
thousands feed the flames, that consume this sorrowful pyre.

This heart which beats to the rhythm of life, now succumbs as
the carnage abounds. It longs to be free from the stench of
death, that pervades these battlegrounds. It wants no more
part in this madness, which mocks the very essence of life. It
yearns only the warmth and tender love, reaching out from
mother and wife.

This youth of England's Glory, ignorant of the horrors to
befall. Flocked like sheep in their thousands, when asked to
answer the call. And now as they die in their thousands, their
life's blood to soak foreign soil. Is it enough to say they were
heroes, is it enough to say they were loyal?

W. E. Fitzpatrick

Summer

Spring came with all her glory, but now she has departed
Leaving the doors open wide for summer to continue what she
started.
So summer with her paintbrush has splashed more colour
everywhere
Not quite so delicate in her touch, but bolder, quite brash, her
beauty we all can share.

The brightest reds, the deepest yellow, purple, orange, gold.
The tightest buds bring big surprise as they gradually unfold,
To beckon all the busy bees their nectar to partake
Whilst dragonflies hover on shimmering wings over a still and
peaceful lake,

The cuckoo has gone; the swallows arrived with their cousins
house martins and swifts.
The lark in full song as it soars all day long, and birds glide on
the winds thermal lift
The trees now clothed in heavy leaf, give shade from the hot sun ray
And in the summer breeze gently back and forth they sway.

The bright clear blue of the summer sky, small feathery clouds
as they drift slowly by.
Hazy days, lazy days, picnics, haymaking and all those things
In her short stay, and in her own way, these delights only
summer brings.

Joan Clearista King

A Lamentation On Nabodiah

Nabodiah, thou spotless bloom;
Fostered by an ecclesiarch.
Thou knew not who they Mum and Dad;
Still folk repeat thy mum a whore.
She went out in a full moon night;
And came she home no never at dawn.
Alas! Thou infant wheatish tint;
Under a roof that swayed in wind.
The heart of priest did melt as wax;
And did the child sleep on his chest.
Oh! Time as horse, yea ran so fast;
And true thou saw green 'teens' so nigh.
But fools are wide and wise so dolts;
And God did prove He called the priest.
Orphan a lass! Yet orphrey thou was;
Often thou sand melancholic tone.
Went out in that full moon night thou;
And saw Michael's friends high above.
From the Throne heard voice 'come child';
Oh! Did thou fly Seraphim's build.

M. J. Gabrial

The Side Show

To sit.
Contemplate.
Fruitless is the sweat that falls from the brow
Falls fast, into the pool of disinterested conclusion.
Life—the show too good to miss?
Too fast to blink!
A young, hulking, huge world where there are no boundaries
not round, not square.
The sanguine glasses are poised on the rosy nose of the
expectant
child, pensively he peers—a chink in the curtain reveals his
audience.
He observes through hazy, cataract eyes—excitement mounts.
The curtain opens.

Time passes.

Conclusion nears—the curtains
Fool!
Warm tributes, proud breasts bursting with accolades
A wilting rose pricks one dirty finger—all that is left of a life's
toil!

To sit
To contemplate . . . no?
To live.

Julia Deats

Spaceology

In this age of technology,
On account of our biology,
A fact that you will see,
Going into the internet, like the bumblebee,
Our fingers do the tapping,
on the processor's keys,
Our minds go a-flapping—
The cursor's gone to freeze!

And as we are waxing lyrical,
Our jargon is oh so physical!
With bits and bytes, and roms and rams,
Words do fight, and other words clams.
Surfing the net, from day to day,
Swim with the tide, but keep some play.
All over the world, an enclosing net,
An electrical field of massive extent!
So treat this machine with the utmost respect,
or we will become another select—!
Remember to use in just moderation,
This will save the ultimate, our nation.

E. McL. Gibb

The Silent Screen

The magic of the silent screen, an era lost in time
When a movie star, without a word, could break your heart with mime
The glamour of La Swanson, flashing eyes and shoulders bare
America's Sweetheart, Mary Pickford, ribbons in her golden hair
The Jazz Age brought the flappers, fluttering to the fore
'It Girl' Clara Bow, and the 'Flaming Youth' of Colleen Moore
The swarthy Latin Lovers, lithe of body, fair of face
Rudolph Valentino making shop girls' pulses race
Daring Douglas Fairbanks, dashing John Gilbert, too
And, oh, Ramon Novarro, how I'm yearning for you
Keaton, Lloyd and Langdon, never failed to raise a grin
Despair and doubt were swiftly cast out, when Charlie Chaplin
    shuffled in
Is that a phantom, a vampire, or a hunchback on his knees?
No, lurking in the shadows is Lon Chaney, if you please
The Gold Rush gave us laughter, and The Big Parade brought tears
And Ben-Hur raced to victory to the sound of silent cheers
The Golden Age of Hollywood, how lucky we were to know
Of those flickering silver images, of so very long ago.

Catherine Baldrey

Reflections . . .

Like the surface of a still pond, the images stare outwards
sometimes the reflections are clouded, not as clear as they
could be yet others can be so sharp; they make you startle at
the visions you see it all depends when and how long you
look out of life's still pond . . .

Like the surface of a still pond, the images stare inwards
sometimes the starkness of the mirror, bears little to the mood
the journey inward takes courage, but brings more rewards
it all depends how honestly you look into life's still pond . . .

Like the surface of a still pond, the image stares through
sometimes three dimensional, creating a distortion
separating the image, bringing in the perspective
it all depends if you seek reality or illusion . . .

Bryan J. Allen

Rainbows

Rainbows dancing on my bedroom wall
Such pretty colours where they fall.
Suddenly appearing like a shower of rain.
Pretty, pretty colours, quickly gone again.
I would like to keep you,
But you will not stay.
Coming back to tease me,
When I don't want to play,
Rainbows falling out of the sky,
Special little presents
From a shower of rain.

Ann Townsend

The Silent Garden

The incandescent sun had left us,
Surprised by the sudden descent of rain
It fled for its nearest shelter.

Creatures enjoyed the moment,
playfully creeping around in the damp.
Rain acted as a relief from the blazing youthful star.

Old, tattered gravestones stood tall and proud,
seeking attention, but finding none.
Outside is a motionless garden of the past,
Sleeping day after day,
Forevermore.

Jonathan C. Wedgbury

Hiatus

In the wake of a blizzard, there is always that
stillness, gently oppressive, starkly serene.
A stillness, raucous of sound,
and crackling presence
where only silence prevails.

From the snow, with its familiar, elusive no-scent,
comes that remembered perfume of forgotten days.
A stinging of the senses,
an all–pervasive smell
which is non-existent.

And all around you, everything is movement, a perpetual
shifting in a ever–changing landscape.
A transient, spectral scene,
from a bustling world
that is utterly still.

In the wake of our lives, there is that eternal
stillness, a quiet oblivion, a careless serenity.
A stillness, empty of sound,
in a silent creation
forever at peace.

William F. Craig

A Whisper Of Truth

Fear not, oh child of life's longing
For the pattern of destiny is but within thy hands
It is for thee to weave its form, prudently
Wash the folly of ignorance from thy self
And rejoice in being in the essence of your own true will
Make light, out of darkness
And see through tomorrow's dreams, thine eyes lest today

Ferry your heart not, in a cup of bitterness
For swift is the gale, that redirects the captains ship
Govern your life's course judiciously
Delay not thy furtherance
And weep not a tear
For the wind of despair, lurks in darkness

Verily you must strive, to shed the echo
Of seemingly distant pasts
Make life anew, each day; fill your cup with hope and verve
For the dawning of truth, is but a thought away
Which no wind in all her immensity can blow not asunder
Tarry not then oh child,
your dreams of hope and desire.

Samsa

My Cat

She walks with grace upon her feet,
and creeps so stealthily,
she's white and fluffy from head to tail,
with black and ginger streaks.

She eats and sleeps and meows and purrs,
and walks about the house.
But one thing she will not do,
and that is catch a mouse.

G. Ecclestone

To Find Reality

How do we define
Between that finest line
Of which we call life and death
Or what it may foresee
For me that is reality
In that we should enlist
But why! Why! I should be so deeply ailing
How long will it be
For that I was once strong as a lion
A man of ways and means
Science was my gift
Please lay an answer at my feet
For when I cry
Help! Help me! To find that new phase in life
To shed my time of pain
To rally round
Contrive it until I gain
That final race
To feel a loving peace
Be it to abide around my gaze.

Iris May

The Search For Love

Yet again my heart is aching;
Being deprived of the love it desires.
Will the hunger ever be fulfilled,
Or will the search for love go on forever.

The faces of past loves pass through my mind,
Like an endless reel of tape.
The memories haunt me constantly,
Tempting my heart to take one more chance,
To risk yet another time of heartbreak,
For the chance of receiving the perfect love.

Marie Beba

Please Forget

"I did not mean it, please forget"
Is all too well known a phrase.
For what is done is done
And what is said is said.

There would be no history if the ills done were forgotten
Good and bad, what we do, is there forever to remain
In the evil of war we see the good of many
Such as Florence Nightingale.

Would it not be better if we paused to think a while
Before an evil deed is done or unkind word is said
Then we need not say
"I did not mean it, please forget".

Margaret Owen Jones

Harboured Memories

A fisherman has waited for the tide to ebb
And get out his waders, he must,
To paint the boat which is his livelihood,
And cover the unsightly rust.
An old man is beckoning
For boat trips around the bay,
Another offers fishing trips
To pass the hours away.
The seagull on the tall ship's mast
Squawking with deafening tones
Swooping down for scraps of food
And leftover ice cream cones.
The houses on the hillsides
Create a pastel hue,
Of pretty shades and colours
Of yellow, pink and blue.
As the day draws to a close
What a beautiful sight,
All the harbour lights come on
To show Brixham off by night.

Diane Lee

Fantasies

Fantasies, fantasies, they are not true,
just unclear thoughts that wait to show through:
They are objects
to cherish
to hold
and to love,
but unlike the real world, they come from above.

Just hoping and wishing
for things that can't be.
That's the way of the real world —
the real you and me.
But unlike all others
we see things differently.

We run —
and we jump
for things too high to reach.
And realize
after,
that dreams are too deep.

A. Edwards

Cobbled Streets

How the winter's rain splatters upon the cobbles,
As the frail old man with walking stick hobbles,
Between the rows of gloomy, oppressive houses,
Where young children play in soiled blouses.

Gossiping wives in dark doorways linger,
Always ready to point that accusing finger,
Shaggy-coated, hungry dogs, always on the roam,
Looking for a little kindness, a meal, a home.

And as the rain along the gutter courses,
Comes the loud cloppings of the drayman's horses,
The excited shriekings of the unworried young,
And the sharp orders from a parental tongue.

All manner of people do pass this way,
At strange ungodly hours of night and day,
In darkness, bold Bobbies patrol their beats,
As unsavoury characters walk the cobbled streets.

Clive Sanders

In The Mirror

It is not you, nor any memory of you,
   Which shades this morning face;
Nor could you, remembering, trace
   A finger through my hair,
Leaving these silver ribbons there.

It cannot be, that in this image now,
   The lines around my mouth still cling;
As if the lips, late answering,
   Shaped to your far-off smile
And lingered, lovingly, a while.

Searching in the mirrored eyes,
   I fail to find them cold or bleak,
Though time's pale kiss is on each cheek;
   Rather does my face reflect
Forgotten dreams—in retrospect.

Sheila Blount

A New Day

The sun rises from beyond the hills,
Lighting the world with a new found joy.

The birds in the sky, swoop and dive,
Singing their morning glories to the world.

The wind wanders freely throughout the trees,
Awakening every last soul.

A silver light creeps through the night's dreams,
Enchanting the world with its splendour.
Morning is here, a new day begun.

Lucy Heming

A Long Dark Tunnel

It is so lonely and dark in here,
so cold and desolate too.
The end is in front that's clear,
but I still have to get through.
As I walk I only see darkness,
a shiver goes down my spine.
My footsteps get quicker and quicker,
I look back, take a breath, as I walk a straight line.

I am half way through the darkness,
my heart is pounding a beat.
There is an eerie feeling inside this place,
as the ground rushes under my feet.
I finally reach the end,
the tunnel is behind me now.
But I've got to walk back through that tunnel,
but how?
I am Claustrophobic.

Debbie Timson

Pam Ayres

Pam we loved your poems
when you read them on TV
we like a lot of fun you see
you were great to make the laughter,
and in your garden you are a grafter,
Pam you now do stand
with your gardening gloves in hand
you gave one almighty shout get the mower out.
Ginger from next door was the first to jump
the fence, falling in the muddy trench.
The mower has gone, he calmly said.
Then I will phone the police said Pam and
called to Ginger, they are on their way, he was
gone to jump the fence again, and taken away by
police. The day has ended sound and clear
Ginger has gone never fear.

Ivy Kisbee

Enchantment

Translucent night in early June
Gentle breezes bring a tune
Music made by dragonfly wings
A chorus of fairies, as they sing
Visions of light in mosses green
Cobwebs of silk, for a fairy queen
It is a dream within a dream
When fairies dance by the running stream
Grasses of shimmering velvet
Sparkling with the dew
Under the spell of the fairy dell
Where dreams can come true

Rita F. Kelly

Winter

The wind that whistles through the trees
No more to hear the sound of bees
The sun is lower in the sky
Sometimes I have to wonder why
The winter has to be so cold
Or is it just, I'm getting old.

It seems as if when winter's here
and thoughts of snow are very near
The winter winds that seem to chill
The leaves from trees that seem to swill
around your feet in paths of gold
Or is it just, I'm getting old.

Day by day and year by year
The frosty mornings bright and clear
I don't like the way it freezes
Or the blustery winter breezes
The winters always seem much colder
Yes I'm sure I'm getting older.

Jeannette Atkins

Strength

Unable to speak with his own voice.
Unaware that he has a choice, but
Sometimes pausing to wonder if his thoughts are his
or just absorbed.
A human sponge, you see, but not a rare breed.
Unwilling, and too afraid, to listen
To his heart; and so it had been moulded like clay.
By pretending craftsmen
Who weren't interested in the finished product.

He journeys through life with barely a scar.
But sits in the back seat of his own car, as
There's always a stranger at the wheel, whose face
Changes every minute, whose eyes
Glare in the mirror.
Who directs the course and crushes obstacles
Created by individuality.
To row one's own boat
Down the river of pain and of hopeless conformity
Requires strong arms—very strong arms indeed.

Jillian McFarland

The Pain Of One's Love

There is a sadness haunting my mind,
Because someone special left me behind.
My heart feels like it has been torn in two,
All because of the pain I've been through.
My feelings have been shattered,
from continuously being beaten and battered.
When raging love with extreme pain,
Produces tears, as floods of rain.
Soon all my memories with part,
so I would have to give in to my heart.
I need to accept my love has gone,
To let go of my undying love and to be strong.

Natasha Peters

Leaving

It does not seem so long ago,
I took you to school, for the first time,
You went in with a kiss, and waved me good bye,
I went home on my own,
It will not be long before you are home.
Then the years went by.
For the time had come, to go to university,
Car all packed, you left me with a kiss and a wave,
But you will not be back so soon,
Then the time came, once more you were to leave,
To the other side of the world,
you left with a kiss and a wave,
How long you will be away, I do not know.
I wish you were the little boy,
I took to school all those years ago.

J. Harley

A Friendship That Will Never End

Lying here thinking about the past,
I wonder why did it end, why so short did it last?
Words trapped deep down in my heart,
I wish I could tell you, but were do I start?
Loneliness creeps inside my soul,
The hurt, the pain, it's out of control,
Why did you leave me? Why did you go?
I wish you could tell me, I really want to know,
Still wishing you were here, sitting beside me,
But now you're just like a photo, a past memory,
I'd get visions of you with every tear,
Dreaming that you were still here,
I know that death takes people every day,
But why you? Why did it have to take you away,
Wishing you were still here, wish you did not die,
But instead you're in a place where the angels fly,
However you are in my heart, and there to stay,
At least death can not take that part of you away.

Dionne Mansell

Jess

The sun has set upon my wild despair
The shadows darken in the skies you knew;
I stand alone tonight and watch the stars.

A sound I hear recalling other years
When you were young, and I a little child:
The stars recede; once more I seem to see
That loving face, those eager pleading eyes.

You journeyed with me down the memorable years;
Dear faithful heart why must you leave me now?

I stand alone tonight and watch the stars.

Mary Coates

Living With Fear

I can feel the fear building up,
Twisting me inside,
Even though, I'm sure it's in my mind,
I need to feel secure.
I'm lonely—I always feel the odd one out,
Confusion—my mind is filled with doubts,
I can't handle the pressure.
As expectancies grow,
Inside I know,
The fear that I live in is changing me.
I need to live life in a shell,
To escape from my living hell.

Shona Alder

Garden Sense

He sits relaxed and contented in his garden chair,
Eyes closed, revelling in the warmth of the sun touching his face.
Smelling the fragrant aromas of the flowers, that he himself
    nurtured from seed,
And that are now filling the air around him with sweet scent.
He listens to the activity in the garden, bees busy gathering pollen,
Birds calling to one another, and crickets, passing messages
    by rubbing their legs together,
Telling each other's plans for the day.
What he does not see, is nature's tactics of survival being put
    to the test,
By the smaller inhabitants of the garden as part of their
    everyday existence.
Or the cat, making itself a cosy retreat on the vegetable patch,
In the cool shade, of the large over-hanging leaves of his
    prized rhubarb.
His taste for life is measured only in comparison, by the
    grandeur, richness, and pride, displayed in his garden.
He sits relaxed and contented in his garden chair,
Eyes closed, revelling in the warmth of the sun touching his face.

W. E. Monaghan

The Answer . . . Is Waiting

Pray! Please tell me this,
You different shades of righteous minds.
Will you kill-maim, and then destroy
Those at prayer in Heaven's shrines,
Or share as one, a love divine
On Heaven's unseen border lines?

Then pray! Please tell me this,
You different shades of righteous minds.
If you share that love divine
On Heaven's unseen border lines
Why is it then that you consign
Vitriolic hate from thoughtless guns
For earthly unseen border lines?
To kill-maim, and then destroy
A different shade of righteous mind,
Who you may meet at Heaven's shrine
And share that perfect Love divine.

The answer you will only find
If you are of the chosen
To enter Heaven's shrines.

James Henry Warren

The Serpent

A glance filled with stifled emotions,
Barely hidden by the maze of unspoken words between us.
A golden halo framing ice–blue eyes,
The apple of temptation to my innocent lips.

A feeling shared,
The serpent,
Beguiling yet forbidden fruit.
My nakedness, so public a confusion,
Belies the eggshell path I have to tread.

A mental crossroads bars my way—
With the devil of my own imaginings I must make a deal.
Happiness, that elusive of companions,
Taunting me,
But which road must I take?

Only my devil knows,
Though neither begging nor pleading
Would bring forth pearls from those twisted maws.
Instead, this deal so cunning in construction,
Is signed in tears and wounding words.

My soul is snatched by the serpent.

Heidi J. Scott-Bruce

Bahamian Experience . . .

Your distant shores were calling to set my spirit free,
to dwell, to laze, to dream awhile, reflect the life in me.
Such days should leave tranquillity emblazoned on my heart,
but no alas, it is not so . . . now restless . . . now apart.

I found not just an island fringed with silken sands of time,
but a pearl within an oyster, in life's essential rhyme.
The seas that oft I've travelled, the cultures I have known,
not one had ever touched my soul, now heart in turmoil thrown.

Your people bedecked in friendship, no false face found to please,
a natural welcome for one, for all, to make all feel at ease.
If I were born of royal blood I know not that I'd find,
such a plethora of life's virtues wrapped up in one mankind.

Now in this English garden I see nought to keep me here,
a yearning to return to you, then heart be full of cheer.
Atlantis cornucopic visions found akin to promised land,
planted deep is this emotion, my heart now yours . . . command.

Yet sleep now eludes existence, no thoughts of life once new,
just memories meandering steeped in euphoric hue.
Someday I pray that I'll return to where I left my heart,
for fate decrees that when I do . . . we shall never part.

Anne Brown

Kilmalooda

When you come from Kilmalooda towards the shadow's end of day,
Bring the shimmer of the meadow and the rustle of the hay
And the sun of a West Cork morning filtering through
    the window pane—
And a Connemara pony skitting shyly on his rein.
Bring the slumber–downy peace of a splendid sleep
In a soft, safe bed in the still-night's deep.
Bring the hymn of heifers hoofing in a circle—forming round
And the echo of the black horse pawing
    the clover–patterned ground.
Bring the hair of the wild, wild donkey determined to be free
And the birdsongs of twilight wrapped in leaves from
    the beechen tree
Bring a skein of wool from hedgerows brushed by the wandering ewe
And mushrooms from the upper field plucked with morning dew.
Bring the silvered voice of countrymen and terriers at play
And a curl from the coats of the silken calves
Clipped at shadow's end of day.
For the city's falling down and makes dust upon the feet
And we long for Kilmalooda where the morning air is sweet—
Where murmurs from the old mill-stream say words that the
    heart would say—
Words we might be saying at the golden end of day.

Mayhew Connolly

Thoughts

Why is it whenever we're happy
and someone demands to know why.
Our elation begins to diminish, as we
Can't explain, however we try.

Why is it there is always someone
who, however obliquely, just cools
the rapturous feelings we cannot explain,
so then we begin to feel fools.

I've decided to look at them kindly
and tell them I'm sorry that they
just can't understand and enjoy what I can,
— there is no more I can say!

E. Tyrrell

Just Rose

Rose took delight in a simple thing,
Faith, family, friends, and a kettle to sing.
She visited many—not feeling so well,
Ran an errand or shopped or just sat for a spell.
She sought out jobs, her time to fill,
Never mastering the art of sitting still,
She did nothing great; just helped every friend,
They knew on her they could always depend,
Rose never smoked, she was no alcoholic,
Hated scented soap, preferred old–fashioned carbolic.
She hankered not for worldly wealth
She even spurned the National Health.
She never really enjoyed the sun,
A crisp wintry day was much more fun,
In the eyes of the world, she was not well blest,
But she cultivated the seeds of happiness.
No foreign travel—just a walk in the wood,
No caviar—just plain apple pud',
No automobile—just a ride in a bus,
Death came, as she lived, without any fuss.

D. E. Galcutt

Gentle Stranger

Do you see him standing there
the stranger with the gentle stare, you don't!
Well, look again and see
the man who died for you and me.

Born upon one Christmas Day
this gentle man was here to stay
to clean up all of man's decay.

Yet for this to be understood
they nailed him to some cruel wood
up high for all the world to see
he hung in pain and misery.
Giving his life for you and me
what pain he took
yet we gave him not a backward look.

A. Marshall

Shadows Of The Future

Long fall the shadows, within the twilight zone,
Racing across the grassland, looking for a home,
If you look among the shadows, deep into the grass,
You may see the face of yesterday, peering from the past.

If you look a little harder at the fleeting sight,
You may even chance to glimpse, a distant glowing light,
For deep among the shadows a message there to see,
Of a new to-morrow, and a long decree.

Drifting with the wind, stirring in the reeds,
Watching out for Man, looking to his needs,
Ripping on the waters, flowing down the stream,
Forming many patterns, awakening to the dream.

To-morrow's dawn is breaking, lightning up the night,
To-morrow's sun is rising, to its greatest height,
Look among the shadows, of the Twilight Zone,
Watch them as they cross the land, and never feel alone.

Jim Wilson

Fearful And Alone

Away from home and in a strange land,
Empty inside and all alone,
People come and people go.
Will they ever really know?

Excruciating pains consume my brain,
Time passing slowly presents a strain,
Upon my bed I sit and wonder;
What life would be like over yonder!

From the depths of my despair;
I have taught myself to shake off fear,
To take on board a positive stance,
If only to have a fighting chance.

Sad but no longer filled with anxiety,
Life takes on a new reality,
The days and nights go swiftly by;
My time no longer spent wondering why.

I'm hopeful now, as courage I have found,
To drive this fear right underground,
No longer fearful, but still alone;
Desperately wanting to be back home.

Glasmine Banton-Douglas

Now And Then

I remember how precious was the time
That we spent with each other entwined
When the whispers of words were heard
When the arms we fell into weren't tired
I remember how long evenings raced
Captured in love's sweet embrace

Spare moments the children now devour
The needs demand time every hour
I take strength from your patience day
And thank God for your understanding way

I regret the times that we exist
Without much more than a kiss
When I collapse in your arms with despair
That I can't always "be there".

From a friend to a lover, to you, grew wife and a mother of two
But I'm still all the things that you dream, and not all the
things that I seem

These words I want you to hear
That come from the love of these years
You're with me in my life, and you'll stay
The first thought in my mind every day.

E. C. Nice

The Last Chime Of Midnight

Shadows whisper to each other
Sieving secrets through the wind
Trespassing with the intention to introduce another whim
As night begins her journey evil settles in the dark
And they prosper from the flattery released by every sin

The shadows march in unison
Shedding lies with every step
Stretching towards tomorrow on the fingers of the moon
And over the silent wilderness they must prostitute their dream
To amalgamate peace and nightmares into an orchestral
haunting theme

With a vile deliberation
They intimidate the weak
Stealing all the solitude while the children count the sheep
With a strategic manifesto every bribe is their belief
They offer out the olive branch and then rake the leaves of sleep

Amid the insomnolent atmosphere
Shadows bathe in the night's perfume
And midnight turns to greet them with a neighbourly interest
The shadows claim the moonlight and discuss their next foray
As the last chime of midnight turns the clock to another day

David Bridgewater

A Real Friend

When I was small,
You took good care,
Now I'm grown,
You're still there,
A helping hand you will lend,
You've always been my best friend.

Although we sometimes scream and shout,
You're lots of fun to have about,
We do the things, that best friends do.
No one could be as special as you.

Some people can be very kind,
But real friends are hard to find,
Through my life, if there's been one,
That's got to be you—my Mum.

S. J. Hill

Getting It Straight

When they're gone, they don't come back,
You just remember,
The times you laughed,
The simple things seem the best,
You seem to forget all the rest,
In your arms with all your charms,
There's nothing to compare,
And all the things we share,
In my dreams they live for ever,
And forget them I will never,
In music I have painted,
The things that can't be tainted,
The memories will live forever,
You can't believe the luck you've had,
So you don't need to feel so sad,
So rejoice and feel extremely glad,
That you're still here, with much more to come,
So get up and go!!! Get off your bum,
There is so very much more to enjoy,
Whether you're a girl or even a boy.

Dennis Mudd

The Sea

Oh beautiful cruel sea —
How deep, how blue!
Sometimes we hate you, sometimes we love you.
On a hot Summer day
You invite us to play.
What wonders are beneath you untold,
Within your bosom you enfold
Crustacean, fish and weed,
You give them all they need.
When the stormy winds blow high,
It sends you into a rage.
Then you go on a rampage.
You hiss and roar, and churn with all your might.
Woe betides all who sail on you tonight.
The storm is gone by morning light;
No-one can tell the unrest of the night.
The sun rays dance upon your face,
The creamy surf edges the shore like lace.
No-one can understand or conquer thee,
Oh beautiful cruel sea.

Doris Hogan

Thoughts

In the garden you are forgiven
Kind thoughts relief the mind of stress
For in seclusion the peaceful existence of nature
Can remedy all.
I have found that you are blessed
To make your findings in life
Be it good or bad to suit your very existence.
Look at life as you wish it to be
Then you will remedy any ill

Frank Gale

Missing

It is very surreal, but something is missing.
A frame for the picture, the chalk for the board.
I am not yet complete I feel like a fraud.
The bowing of the trees are telling me to go ahead and shout
to the world the thoughts in my head.
I am waiting on the pavement it is over the other side, waving
for me to go, with its arms way open wide.
The candle that's inside me needs a match, needs a light.
The person that's within me is shouting, help let me out.
The house needs an insulator.
The baby needs a bed.
I really need this person, this person in my head.

This person keeps me together is a splint for my broken leg.
Is a psychiatrist for my twisted and somewhat maddened head.
The thing that's in my heart is always in my head.
I take it with me everywhere, to school and to my bed.
But life I know must go on until the day I die, and then I know
I may be joined with that person in the sky.
But until that day does come, I will have to wait in vain and
live with these deep painful feelings each and every day.

Danielle Carter

Why?

I had a baby and now it's gone
My love for my child is still very strong
It happened so quickly and made me so sad
Maybe it was God's way of saying it should never have been
It's sad when it didn't live long enough for itself to be seen
The day of the funeral drew near
My head wasn't exactly clear
The melody plays as the coffin of my child is escorted in
Now the priest starts to sing the perfect hymn
He says a few words to try and comfort me through
But he's not the one that will never hear the words
Mummy I love you
The coffin is getting lowered into the ground
You can see the tears and hear the screams
Of people wondering what might have been
One day we shall meet in the sky above
That day we can reunite our love

Cheryl Darrah

Memories Of My Lost Love

Memories are such things of wonder,
Each so different like every clap of thunder,
It makes me feel quite sad,
That so many have to be bad,
Not the bad times that we shared,
Just the bad that changed the way we cared.

Sometimes my memories strike when I don't want them to,
They leave me with the feeling of not knowing what to do,
Still as long as the rain falls from the skies above,
I'll keep the memories of you, my lost love.

For today and tomorrow,
I'll remember all the joy and sorrow,
But I will always feel cheated,
Sometimes even defeated,
For we weren't really given a chance to get started,
Before from each other we were parted.

Susan Stokes

I Wandered This Way

The river runs shallow, the trees mirrored there,
all is so beautiful, all is so fair,
I wandered this way, when my heart in despair
Looked to the heavens for hope glimmered there.
My eyes were at rest with what they beheld,
yet my soul in its torment refused to the quelled.
Where sky meets the earth in a fond embrace
I hoped to reach there though not in haste
for the distance held peace which must be my aim,
until God calls me to his house of fame.

Ann Surtees Robinson

Miracles

Lord ye blessed the loaves an fish,
a humbly ask will ye bless this dish,
the contents to it are very sma,
will ye jist make sure it feeds us a,
an if you yersel wud like tae dine,
jist come doon join me an mine.
We hivny much but were willing tae share,
an Lord could a jist ask yin thing mair,
the corns gone bad on yon tap fiel,
and hardly a tattie frae twenty dreel,
the coos gone dry and the auld mares died,
mony a tear this wee family's cried,
a hivny prayed for a long long while,
am begging ye Lord,
help this auld faither smile.

Janet Evans

I'll Not Be Here

Fresh winds a-blowing in the springtime
Birds a-singing o' what a lovely time,
I'll not be here.
Flowers a-blooming in the month of June,
A baby crying a lady sighing,
I'll not be here.
Leaves a-fallen from the trees, cold nights,
Stormy skies, water in your eyes,
I'll not be here.
Snow a-falling in winter time bells a-ringing,
For Christmas time hearts full of joy for the
Festive time, O'but I'll not be here for I have,
Passed away a long time.

Edward Travers

The Dinner Party (For A Forgetful Man)

The table is set
At the first time we met
Blind date, I think of the show.
It seems so long ago.

Glasses sparkling in soft candlelight
Red wine breathing, so strong yet bright
Smoked duckling plate, a nice starter
Wild mushrooms, herbs much sought after

The sirloin steaks look tender and juicy
Waiting for my love Lucy
Sea salt, mustard and black pepper
Magnificent, this table looks deeper

The taxi arrives
I thank God I'm alive
Oh sh** before I began,
My love of loves Lucy is a Vegan

Michael Faull

Childhood Patterns

Childhood forms the patterns of my life.
Pathways strewn with fragrant apple blossom.
My meadows filled with golden ripe corn.
Raindrops like sparkling diamonds crystal clear.
Waking joy of youths freshly pure delight.
Well springs of strong determined ambition.
Dawning passions of deep seated desire.
Pangs of bitterness and longings of love.

Childhood forms the patters of my life.
Mindless rejection and untold sweet beauty.
Rivers of delight rushing, flowing and ebbing.
Sweet music of lifelong hidden, untold mystery.
Longings, smouldering, throbbing, drifting around.
Unguarded tears, selfish pride, and self pity.
Tangled mixture of colour, and deep dark sorrow.
Long dreamy summer fairs, and swaying maypoles.
A tangled highway, bright with threaded ribbons.

Vanessa Ann Sherwood

Judgement

The land is desolate.
Nothing had survived, and,
As we few survivors emerge
From our hiding places we weep, we cry
For a land that once we knew
And once we loved.
From the bunkers we come,
The last sad vestiges of a species, we
Who have been touched to our souls,
And, no longer innocent, our children
Stare wide eyed at what is left of our world.
Young men sigh, rocked to their very souls,
The aged clutch onto the hands of their loved ones,
Remembering how once it was.
But then the horror, the realization
That all is not yet over;
That it has only just begun.
And the nuclear hellfire
Washes down over us
And purges our souls of our crimes.

Chris Bryden

Reflections Of A Rainbow

Did once a rainbow fall to earth
Colour the flowers and give them birth
Paint the poppies a brilliant red
Splash some gold on the marigolds head
Coloured the violets purple too
Gave tiny forget-me-nots tinge of blue
Seeing the ferns lying in between
Gave them a loving touch of green
So be not sad when the rainbow goes
The colours are always right there at your toes

Joyce M. Chaffer

Cometh The Snow

Now the snowflakes gently falling
Cover land and tree with white;
Reach cool fingers to the windows
In the grey and lilac light.

All the bushes in the garden
Bend like burdened aged men.
Every hill is like a mushroom;
Fairy trees grow in the glen.

Softly, softly fall the snowflakes
From the low and yellow sky.
Softly breathes the wind, then slumbers.
Muted is the owl's first cry.

Oh! What joy it is to waken
To a world of delight.
Every tree and hedge and garden
Hushed with wonder, awesome bright.

Patricia Haynes

My Son

I remember when you were born,
so beautiful you were, bringing twenty
years of smiles and laughter and
sunshine to my world.
Then I remember the day you died,
when God took you away,
then the skies turned grey, taking the
sunshine away.
It would have been so easy to come to
you, it's been so much harder to stay.
But I know in my heart, my memories
and the love I have for you will never
fade away, because time for me will
stand still until we are together again some day.
For I know you are always by my side,
and will patiently wait for me, and I
will see your face again as we meet
in God's bright light.

Cynthia G. Tyler

I Am All The Things Of My Past

I am all the things of my past
The things I remember
The things I did
The things I said
The dreams I had when I was young
I loved those things that I did but now I am boring
And scared sometimes
Sometimes I want to go back to the past
And look at the things I did
And the thing I said
And the dreams I had
I am a young girl I should be having fun
And not be boring all the time
I should be getting out more often
And starting from tomorrow
I am going to get out more often.

Lynsey Gent

Jeremy

I saw you again today.
If only you knew, how you made my life complete.
We talked, as usual, the weather, work, etc., etc.,
That's all it as ever been, and all I ever want it to be
The first time I saw you, I knew, you were someone special.
I broke the ice, by telling you I liked your long hair,
You laughed, embarrassed, but happy.
Briefly our hands touched as you took your change,
As I looked up into your eyes, I felt, I was looking into,
The eyes of my soul mate!
We have exchanged the same look, on numerous
Occasions, but I don't intend to pursue it.
I don't wish to spoil what we have, which is nothing,
But small talk and fantasies, my fantasies.
So I will wait, with baited breath, until I see you again.
Maybe, if I'm lucky, tomorrow

Andrea E. Fazackerley

Behind The Veil And Back

Molehills became mountains
The outlook was grim,
Life's nourishing fountains
Were turned off for him.
Anxious? Depressed? Take a rest or a pill,
Advice is showered down how the void he should fill,
Good intentions abound yet they fall on deaf ears
And do not dispel his disquiet or fears.
Counsellors cajole and parrot their wares
Then go home to tea as the troubles aren't theirs.
Refer him along isn't passing the buck
But helpful to someone who's down on his luck!
Then, ray of light, its source all unknown
Was it something heard, read, that caused seeds to be sown?
That returned him again to life before gloom,
And lifted at last the outlook of doom.

D. P. Downes

The Pond

The pond seemed motionless, the
bridge reflected in the water. 'Ribbit'
croaked a frog that had just leaped
into the cool waters.
The soft pink lilies had recently opened,
and as I walked across the bridge,
I admired their simplicity.

As I leisurely walked across the
bridge, my flowing dress swayed in
the slight breeze. My umbrella shaded
my dark brown hair from the sunlight
My large almond, shaped eyes stared
at the passing butterfly.
I hurried across the bridge, because I
was late for . . .

Claire Wise

The Death Of Hiroshima

Eight fifteen, nineteen forty five
   The day was quiet and warm,
A sudden happening broke through the skies
   And shattered the silence of dawn.

A breath–taking heat swept over the land
   It hit people both near and far.
It burnt people's homes, their bodies, their lives
   And leaving one terrible scar.

Those who looked up saw tall flames and clouds
   Paralysed, they stood with raised heads.
It occurred to them then, the women and men
   That most of their family were dead.

A clearance began and every live man
   Explored all the homes that were gone.
By day and by night they continued their fight
   To pull out the dead and go on.

And still a year later the suffering went on,
   As people recovered from illness.
But nothing replaces the scars on their faces
   Nor that eerie, death–defying stillness.

Elissa Monk

Memories Of An Old Sportsman

I climb to the attic, and sit on the floor,
The things that I see, bring back memories of yore,
The visions are hazy, so long in the past,
I can picture the faces, but not the names of the cast.

I see some wickets, a cricket bat and a ball,
That brings back a memory that I recall,
Of a crumbling wicket that was taking spin,
And the tense excitement when their last man came in.

ThereÆs my old wooden racquet, with strings made from gut,
It looks as though, some have been cut.
The tennis match evenings enjoyed at the club,
Then a walk down the road for a last drink at the pub

I find an old football, made from real tanned leather,
It really could stand all kinds of weather,
I hear the roar of the crowd, as we run out to play,
It seems as if it was just yesterday.

ThereÆs an old pair of roller skates, so tried and trusted,
But the wheels wonÆt revolve now, because they are rusted.
An old pair of running shoes, their spikes still gleaming,
I see that hundred yard sprint, and carry on dreaming.

L. D. Westwood

A Mistake

He slinks about the street
Like vermin in a sewer,
Offering misery and torment
In his little packets of sweets.

He preys on the pathetic and vulnerable,
Like a hawk on a feeble sparrow.
He keeps his lavish lifestyle
By plying his evil trade.

But there comes a time
When he gets caught out,
Not by the law
But by his own guilt.

Seeing the tragic end
Of one of his young punters,
He opens his eyes . . .
And finally sees what he has done.

Family and friends desert him,
He is now so alone,
With drooping shoulders and solemn eyes,
He wants to put right the wrong.

Vanessa Moore

Memories Of Daniel

One day he came into this world to fill your hearts with joy,
A little bundle, full of love, this was your precious boy.

He stole your hearts, he stole your lives, he captured everything.
You never knew of so much love, this tiny child could bring.

You thought you had it all, you thought your life complete,
Until the angels came one night and kissed his tiny cheek.

Heartache, pain and misery you felt upon that day.
Because God had chosen Daniel and he could no longer stay.

Remember that he suffered none, he only closed his eyes.
He plays beside the other babes somewhere in paradise.

When you've finished crying, when your grieving's done.
Put the smile back on your face, you had a champion.

Sandra Robson

Transitory Dream

I saw her etched against a mist of muses,
a rose of haunting, lingering beauty,
to whom my latent feelings came alive
with hopes her life to share in love and care.

Such desires, I knew, were only dreams
for there were ethical restraints,
voiced by that inner voice—that forbids
all thoughts of such encounters.

Its message clear and final.
Your lives can never unify,
so to reality return—and there
not lament the passing of your dream.

Her image by my will I exorcised,
dismissing her forever from my mind
but still the questions linger on
Did she ever care for me?
or even know my presence?

A. Sheehan

Parted Union

Alone I tread our separate ways,
apart now in the space of time,
For I have yet to understand,
how you have distanced our years together.

Feet now twice confused as I
shamble through the sad, wet stones,
That once had glimpsed our ecstasy
and now reflect the remnant
In shards of fractured light.

Deep nurtured in soft needled pain,
entangled in these greening ways,
I seek your laughter, soft as this,
the rainburst drenching of my soul.

And as wet solace speeds away,
I turn away in haste to miss,
Than risk again this liquid hurt,
the parted venom of your tongue.

Michael Millo

"Entrenched in Duncee"

"The banners of the beginning and the end are crossing,
On an overgrown passage in the pinions of time,
Straining at the ever fluent circumference,
Collapsing back to the corporeal centre,
Yet neither yield as is convention,
Weathered faces incapable of retreat,
These sons of Somme again are marching,
Blood flows down a red–veined stone,
And he hath cast it at his brother,
Strangers in this land of plenty,
Where grasses rise as is the order of the age,
And polished harvesters lie motionless by the verge,
Not one can see this passing hour of daylight
Will surely never come this way again."

Patrick Treacy

Dublin—Through My Window

Four a.m. rolls in the dawn,
And with it shades of soft bright light,
From my window I feel her yawn,
Standing proudly a peaceful sight,
But soon that lovely silence breaks,
No more the sound of birds at song,
Instead commotion overtakes,
And carries on the whole day long,
Until at last the darkness falls,
And oh!—it is a wondrous sight,
From out my window no blocks or walls,
Instead a spread of endless light.

At dawn, through night her beauty's found,
Without her people, without a sound!

Fiona Ni Chochlain

Cutting Deeper

She has time to reflect,
watching the blood flow from her pale, delicate skin,
A lonely isolated battle she tries to win.
Desperate cries from the secrets she hides,
her life in ruins on a downhill slide,
as a child cruelly tormented,
far too young to bear,
the desolation with no one to care,
painful memories too strong to fight,
one slash with a razor puts it to flight,
time to reflect, as her blood runs free,
releasing her pain of which no one can see.
Incestuous torture she has endured.
Into pornography she was lured,
self mutilation is her only way,
to help her through another day,
her cries for help, no one to tell,
a quick release from her inner hell.

Susan Brennan

The Refugee

What am I doing?
Looking out at the cold?
Watching for the sunshine,
Waiting to be told.

What am I doing?
Looking at TV.
Waiting for my papers.
Waiting for my family.

What can I be doing?
I'm looking at the war,
Waiting to go home,
But, home isn't home anymore.

This good land gave of its charity.
Here we have hope, so politicians agree.
Begin to think about us.
The worlds family, the refugee.

Betty Van Dusschoten

Lost Friends

The wind is up again!
More pounding for the trees
that brace themselves again the fury.
October hurricanes—
Brought down majestic trees
that stood for countless years enduring!

Can we have roused some anger in the seasons—
Does global warming claim macabre revenge?
Proud forests cut down without reason!
Can the Earth withstand—
Is this the end?

Was once this book of words
that I hold in my hand—
A friend?

Kris Ife

At A Loss

I opened my mouth
not knowing I was saying good-bye
I should have known
women should behave the way they are trained

You said nothing
not knowing you were saying good-bye
and not trained to know

The rest is silence
in which I now watch my words

So
there we are:
Out of joint—cursed spite
for as long as neither words
nor silence
will set it right

Ulrike Wittenborn

Darkness

In liquid form, oozing around,
Closing in on life, drowning reality.
Becoming impersonal, people. Objects.
Relief as it grips. Numbing.

Intensity, feelings echo the depth
Of the nothingness, heightened as shadows
cast from the setting sun, looming.
Loss into grief, conscience becomes guilt.

Solitude, bitter and sweet,
Silence chills loneliness to horror.
Hauntingly beautiful the gloom soothes.
Visions spring up, in light never imagined.

The smooth blanket, gliding, flowing silk.
Warmly enfolding, comforting.
A return to the blackness, once a whole world.
Protected in a dark cocoon.

Elizabeth Kirby

Denied Love

I lived to see you every day,
to see our face, your eyes and more,
but it seems now football's our only goal,
as we are not together anymore.
It only lasted one magical day,
and for you it seemed like the only way.
You asked me out a year ago,
and I gave you a very definite no,
but through the year, I saw I was wrong,
because now I hear you in every song.
I was so stupid, I lost my chance,
and now you won't give me any second glance.
Only my feelings keep telling me how,
I am so sad and lonely now.

Susie Mahon

Death Will Come To Find

I gaze an eye upon your face,
I wonder why death chose you to chase.
I search for life left by mistake,
But none is found, none can be seen to wake.

Living this life, waiting for death,
Is this what is meant by a final breath?
Do we cast our lives upon the waves,
And sit, to wait, to be buried in graves?

Are our lives hunted by death?
Are we all waiting for our single last breath?
Will we cast our net wide away,
Or shrink and shirk and hide for a day?

Humans cannot borrow the wisdom of tomorrow.
We must live life now,
Like a child take a step at a time,
Because all too soon death will come to find.

Kathryn Brown

Snow

The postbox gulps snow. Its times
have disappeared.
From the window-ledge whiteness

descends in a flurry
into whiteness below.
The lane became a wedding at midnight

today branches bend
under their snow-weight.
We wait

for these burdens of light
archetypes of white.
The crow's dark messages

have been confused—
white spaces live inside us.
And now the numbers on clocks and calendars

are buried in whiteness
we pretend to know
where all this time has gone to.

Tricia Corob

Great News

"We'd like to make an announcement", said our son and his
lovely young wife,
"We've something exciting to tell you, it's something that
could change our life!
You're going to be Granny and Granddad", they proudly said
with a grin,
Then they sat back and smiled at each other, to wait for the
news to sink in!

You could have knocked us down with a feather, we never
expected that,
For the chances of that happening this year, I'd have gladly
eaten my hat!
All my friends who are Grannies I've envied, I'd hinted as
much to my son,
But I'd almost given up hoping, that some day I might be one.

Now I'm knitting like there's no tomorrow, the needles stood
idle for years,
Since the early days of our marriage when I knit for my own
little dears.
I drool over baby clothes displayed in the shops, won't mind
if it's pink or blue,
As long as it's got twenty fingers and toes, either sort will do!

You would think that 'twas me who's expecting, but I'm glad
that it's her and not me,
'Cos I've been there, done that, and enjoyed it, now it's on
with the family tree.
So I wear a smug grin now when I meet my friends, no longer
an aboran,
And I'm counting the weeks and the days and the hours,
when they'll make me such a proud Gran!

Margaret Leach

'Life'

As I sit here I wonder, where does it go?
As I watch in silence, the sea ebb and flow.
The coming of dawn, the red setting sun
The start of a new day, the previous one done.

Chimes of the church bells see the new year in
Summer, Winter, Autumn and Spring—
Have characteristics known to us all
A snowdrop's whiteness, radiant colours in 'The Fall'.

The birth of a baby—new life has begun.
Childhood and adolescence signal times of fun.
Adulthood is soon with us—the years fly by
Whilst the leaves on the trees rustle and sigh.

They tell their own stories, as does the sea
Tales of past generations unbeknown to me.
I smile at memories, my laughter lines show
As I sit here and wonder—where does it go?

Deborah Harriet Jones

When The World Was Young

When the world was young my love,
when the world was young—
when mornings were crystal bright
and the air was sweet,
and all the future dazzled at my feet
when the world was young.

When the world was young my love,
when the world was young—
when each new day seemed to take so long
to come, yet every fleeting hour sped by
before it had begun,
when the world was young.

When the world was young my love,
when love was fresh and new,
and all that mattered on this earth
was being close to you,
oh for that rainbow once again
where my dreams, like stars were strung,
that beautiful distant fragment of time
when all my world was young.

Gerald A. Fewkes

Mysteria

A lonely day, oh, hold me dear, the ochre leaves are falling—oh
The trees have spoken to the wind in voices we will never know
In falling snow a diamond glints, the rains are overflowing—oh
The shadows of a million march yet know not where
   they're going—oh
The sunset is as sunrise, dear, the moments are forever—oh
The frosty kiss of morning dew is gentle as we shiver—oh
In breathless wonder, silent awe, the heart beats as it pleases—oh
Intoxicating petals float upon embracing breezes—oh
The memory is fleeting, dear, the hunger in the dining—oh
A passage writ in emerald hand with rainbow underlining—oh
The lightning always just beyond yet ample to be blinding—oh
A constant whim depends upon the magic you are finding—oh
Remember dear, this distant day when wind and
   voice were lovers—oh
Immortal was your every thought, the hopes and dreams
   you cover so
A midday, dear, a midnight clear
The shadowed boughs are calling—oh
Recall me when a tear is born
Whenever you are falling—oh.

Kris Cummings

Wimbledon 96

The crowd was hushed, the players tense,
Even birds were quiet, as they sat on the fence,
Each contestant tried, to calm his nerves,
As he prepared to face, some awesome serves.

Two weeks of strife, before this day,
Many had fallen, along the way,
Sir Cliff had sung, emphasizing his class,
Backed by lovely girls, who excel on grass.

Every fiercely fought point, met with sighs or cheers,
Faces radiating joy, or a hint of tears,
It's a game to love, the umpire cried,
That's very true, the crowd replied.

A young girl decided, to ease the tension,
By showing several things, we should not mention,
Willing hands grabbed her, and held her tight,
She had her moment, but her end was in sight.

On everyone's face, there was a smile,
It even stopped raining, for a while,
The trophy received its usual caress,
For Wimbledon Club, another success.

Malcolm Stones

Suddenly

I am flying through my memories
Waiting for my destiny
I can't think about those things that meant you to me
What if you disagree
You have still got the wrong opinion of me.

I am flying away from my past
leaving my memories, in a place you would only find if
you would not disagree and change, change your opinion of me.

I am crying and flying
Waiting for a place to hide.

Hide from my destiny, a place so suddenly dark,
including my past.

I am flying through my memories.
I think you would agree
if you should lose your pride,
and make me smile,
that to change your opinion,
would be a release,
even if it didn't lead you to me so
suddenly.

Solbjorg Liland

The Evil Soul

There we are altogether,
Enjoying time and imagining forever,
Saying things that made us laugh,
And others, so riff-raff,
Then suddenly, she came and screamed at us,
We listened to her and made no fuss,
With fear, we carried on what we did,
But there our foolish prides, inside us it hid . . .

All of a sudden, our eyes filled up with guilt,
Innocent faces, but prides behind one quilt,
Puzzled in so many ways, we couldn't collect one thought,
Certainly not the kind with the defence that fought,
But where was the faith we built throughout the years?
Was it that weak to get washed away by the tears of our fears?

Nobody knows—but here we are, all alone still in the dark,
Not an illusion, except for a sudden spark,
There it was, Marie's light that held us in its arms,
True it was; a miracle with a sorts of beautiful charms,
Charms that were sent from up above, from the Lord who
Took the evil soul away, for it was here no longer to stay . . .

Racha Daher

Love

Love is a treasure much richer than wealth
Not guarded, my friend, will be taken by stealth.
Bury it deep in the heart let God fit the lock
Time will strengthen the structure, so build on the Rock.

In sharing the increase will bring a surprise,
Invest in love wisely that's a word to the wise.
If neglected love fades, will wither and perish
But carefully tended will blossom and flourish!

Be diligent in seeking, it's not easily found
And the loss would be great if it fell to the ground!
Our heart is the custodian, our mind shows the way
Let your eyes look with clarity—bright as the day.

Find a kindred spirit, a companion for life
A friend to be trusted come peace or come strife.
The devil's deceitful, don't let him get in
So close firmly your door to keep out sin.

God breathed in Eden and man was made
His spirit then shared with a wife to be cared;
Love is a message borne on angelic wings
So keep lookin' and listenin' for blessin' and wee thin's.

Phyllis Andrade

Pharaoh Seti I: British Museum

Oh mighty Pharaoh Seti
God king of the Upper and Lower Nile
Buried in the Valley of the Kings
As a god in ceremonial style

When you looked up at the Milky Way
The celestial Nile of the sky
Did you ever doubt you would join the gods
When your time would come to die?

With all the pomp and splendour of a Pharaoh
Did the thought ever cross your mind
That although worshipped as a god
Maybe you were not divine?

When the Ka boat carried you down the Nile
None of your subjects would have thought to say
That the mighty god King of Egypt
Was only a god of Clay

Oh mighty Pharaoh Seti
Your destination was not to pass
To the celestial Nile of the gods
But your remains on exhibition under glass
    Kenneth Benoy

Have Faith

Like the sun that sets in the evening
Or the light that dims over the lake,
The hope that I have is fading
With every new war–torn day.

As the rusty red leaves fall in Autumn
Or the tears that fall down my cheek,
The people around me are falling,
Never again to speak.

The people I shared my life with,
Who, when I feel gave me their hand
Are dying, because terrorists don't know
What's more important—life or land.

When I see my country covered,
With death as its only shroud,
I wonder where the silver lining is
That should surround this cloud.

But the hope that I have is not gone yet
And like the darkness that turns into light,
Hope is the silver lining
That keeps all through the blackest nights.
    Fiona McGlinche

Two Boys At Play

Heads together, oblivious to the world
Heroes and villains with flags unfurled.
Two boys on a beach under early summer sky
Hunkered in sand, attentions focused, gulls up high.

Horizon heats up, waves come in to and fro
Little feet run hard over sand hills high and low.
Sandy eyed and sun burnt neck, rolling over and under
Crouching on slippery rocks searching for crabs and plunder.
Mountains of weeds and mosses sprawled over rock
Colourful skies reflected in little pools landlocked.

Faces never more happy on an endless day
Tides curl in round logs, where little whitewashed bones lay.
Booty collected and reclaimed from the sea
Head for home, dusty haired, good days work they all agree.

Climbing and crawling over dunes, sun sets on another day.
Up the bendy road, back to civilization where they stay.
Time for a sleepy supper, and then to bed
Dreams of pirates and treasures somewhere in the Med.
    John McLaughlin

Spring

The flowers, the lambs, the warmth of the sun,
Bring everyone out to join the fun.
The buds burst forth, the birds, they sing.
The message is there for every living thing,
It's that magical season called Spring.

The crocuses, mauve, yellow and white,
Huddle together, so close, so tight.
They stand up straight, looking proud and bold,
Because you see, they have been told,
At last, at last, it's Spring.

The daffodils, such vibrant colour,
Seem to be nodding to each other.
They bow and bend, they swing and sway,
And everyone knows they are trying to say,
Come on, come on, it's Spring.

The lambs in the fields, they gambol and prance,
They look so funny, as if trying to dance.
The honey bees too, they are so busy,
Buzzing around, until they are dizzy,
And all because it's Spring.
    Muriel Aird

Paradise Beyond

Not far from where I'm sitting
Lies an Island that time has forgotten
The houses, the sheep, the rough looking seas
Are all part of the Island called Scarp.

Time stops still for this picturesque scene
In summer time the grass is so green
Evil thoughts banished
Kind words spoken
All of this because of my dear Scarp

My life feels incomplete
My soul is bare
My heart is there
All because of the Island of Scarp.

One day I'll go
To that mysterious Isle
To fill my soul
Find my happiness
And visit my people whose spirits remain
On that sacred Isle
Rugged, windswept, misty Island of Scarp.
    Annchris MacLean

Faith

Life is long, so very long
Can I bear the painful slipping,
of existence,
once the spirit has been slaughtered
Hung drawn and quartered.

The shivering, chilling cries of the haunted
Bear no comparison,
to those that drive to escape,
from the battle deep inside
Blocked, as if no man has ever cried.

Faith can keep people going,
bring light from the depths of despair
No faith can pull you down
Faster
Make you believe in disaster.

Once the strength in you has gone,
sunk in the storms of the day
No future to see,
the battle's been won
No need to go on.
    Zoe Carter

My Dog

My beautiful dog was black
I knew I could never have her back
She died so peacefully in my arms
Although I was heartbroken, I had no qualms
She was too ill to keep her alive
The dreaded moment had to arrive
I cuddled her till the very last
When the breath had left her and her life had passed
Time does heal eventually
But she will always live in my memory

Patricia Daniels

Father

I have seen your pictures, I have heard the stories people tell
You were my father from the beginning, but a stranger you
have always been
You saw me as a little girl, but you never saw me grow into so
much more
Although you have gone from my life, you will never be
forgotten
And if I could see you face to face, I would tell you all is
forgiven

You were there when I took my first steps
You were there when I spoke my first words
Then you disappeared through the window to your future
And closed the door to your past

I need to find you and learn about the other part of me
And rediscover that someone I have never known all these years
In your eyes, I may be too young to know all the ways of this world
But, I am old enough to understand

Even though you were never there for me growing up
Just knowing that you are my father will always be enough

Junalyn Corre

Comfort

If you feel a snowflake fall and brush your cheek,
I'll be there, I'll be there,
If you hear a skylark trilling sweet,
I am there, I am there,
When you smell the roses musky scent,
I will be there, I will be there,
If you are lonely touch my empty chair,
I'll still be there, I'll still be there,
And if you glimpse me from the corner of your eye,
Take comfort, as my shadow passes by,
For I will always be there, I will always be there.

B. A. Hynds

"It Breaks Me Up"

You better listen to what I have to say,
life can't go on like this, day by day.
It's time to face wind and rain,
it's time to wash up some of their pain.
It breaks me up to see boys and girls who are so small,
shot down dead against a wall.

It breaks me up listening to those innocent cries,
with tears on their faces, and a question in their eyes.
There's so much pain, it breaks my heart,
think about them, give them a part.
We can give them food, maybe they need a friend,
maybe they want a family, so let's give them a hand.

You see a small child, all skin and bone,
sitting in a corner, all alone.
I wish you could see what I feel,
I want them to hold something which is real.
This is not a story, it's a shame,
this is happening, it's not a game.

You are in the perfect ocean, I know the perfect dive,
if we jump together, they will have the perfect life.

Daniel Cauchi

Wanderings

Walking in the woods on Sunday afternoon
can lead to Tuesdays . . . Fridays . . .
as the dog chases sticks.
A twisted bough recalls a party and a favourite friend
until a footprint, heavy, causes me to think:
Beyond the trees that guard the path
could lie a treasure—if I had the will to check;
Or danger—so I send my men to flush it out
by throwing sticks which seem to fly for miles.
My shoulders are broader here.
The sun upon a brook winks and I stop
to drink the beauty of the ladies bathing
proudly naked until I skulk away
startled by a friendly greeting and another dog.
All too soon tarmac is regained—
Ordered houses, bills to pay, Sunday afternoon.

John Andrew Crawford

The Beast Of The Storm

The chill upon the air cools the fire in my veins,
A beast held check within is sated when it rains.

The turmoil in my heart echoed in the raging skies,
The anguish within my soul beheld within my eyes.

Standing beneath the weeping heavens my tears become as rain,
For I need to know, before it goes; how do I end this pain?

But the hollow skies are empty now, the birds return once more.
The air is clear, the world is bright, yet I turn from the open door.

Again I pace the world of pain, the plains of hurt within my brain,
And, alone, my mind my home, I await the returning rain.

Daniel Green

What Is Love?

It comes from beyond
Somewhere deep down inside,
It's a feeling so strong
One that you could never hide.

It comes from the heart
It pounds in your chest
It's a feeling so strong
Above all the rest,
Every beat, every motion
Could pass any test.

It feels so strong
It feels so deep and true,
It can blind and change the inner you.

Who knows how it starts, how it lives or grows?
But you know when it's there.
When it feels deep and special and ever so real
You know you're in love
and you know that it's true.

Joanna Jane McCudden

A Lady And Her Dog

She stands a silhouette atop the hill
Poised as if at unseen artist's will
She doesn't move, 'tis though she's made of stone
Yet there is life about that figure standing there alone
But she is not alone for sentinel at her side
Her faithful friend her dog and trusted guide
'Tis though she gazes at the scene below
And drinks in all its beauty that she can never know
Her face is wrapped in secret thought
A smile escapes—her hair is caught
By dancing breezes passing by
her faithful dog is heard to sigh
For it seems as though he understands
Yet cannot let her know
That he will never fail her wherever she may go
And standing bravely smiling she sees within her mind
That which her eyes cannot embrace
For she is blind.

Joy R. Wright

Frustration

A pulling and twisting of nerves,
pressing in on my mind until there is nothing else.
My need for a release is great.
Pent up emotion building inside;
a turmoil, brewing and burning,
poisonous in its increase.
This impotency is a physical thing,
an animal rucking and clawing
until I reach melt down.
Limits o'er passed,
primeval screams tearing at my core,
and tormenting my senses.
Evasion is longer an option
as I am devoured by my demons.
Possessed and agonized
I meet oblivion with eager arms
and a desperate desire.
As if a lover I tenderly embrace death
and welcome his icy kiss.

Mandie Wright

Autumn By Moonlight

Gently swaying trees surrounded by a silvery silence
Comforting by starlight.
The moon, weaving her halo of mystery,
Benignly shining on softly–shadowed trees
Spectral shades of Autumn by moonlight.

Slivers of slanting moonbeams
Tinting scurrying creatures of the night
Scampering through the depths of fallen leaves,
Scattering them like a brilliantly–pattered Autumn Snowstorm,
Only to fall again, softly, deeply–lying
Silvered orange, brown, yellow, red.
Colourful shades of Autumn dying.

The stark trees sway but slightly—
Embarrassed . . .
Their crowning glory severed, shorn by an icy–fingered wind.
Their tresses at their feet in solemn mute appeal,
For death strikes harshly in Autumn.

Pamela M. Ramsey

Life Is An Experience

When you make up in the morning after the night before—it's
    an experience
After nine months you bare a child—it's an experience
Oh you'd think you'd learn by other people's mistakes

War after War—life after life—it's an experience
Disease taking hold—people growing old—it's an experience
Nations starving—millions dying—criminal activity—
    politicians lying

Oh you'd think man who creates life—he himself could end
    atrocitites and strife
First kiss—first touch—if only you'd been shown
If you'd never experienced it—you never would have known

Artificial light in the dead of night—it's an experience
Poison and cures we want more—it's an experience
We've learnt too much for our own good—nuclear races we
    never should

Back-stabbing and deceit—old ladies getting beat
Don't you think it's time humanity laid down the law if you
    step out line—you'll do it no more

Army, Navy, R.A.F.—Communist—Right Wing or Left
It's about time we secured our future knowing that it was a
    bloody past
Save the beauty of the world—stop the butcher and try and m
    make it last

Armies marching—dogs barking—children crying—there's no
    denying—it's an experience
Nuclear explosion—passing a motion—spending a penny—
    stuck in a jenny
IT'S AN EXPERIENCE OF LIFE.

C. G. Sanderson

Special Mums

Your mum is someone special,
Somebody who cares,
She's always there for you,
A goddess that shares
her feelings with you.

She makes you feel better,
When you are feeling down,
She nurses you, she feeds you
even though her money's tight sometimes,
You always come first in her life.

Do you feel bad when you ignore what she tells you to do?
When you cause a quarrel
she runs away from you
crying, aching with anger
But she doesn't disown you.

So why does she feed you?
Nurse you?,
Clothe you?,
Why . . . ?
Because she loves you!

Claire Phillips

Daughter Of Egypt
(A Tribute To The Builders Of The Pyramids)

Daughter of Egypt, how you sigh, the long hard days drift
    slowly by,
In heat and dust you toil and strain, come morrow's dawn
    you'll toil again,

Brown sturdy limbs and pretty face, slight of build with
    natural grace
All too soon your youth will fade, for Pharaoh's whim you will
    have paid.

Khufu sits on Egypt's throne, God King of his Memphite home,
His ego he must satisfy, before the shades of death draw nigh,

A mighty mound of stones will rise, and point in triumph to
    the skies,
This monument will grace the ages, and inscribe Egypt on
    history's pages,

No one remembers you my maid, or wonders at the price you paid,
Your flesh is one with Egypt's sands, your bones are touched
    by curious hands,

Khufu's tomb stands to this day, "But who was Khufu?"
    tourists say,
Mere flesh and bones, dear maid, 'tis true, in death he is but
    one with you.

T. Cartwright

Juxtapose

At the theatre,
On a steamy afternoon
Queued up in front of the booking window
Soaked in warm odour of humanity
I grasped a transient moment
Where life had hidden its stunning actuality

Promise of a cool afternoon
Soft music, lilting music
Pop-corns and cokes
Twilight, charged with a vague, trivial expectancy
To see and be seen.

This queue, a civilising restraint
On vulgar sinews does, nevertheless, permit
Irk of the man in front
Distrust of the one behind
Place and time tell after all
The haves from the have-nots

I inched my way up to the bloke
Ticking away sleepily at the seating plan
I put a fiver out; he mumbled and slammed the window shut.
Sold out!

Ijaz Haider

SPLIT

There were two of you. A partnership, a couple.
A team sharing a vision of the future.
Uniting against problems—as yet unseen.

Your nucleus appeared secure. Dynamic, unbreakable.
Strong.
Where did this whirlwind of energy disappear.
With such optimism, why did it all go wrong?

The insidious erosion of trust. Apprehension, doubt.
Suspicion that fed off the clouded circle of certainty,
gorging on the precarious equilibrium.

Uncontrolled tirades of anger.
Masking the guilt caused by prohibited alliance.
Emotions spinning in an abyss of never–ending hurt.
Too late for the bliss of ignorance.

Was our bond so tenuous? Superficial, weak.
Easily broken so that our mutual confidence was undermined
by the wounding words that were spoken.

The unappreciated sanctuary of home. Dissatisfaction, derision.
Discontent like a tangible black cloud of comparison
with your other lifestyle attempt.

Debatable freedom is granted. Separate, divide.
Release from the apparent constraint of family love
to everlasting confusion from lack of inner peace.

Ellis O'Brien

The Blessings Of A Garden

To own a garden is a treasure.
Which fills so many delightful hours.
Planning the landscape is quite a pleasure.
And finding the numerous contrasts of flowers.

Something to plan the whole fear round.
A change of scene in no short measure
Is something that I have always found.
Relaxing for my leisure.
A gift of flowers from one's own garden
The colour and fragrance so sublime.
Can bridge a gap or beg a pardon.
Because it's measured in one's own time.

Hanging baskets and patio pots,
Add essence of summer colour.
Whilst lawns and trees provide
The backdrop for the birds to hover.
The birds if encouraged, will take their fill.
And bees their nectar enjoy.
Insects meander at their will.
Whilst butterflies continue in their joy.

Eileen M. Leake

In A Gentle Place

Somewhere in a gentle place,
Somewhere around her smiling face.
Her bold, blue eyes did shine,
I'd entered in the happy time.

Among the clouds do ravens soar,
And night, cold black velvet wore.
The feeling was all but mine,
I knew, I'd felt the happy time.

How the cool glen air does blow,
And spirits praises awake and grow.
The sway of autumn hair felt fine,
The sweet smell of the happy time.

And when long distance knows the pain
And the sun in the west will fade to rain.
The brief clock of life will chime,
Announces the start of the happy time.

Bright yellow the sight of some men.
Who look over and sigh of when.
They knew a face of sight divine,
To watch only for a happy time.

K. D. Rafferty

Who Am I?

Who am I?
I am who I am
accept me as I am
and I shall be so giving to your every need
Allow me to be me
And I will always be there for you
I am me
In the present past and future
Time cannot change me
I can only be enriched by the presence of time
given to me
With this I shall be allowed to be me.

Jenny Gudmundsson

Technological Divorce

The system has crashed!
Main frame obstructing on–line partners
Buttons pushed, this one, that one
What the hell is wrong?
The system has crashed!
Stagnant communication, locked by inaction
Partners waiting for a result
Statistical gathering, feeding in data,
to achieve a solution.
The system has crashed!
No response! How long no response?
Time unknown
Frustration now at impotence
All lines are down.
Blocked, no button left untried
The system has crashed!
Should we wait it out
or re-boot and clear the screen?
The system has crashed!
No communication.

Fiona Leslie

Down The Pit

While down in the pit a big black cloud
Rumbles across the midnight sky,
Down in the pit,
Men on their hands and knees,
Dust getting down their throats and on their chest,
The smell of rats as they run around,
Down in the pit,
You see a spark of light in the distance,
A spark of light, sending a gleaming glow all around,
Men sit down to eat their lunch,
While rats sit around watching,
While down in the pit,
A cage comes to take the men back to the surface,
Back to breathe some clear air, and take a good bath,
Then it's early to bed,
Ready for another day down in the pit.

Elaine Wilkinson

Reflections

Do not step on my grave young child,
to plant flowers by my side,
I am the glisten in snowflakes falling,
I am the happiness in the person who smiled,
I am the warmth in the sunshine,
I am the colour in the blooming flowers,
I am the sparkle of dew in the morning,
I am the taste of sweet red wine,
I am the tenderness in a mother's love,
I am the deep, deep blue in the sky,
I am the joy and harmony in music,
I am the peace in the sign of the dove,
I am the breeze through the trees,
I am the cool of a stream in summer,
I am the peace in a baby's sleep,
I am the calm of the seas,
I am the laughter of years before,
Abide with me Lord, for I'm earthbound no more.

Sarah Layhe

Woman In Black

I see her sitting alone in black,
   a dead animal draped across her right arm.
She sits staring into space, dreaming,
her dark clothes contrasting with her pale face and red lips.
Glasses clinking, chat, piano playing soft slow tunes,
an occasional laugh from a party of business men.
She's alone, dressed for a funeral in a black veil.
But I notice her wedding ring. Is she widowed, or just waiting?
The animal still draws my attention, its magnetic eyes watching
   me, watching it.
Diamond brooch, fancy hat and that . . . lifeless fur.
Her blood red nails clutch the umbrella, it too, as black as night.
Face done up for a night out, but there, she sits alone.
Dreaming.
part 2 (voice of woman)
flowers, cars, bowing black heads in the grave yard.
Right now they grieve over a life that only I knew.
In the church yard now, wearing black.
They think, pray, cry, without me;
mother, father, Charles and little Chloe.
They watch, watch the miniature coffin.
They will leave the grave regretting, regretting, regretting.

Kirsten Dorman

Wrapped Up In Brown Paper

Wrapped up in brown paper
is the bottle in his hand.
Sitting on a bench,
surveying the land.
Watching the people
go about their day.
Swigging from his bottle,
drinking his worries away.
Not thinking of the future.
Not remembering the past.
Now he has his drink at last.
No worries, no problems, no fears.
A bottle of wine and a can of beer.
Sitting alone with his brown paper bag,
his box of matches and his hand–rolled fag.
Not bothering anyone with his bottle of booze.
Always being hassled, always being moved.

P. J. Raven

My Mirror Of Disguise

I would like a special mirror, I could look into and see.
Not the way I really look, but how I used to be.
Those funny little lines around my mouth and eyes.
Would disappear completely in my mirror of disguise.

The teeth that now are lengthening, would again be pearly white.
The golden hair would look so neat and never look a fright.
My waistline would shrink back, to measure twenty four.
Instead of twenty eight, or maybe even more.

No blotches on my skin, no cellulite on my thighs.
I would always be young and beautiful in my mirror of disguise.
Just think of all the confidence my mirror would inspire.
The trouble is all other mirrors would prove it was a liar.

Elizabeth Wren

Laid Up

I've got a cold, my head's really sore;
My throat is quite dry and feels a bit raw.
I can't get to sleep 'cos I cough in the night;
I'm dosed up so much I'm as high as a kite.
My eyes water up as I'm trying to sneeze;
I walk up the stairs and my chest starts to wheeze.
There's a flow from my nose and I can't really smell;
I'm not very happy—I'm sure you can tell.
But I know it'll go in a days time or two
And then I'll be fit to come and see you.
'Cos it can't be much fun for you sitting in bed . . .
When you've fractured your pelvis and broken your leg!

Susan Davies

Let Me Talk To The Maiden Of Tomorrow

Will I pay with plastic to breathe fresh air . . . will justifiable
   murder seem quite fair
Will I ride a battery bike and talk to who I like
Will we cruise around in bubbles with no more depression troubles
Will we worship vegetation and have drugs for each occasion
Will professional impresarios teach young lovers to speak
While learning to party will be the only tuition of the week
Let me talk to the maiden of tomorrow whose cupped hands
   will toss the destiny of the dice
Will she turn men into mice . . . invent new grains of rice
Will scientific creation seem unsatisfactory or just plain ol'
   matter factory
Will we be forgetful of history as tomorrow's child will say to
   me did they once regulate sexuality
Will we live in even more violent times where everyone
   commits boredom rimes
Will we exist on the ecstatic edge between seduction and violence
Death and theatre flies trapped in a spider's web of silence
Will we live in tiny cupboards stacked on top of malls
Will we make love in cubicle stalls
Will the president of the world live in Hollywood
Will everything seem like Florida, cartoon heaven, or 7-Eleven
Will we never meet, talk through the T.V. screen and forget to
   sing or talk without a machine
Will no one be fat or weird looking
Will no one need remain content without the perfect face . . .
   let me talk to the maiden of tomorrow

Jennifer Lee Potter

Human Prospects

What then, if life be found on Mars?
What difference will that make to earth–born folk?
We cast about but do not understand
that Test–tube babes no creation prove.
From muddle to puddle ourselves we toss
not to resolve but new problems create.
What prospects lure us in this plastic–computer age,
this age of cancer, blood and heart disease?

This is the question dollars cannot answer
not even in sixty and four thousand measure.
But answer it we must if only for survival's sake.
Humans not forever in this environment shall live,
where pollutants, incapacitants with happenstance combine
to inveigle with phoney, instant pleasure which delight and destroy.

Be not afraid to name them all, if you be Squire.
In truth, familiar items they already are
to toddlers, adolescents and teens.
They kill and maim, destroy, malform the unborn.
Let computers across the globe, with data fed, combine
to tell how soon destructive humans will themselves destroy.

Nelson H. Charles

Images

I watch, I see and don't believe,
   My ancient mind just can't conceive.

Yet youngsters take it in their stride,
   Visions flicker in coloured tide.

Children laugh and scream with joy,
   Harks me back to a favourite toy.

Pleasures felt exact the same,
   Truly life becomes a game.

Still I look and still I stare,
   So vastly diff'rent than yesteryear.

I marvel at technology,
   With unreserved apology.

Past is lost, forever gone,
   Now is here, for everyone.

Future beckons inexorably,
   To the realm of Virtual Reality . . .

Colin D. Evans

The Goblins

Listen Children, gather round,
To hear about those ghostly sounds,
The ones you hear all through the night,
Are goblins waiting for a bite.

Those creaks and groans you hear so late,
Are Goblins washing up their plates,
they wait until you're fast asleep,
to nibble toes between the sheets.

Tasty morsels, little toes,
Tastier even than your nose,
So if you hear the house start creaking,
hide beneath the sheets, no peeking.

Daylight sends the goblins running,
Once again you've proved too cunning,
Your nose and toes still firmly fixed,
Even with those Goblin tricks.

This warning is a timely one,
To stop them eating you for fun,
So safety first and burn that light,
To see you, always, through the night.

Jo Curthoys

Oh Lonesome Me

When we were surrounded
By all those lights
We walked along those old sights
The air was cold and damp.
But our hearts were filled with warmth
It was a moonlight night with a cold breeze

I held your jacket
You held me close, when I was cold
And all the warmth inside our hearts

Were out in the open now
The wind and my hair
Blew into your face
You brushed it back
You pressed your warm lips against mine

I felt a fluster and the earth moved
For you and me
I looked away and looked back
And you had gone
Oh I don't know where I belong
But I know it won't last long.

Nicola Cook

A Last Farewell

Such aching sadness fills my heart, the bitter tears I can't restrain
My son has gone, these are dark days, I'll never see his face again
Or touch his hand, or hear his voice, or see his happy smiling eyes
It breaks my heart, for now I know, that we have said our last
goodbyes.
No more he'll walk with dog and gun, through meadows wet
with morning dew
Or see the early rising sun, with glory gild the world anew
Or watch the flocking pigeons rise, or hear the pheasants
raucous cry
A countryman, he loved all this, I weep why did he have to die
He loved so much the Scottish moors, all heather clad neath
Autumn skies
To tread again the springing turf, and hear the grouses'
distinctive cries
Go back! Go back! It calls in vain, but this he'll never hear again
And on the hills and rolling moors, the snow that icy winter brings
Falls soft and through its mantling shroud, there comes the
sound of many wings
Skein upon skein of geese appear, to fill the heavy leaden sky
Their muted voices seem to be, from them, to him, a last
goodbye.
And with them now, his spirit flies, from earth bound pain, at
last is free
And all my prayers and tears I know, can never bring him back to me.

Kathleen Davis

Life is a Journey

Life could be long, or life could be short
So let's be happy with what we have got.
If we could learn to live our lives
To help each other, and to be wise
To share one's burdens and heavy load
As we travel along life's common road
It does not matter our caste or creed
To help someone in their hour of need
To sow some kindness wherever we go
To help someone we do not know
Then God's blessings will be on you and me,
As we wend our way to eternity,
We will then know that life's too short
And just be happy with what we have got.
Then the heavenly skies will be always blue,
And the blue birds of happiness will
always fly with you.

W. Williamson

Upon This Shore

Upon this shore of windswept time,
That with the sun, does in exuberance shine,
The day of beauty to be seen,
In golden land and shimmering sea,
The cloud of white, the sky of blue,
All this seen through light of dawn,
A bird that sings at break of morn,
And natures harmony shows a scene,
With silver rain, that sounds a rhyme,
Upon this shore of windswept time.

Nicholas Simon Monaghan

The Greatest Gift

It's hard to celebrate Christmas, when you're feeling so
confused,
Especially when the meaning has often been abused,
He made sure of everything, all things were planned,
But the world just didn't listen, they couldn't understand.

Yes it's hard to believe, with a world so full of sorrow,
When some of us don't know how to cope with tomorrow,
So many want to be loved, a thought that's often craved,
If only they could get it, so many would be saved.

Let's shed some light on Christmas, what does it all mean?
Many years have past, so much has been unseen,
Please remember when you're hanging stockings on the wall,
That Jesus really is the greatest gift of all.

Samantha Sutherland

Oh My Sweet Lady

Oh my sweet lady, what more can I say?
For I do love thee, beyond care, beyond price
For who cares more for me, if I needed to know?

You lived your life, filled with truth and grace,
And from the offer of your life,
God was able to offer another (life), that of His Son,
So that the hopes of God, of man, might really be one.

Filled with truth and grace, you came to show the way,
To behold the beauty of love and wisdom and truth,
The importance of our motives, and of how we live our lives.

Oh my sweet lady, what more can I say?
Take myself, my hopes and my cares,
And show me how to live, to love and to care,
For your life shows to us the essence of such beauty is to share.

How to comprehend, to contemplate
The magnitude, the treasure of such a life
Is all I ask to do, for the prize in such a sacrifice,
Is more than worth the asking it's For The Telling.

Oh my sweet lady, what more can I do or say, sing or pray?
To live is to love, to love is to give, oh my sweet lady.

John Atherton

Southern Coast

Early morn,
Just past dawn,
Sky dusted,
Village flustered.

Leaves falling from Autumn trees,
Water rippling with the breeze,
This village owns a mysterious past,
Boats sailing with a free flapping mast.

Fishermen continuing their everyday lives,
Returning home late to their dutiful wives,
Tired from working with great effort all day,
Awaiting to receive their rewarding pay.

This village appears to be desperately poor,
Working so hard their feet so sore,
Fishermen's success cannot be told by you nor me,
This secret is held at the depth of the sea.

Louise Ross

At The Beach Hut

At the beach hut where kites rule
And Nick picks his way over the dunes
To the women, reading,
Widows now, taking tea at three,
Talkin' about how things used to be.
Watchin' the white horse,
Come gallopin', gallopin', like the calvary of old,
Only to retreat on the orders of General Moon Face
As a ship sailed into view.
Others contented themselves trawling the pools
Purchasing their nets at the shop,
Together with their ices,—for leaving lookin' like lobsters,
With the sound of the seas ringing in their ears.
As the women packed both brolly and seat
Leaving poor old Pete down among the driftwood.

Andrew J. Fry

Private Clegg

Violent emotions confound the truth.
Reasonable men confound reason.
What is truth?
Truth is manufactured like window sealant,
Pliable, sticky, filling a gap.
More available, just squeeze harder.
It will last, no danger of leaks.
Nothing can pass through it, only violence.
What is justice?
Justice is solid, established, hard as a rock.
Cutting like flint into the soft belly of all it comes in contact with
Nothing is harder than justice, nothing can soften its edge.

John Stirling Watkins

The Monthly Meeting

They sat and talked of this and that
of who should bake, and who should chat
to all the people they hoped would come
to spend their money on home-made bread and honey.

But what is this I'm hearing now
how shall the vote go on acid rain,
and is it right to support the claim
that thirty pounds is far too much
to bury Granddad in the church
where his family have always lain.

Peggy, madam chair, calls to order
all the ladies there,
our delegates must be sure, when at
the Albert Hall they do appear,
all is clear on yeas and nays
so all can say, well done the
women of this constitution
three cheers for Pembridge Women's Institution.

Dawn Rowe

A Sonnet For Sarah

And now it's time for Sayonara
To the lovely Ault called Sara(h)
Her parting leaves us with a void
Sayonara's such a final word
We sure will miss her dulcet tone
As she calls us o'er the phone
Her husband is a clever cunning fox
He stole that gal from off a chocolate box
The Travel Agents say it is a must
To visit on this American beauty rose
Who wears it all without the slightest pose
As long as there are stars in Heaven's vault
We'll ne'er forget the gorgeous Sarah Ault.

Terence J. McGowan

Unrequited Love

It's never too late to-day to
Talk of love that's true
So I will wave my magic wand to
transport my love to you
Transcending all your fears, conventions and portents
To hold you in its arms so warm each
cold and lonely night.

But then how could this be, no
magic wand have I, too late to tell you of my love,
"Too late," I hear you cry.
With aching heart the door I close
Ne'er to relate
This awakening in my heart a love for you alone.

And now I have but dreams to dream
No magic wand need I,
No mystic powers, no spells to weave,
No tricks to catch the eye,
And in my dreams I kiss your lips
and lay you down beside me,
Only to awake and find too late you have escaped me.

Nora Wilks

Cautionary Tale

So Eliot wrote some smutty verse,
And now what is indeed far worse,
Julius says they're puerile, racist, coarse—
The critics, reverent, sad, what's worse
Fear T.S. will topple from his perch,
And downward spiralling will lurch.
So, beware, young man, what you write down
You may dislodge your laurel crown.

Fiona Hiern-Cooke

Old Age

It comes to us all at one time or another,
To sons and to daughters, fathers and mothers.
No one wants it, least of all me
But we cannot avoid the future you see.

We go through our lives we cannot see ahead.
We then fall in love and soon we are wed.
Next there's a child, the years go so fast.
Were's my life gone? Where is my past?

Now Mother's a nanny, my grand-daughter is born.
I look in the mirror; my face wrinkled and worn.
What happens now? I've no one to care;
No one to talk to, no one to share.

Where will I live? Not here anymore.
I can't get up now to open the door.
My family's just been because I'm leaving today
For an old people's home because I'm in the way.

I hope I don't stay long and God calls me above
To live there in Heaven with people I love.
Don't think I'm complaining, I just feel a bit sad;
For the life I've got now to the one that I had.

A. Iommi

Forever

Spending time each day,
Being with you in every way.
Thoughts of you always with me,
And that's the way it will always be.
Since the first time our eyes met,
Forever more I'll never forget.
The way that you make me feel,
I can't believe your love's for real.
The beating of my love filled heart
From our beginning, from the very start.
You've always been there showing me so much love and care,
Before we met I was unaware.
That this sort of love was true,
And could be shared between us two.
You're the best thing that's happened to me,
And I hope we will always be.
So in love together,
Because my love will last forever.

Rachel Rowley

Like a Lark

Like a lark—sky high
One cannot deny that the lark
Is up on a higher level than I

Like a lark—silhouetting its mark
For sure it's up and away
So free for another day
Try as one may
The sky belongs to the lark today

Like a lark—born free to the wind
No traps of time or time to trap for
anything

Like a lark—so flightily kind
Gliding upon air stream flowing rapid
To conquer a cloud—to fly and find
Across the sky—its course it goes
Gently mapping

Like a lark—whistling to the wind
Hark and listen—how does it sweetly sing?

Kevin Watson

Jealousy and Bullying

Oh, the acid is slipping down
I must not respond, I must not fight
Even though my stomach's churning
And the sourness is turning ripe
Now the bitterness is coming up
The hatred, the harsh and the sore
left out, put to one side
It's enough to make any one feel uptight
Abomination, animosity, detestation
It still doesn't describe the hurt in me
But if I look into the future
Some day I will find the light
But what if I don't
But what if they won't
Stop me from becoming jealous
I might as well give up
There's no hope in me
But I won't, but I don't
I'll wait till the scores 10–3
To me.

Richard Evans

Beauty

My garden's bestrewn with cuckoo flowers,
Never—oh never in all the hours
Of my life have I seen such beauty
As there abounds. It is our bounden duty
To preserve the treasures that are given,
For surely they are sent to us as a gift from heaven.

Cyril F. Herbert

Painting A Picture

I stood alone in my garden
It looked so cold and bare
Imagining the picture
I would be painting there
Alone now I stand a spade in my hand
Knowing I would conquer
This desolate piece of land
So many hours of labour
Bent with aching limb
With plants and seeds
I knew my picture would soon begin
So now with tender care I'd toil
Like so many had before me
These lovers of the soil
Now I sit in my garden
Relaxing in idle hours
Enraptured by the beauty of cascading flowers
Each one gentle nods to me
Just as if to say
Oh! Have you seen the picture painted here today

Edward Stackhouse

Melissa

I can't believe that she is mine
This little girl with features fine
Her hands and feet are oh so small
I wonder how she'll ever crawl
But before too long she's on her feet
And running up and down the street
She's so perfect in every way
She brings so much joy each passing day
Into her room at night I'll creep
To watch her as she lies asleep
And when I'm feeling sad or down
Her laugh will take away my frown
Though, I often sit and wonder whether
Times like this could last forever
For she grows so fast as days go by
And soon from the nest I know she'll fly
So I cherish each moment we spend together
For I know the memories will last forever
Just like the love and the overwhelming pride
I have for my little girl who's standing by my side

Bettina Shergold

The Great Illusion

This is not that
But that is the way it is
Don't waste time on this
But live in that

At last the real from the unreal
And it's not the way round you think it is
The unreal is the real

The state is the way
The body is a means of play
Use the body to live in the state
That is there for all to know

I'll be there always.

G. C. Heath

Life

Across the sands of time the winds are softly blowing
As night follows day, each season glowing

With colours bright and gay.
The morning of our youth, chasing rainbows and the truth of life.

At noon we think we have found the secret of life and serenity.
Love, riches and a life full of plenty.
As evening draws on, life changes steadily
Slows its pace, becomes more leisurely
Until as day draws to its close, life ends

Shadows fade and new life begins bathed in glorious brilliant light
As we come from darkness into the kingdom of eternal life

Margaret Mizen

Early Walk

Sunlight shines softly down on dappled meadow,
glinting and glistening—dew making, day dawning.
Young feet through lush grass gliding—
    tapering tails of green pushing between toes unclad.
Nowhere seen is hoof or horn, 'cept their shaped impress made
    on ground rubbed flat by heavy weight.
Young ear hear shrill shriek of lark burst forth from hide,
    where five jewels lay:
    the beauty of creation in fair display waiting—
    for time to herald their show.
Scented air wafts o'er early field, young nose to perceive
    as resin aroma breaks from wrinkled trunk of tree.
Spring colours cascade across green canvass,
    scattered by hand of the Eternal Artist
    to pleasure young eye in yellow and white.
Small grey statue, motionless in thought,
    framed in nature's drama, sits poised for flight
as young heart, beating in delight—
    advances to the gate.

P. A. Goodall

Confess!

I search deep in my soul and feel but cold,
My heart is breaking there's no mistaking,
Forever breaking forever holding the pain
controls always on a hold!

The sun is rising but I keep on hiding with
pain and grief, I feel the breeze,
and fall to my knees waiting for a better life!

Reach out your hand because I am
falling in total darkness and despair, stop
me falling hold me once more, and show that you really care!

My mind is in confusion, and in total
explosiveness how can I show you
how much I'm in distress!

One day I might be happy, or one day sad
but at the end of the day all I want
is peace and happiness.
And my soul not to be stressed!

James Wood

Found An Old Dirty Note Book

Dirty and faded the dust covered old empty wordless note book,
faded and stained with time, not a word on one line,
never been used, it as a blue cover the dirty stained old faded
notebook, purchased somewhere back in time, to be used,
but it never was, the years itself, abused it causing its empty
pages to become perished, so now its empty lines couldn't be put
to any meaningful use, mind you, the note book as a title and a name,
the handy, scribbling tablet, ruled and perforated, British made . . .

R. A. Gardham

Morning Thoughts

Fresh still the dreams within my head
    As I rise to greet the day
Wondering if the way I ache
    Is the price I have to pay
Far past the witching hour
    Sweet sleep released my mind
Gone the dream so rich in power
    Real life is still unkind
Fresh the day another day
    Another life to start
Time to play it other ways
    To brighten up my heart
Is it time to make the change
    This lifestyle I Must shed
Its a must to rearrange
    Stand still and we are dead
One kick is all we get a stab at this poor pretence
A brick to be a chance to grab am I to learn some sense
Half time has come tactics change in this second half
To make it rhyme my sights are set how soon before I laugh.

C. L. Hall

The Riverside

Sitting down by the river, lazing in the sun,
people passing in their boats, having plenty of fun,
the herons are diving, catching the fish in the weir,
baby ducklings swimming, oh there is so much to see here.
A little further up, men are fishing on the bank,
all of a sudden one gets a bite, his rod he gives a yank.

Then with elegance and grace, two swans pass me by,
I throw them pieces of bread, while I'm eating my pork pie,
Canada geese come in groups, such greedy things they are,
up and down the river, they don't worry how far.
All of a sudden I jumped, sitting next to me was a mouse,
full of fear I panicked, I ran back to my house.

I looked out of my window, when it was very dark,
all that could be seen was the trees in the park,
then to my surprise, a badger ran across the grass,
he looked up and saw me, then ran so very fast.
A day I will always remember, it's time to go to bed,
and so I say goodnight, on the pillow I lay my head.

Janet M. Kilmartin

The Olympic Games

The Olympic Games are over now
The competitors have all gone home
Each one to their own country
With the medals they have won.

While others will be disappointed
That they did not win a gold or silver medal
Or a bronze one
To bring home to their country
Or to their loved ones.

To all the great competitors
That took part in the Olympic Games
Regardless of the winning or losing
May each one of them be praised
For all the effort they put into
Winning the Olympic Games.

Most of all for the great entertainment
That all of them did give
And God willing may each one of us
Live to watch it all again.

Eileen Adair

Junior Train Spotter

Eyes saucer-like and little body taut,
Like a dog on a leash, three year old waits
For his beloved train. Sharp ears detect it
in the distance—he is suffused with joy
And his five senses soon work over-time.
So much to see: passengers, signals, track,
Then the strange caterpillar glides away.
He does not hoard his happiness but shares
With staid adults his simple, childlike joy.
Stern faced drivers smile and toot a greeting.
Porters unbend and track repair men wave.
Gladness is infectious, especially when
It stems from shared emotions, quite divorced
From the petty pleasures of acquisition.

Joyce Hallmark

Just Remember—I Am Always Here

Life is a long road, we travel the way we choose
There are no directions we can either win or lose
Things may seem so very bad and the clouds are so grey
It's our friends we need—to keep the shadows at bay.
You feel nobody else can ever feel so bad
At times you seem to be driving yourself mad
With the bad thoughts that never seem to shift
But they will my friend, they will eventually lift
You must remember you are surrounded by friends
They are always there to try to make amends
Life isn't always so hard there is always someone there
So please try to remember that forever—I care.

J. Barton

June Eve

A field of corn in the month of June,
Glistening green in the evening sun,
A gentle breeze from over the hill,
Stirring the leaves above, until
Softly swaying it played with my hair,
Making it dance over here, over there,
Then tiring of me went over to you,
And up and away in a sky so blue,
Taking my thoughts with it, circling round,
Upward and over the hill it was bound.
Outward and onward into the night,
Making me wonder if one day it might,
Return them again on a warm June eve,
Whether they'd matter then, or even please,
Or like my dreams blow hither and thither
Until they are lost from me forever.

Hazel M. Lewis

Jenny In India

Far, far from here, my tall, my dark–eyed daughter
Blooms in bright cloth, a new world in her arms.
And treads the barefoot beaches of her letters,
Or dreams among the feathery palms,
While overhead the monkeys scream and chatter,
And on the blue rim of the bay,
The porpoises and dolphins cleave the water
In arabesques of play.

Will she return in summer? Will she ever
Ride the slim jet across the changing skies,
Beyond the heights where kite and eagle hover
Above an alien paradise?
The stone Gods stretch to grasp their shameless lovers,
And shadow puppets grip the wall.
Will she recall drab fields, and gun–grey rivers,
And will she come at all?

Simon Wood

Heaven Is Here

The Son of Man is the Son of God
Please don't think that rather odd
Our Father reigns in Heaven above
And we must try to share our love
As mirrors that reflect and shine
Or goblets gold that sparkle with wine
Peace serene and tranquil joy
These are meant for a little boy
And children all are what we are

The Son of God is the Father's Son
And we are men who a race must run
Through rain and snow, sunshine and leaves
Though often the journey troubles and grieves
Trial and struggle, wrestling we play
While all along we look for the day
When mental fighting will be done
And we shall serve the Holy One

These are my verses, these are my rhymes
Now we are entering golden times
And I am a poet at last.

Robert William Currie

Memories Of You!!

The first kiss like a butterfly resting on my lips
Lightly, then more insistent
To hold you close was a dream come true
May I never awake
Our love will grow will survive all things
Our bodies entwined are as one together
This love I feel takes me to the highest point of ecstasy.
And to deepest despair when we are not together.
So come let us lie together and make love in all ways wonderful
For you are my life, my reason for being, my very soul
I love you.

M. J. Polkey

Mayhap

Mayhap I'll pen a stave and save the bard from
turning in his grave to wit, I know not what
he'll think as down I lyrically sink into the
murky depths of prose I do not comprehend.

Suppose I pray to his immortal ghost
for guidance?; he may for the most deride and
laughingly inquire why to a poet I aspire? At
which my blushing pen will shake and strive to
rectify mistakes. Oh, snakes alive! what's to
become of me? I feel as if his thumb were
pressing hard and steel myself as ego scarred
fragments to shrapnel. God! this room is
wrecked, my kingdom for a broom! Oh feckless
spirit mine ascend, they noble efforts to defend
with fine and altruistic grain—mayhap
to-morrow, try again.

Ian Castree

Untitled

Curtain of love,
open up and see the light,
let down your guard,
don't put up a fight.
Let me see the love you have,
covered by the outer shell of your heart,
let's not dwell on the past
and make a step for a new start.

Corinne J. Morris

Cats

Large cat, little cat, Fatso and Friday Sootica Lizzie and Sam,
Are all friends of mine, who walk round each day
In search of left over scran.
Friday is my cat, Sootica my neighbour's
Both pampered, well fed and adored Lizzie and Sam have good
homes of their own but often walk round when bored
Little and large were once favoured pets
Until children arrived you see
Then cast out of their home, like gipsies to roam,
Their bed, some leaves under a tree
No friendly lap to purr and cat-nap
No gentle fingers to tickle their chin
Neglected and sad, things looked very bad
Till my neighbour and I took them in
Fatso sweet appealing face, gains him a friend in every place
Tho' a vagabond puss cat is he if when I have left this earthly scene
One night in the garden where moonlight gleams
A ghost is seen gliding, don't blame it on dreams
If it is followed by hedgehogs puss cat and birds
You can bet that ghost will be me.

Dora Clark

Life's Blood

When I bleed on the carpet, bleed on the staircase
Bleed on the blankets, bleed down the phone
Let me die in the morning, die in the evening
Die without whimpering, die all alone.

Make me smile without malice, laugh without crying
Whisper to my ear, give me a sign
Strength for the future, to fight and be fearless
Strength in the present for I feel so alone.

Pluck my eyes from head, replace them with gemstones
That sparkle reflections of the time when the dreams
Were not losing the fight with death and destruction
Pluck my eyes from my head, my head from my dreams.

Give me gospel, not preaching, learning and teaching
Peace and contentment, away from the streams
That bleed in the morning
Bleed in the evening
Show me quiet and safety
Let me come home.

M. N. Gilbert

Death

Come to me, my love.
Allow your silent, healing energy to caress my being.
Hold my soul in timeless sweet surrender,
So gentle, yet somehow vibrant.
In this suspended moment, I am alive,
As I have never been before.
My heightened perceptions, allow me to beat
With the rhythm of the cosmic heart.
I can breathe with the universal breath,
That is the earth, the sea, the sky.
I am free.

Debbie Wander

Black Wave

I've been trying so hard, to get you out of my head.
But I'm stuck in a groove, I'm a shivering wreck.
The black wave that follows me, is catching my stride,
I have no where to run, I have no place to hide.
I keep asking myself where the happiness went,
The laughter, just memories, that seemed heaven sent.
I just can't get up, but I don't know just why,
So I stare at the ceiling, I'm curled up so tight
It clings to me and covers me and drags me right down,
I can't move, I can't breathe, I'm just spiralling down.
It cloaks my emotions, it plays on my fears,
Questions existence, suffocates tears.
I wish there were answers to some of my prayers,
A chance of a better life, a means to an end.

Paul Holloway

Behind The Painted Smile

You hide behind your painted smile
All the hurt and all of the pain
In this circus your happy fora while
It stops you going so insane

Behind those sad and lonely eyes
You keep those memories so deep
All those times they told you them lies
That still haunt you whilst you sleep

As you bring the crowd sheer joy
You bask in the warmth of their laughter
To escape a life for years destroyed
You've now got the love you were after

The search is finally over and done
But the ghosts still rise from the past
You're tired too weak to fight or run
You play well this role for which you're cast

You hide behind your painted smile
All the hurt and all of the pain
In this circus you're happy for a while
It seems to stop you going so insane.

Stephen Mark Allwood

Mournful Stillness

Lingered a mournful stillness to be heard.
Solitude, muffled the song of the distant bird.
Left on broken hinge the tarnished rotten timbered gate.
Overgrown, your once trodden path. A destiny of dying fate
Muted forever the once ringing bell in crumbled steeple.
No longer the sounds of hymns sung by your village people.
Whistled through it the wind a coolness, the air to chill.
Interred on lone desolate forgotten distant hill.
A mournful stillness, a silent moan.
Lie the bodies marked by wilted weathered stone.
In time rendered, forgotten unkept peaceful silent grave.
Echoing the past unsung sons and daughters of the brave.
Scrolled in italics your memorable name engraved to mark your dead
A visible impression of sadness planted above your head.
Lifeless, prostrate in mournful stillness buried here.
A passing generation, forgotten loved once so dear.
Remained to stay a rubble ruin left indented to scar.
A house of God empty and barren, the landscape to mar.

Yvonne Fraser

Another Day

The sweat was pouring down from my head
This morning when I got out of bed
I had a dream that I cannot remember
But I know it was cold in the month of November
So why was I sweating?
Was I ill?
Should I go into the cupboard and take a pill?
Another day to face me ahead
I wish that I could stay in bed
But I have to get up, I got things to do
I'll put on a brave face and struggle on through
My work I can't face so should I phone in sick
I'll put on a cough it might do the trick
But I'm no use at lying so I'll need to go in
My curer today is a bottle of gin
Now I'm ready to face another day
I know it is wrong but it's the only way

Ken Godwin

The Garden Beyond

Slowly, slowly, a feeling of turning around
of being turned. Thoughts and ideals, once so
impossible, now within my grasp. Surely a false
reality being shown to me within a false situation . . . ?
The gate stands wide open—I know not which side
of it I am. Ivy blocks out the light. The shrinking
violet stands so close . . . Breaking through . . . Somehow . . .
Maybe I'll go this way—try, try to break into the
small piece of sky, beyond which anything is possible.
I see colours against a backdrop of blue, but out
of reach unless I pass through the dark leaves
beginning to enfold me. Panic . . . I must escape, but
impossible obstacles—vague, nameless monstrosities
loom out of the light. I back away—too soon.
These shapes—if only I knew the nature, the texture
of these beings. But I sink down without the
strength of will yet needed to fight. The gate remains
intact. The garden remains, as yet, unpenetrated.

Kay Pank

Imagination

He awakens as the morning ripen
with a glint in his smile
joy radiating in his heart.
I feel the thrill of love
on his tight embrace
blood rushing through our veins
as our hearts beat rhythmically to
this tender moment.
A moment I'd long for . . .
a sudden flash there he goes again
sadness overwhelmed my soul as his
figure disappeared.
Will it ever be?
Is the only question I asked.
But until that final day I'll keep
hoping and waiting for my
dream lover to take me in his tight embrace.

Deidre Freemantle

A Day Trip To Swanage

A town of contrasts old and new,
Amusements for many, sunbathing for a few.
The Victorian bandstand stands silent and aloof
Summer is approaching but we need a lot more proof!

A gentle breeze, a hazy sun
A weekend's quiet solitude when work is done.
A paddle in the water an ice cream for a treat,
Candy floss and hot dogs and football in the street.

Children writing poems sitting on the grass
Children playing football and shouting for a pass
People walking, talking, snoozing, what a lovely day
Swanage is a splendid town to spend a Saturday.

Josephine Butcher

Drunken Reality

Conjure up these vodka spills,
Rainbow dreams and faded days.
Living life full of thrills,
colour scheme finally pays.

The Whisky starts to disappear,
Tall bottle, drought is on its way.
Yes, the drink is always near,
tonight's the night, my dear, you'll pay.

With demons round every corner,
You don't really have a say.
With the nightmare just beginning,
The creditor is on his way.

Louise Day

The Old Cottage

Oh listen to me, I'll try to explain,
a walk I took down an old country lane,
I saw an old cottage that wasn't there before
with three young children playing by the door.
One little boy in a sailor suit happily playing with a hoop
two little girls with spinning tops and whips,
over the cobbles in buttoned boots they skipped.
Watching them, so they came to no harm
I saw a young mother, a babe in her arms,
she called to the children, and to my surprise
they suddenly vanished before my eyes.
That is why I shiver with fear
Where they the ghosts of yesteryear?

B. Bonner

It Is Time

It is time for me to go, I leave for another place,
That as yet has no shape or form for me.
It is time to say not good-bye but Adieu, my love,
The flowers that you lay on my chest does not ease
The aching pain that lies within my breast,
For I am no longer there, you hold my hand in yours,
You caress the face you once loved and trace features you
Know well. You whisper fond memories into space an empty
Air, but I hear you, I remember your touch and I feel you.
Have hope a memory of life can keep me living.
Do not be sad think occasionally of what was, do not be
Alone for what might of been, for you and I will never know.
It is time this world is turning cold to me,
And though I feel your love, you are so very far.
Shed your tears but once they have fallen let them be gone,
Do not let them cast shadows over future happiness.
For love is always love, and life is to live.

Ellen Templeton

Silent Tears

The sun has shone her rays upon your face,
And there, gliding down into space, a silent tear.
Red and yellow, pink and blue.
The rainbow in your tear shines through.

I search you face, please make it clear
the reason for the silent tear,
are you sick, feeling pain?
Please my God, make it plain.

Perhaps you want your Mama near,
Is that the reason for your tear?
Or did we through our busy day,
Omit to talk, then walk away?

My tears they flow I cannot speak,
The flame that traps me makes me weep,
I watch you dance and sing and play,
I want to join you on the way.

My thoughts and feelings are profound.
My stomach aches, my head does pound,
I miss my Mama as you do too,
There is no difference 'twixt me and you.

Joan Vass

My Love's Strength

Winter has come to my pen,
The reaper has harvested again,
Death and destruction rape the land,
Different horrors from different hands.

The sun bleeds and dies in the west,
Again and again, denied it rest.
In the north, a lonely baby cries,
In the south, an old patient dies.

A loving mother fights for her son.
The miracle of life, procreation, carries on.
The powerful emotion inside this prose,
Is finite compared to the love my heart knows,
For you.

Mark Barnes

Death Of A Tree In A Kentish Lane

It was early spring, the year nineteen hundred and eighty three.
The tree stood in the hedge beside the lane,
She had stood there for untold years, long before the house,
    but now she had gone for ever dead.

Men with chain saws, ropes and winches came and limb by limb
    the tree dismembered.
Her sawdust blood lay on the ground, her budding branches
    all around.
And in the lane her fine trunk was winched down.

No birds will sing there, insects crawl or fungi grow upon her trunk,
She is dead, gone for ever, the tree, the tree that stood in the
    hedge beside the lane.

Ash was her name.

Sally P. Hicks

Columbia

You with your disappearing beauty:
You with your enchanted dream;
Your instalment of fear by
Your symbolic mystery

Giving way to dismantled faith,
When you should be dismantling your paramilitary troops,
Instead of oppressing, and
Giving rise to depression, and risky work.

Your instalment of fear,
You might just shed a tear,
But where is your self respect and self pride,
In those cold, hate–filled eyes.

There is none there,
Yet beyond that cold stare,
I sense a solution,
Please dismantle your troops
Let us people move.

Give them good work to do
Freedom is coming soon, they need no regime,
Just liberty, honesty, security, respect and care.

Bernadette Vassallo

Peace At Last

Respect is what you should get, when folks see you pass bye,
Down at heart and harassed, don't let them see you cry.
Hold your head erect, and kick the world back into touch,
Even tho' you feel, life gets a bit too much.

Keep a smile upon your face, when you really want to weep,
Don't let them see the path you tread, is really much too steep,
They say your reward is in heaven, how you wish that you
    were there,
But you carry on, regardless as if you have no care.

One day you'll walk the stairway, to life on the other side
And loved ones, gone before you, will be waiting with arms
    held wide,
The pain will drop away from you, you'll find eternal peace,
For "he" will be there, waiting, to hold you without cease.

Rosemary P. Talbot

A Farewell To Man

I am the human race, I am the multiface,
I am the brick, I am the wall,
I am the master of you all.
The rich, the poor, the in between,
of those to come and those who've been.

Multi-language, multi-colour,
multi-father, multi-mother,
multi-sister, multi-brother.
Life's millenniums I do span
Pre-palaeolithic to modern man.

I am your mind, I am your sight,
I am your weakness and your might,
your right, your wrong,
your seed, your need,
so, on and on in everything
I am your crowned king.
But kings do reign and kings do fall
and death is coming after all.
Man's hate and greed has done me in
and man soon shall die from his own sin.

J. I. Howard

The New Baby

"Oh", Isn't he lovely, Isn't he sweet
Just look at his fingers look at his feet.
With his turned up nose and eyes so blue
I think the resemblance is mostly of you.
Or second thought though when I look once again
At his little red face now crumpled with pain
He looks more like his dad or grandfather Ted
The morning he stubbed his big toe on the bed.
Now is that a smile or only the wind
That enhances the deft on the end of his chin
It's so hard to tell when his just one hour old
And the rest of his life it's about to unfold with.

Joan Linwood

Temping Days

Here I am on reception desk again
thinking to myself 'Oh My' what a pain.

At $5.50 per hour I shall do it willingly
until they manage to find a permanent employee.

I'm here for afternoon from 1 p.m. till six
I'd better get these extensions right or I'll be in a fix.

A message here a message there, are they in or out
I wish these lines were clearer then I wouldn't have to shout.

I feel like I've been here hours my I'd love a cup of tea
you have to call someone down when you want to go to pee!

I wonder where I'll be temping next, we shall wait and see
one day I'll get a proper job or win the lottery!

B. Woodbridge

Help! . . .

I receive invitations, I don't want to go.
I search for the answer but I don't really know.
I want to rest, I want to play.
I want to go, I want to stay.

I walk round the room, I sit in the chair.
I can't concentrate so I just sit and stare.
I want to kick, I want to scream.
I want to lie on my bed and dream.

I read my letters, I talk on the 'phone.
I'm surrounded by people yet I'm all alone.
I want to live, I want to die.
I want to laugh, I want to cry.

I look into darkness, I find a friend.
I know I can cope if his arm he will lend.
I want to hear, I want to see.
I want to love, I want to be me.

V. Walsh

Questions

Why, is all this bombing, what do they hope to gain
Why, is all this bombing, causing grief and pain.
Why, is all this bombing, there is no reason why
By killing, maiming, people, blowing buildings to the sky.
Why, is all this bombing, by killers without a thought
Telling themselves "we are right, we are fighting for a cause."
Why, is all this bombing, there's no such thing as cause
Their hateful, evil, murderous deeds
Are just their own mad laws.
But one day they will meet their God
And to him have to tell,
Why they did the bombings
And damn themselves to hell.

M. Farrell

Kevin

You are the sunshine of my shadow
The safest port of all my storms.
You are the reason for my being
And I am safe within your arms.

You tell me stop when I should listen
And make me think when all thought is gone.
You are there to pick up the pieces
When it goes so very wrong.

You taught me to know when I am happy
And wiped out years of aching pain.
Because you cared so much for me
I found the will to live again.

I would wish this for all women
That they could have a friend like you.
The jigsaw piece that makes the picture
And colours life the way you do.

You are the light in all my darkness
The truest right in all my wrongs.
My forgiver and my confessor
And to you my soul belongs.

Gerardine Roulston

Mirror

Looking in the mirror, what do you see?
Reflections of a person, who I thought was me.
Glancing into the corridor, of aspects of you.
Fragments of a life, that I once knew.
Lines of hope, lines of despair, lines of things, which I do not care.
Pools of mystery, only one can be, leaving a body,
that used to be me.
Visions of my dreams, thermals floating away.
Catching that cloud, on the following rainy day.
Deeper than the surface, but shallower than the sea.
That person in the mirror, isn't, no it isn't really me
Only a mask, that portrays my point of view.
The mask I really wear, is to hide my loving feelings from you

Paula Marshall

Soul City

A city that's hazy and hidden,
But still we can see the overpowering standstill
Its liberty and freedom is stylishly tainted,
With splashes of a stunning absence.

A world that's rough and abandoned
Scattered with suburbs here and there
But this city is one of its own,
Singularly unique with a lighter horizon.

Splend'rous skyscrapers reach to the sky,
The turbid towers now in full stretch,
Making it seem atmospheric and calm
From a distance it looks like a picture!

A city that looks sad and subdued
One with a clockwork civilization
Merging colours—coal, black and charcoal
Fulfil one's every potential desire.

Kerry Elsworthy

There Is Nothing . . . But . . .

There is nothing in a tree . . . , but nature.
There is nothing in a rose . . . , but beauty.
There is nothing in the sun . . . , but warmth.
There is nothing in the stars . . . , but peacefulness.
There is nothing in this wind . . . , but strength.
There is nothing in a baby . . . , but pure life.
There is nothing in this life . . . , but joy.
There is nothing in this existence . . . , but you.
There is nothing but love is everything!

Christophe M. P. Aubry

The Audacious Madman

In the heat of the night a voice is calling you
He is stalking you down and you know it too
You look behind as you know that he's there
You feel the strain of his presence pretend you don't care.

The voice of this man is haunting your mind
You think of racing so he can't find
What does he want with you? Why does he care?
What is he after? Why should he dare?

He touches your shoulder then spins you around
Hand extends to his pocket, you subside to the ground
This is it you say, this is the end
You advance to the land where nothing depends

You take your last breath and search for the light
One that will hit you, shimmering bright
The last dregs of all life now drained from your soul
You observe all around you where should you go?

You weren't prepared, not quite ready
And wish that someone would hold you steady
That was my story, this is the end
Of how I lost my beautiful friend

Helen Ellard

Ripples Of Adolescence

When the rare jewels of life pop their heads
And the adolescence is done and gone,
What then? Look to the future or the past?
Though all planned in precise measurements,
Knew life's secrecies and intricacies
Today and tomorrow, that was all. But . . .

Dark dismal depths of the abyss await,
The present of that past which it has led to.
Responsibilities, recriminations.
Thoughts of yesteryear obsess the psyche
Giving strength, though it's false, for survival.

Life's realization that this is all,
Accept or reject; not that it matters.
When all is said and done those decisions
Were made, have been made, all those years ago.
Yet . . . Oh! once more to
Open the door on the jewels of life.

Pauline M. O. Davies

Peace Of Mind

How many times are we all given the chance to start again,
After being low in spirit an easy mind we must regain,
For worry gets you nowhere however bad things seem
Just turn your thoughts toward our God and let his love light beam,
Once more, within your hearts of heats,
    then take his outstretched hand,
Then he'll lead you gently onward toward the promised land,
A land that is not far away you'll see it all around
In the sky, the trees, the landscape, it's just that you'll have found
The way to lift your head up high, with peace of mind in sight,
Your troubles will seem far away when again you see the light,
Look forever forward you have the chance to start again
With God as your companion a joyous life you will sustain,
Your life is like a precious gem that may be dimmed just for a while
You'll make many people happy when once again you smile.

D. M. Williamson

Untitled

Faded the evening glow of westering sun,
And when the silent moonbeams softly stole
Into that darkened, cool, monastic hall,
And painted silver traceries on the stones,
There came the echo of long forgotten tones,
of ghostly voices raised in priestly thrall,
Singing the Kyries—praise to the Lord of all,
And gentle footsteps passing into dark
And hidden cells of purity.
And velvet silence closed upon austerity
And those eternal souls of piety.

S. Lilley

Progress

There were fields here once,
Star-studded in Spring with cowslips,
Clover, birds-eyes and bluebells,
    Flower heads peeping through the
Fresh green grass.
    A rich harvest for Mother's Day,
Short stalks just right for small fat fingers.
    A soft scented bed for weary limbs and heads;
A place for sleep on hot Summer Days.
    Now they are gone.
Covered in concrete, brick and small square boxes.
    The acme of a Builder's dream,
A Planner's Paradise.

Gwendoline Alder

Safron

With red hair, a tattoo and weird clothing
I wonder who she is.

Does she really come from me I ask,
Hopefully it's just a phase.

Perhaps it's something to do with her name
She never did like it.

Boyfriends are too many to remember
Except for her present love.

Gifts of washing she brings each week
Incapable of turning a simple machine on.

Exasperation is what she gives
With the dirty dishes left in the sink.

At twenty three she is my eldest
And I would not change a thing.

For I do love her so very much
Though I never tell her so.

Anne Winstanley

The Piano

Ebony and Ivory; noted for sound
Digital playback; sleight of hand
Songsters echo; vibrant pound
Upright, organ, cottage, grand.

Strings attached, taut with suspense
The Master Key hammers home
Letters of note; chords of tense
Past and present; timed metronome

Naturally played with flat and sharp
Sweeping the board; ayre of nonchalance
Orchestral manoeuvres; performed with harp
Brass and wind; counter balance

Peddled depression; ayre lingers on
Distant wave; caressed . . . pianissimo
Emotive conductor; under the baton
Chorused voice harks; keyed to the piano.

To be read slowly
Verse 2 "The Master Key" refers to the pianist

E. Clark

Dreams!

Dreams, dreams, dreams
Why do we have dreams?

Ghosts, fairies, all sorts of dreams
Happy, sad all sorts of feelings
Children, adults, even animals have dreams.

Dreams, dreams, dreams
Why do we have dreams?

Dreams of winning the lottery
Dreams of being eaten by gorillas
Dreams of falling down cliffs
never coming to an end

Dreams, dreams, dreams
Why do we have dreams?

Dreams that frighten us at night
Parents saying it's alright
Dreams of all sorts of things
Good, bad, happy, sad

Dreams, dreams, dreams
Why do we have dreams?
Do you know why we have dreams?

Davinder Chana

A Wartime Beginning

"Move over little girl, clear off,—out the way."
This command, when mother working ,was what she heard them say.
Climbing stair, laughing there, man in uniform, another one today.
Outside sky, aglow with bombing—and she doesn't know
how to pray,
Left alone as usual—scared witless, sucking thumb,
Clocks ticking, long nights banging, flashing, she wonders
why, and what's to come.
Soldier's hussy mother—cast black sheep of street by some,
'till one day, old uncle in silence, took away the little one,
In new home it's "you just forget your past—not allowed to
mention."
Can't block it out so easily—however good is their intention,
"Stop crying, be grateful, you horrid girl, we'll pray for your
redemption."
She doubted God—whoever he was, could help—so great her
apprehension,
Grey haired uncle and the aunt, watch like hawk observing prey,
"Such worthless origins as hers—we'll keep check—she will obey."
That little root was dumped—in jagged hard–edged clay,
No healing tenderness or loving,—strict times, austere and grey,
Years rolled by–many sigh—but the past still withheld its key,
Secret bolted—always faulted—they still ignored her every plea
Now we're supposed to be, celebratory, of wars fiftieth anniversary,
She's still unloved and searching,—"Does any old soldier
look like me?"

Gillian Randall

Acid Rain

It drops as the gentle rain from heaven,
upon the place beneath.
But unlike the gentle rain that falls,
this rain has acid teeth.
It eats into the greenery
like some gigantic snail.
Destroying life and leaving,
devastation in its trail.
This acid rain created by the greed of man,
Who thinks about tomorrow's world,
and doesn't give a damn.
For when politics and greed are mixed,
they make a deadly brew.
Creating havoc for the millions,
just to benefit the few.
And when tomorrow does arrive,
how barren be the plain.
It depends if it is acid,
or just the gentle rain.

John Lovatt

Reflections Of Drumcree

Barbed–wire politics pollute our nation
As the quest for equality finds, 'no equation'
Madness and mayhem disrupt dialogue
Whilst reason gets lost behind a religious fog

Orangemen and nationalists won't, 'let sleeping dogs lie'.
Honouring traditions of men 'above' vast numbers who die
With constant riots and bombings, none can justify or condone
cause by our self-righteous pride, we've made them our own

Needless destruction of property, distraught communities
Tax-payers, picking up the tab for vandalism fees
Trade and tourism decline, as Ireland's image is lost
'Tis such a terrible waste, forfeiting such terrible cost

Optimism quietens as future uncertainty grows
And it's down the tubes, least for now, the peace-process goes
Cause peace won't be governed by a political rod
But comes 'only' as penitent hearts move the healing hand of God.

P. A. Gray

Silhouettes

Reflections of the moonlight make a silver path across the lake,
where ghostly shadows of the trees dip and bow in night-time's
breeze.
The gentle murmur of a stream echoes softly through my dream
While, all around, day's turmoils cease, and Earth is cloaked in
tranquil peace.
But not for all a time of rest. The barn owl leaves his cosy nest.
The fox and badger leave their home, and through the
undergrowth they roam
This is their world their time to play, while night moves
onward into day
When back into their homes they'll creep, to shelter safely
and to sleep;
Away from mortal's daily round of hustle, bustle, whirl and sound,
With space age travel fast food bars, computer chips, electric cars.
We share this planet side by side, and we must nurture it with pride.
Two words in one so far apart. The silhouettes of Nature's art.

Marilyn Claire Haig

The School On The Hill

My life spreads before me
just like a fan,
from childhood to school day,
when everything was fun.

The old school that stood on the hill,
the yard where we did our drill.

Marching to the signal never out of step.
It used to go click da click.

The bossy Miss, who slapped our hands,
Headmasters who told boys "Bend over!"
Six of the best (swish)

No tears were shed,
just a voice, saying "don't do it again!"

Then the lovely teenage years,
when ribbons and bows came into view.
Black painted shoes with fancy laces.
Toying with make-up. Looking as though we had porcelain faces.

Lips as red as cherries,
teeth gleaming white,
hair styled with pins and combs.
Falling down in gay confusion, in disarray, it will never stay.
Looking through shaded eye lids as the boys pass by,
the demure miss was here.

First balls, dressing for dances,
silks and frills, tightened waist lines,
Spanish heels, tapping out the beat,
Stepping out for the Polka dances and Tango.

The handsome beau taking us for the waltz,
holding hands in dark places
making dates to meet again,
Oh! To live it over again.

Winn Whitfield

The Matriarch's Womb

The tapestry's needle is threaded with care;
in answer to life's longing and her indefinite prayer.
Distant voices, audible bubbling, raw fluids that flow.
I am the arrow that awaits to be sent by the bow.

Liquid confinement, struggling, born yet unborn.
Claustrophobic, I move my tiny form.
Nurturing care, soothing waves of concern from above.
How close the voice that speaks of sweet solace and love

Echoes travel my chamber as I move gently around.
Sharp noises, mechanical whining, musical melodies sound.
Yet when silent, two audible harmonies pulsate as one.
They reassure me that my tapestry's course must be run.

Pandemonium, panic, pulsating heart frantic with dread,
As intense forces bend bones, sending pains through my head.
Intensifying tightness, squeezing from head to toe,
Then released into brightness, I'm sent forth by the bow.

Choking fluids, applied suction, they said "breath," I obeyed.
Assaulted, washed, dried, measured and weighed.
Alien noises surround me, nebulous forms stand and stare,
My matriarch receives me and feeds me with care.

Mervin S. Telford

"You Pulled The Curtain Down On Our Love"

Thank you for the love you gave me, for cosy nights by the
fire, the soft music, the discovery of passion and deep
meaningful kisses. The hugs and embraces that brought
comfort and lightness of my heart, The butterfly feeling of you
can on my mind.

Thank you for the never ending smiles and fun we had, for
rock 'n' roll, and close, warm smoochy waltzes, feeling your
heart beat close to mine, feeling the love we roused in each
other, for flowers and presents, for listening and
understanding, for caring and loving.

Thank you for Sunday treats, walks by the sea, trips to the
lakes, chips out of packets. Thank you for helping out with
family and problems, for being there, for making me realize I
was capable of love, for breaking down barriers.

Thank you for precious moments, memories for the future of a
special time in my life. You made me see buds of Spring of
fresh blooms, fresh starts, thoughts of picnics in the summer,
plans for the future, a new beginning.

How sad that my time is up. How sad I can't feel anymore
fight in me to keep your love. How sad you brought the
curtain down in a sweet, sweet Love.

Veronica Douglass

Time And Dreams

Thrusting dreams in the mind's abyss
A fleeting thought, a plan a kiss.
A surge of conquering spirit fills
Timeless time in the mind's green hills.

Is It the time when time stands still?
The dreams and hopes we cannot fulfil.
Time was when we in high esteem
Joyfully forged life's thronging stream.

Without thoughts hesitation, rejected
Society gives no chance of reformation.
The time has come when ageless energy must be re-directed
Fantasy of dreams an unworked mind from insanity protected.

Activities to cleanse the soul,
Purges to keep the body whole.
The changing scene, the months the years
Lie gloating as supplication nears.

A puppet on the stage of life — strings
Broken, abandoned to dream time fears
Unfettered from the freewill ties
The soul swallowed up in dreams now hides.

Christina M. Clarke

Katie's Day

Eyes of bluest blue,
Her smile is just for you,
Dressed in satin and in lace,
Baby Katie is full of grace.

Golden silk is her hair,
Dimples in her cheeks, so fair,
Her little arms outstretched to you,
Baby Katie we all love you.

Her Godparents smile, and then they coo,
Mummy and Daddy are very proud too,
Nannas and Grandpas and all agree,
Baby Katie is a joy to see.

Julia Ray

Growing Old

Holding hands like two small children,
They stood waving through the window.
For a moment time stood still,
As the anguish of the past and present
Flickered across their lined faces,
For they were not children anymore.

Life had taken its toll, and the ravages
Of time were plain to see.
There was fear, of what the future may hold;
For the past had already been told.
The need for comfort and solace was there.
Time had been lost, there's no more to spare.

May the shackles of pain fall away from their lives.
And may the kingdom of heaven open their eyes
To a love,
Which is greater than anything here.
God rest, and God keep them,
For they are so dear.

Dorothy Pimblett

Holly

Shine green and pike the predators
Who snuffle, scrabble at our doors;
And let the berries of their blood
Dissuade the mob from huff and thud—
To stamp their rage on different floors.

Shine red and ring the victim's crown
Victoriously with renown.
Though the drops redly gathered seep
Past brow and cheekbone, do not weep:
They honour while they stain the gown.

Shine gold and gloriously light
The candles of our Christmas night:
Your points, nor pike or spike, to mime
The antlers racing midnight's chime
Across the world's expectant white.

E. M. Thomson

Born Are We

Unto the world, with my eyes open
I looked to the skies, I do
for all that I'm hoping
for a life to treasure, with days of pleasure
I want to feel all emotions
to succeed in the highest measure
from the start, I found my heart
one that keeps me going
to the place in my mind
the one that keeps me knowing
All I want to give
for all that I see from my eyes
I plead for all creatures to live
being underground or above the skies
we were all born, like a flower
that blooms when a seed is sown
and one day we'll be together as one
when peace is finally known.

Darren Sidney

I See God

I see God through nature;
I see his tenderness in many a creature.

I see his beauty in the flowers;
And in birds of varied colours.

I see his kindness to man;
In giving him woman.

I see his gentleness in the sweet little baby;
A magnificent gift from the belly of a lady.

I see his power in holding up the planets;
And even providing protection for the stinging hornets.

I see his dexterity in forming the body;
Excellent, intricate and of great beauty.

I see his thoughtfulness in giving us delicious foods;
And other precious life–sustaining goods.

I see his care in preserving us from evil;
And rescuing us from many a peril.

I see his love in giving us advice;
Praise be to him for wanting us to be with him in paradise.

Clifton L. Pinnock

A Prayer To My Lord

My Lord, who is ever watchful from the heavens above,
the expansive skies which never end, and neither does your love.
Father come, advise me in my pain,
Still my disquiet—never let me stray from your love again.

My Lord when no other person seems to bear a burden as
great as my own,
Help me to remember that I will never be alone.
Father, give me the courage to smile throughout the day—
I know that in the end, he is the one who will have to pay.

My Lord, let me be your servant here on earth,
Through experience I can tell how much our precious life is worth.
Father, cast away my doubts and make my faith strong.
I realize now—I can come straight to you when things go wrong.

My Lord who has struggled to make yourself known to me,
Now I have found you—now I am free!
Father I know that one day my duty on earth will be done.
Through the clouds my spirit to you, will come.

My Lord, when the time comes for my body to turn to dust,
to you, my soul, I will entrust.
Father, I admit I have been weak, when troubles I have had to face.
I pray you put me to rest, in the assurance of your divine grace.

Francesca Jarrett

The Stage Of Fools

When we are born we cry
that we are come to this great stage of fools
—Shakespeare, King Lear—

In tragedy,
reality mocks man;
in comedy,
man mocks reality
so man and his reality
on this great stage
stand face to face.
There grimacing clowns
and sorrow's stricken shape,
jostle for space,
and horror crashing
laughter's wild shriek collides—
There man enclosed
within his capsule of despair,
locked in his paradox—
must wait for Heaven,
for paradox,
ends there.

Kenneth A. Cossar

The Gift

The golden yellow field is swaying in the breeze,
I quickly clamber o'er the gate and drop down on my knees;
Though distant is the memory, remembrance still is true,
Of the Mother's Day I picked the golden buttercups for you.

As country child both born and bred, 'twas often happy play,
To gather you with childish pride the flowers of hedgerows way,
With happy heart, like butterfly I'd flit from flower to flower,
With sweet content I'd hand to you the yield of happy hour.

The years so quickly sped on by as years are apt to do,
Time came along when time it was to say goodbye to you,
This time at garden rockery I once more bend the knee.
The golden blooms, my last bouquet to give to you from me.

Beth Hall

The Dawn Of A New Era

The light is shining, all is bright,
But this is not day, but the middle of night
Search lights are shining across the sky
Looking for bombers, oh God, why
Can we not learn the lesson of years gone by?

Bright new eras have come and gone,
But someone, somewhere, always comes along
And shatters the peace
Of our hopes and dreams that wars will cease.

Half the world is at war with each other
Innocents suffer, both child and mother.

Let us hope, that in this new millennium
This twenty-first century will silence men
Who will no longer wage a war
That lasts and lasts forevermore.

G. M. Taylor

The Cry Of A Child

In the still of a silent room,
An innocent child meets her doom.
The man picks up a big black stick,
And one by one the bruisers kick . . .
Down it comes again and again,
Is this man cruel or merely insane?
What enjoyment dose he find,
In beating a little child's behind?
What kind of man must he be
To kill a child as sweet as she?
So innocent so sweet and young,
surely this can be no fun.
She had the rest of her life,
What a shame it was ended by the blade of a knife!

Shelley Makin

"Friendship, Courage, Hope"

A chasm bottomless, inky dark, encased by four grey walls,
No naked eye seeing, or ear hearing your despairing calls.
The days lonely, long, bleak, tormented with deadly fears,
Empty, aimless, abject, wearily drying-up helpless tears.
Suddenly a door slowly opens, a friend steps inside,
Have you the tenacity, guts or courage to stumble outside.
Destroy your failures, forsaking the crumbled world around,
Grasp the friendly hand, firmly urging feet onto firm ground.
Courage helps cast your failures, and damned pride aside,
Deeply search your heart, release torments buried deep inside.
Disperse gloomy shadows, dispel the shrouded darkness of night,
Search, seek, until ultimately, firm feet walk a road that's right.
But inspiration is trapped, no words, thoughts inspire you anymore,
Courageously start anew, forsaking the storms that blew before.
Let your reasons for living, shine a light bright crystal clear,
Renewing your spirit, freedom, gives wings strength to fly free.
Yesterdays darkness disappears, the storm has blown itself out,
Your whole being is alight, your friends are hovering about.
Your hearts renewed, filled with hope, searching inside your mind,
Armed with courage and hope, who knows 'what treasures
you'll find.

Agnes Phil Gilbert

411

Steel

If you woke one day to find,
A different world outside,
To the one you had inside your mind,
What would you do?
Is it me or you?
In a world of steel and stone,
Where an ancient wind had blown,
This is all they have left behind for us to find,
Tell me where to go,
If you know,
There is a fine line that divides,
All of the different kinds,
In this world of steel and stone,
How does it feel to be alone?
How does it feel?
Now that it is real.

David Welfare

Time

Oh summer, how soon you
passed, like wind, when we turned our heads.
  The river flows so darkly now
as through the valley wends!
  The trees with leaves so richly
gold, like the summer sun, they
hold you for a moment in their glow.
  The winberry beds lie brightest
red, as home we make our way.
  Lights like swans in flight, the
night is drawing on.
  "Summer is gone."

Rosemary James

The Fight

Yes! Yes! Yes!!!
They shout, punching the air
Victors in the fight
The fight of the Olympics

For every four, the five gather
The rich and the poor, the white and the black
For a friendly fight they gather
Victors they have, losers they lack

They run, they row
They leap, they throw
The Champions in the fight for a medal
The medal of honour that glow

And just as the fight is over
They embrace, they shake hands
The champions, and the champion's champion
In the fight for global unity and peace.

Ibikunle Thomas

"Wondering"

Night shades falling, and I'm recalling
Moments I've shared with you.
Moments tender, sweet surrender
Vowing our love so true.
The night was fair and we were there
Beneath the stars above.
Ours to capture the sweet enrapture
On a night for love.
Oh! Dream of love divine,
Could I hope you'd be mine?
A dream of love divine, could you ever be mine?

Two hearts beating and our lips were meeting,
Lost in the silent thrill,
Knowing you were near to me, so near and so dear to me,
Vowing to love until; all the stars failed to shine,
And the moon lost its glow;
Would you still say you are mine, more than I'll ever know?
Could you still say you are mine, more than I'll ever know?

J. J. Cooke

Snow In Spring

While we slept the white snow crept
over roof and ground—
Concealing all by its soft fall,
a world devoid of sound.

In quietness we rose and dressed,
the birds declined to sing.
The sudden cold made us feel old,
dispelling thoughts of spring.

By afternoon, depressing gloom
yielded to brighter gleam—
The sun grew bold, the roof
dripped gold, wet where the snow had lain.

The warming glow; departing snow
filled us with hope again.
We hurried out with joyful shout
to greet the spring again.

Elizabeth Fennell

Retirement

You're officially retired.
Your working life is done
No more to bold you'll travel
The colliery has won
No more rise at 5 a.m.
To go to yonder pit
To take the coal, the dust, the sweat
You are no longer fit.
Just say no to Arthur Scargill,
When he's laying down the law
Saying are my lads behind me
It's more cash were striking for.
Turn your back on Mick McGahey
You're no longer of their clan
You've lain down your pick and shovel
You're no more a working man

Dedicated to my brother, who was a hard working miner.
Who died September 8th 1988.

Margaret Conway Hilton

For The Lost

Do not ask why. Do not enquire of death
Why you are chosen. Why you must pay this price.
The true assessment of your sacrifice
Lies in the hearts of those who know your worth.
Death takes no heed of innocence or truth.
Death values nothing. Death does not make a choice
to mark the impact of a broken voice
Imploring recognition of your youth
And we—the living, who can move and breathe
And look around us with our ransomed eyes—
We know our debt but dare not compromise
While terror reigns and tyrants tread the earth.
So death wins twice, with equal certainty,
Paid in defeat and paid in victory.

Joan Turville

Heaven

When you go to heaven,
There's no turning back
  you know.
Like you can down here,
From time to time.
Be it fast or slow
What shall be done way up there,
Will there be joyful things to share,
Will we be able to read, write and work; rest;
I wonder who knows, what will be best.
I wonder if there will be a place for me?
  Oh, why worry,
  we will all have to wait
  and see.

Desmond Chapman

The Compost Heap

Every year, about this time, I take a look outside
To the place I call my garden. The place I tend with pride
Has turned into a jungle, a most untidy thing
The flowers that were beautiful, so straight and tall in spring
They've gone away, and left behind some awful yellow string.
Peonies fall, geraniums sprawl, sneaky weeds creep everywhere.
There is no shape, nor style, nor form, no order anywhere
I heave a sigh, I heave the spade, I take a fork as well,
Dig up, dig out, and rake about, oh what the bloody hell!
The compost heap is getting high, I hear my neighbour say—
"Well, you can burn it up next week, because we're going away"
I'm not amused, no time for mirth, I cannot rest 'til all is earth.
I see the soil, here endeth toil and this is why
I sleep so sound, for in that mound and while I slumber
Tiny insects without number, rounded snails, with jelly teeth
Fatted slugs crawl underneath
Chewing, spewing and devouring all that failed or was not flowering.
My efforts here were ne'er in vain,
Come back next year and try again.

Roberta E. Rabson

A New Forest Oak

From a tiny acorn grew, this massive oak.
Braving years of icy cold and blazing sun.
Whose light flickers through bracken
From pale to deepest green.
Until the day is done.
When autumn paints their fronds with gold
The old oak sighs, wrapping its skeleton against the cold
As with the wind it sighs
Adding another ring to those inside it lies.

V. M. Rowland

Madame Butterfly's Lament

Oh, heart within my breast, be still!
Stop beating like a bird's wings till
Your love returns into your sight,
And fills the world with wondrous light!

Oh, eyes within my head, don't stare!
Don't show the world how much you care.
Don't look for him on every street!
Someday he'll make your life complete.

Yet will I hold myself apart,
Upon the beach, with pounding heart,
Not daring hardly I to move,
For fear that I should die of love!

Oh, love within my breast, my heart
Don't burn me out while we're apart
Soon he will come—you'll hear him sigh,
"I love you still, my butterfly"

Dilys Goodfellow

Little Mouse

Little mouse out in the field,
Hiding in the seasons yield.
So still . . . there . . . in the long long grass.
Waiting for the plough to pass.

Here comes the tractor and the plough,
It's got to pass me. I hear it now.
The furrow's deep and hard to cross.
If I get caught, I'm at a loss.

For I, so small a rodent be,
Heading for a lonely tree.
Could easily fall for birds of prey.
They stalk me almost every day.

I hide beneath a large tree root.
Close by me, huntsman meet, to shoot.
Their dogs are sniffing on the ground.
But I can sleep now, safe and sound.

D. A. Grant

Untitled

The summer seems so far away now it is cold and grey
And the darkness lingers on, long into each new day,
And winds blow chill, the sun grows cold as winter comes again,
And icy tendrils of Jack Frost pattern each window pane.
The snow comes down and covers trees, shrubs, ground and flowers
Sometimes for weeks, sometimes for days, sometimes just a few hours
Then comes the rain and watery sun turning it to slush
Next swirling fog, deadening all sound, as if someone said hush
Familiar landmarks lost to sight, nothing looks the same
Then, thankfully, it disappears as quickly as it came
And so the winter months drag on, with everything on hold
But buried deep within the earth, away from all the cold
Until the days lengthen and the sun warms up the earth
Then everywhere new life abounds and spring proclaims rebirth.

P. Ellis

Sitting On A Cold Bench

Sitting on a cold bench of the park,
I threw a bored glance
at the branches stripped by the winter.

They looked like a lot of bony arms
looking for help in the greyness of the sky.

An old man was sleeping
crouched a little further on,
on a flower bed;
but the passers-by
didn't care.

My glance was getting more and more bored
but it wasn't turned towards the trees anymore,
it felt the heart of the passers-by
which was like my hands:
colder than the ice.

Elisabetta Pizzochero

My Last Tear

The happiness in the past seems as if it were only a dream
But things in the past never really are what they seem
They say what they say, they say they do not really mean
And I come to this place and it feels like I've already been
Then I dream of the rain and snow and wake up to another day
I find myself locked up in the prison of tears and wish I could
run away
My mind is clogged up with poison and every day my brain
will decay
And still the doctor of life stands up and tells me I will have to pay

The clouds of my mind blacken and force the heavy rain to fall
I go round and round in circles until I stop and hit a wall
The beating of my heart is slower and I give my Lord a call
But the tears roll on, I'm tired and the pain hasn't gone at all
Once upon a time you loved me and I thought you would
always be here
But now I know that your love wasn't strong enough to stay
my dear
And now I still hold on to the dream that maybe you are still
very near
And I still long for the day to come when I will shed my very
last tear

Neil Curran

Ode To An English Spring

Winter jealous lover lay off those cloths of white
shining sparkling yet concealing violent might
enter spring soar and bloom refreshing air and space
rise-up spring fill all with blossom and with grace
Depart winter disinterested in neither friend nor foe
spring is here in profusion brilliantly aglow.

Flowers abundantly covering nakedness of barren earth
Birds cry—nature's witness to the mysteries of re-birth
Freshly fragrant flowers float freely upon the air
Our delicate English spring needs a treatment of great care
That future generations may always be allowed to bring
Their dreams and aspirations to fulfil an English spring.

P. L. Hunter

Wings Of Glory

As the eagle flies from its safety ledge . . .
Gliding in the winds looking down . . .
As I sit on the mountain top . . .
It flew past me . . .
Searching for its destiny . . .

The wings so large with its spotted white . . .
Creating a shadow of dominance,
Its eyes moving to and from . . .
With quick succession looking down . . .
As she flew into the sun rays, producing a sparkle that is
rarely found . . .
What uniqueness,
What grace,
What great control over its large weight . . .

As she flap her wings over the ledge . . .
Creating a protective shield for the young ones . . .
Tearing at the flesh, with her ripping beak . . .
Creating an opening of sustenance . . .

Then she flew from the safety ledge one more time . . .
Flapping her wings of elegance into eternity . . .

Prince A. Balwah

Untitled

this passing phase of despair has lasted for a thousand years
the water cries its everlasting tears and I supply the sea
I tread with angels but they smile at fear
and truth rains as knives thrown by you
whale song joins the keening
seaweed strangles while the peonies dance
on the shore; shells crushed by the years; did they ask?
I did, but no-one replied

Erica Kimber

The River Of Life

The past is past, the river floweth on
towards its destiny, and so you too
must follow on along the path of life
thro' hills and dales, thro' pastures ever new.

The present is today, the river flows . . .
upon the threshold lift a silent prayer
and plan your course before the current comes
and carries you like driftwood, unaware . . .

The future lies ahead, the river flows . . .
and smaller streams join in to swell the tide,
and pilgrims play their part upon the stage
while others walk along the riverside.

By night and day the river runs its course
while time moves on in measured grains of sand,
and pilgrims travel onward, come what may,
towards the haven of the Promised Land.

Suzanne Low Steenson

Love's Facade

You hate me because it's something to do,
Drawing my attention solely on you,
Hoping I'll stumble as you want me to,
You hate me.

You need me to conquer and to collect,
You know that this hatred has an effect.
But whatever the insult, however direct,
You need me.

You want me, I know beneath this disguise,
Beneath the contempt in your stone grey eyes
Under the insults and feeble lies,
You want me.

But do you know me and do you understand?
You've seen me cry at your command
I could be crushed in the palm of your hand,
Do you know me?

Anne-Marie Carlile

What's So Bad About Me?

I'm not your friend when in need, but I lurk in the
background of every bad deed.
I sit on your shoulder giving instruction, my suggestions
unhelpful, full of destruction.
My dark reign is eternal, my powers undiminished,
my work in this world will never be finished.
I'll give you riches and wealth, it's all within my control,
you can have anything you want, just give me your soul.
Temptation, unfulfillment, regret, self resentment, these are the
emotions you feel as we make the deal. But now it's too
late for feeling self hate as your soul I steal.
Fear me I'm the unholy one, creator of misery and despair,
capable of causing havoc and damage beyond any repair.
My interest in you is totally obscene, my goal is the same as it
has always been, to turn brightness to darkness and make
the unblemished unclean.
I am the force of evil you will never deter, you know who I am
my name's Lucifer.
So please live the kind of life I decree, don't try to behave well.
Feast on a rich menu of sin and debauchery, then spend the
rest of your days in my home sweet hell.

Kevin Costello

Distant Temptress

Tall green pastures sway to and fro,
While the breeze danced 'round the dale.
A haze rose o'er the buttercups bloom,
a calm within my gale.

Temptress   temptress
The heavens cry.
Her soul   her soul,
It does not die.
Hence she comes, stand tall my child.
Be strong in faith,   her powers be mild.

The thunder beckons,
It tears the skies.
The lightning strikes,
It blinds my eyes.

Defeat is no an option here,
there's a hungry wolf and I'm the deer.

All around the skies are grey,
but the shadows net casts wide.

Somewhere up there lies my God,
Mt temptress' soul had died.

Timothy Brookes

To Jesus Of Nazareth, On Good Friday

Today I remember your cross set upon that stark hill,
Where your body was strung up so broken and still;
Oh Son of Man, this was to be your fate,
For the Love that you brought was met with Hate.

As the Prince of Peace and Light to our earth you came;
In the name of the Father, you raised the dead and healed the lame;
Humility was your crown, and Love the sceptre in your hand,
But your message was too spiritual for most men to understand.

You tried to teach us that every stranger is really our brother,
And by your own deeds, you showed us how to love one another;
In your ministry you urged us to spurn material fame and wealth,
For this was the only way to improve our spiritual health.

But rejected by your own people, you were viciously reviled,
Crowned with thorns, spat upon, by men's evil defiled;
Finally, they took you away to Golgotha, to be crucified,
And in all your innocence, you hung there while you slowly died.

Today as I contemplate again that black Good Friday scene,
I no longer see it as something hopeless and obscene,
For amid all the darkness, your purity transfigured that grim
cross of wood,
And as they gazed up at your countenance, some men finally
understood.

Jonquil Tanti Hughes

In Memory Of Laura

I see you in the early morning dew,
and the fragrance of freshly mown grass,
An inspiration for my dreams, not yet achieved.
But to others you are a memory of my past.

A reality for but a precious moment.
the seed of life denied the chance to grow.
My personal failure replaces your departure,
A memory of Laura is all that I will know.

When you were here, I often talked,
about the world, you'd yet to see,
How could I know that at that time,
Your life was never meant to be,

But in the dew, the fragrant grass,
and sun rays you appear to be,
for all good things I live and breathe
will bring a part of you to me

In these words I dedicate
the words I never got to give,
Until my life gives up on me,
In my memory you will live.
Tracy J. Holder

Untitled

The good Samaritan on the phone
Taking all the calls,
Hearing the people's sad little stories
Persuading them not to fall.
But one day whilst he's sitting there
It all begins to pile up,
The constant moaning, the whining voices
Of people out of luck.
Out of work, or out of love,
Looking for a sign from up above.
He tries to sound 'oh so sincere'
But he really wouldn't shed a tear
If they lived or if they died
If they dropped out of the sky like flies.
It just wouldn't make any difference at all.
So who does the Samaritan have to call,
When he gets down or he gets stressed.
Is he alone when he gets depressed?
Kim Green

A Middle–Aged Mum's Lament

How many women just like me,
Stand and wonder while making the tea,
Is this all there is to life?
Just because you're some man's wife.

We scrub, and clean, and cook all day,
With hardly a thank you, and never any pay,
We bring up the kids the best that we can,
With not much help from the husband man.

When they're grown up, married and gone,
Life should be easier, but there you're wrong
Their marriages break up, so what do they do?
They bring home their children and dump them on you.
S. C. Smith

Personal View Of The Deaf And Dumb

To see these people, using their hands,
Is like watching composers, conducting bands.
No music echoes, though not by choice,
For these deaf people, hear no voice.

It seems a shame, they hear no sound,
To use their hands, is a voice they found.
But to see sign language, at its very best,
We need to be with them, and that's a test.

To put ourselves, within their plane,
We use our hands, to try and to explain.
There is a problem, which is not so good,
They get all frustrated, if they're not understood.
Bill Rowsell

Autumn Violins

Sere sedge, fringing the pale pond, quivers
    To quietness as the song begins.
Elfin–sweet through the willow shivers
    The music of autumn violins.
Minuet for the tawny bracken
    Flirting its fronds at a stately sky.
Gay gavotte for the green–gowned grasses
    Swirling their skirts with a silken sigh.

Slow pavane for the treetops, swaying
    Sensuously to the soft refrain.
Listening leaves of exquisite amber
    Hear in the distance, again and again
Melodies wooed by wild wind-fingers,
    Though the pleading branches bid them stay,
Lightly they follow, down woodland shadows
    Dancing their delicate whirlabout way.
Gwyneth Butler

2000 Years

New years eve
New years day
2000 years only thirty to your name
Longing for the change
Longing for the change and resurrection
We've wasted all our time with expectations

We can celebrate and barely see the flames
Eternity belongs to those with ventured souls
Wishing upon wishes for this new years day
2000 years A.D. is not so far away

Holding up our hands
Shaking off the tears
Do treaties for the masses only separate our hearts?
Waiting for the peace
Waiting for the peace of mind not misery
We use up all our strength in security
Peter D. Stanton

Untitled

Rivers of time flowing into the ocean
Memories and mind flowing into the sea
Bridges of sighs empty into the ocean
Empty those thoughts 'tween you and me

The tide it carries us into eddies and whirlpools
Shows us the way it was meant to be
How can we know where our thoughts will lead us
Thoughts speaking louder from you to me

Send me a float drifting down on the memories
Signal the shore that you're carrying me
I do not know where my next thought will spring from
All that I feel is harmony

Words are not said or needed for you
Actions speak louder than vocabulary
Snapshots of minds focusing on your thoughts
Help me to hear—help me to see
David Thompson

Those Wonderful Days

Where have those wonderful days gone?
Those days of long ago.
We as children loved each day then—
of "hopscotch" and marbles we could throw.

We tied our ropes to lampposts to swing around the post.
There was a "season" for each game then,
"Hoops" and "skipping" we loved the most.

Remember the lovely "picnics" and watching "bowling" in the park.
Sometimes we would tie cottons on letter boxes,
We thought this quite a lark!

Where have these wonderful days gone?
Children then got so much pleasure.
No-one can take away our memories
They are left for us to treasure.
Vera Simm

Coming Home To Blackhall

See the boy at the end of the street
Already condemned to a life on the dole
Or the old lady shivering in her home
Because of the price of Gas and Coal
A grey and misty Middle Street
With paper blowing everywhere
Whether there be rain or snow no one really cares
Old people walking in the park
Recalling all the glory days
A colliery village full of life
Smiling children out at play
Kicking footballs in the street
Being chased by the man next door
It seems so sad now looking back
Nothing happens here anymore
Young people they all drift away leaving the old behind
Heading to the brighter lights a better life to find
Those who stay here won't lie down
They swear the place won't die so the daily struggle carries on
While the world just passes by

Jeff Storey

Letting Go Of Someone

They have a smile when they first tell you they're leaving.
Have a party to say farewell with such happiness and galore.
But I know inside they'll soon be grieving.
Why? Because I've seen it all before.

That person might be a family or a friend you loved for the right
    reason or the wrong.
A person with whom you shared everything together,
A person your heart skipped a beat for because they were the
    dream of your life for so long.

The time has come for they have to go, and tears slowly creep
    in your eyes
You tell them to keep in touch a phone, a letter, anything.
And so they hit the road giving a hug and saying their 'byes.
Immediately you have that pang of emptiness, suddenly you
    know it won't be the same no matter how hard you try.

For whatever reason they left either for fortune or even for fame.
That person took a special part in your life which no one can replace.
Letting go of someone always hurts because without that
    person it will never be the same.

Jusna Begum

The Struggle

Born deformed with twisted limbs
Unable to do the usual things
Can't talk to say how I feel
So they think I'm mental as well as deformed
A pat on the head with a half cocked smile
They say 'How is she doing?' as if I'm not there
My brain's frustrated and overworked
Thinking of ways to make itself heard
The people around don't have a clue
And can't understand what I'm going through
I'll keep up the struggle and hope that one day
I will be able to say just how I feel
And until that time happens I'll stay locked away
In my twisted old body without any say.

Maureen Roscoe

Lonesome Retirement

Can you see beyond my smile the pain within my heart?

Do you know just how it feels to never feel a part
of life that is around me, of couples young and old,
Their aspirations hopes and dreams so often being told?
They plan to do so many things, as couples often do
And every time I hear of them the pain cuts in so deep,
It's like I'm in another world, yet I am not asleep.
You see, we too had plans mapped out for our later years
But death has snatched away those plans and left me only tears.
So should you see me turn away, bite my lip to halt those tears,
Try to understand how hard it is, to be alone in retirement years.

Christine Neville

Nigel Watson-Nicholas Or The Mandrill

You may not know what a mandrill is,
well he is a monkey with a very strange phiz.
I know of one, and he is very high class;
goes by the name of Nigel Watson hyphen Nicholas.
His family is rich and of very blue blood
and mixing with hoi poloi is nipped in the bud!
You can tell he's from nobility by the colour of his nose.
It's blue see, and Roman. You know one of those?
Impeccably dressed in white tie and tails,
He's the toast of his club, where he dines on snails.

Nigel goes out shooting on the glorious twelfth.
Not pheasant, that's too rich, he mush consider his health.
He prefers fresh coconuts from high in the tree,
should he shoot one over that may be for me.
So I'll just stand here patiently holding my plate,
I like him a lot, he's my very best mate.
For Nigel is generous and I love him to bits!
But he has just one fault; he is covered in Nits!
So when he has finished we will go home
and I'll give him a good going over with a fine toothed comb.

Avril Maguire

The Tired Oak-Piece

To My Dear Friend Dee

A battered well worn oak-piece stood
against a wall which over looked the
clutter of a huge gigantic hall,

A chippendale stood regal with polish
that shone through, and a chesterfield sat
silently admiring the view,

Then a gathered crowd assembled and awaited
at the back, while the shuttered doors were
opened to a jolly looking pack,

The crystal chimes are ringing and the
chatter it was high, but the battered well–worn
oak-piece groaned a tired sigh,

But soon gasps of admiration sought people
to look down, when a well proportioned lady
she pushed the piece around,

She caught the piece quite firmly, then
heaved it to and fro, and that gave the tired
oak-piece a contented inner glow,

Her inspection, it was thorough no objections there at all,

And soon a contented oak-piece waved good-bye to that
cluttered hall.

Hope is the fuel of one's soul.
No cloud is so black,
But that it finally passes.

E. J. Ward

A Battle

The autumn leaves of red and gold
Stir in the breath of an autumn breeze.
Sometimes they lie like poppies
Or like soldiers in a foreign battlefield.
The leaves may blow to and fro.
But the bodies lie quietly still.
The autumn comes and goes,
But the bodies remain where they have fallen.

Autumn will soon give way to a winter scene,
The land will be covered with snow.
Snow will cloak the graves of the soldiers
Who gave their lives so long ago.
Then spring will come
And everything will burst into life
The children will sing for joy and play,
For they have been saved now the battle has been won.

Stanley R. Devine

A Lost Husband

I lay awake, my eyes are wet,
Where are you now?
My other half, I can't forget.
Where are you now?

The years were long the time has passed
The tears were many the die was cast.
Where are you now?

My hand is empty, as is my bed

My heart is full of tears unshed
Where are you now?

So young we were, the years were full.
Where did you go?
We didn't think they'd end at all
I loved you so.
We rowed as well, with many fights
And now I am alone at night
I do believe you've gone to God.
He loved you too.
Amen.

Teresa A. Clark

Reminiscing In The Park

Late in the afternoon, I sat beneath a tree;
Everyone in the park enjoyed the sun but me,
My heart was heavy laden; an answer I did seek,
After all, I reasoned, I shouldn't feel this bleak!
I needed to divert my mind,
Leave my troubles far behind,
I watched the pretty sunbeams, dancing in the air.
They seemed so very happy, without a single care,
Then I recalled a winter's night, that had passed me by,
When snowflakes, light as feathers fluttered through the sky,
Working silently together, so that by the morning's light,
A dazzling picture was revealed: The world all clothed in white,
Suddenly I felt uplifted; reminiscing in the park,
But I made my way back home, as it was nearly dark.

Sheryl Williamson

The Soul's Long Wished For Rest

Not even a cushioned childhood,
Can prepare for life's great quest.
It merely gives repose to find
Dreams to remember in blissful peace;
When sleepless night, keeps fretting mind
From the soul's long wished for rest.

Not even past love can persuade
Us to relinquish conscious thought,
How thus, and thus it was,
Or might have been — and yet
Would it be less than magic
If seeking love found naught.

Not even the honey–filled hours
Are wasted time. Relish now
For time past, leaves only time to come.
Remember the kiss of comfort from the sun,
The bliss of an ice–cold breeze
With salt upon its breath from seas
Uncharted. Remember these
As the soul waits for its longed for rest.

Olive M. Wood

The Bar Fly

Give me a whisky mac or a rum and black,
And I will thank you kindly,
For it's a cold night out
And a bottle of stout,
Will not put warmth inside me;
I'll thank you for a white wine,
A glass of cider too;
But a whisky mac or a rum and black
And I'll be a friend to you.

M. F. Bones

Country Ways

Darting drafts dance round my feet;
I'll pull on my boots; go out to meet
The cutting wind, and stinging snow,
Which scornfully mock my fire's warm glow.

At break of dawn, a path I made
From my cottage door with my trusty old spade.
But if it is now covered over with snow,
Bravely once more, to my task I shall go,

Returning at last to my dear fireside,
Laden with logs, in which I take pride,
In chopping each morning in wise preparation,
For just such an eve, as this storm does occasion.

I'll turn up the oil lamp, and take up my volume
Of great English poets; a joy to consume!
I envy no townsfolk, who reach out at leisure,
To the flick of a switch—they must pay for this pleasure.

My fuel is abundant, and candles are cheap.
And sufficient to me, cordial company to keep,
Is a well–thumbed old text, worth its weight in gold;
Whilst sturdy oak shutters, keep out the cruel cold.

Jean Mary Brady

Bullied

Some people tease me because of the way I act
and because of my small size I cannot fight back

So I go home crying longing for the day
when they at last leave me alone or bring flowers to my grave . . .

Nigel Shipley

Did I Say It

You have said, that I have said it. How certain are you in
saying that I said it. I may have thought it but not said it, so
you have read my thoughts and thought that I have said it.

In my mind, the thoughts arose and I have thought it. So you
have read my mind and know that I have thought it. You are
in my mind and know my thoughts, how can you be there and
know that I have said it.

I can, in words my thoughts express to say it, so if you are in
my mind and thoughts, how could you hear it. My ears
explain the way that I would say it, but you will insist and say
I said it.

I have asked myself, how could I have said it, it was in my
mind I knew that I had thought it. You still maintain that I
have said it, which makes me to wonder, did I say it.

I thought and rethought, how could I have said it. My mind
and thoughts, are mine to know it. Yet you have said that I
have said it.
How I wish that I had never thought it, so that you, no longer
could remind me, that I had said it.

Leslie George Platt

Voices In The Wind

The pyramids of "Giza", an awesome sight
When seen at night added by sound and light
I long to be there,
To see the "son-et-lumiere"
Truly magnificent, the "colossi of memon"
Once guarded by asps filled with poisonous venom
We walk the land of "kings and queens"
Invading their tombs, enthralled with the scenes
Ancient hieroglyphics in striking colours
Adorn the walls and the ceilings above us.
"Abu Simbel" the temple of "Ramses" II
The grandest monument, its sight awaits you
The chatter of locals discussing their day
Smiles all around as you make your way
Destination reached, our cruise complete
We reflect on our visits, an accomplished feat
As we rest in the heat with the sun God "Ra"
Was that the wind again? Or "Pharaohs" voices from afar . . .

Pauline Giles

A Deceptive Journey

The world is full of human beings,
then why does loneliness strike each one?
Everyday he lives and dies,
but still disappointment attacks each man.
He walks, smiles, a grief that he conceals,
a numbness in eyes,
what is on the lips, what does he reveal.

Every man feels the same,
all experience and shudder with pain,
know defeat, determined to fight,
only if he knew it right,
walk hand in hand,
remove storms to come,
fellowship will all succumb,
but he carries his burden,
accustomed to isolation, ultimately
draws his last breath.

Such is his life, begins and passes unknown,
disillusioned by its own role, remains alone.

   Beenish Nafees

"Forbidden Love"

The days go by so slowly whenever we're away from each
other, can't get you out of my thoughts. Each passing day,
each crippling moment, I experience the fear that we may never
get the chance to fuse together the innate passion we have
found. I feel stifled, and choked by the fact that God has
bonded our soul to this point, a feeling so pure, so wonderful,
so unique and so strong, yet so wrong . . . How can some-
thing so right be considered so wrong? . . . I want to relin-
quish the needs of my excessive sexual desires, but how can I
. . . It's all I have of you and of wanting to be with you . . .
I'm only human after all. The physical pain, the spiritual
needs, I don't ever know if anything could ever compensate
for the emptiness I feel; not being able to be with you the way
we should not being able to express what we feel for the fear
of being tarnished by societies stereotypes. I want to stream
out as the frustration is unbearable but who will console me?
How can one be open minded to something one declares
morally unacceptable and distasteful. We cannot choose
when we fall in love or with whom, but can choose what we
are to do with it when it happens. Do we suppress it so deep,
it makes us behave as a recluse? Or do we release it fulfilling
life's mission, "to love and be loved". I accept simply, that
caring, talking, even sharing a part of your life and you I'm
grateful to do but . . . I still wait earnestly in hope for the
chance to be set free.

   S. Wildman

Sarajevo 1995

Terror, horror, panic stricken
Running around like a headless chicken
A bomb's gone off, there's people down
A mortar has landed in market town,

A mother's scream, a little child's cry
They hear their fathers' last goodbye
A motionless woman, those staring eyes.
Her husband gone, no time for goodbyes.

A racing pulse and soaked in sweat,
I help a woman I've never met.
I want to shout, and scream and cry
Why do innocents have to die.

3 Miles away behind their lines
Factions laugh as their mortars whine.
For they are safe in their dingy hole
As they strip the town of its precious souls.

37 dead and many maimed, from a mortar that wasn't even aimed.
"It's from the Serbs", the people say. "They'll get theirs, one
fine day."

But until that fateful time the town's church bells refuse to chime.
37 dead and many maimed, from a mortar bomb that wasn't aimed.

   Patrick Robinson

Cats

Cats walk dignified, they walk tall.
They walk accurate and smooth.
Cats sleep slumped near a cosy spot
In the sun.
They sleep peacefully, silent and while they are
asleep they lie looking smooth, silky and sleek.
Cats jump in twists and stretch their snaky tails.
Cats sit proud, looking at anyone who passes them.
They sit smart, in a world of their own.
Cats walk.
Sleek cats don't creak.
Cats walk boastful and sly.
At the end of the day cats sleep quiet in dreams
of their own.

   Maria Obasi

Mind How You Go Little Children

Mind how you go little children as you go out to play,
Take notice of your mother when she tells you not to stray.
But that garden gate is open, you go out and run.
Mind how you go little children as you go down to the park,
Make sure you are home long before it gets dark,
Don't get into mischief as you have your fun.

Don't talk to that stranger watching you swing and slide,
They are not all like your parents who laughs when you hide,
He might have nasty thoughts and wait until you are alone.
So keep together little children, and you will have nothing to fear.
It doesn't matter if your clothes are torn and have a dirty ear.
It's getting dark little children, time to be going back home.

Mind how you go little children as you make your way home.
Keep with someone, that stranger is still waiting when you're alone.
Your mother will be watching that open gate with a little fear.
She will sigh with relief as you run up the garden path.
She will shout at the state of you, and make you have a bath.
But she will hug and welcome you home with a happy tear.

   Charles S. Layton

'Missing You'

I miss you more than you'll ever know
Mr. Magic Man I love you so
Can't you see how much you're hurting me
Can't you see how much I care
I thought we shared a love so rare.

You left me when I needed you most
You just left and walked away.
Please come back I beg you
I need you more each day.
Every day my body aches for you
I miss you more than words can say.

I love you, need you, want you
Please come back to me today
I promise that I will always be true
If only you would love me too
I wonder if you're missing me as much I miss you.

   Lynn E. Boleyn

The Arctic Fox (Otherwise Known As The Ice Fox)

The ice-fox is a scavenger,—It's the key to their success,
It's their lone fight for survival, that make them—the very best.
They live on the Artic Coastline,—and they guard their territory,
Cold climates do not bother them,—through blizzards they still see.
The Artic-fox will often eat,—almost anything,
From shredding reindeer antlers,—to gulls, chicks, and crabfish.
The Artic-fox will often climb,—to get his long watched prey,
He sniffs the ground, then prowls around,—and pounces in a way.
The animal it seizes, is dead within an instant—
The fox's teeth are sinking in, and tearing it to pieces,
His diamond eyes are dark and shrewd—
Tho' very glassy when hunting food,
He has a big fur coat and pointed ears—and can live as long
as seven years.

   Marie Angela Dolan

The Old Green House

The old green house is very old
it has been here since my granddad was alive
My granddad died at 73 and he loved his old
green house
He kept his long hose in the old greenhouse
he had his plant's pansies, daffodils, primroses too
The old greenhouse is still here now dirty and
battered but still alive
I'm just glad it's still here
My granddad loved the old green house just like me
He told me about it when I was 3
I never will forget that day about the old
green house

Rachel Clements

The Tears The Heart Cannot Hide

The tears the heart cannot hide,
The floods of pain the love that died,
The heart bleeds hurt rivers are cried,
The streams of sorrow the red seas are wide,
The stormy oceans the high heavy tide,
Thunder bolts strike hit from every side,
Thunder storms in this life I do ride,
Waiting for justice to be my bride,
For love has grieved me tears have not dried,
Injustice is rife sin is never satisfied,
For righteousness the Lord God knows I've tried.

Brian Noel Degnan

Humanity

Oh little Angel, how well you sleep.
Garrulous, and chaotic only moments ago.
You make my life so complete, so I've just
popped in to your room for a little peep.
Amidst the hurricanes of life's turbulent mist.
You guile the anger that swells inside.

Of so precious a child, Gods only gift, go missing,
We love them all, I must insist.
Now dark black days, of all hope gone, the
tears we now shed.
The little children that really shone, leaving
the path of life, we must now tread.
Of life's biggest blunder, we must put asunder.

Life, loves, treasures we all cherish, plants,
weeds, litter are here to perish.
Not us, no, we have to be strong. Oh love
these little Angels guide them along.
As we go on our daily task, send us a moonbeam,
and fill are hearts with tenderness, say a
prayer for our missing Angels, we've missed them for so long.

Jenny Butters

General Jim

As the turgid noise of tanks went on
somewhere in the distance light
shone through, like the angel of death, and there was you too.
1996, the wheels go on, more than one
man makes in a lifetime, turning
about I ain't supposed to be, hear? But I was.
Soon the smell of iron and salt
would consume the senses.
What's it all about, as behind us
mushroom monstrosities confined
any possible retreat, well.
Destined to second band daylight, are we safe, hear?
No, but surely stoned by men in
blade clothes, who have shelters for themselves.
Up the royal mile, machine guns
and artillery, blowing buck out of
us, and my be Jesus to
does that mean I have to spank the monkey again?
Then I woke up, caught in the middle of a horrible dream
my sister was a spastic but my books were clean.

Jeremy Charles Gallacher

Pharaoh's Island . . . (Summer 1944)

A paradise for youngsters providing they can swim.
With skiffs and punts and kayaks and sailing boats to trim.
The barges in the middle, to prevent the sea plane's land
With German spies, or other things, the Germans may have planned.

The barges were the ideal place to smoke a "Weight" or two.
Where adults couldn't find the naughty "Pharaoh's Island Crew".
Our heroes were the fighters, in air, on sea, or land;
Glen Miller, Eric Winstone, or Vic Sylvester's Band.

The swans would nest in Sphinx's creek and heaven help the fool,
Who tried to steal the cygnets and break the river's rule.
And once a year the "uppers" came to mark them with a `ring',
For they belonged to George VI, as George VI was King.

'Matric' and 'School Certificate' were over, thank the Lord.
No more mathematics, no more children getting bored.
Your whole life still ahead of you, a war still to be won;
Excitements and disasters with years and years to run.

There was a certain magic in that Island on the Thames.
Two houses and some chalets, all with Egyptian names.
A widow made a fortune when her greyhound won first place
And named the Island 'Pharaoh', to commemorate the race.

Ann Fitzmaurice Creighton

A Widowed Mother

Gnarled and twisted with arthritic contours
Grasping the ochre arms of the chair
The wood and flesh infuse as one, each blending with the other
As pock–wormed, score–marked oak
Meets callused skin and brittle bone

And varicosed legs stretch from a withered trunk
And numb-sleep by the dying hearth
In antiquated slippers, soft with dust
Begging reprieve from toil
Too long have walked the earth

Rivulets of bitterness extend from age thinned lips
And furrows, scored by tears, mark the emaciated cheeks
While cavernous grooves enfold myopic eyes,
With glimmer long since gone
Isolated decadence reeks

Narrow mindedness has alienated.
Her rosary, calumny and detraction
Reflect the lifelong path she's worn.
Self pity reeks from this rotting shell as extreme unction looms.
She waits for that for which she has been born.

Tess Good-O'Brien

Sound—The Omnipresence

The background of our lives is shadowed by sound.
It can be loud, quiet, noisy, even bordering on silence.
Wherever we go, it reverberates around and around.
Whatever we do, our ears can be battered by its violence.

Every place has its own acceptability of amount.
A swinging clock pendulum makes us number its ticks.
A travelling train, a steady speed means a regular count.
A crying child, a mother thinks again, "he's up to his tricks".

The penetrating, persistent hum of traffic on a modern motorway,
Increasing in those hours when we 'rush', our money to earn,
Also when we 'rush' away from work, needing time to play.
The squeal of brakes, the screech of collisions, pain, will we
    ever learn?

Did nightingales really sing in Berkeley Square?
We listened to their song in the trees, around the lake, on one
    country estate.
The trees have gone, houses and roads now encircle that lake,
    no bird is there.
Without human help, even Nature is unable to keep its natural state.

But with all the extremes of unremitting noise,
When we think the whole world has got it wrong,
Before the storm breaks, we can look up into the darkening skies,
And listen to the faithful blackbird start up his warning song.

Albert G. Willis

Nature And Spring

As I walk down a country lane, thinking of the past.
The world has changed, and troubles cast.
But nature and growth, remain the same.
A thrush is singing, perched on chimney high.
The sun is shining, there's a clear blue sky.
A startled bird flies from its nest,
As I look, it's a robin red breast.
Blackbird calling to its mate,
That's perching on the farmyard gate.
Cattle in the fields are grazing,
A cockerel crows, a horse starts naying.
The cows are waiting to be milked,
A farmer comes to guide them in.
As I walk and see these things,
My heart gives just a little twinge.
Nature and love, "they are a beautiful thing,"
We feel this most, "with the approach of spring."
Flowers bloom, bees pollinate the various plants.
This is the time that nature calls,
When born are creatures, "great and small."

E. D. Shaw

Christmas At St. Joseph's

St. Joseph's is a holy place,
    Where Mother Mary stands in grace,
To guard the patients in her care,
    and show that love is always there.

With picture cards of the son she bore
    as they stand in silence on the door.
The Xmas tree lights up the hall,
    and trimmings bright on every wall.

From tranquil beds the angels shine,
    alighting on the window pane.
Then the snowman and fairies come
    To bring us hope and say 'well done'.

To Sister, doctors, nurses, all.
    Who are always there at a patient's call.
We wonder how they sometimes cope.
    But our Lord and Saviour gives us hope.

Rona Morley

Untitled

As I sit and watch T.V.
I wonder if love will ever find me,
I dream of life as a couple,
"Maybe I am better off without the trouble",
Then out of the blue,
A wife, 3 kids and a dog too,
At last I am happy this will do,
Then for months it's D.I.Y,
With the wife's ever present eye
As I stand back and say "that looks fine",
She reply's "it's O.K. If not a little out of life".

Elliott Garner

Untitled

Do not live in despair,
Just sit quietly, remember God does care.
That miracles do happen in a wonderful way.
Even when ups and downs happen each day.
Have enough faith, hope and love.
Put your trust in God above.
Kneel down and say a prayer
I know for sure God will be there.

Listen? What do I hear?
A voice of one so dear.
As I close my eyes tight,
And ask God to guide me in his sight.
I sure feel relief.
To know it's God that I believe.
In a time of distress
God will listen, and you he will bless.

Rita Dandridge

'Breathing'

It surrounds us, heaving, breathing,
What keeps us alive? And apparently sane.

What is this that caused us so much pain at times?
Yet alternatively produces so much happiness,
It can make us smile, or cry, or at spaced intervals both.

And at peaceful interludes help us to reflect,
And to dream, and to remember that we are alive,
That is the way life is,
And why that is?

What if for a time that something special goes missing?
We feel that we can't go on with life?
We feel that, that is gone.
Our life for a time is devoid of meaning.

We scream, we shout for it.
For what our mind is screaming?
It is for?

We calm down and recover for all of us know.
Whether we realize at the time that it is true.
That it is love that surrounds us heaving and breathing.

Clare Martin

'Wooden Books'

Trees are special, books are good,
Both are made of solid wood.

Trees sacrifice their life for you,
So you can read a book or two,
In this matter they have no choice,
They cannot speak, they have no voice.

Books are special, trees are good
Both are made of solid wood

Books are precious so take care,
When turning pages, not to tear,
Think! How a tree would shake with rage,
To see your scribble upon a page,

Trees are special, books are good
Both are made of solid wood,

Books from trees? Yes it's true!
Their lives are taken just for you,
Do trees have feelings, feel pain and strife?
Yes! Look after books, they cost a life.

Tony Murphy

Fathers Day 1996, Manchester

Hopes were high on the city streets, one sunny summer's day,
Happy voices could be heard, all hearts were light and gay.
Wives and mothers, sons and brothers, made up the happy crowds,
Chatting cheerily to each other, they spoke their thoughts aloud.

The stores were packed with endless queues,
    for all were there to buy,
A watch, some gloves, a pair of shoes, maybe a lovely tie?
But no-one there suspected then, of someone's wicked will,
Their evil minds planned to destroy, to bruise, to maim or kill.

A hidden bomb began its work, and like a roar of thunder,
It seemed to split the world apart, and tore the streets asunder.
Then suddenly all hell broke loose, and flames shot to the sky,
Great buildings crashed down to the ground,
    smashed glass began to fly.

Twisted steel and concrete walls, were hurtled through the air,
Escaping gas and shattered glass, and fires spread everywhere.
Both old and young were stained with blood,
    young babes in prams survived,
For help came quickly to the scene or hundreds could have died.

No doubt all dads received their gifts, maybe a little late,
Some anxious thoughts were on their minds, on that terrifying date.
As we reflect upon that scene, and hope all strife will cease,
We pray that wise men can prevail, to bring us lasting peace.

Walter Scott

Free-Fall

In a normal street on a normal day
In a normal city where the bankers play.
With the sun in the sky, and the moon hidden too,
Everything the same, nothing ever new.

One day when the workers filed in crooked human lines
Down the street, expressionless zombies of commercial time,
Their progress was stopped and they weren't even warned
By a whirlpool of people, round and round they swarmed.

Each one was looking with mouth open wide,
Some gasped, some screamed and some even cried.
And they followed their eyes heavenward, ten stories high
To see white figure leaning on the sky.

Like the sails of a ship resting on the seven seas
Her pure white grown lifts slowly on the breeze.
She stands in the window like a picture in its frame,
A free spirit that no one could ever hope to tame.

The angel on the tower-block reached out to the air,
Behind her streamed the golden banner of her hair.
With one step she reached a plateau which nobody could see.
Finally, finally her soul was free.

Nicola Baughan

Fortress My Guard

No-one can take a hurt more than once,
Deeply that is.
So protection is built to preclude the chance,
If change there is.

Awkward and crusty one seems to become,
Briefly—hard.
The walls must be built of stone driven home,
Fortress my guard.

Within these stone walls so apparently strong,
Dare I hope?
I may live out my life safe from all wrong.
Can I cope?

Whatever I feel must never be shown,
Bearing rein tight.
Whatever I need must not become known,
Never see light.

Outwardly cheerful must I always seem,
Sunnily smiling.
Whilst behind this false mask nightmares I dream,
Partially dying.

Jean Brumpton

Ladder Of Love

The prospective young lover looks to the sky,
And sees the love ladder towering high,
It stands still and long, revealing a life,
Of embraces and tiffs, a husband and wife.

They come in huge numbers every day,
To find out what the ladder will say,
Climb ten rungs for beauty and what do you see?
A pretty, sweet girl is smiling at me.

Ten more if your flesh is in the right place,
Five if it's not; move behind in the race,
Turn to your left, what do you find there?
My eyes are in line with the bottom of her hair.

Are you bad tempered? Then climb only four,
You say you're romantic; jump on a score,
Naughtiness, do you fare well in bed?,
I now look down on top of her head.

Last now and some would say least,
Can you offer your partner a feast?
A Rolls Royce, yacht or gold leafed oak tree?
Look across tell me, where may you be?

Scott J. S. Stewart

Nanny—A Memory

In Memory of Vivian Dorothy Birchall
Born 12 July 1920, Died 21 March 1996 R.I.P.

Nanny
    You searched through bombed rubble searching for life
Now I search and I'm searching for you,
All that you stood for is all that you are,
Nanny you're everything now I stand for you,
Whenever I think I'll think of you,
Whenever I write I'll think of you,
When I hear of bravery I'll say your name,
I watched you suffer with tears in my eyes,
True courage I've seen you perform,
You kept me smiling through thick and through thin,
Now when I smile I'm thinking of you,
You will live on through me I swear to you,
You are now linked with Poppy.
One day I'll link with you too
Nanny I live for the day when we'll join hands again,
We'll walk on together with no cracks in our chains
But today I'll keep on smiling just like you showed me,
Until tomorrow when we meet again.

Katie Vivian Birchall

"Earth's Body"

The spring has sprung from winter's grasp, earth's body
gives life to dormant seed the snow drops stand proud for
moments few,
The daffodils and tulips in golden hue
All life is filled with hope and promise,
the sun is warm the rain is light,
It's all so green a wondrous sight.
Like life itself a start so pure, everything new beyond
comprehension,
Walking to summer with full bloom of youth, but facing the
autumn with
Some apprehension.
The winter arrives all but too soon, but we need not have
worried as we lay down to sleep,
Earth's body will keep us till we rise from the deep.

W. Edwards

True Love

    True love is letting go of fear,
To be cradled in a heart so dear,
This rainbow in ones heart does glow,
Its eternal beauty will make you grow,
In every colour there shines a light,
Please set it free to take its flight,
To put splashes of colour in hearts full of pain,
To put glorious sunshine in their lives again,
So let your tears come let them water your soul,
For this true love will make one whole,
Cup it in your hands and set if free,
For without this love where would we be?

Nicki Campbell-Barker

Dancing With Astaire

I'm seen at family parties sitting with the other "grans."
You'll know me by my thin grey hair and thick rheumatic hands.
Yet, deep behind my faded eyes my mind still has its zest.
And I'm out there in the middle rock n' rolling with the rest.

Sometimes at school on sports days you'll see me in the crowd,
Willing children to the finish, though my cheers no longer loud.
But still my heart is pounding as I leave old age behind.
And I'm in the "young Mum's hundred yards" and running
like the wind.

My partner is immaculate in top hat, tie and tails.
The tapping feet, the music. Oh! The magic never fails.
And my slippered feet are twitching as I snuggle in my chair.
'Cause I'm slim! And blonde! And twenty! And I'm dancing
with Astaire.

Pamela Baker

The Gentle Face

I saw the laughter in her eyes,
A gentle face a loving smile,
She was the apple of my eye,
That gentle and most loving child.

Today she starts out in life.
In a big sad world full of strife,
But the gentle smile full of grace,
Will take her through from place to place.

The day has come for her to leave home,
To start a new life on her own,
I see not the laughter or the smile,
As she sets out on that second mile.

Three years have passed since she went away,
I never will forget that sad day.
When the laughter and the loving smile
Had died in that gentle face.

Carole Slade

Untitled

The world spins by and day turns to night,
The moon goes down, and soon there is light,
Birds sing in trees by God's hand that were planted,
But man looks on, he takes everything for granted,
He does not appreciated the joys of living,
The simple things we all could share,
Our love that's for giving,
The warmth of a smile could say so much,
To say that we care by a simple touch.
As seasons come, and seasons go,
Will we ever appreciate the breezes that blow,
The new leaves of spring that always appears,
It's God's way of telling us rebirth is here.
But man to himself is his worse enemy,
Evil through out and always will be,
And one good example of one man insane,
And God bless his victims, the dead at Dunblane.

M. Nash

Have A Nice Day

A robin stands by the garden pond
And looks around at what's going on
The goldfish are swimming, safe and sound
And a puppy dog barks, at the postman found
Tall trees are waving in the gentle breeze
Bringing down the first autumn leaves,
Smoke from a cottage twists and turns
From an open log fire that burns and burns,
The milkman is calling with a tune
He's always so cheerful, even afternoons,
The sound of traffic on the motor way hums
And the sight of an athlete, who takes off and runs
Children are awaking, and having their say
As the robin flies off, have a nice day.

Sonny Blackwood

Rewards

Rewards are of many shapes and sizes,
all can bring so much joy,
love freedom, peace can be valued prizes.

Rewards can be seen everywhere all around,
size should not be important,
it's the happiness that comes when they are found.

Rewards do brighten a sad and dull life,
make us smile and laugh,
take away the harmful strife.

Rewards come from out of the blue, such a great high,
surprise, shock, pleasure,
feelings that have happened to you and I.

Rewards help us to learn and to grow,
understand, feel,
all that is so very necessary for us to discover and know.

Kaz Holman

Sheila's Song, To Be A Widow Long

The Lord God said, "Put me not to the test",
In matters of marriage, same age partners must be best,
Psalm Ninety advises upon the expectancy of life,
So why have a husband, much older than a wife?
In matters of life, the weaker sex is stronger,
As an actuary will tell you that women live longer,
Then talk to a doctor, the scenario becomes quite mad,
Twenty more years allowed, for a man to be a dad,
Was it Freud or Greer who drove women into careers?
Should they listen to God and avoid all the tears,
Thinking aright is a very good prevention,
Rather than seeking a miracle and biological extension.

Adrian B. Rimington

Believe

If you believe in yourself, as you go from to day
    You will find that life will lead you on your way
So don't despair when things get tough and hard
    It's a way of understanding life's pathway to the stars,
Without the downs, there won't be ups; for us to live and learn
    We must have balance in all we do, so trust for your return
Make every day a learning day, so use your magic power
    To keep you on your guidance watch your thoughts by the hour
Thoughts, they are such powerful things, so watch them come
and go
    Are they good, are they bad? only you will know.
Follow all the good ones and learn from the bad,
    It's not this moment you can see the way that things will turn
It's only later that we see our lessons here to learn.

Margaret Skinner

Worry

Why do you come whispering, sounding in my head
When I was fast asleep and all my cares had fled?
You show me what I cannot be
You speak of things long dead
You whirl and dance and undulate round about my bed.
You drive me to a frenzy
I cannot see for tears
Regrets and old defeats replaying loudly in my ears.
You rob me of my logic
You steal from me my peace
You lie, exaggerate and cheat, make all of it seem real.
Then just as dawn is breaking
When I need my strength to rise
You twist into the shaft of sun that shines into
my eyes.

Judith Climer

The Tyke's Lament

The Cricketers of Yorkshire over the years have
had so little joy and too many tears.
The plight of our team was for all to see, the
laughing stock or so it appeared to me!

One night I had a dream a newborn son—the
future captain of our team. I spoke to my wife
and she agreed, we should try for a son so we might succeed.

A left arm fast bowler who would give them a
hiding, so I convinced my wife she must stay in
the Riding. He must be Yorkshire born and bred
to bring back a dream once thought dead!

But alas my friends although I prayed daily, the
love of my life gave birth to our Hayley. And so
good people it wasn't to be, no sign
of a Trueman, Rhodes or Ve-ri-ty!
"Paul, all is not lost," my wife said to me,
as she handed me a daughter, now that made three.

"Do not be melancholic the future is bright!
For girls can have sons to continue the fight."
So fellow Tykes do not despair for the Yorkshire Rose,
with the help of our Hayley, we'll have another Bowes!

Paul Gowland

The Man In The Street

Often watching discussions, on my T.V. screen.
I find remarks by "experts", quite often do demean
They sit there po–faced, in the studio heat.
And denigrate this person. "The man in the street".
"He wouldn't understand, it's well above his head"
As if he's a moron and half his brain is dead.
Who is this man? It sounds like he's tramp
Living in a cardboard box, outside there in the damp.
But no! He is educated, maybe no degree,
And through their manifestations, he can easily see.
In long words they couch their statements. It really is an art
Like quintessential. The most essential part,
He sees them pontificating, a long word for me.
Hoping to impress their peers and gain another fee.
The man in the street, probably has a wife.
And he's learnt really well, in the school of life.
He certainly isn't ignorant and definitely not obtuse
His knowledge at his work place and hobbies put to use
I'm glad I'm not an expert, with a narrow minded view.
For I'm in the man in the street, or possibly it's you.

Peter Madle

Beyond Imagination

Drifting into a silent sleep
Floating above clouds and mountain peaks
Minds eye reflecting a new world to see
Superior beings watching over you and me
Colours of the rainbow transpired visions
beyond imagination
Powerful faces strengthening our minds
limitations spiritual awakening beyond all knowledge
of mankind
A unique infinity for us all to find

Nicola Jayne Richardson

In The Papers

I saw it in the papers, I see it every day,
The tiny little children they grab and steal away,
Is it a reflection of our times, our gloom and apathy,
Or has it always happened, though not to you and me.

Could it be your baby, your sunshine happy face,
Turned to tears by hatred how strange this human race,
Most of us are loving, most of us are kind,
It only takes an in balance to sway a once sane mind.

No one knows what sparks the person who offends,
Perhaps our world's the villain, a world we need to mend,
We all have a threshold over which we dare not step,
Do you know your limit? Or just what establishment expects!
Just before you judge them, about their awful deed,
Take a minute to reflect, what it was, their need,
If we could have helped, or stopped that final step,
That took them over the edge, we could with love—I bet!

Auril Smith

Put On A Face

Put on a face and pretend
You're as good as they all say
Your fear hidden by a smile
Will force you to that room
They're all taller of course
And some of them seem to smirk
Weighing you up
And you who have trouble
With names
And always those who communicate whispering
And always those who star through windows
And always those already bored
Imagined contempt?
A kind of shared confidence there
Which undermines your own
Get them to open their books
And
Put on a face.

Colin Park

A Sense Of Real Freedom

Free in your confine, a natural habitat,
How free would you be?
Once removed from your natural habitat,
'Twas so with Man;
He, too, was free like you
In his natural habitat,
Until that time when Man
Deriving knowledge, misused,
Confined Man into that which is based
On some assumption apparently true; yet false

Yes, Oh lesser creatures
Free by your physiology;
Not yet tampered by Man,
How does Man envy you;
You move from place to place
In your own time and space,
With your only Lay by Nature given;
No wonder the Robin continually sings
Its natural songs with a sense of real freedom

Alphonso Charles

Beaches

Always at the end of land,
Beaches are covered in stones and sand.
Peaceful places where you relax,
You lie there, but lets face the facts;
Ships go by, polluting sea and sky,
The oil leaks out over birds, not letting them fly.
The oil washes out onto the shore,
Making it dangerous to explore.
Is this the way that it must go on?
It has to stop before too long.

Sarah Trickett

Here Comes Summer

Suddenly it's summer—blue skies and blue seas
Leaves of brightest green are clothing all the trees.
Roses, clematis, pansies and pinks,
All at once are blooming—and methinks:
"This is what we waited all the winter for"
Summer joys in plenty for us are now in store:
On a hot June afternoon—Strawberries and cream,
Time to sit in the garden and there to dream
Of faraway places, the turquoise sea
With a white sandy beach inviting you and me.
Warm summer nights for going out strolling,
Eating "al fresco", watching the ocean rolling.
For lucky old me, it's not just a dream,
For we are lucky enough to have already been
For two lovely weeks we've been away
During June on our summer holiday.

Jackie Holland

A Day At The Seaside

Here we all are in our favourite spot,
quick bring out the sun cream it's going to be hot.
The children can't wait to run to the sea,
Just look at them splashing around with glee.
Two happy faces with smiling eyes,
I'm feeling content with family ties.
Chicken sandwiches and potato salad—home-made,
some fruit, brownies and lemonade.
A flask of tea and one of coffee.
also yogurt flavoured caramel toffee.
Up the steep steps to the top of the cliff,
where the grass is green and the elderly sit.
Pass rows of hotels with long fronted lawns,
where flowers, lanterns and fairy lights adorn.
Giant hollyhocks and sunflowers sway in the breeze,
there's an ice cream parlour beyond those trees.
Up cobblestone streets to curiosity shops,
selling gifts made from shells and all kinds of what-nots.
One last treat at the end of a perfect day,
eating fried fish and chips overlooking the bay.

Maureen Coughlan

Shattered Dreams

You plan your lives together and share your hopes and dreams.
You think you know each other but things aren't what they seem.
The years you are together are built on love and trust.
And then he tells you something and your dreams are turned to dust.

He's found another woman and he loves her more than you.
Your life is now in ruins, what are you going to do?
How do you tell your little girl, her daddy's gone away,
He doesn't love her mummy but he loves her more each day.
We told her she was special, she was our 'chosen' one,
We'd always be there for her, no matter what she'd done.
So now her daddy's gone, away, how do I explain—
He's not a 'bad' daddy when he's causing so much pain.
So now, for her I must be strong.
It's for me to teach her right from wrong.
I'll do my best, do all I can,
I'll prove to him how strong I am!

Tracey Mills

Sympathy

It's hard to find the words to say,
When someone you love just slips away.
You carry the burden through the years,
And smile when you're really near to tears.
It's very sad to say, "Goodbye"
And, no matter how you try,
You can't see the reason or the rhyme
But maybe you will in God's good time.

N. Pepper

A Tree

I once stood tall upon a hill, a place for birds to nest
My branches offering shelter to walkers when they rest

Over many years I've watched the ever–changing seasons
And wondered at the acts of Man, what can be their reasons?

For on one day the lorries came with cutting gear and rope
They tore off all my branches and hauled me down the slope

Now in a timber yard I lie, stripped of bark and twigs
Instead of gentle bird song, all I hear are mechanical rigs

They measured me and sliced me, they painted me dark brown
They attached me to some iron and wonder why I frown

In place of knots and gnarls I've now got screws and studs
I'm so smooth and lacquered I'll never sprout any buds

But wait, I think I see now what they've made of me
I've been turned into a garden seat and placed beneath a tree

Is that a bird above me? Could it be a lark?
And what is scattered under me? I think it is my bark!

Helen E. Urquhart

Judgment's Been Made

Lenders say No! Your debts are too long,
Items belonging to you are sold for a song.
Name and address, well they already have it,
Don't bother trying to plead for more credit.
An express clearance is the way that it's done.
Court judgment been made on you by someone.

Our dreams all are shattered, by sorrow and pain,
Lost in the wrangle of one loan shark's claim.
Easily all happiness, was quickly effaced,
Meeting incapacity, though no crime the same taste.

Ah heavy are the footsteps of such a disgrace,
Nothing to prevent it, your home contents erased
Which in turn will cost far more to replace,
Receivers have power, since you lost the case.
Often owning a little means little to lose,
Trust in yourself seems the best way to choose

Expect what you earn will one day be sufficient,
Though however for now, it appears that it isn't.
Have faith in your ability to overcome,
If possible be glad that it's over and done.

L. Coleman

"Metaphorically Speaking"

What are we people, in this vast unknown,
We are mere drops in the ocean,
flakes of snow,
blades of grass,
seeds, with love to sow.

We are stars in the night sky,
grains on a beach of sand,
pebbles on a lane,
trees in a wood of no-man's land.

We are doors, that open and close,
our lives are stories that end and begin,
We are windows, as to see the perfect world,
yet we are locks, to stop us getting in.

Bronagh Curran

Jigsaw People

Plastic personalities on a polystyrene face
and with cardboard emotions they entered the human race

Running up the road is the face that you sold
and running after him is an empty human mould
and running even faster is the blue print that you 'stole'

And they all get cut up into pieces of jigsaw
but the box is not full yet and they still need some more

So they have these jigsaw pieces and they join them with the rest but
they will not fit back together they have all tried their best

Now the jigsaw is unsolved and they have all gone to sleep
and in their dreams there is an ocean where they all sink
into the deep

So now they can't wake up but their jigsaw souls can't weep
and at the bottom of the ocean are jigsaw people fast asleep

This is red tape of the unconscious law
now they are jigsaw people they won't worry any more
with their photocopied perceptions and their silicon minds
they can leave their conscious life far far behind.

Shannon Crews

The Nature Of War

Turn around for nothing look back no more
For Man is coming and with him war
Take with you only the petals you need
And buds sufficient to plant new trees
You saplings now in the ground so low
Take care may in purer gardens you grow
Insects and beasts of the earth around
The time has come for new grazing land
In peace we have lived until this sad day
Now Man comes to fight each other as prey
Their darkness now falls upon this our home
On all we have loved and all we have known
But we shall return and this sign you must heed
New life shall begin with a red poppy seed

Gary Baugh

Forget-me-nots

Wild flowers and sun shadows
Lie scattered on the mat
Just inside your back door
Left open for the cat

Your cat is a hunter
He stalks the wood at night
Beside the churchyard softly
Where I lie out of sight

Your cat is now my cat
A sentry on my grave
He watched your teardrops fall there
For a love that will not fade

He took those flowers you picked for me
Returned them to your door
From me to you eternal
Our love forevermore

Lisa Callan

The Calm Of The Evening

I gaze, almost in a dream
Waiting for the calm
Of the evening.
The sunsets each and everyone different
Yet so breathtaking.
The colours and changing cloud formations,
Sea, hills and sky meet—enraptured in a
purple haze with gleams of gold and silver
and clouds of darkest grey.
But oh—to capture and to hold
Would be true heaven.

Ann Fletcher Campbell

Empty Promises

The love of a child took you away, you just packed and left
when you'd promise you'd stay.
I smile a sad smile, my feelings to hide, you'd taken away
everything except my pride.
You promised to love me, to cherish me for life, said you'd
only be happy with me for your wife.
But when the time came, alas you were weak, and I was so
stunned I could hardly speak.
Or cry the bitter tears which rained in my heart, which would
show you broke me apart.
You made me trust you by your thoughtfulness and care, but
of your love for your daughter I was only too aware,
That this was a fight I couldn't win, no matter how I tried, so I
closed the door behind you, and I cried, and I cried.
The world you'd built around me, shattered beyond repair, so
where do I go for comfort now?—For someone to love and care?
I am sad and alone, retreating back to my shell, back to a life of
emptiness which I remember, oh, so well;
To cry my bitter tears and drown in my sorrow in my sorrow,
not even caring if there is no tomorrow.
So, little girl—please look after my Jay, the man who I loved,
and you took away,
Please care for him with a love divine, and don't break your
heart . . . the grief it all mine.

H. Jean Lewis

War In The Gulf

As sleep descends silently, like a dense fog, to envelope the city,
The old and the young, in homes and hotels, relax in warm luxury,
Suddenly, all around, screaming sirens spear the Arabian tranquillity,
Brutally shaken, men, women and children listen to impending anger,
With beating hearts they scramble through a maze of confusion
   to safety,
The more cautious with gas masks; the less fortunate, with
   wet towels,
Earth–shattering sounds reverberate, as they watch in horror
   and anxiety,
Different nationalities, together today, bound by fear but
   united in hope,
As silent prayers escape from parched throats to seek the
Almighty.

Pratap P. Jayavanth

Brief Interlude

The stillness of the darkened night is broken
As strong winds sob outside my window pane:
I cannot sleep, as restless in my bed I lie;
Nor yet dream nor fantasize
As time goes slowly by!

At my left, upon the bedside table
My clock tells me it's long before the dawn.
I scarce have slept beyond an hour or so
And now my thoughts form in my head, like phrases
Written on a blank page, deliberate and slow.

Ah . . . drowsiness and sleep may overtake me,
The lids close heavily upon my eyes,
Outside the sheets seems cold and uninviting,

The bed is warm: Wakefulness slowly dies . . .
I lie back and snuggle in the pillows.

Joyce Parker

True Harmony

Everything in the Universe is conscious,
Whether it knows it, or not.
Trees and streams, stars and stones,
All pulse with life and electricity.
As we see them in everyday life,
They are beautiful—but familiar!
But, if we could see them truly—
At sub–atomic level—shall we say?
How much more brilliant, scintillating,
Blinding—almost—would be their hues!
And restless, constant, motion would be seen:
Vibrating, pulsating, zephyr-like activity . . .
Our human forms would radiate and pulse,
In perfect tune with trees and streams, stars and stones,
In one glorious, God–given, melodious, vibrancy . . .
Our souls would then experience true harmony,
Existing at the core of everything.
That greater beauty, that is now invisible to us,
Will be revealed, when we shake off this mortal coil,
To merge with all other, conscious things in our Universe.

Joan Porter

Life

A long windy path leads into a lonely field,
This is the path of life
There is no turning back.
Here you are born, the field empty
But slowly it fills.
You are at the middle of the road
You view the past and search the future.
You follow until the end.
Ahead is black, unknown
Back is a field filled by your past.
There is no more room
This is the end of life.

Zoe Ellen Woodcock

Blue Gems

Beautiful blue sprinkled with gold
Twinkling like the night
Deep within the earth unfold
Treasure to delight.
This stone so blue where does it lay
High in the Andes mountains
A pleasure and a joy to see
Mined by a master worker.
Surpassed by beauty oh so rare
This beautiful blue gem
Is cut and polished with precision
With thought and care and great decision.
If you want to come and see
Where these gems are found
Upon a mule you'll have to go
As snow lies thickly on the ground.
Lapis Lazuli the beautiful gems
Prized so long go
Deepest blue with twinkling eyes
Where they come from now you know.

L. M. Carter

The Surgeon

Robotic, neurotic in his primary function,
Is this psychotic ape, bent over a scalpel,
Ready to cut flesh, incise a gaping wound,
With a scientific proficiency.

Operate, deliberate against the laws of time,
Give haste to the conveyer belt of life,
Bring forth another slab of meat,
To dine with the master of the knives.

Patient, subject his programme undefined,
Input knowledge to the neurons of science,
Prolong life to the maimed, deformed,
And torment them in the name of ethics.

Colin Moore

Contented Collies

My name is Misty, my brother is Storm,
And three years ago when we were born,
Our lives began living rough in a shed,
But a newspaper advert by people was read.1

They came to see us, and took us away,
To live in their house where we would play,
Walks are to us given twice a day,
And a large quilted duvet on which to lay.

We're glad that these human beings can read,
Because living with them we have all that we need,
The only dislike in our lives so far,
Is when we are told to get in the car.

This means our yearly injections are due.
Then sure enough right on cue,
The needle goes in, we wince with pain,
And vow never to visit vets again.

Apart from that, our lives are great,
So glad that advert decided our fate,
As two border collies we're happy to live,
With this family, who, to us, so much love do give.

Mary Rowe

Chiaroscuro

Here, winds chase the rain, and both are strong.
In Spring daffodils are lashed in fury, bent beneath the rain,
Until the sun dries off their tears and lifts their heads again.

There—Spring disguised, comes hurriedly. No rain. A sudden
Show of flowers. Flamboyant. Heady. In flagrant bowers
Droop until night's heavy dew lifts their heads again.

Here, in June, between the showers the sun is warm
And twilights long golden hours usher in the gentle night.
There all is deep unrest. The fiery sun has set and nocturnal
Quests begin as tooth and claw raise up their head.

Here, rain persistent, streams from leaden skies.
There the unholy power of rain defies the puny strength of man.
Day after day the deluge falls, then suddenly will cease—
And birds' frenetic calls signal reprieve before night falls.

God. How I am torn between East and West
That land which gave me birth. This which I know best.
There were my roots go deep. Here where my duty lies.
How can I choose between soft, gentle blue
And violent sun–drenched skies?

Letitia M. Davies

"Depression"

It's an illness people "don't understand"
So no one wants to "be around".

You're trapped inside a tunnel of dark, there's
"No way out", "without a doubt".

On days it's all "doom and gloom",
Sitting alone "in your room."

You find it hard to "face another day,"

But something makes "you find a way."
No one can help "that's true",
In the end it's "up to you".

Time just drags "on and on",
And you just want "to belong".

Then one day "God", "above",
Reaches out a "hand of love"

He sends someone to "help you through",
With a friendship "warm and true."

It's been so long "without the light:,
Now things are starting "to look Bright".

I had been asleep "for a long while",
At last I'm learning "how to smile"

Janet Rose Marsh

The People Watchers

We can sit and look, we People Watchers.
Wonder about folk, guess a bit.
Why so curious of others?
There really should be less of it.

We go about our daily business.
We People Watchers, harmless fun?!
Look quickly away, that's what we do.
Should we be caught, what would be done?

We mean no harm, we People Watchers.
No disregard, no malice there.
We all do it don't we?
There's People Watchers everywhere.

Some authority on behaviour somewhere may say,
'Something is lacking in one's life, go to therapy.'

It's no big deal, that's my view.
No 'inner meaning' lurking, just something People Watchers do.

To sum it up, it's no sad thing.
No-one's perfect, life isn't always rosy.
As for 'therapy needing People Watchers',
well actually it's just being nosey!

Paula Osbaldeston

Watching Allotment Veterans

Year by year, as I pass
The dry rotted shanty huts,
Why is it that I begin to wonder
A little more if the regimental-like
Tenders fight on new fronts?

Here I witness them unarmed,
Decorated only by once rain–swept
Promenade deck chairs; bores and bayonets
Exchanged for gently swaying hip flasks:
They seem to have found a new El Dorado.

The welcoming communal pipe rifts,
Which interrogate the evening air
Into a form of silent suffocation, suckled
Through a myrmidon owner's half–crescent mouth
I begin to see ten-penny lids fall and lye black.

I pause to see the billowing smoke rising from the bonfire
Rocking, unrolling its way into the freedom of a gratis night sky,
I begin to realise these men are like sheep being put out
to graze on a voluntary basis, a new form of high noon.

Glenn Freeth

Misty Darkness

Grey veils of misty darkness, are closing in on land,
The hills of distant islands, are covered where they stand,
The night grows dark and silence comes, with the eerie misty shroud,
An awesome shriek from a lonely bird, is fearsome and so loud.

No light to see the lonely roads, no moon to light the way,
No stars of comfort sparkle, as it nears the end of day,
This veil of darkness hanging there, is eerie, damp and cold,
It twists and swirls and billows, as though trying to unfold

This misty veil of darkness, covers all things in its wake,
Descending like a deathly shroud, from which there's no escape,
This misty shroud of darkness, will cover all the land,
And close and tighten round it, like a fearsome evil hand.

The night will seem to never end, as the misty veil goes by,
Unfolding over everything, hiding moon and stars and sky,
But as the night is ending, and light comes creeping through,
This misty veil of darkness, will be replaced by something new.

The light will chase this frightening shroud, and all evil will
    pass by,
The fear will lift and peace extend, from the comfort of the sky,
The distant mountains will be seen, as the light of day shines
    through,
And peace will follow the misty shroud, with a sky so bright
    and blue.

Marjory Davidson

Lament For A Hunter

What will they do, when they have done
with knife and trap and cage and gun
When all the animals are dead
With a bullet to the body or blow to the head
Or torn to pieces by packs of hounds
except when their skin may be worth a few pounds

When the song of a bird is no longer a sound
that the hunter hears as he tramps the ground
The sight of a Pheasant, a Rabbit, a Hare,
are no longer seen, are no longer there.
To catch a fish in polluted streams
is something he does in occasional dreams.

What will he find to shoot at them?
Will he continue to shoot at men?
The Hunter hunted, the Trapper trapped
until all life in the world is sapped

Will the last man turn to God and say
Why did you let it happen this way?
Will he say to God as he holds his gun,
you know that the Hunter enjoys the fun.

Leonard G. Renwick

Judy II

She was waiting at the window as I reached the garden gate
and was just a little anxious for she knew that I was late.
Then with tail a-wagging gladly she goes bounding to the floor
and with bark of merry welcome comes to greet me at the door.

She is such a grand companion in her little doggy way
and understands exactly such a lot of what I say,
for she barks in approbation and her eyes and "rudder" talk
if she hears "the paper" mentioned, or "some supper" or "a walk".

How she revels in her freedom with some hedgerows to explore
or to scamper in wide circles all the grassy meadows o'er.
Then she trots home with contentment as her padded footfalls tire
and with sighs of weary pleasure falls asleep before the fire.

With her paws upon the fender and her nose upon her paws,
she continues happy hunting in the lands that know no laws;
when a sudden, brief excitement breaks the rhythmic breathing tone
as she dreamt she chased a rabbit or was playing with her bone.

There are times when she is naughty but she knows
    that she's done wrong
and repentance shows so clearly that she's pardoned before long;
then she comes and prods me gently with a soft enquiring nose
for a pat upon the shoulder before sitting on my toes.

.   .   .   .   .   .

When the trumpet sound shall call her and she passes from my sight
she will surely go for ever to those realms of endless light,
and in Heaven, if I win there, I shall hear her bark again
and see her sniffing sweetness in a scented heavenly lane

Eric Harry Clarke

My Land In Autumn

The September summer sun is fading
Warmth is replaced by wind whistling through the valley.
October heralds the dawn of damp, dank mornings,
hoar frost, drizzle rain and dark cold afternoons beckon as
November proceeds.

A myriads of colour flutters in the fast failing sunshine,
reds, golds, yellows are the colours of the leaves,
as they tumble in a flurry from deciduous trees.
The nearby cockerel begins to cry out
awakening the birds huddled in skeleton trees.
A carpet on the ground is strewn,
the barren hillside now looks bleak.

Seasons of ageing brings with it dreariness, depression,
despair and death to my land.
Misty mornings and rain make me despondent, people stay in.
All I get older like this season,
In hopeful anticipation I wait for Christmas, Spring and the
re-birth of my Nation.

Andrew Blewden

Absent Friends

I still remember friends we left behind,
In shallow graves, we hoped someone would find,
And bury them in a hallowed place.

I still remember everyone, can recall every name
Their countenance of youth, despite the years remain the same
I close my eyes and I see every face.

I still remember, after all these years
How we all acted, just to hide the fears
That every soldier knows but dare not show.

I still remember and never will forget,
The cease-fire called to end the war, and yet
The friends we left behind will never know.

I still remember, the Stuka's whining sound
Still see the bomb exploding on the ground,
The bomb that killed the friends we left behind.

I still remember, time and time again
The carefree youths, war changed to fighting men
The friends that live forever in my mind.

James Inverbeg Smith

Extinguished Not Distinguished

Lurking, danger; green barter
White exchange or any colour
Love your lover? Be smothered.
Pity your smile mind.

This exchange is greater
Than you'll ever remember.
Pity your smile mind.

Pity your fall.
When all you did was blame others.
Pity your self-pity
That belittled
Others love so little.

Sorry, state:
You lost before you even played the game.

Pity your smile mind.
Pity your smile mind.
A circle untouched?
Fools!

T. H.(c)3.2

My True Love

In Scarbourgh looking at a seaside view,
That was the place I fell in love with you.
In amongst the sea and golden sand,
You looked at me and I took your hand.

We've being going out ever so long,
Because our love is every so strong.
We've been through so much together,
Because I want our love to last forever.

I think of you all the time but that's cool,
Because my love for you is a bottomless pool.
You're constantly on my mind because I care,
As long as there's a me and you I want you there.

You are the only one on earth for me,
My heart's all yours, you hold the key.
Your kiss send shivers down my spine
A cuddle makes me glad you're mine.

Helen Abel

Mother

Oh, why, why, why, did I not know a mother
It was not meant to be to know a mother
The instinct of a child to love a mother
Oh, why, why, why, did I not know a mother
When I was at school the kids would talk of mother
I felt lonely and would walk away from them
And I had no mother there.

Doris Gertrude Parry

October's Child

Autumn wooed October fair
Courted her with colours bright
Wrapped his gift of misty veils
To hide her from old Summer's sight
Painted her trees with red and gold
Bestowed her hedgerows with berries sweet
Collected the fallen leaves to make
Rustling carpets for her feet
He sprinkled her fields with frosted gems
Brilliant and cold in the dawning light
Hiding them with his sun–warm glare
To reveal again in the star–lit night
He took October with gentle grace
And as she succumbed to Autumns charms
He made her the Mother of Winter's needs
Reaping the harvest within her arms.

Helen Hyatt

Box Of Gold

I have a little box I lock it with a key.
It is a box of gold and it belongs to me.
For the riches in that box are memories divine.
Memories of you locked within this heart of mine.

The gold within that box is the love within my heart,
that only I can unlock whenever we are apart.
So I never feel alone dear when you are not about,
I just open up my box and let the memories flood out.

We have had our trouble and we have had our strife,
But we know the love that lingers, with a loving man and wife,
that is all the gold I need and it's safe I have the key,
safe within my heart our golden memory.

V. Howells

A Foster Child

Oh, little girl with eyes of blue,
You're very small and only two.
I have three daughters of my own,
But still the passing time has shown
My heart had room for you.

I've tucked you up in bed at night,
Your eyes so tired, but still so bright.
I've watched you grow and learn to walk,
And thrilled to hear you when you talk.
You're such a precious mite.

Now that you're gone. God how I miss;
That great big hug. That baby kiss.
The happy smile. The joyous shrieks.
And sobs as tears rolled down your cheeks.
It hurts to think like this.

I can't forget, but never mind.
Life must go on, look not behind.
I've loved you like you were my own,
I hope to see you when you're grown.
Perhaps, if God is kind.

R. Searle

The Angels Sing Holy Holy!

Lord, I love the silence, the silence that you bring.
The waves of peace that come, awesome stillness, deep within.
Love, so unconditional, one weeps with tears of joy!
Oh! the wonder of your faithfulness, in the face of sin.
Astonishment at such a love, a holy God suspended on a cross!
A mind that planned a life given freely, all for us.
Life–giving words "Yes, I will, be thou healed"!
Truth and grace and mercy so lovingly revealed.
He has shown the way, his hand beckons "Come walk with me"!
There is a path of beauty where restoration flows for you—just see!
But child, can you die to all you want to be?
The meekest in all the earth, our God, walked this path, great
glory, great power, in sacrificial love.
To shine, thro' any darkness, to overcome the worst Satan can bring.
Is this not a calling to make the angels sing!

Mary Comley

Kindred Spirits

Dedicated to Donald

I opened up my heart today and took a look inside
By looking out, I looked within
Now let the journey begin.

Don't look to the future and what might be
Grasp the now and what can be
For we make our own destiny.

Take my hand, I'll lead you through
Take my heart, to you I'll be ever true
Love will be our guide, love our strength
And love our immortality when our mortal time is spent.

When life gets dark
I'll hold onto you
When the night comes and it looks too stark
Hold onto me, let me be your rock.

For nothing is impossible to love and faith
The heavenly twins that decree our fate
Nothing is impossible to love and faith
Together they transcend time and space.

Sarah Musson

The Garden Urns

They always stood together in the tiny garden plot
That was my mother's garden, a special little spot.
They were old and rugged and weathered standing on their base
Giving to her small garden a dignified sort of grace
The flower design, a tulip with petals open wide
And leaves so delicately fashioned abound on every side.

Mother tended her garden urns as precisely as she chose her clothes
Selecting the colours carefully, matching her bulbs in pinks
    and mauves,
Exquisitely shaded hyacinths and crocuses bright and gay
To lighten up her garden, each year on Easter Day.
And summering flowers, the special ones she always loved so much
Geraniums and asters enhanced by her artistic touch.

And now those precious garden urns stand side by side
    at my front door
Lovingly tended now by me as Mother did in days of yore
Watering them every evening the yellow daffodils
I remember in my childhood growing wildly on the hills
And amongst the yellow trumpets in those sentimental pots
I will grow so very specially some blue forget-me-nots
Admiring them from my window, yet they will never be the same
As when they adorned my mother's garden, by the rookery,
    down the lane.

Joan Smith

"It's Time"

The Innocent Earth through mankind greed
Is losing nature's skin
Without its strong protection
There'll be nothing left within.

Now it's our turn to make amends
We've had it all our way
To give back what we've taken
And to look beyond today.

This is our home we can't escape
There's nowhere after here
When this is gone, then so are . . .
To late to shed a tear

Don't close your ears and shut your mind
And look the other way
It's time to do some reckoning
It's time to have your say.

Survival of the world as one
United we must stand
The war that all of us must win
To save our precious land

Pauline Jones

Forest

Walking dreamily among the forest greens,
   above a canopy of the shadiest leaves.
Animals hide to daringly peep at me,
   while birds fly high above the trees.
Beneath my feet the undergrowth conceals,
   a treasure-trove of secrets.
Splashes of colours appear here and there.
Towering above me the trees and their tall, wide, brown trunks.
Beasts roam freely and seem not to have a single care.
Farther on, a little pool with the prettiest flowers I have ever seen.
Fish glide lazily around the reeded edges.
Lilies and their lily pads float on the surface, clear and clean.
Around this glade a whole range of colourful hedges.
"Dream on." They said, "for man does destroy.
Through mankind's greed such glades have gone.
Trapped in time these pretty glades are hidden.
Buildings now stand where the sun once shone."

Cheryl Clark

"Working Man's Wage"

Poverty! Poverty! Everywhere,
So many people living in despair,
Don't know which way to turn, how will I cope?
When you're living a life of fear and hope,
Budget my pennies and keep the family strong,
But it's hard to keep going when things start to go wrong,
Not a bit of work coming my way,
I would be grateful for a working man's pay,
The mines are long gone but I'm still here,
Scraping every penny which might occur,
Muscle and sweat was the answer to my life,
I was bringing in money for my children and my wife,
The coal has marked my body, scarred! Till the day I die,
But in them days I had my pride,
And I could hold my head up high,
Another day is here but I'm all gone,
Can't sleep no more the nights are so long,
My body's my disguise cause inside I've aged,
God! I would do anything for a working man's wage.

Lance Reed

Night Feelings

I'm in bed with my pen and paper,
Thinking what's on T.V. for later.
My mind is full and my heart is hurting,
When I'm asleep I'll be tossing and turning.
My room is quiet as a dolly,
Outside is nice, full of poppies
I'm looking now at my shelf,
There are pictures of family and myself,
My eyes are falling,
My head is going,
I'm counting sheep,
Now I'm asleep.

Elizabeth Broadhurst

Christmas Time

Beware of Jack Frost beware
For now is the time we shiver,
As snowballs are tossed in the air
And children await Father Christmas with a quiver.

The snowman is taller than the hedge
As the children are out playing on their sledge.

There are snowflakes falling as the cold winds blow,
Winter is calling and the ground is thick with snow.

Church bells ring to the sound of joy and laughter,
As carols people sing as they give thanks to our Lord and master.

The turkey is stuffed and cooking,
The Christmas tree shines and gleams,
As presents we are wrapping for all our children's dreams.

Now is the time of rejoicing,
Christmas is here, ain't that something.

Philip N. Dawson

Home

I wish I were a bird, that I
Might take to wing and soar and fly.
Above the land that holds my heart
Across its miles, its beauty stark.
To have no need for plane or bus
To go at will, without a fuss.
To watch the dawn break, from a cloud
As mountains peep through misty shroud.
I'd love to sit and watch the spring
Burst forth and colour everything.
And then to glide down to the glen
To carpet green, then up again.
To feel the sun's warm, golden rays
As summer brings its sultry days.
Then winter takes its magic brush
And paints the landscape in a rush.
One moment green, with trees so bare
The next, white diamonds everywhere.
This special place, my home, is grand
There's nowhere quite, like my, England.

Christine Stubbs

Terminations

Every one of us, at one time or another,
Have had to endure life's tribulations,
As sharp as a knife, they cometh,
Sudden or gradual terminations.

Some of us may have been quite happy,
enjoying the fruits of their occupations,
When suddenly, and perhaps without reason,
Employers decide on workers terminations.

Others may have ventured into matrimony
A blissful life being their main intention,
Alas, quite often, their marriage turns sour,
Succumbs to disillusion, leading to termination.

Nimble creatures, in their mothers wombs,
Whose cries are unheard; and whose rights deprived,
considered to be society's unwanted bearings,
anguishly muffle their unjust termination.

Much have we grieved for loved ones departed,
who left this earth with quite some contention,
whether we like it or not, such is the system,
the good life must also conclude in a termination.

Raymond Sammut

Dunblane

God must have gone to sleep on that fateful day in March.
Must have gone to sleep, when our children safe he was
supposed to keep.
But now he has them, wrapped up in his love, they can laugh,
sing and play, in the now and forever. For there is no need to
cry, in your kingdom in the sky, for they are all living safely
and laughing altogether.
Let them have no thoughts of the world they left behind, but
let their souls roam free, happy and at rest. For they are now
free of the cruelty and evil that dealt them such a wicked blow,
on this earth far below. Mum, Dad don't grieve for me, for
now I am happy and spiritually free, I have gone to Heaven
and now Jesus watches over me. Sister Brother please don't
grieve for me, I am now at peace and running free. So I say to
all of you who are suffering such sorrow, and asking the
question why, don't worry we didn't really die, we are waiting
for you on our cloud in the sky. Mummy don't cry at night
when the bedroom lights go out, I really didn't mind when
you used to shout. Sister Brother please don't cry, I didn't
mind when we used to fight, for I am now at peace wrapped up
in God's love, now and every night. So don't weep over the
place where I lie, for I am not there, I did not die. Instead of
grief you should feel relief, for we are altogether now happy in
our peace. So when the pain becomes too much to bear and
you feel the need to cry. Stop and look to the heavens up
above, and if you really pray you will see us dancing around
the heavens up in the sky. For you see we did not really die.

Tony Bambrough

Soldier's Prayer

Oh Lord we ask Thee, hear this our special prayer,
A prayer for our soldier's fighting out there.
There in a war, one that should never have been.
A war that will make, many soldier's heart bleed.

Give them your strength Lord, your courage and shield,
Let me know you are with them, whilst out in the field.
And, if any soldier, stumbles and falls,
Then Lord, pick him up, in those loving arms of yours.

We pray for their families, and loved ones left behind,
Who pray their own prayer, with tears in their eyes.
Touch them Oh Lord, let them know you do care,
May your Spirit of Peace, conquer anger and fear.

When the war is over, help us find room in our hearts,
For compassion and forgiveness, to those whose fault the war was.
Oh Lord we ask Thee, hear this our special prayer
A prayer for our soldiers, fighting out there.
D. Skittrall

Waiting

The child sat, balancing on the window sill,
tendrils of wispy hair
pressed hard to her forehead by the glass.
Button nose, red and cold, squeezed against it.
Blue, tired eyes scan the frosted roof tops.
Waiting.
"Won't come while you're awake."
Mummy says. Kindly, lifting the small chilled
form back to the warmth of the blankets.
"I want to see him."
Sleepy now.
Mum's gentle hand strokes her wayward locks,
as blue eyes droop and lashes brush her cheeks.
Waiting.
Mary Loretto Walsh

The Wind Has Taken You

The wind it has taken you
Taken you away
Releasing you forever
You are now free
Why does the breeze have to be so unkind
It wreathes itself inside of my mind
Making me realize that you're gone, the one I live for
Because the wind has taken you
You will be the breeze forevermore.
Sarah Eddolls

The Emotional Prostitute
(Quo Animi Motus Publicane)

I'd give you my all,
I'd sell my soul . . . gladly for the chance,
the chance to be in love and be loved.

My heart is like a tacky neon sign, an
advertisement of my lonely existence.

The smiles that hide the pain of the
failure to communicate, have you ever
the need to wonder why love is a
four letter word?

The orchid in the desert, the fool
that wears the crown I am, I would
gladly give the shirt from my back . . .
and live out in the rain . . .
    If only I could be understood!

You could take me and leave me naked,
in the tears that I bleed . . . and
you often do! . . .

So sit I, crucified by my own feelings,
The emotional prostitute.
L. Edwards

Immortal Pride

Crushed in a lightless cell, all eyes staring,
Not able to move, still staring.

Too scared to speak,
But through frightened eyes,
Silence all around us,
Apart from my silent cries.

Pointless joy, still carries on,
Cold with terror, lazed with anger.

The blow of a rifle butt,
Plus One Sharp Push,
Into the stench of the dead,
Whose prides were murdered.

Sly animals still growling,
Devious and filled with death,
Tie like a puppet on a string,
Handled with hatred and fury.

All dazed from the torture,
But courage still holds me,
For my teaching is to be free,
And some day I Will Be Free.
Stacey Moore

Hine Moa And The Resting Pool

When the waters of Rotorua
guided Hine Moa to the resting pool, she found true love.

Unannounced, Hine Moa fled her tribal fold
to tame the boldness in her heart.

She sought the resting pool and its buoyancy,
to imitate lover's heaven.

With interference Hine Moa
caught the attention of Tutanekai, she took his calabash

From which he drew his water from the resting pool,
and broke it against the rocks.

Furious Tutanekai was, as he reached
around the pool to find the one
responsible for breaking his calabash,

But his anger was swayed when his
hand met the caress of Hine Moas
gentle hands, guiding him to love.

And as they walked with passions entwined,
away from the resting pool,
so ancestral presence made a legend's claim,

To keep in the heart of the people, the
love story of Hine Moa and Tutanekai.
Simon Thomas Jacobs

A Study Of Life

Morning thrusts itself like a wild tornado
The sand swirls back to the sea,
Rain is pounding as if in bravado,
Summer is long gone for me.
I remember this beach, when all was calm,
And like life, still and warm,
Whatever happened to peace and tranquillity
Before the advent of the storm.

I remember that night, when life was so bright
And we took all life's pleasure for granted,
How could we know, life was short in its flow,
And one day it would end as it started.

But happiness is in the mind,
It is the call of a bird,
At fleeting glimpse of another kind
Of life, beyond the herd.
Happiness is a child at play,
Content in all its ways,
We can't go back, but must go on,
Through all our future days.
Dorothy King

"Lost!"

An angel held out a silver wand—
Between her and the child, the bond was strong,
Within the child's eyes . . . She saw a true friend—
So she waved her wand . . . for the bone to mend,
"you must go home!
For too far, you have roamed—
Your mummy will be afraid—
when she finds you have stayed!"
The child asked, "Please won't you come home with me?"
"No, heaven's where I've got to be!
But, never fear . . . my little dear—
My heart will always be near . . .
Go quickly now, it's getting dark!
Just follow the sound of your puppy's bark!"
"Bye-bye" the child said—her smile quite gay—
As slowly . . . the angel faded away!

Meg Gaspar

Without Love

No one can live without loving someone,
No one can live without love.
Love for a mother, a sister or brother,
No one can live without love.
No one can live without someone caring,
Sharing your troubles and joys;
Sharing your heartbreak,
Your each little heartache,
No one can live without love.
Love will find an answer, to hope and despair,
When you know that someone
Will always be there.
No one can live in a world of darkness,
Clouds always looming above;
So, just follow your light side,
And look on the bright side,
For no one can live without love.

L. J. Stopher

After The Passover

Should we go or should we stay?
Can we possibly find the way?
Should we stay or should we go?
After all that happened, I don't know
Outside is a rough and urgent voice,
"Away you go! You have no choice
My father my brother and my son
Lie dead! Is this what your God has done?

Other voices join in this hear felt cry
Go quickly before the rest of us die
Gather your goods and your cloaks, don't wait
Moses told us to meet at the gate
Such strange things happened through the night,
I was heartily thankful to see the light
Moses told us that God will be our guide,
Let us trust him and in his strength abide
Come we must be leaving for we have far to go
God is ever near us, his presence we will know.

Janet M. Lewis

Letting Go

You look around you and what do you see?
Everything's dark and full of misery,
Life, it doesn't seem worth living anymore,
But in reality 'he's only gone next door.

At this time you're probably weeping,
For you're loved one who's eternally sleeping,
But time will heal the sore,
And you, you'll cry no more.

You'll remember all the things you've been through,
and the special times between him and you,
and when you're time comes, long or soon,
You too will enter that special room.

Edwina Dewart

Prejudice

It is so rife it is so profound
Just open your eyes and look around
See how the people stop and stare
At the person in the wheelchair
Watch as they cross over the street
So the homeless they do not meet
Hear how the children so taunt and tease
The other children born obese
Listen to what the hushed whispers have to say
Against those among us who are gay
Watch the hatred rising from within
Unleashed upon the races of coloured skin
Hark at the many angry voices raised
When the same belief is not praised
So what closes so many, many open doors?
And causes so many bloody religious wars?
We all know just what it is
It's our own petty prejudice
Just be thankful for the variety nature has to give
And for you own God's sake.
Live and let live!

C. C. Harris

ThoughtsAboard

Driver accelerates bus
Listless and unsuspecting heads pull back in unison
Necks quickly react and restrain
Girl looks out of window
at grey man
trying to keep his Englishness in the rain and wind
  Bus stops
    Grey man boards bus
Purple coated old-dear looks into . . .
    space
And visualizes macaroni cheese for her Arthur's tea
Guy fails to keep his stereo personal
  "Dance to get high, look to the sky"

  Fellow passengers,
    Have you ever lived
    Or have you never lived?

Bus travels on . . .

Elizabeth A. Hirst

Shooting Stars

Actors of screen and stage
From Cary Grant to Nicholas Cage
Everyone wants to be someone
To be proud of what they done
Film stars from here and there
Coming in from everywhere
Looking back through years of greats
Hoping they got what it takes
Men and women who have sealed their love
Who flew off like a pair of doves
A year later after they fought
They were on their way to the Divorce Courts
When a young actor gets a job with lines to read
They will make sure that love and liberty is all they need.

Carolyn Anna Lloyd

We Will Remember

Standing tall against an unblemished
Sky, mourning figures curled helplessly
Defending against pain. Loss scarred in the
Unhealed wounds of buried soldiers. Fear
Fossilized in the smooth–cut marble. Names
Carved in bricks like death into war. Embedded
Hate concealed by beauty. Where the white
Columns stand are pillars of love and courage,
Bonding the dead to the living. Connecting us
All to heroes of war—now dead, forever gone.

Clarissa Chase

431

Submit

Strong winds blow out the candle
And inspire desecrating clouds to suffocate the moon.
Particles of dust, with masculine vigour.
Blind and force salty tears to the ground.
It is dark.
I cannot see.
And nature remains all painful.

Emma Sinclair

Coming Of Age

Worry not little one,
Human emotion can not be denied
But your time will come
It is now time to decide

It is a decision not made lightly
To contain your love and behold from afar
The different ones who exist no less rightly,
To bottle up the anger to keep on par
For deep inside you know you were born to travel

These others are not of your ilk,
The intricate mysteries of time and space, love and death
  are yours to unravel
The coming of age arrives as strident as a mustangs gallop;
  as smoothly as silk
So come now take the gamble
It is time for you to ramble

R. K. Paul

The Black Child

Am I not changed
Since the advent of conflicts and wars?
Conflicts and wars erupting through greed for power
When strong men besiege the weak and innocent
Without law, grapple and seize power for itself
I heard booms and rattles here and there,
And fled with others helter-skelter
And at last I wander about far from home
Seeking safety amidst the greens; starved for food and water
O am I not changed
What peace can be found
The assurance to live together with my dear
The love and harmony?
My love is gone
No human is gone
No human is link I ever enjoyed
Ah but life there in sadism abound,
Lust, crime and unhappy love, callousness and
sanguinariness
of massacre.

Yet an end to such cruelty?

Raphael Kuagbenu

Bare Flower

He loves me,
I peeled a petal away
from the flower he gave me
On the very first day we met.
He loves me not
he blew another away with a kiss
to a girl, I didn't know.
He loves me again
I plucked another one off
his embrace so warm, his touch so soft,
he loves me not, the flower was shook
a petal lay on the ground, I was shook
lay on the ground, I was hit—
Warned not to make a sound.
He loves me still, we had made the love, he said
with a grin and some cheap perfume.
He loves me not
the rose thrown on the floor
he is gone
I'm not naive anymore.

Rachel Cullen

Aromatherapy

Tranquillity, Sensuality, Vitality,
In fragrant bottles of wondrous hue,
Smelling of heather and the morning dew.

Essential oils he gave me
To renew my drooping spirits,
And revitalize my life,
When all I longed for
Was the touch of his fingers
Slip sliding delicately
Down the slopes of my desires.

Sitting in splendid isolation on my couch,
He preened himself like a peacock,
While I admired his Gucci boots,
Armani jeans and slinky rib-knit Polo,
The Quintessential Sensuous Man.

He gazed despondently at his sun–tanned wrist,
Where that Tag Heuer watch should lie,
While I, his dull obsequious hen
Waited in silent trepidation,
For the touch of his wings to bring
Tranquillity, Sensuality, Vitality.

Kitsy Brady

The Wheel

Without stay, or pause, the wheel turns
and we, willy nilly, follow its course
until our own cycle we have run,
and end! Or is it just begun?

How oft have I felt, in some strange, unused moment,
the intangible knowing that this place
and these people, whom I know not, are yet
a close part of the pattern, set.

For one brief second is the veil rent
on a life that long ago I lived, or is it still to come.
Did the wheel hesitate and I glimpse past, or future,
what a thought to nurture.

Have I lived another life before taking this garb I wear,
or is it a fleeting look at what is still to be,
but whether past or future it is still I
who rides the eternal wheel. Never to die

But interlaced relentlessly
into a tapestry still to weave,
or a pattern already spun.
One life fulfilled, or another still to run.

Helen M. Colthorpe-Parker

God's Wonderful Love

Deep deep as the ocean
Is God's wondrous love
Deep deep as the ocean
God as gentle as a dove

We see His love in Jesus
We see God's wonderful gift
We see God's gift of creation
It gives us all a lift.

We see His love in redemption
We see The Creator's power
We see His love at Calvary
It is God's finest hour

We see God's love in grace
We see His mighty hand
The rainbow and the clouds
Echo God's praise throughout the land

The whole earth is full of His glory
That is the start of the story
When all God's people will enjoy heaven above
Then we will all sing of God's wonderful love.

Richard Shurey

432

Why

Why do they use the bomb and the gun
Is it for pleasure? Or maybe for fun?
How do they feel when they take peoples lives
Do they not care about another's cries
Loved ones who suffer, weighted by cares
How would they feel if the suffering was theirs?

These men with the bomb and the gun
What good do they think they have done
It seems what they most achieve
Is to hurt many people and make them grieve
War creates fear and does not hasten peace
When will they learn and when will they cease

How did hate invade that mind
How could relations be that blind
I cannot understand however I try
Again I cry why? Why? Why?

  P. A. Murphy

Fame

A life of fame
To aspire, a game
In one foul swoop
To capture, maim
Your purpose to be.
And but only one foresee,
For a time at least
And a half.
What is this aspiration,
And desire to fulfil temptation
In proud prowess for yourself, your nation,
Your name or a girl?
So why stick your neck out
When you know of the Golden Goose?
I suggest you use a pit of sand
And not a knotted noose.

  Scott T. Fitz-Gerald

Anger

A scarlet oblong face lit like a burning candle,
A face as red as a tomato,
Cheeks as lustrous as roses,
Flickering flames of fire trickling up my face,
A sweltering face about to explode with words
of revenge floating out of my head,
My face beats like the hoof of a stamping horse,
Rushes of blood crossing my face like a sea
full of waves,
It's the look of a glowing sun lying upon earth,
It's a velvet red smeared across my face,
My face looks like the crippling red leaves in the
Autumn,
I'm as fierce as a bull,
Fumes of green smoke puffs out of my ears in great big clouds,
I'm angry with rage,
A beastly spirit inside me can't control it self much longer.

  Nadia Khan

A Love

Why did you go away
Why did you make me sigh
Why did you walk out the door
When I began to cry
You knew I really loved you
You knew I really cared
I thought our love was shared
I thought you were the one
The moon stars and the sun
Now you have gone
I know this to be true
How can I go on living, without you
Now in our room, cold empty and bare
I sit thinking of you, but you not there

  Gillian Pattinson

For Cat Lovers
'Ziggy'

She leaps and prances up and down,
She bounces like a rubber ball.
She flings her pliant body
Here, now there,
With infinite grace. As light as air.

Luxuriant whiskers crown her brow,
Her coat is jet, her paws are white.
Each pad, the palest pink—on each,
a spot of black,
How delicately fashioned is this cat.

Pale is her chin, her eyes are green,
At her tail end a puff of snow,
Reaching for wind blown leaves
Imaginary foes.
She stands and dances on her toes.

She crouches in the grass, she springs.
She rolls upon her back with joy.
She climbs,
She stalks a hurrying ant, until dead beat,
Quite suddenly, she drops, and falls asleep.

  Leslie Grant

Woodland Weeping

The tree stood solid, proud and old
In woodland green and mellow.
Its leaves, rich green, bowed to the cold
And slowly turned brown–yellow.

The snow dressed our friend in white,
In still and quiet she rested.
Then slowly buds embraced the light—
Of Spring, and song birds nested.

Of blossom, chicks and busy flight
New leaves and insects rustling,
The tree was bursting with delight
So rich with new life bustling.

Rain clouds gathered as if they knew,
As axe struck wood with force.
The birds in fear and panic flew
As fate took its dreadful course.

People rushing through the day
Using paper as they please
Then tear and burn and throw away.
Unthinking for the life of trees.

  P. T. Marshall

Pearls Of Memory In A Whelk Shell (1986)

I grasp the shell.
The inside is dreamily smooth and pearly pink.
Mysteriously twisted . . .

Like a staircase
Where steps melt away at every step.
Almost vertical . . .

On a turret
Solitary with fluffy clouds surrounding it.
One bears a face . . .

That departed
Two days before my birthday
Last year . . .

Now gone
Back to the world that is always 19 February
And always 1985 . . .

Like the horizon
That is far beyond reach of any ship
And bears a secret . . .

That hushes this world.
Obey it . . . be silent.

  Louisa Radice

Eventide

There's a stillness that comes with the close of the day
As the sun slowly sinks in the west
A stillness that brings such peace to my soul
As the birds start to sing by their nests
This melodious sound at eventide, like no other sound of the day
Makes my soul take flight, like a bird on the wing
Like a traveller, wending his way
At eventide, when the wind settles down and the leaves
become still in the trees
When the sounds of nature are clearly heard
The grasshoppers, crickets and bees
I feel such peace . . . and gratitude that I can see and hear
And walk through the quiet countryside
At this wonderful time of year

Some like the morning—the break of the day
A challenge—appointments to keep
But I love the evening—the "tapering off"
When the earth settles down to sleep.

Joy Wingrove

Born Into War

My grandfather alas I never knew,
Killed by a bomb blast in world war two.

My grandmother, I owe my life to, they said.
Although to small to remember,
She made sure I was fed.
I returned from convalescent home
to find her quite ill,
And before I could thank her
she to was dead.

My mother had left some time before,
Divorced by my father when he returned from the war.

My father, as we celebrated victory,
Had an extra problem to contend with.
He was saddled with me.

As we grow older,
Certain feelings we learn not to show,
Happier now, still I retreat now and then,
To the roses I grow.

Alan Pilgrim

Precious Moments

Enjoy each moment of your life,
Forget about the family strife,
Time to think of important things of day,
Like birds and flowers and making of hay,
Our doggie friends, and loving cats,
Happily sitting upon our laps,
Our friends sincere, we hold most dear,
There is no time, to sit and fear,
All beauty which surrounds us,
Thankfully, blots out all hurts and fuss,
There's more to life, than bearing grudge,
As God will be our final judge.

Elsie Joyce Cranfield

Forbidden

Forbidden to know the things I would
Forbidden to see the things I should
Forgiveness denied for sorrow I cry
And with this loneliness I now must die.

Forbidden to help me see the light
Forbidden to make things right
All faith becomes dim, for within
Ever forbidden to be giving sight.

Forbidden past, forbidden time.
The broken heart, the unchanged mind.
A soul so much with sorrow filled
A death so sudden could not be willed
The passing heat will scorch the vines,
And melt the ice that has frozen the minds.

Jenny Gayle

Apartheid

Shout aloud; spread the news; so the world will know
There is no need to fight
When we stand face to face with our neighbour
And see both day and night
Search the eyes and reflect, that they mirror the thoughts
Sharing God; hope and joy; can't be wrong
So think for a while, does it matter at all
We're not on this earth very long
So cry out for love, and a peaceful existence
Why live in a world of despair
Roused from sleep in the womb, to a dark stinking grave
Peels the skin; leaving bones that are bare
Then we'll all look the same, and unable to tell
If our neighbour is black, white or red
When the flesh has decayed, as we lay side by side
We'll be equal, when we are all dead!

Ken Williams

The Acquaintance

I phoned, to ask a question,
'Did you know my father?'
Some half forgotten memory had arisen,
as you are getting older
you were hard of hearing.
Who I am,
'Are you the lady friend of Brian?'
'Yes, that's me!'
It seemed expedient to ask you,
so I did,
time rushes by.
When I got the message over,
and about to replace the receiver,
you suddenly said, 'I'm leaving'.
'You're leaving!' I repeated in surprise,
'I'm going away to stay.'
'You'll be missed terribly.'
I heard myself say.

Irene Grant

Uneaten Chocolates

The bottles unopened, our photo's been broken,
The chocolates lie still in the fridge;
The candles are quenched, my teeth clenched
As I watch you walk over the bridge
My heart madly thumping, nerves wildly jumping,
And I picture our happier days.
Your heels are dragging, your head sagging
As you silently go your own way.
While our bodies were lifted, our minds drifted
And our hearts went to some other place;
Our separate lives and sweet goodbyes
Now, the hurt look on your face.
Our eyes meet, our lips not wet
We recognized adieu.
My heart saddened, but spirits gladdened
And I said farewell to you.

Jayne Moran

She Appears

My mind awoke to pleasures anew.
The comfort of patience. The radiance of you.
Wrapped in the sunlight. Sheets left half open.
Waiting for me to enter the hue.
Numbed by your body and by your thought,
Speechless I followed and lovingly caught
You held me and told me what I should do.
Transcending all feelings I gazed into you.
Interruptions then happened you thought only of us.
A man at the window, a woman at the door,
You soon saw them go.
The stillness returned.
You held me once more.

When I awoke your face had gone, your presence had dimmed.
But still you comforted me.

Niall J. L. Urquhart

The Last Journey

War has taken your Grandad away
To the lines of Picardy,
A khaki uniform he wears
And puttees to his knee.
A flat cap for the infantry
And a loaded magazine
Are all the wordily good he needs
And to keep his riffle clean.

Nana said that you didn't make it
You were gassed at the break of dawn
By the rolling clouds of mustard gas
With the friends you couldn't warn.
And the earth that you'd grown so close to
Is now a closer friend
Than any of those you left behind
To fight for and defend.

Christine E. Tandy

Only A Heart Beat Away

I won't shed any more tears of love,
Because you're only a heart beat away,
I'll smile when you're near me in the evening,
Because you're just out of sight through the day.

You're watching when I am sleeping,
Hearing me when I pray,
Sending your love to be near me,
Because you're only a heart beat away.

I'll dry my tears and smile again, love,
Remembering the happy times we've known,
Guarding the joy we discovered,
Like the love that was planted and grown.

The road will be lonely without you, love,
The future before me looks grey,
But I won't travel the road alone, dear,
Because you're only a heart beat away.

Florence Turner

Picture This

Figures from a mural stand tall upon a screen
So slender and so gaunt, an anorexic's dream
These figures look so lifelike, carved from flesh and bone
But not from wood like artifacts, these figures have been grown
Children lie like kindling on a rag upon the ground
They cry with eyes and mouths so wide, not making any sound
The world unites, sends food and tools, money, goods and care
Further down the river it's all stolen for a dare
Too sick to walk a grandmother crawls to look for help
Her loved ones died a week ago, she knows she'll die herself
A nurse picks up a child, she's six years old we're told
The girl looks on pathetically with eyes that have grown old
Flies like vultures hover round, feasting night and day
The corpses wrapped against them in sacks all torn and grey,
Our animals have better in countries to the west.
And most of us ignore these facts, some say 'It's for the best'.

Sherrilyne Hosler

Nature's Heavenly Jewels

Come with me on a journey to the sky,
And see the beauty of Nature's heavenly pearls,
They will be dancing and sparkling in a timeless zone,
An eternal tapestry crowned in Wondrous jewels.
White silky clouds will be kissing the setting sun
That shines through a golden ring of endless light.
You may see coloured beads of falling raindrops,
Following the band where the rainbow ends.

Imagine the sky all draped in black,
As though covered by angels' mantles in upward flight,
Stars like diamonds will be as twinkling lights
Guiding travellers to their homeward shore.
Come with me down the pathway of the moon,
You will be bathed in a pale silvery light,
And all will be calm in her warm embrace
Like Eternity, the home of your heavenly soul.

Anthony Lount

Edinburgh

I live in a beautiful city
the scenery is divine
and as I was born and bred here
I think of it always as 'mine'

The seaside, the hills and the lochs are nearby
The castle stands proud on its rock
Princes Street gardens are laid out below
and the wonderful floral clock

Pentland Hills, Swanston Village and Cramond
and Silverknowes walk by the sea
Queensferry with both the Forth Bridges
There's no better place you can be

The people are kind and they're friendly
There's plenty to see and to do
and this Capital City of Scotland
is ready to welcome you

The old town is brimful of history
with the castle, royal mile and the shops
The new town is known for its grand architecture
no wonder that Edinburgh is tops.

Margaret Lynch

Untitled

I'd much rather have a G and T to sip.
Then lie on this bed, attached to a drip.
Just you relax, if you need us just ring,
Your treatment is about to begin.

I'm feeling quite poorly, I must admit,
Hope it's not long before I can, again knit,
The ward isn't bad,
Except the others are confused or mad!

The nurses are really quite sweet,
Until they come and jab you in the seat,
Listen to the lady in bed number 3.
Says she's dying to do a wee.

Nurse! The commode please if I may,
Whoops! Sorry too late, she says.
Out comes the mop, you have to smile,
Another bell rings, I'll be there in awhile.

As I lay and observe here in my bed,
Prodded, examined, I'm past going red.
When I leave here, I'll go doo-lolly,
Especially as she in the corner, keeps calling me Sally.

P. L. Cannon

The Artisan (For Want Of A Nail?)

I am merely a carpenter but good at my work,
here, just look at this craftsmanship
and tell me if I shirk!

Beautiful wood—the very best timber,
it has to look right
so that people remember.

I have thought about engraving my name
on the vertical,
but my client says it's vain and fickle.

I have to keep my customers sweet,
it's all "width at the arms
and narrow at the feet".

It is almost complete, but before I exhale.
the recipient has got to be brought from the gaol;
"A blasphemer and a charlatan,
you should hear his 'Hallel'
a crown of thorns and a heart of vermeil".

I am almost done, I shall not fail,
with a wife and six children I have to travail,
or lose this work for want of a nail.

B. Wood

Memories Past Poem

Shipley Glen and Leeds.
Were happy days. In the 70's.
Way back then. When we laughed and played.
Myself and sister Ann Mum dad and Auntie Anne.
On the grassy rocks in Shipley Glen.
On what happy days, way back then.
Dad would sit on the grass.
Watching people go pass.
Myself Anne and Dad would walk to Baildon.
Oh we had happy memory days back then.
Sun would always shine.
Happy golden days.
I didn't want them to go away.
Golden memories to have and treasure.
They will always remain precious.
In my heart and my memories.
Of Leeds never to part.
Going to the bowling alley in Leeds
With Dad are memories I am glad to have.
Long may they remain and always stay the same.

Marie Bernadette Brosch

Ireland

Land of Saints and marching bands
I watch you tear yourself to strands
Your scenic beauty, your gentle hills
Despoiled by angst and other ills

The good who dwell are sorely pained
Vain hopes and dreams, dashed and drained
Such pursuits of common sense and hope
Destroyed by a multitude who will not cope

A world is watching, but does not care
Because we're here and just not there
Many will die of want this day
Intransigence wins, dealing death whatever way

Humanity, will just not learn, from evil past
What strange creator made this cast
Perhaps they're willing for time to unfold
A lesson that we might all behold

Alas that road is not yet in sight
When honest folk might see some light
Pray that sanity might deliver to all
A common good, a peace with love, albeit small.

Francis Gillies

Reflections Of A Night Nurse

In the quiet hours of night,
We make sure for you, all is right.
Wanting to make you aware,
That, while you sleep, we do care.

Quietly, around we creep,
Checking that, you are asleep.
If we find that you are not,
A drink we'll make, soothing and hot.

Should you need your bell to ring,
Help, and kindness we try to bring.
To help you on to slumberland,
We are willing, to hold your hand.

Sounds, and shadows, so different seem,
Perhaps you wake up from a dream.
When morning dawns, you will see,
A smiling face, with a cup of tea.

As day draws on, into the night,
Do not worry, or have a fright.
You are in God's hands, and His keep,
We watch by, as you lie asleep.

June F. Allum

Visual Artifice

And then, I turned another page,
And there was a picture of a pouting girl,
Pretending to simmer with rage.
She was exploiting the new colour.

Her eyes were shining,
but I did not see the light.
Her smile was seductive,
but I did not see the deceit.

And now, I flick passed some more articles,
And only two pages later I arrive again,
At another illumination of an ordinary girl.
She is smiling, but does she feel pain?

Does she suffer too although
her glossed lips are remarkable but removable?
Does she care like I do, even though
her waist is visible, but disappearing?

Somehow I think she does,
but for now she makes me not belong.
Somehow she makes me take thirteen steps back,
but I wonder, could she possibly be me?

Jillian Paterson

The Garden

From tangled web of massed prolific weed
emerging slowly with such loving care,
a beauty to behold, fulfils a need
where once a blossom was so rare.

And now in all her glory
'tis worth the toil, with satisfaction gaze
and sit and muse, to see it grow
where thorns hung deeply left unscathed.

Now blaze with each and every hue
clusters forming billow gently in the air,
scented sweetly in the morning dew.
Peace. Tranquillity, a haven to compare.

Stone rockery and rippling fall
in cottage garden 'mid the trees
hollyhocks and ramblers nestle 'gainst a wall.
An arbour of contentment in surroundings such as these.

Pamela J. Hickman

A Little Welsh Town

The hearth with flame aglow
Reflected on the mistletoe
Its waxen beads of purest white
Amidst the golden candlelight
On that happy Christmas Day
I paused and thought of those I'd met and loved
And those so far away

Memories so near and dear
Sharing happiness and tear
Of sad and smiling faces, in a multitude of places
Acquaintances who keep in touch
And others you have loved so much
A host of friends so bountifully cherished
A treasured few, alas, so sadly perished

Through all the years of hopes and dreams
And striving to achieve what seems
To be a glorious world within a soul
Far reaching for its endless goal
At last I find a tranquil place, so full of harmony and grace
A haven wherein love and peace serenely dwell
That little bit of Wales—Llandrindod Wells

Nicholas Bryans

"Little Beth"

I feel helpless now just lying here.
While everyone stands and sheds a tear.
I lie so still but not from choice,
And in my head I hear the voice.
The voice of sadness, the voice of sorrow,
With lots of hope it will be gone tomorrow.
There's people all around, I don't know what to do,
Just look at their faces they seem so blue.
I ask what's wrong but no one cares,
They want to speak but no one dares,
I ask what's wrong as they all cry,
But all they do is say goodbye.
The voice has gone, there's not a sound,
There's no one in sight to be found.
Now I've realized what I've done
But to them it's harmless fun,
It's now my fault I'm lying here
The driver had drunk too much beer.

"Too much booze can end in death
And that's what happened to little Beth."

Claire Sewell

Students First Assembly

Decisions are made, and foundations now laid,
Good luck, and goodbyes in the past.
With mixed feelings of hope and possible fun.
As now a new chapter of life has begun.

The day has dawned you're here to stay.
Hello! To work begone dull play.
Your caps of thought you now must don
And be prepared to keep them on.

With pen and paper always ready.
Plus books galore for you to study,
Discussions there, opinions here
You really haven't a thing to fear.

So, if at first you're all at sea
When nothing seems right not even tea,
You'll soon forget your little woes
As week by week your knowledge grows

Then, before the final term is through.
I hope you'll all know what to do
But, if frustrated, is how you feel
Give all you've got to the "Durham Reel."

G. L. Lister

Tortured Heart

Look at this woman,
you may always see a smile.
Look deep into her eyes,
You may see so much pain, such frustration.
A time gone by, so much agony.
Something missing, a wide open space.
Show her a child and within her eyes,
you will see a twisted heart.
Showing joy, but also pain.
Her babies taken away before they grew.
The frustration of being unable to protect them,
knowing she couldn't.
And the love she still holds for them.
Her grieving shall continue all through her life,
because she never had the chance to say goodbye.
Nowhere to go and talk to them,
No headstone no grave,
Just her own made up memories
of what may have been.

M. F. Carty

Halloween Spell

Frog's legs . . . Bat wings,
Spicy curry . . . A lady's rings.
The fur of a big fat cat,
A car, a dog, a panama hat.

Kylie Minogue should go in,
She'd probably fit 'cos she's really thin.
Someone's dandruff is a good idea,
A fish, a rose, a pint of beer.

A boy's left ear, a wolf's tongue,
Someone's brain, someone's lung.
An eagle's eyes, a blind worm's tail,
A dead turtle, a dead whale.

An old man's stick, an old man's wig,
Pamela Anderson's chest (. . . or is that too big??)
I'd also put in Belinda Carlisle,
She'd add class, she'd add style.

Now there is a combination to scare the demons from hell,
But, here, my friends, I must end this spell.
"Bubble, bubble . . . toil and trouble,
Fire burn . . . cauldron bubble."

Qaiser Talib

Life With A Ghost

Far into a marshy forest the two boys went,
For the regular woods around were all burnt;
And fire–heating live trees their work at dry season.
In the marsh stood a wood huge and high.
Climbers and thorny weeds entwirling as well high;
And to fell the wood each boy pulled a climber.
Shaking and shaking a crack sounded from the root,
And shaking again, down fell the wood.
Escape direction was never their thought;
And down on the head and chest of the younger boy it fell;
The older in extrication bid a failure.
Hope lost, and dying, a message to the uncle he sent.
'God forbid', said the older boy, inspired or frustrated;
But later escaped into a bush, leaving the 'dead'
And the 'dead' under a palm tree for hours painfully slept.
'How?' He couldn't explain, staggering to the tent.
The uncle arrived, amazed to see him shiver,
But dreading a further torture, the boy replied, 'Fever'
Louder shouts brought out the older boy from hiding
And since then with a 'ghost' had been living.

J. Ayo Aderibigbe

Lost Love

The mists of time have blurred your face
I no longer call your name
My memories are kept in place
The years have cooled the flame

Your photo lies within a drawer
And with it lies a rose
It shows a dream I had before
And not the life I chose

Sometimes I hear our favourite song
And my heart skips a beat
Although I know it to be wrong
I feel your body's heat

Our love was never meant to be
I know that this is true
But when you walked away from me
I kept a part of you

Time heals all wounds or so they say
And this I've found so far
But memories are meant to stay
Wounds always leave a scar.

Jackie Johnson

437

Summer Month

Alive and vibrant,
precious and beautiful.
Her presence is like,
a brilliant fragile image.
Her fleeting grace surrounds you,
soft warm and inviting.
Her welcoming clear pools
are blue pure and enticing

Her days are long and warm,
none of Autumns tears will fall.
Her nights are bathed in shafts of gnostic moonlight,
so perfect, owned by none, desired by all.
Where are you to be found?
Mystic jewel that I seek.
Like the cries of all mere men in love,
my words are un-unique.
But this un-unique display,
born of a heart that's true.
A humble gift to share between two souls,
for my heart is true to you.

Michael E. Rawson

Of Reckoning And Reason

Why must we grieve when we deeply believe
That the system is wrong; that those who are strong
Are corrupt, and belong to the confines of hell;
Those doyens of gloom, who think they're immune
From the death-knell of doom. In towers of power
They plot and they cower, secure in the law,
Wealth in great store, they go to great lengths
To inflict their strength on mortals like us,
To keep us in line, save their greed from decline,
To feather their nests at our lowly expense,
So that they may climb the ladder of slime
Down which society slips in the coming of time;
And we stand by and watch, and tamely accept
These afflictions of shame as we play the great game
Of living and life. No wonder good mother
Will one day recover her brood, and discover
The beauty and grace of this once wondrous place,
Where meek will inherit, and earth will exhibit
The justice of reason from season to season,
Where no longer man's treason can sully her soil.

Steve Freeland

Bridge

Now we have reached 'middle age' . . .
Of life we have turned another page.
An interest together we must find,
A game of cards comes to mind.

To learn Bridge we took lessons,
Each week we took hourly sessions.
Then came the day we were free . . .
To play in matches for the NCB.
1 No Trump, 3 Hearts, . . . Double,
Now I am in a lot of trouble
Do I respond? Can I respond? . . .
I am in the 'Slough of Despond'.

On the way home the inquest starts . . .
Why did you leave me in 3 hearts?
I am upset, I 'pipe my eye'
It must have been easier to cross the 'Kwai'.

Another week has rolled round again,
I am now beginning to take the strain
Now I could play both night and day,
This darned game I just Love to play.

Joan May Gammons

Child's Play

A Child runs out and starts to play
But a voice rings out
The Child listens to what the voice has to say,
"Go back to your home. You haven't much time
For the Army have discovered an unexploded mine."

As the Child runs along with his head bent low
He asks himself, "Just where can I go?
For this is my Homeland and woe is me,
To think this could happen in a land of Christianity.
For no one will give in, or live and let live
The kind of life that God to me did give."

Trust is what one needs today
"But whom do we Trust?", the people will say,
And love of one's neighbour is badly needed
But where do you start when Hate has therein seeded?

So wake up my foolish folk
Before it's too late,
For all can be lost
Through too much hate.

E. Alwell

Persistent Vegetative State

There she lies, silent and still,
Wreathed in the darkest depths of sleep, until
I decide what her fate must be—
To release her to eternity
Or keep her alive, to stay with me.

Can she sense that I am here,
Hoping and waiting night and day?
Does she know how much I care,
Day after weary, lonely day?

She opens her eyes, but can she see?
Her thoughts are quite unknown to me.
At last I can speak to her—gently
And hope that now she will hear me,
Not as close to death as she could be.

For who are we, at God, to play,
To decide to take her life away?
Please, leave her alone, to sleep and dream
For at least another weary day.

Helen Lyon

Poor Mortal

A dark hand of shadows upon him was cast,
As to emphasize the light in contrast.
In a bad atmosphere with a sterilized smell,
Into a cage of extreme agony and pain he then fell.
Like an innocent child huddled up in a ball
He was taken over by a spasm until his soul took back control.
Medical treatment onto him they did enforce.
But the idea was abstruse, he was letting nature take its course.
His head was spinning with an increase of fever,
The medics were no help for, his life he did endeavour.

With no friends and no family there was no sign of supports,
He had to fight on his own just as he had thought.
A million images were spinning in his head
His life would end soon which he very much did dread.
The thoughts were eternal and would not come to a halt
Like an irritant alarm clock except with a fault.
From each second to each minute he held onto inhale and exhale
But as he took each last breathe he became more pale
As the mighty figure of the grim reaper did creep
So fell the poor mortal into his deep sleep.

Fateha Begum

Flowers Look Better On Fences

This is a sad place,
The trees will keep their secret,
Softly whispering in the gentle summer breeze,
Whispers of a winter's night,
A cold and stormy, ill met, ill lit, tragic night.

Sadness and badness linger here
And fear and the shame that honest men have,
For not a man, but a nothing.

A wooden fence divides the trees,
It leans a little now as old age takes its toll
And by the fence a path, smoothed by good shoes,
Smoothed by bad and smoothed by those who want to look,
Those who are so sad.

Someone cares, someone loves,
Maybe, someone cries.
On the fence are flowers, fresh and bright,
As fresh and bright as the last time,
As fresh and bright as every time I pass,
This sad, bad, cared for place.

Douglas Smith

The British Warriors

Near and far, wherever told,
they go to battle, brave and bold.
They fight on land, at sea, in the air,
where there's strife, you'll find them there.
For several years I too was one
but I came home, my service done.
Their graves are found in many a land,
in steaming jungle, desert sand.
Some unmarked, are just a mound
but still a piece of British ground.
Some bear number, rank and name
but all were heroes just the same.
They give their all for other's gain
and never to return again.
Although they lie in foreign parts,
their memory lives in loved one's hearts.
In scorching heart and freezing cold,
in recent times and days of old.
They died on hill, on plain, in valley
and sleep now till the great reveille.

Robert Hogg

I Believe! (An Ode To Ex-President, Jimmy Carter)

There is a man, a man who sees things grow;
A man of faith who builds on dreams
And spoke those words we love to hear: "I believe!"
A man of peace who believes in people;
No longer at the top; but, still, the same sweet guy!
To those who speak of doom, how can this be
With words like these echoing over the land
And across the sea and on the waves of the air:
Yes, I believe! Do you?

There is a man, a man who says what he feels,
A man of hope who never said: "Die!"
And remember this: He never gave up the fight
For what is just and true, battling against the odds,
At the same time, understanding his oppressors!
A man of fruitful endeavours, a farmer at heart!
"I believe" are the words of a man of vision—
A man for the future who believes in people!
Yes, I believe! Do you?

Catherine Flint

Kismet

Two strangers in town pass by on the street
never to glance, never to meet

Never to know, for who is to say
their best chance of happiness walked by today

He the poet, chained to the mill
she the artist, who never will

A perfect match, did they but know
a secret hidden from mortals below

Sport for the gods who watch from above
never to speak, let alone love

Back to the life she lives on her own
back to his wife and comfortless home

Just a quick glance and a smile in reply
a momentary pause and meeting of eye

A stammered word could have broken the spell
leading them both where none could foretell

But when strangers to town pass by on the street
if they never glance, they never will meet

Roy L. Smith

Heaven's Gate

Mocking leaves in autumn break, as if laid before heaven's gate,
To clown about with life's great skill,
With words of rhyme so full of chill,
Bare out the mind and heart within,
So caught in thought never running thin,
Mere particles of dust carried by the wind,
On through reason swept through time,
With end in sight but no door can find,
Who is to say you're merely blind,
With passages of love that tears frequent,
To wish a moment not to be spent,
Lay of hand to what route you take, sound of a footstep is it
    too late,
To the flicker of an eye before the gate,
To roars of laughter with mocking birth,
To cradle rock no child within, to growing up with schooling learn,
With riches of work in hours of toil, not yet time to go back to soil,
With times reward yet to foil, a burden carried but no burden gained,
Is life but a number in what we aim,
To spin thee wheel what path to take,
Down through the highway to heaven's gate.

A. C. Gates

The Village

I go down to the village at the end of the day.
Sea smashing against rock in a glorious spray.
A friendly smile, a cheerful face,
A slender old lady full of grace.

The memories roll on with the frolicking sea
Salmon shimmer 'neath the surface bringing thoughts back to me
A pipe–smoking man, a woman in a shawl.
A fisherman pulling in a generous haul.

The old seafarers laugh on an old battered seat
Swapping tales of foreign lands with unbearable heat,
A swan swims on by, a lark cries out loud
A clear sky above with no sign of a cloud.

This place is so beautiful and yet so carefree
There is no place in the world that I would rather be.
A butterfly floats by, a seal splashes in the bay.
Now you know why I go the village at the end of the day.

M. W. Connolly

Castle Of Night

Rebuild them.
Pile the boulders high.
Fill the cracks,
Watch the motor dry.
Re-shape the battlements.
Arm the turrets.
Give teeth to these,
Cold stone walls,
That reach so high.

Shut the gate,
Slam the bolt.
Entomb those eyes of day.
Banish the light,
So all I can live is the night.
Never to come forth again.
Never to open my gates.
Let me remain enclosed, alone.
Where no one can see me, no one can plague me.
As I sit upon my regal throne.
King of my self made castle of might.

Duncan J. E. Hooley

Holocaust

A race we breed to be so malicious
That man to man could be so vicious;
It seems really impossible to me
That such a dreadful thing could be
But its happening is a true fact
To such inhumanity how can I react?

It made no difference, man, woman or child,
They were all so tragically reviled,
Death we know must come to us all,
Those poor people didn't get their call
by our God's usual chosen way,
But for them the whole world did pray.

Such ways of suffering and death
Made it so hard to take a simple breath.
The pain and tortures those chosen people bore
Sent them to heaven through a wide open door.
The star of David guided all their souls,
For them the journey straight, there were no tolls.

P. M. H. Wood

The Walk Of Life

Far below is an avenue
The winter sun penetrating through the trees.
Looking up towards the horizon.
Trying to get a glimpse of dawn.

As we keep moving on
The past and the dark shadows are finally gone.
We begin to wonder how does it come,
Where does it go, till later we realize
Life's like that.

There are many out there looking for hope.
Some are good many who can't cope.
With guilt, suspicious and lies
We live with tongues that are bitter.

And faces that glitter.
The world has come to a point, for once we are born
There is no return.
We face what has been done
What's going on and what's coming.

For in life
expect the unexpected.

Melvin Patten

Living In The Past

Each day, sitting by the window,
There she is, ever so transparent,
With all the sweet memories
Flooding through her face:
Wondering whether it was really over.

Living in the past
Livens her face and transforms her world:
But the pain is still there.

Living in the past
And remembering the pleasures of yesterday:
When time ticked away slowly,
There was no need for her to talk,
Her eyes said it all.

Living in the past
Keeps her heart beating
drives her fears away—
Oh! If it were possible to turn the clock back,
How simple life would then be.

Living in the past
Is all she ever does.

Gisela Abbam

On Being Deaf

If you have your sight, sound limbs and can hear,
Then count your Blessings, for you don't live with fear.
I had good hearing in younger days,
Enjoyed opera, music and going to plays.

I started going deaf, when almost twenty three,
But was told, they couldn't operate on me.
Bone conduction deafness, they said I had,
It was hereditary, passed on from my dad.

Many tests followed and plenty of pain,
Hospitals, doctors, and what did I gain?
Just help and advice, to live with my fear,
Knowing—it will get worse—year by year.

Friends have helped in many ways,
Giving me comfort on bad days,
Now I have hope, and it's fun to share,
A laugh and a joke—with those who care.

Try to understand, when I don't reply,
Don't walk away, or say "Goodbye",
I can lip-read a little, and will try,
To hear your words.

Ethel Georgina Wallis

The Song Of The Storm

With a clash of thunder the storm comes alive,
Sea meets sky, day moves into night,
The reds and yellows, the pinks and whites,
The spectacular cloud forms, that reach to great heights.

As the sun disappears, moon comes into view,
The clouds that were red, turn into blue,
Sea starts to fight and the waves collide,
The rocks disappear, by the furious tide,

Thunder and lightning take turns to perform,
The rattles and rumbles, the song of the storm,
Torrential showers blanket the ground,
An orchestra of nature, create a wonderful sound.

As the storm dies down, the noise fades away,
Night progresses to morn, birth of a new–born day,
Sun rises and shines and burns so bright,
Disappears, all evidence of the storm by night.

Janice Walker

Always Remember

Always remember how our gallant men fought
To make a land much better for all
Don't let it be in vain and for nought
They left all they loved when they answered the call

We who are old do not forget
The sacrifice they gave
And so many that we never met
Lie in a foreign grave

At the D-Day Celebrations
Our heroes did us proud
They came from many nations
And we cheered them long and loud

Don't remember them just for a day
They deserve much better you know
Give them respect in every way
And remember they beat the Foe

So when Remembrance Day comes along
When you see the blind helping the blind
Remember they helped put right a wrong
And did their best for mankind

Molly Andrew

Escapology

I sent myself to sleep as a last persuasive gesture
to undergo a rebirth, a re-entry to the womb,
a necessary deactivation of my hopes, my thoughts and dreams
which had become embittered, twisted by my gloom.
A journey which was to take me to an inner sanctum
which nobody else could reach, a sanctity embound.
But this re-foetal transformation caused agony untold
yet no more than my mother suffered on my first time around;
for whilst penetrating hard into a dark vacuous void
I saw remnants of a time gone by, vistas from my past
bearing witness to the error of my ways as if on a TV screen,
with painful recriminations of regret which would always last.
But once I'd broken in, like the sperm into the egg,
I was back at the beginning, a chance to start again.
So warm in there, so clean and safe
the ideal place to incubate a positivity so plain.

It is escapology which ingratiates a meaningful life to lead
with freedom from societies uptight trivial goals;
allowing the ideal chance to nurture an existence simple and pure
for living life without complications of desires not based on greed.

Richard A. Featherstone

Untitled

As I was out walking late one night.
Out of the blue there came this light
and the light said, "relax and don't take flight"
then all of a sudden I didn't exist as me.
 I was the birds
 I was the bees
I was the whistle in the breeze
I was the stars in the sky
I was the clouds floating by
 I was the rivers
 I was the seas
 I was the grass
 I was the trees
and I existed as everything but not as me
But when I thought that this can't last
Then there I was stood back on the path
if that's enlightenment
without any shadow of doubt
Please light shine on me
whenever I'm out

G. J. Crowley

Have I Lost You Forever?

Have I lost you forever?
Can we not work things out?
There's no need to scream or shout,
Just hear me.
Is my voice silent?
Are my screams just whispers?
There's no-one here to wipe the tears
That fall from my eyes when I
Dream about you.
And what of that tear?
Like you, it is lost forever,
Another lost tear.
Another lover lost.

Pain will achieve nothing.
My tears are just a raindrop in the storm;
A snowflake in the blizzard.
But that snowflake is your smile.
A faded smile, frozen in time.
In my mind, I'll remember . . .
You taught me how to cry.

Karl Woods

The Majestic Land

As I reach the summit,
take a look around,
at the beautiful mountain theme,
and the sun beats down
on the deserted woodland
sending up a haze of heat
which seems to bathe
the place in drowsiness.
The thyme is sweetly blooming
as is the heather.
I reach a peninsula and
score the land below me,
bogs, marches and swamps
add to the wonderful scenery.
I see children playing,
mothers at cottage doors and men working on farms.
But I knew nothing of them nor they about me,
they were each a glimpse and gone forever.
I am alone in this beautiful majestic bewilderment
with nature around me and God in harmony with me.

Colm Cosgrove

"Where Are You Now My Son?"

I let the Sun set on my wrath, never said that last goodnight;
and on the morrow you were gone.
Where are you now my son? Where are you now?

I spent a lonely vigil through the night beside your
lifeless form, until the dawn that brought no light.
Where are you now my son?

No more to see you smile, hear your boyish laugh, feel your
tiny arms enfold me tight:
My will to live has vanished like the chaff.
Where are you now my son?

Have you been reborn of another womb: an infant smiling at me,
Someone passing me by without a glance, a bird soaring in the
cloudless sky? Or are you in the falling rain, soft white snow,
silent winds that cool my brow: a waterfall, or pink and blue
lobelia cascading down a garden wall? Have you learned what
lies beyond the grave, met the unknown God face to face? Is this
earth all there is, or is there yet another time and place?

Each night I lie upon my bed and sigh for never having said
that last goodnight; and then my heart in anguish cries,
"Where are you now my son? Where are you now?"

Cyril O. Thornton, M.C.

Shades Of Love

It was just a television scene,
I hear you say
Just what it was meant to be
A mirage of reality
An orchestrated illusion
With no actual experience,
No real thought of mind in action,
No depth of feeling, or was it?

Was it just a pale shadow of the real thing
Or, was my intuition powerfully accurate?
Was the very way she slid into his arms
Exactly what it was supposed to mean?
He placed his arm gently and tightly round her waist
As if done so oft before—
An act so daring in its innocence.

For idle moments, they were so tantalizingly close.
Did they know any more than I?
Were they, like me, fooled by the act?
I stopped and thought . . .
And then put pen to paper!

Naomi Anne Kloss

Autumn Leaves

Sunlight sifting through the trees,
Branches swaying in the breeze,
Autumn leaves, green, yellow, gold and brown,
Watch them tumble gently to the ground.
Take a walk along a wooded path.
Capture the glory that will not last.
Rustling leaves beneath your feet.
Stop! Look around and give your eyes a treat.
The trees are displaying there final show.
Before they are sprinkled with winter snow.

Freda G. M. Harris

Free Spirit

The clock is chiming in the hall,
Evening shadows start to fall,
Sounds of barking, scratching, bangs against the wall,
Leashes hanging, chains jangling, ready for a walk.

The Master's coming, here we go,
Mother and Son, the Springers, bobbing to and fro.
There's just the two dogs now,
Once there were three.

The Father of Moss and Holly's pal,
His name was Todd, a lovely dog,
He went to sleep last year,
His spirit now is free.

There they go the pair, racing, stopping, listening,
Sniffing out a lair,
Rolling in the puddles, it seems without a care,
They race across the meadow, the wind in their fur.

Do they know something? Is it their king?
Running and racing with them, in the wild wind.

Joyce May

The Last Warrior

Out on the plains a warrior stands,
Feathered headdress and braided bands.
This man was once the chief of a tribe,
A happy people filled with pride,
They lived in peace and were bold and true,
Their spirits going where the wind blew.

He looks out now upon the land,
Everything gone like grains of sand,
Only memories of hurt and pain,
Echo to him now from across the plain.

Out on the plains a warrior stands,
Feathered headdress and braided bands.

S. Simon

The Fox

Red coated riders, are gathered here,
For the weekly hunt, for a fox is near,
A blast on the horn, and they gallop away,
Through peaceful country, they chase their prey,
Across fields, and meadows, see them charge,
A demented chase, for a fox at large,
Hounds in a fever, blood lust for all,
So much hype, for one so small,
The fox breaks cover, and runs like hell,
Jumps over a stream, and down through the dell,
Confused hounds, have lost the scent,
No one can tell, which way he went,
Angry hunters trot, around hedges to look,
For the golden haired terror, they lost by the brook,
The fox lies still, with a thumping heart,
To move now, is to be torn apart,
Time goes by, but he remains still,
Watchful, as they hunt, for their elusive kill,
The hounds are called off, that enough for to-day,
That wily old fox, has got clean away.

Colin Dudley

Farewell

Today will bring you heartache; Today will bring you strife,
Forgive me, my sweet love, for Today I end my life,
Cry not that I will move no more, for pain I shall not know,
I'll rest my head, close my eyes, and whisper to my soul to go.

Remember me tomorrow, when the sun shines overhead,
Think of how we laughed at the silly things we said,
Cast back your mind to happy times, of dreams and things
long past,
Think not of pain or illness, or my torture to the last.

When next week comes be happy, throw cares into the sky,
Force from the archives of your mind, sad thoughts of you and I,
Make haste to build a new life, and yearn no more for me,
For next week is the beginning of all eternity.

When springtime comes around again, carrying fresh life for
all things,
Welcome her with open arms, cast sorrow out on wings,
Pick one small flower for me, and plant it in your heart,
Let it grow and prosper steadfastly, for the new life you will start.

Jacqueline S. Handyside

The Burngrange Disaster

Deep, dark, down the mine
One lantern, lots of lives
Fire caused, frightened people all because, of one lit lantern
Worried, surprised, desperate cries.
Deep, dark, down the mine.
Times up, lights out
Scurrying footsteps down below

Fire burning, hot sparks running down the passages
Minds all wiped out, dreams swallowed up.
Open mouths, as if to say, remember us in a special way.

Digging hard for shale and pay.
Crying, weeping, their families sad.

Spending their last minute of life frightened to death
Deep, dark, down the mine.

While they lie there dead in the pit
Not recognized but remembered.

All the men who died, had to be identified.
Their mouths open and desperate
But they will never be forgotten.

Heather Connell

Star

I'm the brightest star—that shines at night
My eternal glow extends
Sparkling, twinkling high above
To you I only lend . . .

My spark, my gleam
That stirred me on, to tackle all I've done
Is now all that I can offer
To you, my special one.

Look high into that deep, dark night
In which I float around
I can guide you now in times of need
And never let you down.

I'm forever in the night sky
You only have to see
I am so far, and yet so close
My guidance is your key.

As some time—long in the future
You, too, will one day find
You can look down on this misshaped world
Because your spirit'll be with mine.

Lisa Walsh

Disability

Disabled people are special people
And a joy to have around
A nicer, kinder, understanding lot
You'll never find
Some of us are deaf, some of us are blind
But a friendlier lot we try to be.
Each of us are handicapped in a different way
Our lives we try to lead every day
Every minute of every day is a challenge in itself
Nothing to do about it or we'll get left on the shelf
Doing jobs and bringing up children
Just like healthy people do
No easier, maybe harder, depending on me or you
We love, cry, laugh and feel pain
Just like everybody else
Give us a chance to be accepted as equals
Is all we ask
To help us not hinder us is no hard task
To belong in society in our rightful place
And to be a part of the human race.

Christine E. Burnett

Home

Enter this seedy place, heave with nostalgic sickness.
Pull back the covers, take a good look at the sheets.
Stained with passion and carelessness: Plenty of feeling;
Doused with wishes, and bodily heat.

Lie back gently and observe the jaundiced ceiling,
Caressed by cigarettes, and smothered, abused air.
The dimly glowing light is buzzing with movement, thinking:
'Here we go again, but who said life's fair?'
(Think of the time, lying elsewhere,
In a different world, where sun filters through the patio,
Fresh air sprayed with coffee, smooth kisses for a while.
Someone else to cling to in the depth of the night,
Lips crease to show contentment, yet through the eyes: No smile).

Claim back your emotions from Heaven, as you smell the bodily fluids,
Grab your clothes and shudder, thinking of all the other men.
Turning away from the paint–stripped door, turn back for a glance;
Say a word: Say any words, whisper; "Until we meet again".

Natalie Kristina Kelsall

Flowers

Golden Rain, Golden Showers
What lovely names we give to flowers
Ragged Robins, Lady's Lace
The Pansy with its pretty face

Larkspur pink, white and blue
Ladies Slipper, Ladies Shoe
Pimpernels and Poppies too
Buttercups and Cornflowers blue

Lavender and Love-in-the-Mist
Haste to the Wedding, and Lover's Kiss
Candytuft of every hue
Primroses, Violets and Heavenly Blue

Sunflowers, Moondaisies, Bethlehem Star
Rosemary for remembrance wherever you are
Sweet William, Sweet Rocket, Sweet Peas climbing high
Granny's Nightcap and Traveller's Joy

Harebells ringing in the rain
Daisies to make daisy chains
Oh, I could sit and think for hours
Of the lovely names we give to flowers

Rose Anderton

Imprisoned By My Inner Self

Obscurity conceals my only light,
Clarity is no more.
I know not of who I am or why I am.
To drown my sorrows is impossible,
For they have learnt to swim.
I push them down and as I try to obliterate their being,
Still they return.
To face myself is to face my conscience,
An infinite argument between right and wrong, good and bad,
Yes and no.
Where do I belong?
If I cannot face my true self, who can face me?
Why am I trapped in this vigorous cage created only by myself?
Questions that possess no answers, or do they?
Who is here to answer them?
Here I lie still and alone, 'Imprisoned by my inner self.'

Janine Cain

Death On The Road

There's death all around us . . . there's death on the road.
the squirrel the rabbit and even the toad.
The magpie the pigeon . . . no one is spared;
As the cars speed on through I wonder who cared.

You drive so fast all through the night,
The animals that wait there you give such a fright.
All the heartache and misery and death that you bring.
With your stereo full on you don't hear a thing.

You don't hear a thing . . . the scream . . .the thud
As you leave them all there squashed in the mud.
Their eyes are wide open, with panic they stare
But you just speed along and don't even care.

The mothers . . . the babies . . . they're all left behind.
A new Daddy they will now have to find;
For Daddy's lying dead and squashed in the road,
Along with the squirrel . . . the rabbit . . . the toad.

John D. Fountain

"Old Smoky"

She came to freystrop all tired and worn,
Her body in pieces, some twisted and torn.
Hydraulic equipment lifted her carefully in,
To the garage, for necessary work to begin.
Plenty of people tended her there,
Working long hours with loving care.

Today "Old Smoky" stands on show,
All newly painted and steaming to go.

Gwyneth John

443

White Satin Never Falls

The whiteness of the purest flower flies upwards with grace,
The softness of the snowflakes falls gently with its lace.
The blossoming of a newborn's smile goes forever on and on,
The melodies and harmonies of that sweet sounding song.
The sun shining on the morn carries the gift of life for all,
The splendid face of a tree standing graciously tall.
The sound of flapping from the truest dove up high;
The forming of the cotton clouds in the light blue sky.
The flowing of the silent stream, wending its way home,
The buzzing of the bumble bee, the pollen is now sown.
The settling of the rain, as it flows from the roof,
The clopping of the horse, as it puts down its hoof.
The whistling of the wind, as it races through the land,
The sweetness of the container, honouring its jam.
The sighing of the balloon, as it's released in the house,
The munching and running of the little field mouse.
The fairest of the rainbows shining, personally pleased,
The cropping of the cornfield, as the farmer sees.
The rising of the hot air balloon . . .White satin never falls.

Caroline Anne Barker

A Child's Eye

Do you wish to know what Christmas is about?
Then look into a child's eyes for here you will find out.
There are many things not clear to you and I,
Which become plain and simple through a child's eye.
We look around and see things every day,
Then in our minds are altered and described in disarray.
A child will look straight-forward and see the very same,
Then tell it to us as they saw disregarding any shame.
We teach them to change things round and even to tell lies,
We muddle-up their simple minds and loving child's eyes.
It surely is a pity we cannot leave these as they are,
For then we would all think so clear and see so very far!

C. S. Murphy

Untitled

It's good to be contented,
and free from troubled mind,
God is good to all who seek,
and loving to all who find,
he certainly has no favourites
and gives good gifts to all
such as sun, rain and fresh air
many cannot buy these things
they just come to us by call,
we but are in service were passiveness never been
able to work but do voluntary kindnesses to all
Mr. and Mrs. S. J. Gess
Yes I believe in God's goodness.

M. Gess

Choirboys

Within the dark, faint eerie light,
White walls flawed with crumbled damp,
Air, rich with old dry wood, and dusted stone,
Wax polish, a dead and distant furnace,
Weeping resin from a knotted pew,
Long faded flowers, dead lilies, two.

Light oaken walls, and closets, four,
With surplices behind each door,
An ancient rug upon the floor,
Where boys, small boys, not angels tore,
Around! Around! 'til tempers soar,
Made elders quell the wild furore

Oh whistling wind of windswept spire,
You sing a song of your desire,
Such purity of note, so true,
No matter that there are so few,
What is the song that they should sing?
The song that will proclaim Him King.

Elliott Gibson

Involuntary Euthanasia

At first a smile, then a tooth, now just one more step
Kindergarten stories, look mummy a gingerbread man
Next to school, bag in hand, excel (not just your best)
One hundred percent essential
Daddy I can't (you're my son) I know you can.
From school to university down life's production line
A puff of smoke devours your teens the dreaded midnight oil
   Cap and gown jewel in your crown
      Of never ending toil.
Husband, house, father, holidays and cars.
Heart attack you made them proud
Still reaching for their stars.
So now the stars belong to you
You stand at heaven's gate
No second chance, your children's children
For them it's all too late.
So beautiful, so delicate, so short a life on earth
So fulfilled and undemanding seen but never heard.
To give to man, what man can't see through life's distorted eye
If this be life, Dear Lord, I pray next time a butterfly.

Carole Ann Harding

Soul Of The Sea

A shimmer of colour, beneath a fake sea,
Holds a beautiful secret only meant to be free,
As he spins and he turns a body appears,
And he leaps through the air to the sound of great cheers.
He jumps through a loop at the command of a bell,
He is fed a small fish, his job was done well.

This creature, this soul, this spirit so free,
Is held captive, so cruel, away from the sea.
He swims around in circles and does what is said,
He wishes for freedom and to choose what he's fed.
This creature, this soul, this spirit so sad,
Wishes for freedom when he once was so glad.

He dreams of the sea, his natural home,
With others like him, when here he's alone.
This spirit of the deep, this soul of the sea,
He's a beautiful secret only meant to be free,
This life he lives now is a life that's not his,
He dreams of the sea, the freedom, the bliss.

Kathryn Connor

The Rainbow

Colours are all around us colours dark and bright
I thought about colours of a rainbow and they gave me the light
For they are sent from Heaven for all of us to see
So I would like to tell you of what they mean to me
Red so bold and vibrant it generates its glow
So I put this all around me when I am feeling low
Yellow the colour of sunshine it radiates its heat
It gives me warmth and comfort when I am feeling beat
Pink so soft and gentle I think of when I'm fraught
It calms my nerves and silences my very angry thoughts
Blue the colour of spirit with its healing light
To penetrate my body it makes me feel so bright
Orange the colour of sunset that glows across the sky
It lifts away my sorrow when I feel I want to cry
Purple deep and rich like the silence of the night
A cloak of velvet round me then there's not a pain in sight
Green the colour of nature a colour to make me grow
Into a better person to help the folk I know
So look too the colours of rainbow and take the colour you need
And through all life's tribulations I'm sure you will succeed

P. G. Greenwood

My Friend

I miss you and wish I could be with you on this day,
and think of you even, if I am miles away,
and I hope to see you again sometime.

Do you remember the walks we took,
and read together some poetry and books?
The sun was shining and your gentle smile,
gave pleasant times just for a while.

The comfort you gave me was as from a mother,
and little secrets we told each other
often came back into my mind,
and left some lovely memories behind.

You will always be a dear friend to me,
whatever the future may be.
You've done so much for me in the past.

Therefore, I pray to God for your happiness and health,
for this will be to you the greatest wealth,
God bless you now my dear and I hope good fortune will be near,
I send to you with all my heart this gift,
and like to show you we have not floated adrift.

Helene Kolonko

Springtime

The winter cold at last has gone,
The world is waking to the sun,
Soft as a sigh the gentle breeze
Like thistledown in the trees.

In the wood down the lane,
Bluebells are come again,
Their fragrant scent and nodding heads
Fills my heart with sweet content.

Sweet cherry blossom on the bough
Swaying gently above me now,
Apple blossom, lilac too
Spring flowers of every hue,

Birds on the wing, song of the thrush,
Far too busy to notice us,
The babbling brook hurries on its way
Adds to the sounds of a lovely day.

Lambs skipping, playing, close to mother,
Fluffy little rabbits chasing each other,
Oh what a lovely world to see,
Our Lord made it all for you and me.

Irene Webley

Summer

On a peaceful summer's day
When farmers are busy bailing the hay
Sitting alone in the peace of the garden
One really has a sense of pardon
Listening to the song of the thrush
When all around there seems a "hush"
Poppies growing in the fields
Remind us all of what nature reveals
Bees are busy in the flowers
They are at work for many hours
The baby birds from their nests have flown
And now have learnt to feed on their own
The caterpillar that seemed so shy
Has turned into a lovely butterfly
Children playing on the seashore
Are saying they could not ask for more
This truly is a wonderful time
It should make us all feel sublime

M. A. Emsden

My Dog Mick

You wake up in the morning, just like the lark
The binmen call, and they get a friendly bark,
But the postman, with his swinging bag,
Is treated like a burglar with his swag.
You bark, and bark, as though to kill,
Then watch him, until he is out of sight,
Sometimes you sit down there and wait,
Hoping he will walk through the gates.
I feel convinced you would have his leg
If he did not stroke you, as you sit and beg.
One morning through the gates he came
You looked at me, and then at him,
As much as to say, "Shall I have him Jim?"
I said "Good boy" and the postman smiled,
He patted your head, I thought him brave.
Two days later I was woken from my bed, a constable said,
"The burglar is half dead, he walked from your house,
He carried a stick, and his loot, and met Mick."

James Fernridge

Island Of Love

In my dreams, I dream of you each night.
I'm floating over meadows and woods,
    flowers spring beneath my feet.
I float to an open sea, a ship is waiting for me.
Bright white sails, on a emerald sea, and above a silent moon,
This ship is taking me to the island of love.

The ship sails into the island, where you're waiting for me.
We run towards each other, your lips touch mine with a kiss.
"Now I know I'm home at last" on our island of love.

We walk hand in hand, leave our footprints in the sand,
We talk for hours, as we sit down under the swaying palms.
Exotic fruits we eat, and the flowers you gave me
Smell sweetly, as you put one into my hair.

Birds singing gaily, and the mountain waterfall sparkles,
    as it falls into streams.
The breeze blows gently on my face, and we haven't a care at all.
We hold on tightly to each other, as we whisper words of love,
We are happy and contented,
In this never, never land paradise island of love.
We vow our love to each other, under the swaying palms,
That our love will last for a life time, on our island of love.

Elizabeth Barnett

Waiting

Miss Mutton and Miss Green
Sitting in the still bright evening sunlight room
Talking, waiting in the still bright cold bright evening room
Talking as they had talked for fourteen years.
Long shadows extending time as the angular
Mrs. Hughes Cucks along the endless corridor
To the kitchen, hesitates, and clicks back again unbent, waiting
Elsewhere ethereal visitors take tea and others
    sit unrecognized once more.
Clothes lay scattered, rooms shine, empty waiting.
Light fades and shadows move across others
And into others, slowly and with pain.
Some will return,
All will change.

B. R. Vigour

The Man On His Own

He looks out of the window people pass by no one sees him
looking at them though the window of his solo. The man with
no name because no one knows it but then no one cares. He
turns away from them and the world outside and goes back to
the TV world in which he likes to live a life full of love and
happiness but he knows that his life is not going to be like
that no love no happiness nothing but sad and lonely
thoughts. So if you see a man looking at you out of a window
one day give him wave it may be you one day.

Martin Robb

The World's Garden

As I walk through the garden,
My eyes take in the beautiful colours
From which the petals glow.
Everything looks so perfect
Yet there's something underneath.
I reach down and touch the death,
As I look at the limp flower.
I see it has been pushed from the garden
By the stronger, powerful plants.
Searching along the ground
I find another, and another death.
Soon I have a collection.
Each tiny body has been prevented from life,
They have been starved of water,
And the plants above have ignored their cries.
As I stand and go to the gate,
Carrying the bodies in my arms,
I realize that I'm no longer in the garden
Instead, I'm walking through Africa, Bangladesh, Ethiopia,
This is the world's real garden.

Lucy Ablitt

Poster Child

I see you standing alone and
afraid, so close I feel I
can touch you, and wipe away
the tear that wets your weary cheek.
But yet you are so far away . . .
You stand in a world
so distant from mine, as I
stand in the rain looking
up at you on a Shopping Centre's notice board.
I can't help but feel selfishly relieved
that I am the one who is getting wet from rain.
I am weary from shopping, you are weary from
walking an eternity. I know we are both hungry
but I am the one who had breakfast this morning.
Did you have anything? I can't be sure.
Your skin is like transparent paper—
your bones showing through.
Your eyes watch me as I watch you. I feel
almost close to you but what can I do—
poster child?

Laura Brennan

Age On The Beach

Sea shells on the seashore,
He picked them one by one
From early dawn to rise of sun,
And yet his task was on.

Full eighty years he seemed to me
As frail he trod the strand;
His voice a childish treble was,
His hand held light the brand.

With fragile net he dared the waves
To snatch from them his ware;
The little things that make life gay
For these poor souls of care.

The shells he'll burn for his white line
To take his betel chew
And in the evening by his fire
Perhaps dream dreams anew.

For sea and man appeared to be
In perfect harmony!
The one his long life's secrets kept
The other its awful symphony.

Nalini Elapata

Free ME

I'm journeying through a wood covered in thorns
The thorns cover and strangle their beautiful flush of roses
The roses are keys, so very important, necessary, so very
difficult to find
If I gather enough roses I may just catch a glint of light from above
If the light comes it is easier to see where the roses lie

Sometimes it stays so completely dark that the roses wilt and
die in my arms
How can I fight with a life that's so slight
A pulse barely beating, a life that is sleeping
I have no might, no fight with a life that's so slight.
Just the memory, not the reality.

Still I persist and my technique strengthens
It takes a shorter and shorter time to catch the roses
I know one day I will have a strong and beautiful bouquet
That fills me with such love and strength that I am able to run free,
at last from the cruel thorns.

I'll be left with scars, but I will be free, I will know peace, I
will know life.

Suzanne Scambler

The Paseo (Promanade) Estepona, Malaga, Spain

At all times of day the place is alive,
Early morning brings joggers with pets by their sides.
Next, come the men with their journals and mail
Stop for a coffee, and tell the tale of days gone by
When they used to work and the word relaxation was almost
unheard.
At lunch-time the place is a maze of delights as children leave
school on skateboards and bikes.
Mothers and babies come out for a stroll when the hustle and
bustle has quieted down.
In late afternoon small children must play—on swings, slides
and roundabouts—such a melee.
As evening comes and the sun goes down the young and the
old may again take a stroll,
Or sit and chat of the days events, enjoying the aromas and
evening scents.
The light quickly fades, friends say farewell.
The paseo now quiet is calm and still, awaiting the dawn,
another day to fulfil.

Ann Christine Blair

Morning

It's 7:30, I must get up
And the clock ticks like nails
But the hand of the carpenter
Is so clumsy

I'm face to face with the day
Which pours through my curtains
The sun doesn't know that I'm waiting
For one beam which is mine

It's razor sharp
It breaks down molecules
It'll wake me up
But nothing else and it's enough

He tells me why to get dressed
Water drips from my broad shoulders
Looking for a towel
Swearing at the swine who every morning hide my glasses

Jump onto the bus
And wait again
For the next
Morning

Victor Tarskikh

Transitory

Opiate flower grow in my head
Blossom for the living dead
If you live in every corner of every room
Where can I look?
If I close my eyes the silence gets louder
I hear your voice here
The only way in is out
I may by poorer, maybe wiser
Nurture my disease, please

The weather is an omen
Crystallized my tears again
Do not call my name
Do not read a word I write
Right or wrong
Just absolve me of my insecurity
I was taught to be taut
To stare at the sky
Though it fills me with fear
I'm so happy, I've finally found a friend
She's somewhere else

William R. Stevenson

My Spirit Is A Temple

I'm sitting on my bed,
I don't hear a sound,
I lie on my bed,
looking around,
I look out my window, to see if I can see
 a bird,
A bird with its beauty as it flaps its
 wings and whistles its tunes,
But there is nothing,
And why?
As I get up on stage and in my stomach
 butterflies are trying to kill me,
But the atmosphere in the world, the
 pollution, the fighting, the killing, the
 wars, the starvation has done it,
Not the nerve raking pain of fragile
 wings inside my temple, as the
 humans have filled them.
And I'm the wondering spirit left
 alone to be free.

Anita Hakhnazarian

Because Of Drugs

Behind locked doors you've been shut away
But you're in my thoughts every night and day.
Because of drugs, that's why you're there
Could this be the answer to my prayer?
We tried to help, but you turned away
'I don't need help. I'm happy', you'd say
But day by day, as time passed by
The pain got worse and you'd sometime cry
Days when on your clothes the smell still lingers
I could see your life slipping through God's fingers
To hospitals and doctors, I've asked, 'Help him please!'
I've begged, prayed and pleaded upon my knees.
They'd give you more pills saying 'take these for now'
That wasn't what you needed, it was help—but how?
Heroin, methadone, tablets and more.
Strangers now knocked on our door.
Evil drugs all sent from hell
But now you're better, fit and well
God's answered my prayer, this must be the way
When you're home again son, you'll be home to stay.

Moreen Travis

The Day The Swans Flew

The ships of steel, once landed here
They glided in, as gracefully as swans,
Their rusted, salt beaten hulls
The smell of men's toil, and the winch's oil.

The coloured flags of foreign shores
Their eerie wails as they strain to moor
The hope they brought to a Northern town,
The food they put on tables
Gave a shining light, so true and bright
Just like the vessel's cables.

But that was once, it is not now
The swans they have migrated,
And families wait, and try their fate
While their future is debated
In the corridors of power.

The news, we knew, we could only rue,
As the shipyard was closed down,
No prosperity, hope, or steel built swans
Again to grace this town.

David Biggins

Night Thoughts

I hide in the wind of the night,
And squat in the echo of decrepit words.
I crouch in the sounds of crushing voices.
Shrill and cruel, in savage whirls,
They pierce my mind,
And, while I glean among the random ones,
I hazily perceive
The wonted words of love
Of far-gone nameless lovers:
Frayed remnants of remote pale dawns,
Bright noons and deceiving twilights
That no longer mar my peace.
I don't deny my past or any choice I made.
I am the woman I have been so far
And wistfully await in solid darkness,
The silent sublime night,
which will lay me down, at last,
On the arid threshold
Of a longed-for, peaceful
Nothingness.

Laura Marocco Wright

The Train

Birmingham, Brighton, Liverpool and Leeds,
Manchester, Maidstone, Dover and Durham,
Winchester, Whitby, Colchester, Cambridge and Plymouth.

With a huff and a puff,
And a cloud of smoke,
Down the track it goes,
Under tunnels over bridges,
Past rivers, oceans and sea
happy faces, laughs and smiles,
Water to cool the engine down, a bag of coal
Pushed in the engine's hole,
it goes on and on till the coal's all gone.
It's slowly down to a huff and a puff.
The day's finally at an end,
Children awake children asleep children with
wet sandy feet.

It's a day to remember until next September.
Riding on a train is clearly the best way
to enjoy yourself on a sunny day.

Donna Hunt

Freedom

Those who live midst hate and fear,
Deprived of all they held so dear.
Can only dream and hope and pray.
That freedom will come, Oh Blessed Day.

How can we who live in this fair Land,
Really know and understand,
The Satanic forces far and wide
Imprison body, soul and mind.

In dungeons dark with chains and bars.
How long to wait? Until they behold the stars
And walk in peace through pastures green,
Where in the distance home is seen.

Frances Young

As I Bow My Head To Cry

Drifting around, with no life to live
Drifting around, with no love to give
The emptiness grows stronger as each day passes by
The loneliness seems longer as I bow my head to cry
Dreaming of someone, but that someone was never there
Dreaming of someone, but that someone doesn't care
The tears fall down my cheek, I just wish I could die
I find it hard to speak, as I bow my head to cry
Life is never ending, without Jesus as your guide
Life is never ending, without a friend by your side
For now, I'll face on my own, because I am so shy
I just hope I'll never be alone again, as I bow my head to cry

Adele Bird

Odd Socks

Is there a place called odd-socks
Where all the odd-socks go,
I'm sure it's out there somewhere
Does anybody know.

Six pairs on a Monday
by Friday down to four,
I've searched from top to bottom
And emptied every draw.

Do aliens swoop in, with one leg
To snatch a sock, and leave the peg,
Do rodents pick them from the floor
To line a nest, return for more.

The wind might take them, day or night.
Is there a sock tree, out of sight,
Maybe a kinky thief out there
With one foot covered, one foot bare.

Will anybody help me
To end this tale of woe,
Can someone solve the mystery
Of where the odd-socks go.

J. W. Scatcherd

Gone . . .

Whenever I come to see you,
I can just imagine you there,
I could remember all the things we did,
and all the secrets we shared.
I could remember you cracking up 'cos of
the jokes I pulled, I could remember
when you hugged me when I was so cold . . .
I really loved that smile of yours, it
dazzled all the time,
I just wish you could live again,
just to say you're mine.
But as long as you're in my heart, I know
you'll never die,
the photo I've got is so tattered and torn,
but who needs photos when the
memories are still very strong.

Melanie Dewe

Peaceful Child

The child lies sleeping,
peaceful and content.
Oblivious to the perils
of the world to which he was sent.
Cuddling his teddy bear,
Sucking on his thumb,
He's so much to face,
on this road he's just begun.
Violence, cruelty, hate and fear,
Words of venom whispered in his ear.
Love, hurt, smiles and tears,
he'll have to face this through the years.
The child stirs and whimpers,
his momma's at his side.
She comforts him, and loves him,
her worries from him she hides.

He's got his momma now,
good care of him she'll take
But one day soon, she'll have to let go,
and mistakes he'll have to make.

Donna Semark

Holiday Dreams

I saw a plane flying high today
It flew over my house and far away
I wonder'd if it flew to a distant land
There palm trees, sea and a golden sand

Where holiday makers enjoy the sea air
Sunbathing without a thought or a care
Relaxed whilst lying in sweet repose
In swim wear unlike their usual clothes

The children in the water learning to swim
We've given them a safe inflatable ring
Splashing about they will make such a noise
Both the two girls and then the three boys

Some people seated along the promenade
Seen drinking hot tea or ice cold lemonade
Others seems busy eating strawberry ice cream
Children on the sand run about and scream

Suddenly I awaken from a deep deep sleep
It's now that things impossible seem
That all reality subconsciously then
Was merely just a part of my dream.

S. Arrowsmith

Two Together

I touch your body
As I touch my own
I hold you,
As I hold myself.

I lie with you
As you lie with me
You breath
We breath in time.

Your heart is mine
As mine is yours
Your hand is open for me to hold.

Your eyes follow me.
My love is blind.
When you are lost, it is me you will find.

You are here, as I am there
Still it is you I long to be near
Within my thoughts forever clear

Your life is mine, as mine is yours
I look at you, sit then pours
For to you I have given my soul.

Cerys Furwess Davies

Trees

When love converts into a tree,
her roots suck earth's sweet marrow,
and her arms reach out to see,
the gold and warmth of her tomorrow.

Love and trees don't change completely,
for still they eat and seek the same,
though seasons let appear them strangely,
as if there were for one—a hundred name.

A tree may find by lightning death,
and so does love through shame and cowardice,
so now with strength, defending inner depth,
with swords transform thy love into a kiss.

Then note how close are love and battle,
the right without the wrong would fail,
and if you flee from combat's rattle,
your boat with love will never sail.

Kai Teckentrup

Memories Of Loss

Though the touch of flesh be welcomely warm,
and the heart be of the kindest.
The darkness brings forth the mourning,
in memory of those dear departed.
As one's visions begin rekindling,
smiles slowly fallow and partake of gloom.
The thoughts of a loved one dear departed,
leashes a cold chill circulating the room.
As special memories immerse with gladness,
and one's lips react and forms some smiles.
The solitude and darkness then, so sadly,
brings emptiness, and tears to one's eyes.
To heaven we extend a pleading look,
and mutter prayers that our heart be lightened.
We pray for the peace, offer love, to those who are took,
and beg togetherness through life's recycle.

Ronald Henry Lamper

Friendship Failure

You said I was your very best friend,
I'd hoped our friendship would never end,
I don't know what I'm supposed to have done,
But please don't take it out on everyone.

When you felt down, I was always there,
I stood by your side but did you care?
I offered a shoulder, one you could cry on,
I tried to be someone who you could rely on.

You even told me that I didn't belong,
That made me think that I had done something wrong,
Why did you use me and call me your friend?
If all you're going to do is lie and pretend.

If you don't like me, then fair enough,
"Goodbye my friend", and all that stuff,
But if you do, deep down inside,
You might feel saying "Sorry" would affect your pride.

Let's just forget it and make a new start,
friends like us should never part,
We can get it back to how it used to be,
Here we come—you and me!

Penny Tucker

Pastures New

You're off to pastures new
No more feeling blue
May the road ahead be paved with gold
Good luck surround you as the years unfold
A bright new tomorrow is in store for you
I knew it, I felt it and I prayed for you
Now there is nothing more for me to say
But to wish you godspeed on your way

Joyce Roberts

The Lottery

When I was a child at school
I hated maths but now it figures.
Today, to my dismay, numbers rule the world

Yes, the lottery is here
Yes, the lottery is here to stay.
The daily papers leading the way.
Bingo, scratch cards every day,
Scratch, scratch to match the cash.
Yes, lady luck says yes at last.

Every week we pick the six to make us rich
Maybe to be the next millionaire
Which boosts the world of art
With their very needy ventures and tasks

Yes, this is my day, no more worries.
The money is in the bank
I can now join the upper-crust
A life of ease or is it all make believe in my confusion
Is it an illusion or just a dream.
Cheers.

J. R. Molr

No Goodbyes

I sigh we never say goodbye.
Not yet, not till our love has no more to give
That is never no ending
Drenched in warmth
A love so sweet, so tender
Two souls complete within one heart
I look, you look at me
We see only one another
Nothing else exists
A love so deep no others to compete
I can hear your very thoughts
Your heart beats so fast when we are alone
Together
Your arms warmly enfolding my body
Tender loving giving all
This gift of love, no goodbyes.

Helen Nelson

Newborn

They came from all around to gaze upon
My beautiful, flawless child;
A miracle child,
Newly delivered into this world,
Yet not belonging,
Still transitional, unworldly, spiritual;
Too good for us.
Enveloped in a golden aura
Of strange, silent mysticism,
Lying there, in my arms, an ancient man
Wearied by his difficult passage into
Life.
And I knew, at that moment,
You were special, and
Different.

R. A. Mitchell

A Day Too Late

A smile.
A helping hand when needed,
If only we, the world had heeded,
But no, we, just break out in song,
Pretend that things have not gone wrong,
The world we love, we let decay,
Then still sing on, as if, to say,
Tomorrow's just another day,
When someone else, can take a stand,
And as they hold their baby's hand,
See red sun rising, in a murky sky,
Not knowing, the day has come
For a lovely world to die.

Tom Leech

Memories Of You

The glory of the morning sunrise
Awakening the world anew
Is but a gentle memory
Of a tender love we knew

I remember walking hand in hand
Through valleys wet with morning dew
Promising to love and understand
Each other's point of view

Love we thought was ours alone
Never dreaming we would part
I was King on a Golden Throne
Until darling you broke my heart

Through the sun–kissed valleys I walk alone
My tears matching the morning dew
For memories now are all I own
Sweet memories of a love I once knew
Memories now are all I own
Sweet memories of you
Sweet memories of you

J. H. Hughes

Ode To My Great Grandson Or Immortality Breached

At last I've held my future to my breast:
It was a humble 'thought moment proud.
My sojourn in this life has reached its crest.
With an honour that I was never owed.

Granddaughter you have travelled far and long,
To introduce me to your lovely child.
I'm blest that our family tie so strong
Goes on through time with the love that will abide.

Rhys lad, you're the pinnacle of dreams and genes:
The fruit of a million years of lives,
And the merger of the customs of two scenes,
Moulded like steel, through centuries of strife.

Italy, Scotland, England, Wales and Middle East
Make up the history of your heritage.
Some good, some bad, some lazy, though not the least
is love of life from which your eyes (like mine) so emanate.

Your loving parents have a glorious task,
To teach you all the things that life holds dear.
Living a little longer now is all that I might ask:

So that when you too are old, memories of me stay clear.

Rees Thorley

Naomi

My sweet dear little Naomi, the greatest achievement of my life.
Always so precious to Mummy, during times of peace or strife.

So sweet, so beautiful, so kind, my daughter, my present, my prize.
The sacrifices; the worries in mind, the scars on tummy and thighs.

I'll always be proud of you baby,
    through good or bad you're mine.
My angel, you've reached two years already,
    dear God; my Naomi, so divine.

To you, I'm eternally thankful, Dear God,
    you awarded me such a beautiful daughter.
What did I do to deserve her, Dear Lord?
    I'm so grateful for being her mother.

Precious Naomi, through your tantrums and smiles,
    we've survived off one another.
We feel loved looking into each other's eyes,
    without even saying it to each other.

Since the first time I ever held you, baby,
    since the very first moment we met.
I always realised, dear Naomi,
    I would love you till the end of time; no sweat!

Ilta Inkeri Collins

My Brother—Man

When man stood erect
And looked around
No longer gazing at the ground
Then he gestured—then he spoke
What passions—and anger—that could invoke
He needed clothing—for the weather?
Or for when he went shy?
It's not really changed that much—
As time has gone by—
It's when he found flint and stone—
For marking his cave wall
It made him feel pride—and fulfilment—
It made him feel tall
Will my pen on paper last all that time?
Will someone see my enjoyment—in writing in rhyme
We've one thing in common though—one thing overall
When I read what I've written—
    Yes! It makes me feel tall!

Norbert Atherton

The Snowdrop

The demure head fringed with green,
Symbol of innocence and simplicity,
Yet in that downcast face there's beauty seen
To enhance its diffident frailty

Unaware of its intrinsic beauty,
It hangs its head in sheer modesty,
Yet far within that demure frailty,
There is grace and purity

Trace that shy beauty down to earth,
To the hostile coldness whence comes its birth,
Up through the stem from bitter cold,
By divine magic comes the stamen's gold.

And so it is with many a one,
Nothing to see until you scan,
By lifting the face and seeing the grace
By peering at the inner man.

Llyfnwy Eynon Davies

Resting Place Of Giants

Walled in, fettered there
Stoical brooding immortal frailty
Ringed in bands of steely fists.
Piano–playing dominion's grandeur;
Pool of light, back–dropping bastion's form.

Dawn awakes! Unleashed power
Leaving through the crust of earth.
Blows clench the fathom's inch
Against the caldron's boiling spit.
The weight of man's creative power
Poles to nature's slating hand.

Tireless influence denudes the mortal's form;
Man's washed in, framed still, goes pale;
Ebbing flowing tidal race;
But a fleeting glance in time.
From heedless slumbering—almost nothingness,
Pool of light, back–dropping bastions form.

Douglas Riley

The Thought Of A Fly

Little fly thy summer's play,
    my thoughtless hand has brushed away.
Am not I a fly like thee,
    or art not thou a man like me,
For I dance and drink and sing,
    till some blind hand shall brush my wing.
If the thought is life and strength and breath and the
    thought and want is death,
Then I am a happy fly if I live or if I die!

Alison O'Brien

450

The Donkey's Part

Hurry little donkey, along the frosty road; you're almost there!
I wonder if you know how precious is the load you bear.
All your life you've toiled and served, a scorned and lowly beast.
But tonight you're very special; a Prince at least!

In a dreaming, sleeping Bethlehem, before the dawn;
Warmed by you, in stable bare,
The Christ Child will be born.
Sent by God to free men from the burden of their sin,
That love may enter in.

So hurry little donkey, don't delay.
There's a resting place awaits you in the hay.
The child will share your manger,
For there's no room at the inn.
Make haste! You have a part to play.

At journey's end, by yon bright star,
Kings will come from lands afar,
And humble shepherds kneel.
There you will gaze on Jesus Christ,
And know "Your Lord" is real.

Jennifer C. Wellings

The Rape

"Strip her naked!"
Paused.
Silence spread her gown
Glances here and there
They confided and loot her
I wept for her
Conscience! My throat!
I gasped for breath and troth
"Indifference to humanity",
Wondered I.

"Strip her naked! Strip her naked!!"
Voice of tyrant, rapist leader
Came again, "Who cares."
My tears! Mopped and sobbed
Endlessly for my beloved
Her beauty robbed
Possessions devastated
Inhuman absurdity
Subjected she is
She is raped . . . raped nakedly . . . oh gawd!

Bamidele Adegboyega

Phone Call At Midnight

A phone call at midnight, loved one has died,
Life snubbed out on a motorbike ride.
Feelings of shock, disbelief, cold,
This doesn't happen if you're not ill or old.
Unless a man's in a hurry and late for a date,
Gives no indication and has no time to wait,
With one lapse of concentration and no harm meant,
Just one second and it's over, young life's spent.
Only it's not life, it's a whole lot more,
An entire families hearts, minds and spirits,
Torn apart at the core,
No children left behind, and none to come,
Never to be a father, his role was cherished son.
And the man in the car,
With his points and his fine,
Will his guilt ease for him,
As our pain may, with time.
I Think Not.

J. Barry

The Blue Heap

The days I remember
and treasure so dear
was as a small child without any fear
Claiming the quarry tops
high as could be the wind was so strong
I thought I could fly
Sometimes a witch I'd
pretend to be throwing
my broomstick high as could be
My slidey costs nothing
but still was a treat to sit in an old bath
Tin and fly down the heap
I made my own kite with paper and sticks
I could fly it real high and no need for a lift
My bon shaker bike no brakes or no chain
still got me down the blue heap again
The house where I lived has since been pulled
down but the blue heap still stands at Pridham
with pride and I hold these memories of being a child

Marjorie Hubbuck

"Valentine"

I remember a girl, I first kissed long ago,
I remember the question, when her dad's answer was no,
Come back when you prove, you love her as I do,
Don't worry . . . I thought . . . I'll soon show you
Time passed . . . I returned . . . his message to me,
Your love for my daughter is plain to see.
My blessing you have . . . were words that he said,
Her hand I will give . . . go on . . . get wed.
The years soon passed, our love grew stronger,
I must tell you right now . . . I can't wait any longer,
This message I have, I can tell you is true,
The love I have given, has only been for you,
All these years we've been together . . . I know I can say
I just wouldn't have wanted it . . . any other way.
With my hand on my heart, I can tell you right now,
I will be with you forever, if God will allow.
My life with you darling as worked out just fine,
To me you are, and will always be, my one and only
Valentine . . .

A. J. Nabbott

A Sonnet of Quiescent Love

Rouse not my heart, for 'tis a dormant dove,
That 'pon your step would rise with flutt'ring beat
To circumfly the aura of your love
And light, a-craving-crumb, before your feet.
Then timidly, should you but morsel cast,
'twould weigh askance and sidle to partake
A peck from Aphrodite's sweet repast,
Ere becking unrequited in your wake.
But your lorn pigeon's crop you'd not replete,
For soon, to gleam your eye and blush your bloom,
Some vainglorious, strutting, beau you'd meet
And ne'er could fantail best a peacock's plume.
So would a broken heart, no bill to bill,
Coo love-losts' plaint from life's forsaken sill.

Catesby Allers

Reincarnation Or . . . ?

Sitting here confined to gloom,
Sensing something has gone away.
Never returning to face this earth,
Nor planting hope for future year.
Luck turns sour, there's now here,
To clutch what remains to be held.

For those who dream of building a dawn,
Their thoughts are christened with fear.
Colours of black swirl around their heads,
An edge of darkness to play.
Darkness, madness, a twist of insanity,
And a memory will play no part here.

Trouble lurks around every corner,
To escape, but not to outlast.
They'll come back to this earth one day,
To suffer the fate once again.
For a time spent away to be stronger,
Still cannot be released from the cycle.

Sharon Louise Thomas

A Prayer

It was God that made the earth and sea.
He made the sunshine and the rain.
He gave us eyes to see, and ears to hear
He knows our every ache or pain.
He made a new-born babe to cry
He taught the birds how to fly
He made the mountains and the sky
He taught us how to laugh or cry.
Take a walk if you feel down
in the country, not in town
you will see things God has made:
Trees, flowers or a lake.
Look at the sky, and see the sun
only God knows how things begun
so say a pray and keep in touch
He would be pleased if we would say
thank you God, for every day.

E. Barber

Your vibrant colours beckon me,
wanting me to come close.
Your smooth silken body,
pulling me towards you
even though we both know
I should not.

Your eyes probe me,
deep into my soul
forcing me to surrender
to your touch,
even though we both know
I should not.

You tempt me with your
irresistible walk and charms.
I cannot hold back any longer
as your magic becomes stronger
I just *have* to pick one of your feathers.

The Peacock

Shanty Begum

There Is No Sin

There is no sin in the world you see, all is a learning to set us free
I look inside and as I speak, words of wisdom are all I seek
I search inside and I want to know, the truth I seek that I may grow

There is no sin we shall all see, this words been used to torment me
To make me feel guilty, to take my faith,
so others could use me, and take my place

Now I am trying to gain my faith, by looking inside and taking my
place as a beautiful member of this human race

There is no sin inside of me, whatever I have done, let it be
I except this as learning, I now set myself free
Moving onto better things, knowing God is with me

And every time I've learnt, and see what I have done, in my
realization, I know we are all one
I give my learning with love and grace, This is the input I offer to
the whole human race do not have pride, and do not have fear, wisdom
from within will make it all clear

There is no sin inside of me, there is no fear for I am free
There is no pride that I might fall, everything is learning so I stand
tall knowing that it's wisdom I seek, and sharing wisdom when I speak
Never to judge, this is not my place, standing with lover for the
human race now all take courage and set yourselves free, never judge
of fear or speak ill of thee for we are all one, just let us all be.

Veronica Anne Blunden

Night

It is Spring moonless night in the small town,
Starless and bible-black, the cobble street
Silent and the hunched couters'-and-rabbits'
wood limping invisible down to the sloe black,
slow, black, crowblack, fishing boat-bobbing sea.

The houses are blind as moles though moles
See fine night in the snooting velvet dingles.
And all the people of the lulled and the
dumb found town are sleeping now.
Look it is night, dumbly, royally
Winding through the dark street.

Asima Rafeeq

Miserable Child

Oh miserable child, who walks day and night on the road of life,
Searching for food and drinks, in a ragged old cloth which has been
torn into pieces. No one to look after you, no one to love and
cherish you, to talk to you, adore and console you.

Oh miserable child, searching for someone to love as a father, and
someone to love her as a mother, oh where, oh where, can they be
found? In this terrible world of darkness where death can occur
anytime. What are you doing child? The road is long and there are
dangerous paths to cross, though you have taken many blows, fate has
been unkind to you, do not despair and lose hope. In your loneliness
you have witnessed the days gone by, in your wakefulness you have
listened to the weeping and laughter of the others like you.

Child have courage, there is a better world beyond this present one.
The shadow of life will bear a light upon you, affection will come
your way, and everyone will stand and reveal before you what you have
missed. Child, give your heart but not your soul, share your thoughts
and mind to others when you have the chance. The hour will come when
you will be joyous, your cup will be filled with drinks and your
stomach full.

Child who can you trust and have faith as a friend, when everybody
mocked at you, how sad, painful to see someone giving you a big smile
but deep down in their hearts only hatred. Why make the child suffer,
why ignore and destroy her, when life seems really hard for her to
face? Have courage and gain strength. Child, someday your call will
be answered and you will be the happiest child in this world.

Jacqueline Hoareau
The 22nd day of August 1996

I Remember

My mind goes back
To the past
I remember gong for soup
If you went first
You got water
If you went last
You got a potatoes
And horse meat
I remember Leipzig
The vapour trails
In the blue sky
The sound of planes
Coming closer and closer
No shelter for us
We ran and ran
Like chickens on a farm
I will always remember that

John Rudd

Why? I Don't Know

What was that noise Mother
In the middle of the night?
Was it the telly blaring?
Or the tom cats having a fight?

Why are your eyes red Mother?
And your hair looking a fright?
Where is father's motor car?
And why does the place smell of tar?

Why are you crying Mother?
Don't you know I want to know
Why you're in such a bother?
And don't say I'm too young to know

I heard a loud noise Mother
I woke up to such a scream
But why do you say Mother
It was no more than a bad dream?

Maybe you're in pain Mother!
Or are you going insane?
Oh, look! The police Mother,
Why are they coming back again?

Ann-Marie

The Dark Room

It's dark and cold
I see you
Yet I can't touch you or feel you
I can hear you
and sense your presence
Yet I am afraid to call out
your name
When I take a step towards you
A tear falls down my cheek
Then my body feels faint
Suddenly I fall
When I awake I am back
where I started
In a dark corner
where I seem
to belong.

Sue Kuti

Water

Water is the spring of life
we need it every day
To wash our clothes and bodies
And to clean our germs away.

We used to fetch it from the well
Some many years ago
But now we have it piped indoors
And think its very swell,

We fill the kettle and make our tea
We cook our meals as well
But do we thank God for water
Which he gives to us all for free.

Do we stop to think what we would do
If the spring of life ran dry.
Where would we go to get this gift
That's so precious to you and I.

We take it all for granted
As if it were our right
With not a word of thanks to God
For all his power and might.

M. T.

The Value Of Love

To love and to be loved
Is the greatest gift of all
It grows so very quickly
From something very small
It wraps around your body
Just like a second skin
And unleashes many feelings
That where hidden deep within
It brings happiness and comfort
And a certain peace of mind
So hold on to it if you have it
For it's so very hard to find
Only those who are very lucky
Shall find this love so great
And through ignorance they may lose it
And only realize when it's too late
You cannot own it or buy it
Its depths you can not measure
But receiving it from someone
Will bring you untold pleasure

C. Dalton

P.S. I Love You

I look at him everyday
feeling the same way
I see him walking around
but I hear no sound,

Her smile is like a
secret file,
His voice is as hard as
a tile,
he has the bluest eyes
and wears the best ties.

There for I love him dearly
So I feel so teary
but I'll give my life
to be his wife.

I wonder one day
if I have to pay
for the love I keep which is so deep.

Ozlem Ozkan

Hand On Heart

Listen. Silence is seldom heard.
A paint beat
Of a constant heart,
At peace and at a distance.

A thud of recollection
Can I relate
Or will it remain,
Still distant, still

Craving attention,
But not ravenous enough
Just an industrious worker,
No head for ambition

But a head of thought
Is of little use—
Considered troubles
Are only replaced.

A sweetness in maturity,
A rhythm hoped for,
And remembered

When must it stop?

Haydn Lewis

"Leets"

The equinox of our soul
lies here.
Wake up and see the
shadow cast by light.

What body separates
our thoughts.
What is it makes one
wrong, one right.

Yiannis Antoniou

Nan's Christmas Fare

A box of last year's Christmas lights
A trailing on the floor
I plugged them in and nothing there,
I can't afford, no more,
It happens every single year,
It really makes me mad,
I guess, I'll have to buy some,
And then, I will be sad,
I get them home from shopping,
And put them on the tree,
I plugged them in and lo, and behold
They lit up just for me,
I'm happy once again, you see
I feel that Christmas is here
I'll fill up all your glasses
With lots, of "Christmas cheer"
The turkey's on the table
The pudding's in the pan,
The carollers outside and singing,
I am a lucky nan.

Honor Walmsley

Most Lovely

She like blossom glowing, dreaming lovely girl of mine
Passion ever flowing, simple yet divine
My woman I'll always love you
Caress our precious lives
And dance through life's adventures
Two together will survive.

She like summer rainfalls, dancing flickering of light
Rainbow colourings surround her, like some lovely bird in flight
My woman I really love you
Preserve our happiness
And hold us both together
Whilst embracing this loveliness.

Peter Seaman

Education

It's something you cannot buy,
But everyone says bye;
It's something which you cannot sell,
Education is not like a smell,
To smell it and throw

Education can come high in future
Money can be destroyed by nature
Education is also not leisure,
Don't take this as a mixture;
Because education shows your picture.

Everyone can make wealth,
But without education it will be a weight,
So people fight for money;
But money will disappear like honey.

You need education forever;
Not like you say of never,
It's important to life,
Although you don't like.

M. Fazloon Maqsood

The Poisoned Garden

Doubt is a garden, where deceit and lies will grow
If left unchecked, they multiply to poison all you know.
For they are strong, invasive blooms, with scented wild cascade.
Strangling the innocent truth, destroying the plans you've made.
Their Heady perfume joins the breeze, is carried on the air.
It's in the bedroom, preventing sleep as you lie tortured there.
Why did she plant this creeping weed?
    Truly Satan's flower.
Was not my kiss her garland?
    And all my love her bower?
She will not explain its origin, so with no one else to blame
You tend the others, your favourite blooms,
    but the garden's never the same.
Now she visits another garden, somewhere secret to plant her seeds
I am left with faded flowers, the mosses and the weeds.
Somewhere lies the hidden root concealed beneath my feet.
Invasive, destructive, poisonous the evil growth—deceit.

M. Hood

A Dream Of The Welsh Countryside

I'm moving to the hills. I am,
Up to the land of fluffy lambs.
Where the air feels fresh and clear,
and less noise on the ear.
Where towering mountains touch the sky,
and rare red kites sometimes fly,
winding, narrow country roads,
and tall old trees topped with cawing crows.

But for the moment I'm stuck here in my flat.
In a busy town by a railway track.
I'll move there someday, someday soon,
and when I do I'll be over the moon.

Rosemarie Fletcher

I Stand Up And J'accuse I Accuse

I stand up, raise my voice and I accuse j'accuse
Men of many nations, before Our Amazin' Good Lord,
For all sorts of injustice and other abuse,
Which brought threats of death to our world . . .

Selfishness, greed for riches in silver and gold,
Their evil striving, for things of no good use,
Brought all the suffering, j'accuse I accuse,
All those who persecute good, just and bold . . .

This world would be, so much a better place,
Were they never born on its once pretty face!
This earth of ours, that was so full of grace,
Thanks to them may disappear without trace . . .

Oh, God how much better-off we all would be!
If Evil Force never made, that wicked race,
How much more all the good men would be free!?
But instead of freedom, slavery is their case . . .

Instead of our sun's glorious and shiny light,
The darkness rules in eternal starless night . . .
Instead of life earth will be empty and dead,
The place of love will take hatred and dread . . .

Then, even, on my dead lips, read—j'Accuse, I accuse!!

Georgie Zoriastro

Days Roll On

The sun comes up,
The sun goes round,
The sun goes down.
I come up,
I go round,
I also go down.
Black clouds drown the sun
So it can't continue shining on
Black clouds also drown me,
So I can't continue shining on
No matter how hard the wind blows,
No matter how the rain come down,
The sun will always carry on,
So, so will I, I won't, I refuse to stay drowned
Forever by the wind blowing at me
And the rain that never stops coming down.
If a burning red ball of fire can carry on,
For as long as God desires,
So can I a human being I can carry on,
One day the sun and I will rest in peace.

Sarah Walsh

Faith, Hope, And Charity?

On the seventh of July, shreds of peace crumble.
But there seems a light at the end of the tunnel, negotiations get under-way.
A march was banned, down an area that would cause pain, conflict and defeat.
But defiance, anger rose at a ban on the Queens highway.
Threats of a blood bath forced a U turn to happen.
But in the U turn a minority culture knew betrayal, defeat, oppression from the greater majority threat.

Fires ripped across Northern Ireland,.
A bomb in Enniskillen, people all backgrounds intimidated out of their homes.
A sensitive, political decision, left to a police man.
Two die in Ulster, the casualty wards are full.
Injuries cross the divide, from security people to civilians on both sides.
But life comes cheap in Northern Ireland.
Who will be the scape goat?

Mary C. McHugh

A Walk In The Woods

The sky is getting darker, clouds gather from the West
A breeze, in little flurries, dance, as in jest.
As rain begin to splatter on fallen leaves below
The trees, dripping circles, as the stream begins to flow.
On the muddy woodland track puddles form and then expand
To make a mockery of walking on once dry land.
With collar up and hat pulled down I squelch along the path
Thinking wistfully of teapot, crumpets and a glowing hearth.
Dogs play uncaring, splashing mud upon my skirt,
Unworried by the gloom and rain and dirt.
I trudge along in silence and then decide to turn
But become entangled in a grabbing, prickly fern.
Seeing my intention the dogs rush back to the car
While I slip and slide and wish it weren't so far!
As I reach the car and let the dogs clamber in the back
I think again, I wish I'd brought my willies and my mac!

Shelagh Kliczczewski

Untitled

The hypothalamus in our brains sends messages down our spine,
the nervous system it reacts but today I don't feel fine.
Mother nature intervenes,
my moods begin to warn her.
Flowers bloom and songbirds sing,
for there's love around the corner.
When things don't always run smoothly
and life seems no more than a curse,
pause in your tracks and think again
for there's always someone worse.
I think to myself
"has it all been a dream,"
when I wake up in the morning.
Everyone's lives go up and down,
and sometimes without a warning.

John Taylor

Finding Out

Who predicted this clouded day
That brought rain upon my window sill.

Who asked the gull with its mournful cry
To float endlessly above my head

Who told the music to carry on
When all I needed was peace and quiet

Who said that she would never cry
And yet the tears flow freely now

Who enticed me into writing these lines
For they are real make no mistake

Who shall end this plaintive song
The writer with his inquisitive pen.

Alexander Kovell

Dreams Or Reality?

One more dream is gone, leaving my soul alone.
I dreamt I was a Pharaoh sitting on a golden throne.
I was rich, arty, powerful, but extremely sad,
I was there, alive, but truly my heart was dead.
In my whole brilliant empire I was searching
not for channels, proceeds, just for a love thing.
I looked around a lot there was nothing good
I've just seen struggles, rumours—people were so rude!
And even the sky, with its purity, was grey and weeping
And I realized that with our envy we've done nothing.
All I wanted was to escape from that miserable world,
Not to be a king, just a brave knight with a shiny sword.
And then, I finally woke up and I was pretty glad
That I have escaped from that world which was so bad.
But soon I realized our world was the same, even worse,
Full of hatred, anarchy—a chaos in which we do nothing, but curse!

Nanu Irina Roxana

The Land Of The Lake

I long to sit by the lake and brood
getting to know its every mood
Sometimes serene, gentle and calm
filling me with its healing balm
other times angry and very rough
telling me it can be strong and tough.

This lake of ours is full of surprises
presenting itself in various guises
At morn it is dressed in silvery hue
rapidly changing to green or to blue
the sun sending rays of wonderful light
creates in the middle a pool gleaming white.

The fishermen, too, are intriguing to watch
As they row out in search of a bountiful catch
their fragile canoes battling the waves
Against current so strong they need to be brave.

Returning at dawn with the fish they have caught
Willing hands ready to haul them to land.
Where nets are laid carefully out on the sand,
Small fish are spread in the sun to dry
While others are put on the spit to fry.

Sue Moss

England

A land green in beauty with views that touch the heart
and course the soul to rise in wonder.
She is apt to neglect her older citizens, the offspring of
those who died to free the many nations, whose children
weep on her shoulders and receive comfort.
She is blessed with workers, who will sacrifice much
to keep her great. She gives an allowance to the
mothers of her children, and an abortion to the play things
of their fathers.
She has a freedom envied the world over. To the sick and
afflicted she gives medical help and care that only those that
have received would understand. She will survive, for she tries
to live as God intended.
Alas, many of her people can never see her beauty they are
shut in, trapped, by poverty or ugliness of man's making. She is
inclined to be selfish over the seas that surround her, forgetting
the needs of lands that rely upon them. She is too eager in her
dealings abroad, regarded as a soft touch by many.
England sporting champions, England my homeland
land of my birth, where dear ones, rest in your soft rich earth.
    To me you stand for life itself
        Just home.

Margaret Vinall-Burnett

Darwin Or God

Where are we?
Mix with animals in a kingdom,
Whirling in space around and around,
The sea and the sky meeting and mingling,
A fantastic planet where much is found,
To meet our needs,
Who needs the human race and creatures?
Growing and living by strange power of will,
A creation most strange,
And yet we've reaped this earth,
And brought forth wheat to mill,
What is this world so full of life,
Not like other stars,
Our earth alone seems to have a written face,
Covered with buildings modern scientific artifacts like cars,
From our earth minerals are brought to the surface
As though it were all arranged
That it was there for our use,
A strange extraordinary miracle that is hard to explain
Who shall we believe Darwin or God?

Anna Parkhurst

If Only

If only there were no differences, if only there was no greed,
If only everyone realized keeping peace must never go to seed,
If only this could happen, wouldn't it be an achievement,
perhaps then there would be no more wars and no more mass
bereavement.

We must not destroy ourselves, we must not destroy our planet,
otherwise there could be nothing left except coarse grit and granite,
if only we could prevent crime, if only we could say 'we will'
given time,

Fortunately there is more good than bad,
let's pray it stays that way so there aren't many sad,
if only our creed and nationality didn't matter,
or the colour of our skin,
as what is most important is how valuable we are within.

If you cannot see another's point of view,
a day in their shoes might help you see it too,
nothing can be black or white,
there's always an area which is blurred,
so why can't we sometimes compromise, or is that too absurd?

If only it was realistic to hope for a world at peace,
If only the crime and fighting would once and for all cease,
I know some of us can stand tall and some of us have to fall,
but this wonderful world was definitely made big enough for us all.

Linda Blake Trussler

Pointless Killing

Soldiers crouching, soldiers crawling,
Soldiers shooting, soldiers falling,
Winners leaping, losers crying,
Winners living, losers dying.

Soldiers eat, the food's disgusting,
But it's either that or nothing,
Men still hungry, men still looking,
Nothing left, there's nothing cooking.

Down the trenches, soldiers writing,
Guided by the candle lighting,
Writing to their sisters, brothers,
Aunties, uncles, fathers, mothers.

Soldiers stretching, soldiers yawning,
Welcome to another morning,
Some aren't moving, but instead,
They're lying still, they're lying dead.

"Come on boys, take up positions,
Set to work, you know your missions."
Bored of all this mournful drilling,
Soldiers start the pointless killing!

Michael Smith

Magic Shoes

I have a pair of "magic shoes" and with them I can fly.
All I do is put them on I rise up to the sky.
Tho' one thing's unusual. There is not left or right.
And when I go to bed they glow all through the night
Becoming ever brighter at every passing you're
As if collecting energy, to give them 'lift off' power.
The other day. When it got dark and no-one was about
I took them to the local park—thought I'd try them out!
No sooner had I put them on. I rose up in the air.
Luckily at 'lift off' there was no-one there.
Although I'd no sensation of flying high so fast.
Below could see the city lights St. London as I passed
Then to my amazement, I saw the royal palace
Where 'tis said in nursery rhyme—"Christopher took Alice"
As I felt a fall in speed—I'd more chance to look around.
Then descending very slowly—gently touched the ground
Landing near the palace gates at the changing of the guards
I saw a smiling prince of wales—who gave me his regards
When I told him about my shoes—tho' not easy to convince.
He then asked to try them on—and no-one's seen him since.

G. W. Dobson

The Visitation

A purple crocus flower has broken
from its bulb
And filled the room with
fragrance so divine.
Gladness thrills my heart, for this
beautiful thing is mine all mine.
I sit and weep at such a sight.
It came so still and silent,
whilst I was asleep last night.
The tears fill my eyes to overflowing.
The purple blurs and casts a
wondrous transparent light.
A stained glass window could not
radiate such a vibrant glow.
What a marvel dear Nature you
have bestowed on me.
How can I repay you for such a
well shaped jewel?
When funds are high and the spirit is low
I will buy and watch more flowers grow.

Tom Clarke

An Ode To The Sea

I sat on the wall by the sea today
And I heard the most beautiful sounds
Of the waves, gently lapping the shore.
The sea itself was blue today
Reflecting the blue of the skies,
And the rays of the sun, filtered down.
One or two grown ups quietly jobbed
Two or three children at play,
And I felt such peace, in my heart
As baby gulls, unafraid, also played.

I knew in this moment, of lingering peace
That this was the place for me
As my eyes slowly traced, in the distance
The rise of green hills o'er the bay.
I'd be happy to drift far away on the sea
In a boat with a sail, and, a rug for my knees,
The sea holds the key to life on earth
And I feel she could carry me, to those I have loved,
My soul I have lost to the sea today,
My soul I have lost to the sea!

Olive M. Robinson

The Queen Of The Isles

The Queen of the isles to me no island compares
Oh Islay, thy charm enraptures all unawares
Thy beauty, thy peace! Thy breath's the purest of air
Unique is thy power, the Isle where every one cares.

Sweet solace, and love brings joy all over this land
The island's renowned for geese that thrive off the land
The tang of the sea, and shores of glorious white sand
Where others cavort, carefree on each distant strand.

High crags, and deep caves hold wealth in tales told of yore
From Jura the stags in pleasure swim to thy shore
Tides tumble the gems at Sanaig mind oceans roar
Unique is thy charm, my island, thee I adore.

Where fresh water flows the salmon's never at rest
In quest of their prey grey seals cull always the best
The eagles soar high o'er spacious moors at the west
Where cliffs and lone crags have caves that cradle each nest.

Fair Queen of the isles, thy music sounds through the air
The pipes, from the glens pour forth their sweet highland air
Oh! Islay, mo chridh; no island yet can compare,
Unique is thy joy, the isle we all love to share.

Lily (Fish) MacDougall

Part Of Him

He sought the animal within,
a countryman who couldn't milk or plough,
dodged the huge fetlocks and fly–maddened cows
and couldn't tell the teazle from the grain;
no, they were not for him.

And yet at night the great feet rang
hard in his head, and bulls and horses drove
stampeding through the grain and mopped and mowed
at their reflection underneath his skin,
till they were part of him.

By day he made them sing—
Anubis, Chaeron and the minotaur
and glory in the human masks they wore,
but kicked the old stray whining to get in—
it wasn't part of him.

Dilys Frascella

The Bar Fly

Terrible is the set stare,
that wanders an ocean of noise,
seeking a moments response in a sea of eyes,
and finding none,
returns to the solace of the dark swirling liquid,
gripped in a claw of glass.
It was not always so!
Once this poor battered fool touched love.
Drank deep of its warmth.
Laughed loud in its company.
Sought a different oblivion.
Now all that remain are memories,
Breaking waves, pounding the shores of consciousness.
Drowning the already dead.

David Golightly

Wild Harvest

Cobnuts clad in soft green mantles
Cluster each slender hazel twig.
Rough brown beech masts split asunder
Fodder for the snuffling pig

Gold crab apples tinged with scarlet
Shaken from the stunted tree
Country wives make amber jelly
From a well–tried recipe.

By the oak tree's acorn crop
Sycamore wings twirl down on the winds
Ash keys fly across the meadows
And somewhere a new forest begins.

Fruit of hedge and tree and briar
The nutting squirrels harvest home,
A time of richness, ripeness, plenty
All gathered and stored ere winter's come.

Florence Wayles

The Slow Lane

Black car glides slowly, oh so slowly.
Woman, gaunt, grey, grips wheel.
Road is narrow, twisting, turning,
Hedged by golden gorse and may.
Cars behind crawl slowly, oh so slowly;
Drivers hoot, fret, fume, and pray
For deliverance from suffering
Mile upon mile funereal file!
Black car stops sharply, pulls in neatly,
By a graveyard close to church.
Brakes are squealing, bumpers touching,
Drivers curse both woman and way.
In shattered peace she then emerges,
Stepping slowly, oh so slowly,
Clutching roses red as blood;
Stands aside as ten cars pass her
Moving quickly, oh so quickly;
But from her eyes the tears flow slow.

Eileen Williams

Poet

He sits,
Words dripping deftly from his pen
His aim, to flummox mortal men
Who pore and ponder, peruse and then
Thoroughly baffled begin again
To decode the cipher, some meaning find
In enigmas unleashed by the wordsmith's mind.

He watches,
Boffins browsing, like huddled crows,
And sceptics seeking in vain for flaws,
Till a titled pedant draws wild applause
Extolling this "gem of perfect prose".
The author smiles on the sheep he loathes,
Who fear to disclaim the 'Emperor's clothes'

He knew,
When cultural snobs communed and fused
And pundits proffered rave reviews,
They would drown in his tome of obscure text
Whilst he, at his ease, prepared for his next
Position. Confound the elite—exploit their gaffes,
This future laureate preens and laughs!

Jean Crowther

Penelope's Children (Waiting For The Hero To Show)

The dark side of the moon
Draws down the violent and the damned
Depressing on the wounds
Of swift flow, heart bleed, agonies
Of mind stealth, warp weavings
(Slash/cut the thread
that was a stitch in time)
To unravel the accomplishment of days
Spent shuttling sense into meaning
And a patterning into life

In the timeless bound of dark moon
No reflection can emerge no containing be seen
Just endless now of no light at point of no return
The remedy but end to conscious pain
And all alone in the dark

Time to spin and dangle on the thread.
Grandmother spider teach me how to feel the web,
How to sail till morning on cast off lines
Of hope, to trust in the buffeting breeze
And tempest tossed remain aloft.

Lesley Vann

The Inevitable Blues Without A Cause

A jazz bar. The blues, funky beats,
Smoky atmosphere. Blue moods and pink cocktails,
She stood there, in a little black number,
Her dreams bigger than her reality,
Passive smiles, yet knowing all,
Men. Attractive to say the least,
The bass conducted the hum of conversation,
When there was any. Failed dreams. Moody,
Her slender finger nails subconsciously tapped to the beat,
The cigarette smoke drifted across her face,
Like a snake of the orient,
Why was she so blue?
Remoteness. Sadness. Uninterrupted by the bar man,
She sat there thinking. Of what?
Of what she had been or would become,
Vibes. Subliminal beats. A stage for thought,
At a small jazz bar, down town,
Lit by the energy of a neon sign above the door,
Down the steps, a haven for lost souls,
Black and white with a hint of blue in the air.

Louise Young

"The Champion's Pep-Talk"

"Quiet please!" The game has started.
Throw the ball up, hit it hard!
Wiggle bottom, shift the balance . . .
The ball is out by half a yard.

Blow on fingers, clench the racquet,
Wipe the sweat with wet wristband;
Adjust the headgear, tuck the hair back,
Bounce the ball with steady hand.

Breathless, gasping, pluck the shoulders,
Examine racquet, straighten strings;
Bang with palm to check the tension . . .
Clear the mind of other things.

Gaze at trainers, check the laces,
Psych the mind up, clench the fist;
Set the jaw in sheer aggression . . .
"Deuce", another ace is missed!

Sit and drink, and plan the winning;
Towel the head, and focus "POWER!"
Relax with eyes and thoughts towards heaven.
Then win the match in half an hour.

Joan S. True

Timedance

One second.
A howl in a gale,
and a rhapsody
of dialectic chirps.
'Something coming, something running.'

Enter light,
reliable light,
a dawn of colours,
a symphony of yawns
from the gasps of coffee drinkers.

Tannoi speech.
A train awaits each
anonymous soul,
to study the form or
deal with the mail then head for home.

'Something missing, something showing.'
Letters to write, a kiss
for the wife, then off
to bed, to sleep, the
moon, darkness . . .

Philip J. Taylor

The Bronze Statuette

Gaunt as the waning minon-ette
Peruse of what you think is best,
Joined only by hard pleated folds
That swaged between and gripped your souls,
A lank arm bent across a knee
Crabbed hands that clutched a filigree,
Dark holes of eyes in sockets bare
That keep deep corners in despair,
Ungainly feet that interpose
And touch secure the ground below,
A sense of peaceful aged repose
Etched in the lines that hold the face,
And mirrored in the friend beside
Who sits ungainly at your side,
Intent upon the book she reads
Deep cradled in her bony knees,
No words need pass between the two
The many years are but too few,
Long reconciled upon their fate
To long, to few, to meditate.

Kevin Garratt

Rooks In The Churchyard

He shivered a really delicious shiver,
that travelled the length of his back, to a dusty tail feather,
how proudly he preened in mud sodden ground,
with a crown on his head, rags to his back,
the king of the rooks, silenced all as he spoke,
slowly his neck, he craned to one side,
rested his lid, caused a blink in one eye,
he opened his beak and called to his friends,
who high from the church tower, in pairs did descend,
they pawed with their claws, scratching initials in mud,
screaming like demons, hungry for blood,
spreading his wings, the king of the rooks,
from under his mantle sends the meanest of looks,
his cold heart of treason, keeps death's sweet surprise,
he orders his henchmen to take to the skies,
with wing's making thunder, in pairs they ascend,
back to the belfry, their church to defend,
what is the secret, why is it so,
no further then the graveyard do the brotherhood go

Z. Cromie

Uncertain Though Within This Deepset Heart

Distinction between art and people, therefore from art,
reflected in the light of present pressure,
I give to you the reason that demands your presence
from another place where twice I have shown my disinterest
in the nature of the struggle between opposites
the sense loud that hurts by confecting enemies

This could not be art although it could not be denied,
denunciation ripping off its red cap waving frantically
in the perfume of mists and loneliness a wild cornflower
faint against the strong blossoms of cultivation
weak by naive ardour loses presence to the refute in
everything for lovely praise of dipping ghosts

In this dim and rise a coronet of new found hazel nuts
in this glass case I offer you an absent fellowship
for our legs have been leaded by stray bullets
we, some who were kings and princesses, the scavengers of old
words wrenched from our daytimes, screens rammed into our vision,
retrieved for selected short stories that eat into tapeworm
with the hideous recommendation of a comforting rival
who holds the inevitable gesture between finger and thumb.

Grace Lake

Escape To Freedom

Far from the teeming rivers of mankind,
Whose seething waters flood but soon decline,
Far from the brief–lived empires of the mind,
I seek forever that eternal shrine.

Where gently blows the sea–washed scented breeze
And graceful gulls forever dive and soar,
Where Summer skies reach down to azure seas,
And limpid tides lap softly on the shore.

Here let me rest upon the golden sands,
Steeped in the sun–warmed bosom of the earth
Where God and Nature clasp eternal hands,
And drink the sparkling nectar of rebirth.

Here lie the tranquil seas of ageless peace,
Whose muted voices whisper timeless dreams,
Here, Time's unending motions never cease,
Replenished from life's deep immortal streams.

Derek Dodds

From Glory To Tears

New Year's day morning, in nineteen nineteen
A tragic disaster, the world never seen
Returning from battle, to a fate so unfair
More than two hundred perished, on HM Iolaire

Survivors were few, when the Iolaire went down
Twenty yards from the shores of Stornaway town
Pride and the glory, turned to cries in the air
As news spread through Lewis, of the wrecked Iolaire

The great war was over, home was in sight
A welcome so warm, a future so bright
Stories to tell, round the fireside chair
Was denied to the brave, on board the Iolaire

They died not in battle, nor a land far away
But perished near Lewis, outside Stornaway
A piper's lament echoes, through peat misty air
In remembrance to the sons, lost with the Iolaire

An island left weeping, asking God, "Tell us why
Did the cream of the highlands, come home just to die
No embrace nor goodbye, no tears we would share
With the loved ones who perished, on the HM Iolaire.

William McKechnie

Dreamtime Billabong

there is a secret everyone knows . . .
bubbles from the depths
fish feed on insects water-skating billabong
birds chased out by dragonflies circling crimson
seeking sentinel post policing area with silent siren

there is a secret everyone knows . . .
hovering hawks air current gliding
billabong sun bright disc in the water
brushed by motion of flies' circular ripples
that fray the water canvas sheet
and when the disc is obscured by cloud canvas also fades
then there is no canvas until it comes alive again with sun

there is a secret everyone knows . . .
snake lizard wallaby surrounded by rustle not always the wind
a tree leans over to touch the sun that becomes a meteor to score across
as a dragonfly hits bulls eye another skates its last
and then the meteor loses its tail its speed and everything slows
and dry stalks by the edge rasp simply a block of stone

Alan J. Summers

Carnac

Sun-blind we enter,
Moisty blackness and shiver of cold stone
Pricked in three points by cool gold
Dripping white wax on damp fingers.
Bending low beneath the earth,
Whispering our awe,
We follow him who chants.
They are here on all sides watching our passage as we stumble
  through their hallways.
They have lain for millennia behind these blocks of stone,
Great chunks of the earth that seal their rooms from eyes of
  another time.

But empty sockets have no need of light.
Bare bones know the weight of the earth.
We peer and touch and smell and the faint odour of fear belies
  our trespass.

Our senses, dizzied by the dark, swirl in us
Until a curve reveals dim light poking fingers through the black.
And as we pass into our world, the breath of soft sighs is cool
  upon our cheeks.

Sally A. Fitz-Gibbon

Fin de Vacances

To this our frail and melting earthliness
we clung like demons till she soared away,
trailing the sad satiety of that day,
our limbs' communion, and each deep caress.

The cool of evening offered some redress
along the shore, where lengthening shadows stray,
and we walked there wordless, with no more to say,
our spirits chastened by flesh-torn distress.

Now alone on the shore in the light of the moon,
like wraiths, hand and hand, we still silently roam,
and the cliffs, in suspense, in an ocean of foam,
float by us like clouds in the deepening gloom.

We, as nature communes, our transgressions replay,
when the first stars emerging intrusively shine;
but the lengthening shadows her face hides from mine,
while the waves from the sand our prints wash away.

Frederic J. Jones

Enigma

On her best days,
She'd smile lying beautiful,
Reading listlessly alone.
Flowing brushed hair passing paper people,
Occasionally watching,
Listening,
Yet still centre of her own attention.

On her worst days,
She'd be caught.
Rushing, tense,
Fleeting and flustered amongst others.
A different,
Yet still,
Alone.
The silver moon on a pool of water,
Longing to be still.

Russel Lewis

Saga Of A Field Trip

The wind of Armageddon roars across the field,
I struggle towards the village—unwilling to yield.
Give in to this haradon—elemental, fearsome foe?
I need to get some cat food—to the grocers I shall go!

Oh No! You mighty gale force—"Winds of Hades" hither—
Do your worst, yes, throw down rain, and hail, and torment gather,
I shall not bend, or break, or tarry, nor my backbone wither!

And now the sound of wind does change,
The roaring fades and whistling begins—
Like a chorus of owls, eerily singing, "take care small human—
Here nature reigns."

It speaks to me, this wild a-wooing, "You'll get to the village
  sooner than planned,"
—It chimes to me, "A mile a minute is easily reached with a
  helping hand."

No locals venture out in this—only foolish tourists and wayward
  girls,
The price? It's nothing too disastrous, just ruined shoes and
  tangled curls.

The experience I'll soon repeat, in spite of being now un-shod,
I'll look for wonder in the lanes again
And in that wonder I'll find my God.

Elaine Whyte

Fight The Good Fight

I look for a hero but find only a thief,
A quest for romance which ends only in grief,
I yearn for the past, of ages expired,
Stolen by the advance of human desires.

These human desires have corrupted and led
To indolence and insolence which now is inbred,
What happened to valour, honour and trust,
Which has now been replaced by deceit, hate and lust.

As innocents we were fed with Drake and King Arthur,
Ivanhoe, Robin Hood, Homer and Chaucer,
But now we bloom into the 'latest' young men,
Tainted by 'self' in the capitalists' den.

A cynic I am and that I will stay,
I fight for my past but lose every day,
This battle is lost, for the victor is time,
The future is yours my son, it's certainly not mine.

J. D. Boyles

Sensorium

The shadowed leap at my command
Eternity's arrow in blazing hand
Through a trellis-work of phantom fire
Impaled on dreams, I know desire.
All this is mine to convey
You are Lord and Master of all I survey
Sensorium, time capsule, layered contradiction
Lip service is over, you await benediction . . .
You feel no pain, though I must suffer
No words or religion, no prayer can I offer
What serpents do crawl through those monochrome spires
Cold, reptilian cathedrals where forbidden fruit lies?
Do you carry the burden of every man's sin?
Count the demons that jostle on the heads of dull pins
Kiss my eyes, dreaming lizard, where the coins bruise and scar
In the pit, I am lucid and scared
There's a sound near the ceiling like a long swishing gown
Then the pendulum starts to come down . . .

Barbara L. Richards

Precious Time

As I sit and watch the resting pair
Content in their equilibrium,
Washing their limbs with tender care
A sideways glance, a knowledge shared.

A tender touch of nose to face
Offers friendship, love, an accepted place,
An understanding, a bond unknown
To those which spend their time alone.

I wish I could share with them
That special secret, that special trust
Formed slowly from their first wary touch,
An intrusion became a unity.

If I could cross the boundaries to reach their minds
And break the shackles of Mankind,
I'd curl up there, beside my friends
And while away that precious time.

Vicky Atkinson

Caledonia

Summer's heady thrill lured me north
To watch the dancing, dazzling light
Of the dark and murky lochs
Where blue plunges into black
Treacherous deadly depths

In the city people rushed homeward
Glancing fearfully at the gathering cloud
Over the hills where Summer's sultry beauty
Masked a storm

Later, in the velvet twilight of the longest day
I sensed something slip into the soft night air
A pale light dwindling on the horizon
And I knew you were gone

Like the slow drawing in of the nights
Casting shadow over the earth
The relentless pull towards Winter
Chills all Summer has scattered in her wake

Midsummer so brief, so glorious
We will never know this time again.

Maggie Ayre

Siamese Twins

As you sat, cross–legged, in that humid, fragrant Bangkok twilight,
working on a now long–discarded handiwork,
the rain began to fall outside, hot, dense, liquid black
on the paths and alleyways,
pounding and testing your timber dwelling, but doing so
almost unnoticed by yourself,
as your tongue weaves in benign Siamese tones, the
important issues of the moment, to your companion.

And as the night assumed the tone of your hair,
and the rain gradually stopped,
for a moment, you wondered what would become
of all and everything around you,
Your coffee–brown countenance creased in wonderment;
dark almond eyes, so very much alive,
unrivalled at any time, anywhere, in beauty, gazed upwards.

Strange, so very strange, that nigh a century-and-a half
later, I should think of you,
on that night, in that land of smiles.

Colin G. Black

Words To Press

Prolix discussions of nothings
Plained people in accord
That naught be done and
Nothing come
Of jejune plans and promises

Recorded
Words pressed
Dull and flat
Lie as filed

Drear inkswells swirling exotic cocktails
Foxtrot fancies up and down the page
Roues casting lines about
For a faux pas
Centre stage

Reported
Words to press
Dull and flat
Lies piled

Morwenna Morrison

The Mouse's Reply To Robert Burns

Ye muckle hammerin
Fitted chiel
Ye maun think
This mouse is feel
Tae big a nest
Far ye mak a dreel
We yer muckle ploo.

Maybe this ground
Belongs tae ye
Bit I've a richt
Tae be here tae
At we nest
Wis nice an warm
Tae keep me awa'
Frae winters harm
Now I'll hae
Tae big anither
Nae thanks tae you

Douglas Parley

Untitled

Behind them, behind you,
Another one first.
At the bottom of a glass.
The bit that gets left,
And tipped away.
Gone sour, too warm, not good enough,
Or just not wanted.
An old jumper,
Because it was all you could find.
A song played,
That has to suit the mood.
Go without lunch,
You didn't have enough time,
You were meeting someone.
You don't bother to phone,
You might bump into me.
Use my hand to write their numbers,
Use my company when they're not around,
Use me,
because you won't use them.

Alexandra Evemy

Early Warning

Drunken
    scrubby landscape
        leaning and veering

raffish blacks and browns

      slipping horizons

scratchy doormat subsistence

    three bridal domes laid on
    like wens on a horny hand.

I swallow the sight
    without tasting

      tipsy as a boozer

eye warped out of meaning

slopping a froth
    on the pains of knowing

dead

    to the world in the morning.

Teresa Howell

Here Today Gone Tomorrow

Morning wakes, veiled light,
Snowfall married in the night,
To the earth beneath my feet,
Dawning of the day complete.

Footprints they were spoken,
Echoed in the snow,
The morse of hungry rodents,
Round and round they go.

One alone, stood silent,
Amid this vortex of despair,
Brown and strong, ears long,
A proud but hungry hare.

Einstein wasn't needed,
To understand this plight,
I dug until I reached the green,
To compliment the white,

Twitching nose, ears high,
I swear that hare winked an eye,
Morning woken, no remorse,
Snow and earth, quick divorce.

John P. Lloyd

Domestic Tomb

I used to see them holding hands,
For years I've seen that golden band,
Their love was like a jigsaw,
Now the game is over,
Loves now familiarity.
And as they walk,
About, not hand in hand,
I can hear them talk.
No effort to impress,
No rich tapestry,
Just discussing,
The price of fish fingers.

Yvette Monique Ogden

Biographies
of
Poets

ABBAM, MISS GISELA
[p.] Eileen Abbam, Peter K. Abbam; [ed.] Middlesex University; [occ.] Freelance Consultant; [memb.] Association of Masters in Business Administration (AMBA), Oxfam Charity; [hon.] Master in Business Administration (MBA) BEd (Hons) Award for Excellence in English Literature; [oth. writ.] Three academic publications, wrote plays for local club performance; [pers.] I believe that by being determined and always persevering, there is very little one would not achieve. My poetry reflects my innermost thoughts.; [a.] London, UK, SW16 5QE

ABDULLA, ELIZABETH MCFARLANE
[pen.] Elizabeth Abdulla; [b.] 1 October 1952, Wimbledon, London; [p.] Catherine and Duncan McFarlane; [m.] Professor Y.M.H. Abdulla Scientist/Pathologist, 1 April 1972; [ch.] Sara Abdulla (23); [ed.] Pelham School for Girls Wimbledon, Guy's Med. School, Lond. Univ. Msc Immunology, Ph.D in Neuroscience Univ. London (imminent); [occ.] Research in Neuroscience at The Inst of Psychiatry: magnetic field and the nervous system; [memb.] Royal Academy of Art, National Trust, Royal Horticulture Society; [hon.] Financial Times Christmas Poetry Competition 1992; [oth. writ.] The first of many scientific publications was in 1970 with my husband and recently with my colleague and supervisor, Reader in Neuroscience, Iain C. Campbell. I have been offered publication of a personal anthology of poems by Quartet Books.; [pers.] In my Scottish Presbyterian home (in Wimbledon) I was one of six siblings with manic-depressive genes. I married an Egyptian Aristocrat and Scientist whose family religion was Moslem but whose philosophy was logic and compassion. My angle on the world has always been peripheral but I have been lucky to receive and give love and to receive constant encouragement.; [a.] Beckenham, Kent, UK, BR3 6RD

ABLITT, LUCY
[b.] 27 July 1980, Isle of Wight; [p.] Paul and Julia Ablitt; [ed.] Medina High School, 6th Form; [pers.] I enjoy poetry very much and have been inspired by the late poet William Blake.; [a.] Newport, Isle of Wight, UK, PO30 2JX

ACKERMAN, DAVID
[pen.] Henry George; [b.] 4 May 1972, Swansea; [p.] Brian Ackerman, Ceinwen Ackerman; [occ.] Entrepreneur; [hon.] Mensa; [pers.] I first got into poetry when I read a book from a man who was from the same city as myself, "Dylan Thomas" the book's title was, "Dylan Thomas Letters"; [a.] Swansea, W-Glam, UK, SA5 7HS

ADAMS, MR. JAMES
[b.] 9 June 1937, Balham, London; [p.] Edward Adams, Lily Adams; [ed.] Secondary Modern School; [occ.] I cannot work as I am registered disabled and was an auctioneer assistant; [oth. writ.] I have written several short stories. They are unpublished to date; only one other poem. (Unpublished); [pers.] I like writing about past events in my life. But I've weakness now in my hands. I am fifty nine years old and now disabled. (Registered); [a.] Tooting, London, UK, SW17 0LD

ADAMS, JILL
[b.] 17 February 1958, Hackney, London; [p.] Gordon and Dorothy Adams; [occ.] Legal P/A; [memb.] The Poetry Society, Redwings Animals Sanctuary, The Labour Party; [hon.] Poetry Competition Commendations; [a.] Wembley, Middlesex, UK, MA9 9TG

ADERIBIGBE, MR. JAMES AYO
[pen.] Olorun Ara; [b.] 17 April 1937, Gbongan; [p.] Mr. and Mrs. S. A. Aderibigbe; [m.] Phebean Olufunmilayo, 17 December 1966; [ch.] Adesola, Olusayo, Oyedunton, Subomi; [ed.] St. Paul's Primary School, Gbongan, Nigeria, St Andrew's College, Oyo Nigeria; [occ.] Gardening; [memb.]

1. Christian Benevolent Group, St Paul's Cathedral, Gbongan. 2. Nigeria Union of Pensioners Ayedaade Branch, Gbongan; [hon.] Teacher's Certificate grade two.; [oth. writ.] Novels (1) "Robbery In God's Name," and (2) "Angelina." poetry (1) "The Dais" (narrative epic) (2) Dozen poems on various topics. History: "Here So Far" (auto-biographical essay.) All the above unpublished due to unfavorable conditions, unconducive environment.; [pers.] "The Still Small Voice.";
[a.] Gbongan, Ayedaade

AFIFI, AHMED
[b.] 26 November 1979, Kuwait; [m.] I can't wait for that, not until I'm 35 years or older; [ed.] I finished my IGCSE examination in November 1996 and I am willing to study Computer Science in the U.S.A. and my goals in life is to be the world's greatest programmer; [pers.] A special thank you goes out to Ms. Jenkins, my English teacher, and if she ever reads these words I would like her to know that I enjoyed every second in the English classes. To everybody who tried writing a poem before, in order to make it a good successful poem that people would enjoy I advise you to write about your true feelings... "I really wanted to go to the beach with the girl that I loved where we sit together watching the sunrise starting a new day, a new day in our relationship, beside staying close to her till the last day in my life. To my love, I'm not sure if she would read this because she is not into poetry but if she does. I want her to know I wrote this poem for you and to prove to the world that my love is true.

AGIRBAS, CAROLINE
[b.] 11 January 1959, Kent; [p.] John Clifton, Sonia Clifton; [m.] Sahin Agirbas, 3 August 1982; [ch.] 4 children, 2 boys and 2 girls; [ed.] State schools; [occ.] House wife; [oth. writ.] Poetry but none published before.; [pers.] I hope to convey through my poetry that all of life is precious, that we should appreciate the simple things in life, that so many of us often take for granted.; [a.] Carshalton, Surrey, UK, SM5 1BS

AGIŬS, MARIA
[pen.] Ria Scann; [b.] 9 May 1971, Sliema, Malta; [p.] Emmanuel and Paola G. Mifsud; [m.] Kevin Christopher Agius, 20 September 1993; [ch.] Amy, Emanuela; [ed.] Maria Ass. High School; [occ.] Shop Manager; [memb.] Vittoriosa Lawn Tennis Club; [oth. writ.] Small articles published in local magazines; [pers.] Writing gives me the freedom to express myself. Even sometimes trying to pass over messages to people.; [a.] Fgura, Malta, PLA 18

AHMED, NURZAN
[b.] 16 January 1974, England; [p.] Gous Ahmed and Sumirta Ahmed; [ed.] Mulberry School for Girls, Richard Street, Commercial Road, London E-1, 2JP; [occ.] Dental Nurse; [pers.] I have always enjoyed English poems and this therefore influenced me to give it a go. Poems reflect on all kinds of feelings like love, sadness and loneliness. Everybody comes across these once in the lifetime.; [a.] East London

AHMED, SONIA
[b.] 26 June 1983, London; [p.] Hashem Ahmed, Nilufa Ahmed; [ed.] Eldon Juniors (Edmonton), Winchmore Hill Senior School (currently going to); [occ.] Student; [pers.] I try to express my feelings in my writing, as it tends to sound more passionate that way. But if I don't write what I'm feeling, I use my creative imagination instead.; [a.] Edmonton, London, UK, N18 1XL

AITKEN, CHRYS
[pen.] Christina Corbyn; [b.] 16 September 1937, Woodford Halse, Northamptonshire; [p.] Kathleen Rose and Stanley Westgarth Leonard; [m.] Mike R. Aitken, 21 April 1965; [ch.] Mark; [ed.] High School for girls, Brackley, London University; [occ.] Ret. English Teacher, now

Development Manager, Young Enterprise; [memb.] Several animal- and countryside-related societies, Business and Professional Women's Association; [hon.] The usual professional qualifications, Triple Distinction on Teacher's Certificate, Young Enterprise Gold Award; [oth. writ.] Poetry published in magazines and other anthologies. A few short stories for children.; [pers.] Our world is beautiful, man alone destroys that beauty. We must learn to cherish it.; [a.] Bideford, North Devon, UK, EX39 3PY

AKHTAR, SHAMSHAD
[pen.] "Light of the World"; [b.] 14 April 1957, West Pakistan; [p.] Nazir Ahmed, Ramzan Bibi; [m.] 8 November 1977; [ch.] Muhummed Akhtar; [ed.] C.S.E. and G.C.E. Level in variety of subjects, Qualified Paralegal in Criminology Level 1: The Sociology of Crime and Deviance; [occ.] Law Student; [memb.] Have served as school governor and on Local Mental Health Committee, member of Socialist Workers Party, Workers Revolution Party; [hon.] Community Sports Leadership Award; [oth. writ.] I am a known established community and union resource: my unpublished work is to be found Internationally within our Community and the world.; [pers.] I support and uphold the weak and vulnerable, encourage goodwill and protect the essence of life, beauty and nature.; [a.] London, Peckham, UK

ALDER, GWENDOLINE
[b.] 15 August 1920, London; [p.] Elizabeth and Lionel; [m.] Albert Alder Osborne, 12 December 1942; [ch.] Michael, David and John; [ed.] Various Army schools, St. Frideswide's Girls School, Didcot, Oxon; [occ.] Housewife; [memb.] Milverton and Eitzhead Horticultural Society Fitzhead and Milverton Conservation Society; [oth. writ.] 3 other poems published by International Library of Poetry; [pers.] My poems are spontaneous and from the heart.; [a.] Taunton, Somerset, UK, TA4 1QX

ALDRIDGE, KATHLEEN
[pen.] Katie; [b.] 16 May 1923, Stalham, Norfolk; [p.] William Woodbine and Rachel Althea Sandell; [m.] George Aldridge, 25 March 1978; [ch.] Graham Stuart Leslie 49 yrs., Vanda Kathleen 47 yrs., Trevor Stanley 43 yrs.; [ed.] Northwalsham (Norfolk) High School, (Gilian Shepherd - Minister of Education, also attended later!), Gained - Cambridge School Leavine Certificate 1939; [occ.] Retired; [memb.] Cambridge and District Co-Operative Society Retirement Fellowship; [oth. writ.] "Eastern England" published in "Poetry in Motion - Eastern" 1994 (Page 78), "The Pig on the Wall" published in "Islands Moors and Reflections 1995 (page 16); [pers.] "Time" is the most valuable asset anyone can have - I strive to make my beloved husband, and - my children, my family and all my friends, understand I dearly love and care for them.; [a.] Cambridge, Cambridgeshire, UK, CB4 1RB

ALGHOUL, LIDIA
[b.] 31 December 1975, Palestine; [p.] Tajeddin Alghoul, Nadia Obeid; [ed.] Communications Major, American International University in London; [pers.] "I have a very sincere appreciation of the more spiritual elements of human life and I do like lending a great deal to helping others to understand them through my writings. The whole matter draws me and I see it as one area in which I find a channel for my finest feelings.; [a.] Richmond, Surrey, UK, TW10 6EX

ALJUNIED, AHMAD FAISAL SALEM
[b.] 3 April 1966, Singapore; [p.] Salem Aljunied and Zainab Bin Sahel; [m.] Salwah Alsree; [ch.] Aseel; [ed.] Fourth Level Student (University Ummal-Qura) in Makkah in the English Department; [occ.] Student; [pers.] Love for others what you love for yourself and hate for others what you hate for yourself.

ALLARD, MR. JULIAN
[b.] 8 December 1966, Eye, Suffolk; [p.] John and Eileen Alland; [ed.] Stowmarket High School, Suffolk; [occ.] Unemployed; [oth. writ.] My poem "Sides" published with The International Library of Poetry - semi-finalist 1995; [pers.] I regard my poems as songs, being hugely influenced by song lyrics. But I haven't done anything to put them to music!; [a.] Ipswich, Suffolk, UK, IP2 8AD

ALLBEURY, RICHARD
[b.] 4 March 1947, Dartford; [m.] Phrosa; [ch.] Andreas and Christopher; [ed.] Dartford East Secondary School; [occ.] Lead Specialist; [pers.] I write for my own pleasure about me or those around me. I find great pleasure and real surprise at any praise my stories or poems gather along the way.; [a.] Chingford, London, UK, E4 8PN

ALLDEN, PHYLLIS
[pen.] Phyllis Cannon; [b.] 23 June 1961, Meriden; [p.] Michael Cannon, Sheila Cannon; [m.] Michael Allden, 11 May 1996; [occ.] Nurse; [pers.] From a privileged view point I am able to witness very personal moments and emotions which I strive to reflect in my writing.

ALLISON, DAWN P.
[b.] 1 September 1974, Kirkcaldy; [ed.] Viewforth High, Kirkcaldy, University of Stirling, Telford College, Edinburgh, Fife College; [occ.] Student; [memb.] Youth Leader, Percussionist, Christian, various sports; [hon.] Sound Control Trophy, Senior Perfect, Year Representative at University; [oth. writ.] My writing continues to be published, exhibited and read by many people, from all walks of life.; [pers.] My aim in writing is to give God the glory and honour. He gave me the gift in the first place. There's a great communication in writing a lot of emotions and sentiments can be expressed. I view my writing as a means to reach out and educate others.; [a.] Kirkcaldy, Fife, UK, KY1 2YU

ALLWRIGHT, JANET
[b.] 28 August 1948, Guildford; [p.] Mr. R and Mrs. O. M. Simms; [m.] Keith, 20 September 1988; [ch.] Andrea, Linda, Michelle, four grandchildren; [ed.] North Secondary School for girls; [occ.] Disabled Housewife; [memb.] D.D.A.; [oth. writ.] Poem in village magazine poems published in six other books; [pers.] Writing poetry has transformed my life, and given me something interesting to do, makes my living worthwhile, my aim is to win a competition one day. And maybe to publish my own book.; [a.] Feniton, Devon, UK, EX14 0EQ

ALMSLEY, MRS. HONOR W.
[b.] 8 July 1962, Rochdale; [m.] Deceased, 17 July 1948; [ch.] Elaine, Shirley, Yvonne; [ed.] Glenbank Elementary Prefect; [occ.] Widow; [a.] Rochdale, Lancashire, UK, OL11 3JU

ALWELL, ELIZABETH
[b.] Armagh; [occ.] Retired; [oth. writ.] One poem published in another anthology.

ANDERSON, KATRINA M.
[b.] 7 December 1947, Springfield, Fife; [p.] Margaret and Zygmunt Tomaszewski; [m.] William Anderson, 13 July 1984; [ch.] Edward 31, Loma 26, Tanya 19; [ed.] Bell-Baxter Junior and Senior High, Cupar, Glenrothes College (HNC) Social Sciences University of Dundee, M.A. with Honours (English Education); [occ.] Full time student 2nd year University of Dundee; [memb.] Lifetime Royal Patronage Principality of Hutt River, Queensland, Australia; [hon.] Patronage WNFERS The Title of Honorable (the Shortened to hon.) before me. And soon to be a member of International Honor Society; [oth. writ.] Previous work published by International Library of Poetry. Poem printed in college.; [pers.] In poetry I am free to be myself.; [a.] Glenrothes, Fife, UK, KY6 2BN

ANDERSON, LYNDSEY
[b.] 24 March 1984, Bangor, County Down; [p.] Alison Anderson; [ed.] Grosvenor Grammar (1995-); [occ.] Student; [a.] Belfast, Down, UK, BT5 7NA

ANDERTON, ROSE
[b.] 9 April 1909, Bury St. Eds; [p.] Frank, Martha Newman; [m.] Dudley Bower Anderton, 22 May 1971; [ch.] Christopher John - Rosemary Anne; [ed.] Chevington Bury St. Edmunds; [occ.] Retired; [oth. writ.] Poems of the South West 1993, Winter poets 1992. Poets around Britain. West Country Poets 1995. Poetry now. South West 1996. Triumph House Collection 1996. Animals Forever, My Favourite Things, 20 Anthologies.; [pers.] My aim in life has always been to give rather than receive. Maybe that inspired me to knit over 2,000 garments for Oxfam and Rwanda babies. I have always been in church choirs and have sung in the Royal Albert Hall with the London Emmanuel choir.; [a.] Frome, Somerset, UK, BA11 4JS

ANDRADE, PHYLLIS DOROTHY NOUCHETTE
[pen.] Ruth; [b.] 7 June 1917, Kingston, Jamaica; [p.] Cyril and Minna Levy; [m.] Neil DaCosta Andrade, 23 April 1937; [ch.] Two; [ed.] English Secondary Schooling; [occ.] Retired housewife, author and publisher; [memb.] Promoter of the 'Christian Child Education Project,' Editor Dr. Bob DeMercado, presently acting editor, Winnie Foster Lewis for new edition, "Gemo by Ruth", 38 poems; [hon.] "God's Little Sparrows" by Ruth was entered in the Winter edition '86, Vol 4, American Poetry Anthology by John Frost, Editor; [oth. writ.] Book Marks, Hangers, Booklets: Rainbows and Reflections," "Sunshine and Promises," "Gems". Just launched locally and have copywright 1996, ISBN 976-8138386; [pers.] I trust that my poems will continue to cheer, guide and bless the lives of many folk of all ages, as they are influenced by the bible teachings.; [a.] Kingston, Jamaica, West Indies

ANGUS, ROBERT DUNSMUIR SHIELDS
[b.] 17 February 1912, Wishaw; [p.] William and Bethia Angus; [m.] Jean Davidson Millar (Deceased), 14 February 1953; [ch.] Two sons and one daughter; [occ.] Retired; [oth. writ.] "The New If", "Granny", "Four Seasons For The Young", "Joe Irish Lass", "Special Christmas", "Next Time Round", "To My Dear Wife", "To End Your Valentine", "Only A Dream"; [pers.] As you will observe because of my age my poems were written a few years ago; those mentioned above are all I remember and I mainly wrote to my wife on anniversaries.; [a.] Wishaw, Lanarkshire, UK, ML2 8PX

ANYALEWECNI, IKECHI
[b.] 11 November 1974, Manchester; [ed.] Burnage High School, Manchester, Shena Simon Sixth Form College, Manchester; [occ.] Student studying politics and philosophy at Middlesex University; [memb.] Amnesty International considering joining 'New Labour'; [oth. writ.] A poem, 'Here I Am' published in a compilation by Arrival Press in 1993, A 'Considerable' amount of music for recorder and violin; [pers.] I would like to thank my ex-history teacher, Chris Chisnall, who gave me the confidence to write again, and to Murium Gulam, who continues to lend me her ears; [a.] Manchester, Lancashire, UK, M16 0BP

ARNOLD, MARIE
[b.] 16 January 1975, York; [ed.] Lowfields Secondary School, York College of Further and Higher Education; [pers.] When the skies are no longer blue and the shadows stand bold and the key to the door is lost, remember, to be strong and keep holding on.; [a.] York, Yorkshire, UK, Y02 4UU

ASHLEY, MARJORIE EDWINA
[b.] 19 March 1933, Bolton; [p.] William Ashley, Winifred Castille Ashley; [m.] Deceased; [ed.] Local School Bolton; [occ.] Registered Blind Retired; [memb.] Formerly member of Bolton and Blackpool Art Societies; [hon.] Nursery Nurses Diploma, Teaching Diploma for Handicapped Children, Diploma from Keith Maklin; [oth. writ.] Poem - My Special Dog publ. in last two years in new poetry book in Animals, poem - What a Mess sent to Poetry Today; [pers.] I was born in Bolton, my father a Dental Surgeon. I looked after 18 blind/deaf children for 22 years, moved to Blackpool to look after mentally handicapped. After 5 years was attacked by a Schizophrenic boy and since have lost my sight now registered blind with guide dog Donna - more overleaf.; [a.] Saint Agnes, Lancashire, UK

ASHTON, MISS ANDREA M.
[pen.] Andrea M. Ashton; [b.] 21 June 1956, Chester; [p.] William Ashton, Margaret Ashton; [ed.] Lymm Grammar and Altringham Grammar, St. Mary's College, Bangor, N. Wales; [occ.] School teacher (retired on medical grounds); [memb.] Lewis Carroll Society, Daresbury, Elizabeth Gaskell Society, Knutsford, Beatrix Potter Society, London; [oth. writ.] Six poems published in Contemporary Poets of 1979, Children's story in an Oldham newspaper. Author of children's book yet to be published (China Hall).; [pers.] I have been influenced by the Brontes and various romantic poets. I like to reflect the beauty of nature in my writing.; [a.] Lymm, Cheshire, UK, WA13 0PB

ASKEY, VIOLET
[pen.] Vi Askey; [b.] June 4, 1919, Acton W3; [p.] Rose and Bert Streams; [m.] Charles Askey, June 4, 1938; [ch.] Daughter - Yvonne; [ed.] South Acton Girls School; [occ.] Retired; [hon.] Swimming and Life Saving Certificates, 1st Certificate for Garden, a letter from the queen on behalf of writing to her for the children of Ruislip Gardens School for her Majesty's Jubilee June 1977; [oth. writ.] I am hoping before I leave this world to one day maybe get a small poem book printed for my two wonderful grandchildren "Sally Jane" and Stephen.; [pers.] I write many poems all of which are true to life past and present harmonious and sad something of which I and many others feel and see at times.; [a.] Ruislip, Middlesex, HA4 6PG

ASTON, VIVIAN
[pen.] Poupee; [b.] 14 August 1939, Paris France; [p.] Eta and Max Aston; [ed.] Brussels, Montreal Canada, Boarding School England, Royal Academy of Music, Trinity College of Music, McGill University; [occ.] Musician, poet; [memb.] Friends of the British Federation of Festivals for Music Dance and Speech, Royal Academy of Music Club; [hon.] Cups, medals and certificates in piano, medals, plaque and certificates in poetry, certificates in music composer medal for essay; [pers.] I strive to be a good poet. I like to write about philosophy of arts.; [a.] London, UK, NW2

ATHERTON, JOHN MICHAEL
[b.] 24 August 1956, Leigh, Lancs; [p.] John and Pat Atherton; [ed.] De La Salle Grammar, Salford Wigan College of Technology, Derby Lonsdale College, Wilmorton College, Derby; [occ.] Assistant Accountant/Production Cost Technician; [memb.] Association of Accounting Technicians; [hon.] I cycled from Motherwell to Derby, June 1994 to raise funds for an Orphanage in Bosnia, (2000) over 6 days.; [oth. writ.] Does It Really Matter, What's The Reason For?, The Question, The Transfiguration, The Sorrowful Passion, So Much Love; [pers.] This poem was inspired by Mary, mother of Jesus (Our Lady), and my desire to express admiration for the life she lived, the work she did, her response to the word of God, and the love she showed to others.; [a.] Derby, Derbyshire, UK, DE1 3EE

AUBRY, CHRISTOPHER
[pen.] Christopher Aubry; [b.] 16 December 1969, Troyes, France; [p.] Michael and Franquoise Aubry; [occ.] Planning and feeling for future writing.; [oth. writ.] First timer into publishing achieved work of art. A lot of already written pieces unrevealed still. A first book on its way and who knows! Perhaps more!!!; [pers.] I admire life surrounding me, I feel so lucky, fulfilled with passion, human being, and this life, now is for me the top of the list of my topics. Being alive, being real, being awakened, is what we all remember beyond the every day doing.; [a.] Brighton, East Sussex, UK, BN2 5LH

AXWORTHY, JILL MADGE
[b.] 15 January 1937, Plymouth; [p.] Phyllis Dewaney, Horace Dewaney; [m.] Anthony Axworthy, 14 April 1962; [ch.] Andrew; [ed.] Secondary Modern (Laira Green) Business College; [occ.] Retired/Housewife; [oth. writ.] Several "unpublished" 'occasion' poems for family and friends in times of joy or sadness.; [pers.] I feel poetry can bring a smile to the face, a tear to the eye, and comfort for the soul.; [a.] Plymouth, Devon, UK, PL3 6DP

AZIM, SARAWAT
[pen.] Sarawat Azim; [b.] 6 November 1979, Rochdale; [p.] Mrs. N. Kauser, Mr. Azim; [ed.] Spotland County Oulder Hill School and 6th Form 8 GCSE's A-C's; [occ.] Currently studying A' Level English, Law and Psychology; [hon.] Various awards of merit and distinction; [oth. writ.] I have had a number of poems published in school magazines. I am constantly writing short stories and scripts.; [pers.] I write for comfort, warmth, and healing. Hoping I can reach out to others through my words.; [a.] Rochdale, Lancashire, UK, OL11 1QG

BACHE, SARAH
[b.] 4 November 1980, Birmingham; [p.] Peter Bache, Margaret Bache; [ed.] Kingsbury School; [occ.] Full time student; [memb.] Irish Fancy Canary Club - UK and Eire Junior Bird League Birmingham A.S.; [hon.] (G.C.S.E's to be taken in 1997) West Midlands Junior Canary Champion; [oth. writ.] Article in Cage and Aviary bird paper; [pers.] I am influenced to write poetry on how I see the world was a teenager who has her whole life to live to confront the good and bad sides of the world.; [a.] Birmingham, Warwickshire, UK, B24 0LA

BAILEY, ANDREW JOHN
[b.] 18 July 1973, Fleetwood; [p.] Heather and John (Divorced); [ed.] Fleetwood High; [occ.] Box-Man, Crisp Factory, Bensons Crisps, Kirkham, Lancs.; [oth. writ.] None published; [pers.] I try to write with everyone in mind, showing both good and bad, balancing all on the scales of human justice.; [a.] Fleetwood, Lancashire, UK, FY7 7LY

BAILEY, JOANNE MICHELLE
[b.] 30 April 1973, Bradford; [p.] John Triffitt, Jean Triffitt; [m.] Anthony Stuart Bailey, 17 September 1994; [ed.] Rhodesway Upper School, Bradford; [occ.] Switchboard Operator/Receptionist; [pers.] "Sometimes" is the first serious poem I have written based on feelings shared by myself and those of close Christian friends.; [a.] Bradford, West Yorkshire, UK, BD2 2HW

BAKER, COLIN
[pen.] Lancashire Lad; [b.] 25 May 1939, Bury; [p.] Deceased; [m.] Brenda Marian Baker, 1 September 1992; [ch.] Step children, one girl, three boys; [ed.] Secondary modern school; [occ.] Bus Driver (Blackpool) which I have done over the past 30 years on and off; [hon.] Life Saving Award (letter) in the Liverpool Shipwreck Society; [pers.] Personally, I like to write verses on birthday, or anniversary cards or write something down which comes to mind and keep at one side just in case of an event.; [a.] Blackpool, Lancashire, UK, FY4 5RQ

BAKER, DEBORAH
[b.] 22 June 1963, Cheshunt; [p.] Janet and Allan Hatchett; [m.] David Baker, 26 May 1984; [ch.] Sarah, Stephen and Hannah; [occ.] Housewife and mother; [oth. writ.] This is my first poem; [pers.] I love the simplest things in life, nature is a wonderful thing. The colours and expressions of animal and plant life, and the joy and beauty children bring.; [a.] Bishops Stortford, Herts, UK

BAKER, LESLEY
[pen.] Maddy Thomas; [b.] 24 June 1945, Hillingdon; [p.] Victor and Jean Cooper; [m.] Raymond, 31 July 1965; [ch.] Simon Dominic, Andrew James, and Lisa-Jayne; [ed.] Harlington Secondary Modern; [occ.] Admin. Assistant; [memb.] St. Mary's Flower Guild, Secretary Glastonbury Pilgrimage Committee (R.C.); [oth. writ.] Several poems published in anthologies - local magazines.

BAKER, PAMELA
[pen.] Pamela Baker; [b.] 26 February 1932, Guernsey, Ch. Isles; [p.] Walter Realey Fallaize, Violet Fallaize; [m.] Leonard George Baker, 29 May 1952; [ch.] Brian Baker, Andrew Baker; [ed.] St Martin's Parish School and States of Guernsley Intermediate School for Girls.; [occ.] Retired Proof Reader, Lifetime Singer/Entertainer (Amateur); [memb.] Former Member of Whatkatane Operatic Society and Whakatane Music Club in New Zealand, Former President and member Western Morning Women's Institute, Guernsey. Current member Daberaeron Yacht Club.; [hon.] Only One! I won the Contvalto Solo Cup in the Guernsey Eisteddford in 1984; [oth. writ.] Bits and pieces for the local paper in Guernsey when I lived these and recorded some poems and prose for Radio Guelnsey before we retired to Wales.; [pers.] Music is my life. Words were my living. Life and living combine in my poetry. People's feelings, hopes, joys, sadness. I like in my singing as in my poems to make people laugh or cry.; [a.] Llanon, Ceredegion, Wales, UK, SY23 5UH

BALDWIN, PATRICIA TUNE
[pen.] Patricia Tune Baldwin; [b.] 22 September 1948, Lancashire; [p.] Nelson Baldwin, Jean Deeble; [ed.] Secondary Modern Swindon General Nurse Training - Swindon Post Grad Tranining - Psychiatric Nursing, District Nursing Fil; [occ.] Medical Sales Executive; [memb.] Amateur Dramatics; [hon.] Amateur Dramatics; [oth. writ.] Poetry published in three volumes of modern poets.; [pers.] Inspired to write from the age of 10 and continue to find beautiful services in this changeable sometimes success world.; [a.] Watford, Herts, UK, WD2 5BY

BALDWIN, SYLVIA
[b.] 5 July 1944, Watford, Herts; [p.] Grace and Arthur Bugbee; [m.] John Baldwin, 3 October 1964; [ch.] Avril, Simon and David; [ed.] Victoria Sec. Mod. School for Girls, Watford, South West Herts College of Further Education, Watford; [occ.] Housewife and Hot Air Balloon Crew; [memb.] British Balloon and Airship Club; [oth. writ.] Several poems as yet unpublished. One 'Goodbye Gran' to be published in "Awaken To A Dream".; [pers.] In writing poetry I am expressing emotions that surface when I look at a situation, and hope others can relate to and draw comfort and pleasure.; [a.] Watford, Hertfordshire, UK, WD2 7AP

BALL, J. MARTIN
[b.] 27 March 1977, Newcastle-under-Lyne; [p.] Jean Ball, Terry Ball; [ed.] Endon High School, City of Stoke-on-Trent Sixth Form College, The University of Sheffield; [occ.] University Student; [memb.] British Sub-Aqua Club, National Student Industrial Society, Anchor Road Bowling Club; [hon.] 8 GCSE passes including Grade B English, Grade B English Literature and Grade 3 Oral Communication. 5 A level and A/

S level passes including Grade A English Language; [oth. writ.] Two poems published in West Midlands Poetry Now 1996 and 1997 anthologies.; [pers.] Life is excited by diversity. I endeavour to create this in my writings. A unique quality of reflecting harsh realism on a surreal background. Many thanks to my family, english teachers, the influence of Michael Jackson - the king of pop, and all my friends.; [a.] Stoke-on-Trent, Staffordshire, UK, ST2 7JN

BALLARD, EDNA F.
[b.] 1 January 1906, Acocks Green; [p.] Cyril and Frances Lloyd; [m.] Norman H. Ballard, 29 August 1936; [ch.] Roger L. Ballard; [ed.] Yardley Grammar School; [oth. writ.] Several poems accepted by magazines. This October my poem "Getting Old" accepted by Anchor Books for their edition of "Inspirations from the West Midlands"; [pers.] From early years I have written poems mostly for my family, special events, birthdays etc. The poems all bring back fond memories now that I am 90 years old.; [a.] Birmingham, UK, B68 9JQ

BALWAH, PRINCE
[pen.] Prince A. Laveau; [ed.] 7 London GCE passes, Diploma in Process Operation/Natural Gas Tech Financial Control/Business Administration Degrees/Cert. Counselling; [occ.] Hospitality Personnel; [memb.] Fellow: Association of Financial Control and Administration Member: Corporation of Exec. and Administrators Member: Instruments Society of America; [hon.] Mensa Challenge Certificate, honoured for work done with children 3 yrs. with Ichthus Christian Fellowship; [pers.] Life is filled with negative and positive, use every negative situation to build one's character and every positive situation to further uplift oneself. For true success comes when the generation behind progressed above you.; [a.] Nunhead, UK, SE15 3DY

BAMBROUGH, TONY
[b.] 27 March 1955; [m.] Josephine, 23 December 1975; [ch.] Two girls, Carina, Karen; [ed.] Oxted County, Military College; [occ.] Instructor in The Transport Industry; [memb.] I Mech IE, The Institution of Mechanical Incorporated Engineers; [hon.] Three Military Awards, LS and GC Medal Falklands Medal, Northern Iraq/Turkey Medal; [pers.] I try to reflect in my writing, both the suffering and hope that I have witnessed whilst operating in various places around the world.; [a.] Plympton, Devon, UK, PL1 3XQ

BARCLAY, RUTH
[b.] 21 September 1919, Bradford; [p.] Jack and Minnie Kirk; [m.] Peter Barclay, 9 August 1957; [ch.] Susan and Lee (from 1st marriage); [ed.] Marlborough School in Dewsbury and Harrogate Ladies College, Portsmouth Art School, Open University; [occ.] Retired; [memb.] The National Trust, N.A.D.F.A.S., The Ramblers Association, The Woodland Trust, RSPB, Lifeboat Institution (Life Governor), Hampshire and I.O.W. Wildlife Trust; [oth. writ.] Poem published in "Prize Winning Poetry", Highlands Arts Society; [pers.] Written many poems but have never had the confidence to offer them for publication (apart from above publication and the present Library of Poetry one.); [a.] Lee-on-Solent, Hampshire, UK, PO13 9DT

BARKER, MISS EUGENIE
[b.] 1 July 1927, Myerscough, Near Preston; [p.] Kathleen (Halstead), William Barker; [ed.] Lancaster Girl's Grammar School, St. Mary's College, Cheltenham, Glos; [occ.] Retired Teacher; [memb.] W.I., U.S.P.G., Cats Protection League, Raynaud's and Scleroderma Association; [oth. writ.] A number of poems published in various anthologies. Two published in the United States of America; [pers.] I tend to bear to writing 'Christian' poetry. I try to write a few light hearted, humorous ones too.; [a.] Carnforth, Lancashire, UK, LA5 9TA

BARNES-DOWNER, CLAIRE
[b.] 11 December 1083, Aldershot, Hants; [ed.] Schools - Waverley Abbey, Farnham, Bohunt Community School, Hants.; [occ.] Student; [pers.] I find that writing relaxes me a great deal, and through the written word I can express anything. It is my dream to see my work in print.; [a.] Liphook, Hampshire, UK, GU30 7JR

BARNETT, PAULA-JANE
[b.] 29 June 1963, Oldswinford; [p.] Kenneth Percival and Beryl Qwendoline Pethrick; [m.] Michael Barnett, 16 October 1995; [ed.] Valley Road Secondary School; [oth. writ.] Poems and novel in progress; [pers.] Through the patience of my parents and the unfailing love of my husband I have finally discovered love and contentment. I hope my writing can reflect the power given to oneself by another's faith and belief. For they open many doors within and in our future lives.; [a.] Lye, West Midlands, UK, DY9 7EY

BARRON, YVONNE MARGARET
[pen.] Yvonne Barron; [b.] 15 March 1945, Swanland; [p.] George and Doris Gant; [m.] Alan Eward Barron, 23 March 1984; [ch.] Alison, Steven, Robert; [ed.] Hessle High School, Kingston upon Hull, College of Technology; [occ.] Housewife; [memb.] Hornsea Art Society; [hon.] The British Ballet Organization, Operatic Dancing Teachers Society, awards for ballet, Trinity College of Music, London Awards for Speech City and Guilds for Hairdressing Award of Merit; [pers.] I find that writing poetry helps me to explore my more deeply felt emotions and thoughts.; [a.] Hornsea, East Yorkshire, UK, HU18 1BT

BARRY, JACQUELINE
[b.] 7 November 1964, Dagenham; [p.] Eileen Hammon and Laurence Hammon; [m.] Kevin Barry, 31 August 1985; [ch.] John, Cristi, Clark; [ed.] Robert Clack Comprehensive School; [occ.] Housewife; [pers.] Phonecall at Midnight was written following the tragic death of my cousin Keith, killed outright in a road accident in summer of '95. The driver of the car received penalty points and a fine. Keith's family received a life sentence.; [a.] Basildon, Essex, UK, SS15 5QS

BARTON, JOANNE
[b.] 1 April 1972, Rochford; [p.] Mrs. Anne Bicknell; [ed.] Comprehensive Schooling; [occ.] Bank Clerk; [pers.] My outlook on life is something far beyond that which you can physically see and optimism is they key word of life.; [a.] Southend-on-Sea, Essex, UK, SS1 2QU

BATES, MAUREEN ANNETTA
[b.] 6 February 1958, London; [p.] Constantine Bates, Olive Bates; [ed.] Silverthorne Secondary, Brixton College, West London Institute, EN, RMN, RGN, DN; [occ.] District Nurse; [memb.] Calvary Temple United Pentecostal Church, 'Conquerors Choir', Nurse's Dept. C.T.; [pers.] "Lo, this only have I found, that God hath made man upright, but they have sought out many inventions."; [a.] London, Penge, UK, SE20 7TJ

BAUGH, GARY JOHN
[b.] 1 May 1960, Woolwich, London; [p.] Terry Baugh, Jean Baugh; [m.] Deborah Jean Baugh, 26 May 1989; [ch.] Martyn, Zoe, Jonathan, Rebekah, Daniel; [ed.] Strathaven Academy, Larkhall Academy, Lanarkshire Scotland; [occ.] Day Care Officer for Learning Disabilities; [memb.] Born Again Christian; [pers.] Debbie, Mum and Dad, Sharon and Wayne thank you for believing in me; may I also now start to believe.; [a.] Billericay, Essex, UK, CM11 2AX

BAUGHAN, NICOLA
[b.] 21 August 1979, Wycombe; [p.] Michael Baughan, Pauline Baughan; [ed.] Dr. Challoners High School; [occ.] Student (A-Levels); [oth. writ.] Poems published in two other anthologies; [pers.] I believe that poetry enables the author to share those feelings that would otherwise remain buried deep inside; [a.] Chesham, Bucks, UK, HP5 2QR

BAXTER, BERNARD W. J.
[p.] Kathleen and Frank Baxter; [m.] Denise; [ch.] Tony, Graeme, Ben; [ed.] Nottingham and Leeds Universities; [occ.] Teacher and Lecturer; [hon.] Justice of the Peace; [oth. writ.] Articles on education and society, operatic play 'John' performed in Newcastle upon Tyne, various poems; [pers.] I prefer writing longer poems; [a.] Stotsford, Hexhamshire, UK, NE47 0HP

BEER, DELPHIA
[pen.] D. Beer; [b.] 28 May 1918, Minster, Kent; [p.] Fostered by Mr. and Mrs. Dennett of Bexhill on Sea; [m.] Raymond Beer, 30 December 1972 (2nd marriage); [ch.] 9, 6 girls and 3 boys; [ed.] Elementary and self-educated; [occ.] Housewife; [memb.] Was a member of Wandsworth Fostering. I used to foster teenage lads; I have an autistic son.; [oth. writ.] I have a poem to be published in a book "On the Ball" about X'mas time. I have been asked also to write an article on the old times of Bexhill on Sea (how it has changed).; [pers.] Kipling, Dickens: I love reading their poems. They have stories in them. I find many ordinary people like this kind. Because they understand them. I like writing this kind as well.; [a.] Crawling, West Sx, UK, RH11 0DN

BEEVERS, MARGOT COLLINGBOURN
[b.] 2 February 1931, London; [p.] Grace Collingbourn, Robert George Brown; [m.] John Nigel Beevers, 20 August 1975; [ch.] Pauline Mary, David Christopher, James Robert Gerard, Madeline Mary Carmel; [ed.] Brondesbury and Kilburn High School for Girls, Garnett College, Univ. of London, Birkbeck College Univ. of London, Birkbeck College, Univ. of London, Brunel University; [occ.] Part-time Lecturer (Retired former College Principal) Running courses for rehabilitation for mental health clients (Social Services); [memb.] Royal Horticultural Society, Royal Academy, National Trust, Formerly: Royal Society of Arts, British Institute of Management, Dyslexia Association for Teachers; [hon.] MA, Dip Ed, FRSA, MEIM; [oth. writ.] Winner of poetry competition in Times Educational Supplement, Contributor to local poetry anthology, Contributor to Business Magazines; [pers.] My writing of poetry is always influenced by a.) a sense of the 'magic' existing in certain word relationships and b.) a personal religion/metaphysical sense of 'being'. I have been exhilarated by John Donne, Gerard Mandy Horkins and Dylan Thomas.; [a.] Cheltenham, Gloucestershire, UK, GL50 2EZ

BEGLEY, LYNN
[b.] 20 June 1968, Elderslie; [p.] Allan Ferrier, Betty Ferrier; [m.] Tommy Begley, 24 June 1995; [ed.] Park Mains High School, Clyde Bank College, Langside College; [occ.] Nursery Officer, The Glen Children's Centre; [oth. writ.] Short story for nursery age children published in "Nursery World" magazine, poem "Father of the Bride" published in book "Poetry Now Scotland 1997."; [pers.] My writing is inspired by personal experiences and the love I have of working with children. "Imagination is infinite, when seen through the eyes of a child"; [a.] Kilwinning, Ayrshire, UK, KA13 7JZ

BEGUM, FATEHA
[b.] 14 January 1981; [p.] A. Motlib and B. L. Khanom; [ed.] Denbigh High; [hon.] Won Bedfordshire (French) Poetry Competition; [oth. writ.] Collection of poems for my own keeping; [pers.] I compile different thoughts and views of mankind in my writing. I would like to thank my family and friends for influencing me to write.; [a.] Luton, Bedfordshire, UK, LU1 5QH

BEGUM, JUSNA
[b.] 15 November 1982, Northampton; [p.] Mr. Tera Miah, Mrs. Jahanara Begum; [occ.] A pupil at Trinity Upper School Northampton; [memb.] Was a member of the school netball team in previous middle school called St. Georges Middle School N'pton; [hon.] A medal was awarded to my netball team and myself for coming third at a girls' netball tournament held at Kings Health All Weather Pitch in April 1996.; [a.] Northampton, Northamptonshire, UK, NN1 3BG

BEGUM, SHANTY
[b.] 11 July 1979, Rochdale; [p.] Mr. Abdul Bark and Mrs. Kachon Bibi; [ed.] Howarth Cross Middle School, Falinge Park High School, and at present at Oulder Hill Community School, 6th Form.; [occ.] A full-time student, Studying 'A' levels at Oulder Hill 6th form.; [a.] Rochdale, Lancs, UK, OL16 2JS

BEISSER, SANDRA ELIZABETH
[b.] 4 January 1978, Cambridge; [p.] Brenda and Philip Beisser; [ed.] Sandy Upper School; [occ.] Part-time news agent; [memb.] Lonely Planet Publications (for whom I plan to write articles, when I travel around the world); [oth. writ.] I've written short stories and various poems, but "the travel bug" is unique in that I've never shown my work to anyone, previously.; [pers.] I use poetry to pinpoint everyday issues that need to be acknowledged rather than ignored. The poetry of Sylvia Plath has greatly influenced my work.; [a.] Sandy, Bedfordshire, UK, SG19 1EB

BELL, GILLIAN
[b.] 24 August 1979, South Shields; [p.] Lynda Bell, Leonard Bell; [ed.] King George Comprehensive School; [occ.] Electrical Engineer; [oth. writ.] Poems published in an anthology and small children's book; [pers.] I write poetry for my own pleasure but it is an even greater pleasure when other people read and enjoy it.; [a.] South Shields, Tyne and Wear, UK, NE34 8HR

BENACS, PHILIPPA C.
[pen.] Philippa Benacs; [b.] 7 May 1944, Birkenhead; [p.] William G. Townson and Ethel Townson; [m.] George Benacs, 14 June 1986; [ch.] Mark Edward, Kathryn Jane; [ed.] Secondary school and Carlet Park College of Further Education; [occ.] Rest Home Proprietress, Bunkers Bounty Rest Home; [pers.] To share one's thoughts with others through the expression of rhyme can be truly gratifying.; [a.] Blackpool, Lancashire, UK, FY6 9AN

BENNETT, DAVID
[b.] 26 April 1954, Belfast; [p.] James and Elizabeth; [m.] Fiona, 14 May 1994; [ch.] Andrew English (Stepson); [ed.] Regent House Grammar Queens University Belfast; [occ.] Certified Accountant; [memb.] Chartered Association of Certified Accountants, Society of Insduency Practitioners; [pers.] Say (write) what you mean.; [a.] Comber, Down, UK, BT23 5ES

BENNETT, LAR
[b.] 12 June 1969, Newcastle upon Tyne; [p.] Dorothy Jean Burdis and Ralph Burdis; [m.] Benji Bennett, 10 December 1993; [ch.] Sophia Bennett; [ed.] Heworth Grange Comprehensive; [occ.] Florist; [pers.] Be true to yourself and happiness will follow.; [a.] Elgi, Moray, UK, IV30 2TF

BENOY, KENNETH
[b.] 5 April 1920, Plymouth; [p.] Lievt. William Benoy MBE, Katie Benoy RN; [m.] Rosemary Benoy, 4 June 1954; [ed.] Southern Polytechnic, Portsmouth School of Architecture; [occ.] Retired; [memb.] A.R.I.B.A. (Resigned) on retirement 1987; [oth. writ.] Poems included in many anthologies by Poetry Now W. Midlands and Anchor Books of Forwards Press; [pers.] Influenced by an artist, Russian mother, my life has been dominated by the arts. After serving in the army in India in World War II, I qualified as an architect in '52 and on my retirement in '86 returned to my first love of painting but on being reg. blind in '93 I began writing poetry.; [a.] Solihull, West Midlands, UK, B93 8DW

BERE, GWYNETH M.
[b.] Plymouth; [p.] Gwyneth J. Morris and Frederick W. Lewis; [m.] Thomas G. Bere (Deceased), 23 December 1963; [ed.] Saltash Grammar School, Cornwall, London University, University of Wales; [occ.] Retired English Teacher (schools); [memb.] Plymouth Athenaeum M.E.N.S.A. (1964) Assoc. of Stress Consultants, National Federation Spiritual Healers; [hon.] Teacher's Cert. London University, Associate of College of Preceptors, London (A.C.P.) fellow of College of Receptors, London (F.C.P.) Diploma in Art and Craft University of Wales; [oth. writ.] 50,000 word bound thesis on the development of schools in Plymouth from 1571 to 1972 (F.C.P.) (Educ. History Research); [pers.] "The creative and intuitive side of ourselves helps us to be at peace and calm."; [a.] Plymouth, Devon, UK, PL6 6AZ

BHASI, MAVILA KUNJUSANKARAN
[b.] 22 April 1930, India; [p.] Kunjusankaran and Bharathi; [m.] Suleikha Bhasi, 1956; [ch.] Three Rajeev, Rinam Renu; [ed.] B. Sc. (Chemistry); [occ.] Retd. Vice-Principal Ministry of Education, Singapore; [memb.] Member, Society of Singapore writers; [hon.] Kerala Kari Samajam Award - 1995, Outstanding Malayalee Award for contribution with distinction to the Singapore Malayalee Community - 1993 from the Singapore Kerala Association, Kaumudi Award for poetry - 1952; [oth. writ.] Rainbows - Collection of poems in Malayalam, Ajanta - collection of poems in Malayalam; [a.] Singapore, 575019

BHATTI, SUKAWANT
[b.] 5 December 1979, Southampton; [p.] Narinjan Singh Bhatti and Suhag Wanti; [ed.] Regents Park girls school nine GCSE passes including English and English Literature and History; [occ.] Working in the Dispensary in Oceanic Chemistry (not perminent); [pers.] I find writing out feelings poetically, not only helps you feel better but creates beautiful emotional poetry, too.; [a.] Southampton, Hampshire, UK, SO14 0BP

BICKNELL, THOMAS GEORGE
[pen.] Rocky; [b.] 1 August 1941, Balham; [p.] Tom and Maisie; [m.] Ann Josephine, 26 March 1968; [ch.] Ken, Jason, Melanie; [ed.] Secondary Modern School, Tranmere Road Earlsfield SW18, No 'O' or 'A' levels; [occ.] Security Officer Stationary Office Vauxhaul 51 Nine Elms Lane; [memb.] R.A.O.B. Ye Olde Oxford Lodge, The Poetry Society, C.I.U member, Qualified Boxing Instructor A.B.A, First Aid Certificate; [hon.] Poem accepted for, and printed, in 'Passage in Time' (Anth), Editor's Choice Award (Cert), City and Guilds in Security (S.I.T.O.), article printed of achievement in Wandsworth Boro News on my sonnet, for a Passage in Time. I have written over fifty sonnets so far, and, other poems. I myself have only been writing poetry for about three years.; [pers.] Every poet, is a gem on their own as is the same, with a painter your talent, from God, is on loan. Give of your best, now, not later. My main influence is Shakespeare.; [a.] Battersea, London, UK, 2BA

BIGGS, PATRICIA
[b.] 3 December 1937, Sheffield; [p.] Thomas and Nellie Holland; [m.] Ronald Biggs, 28 June 1958; [ch.] Steven Andrew, Adrian Paul; [ed.] Whitby Road, Secondary Modern School; [occ.] Housewife/Carer; [pers.] My poem was a release from pent up feelings, after caring for children with special needs for eighteen years, and my mother who has suffered several strokes, the poem is for her; [a.] Rotherham, South Yorkshire, UK, S63 7JL

BINGLEY, GARY
[pen.] Gary Bingley; [b.] 17 May 1955, Shipley; [p.] Arthur Bingley, Joan Bingley; [m.] Lorraine, 5 July 1980; [ch.] Gavin David, Christopher John; [ed.] Bradford Boys, Grammar School; [occ.] Civil Servant, H.M. Inspector of Taxes;

[memb.] British Mensa Since 1989; [oth. writ.] 2 pieces in the school magazine; [pers.] I believe the importance of the written word cannot be overstated, and the timeless beauty of poetry will shine like a beacon when all seems darkness, bringing inspiration across the years.; [a.] Shipley, West Yorkshire, UK, BD18 3BZ

BIRCHENOUGH, SUSAN A.
[pen.] Suzette Raw; [b.] 15 September 1956, Lancs; [p.] Deceased; [m.] Dr. Paul Birchenough, 3 June 1989; [ch.] Jennie (21), and Chris (18); [ed.] Comprehensive to sixth form Army Training (WRAC) World Travel With The Army. Oxford College 3 yrs. to certified social work (as a mature student); [occ.] Proprietor Home Care Agency, Counselor and Advocate; [memb.] Full Member of United Kingdom Home Care Association; [hon.] No major awards to date; [oth. writ.] Various radio readings and internal social work magazines. First book "A Student Of Life" is almost ready and I will be seeking a publisher.; [pers.] As a child of the 50's and one of eight children, my life has been hard; my parents cruel and my environment aire. I write to control these experiences and to go forward. Positively.; [a.] Didcot, Oxfordshire, UK, OX11 9RN

BIRKENFELD, JENNY FRAUKE
[pen.] Jenny B. Gall; [b.] 20 August 1964, Kirchheim/Teck; [p.] Rose Birkenfeld, Max Birkenfeld; [ed.] Morike - Gymnasium, Ludwigsburg Stuttgart University, Inlingua Language School; [occ.] Foreign-Language Secretary; [memb.] Greenpeace, Animal Welfare, Singer with German Band "Mystery", MTV Jazz dance group "thirty-up"; [hon.] Various prizes at school competitions (writings, sports, photography); [oth. writ.] Song-lyrics for "Mystery", various unpublished poems and stories, readers' letters published in newspapers and motorsport magazines.; [pers.] Writing, to me, is the best way to convey my deepest wishes, thoughts, feelings and also social criticism to a society that has largely lost its sense for real beauty in a world reigned by materialism and blind consumption.; [a.] Ludwigsburg, Germany, 71638

BISHOP, ELSPETH
[pen.] Elspeth George; [b.] 2 March 1938, Shadox Hurst; [p.] Edwin Beeching, Emily Beeching; [m.] Peter Bishop, 29 March 1958; [ch.] Ian George, Peter John; [ed.] Local Primary School, Ashford Technical College; [occ.] Laundry Assistant at Benenden School; [oth. writ.] My Brother, My Dream, Yellow Is My Colour, all poems, none published; [a.] Cranbrook, Kent, TN18 5PU

BISHOP, LAURA L.
[b.] 28 February 1980, Norwich; [p.] Angela Bishop and John Bishop; [ed.] Earlham High School, West Norwich Sixth Farm; [occ.] Student; [oth. writ.] Poem published in school prospectus; [a.] Norwich, Norfolk, UK, NR5 9DQ

BISS, MISS KATIE SARAH
[b.] July 5 1984, Hounslow; [p.] Paul Biss, Gaynor Biss; [ed.] Longford Community School, Bedfont Middx; [occ.] Pupil; [memb.] Bedfont United Foot-ball Club for Girls; [oth. writ.] School Magazines, Local Paper; [pers.] I love to write about cats, after losing my beloved cat, Fred, my poems are based on personal observations.; [a.] Feltham, Middx, TW14 0DB

BLACKMAN, STEVE
[b.] 9 October 1959, Crowborough; [occ.] Railway Sales Person, Connex South Central, Crowborough; [oth. writ.] Editor/Compiler Oxted line newsletter. Poems and stories in various railway publications.; [pers.] Attempt to stir the soul by putting pen to paper.; [a.] Crowborough, East Sussex, UK, TN6 1JH

BLAKELY, MRS. JACQUELINE
[b.] 21 March 1935, Colchester; [p.] Freda and William Summerbee; [m.] Donald Blakely, 16

April 1991, Widowed 25 August 1994; [ed.] Edgehill College, Bideford, Devon, North East Essex Technical College, where I qualified with secretarial diploma and "O" levels. Rolle College, Exmouth - teaching diploma; [occ.] After teaching in Chelmsford, Germany and Wiltshire, retired 1983; [memb.] Hyde and Frogham WI - which leaves little time for other things.; [oth. writ.] Stories for children; [pers.] Hobbies - knitting, crochet, cross stitch. Now living in the New Forest; [a.] Fordingbridge, Hants, UK, SP6 2QH

BLAKENEY, MAVIS
[b.] 7 November 1937, Cambridge; [p.] Walter Maltby, Helen Maltby; [ch.] Ian Geoffrey, Helen Carole, Wendy Mavis; [memb.] Spiritual Church, Sequence, Line, Dancing; [pers.] Life's experiences, it is not what you go through, your just reward comes from how you have dealt with it.; [a.] Cambridge, Cambridgeshire, UK, CB4 2NP

BLEWDEN, ANDREW
[pen.] Blue-Rab; [b.] 11 June 1981, South Wales; [p.] Carol; [ed.] Blackwood Comprehensive School; [occ.] Student - GCSE's; [memb.] Army Cadets; [oth. writ.] Poetry: Speed Demon, The Appointment, All News is Bad News Now, and several others for G.C.S.E. English. Short story: The Haunted House.; [pers.] All experiences in life are never wasted, they make us more tolerant beings. I look around me and strive to succeed.; [a.] Blackwood, Gwent, UK, NP2 0SF

BLUNDEN, VERONICA ANNE
[b.] 28 September 1957, Chertsey; [p.] Fredrick and Patricia Cooling; [ch.] Stephen and Karen Blunden; [ed.] St. Pauls Addlestone SY; [occ.] Healing Consultant; [memb.] N.F.S.H. and The Addlestone Healing Centre; [oth. writ.] Many yet to be published.; [pers.] My poems are written in communication with my sole. Reflecting my understandings of this time. And as all things change from moment to moment they are but one moment in time.; [a.] Addlestone, Surrey, UK, KT15 2HH

BLUNDUN, SHEILA
[b.] 3 July 1930, Surbiton, Surrey; [p.] Bernard Blundun, Nora Blundun; [ed.] Clark's College, Romford, Essex; [occ.] Retired; [oth. writ.] Autobiography "I Chose To Live" was asked to write this, as she was the oldest person in this country to have a hole in the heart operation in 1957, the pioneering days, at Guy's Hospital, London; [pers.] The miracle being that she had survived 27 years with this condition. It was her own will power and the love and care of her parents.; [a.] Exmouth, Devon, UK, EX8 3BX

BOLEYN, LYNN E.
[b.] 21 September 1957, Kidderminster; [p.] Ted and Edith Boleyn; [ch.] Benjamine Edwin Boleyn (20 January 1996); [ed.] Bilston Girls High School; [occ.] Secretary Midland Bank PLC. Stourbridge; [pers.] Interested in emotional romantic poems and songs.; [a.] Wall Heath, West Midlands, UK, DY6 0HS

BOLTON, WILLIAM
[b.] 28 August 1957, Blantyre; [p.] Thomas K. Bolton, Jane Craig Honeyman; [m.] Nancy Hargrave-Bolton, 28 June 1980; [ch.] Murray William, Graeme Thomas; [ed.] Bellshill Academy, Motherwell College, Coatbridge College; [occ.] Warehouse Supervisor, Salvesen Food Logistics Bellshill; [memb.] Institute of Logistics (Amilog); [hon.] C.P.C. National; [oth. writ.] None published before in this form: Poem was printed in Motherwell F.G. Match Day Magazine Jan. '86 to celebrate centenary of Motherwell F.G. other titles "Silent Outcry" and "On The Other Side" influenced by my belief of man's search for immortality.; [pers.] I believe that there is goodness, even in evil, and that there exists a greater force than we can imagine guiding our destiny. I believe all men and women are equal.; [a.] Mossend, Bellshill, Lanarkshire, UK, ML4 2RL

BONES, MARTIN FRANCIS
[b.] 8 November 1938, Ilford, Essex; [p.] George Henry and Bridget May; [ed.] St. Peter and Paul, Ilford, St. Ignatius College, N15; [pers.] The three hardest things that ever were known begging, borrowing or receiving one's own!; [a.] Braunton, North Devon, UK

BONES, STEPHANIE KAREN
[b.] 27 December 1960, Dartford; [p.] Mr. and Mrs. P. Young; [m.] Kenneth Leslie, 16 February 1991; [ch.] Marc and Tracey Mercer; [ed.] Attended Uptergrove Public School in Canada. Then O.D.C.V.I High School in Orillia, Ontario, Canada; [occ.] Housewife; [memb.] Belong to Poetry Now and the National Poetry Society, Betterton Street, London; [oth. writ.] Have had another poem "Distant Love" printed in anthology "Between a laugh and a tear" and "Oh! for the vanity of man" in anthology "Respect Too". Careless Creature published in "Politically Correct" by anchor books; [pers.] Writing to me is a form of relaxation and let my inner feelings escape.; [a.] Saint Leonards, East Sussex, UK, TN37 7BX

BOTTER, ALEIDA EATON
[b.] 9 October 1946, Den Helder-Holland; [p.] Abraham and Gladys Botter; [m.] Divorced, 1965; [ch.] Darren, Joanne and Daniel; [ed.] Elliott Comprehensive School - Roehampton, Blacknell Technical College; [occ.] Company Director; [hon.] Qualified as part time youth worker and youth counselor; [oth. writ.] Only written for my own pleasure; [pers.] I find writing poetry very therapeutic especially in times of extreme stress; [a.] Wokingham, Berkshire, UK, RG40 1TN

BOULTON, JANET
[b.] 21 March 1949, Bognor Regis; [p.] Olive Boulton, Frederick Boulton; [ed.] Villa Maria in Bognor Regis; [occ.] Police Officer; [memb.] British Horse Society; [oth. writ.] A few poems published by small pointers.; [pers.] Money and possessions are not the route to happiness, they can help, but happiness comes from within. The more you put into life, the more you get out of it.; [a.] Billingshur St, Sussex, UK

BOURSNELL, SALLY
[b.] 6 April 1976, Chelmsford; [p.] Thelma Boursnell, Alan Boursnell; [ed.] Boswells Comprehensive; [occ.] Sales Assistant for 'Andys Records'; [oth. writ.] Unpublished as yet: 1.15 am, Occurrences, The Uncertainty of Preference, The Absence of Light, This Perfect Illusion, A Certain State of Perfection; [pers.] I wish for people to see my writing as an open and honest account of my own personal reality. "Do not seize my mind without consent, it makes more sense to be in my trust".; [a.] Chelmsford, Essex, UK

BOWDEN, MARY
[b.] 19 September 1917, Warrington, UK; [p.] Aaron Veale, Emily Tyrrell; [m.] Harold Bowden, 11 August 1939; [ch.] Gerald; [ed.] Warrington High School; [occ.] Housewife and carer, husband in wheelchair for ten years; [memb.] St. James Church Warrington; [oth. writ.] Articles accepted in three magazines; [pers.] Met so many loving, caring people over the last ten years. In my writings tried to express how much kindness still abounds in the world.; [a.] Warrington, Cheshire, UK, WA4 6AL

BOWEN, LUCINDA
[b.] 28 March 1980, London; [p.] Steve and Amber Bowen; [ed.] Holy Cross Convent School, New Malden, Surrey; [occ.] A-level student; [memb.] The Royal Mail Stamp Collectors Club; [pers.] The essence and concept behind my poetry stems from the ability I have to empathize with others, and my general awareness of my emotions. I want people to find my poems challenging towards issues, but at the same time amiable.; [a.] Cheam, Surrey, UK, SM2 7LN

BOYLE, MR. FINNAN
[b.] 1 October 1960, London; [p.] Patrick Boyle, Therese Boyle; [ed.] Maths School Rochester, Dominican College, Portstewart, Manchester University, Magee College, University of Ulster; [occ.] Artist; [memb.] RoeValley Arts Society Limavady, Coleraine Art Society, NI; Town Planning Community Development; [oth. writ.] Several poems published by Anchor books, Peterborough; [pers.] I strive to highlight social issues. I have been influenced by the social writers of the Victorian Era.; [a.] Limavady, Londonderry, UK, BT4 9AT

BOYLE, KATIE L.
[b.] 13 August 1982, St. Joseph's Orange, CA; [p.] Steve and Trish Burgess; [ed.] Freshman in High School (9th grade); [occ.] Student (minority-14 yrs. old) and First Sergeant/Teach Sgt 88 - USAF Auxiliary; [memb.] Zoological Society, Civil Air Patrol (United States Air force Auxiliary), Aircraft Owners Pilots Association, El Toro Aero Club, El Toro Marine Base; [hon.] Gate Gifted and Talented education program, 6 November 1996 American Legion School Award for Community Service, 6/96 Presidential Education Awards for outstanding Academic Achievement, 6/96 Outstanding Student of the Year award in Art, 6/96 Cadet of the Year - Civil Air Patrol United States Air Force Auxiliary, 10 February 1996 - Science Student of the Month, San Clemente High School; [oth. writ.] Numerous poems - unpublished.; [pers.] Of the many components of life, love is what affects my decisions, it is the basis on which everything is built and the thing upon which everything depends.; [a.] San Clemente, Orange County, CA, 92673

BRADBURN, FRANCES E.
[pen.] Frances Nelson; [b.] 19 June 1939, Manchester; [p.] Joseph/Eileen Wright; [m.] Roy Bradburn, 31 July 1965; [ch.] Jonathan, Jeremy and Joanne; [ed.] With the F.C.J. nuns at the Catholic Grammar School for girls in Fallowfield - Manchester.; [occ.] Lecturer in further education; [memb.] Photographic Society Music Society; [hon.] I was the North West "Mum of the Year" in 1993, I was invited to Buckingham Palace - to the Garden Party to celebrate 150 years of public education date 1989; [oth. writ.] A poem about our pet cat was published three years ago in a national magazine; [pers.] I strive to find the goodness which exists in each one of us. I treasure my family and friends and my world is a better place because they are in it; [a.] Southport, Merseyside, UK, PR8 2RG

BRADFORD, MARY P.
[b.] 23 February 1943, London; [p.] Agnes and Charles Harris; [m.] Roy Bradford, 17 February 1962; [ch.] Kim, Robbie and Kerry; [ed.] Fairmead Secondary M. School, Loughton, Essex; [occ.] Housewife; [oth. writ.] Inspirations from favourite poets, patience strong, Robert Burns.; [a.] Buckhurst Hill, Essex, UK, IG9 6JX

BRADLEY, DHE
[b.] 24 October 1927, Swindon, Wints; [ed.] Retired; [oth. writ.] 'Taking the Epistle' 1985: Poetry Merlin Books Ltd. Braunton Devon. 'More Moronic Rubbish' 1986. Merlin Books Ltd Poetry, 'Nutty Notions' 1986. Poetry Merlin Books Ltd., 'Random Ruminations' verse. 1987. Vantage Press Inc. NSW York 10001; [pers.] 'A Wealth of Words', 'A Diet of Dictionary'; [a.] Cheltenham, Glos, UK, GL53 0NB

BRADLEY, TONY PATRICK
[pen.] Tony Patrick Bradley; [b.] 25 November 1950, Plymouth; [p.] James and Queenie Bradley; [m.] (Widowed) Sandra Mary, 31 March 1970; [ed.] Secondary Modern (Quernsey) City and Guilds Construction Technician (With Credit); [occ.] Semi-Retired Commercial Artist/Design Consultant; [memb.] Man UTD. Supporters Club; [hon.] None (except C and G above) Runner-up in local poetry competition

(not Poem), Prize Winner in local letter writing competition, Story writing prizes in Junior School; [oth. writ.] Nothing submitted for publishing; [pers.] I was badly abused as a child in a 'respectable' family and bore the mental scars into my teens, but was lucky to meet and love a caring person, whose devotion and needs released me from my traumas and phobias and instilled true values in me.; [a.] Guernsey, Channel Islands, GY4 6DU

BRADY, JEAN MARY
[b.] 19 October 1950, Bark Island, West Yorkshire; [p.] Pauline and James Wheelwright; [m.] Divorced; [ch.] Gail Louise, Diane Carol, Kathryn Rose, Christopher Michael, (Grandson Arron Halton); [ed.] The Grammar School, Elland, W. Yorkshire, Manchester Metropolitan University; [occ.] Teacher (of English); [hon.] BA (Hons) Degree Humanities/Social Science. Presently completing first year of MA - History of the Manchester Area; [oth. writ.] Picture script stories for children, children's poetry and stories - 'Twinkle' comic and 'Perples Friend' have published my work. A poem accepted for publication by the International Library of Poetry for a previous anthology.; [pers.] The best poetry comes from the heart - when the writer has something important to say and to share.; [a.] Gorton, Greater Manchester, UK, M18 8DH

BRADY, PAUL
[b.] August 7, 1955, Derby; [p.] Vincent Brady, Marie Brady; [ch.] Toni Louise, Haydn, Mark-Anthony; [ed.] Sturgess Comprehensive; [occ.] Full time Dad single parent; [pers.] Take life as it comes; [a.] Derby, Derbyshire, DE22 3WD

BRAHMBHATT, SEETA
[b.] 4 May 1982, Harrow, Middx, UK; [p.] Bali Brahmbhatt, Shiela Brahmbhatt; [ed.] Preparing for my 'GCSES' studying in Hatchend High School in year 10; [occ.] Student; [hon.] Swimming and Indian Classical Dancing Awards; [oth. writ.] "Is There Something Wrong With Me" is my first ever poem; [pers.] 'It's fun to do something you enjoy doing. It's fun being able to express views and feelings.' 'Poetry is fun!'; [a.] Harrow, Middlesex, UK, HA1 1TN

BRAILSFORD, DEAN MARC
[pen.] Dean Marc Brailsford; [b.] 12 December 1971, Worksop; [p.] Mick Brailsford, Jean Brailsford; [ed.] Clowne Comprehensive Clowne College, Chesterfield College, Manchester University; [memb.] Equity; [pers.] What we are today comes from our thoughts of yesterday and our present thoughts build our life of tomorrow. I am influenced by my mother in my work and thinking.; [a.] Worksop, Nottinghamshire, UK, S80 4QB

BRAITHWAITE, LYNNE JANINE
[b.] 1 July 1934, Nr Sawrey, Hawkshead, Lancashire; [p.] George and Elizabeth Braithwaite (Deceased); [ed.] Hawkshead County Primary School, Royal Airforce; [occ.] Retired/Unemployed ex Royal Airforce (39 1/2 yrs.); [memb.] "All now ceased", Society of Licensed Aircraft Engineers and Technologists. Jim Russell Racing Drivers School (Snetterton) Institute of Advanced Motorists. Registered Silver Smith-Sheffield Assay Office. Royal Airforces Association; [hon.] Long service a good conduct medal with clasp. British Empire Medal; [oth. writ.] Non published! 1. An Ode to Life or Two Into One Will Go 2. The Cards 3. An Ode to Survival 4. To Aunty Doris 5. What Patients Charter? L.J.B. Life Vol. 1 Vol. 2 Vol. 3 In progress of being written; [pers.] Being born and educated in the Hawkshead area of the Lake District gives one a real sense of beauty that lives with you forever. This followed by 39 1/2 yrs. in the R.A.F. suitably enhanced my education in the "University of Life". Undergoing a change of gender at the age of 59 1/2 compels one to look in great depth at one's life, past, present, and future.; [a.] Morecambe, Lancashire, UK

BRAUN, GABRIELLA
[b.] 12 October 1970, Plymouth; [p.] Rosemary Braun, Gerhard Braun; [ed.] Devonport High School for Girls, Plymouth University of the West of England, Bristol; [occ.] Reporting Administrator, BT; [hon.] BSC (Hons) Construction Management; [pers.] Writing provides me with immense pleasure, and enables me to escape the stresses and strains of everyday life. I like to lose myself in my imagination.; [a.] Bristol, UK, BS12 7HT

BRAZIER, DEBBIE JEAN
[b.] 5 November 1964, Shropshire; [p.] Kathleen Copsey, Michael Copsey, Phillip Brazier; [ed.] John Hunt School - Comprehensive, School of Nursing - Kingston Hospital; [occ.] Senior Staff Nurse, Day Surgery Unit - Royal Gwent Hospital; [pers.] I began writing poetry as a teenager, for pleasure, as a means of expression and at times a reflection of personal experiences, keeping all hidden from view. I am thrilled, now that I have let others see my work, to be published and the pleasure of writing will be ever greater now.; [a.] Newport, Gwent, UK, NP9 0BS

BRENNAN, SUSAN ANN
[b.] 11 March 1959; [p.] John Gould and Margaret Gould; [m.] Frank Brennan, 27 October 1984; [ch.] Sarah Veronica, Gareth Francis; [ed.] Hillstone Primary and Junior School, Longmeadow Girls Secondary School. At present home correspondence course, with writing school, London; [occ.] Mother, Housewife and Student; [hon.] Two Editor's Choice Awards presented by The International Society of Poets; [oth. writ.] Published in, Poetry Now anthology 1995, Rhythms of Love - love is all around - 1996 British Poetry Review - Mystical Wanderings - A Passage in Time - Poetry Now magazine - The Other Side of the Mirror - Funny and Strange Situation - Images of Thought - 1996 Summer Poetry Review; [pers.] Poetry enables me to express my most inner thoughts and feelings. And I always strive to perfect a distinct originality in my own written work.; [a.] Birmingham, West Midlands, UK, B34 7SD

BRETT, PATRICK
[b.] 5 May 1960, Liverpool; [p.] Henry Brett, Patricia Brett; [m.] Carole Maddock, 20 November 1992; [ed.] St. Mary's Grammar School for Boys - Liverpool, Huddersfield Polytechnic, Leeds University Business School; [occ.] Personnel Manager; [memb.] Member of the Institute of Personnel and Development, Great Crosby Great Local Poets Society; [oth. writ.] Priest - King, Rest, My Brother's Garden, Mansion House, Musselmen - The Soothsayer Way; [pers.] Blessed are the meek for they shall inherit the earth.; [a.] Birkenhead, Merseyside, UK, L43 8ST

BROADHIRST, ELIZABETH
[pen.] Elizabeth Broadhirst; [b.] 25 March 1984, Leeds; [p.] Roslind Broadhirst; [ed.] Cardinal High School Second Year (year 8); [occ.] School girl; [hon.] Poetry award, Art award; [oth. writ.] Other poetry; [pers.] My artistic nature tends to make me aware of environmental issues. I'm also very much a family girl.; [a.] Leeds, UK, LS8 2NT

BROOKES, TIMOTHY
[b.] 16 January 1980, Davyhulme; [p.] Jerry Brookes, Janice Brookes; [ed.] J. J. Sale Moor Technology College; [occ.] Student; [oth. writ.] Growing collection of poetry and short stories.; [pers.] Poetry helps us all escape conformative society and explore the creative imagination which is often forgotten.; [a.] Davyhulme, Manchester, UK, M41 8DF

BROOKS, THELMA JOY
[b.] 13 March 1936, Birkenhead; [p.] John Olive Murphy; [ch.] John Debra; [ed.] Kirklands Secondary School "Ornum College" Birkenhead Nursing and social work with children; [occ.] Caring for mother; [hon.] O'level English; [oth.

writ.] Children's poems, local paper short story published in national magazine. I hope to write a book titled, Somewhere Under the Rainbow, my experiences of preparing the way for Christian Radio UCB.; [pers.] From an early age I loved books. I was encouraged by my mother to work for the benefit of mankind.; [a.] Newcastle under Lyme, Staffordshire, UK, ST5 2SY

BROSCH, MISS MARIE B.
[b.] 30 April 1965, Bradford; [p.] Mary and John Brosch; [oth. writ.] To my Dad, John Brosch, I want to say thanks for all the happy times we had together. Miss you every day, God Bless, from your loving daughter. Marie Brosch.; [a.] Belfast, Northern Ireland, BT11 8BL

BROTHERTON, ANNETTE
[b.] 24 October 1937, Birmingham; [p.] Winifred and Eric Brotherton; [ed.] Convent School Birmingham Road Sutton Coldfield, St Joseph's Kenilworth; [occ.] Unemployed but I was in UDU, operator at Delta Metal Company Nechels, Birmingham; [pers.] This is my own work and writing. I hope my work will be successful.; [a.] Castle, Vale Bham, UK, B35 7HS

BROUGHTON, MALCOLM CARL
[pen.] Xanadu; [b.] January 1956, Scunthorpe; [ed.] Frederick Gough Grammar, Birmingham Polytechnic; [occ.] Maintenance Electrician; [oth. writ.] 1989, The Axeman Cometh, Cinderella and the Three Bears, (none published/printed); [a.] Wednesbury, W. Midlands, UK, WS10 7SL

BROUW, THEA OPDEN
[pen.] Tristen Niknar; [b.] 12 September 1982, In An Ambulance; [p.] Leo Opden Brouw, Kim Opden Brouw; [ed.] Mallacoota College; [occ.] Student; [memb.] Youth Sports Club, Mallacoota Surf Riders Club; [oth. writ.] One other poem printed in local book called "Inlet"; [pers.] Don't follow the world, follow your dream. If that fails, trust your heart and follow love wherever it may take you; [a.] Mallacoota, Australia, 3892

BROWN, MRS. IRENE SYLVIA
[b.] 17 March 1916, London; [p.] Alfred and Lily Williams; [m.] Frederick Charles Brown, 13 August 1949; [ed.] Carlisle Secondary, Chelsea, S.W.3, London; [occ.] Retired; [memb.] Harpenden Society RSPCA - RSPB - MENCAP - I grow plants for the charities selling them at their fairs and bazaars; [oth. writ.] Autobiography, One Woman's War, Poems - Falling Bombs - Falling Sight - Grief For A Sticken Farm - Requiem For Sammy - Finale - Ballerina Assoluta - Waterferry; [pers.] I grow older and sadder because of the crime, cruelty, viciousness in this lovely world. We are nearing the year two thousand and should have learned by now how to live amicably and peacefully one with another.; [a.] Harpenden, Hertfordshire, UK, AL5 3AG

BROWN, JEAN
[b.] 15 February 1948, Burnley, Lancs; [p.] Jennie and Denis Smith (Divorced); [ch.] Son - Andrew James; [ed.] 6 A Levels, Diploma and Art and Design Member Royal Photographic Society; [occ.] Business owner; [memb.] Member Business Professional Women; [oth. writ.] None published; [pers.] "I cannot know what you know unless you tell me."; [a.] Simonstone, Lancashire, UK, BB12 7NX

BROWN, SARAH HELEN
[pen.] Kia Sampson; [b.] 25 September 1944, Oswestry; [p.] Reginald Sampson, M. Helen Sampson; [m.] Gerald O. Brown (Deceased 1968); [ch.] Rowena Helen and Alistair Allen; [ed.] Oswestry Girls High School, Cartrefle Teacher Training College, P.E. and English; [occ.] Sport Instructor (Sale and Altrincham Leisure Centre); [memb.] Altrincham Golf Club, Timperley Tennis, Forest Badminton Club, Rostherne

School of Equitation; [hon.] Lady Captain - Altrincham Golf, many awards for sporting activities, A.R.B.H. Award for Excellence; [oth. writ.] Rhyming pictures books for children (yet to be published), verses commissioned by friends for special occasions.; [pers.] My poems reflect my own experiences of life and of those dear to me.; [a.] Altrincham, Cheshire, UK, WA15 6QU

BRUCE, MRS. GAYLE
[b.] 2 February 1960, New Barnet; [p.] Maureen and Lionel Herscott; [m.] Mr. Les Surry; [ch.] Sueellen, Stuart and Terry; [ed.] St. Peters Comprehensive School, Burnham-on-Crouch Essex, Southwalk College, Waterloo, London; [occ.] Secretary to Capt. Steve Winter at Cable and Wireless Marine Ltd.; [pers.] I dedicate this poem to a very special friend, Bob Smith.; [a.] Witham, Essex, UK, CM8 2PE

BRUMPTON, JEAN
[pen.] Lynsay West; [b.] 6 October 1926, South Willingham, Lincs; [p.] Geraldine Brumpton and John Brumpton; [ed.] Minimal but continuing; [occ.] Retired S.R.M. S.C.M.; [oth. writ.] One poem published in a book by Dr. Dorothy Rowe "Depression: The Way Out Of Your Prison" Routledge and Keegan Paul 1983.; [pers.] It was Dr. Rowe who suggested I try writing - 1968 during a period I had of depression. Her guidance and friendship have been an inspiration and this continues. I will endeavour to use this experience, to try and help others, who like myself, have found burdensome the difficulties of life through.; [a.] Gainsborough, Lincolnshire, UK, DN21 5LD

BRUNNEN, JOHN G.
[b.] 25 August 1941, Southampton; [p.] Walter John, Dorothy Brunnen (Deceased); [m.] Margaret Rosina Brunnen, 17 April 1965; [ch.] Roger J. and Susan M. Brunnen; [ed.] Bitterne Park Secondary Modern School; [memb.] Life member Royal Signals Assn.; [oth. writ.] Compiled "The History Of Stour Provost" published February, 96 also a selection of works - written or collected by - J.G.B. available only from the author.; [pers.] My works are usually a reflection on life and its problems - it is hoped they provide food for thought and amusement.; [a.] Stour Provost, Gillingham, Dorset, UK, SP8 5SD

BRYANT, JACQUELINE
[b.] 5 April 1967, London; [p.] John, Josy Heywood; [m.] S. P. Bryant; [ch.] Natalie and Reece Bryant; [occ.] Homemaker, Wife, Mother, Poet; [oth. writ.] Currently writing a book of poetry; [pers.] For the bad that man does, the punishment he shall receive is the guilt that he feels for the rest of his life.; [a.] Brighton, East Sussex, UK, BN2 4JN

BRYANT, PATRICIA
[pen.] Pat C. Carter; [b.] 29 February 1956, Mitcham, Surrey; [p.] Henry Carter, Jadwiga Carter; [m.] Paul Henry Bryant, 21 February 1975; [ch.] 4 children; [ed.] Pollards Hill High School, Mitcham Surrey; [occ.] Negotiator, Wates Estate Agency, Norbury SW16; [hon.] Honours (Imperial Society of Dancing), Adult Tap Dancing grade I; [oth. writ.] Has written many poems and is now currently writing a book. Entitled "A Difficult Situation" she hopes to further her work in biographies.; [pers.] To put one's thoughts on paper, in order to enlighten or inspire others, is truly a wonderful feeling!; [a.] Mitcham, Surrey, UK, CR4 1EL

BUFF, MRS. PATRICIA DAWN
[pen.] P. Dawne; [b.] 17 December 1956, Liverpool; [p.] Ivy Elder, Bruce Elder; [m.] Kimberley C. J. Buff, 9 June 1979; [ch.] Martin John, Karl Lyndon; [ed.] Oxley Senior Comprehensive, 8 O'Levels and 1 A'Level, Birkenhead College of Technology - BEC National Certificate in Business Studies; [occ.] Sales Assistant for a retail distributor; [hon.] Deputy Head Girl

at School, won a book prize every year for attainment; [oth. writ.] I had a poem printed whilst still in primary school. It was called "The Wonders Of A Spider's Web", and I can still remember the words even now; [pers.] Writing poetry releases all the clutter of emotions/thoughts within the mind. It's relaxing, enjoyable, and definitely recommended.; [a.] Chaddesden, Derby, UK, DE21 6HQ

BURDON, RICHARD H.
[b.] 11 September 1922, London; [m.] Deceased August 1995, 31 July 1961; [ed.] At private schools and coaching establishments; [occ.] Retired teacher of EFL; [memb.] Local Gardening Club - Bowls Club - Art Groups; [oth. writ.] Dinner Tete-A-Tete anthology - Symphonies of the Soul - Poetry Guild and others in various publications; [pers.] I write on the wonders of nature and the vagaries of life - Love, travel, human situations, philosophical insights - romantic attitudes; [a.] Newport, Pembrokeshire, UK, SA42 0SY

BURGESS, PAMELA TENNIEL
[b.] 17 June 1957, Nairobi, Kenya; [ed.] Edgehill College, Bideford Exeter and District Riding School, Ebford (BHSAI); [occ.] Quality Controller; [oth. writ.] Two children's books published, "The Dreamer" and "The Guardian Of The Valley"; [pers.] I Corinthians Chapter 13 Revised standard version of the Bible; [a.] Beaford, Devon, UK, EX19 8AB

BURKE, NIAMH
[b.] 22 October 1983, Drogheda; [p.] Tom (Deceased 31st August this year) and Marie Burke; [ed.] St. Brigids Secondary School, Tuam, Co. Galway; [occ.] Student; [oth. writ.] Written many poems and short stories. This is the first poem entered for publication.; [pers.] When I feel strongly about something I pick up a pen and put my thoughts into words.; [a.] Tuam, Galway, UK

BURNETT, MARGARET VINALL
[b.] 3 October 1913, Haslemere, Surrey; [p.] Arthur and Frances Benneyworth; [m.] Albert Vinall, 1940-42, Robert Burnett, December 1945-75; [ch.] Nancy, Albert, Corolina, Rosalind, Robert, Dorothy, Jeffrey Kenneth; [ed.] Cross-in-Hand Village School, left 14 for domestic service; [occ.] Writing Disabled Community Work; [memb.] N.A.L.D. Access Disabled Act; [oth. writ.] Disabled Mags, Anchor Books, P.I.B.I., Deven and Dorset Poetry Club, Poetry Now, Sussex Poems, Mencop (70's); [pers.] As a long time disabled ambutee, I write to keep my mind alive, and to fill sleepless nights, also like to take a dig at injustice.; [a.] Eastborough, Sussex, UK, BN22 7DE

BURNS, CHRISTINE
[pen.] Christine Dalton; [b.] 18 February 1963, Birmingham; [p.] James Joseph Dalton, Pat Hicken; [m.] Peter Burns, 16 October 1986; [ch.] Peter, Shaun, David, Seamus, Christina; [ed.] Cardinal Wiseman R.C. Secondary School; [occ.] Housewife; [a.] Birmingham, Warwickshire, UK, B12 9QD

BUSH, ANNE
[b.] 2 February 1952, Johnstone, Scotland; [p.] John and Maria Canney; [m.] James Bush; [ch.] Paul, Gayle; [ed.] Holy Family Primary, St. Stephen Secondary School, Port Glasgow, Scotland; [pers.] I have been writing poetry since childhood, and quite a lot of my poems reflect my emotions at the time.; [a.] Luton, Beds, UK

BUTCHER, JOSEPHINE
[b.] 1 January 1947, Weymouth; [p.] Joseph and Mary Maddern; [m.] Paul Butcher, 19 December 1970; [ch.] Beverly-Jo; [ed.] Weymouth Grammar School, B.Ed (Hons) Southampton University; [occ.] Teacher at Holy Trinity Junior School, Weymouth; [oth. writ.] Some poems published in anthologies and in a poetry maga-

zine. Editor of Holy Trinity Church Parish Magazine.; [pers.] I want to write poetry which everyone can understand and to which they can relate.; [a.] Portland, Dorset, UK, DT5 1LU

BUTLER, MRS. AGNES
[b.] 12 November 1932, Airdrie; [p.] James McKinlay, Agnes McKinlay; [m.] John Butler, 21 January 1955; [ch.] Allan; [ed.] Albert Primary, Airdrie Central; [occ.] Part Time Receptionist; [memb.] Local Writer's Club, local choir; [oth. writ.] I have written many poems, but "The Highlands" is the first one to be submitted to a competition.; [pers.] I look at the beauty all around me, and try to portray what I see in my poetry.; [a.] Cumbernauld, Strathclyde, Nr Glasgow, UK, G67 1LG

YRNE, LYN
[b.] 5 January 1977, Carlow, Ireland; [p.] Anthony and Angela Byrne; [ed.] St. Mary's College, Arklow, Co. Wicklow, R.T.C., Co. Carlow (Ireland); [occ.] Student of International Business and French; [pers.] We search for so long to find our souls under a grave of sniggering pebbles. I would like people to undress my poetry as they would undress their own feelings. I strive to write beyond fears.; [a.] Arklow, Wicklow, UK

BYRNE, SUSAN
[b.] 5 February 1949, Somerset, England; [p.] Harry - Ruth Regan; [m.] Thomas Patrick Byrne, October 1971; [ch.] Mark - David Byrne; [occ.] Housewife Writer for Pleasure; [memb.] Fingal Writers Club Coolock, Dublin 5, Ireland.; [oth. writ.] Have been published in group book called Woven Threads, also, had poem published in magazine called Mischief, I have also written several books, but as yet waiting to be discovered.; [pers.] I would like to dedicate this poem to my dad who died January 1989. His name Harry Regan, born in Kent, England.; [a.] Swords, Dublin, Ireland

CAHILL, KENNETH
[b.] 17 December 1978, Trim, Co. Meath; [p.] Miriam Cahill, Pat Cahill; [ed.] Junior Cert., Cannistown National School, Community College Navan Co. Meath; [oth. writ.] Love, Your Dream, Together Forever, Wish You Were Near, All Alone, Would I Be Wrong; [pers.] My reasons for taking to poetry are basically feelings and on all the hurt in life. I also love poetry, for I think poetry shows the true meaning in a person.; [a.] Navan, Meath, Eire

CAIN, CAROLINE A.
[b.] 10 December 1977, London; [p.] Briony and Alan Cain; [ed.] Llandovery College (1989-1996), University of Wales, Cardiff (1996); [occ.] Undergraduate student of English Literature; [a.] Llandybie, Wales, UK, SA18 3NG

CAIN, JANINE
[b.] 21 May 1983, Ormskirk; [p.] John and Pauline Cain; [ed.] High School Student; [hon.] English Speaking Board Exam - Distinction; [oth. writ.] Further unpublished poems.; [pers.] I try to express a lot of feelings in my poems. Also, because I belong to the younger generation, I see much through the eyes of a child. The actions around me affect my writings greatly.; [a.] Ormskirk, Lancashire, UK, L39 6SS

CAIN, RENE
[b.] 24 May 1921, Dunscar, Lancs; [p.] Frederick Earnest and Nell Onley; [m.] Eric, 30 July 1942; [ch.] Shirley Anne - Robert Eric; [occ.] Retired; [oth. writ.] Writing a novel which drives me mad at times.; [pers.] Hope to finish novel before 'going to heaven' time looms.; [a.] Hessle, N. Humberside, UK, HU13 0HU

CAJEE, YASMINE
[b.] 30 April 1960, London; [p.] Valery Wilkinson and Abe Cajee; [ed.] St. Martins Preparatory, Mill Hill London, Kingsbury High, London, American International Schools and Private

Tutoring, Ibiza, Spain; [occ.] Travel Agency Admin. and Student of Astrology; [oth. writ.] More poems, am currently working on the concept for a novel. No publication to date; [pers.] I hope, that the "Age to Come" won't say "This Poet Lies"!; [a.] Ibiza, Spain, 07800

CALDWELL, JAMES A.
[pen.] Ayrshire Jimmy; [b.] 1 May 1927, Maybole; [p.] James A. Caldwell, Annie Caldwell (Nee McCulloch); [m.] Jean McNab, 25 September 1957; [ch.] Three; [ed.] Carrick Academy, Maybole; [occ.] Retired Blacksmith; [hon.] Keostler Awards, 1976 - Proses - Highly Recommended, 1977 - Short Story - Highly Recommended, 1978 - Autobiography - Equal 1st Lis.; [pers.] Wasted Life - some poems 1935-40, became an alcoholic and drug addict, 1975 became Reborn Again Christian, the real me through my experiences would help others. Now 50 poems on different subjects.; [a.] Paisley, Renfrewshire, UK, PA1 2LS

CAMPBELL, ANN FLETCHER
[b.] 21 February 1945, Wolverhampton; [p.] Frederick Slocking; [ch.] John Anne E. Keith; [ed.] Girls School; [occ.] Researcher (for all Markets); [memb.] Market Research; [oth. writ.] A few published in other books ie: Wish You Were Here, Trees; [pers.] I write about the themes that reflect the way in which I view love and nature, dreams and desires.; [a.] Wolves, Staffs, UK, WV6 7SZ

CAMPBELL, BRU
[b.] Clydeside, Greenock; [m.] Helen; [ed.] My professional background includes psychiatric and general nursing before developing into management. I had a long and successful career in the NHS which took me to Birmingham and culminated in the post of Director of Nursing Services in Aberdeen where I now live with my wife Helen. I did a Masters Degree at the University of Edinburgh (1983-84) as a post graduate student. My dissertation was an observational study of coping strategies, violence. Some of my poetry expresses feelings about violence and mental illness.; [occ.] Since retiring from the health service I have managed a project for single homeless people on behalf of Aberdeen Cyrenians which I enjoyed very much and I have written some poems about this experience. I am currently employed as a Manager of a Residential Home for the Elderly run by the Church of Scotland.; [memb.] I am a committed Christian and Church of Scotland elder, although my mother's side of the family are devout Roman Catholics of Irish descent. There is a very strong influence here in much of my writing.; [oth. writ.] I sing with the Garioch Musical Society. I also enjoy a wide range of music, cinema and sport. I have written poems on these subjects too.; [pers.] Poetry to me is a kind of compulsion, a need to communicate which I can avoid but as soon as I begin to write I cannot stop until it is finished.

CAMPBELL, MARY IRENE
[b.] 13 March 1938, Swansea; [p.] Lavina and Edwin Holledge; [m.] Allan Malcolm Campbell, 31 October 1959; [ch.] Three - one daughter, two sons; [ed.] Danggraig and St. Thomas School, Swansea; [occ.] Housewife; [memb.] City and Guild in Sugar Craft Kensington and Chelsea College; [hon.] LOCF in Sugar Craft; [oth. writ.] Have written - told stories but never had any published; [pers.] My husband and children have always been my inspiration in being creative; [a.] London, UK, SW1 54DA

CAMPBELL-BARKER, MS. NICKI
[pen.] Nicki Campbell-Barker; [b.] 10 October 1968, Rugby; [p.] Paul Catchpole and Leona Campbell-Barker; [ch.] Callum; [ed.] Lutterworth High School, and Lutterworth Grammar School; [occ.] Dance student; [oth. writ.]

Currently writing a book. I've never sent a poem into a competition before and had always used writing as a personal form of self expression.; [pers.] I strive to bring out the inner beauty and creativity from within the hardened hearts of people in a crying world. I truly believe that we must daily search the pit of our souls and reflect on the goodness within, thus teaching and setting free the light, truth and a pure love to bring joy and freedom into the lives that are filled with darkness and inner torture. Goodness and love comes from above. God can only be in the eternal.; [a.] Forest Hill, London, UK, SE23 2SS

CANE, JESSIE C.
[b.] 11 April 1927, Carlisle, WA; [p.] Archibald and Jessie Paton; [m.] 4 June 1949 Divorce; [ch.] Two sons; [ed.] To eight standard then on to Business College; [occ.] Retired - home duties; [oth. writ.] Only the few poems I have sent to you being "that", "My Garden", "Noise", and "Sleep", "The Spider" and "Tears".; [pers.] My poems are just about everyday life - very plain, just learning.; [a.] Geraldton, Greenough, 6530

CANNING, MS. MARY-JANE
[pen.] Jane Canning; [b.] 26 May 1954, Cleethorpes; [p.] John Green, Mary New; [m.] Divorced; [ch.] Kylie Jane, Lydia, Liam Francis John; [ed.] Wintringham Grammar, Grimsby, Liverpool University; [occ.] Unemployed single parent; [hon.] Combined degree (Hons) French and Sociology, Cercle Francais Prize 1st year university; [oth. writ.] Several unpublished poems - most too personal for publication - specialize in satire.; [pers.] Still hoping, for once in my life, to be in the right place at the right time.; [a.] Liverpool, Merseyside, UK, L21 6NZ

CANNON, PAT
[b.] 30 November 1933, Surrey; [p.] Deceased; [m.] Deceased, 1 September 1956; [ch.] 3 girls, 1 boy; [ed.] Comprehensive; [occ.] Retired; [pers.] Owing to ill health - my limitations are not good - therefore I 'Amuse' myself by playing with words etc - and knitting; [a.] West Molesey, Surrey, UK, KT8 2LZ

CARBY, RONALD D.
[pen.] Ron Carby; [b.] 19 September 1929, Jamaica; [m.] 1959; [ch.] Timothy, Helena, Jonathan Carby; [occ.] Retired; [oth. writ.] Poems: The Drunk, The Blind, We Suffer Long, Bench Sitters, Old Lady By Her Window; [pers.] Is this 'Life' all there is? My influence for writing comes from my observation of what mankind has done to himself.; [a.] London, UK, NW10 4JU

CAREY, CAROL
[b.] 18 June 1969, Glasgow; [p.] Thomas Carey, Margaret Carey; [ed.] St. Columba's R.C. High School, Clydebank College; [occ.] Unable to work due to disability; [memb.] Scottish Spinal Injuries Association; [hon.] City and Guilds (Catering); [pers.] From personal experience, as a victim of a R.T.A. I reflect on the positive side of life rather than dwell on the insecurities that life bestows on us. "Life is for living".; [a.] Clydebank, West Dunbartonshire, UK, G60 5NF

CARLILE, ANNE-MARIE
[b.] 27 April 1955, Blackpool; [p.] Jean and Ray Carlile; [ed.] Keele University, Staffordshire, Psychology, English, Astronomy and Greek Studies 2nd class honors; [occ.] Advertising Director; [oth. writ.] 45 other poems and a 1 act play, Member of South London Theatre GP, Ruskin Players and Sutton Amateur Dramatic Society.; [pers.] My poetry has immediacy; it is written as emotions strike me.; [a.] Blackpool, Lancashire, UK

CARPENTER, MR. PETER JOHN
[pen.] Moon Man; [b.] 18 October 1951, Portsmouth; [m.] Anne Carpenter, 24 July; [ch.] Tracy and Suzanne; [ed.] North End Secondary Modern School for Boys; [occ.] Able Seaman Serco with Portsmouth Naval Base Tugs; [pers.] I try to make a point, of how much love we need, in this hostile world of ours. As a 60's child I was influenced by the words and music of the Beatles, their songs carried my thoughts at that time and still do; [a.] Portsmouth, Hampshire, UK, PO1 4PS

CARR, JOHN
[pen.] John Harrison; [b.] May 14, 1941, Nottingham; [p.] Lancelot Harrison and Vera Harrison; [m.] Frances Carr (Nee Russell), September 18, 1980; [ch.] Gary, Robert, Amanda, Jacqueline; [ed.] Abingdon (John Roysse's) School, Berkshire; [occ.] Document Courier; [oth. writ.] Various, including short pantomimes, dialogue, prose and poems of which one entitled "The Tree" sent to the Green Party and to The Woodland Trust in Grantham, Lincolnshire.; [pers.] I believe "Life is now". If we worry too much about the future we can't enjoy the present therefore we have no past. The present shapes the future and creates the past.; [a.] Chorley, Lancs, PR7 1UD

CARTER, DOUGLAS
[b.] 4 December 1911, Bradford; [p.] Albert and Mabel Carter; [m.] Alice Le Mesurier (d. 1986), 20 April 1935; [ch.] 3 sons, 1 daughter; [ed.] Bradford Grammar School, St. John's College, Cambridge; [occ.] Retired; [memb.] Many Bridges Clubs Clubs Travellers Club, London (1961-71), Walton Heath Golf Club (1971-93); [hon.] B.A. Cantab Companion, Order of the Bath; [oth. writ.] Articles in the Board of Trade journal and some bridge magazines.; [pers.] Crough translation from Latin, 'card games are good when played courteously and without money' (Frater Johannes, Ludus Cartarum, 1377).; [a.] Beccles, Suffolk, UK, NR34 9TQ

CARTWRIGHT, TOM
[b.] 17 February 1931, Bury, Lancs; [p.] Stanley and Elizabeth Cartwright; [m.] Barbara Martin-Abad, 15 September 1957 - Zaragoza Spain; [ed.] Wellingboro Grammar (Northants); [occ.] Retired; [memb.] 1. Association Para La Defensa De Los Drechos Del Animal. (Spanish Animal Welfare Organization), 2. Sports Clubs; [hon.] Long Service Award Canadian Federal Government; [oth. writ.] Sundry articles of topical interest for magazines and social organizations.; [pers.] The poem is designed to reflect the anonymous people throughout the ages who have contributed in their own way to the advance of civilization, dedicated to my Spanish wife, Barbara, to commemorate 40 years of marriage and life in 9 centuries together.; [a.] Zaragoza, Spain, 50008

CARTY, MANDY FRANCES
[b.] 3 May 1970, Leeds, W. Yorks; [p.] Doreen and Francis Carty; [m.] Robert Lee; [a.] Leeds, West Yorkshire, UK, LS14 1JQ

CASTREE, IAN
[pen.] Cass Casstree; [b.] 20 July 1945, Bury; [p.] Sid and Betty; [m.] Marion (3rd), Catherine (2nd) and Christine (1st); [ch.] Noel (1st), Natalie, Lucy and Anne (2nd); [ed.] Bury Grammar School and The Soul of Life; [occ.] Professional pianist/singer/entertainer/songwriter and poet?; [memb.] Equity and the A.A.; [hon.] 5 "0" levels grade in Piano; [oth. writ.] One album (C.D.) of songs "Mixed Emotions" 1990 and hundreds of verses for friends and family and "We need a poem, let's call Cass".; [pers.] I write as I feel. If it feels right, I write it. I like to love and I love to be loved. Ambition for my children to respect me as I do my own mother and father.; [tn] Bury; [cnty] Lancashire; [a.] BL0 9YR

CASTREE, STEPHEN MAURICE
[pen.] Goshawk; [b.] 6 July 1956, Wolverhampton; [ed.] In Wolverhampton at Smestow Secondary Modern School and at Bilston College and Old Hall Street Adult College; [hon.] Previous semi-finalist in an International Society of Poets Competition with "Aeroplane Jet Winds: Outside" consequentially published in the Other Side of the Mirror; [oth. writ.] Occasionally I do delve into short story writing and have had one or two published in college magazines. I have entered many short story competitions. However I have not been successful so far.; [pers.] I stage myself as a nature poeteer, as that is where my appetite lies in the wild life and the natural environment due to being raised in a semi-country area. I am looking to win a major competition to finance my first book of poetry.; [a.] Wolverhampton, West Midlands, UK, WV3 7LX

CATHERINE, MARY
[pen.] Mary; [b.] 10 December 1957, Fintona; [m.] Eugene, 1 June 1974; [ch.] Declan, Deidrie, Seamus, Sharon; [ed.] St. Johns High Dromore, F.C.F.E. Enniskillen, open university, University Ulster Magee College; [occ.] Classroom Training for Teachers Certificate; [memb.] Chair Person Students Union in Fermanagh for O.U.; [hon.] Medals for singing in Fermanagh Feis, Ju Jitsu Certificate, N.E.B.S.M. Certificate, studying for BA Degree; [oth. writ.] Unpublished poems, Stones, Songs; [pers.] If we could all give one drop of praise to each other every day, what a world would emerge, what potential for the human race to rise to a greater plains.; [a.] Enniskillen, Fermanagh, UK, BT74 4AG

CATTLE, ARTHUR
[b.] 13 November 1915, Flinton, Yorks; [p.] Mr. R. B. and S. Cattle; [m.] Edith Louise, 19 February 1942 (Divorced - 17 January 1996); [ch.] Steven and Patricia; [ed.] Primary School (Till age 14); [occ.] Retired Hull University, Head Groundsman; [memb.] Loten Luncheon Club, also my story of "Gateway To The East" in the book "Our Ever Present Past" edited by my tutors Audrry Dunne and Alec Bill; [hon.] 5 Athletic, Holderness Junior Schools Awards, also the Hull University Centre for Continuing Education, Development and Training, Certificate of Course Completion, 20 Credits - to University Foundation Award by Completing The Module, "I remember when" in March 1995; [oth. writ.] "I Remember When" as a school boy, teenager and up to age 22. Early life. 12 years in the Royal Marines. 12 years, as a potter, and 12 years on Hull University Grounds Staff.; [pers.] Due to rheumatic fever at (13) weak heart 58 years. 1987 Dren Heart Ope, feel 20 yrs younger. (Age 81 13/11/96) Still love to play the Larry Adler Harmonica. 6 brothers, one sister, and man all played. Dad's was the Accordian.; [a.] Hull, Yorkshire, UK, HU5 5ST

CAUCHI, DANIEL
[pen.] Moon Walker; [b.] 10 January 1979, Malta; [p.] Alfred and Anna Cauchi; [ed.] Finished all secondary school; [occ.] Cashier; [hon.] 1st prize for completing a story for an international fan club; [oth. writ.] One of my stories was chosen and published in an international magazine.; [pers.] I know that a poem can't change the world, but maybe it can change someone's heart, and that could make a little difference for a better place.; [a.] San Gwann

CEMAL, BAHAR
[pen.] Janie Kamber; [b.] 1 May 1979, Lewisham; [p.] Mr. Ismail and Mrs. Destine Cemal; [ed.] Hillview Comprehensive School, West Kent College and hoping to go to University; [occ.] Student studying Business Adv GNVQ and French (3 1/2 A levels); [memb.] I currently am a member of a Film Extra Agency called Lorraine Dior, who also specialize in adverts and modeling; [pers.] To write poems expresses strong feelings of anger, depression and hopefulness of somewhat a better life. The goodness it brings out of me is strength and power of soul and of the mind. Sometimes writing things on paper is the only way of seeing the light and turning bad into good, today and tomorrow and a dream into a reality.; [a.] Townbridge, Kent, UK, TN9 1TN

CHADWICK, JOYCE
[pen.] J. Chadwick; [b.] 5 November 1937, Tunstall; [p.] Robert and Elizabeth Chadwick; [occ.] Enamel Kiln Cranker; [oth. writ.] Bob-the-Collie (first poem), Bob-the-Collie (Holiday Time); [a.] Tunstall, S-o-T, Staffs, UK, ST6 5ND

CHAMBERLAIN, MRS. JULIA
[b.] 29 October 1956, Bolton; [p.] Edmund Pilling, Anne Pilling; [m.] Timothy Mark Chamberlain, 19 June 1981; [ch.] Sara Marie, Emma Clare, Mark Francis; [ed.] St. Cuthberts R.C. Secondary School, Bolton Nursery Nurse College; [occ.] Nursery Nurse at St. Peter and Paul's Primary School Bolton; [memb.] Member of Manchester and Lancashire Local Family History Society; [oth. writ.] Written a children's Christmas story entitled "Father Christmas and the Ace-Racer": (unpublished); [pers.] I believe my writings carry a moral way of looking at life, whether it is in story or poetry form.; [a.] Bolton, Lancs, UK, BL1 5LA

CHANA, DAVINDER K.
[b.] 27 March 1980, Perivale; [ed.] 1. Hambrough First and Middle School, 2. Villiers High School, 3. Uxbridge College; [occ.] Student; [memb.] Alton Towers Club, Ribena Club, Crackerjack Fitness Club; [hon.] I have entered many competitions such as help the aged and Blue Peter Competitions, and a lot that come on teletext and in magazines. I have lots of certificates and prizes.; [oth. writ.] Poems published in school magazines and stories for young children.; [pers.] I haven't always been fond of English, especially when it comes to poetry and I have been told too many times in my high school years that I haven't got many ideas and I don't explore them, but after my poem being chosen I don't agree with what I was told.; [a.] Southall, Middlesex, UK, UB1 1LF

CHAPMAN, ANTHONY G.
[b.] 17 September 1974, Barnsley; [occ.] Factory Operative; [oth. writ.] This is my first poem to be published therefore I feel proud of my accomplishment.; [pers.] I get most of my inspiration from music. I have been greatly influenced by Freddie Mercury and John Lennon's work. I strive to reflect life and honesty in my writing.; [a.] Barnsley, South Yorkshire, UK, S75 5PD

CHARALAMBOUS, STELLA
[b.] 19 January 1957, Mykonos, Greece; [p.] Spyros, Irene Charalambous; [m.] Nick Kalogridis, 29 November 1981; [ch.] Basilios; [ed.] English Literature; [occ.] Private Lessons; [oth. writ.] Several poems in Greek; [pers.] Life is so precious, so beautiful however hard it maybe. I thank all the people I have met and those I'm going to meet, for their existence makes life meaningful; [a.] New Heraklion, Athens, Greece, 14122

CHARBIT, ANNABELLE
[b.] 28 April 1974, London; [ed.] Fracis Holland School. University of Reading; [hon.] BA in Philosophy; [pers.] I once asked an old friend how he manages to write good poetry. And he told me to look into my eyes and write down exactly what I see, for the best poet is the one who is the most honest with himself. I believe that "The Child" reflects something true of all of our lives, though few of us would care to admit it.; [a.] London, UK, SW1 W9EA

CHARD, GARY
[b.] 21 May 1969, London; [p.] Derek and Susan Chard; [m.] Lisa Chard, 19 August 1992; [ch.] Daniel, Kayleigh, Natasha and Gary; [ed.] Southfield School; [occ.] Self-employed; [oth. writ.] I have written loads of poems, I have never sent any away to be published. Short list of some, gone of know: State of mind Pts. 1, 2, 3, and 4 Mother Earth, Death of a Working Class; [pers.] I live my life for my wife and children. If you can write you can be a poet.; [a.] Milton Keynes, Bucks, UK, MK12 6AP

CHARLES, MR. ALPHONSO
[b.] 17 September 1933, Portsmouth, Dominica, WI; [p.] Alfred Peter Charles, Eutina Charles; [m.] Madonna Charles, 26 April 1956; [ch.] Adrian, Anthea and Anthony also Aldith; [ed.] Portsmouth Government School, Dominica Grammar School in Dominica, West Indies and Regent Street Central Polytechnic in London, England; [occ.] Early voluntary retirement from British Telecommunications PLC "to pursue voluntary community work"; [memb.] Founding-member of Dominica Oversea Nationals Association (DONA), in Britain, in attempt to achieve my idea, the "Triangle Connections" by organizing Dominica Nationals living in the United Kingdom, Canada and the United States of America to develop the island of Dominica Commonwealth of Dominica, West Indies, on the basis of self-help, self-service and self-sufficiency. Also attempted to organize the West Indian Standing Conference, an umbrella organization, in Britain, to be of effective service to the black community, in Britain.; [oth. writ.] Completed five manuscripts, namely: "Self Experience", "Attempts to Move a Standing Giant", "Commonwealth of Dominica, the Dominica Oversea Nationals Association (DONA) and Me", "Land of Hope and Glory?" and "My Imagination", for possible future publication.; [pers.] "I believe in the idea of the "Brotherhood of Man". I see mankind as being placed in a "Universal Womb", where our sameness is determined by the natural fact that all human beings eat the same foods, drink the same water and breathe the same air for our survival. And because of these basis requirements, we must strive to live together, as brothers and sisters, irrespective of color, creed, race, sex, through sharing, because this is the only way forward".; [a.] Poplar, London, UK, EL4 7AR

CHASE, CLARISSA
[b.] 22 November 1980, London; [p.] Robert Chase, Chaltali Chase; [ed.] South Hampstead High School for Girls; [occ.] Student; [pers.] This poem was inspired by a trip to Belgium in 1995. There we saw thousands of unmarked graves and memorials of those first World War soldiers who "gave their tomorrow for our to-day". I wrote the poem to remember them.; [a.] London, UK

CHASE, EMMA
[b.] 15 September 1979, Southampton; [p.] Gerald Chase, Carolyn Chase; [ed.] Ballakermeen High School, Isle of Man; [occ.] Student (A-Levels), Part-time Staff in Bookshop; [memb.] Air Training Corps (440 Sqn), British Sub Aqua Club (Ramsey Branch) Amnesty International (School Group); [oth. writ.] Many poems although none are published.; [pers.] I know I can't change the world with my poem - but one person's thoughts is world enough for me.; [a.] Onchan, Isle of Man, UK, IM3 2EA

CHURCHILL, MRS. FIONA
[b.] 26 October 1962, Edgeware, UK; [p.] Joyce Musgrove and (the late) Ian Musgrove; [m.] Allan Churchill, 8 June 1991; [ch.] Katrina Louise, Mark James; [ed.] Windsor High School - NSW Australia, currently a student at the University of New England - Australia; [occ.] Casual bar attendant, Goulburn Golf Club, wife and mother; [memb.] Lieder Theatre Society, Goulburn, Goulburn Golf Club, UNE Sports Union; [oth. writ.] Several poems published as a child in local papers, year award in creative writing, 1980 Windsor High School, a one act play "First Kiss" written by me and performed by the Leader Amateur Theatre Society - 1996.; [pers.] I always strive to write with a mixture of pleasure and challenge. The pleasure, my love of nature. The challenge, to construct a piece in the absence of one of the vowels this time.; [a.] Goulburn, Australia, 2580

CLANCY, ELIZABETH
[pen.] B. B. Clancy; [b.] 7 January 1923, Mooresfort; [p.] John and Lena Halligan; [m.] Michael Clancy, 7 March 1959; [ed.] 3 years of 2nd Level Education; [occ.] O.A.P.; [oth. writ.] Contributor to "No Shoes In Summer". Compiled, by the over all, winners in the Cathe Gory, of the 1995 Guinness living Dublin, awards in the Mansion House Dublin; [pers.] All my poerty comes from my personal feelings. When I am under the influence of some deep trouble, the pressure impels me to an outburst of poetry. I do not burst out in wild denunciation of fate or human misery; [a.] Tipperary, UK

CLARE, MRS. LOUISA
[pen.] Louisa Clare; [b.] 18 April 1928, St. Helens; [p.] The late Mr. and Mrs. T. Davies passed away 1971; [m.] The late Mr. A. Clare, 11 February 1950; [ch.] James Anthony, Francis Gerard, Anglela Mary, Theresa Marie; [ed.] I was educated St. Mary's School Blackbrook, St. Helens; [occ.] Retired 1980, Clerical Worker; [memb.] Pilkingtons Choral Society; [oth. writ.] Wrote some play scripts; [pers.] I left school at thirteen, war years 1941, educated myself thereon and brought my brother up (mother working war-work).; [a.] St. Helens, Merseyside, UK, WA10 6PS

CLARK, MR. A. A.
[pen.] A. C. Gates; [b.] Aberdeen; [p.] Deceased; [occ.] Care worker; [oth. writ.] 2,162 poems to date, 2 short stories, 3 novels, still to be completed 1 epic poem, 5 chpt of A and, over 6,000 lines still working on the other 5, chpt, 1 play working on! None of my writings have been published yet to my knowledge!; [pers.] It is only through grief that I started writing from 1990, onwards, once the above is finished, I shall write no more. I myself, deem my waiting, whether personal or otherwise, only as...("as voice and nothing more".); [a.] Leicester, Leicestershire, UK, LE5 3FJ

CLARK, BERYL
[pen.] Maria; [b.] 7 November 1907, India; [p.] Mr. and Mrs. Palman; [m.] Mr. George S. Clark, 19 December 1931; [ch.] 5; [ed.] Convent; [occ.] Retired; [memb.] Age Concern; [oth. writ.] Book of poems for my local church; [a.] Christchurch, Dorset, UK, BH23 2LA

CLARK, CHERYL
[pen.] Ryl Clark; [b.] 20 February 1975, Guildford; [p.] Sue and Trevor Clark; [ed.] Guildford County, Secondary School; [occ.] Sales Assistant; [pers.] I have been writing poetry since I was young. It seems to just flow from out of nowhere through my fingers and onto the page. It seems really natural to me.; [a.] Guildford, Surrey, UK, GU1 1LR

CLARK, MRS. DORA
[b.] 8 March 1910, Rochester, Northumberland; [p.] Robert and Jane Snaith; [m.] John Edward Clark (Deceased), 20 September 1933; [ch.] One son, one daughter married; [ed.] At the Village School Bellingham, left at 14 to earn my living as domestic help; [occ.] Retired but help with various charities, visit blind and write letters and fill forms etc.; [memb.] U.R. Church, Senior Elder Local over 60 Club; [oth. writ.] Lots of letters to the papers a few short and amusing poems in local papers and church magazines. Two songs with lyrics and melody composed by myself published and recorded. Love wildlife and nature and all animals.; [a.] Longframlington, Northumberland, UK, NE65 8EP

CLARK, TERESA ANN
[b.] 19 June 1943, London; [p.] Mr. and Mrs. Ludkins; [m.] On a widow, 14 October 1960; [ch.] Three; [ed.] Grammar School; [oth. writ.] Other writings, short stories, poems have been purely for myself. My husband made me wish to write how I felt and enter this competition.; [a.] London, Chingford, UK, E4 9DH

CLARK-STEEL, C. MAXWELL
[pen.] Leets; [b.] 8 December 1936, Astwood Bank; [ed.] Glasgow College of Building (Amongst others); [occ.] Creative Builder Inventor and Painter; [memb.] Fellow of the Faculty of Building, Fellow of the Institute of Retroleum, Fellow of the British Inst. of Mgmt, Member of the Inst. of Industrial Mgrs; [oth. writ.] Numerous poems and song lyrics. (Private) Many Technical Articles and Professional Papers. (Published); [pers.] A writer is a soldier whose first duty is to thrust the sword of truth through the armour of hypocrisy.; [a.] Wadi, Kabir

CLARKE, CHRISTINA M.
[pen.] Christina M. Lomax; [b.] 18 January 1944, Birmingham; [p.] Gwendoline Dolphin, Donald G. Lomax; [ch.] Lewis, Anthony, Gary Clarke; [ed.] Yardley Secondary Mod School for Girls, Birmingham Technical College Wiltshire; [occ.] Assistant Manager for Charity-Oxfam Fair Trade Co-Cirencester; [memb.] Cirencester Operatic Society; [oth. writ.] Several poems published by Arrival Press; [pers.] I seek to fathom life and its mysteries. Those inner feelings that we all have but express. Bringing comfort and reassurance to the reader as only the written word can!; [a.] Grencester, Gloucestershire, UK, GL7 1TB

CLARKE, MARICA DRUSKOVICH
[b.] 1 June 1964, Jugoslavia; [p.] Toma and Frana Druskovich; [m.] Roger Jardine-Clarke, 12 January 1994; [ed.] Our Lady of the Missions Ladies College. Fromantle Australia Murdoch University - Australia; [occ.] Private Business Consultant; [memb.] Tanglin Club - Singapore; [hon.] Ran for Parliament when a student in Australia (against labour)!!; [oth. writ.] Deer Feeding: short novel of young married woman in foreign country remembering her mother. The becoming of woman from source.; [pers.] I believe all things are possible by the grace of God and a clear and open mind, a warm heart and a smile.; [a.] Abbascombe, Somerset, UK, BA8 0HE

CLATWORTHY, FRANK
[pen.] Edit; [b.] 15 January 1953, Taunton; [p.] Geoffrey and Francis Clatworthy; [m.] Marion Patricia Clatworthy, 25 October 1984; [ch.] Samuel Luke, Joshua Matthew; [ed.] Washford Primary, Williton County Secondary; [occ.] Landscape Gardener; [hon.] LRPS Royal Photographic Society 1983, 1985 Domesday Project country life winner, 1985 Amateur Photographer of the year vivitar, Award received from Lord Lichfield 1989 Schering Agri, Farming News; [oth. writ.] Published poem Poetry Now anthology southwest 1990 and 1993. Also local paper.; [pers.] The wonder of nature through my words, my camera, my poems that I simply care. Thank you mother earth, only time will tell.; [a.] Taunton, Somerset, UK, TA1 4DQ

CLAYTON, ROBERT
[b.] 3 November 1943, Ashton-u-Lyne; [p.] Stephen and Annie Clayton; [ch.] Kalvin; [ed.] Westend Secondary Modern A-u-L; [occ.] Career; [memb.] Making Space - North West; [pers.] I believe in the spirit of life and the love therein.; [a.] Ashton-u-Lyne, Lancashire, UK, OL7 9ER

CLEMO, KEVIN MARTIN
[b.] 9 June 1971, Green Bank, Plymouth; [p.] Mr. E. J. C. Clemo, Mrs. S. Clemo; [ed.] Torpoint Comprehensive and Plymouth College of Further Education; [occ.] Night Club Cloak Room - Attendent Poet, Marine Engineer, Carpenter; [oth. writ.] 22 writings published in various books by Poetry Now, Peterborough first published 30 February 1995; [pers.] I strive to reflect the thoughts and guiding forces in my life and others. I have been influenced by poets old and news life, partake of the fruits of my labors, immerse yourself and be creative.; [a.] Torpoint, Cornwall, UK, PL11 2DV

CLIMER, JUDITH
[b.] 28 December 1954, Cardiff, Wales; [p.] Joyce Powell, M. Dennis Climer 1 February 1947; [ed.] Howardian High School; [occ.] Novelist; [oth. writ.] Novel entitled 'The Taking of Dennis Dover' published May 1996; [pers.] I like to entertain in my work and make people happier. A little humour goes a long way.; [a.] Cardiff, South Glamorgan, UK, CF3 8DU

COATES, PAUL
[b.] 22 January 1965; [m.] 1 July 1989; [ed.] Bray Technical College, Bolton Street College of Engineering; [occ.] Fitter/Turner; [pers.] 'With time, everything!'; [a.] Wicklow, Wicklow, UK

COATSWORTH, NIGEL GEORGE
[b.] 8 October 1939, Consett; [p.] George Coatsworth, Pelly Coatsworth; [m.] Deborah Coatsworth, 4 July 1992; [ch.] Rebecca, Naomi; [ed.] Rossall School, Trinity Hall (Cambridge Univ.) Cuddesdon Theological College; [occ.] Parish Priest Selattyn and Weston Rhyn; [pers.] In my poetry and songs I seek to reflect on my experience of God and his love and to communicate his compassion to others.; [a.] Oswestry, Shropshire, UK, SY10 7DH

COBBAN, ELIZABETH
[pen.] Elizabeth Cobban; [b.] 11 October 1921, Edinburgh; [p.] John and Wilhelmina Andrews; [m.] George Florence Cobban, 7 November 1943; [ch.] Elizabeth, Michael, Maureen; [ed.] Hamilton Academy, F.E. Classes, W.A.A.F. and Life; [occ.] Retired/Volunteer/P.R.O. Island of Arran C.P.L. group (Cats Protection League); [memb.] All are charities - nothing illustrious. S.S.P.C.A., C.P.L., P.A.L., Marie Curie, N.T.S., Life boats, R.S.P.B.; [oth. writ.] Jottings everywhere in notebooks and on sundry pieces of paper, none submitted except nonsense poems to local weekly.; [pers.] I've taught myself patience and, I hope, diplomacy, or I would have wasted all these years. Poetry and many poets help considerably, and delight, and sadden.; [a.] Brodick, North Ayrshire, UK, KA27 8AT

COBBETT, DAWN ANN
[b.] 26 October 1968, Chiswick; [p.] Yvonne and John Ravenhill; [m.] Stephen Andrew Cobbett, 3 May; [ch.] Two sons - Luke and Samuel; [ed.] St. Teresa's R.C. Girls School, Sunbury Upon Thames; [occ.] Staff Nurse, Intensive Care, Kingston Trust Hospital; [memb.] Tolworth Recreation Centre: Gymnasium and Dance Classes; [hon.] ENB 100 Intensive Care Course, SNB 998 Teaching and Assessment Course; [pers.] I would like to dedicate my work to Richard Sanders, the best friend a poet could have. He provided me with inspiration, encouragement and strength to believe in myself.; [a.] Worcester Park, Surrey, UK, KT4 8JF

COCKBILL, KIM J.
[b.] 4 March 1962, Oldbury; [p.] Mr. B. Brady and Mrs. D. Brady; [m.] Mr. P. R. Cockbill, 24 July 1980; [ch.] Master J. Cockbill, Miss J. Cockbill; [ed.] Rounds Green Junior School, St. Michael's C. of E High School; [occ.] Micro-film Camera Operator; [memb.] Warley, Martial Arts; [oth. writ.] Whilst You Sleep, Scared In Bed, Space Friend, What A Catch, The Last Time, Mother's Thoughts, all as yet unpublished; [pers.] This poem was written in memory of someone dear, who although no longer with us, is forever in thought. Written as a present for Mrs. J. Cockbill, hoping it would give some comfort.; [a.] Oldbury, Warley, West Mids, UK, B69 4TG

COLE, ELIZABETH
[b.] 13 July 1981, Jersey; [p.] Jill Cole, Christopher Cole; [ed.] First Tower Primary School Jersey College for girls; [memb.] Jersey Intermediate Wind Band, Les Mielles Tennis Club, Asthmas Society; [hon.] Baden Powell Award for Girl Guides, Community Service and Personal Challenge for Project Trident, Basic Level Abseiling.

Second Class Certificates for French Verse and English Speaking in the Jersey Eistedfod; [oth. writ.] Played the flute for five years and have begun working on a portfolio of poetry hopefully to be published one day.; [pers.] I write my poetry in view of everyday experience and I like it to relate to the feelings of teenagers and young people today.; [a.] Saint Lawrence, Jersey, UK, JE3 1JW

COLES, MARTIN
[b.] 1 November 1957, Rochford; [p.] Micheal and Eileen; [m.] Fiona Coles, 19 October 1984; [ed.] King John Secondary School Essex; [occ.] Builder/poet wood Sculpter; [memb.] Rotorua Mad Poets Society Ngongotaha AFC; [oth. writ.] Yet to be published books words on my mind how the hell did I get here unravelled freds.; [pers.] To be out of your head with no thoughts or feelings, is to be totally free, and totally imprisoned at the same time.; [a.] Ngongotaha, New Zealand, 3202

COLLIER, JOAN
[pen.] Joan Collier; [b.] 11 March 1934, Birmingham; [p.] William Lesley Keen and Gladys Keen; [m.] Gordon Collier, 10 December 1976; [ch.] Andrew McNamara and Valerie Harwood; [ed.] British School of Commerce; [occ.] Retired Financial Advisor; [memb.] The George form by Society; [oth. writ.] I have many unpublished poems which I have written over the years.; [pers.] My favorite poets are Robby Burns and Rudyard Kipling and I have always wanted to become a writer from a very early age. My hobbies are reading, playing banjo, ukelelee, gardening; [a.] Birmingham, West Midlands, UK, B44 8HA

COLLINS, DIVENA NOREEN
[b.] 29 October 1940, Bellshill, Scotland; [p.] Deceased; [m.] Derek William, Frederick Collins, 4 June 1960; [ch.] Peter and Roy; [ed.] Bellshill Academy; [occ.] Proprietor in partnership with husband, in a Calor Gas Shop; [pers.] Writing poetry is very rewarding to me, I enjoy reading other poets' work, and the poems I write are purely from the heart.; [a.] Watford, Hertfordshire, UK, WD2 6NY

COLLINS, EILEEN
[b.] 16 December 1916, N London; [p.] Reg and Betty Read (Deceased); [m.] Ted Collins (Deceased), 23 March, 1940; [ch.] Allan, Janet, Andrew, Murray Collins; [ed.] Various London Junior Schools owing to family movings - ultimately to Morley College, Westminster Bridge Rd for a Secretarial Course; [occ.] Retired but worked for Margaret Thatcher's Office 1958-61 (not Conservative) then 17 years as H. M.'s Sec, at Chatham Tech. High for Boys; [memb.] Operatic Society at a London, Polytechnic - Chorous Master, Leslie, Woodgate so sang with BBC Singers at Odds Zends of Times (1938) at present a member of 2 local choral societies in Bognor Regis; [oth. writ.] Several poems published by "Poetry Now" or "Anchor Books". My first winning writing was with "Tiger Tims" comic in 1923 when I was 7 (seven) years old!!!; [pers.] My thoughts are always "Do-as-you-would-be-done-by". My own love of words and poetry were nurtured by a teacher of english when I was between the ages of 12 to 16 years.; [a.] Bognor Regis, West Sussex, UK, PO21 5DP

COLLINS, KEVIN P.
[b.] 4 November 1945, High A Walton, Nr Preston, Lancs; [p.] Peter and Catherine Collins; [m.] Eileen Collins, 12 November 1994; [ch.] One daughter, one step daughter, one stepson, six grandchildren; [ed.] St. Marys Sec/Modern Bamber Bridge Nr Preston Lancs; [occ.] Security Officer; [hon.] Editor's Choice Award, International Society of Poets; [oth. writ.] Several poems published by "Anchor Books", Peterborough - Triumph House Peterborough and Anchor Book Anthologies; [pers.] My poems are a reflection of life which consists of pain, sorrow, love, and happiness which we all experience.; [a.] Melbourn, Hertfordshire, UK, SG8 6HX

COLLINS, TRISHA
[pen.] Rosey Neverland; [b.] 17 October 1949, Potton, England; [p.] Peter Wilkinson, Ilse Wilkinson; [m.] Divorced, 23 September 1966 to 6 June 1995; [ch.] 2 sons, 28 yrs. and 29 yrs.; [ed.] Robert Bruce (State), Ordinary State Education; [occ.] Farm Secretary; [memb.] Guild of International Songwriters and Composers; [oth. writ.] Other poems, stories, song writing and composing; [pers.] If you believe you can do it and don't try you have failed. I believed I could do it and will succeed. We all have a talent so use it. Let your inside come on out!; [a.] Staughton Moor, Cambridgeshire, UK, PE19 4BT

COLLINS, VERA M.
[b.] 18 January 1943, Wolverhampton; [p.] Arther Tyrer, Blanche Tyrer; [m.] Henry Collins, 30 August 1966; [ch.] Jacqueline, Diana, Christopher; [ed.] Kinver Secondary Modern, Further Education, Office Technology Course, Computer Training Course, in Information Technology N.V.Q. Level 2; [occ.] Housewife; [memb.] The Official International Wade Collectors Club; [hon.] English Art, Music, Certificate of Appreciation, Volunteer Work. British Heart Foundation, City's Guilds NVQ Level 2 using Information Technology; [oth. writ.] A collection of poems which I would like published; [pers.] I enjoy writing poetry, in my spare time and I am committed to write for family and friends. I get my inspiration from life. I love my home and large gardens, which is a listed building associated with Biddulph Grange.; [a.] Biddulph, Leeks, Moorlands, UK, ST8 7PN

COMLEY, MARY
[b.] 3 April 1928, Cuckfield, Sussex; [p.] Nell and Lionel Peake; [m.] Robert Comley; [ch.] Stephen, Anne, Clare; [ed.] Convent Educated. Lourdes Mount, Ealing, Middx St. Josephs Convent Reading, Berks; [occ.] Homemaker-along with Bible study and writing poems.; [hon.] I won a cup for running at my school cert. other sports, first teams medal elocution. Distinction in religious exam.; [oth. writ.] Articles in Reading Evening Post - human relationships. Very many letters published in the same. Publication one poem published years ago. I have never submitted my poems - until this year!; [pers.] I had a disastrous upbringing - resulting in various traumas and tragedies. I survived when I met the person of Jesus of Nazareth in an encounter of great grief. I learned how to respond from healing - not, pain - to learn and not grieve! I wish to try to bless and encourage others with the person who blest and does continnually bless me! That's what my poetry is all about!! Along with a ministry to hunting people "what God has done for me - He can and will do for you"! I say many times, to many people.; [a.] Glenthompson, Victoria, Australia, 3293

CONBOY, MAURICE
[b.] 23 May 1945, London; [p.] Maurice B. Conboy, Elizabeth Conboy; [m.] Alison Mary Conboy, 1979, Widowed 1994; [ed.] Convent school, later SM School in North London; [occ.] Salesman working in Manchester; [memb.] Lay Minister in spare time, Member of St. Vincent De Paul Charity Workers, Golf, Citess; [hon.] English Language, English Literature; [oth. writ.] This poem is my first written work; normally my first interest is painting; [pers.] I think poetry gives words life. A poet to be admired is Siegfried Sassoon for his realistic war poems. It is nice to hear about poetry that deals with recent history.

CONNOLLY, MARK
[pen.] Cossack; [b.] 11 November 1968, Kinsale; [ed.] Associate of the Chartered Insurance Institute; [occ.] Insurance official; [memb.] Kinsale Historical Society Insurance Institute of Cork; [hon.] Insurance Examination Awards; [oth. writ.] Various articles on insurable matters, song writing; [pers.] A few pints of Guinness does wonders for the imagination; [a.] Summercove, Co. Cork, Ireland

CONNOLLY, MAYHEW
[b.] 18 October 1937, Dublin; [p.] Dr. Samuel Connolly, Dorothy Connolly; [m.] Ravinder Singh; [ch.] Tapan, Amala, Ranjana; [ed.] Sunny Hill School Bruton, Southampton Univ. and Mysore Univ. M.A. (Indo-Anglian Lit.) Cert. Soc. Studies, Dip. TEFL and German; [occ.] Environmental worker animal; [memb.] Blue Cross of Hyderabad, India, Blue Cross of Madras India; [hon.] Not interested; [oth. writ.] Co-author 'Kipling' centenary pub. Dhyvanaloka, Press, Mysore. Author The Lough Ine Mystery (awaiting pub.) Many articles in Asian journals including the Crescent (pub. Kerala).; [pers.] While an author must easiness the nobler sentiments of his/her Jaire in language that can be spoken in everyday places, he or she must maintain literary standards if the common parlance is deteriorating all around us.; [a.] Hyderabad, India

COOK, SANDRA ELIZABETH
[b.] 15 November 1961, Taplow, Bucks; [p.] Ronald Cook, Amelia Margaret Cook; [ed.] Altwood Comprehensive School, Maidenhead, Berks. Windsor and Maidenhead College of Further Education. From Windsor and Maidenhead College on day release from Southern Electric B.E.C. National Certificate in Business studies. B.E.C. Higher National Certificate in Distribution.; [occ.] Senior Pensions Clerk, Southern Electric Plc, Head Office, Littlewick Green, Nr. Maidenhead, Berks.; [memb.] The Cinema Organ Society, American Theatre Organ Society, National Traction Engine Trust; [oth. writ.] An article on a musical evening for the Cinema Organ Society Quarterly Journal, where the London District Secretary performed on an organ and a pupil on a piano.; [pers.] To have a go and do my best. Be it at work, home, helping other friends or even when on holiday in Scotland climbing some of the high hills.; [a.] Slough, Berkshire, UK, SL3 7TE

COOKE, JOHN JAMES
[b.] 1 August 1915, West Gorton Manchester; [p.] John Edward Cooke, Gertrude Cooke; [m.] Now deceased, August 2, 1991, 22 August 1936; [ch.] (Two) Pamela, Howard (Both married); [ed.] Elementary-cum Secondary Municipal School, Birley Street, Manchester (school now demolished); [occ.] Now retired ex. R.A.F. Service, 24 yrs. and Technical Civil Servant 12 yrs., retired August 1980, N.R. ex chief Technician (R.A.F.), Civil Service Retirement Fellowship; [hon.] Made Chief Liaison Officer by the 3rd American Air Force in Ruislip Surrey Coordinating with R.A.F. on the American Phantom A/C and Hercules A/C, Awarded C. in C'S Commendation 1968 for Designing/Inventing 220 pieces of ground support equip. for compatibility between British A/C equip. and U.S. Airforce equip., awarded six cert. of merit plus monetary, awards for taking six 1st prizes in art (Water colours and the R.A.F. B1-Annual arts/crafts exhibition 1968; [pers.] By believing in one's self and realizing the capabilities that one can achieve by so doing. I believe in self denial. Too, for the true meaning of happiness and deep contentment, and to never make money one's God, and all my life has been influenced by my love for music. But I cannot stand this "Up to Date" Cacophony. Any "Easy Listening - "Yes" since 1992, - Chippenham and the Swindon Area. "To my dearest "poppet" (Jean) for all her love and care, during my most traumatical hospital experiences." God Bless you Love.; [a.] Wiltshire, UK

COOPER, ANNE
[pen.] Anne Marie; [b.] 27 December 1916, Maryport, Cumb; [p.] John and Jane Minkella; [m.] Herbert Cooper, 28 August 1940; [ch.] Carl; [ed.] Church of England School; [occ.] Retired; [oth. writ.] Various poems published.; [pers.] Inspiration for my poems stems from years spent

in the English Lake District. The philosophy of spiritualism also helps me to write spiritual verse and "To serve others to the best of my ability".; [a.] Carlisle, Cumbria, UK, CA1 3QA

COOPER, NORA KATHLEEN
[b.] 14 September 1934, Glossop, Derbyshire; [p.] Edgar Hallam, Ellen Hallam; [m.] George Ernest Cooper, 11 July 1953; [ch.] Norman, Leslie, Derek, Joy, Diane, Roger; [ed.] West End School, Glossop, Derbyshire; [occ.] Farmer's Wife; [oth. writ.] Several poems in various anthologies, I am just happy to have my work published, I hope whoever reads my poems will enjoy them.; [a.] New Mills, Derbyshire, UK, SK22 4QN

COPLEY, MRS. VALERIE KAY RICHARDSON
[pen.] Laraine Kay; [b.] 16 February 1950, Gateshead; [p.] Mollie and Sidney Richardson; [m.] Frank Brian Copley; [ch.] Mark Edward and Kay Laraine; [ed.] Elland C of E Junior School, Elland Brooksbank School, Percival Whitley College Halifax; [occ.] Customer Services; [memb.] All Saints Church Elland Music group and choir; [oth. writ.] A book of religious poems sold locally to raise funds for church fabric appeal. Song set to music and sung at a church service written in memory of a friend who died.; [pers.] I was first inspired by a saying of a dear friend who died, so much so that I wrote a song in his memory. I have since written many poems, all with religious themes inspired by my faith in God.; [a.] Greetland, W. Yorks, UK, HX4 8QD

CORCORAN, MICHAEL
[b.] 28 November 1961, Ireland; [p.] Michael and Kathleen; [m.] Shanti, 27 June 1992; [occ.] Pain Management Nurse/Therapist; [pers.] The most inspiring word in my vocabulary is a name. The name is Shanti. The most beautiful sound is that of her heartbeat.; [a.] London, UK

CORDINGLEY, JANINE DEBRA
[b.] 17 July 1962, Leeds; [p.] Peter Hirst, Maureen Hirst; [m.] Paul Cordingley, 4 June 1982; [ch.] Daniel, Shellie, Nichola; [ed.] West Leeds Girls High School; [occ.] Student in Applied Social Studies - Bradford University; [pers.] I have found that poetry inspires deep thought and affords me the opportunity to reflect, and transfer those thoughts into expressive language.; [a.] Leeds, Yorkshire, UK, LS13 1AW

CORMACK, RON
[b.] 11 September 1956, Aberdeen; [p.] R. Cormack (Snr), Joyce Cormack (nee Duncan); [m.] Shona Cormack (nee Murray); [ch.] Leanne, Kayleigh; [pers.] This poem was written for and dedicated to my wife, Shona.

COROB, TRICIA
[ed.] BA Honours English, University of London, MA Drama and Theatre Studies, Univ. of London; [occ.] Workshop Leader/Lecturer in Theatre and in Meditation and Mysticism; [hon.] Caroline Spurgeon Shakespeare Memorial Prize; [oth. writ.] Articles on and reviews of poetry, poems in the Dybruk of Delight, an anthology of Jewish women's poetry, poems in other anthologies and in magazines. A forthcoming collection published by Amber Press; [pers.] I would like modern poetry to include more about the spiritual dimensions of ourselves in language that is taut and muscular and of our time.; [a.] London, UK, NW3 2PL

CORRE, JUNALYN
[b.] 30 June 1977, Hackney, London; [p.] Father - Leopauldo Corre, Mother - Nardita Cabatit; [ed.] Radcliffe School Milton Keynes College, (Woughton Campus); [occ.] Data Input Clerk, ICS, Milton Keynes; [oth. writ.] Short stories, song, lyrics and several other poems. None of these have been published.; [pers.] (Writing is my release from the grind of everyday life). I write through inspiration, writing either about

things close to me or otherwise. I usually use a mix of empathy and personal experience.; [a.] Milton Keynes, Buckinghamshire, UK, MK11 1NN

CORRIGAN, MOONEEN
[pen.] Mooneen De-Burgh; [b.] 24 August 1947, Gillingham; [p.] Thomas Canning, Kathleen Canning; [m.] Francis Corrigan, 23 August 1969; [ch.] Susan and Sannine; [ed.] Camberley France Hill Swindon College Wiltshire; [occ.] Artist; [hon.] Social Psychology, Developmental Psychology, Environmental Psychology, Information Technology, English Language; [oth. writ.] Compiling collection of own work, short stories, poems, paintings, drawings.; [pers.] Life is a journey, an experience, to live the experience is to know that journey for the experience shapes man.; [a.] Swindon, Wiltshire, UK, SN5 9SS

COSGROVE, C. A.
[pen.] Cathie; [b.] 19 September 1912, Scotland; [p.] Deceased; [m.] 1 August 1939; [ch.] Six - 5 daughters and 1 son; [ed.] Ministers 2, Model 1, shop owner 1, School, 1 Teacher, Son; [occ.] Housewife, MED Centre Employee; [memb.] 12 yrs.; [hon.] University Degrees; [oth. writ.] Six not published; [pers.] I am delighted my poem has been chosen.; [a.] Scotland, G07 1EP

COSGROVE, COLM
[pen.] Colm; [b.] 27 May 1980, Limerick; [p.] Tom and Helen Cosgrove; [ed.] Student at the Abbey C.B.S., Tipperary Town. Ireland; [occ.] Student; [memb.] Tipperary Golf Club, Clan William Rugby Club, Bansha Athletic Club, Bansha Ju-Jitsu Club; [a.] Tipperary, Tipperary, UK

COSTELLO, AUDREY
[b.] 10 November 1971, Glasgow; [p.] Charles and Elizabeth Moore; [m.] Duncan Costello, 28 August 1992; [ch.] Kelly and Glen Costello; [ed.] Penilee Secondary School, Glasgow; [occ.] Housewife; [a.] Glasgow, Strathclyde, UK, GS2 4BD

COTTERELL, LINDA
[pen.] Catherine Cloud; [b.] 6 December 1946, East London; [p.] Deceased; [m.] Ron Cotterell, March 1967; [ch.] Two grown up daughters; [ed.] Secondary Modern School; [occ.] Administration Assistant

COUGHLAN, MAUREEN
[b.] 20 September 1934, Essex; [p.] Robert and Edith Martin; [m.] Cyril Coughlan, 30 March 1968; [ch.] Martin, Tracy and Matthew; [ed.] Catholic School; [occ.] Housewife; [oth. writ.] I have done other writing and poems. But have not had them published as yet.; [pers.] When inspiration takes me, I find I can select a subject or place and commence to write without difficulty. I am often without difficulty. I am often inspired sitting in my garden or listening to music.; [a.] Charlton, London, UK, SE7 8SS

COWLEY, JOHN
[b.] 2 March 1927, Westmeath; [p.] Joseph and Anne Cowley; [m.] Ann Cowley, 20 April 1949; [ch.] Anne Heraty, Carmel Lahart Joseph Cowley, Maura Clarke, Deirdre Doody; [ed.] St. Patrick's Primary School, Ballinagore Co. Westmeath; [occ.] Retired farmer; [memb.] Comhaltas Ceoltoiri Eireann - Castletown Geoghegan G.A.A. Club Scor Sinsir - Motte and Bailey, Pitch and Putt Club; [hon.] All Ireland Champion Story Teller Comhaltas English and American Tours as Story Teller and fear a Ti - Leinster Scor Winner in Recitation and Sketches; [oth. writ.] An Seanchat - a book of verse, several poems published in local newspaper, poem published in "Tyrells Pass Past And Present" two poems published in Ballinagore G.A.A. Booklet; [pers.] I write for my own pleasure and to bring laughter and enjoyment to others.; [a.] Mullingar, WestMeath, Ireland

COWX, AMANDA JAYNE
[b.] 19 November 1966, Workington; [p.] Raina Cowx, Alan Cowx; [ed.] Workington Grammar School, Workington Technical College; [occ.] Hair Stylist, Raina's Hair Design; [pers.] I find great peace of mind in expressing my inner feelings in the form of poetry.; [a.] Workington, Cumbria, UK, CA14 2NY

COX, MANDY J.
[pen.] For My Artwork - YDA; [b.] 3 November 1975, Lewisham, London; [p.] Debbie Cox, Stephen Cox; [m.] Jason Priday, (Met May 1994); [ch.] 3 years old daughters; [oth. writ.] Many other poems but none published.; [pers.] All my poems are influenced by the emotions I feel for the people and things around me. I find it easy to express myself in writing.; [a.] London, Nottingham, UK, SE9

COX, MELANIE
[b.] 30 December 1978, Weymouth; [p.] Stephanie Cox, Barry Cox; [ed.] All Saints Cofe, Weymouth, Weymouth College; [occ.] Student; [pers.] My inspiration is my boyfriend and the courage is from my family who have never let me forget that I can do anything I want to.; [a.] Weymouth, Dorset, UK, DT4 9BJ

CRACKNELL, MARIA
[b.] 9 October 1975, Welwyn Garden City; [p.] Dick and Sue Cracknell; [ed.] Presdales Secondary; [occ.] Trainee Manager, Shop in Ware Town; [oth. writ.] Several poems in various books and anthologies.; [pers.] I would like to thank all my family Dick, Sue, Eve Cracknell and Lee, Hannah and Emmie Davey. Not forgetting my friend Dean, for his inspiration.; [a.] Ware, Herts, UK, SG12 7HN

CRADDOCK, ROBERT CHARLES
[b.] 4 December 1942, Plymouth; [p.] William Craddock, Beatrice Craddock; [m.] Geraldine Craddock, 28 March 1964; [ch.] Robert, Stephen, Martin, Teresa, Michelle; [ed.] Stone Secondary Modern; [occ.] Electrical/Data Engineer; [oth. writ.] Several Poems; [pers.] Inspired by thoughts of youth encouraged by knowledge of age fulfilled by the life of words; [a.] Portsmouth, Hampshire, UK, PO9 4DY

CRAIG, DOREEN
[b.] 19 July 1936, Larne, Co Antrim; [p.] Samuel Perry, Agnes Perry; [m.] William Craig, 2 April 1955; [ch.] William Craig, Trevor Craig, Karen Craig; [ed.] Public Elementary School Mullagh Mossin, in Magheramorne Primary School Sullatober in Milebush Carrickfergus; [occ.] Housewife; [oth. writ.] In 1980 I had a book of my poems entitled "Be of Good Cheer" published by Graham and Hyslop Dublin Rd Belfast. In 1995 I wrote poem "Power in Thought" and it was published in book "Christian Poets from Nr Ireland" Triumph House Poetry Now. In 1996 I wrote poem "Peace Will Reign" and it was published in book. "The Road to Peace" Triumph House Poetry Now, and since 1979 I've been writing a poem each week for local newspaper "Carrick Times"; [pers.] My desire is to bring a little cheer, warmth hope and encouragement to others. To express the goodness and love of God in my writing with the assurance that God loves each of you personally, and will give you peace and strength beyond your own as you trust him.; [a.] Carrickfergus, Antrim, Northern Ireland, BT38 8NS

CREWS, SHANNON
[b.] 8 January 1972, Torbay; [p.] Fred Crews, Joy Phillips; [ed.] South Devon College Worcester College of HE; [memb.] Animal Aid; [hon.] BSC Psychology with honors; [oth. writ.] Several poems published in books, articles in college magazines; [pers.] I owe the creativity and depth of my work to the 5000 dreams which I have recorded over the last 11 years. These dreams are clearly the foundations of my work.; [a.] Torquay, South Devon, UK, TQ1 2JA

CROAD, JOAN
[b.] May 1936, Halifax; [p.] Phyllis and Leslie Daws IV; [m.] Peter Croad, 1 October 1960; [ch.] Ian, Jill and James; [ed.] Princess Mary High School; [occ.] Retired Nursing Sister and part time work in a private nursing home; [hon.] Registered General Nurse, State Certified Midwife; [oth. writ.] Other poems and biography - not yet published; [pers.] I only ever wanted to be a mother and a nurse and have the honour of being both. When writing I strive to pass on the joy and blessing of the love I get from my children and grandchildren and from the patients past and present, and I strive to show that mother love is the greatest and must powerful gift one can have and that children are truly a gift from God.; [a.] Halifax, West Yorkshire, UK, HX1 3UL

CROFT, VERA
[b.] 6 March 1923, Birmingham; [p.] Adoptive; [m.] Widow, 7 June 1944; [ch.] Two; [ed.] Convent High School Standishgate, Wigan; [occ.] Organist, St Pianist, Vocalist, Entertainer; [memb.] Equity, Musician's Union, Retired; [oth. writ.] Four Seasons, One Golden Moment. Twice a Miracle, We May Be Missing Something, I'm So Glad That I Found You, Mystery of Phantom Bus 41; [pers.] Went to Yorkshire after losing money in hotel business. Weren't professional on stage and clubs and reads my name as Verina. Singing and playing comes back to Blackpool in 1968 and continued. Now play all over for over 60's.; [a.] Blackpool, Lancashire, UK, FY4 4YB

CROLL, JIM
[b.] 16 September 1945, Hartlepool; [p.] Sybil and Jim (Watson-Stepfather) both deceased; [m.] Mandy Rose, 25 June 1988; [ch.] James (7), David (4), Michael (2), (Victoria, Deceased); [ed.] Secondary Education; [occ.] Process worker 1-C-1- chemicals and polymers; [oth. writ.] Other poems and series of children's stories (as yet unpublished); [pers.] My poetry and writings reflect my true feelings - I couldn't sit down to write a poem without reason - when a situation demands it, the poem writes itself. I believe that feelings should always be given expression.; [a.] Hartlepool, Cleveland, UK, TS25 5QA

CRONIN, DENIS
[b.] 23 June 1922, Portsmouth, England; [p.] Cronin and O'Neill; [m.] Helen (Nee Unford), 1956; [ch.] Two grown-up sons; [ed.] First-Class Hons, Mathematics Trips, Cambridge University; [occ.] Retired Chartered Engineer; [memb.] F.I.E.E. M. Inst. Management, Farnham Town Council, Farm Public Art Trust, Farnham Society; [hon.] (M.A., C.Eng., Flee, M. Inst M); [oth. writ.] (Well, lots of professional reports!); [pers.] 'The Tune' was written in 1946 when I was serving in the R.A.F. at ABU Sueir in the Suez Canal Zone. It echoed the fashionable way in which show-bands were presented. I sent it to my sister, who died several years ago. It has never previously been published.; [a.] Farnham, Surrey, UK, GU10 4NS

CROPPER, LYNSEY ANN
[pen.] L. Cropper; [b.] 27 November 1984, Whiston; [p.] Debra and Howard Cropper; [ed.] I am a first year student at Sutton High Senior School; [occ.] Student; [oth. writ.] I have written several poems but 'The Life of a Boy' was published in the book 'Girls on Boys' in 1996.; [pers.] I write poetry for fun and I enjoy reading poetry by other poets. I hope that people will enjoy reading my work. I also like writing stories and reports. When I am older I hope to be a journalist and a part time poet.; [a.] Rainhill, Merseyside, UK, L35 4PZ

CROSS, IRENE
[b.] 25 December 1919, Blackburn; [p.] Courtney and Bertha Boyle; [m.] William Cross (Deceased 21 December 1994), 8 August 1945; [ch.] Melvyn and Peter; [ed.] Queen Mary School - Lytham

Manchester University - where I met my husband; [occ.] Retired; [hon.] B.A. Honours degree in French, Manchester University, B.A. Honours degree (external), London University, Spanish; [pers.] Shortly after the death of my husband, after almost fifty years of a very happy marriage, I was inspired to write this poem one day when I was feeling very low. It lifted my spirits and gave me new hope.; [a.] Todmorden, Lancs, UK, OL14 5NJ

CROSSLAND, MARTIN
[b.] 20 October 1960, Cheshire; [p.] Jean Wardle, George Crossland; [m.] Tracey Crossland, 10 May 1991; [ed.] Westhill Boys School, Stalybridge, Cheshire; [occ.] Engineer, Self-Employed; [oth. writ.] This is my first publication; [pers.] I write for the minute then crawl inside time.; [a.] Stalybridge, Cheshire, UK, SK15 3BL

CROWLEY, G. T.
[b.] 21 October 1965, Bradford; [p.] Bridie and Patrick; [ed.] Milton Grange School; [occ.] Currently out of work; [oth. writ.] One other as yet unpublished poem.; [pers.] The way things are going and of this theirs know dought all religions need to look deeper than the structures of a book?; [a.] Bradford, West Yorkshire, UK, BD5 7PT

CUBITT, ANN
[b.] 21 January 1922, Wimbledon; [p.] Wilfred and Clarissa Stephenson; [m.] Willoughby Cubitt, 4 March 1944; [ch.] Willoughby David, Richard Geoffrey, and Elizabeth Mary; [ed.] S Mary and S. Anne's School Abbot's Bromley, Froebel Educational Institute, Roehampton; [occ.] Retired; [memb.] North Forest Written Circle, Avon Way Community Centre, Fordingbridge Historical Society; [oth. writ.] Poems submitted for reading to a U.S.A. Poetry Circle Poems and short prose articles for local magazines and county W.I. and published poem in "Sing a Song of Christmas" Triumph Poem.; [pers.] I write poetry when I am deeply moved by sorrow or joy, and I would like to convey to others the pleasure and pain of such moments.; [a.] Woodreen Fordingbridge, Hants, UK, SP6 2QU

CULLEN, RACHEL
[b.] 14 November 1982, Co. Cavan, Ireland; [p.] Mr. and Mrs. Benny and Joyce Cullen; [ed.] Secondary School student, "Royal School Cavan"; [pers.] I get inspired by life in general. The themes of my poems display simplicity; this way everyone can relate to them in one way or another eg. death is associated with sadness, you don't have to experience death to feel sorrow and regret. Passage I always remember - "Good writing is something you've always known, but were never able to express," there is a poet inside each of us!; [a.] Looh Gowna, Co. Cavan, Rep of Ireland

CUMMINGS, KRIS
[b.] 21 August 1978, Ayrshire; [p.] George Cummings and Shirley Cummings; [ed.] Glen Cairn Primary School, Auckenharvie Academy.; [occ.] Student, Glasgow College of Building and Printing; [memb.] Glencairn Fitness Club, Mike Oldfield Fan Club; [hon.] English, Frency, German, History, Art and Design Awards throughout secondary school career; [oth. writ.] Numerous songs and poems of personal pleasure.; [pers.] No-one is ever truly alone. We all hold inside of us that most human of abilities, that which allows to create and dream, to chase away the shadows when they call our names at night.; [a.] Stevenston, Ayrshire, UK, KA20 4HD

CUNNINGHAM, GEORGE
[b.] 25 December, Statue, Co. Syrone; [p.] John Derler, A. Nelle Devler; [m.] Elizabell, 15 August 1949; [ch.] Two children; [occ.] Labor; [oth. writ.] In A Lost Talker, and A Lot Reader, and Fort Reader In The World, I have been on TV several years; [pers.] They told me on TV I have great talent that comes from all producers and stars and all the people that watch me on TV says, George, you're a great star.; [a.] Strobone, Tyrone, Northern Ireland

CURRAN, ANNEMARIE
[pen.] Samara; [b.] 20 June 1981, Dublin; [p.] Rosemary Curran, Patrick Curran; [ed.] P.C.C. Secondary School, Falcarragh Derryconnor National School; [occ.] Transition Year Student at P.C.C. Secondary School, Falcarragh; [memb.] Criost RI Drama Group, P.C.C. Transition Year Drama Group; [hon.] Numerous local competitions; [oth. writ.] Several poems published in local magazines - poem featured in the recent book of poetry compiled by internationally recognized poet "Cathal o Searcaigh"; [pers.] "Peace will come only, when we surrender our fears. Through my writing I surrender all". Simplicity and love has always inspired me to write, for it was by the simplicity of love that we were brought together. I have great admiration for Seamus Heaney.

CURRAN, BRONAGH
[b.] 7 August 1981, Dublin; [p.] Paula and Thomas; [ed.] Gilson National School Oldcastle, St. Oliver's Post Primary, Oldcastle Co. Meath; [occ.] Student; [hon.] Prize winner for poetry - The Michael Walsh Memorial Competition, Fore Co. Westmeath; [oth. writ.] Collection of personal poetry.; [pers.] My poetry reflects the aspirations I have for mankind to live in peace and harmony. I am influenced by modern poets such as John Lennon and Jim Morrison; [a.] Old Castle, Heath, Eire

CURRAN, NEIL
[b.] 17 September 1976, Dundee, Scotland; [ed.] 1. Crakie High School, Dundee, 2. University of Abertay Dundee, 3. I.U.T. Orleans, France, 4. Kachhochschule, Dartmund, Germany; [occ.] Student; [memb.] Scottish National Party; [pers.] I write poems and songs for my own pleasure and therapy, but it makes me very happy if other people can gain something from them.; [a.] Dundee, Tayside, UK, DD5 1PU

CURRAN, SARAH LOUISE
[b.] 19 September 1978, Winchester; [p.] Patricia Curran, Dereck Curran; [ed.] Mudeford Infant and Junior School, The Grange Comprehensive, Bournemouth and Poole College; [occ.] Student at Bournemouth and Poole College Studying A-level-Eng. and Art; [memb.] Ballet School with Mrs. Jean Hayter, Art class with Anna Hills, participated in a band 'Xantai' playing electric and acoustic guitar and sang for 3 years; [hon.] Grade IV Flute, Grade II Ballet; [pers.] After reading Michael Jackson's 'Dancing the Dream', my emotions have been haunted by his wonderful, profound and peaceful soul. His provident views reflected in his prose, poetry and reflections on life, have influenced me tremendously.; [a.] Christchurch, Dorset, UK, BH23 3TN

CURRIE, ROBERT WILLIAM
[b.] 20 September 1955, Galashiels; [p.] Robert Currie, Jean Currie; [m.] 23 August 1986; [ch.] David Robert Wallace, Peter William; [ed.] Galashiels Academy; [occ.] Student; [memb.] Associate Member of Jewish Vegetarian Society, Scottish National Party; [hon.] MA in History and International Relations; [oth. writ.] Zion (in process of publication), a short pamphlet on the ideal of religious unity. Regular letters to local newspaper, a ballad on local borders history.; [pers.] I am still a child, and I am the master of my own life at last. Peace and blessings to everyone, especially the sick, the bereaved, the ill and the dying, those who are poor and those who are not.; [a.] Galashiels, Scottish Borders, UK, TD1 2UB

CURWEN, FELICITY
[b.] 9 September 1980, Lancaster; [p.] Janet Curwen, Bernard Curwen; [ed.] Norton Hill Comprehensive School; [occ.] Student; [memb.] Young Leader with the Guides, Banes County Saxophone Ensemble Norton Hill School Concert Band; [oth. writ.] Article published in the local paper, an unpublished novelette, and other po-

ems.; [pers.] I draw inspiration from life and from the people that I know.; [a.] Bristol, Bath and Northeast Somerset, UK, BS18 5LB

DAHER, RACHA
[pen.] Racha Daher; [b.] 17 May 1983, Dubai; [p.] Mohammed Daher, Laila Daher; [ed.] Rosary School, Al-Mawakeb School; [occ.] Student in year 8.; [hon.] 5 School Merits and 1 Distinction Award. Best Handwriting and Best General Knowledge Award of 1995 at school.; [oth. writ.] 12 other poems and a few songs.; [pers.] I've always worked hard believing that I shall reach somewhere, but within myself know that I have a high place and talent that I should be proud of.; [a.] Sharjah, UAE

DALLING, MARGARET LILY
[pen.] Bunty, James; [b.] 12 September 1932, Glasgow; [p.] Alexander Jamieson, Agnes Jamieson; [m.] George Dalling, 13 April 1957; [ch.] Stephen, Richard; [ed.] Now Top School Motherwell, Central High Motherwell; [occ.] Retired; [oth. writ.] Book published, articles in local papers; [pers.] This poem says it all (not mine) you will never grow old if you have a goal and a purpose to achieve you will never grow old if you have the power to dream and believe.; [a.] Bournemouth, Dorset, UK, BH5 1BE

DANDRIDGE, RITA
[b.] 14 April 1938, Aldershot, Hampshire, Eng.; [p.] Both Deceased; [m.] 9 January 1960 (1st marriage), 14 December 1992 (second marriage); [ch.] Four by 1st marriage, no children 2nd marriage; [ed.] Secondary School, Hartley Wintney Hampshire; [occ.] Widow/Home Duties; [oth. writ.] In church magazines; [a.] Yateley, Hampshire, UK, GU17 7XF

DANIELS, LYNNE
[b.] 9 April 1970, Middlesbrough; [p.] Shiela and Ian Daniels; [ed.] Rye Hills Secondary School, Cleveland Technical College, Stockton and Billingham College, Glamorgan University; [occ.] Student; [pers.] My poems are a way of expressing emotions otherwise hidden.; [a.] Pontypridd, Mid-Glamorgan, UK, CF37 4DA

DAULBY, LISA
[b.] 17 May 1979, Liverpool; [p.] Linda and Edward Daulby; [ed.] St. George of England High School Bootle; [occ.] General Assistant in the Buckingham Bingo (Bootle); [pers.] In my writing I try to bring across the simple message of everyday life. In my own opinion the best forms of poems are those unexpected to the mind.; [a.] Bootle, Merseyside, UK, L20 81Y

DAVEY, JANET
[b.] 3 June 1933, Kings Lynn; [p.] Albert Krill, Kitty Krill; [m.] William Davey, 28 November 1953; [ch.] Jane Ann, John William, Colin Thomas; [ed.] St. Mary's Roman Catholic School, Gaywood Park Secondary School; [occ.] Retired; [memb.] Prodogs and P.A.T. Dogs National Charity. Also, S.C. Bearded Collie Club; [oth. writ.] Personal verses for friends' birthdays etc., various verses and articles published in Beared Collie Magazine, and Woman's Magazine.; [pers.] My verses are intended to amuse. I greatly admire Pam Ayres and envy her talent.; [a.] Kings Lynn, Norfolk, UK, PE30 5RX

DAVIDSON, SARAH LOUISE
[pen.] Sarah Davidson; [b.] 15 July 1983, Burnley; [p.] Mrs. L. M. Davidson, Mr. G. C. Davidson; [ed.] Habergham High School Burnley; [occ.] School pupil; [memb.] Guides; [hon.] Mensa Certificate, gold, silver, and bronze badges for swimming.; [pers.] I love writing poetry. I get influenced by what's going on in my life. My mum and dad are really proud of me for getting my poem published. I would just like to thank my family and friends for supporting and encouraging me to write.; [a.] Burnley, Lancashire, UK, BB11 3QE

DAVIES, MR. DENNIS N.
[b.] 20 February 1937, West Bromwich; [p.] William and Edith Davies; [m.] Marie Davies, 16 June 1960; [ch.] Jason Davies; [ed.] Church of England; [occ.] Production Worker; [oth. writ.] Anchor books - Poem - Goodbye Friend. Plus several more International Society of Poets books. - The Other Side of the Mirror - Poem - Inner Peace; [pers.] Serverd in army as a driver in R.A.S.C. - 1955-57. Work at GKN Sankey for 30 yrs. Started writing poetry when my dog - (William) died. Found writing poetry enjoyable and natural; have lived in Telford for 30 yrs. Moving from West Bromwick.; [a.] Telford, Shropshire, UK, TF2 6RA

DAVIES, MRS. JEAN ANDERSON
[b.] 2 July 1921, Durham; [p.] Mr. and Mrs. J. Lock; [m.] Stanley Charles Davies, 1944; [ch.] 3 daughters and twin sons; [ed.] Modern Secondary; [occ.] Housewife; [oth. writ.] A little book, I have kept over the years poems of so many things in my life.; [pers.] I write my poems for family and friends, any special occasion brings my thoughts into words. They treasure them and I feel honoured they like them so much; [a.] Crawley, Sussex, UK, RH10 1JN

DAVIES, LILLIAN BEATRICE
[b.] 11 April 1908, Barry; [p.] Lillian and Alfred Taylor; [m.] Ronald T. Davies (Deceased 1981), 28 May 1927; [ch.] Ruth and Audrey; [ed.] Barry County Grammar School; [occ.] Retired; [memb.] Barry Choral Society During 1958-1981, Ladies Choir 1982-1996; [hon.] Several awards for baking, receiving diploma from Kardov Flour Co. in 1968; [oth. writ.] Main interest in my life, Barry Co-operative society. Elected to management committee board, delegated to conferences all over the country, member of education committee.; [pers.] Secretary of women's co-op guild for many years, until disbanded. Hobbies: knitting, swimming, walking, singing, dancing (old tymb).; [a.] Barry, S. Glam, UK, CF62 7HN

DAVIES, LLYFNWY EYNON
[pen.] Llyfnwy; [b.] 16 February 1909, Nantyffyllon; [p.] David and Ellen Davies; [m.] Ethel (Nee Sutton), 5 June 1938; [ch.] Michael and Hilary; [ed.] Elementary at Nantyffyllon, Elementary School in the Llynfi Valley Maesteg Bridgend Mid-Glam, South Wales; [occ.] Retired, life time occupation - Bootmaker and Repairer; [memb.] United Reform Church, Bridgend Mid-Glam; [oth. writ.] None other than poetry in a book entitled "Two Valleys" edited by Vernon Evans and Clive Smith both from the valley where I was born in South Wales.; [pers.] I like the simple things of life, and I always have ringing in my ears the well known lines from Shakespeare's 'As you like it' Act 11. Spoken by the Senior Duke, which end: -Find tongues in trees, books in the running brooks, and good in every thing.; [a.] Malvern, Worcester, UK, WR14 4BX

DAVIES, PAULINE MARY OLIVE
[b.] 19 October 1961, Cardiff; [p.] Rev. William and Phyllis Davies; [ed.] BA (Hons) Modern English Studies (Swansea University), MSC Historic Conservation (Oxford Brookes University), PGCE English - Secondary (Plymouth University); [occ.] Teacher of English (Secondary); [memb.] Association of Conservation Officers, Swansea Civic Society; [pers.] I have been greatly influenced by late eighteenth and nineteenth century literature, specifically the romantic poet Keats and the novels of Hardy. These artists have shaped my approach to creative writing and the mysteries of life.; [a.] Swansea, W. Glamorgan, UK, SA2 7RP

DAVIES, SUSAN
[b.] 8 December 1966, St. Asaph; [p.] John Davies, Edwina Davies; [ed.] Holywell High School; [occ.] Legal Assistant; [a.] Holywell, Flintshire, UK, CH8 7EX

DAVIES, MRS. UNA VIOLET
[b.] 23 July 1907, Wells, Som; [p.] Deceased; [m.] Deceased, 6 June 1965; [ch.] 2 children, a girl and boy; [ed.] Won Scholarship, Wells Blue School; daughter a teacher; son emigrated Australia; [occ.] Retired Senior Citizen; [oth. writ.] Nothing published; [pers.] I have been to Australia four times; [a.] Melborne Port, Nr. Sherborne, Dorset, UK, DT9 5HN

DAVIS, KATHLEEN
[b.] 18 November 1915, Winchester; [p.] Hugh and Violet Groves; [m.] John Colin Davis, 27 August 1938; [ch.] Three sons - Simon, Neil, Peter; [ed.] Winchester County High School for Girls; [occ.] Housewife; [oth. writ.] Poems written on country subjects for the amusement of my grandchildren.; [pers.] I find that deep feelings of sadness can more easily be expressed in verse than in usual speech. There seems to be a depth of beauty that can be a gentle consolation when the heart is so sore from loss.; [a.] Farnham, Surrey, UK, GU10 2BN

DAVISON, ANNE
[pen.] A.M.E.; [b.] 8 August 1961, Dublin; [p.] Thomas Fetherston, Catherine Fetherston; [m.] Philip Davidson, 21 August 1987; [ch.] Stephen age 6, Lauren age 4; [ed.] St. Paul's Secondary School, The Free University of Ireland; [occ.] Assistant Music Kindergarten Teacher; [memb.] HXT Musical Society Now and Then Production Co., Shadow of the Cross Folk Group, Greenhills; [hon.] Gold Medalist with the London Academy of Music and Dramatic Art in Drama and The Speaking of Verse and Prose; [oth. writ.] Have written some prose but my main emphasis is now on poetry.; [pers.] Poetry is a reflection of life that transcends the everyday living of it, lifting us to a state of spiritual and emotional beauty, my thanks to those who inspired it.; [a.] Dublin 16, UK

DAVISON, RITA
[b.] 5 April 1962, Malta; [p.] William and Josephine Davison; [m.] Francis, 4 April 1982; [ch.] Hurston and Arlen; [ed.] St Maria Goretti Sch., Higher Secondary; [occ.] Secretary; [memb.] Geres, Health and Fitness Gymnasium; [hon.] English Language, Mallese Language, Social Studies, Italian Language, Typing, Computer Skills; [oth. writ.] "My Love", "Dreams", "Resolutions", "How could it be", "Thank you oh! Jesus", "Broken Hearted", "Love", "My wish", "Valentine's Day"; [pers.] All my poems were written while I was feeling very lonely, and heartbroken. All the words seem to flow up by themselves as a sign of consolation.; [a.] Paola, Malta, PLA 02

DAVISON, RUTH
[b.] 18 November 1960, London; [p.] George Davison, Sheila Davison; [ed.] Ilford County High School for Girls; [occ.] Music Copyright Admin.; [oth. writ.] Articles and research for U.S. based magazine, Barbrabilia, and UK based all about Barbra - both are fanzines on Barbra Streisand; [pers.] I draw inspiration from people and events in my life. Writing poetry has always given me great pleasure.; [a.] Ilford, Essex, UK, IG4 5DA

DAWSON, M. E.
[pen.] Marjorie Dawson; [b.] 13 April 1920, Bradford; [p.] Deceased; [m.] Deceased, Two marriages 1946 and 1970; [ch.] One daughter; [ed.] Elementary Education - Village School and leaving at age 14. Worked in Woollen Industrial Mill until 1940. Worked in Munition Factory until 1946.; [occ.] Retired; [oth. writ.] I have written many poems and prose over the years, often wrote scraps of verse in early years but did not take it seriously until later in life. My poems are on spirituality, philosophy, everyday experiences, children and animals; also composed a number of songs.; [pers.] I love children and animals, I love people, there is nothing in the

world so complex, so strange, so irritating or so very wonderful as people. All have one great need and that is to love and be loved. Without love a vital spark dies within us. We cannot truly live without love.; [a.] Halifax, West Yorkshire, UK, HX1 4DN

DAWSON, MRS. CLARE
[b.] 26 February 1970, Skegness; [p.] Michael and Maureen Carpenter; [m.] Stephen Dawson, 25 September 1993; [ch.] Michael Anthony Dawson; [ed.] Maypole House Prep School, Horncastle, King Edward VI Grammar School Spilsby, Boston College of Further Education, Boston; [occ.] Partner in a family business; [pers.] I like to write poetry about everyday ordinary things that are often taken for granted or go un-noticed.; [a.] Spilsby, Lincolnshire, UK, PE23 5LQ

DAY, LOUISE
[b.] 4 September 1976, Birmingham; [p.] Mr. Derek and Mrs. Karen Coris; [ed.] Baverstock G. M. School, Derby University; [occ.] Student, studying for a degree?; [pers.] My writings are an expression of my inner feelings and emotions. I hope I write from the heart so people can relate my poems to emotions they've experienced.; [a.] Birmingham, West Midlands, UK, B14 5HT

DE ROO, SHIRLEY ANNE
[b.] 9 October 1935, England; [p.] Louisa and Reginald; [m.] Eelze, 18 November 1969; [ch.] Debra Malcolm Della; [ed.] Secondary School; [occ.] Housewife; [a.] Mount Albert, New Zealand

DEACON, SIMON JUDE
[b.] 7 July 1976, Ipswich; [p.] Mr. and Mrs. M. L. Deacon; [ed.] Orwell High School, Felixstowe Sixth Form College, Leicester University; [occ.] Student; [pers.] A poem is merely born in the poet's mind, for it to mature it is dependent on the reader. It is here the beauty of a poem is, with no objective truths it becomes a multi personality leaving the confines of the poet's personality through the reader's imagination.; [a.] Felixstowe, Suffolk, UK, IP11 9EA

DEATS, JULIA
[b.] 27 October 1970, Kent; [p.] Gwendoline and Michael Downs; [m.] Gareth Deats, 28 July 1995; [ed.] Holy Cross Convent School, New Malden, Southampton University; [occ.] Music teacher and performer; [oth. writ.] First attempt at writing.; [pers.] I enjoy writing poetry as a means of exploring deep self-expressions a process to cleanse, a way of thinking around a wide spectrum of subjects.; [a.] Reading, Berkshire, UK, RG4 8HJ

DELIENS
[pen.] Tonia Jenny; [b.] 20 December 1972, Vilvoorde; [ed.] No qualification or anything of that sort. Due to some personal problems, I have gone to the Hotel school in Leuven. After that I tried tourism.; [occ.] None. I have been unemployed since I left school; [memb.] I am member of the Dutch Tempest Force which is the fan club of Joey Tempest; [hon.] None, this is my first competition; [oth. writ.] I have written many other poems and lyrics. Unfortunately, there are no other poems published before. I hope that I can do something with my poems and lyrics.; [a.] Zaventem, Belgium, 1930

DENHAM
[pen.] Robert; [b.] 3 October 1931, Hampshire; [p.] Robert Denham, Charlotte Denham; [m.] Jessie Rogers, 12 March 1955; [ch.] Alan, Lynne, Julia, Jane; [ed.] Eastleigh Toynbee Secondary School, Southampton Tech.; [occ.] Retired; [oth. writ.] Several poems various anthologies; [pers.] Poetry based on Philosophy, acquired by my own life's experience. Still collecting gems of wisdom, accompanied by my dog. (Bess).; [a.] Eastleigh, Hampshire, UK, SO50 5BA

DESIR, ANDERSON PETER STANLEY
[b.] 12/12/38, Grace, in the quarter od Vieux Fort, St. Lucia; [p.] Mrs. Alicia Husbands, R.I.P. & Mr. Godfrey S. Desir, R.I.P.; [m.] single; [ed.] Soufsiere Junior & Primary; Castries R.C. Primary; St. Mary's College, Castries; St. Lucia Teachers' College; University of the West Indies Library of Liberal Arts and Sciences; (retired school principal); [occ.] Free Lancing, tutor in adult education (literacy); tutor in Family Life Education; [memb.] Honourable member Castries Cricket Association; International Transcendental Meditation Society; S-T-O-P Club Educational Institute; St. Lucia Association of Poets; Board of Management of the Frances Memorial Home for the Elderly; Parent/Teacher Association Memberships; St. Lucia Teachers Union; [hon.] B.B.C. Poetry Award (1980); Publication work in the London Times (1983); Peat Marwick International Prize for Poetry (1984); Geest Industries International Prize for Prose (1985); M & C Fine Arts Awards Council Overall Prize for Poetry (1991); Prize Waterhouse International Prize for Poetry (1993); The Saint Lucia Medal of Merit (S.L.M.M.) Silver Class for Meritorious Long Service in the field of Literature (1990); [oth. writ.] Several poems published in local magazines and newspapers. Poems published in "The Caribbe Writer" of the U.S. University of St. Croix, Virgin Island. Poem - "The Flag of My Country" - published by Heinnemann Publishing Educational Books, London 1983, Tribute to Simon Bolivar (1983); An Eclogue for Christmas (1994); Desire's Cricket Satire - 1996; Calypso Poetry 1995; short stories"Death By Disappearance" submitted to the British Commonwealth of Nations in London. "Back to Calvary" - a B.C.C. Special Award Poem 1980, etc.; [pers.] I have been writing poetry and short stories for about twenty-eight years. I have been greatly influenced by Derek Walcott, the St. Lucian Poet and Nobel Laureate. I also read a lot of Keats and Shelley, Robert Burns, T.S. Eliot, R.L. Stephenson, W. Shakespeare, Milton and others. I believe that poetry is one of the highest forms of art which people should study and review. It makes one's life richer. The stronger the imagery, the stronger the feeling of poetic artistry. I am an international poet. [a.] Oastries, St. Lucia

DESMIER, GWENDOLINE
[pen.] Gwen; [b.] 26 June 1938, India; [p.] Paul and Marjorie Wilfred; [m.] Leonard Desmier, 1 June 1961; [ch.] Eileen, Roland, Glen, Dale, Derek; [ed.] Matriculation Diploma in General Nursing; [oth. writ.] Several poems published in "Southern Asia Tidings" (a local church magazine). Some country style songs.; [pers.] I strive to immortalize a true story, and by a moral, or draws a comparison in simple poetry, so that the reader automatically memorizes the poems, as part of it, and in so doing memorizes the truth.; [a.] Hubli, India, 580020

DEVANE, EMMA
[b.] 17 April 1972, Llangollen, N. Wales; [p.] Shelagh Butler, Allen Butler; [m.] Brendan Devane, 28 October 1995; [ed.] Ysgol Rhiwabon, Ruabon, Wrexham, Clwyd, N Wales; [pers.] I would like to dedicate my poem to my husband, Brendan Devane, who works as a fisherman, in our Connemara home.; [a.] Roundstone, Co Galway, Eire

DEVINE, MISS IRENE
[b.] 10 August 1952, Dunfermline; [occ.] On capacity benefit I was a Production Manager till I was ill; [hon.] After my operation in March 1992, I went to Lauder College Halbeath I achieved: Scotvec National Certificate Modules 8111001: Information Technology 1 (Computers), 7180211: Numeracy 2 (Maths), 81228: Job Seeking Skills 1, 7180321: Core Mathematics 3, not bad with a value (shunt) in my head!, complete items Nov. 94 (1), Dec. 94 (2), March 95 (3), June 95 (4); [oth. writ.] One of my poems was published by you. The one "Aspects of

Trying to Rhyme Again" I got the Editor's Choice. And the poetry book was "A Passage in Time"; [pers.] In 1992 I had a brain hemorrhage operation and I was in hospital in Edinburgh for about 12 weeks. I could not read, write or speak but with a hard slog I am getting better. I do not work but I went to Lauder College Dunfermline to start again. I lost my poetry but I hope to start again.; [a.] Cowdenblath, Fife, UK, KY4 9EZ

DEVINE, STANLEY ROBERT
[b.] 10 July 1943, Belfast; [p.] James and Mable; [m.] Divorced; [ch.] Two girls (Teachers); [ed.] Boys Model Secondary Intermat; [occ.] Retired, former hospital worker; [hon.] R.S.A. Stage I; [oth. writ.] Poem "Seasons" short story "Farewell", "The Message". The Message was published in a local creative writing group where stories and poems were made into a magazine.; [a.] Belfast, Antrim, N. Ireland, BT14 8HH

DEWART, EDWINA
[b.] 8 February 1980, Cavan; [p.] John and Deirdre Dewart; [ed.] Arva No. 2 NS, St. Patricks NS Gowna, Royal School Cavan; [occ.] Student; [oth. writ.] Essay printed in local paper and articles for school magazine.; [pers.] Poetry is like a jewel so beautiful and we can do what we want with it.; [a.] Gowna, Cavan, UK

DIWAN, SAM I.
[pen.] Fred The Dread; [b.] 23 May, 1977, Burn, UK; [p.] Ismail Diwan and Zebeda Diwan; [ed.] Will attend Bradford and Ilkley Community College in Sept '97 (BA) hons youth and community work; [occ.] Student; [memb.] Little Harwood Youth Club (senior member), (B.K.F.A.) British Kung-Fu Association; [oth. writ.] Short stories "The Boiler Room". Poem inc. "A day in the Life of Trip", and other; [pers.] I write from personal experiences, a teenager in perception of everyday life. I am true to myself and others and gain my inspiration from people around me; [a.] Biburn, Lancashire, UK, BB1 5NR

DOBSON, GEORGE WALTER
[pen.] George Montgomery; [b.] 20 September 1927, Darlington; [p.] Mr. Geo W. and Mrs. Lavinia Dubson; [m.] Mrs. Jean Mary Dubson, 29 December 1994; [ch.] Two stepchildren; [ed.] Elementary, Technical Colleges, and private (Business Studies); [occ.] Retired (Semi-Senior) Accountant; [hon.] Poems accepted and published in English heritage magazines and local newspapers; one recognized personally by the 'The Prince of Wales'; [oth. writ.] Over 170 each demands to be read. They vary from serious comment to happy-go-lucky. Others qualify as light verse. A poem's an artistic expression of mind relaxing to read, and so help you unwind; it can be inspired by a beautiful scene, an unusual happening, or events that have been. It's a collection of symbols written in rhyme for all to enjoy. Whatever the time 'tis hoped what is said, will strike up a chord and awaken memories. Your mind has long stored its aim to enlighten, brighten from its verse reflecting on things. Real and diverse. Saying what is felt. When truly inspired can only be helpful. The not always admired; [a.] Stockton-on-the-Forest, York N. Yorks, UK, Y03 9UL

DOBSON, MRS. JOYCE
[b.] 18 March 1929, Stoke-on-Trent, Chell; [p.] Deceased; [m.] Deceased, 18 March 1975 (2nd marriage); [ch.] Two; [ed.] Council School - Chell, Grammar School - Brownhills, Commercial School - Bursley; [occ.] Retired, nursed for forty-two years; [memb.] Cruse, Keep Fit Club, Swimming Club ex. NHS Club; [hon.] S.R.N. Q.I.D.N.S., (certificate) silver award for my ward in the Salford Area Health Authority; [oth. writ.] Other poems. Imagination, published in "Passage of Time".; [pers.] I write what I feel and think about everyday life.; [a.] Worsley, Manchester, UK, M28 3PH

DODWELL, HAYLEY
[pen.] Hayley Dodwell; [b.] 20 October 1979, Market, Harborough; [p.] Joan and Christopher Dodwell; [occ.] Writer/Poet; [hon.] Many trophies for dancing, Three Cross Award in Emergency Aid, English Merit Award; [oth. writ.] Several poems published in local newspaper, articles for magazines.; [pers.] I am greatly influenced by the stars of golden Hollywood, especially Shirley Temple and Mickey Rooney. I want my work to make people happy, just like they did.; [a.] Kibworth, Beauchamp, Leicestershire, UK, LE8 0SD

DOLAN, MARIE ANGELA
[b.] 29 March 1964, Birmingham; [p.] Mary and Philip Dolan; [m.] Andrew Sirrell; [ch.] Michelle, Kevin, Richard and Mark; [ed.] Blessed Humphrey Middlemore Secondary School and Saint Philips College Edgbaston; [occ.] Housewife; [hon.] None as yet, but I have been told that I have a talent for writing and hope one day to be recognized for it.; [oth. writ.] I wrote poem called "What is Love" and it is getting published in a book called "Whispers in the Garden" an anthology.; [pers.] I have been writing poetry on and off for several years now, The Artic Fox was the first poem I sent off for in a competition. Words and life inspire me to write.; [a.] Birmingham, West Midlands, UK, B32 1RN

DONALDSON, STUART
[b.] 20 January 1965, Edinburgh; [p.] Robert Donaldson, Alison Donaldson; [ed.] James Gillespies High School, University of Life!; [occ.] Customer Service Representative - Standard Life; [memb.] Standard Life Athletics Club; [hon.] None to date but still hoping!; [oth. writ.] Nothing published as yet as I've never submitted my works before. Have written hundreds of poems, a few short stories and one novel.; [pers.] I believe in trying to expose the beautiful side of human nature. I am influenced by Byron and Shelley and the novels of Thomas Hardy.; [a.] Edinburgh, Lothian, UK, EH16 6NQ

DONEGAN, MISS ANNA-MARIE
[pen.] Anna-Marie Donegan; [b.] 16 October 1971, Manchester; [p.] Laurence Donegan, Maureen Donegan; [m.] David Mulligan; [ed.] The Barlow RC High School (Formerly the Hollies FCJ). Xaverian College, City College Manchester (Fielden Centre); [occ.] Customer Services. Dollond and Aitchison.; [oth. writ.] None published.; [pers.] Poetry gives me a way to relax. A 'time out' from the stresses of everyday life. Through poetry I can express my inner thoughts as well as my experiences of life.; [a.] Manchester, UK, M16 7JL

DOUGALL, SHEILA
[b.] 22 August 1960, Aberdeen; [p.] Jimmy and Margaret Alexander; [m.] Graeme Buchan Douglas, 30 May 1980; [ch.] Heather and Craig; [ed.] Skene Street Primary School, Harlaw Academy, Aberdeen Technical College; [occ.] Supervisor Cook; [memb.] Newhills Ladies Darts, Tillydrone Community Centre, Grampian and Highland Cat Lovers, Fluffsfield Donkey Sanctuary; [hon.] City and Guilds, First Aid, dart trophies; [oth. writ.] Several unpublished unseen poems; [pers.] What I write about expresses life as it comes to me and captures the moment of escapism as it arises.; [a.] Dyle, Aberdeen, UK, AB21 7LL

DOUGLAS, GLASMINE BANTON
[b.] 12 April 1949, Jamaica, West Indies; [p.] Laban Banton and Corgena Johnson; [m.] Barrington Douglas, 24 November 1979; [ch.] 3 Sons; [ed.] Clarendon Academy J'A', Mid Kent College of Higher and Further Education, University of Kent (Short Courses); [occ.] Probation Officer; [memb.] Writers Bureau, Manchester; [oth. writ.] Number of unpublished poems; [pers.] My writing is a reflection of some of my innermost thoughts and feelings. I am indeed humbled by this recognition.; [a.] Chatham, Kent, UK, ME5 9QQ

DOUGLASS, VERONICA MARY
[b.] 8 March 1942, Hebburn-on-Tyne; [p.] John and Margaret Douglass; [m.] Divorced, September 1968; [ch.] Chad and Jason (Feldwick); [ed.] Roman Catholic Secondary Modern - Felling-on-Tyne St John's; [occ.] Branch Manager in Retail; [hon.] Various medals and championships for Irish step dancing. Qualified Irish dance teacher; [pers.] My poems and short stories are reflections of my inner emotions, of my life and inspirations and people I loved.; [a.] Thingwall, Wirral, UK, L61 9PL

DOWELL, TINA MARGUERITE
[b.] 26 March 1975, Gillingham; [p.] Jill Dowell, Patrick Dowell, [ed.] University of the West of England (Bristol); [occ.] Student, Environmental Health Officer; [memb.] British Conservation Trust for Volunteers, Chartered Institute for Environmental Health; [a.] Rainham, Kent, UK, ME8 7BP

DOYLE, JOHN
[b.] 6 July 1931, Uxbridge, London; [p.] James and Eileen Doyle; [m.] Helen, 10 September 1955; [ch.] James, Elizabeth, Graham, Kevin, John; [ed.] Born London, went to school until I was eight years, but cannot recall the name of the school in Uxbridge Educated. 1940 to Grandparents in Ireland...Killishal National School, School Leaving Certificate, After the war came to Scotland...Ardrossan Academy "0" levels at "Highers" trained as Chiropodist 1954, trained as Nurse 1975; [occ.] Registered nurse in the private sector; [memb.] Life Member Royal Air Force Assoc., Member Springside Bowling Club, Irvine Angling Club, Ex Toastmaster. Gold club and riffle shooting club membership lapsed re lack of time; [hon.] R.G.N., L.V.Ch.C., R.N.M.H.; [oth. writ.] Have written many poems over the years and short stories for children: nothing published as it was a hobby. Much of my writing at present is factual "eg" abstracts for work and/ or letters for people who give me basic data for me to draft for them.; [pers.] I try with simple language to reflect an aspect of life. "Taking The High Road" warns of bad driving. "The Weeping Rose" reflects nature, "The Point of Life" is a reminisce. A man in a nursing home tells what he has done with his life.; [a.] Springside by Irvine, Ayrshire, UK, KA11 3BT

DRIVER, NORMAN MITCHELL
[pen.] Norman Mitchell; [b.] 27 August 1918, Sheffield; [p.] Walter Arnold and Elizabeth Driver; [m.] Pauline Margaret Southcombe, 31 July 1946; [ch.] Christopher Mitchell/Jacqueline Mitchell; [ed.] Carterknowle Council School, Nether Edge Grammar, Sheffield University, Weston Bank, Guildhall School, Music and Drama; [occ.] Actor/script writer; [memb.] Savage Club, BBC Club, Royal British Region, Monte Cassino Veterans, British Actors Equity Assoc., Cinema and TV Veterans/Assoc. Green Room Club, Emile Zola Society; [hon.] Licentiate and Guildhall School of Music and Drama (Elocution); [oth. writ.] "Amos Goes To War" - novel adaptation of Emile Zola's, "La Bete Humaine" for theatre "Regency Revolutionary" - Historical Novel; [pers.] I strive to interpret life as it is.; [a.] East Molesey, Surrey, UK, KT8 9LT

DUCKWORTH, EILEEN
[p.] James and Marjorie Duckworth; [ed.] Bridgnorth Grammar School Hockerill College Warwick University M.Ed.; [occ.] Her Majesty's Inspector (H.M.I.); [memb.] Geographical Association; [oth. writ.] Several unpublished poems.; [pers.] The education of children is central to my life. Education to enable an awareness of life which, in turn, fosters knowledge. Knowledge creates awareness. I try to reflect this in my writing.; [a.] York, UK, YO5 8LR

DUDGEON, EILEEN RACHEL
[p.] Mr. and Mrs. W. Siddons; [m.] Mr. A. R. Dudgeon, MBE (Deceased), 27 March 1959; [pers.] A kind deed is never wasted.; [a.] Umberleigh, North Devon, UK, EX37 9AH

DUFFY, BEN
[b.] June 1963, Dublin; [m.] Linda; [occ.] Civil servant

DUGDALE, MRS. PEGGY DOREEN
[pen.] Duggie; [b.] 9 September 1924, Tonbridge; [p.] Mr. and Mrs. W. Morris; [m.] George Arthur Dugdale, 21 September 1957; [ch.] Two daughters; [ed.] Comprehensive School; [occ.] Housewife; [memb.] Old People's Association called Pensioner's Eye; [oth. writ.] My Home Town (Poem) was accepted for Inspirations of the South poetry book; [pers.] Just love doing verses, whether serious or humorous.; [a.] Tonbridge, Kent, UK, TN10 3ES

DUMMETT, ROBERT LOUIS
[pen.] Robert Louis Dummett; [b.] 11 November 1948, St. James; [p.] Gloria Dummett and Louis Dummett; [m.] Pamela Dummett, 7 May 1974; [ch.] Paul David; [ed.] St. James Modern Secondary, Teesside University; [occ.] Self-Employed Quality Consultant, Formerly Q.A. Manager Bouygues Offshore; [memb.] Darlington's Chess Club; [hon.] M. Sc (Mech. Eng.), DMS. member of Asme, member of Astm, English Literature; [oth. writ.] Extensive journal publications in "Quality Matters" monthly magazine and "Metallurgy Today" monthly magazine. Poems published in "Through The Eyes of The Poet", an anthology. Poems published in local press and magazine.; [pers.] Images, pleasant sights, sounds and much more are vital parts of fine poetry, but the sum of the whole is music. A government health warning should be labeled to all verse: Musing the muse is bard for your health.; [a.] Darlington, Durham, UK, DL1 4PD

DUNCAN, EDNA
[b.] 13 October 1950, Sunderland; [p.] Daisy and Jack Rogerson; [m.] Malcolm; [ch.] Michael, aged 7; [occ.] Teaching Auxiliary - special educational needs - Cramlington High School; [oth. writ.] Various writings, compilations towards personal anthology; [pers.] I strive to reflect and balance the personal and unique qualities I find in people and in God's creations, surrounded by and captured in the 4 seasons of life: spring, summer, autumn and winter; [a.] Blyth, Northumberland, UK, NE24 5LE

DUNICAN, ELIZABETH
[b.] Armagh, NI; [p.] Eta Maginnis, James Maginnis; [m.] Christopher Dunican; [ch.] Paul, Kathy, Chris, Juanita; [ed.] Primary School Level; [occ.] Productive Operator; [hon.] Award winning essay on Canada; [oth. writ.] Several poems written and songs, not published.; [pers.] I strive to reflect the realistic nature of mankind in my writing. I have great fascination for early poets of sincerity and humour.; [a.] Clondalkin, Dublin 22, UK

DUNKLEY, GWENDOLINE TALLON
[pen.] Gwendoline Tallon; [b.] 21 June 1916, Wrexham; [p.] William Tallon and Elizabeth Tallon; [m.] George Edward Jones, 3 August 1940; [ch.] Cynthia Gwendoline, Rosalind Carole, and John Edward Tallon; [ed.] Victoria School, Wrexham Clwyd North Wales; [occ.] Retired, reside - overlooking North Sea Sheringham. Widowed, Married, John William Dunkley, 16 December 1989; [memb.] Wrexham Writers' Circle, St. John Ambulance Brigade, Divisional Superintent of Nursing Cadets Brymbo Clwyd, North Wales; [oth. writ.] Articles published in periodical Maldon. Essex. Several poems published in local community newspaper.; [pers.] I acquire pleasure whilst dancing in Spain - Wintertime. I am inspired by the realistic depth of W. Shakespeare's sonnet "True Love". I find a sense of humour is a Godsend when meditating on life's human frailties.; [a.] Sheringham, Norfolk, UK

DURU, SHEILA
[b.] 21 June 1949, London; [p.] James Dickson, Vera Blanche Dickson; [pers.] Poetry is the power of thought transmitted to the pen: stimulating the senses.; [a.] Cambridge, UK, CB2 2AJ

DYER-RICHIE, ROACHFORD
[b.] 25 April 1956, Montserrat; [p.] Divorced; [m.] Separated; [occ.] Self Employed Tarot Advisor, Retailer; [oth. writ.] So far unpublished manuscripts of novels and poetry.; [pers.] I am, I think, I breathe: woman.; [a.] Ladywood Birmingham, West Midlands, UK, B16 0BT

DYMOND, MICHAEL
[pen.] Vince Everett; [b.] 8 October 1961, England; [p.] Kath and John Dymond; [m.] Julie Dymond, 23 July 1994; [ch.] Michelle Dymond; [ed.] St. Anslem Secondary School; [occ.] Warehouse Operative; [oth. writ.] I had a poem published in the works magazine.; [pers.] I like writing poetry because I can show my feelings, what I think about life, people and the world around me in my poems.; [a.] Oldham, Lancashire, UK, OL1 4BN

EBERHARDT, JOAN
[pen.] Joan Bovell-Eberhardt; [b.] 11 July 1946, Glasgow; [p.] Deceased; [m.] Helge Eberhardt, 26 July 1969; [ch.] Meike, Peter; [ed.] Honours Degree in Modern Languages and Philosophy University of Leeds, later also Psychology and Diploma in Creative Writing; [occ.] Head of English Dept., Adult Education College Kiel; [memb.] Society of Authors, Regular Contributor to 'Writer's Forum'; [hon.] Ford Essay Prize; [oth. writ.] Miss Sophies Past and Other Lives (Oxford Univ. Press) 1994 Pandorah's Package and Other Stories (Minerva Press 1995) 'Isabel's Choice' (Novel), (The Book Guild 1996); [pers.] I hope to create a medium for reflection for the reader, allowing an individual perspective. I have been influenced by many aspects of European Languages and Literature; [a.] Kiel, Germany, 24145

ECKHARDT, PAMELA
[b.] 27 April 1922, Bromley; [p.] Harold Ewens, Trissie Ewens; [m.] Eduard Eckhardt, 16 February 1950; [ch.] Michael, Jennifer, Peter Derek and Grandson James; [occ.] Retired; [memb.] The Orchard Encore Theatre; [hon.] Medallion for poem in a book called 'Veterans of Victory' and a Certificate of Merit for a poem.; [oth. writ.] 21 poems published in books by Poetry Now, Arrival Press, Anchor Books and Triumph House; [pers.] I found inspiration in the everyday aspects of family life and the wonders of nature which are all about us and which each and everyone can identify with in the easy writing of my poems.; [a.] Swanley, Kent, UK, BR8 7TU

EDEN, JOHN
[b.] 17 October 1949, Surrey; [p.] Josephine; [m.] Jenny, 20 July 1996; [ch.] Robert (22) and Michael (13); [ed.] Bournemouth School; [occ.] Retired Police Constable now Library Assistant; [hon.] Police Long Service and Good Conduct medal; [oth. writ.] Compiler of crosswords published in various in house magazines for home office, securicor, met. Police etc.; [a.] Finchley, London, UK, N3 1BE

EDMONDS, MARTIN EDWARD
[b.] 24 July, Devonshire; [p.] Edward Edmonds; [m.] Elizabeth J. Edmonds; [ed.] College of St. Mark and St. John, Plymouth; [occ.] Student/ Local Broadcaster; [memb.] The Hell-Fire Club; [oth. writ.] Short stories and prose - poems published in small circulation journals.; [pers.] Well known locally for his role as "Master of the Macabre" on regional programming. Poetry is a relaxing diversion.; [a.] Plymouth, Devonshire, UK, PL3 4LE

EDMUNDS, BARRY
[b.] 17 June 1942, Woodbridge; [p.] Philip and Nellie Edmunds; [m.] Patricia Ann Edmunds, 26 June 1967; [ch.] Sheena, Karen; [ed.] Leiston Grammar S.E. London Tech. and Cambridge Col. of Arts and Tech. (applied Physics); [occ.] S.E. Auto Engineer; [oth. writ.] Technical tips published in woodworking magazine; [pers.] I try to influence everybody to appreciate and care for the wild life and its environment.; [a.] Carmarthenshire, UK, SA14 6HF

EDWARD, MARTIN MCKENZIE
[b.] 30 December 1963, Dundee; [ch.] Nalatie, Marie; [ed.] Harris Academy Dundee; [occ.] Full time student, B.A. Communications Bournemouth; [pers.] The poem is dedicated to Jean McKay Weir, a very special person; [a.] Bournemouth, Dorset, UK, BH1 4PN

EDWARDS, LEE
[b.] 26 June 1967, Birmingham; [p.] John and Ann Edwards; [m.] C. Deakin; [ch.] Belinda and Jake; [ed.] Kings-Heath Tei and Handsworth Technical College Birmingham; [occ.] Reluctant Security Officer; [oth. writ.] A collection of my poetry (Enough for a Book!?) titled "Thoughts in the Kitchen" (not yet published) a science fiction novel, in progress "Folk Tales" and many other scribblings.; [pers.] I like to write in a manner that `shocks'! or stirs the imagination, makes people think.; [a.] Birmingham, West Midlands, UK, B45 0BQ

EL-ALI, MARWA
[pen.] Marva; [b.] 16 April 1977, Sierra Leone; [p.] Hilal El-Ali, (F) Siham El-Ali; [ed.] The European University in Antwerp. A student in Social Science, in the 2nd year...; [hon.] The ECIS Award for International Understanding, Organizing International Day June 1994 at E.E.C. International School, Basketball Competition May 1994; [oth. writ.] Several poems published in my school yearbook from 1993-1995, "3 years" Editor of my school yearbook, and in some students' magazines. A book about my experiences and life... Not yet finished...; [pers.] "I am myself, Yet myself is still unaware of itself" I was born in Africa, where I grew up witnessing real nature (before man cut down all trees). Then moved to Europe where (History repeats it-self). Though I am originally from Lebanon where my "blood runs and thoughts could never escape". In a way, all three different cultures are a part of me. Do not know where I belong and can never be fully accepted in any of them. I feel so lost, yet gaining a lot. "I am the shadow that longs to capture your consciousness..."; [a.] Antwerp, Belgium, 2018

ELKINS-GREEN, UNA
[pen.] Una J. M. Elkins-Green; [b.] 22 July 1942, Oxted; [p.] Fredrick Atkins, Ivy Atkins; [m.] Anthony Elkins-Green, 10 March 1962 (1st) Widowed, 21 August 1991 (2nd); [ch.] Andrew Neil, Nicholas Michael, Karen-Marie; [ed.] Oxted County Grammar; [occ.] Manager Croydon College Bookshop; [hon.] English Language; [oth. writ.] Several poems published in magazines. Children's stories published in magazines.; [pers.] On writing poetry - all my poems are drawn from real life situations, or pure imagination. A most satisfying pastime with a sense of achievement.; [a.] Billinghurst, West Sussex, UK, RH14 9PL

ELLARD, HELEN
[b.] 9 August 1976, Meriden; [p.] David Ellard and Georgina Ellard; [ed.] Lasswade High School; [occ.] Clerical and Financial Assistant, University of Edinburgh; [oth. writ.] 2 poems in other anthologies: 'Why?' is in the 'The Forbidden Fruit', 'Dares' is in 'Rage and Rebellion' both published by Poetry Now; [pers.] I try to write from my heart and mind in a bid to rationalize my thoughts and feelings in the hope that I can learn from them.; [a.] Bonnyrigg, Midlothian, UK, EH19 2JE

ELLIOTT, EDWARD JAMES
[pen.] E. J. Elliott; [b.] 27 August 1955, Glasgow; [p.] James Elliott, Sarah Elliott; [m.] Susan Elliott; [ch.] Marc, Edward, Paul, River; [ed.] St. Johns, Gorbals, Glasgow, St. Brendans, Linwood Renfrewshire; [occ.] Carer to my father; [hon.] Football and swimming awards; [oth. writ.] 'Innocence', published in a 'Invitation to Poetry', 'Anchor Books'. Other writings, but have never published, currently engaged on the works of Jack, Denzel, and me.; [pers.] To make happy,

that which of mind, yearns and longs to God. The wynds of the imagination.; [a.] Newton-le-Willows, Merseyside, UK, WA12 9BY

ELLIS, SANDRA ELIZABETH
[pen.] Sandra Ellis; [b.] 28 October 1943, Wickford, Essex; [p.] Ruth (Nee Carter) and Leslie Flexman; [m.] Kenneth Peter Ellis, 28 September 1963; [ch.] Tracy Jane, Kerry Ann and Kristy Ruth; [ed.] Brentwood County High School for girls, Mid-Essex Technical College and School of Art, MALA School of Dancing; [occ.] Secretary - S. Essex Health Authority (Following 12 years in Banking); [memb.] Member of the Royal Academy of Dancing, Fellow of the Imperial Society of Teachers of Dancing (Operatic Ballet and Stage Branch), Hon. Secretary - Wickford Lawn Tennis Club, Member of the Institute of Advanced Motorists; [hon.] Cadburys Junior Writers Award; [oth. writ.] Various poems - school/church magazines etc. Biography - (with pinch of salt!) "Little Potatoes Are Small", (The Carter Family in Wickford from 1907) - unpublished; [pers.] I have always loved writing - even letter-writing is a literary challenge and one that I hope delights the recipient.; [a.] Wickford, Essex, UK

ELSWORTHY, KERRY
[pen.] Lena; [b.] 23 November 1979, Taunton; [p.] Lynne Gillian Elsworthy; [ed.] West Somerset Community College, Somerset College of Arts and Technology; [occ.] Waitress, Premier Restaurant, Minehead; [oth. writ.] Two poems published in "Poetry Now Young Writers": "Dorset and Somerset" and "Carousel".; [pers.] I like my poems to express a feeling of true meaning and depth. To allow the reader to focus on my way of thinking!; [a.] Williton, Somerset, UK, TA4 4SD

EMSDEN, MARGARET ANN
[b.] 23 March 1944, Eyke; [p.] Mr. and Mrs. S. Fordham; [m.] Mr. Richard Emsden, 1 April 1967; [ch.] Two boys; [ed.] Hadlegh High School, Ipswich College; [occ.] Doctor's Receptionist; [hon.] Pithans shorthand and typing; [oth. writ.] Poem published in local magazine and for colleagues on their retirement from work etc.; [pers.] It gives me great pleasure in putting my reflections down in the form of a poem.; [a.] Bildeston, Suffolk, UK, IP7 7BG

ESCOTT, BERYL E.
[b.] St. Johns, Newfoundland; [p.] Ernest and Anne Escott, [ed.] Guernsey Intermediate Chorley Grammar, Saltburn High, Kings College, Durham University; [occ.] Retired WRAF Officer now - writer Historical (Non fiction); [memb.] Member of Institute of Management, Life Member of National Trust and English Heritage. Member of Royal Shakespeare Theatre Society, Friend of Shakespeare Birthplace Trust, Member of Society of Authors, Off Pension Soc, RAF Club, WRAF Off's Assoc, Committee Member of Area Community Educ. Council, Shakespeare Club, Halls Craft Club, Embroiders Assoc., member of NADFAS; [hon.] BA, MIMgt; [oth. writ.] Editor (contributor) to many RAF newspapers and magazines - latterly the Haltonian 1981-5 publications: 1968 History of Headquarters Bomber Command 1984 - story of Halton House and Alfred de Rothschild, RAF PUb 1989 - Women in Airforce Blue (Hist 1918-89) Pub Patrick Stephens, 1991 - Mission Improbable WARF in So E. Pub Patrick Stephens, 1993 - Means of Victory contributed article on WW 2 WAAF - Bomber and Ass, 1995 - Our Wartime Days (WW 2 WAARF) Pub Sutton. Presently researching for new book 'Bravest of the Brave' pub. Sutton; [pers.] History is my love, poetry is my pleasure. It is good sometimes to turn from the world of fact to the world of imagination.; [a.] Stratford upon Avon, Warks, UK, CV37 6RB

EVANS, JANET
[b.] 5 November 1936, Corsock Village, Kirkcudbright; [p.] Robert John and Emily Jane

McClymont; [m.] Divorced; [ch.] Tanay, Amanda Jayne; [ed.] Kirkcudbright Acadamy, New Abbey Secondary; [occ.] Retired

FAIRLESS, OLWYN
[b.] 21 May 1936, Middlebrough; [p.] John and Lilian Moore; [m.] John T. Fairless, 9 December 1967; [ch.] Gillian, Simon, Andrew; [ed.] Ayresome Girls School; [occ.] retail security; [oth. writ.] Many other poems but this is the first time I have ever entered any sort of competition.; [pers.] The daily business of life is a script waiting to be written.; [a.] Middlesbrough, Cleveland, TS5 7DB

FAIRLEY, JAMES T.
[pen.] James Fairley; [b.] 2 December 1936, Edinburgh; [p.] James Fairley, Margaret Fairley; [m.] Margaret Fyfe Fairley, 1 March 1958; [ch.] Loraine, James, Michael, Ian, Jeffrey, Gail, Claire, Gregor; [ed.] St. Columba's Cowdenbeath Fife; [occ.] Retired Police Officer, Strathclyde Police and now a part-time Library Attendant, Milton, Glasgow; [hon.] O.N.C. Electronics; [oth. writ.] Only privately; [pers.] I enjoy helping other people - "We are all but passing through this life."; [a.] Glasgow, Strathclyde, UK, G22 6NY

FAIRWEATHER, DORIS
[b.] 18 August 1926, Renfrew, Scotland; [p.] John Taggart, Isabella Taggart; [m.] W. Ron Fairweather (Now Deceased), June 22 1971; [ed.] Govan High School, Royal Scottish Academy of Music; [occ.] Retired Teacher of Singing; [memb.] Glasgow Cathedral Choir - formerly as Principal Soprano - now as Voluntary Chorister; [hon.] F.T.C.L., LRAM, ARCM, (Singing, Performer and Teacher); [oth. writ.] Articles and poems for church magazine - but mainly as a pleasurable pursuit.; [pers.] Inclined toward descriptive writing based on a combination of past experiences and observation of human and animal behaviour in everyday life.; [a.] Glasgow, Strathclyde, UK, G41 5AA

FALKENLOWE, MICHAEL BARON OF RUTZ
[pen.] Michael Rutz; [b.] 2 August, 1942, Copenhagen; [p.] General Falkenlowe, Baron of Rutz; [ed.] Archus Univerastet, Faculty of Journalism; [occ.] writer (and Baron); [memb.] Danish Writers Assoc.; [hon.] Knight of the Most Venerable Order of Malta; [oth. writ.] 16 books, novels, poems, short stories, plays and 23 years of journalism in Danish media; [a.] Hadsund, Denmark 9560.

FARLEY, MRS. CLARE MARY
[b.] 4 February 1948, Swindon; [p.] Ruby Maller, Colin Maller; [m.] Richard Brian Farley, 12 April 1979; [ch.] Nic, Stephen, Caroline, Trish; [ed.] Brockenhurst Grammar, Philippa Fawcett College of Education, Reading University, Working with Graham Bevis; [occ.] English teacher Richard Aldworth Community School Basingstoke; [memb.] RSPB; [hon.] (Distinction) MA in Education; [oth. writ.] Several articles in county and national publications, co-editor of "User Friendly" county periodical, contributed to "Language in Contest" and "Creative Language".; [pers.] Life is not a dress-rehearsal.; [a.] Basingstoke, Hants, UK, RG22 5EN

FARRELL, GERALD LEO
[b.] 23 August 1930, Manchester; [p.] Mr. Thomas Francis Farrell, Mary Agnes Farrell; [m.] Emily Farrell, 11 June 1960; [ch.] Angela, Lynne, Elaine, Jo Anne, Denise, Sharon; [occ.] Retired; [memb.] R.A.F.A. Sale; [pers.] To make people aware of the beauty of the country side for all mankind and not to abuse this wonderful gift.; [a.] Manchester, Lancashire, UK, M31 4PP

FARRELL, HELEN
[b.] 21 December 1982, Eccles, M/CR; [p.] Peter Farrell, Ann Farrell; [ed.] Stretford Grammar; [occ.] At School; [pers.] In my poetry I strive to put my views on the complicated world into simpler terms for myself and others around me.; [a.] Eccles, Greater Manchester, UK, M30 0FX

FARRELL, MARGARET
[b.] Pensioner, Liverpool; [p.] John and Ann Gannon; [m.] Charles, 19 May 1956; [occ.] Retired

FAULKNER, ROSS
[pen.] Ross Faulkner; [b.] 7 May 1966, Sidcup, Kent; [p.] Marjorie Faulkner and Graham Faulkner; [m.] Gabriella Faulkner, 29 October 1994; [ed.] Homewood School Tenterden, Kent, North Sydney Tech. Australia; [occ.] Proprietor of Decorating Business; [oth. writ.] At 19 I had a dream, so vivid and real it seemed more like a memory. That's when I realized there is more to life than meets the eye. So much more. So we write for those who cannot see so they may know the magic.; [pers.] Langton by Wragby; [a.] Lincoln, UK, LN3 5QB

FELDMAN, HILARY ROSALIND
[pen.] Rosie Kinsler; [b.] 28 February 1947, Hampton, Middx; [p.] Anne Stricker (Nee Kinsler), Alec Stricker; [m.] Divorced; [ch.] Julia Louise, Robert Mark; [ed.] Mount Pleasant Secondary Modern, Mount Pleasant Lane, London E5; [occ.] School's General Kitchen Assistant (Dinner Lady); [pers.] To congratulate yourself, one needs to be the cat and come up to scratch.; [a.] Ilford, Essex, UK, IG6 1AG

FEREK-PETRIC, MARGARETA
[b.] 20 December 1982, Zagreb; [p.] Ivancica (Mother), Bozidar (Father); [occ.] The pupil of the final grade of the school "Gracani"; [oth. writ.] Two prose stories and a poem in the school papers "Cvrcak" (The Cricket), published in Croatian. I write lyrics and poems in Croatian and English language.; [pers.] This world is a cold place and I think that writing is the sun keeping us warm. I like to write lyrics and to listen to the music. I would like to be involved in the struggle for peace and freedom.; [a.] Zagreb, Croatia, 10000

FIRTH, EMERYL
[b.] 13 April 1982, Barnsley; [p.] Sylvia Barker, Shaun Firth; [ed.] Wombwell High School; [memb.] WWF; [pers.] I am a school girl of 14 years old and love to put my thoughts down in writings such as poems. I hope to be able to do many more in my future.; [a.] Barnsley, Yorkshire, UK, S73 0EJ

FISHER, SIDNEY RICHARD
[b.] 11 December 1910, Gravesend; [p.] Florence M. Fisher, Edward J. Fisher; [m.] Kathleen Mary Fisher, 7 May 1938; [ch.] Sally Fisher, David Fisher; [ed.] Gravesend County School for Boys; [occ.] Retired - Civil Servant; [memb.] Curry Rivel Footpaths Group-Life Member, Saffron Walden Footpath Group-Life Member, Seekers Association, Friends Fellowship of Healing, Religion Society of Friends (Quakers); [hon.] Fellow of Chartered Insurance Institute (FCII), The Universal Order - Second Degree Neophyte (Fellow); [oth. writ.] Dust and Stars (Prose and Poetry), 6.95 pounds published: Avon Books 1995 A Spiritual Autobiography, pamphlets and booklets: Avifauna of Alnwick Northrambeland (Wild Flowers of Curry Rivel), Walks Around Saffron Walden (Public Footpaths of Curry Rivel), Rambles Around Saffon Walden "Northern Lights" A World Citizen newsletter etc., Quaker (Religious Society of Friends: Briton Yearly Meeting) Pacifist, World Citizen, Mystic and Universalist; [a.] Carry Rivel, Sumerset, UK, TA10 0PU

FITZ-GERALD, SCOTT
[pen.] Scott Fitz-Gerald; [b.] 27 June 1979, Cardiff; [p.] Lyn and John Fitz-Gerald; [ed.] 6 GCSE's, and due to complete a level English Literature and a level Theatre Studies, hoping to study drama as a degree, studied at St. Teilo's C/N High School; [occ.] Student, and part time amateur actor/writer; [memb.] Welsh Literary Academy; [oth. writ.] I've a collection of over 50 poems. 20 sketches, 3 plays, but as of yet but none has been recognized.; [pers.] Life is not a crossword puzzle, not everything that makes sense and links conveniently is necessarily right. You need to find what you think is the answer and ask why? And once you've found that answer you question again and again, for words are only pen and paper, their meanings are far more fickle, and are lost with time and tide.; [a.] Cardiff, S. Glamorgan, UK, CF3 8AA

FLAHERTY, PEGGIE
[b.] 23/9/35; [p.] Bartley OMalley & Norah OMalley; [m.] 18/1/53; [ch.] ten; [ed.] Third level education; [occ.] Housewife & writting; [pers.] Inishtrawar, Scholar and Beaghye;

FLEMING, PETER MARCUS
[b.] 3 November 1952, Plymouth; [p.] William Travers Fleming, Eva Fleming; [ed.] Plympton Secondary School, M.O.D. Devonport Deckyard Technical College, Plymouth College of Further Education, Plymouth Polytechnic.; [occ.] Communication Engineer - Works at Home; [memb.] The institute of Patentees and Inventors, The International Songwriters Association; [hon.] ONC in Naval Architecture and Ship Building, Technician Education Council Diploma in Electronics, and with distinctions.; [oth. writ.] I have written over sixty songs and a lot of poems. (all unpublished); [pers.] In my poetry and song writing I try to create energies that could uplift and enrich people's lives. I have been influenced by Peter Gabriel, the Moody Blues, the Beatles and some poets and philosophers throughout the ages.; [a.] Plymouth, Devon, UK, PL6 5XD

FLETCHER, ROSEMARY ANNE
[b.] 19 September 1983, Leamington Spa; [p.] David and Anny Fletcher; [ed.] American School, Nouakchott French School, Bujumbura, French School, Antananarivo, Dean Close School Cheltenham; [occ.] Student; [hon.] School award for poetry recital; [oth. writ.] Poems and short stories; [pers.] I enjoy reading and reciting poetry, as well as writing it.; [a.] Cheltenham, Gloucestershire, UK, GL51 6EB

FLINT, CATHERINE
[b.] 12 April 1929, Devonport; [memb.] B.A.S.C.A.; [hon.] Mensa Cert.; [oth. writ.] I love singing and have written many kinds of songs, including gospel and children's songbook. Also: stories and teaching manuals in connection with alternative health and rejuvenation, Yoga, singing and dressmaking. I have had poems published in several anthologies and a hymn in Dame Thora Hird's book for help the aged.; [pers.] As a woman, in my poems, I often like to put myself in the shoes of children and men and sometimes, animals. I have a very special sympathy for all kinds of animals who are cruelly treated and misused and have written an appropriate song on their behalf which needs to be published to raise money for this kind of charity!; [a.] Harrow, UK, HA2 0RS

FLORES, CHARLES
[b.] 6 March 1948, Malta; [p.] George and Catherine Flores; [m.] Margaret Nee Ciantar, 9 December 1973; [ch.] Rona and Davida; [ed.] Stalbert's, Malta, De La Salle College, Malta, Syracuse University (U.S.A.), University of Malta; [occ.] Journalist/Broadcaster; [memb.] Maltese Literary Academy; [hon.] Winner of various national literary awards for works in Maltese. Winner (Europe and Canada Region) of Commonwealth Short Story Competition; [oth. writ.] Various novels and theologies in Maltese and English (personal and shared). Writers also for "The European" and Associated Press. Newspaper Columnist.; [pers.] I associate writing with pain but not in the escapist manner. It is more a quest for inner truths and their sharing.; [a.] Birkirkara, Malta, BKR 08

FOLEY, PATRICK J.
[b.] March 29, 1969, Stepney

FOORT, CHRISTINE ELIZABETH
[pen.] Christine Foort; [b.] 19 May 1958, London, Woolwich; [p.] Mr. Kenneth and Mrs. Edna Foxon; [m.] Roger Foort, 18 August 1990; [ed.] Upton County High School St. James Avenue Upton-by-Chester, Cheshire; [occ.] Housewife, also p/time carer; [memb.] North West Afghan Racing Club; [oth. writ.] A novel entitled The Dark Side of Rashid published by Minerva Press. Publishers 1 Cromwell Place, London, SW7 2JE; [pers.] Write from the heart; [a.] Chester, Cheshire, UK, CH3 5RU

FORGE, MARTIN
[b.] 16 May 1945, London; [p.] Edward and Wilhelmina Forge; [m.] Wendy Annette; [ch.] Elliott Martin, Kristian Martin; [ed.] Henry Compton School London; [occ.] National Accounts Manager; [memb.] Finch Coaster Running CLub, Yateley Aikedo Club; [hon.] Marketing Diploma; [oth. writ.] Poems and short stories. None offered for publication; [pers.] I believe that poetry is just a form of communication. My poems reflect my views on real life including the harshness, stupidity, greed, compassion and love in mankind and nature.; [a.] Camberley, Surrey, UK, GU17 0AP

FOWKES, ALAN S.
[pen.] Sekwof; [b.] 15 April 1970, Wolverhampton; [p.] Ken and Linda Fowkes; [ed.] Springs Central (South Africa), Smeston High (Wton), Wulfrun College (Wton); [occ.] Marine Engineering Electrician; [oth. writ.] Various poems North Published.; [pers.] A toast to the future however uncertain - for one day it will all be sorted out, won't it?!; [a.] Wolverhampton, West Midlands, UK, WV3 7BN

FOX, ELIZABETH
[b.] 2 March 1979, Ipswich; [p.] Graham Fox, Veronica; [ed.] Copleston High School, Northgate Sixth Form; [occ.] Student; [mcmb.] Northgate School Choir, Copleston School Choir, Wing and A Prayer Theatre Company, St. John's Church Music Group Ipswich; [pers.] I visited some battlefields on a school trip in October 1994, and it provoked such deep emotions in me that I decided to write them down in this poem.; [a.] Ipswich, Suffolk, UK, IP4 4RP

FRAME, PAUL
[pen.] Paul Wardle; [b.] 17 May 1948, South Shields; [p.] John Thomas Storey Frame, Agnes Middlemost Wardle; [ed.] South Shields Grammar Technical School; [occ.] Writing; [oth. writ.] Various poems in newspapers and one spoken on Tyne Tees television, religious epilogue, together with poems in book anthologies.; [a.] South Shields, Tyne and Wear, UK, NE34 0HP

FRECKLETON, SAMUEL
[b.] 31 March 1944, Manchester, Jamaica; [p.] Eurelda and Cyril Freckleton; [m.] Mrs. Gleneta Freckleton, 28 May 1980; [ch.] Mark Phillips Freckleton; [ed.] Elementary; [occ.] Mechanic; [memb.] Church of Jesus Christ of Latter Day Saints; [oth. writ.] Unpublished TV plays, unpublished book, unpublished TV sit comedy; [pers.] I am very happy to learn that my poem The Long Dark Road had been chosen, I am very grateful to the selection committee who judged, with such precisement, I still can't comprehend.; [a.] London, Wembley Middx, UK, HA9 9UL

FREELAND, STEVE
[b.] 29 December 1948, Aden; [p.] Henry Douglas and Gladys Mary; [m.] Twice married and divorced; [ch.] Paul Andrew and Suzanne Jane; [ed.] 1957-1965 Merchant Taylors', Crosby, Nr. Liverpool; [occ.] Landlord of the Concle Inn; [memb.] Numerous amateur dramatic and operatic societies and sporting activities.; [hon.] Best Performances as an actor for 'Twelfth Night' - Feste, and for 'Dick Deadeye' in HMS Pinafore, and Player of the Year for a local football team.; [oth. writ.] A few songs for Guitar Accompani-

ment Inc. 'It's Too Late For Me', and numerous personal poems about life and the world.; [pers.] I am a soul in torment over humanity's treatment of each other and of the world in which we live. I fear the headlong plunge we are making toward oblivion - sooner than we dare believe I feel.; [a.] Barrow-in-Furness, Cumbria, UK, LA13 0PU

FREEMANTLE, DEIDRE
[pen.] Keisha Murphy; [b.] 19 August 1979, Jamaica; [p.] Beverly Smith and Patrick Freemantle; [ed.] Ocho Rios High, Jamaica and Croydon College (Farfield); [occ.] Student (Croydon College); [memb.] Logos Bible Church; [hon.] G.C.S.E. (English Language, English Literature grade B).; [oth. writ.] I have written poems and songs which have never been published,; [pers.] In my writings I try to bring across inner feelings most people are afraid to explore. I have been influenced by the Christian faith and my past and present English Literature teacher.; [a.] Croydon, Surrey, UK, CR0 8JT

FREETH, GLENN
[pen.] G. C. Freeth; [b.] 15 December 1971, West Bromwich; [hon.] If I were to win some money then I would spend it on buying the book with my poems in.; [oth. writ.] I thought my background not suitable to write poetry. I saw it as the antithesis of what I was after leaving comprehensive school with no significant knowledge or trades and a council estate upbringing; I didn't seem poetry material, but I have proved myself wrong. I have been given the conviction to carry on writing poetry. Which I find a somewhat uneasy process within the framework I live in.; [pers.] I strive to relate in my poetry to a universal self which is all man and to play a small part in breaking down barriers. I would like to dedicate the poem to my deceased father.; [a.] West Brom, Black Country, UK, B71 3EU

FRENCH, JULIE-ANNE
[b.] 12 January 1976, Waterford; [p.] Eleanor and John J. French; [ed.] Cathal Brugha Street, The Dublin Institute of Technology; [occ.] Student; [memb.] Book Club of Ireland; [oth. writ.] Short stories and poems; [pers.] The poets who have had the most influence on me include Percy B. Shelley, William Wordsworth and Patrick Kavanagh; [a.] Dungarvan, Waterford,

FRY, ANDREW JOHN
[pen.] Andrew J. Fry; [b.] 29 July 1961, Torquay; [p.] David and Joy Fry; [m.] Jean Fry, 3 December 1993; [ed.] Bluecoat School Pilton and Pilton Comprehensive Barnstaple; [occ.] Writer and Voluntary Worker; [memb.] Evangelical Alliance Labour Party and CMS Westcountry Writers Assoc. D.A.U.N. Amnesty Deo. Gloria Trust; [hon.] NLP Course, Myers-Briggs Course; [oth. writ.] Badger Books, Disability Now papers, local paper articles, published three vol. Poetry Inc. in five anthologies; [pers.] And the lame man walked.; [a.] Barnstaple, Devon, UK, EX31 3QX

FULLSTONE, RAYMOND
[b.] 2 February 1962, Forest Gate, London; [p.] Ronald and Elsie Fullstone; [m.] Angela Margaret, 10 August 1985; [ch.] Zoe Anne; [ed.] Brampton Manor Comprehensive, Eastham London, E.6; [occ.] Unemployed; [oth. writ.] Nothing published; [pers.] I believe we should make the most of what we have now, rather than progress blindly into the future without care or thought.; [a.] Barking, Essex, UK, IG11 9HG

FUTER, DONALD
[b.] 18 January 1929, Edenham, Lincs; [p.] Joshua and Ethel Futer; [m.] Constance Elizabeth Futer, 21 August 1954; [ch.] Pamela Mungroo and Julie Ward; [ed.] Grammar School, Bourne, Lincs; [occ.] Retired Police Officer; [oth. writ.] Poem, Twilight Dream, being published in 'Sands of Time' Penhaligon Page Poetry/Today. 'Ode to the Cathedral Builders of

Lincoln', being published in 'Images of Thought', Hilton House Publishers, 'The Stinging Nettle' in whispers Norwich. In the Garden, by Poetry Guild.; [pers.] Resides near birthplace of Alfred Lord Tennyson in Lincolnshire, inspired by his works. Attempts to remind people of the values of small and simple things often taken for granted.; [a.] Lincoln, Lincolnshire, UK, LN3 5UD

GABB, IAN A.
[b.] 30 April 1954, Lewisham; [oth. writ.] "Lambs To The Slaughter"; [pers.] I dedicated this poem to my father, your wisdom follows me.; [a.] UK

GABRIAL, JOSEPH
[pen.] Gabrial M. J.; [b.] 2 June 1964, Anachal Kerala, India; [p.] Ouseph Joseph, Annakutty Joseph; [ed.] M.A. (Political Science) University Of Kerala, India.; [occ.] Product Designer; [memb.] Gandhi Peace Foundation Library, New Delhi; [hon.] NIL.; [oth. writ.] Written poems in english, several poems and songs in Malayalam, one of the Indian languages.; [pers.] In my writing, I'd like to say this must "Just think..." I have been greatly influenced by the poems of Keats and the philosophy of Socrates and Mahatma Gandhi.; [a.] Anachal, Kerala, India, 685565

GABRIELA, GREATWOOD
[pen.] Gaby; [b.] 20 February 1955, Macaresti, Romania; [p.] Micu A. Melania, Micu N. Aurel-Vasile; [m.] I am separated since 1986, 17 October 1982; [ch.] One boy - Greatwood Terence-Petre; [ed.] I followed studies ay the Lyceum, Mihai Eminescu Nr 2 in Iasi Town - Romania 1965-1973 when I obtained my diploma of Bacalaureat - I studied at the University Al.I. Cuza - Iasi - Romania 1976-1980 when I obtained my diploma a teacher in English and French; [occ.] Poet - Writer; [hon.] My teaching diploma - of a teacher in English and French, I am; [oth. writ.] The anthology of poems entitled "The Eye Of Life" (1996) a volume of poetry with over 400 poems - entitled - "I Am The Running River" (1989-1996) - volume - title - a volume of poetry entitled "The Bribary of Life" - (1982) a volume of poetry entitled "The Burning Star" That Glitters In The Night Into The Glitter Of My Soul - (1992); [pers.] I love the words I write - into the beauty of my soul filled up into the beauty of the words I write - the pleasure of writing is the joy of my life - into the red wine of the lips I drink forever; [a.] Isleworth, Middlesex, UK, TW7 4NY

GALE, CHRISTINE
[pen.] Christine Neville; [b.] 30 March 1939, Bristol; [p.] George and Joyce Osborne; [m.] The late Peter Neville Gale, 16 December 1961; [ch.] Jo-Anne, Anton and Melvin; [ed.] Victoria Commercial Institute Trowbridge Wilts; [occ.] Retired Secretary and Book-Keeper; [oth. writ.] Life's Awakening After Death's Sorrow published in - "Voices On The Wind" 1996. Other poems written but not sent anywhere to be published.; [pers.] Lonesome remember in an expression of my feelings of life without my husband who died suddenly after 30 years of a wonderful marriage.; [a.] Bridgewater, Somerset, UK, TA7 9AF

GAMBLES, STEPHEN
[b.] 6 March 1962, Sheffield; [p.] Derek and Audrey; [m.] Janet, 4 August 1995; [ch.] Stefan and Tammy; [ed.] Bluestone, Infant and Junior School, Ashleigh, Comprehensive School; [occ.] Painter and Decorator; [memb.] Blades, Revival, Season Ticket Holder at the above; [oth. writ.] The Party, Tableau of Beauty, The Inspiration, Papover Rhaeus; [a.] Sheffield, South Yorkshire, UK, S12 4ED

GARCIA, EDITH
[b.] 30 June 1925, Denton, M/C; [p.] Fred Barlow, Edith Barlow; [m.] Leonard Garcia (Deceased), 4 August 1970; [ed.] Denton St. Lawrence Cofe,

Manchester Conservatoire of Music and Drama; [occ.] Retired; [hon.] Diploma and Merit - Voice, Production and Solo Singing, Diploma and Merit - Guitar and Musical Theory; [pers.] The beauty of nature is my inspiration.; [a.] Blackpool, Lancashire, UK, FY4 1HE

GARDHAM, RICHARD ALAN
[pen.] Richard Gardham; [b.] 21 August 1941, South Elmsall; [p.] Jabas Joshef, Ceilia; [ed.] Westfield Lane, Secondary Modern School; [occ.] Builders workman; [oth. writ.] Unedited manuscript 8 inchs high, 35 years accumulation; [pers.] Sufi; [a.] South Elmsall A Village, Yorkshire, UK, WF9 2XA

GARDINER, TOM
[b.] 20 July 1968, St. Andrews; [p.] Jack Gardiner and Sheila Gardiner; [ch.] Rachel; [ed.] Kirkland High School, Methil, Fife; [occ.] Dispatch Administrator; [memb.] Bass Player and Co-Songwriter in an amateur rock band!; [hon.] High School Dux Award in German and Modern Studies (1985); [oth. writ.] No previous compositions submitted for publication (prefer song writing); [pers.] I would like to dedicate my writing to all those around me, loved or otherwise, as they are my inspiration.; [a.] Windygates, Fife, UK, KY8 5DU

GARDNER, CHRIS
[b.] 24 September 1964, Preston; [p.] James Jesse and Diana Gardner; [ed.] Southmoor Comprehensive, Manchester Polytechnic (School of Theatre); [occ.] Actor, Writer and Director; [memb.] SGI-UK, Amnesty International Equity, Actors Benevolent Fund; [hon.] Theatre studies (1st class honour with distinction). Diploma in European History; [oth. writ.] Theatre and radio plays as well as other poems - unpublished at present!; [pers.] True happiness is not a life without problems, but is having enough wisdom and courage to turn them into an advantage.; [a.] Richmond, Surrey, UK, TW9 2EW

GARDNER, ENID
[b.] 26 October 1943, Wigan, Lancs; [p.] Norman Harter, Doris Harter; [m.] Alex Gardner, 30 March 1966; [ch.] Alan Gardner; [ed.] Leigh Technical College, Leigh Lancs, Left with Secretarial and Bookkeeping Qualifications; [occ.] Personnel Officer, Royal College of Surgeons of Edinburgh; [memb.] IPD, Edinburgh Branch of National Assoc of Secretaries, Kings Theatre Club; [oth. writ.] Several poems published in other anthologies (Stylus 1486) and a collection of children's poetry in a small booklet.; [pers.] I have loved poetry since I was a small child. It has always delighted me the way a thought or a moment can be encapsulated in verse. I am greatly drawn to the Shakespeare sonnets and Wordsworth's poems.; [a.] Edinburgh, West Lothian, Scotland, EH10 4AG

GARDNER, MELISSA TELERI
[b.] 14 January 1976, Carmarthen; [p.] Ian and Sue Gardner; [ed.] Bacon's City Technology College, Lambeth College; [occ.] Toy Analyst; [pers.] In my poetry I try to reflect feelings that could be true to many people, making it not personal but an expression of the life being lived by so many around us.; [a.] Peckham, London, UK, SE15 4HX

GARDNER, TREVOR ARTHUR
[pen.] T.A.G.; [b.] 2 April 1952, Bournemouth; [p.] Myra Esme Gardner, Edward George Gardner; [ed.] Winton Boy's School; [oth. writ.] I have written poems over the last ten years, this is the first to be seen by anyone.; [a.] Bournemouth, Dorset, UK, BH9 3NR

GARNER, ELLIOTT C.
[b.] 20 October 1968, Peterborough; [p.] Steve and Carol Garner; [m.] Helen Garner, 1 April 1996; [ch.] Wendy, Mark, Luke; [ed.] South Axelholme Comprehensive, South Humberside;

[occ.] Self-employed Company Director; [memb.] Kawasaki Riders Club; [hon.] English Literature, (C.S.E.), English Language (C.S.E.), Basic Engineering (Distinction), B.S. 5750 Part 2; [oth. writ.] Articles in local papers, features such as my work within the company and the various services we provide to industry.; [pers.] Don't walk in the shadows of others, you'll only come second!; [a.] Sheffield, South Yorkshire, UK, S30 3NB

GASKIN, JO ROSSON
[b.] 21 February 1925, Tamworth; [p.] Deceased; [m.] Frank Gaskin, (second) 1963; [ed.] 9 different schools due to circumstances, college: German Language Painting and Modelling; [occ.] Retired - writing; [memb.] 'Poetry Now', 'Flair for Words'; [hon.] Special commendation for "The Wolf", National Poet of the Year/96 - Hilton House; [oth. writ.] Published in 8 anthologies; desperately trying to get published in children's stories and adult reading.; [pers.] Born into the circus and had an awful childhood. Eloped when 20 years old but my husband died young. Have written biography.; [a.] Solihull, West Midlands, B91 1UB

GASPAR, MRS. M. E.
[pen.] Meg, Lulu, Hot-Hot Lady, Tosca, Shortie, Alien, Ding-A-Ling; [b.] 24 August 1947, Rhodesia now Zimbabwe; [p.] Jack Donald Baked (Deceased), Sophia Elizabeth Earl; [m.] Manuel Domingues Gaspar died April '93, 6 August 1968; [ch.] Mandy Elizabeth (15) adopted, Anthony Manuel (29) our own; [ed.] A total of seven years and two months - education, 7 years Junior School but missed one full year due to illness - 6 years Junior School and one year and two months in high school; [occ.] Live-in/ Home-Care: Serve to mankind. Handcrafts/ Baking/Poetry; [hon.] (OH) This amateur poet won first prize in Africa - for the first poetry competition she entered!; [oth. writ.] To magazines and newspapers - I love to push a pen over paper! Can empty a ballpen in two days.; [pers.] Of essence - I am a philosopher in the true sense, with hope, no matter what - God and his son Jesus are the ones who give me hope, even in the darkest times - no matter what: I do not attend any church - as those I tried were without God and Jesus; [a.] Witham, UK, CM8 2LJ

GATENBY, JULIE
[b.] 3 March 1965, Durham; [p.] Patricia Rivett, Leslie C. Rivett; [m.] Nigel Ronald Gatenby, 2 July 1983; [ch.] Thomas, Matthew, Anna; [occ.] Playgroup Helper, Housewife, Mother; [a.] Harden, West Yorkshire, UK, BD16 1LQ

GELDART, E. M.
[b.] 29 July 1916, Audley; [m.] Widow, 12 May 1944; [ed.] Local Schools; [occ.] Retired; [oth. writ.] Yes; [a.] S-O-T, Staffs, UK, ST78 ETY

GEORGE, LINDA
[b.] 17 February 1951, Gower, S Wales; [p.] Anna and Robert William Phillips; [m.] Divorced; [ch.] Gaynor George, Anna George and Helen George; [ed.] Mynyddbach Comprehensive School, for girls in Swansea, S. Wales; [occ.] Secretary Administrator; [memb.] Runrig fan Club member; [hon.] Several passes in G.C.S.E. and typewriting and Secretarial Studies. I also now hold a certificate for poetry issued to me for outstanding achievement in poetry (Editor's Choice Award) from International Society of Poets; [oth. writ.] "That Special Moment" published in "The Other Side Of The Mirror", "Forbidden Love" published in "Quiet Moments", "Holy Waters" to be published in "Jewels of the Imagination". I have written 50 poems to date.; [pers.] I was originally influenced to write, by Stuart, the love of my life. I now write about most subjects that I have strong interests in. I have had several misfortunes in life but God walks with me and picks me up. Besides having my poems all published in one book I would like

to sing to a live audience. I have been auditioned and thoroughly enjoyed it. I love music as well as poetry. Finally I am now planing on writing a romantic novel.; [a.] Swansea, W. Glam, UK, SA6 7NZ

GERRARD, STEVE
[b.] 26 October 1958, Bolton; [m.] Janet Birchall, 26 April 1986; [ch.] Silvannen Rebecca, Alexander James Steven; [ed.] Walkden High, Eccles College Manchester Polytechnic; [occ.] Self Employed; [oth. writ.] Novel in progress; [pers.] The 'Watcher' I dedicate to my wife and children. 'The True Gift of Life is the Wonder of Nature'.; [a.] Walkden, Lancashire, UK, M28 3RF

GHURA, ANTOINETTE
[pen.] Antoinette Giles; [b.] 13 June 1957, Italy, Bari; [p.] Balwant and Luigia Ghura; [ed.] William Morris Senior High, Southern Training College, Sussex London Art College, Bristol Southgate College, Writers Ring, Shropshire; [hon.] Art, Library and Information, Nursery Nursing, Community Studies; [oth. writ.] Several articles published in magazines and newspapers, - Daily Mirror, Evening Standard, Woman's Own, People's Friend, Money Magazine.; [pers.] I enjoy writing about the positive experiences in my life, that make it so special, worthwhile and magical to me.; [a.] London, UK, EI3 9DA

GIBBONS, DAWN MARIE
[b.] 26 December 1978, Waltham Forest; [p.] Christine Colyer, Roger Gibbons; [ed.] Highams Park G.M. School 1990-1995, Highams Park 6th form College 1995-1997; [occ.] 'A' level student; [oth. writ.] A few poems published in 'Poetry Now' anthologies.; [pers.] It is incredible that such a beautiful thing as poetry can come from a time and place which is filled with so many destructive influences.; [a.] Chingford, London, UK, E4 9BD

GIBSON, ELLIOTT JAMES
[b.] 3 September 1944, Gateshead; [p.] Elliott Gibson, Martha Gibson; [m.] Marian Gibson, 13 October 1965; [ch.] Sharon Elizabeth, Jennifer Vivien; [ed.] Beaconsfield Grammar School; [occ.] Retired Police Sergeant; [memb.] 'Springs' Health and Fitness Club, Gateshead; [hon.] Diploma in European Humanities (OU), (Pending Final Exam Result BA (Hons) Open University); [oth. writ.] Nothing published; scripted series of cameo's for 'in house' training video.; [pers.] It is regrettable that it has taken the death of a good man to promote the necessity for good citizenship to be included in the school curriculum. The increasing absence of reasonable parenthood has made those obvious for several decades, ask any policeman.; [a.] Gateshead, Tyne and Wear, UK, NE9 5RE

GILBERT, AGNES P.
[pen.] Cathy A. P. Cregan; [b.] 15 September 1934, Limerick; [p.] Agnes and Patrick Cregan; [m.] James Gilbert (Separated) 20 years, 21 November 1954; [ch.] Theresa, Stan, Glona Kyran, Maurice Geraldine; [ed.] Boarding school. 1940 to 1952 Brigidine Convent Mount Rath. Co. Leix. Ireland.; [occ.] Retired 20 yrs. ago due to accident., wheelchair confined.; [memb.] Reg. Mem. Irish Wheelchair Association Elected Member of "Council for the Status of People with Disabilities". Ass. Sec. Ir. Wc. Ass. Local Branch.; [hon.] Discovered a flair for writing unexpectly in 1993. 1st article, "European year of Solidarity between the generations" for a seminar. 10 articles on disability etc. Published Integration and Participation in Society.; [oth. writ.] Wrote 2 short stories. "Why Truth", well recommends. "A shattered dream", about 20 poems published since 1994. Book, "Ready for publication" summer 1997 title "A Blinkered Life" fact, not fiction; a 'Pen name' Cathy A. P. Cregan.; [pers.] Due to accident my priorities in life completely changed. Money, status, success etc. are meaningless. Poverty, pain and

suffering brings you life, you see beauty in broken bodies, love in sightless eyes.; [a.] Charleville, Co Cork, Ireland

GILBERT, MARTIN N.
[b.] 22 February 1951, Mortlake; [m.] Sally, 15 July 1978; [ch.] David, Paul, Jonathan; [ed.] Wimblendon College, Polytechnic of North London; [occ.] Librarian; [memb.] Library Association, Richmond Shakespeare Society; [hon.] B.A., A.L.A.; [pers.] I write as a means of expressing my inner feelings.; [a.] Strawberry Hill, Middx, UK, TW1 4PD

GILES, PAULINE
[pen.] Pauline Giles; [b.] 18 November 1959, Bishop, Auckland; [occ.] Residential Care Officer; [oth. writ.] Various unpublished poems, children's stories; [pers.] I write on impulse, I am at my best when writing.; [a.] Bishop Auckland, Durham, UK, DL14 8QX

GILHOLM, MRS. D.
[b.] 5 October 1919, Newbiggin-by-the-Sea; [p.] Mr. and Mrs. T. Peel (Deceased); [m.] George Norman Gilholm (Deceased) 1990, 1 January 1940; [ch.] Norman, June, Dorothy; [ed.] Northumberland County School, left aged 14 yrs.; [occ.] House-wife, retired; [oth. writ.] Several poems. Started writing after being widowed in 1990. One poem published. Arrival Press Peterborough 1995 My husband was an Assistant Electrical Engineer at NCB where I still live, 55 yrs. in same house, Ellington; hoping to go to Australia from February–May 1997.; [pers.] Thank you for your correspondence and encouragement. I am a member of an over 60's local club. I sing and read my poems, as I am a member of the over 60's choir. We visit other over 60's clubs. This I enjoy: I like attending and singing in the local church.; [a.] Ellington, Northumberland, UK, NE61 5HF

GILL, RUSSELL
[b.] 8 March 1958, Neath; [p.] Denzil Gill and Adeliene Gill; [m.] Annette Gill, 17 January 1978; [ch.] Stephanie Gill and Helen Gill; [ed.] Glan Afan Comprehensive Port Talbot; [occ.] H.G.V. Driver; [oth. writ.] Short Stories for Good Morning T.V. (unpublished), a poem entitled The Hero, to be published in Quiet Moments.; [a.] Port Talbot, West Glamorgan, UK, SA12 9YN

GILLIES, FRANCIS
[b.] 29 August 1944, Leith; [p.] Francis and Rose Gillies; [m.] Anne Gillies B.Ed., 13 August 1966; [ch.] Rosanne, Tony, Emma, Claire, Maddy; [ed.] St. Marys Star of Sea, Leith, St. Anthonys Leith, Fire Service Technical College; [occ.] Retired Fire Officer, sometime artist and poet; [memb.] Blackness Boat Club "Harbourmaster", Livingston Rugby Club; [hon.] Coastal Skipper R.Y.A. Certificate of Excellence in recitation of Burns Literature; [oth. writ.] Various unpublished plays and poems; [pers.] I strive to put on paper the jollys of mankind, and my own that my family might understand my thoughts. If only a mark that I passed this way.; [a.] Livingston, W. Lothian, UK, EH54 5NR

GILLMAN, DULCIE BEATRICE
[pen.] Dulcie Beatrice Gillman; [b.] 21 October 1922, Plumstead; [p.] Mr. and Mrs. Arthur W. Hill; [m.] Mr. William S. L. Gillman, 29 July 1944; [ch.] Two; [ed.] Welling Central School; [occ.] Retired Housewife/Artist and an interest in pottery; [oth. writ.] 'Granny's Lace' is my first poem but now I know where to send my poems; thanks to The International Library of Poets I am inspired to write more.; [pers.] I wrote Granny's Lace for my five grandchildren to remind them of our holidays in Leysdown. I showed them the wild flowers, in particular granny's lace, to make them aware of the wonders of nature, even the common cow. Parsley has its own beauty with its lace like flowers.; [a.] Abbey Wood, London, UK, SE2 0BN

GINN, EMMA LOUISE
[b.] 23 October 1986, Bolton; [p.] Terence Ginn, Pauline Ginn; [ed.] Devonshire Road Primary School; [hon.] RAD I RAD 2 Sign Language Certificate, North Manchester Charity Princess; [pers.] I enjoy writing poetry and making people smile.; [a.] Bolton, Lancs, UK, BL3 4RT

GODWIN, KEN
[b.] 28 February 1970, Clydebank; [p.] Beatrice Godwin; [m.] Lynda Godwin, 2 June 1995; [ed.] Clydebank High School; [occ.] Garden Centre Supervisor in Erskine Hospital for Disabled ex service men; [pers.] I have so far, written 65 poems. I started writing poems April 96. I try to make my poems as funny as I can. My influences came arm in my head on past experiences. I also write songs for the band I'm in. I sing and play Creator/Bass/Synthesizer.; [a.] Clydebank, Dunbartonshire, UK, G81 4QE

GOLDEN, PAT
[pen.] Pat Golden; [b.] 10 August 1939, Temple Bay, Co. Sligo; [p.] Peter Paul and Mary Golden; [m.] Mary Kelly, 3 April, 1961; [ch.] Christine, Vera, Peter; [occ.] Carsales-man; [oth. writ.] Songs awaiting publication: title Growing Old, Has Never Been A Sing; song, title: The Irish Politicians; [a.] Enniscrone; [pers.] Sligo

GOLDSMITH, MRS. VALERIE
[pen.] Valerie Braithwaite; [b.] 18 April 1938, Surrey; [m.] David Goldsmith, 6 April 1964; [ch.] Damon Lee (one son); [ed.] Aida Foster (Stage School) Golders Green; [occ.] Dance/Acrobatic teacher; [memb.] Equity (Actor's Union) Acrobats Assoc. B.M.H.S. (British Music Hall Society); [oth. writ.] Several articles published on dance/acrobatic, in UK and U.S.A. Poem published in the late actress Beryl Reid's Book, "The Cat's Whiskers".; [pers.] Whenever I have any spare time, I enjoy writing poetry, short stories and children's verse. I have also written several plays for children.; [a.] Harrow, Middx, UK, HA3 6RZ

GOLIGHTLY, JOHN
[b.] November 26, 1963, South Shields; [p.] Irene and Edwin Golightly; [m.] Clare Golightly, May 7, 1994; [ch.] Ragan, Shanelle, Ebony, all girls; [ed.] Chuder Ede Comprehensive; [occ.] Train driver at Newcastle Central Stn; [oth. writ.] Just personal poems and stories for own satisfaction; [pers.] I'm to laid-back to be philosophical, I just enjoy reading what my right hand and pen create in ink.; [a.] South Shields, Tyne and Wear, NE34, 9AS

GOODWIN, MAVIS
[b.] 17/05/41, Northampton; [p.] Thomas Middleton & Dorothy Middleton; [m.] Arthur Goodwin, 17/04/65; [ch.] Annanea Kim, Hehayna Dorothy Marjory; [ed.] Brookfield Central, Highgate, part time St. Martins Art School, various furthur education courses in publishing, ecitorial and computer skills and graphics; [occ.] Legal secretary, but would love to be a travel writer; [memb.] CSMA, coordinator neighborhood watch; [oth. writ.] Various articles in local newspapers including poetry and current issues, poem published 1995, editor monthly newspaper local group CSMA, currently writing novel, written illustrated book with equiptment becoming alive and magical aimed at educating children in office technology and practice yet to be published; [pers.] I am a romantic at heart but most of my poems reflect my moon, situation, experience etc. of the moment therefore cover all experiences of life. Wordsworth is my mentor.; [a.] Hoddesdon, Herts.

GOODWIN, VALERIE M.
[b.] 22 May 1943, Bishop Auckland; [p.] M. and S. Smith; [m.] David, 16 January 1971; [ch.] Two Daughters; [ed.] Secondary School; [occ.] Staff Nurse; [hon.] R.G.N. O.N.C. (Nursing Qual.); [oth. writ.] Numerous poems that I have never submitted for publication anywhere; they have been read only by family and friends due to lack of confidence in my talent.; [pers.] Poetry enhances my spiritual perception on life.; [a.] Sunderland; [Cnty.] Tyne and Wear, UK

GORDON, TAMMI LOUISE
[b.] 14 October 1983, Wellingborough, Northants; [p.] Paul and Debbi Gordon; [ed.] Kesgrave High School, Kesgrave, Ipswich, Suffolk; [occ.] School student; [pers.] I am influenced by my love of playing the piano and by my family.; [a.] Ipswich, Suffolk, UK, IP5 7TQ

GORMAN, TIMOTHY JOHN
[b.] 26 December 1967, Southampton; [p.] Sharron and Tommy Gorman; [ch.] Jason Aaron Gorman; [ed.] St. Mels College Longford Rep. of Ireland; [occ.] Bar Manager; [pers.] I write poetry as a hobby. My writing is always based on my own experiences and feelings; this is the first poem I have ever had published and is dedicated to my beloved son, Jason; [a.] Islington, London, UK, EC15 0BT

GORMLEY, ROBERT J.
[b.] 22 December 1955, Barrhead; [p.] James Gormley, Annie Smith; [m.] Catherine Ann Robinson, 11 October 1980; [ch.] Fraser James, Lisa Unity, Ross Murray; [ed.] John Neilson High School, Paisley Strathcylde University, Glasgow; [occ.] Multiple Grocer Sector Controller - Wines and Sprits; [memb.] Murrayshall Golf Club, Scone, Perthshire; [hon.] 'Break Through' Award from largest spirit of individual initiative that delivers "break through" in performance; [pers.] I have always believed if you want something in life, you should go for it. If you don't ask, you don't get; if you don't try you'll never succeed. "Whatever you can do or dream you can, begin it. Boldness has genius, power and magic in it" (WH Murray); [a.] Perth, Perthshire, UK, PH1 2SG

GOULDEN, BONNITA
[b.] 13 February 1978, Pembury; [p.] Jackie Forward, Colin Goulden; [ed.] Jarus Brook C.D. Green Lane Beacon Beacon C.C. West Kent College; [memb.] National Trust Camping and Caving Club; [hon.] English Lit.; [oth. writ.] A poem published in 'Wot Not', Poetry Now.; [pers.] Many of my writings are from personal experience and the society around me. I place myself in someone else's mind and try to write what they might feel.; [a.] Crowborough, East Sussex, UK, TN6 2EX

GOWHARJI, NOUR
[b.] 10 October 1978, Jeddah, KSA; [p.] Fathi Gowharji, Philomena Kelly; [ed.] Graduate of Jeddah Private School Undergraduate at King Abdul Aziz Dental School; [occ.] Dental Student; [oth. writ.] Medical City Magazine, high school magazine, intend to write book.; [pers.] Strive for the stars that you seek in the deepest of your dreams.; [a.] Jeddah, Saudi Arabia, 21423

GOWLAND, PAUL CHRISTOPHER
[pen.] P. C. Gowland; [b.] 13 November 1958, Leeds; [p.] Sheila and George W. Gowland; [m.] Deborah Gowland (Nee Pollard), 11 January 1986; [ch.] Zoe, Kerry, Hayley, Oliver; [ed.] West Leeds Boys High School (Armley); [occ.] Teacher - (Adult Education) North Lincolnshire College.; [memb.] Amnesty International, Green Peace; [hon.] Articles and poems published in magazines, newspapers; [oth. writ.] Currently researching for a novel about the miners' strike 1984-85.; [pers.] To empower every individual to reach their full potential through educational. To help make equal opportunities a reality.; [a.] Theddlethorpe, St. Helen, Lincolnshire, UK, LN12 1NW

GOWLING, ELSIE
[b.] 2 February 1920, Lowestoft; [p.] Leonard Felgate and Rose Felgate; [m.] Edward Gowling, 14 August 1943; [ch.] Three daughters; [pers.] Now a widow and housebound, having Rheuma-toid Arthritis. I started writing poems thirty five years ago. Most have a Christian message and have been published in church magazines, local newspapers and Christian Herald. My aim is to promote understanding and peace.; [a.] Crieff, Perthshire, UK, PH7 3SE

GRAFTON, KARL
[b.] 2 October 1964, Manchester; [p.] Diane Grafton, James Anthony Grafton; [ed.] North Manchester High School, Adult Education College, Manchester, Manchester Metropolitan University.; [occ.] Bus Driver (part-time), Semi-Professional Golf Player; [memb.] Churston Gold Club, The Rotary Club of Great Britain, (Brix Division.); [hon.] 10 Cub Scout Profficiency Badges, first aid certificates, B.A. English and history (hons.); [oth. writ.] Poems published in Writers News, and 'A passage in Time' anthology. Articles for local resident's newsletter, and poems put on Sarah's bedroom wall, my girlfriend.; [pers.] I write for myself, for the judgement of history, and posterity, but mainly because most T.V. is boring and I like to fill the gaps between episodes of Eastenders and "Corrie".; [a.] Brixham, Devon, UK, TQ5 9SQ

GRAHAM, MS. SHEILA
[b.] 1 April 1942, Carlisle, Cumbria; [p.] Jean Graham, Charles McKenzie-Graham; [m.] Kenneth W. Brunning (Both divorced); [ch.] David, Suzanne, Leane and Glynn (4 children) (By former 2 marriages); [ed.] Thursby Jnr. Sch. Cumbria Wigton Secondary Modern School Cumbria; [occ.] College Catering Servery Supervisor, Cleaner; [oth. writ.] Poems: this is my first to be published. (Thank you for the honour and for making me a semi-finalist in your poetry competition).; [pers.] I like composing and writing poetry and reading other people's poetry: My father also writes poetry, short stories, and has had his wartime diary published.; [a.] Cambridge, Cambridgeshire, UK, CB4 2TZ

GRANDON, ADELE
[pen.] Adele Meekins; [b.] 8 June 1966, London; [p.] Barrie and Paola Meekins; [m.] David Grandon, 22 October 1994; [ch.] Connor Grandon; [ed.] The King Alfred School, London; [occ.] Full time mother; [oth. writ.] Three poems published in the series of 'Poetry Now' anthologies.; [pers.] I owe a great deal to the three magical influences in my life: David Jordan, my incredible english teacher, Pauline Keep, who guided me through a life altering journey of self discovery, and finally, my wonderful family.; [a.] West Drayton, Middlesex, UK, UB7 9AG

GRANT, DAVID A.
[b.] 12 July 1929, Heston Middlx; [p.] Deceased; [m.] Josephine Ann (Deceased), 9 September 1950; [ch.] Two boys and one girl; [ed.] Basic in England. 4 1/2 years in Winnipeg Canada during WW II, Sir Isaac Brock and Lord Kitchener High; [occ.] Retired ex Workshop Supervisor, British Telecom; [hon.] Mentioned in Despatches Ref Royal Air Force Police 1947-1955; [oth. writ.] Few poems not published; [pers.] My intent was to reflect my visions in writing to please others.; [a.] Bristol, South Gloucestershire, UK, BS16 6EX

GRANT, IRENE
[b.] 19 July 1941, Aberdeen; [p.] Lilian Smith, Francis Grant (Adoptive); [ed.] Newbold College Berks, Commercial College Aberdeen Further Education; [occ.] Carer; [memb.] Cats Protection League National Trust; [hon.] Audio Typist Diploma GCE's English; [oth. writ.] Poems in a number of collections, articles for Adventist 'Messenger' and local press.; [pers.] I was influenced by Christina Georgina Rossetti's 'Remember Me', and 'Snow in the Suburb's', by Thomas Hardy, to enjoy poetry, for the first time.; [a.] Aberdeen, Aberdeenshire, UK, AB15 8EJ

GRAVES, YVONNE
[b.] 5 February 1958, Warrington, Cheshire; [p.] George Latimer, Brenda Latimer; [m.] Walter Graves; [ch.] Kelly Anne O'Neill, Emma Jane O'Neill; [ed.] University of Life and still being educated; [occ.] Warden Sheltered Accommodation; [oth. writ.] Several poems about own life concentrating on humorous stories.; [pers.] I dedicate this poem to my beautiful daughters Kelly and Emma - Long may they bloom and grow.

GRAY, PAUL ANTHONY
[b.] 29 June 1958, Coleraine; [p.] Thomas Gray, Jeanette Gray; [m.] Eunice, Kelly Gray, 16 April 1988; [ch.] Anthony, Christopher, Aaron; [ed.] St. Joseph's High School Coleraine; [occ.] Fitter/Welder; [memb.] T.B.E. Thompson Golf Society, Ballysally Presbyterian, Indoor Bowling Club; [oth. writ.] Several poems published in local papers, national magazines, church magazines E.C.T.; [pers.] My endeavour is to be an ambassador of God's love and mercy, proclaiming the good news of the gospel to whosoever has an ear to hear.; [a.] Coleraine, Londonderry, UK, BT52 2QL

GREEN, DANIEL PAUL
[pen.] Kurt or Jarret Jaeger (Vlowenski); [b.] 13 December 1976, Edgeware; [p.] John Green, Patricia Green; [ed.] Dame Alice Owens School, Oaklands College of Arts and Sciences, St. Albans; [occ.] Student; [memb.] RSPCA, RSPCC, WWF, RSPB, Labour Party; [hon.] None yet - I'm working on it!; [oth. writ.] Science fantasy, a Historical fiction, short stories and novels, awaiting publication urgently.; [pers.] To honour my mother and my father's memory in all I do. To Lisa, all my love, always. My friends: Thank you for believing.; [a.] Borehamwood, Hertfordshire, UK, WD6 5AU

GREEN, JONATHAN KIM
[pen.] Kim Green; [b.] 7 January 1977, London; [ed.] Uxbridge High School, Liverpool John Moores University; [occ.] Student; [pers.] All anyone can strive for in this life is to get noticed and make a difference.; [a.] Uxbridge, Middlesex, UK, UB8 2DL

GREENE, JAMES
[b.] 8 June 1951, Motherwell; [p.] Patrick and Elizabeth; [ch.] Louise; [ed.] Secondary School; [occ.] Unemployed; [memb.] Green Peace, I.F.A.W., W.W.F.; [pers.] Some people choose to sip from Shallow Pools, I choose, the Deepest Wells.; [a.] Eltham, London, UK, SE9 6TX

GREENWOOD, CARON LUCY
[b.] 23 April 1975, Exeter, Devon; [p.] Bob and Judy Greenwood; [ed.] Knowles Hill Comprehensive School, South Devon Technical College; [pers.] Caron had a short life, passing away 2 months before her 21st birthday. She had a great love of life and a tremendous compassion for her fellow humans. She had a great sense of the spiritual which came through in her writing.; [a.] Newton Abbot, Devon, UK, TQ12 4AF

GRIFFIN, LINDA
[b.] 15 August 1979, Limerick City; [p.] Margaret and John Griffin; [ed.] Salesian Secondary School, Limerick City (Principal - Sr. Bridget Dowling); [occ.] Secondary School Student (in my final year); [memb.] School debating team, School Magazine, School Bank, Senior School Council; [hon.] Deputy Head Girl for school, Semi-finalist in University College Cork (UCC) Debating Championships; [oth. writ.] Several poems published in local papers and magazines; [pers.] Although my poetry seems to dwell on futility in life, I believe that it highlights the strength and beauty of the human character; [a.] Limerick, UK

GROTE, JOANNA
[pen.] Joasia Jowashi; [b.] 16 November 1981, Taplow; [p.] Mr. John Grote, Mrs. Basia Grote; [ed.] 1987-91: I.S.S.H. Tokyo 1991-96: A.I.S.B.

Budapest 1996-United World College of South East, Singapore; [occ.] Student; [oth. writ.] Poems and short stories published in school magazines.; [pers.] Thanks Mr. Clarke, this one's for you.; [a.] Singapore, Singapore, 248506

GROVES, CHARLOTTE
[pen.] Charlotte Weldon Groves; [b.] 1 April 1931, Glasgow; [m.] Denis Groves. 3 March 1953; [ch.] John Alistair, Stephen, Alexander; [ed.] Glasgow University; [occ.] Housewife; [hon.] Redruth, Cornwall; [pers.] Got bored at bingo, started writing poems in Slough. I now live in Cornwall. The bingo, it was boring. The numbers went out of my head so I used the back of a ticket at wrote a poem instead.; [a.] TR15 3XQ

GRUNBERG, NATASHA
[b.] 13 September 1985, London; [ed.] Channing School, Henrietta Barnett School; [hon.] Won the Young Writer's WH Smiths award 1995. Work/poem published in book. Awarded Commendation Certificate WH Smiths 1996.; [oth. writ.] "I Wonder" In Walk The High Wire 1995; [a.] London, UK, NW11 6PB

GUIVER, SYLVIA
[b.] 27 September 1937, Brentford, Middlesex; [p.] Edith and Thomas Cook; [m.] Kenneth Guiver, 6 April 1969; [ch.] Sheran Elizabeth, Sarah Emily, Simon James; [ed.] Wood End secondary school Greenford Middlesex; [occ.] Swimming Instructor and Aromatherapist; [memb.] Amateur Swimming Ass., Guild of Complementary Practitioners; [hon.] I.T.E.C. (International Therapy Examination Council) Diploma in Anatomy, Physiology, and Body Massage, I.T.E.C., Diploma in Aromatherapy, A.S.A. (Amateur Swimming Ass.) Advanced Teacher and Tutor.; [pers.] May my entry embrace you, body, mind and spirit. God Bless You; [a.] High Wycombe, Buckinghamshire, UK, HP13 6UQ

GULLIVER, IRIS
[b.] 1916, Leamington Spa; [p.] Major O. Underhill O. B. E. and Mary Ann Corbett; [m.] Peter John Gulliver, 1937; [ch.] John Byron (Deceased), (three Grandsons) Paul, Jason and Richard, one great granddaughter Melane, 3 great grandsons Martin, David and Adrian; [ed.] Wembley Hill School Middx; [occ.] Retired; [hon.] Lots but in the Doggy World Best in Show's and Cups, etc., Sociedad Canina, Mallorca, IBIZA Palma de Mallorca 1977 Mejor CRIA de Espana (my prefix) Iverhill Pekineses 4 pekineses, my breed; [oth. writ.] I have written poems all my life and have books full, but have never entered a comp. before or published any until now. I am very proud.; [pers.] Left UK 1965 rtd. to Mallorca created, "Casa Florentina 5 Bone Hotel" pets for 20 yrs well known as Florentina, Pedro - 10 yrs ago after death of only beloved child, John Byron, decided to sell and retire to France. Found a tumble down old farm house which gave me my inspiration for "Paradise Found". We gave it the promised face lift, and it now "lives again in beauty"; [a.] Duras,, France, 47120

GUNTRIPP, CHRISTINE
[b.] 1 March 1960, Woolwich; [p.] Reginald C. Edwards, Germaine Edwards; [m.] Stephen Guntripp, 4 October 1980; [ch.] Lynne, Martin, Alan and Benjamin Guntripp; [ed.] Grays Convent School, Thurrock Technical College; [occ.] General Assistant/Housewife; [memb.] Keep Fit Association, Lainson Communist Centre; [hon.] I had a chance for a career as a singer (rejected contract) with R.C.A. record company; [pers.] This poem was written and based on my true feelings. About this lovely celebrity whom I have met several times. I have expressed my inner feelings through the poem. And Michael does have a copy of this poem.; [a.] Basildon, Essex, UK, SS16 6EA

GUTTERIDGE, MAXINE
[b.] 18 February 1958, Northampton; [p.] Albert and Evelyn Howlett; [m.] John Gutteridge, 19 February 1977; [ed.] Moulton Secondary and Open University; [occ.] Local Government Officer; [memb.] Association of Accounting Technicians; [a.] Northampton, Northants, UK, NN5 5NJ

HABERLIN, MARGARET
[b.] 29 March 1981, Cork, Irl.; [p.] Noreen and Michael Haberlin; [ed.] Attending second level; [memb.] Cork Harlequins, Hockey Club, Colourbox Club; [pers.] I wrote "Walking the Fields" in memory of my Grandfather and of all the happy times we spent together; [a.] Carrigaline, Cork, Ireland

HADDIJATOU, JACK
[b.] 25 February 1982, Banjul; [p.] Abdoulie and Maimuna Jack; [ed.] Marina International School; [occ.] student; [pers.] I enjoy writing a lot. It helps me express my thoughts and feelings.; [a.] Pipeline, Gambia

HAKIM, FARZANA
[b.] 25 May 1983, London; [p.] Razia Hakim and Shamim Hakim; [ed.] Mellow Lane School, Hayes; [occ.] Attending secondary school; [memb.] Clarinet School Band; [oth. writ.] Poems in local paper, school concert recitals, poems in school magazine; [pers.] I love poetry and appreciate the art of weaving words. I try my best when writing and hope this is recognised by others.; [a.] Hayes, Middlesex, UK, UB4 8DN

HALFORD, ANDREW GEORGE
[pen.] Hat; [b.] 31 May 1958, Bradford; [p.] Edith and Eric Halford; [m.] Myrtle, 25 May 1996; [ed.] Queensbury and Shelf Secondary Modern School; [occ.] Joiner-Former Professional Iceskater; [memb.] British ICE Teachers Association (BITA); [hon.] City and Guilds in Joinery 2nd class figures and free skating. 3rd class ice dancing; [oth. writ.] Lyrics when performing for rock bands in Bradford. Other personal unpublished poetry.; [pers.] I always endeavour to be helpful to others. Writing poetry is a way of expressing my feelings to others; [a.] Bradford, West Yorkshire, UK, BD4 6LB

HALL, DENISE M.
[b.] 1 September 1970, Shipley; [ed.] Studying at the moment, gained Geses and A level Law Shipley College; [occ.] PT student, PT worker; [oth. writ.] First publication! But I have been working on other poems too.; [pers.] On writing this poem I hoped to bring people's attention to the immense problem of being homeless and having no real chances in life, or any real choices either.; [a.] Shipley, W. Yorks, UK, BD18 1JH

HALL, SARAH
[b.] 12 June 1926, Ireland; [p.] Patrick and Ann Russell; [m.] Ralph Hall, June 1948; [ch.] Five; [ed.] Good general education; [occ.] Retired Nurse; [pers.] Life takes a long time to live, "I look through in silence" and my mind travels over almost all of it, in short space of time. "Short Enough"; [a.] Tipton, West Midlands, UK, DY4 0TG

HALL, SARAH
[pen.] Sarah Louise; [b.] 5 February 1978, Kettering; [ed.] At Oxford Brookes University studying for a teaching degree for infants; [occ.] Student; [memb.] University Orchestra; [pers.] 'The secret in love is not to be secret' beautiful love was inspired by my surrounding countryside; [a.] Glendon, Northants, UK, NN14 1QE

HALLIWELL, ANN
[b.] Northumbria; [m.] Peter Halliwell; [ch.] Four sons, 1 daughter; [ed.] Secondary Modern; [occ.] Retired, Volunteer work, Stroke Ass.; [memb.] Carlisle Ladies Speakers Club, Woman's Institute; [hon.] A.S.C. Certificate of Achievement, R.S.A. Advanced Spoken English; [a.] Carlisle, Cumbria, UK, CA3 0BD

HALLMARK, JOYCE
[b.] 10 January 1943, Stockport; [p.] George Ridgway, Edna Ridgway; [m.] Alan Hallmark; [ch.] Stephen 18 years; [ed.] Cheadle Hulme School, Manchester University; [occ.] Early retired Teacher; [memb.] Manchester United Supporters Club, Voluntary Literacy Tutor, CVS; [hon.] BA English, Cert. in Education; [oth. writ.] "Overcome the Spelling Block" Hallmark and Withers, ed Foulsham; [pers.] I believe strongly that children's hearts should be lifted by beautiful things - I deplore the urban decay/protest/politically correct literature syllabus, also deplore fear of knowledge.; [a.] Macclesfield, Cheshire, UK, SK11 8LU

HAMILTON, ELSIE M.
[b.] 13 September 1923, Manchester; [m.] 1951; [ed.] B.A. Hon. Eng, Lit (M/C University) B.Ed.; [occ.] Retired.; [memb.] Envoi Mag. Ver Poet, Outpost. Poetry Digest.; [hon.] 3rd prize in a Ver Poets competition. Several commendations in other competitions.; [oth. writ.] Envoi Magazine. Poems published in these anthologies: Poetry Now - N West 1994. "Not Alot To Ask" Ver poets 1995. Poetry Now "Home is Where The Heart Is" 1996. "Voices" Ver poets 1996 "Vision On" 1992 5 and 6 Love Poetry - Poetry Digest '94 and '95.; [pers.] Some of the poems I write arise from personal experience - joyful or painful. Others are inspired by articles, a T.V. program about larger issues. I have written poems since I was a child but appear both a slow-developer.; [a.] Manchester, Lancashire, UK, M35 0DY

HANCOCK, JOHN HENRY
[b.] 26/05/48, Sheffield; [p.] Lois Bell & Des Bell (Step father); [m.] Divorced; [ch.] Cara Elyse & John Kristian; [occ.] Senior QA/QC Engineer; [hon.] Peace Keeping Medal for serving with the United Nations Forces in Cyprus (U.N.F.I.C.Y.P.); [oth. writ.] Several unpublished poems; [pers.] Dedication - To my daughter Cara, my son Kristian and my mother Lois. Thank you for all your love and support. [a.] Sheffield, South Yorkshire, S2 3SP

HANDYSIDE, JACQUELINE
[b.] 15 January 1961, London; [p.] Dennis Frederick Handyside and Louise Handyside; [m.] Raymond King; [ed.] Lanfranc High School, Croydon, Surrey; [occ.] Aromatherapist; [memb.] ISPA, RQA; [hon.] Diploma of Holistic Aromatherapy; [a.] Walton on Thames, Surrey, UK, KT12 5ER

HANSON, PETER BARRY
[b.] 26 January 1969, Derby; [p.] Barry Hanson and Carol Hanson; [m.] Sharon Hanson, 31 July 1993; [ch.] Jonathan Hanson; [ed.] Swanwick Hall Grammar School; [occ.] Storeman at local car bodyshop; [memb.] Mensa Membership, Alfreton Snooker Club; [hon.] "O" levels at school in English Lang and Lit; [oth. writ.] None to speak of but would love to write for a career; [pers.] I believe I have a hidden talent for poems and short stories, but need guidance on how to get started (can create a poem without hardly thinking about it).; [a.] Alfreton, Derbyshire, UK, DE55 7LF

HARDING, CAROLE
[b.] 25 September 1945, Cheshire; [p.] Georgina Lowe; [ch.] Amanda Jane, Julie Ann, Lynne Maria; [ed.] Hartford Secondary School; [occ.] Self employed interior designer; [memb.] A member of the Free Spirit Society; [hon.] The honour of being the mother of three very intelligent and beautiful daughters, who have been my inspiration; [oth. writ.] A book of private and precious memories entitled: Every Picture Tells a Story, These are Mine.; [pers.] Brains, beauty, integrity can all save the day. But a flash of true inspiration can save the soul.; [a.] Middlewich, Cheshire, UK, CW10 0AT

HARMAN, JOY
[b.] 7 February 1931, London; [p.] Dorothy and Alexander Drummond; [m.] Gerry, October 1959; [ch.] Russell and Jacqueline; [ed.] Preston Manor Grammar and Pitman's College, London; [occ.] Legal Secretary; [oth. writ.] Two poems published in Anthologies - 1992 "Voices of Love" poem entitled "Old Friends" and 1996 - Between a Laugh and a Tear" poem entitled "The Thief"; [pers.] My grand-daughter, Courtney Shaw, was the inspiration for the poem in this book.; [a.] Flackwell Heath, Buckinghamshire, UK, HP10 9LG

HARMEN, MRS. LOVEDAY
[b.] Southampton; [p.] Frank, Daisy Ramshaw; [m.] Ronald Harmen, 29 March 1944; [ch.] Tessa; [ed.] Granville Coll. Southampton Philippa Fawcett College of Education, Open University (BA); [occ.] Retired Head Teacher, Governor of local Infants school; [memb.] M. ENCAP., Dining Clubs, Huvru Flying Club, (Bownermouth Airport); [hon.] L.R.A.M. (Speech Drama), B.A. Open University, (Hon) Fellow of College of Preceptors; [oth. writ.] Poems and articles on Education, On Panel for MacDonalds "Starters", (Children's books); [pers.] When I write I am sharing my thoughts with others in the hope that they may see ordinary things in a different way.; [a.] New Milton, Hampshire, UK, BH25 6PQ

HARRIS, CHRISTOPHER
[pen.] C. C. Harry; [b.] 3 July 1962, Veryan; [p.] Peter And Iris Harris; [m.] Rosemarie Harris, 14 March 1981; [ch.] Chris, Leah and Tanya; [ed.] Roseland School; [occ.] S/E Builder; [oth. writ.] Numerous finished and unfinished poems and books. All as yet not submitted for publication.; [pers.] The infinite boundaries of imagination can only be truly captivated by the written word.; [a.] Truro, Cornwall, UK, TR2 5QN

HARRIS, JILL
[b.] 18 June 1954, Chelmsford, Essex; [m.] Kevin Harris; [ed.] Great Baddow Comprehensive; [occ.] Nature Student; [memb.] The Little Theatre; [oth. writ.] Several unpublished poems; [pers.] "Poetry is inside all of us; it takes life to bring it out".; [a.] Leicester, Leicestershire, UK, LE2 0HF

HARRIS, MICHAEL
[b.] 10 April 1951, Gainsborough; [p.] Kathleen and Roy Harris; [m.] Melanie Jane, 4 November 1994; [ch.] B. J. and George (Pets); [ed.] Various establishments; [occ.] Technician; [memb.] H.O.G.; [oth. writ.] Poems and various songs mainly for friends.; [pers.] My poetry is based mainly on personal experiences.; [a.] Pease Pottage, W. Sussex, UK, RM11 9BB

HARRIS, RALPH LESLIE
[pen.] Ralph L. Harris; [b.] 26 January, London; [p.] Mark Harris, Annie Harris; [ed.] Central Foundation Sch. of London, Matriculation, open University; [occ.] Company Director; [memb.] Member of Institute of Patentees and Inventors; [hon.] 3 U.K. and 2 U.S. patents, several achievement awards as Financial Consultant. Documented as being in top 3% by British Mensa Ltd.; [oth. writ.] Other poetry published in local press, and 'Awaken to a Dream'. Instruction Manual for playing Snooker.; [pers.] Prefer light-hearted poetry, but also write more serious work. Enjoy solving crosswords, bridge problems, coding problems and Mensa-type problems.; [a.] Luton, Bedfordshire, UK, LU2 7BD

HARTLEY, DOREEN
[pen.] Doreen Taylor-Smith; [b.] 20 March 1938, Doncaster; [p.] Deceased; [m.] Philip David (2nd husband, widowed for 10 years), 2 March 1996; [ch.] Two sons and 1 daughter (all adults); [ed.] Secondary Modern School (Woodlands, Doncaster) RAF, WRAF, and Police further education, 50th Home, Traveled Far East, Mid-East Europe once Piloted, Hercules and appeared on 'Blind Date'; [occ.] Temp. (Clerical,

switchbrds, etc.) for an agency; [memb.] Royal British Legion (where I used to work - H.O.); [hon.] I know that I have great ability stowed away, untapped; [oth. writ.] About 20 poems published years ago, by British Forces paper in the Malta. Peoples Friend published one poem (paid $5) and Woman Magazine showed some interest in short stories over 1500 words years ago - unpursued as abroad at time.; [pers.] I believe that in every word there is poetry, and that every word of poetry could be a song.; [a.] Erith, Kent, UK, DA8 1NL

HARTUP, REBECCA
[b.] 25 October 1981, Sidcup, Kent; [p.] Irene and Bev Hartup; [ed.] I attend Fishguard High School; [oth. writ.] Poem published 'A Perfect Country' published in Nature's Way; [pers.] I get the inspiration for my poetry from the beautiful countryside where I live.; [a.] Fishguard, Pembrokeshire, UK, SA65 9AX

HARVEY, JOYCE
[b.] 4 May 1954, Southend-on-Sea; [p.] Kitty Tanner and Albert Tanner; [m.] Michael Harvey, 1 September 1972; [ch.] Paul Michael and Claire Susan; [ed.] Westborough High for girls, St. Mary's C. of E. School; [occ.] Housewife; [memb.] IFAW Pet Rescue; [oth. writ.] Unpublished poems for own amusement.; [pers.] Poetry can amplify a small voice within you. Imagination can heal an open wound.; [a.] Southend, Essex, UK, SS0 0NL

HARVEY, VAL
[pen.] Val Harvey; [b.] 18 March 1945, Amersham; [p.] William and Florence Podbury; [m.] Brian Harvey, 1 July 1967; [ch.] Belinda Harvey; [ed.] Dr. Challoners Grammar School - Amersham; [occ.] Residential Social Worker; [oth. writ.] Poems including The Mists of Time and Profound Thoughts. Several short stories, several works published.; [pers.] Born under the sign of the poet, I have a profound love of nature.; [a.] Chesham, Bucks, UK, HP5 3LD

HARVISON, PAUL
[b.] 5 July 1978, Crew; [p.] Norman Harvison, Pauline Harvison; [ed.] Rudheath High School, Sir John Deane's College, Keele University; [occ.] Student; [memb.] Keele Writer's Society, The Gothic Society; [oth. writ.] Poems and editorials for Keele Writer's Society Magazine.; [pers.] I have been heavily influenced by the gothic and Romantic movements. This shows in my work as I try to express the darker side of man.; [a.] Northwich, Cheshire, UK, CW9 5RQ

HAWKINS, PAULA-ANNE
[b.] May 14, 1964, London; [ed.] La Sante Union Convent Highgate-London; [occ.] Air Stewardess/In-structor United Airlines; [memb.] Royal Academy, Clipped Wings; [oth. writ.] Poetry published in various anthologies; [pers.] Everything I write, I write from the heart. The goods, bads, highs and lows—total polarity. I'm thankful for all my diversity. It's created a kaleidoscope of concepts and impressions—within me. As the song goes ... "It's a Wonderful Life"; [a.] London:, SW3 5TJ

HAYDEN, ALEX S. R.
[b.] 5 December 1948, Reared in Shropshire; [p.] Winifred and Alfred Park (Adoptive); [ed.] Grammar School, Kennington London; [occ.] Smallholder Painter - Writer of songs and poems; [hon.] NCA Records Nashville, Top Ten Award for Lyrc - Composition; [oth. writ.] Collection of yet to be published poems/books and mini series hopefully for TV, one set of children's books.; [pers.] Hayden Alex, pay attention to the important things in life, respect others as you would have them respect you, reach into your soul to find inspiration and only then, put pen to paper.; [a.] Welshpool, Powys, UK, SY21 8AS

HAYWARD, MR. LEE
[b.] 6 October 1957, Rochford, Essex; [p.] Mr. and Mrs. Hayward; [ed.] King John's School, average examination results. I preferred and was good at practical subjects, especially carpentry.; [occ.] Care Assistant; [oth. writ.] I have written over two hundred other poems, on all kinds of subjects, some drawn from personal experience, some from imagination, some philosophical and ecological.; [pers.] I am not formally religious, but I strongly believe in the sanctity and necessity of all forms of life, including especially all wildlife and the environment, such as rainforests, for instance.; [a.] Southend, Essex, UK, SS1 2TZ

HEATH, MR. GARY CHARLES
[pen.] G. C. Heath; [b.] 15 April 1953, London; [p.] Mr. James C. Heath and Mrs. Lilian Heath; [m.] Sharon Heath; [ch.] Jamie Heath (16), Adam Heath (11); [ed.] Parmiters Grammar School, Private Music Tuition through the London School of Music, The Churchill Centre; [occ.] Living; [memb.] Life Itself; [hon.] To be; [oth. writ.] Children stories (unpublished), poems published in other anthologies, other poetry no one has read to date.; [pers.] I am that I am.; [a.] Bow, London, UK, E3 2EZ

HELLAWELL, SUZANNE
[b.] 26 July 1967, Woking; [p.] Margaret and Michael Hellawell; [ed.] Sheerwater School, Woking; [occ.] Self Employed Cleaner/Housekeeper; [memb.] Whale and Dolphin Conservation Society, Fox Appreciation Society; [oth. writ.] A small anthology of poems published called "The Words In My Mind", in 1992.; [pers.] I try to reflect my own hobbies and interests, but also enjoy writing about real life. Life itself is a great influence.; [a.] Woking, Surrey, UK, GU22 7HL

HEMMINGS, MRS. E.
[b.] 30 August 1932, Cumbria; [p.] Dorothy and Wesley Rumney; [m.] T. Hemmings, 12 February 1955; [ch.] Peter, Carole, Craig, Patrick; [oth. writ.] several poems published; [pers.] I always start off writing a novel and end up with a poem.; [a.] St. Breglade, Jersey, JE3 8BA

HERBERT, MARY
[pen.] Mary Purcell-Herbert; [b.] 19 January 1928, Saul., Gloucestershire; [p.] Ivor and Grace Purcell; [m.] George Herbert, 14 May 1949; [ch.] Lorna Jane and Nigel (R.A.F); [ed.] Saul Village School, Stroud Central School for girls, Stroud, Glos.; [occ.] Retired Nurse; [memb.] Royal College of Nursing; [oth. writ.] Poems published in parish magazines and local newspapers. Article for school achieves. Poem published in your anthology "Quiet Moments" 1996.; [pers.] Elusive dreams - my late father's aspiration to become a keeper of the light, gone forever.; [a.] Dawlish, Devon, UK, EX7 0PN

HERRON, MARY JOSEPHINE
[pen.] Jose Herron; [b.] 6 June 1929, Scunthorpe; [p.] Mary Spencer, Harry Spencer; [m.] Tom Herron, 10 July 1948; [ch.] Marie, Michael, David, Moira; [ed.] Ashby Girls School "University of Life!"; [occ.] Housewife, Retired Accounts Supervisor; [memb.] Scunthorpe Baptist Church; [hon.] Swimming (Life Saving), Voluntary NAAFI Work 2nd World War; [oth. writ.] Poems published in 'Poetry Now' anthologies. Articles in Christian Magazines, woman's magazines and local papers.; [pers.] Education obtained from reading continues throughout life. Writing is a gift to be cultivated. Modestly, I like to think my 12 grandchildren have inherited that gift from me. 3 have already had worked published.; [a.] Scunthorpe, North Lincolnshire, UK, DN16 2QF

HEYWOOD, GEORGE SAMUEL
[b.] 10 October 1941, Blackpool; [p.] Alice and George Heywood; [m.] Patricia Heywood, 25 July 1964; [ch.] Gary, Stephen, Nicola Heywood;

[ed.] Leads High School; [occ.] Ret. Police Officer. now Security Supervisor.; [memb.] None at the present time.; [hon.] Liverpool Shiprock Human Society for Bravery. Numerous police commendations, for police work and bravery; [oth. writ.] None published.; [pers.] I write for my own, or other people's, pleasure. To write poetry, artistic or comical, relaxes me, and gives me fulfillment to see the pleasure on other people's faces, which in this day and age, is deemed to be lacking.; [a.] Blackpool, Lancashire, UK, FY4 1LF

HICKLING, CHRISTINE
[b.] 3 November 1952, Liverpool; [p.] Sarah Duncan, Leslie Duncan; [m.] John Kay Hickling, 21 March 1986; [ch.] Gillian Christine, Elliot Gareth; [a.] St. Helens, Merseyside, UK, WA10 6RA

HICKMAN, PAMELA JOYCE
[b.] 14 June 1931, Sevenoaks, Kent; [p.] Alfred Braban, Alice Braban; [m.] Ronald Jack Hickman, 3 June 1953; [ed.] Church of England School (Village) Sundridge; [occ.] Semi-Retired but run a B&B business with my husband; [memb.] Selsey Horticultural Society; [oth. writ.] One poem published. Stories for children and other short stories but none published.; [pers.] I try to write what I feel and hope that other people will enjoy what I've written.; [a.] Selsey, West Sussex, UK, PO20 0QE

HICKS, SAMANTHA
[b.] 1 February 1982, Bristol; [p.] Pam Hicks, Gordon Hicks; [occ.] School, student of Marlwood School, Thornbury; [pers.] I enjoy all types of music and write songs for a hobby. Also I enjoy reading a wide range of literature from magazines to novels, Stephen King and Len Reighton.; [a.] Little Stoke, Bristol, UK, BS12 6LG

HIERN-COOKE, FIONA
[pen.] Fiona Hiern-Cooke; [b.] 12 January 1927, Infield, Middx.; [p.] Margaret Duncan-Best (Nee Steele) (Deceased), Cecil Douglas Duncan-Best Royal Navy; [m.] Tiles Hiern-Cooke (Deceased), 21 October 1949; [ch.] Francesca, Kirsten, Stuart; [ed.] School for Naval Officers' Daughters, Haslemere Surrey, University Trinity College, Dublin, Eire; [occ.] Retired Psychiatric Social Worker, currently writing at home; [memb.] None, I'm not really a 'Joiner'. More an interested and sympathetic observer.; [hon.] Social Science Diploma Trinity College, Dublin, Eire 1947; [oth. writ.] Magazine articles on countryside and folklore, poetry, a few poems published in magazines.; [pers.] Having many varied interests, music, modern pop and classical, also painting ancient and modern, and literature. Being fascinated by people, and what makes people tick, I relish my interest in psychiatry, and study of the brain, emotions, and conflicts. I admire Constable Turner, Zelda Fitzgerald, Emily Bronte and Emily Dickenson, the complicated, fascinating, women writers.; [a.] Heathfield, Sussex, UK, TN21 9ET

HILL, MRS. AMELIA
[b.] 30 August 1919, Rome, Italy; [p.] Joseph and Dorothy Nathan; [m.] Roland John Hill, 21 December 1996; [ch.] One; [ed.] Bedford House College, London Convitto Wazionale Di Tivogi, Rome; [occ.] Founder Chairman of AAA (Action Against Allergy); [memb.] Society of Environmental Medicine - Action Fable. ME. Association - Osteoporosis Society - Association Anti Allergic, Society Italiana Doxologies Clinica British Society for nutritional medicine; [hon.] Honorary medal, Order of Malta, Italy 1981. Signum Amiciziae medal, Collegium Biologicum Europa, Italy 1981. Medal of Honour, Giornate Medicine International, Italy 1981. Woman of the Year Award, Adelaide Ristori, Rome 1983. Literary Award, Collegium Biologicum Europa, Valentia, Italy, 1982.; [oth. writ.] Poem in voices 69 - against the unsuspected enemy - all above allergies for beginners

- do it yourself biofeedback - other 3 books be published - many papers and articles and translations; [pers.] My writings are mainly on allergies, M.E. (Chronic Fatigue Syndrome) and religion and healing.; [a.] London, UK, SW19 4AT

HILL, JOHN ROBERT
[b.] 26 January 1979, Runcorn, Cheshire; [p.] Robert Hill, Susan Hill; [ed.] Frodsham High School, Frodsham Sixth Form College; [occ.] Student; [oth. writ.] Poems and prose as yet unpublished.; [pers.] You must look deep within yourself in order to find your own dream, that being the idea of which you are made. When you find this dream you must follow it for as far as it takes you, in order to find your true happiness.; [a.] Runcorn, Cheshire, UK, WA7 3BD

HILTON, LINDA
[pen.] Linda Hilton; [b.] 29 October 1952, Clapham; [p.] George and Violet Hilton; [m.] Fiance and future husband Ray Sibley 20 December 1996.; [ch.] Robert, Mark and Tracy Davison, future stepson Lee and step daughter Samantha.; [ed.] Sutton Common Country High School for girls. Sutton Arts College.; [occ.] Nursery Nurse; [hon.] Diploma in Child Care. Full first Aid certificate.; [oth. writ.] A Mother's Bond, published in the "Other Side Of The Mirror. True Love to be published in "Quiet Moments." And many others written for pleasure.; [pers.] It was my mother's dream for my poems to be published. Unfortunetly she died of cancer. I still feel her near and I know she is proud. I may not have won a prize but to have my work published is a great sense of achievement.; [a.] Tadworth, Surrey, UK, KT20 5LD

HILTON, MANDY
[b.] 27 August 1963, Holyhead, Anglesey; [p.] William and Elizabeth Millward; [m.] Stuartneil Hilton, 3 May 1986; [ch.] Clair - 4, Christopher - 2; [ed.] David Hughes Secondary School. Also gained for 3 yrs and gained my R.G.N. (Registered General Nursing) qualification at Ysbyty Glan Clwyd Badelwyaddan.; [occ.] Housewife, but also company secretary as we have a limited company; [memb.] Belong to the National Trust, also a children's book club (Red House) as I have always loved reading and hope my children will also be the same.; [hon.] Never received an honour or award; [oth. writ.] No precious writings; [pers.] I just hope that my poem may bring a smile to someone's face, and that other Mum's can identify with the feelings in my poem.; [a.] Truro, Cornwall, UK, TR3 6BT

HIRST, ELIZABETH
[b.] 20 June 1975, Aldershot; [p.] Terence Hirst, Catherine Hirst; [ed.] Ash Manor Secondary School, Ash, Farnham 6th form college, University College of St. Martin's, Lancaster; [occ.] Student - studying BA hons QTS (Art) yr. 4; [pers.] Living - sleeping or awake - is a sensory feast. Through writing, I attempt to express the impressions of life that resound in my head.; [a.] Ash, Surrey, UK, GU12 6SJ

HOAREAU, MARIE CLAUDE JACQUELINE
[b.] 18 November 1967, Victoria; [p.] Octave Hoareau and Izabelle Hoareau; [ed.] Seychelles Polytechnic School of Secretarial and Clerical Studies; [occ.] Secretary; [pers.] Due to the poverty which the world is facing today. This struck me to write and express what I feel. I would also like to thank God for having given me faith and courage in whatever I attempt to do in life.; [a.] Victoria, Seychelles

HOBBS, LYNDSEY DONNA
[b.] 23 September 1982, Consett; [p.] Denise Hobbs, Norman Hobbs; [ed.] Stanley Comprehensive (still attending); [memb.] Pupil at Stagecoach Theatre Arts; [hon.] I won an award at school out of 200 for best project, and at the age of eight years, I won first prize in a local colouring competition to celebrate opening of

'The Ultimate' at Lightwater Valley.; [pers.] My inspiration came from knowing about the beautiful island of Australia and their sunny beaches which I hope to visit one day.; [a.] Stanley, Durham, UK, DH9 7RP

HOGBEN, REBECCA
[pen.] Megar Plowright; [b.] 7 January 1981, Bedford; [p.] Ron and June Hogben; [ed.] St. Andrews School for girls, 3 years - 14 years, Bedford, Bidderham Upper School, 14 years - present day; [occ.] Student; [hon.] Several Highly Placed Awards in the Bedford Speech and Drama Festival; [oth. writ.] Private diary of poems only.; [pers.] I enjoy writing poems on many subjects but more often than not it is a way to relieve tension!; [a.] Bedford, Bedfordshire, UK, MK41 8NT

HOLDER, TRACY J.
[b.] 24 May 1966, Birmingham; [ch.] Harry J. Byrne; [pers.] A child will ignore words of experience. Those in need find love and consolation. If we can cure the child's ignorance perhaps there will be no needy.

HOLLAND, SEAN KEVIN
[pen.] Fuzz; [b.] 14 August 1963, Grimsby; [p.] Richard and Rita; [m.] Helen Elizabeth, 16 July 1987; [ch.] Karl, Jenna, Rebekah, Leah, Ruth; [ed.] Beverly Grammar School for Boys; [occ.] Chemical Process Worker; [hon.] 0 levels in English, Physics, Geography, Biology, French; [oth. writ.] Numerous personal love poems to my wife and family; [pers.] Let the world unite and talk and live as one people, not continue to kill and make war to no end.; [a.] Beverley, UK, HU17 9DZ

HOLLAND, TAMSIN
[b.] 15 June 1973, London; [p.] Maggie and Tony Holland; [ed.] St. Mary's Convent Hills Road Sixth Form College, St. George's Hospital Medical School (London); [occ.] Final Year Medical Student; [hon.] Hilary Gornell Prize for English Literature, college prize for theatre studies; [pers.] My Grandfather (Gerry Hamill 1919-1995) had the greatest influence on my confidence to write.; [a.] Tooting, London, UK, SW17

HOLLIS, MRS. ELSIE
[pen.] Elsie Hollis; [b.] 25 July 1937, Tideswell; [p.] Benjamin Walter, Ella Wrag; [m.] John Hollis (my lovely John), 9 February 1957; [ch.] Elizabeth Oulsnam, my daughter; [ed.] Bishop Pursglove Cofe School, Tideswell, several diplomas in the school of life. I left school at the age of 15; [occ.] Resident Manager of a Sheltered Housing Complex; [hon.] Seven Caring Awards Dealing with Disabilities in the Elderly; [oth. writ.] Lots of poems, plus children's stories up to now, none published.; [pers.] I write about the aspects of life as I experience them. This poem is dedicated to my husband John (my lovely John) who died November 27, 1995. My favourite poets are Christina Rosetti and Malcolm Wilson Bucknell.; [a.] Tideswell, Derbyshire, UK

HOLLOWAY, PAUL
[b.] 21 November 1974, North Shields; [p.] Norman Holloway, Lovaine Holloway; [ed.] Whitley Bay High School; [occ.] Senior Assistant, Sainsbury's; [oth. writ.] Several poems, as yet unpublished.; [pers.] 'Tomorrow Is Too Late', dedicated to Katherine Oliphant; thanks for you support.; [a.] Whitley Bay, Tyne and Wear, UK, NE25 9LN

HOLMAN, KAZ
[pen.] Kaz, Raven; [b.] 14 June 1964, Weybourne, Norfolk; [p.] Jr. and Sr. Clarke; [m.] David Holman, 26 March 1988; [ed.] Sheringham Secondary Modern 11-16 years Kelling Primary School (Infants) Gt Yarmouth College 1988-89; [occ.] Tarot Consultant of 10 years, Care Assistant Cross Roads Care Agency. Party Hostess; [memb.] Poetry Society. Swords of Pendragon Arthurian Reenactment Society (Secretary).

Psychic and Clairvoyant Society (member). International Guild of Psychics (member) Qualified in psychic arts; [hon.] Poems published as follows: semi finalist with "The Awareness We Need" published by International Library of Poetry in the anthology "A Passage In Time". Other recognitions for work in the following anthologies: "People Like Us", "Perceptions", "The Traveller's Friend", "Good Moods", Reflections, "East Anglian Poets", "Poets Around Britain", "Life's Like That"; [pers.] Poetry is an expression of all emotions and it is a lovely day to communicate. In my poetry I try to give the reader love, hope, joy, confidence and foresight. The word poems - means to me P = perception, O = strength, E = enlightenment, M = messages, S = strength. It says it all.; [a.] Gt. Yarmouth, Norfolk, UK, NR31 8LP

HOLMES, CHRISTINA IRIS
[pen.] Tina; [b.] 23 February 1945, Smithdown Place, Liverpool; [p.] John and Christina Cooper; [m.] Edward Victor Holmes, 17 July 1979; [ed.] St. Gregory's Comprehensive School, Kirkby, Merseyside; [occ.] Kitchen Assistant; [memb.] Lifestyle Gym.; [hon.] English Language, English Literature, RSA Maths Admin Course, Adult Tutor Training; [oth. writ.] Short, very short stories; [a.] Liverpool, Merseyside, UK, L13 1BS

HOLMES, JOSEPHINE
[b.] 21 July 1940, Cockermouth, Cumbria; [p.] Henrietta and Leslie Wilkinson; [m.] James Holmes, 21 March 1964; [ch.] Barry, Sandra, Karen, Andrew; [ed.] Avondale Sec. Mod.; [occ.] Housewife; [oth. writ.] "God's Great Gifts", "Mother"; [pers.] My hope and wish that we all take head, before we destroy the very things we need.; [a.] Darwen, Lancashire, UK, BB3 3AZ

HOLMES, RICHARD
[b.] 10 October 1974, Scunthorpe; [p.] Derek W. Holmes (Deceased) and Gloria Holmes; [ed.] South Axholme Comp., North Lindsey College; [occ.] Unemployed; [oth. writ.] I write songs with a friend for our ever-hopeful band, and am currently working on my own book of poems and prose.; [pers.] If I reach one person with my poems, I have done my job well.; [a.] Barnetby, North Lincs, UK, DN38 6EW

HOLNESS, A. L.
[b.] 20 August 1962, London; [ed.] Catford County Girls School; [occ.] Local Government Officer (London); [oth. writ.] Several poems unpublished.; [pers.] I would like my poetry to be able to move people. Sometimes out of misery comes happiness; [a.] South London, UK

HONES, MARIA
[pen.] Maria Hones; [p.] Capt. Arthur G. Lilliman Hewson and Maria Anna Hewson; [m.] Arthur James Hones, 3 August 1939; [ch.] Julia Anne, Ailsa Marie; [ed.] Pontefract Girls High, and thence to a London University College to study Music and English, there gaining an award (piano performance) to R.A. Music; [occ.] Head of Music Dept. (Now fully retired) Sedgehill Comprehensive ILEA; [memb.] Life mem. Burmese Cat Club, Vice Chairman Men and Women of Today Club - a Literary Luncheon Club then under the chairmanship of the late Lord Donegall, and similar to Christina Foyle's, in which I often proposed toasts to guest speakers; [hon.] Music fellowship, Gold Medallist, London University Teaching Diploma, studied course in practical criticism at Homerton College, Cambridge University under W. H. Auden - specializing in Eng. Lit.; [oth. writ.] Some short stories. Presently compiling an anthology of selected poems - These We Have Loved - to be published in Spring 1997, with illustrations; [pers.] I have written verse since early school days when my poem, The Seasons, was selected for the school magazine. A lover of nature, and the world around me, and with a family sea-faring tradition, I have

travelled extensively. I write from the heart, I hope with truth and sincerity, as events move me, or when reflecting on people - places - or my beautiful Burmese cats, which I breed, and adore.; [a.] Wolverhampton, West Midlands, UK

HOOD, KIMBERLY ERYNNE
[memb.] National Honor Society (11th, 12th), Key Club (10th, 11th, 12th), Interact Club (9th, 11th), Fellowship of Christian Athletes (11th, 12th), Junior Varsity Cheerleading, Captain (9th), Varsity Cheerleading (10th, 11th), Junior Varsity Volleyball Team (9th, 10th), Soccer Team (10th); [hon.] National Honor Society (11th, 12th), Honor Roll, ABC Award (Above and Beyond the Call), Who's Who Among American High School Students, Biloxi Regional Medical Center Outstanding Citizenship Award, DAR Essay Contest, District Award and State Finalist, United States Achievement Academy all-American Scholar

HOOLEY, DUNCAN JOHN EDWARD
[b.] 15 March 1972, Manchester; [p.] John P. Hooley, Jean Hooley; [ed.] Hereford Cathedral School, New College, Telford, Reading University; [occ.] Internal Sales Executive; [hon.] Bachelor of Arts in Ancient History/History; [oth. writ.] One poem published in an anthology entitled "Voice of The People", poem entitled "Proud and Tall".; [a.] Reading, Berkshire, UK, RG1 2AA

HOOPER, ROGER
[pen.] Alice Jacks; [b.] 14 October 1945, Canada; [p.] Nora and George Hooper; [m.] Anita, 22 May 1977; [ch.] Susan and Jenni; [ed.] Canadian Defence School, Canada and Germany, South London Poly.; [occ.] Retail Sales Manager; [oth. writ.] Many poems written but as yet none published.; [pers.] I was inspired by my grandchildren, Jack and Alice, who live in America, to start writing again. My hope is to have my poems made into children's books. Dedicated to my grandchildren.; [a.] Basingstoke, Hampshire, UK, RG24 9EN

HOPKINS, TERESA CHRISTINE
[pen.] Teresa Murphy-Hopkins; [b.] 20 December 1955, Essex; [p.] Stephen Murphy, Ellen Murphy; [m.] Michael John Hopkins, 5 July 1975; [ch.] Michael Steven, Cheri Teresa; [ed.] Eastbrook Comprehensive School; [occ.] Foster parent; [oth. writ.] Asked by Jonathon Clifford to join MEPS 18 years ago, after entering a poetry competition, but the children were young, money was scarce, the 7 men fee was like trying to reach for the moon, I was unable to, 1 of life's big regrets.; [pers.] All my life I have written poems that express my feelings at that time, hardship, happiness, pain or joy. Blessed with two of the greatest teachers, my mother and father, my love of life, I owe to them.; [a.] Spalding, Lincolnshire, UK, PE12 9RQ

HORNBY, MARIE CHRISTINE
[b.] 8 June 1939, Stonyhurst, Nr Blackburn; [p.] James and Maria Holden; [m.] Bill Hornby, 14 October 1961; [ch.] 3, 2 girls 1 boy, Julie and Gillian and Ian; [ed.] Sec. Modern and Further Education; [occ.] Housewife; [hon.] Certificates for Open College Grade A - English Literature - 1995, Grade A - Psychology 1996, Creative Writing - Grade B - Open College - 1992, Exam - Passed; [oth. writ.] Six other poems published in other anthologies. Wrote a play for T.V. (Unsuccessful), entered a competition in a national newspaper (short story). 'Only one winner - not me!'; [pers.] "Writing, especially poetry, brings me closer to the meaning of life on a spiritual level, making me more aware of the reasons why we are here at all."; [a.] Blackburn, Lancashire, UK, BB1 9AU

HOROBIN, SANDRA MARY
[b.] 8 August 1955, Stafford; [m.] David Bryan Horobin, 9 February 1974; [ch.] Emma Marie

and Ivan Lee; [ed.] Oldfields Hall for Girls, Bramshall Road in Uttoxeter; [pers.] Was brought up by my gran, Alice Bertha Smith (formerly Ault), lived at 62 Park Avenue Uttoxeter, until her death in 1971; [a.] Uttoxeter, Staffordshire, UK, ST14 7EX

HORTON, MS. CARLY
[b.] 13 September 1975, Crawley; [p.] Steve Horton and Elaine Horton; [ed.] Park Hall School, Birmingham - Tamworth College; [occ.] Training to be a Chef; [oth. writ.] I am currently working on a fictional novel and other poems.; [pers.] My writing has been influenced and encouraged by my family from a very early age, especially by my granddad. I hope to continue writing for many years to come.; [a.] Tamworth, Staffordshire, UK, B77 2QW

HOSLER, SHERRILYNE
[pen.] Sherrilyne Rigg; [b.] 11 November 1964, Buxton; [ch.] Two; [occ.] Housewife/Student; [pers.] Even now, do unto others as you would be done by Queue from Anne Agnostic; [a.] Stockport, Cheshire, UK

HOUGHTON, REBECCA BRIGID ELISABETH
[b.] 12 June 1983, Bath; [p.] Peter and Brigid Houghton; [ed.] Warminster School, Port Regis School, St. Mary's School Shaftesbury; [occ.] Student; [hon.] Winner of a school poetry competition and other small awards; [oth. writ.] Other poetry and English essays; [pers.] I believe poetry is something that cannot be written to order, but only when it is inspired.; [a.] Warminster, Wiltshire, UK, BA12 0AN

HOWELLS, AUSTIN K. C.
[b.] 1 December 1943, Pontypridd; [p.] Tudor and Doreen Howells; [m.] Maureen Howells, 29 August 1964; [ch.] Anthony and Angela; [ed.] Lanwood Secondary Modern School and Treforest Technical College; [occ.] Panel Beater and Sprayer; [memb.] South Wales Sunbeam Motorcycle Club, Affiliate Member of the British Motorcyclists Federation; [oth. writ.] I've written a number of poems, but for my own enjoyment.; [pers.] I am 52 years old and have never had any interest in poetry, but in February 1996 I awoke one morning at 3 a.m. and simply picked up a pen and paper and started writing. A bit spooky really.; [a.] Ynysybwl, Glamorgan, UK, CF37 3HH

HOWELLS, VALERIE
[b.] 4 April 1944, Rugeley; [m.] Jim Howells (Deceased), 31 March 1962; [ch.] Gillian Smith; [ed.] Aelfgar Secondary Modern Girls School; [occ.] Disabled; [memb.] Rugeley P.H.A.B. Club, Rugeley Pheonix Club; [hon.] Trophies and medals for disabled sports, mainly bowling. Some discus and some javelin throwing.; [pers.] I started writing poetry when I became disabled. I found it a good way of relaxing and making my feelings felt.; [a.] Rugeley, Staffordshire, UK, WS15 2LA

HUBBUCK, MARJORIE
[b.] 16 February 1929, Fourstones; [p.] James and Jane Mayhew Hodgson; [m.] John Ronald Hubbuck, 1950; [ch.] Two; [ed.] Newbrough C-E School and Shafto Trust School, Haydon Bridge Hexham; [occ.] My first job: Warden Paper Mill, housewife now and Bus Conductress, also I worked at Prudhoe Hospital 17 years as a Nursing Assistant; [hon.] None award, but I did give the Queen Mother this poem when she opened Thomas Bewicks Museem and I got a letter back within 3 days that said she was touched why I should give her this poem.; [oth. writ.] I have had about 4 or 5 more poems put in books.

HUCKIN, DIANE
[b.] 10 October 1959, Swindon; [p.] Mary and Ron Bastin; [m.] Glen Huckin, 25 September 1982; [ch.] Hayley Louise Huckin (13); [ed.] The Commonweal School, Swindon and Swindon

College; [occ.] Freelance Interior Decorator and part-time Bar Person at Morris St. W.M.C. Swindon; [memb.] The Caravan Club; [pers.] I wrote the poem "My Little Girl" while on holiday in my touring caravan at Woolacombe in Devon.; [a.] Swindon, Wilts, UK, SN2 2HE

HUGHES, DAVID R.
[pen.] Dei Hughes; [b.] 7 March 1938, Criccieth, N. Wales; [p.] John W. and Annie May Hughes; [m.] Divorced; [ch.] 3 children, 4 children, and 1 adopted; [ed.] Diploma in Psychology and English, B.A. in Social Psychology, M.A. in Counselling; [occ.] Sculptor/Counsellor/Poet; [oth. writ.] Books of Poets Slate 1972 (Stimulate) Gone to Earth (Unpublished) 40P 197 Rose and the Atom single poem. Ireland 3 poems. Earth ascending anthology.; [pers.] "I believe that poetry speaks with a voice that couldn't speak in any other way, because like a spider's thread between trees it has a special way with the heart." Bryn, Croesor, Penrhyndeudroeth.; [a.] Gwynedd, UK, LL4 8SS

HUGHES, PAUL ROBERT
[b.] 1 March 1967, London; [p.] Eric Hughes and Sheila Hughes; [m.] Lisa Christina Hughes, 23 May 1992; [ch.] Kurtis Paul Hughes/Frazer Paul Hughes; [ed.] Bromfords Comprehensive School - Wickford, Essex; [occ.] Welder (Aviation); [oth. writ.] One other published in the Quiet Moments anthology; [pers.] This is dedicated to my wife and sons.; [a.] Chelmsford, Essex, UK, CM1 2RH

HUMPHREY, CHRISTOPHER
[b.] 4 April 1978; [occ.] Student; [pers.] One day I'll create a piece of writing so brilliant and so full of meaning that it will be recognized as the greatest piece of work the world has ever seen and the greatest piece of work the world will ever see.; [a.] Horley, Surrey, UK, RH6 8RX

HUMPHRIES, JOANNA
[b.] 4 August 1984, Greenwich; [p.] Julie Humphries, Nicholas Humphries; [ed.] Bexley Heath Comprehensive School; [occ.] School (pupil); [pers.] I dedicate this poem to my grandad who I dearly love and miss.; [a.] Plumstead, London, UK, SE18 1RL

HUSSAIN, SABERINA
[b.] 1 May 1970, Hammersmith; [p.] Nazar Hussain, Chano Hussain; [m.] Aftab Umar, 7 May 1987; [ch.] Nabeel Umar, Shaan Umar; [ed.] William Gladstone Secondary High School; [occ.] Housewife, Mother of my children; [hon.] BTEC National Cert in Business and Finance and a special award for the achievement for my chosen field.; [oth. writ.] I have written many poems and been to poet functions, but this is the first time I feel I have a achieved my goal.; [pers.] No matter how small you are, as a poet, but if you think small you won't achieve your goal. Think big and you will be successful.; [a.] Willesden Green, London, UK, NW2 4QN

HUTCHINSON, LINDA
[pen.] Valley Michaels; [b.] 24 November 1978, Birmingham, England; [p.] Diana and Sammy; [ed.] St. Albans Secondary, now at Joseph Chamberlain 6th Form College.; [occ.] Student at Joseph Chamberlain College, studying media, English a-levels language and Literature and Photography.; [memb.] Gold Star Member of 'MJ News International' - It is a Michael Jackson fan Club.; [oth. writ.] I write poems from my heart.; [pers.] After, when I look at someone I try to put myself in their shoes, feel their feelings and experience their pain and anger. This fictional quantum leap into their shoes because my truth that I express through my poetry. Michael Jackson is my inspiration, my bright star, rolemodel, my teacher of creation. I love you Michael.; [a.] Quinton, Birmingham, UK, B32 2NT

HUTCHINSON, MONIKA TRAUB
[b.] 19 September 1953, Riedlingen, West Germany; [p.] Hermann Traub, Gerda Traub (Nee Lemke); [m.] John Elwyn Hutchinson, Summer 1981; [ed.] Wirtschafts Schule Sigmaringen St. David's University of Wales, Lampeter; [occ.] Investment Advisor; [pers.] Knowledge is felt; [a.] Maindenbower, Crawley, West Sussex, UK, RH10 7JT

HYMAN, DAVID
[pen.] David Black/Sonny Blackwood; [b.] 15 May 1943, Isleworth; [p.] Andrew Hyman, Emma Hyman; [m.] Barbara Hyman, 17 October 1963; [ch.] Lynn Michelle, Dean Vincent; [ed.] Ashford Secondary Modern; [occ.] Gardener, Imperial College, Ascot; [memb.] R.S.P.B., Tree Spirit, British Country Music Association; [oth. writ.] Several songs published, other poems published.; [pers.] I think that I draw from my love of the land.; [a.] Ascot, Berkshire, UK, SL5 7YZ

IBITOYE, BABATUNDE O.
[pen.] Babs O. Ibitoye; [b.] 28 August 1963, Lagos, Nigeria; [p.] W. Akanni Ibitoye, Abeni Ibitoye; [ch.] Olawale Ibitoye; [ed.] Lagos State College of Science and Technology, West London Institute of Higher Education and Thames Valley University, Ealing.; [occ.] CSSD Assistant, Charing Cross Hospital/P.T. LLB (Law) student Thames Valley University; [memb.] Kakaaki Performers International Drama and Cultural Club, Lagos, Nigeria, West-Africa. Comedy Junction (Brent).; [hon.] Talent Scholarship United States (school of performing and visual arts) San Diego, Trophy won for Outstanding Contribution to Drama (Kakaaki Society); [oth. writ.] Several poems published in local magazine (England) and in national dailies in Nigeria, West Africa. Short stories and staged plays, one recently presented on stage in Lagos.; [pers.] My poems could be compared to my working diary or my personal experiences in life as I go out in pursuit of survival and fulfillment.; [a.] Charlton, Greenwich, UK, SE7 7EH

IGHODARO, ISOSA
[pen.] Wilfred Ighodaro and Dr. Esohe Eno-Mark; [b.] 3 August 1981, Wimbledon; [occ.] Student at Rathdown School; [oth. writ.] Many other poems; [pers.] I write to express myself, all my poems have a great deal of sentimental value to me.

INAM, MS. SONIA
[b.] 14 March 1980, Edinburgh; [p.] Mohammed Zaheer Inam, Misbah Inam; [ed.] The Mary Erkshire School, Edinburgh; [occ.] Student; [oth. writ.] Poems published in school magazine:- 'Responsibility', 'Poison' and 'Orienteering'.; [pers.] I strive to express the monotony of everyday life together with the lack of individuality within society in my writing. I hope to create a greater awareness of equal rights for all and to eliminate feelings of inhibition when expressing oneself.; [a.] Edinburgh, Scotland, EH15 3LW

INGLE, NATALIE
[b.] 12 June 1984, Liverpool; [p.] Annette Ingle, Richard Ingle; [ed.] Savid High School; [memb.] Local Guides Group; [pers.] I write to express the dramatic scenes of life, in which I reflect the good and bad events, which I see through my eyes as a child.; [a.] Bootle, Merseyside, UK, L20 0BA

IRVING, HENRY
[pen.] Henry Irving; [b.] 21 February 1924, Manchester; [p.] Henry Irving, Lily Irving; [m.] Maureen Irving, 1 February 1963; [ch.] Jean, Alan, Neil; [ed.] Elementary Wife and I Comprehensive Children, Jean Doctors typist. Alan Manager, Neil, Electrician Cg 1/2 Am 1/2 Btec Electrical Engineer, Foreman; [occ.] Retired; [oth. writ.] At present writing a book based on experience of service with Royal Marines and fiction; [pers.] Service in the 42 Commando, Royal Marine taught me life is precious, so to take whatever comes day by day.; [a.] Prestatyn, Clwyd, North Wales, UK, LL19 7ED

ISELEY, COLLEEN MICHELLE
[b.] 11 January 1981, Ripon; [p.] John Iseley, Anne Iseley; [ed.] Ripon City School; [occ.] Student; [oth. writ.] Step Out of the Rain, Life After Love, Look at Me, All Alone, Always Changing, That's Life, Help Yourself, etc. None that I've tried to publish.; [pers.] I reflect some of my poems on my life and life in general. Also everyday happenings that add to the poems' intensity.; [a.] Ripon, North Yorkshire, UK

IVES, GWEN
[b.] 30 April 1931, Harwich; [p.] Beatrice Silburn, Joseph Silburn; [m.] Kenneth Ives, 6 September 1952; [ch.] Susan, Jennifer, Matthew; [ed.] Hill School for Girls, Suffolk College; [occ.] Retired; [memb.] Stowmarket Choral Soc., Thames Barge Sailing Club; [oth. writ.] Poems and articles published in magazines; [pers.] Reading and writing poetry are the loves of my life.; [a.] Stowmarket, Suffolk, UK, IP14 5PA

JACKSON, BERNIE
[b.] 8 December 1960, Richmond, Surrey; [p.] John Geraghty and Mary; [m.] Greg Jackson, 1980; [ch.] Fintan, Lisa, Grey; [ed.] Rehins NS, Ballina Convent of Mercy; [occ.] Company Director of Greg Jackson Properties/Housewife; [memb.] Ballina Salmon and Arts Festival, Ballina Golf Club; [oth. writ.] Force 10 - editors Dermot Healy, 3 radio plays, various magazines. The Mayo Anthology 4. New Writings from the West. Western People. songs/lyrics ect.; [pers.] I write because I enjoy it and enjoy the people I meet that have the same interest.; [a.] Ballina, Mayo, Ireland

JACOBS, RONALD
[pen.] Alexander Kovell; [b.] 18 November 1945, Woking, Surrey; [occ.] Ambulance man; [oth. writ.] Another poem "Nibs" in Awaken To A Dream.; [pers.] It was inspiration that created the writer in me.; [a.] South Lancing, West Sussex, UK, BN15 8ED

JACOBS, SIMON
[b.] 5 November 1973, Manchester; [p.] Ann and Charles Atkinson; [ed.] Manist College, Canberra Australia, Lake Tuggeranong College, Australia; [occ.] Barman at the 100 Club, London; [oth. writ.] I have two photo copied booklets in circulation, which were distributed freely, and several articles published in college newsletters.; [pers.] I believe I have a great deal of work to do, before I achieve a level of personal success in my writing.; [a.] Draperstown, Derry, UK, BT45 7LW

JAMES, MICHAEL
[b.] 29 January 1954, Cardiff; [p.] Ron and Frances James; [m.] Carol James, 8 November 1985; [ch.] Simon and Ellen; [pers.] I would like to dedicate this poem to my father Ron who died 5 May 1996. His love and devotion to his family prompted this poem in recognition of his life.; [a.] Cardiff, Glamorgan, UK, CF3 9TB

JAMES, PAMELA
[b.] Cornwall, UK; [p.] Doris and Jack Pitts; [m.] Jimmy James; [ch.] Sarah Jane; [ed.] Private School, Birmingham, UK; [oth. writ.] Poetry and short stories unpublished; [pers.] I like to remember John fleming who was chairman of our voluntary group who encouraged me to write my poetry and entertain the senior citizens and the less fortunate people in South Africa; [a.] Walkerville, Gauteng, SOUTH AFRICA

JAMES, ROSEMARY
[pen.] Rosemary Gwatkin; [b.] 27 August 1946, Nantyderry; [p.] Reginald and Winifred Gwatkin; [m.] Merlyn James, 9 October 1965; [ch.] Matthew James; [ed.] Llanover Primary School, Grofield Secondary School, two years training as (1968) state enrolled Nurse (second level); [occ.] Retired five years ago due to ill health; [memb.] Govilon Village, Swimming Club; [hon.] Only Nursing certificates; [pers.] I have always been able to rhyme words together. But it has to mean

something that I know well. (A bit of inspiration) the piece I sent you was about the Blorenge mountain on which Blaenavon sits. I lived there for 16 yrs.; [a.] Abergavenny, Monmouthshire, UK, NP7 9RL

JARRETT, FRANCESCA
[b.] 19 July 1978, Kingston-upon-Thames; [p.] John Steven Jarrett and Vanessa Jarrett; [ed.] The Queen's School Chester, Upton-by-Chester County High School; [occ.] Student (French BA/QTS) training to teach in primary school; [mem.] Member of Guilden Sutton Players, Nina Gaskill School of Dance; [hon.] Elementary Rad Ballet; [oth.writ.] Several poems written for personal satisfaction and expression.; [pers.] My poems are a reflection of my personal experiences, feelings and emotions. I believe poetry is the greatest means of expression and invaluable for our greater understanding of life.; [a.] Chester, Cheshire, UK, CH3 7HQ

JAVID, BAHAREH
23 April 1980, Iran; [p.] Azemat Navadeh and Hossein Javid; [ed.] Nine G.C.S.E.'s and three A-Levels; [occ.] Student; [oth. writ.] "Last Whisper", "Ocean's Distant Cry", "Heaven's Calling", "Escape", "Candle In The Wind", "Another Tomorrow", I have been writing since the age of thirteen.; [pers.] Through poetry I feel the desire to create an image of an insubstantial place of misery. We are all prisoners of fate, living a tempestuous life in the embrace of inhumanity. Life is merely a passing phase. This earth shall never be healed. Darkness is the only winner on earth. Poetry is our only salvation.; [a.] Middlesex, UK

JAYAVANTH, DR. PRATAP PREMANAND
[pen.] Prem; [b.] 29 July 1946, Madras, India; [p.] Col. Jayavanth, Ranjini; [m.] Vedha, 11 September 1975; [ch.] Deepak, Ashwin, Kiran; [ed.] St. Xavier's Jaipur, Madras Christian College, Madras, AFMC, Poona, WNSM, University of Wales, DPHS, University of Edinburgh; [occ.] Physician, with the United Nations Development Programme previously. Served under the Ministry of Health in Saudi Arabia during the Gulf War.; [memb.] Poetry Society, Edinburgh Unv., Fellow of the Royal Society of Health; [hon.] English Literature, Editor's Choice Award (1996); [oth. writ.] Several poems and articles published in local newspapers and journals in India, New Zealand and in the UK. "Mirage in the Desert" published in A Passage in Time (1996).; [pers.] I wish to capture the various aspects and different moods observed in everyday life. Equally adept in writing serious poetry and humorous limericks. I seek inspiration from life and my experiences.; [a.] Glasgow, UK, G42 9SA

JEFFERIES, FREDDIE
[pen.] Freddie Jefferies; [b.] 14 November 1925, London; [m.] Stephanie Jefferies, 26 March 1955; [ch.] Jonathan, Joanna, Elizabeth; [ed.] Technical; [occ.] Designer of prints to commemorate famous historical events with verses; [oth. writ.] 12,000 words - Children's Books (6) Bunny The Boat, current verses print enclosed ready now for marketing. Bannockburn verses by Robert Burns. Culloden by myself. Others in hand for finalizing and publication.; [pers.] In the field of creation, fulfillment lies in the unknown that unfolds itself in the evolution of the work. I am often reminded of the words of the late Malcolm Muggeridge referring to his public speaking! I often wonder when I speak, what I am going to hear myself say!; [a.] Woking, Surrey, UK, GW21 1JJ

JENKINS, STEWART
[b.] 25 October 1952, Hereford; [p.] Irene Jenkins, Tevor Jenkins; [ed.] Lord Scudamore Boys School, Whitecross High School; [occ.] Forestry Contractor; [memb.] IFAW International Fund for Animal Welfare, WWF - World Wildlife Fund; [hon.] Champions of Animals Award from the

IFAW; [pers.] I strive to tell in my poem, that the goodness of nature, is there for everyone to see, if they look for it. I was influenced by my working outdoors in the woods, all my life.; [a.] Hereford, Herefordshire, UK, HR2 6DS

JENKINS, SUSAN
[b.] 30 March 1965, Ystalyfera, South Wales; [ed.] Bishop Wand Secondary School, Sunderland Polytechnic, Aberdeen University; [occ.] Mental Health Social Worker, Hornsey Lane Registered Care Home, Islington; [memb.] British Association of Social Work, North London Buddhist Centre; [hon.] B.A. (Hons) Social Sciences, C.Q.S.W. and Certificate in Applied Social Studies, Foundation Training in Core. Process. Psychotherapy.; [pers.] My writing aims to explore the human condition, the nature of suffering and joy. I am interested in how life touches us (emotionally, physically, mentally and spiritually) and I am fascinated by how life can be a struggle against impermanence. The uncertainty of life is all that is truly certain.; [a.] Crouch End, London, UK, N4 4AJ

JENNENS, GRAEME LESLIE
[b.] 9 June 1965, Ormskirk; [p.] Gordon Jennens, Patricia Jennens; [ed.] Boldmere School, Sutton Coldfield David and Charles Writers College; [occ.] Sales in Motor Trade; [memb.] Performing Rights Society, Pamra; [oth. writ.] Several poems published in various anthologies nationally, two commercially recorded albums of songs. Published and released internationally.; [pers.] I take great inspiration from Coleridge and the romantic poets, and from my ancestor Charles Jennens whose poetry and writings gave Handel the inspiration to write the Messiah and other works.; [a.] Atherstone, Warwickshire, UK

JENNINGS, BRENDA
[b.] 4 January 1950, Cheltenham; [p.] Leslie Lackie, Simone Josephine Lackie; [ch.] Lewis Jennings, Rona Jennings; [ed.] Jarrow Grammar School - Northern Counties College of Education; [occ.] Senior Teacher Williamston, Primary School Livingston; [memb.] Member of Mensa; [oth. writ.] Poems published in several anthologies. Poems, letters and short articles published in local papers. Runner up in Hilton House National Poetry Competition. Third Prize winner in Hilton House Open Poetry Competition.; [pers.] My writing is fired from the heart - I hope it finds its target.; [a.] East Calder, West Lothian, UK, EH53 0QA

JEWELL, VERONICA
[b.] 28 April, Birmingham; [p.] Edward Capewell, Gladys Capewell; [m.] Raymond Jewell, 22 August 1970; [ch.] Katherine Sarah; [ed.] St. John's Primary School, Moseley Modern Secondary School; [occ.] Self employed - personalized printing and promotional lines; [memb.] British Ju-Jitsu Association; [hon.] Speech and Drama, Black Belt Ju-Jitsu; [oth. writ.] Advertising articles and newsletters for martial arts clubs; [pers.] When writing I try to express different ways of looking at things.; [a.] Solihull, West Midlands, UK

JEYARAJ, PRAVIN
[b.] 11 July 1977, Harrow; [p.] Ponnampalam and Kaushalya; [ed.] Wilson's School (Wallington), University of Surrey (Guildford); [occ.] Student (Maths); [memb.] Poetry Society, National Union of Students (NUS); [hon.] Grade four Piano, grade four Violin; [oth. writ.] Several poems written but none so far published.; [pers.] My poems let me express my feelings that would otherwise be laughed at. I strive to show the best and worst parts of being a young adult in a shocking world.; [a.] Sutton, Surrey, UK, SM2 6JU

JIGGENS, MRS. LYNDA
[pen.] Lynda Jiggens; [b.] 11 April 1952, Hornchurch; [p.] Kenneth Saunders, Doreen Saunders; [m.] Sydney Jiggens, 27 June 1970; [ch.] Shane Jiggens, Wendy Jiggens; [ed.]

Fitzwimarc Secondary School; [occ.] Housewife; [hon.] Music Competitions; [oth. writ.] Musical scores, published in Tech-Plus Magazine; [pers.] The greatest influence in my writing stems from past experiences during my life, and my attempt to communicate in a shorter more direct manner than story telling.; [a.] Benfleet, Essex, UK, S57 3YT

JINKS, REV. KENNETH E.
[b.] 4 December 1910, Birmingham; [p.] Ernest Jinks and May Jinks; [m.] Gwendoline Tharne, 29 July 1939; [ch.] Jane Sargent; [ed.] King Edward VI Grammar School, Aston, Birmingham, Richmond Methodist Theological College, London University Manchester Univ.; [occ.] Methodist Minister (Retired); [memb.] RSPB (Fellow); [hon.] Academic diploma in Theology, London University. M.A. Degree (Psychology), Manchester University; [oth. writ.] Articles on different aspects of the work of the ministry. Articles on spiritual healing. All have been published.; [pers.] The poem The Emmaus Road - is an expression of my personal faith.; [a.] Llandudno, Gwynedd, UK, LL30 3EU

JOHN, BRETT
[b.] 24 February 1963, Newport; [p.] Aeron John, Dawn John; [m.] Michiko, 13 February 1995; [ch.] Kenny; [ed.] Croesyceiliog Comprehensive, King Alfred's College Winchester; [occ.] English Language Teacher, Saudi Arabia; [memb.] Lawn and Indoor Bowling Club (Cumbria and Torfaen); [hon.] B.A. (Hon) 2i in History and English; [oth. writ.] Short stories and poems for local magazines and literary societies.; [pers.] Influenced - mythology and legend, especially the writings of Tolkien and Poe.; [a.] Cwmbran, Torfaen County Borough, UK, NP44 2AN

JOHNSON, ERIC A.
[pen.] Ras Ayandele; [b.] 12/02/73; [hon.] Currently studying a Bso Honours in Business studies at Greenwhich College; [oth. writ.] A self publishes book titled "You Fi Know This" release date July 1996 ISBN 0-9528681-0-5; [per.] To influence positive action and thinking throughout the world.

JOHNSON, PAT
[b.] 12 May 1953, Evesham, Worcs; [p.] Fredrick John and Mary Alice Keen; [m.] Barry Johnson, 26 November 1983; [ch.] Shellie Keen (Love child born 1972); [ed.] Ashton-under-Hill Primary, then Bredon Hill Middle School; [oth. writ.] Book of poems, unpublished and several poems published in local magazines.; [pers.] Do not dwell in the past. Do not worry about the future. Do something worthwhile and enjoy today as if it were your last. One day it will be!; [a.] Evesham, Worcestershire, UK, WR11 6SW

JOHNSTON, BRENDA
[b.] 28 September 1950, South Shields; [m.] Brian Johnston; [ch.] Phillip Paul Kevin; [ed.] Redwell Co. Secondary; [occ.] Housewife; [pers.] I started writing poems in secret at the age of 15, 'Lost Love' being the first of many. I have remembered these poems over the years but only recently decided to write them down. I hope to write more.; [a.] South Shields, Tyne and Wear, UK, NE34 6EF

JOHNSTONE, MARGUERITA JANE
[b.] 27 July 1919, Inverness; [p.] John and Janet Henderson; [m.] William Alexander Johnstone, 3 April 1959; [occ.] Retired, (Widow); [pers.] There is an answer I have sought and cannot find; there is a truth, beyond my mind; [a.] Inverness, Inverness-shire, UK, IV3 6HS

JOLLEY, MARTIN
[b.] 15 October 1950, Cork, Ireland; [p.] Mary Jolley (Snr), Tom Jolley, (Deceased, RIP); [m.] Mary Jolley (Jnr), 27 July 1977; [ch.] Joseph; [ed.] Advanced City and Guilds of London, HNC (BTEC) "Motor Vehicle Management", Miame (Australia), Advanced Cert. (Automobile), Ireland; [occ.] Lecturer, grade 1; [memb.] Miame

(Australia) LCGI (City and Guilds of London); [hon.] Silver Medal Winner for achieving 1st place overall in the city and guilds of London Examination "Diagnostic Techniques" (Engines) - 1982.; [oth. writ.] Part-time motoring correspondent. Researched and compiled history of DKW car assembly, in Ballincollig (1950-1963), Co Cork, Ireland.; [pers.] I have been greatly influenced by my Uncle Jim (Cooney), of Rylane, Co Cork and Tipperary (now sadly deceased RIP), Rudyard Kipling also left a great influence on me.; [a.] Ballygroman Ovens, Cork, Ireland

JONES, BARBARA HARVEY
[b.] 13 August 1946, Mancot, N. Wales; [p.] Hector and Gwendolen Harvey (Both Deceased); [m.] Grevin Jones, 16 August 1969; [ch.] Twin daughters - Dawn and Claire (25 yrs old), Son Grevin (21 yrs old); [ed.] Holywell Grammar School, Wrexham and Oswestry School of Radiography; [occ.] Retired Radiographer; [memb.] Member of Society of Radiographers, member of several environmental action groups; [hon.] Qualified Radiographer (DCR); [oth. writ.] I have written many poems, particularly during my student days and prior to starting a family. Several have been published in a local journal, 'Country Quest'. Since my children have become independent, I am finding more time to express my thoughts through the medium of poetry.; [pers.] I enjoy using words and rhythms which are spontaneous reflections on personal and general feelings.; [a.] Wrexham, Clwyd, UK, LL14 1TG

JONES, DONNA
[b.] 17 November 1982; [p.] Roy Jones, Patricia Jones; [ed.] Currently attending Dunraven Secondary School; [occ.] Pupil; [pers.] I would like to dedicate my poem "Now You've Gone" to my man who died suddenly of a heart attack in March, 1996; [a.] Streatham Vale, London, UK, SW16 5SS

JONES, MRS. JOY F. E.
[pen.] Joy McJones; [b.] 14 March 1938, Jos. N., Nigeria; [p.] Roland and Ethel McCullagh; [m.] The late James H. Jones, 8 August 1962; [ch.] Matthew P. Jones; [ed.] Emmanuel Grammar School, Swansea, Swansea University; [occ.] Retired Teacher; [memb.] Haverfordwest and Dyfed L.T.A's, Milford Operatic Society (Choreographer) Cambrensis Society; [hon.] Ex. Wales Hockey International (World Cup 1967), Ex. County Tennis Champion, Advanced Dance Cert., Worcester College, Member Instructor of American Line Dance Assoc., UK; [oth. writ.] Nothing printed, but a play script in the pipeline.; [pers.] Until recently, my teaching career and family commitments have kept me from writing. I enjoy sport, travel and the creative arts. Whilst I do find computers useful, I do think that society should not rely entirely on them. Chaos could reign in 2000! Let us strive to be thoughtful and creative and less machinated and robotic.; [a.] Milford Haven, Pembrokeshire, UK, SA73 1EP

JONES, MARA LESLEY
[b.] 10 September 1957, St. Asaph; [p.] Henry Jones, Marion Jones; [ed.] Ysgoly Castell Rhuddlan Ysgol Emrys Ap Iwan Abergele; [occ.] Administration; [memb.] British Mensa; [oth. writ.] Many other poems, as yet unpublished.; [pers.] Gathers her inspiration from the countryside, people and history around her.; [a.] Rhuddlan, Denbighshire, UK, LL18 2TR

JONES, NADINE
[b.] 16 February 1972, Hull; [p.] Linda Jones, Robert Edward Jones; [ed.] Andrew Marvell Senior High, Hull College of F.E. Blackpool and Fylde College of Higher and further Education; [occ.] Finishing Assistant, Computype, Hull; [memb.] International Tiger Protection Team, Care for the Wild Tiger Trust. WWF; [hon.] BTEC 1st Dip. Graphic Design BTEC Nat. Dip. Graphic Design, BTEC H.N.D. Scientific and Natural History Illustration.; [pers.] I believe

everything has an earthbound right to live whether human, plant or animal. I will try my very best to protect those who need it most.; [a.] Hull, E. Yorkshire, UK, HU5 1NQ

JONES, PAULINE
[b.] 20 January 1952, Clatterbridge; [p.] Arthur and Ruby Sherratt; [m.] Steven Jones, 20 October 1973; [ch.] Robert Gareth and Nerys Patricia; [ed.] Newton Secondary School Carlott Park College; [occ.] Snr. School Assistant Hill Top Public School, NSW, Aust.; [oth. writ.] Personal poems for friends and special occasions, children's book, several songs.; [pers.] I write for personal pleasure and fun about events or people who inspire me.; [a.] Hill Top, New South Wales, Australia, 2575

JONES, RODERICK FRANCIS
[pen.] Rory McEoin; [b.] 19 October 1944, Dublin; [p.] Jones/Sharp; [m.] Margaret Louise (nee McKenzie), 11 October 1991, Dornoch; [ch.] Brigitte, Patricia, Sara-Beth, Tracey, Robert; [ed.] Irish Leaving Cert. - 'A' Levels, Various Computer Studies Certs.; [occ.] Retired Banker Computing; [memb.] Royal Marines Ass.; [oth. writ.] Amateur song writer; [pers.] To love, to respect, to be considerate, to enjoy all the Almighty has given, good or bad.; [a.] Bournemouth, Dorset, UK, BH9 2TR

JONES, SHEILA YVONNE
[b.] 16 October 1934, Stafford; [p.] George and Ada Staley; [m.] Robert Vaughan Jones, 19 December 1953; [ch.] John, Glyn, Robert, Alexander; [ed.] Riverway Secondary Modern Girls School, Stafford; [occ.] Housewife; [memb.] Kennel Club for Dog Showing; [oth. writ.] The Mouse on Laurel Corner, The Move. Several poems, including 'No More' published last year (1996) by International Library of Poetry in The Other Side of the Mirror; [pers.] I like to write sensitive poems and stories and hope that they give the reader a sense of warmth and an inner glow. I admire William Wordsworth.; [a.] Wolverhampton, Staffs, UK, WV9 5AA

JONES, STELLA
[b.] 3 July 1940; [m.] Dennis Jones, 8 July 1961; [ch.] Four; [ed.] Leicester University; [occ.] Housewife; [hon.] Politics; [oth. writ.] Short stories, T.V. games; [a.] Wellingborough, Northants, UK, NN8 4EW

JORDAN
[pen.] Julie Ann; [b.] 18 April 1952, Bath; [p.] John Regan and Eileen White; [m.] David Jordan, 5 August 1972; [ch.] Paul Matthew and Weena; [ed.] Ralph Allens Comprehensive; [occ.] Housewife and Mother, who in her spare time draws and paints; [oth. writ.] Frequently writes to magazines; [pers.] Started writing down my thoughts and feelings for self therapy. Always liked blank verse and poetry at school.; [a.] Trowbridge, Wiltshire, UK, BA14 9TY

JUDE, PHILLIP D.
[b.] May 17, 1938, City of Westminster; [p.] Eva Jude, Daniel Jude, Deceased; [m.] July 7, 1962; [ch.] Phillip Jude, Angela Jude; [ed.] Sec. Enfield College, City of Guilds for Engineering, Physical Training Instructor HMS; [occ.] Unemployed; [hon.] City of Guilds; [oth. writ.] I have written many more poems but never tried to have them published before this time.; [pers.] In the reality of my perception, I am free and in my freedom, is my enlightenment.; [a.] London, Middx, 6BL

KAMSLER, MATTHEW
[b.] 6 July 1920, London; [p.] Edward and Cecilia Kamsler (Deceased); [ed.] College Education; [occ.] Independent Means; [hon.] (1) Medal for Meritorious Service of the Order of the British Empire, (2) Mentioned in Despatches (London Gazette); [oth. writ.] (1) The Green Huntsman (Reader's review enclosed) Genealogical Breakdown of (2) Honours created after the Norman Conquest of families who survived the Battle of

Senlac (Neither has yet been published, unfortunately) an anthology of poems (150) has gone astray; some poems however were published in Atlantic Press, Regency Press and Literary Editions.; [pers.] Service in R.A.F. Volunteer Reserve June 1940 to April 1946 (Overseas) British Embassy Athens Sept 1946 to April 1947 (Temporary) Assistant Community Schools for 16 years until August 1965. Recommended after the war for promotion to commissioned rank; [a.] Athens, Greece, 10437

KANE, ANDREW
[b.] 16 June 1978, Belfast; [p.] Andrew Kane, Elizabeth Kane; [ed.] Grosvenor Grammar, Belfast, currently at Queens University, Belfast; [occ.] Student; [oth. writ.] This was the first poem that I had ever written.; [pers.] I try to reflect the sincerity of my feelings in the words that I write.; [a.] Belfast, Antrim, UK, BT6 0EU

KANE, LESLEY
[pen.] Lesley; [b.] 1 April 1971, R.A.H.; [p.] Jean and Pat; [m.] Stuart; [ch.] Nicole - 3 years old; [ed.] Park Mains High; [occ.] Full-time Mother; [memb.] At the moment I am looking into joining a writing school.; [hon.] Scotvec and diploma for Business Administration and Computer Studies; [oth. writ.] I have a selection of poems that I have been doing for a few years now.; [pers.] When writing poetry, it is what you feel inside at the time. When you feel sad, happy or excited inside then you can write a good poem.; [a.] Bishopton, Renfrewshire, UK, PA7 5LG

KANE, MARY GWENDOLINE
[pen.] Mary G. Kane; [b.] 5 October 1925, Neath, S. Wales; [p.] Luke John, Gwendoline John; [m.] William Edward Kane, 28 August 1948; [ch.] Paul, Andrew, Deborah, Sharon; [ed.] Elementary, Clyne/Neath Glasgow (name of school forgotten) Cardiff (also forgotten) two schools in Birmingham one was "Cherrywood Rd"; [occ.] Retired, House Wife part time Child Care and Cleaner; [memb.] Fellowship of Christian Writers.; [oth. writ.] Twelve poems published in new anthologies, published by Triumph House (Forward Press) since I started writing in Jan. of this year, also one of these poems published by Arthur H. Stockwell.; [pers.] My purpose in writing is to reflect the beauty of nature, the goodness and severity of God, and to uplift the thoughts and desires of mankind to a higher, nobler sphere. My main inspiration has undoubtedly been the Bible.; [a.] Swansea, West Glamorgan, UK, SA3 3EY

KANU, OKORO PAUL
[b.] 7 July 1927, Arochukwu, Nigeria; [p.] Paul and Ola Kanu; [m.] Patricia R. Mitchell, 1960; [ch.] Ola, Uzoma, Aviazu, Kanu, Ogonnaya (Deceased); [ed.] Birmingham University, England (English Lang and Lit.) Stanford University, USA (Business and Educ. Adminstr.) California State Universities and Colleges (Consortium), USA (Public Administration); [occ.] Retired Teacher/Administrator; [memb.] Member - British Institute of Management (MBIM) Member - American Institute of (AIM, PC) Management, President's Council; [hon.] First Class Certificate/Certificates of Merit for Poetry in English and Igbo (Nigerian Language); [oth. writ.] Policy papers for educational administration in Nigeria; [pers.] Summed up by Longfellow: "Not enjoyment and not sorrow is our destined end or way but to act that each tomorrow finds us further than today"; [a.] London, UK, N11 1EE

KARIM, SHAILA
[b.] 22 August 1979, Edgware; [p.] Aslam Karim, Umme Kulsum Karim; [ed.] Copthall School, Barnet College; [memb.] Duke of Edinburgh Awards; [hon.] Bronze, Silver, Gold Duke of Edinburgh Awards; [oth. writ.] Won a poem competition in a magazine; [pers.] I really enjoy writing poems because I am able to express my feelings and ideas. I also enjoy reading poems written by others. I have been greatly influenced by my parents, sister, friends and others around me.; [a.] Edgware, London, UK, HA8 0JG

KARPE, MRS. SALLY
[b.] 1 January 1963, Wisbech, Cambs.; [p.] Sydney Clifford Bower and Joan Bower; [m.] David Edward Karpe, 21 April 1984; [ch.] Matthew Lee Karpe (10); [ed.] March Hereward Comprehensive, further education at Neal-Wade Community College; [occ.] Hairdresser, also studying to become a medical herbalist; [memb.] None at present. Used to belong to the local Writer's Circle; [oth. writ.] Short story published in "The Write's Rostrum". Have entered Ian St. James Awards, but nothing else published so far.; [pers.] Poetry is immortal and has the ability to touch the lives of many generations without ever losing its original sentiments. It is a living thing. I feel this to be profoundly true whenever I read the work of Emily Bronte.; [a.] March, Cambridgeshire, UK, PE15 9DB

KAUR, HARINDER
[pen.] Harry; [b.] 28 June 1975, Wolverhampton; [p.] Jagtar Singh and Ajit Kaur; [ed.] Colton Hills Comprehensive School; [occ.] Customer Service Assistant - Private Sector; [hon.] 'Gold' Youth Award Scheme. First person in Wolverhampton to complete such an award.; [oth. writ.] Poems selectively written for friends and family.; [pers.] The pen is mightier than the sword. There is no more powerful way to express oneself and feelings within, and toward others, than through poetry.; [a.] Wolverhampton, West Midlands, UK, WV2 1JA

KEECH, MARIAN
[pen.] Martinella Brooks and Agnes Mae; [b.] 31 August 1938, Southampton; [oth. writ.] Poem 'Sorrow' in book entitled 'Quiet Moments', The International Library of Poetry. Oct/Nov 1996, Poem 'Peace' in book entitled 'Days Gone By', Anchor Books, Peterboro, pub Jan 1997., Poem 'No Brighter Light' in book entitled 'Heroes And Villans', Anchor Books, Peterboro, pub Nov 1996., Poem 'Adam' in book entitled 'Treasured Memories', Anchor Books, Peterboro, pub Nov 1996, Poem 'Rainbow Lady' in book entitled 'Sands Of Time', Poetry Today, Upper Dee Mill, Llangollen, pub November 1996. Poem 'Wishing' in book entitled 'World of Words', Anchor Books, Peterboro, pub end Jan 1997, Poem 'Oh! Lucky Man' in book entitled, 'Bundles of Joy!', Anchor Books, Peterboro, pub end Jan 1997, Poem 'Snow' in book entitled 'Poet's Premiere', Arrival Press, Peterboro, pub Jan 1997.

KEIGHLEY-BRAY, CLAIRE
[b.] 13 September 1977, Stockport; [p.] Margaret and Adrian Keighley-Bray; [ed.] Trinity C of E High School Loreto College, Manchester; [occ.] Student; [memb.] GKR Karate International; [oth. writ.] My Release - book of poetry published by Minerva Press.; [pers.] My poetry is my release and an outlet for my bereavement of the death of my sister. I hope it is of assistance to others in a similar situation.; [a.] Stockport, Cheshire, UK, SK4 2BZ

KELLY, CELINE
[b.] 17 September 1981, London; [p.] Colette Kelly, Paul Kelly; [ed.] Brentwood Ursuline Convent High School; [occ.] School girl; [oth. writ.] Another poem published in a young writer's book, 'Rise and Shine', The Writer of This Poem; [pers.] I use poetry to express how I view, feel and see things clearly; [a.] Blackmore, Essex, UK, CM4 0QN

KELLY, JAMES
[b.] 3 November 1971, Wicklow, Ireland; [ed.] Presentation College Bray; [occ.] Sales Executive; [memb.] Astronomy Ireland, Amnesty International; [hon.] All Ireland Accordion Champion, Diploma in Foreign Trade; [oth. writ.] Various poems and short articles; [pers.] I believe in peace and harmony in the world through words, music and pictures - communication is everything. Live life!; [a.] Bray, Wicklow, UK

KELLY, JANINE
[b.] 3 May 1967, Lancaster; [p.] Lilian and Brian Pearson Kelly; [ch.] Expecting: due April, 1997; [ed.] Our Lady's High School, Lancaster; [occ.] Registered Nurse for the Mentally Handicapped; [hon.] R.N.M.H. Nursing; [oth. writ.] Working on personal anthology of poems and collaborating with Artist R. Calderbank on a fantasy story.; [pers.] I am strongly influenced by earth issues and aim to instill a lasting love and respect for all things living in all my readers. Merry Meet!; [a.] Birmingham, West Mids, UK, B34 6BG

KELLY, TRICIA
[b.] 28 December 1965, Leamington, Warwickshire; [p.] David and Margaret Kelly; [ed.] Trinity School (Bishop Bright Hall) Leamington Spa; [occ.] Care Assistant in a nursing home; [pers.] I try to reflect my own personality in my poems.; [a.] Leamington Spa, Warwickshire, UK, CV32 6PA

KELSALL, NATALIE K.
[b.] 28 August 1977, Newcastle under Lyme; [p.] Stuart Kelsall, Valerie Kelsall; [ed.] St. Thomas More High School (obtaining II GCSE's) and Dover College (obtaining 4 'A' levels); [occ.] Model, and also working on my own book of poetry; [memb.] Stoke-on-Trent Writer's Group, Reynolds School of Dance.; [hon.] Honours for French and German (whilst studying 'A' levels); [oth. writ.] Several short stories published in college magazine, poetry published in local magazine, also working on a novel.; [pers.] I strive to be the best I can be in everything. I have no tolerance for 2nd place. My aim in life is to keep on writing as my main profession and eventually teach poetry. I know know that without faith in myself, I would be nothing, and that's why I have the confidence to win all that I choose in life.; [a.] Stoke-on-Trent, Staffordshire, UK, ST3 2EH

KEMP, ANTHONY
[b.] 10 April 1973, Birmingham; [p.] Joyce Stevens, Brian Kemp; [ed.] Great Barr Comprehensive; [occ.] Unemployed; [hon.] 1996 Award for Outstanding Literary Potential, Walsall Short Story Comp; [oth. writ.] Numerous poems and short stories. None published.; [pers.] I am fascinated by human behaviour, and by writing I hope to challenge it. Without this challenge my ink would run dry. I am influenced by anyone who challenges this law.; [a.] Kingstanding, Birmingham, UK, B44 0IJ

KEMP, LINZI
[b.] 16 March 1981, Bradford; [p.] Lynne and Fraser; [ed.] Hanson Upper School. I am studying the following GCSE subjects with a home tutor - English Lang., English Lit., Business studies, Art; [occ.] GCSE student; [hon.] House Vice-captain, Stable Management Stages I and II, various show jumping achievements; [oth. writ.] As yet unpublished personal writings, including poetry, song lyrics and imaginative pieces.; [pers.] My writing is inspired by events in my life. I believe it to be evocative and thought-provoking. I admire the descriptive style of the late Charlotte Bronte.; [a.] Bradford, W. Yorkshire, UK, BD10 8JQ

KENDALL, RACHEL
[b.] 18 March 1975, Tameside; [ed.] Fairfield High School, Ashton II Form College, University of Central Lancashire; [hon.] BSC (Hons) Psychology; [oth. writ.] Poem published in an anthology called 'Loose Change'; [pers.] In my writing I try to emphasize reality as well as fantasy and I feel that any experience in life is valuable material for poetry and should never be dismissed.; [a.] Manchester, Lancs, UK, M34 3TB

KENDRICK, MR. WILLIAM
[b.] 18 December 1938, B'ham; [p.] William and Winifred Kendrick; [m.] Mrs. Joan C. Kendrick, 2 April 1960; [ch.] William, Carl, Alan and Sharon; [ed.] Sladefield Rd. Sec. Mod. School; [occ.] Retired (Disabled); [memb.] Labour Party; [oth. writ.] Poetry: 'Alone', 'No Time', 'Chelsea May', 'Ode to a Faulkland's Hero', 'Love Lost' etc. Also working on an autobiography entitled "It Don't Matter - Does It?"; [pers.] As a lover of art and music I try to harness the emotions of romance, passion, anger in both my paintings and writings; as a child I was deeply influenced by Rudyard Kipling.; [a.] Birmingham, West Midlands, UK, B36 8NP

KENNARD, LISA
[b.] 7 December 1981, Brighton; [p.] Brian Kennard, Alison Kennard; [ed.] Grays Infants, Southdown Junior, Tideway Secondary; [occ.] School Pupil; [oth. writ.] One poem published in local newspaper. Several more in personal collection.; [a.] Peacehaven, East Sussex, UK, BN10 7SE

KENTON, MISS DEBORAH
[pen.] Miss D. M. C. Kenton; [b.] 23 April 1970, Stratford-on-Avon; [p.] William Kenton and Marie Kenton; [ed.] Stratford High, Leamington College of F.E.; [occ.] Wigs and Make-up Assistant R.S.C., S.O.A.; [oth. writ.] Years of personal poems (not published); [pers.] My inspiration comes from the only true beauty in this world - nature and the way man continues to fight her.; [a.] Stratford-on-Avon, Warwickshire, UK, CV37 9SH

KEOGH, KATHLEEN
[b.] 2 September 1929, Boyle, Co. Roscommon; [p.] Robert, Mary Toney Cliffe; [m.] John Keogh, 31 December 1956; [ch.] Eight; [ed.] National School Primary Convent of Mercy Boyle Co. Roscommon Eire; [occ.] Housewife; [a.] Donnybrook, Dublin 4, UK

KERN, LAKSHMI
[b.] 24 January 1957, Cincinnati, OH; [pers.] I strive to express the beauty of human feelings, passions and loves in my writing. Ancient Indian poetry and Japanese verse have inspired me; [a.] Fribourg, Switzerland

KERR, ALAN D.
[b.] 2 May 1948, Glasgow; [ed.] Allan Glen's School, Glasgow, University of Stirling; [occ.] Government Service; [oth. writ.] Prize Winner - Keith Wright Memorial Poetry Competition 1985, short story 'When The Hard Rain Falls' in Scottish Short Stories 1985; [pers.] When it comes to writing, I am a lightweight, but have been known to take the odd pot - shot at posing or pretension; [a.] Stirling, Scotland, FK7 9HD

KERR, MARGARET
[b.] Glasgow; [p.] Violet and William Campbell; [ch.] Two sons and two daughters; [ed.] Rothesay Academy - Rothesay North Kelvinside Academy Glasgow; [memb.] Three Town Writers Group Saltcoats. Art, oils and water colour. "Focus" Saltcoats; [hon.] Blue Ribbon in Ballroom Dancing; [oth. writ.] Articles in newspapers, three short stories to be published in the "Three Town Writers" book, either by Christmas or spring of 1997, 300 copies only.; [pers.] We can only live one day at a time, so be happy in it, and leave all your worries till...tomorrow.; [a.] Kilwinning, Ayrshire, UK, KA13 7JH

KEYS, MAURICE
[pen.] Rupert Sykes; [b.] 2 October 1960, Southampton; [p.] William Keys and Esther Keys; [occ.] Civil Servant; [pers.] I write for pleasure for others to enjoy.; [a.] Catford, London, UK, SE6 1BX

KHAN, NADIA
[b.] 10 March 1985, London; [p.] Farah Khan and Amjad Khan; [ed.] Brookland Junior School, Hampstead Garden Suburb, London NW11 6EJ; [memb.] Netball and Water Polo; [a.] London, Hampstead, UK, NW11 6LH

KHAN, ROXI
[pen.] Sara Roxana; [b.] 20 December 1980, Sutton Coldfield Hospital; [p.] Father - Arif, Mother - Shamim; [memb.] The Star Trek Fan Club of the UK, The Young Telegraph Club, Brownie Guides, at school: Gymnastics club, history club, Junior Cornerstones and Senior Cornerstones (both are drama clubs); [hon.] Two badges and a certificate from 'The Children's Channel' for winning a national art competition, a mug and watch from 'The Young Telegraph' for writing two articles, one of them being on burglaries and the other on the beauty of poetry.; [pers.] Following consecutive attacks of mumps and measles at two years of age I was 'deaf' (the nerves in my ears were damaged) so I'm particularly pleased to have achieved publication of a poem, as I've spent most of my life trying to catch up on those two critical years.; [a.] Burton-on-Trent, Staffordshire, UK, DE13 8NF

KHAN, SARA
[b.] 3 February 1983, Stafford; [p.] Khaja Khan, Sally Khan; [ed.] Stafford Independent Grammar School (1995), St Mary and St Anne's, Abbots Bromley (1994-95), Brocksford Hall (1991-94), St Dominics, Store (1986-91); [occ.] Student; [memb.] Ingestre Riding Club; [hon.] Form Prize (1993); [oth. writ.] Several poems and stories written from the age of 11; [pers.] I am inspired by my surroundings and attempt to portray my emotions in my writings, which generally revolve around various aspects of life. I am much influenced by the works of Oscar Wilde, Thomas Handy and Wordsworth; [a.] Stafford, Staffordshire, UK, ST17 0TZ

KHANOM, SOKINA
[pen.] Liz Jones; [b.] 27 February 1982, Manchester; [p.] Shotiqul Hoque, Dulara Khanom; [m.] Will soon marry, in two years time; [ed.] Still in High School, year 10 upper school of Hyde Technology School, in Hyde; [memb.] Joined a few book clubs and magazine clubs; [oth. writ.] Done a few short stories for school paper. Also, for english assignments; [pers.] It is an honor for a 14 year old's work to be published in an anthology. I hope to be a writer soon, and this is a great start! Writing is the only thing I'm great at, not useless.; [a.] Hyde, Cheshire, UK, SK14 1HT

KIEL, ROBIN TIMOTHY
[b.] 25 August 1949, Hampstead, London; [p.] Jean McKay Kiel; [m.] Laura Patricia Dymond, 19 September 1991; [ch.] Alexander Rhiann; [ed.] Downer Grammar, Edgware Trinity College of Music, London; [occ.] Civil Servant, Department for Education (Independent Schools); [memb.] Darlington Poetry Club, The GAIA Society; [hon.] Ascherberg Composition Prize; [oth. writ.] Original Musical Compositions, Several Poems Published in Local Papers and Anthologies; [pers.] My interest is in the human condition and I write in a tradition which is part romantic and part celtic.; [a.] Darlington, Durham, UK, DL3 0DX

KILLELEA, KATHLEEN
[pen.] Kathy Finn; [b.] 20 July 1947, Roscommon, Eire; [p.] Tom, Mary Kate Lottus; [m.] Patrick Killelea, 27 September 1984; [ch.] Four, two boys and two girls; [ed.] Primary School Lisacul, Vocational Schools, Ballaghaderreen and Castlerea; [occ.] Housewife; [memb.] A steward of a trade union, member of fine geal political party; [hon.] Domestic Science Music Honours; [oth. writ.] A collection of poems; [pers.] I just love writing inspirational poems, about life and nature.; [a.] Castlerea, Roscommon, UK

KILSBY, MISS KERRY
[b.] 18 May 1973, Leicester; [ed.] B Tec 1st Diploma in Care, National Diploma in Nursery Nursing; [occ.] Nursery Nurse; [pers.] I believe that poetry is something in which we can all relate to in one way or another.; [a.] Leicester, Leicestershire, UK, LE2 9UJ

KIMBELL, MISS B. C.
[pen.] Betty Celia Kimbell; [b.] 18 April 1910, New Zealand; [ed.] I was a day girl at Chilton Saint James School Lower Hutt New Zealand Head Day Girl Tennis Champion and won the school's 1st literary prize; [memb.] NZW Association, London we meet most months in the penthouse of the New Zealand high commission London; [hon.] One at school tennis champions 1st literary prize head Dansford etc; [pers.] I have written off the cuff poems over the years when I felt distress as I have a fractured ankle and leave valued several times because of properly take down to make realizes into bigger flets etc.; [a.] London, UK, SW5 0HF

KIMBER, ERICA
[b.] 7 September 1972, Hull; [p.] Malcolm Kimber, Patricia Kimber; [ed.] Whitelands School Ellesmere/North Shropshire College/Edge Hill University College; [occ.] Post - Graduate Student in Women's Studies at Edge Hill University College; [hon.] BA (hons) History and Women's Studies (2I); [pers.] Writing keeps the madness away. Writing keeps me sane in the insanity of modern living.; [a.] Ellesmere, Shropshire, UK, SY12 9HX

KING, RAYMOND
[b.] 2 April 1928, Eccles, Manchester; [p.] James and Isobel; [m.] Jean, 5 August 1950; [ch.] Malcolm and Allison, son and daughter; [ed.] Winton Secondary School at Winton Eccles Manchester; [occ.] Just retired Plumbing and Building Contractor; [memb.] National House Building Council, The Institute of Plumbing; [hon.] Eng. Tech. MIP, RP; [pers.] I am inspired by the fact that most beings are possessed with a deep sense of permanence that cannot be denied. Root feeling that they always were and always will be locked within a scheme of past, present and future. Our finite mental ability, precludes even a glimpse at the cause behind infinite relativity. However this manifests itself in an abundance of fantastic ways with convincing evidence that humanity is much more than a multitude of physical bodies.; [a.] Swinton, Lancs, UK, M27 0AQ

KING, SHEILA BEATRICE
[b.] 5 October 1929, Bromley, Kent; [p.] Archibald and Hilda Rumph; [m.] Stanley King, 4 April 1953; [ch.] Williams and Matthew; [ed.] Bromley County School; [occ.] Principal Executive Assistant: Bromley Magistrates court 1974-89: Retired 1989; [oth. writ.] Several poems and letters published.; [pers.] I acclaim the genius of D.H. Lawrence and applaud the writings of V.S. Naipaul. My life is entranced by reading their brilliant works.; [a.] Bromley, Kent, UK, BR1 3DL

KIRBY, ANGELA
[b.] 9 February 1928, Stafford; [p.] Rev. and Mrs David Sykes; [m.] William Kirby, 1 September 1958; [ch.] Three girls; [ed.] Ashford Girls' School, Ashford, Kent Kendrick School reading Salisbury D.T.C.; [occ.] Voluntary Attending Courts with Litigants in person. Was teacher of English with astonishing results. Antique dealer (5 shops); [memb.] Labor Party; [oth. writ.] Many: Not sent anywhere until now: 3 sent and 3 accepted. At College, poem published in Bristol University Magazine.; [pers.] My writing is influenced by literature. I love aesthetics and a ridiculous sense of humor. I am young at heart and hope I never grow up.; [a.] Winchester, Hampshire, UK, SO23 8EB

KIRBY, SHEILA JOAN
[b.] 5 May 1935, Cheddar; [p.] John and Edna Hillman; [ch.] 2 girls, Lynn and Sharon; [ed.] Local Comprehensive, Filton Bristol, La Le Trait Convent School Bristol; [occ.] File Maintenance Operator; [oth. writ.] 3 poems published in book, poems for the open mind, 1 poem, International Poetry; [pers.] I heal, people say! Or poetry's a bit over my head, and sometimes they are right, one day I would like to write a book of poetry, for everyday people so everyone can enjoy.; [a.] Farnham, Surrey, UK, GU9 7UF

KIRKHAM, WENDY ANN
[b.] 25 February 1969, Stoke-on-Trent; [p.] Gerald Kirkham, Ursula Kirkham; [ed.] Edward Orme High, Newcastle under Lyme; [occ.] Care Worker; [oth. writ.] Two poems published in local book 'Pottery Poetry'; [pers.] There are two sides to every coin. I am influenced by life - as I perceive it.; [a.] Crewe, Cheshire, UK, CW3 9EA

KIRKLAND, ANDREW EDWARD
[pen.] Jon Disney; [b.] 25 January 1961, Derby; [p.] Leslie William, Margaret Ann; [m.] Christina Janet, 24 May 1986; [ch.] Jonathan William, Matthew David, Benjamin Andrew; [ed.] Derby University; [occ.] Senior Local Government Officer; [memb.] The institution of Civil Engineers. Institute of Highway Incorporated Engineers; [pers.] I have been greatly influenced by the natural beauty of the surrounding countryside of Derbyshire where one can unwind and relax with one's own thoughts.; [a.] Derby, Derbyshire, UK, DE7 6JF

KIRKMAN, MICHAEL
[b.] 16 August 1963, Bolton; [p.] James and Katherine Kirkman; [m.] Sallyann Whitlock, 12 April 1986; [ch.] Oliver James; [ed.] St. Annes R. C. High; [occ.] Work for Whitbread P.L.C. Beer Co; [memb.] Member of the National Field Archery Society; [oth. writ.] Several short stories and poems, as yet not submitted. Also work in progress includes my first novel length piece.; [pers.] "My Wish," is the first piece of work I have submitted for publication. For five years I have written for personal pleasure. I feel it is now time to take my work seriously (influences Poe, Barker and King); [a.] Darwen, Lancashire, UK, BB3 2MP

KLICZCZEWSKI, SHELOGH GTIMSHAW
[b.] 30 July 1943; [p.] Major J. N. and Mrs. Sixachan (Deceased); [ed.] Convent, degrees in Psychology and Psychotherapy, Qualified Aromathenapist; [m.] 3 Times in UK, 2 in Nigeria, Present Husband 18 yrs junior, Andrew; [ch.] Two adult, both married, six grandchildren; [oth. writ.] Autobiography - unpublished, various short stories (adult and children), thousands of poems, (only a few published); [pers.] Since becoming disabled in 1992 (and losing home and finance at that time), I have followed the basics of Taoism - and I wrote on the idea that if it's meant to happen then it will and if you can other something you don't like then do so, if you can't then accept it; also don't flounder in a sea of doubt - sit back, do nothing, let it wash over you!; [a.] Winkleigh, Devon, UK

KLOSS, NAOMI ANNE
[b.] 4 September 1973, Kent, England; [p.] Kenneth and Gladys Kloss; [ed.] I was Educated in Kent, presentation, Wexford, Ireland Institute of Education, Dublin and Graduated from University College Public with a Master of Arts; [occ.] Student Teacher; [hon.] I have won drama awards and was a finalist in the Soroptimist Public Speaking Competition in 1990; [oth. writ.] Poetry (Imaginative Philosophical), short stories and currently working on a novel.; [pers.] Poetry, for me, is a means of expressing innermost thoughts, feelings, imaginings and dreams which would otherwise remain unrealised and unspoken.; [a.] Wexford, UK

KNAPMAN, SHIRLEY
[b.] 6 March 1943, Birmingham; [p.] Walter Perkins, Lucy Perkins; [m.] Alan Knapman (Divorced) 30 May 1964; [ch.] Darren John, Andrew Stuart; [ed.] Great Barr Comprehensive, Brooklyn Technical College. (Birmingham).; [occ.] Community Psychiatric Nurse. (East Devon); [hon.] English Literature. Psychology Counseling.; [oth. writ.] Several poems published in other anthologies. Book: 'We'll Gather Lilacs' (Awaiting publisher).; [pers.] My writing comes from deep within my soul. Purely from observation and emotion I strive to paint a picture in words for all to see and feel. Ottery - St.; [a.] Mary, Devonshire, UK, EX11 1TF

KNOWLES, GWEN
[b.] 3 October 1938, Manchester; [p.] Mavis Thompson, John Thompson; [m.] Divorced; [ch.] Mark and Julia; [ed.] Millom Commercial St Lukes College, Exeter; [occ.] Psychotherapist; [memb.] Voices in Common Folk Choir, Local Art Group; [oth. writ.] Several poems; [pers.] My poems are quiet in the moment reflections usually about my physical/spiritual relationship to the natural world.; [a.] Exeter, Devon, UK, EX2 8XX

KNOWLES, HONOR
[b.] 25 December 1949, Hertford; [p.] Norreen and Robert Lindley; [ch.] Julie and Tony McGuigan; [ed.] Comprehensive; [occ.] Sales and Marketing Manager; [oth. writ.] Several poems written and collected but I have never attempted to get any published or sent any off until now.; [pers.] I write about everyday life of myself and my friends, as I see it, with humour and irony and above all fun!; [a.] Hadleigh, Essex, UK, SS7 2AY

KNOX, H.
[b.] 9 August 1922, Sunderland; [p.] Elizabeth Knox, Harry Knox; [m.] Joyce Knox, 26 December 1953; [ch.] Stephen, Graham, Charles Knox; [ed.] Secondary; [occ.] Retired; [oth. writ.] Occupied for several years, now in penning a book, a work of fiction with an authentic background from 17th century. My poem, "Durham's Dark Stones" summarizes the book (as yet unfinished).; [pers.] At school: Shone at Essays and Spelling - and little else! Cannot remember ever finishing an essay - I just wanted to wait and wait!; [a.] Tottenham, London, UK, 7DJ

KRYZANIWSKY, MICHAEL
[pen.] Spike; [b.] 7 April 1953, Edinburgh; [p.] Michael, Agnes Kryzaniwsky; [ch.] Vaila Karin, Jennifer; [ed.] London Street Primary, Belle-Vue Secondary, Edin. Cardonald College, Glasgow.; [occ.] Volunteer Tutor; [oth. writ.] Several poems and short stories published in writers' workshop magazines, both here in Glasgow and Edinburgh.; [pers.] my writings are attempts to communicate the non-verbal using verbal tools. My main influence is the potential of the imagination to further understanding of myself and others.; [a.] Glasgow, Govan, UK, G51 3SL

KUAGBENU, RAPHAEL
[pen.] Jude Timon; [b.] 17 April 1967, Acora; [p.] Philip B. Amoul Kuagbenu, Celestine Kuagbenu; [ed.] Advance Level - GCE; [occ.] Part-time Teacher, Part-time Clerical Officer Rock Management Associates; [memb.] IFL British Section, American Philatelic Society (APS). Ghana Boy Scout, Child Evangelism Fellowship. Child and World Foundation, Martin Luther King (Jr.), Library - USIS. Ngunnagan Club Australia; [hon.] Distinguished National Service Meritorious Certificate of National Mobilization Programme. International Olympic Committee Certificate of the 1st Olympic Day Run; [oth. writ.] Poems recited on the 3rd all Africa Scout Jamboree 1994. Article for Ridge Church Newsletter.; [pers.] I continue to relate all mundane affliction of the underprivileged through poetry, a grievous situation that receives no regard. The words of poets are indeed inspiring, touching and classic.; [a.] Accra, Ghana

KYRIACOU, MRS. STELLA
[b.] 23 February 1962, London; [p.] Nicholas and Maria Anastasi; [m.] Thomas Kyriacou, 4 April 1980; [ch.] Dora, Nicholas and Maria; [ed.] High Cross School for Girls and Waltham Forest College; [occ.] Housewife; [pers.] Lifes' events, whether good, bad, happy, sad are my true inspirations.; [a.] Larnaca, Cyprus, 7040

LAIDLAW, MISS DEBRA JOY
[pen.] Lady of Mann; [b.] 18 May 1966, Douglas, Isle of Man; [p.] Arthur Charles Cranston, Brenda Frances Laidlaw; [ed.] Douglas Junior and Senior High School, I.O.M. College of Further Education, Royal Naval Medical Staff School; [occ.] Operating Department Practioner, Nobles Hospital I.O.M.; [oth. writ.] Various inspirational verses, many written for family and friends. "Look to God" written for grandmother Elsie Johnson; [pers.] Through my poems I aim to comfort and inspire the individual.; [a.] Douglas, Isle of Man, UK, IM2 5AD

LAKE, ANDREA LOUISE
[b.] 16 March 1971, Paddington; [p.] Anthony Lake, Georgina Lake; [ed.] St. Pauls Comprehensive University of Greenwich; [occ.] Care Assistant, St. Aubuns Nursing Home; [hon.] Sociology BA (Hons); [pers.] The message of the poem is to remind us all that more tolerance and less ignorance is the only way forward. This also reflects my own philosophy, well, I try anyway.; [a.] Welling, Kent, UK

LAMB, CHRISTINE
[b.] Darlington; [p.] Deceased; [m.] Lloyd, 1 April 1961; [ch.] Three children; [occ.] I work in the community as Auxiliary Care Nurse; [hon] Sociology, English Language; [oth. writ.] Poet of the month in Darlington Crown Library. "My poems read out on Radio Cleveland."; [pers.] I began writing poetry in 1983. Mainly for my mother, who had a terminal illness, it gave her great, pleasure to listen to my poetry read out aloud. My poem "Leaving to Cope" was read aloud at my mother's funeral.; [a.] Darlington, Durham, UK

LANDON, EILEEN J.
[pen.] Josephine Patterson; [b.] 29 May 1924, London; [m.] Frank Landon, Previous 1946, 1953, Present 1973; [ch.] Hugh, Jenny, Stephen, Rosemary, Edwina and Martin; [ed.] Edmonton Latymer - London; [occ.] Disabled and Retired; [memb.] WWF, RSPB ICAFW, PDSA Slimbridge Woodland Trust; [hon.] Matriculation 5 Subjects 1940; [oth. writ.] Nostalgia - Prose Poem - To BBC Several articles on life bringing up 6 children along to Annabel. Send-up on Slimming To Slimming Magazine. Children's story to people's friend, now tidying up book base on my life; [pers.] Have had a very troubled life - being illegitimate and partly coloured was rough back in 1920's. Have great faith in God, that and lunatic sense of humour helped me after I got police protection in 1958; have inoperable heart failure and osteo-arto still smiling.; [a.] Watton Driffield, E. Riding, UK, YO25 9AW

LANE, MRS. A.
[pen.] Ada Lane; [b.] 7 May 1928, Forest of Dean; [p.] Myra May Fortey and Harry Walter Fortey; [m.] Melvin Ivor Lane, 29 April 1950; [ch.] Brian, Melvin, Cheryl, Katherine; [ed.] Council School; [occ.] Housewife, Gardiner; [hon.] Four First Three Seconds in Garding Mag, One Second in Garding of the Year; [oth. writ.] Poems and short stories in village mags. poems in joyful harvest for charity.; [pers.] And army for six years; open garden for people every year for church and charity.; [a.] Hanley Swan, Worcester, UK, WR8 0DL

LANE, CAROL LESLIE
[pen.] Carol Cilmeri; [b.] September 24, 1941, Ross-on-Wye; [p.] Emily Rose Stephens and Alian George Stephens; [m.] Graham J. Lane, August 27, 1960; [ch.] Joanna Martha and Catherine Pamela; [ed.] Ross County School, Gypsy hill College, Head teacher - Surrey, Head teacher - Kingston Upon-Thames.; [occ.] Retired Head teacher; [pers.] The growth of love for poetry began in childhood alongside the love of music I would like to write poetry which leaves the reader longing to read and investigate farther.; [a.] Merstham, Surrey, RH1 3DN

LANE, LORRAINE ELIZABETH
[pen.] Lorraine Lane; [b.] 22 January 1959, Alton; [p.] Michael and Diana Harding; [m.] Simon Michael Lane, 23 June 1990; [ch.] Sonia-Marie, Carla-May, Lauren Diana; [ed.] All-Saints

School 1964-66, Saint Lawrence School 1966-70, Amery Hill Secondary School 1970-75; [occ.] Registered Childminder; [oth. writ.] Contributions, to inspirations from Southern England, A Mixed Bag, On Mother Natures Doorstep (3 separate books) by Anchor Books. I've also had poems in local papers and I write poems for family and friend; [pers.] I believe that if the words that come from my heart, can touch another, its poetry.; [a.] Alton, Hampshire, UK

LANSDOWN, VIVIENNE
[ed.] Forest Lodge; [occ.] Education Department, Essex County Council; [memb.] MG Owners Club; [oth. writ.] I have had some poems and a couple of articles published in Women's Magazines. One poem was used by a teacher in 'East Germany' to demonstrate 'The Spirit of Christmas'; [pers.] I use my poetry as a modern day tool to express my feelings and reactions to life today!; [a.] Witham, Essex, UK, CM8 2TU

LATHAM, PAUL
[b.] 17 September 1947, Frome, Somerset; [p.] Father (Deceased), Mother still living; [m.] Divorced, 1969; [ch.] 3 Sons; [ed.] Selwood Secondary School, Frome; [occ.] State Benefits; [oth. writ.] Church poem printed in church magazine; [pers.] A poem should reflect what he feels and sees. When an artist paints a picture he paints what he sees.; [a.] Frome, Somerset, UK, BA11 5AR

LAWLOR, EILEEN
[b.] 17 June 1947, Clare, Eire; [p.] J. B. S. and Bride Lawlor; [ed.] Leaving Certificate (Honours) Diploma of Society of Radiographers Diagnostic and therapy; [occ.] Retired Radiographer; [memb.] Allingham Society Drama Society; [hon.] Overall winner of cookery competition in Irish Times. Best Selection of Photographs, Yeats Society Photography competition; [oth. writ.] Compiled collection of William Allingham's poems. 2 Cookery books. Book of poems (not published); [pers.] When I feel a poem in my heart, I feel God in my soul for the true self comes forth, and the true self is from God.; [a.] Bundoran, Donegal

LAWRENCE, ALICE CORINNE
[b.] 16 December 1945, The Wirral; [p.] Archibald Taylor, Norah Taylor; [m.] Robin Lawrence, 24 July 1971; [ch.] Richard Owen, Nicholas Robin; [ed.] Stockport Convent High School The Northern School of Music (Drama Department); [occ.] Speech and Drama Teacher The Grange School, Hartford Northwich, Cheshire; [oth. writ.] Mostly poetry - all unpublished, and of a variety of subjects, although some of it is religious, having been written as an aid to the teaching of religious studies; [pers.] The english language is sensuous and malleable - a perfect vehicle for verse. My writing stems from a special love of Shakespeare.; [a.] Stockport, Cheshire, UK, SK7 1LR

LAWSON, AGNES BURNS
[pen.] Mrs. Weeks; [b.] 29 December 1919, Scotland; [p.] Margaret and James Lanson; [m.] Desmond E. Weeks, 22 February 1946; [ch.] Roger, Yvonne, Patricia; [ed.] Secondary; [occ.] Housewife; [oth. writ.] Thoretic Theology, Mythological "Poetic", Lyrics - Children's Stories - Love Story - Proverbs - Citations - etc". I read poems to music and tape.; [pers.] An uncultured Women is like an imitation Pearl. A special one is man's progress is his own destruction.; [a.] Hillingdon, Middlesex, UK, UB8 3EQ

LAWSON, MISS SARAH
[b.] 30 September 1978; [p.] Eric Lawson and Eileen (Divorced); [m.] Darren Bell (Partner); [ed.] Haydon Bridge County High School, Mexham, Northumberland; [oth. writ.] "Farewell Azure Sky," published in a creative writing book named "Tyne Gap," The short story is about divorce and nuclear war; [pers.] The three most important factors that have influenced my writing have been family, and feelings of great

happiness or sadness. Indeed most of my best pieces of work have been based on my own life experiences. With real life experiences you can put your heart and soul into descriptions and feelings because you have been there and done that. I have not been influenced by any poets as such, but quite like Keats and Burns, my favorite artist is Salvador Dali, I think the encouragement and praise, and interest people genuinely take in my writing keeps me enjoying, improving and keep writing.; [a.] Haltwhistle, Northumberland, UK, NE49 9BL

LAYTE, ANDY
[b.] 30 December 1977; [ed.] Shipley College and Calderale College; [occ.] Student; [memb.] The Eccleshill Horticultural Society; [pers.] Loneliness can last forever, no matter how strong - no matter how clever.; [a.] Low Moor, Bradford, UK

LEACH, VALERIE A.
[b.] 7 January 1946, Hereford; [m.] David Leach, 20 December 1969; [ch.] Sally and Richard; [ed.] Braintree Country High School, Essex and Wall Hall Training College, Herts; [occ.] I manage my husbands Dental Practice; [memb.] Member of N.A.D.F.A.S. Member of Theatre Club of Great Britain. Member of Sarratt conservative main and social committees.; [hon.] Teaching Diploma; [oth. writ.] 'Automation Out of Perspective' published in a 'A Passage in Time' 1996. Poetry and prose written and waiting to be published.; [pers.] My poems are often inspired by nature, death, or poignant moments in a relationship.; [a.] Rickmansworth, Herts, UK, WD3 4NH

LEADBITTER, ANTONY BOULTER
[b.] 25 April 1971, Southampton; [p.] George Walter Leadbitter, Fay Pamela Leadbitter; [ed.] Ridgeway Comprehensive Plymouth; [occ.] Royal Mail Postman; [oth. writ.] Several poems written only for Friends and Family.; [pers.] If you ever point a finger at someone, think about the three fingers pointing back.; [a.] Plymouth, Devonshire, UK, PL1 3BT

LEAKE, EILEEN MAVIS
[memb.] Shifnal Golf Club, Berkswich Church Women's Fellowship; [pers.] I am influenced by the natural beauty of my surroundings.; [a.] Stafford, Staffordshire, UK, ST17 0LX

LEE, DAREN JOHN
[pen.] Deejay; [b.] 1 October 1966, Bury, Lancs; [p.] Martin Lee and Isobel Lee; [ed.] Siddal Moor High, Hopwood Hall College, Derby University; [occ.] Versatile; [hon.] Creative Writing Film and Television Studies, Drama; [oth. writ.] Unpublished stage plays for theatre.; [pers.] For Luciano Canale whose encouragement, praise and enthusiasm inspire me! A remarkable person; [a.] Bedford, Bedfordshire, UK, MK40 4NF

LEE, DIANE
[b.] 5 July 1962, Salford; [p.] Jack Joynson, Doreen Joynson; [m.] Robert Michael Lee, 30 March 1988; [ch.] Mandy Emma, Michael Richard, Dale Nathaniel; [ed.] Joseph Eastham High School, Worsley, Manchester; [occ.] Housewife; [oth. writ.] I have written hundreds of poems, mainly for other people to use as gifts.; [pers.] 'Harboured memories' was inspired by my favorite holiday resort, Brixham, which was where I first went on holiday with my husband. Unfortunately I had to reduce this very long poem to 20 lines for publication.; [a.] Worsley, Manchester, UK, M28 0HP

LEE, MICHAEL
[b.] 27 July 1932, London; [p.] Frederick Lee, Kathleen Lee; [m.] Gwendoline Holland, 27 December 1956; [ch.] Mark, Gabrielle, Edmund; [ed.] Wimbledon College London School of Economics; [occ.] Consultant Economist; [memb.] City Literary Institution Poetry Club; [hon.] Open poetry competition winners anthology

puras 1995; [oth. writ.] (Editor) poems in the waiting room (1996); [pers.] My writing explores the transcendental in the Mundane; [a.] Richmond, Surrey, UK, TW9 4DE

LEECH, MURIEL
[b.] 30 June 1914, Wath-on-Dearne; [p.] Charles Percy and Edith Emma Jones; [m.] Henry Leech, 6 July 1940; [ed.] Doncaster High School, Brighton Teacher Training College; [occ.] Retired, (Teacher 1932-1977); [memb.] Doncaster Council for Voluntary Service, V-President over - 60's Clubs Council (Chair); [hon.] M.B.E. January 1987; [a.] Doncaster, S. Yorkshire, UK, DN12 1JA

LEONARD, DENIS
[pen.] D. Pool; [b.] 1934, Ireland; [occ.] Retired Airline Captain; [memb.] Royal Dublin Society, The Scribblers; [hon.] Scroll of Merit Awarded by the International Federation of Airline Pilots Associations; [oth. writ.] Novels: When Three Bells Tolled, No Apples In Eden, Lych Gate Vigil, Various Aviation Technical Items, and some poetry and short stories; [a.] Brighton, UK, BN1 5JN

LEWIS, ANDREW
[b.] September 6, 1955, Cyprus; [m.] Helen Lewis, March 27, 1975; [ch.] Jayson, Olivia, Marios; [ed.] Downhills Park Comprehensive Tottenham; [occ.] Driving Instructor; [memb.] Royal Society for the Prevention of Accidents, Institute of Advanced Motorists; [oth. writ.] Many written - none published; [pers.] I always try to mean what I say, and say what I mean, then I will never be sorry for what I have said.; [a.] Cambridge, Cambridgeshire, CB1 3QY

LEWIS, BENJAMIN THOMAS
[b.] 8 January 1930, Sheffield; [p.] Ben and Aileen Lewis; [occ.] Retired; [pers.] I believe humanity must turn to religion and especially to Jesus Christ, who proclaimed the coming of God's Kingdom on earth. It is up to humanity to bring God's Kingdom about and drive out Satan.; [a.] Penarth, S. Glam, UK, CF64 3DA

LEWIS, EDWARD LLOYD
[pen.] Lloydie; [b.] 23 June 1936, Llangranog Cards; [p.] Deceased; [m.] Deceased, 22 September 1975; [ch.] Four children; [ed.] Secondary School; [occ.] Labourer; [a.] Whitland, Carmarthenshire, Dyfed, UK, SA34 0AW

LEWIS, HAYDN
[b.] 3 October 1976, Stockton-on-Tees; [p.] David Haydn and Sheila Elizabeth; [ed.] Kader Primary, Yarm School, York University; [occ.] Student of English at York University; [memb.] University Theatre Society, Uni. Badminton Club, Uni. Conservation Society; [hon.] 10 G.C.S.E's and 4 A-levels - 2 at grade A., at present studying for a degree in English at York.; [oth. writ.] Several prizes in school creative writing competitions. Edited school magazine. Article published in local magazine.; [pers.] I aim to seek further self-knowledge through my writing and to have universal appeal.; [a.] Middlesbrough, Cleveland, UK, TS5 8NA

LEWIS, HAZEL MARJORIE
[pen.] Hazel Marjorie Lewis; [b.] 26 June 1916, Hampstead; [p.] Austin and Sidella Brandon O'Halloran; [m.] W. H. J. Lewis, 20 November 1986; [ed.] All Souls C-of England School London, W. I. and Private; [occ.] Retired Secretary; [hon.] Editor's Choice Award - The International Society of Poets 1996; [oth. writ.] Collection of poems various subjects. Mostly Nature. Greatly influenced by Wordsworth's nature poems. Many based on experiences throughout my life.; [pers.] I have a reverence for all life, a Christian Ethic to individuals as persons, not part of the masses.; [a.] Swansea, West Glamorgan, UK, SA4 1EL

LEWRY, MARGARET
[b.] 10 April 1935, Gosport; [p.] Sidneys Hilda Hayes; [m.] Trevor Lewry, 19 December 1953; [ch.] Three; [ed.] Secondary Modern, former nurse. Twenty years trained at Knowle Hospital; [occ.] Very buzy retirement; [memb.] 'W.I.' 'Flower Club', Affaiated to Nafas (Curdridge) Stubbington W.I., singers; [hon.] I was proud to receive a letter from her majesty The Queen, in answer to mine. Now framed on my wall; [oth. writ.] Children, Friends, poems written and read for W.I. singers. Poetry book. 'Something for Everyone'. Vanity, prine sold to air the 'Jennifer Trust'; [pers.] I just enjoy writing, about people and things that happen. The best things that come from this are the wonderful long time friends Que Made. I have 8 grandchildren and one great granddaughter.; [a.] Curdridge, Nr. Southampton Hants, UK, SO32 2DP

LEYS, CHERRON
[pen.] Cheryl Gray; [b.] 13 November 1971, Aberdeen; [p.] William and Sheila Leys; [occ.] Phlebotomist; [oth. writ.] Short stories and other forms awaiting publication or as gifts to friends; [pers.] To Mrs. Fraser, thanks for keeping all that I have written all this time. And Joe for your enthusiasm, most of all mum for being you.; [a.] Aberdeen, Grampian, UK, AB21 9NA

LILAND, SOLBJORG
[pen.] Sol; [b.] 15 November 1979, Voss; [p.] Grete and Sigurd Liland; [oth. writ.] Poetry published on a radio channel in Norway, P3 NRK; [pers.] To me writing is the best form for therapy, and I mean good poetry can never be too personal. Music has influenced my writing a lot, and it's a key to the creative mind.; [a.] Voss, Norway, 5700

LILLEY, BRENDA
[pen.] Charlotte Evans; [b.] 22 May 1938, Runcorn; [p.] Eliza and Joseph Ellis Lowe; [m.] Orlando Lilley, 21 November 1970; [ch.] Andrew Micheal; [ed.] Tonge Fold Secondary Modern; [occ.] Accounts Manageress; [oth. writ.] A collection of verses by Charlotte Evans, due out Spring 1997, this is my first book and it will be published by Avon Books, this poem is part of "The Collection".; [pers.] I have written poetry for the church magazine and have had several poems published in the Bolton Evening Newspaper. I try to state my sense of true values which are the simple things in life. Love and Christian beliefs.; [a.] Bolton, Lancashire, UK, BL1 3ST

LILLEY, KIMBERLEY JANE
[b.] 10 August 1983, North Ferriby, N. Humberside; [p.] David and Jan Lilley; [ed.] North Ferriby C of E infants, Swanland County Primary School, South Hunsley School; [memb.] Whale and Dolphin Conservation Society.; [oth. writ.] A prolific writer Kimberley was a grade 'A' student; [pers.] Kimberley enthusiastically lived her life through her philosophy of helping those less fortunate than herself, whether human or animal.; [a.] Swanland, East Riding of Yorkshire, UK, HU14 3NE

LILLEY, SANDRA
[b.] 9 July 1943, Horsham, Sussex; [p.] Percy Lilley and Gladys Lilley; [ed.] Convent of the Immaculate Heart of Mary, Summers Place, Billinghuest, W-Sussex, Mature student music BA Hons (Darlington College of Arts, Totnes, Devon); [occ.] Music Teacher/Taxi Driver (Self-employed); [hon.] Music, Art; [pers.] I like the Victorian poets, but read little poetry nowadays. I should like to "paint pictures" with words, I admire Shakespeare's mastery of words, Conan Doyle, Peter Cheyney, Mary Stewart also and others.; [a.] Tremar Coombe, Cornwall, UK, PL14 5EG

LILLIE, JEAN
[b.] 16 May 1947, Gainsborough; [p.] John Lillie, Winifred Lillie; [ed.] Gainsborough Girls High School; [occ.] Shipping; [memb.] World Parrot Trust, Lincolnshire Lancaster Association.; [a.] GT Yarmouth, Norfolk, UK, NR30 2RL

LINDSAY, ROBERT
[b.] 10 May 1944, Belfast; [p.] James William and William Lindsay; [m.] Thelma Edwards, 1 April 1967; [ch.] James Israel, Joel and Selina; [a.] Carryduff, Down, Northern Ireland, BT8 8EA

LINNEY, BARBARA ANN
[pen.] Barbarella stage name; [b.] 29/08/37, London; [p.] Deceased; [m.] Single; [ch.] David, Charles, Christopher; [ed.] A in Art Design, A model in fashion art; [occ.] At college at the moment; [memb.] Library at Kiddy College; [hon.] Publication of Spiritual Moma [oth. writ.] The story of my life: Life and Times of Barbarella.

LINWOOD, MRS. JOAN
[pen.] Sam Laura Linwood; [b.] 31 July 1936, Enfield; [p.] Kathleen and William Brett; [m.] Frank Frederick Linwood, 24 September 1955; [ch.] 3 Sons and 1 Daughter; [ed.] Secondary Modern, Suffolks School now called Bishops Stopford Enfield Highway middx.; [occ.] Housewife; [oth. writ.] Have two poems published in 1 poetry now (London 1996 anthology) also 1 'A Moment in Time' 1966. Poem titles "Feelings" "I am a Skip Lorry"; [pers.] I am to provide a little ray light of happiness to readers of poetry; [a.] Enfield, Middx, UK, EN3 4NZ

LISTER, GLADYS LILIAN
[occ.] Retired; [pers.] My first submitted poem, I'm not prolific, but greatly enjoy a love affair with words and like love, the outcome can be frustrating, optimistic, satisfying and sometimes a productive bonus is the icing on the cake.; [a.] Cockermouth, Cumbria, UK, CA13 0EB

LLOYD, ANNA
[b.] 19 November 1967, Gravesend, Kent; [p.] Roy Baines (G.M.), Corinne Baines; [m.] Martin Lloyd, 22 May 1995; [pers.] This poem came truly from the heart and is dedicated with total love to my Dad. A father and his daughter-there is no greater love.; [a.] Gravesend, Kent, UK, DA12 5ED

LLOYD, CAROLYN
[pen.] C. A. Lloyd; [b.] 3 March 1980, Neath Gen Hosp.; [p.] Mother - Julie Sneade, Stepfather - John Sneade; [ed.] Does in GCSE in Ceon Sorson Comprehensive School, Cimia, Neath; [occ.] Media studies first year student at Neath College; [memb.] I am a Member of the Radio Times Presspock, which is with Newsrand on BBC 2 and the Library; [hon.] Distinction in Keyboarding Skills; [oth. writ.] Poem called 'Beverly Hills 90210' published in a book named 'Inspired by Life'; [pers.] I was very influenced by William Shakespeare's portrayal of poems and plays especially Romeo and Juliet which inspires me and my work; [a.] Neath, West Glamorgan, UK, SA11 3HR

LLOYD, M. J. E.
[b.] 9 September 1921, Carmarthen; [p.] Deceased; [m.] Deceased; [ch.] Kim Benbow Lloyd; [occ.] Retired School Teacher; [oth. writ.] I have written quite a few poems, but this is the first competition I have entered, many thanks for your letter very encouraging.; [a.] Carmarthen, Carmarthenshire, UK, SA31 3ER

LLOYD, RICHARD
[pen.] Richard Lloyd; [b.] 1908, Mardy Rhondda, Mid-Glam; [occ.] Retired (Pensioner); [oth. writ.] Reflections, Reality of War, Crazy World, Quality of Life (by 86 year old); [pers.] Quote: Time is not measured by the years we live but by the kindness we give.; [a.] Hirwain, Mid-Glamorgan, UK, CF44 9PW

LOFTS, JASON
[b.] 28 July 1959, Christchurch, New Zealand; [ed.] Christ's College, University of Canterbury; [occ.] Lawyer, Vaduz, Principality of Liechtenstein; [memb.] The Offshore Institute, British-German Jurist's Assoc.; [oth. writ.] Various Legal Articles and Translations; [a.] Nendeln, Liechtenstein

LOGAN, MRS. ELEANOR
[b.] 25 December 1938, Barking, Essex; [m.] George; [ch.] Dawn and Linda; [ed.] Comprehensive School; [occ.] Typist; [hon.] English Literature, English Language; [oth. writ.] Three poems published with arrival press.; [pers.] My poems are often inspired by strong feelings and emotions from within, and a love of nature.; [a.] Barking, Essex, UK, IG11 0RB

LONG, HELEN
[b.] 2 September 1963, Germany; [p.] Raymond Hardie, Stella Pearce; [m.] Brian Long, 9 December 1980; [ch.] David, Ian, Richard; [ed.] King Edward VII Grammar, Melton Mowbray; [occ.] Credit Controller for Pedigree Petfoods; [pers.] This is the first poem to be printed. I usually write to entertain my children and friends, using life situations they can relate to.; [a.] Melton Mowbray, Leicestershire, UK, LE13 1TZ

LOOSELEY, CHRISTINE
[b.] 1950, Farnborough, Kent; [m.] 1972; [ch.] One daughter, three sons; [ed.] Torquay Girls' Grammar School, Bristol University, London University; [occ.] English Teacher; [memb.] Dyslexia Associations; [oth. writ.] Mainly on spiritual themes. 'Hymn to God the Father' published 1996.; [pers.] I am heartened by the ways in which spiritual truth appears in the most unlikely places.; [a.] Cranleigh, Surrey, UK

LOSTY, GERALDINE
[pen.] Judy Gerald; [b.] 16 July 1943, Shrewsbury; [p.] Orphan; [m.] Divorced; [ch.] Paul, Mark, Michelle; [ed.] St Angela's Ursuline Convent, Forest Gate, London; [occ.] Office Administrator; [memb.] T.G.W.U.; [oth. writ.] Several philosophical poems in church and local press; [pers.] The many moods of people and changing times have been the over-riding influence in my poetry; [a.] Romford, Essex, UK, RM6 5ET

LOVATT, JOHN
[b.] 8 March 1933, Liverpool; [p.] Eric and Eileen; [m.] Nancy, 3 April 1956; [ch.] David, Martin, Simon, Virginia; [ed.] Alsop High School, Queens Drive Walton Lipool; [occ.] Landscaping; [memb.] Only clubs as I enjoy the odd pint or two; [hon.] As a keen sportsman, I have won many awards at several sports; [oth. writ.] I have written dozens of childrens stories, but have never done anything about publishings as I am useless at pushing myself I published a book of poetry titled The Thoughts of Me and sold the five handled copies in three months everytime I have send a poem to magazine the have been published.; [pers.] I love life, everything and everybody, I feel very lucky to have been born in the beautiful country. Two years ago I conforted Necrotising facietus which devoured my leg, and was very lucky to survive the ordeal, to till have to have never had a days illness until then.; [a.] North Merseyside, Lancashire, UK, L37 4DD

LUIS, PEDRO DOMINGOS
[b.] 7 January 1968, Angola; [p.] Domingos Nguvulo, Isabel Joaquim; [ed.] Institute Polytechnic of Economics - Int. Peredo (Cuba); [occ.] Student, Access Course at Croydon College; [memb.] Angolan Student's Union, member of youth Brigade of Literature (from 1987-90) Isla de la Juventud - Cuba, Isla; [hon.] Special distinction at the 3rd Municipal Competition of amateur writers and poets of students - "Isla de la Juventud" 1989; [pers.] Although I am a very optimistic person, in my writing I try to reflect the sadness, the suffering and the anguish of mankind. At the same time however my message looks towards the future with confidence and optimism.; [a.] London, UK, SW16 2DY

LUKER, NATHAN
[pen.] Billy Biscuits; [b.] 17 October 1975, Bury; [p.] Mike Luker, Sue Luker; [ed.] New Wellington High, Mid Cheshire College, Falmouth College of Arts; [occ.] Student - Graphic Design; [oth. writ.]

Various poems and songs to amuse friends and myself.; [pers.] That which may seem insignificantly tiny may be an incomprehensively big part of the answer.; [a.] Northwich, Cheshire, UK, CW9 7BB

LYNDON, GLADYS
[b.] 9 November 1911, Birmingham

LYON, JAMES C.
[pen.] James C. Lyon; [b.] 6 July 1969, Dundee; [p.] Patricia Dinnie, James C. Lyon Sr.; [ed.] Caselton Primary, Fettercairn Andover Primary, Brechin, Brechin High School, Northern College of Ed. (Dundee); [occ.] Primary School Teacher - Borrowfield Montrose; [memb.] Scottish Football Association, Referee; [hon.] B.Ed Degrees; [oth. writ.] None as such - this is first venture!; [pers.] When any idea comes to mind, capture it in ink - record it on paper and soon a poem emerges. Anyone of any ability can do it. So give it ago - it's fun. The influence for this poem comes from my dad as a gardener, Robert Burns Poetry and bitter experience!; [a.] Brechin, Angus, UK, DD9 6YA

LYON, RICHARD
[b.] 9 September 1971, Hull; [p.] David and Linda Lyon; [ed.] Great-Field High School Studying of Photography, at Local College; [occ.] The Cleaning of the City Transport; [hon.] Several Certificates in the Area of Music Courses I have attended, and Guitar playing; [oth. writ.] I have written a book full of writings called "To be obscure is to be normal".; [pers.] I've been writing for a while now, I'm not a great writer but do and guess always continues to write.; [a.] Hull, E. Yorkshire, UK, HU9 4NP

LYONS, DIANA
[pen.] Selena Sutton; [b.] 7 July 1942, Weybridge; [p.] Geoffrey Doel (Deceased), Ruby Doel; [m.] Michael Lyons, 25 February 1973 (Divorced 1984); [ch.] Timothy Fletcher, Kay Anne, Martine Joy (by Peter Martin); [ed.] Oakdene School, Beaconsfield South Herts College of Further Education Prince of Wale's School of Physiotherapy, Tottenham; [occ.] Senior Physiotherapist, Lincoln county Hospital; [memb.] Sutton Theatre Company (Sutton-on-sea, Lincs); [oth. writ.] Several Short Stories and poems published in local newspaper (Newbury) poem "The Restless Wave" published in "An Eastern Anthology" 1993. Story "I must go down..." Runer-up in Lincolnshire short story competition 1995, winner BBC Radio Lincolnshire "Write a Poem for our Carol Service" competition 1995 (read on air). 3 Pantomime Scripts for sutton Theatre company.; [pers.] I am baffled why anyone should want to read my scribblings. Far less enjoy them. But, as a spiritualist, I believe that I am inspired by friends who have passed over "Co-llab-oration" was written in new quay (Wales which has Links with Dycan Thomas. I hope for a second career in writing when I retire from physiotherapy.; [a.] Lincoln, Lincolnshire, UK, LN5 9BP

LYTTLE, JEAN-NOELLE
[b.] 24 December 1932, Australia; [ed.] Left School at fourteen office worker a Levels at night School Teachers College Armidalein (NSW) University; [occ.] Retired Teacher; [memb.] Manchester Scottish Singers ASA swimming Teacher, South Lakes Music Festival Patron; [hon.] Psychology and Education Honours; [oth. writ.] Unpublished.; [pers.] Make a bouquet of flowers from those nearest at hand.; [a.] Cheadle, Cheshire, UK, SK8 1NX

MACDONALD, BERNADETTE
[pen.] Angel or Gismo; [b.] 17 May 1950, Dublin, Ireland; [p.] Angela Fleming; [m.] Mick MacDonald, 29 July 1995; [ch.] Eight, seven girls and one boy; [ed.] Holy Faith Covent Glasnivin and Dominic St., Dublin, Ireland; [occ.] Auxiliary Nurse Care of the Elderly; [hon.] I

have never received any awards in my life. That is why this publication means so much to me.; [oth. writ.] I have written many other poems, but this is the first time I have send one away.; [pers.] I love to write. It's a great way to express how I feel about things that have happened to me. Personally, and about people that I have.; [a.] Edmonton, Middlesex, UK, N9 0PT

MACDOUGALL, PETER
[b.] 25 March 1972, Glasgow; [p.] Andrew MacDougall, Linda MacDougall; [ed.] Waverly Secondary; [oth. writ.] Several poems and songs not yet published; [pers.] I write and leave the reader to decide. I am inspired by life.; [a.] Glasgow, Lanarkshire, UK, G13 3YX

MACKENZIE, MRS. VENETTA
[b.] 30 July 1943, Bangor, N. Wales; [p.] Thomas and Violet Smyth; [m.] James MacKenzie, 22 February 1964; [ch.] James, Valerie, Keren, Andrew; [ed.] St Gerards Convent School Bangor N Wales; [occ.] Bookshop Assistant; [memb.] Elgin Embroidery Guild; [a.] Elgin, Moray, Scotland, IV30 3HQ

MACLACHLAN, PENELOPE
[pen.] Caroline Perry, Vivian Brown; [b.] UK; [p.] Thomas and Audrey Cammiade; [m.] Alastair Maclachlan, 1986; [ed.] BA Hons English Brazilian MA (Mestrado) Universidad de Brasilia; [memb.] Mensa Society of Women Writers and Journalists; [oth. writ.] Articles in Mensa magazine, The Times, The Daily Telegraph, Chartered Institute of Building yearbook; [pers.] I am writing a play which I hope will one day be performed. I am planning to become a full-time freelance writer of magazine articles.; [a.] Hanwell, London, UK, W7 3BW

MACLEAN, ANNCHRIS
[b.] 8 September 1982, Harris; [p.] Donald and Marion Maclean; [ed.] 3rd Year Secondary School Pupil; [occ.] Still at school; [oth. writ.] 3rd prize awarded in T.V. Sponsored Writing Competition - 1993; [a.] Tarbet, Western Isles, UK, HS3 3DL

MACLEAN, MR. ALEXANDER
[pen.] LAL; [b.] 16 September 1964, Bury; [p.] Helen and Ian Maclean; [ch.] Blaine aged 8, Connor aged 3; [ed.] Local High School; [occ.] Poet and Songwriter; [oth. writ.] "A Cry from the Sand," "A Cry for Mankind," "Since Time Began and Ever on Entwined", "So Blows the Dust," "Silence," "Maternal Pleasure," "Mother Natures Miracle", "Little Monsters", "No Return in Time" (many others to numerous to mention).; [pers.] To be rich is to have life, to have life is to be rich. I play for fun where the sun don't run.; [a.] Radcliffe, Manchester, UK, M26 3GT

MACMILLAN, LEE-ANNE
[b.] 16 May 1972, Perth, Scotland; [p.] Alistair and Anne Cameron; [m.] Alexander C. R. MacMillan, 27 May 1995; [ed.] Perth Grammar School, Foresterhill College; [occ.] Special Needs Nurse - R.N.M.H.; [oth. writ.] Personal Collection of poems; [pers.] Memorable events in my life have inspired me to write, my first ever, entered and shared - what a reward!; [a.] Pilling, Lancashire, UK, PR3 6AB

MADLE, PETER
[b.] 8 August 1930, Strood, Kent; [p.] Sidney Stephen and Kathleen Mary Madle; [m.] Audrey Joan Medhurst, 24 May 1958; [ed.] Rochester Technical School and H.M. Dockyard, Chatham. College; [occ.] Retired. Ex Diagnostician Gunnery and Missile Systems. M.O.D.N.; [hon.] Mathematics; [oth. writ.] Several poems published local papers Several poems written for friends. Some poems written for people retiring to raise money for local Hospice.; [pers.] Poems should be written for the general public especially children. I write funny poems to my friends and about my friends to bring laughter into their lives.

Influenced first by nursery rhymes and poems from my father on 8th Birthday also Kipling Wordsworth, Tennyson when young.; [a.] Rochester, Kent, UK, ME1 2UA

MAGUIRE, AVRIL
[pen.] Yellow Sky Maguire; [b.] 15 October 1946, Croydon; [p.] Evelyn Sturgess, Frederick Sturgess; [m.] James Patrick Maguire, 1 December 1971; [occ.] Housewife; [memb.] Christian Spiritualist Society of Healers; [hon.] Studying for a Degree in Gastronomy from Pre History to the End of the Middle Ages 1603; [oth. writ.] Poems and short stories for children none published as yet.; [pers.] I like to bring peace, happiness and laughter to people's lives.; [a.] Penrhiwllan, Llandysul, Ceredigion, UK, SA44 5NY

MAGUIRE, JACQUELINE ANN
[pen.] Jacqueline A. Maguire; [b.] 9 August 1977, Enniskillen; [p.] John and Anna Maguire; [ed.] Mount Lourdes Convent Grammar School, Enniskillen, The Queen's University of Belfast; [occ.] Student; [memb.] Amnesty International Greenpeace; [oth. writ.] Poem published in regional anthology; [pers.] Poetry is escape and indulgence: It is my pleasure.; [a.] Lisnaskea, Fermanagh, UK, BT92 0FR

MAHONEY, STEPHANIE
[b.] 20 September 1986, Belfast; [p.] Sharon and Gerard Mahoney; [ed.] Primary School P6, Deanby Gardens BT14 6NN (Our Ladys)

MAKIN, SHELLEY
[b.] 28 January 1981, Barnsley; [p.] Marian Makin; [ed.] I am currently at the Foulstone Darfield and hope to go and do 2 years in college to be a Nursery Nurse; [hon.] I have 2 drama exam passes; [oth. writ.] Dedicated to grandad, Christmas Time, Winter, Mother, Schools, Joy-Riding, I have all the questions but who has all the answers; [pers.] I am 15 years old. I love drama and children and I hope to become a Nursery Nurse and one day have a family of my own!; [a.] Barnsley, South Yorks, UK, S72 0AN

MANDILA, LANA
[b.] 3 April 1953, Lagos, Nigeria; [p.] John B. Mandilas, Theodoti Mandilas; [ed.] Moraitis School, Athens, Political Sciences and Philosophy Universities of Athens and Bonn - Law, Athens Law School and Stage at the European Commission, Brussels; [occ.] Lawyer; [memb.] Athens Bar Association, Yacht Club of Greece, Baden Powell Fellow (World Scout Foundation); [oth. writ.] Poems published in a literary magazine, Greece.; [pers.] The ultimate aim: To become better everyday. Computers and money are there to serve mankind not for mankind to serve them. I have been influenced by C. Cauafy, R.M. Rilke and T.S. Eliot; [a.] Athens, Attica, Greece, 154 52

MANN, DEBORAH L.
[b.] 6 September 1976, Norwich; [p.] Geoffrey Edwin Mann, Kathleen Mann; [ed.] Hethersett High School - 9 GCSE's (8 A-C) Wymondham College 3 'A' Levels; [occ.] Clerical Assistant/ Receptionist at Local Advice Centre; [hon.] RSA Word Processing 1, RSA Text Processing 1; [pers.] It is my aim to reflect personal experiences and social issues in my poetry, my main form of release. I worked tirelessly despite health problems towards my plan from 1993 and I was devastated not to be able to accept a place to read law due to financial hardship.; [a.] Norwich, Norfolk, UK, NR9 3HT

MANN, MRS. LYN
[pen.] Mrs. Lyn Mann; [b.] 16 January 1970, Plymouth; [p.] Maureen Earle, David Earle; [ch.] Denise Helen, Jake Ryan; [ed.] Fakenham High School, and Wymondham College; [occ.] Full time mother by choice and love; [pers.] Modern society does not encourage us to appreciate what we have, therefore, its value isn't recognized until it's no longer ours. Be it love, money or power.; [a.] Fakenham, Norfolk, UK, NR21 8NG

MANUEL, HOLLY
[b.] 3 January 1984, Nakuru, Kenya; [p.] George and Janet Manuel; [ed.] Pembroke House School PO Box 31 Gilgil 1990-1996; [occ.] School Girl; [memb.] Nakuru Players Theatre. East African Wildlife Society. Wildlife Clubs of Kenya; [oth. writ.] Many poems unpublished.; [a.] Njoro, Kenya

MAQSOOD, M. FAZLOON
[pen.] M. Fazloon Maqsood; [b.] 23 October 1975, Sri Lanka; [p.] Mohamed F. & Naema A.; [ed.] Ecole Internationale, Kandy, Sri Lanka; [occ.] student; [memb.] Sunday Island, Youth Colombo Sri Lanka; [hon.] London O/L English-pass, 1995 International Competitions for Schools Credit-pass in standard 10, poetry awards from Ecole Internationale-Kandy, Sri Lanka; [oth. writ.] several poems published in local newspapers and magazines; [pers.] My ambition is to become a great poet of the world and a song writer to prove what life means to us through my writings.; [a.] Matale, Sri Lanka 21000

MARCHINGTON, ANDREW JAMES
[b.] 15 March 1967, Buxton, Derbyshire; [ed.] Public Schools to 16, 16 to 18 Bicton Agricultural College; [occ.] Farming; [memb.] The British Horse Society; [hon.] Farmers weekly, 1992 Farm Invention Competition; [pers.] Purly for love but unlucky for me.; [a.] Crediton, Devon, UK, EX17 5HJ

MARKBRIDE, TREVOR
[b.] 18 August 1956, Stamford, Lincs; [p.] Leonard and Ivy Markbride; [m.] Susan Theresa, 9 December 1978; [hon.] Editor's Choice award presented by, The International Society of Poets 1996; [oth. writ.] Poem published in "The Passage Of Time"; [pers.] I feel that I can express my emotions through writing poetry.; [a.] Saint Bees, Cumbria, UK, CA27 0DE

MARMONT, MARY-ANN E.
[pen.] Mae Edlington; [b.] 3 January 1952, Hunt. Sta. L.I.; [p.] Louis Pipolo, Margaret Procino; [m.] Jean-Jacques Marmont (Canada), 4 December 1976; [ch.] Christina Danielle, Elizabeth Therese, and Michelle Clare; [ed.] C.A.T.'s points in Psychology, Religious Studies, Politics (Oxford University Dept. Continuing Education) (DUDCE); [occ.] Student, Via Henley College for I.T.E.C., Studying to be a Physiotherapist; [memb.] I sing in choirs, compose songs and poetry. And I enjoy "Reciting" my poems publicly. (Bit of an actress in me); [hon.] I was selected to represent my class of 600 students as the "best soprano" to send to the State-level (6th Formers) Musical Conference of a Choir comprising 17 and 18 years old in year 12-13. We were recorded in concert. A record given to each of us.; [oth. writ.] Never attempted to get my works published previously. Currently writing my autobiography, "A Way Given To The Way Once Hidden" and "Deeper Meanings To Behold" poetry of Mae Edlington; [pers.] The gifts of "Versatility" and "Similarity" are themes woven like a tapestry within and outside of our world, at every level of existence, things visible and invisible. To lovingly embrace both is to, at least, progress toward peace.; [a.] Carterton, Oxfordshire, UK, OX18 3LQ

MARSH, JANET ROSE
[b.] 5 February 1959, Poplar; [p.] Jessie and Herbert Marsh; [ed.] St. Pauls Way School Bow E. 3.; [occ.] Receptionist "The Gentry Canary Wharf"; [oth. writ.] Several poems written from the heart about life and people in general.; [pers.] This poem was written at the lowest point in my life. "But I've found the Light". "Thanks to Robert".; [a.] Bow, London, UK, E3 4NQ

MARSH, JASON
[b.] 3 November 1968, Cardiff, Wales; [p.] John Marsh, Pamela Marsh; [m.] Tracey Thomas; [ch.] Sebastian Jay; [ed.] Cardinal Newan School; [occ.] Musician/Bass Player; [memb.] The

performing right society; [oth. writ.] Catalogue of unpublished poetry/writings. Experiences several C.D. album credits, independently released; [pers.] My poetry is an account of observation made on myself and the love and hate I feel. "One Morning" is love.; [a.] Blackwood, Gwent, UK, NP1 4PR

MARSHALL, MRS. A. J.
[b.] 22 March 1939, Kiddeminster; [p.] Dead; [m.] 1957; [ch.] Three, two boys one girl, William, Gordon and Julia; [ed.] Church School, Middle School, Sharnbrook Gordon Julia; [occ.] Housewife the disabled; [memb.] Cats Protection League; [hon.] No honours only for bible study years ago certificates from VOP Stanborough Park five in all finished with diploma of graduation for advanced course Daniel and Revelations in June 1965; [oth. writ.] Several poems published this year in Anlho. This year Anchor Books Peterborough; [pers.] I write what I feel and what I see. I have always wanted to write but poor education held me back until my first grandchild was born. Influenced by reading (Dillon Thomas) under milk wood he was magic.

MARSHALL, CAROLYN
[b.] Dumbarton, Scotland; [p.] Gwendoline and Alistair McIndewar; [m.] Robert Marshall, 26 September 1975; [ch.] Andrew and Pamela; [pers.] Favorite poets and writers. John Donne - Shakespeare - Robert Burns.

MARSHALL, JOHN
[pen.] Struan Yule; [b.] 9 December 1914, Glasgow; [p.] Anne Louisa Robert Sua Yule and James Marshall; [m.] Hilda Evelyn Harper, 29 March 1949; [ch.] One son; [ed.] Whitehill Secondary School Glasgow University; [occ.] Retired; [memb.] National Trust for Scotland, World Wild-life Fund, Royal Society for Protection of Birds; [pers.] I was financial journalist or staff of the Glasgow Herald but on retirement took up oil painting and later started to write Limericks on topical subject for friends. This led to a build up of writing in verse and my interest in poetry in my superannuation years.; [a.] Glasgow, Lanarkshire, UK, G46 6DH

MARSHALL, PAMELA
[pen.] PammyLee; [b.] 29 June 1943, Saint Albans; [p.] Albert and Violet Taylor (Both Deceased); [m.] Lee, 29 June 1993; [ch.] 2 from previous marriages, Tania and Gary plus 3 grandchildren: Tasmine, David and Liam; [ed.] Watford Technical High School; [hon.] The lovely letter you sent me!!!; [oth. writ.] All unpublished, The Life of a Twitchers' Shadow, "Ripples on the Pond" - unfinished "Are You There Ma?" - Poem, Lucky 13 - Poem; [pers.] I love the countryside, animals, reading, painting, drawing and of course writing poems and stories. The spiritual awakening - going into the millennium can only do good. I want to make people aware of what selfishness and ignorance does to the environment.; [a.] Harpenden, Herts, UK, AL5 1LU

MARSHALL, PAULA MARY
[b.] 2 March 1968, Doncaster; [p.] Philip Marshall, Sandra Marshall; [ed.] Hatfield High School; [occ.] The British Army; [pers.] My life and the people who are in it, reflect in my poetry. To my family.; [a.] Doncaster, South Yorkshire, UK, DN7 6AZ

MARSHALL, RENEE
[b.] Brynmawr, S. Wales; [p.] Albert Charles Williams, Gertrude Williams; [m.] John Stuart Marshall, February 20, 1960; [ch.] Chris - Jane - Lynne - Diane - John and Joy Marshall (6 children); [ed.] Girls - Rugby High School Boys - Ashlawn Grammar; [occ.] Retired; [oth. writ.] Several poems printed in "Muse of poetry" and "Mainly for children" also in the local paper about the village green in Bilton; [pers.] I write for Sheer Joy - about life - my children and nature.; [a.] Rugby, Warwick, CV23 9DJ

MARSHALL, SARAH
[pen.] Sarah Marshall; [b.] 18 June 1965, Devizes; [p.] Rose and Derek Hillier; [m.] Gary Marshall, 7 January 1989; [ed.] Devizes Comprehensive; [occ.] House Keeper; [memb.] Library, Leisure Centre; [oth. writ.] I have written a few poems but not really thought that they would be valued by anyone.; [pers.] I write poems when I am sad or happy. Each one is very different. It gives me pleasure to come up with something new.; [a.] Devizes, Wiltshire, UK, SN10 3DS

MARSHALL, STEPHEN P.
[b.] 24 January 1956, Halifax; [p.] Kenneth Marshall, Isabella Marshall; [m.] Denise Marshall, 4 October 1986; [ch.] Katharine-Elizabeth; [ed.] Various short stays; [occ.] Disabled; [pers.] I perceive humour in the Mundane, because sadness is often around the next corner.; [a.] Halifax, West Yorkshire, UK, HX3 9AP

MARSHALL, WENDY
[pen.] Wendy Marshall; [b.] 14 June 1972, Chalfont, St. Giles; [p.] David and Monica Marshall; [m.] Working on it; [ed.] Chesham High School, Langley College; [occ.] Retail Assistant; [memb.] Ant News Today (Official Adam Ant Fan Club); [oth. writ.] None - this is my first and is actually a small part of a very much longer poem.; [pers.] This poem was inspired and my heart was broken by Mark Banford, my one and only love. He will remain in my heart forever.; [a.] Chalfont, St. Giles, Buckinghamshire, UK, HP8 4JZ

MARTIN, CLARE P.
[pen.] Clare Martin; [b.] 20 September 1970, Enniskillen; [p.] Frank Martin and Alice Martin (Deceased); [ed.] St. Fanchea's Secondary School Enniskillen, Mt. Hairless Grammar School, Enniskillen, St. Teresa's Privacy School, Enniskillen; [occ.] Office Trainee, to Enniskillen; [memb.] Enjoy going to cinema, music especially 'Blue' 'Bitzone' like walking.; [hon.] GCSES in English, English Lit, Business Studies, R.E., Biology, Rency, Maths, Art, RSA and Pitman typing exams, plush French graded objective exam. Currently doing an NUQ in 'Business Admin.'; [oth. writ.] Romantic novel 'The Silence' as yet unpublished in local Fermanagh newspapers.; [pers.] Live each day as if it's your very last, remember the world is your universe. Don't look back at your past life in anger.; [a.] Eniskillen, Fermanagh, UK

MARTIN, KERRY
[pen.] Kerry Louise Martin; [b.] 23 March 1970, Crowthorne, Berkshire; [p.] John and Averil Martin; [ed.] Howard of Effingham School, Effingham Surrey; [occ.] Nurse; [oth. writ.] I have written approx 50 poems none of which I have ever sent to be published as I never thought I was talented enough.; [pers.] I write poetry and songs as a hobby. Many are based on personal experiences throughout my life. I find that writing helps me to overcome events that I face in life. No matter how tragic.; [a.] Epsom, Surrey, UK, KT19 9DP

MARTIN, NORMA
[ch.] Michele Julie (RGN) Andrew Martin (RGN) Grandchildren - Daniel (6), Baby India May (4 Wks); [ed.] Rivington and Blackford High School Cooperative College Loughborough; [occ.] Community Care Manager worked in UK and Guerseas/ West Africa and India-Calcutta, Bangladesh, West Bengal; [memb.] Horwich Little Theatre (Amateur Dramatic Society) Appellation Dancing Team; [hon.] Social Sciences Award Information Technology Award Calligraphy; [oth. writ.] "Great Grandmother" - "Leaves and Evergreen" - Several other poems relating to life's experiences one or two published in "Poet's Corner", in the local "Bolton Evening News", paper.; [pers.] Enjoy poetry inspired by the sanctity of the moment. Be it a sunset, sea, flowers, etc. or the human frailty and rights of

my fellowman especially in the third world. The common thread of humanity that binds us all. Shallom.; [a.] Horwich, Lancashire, UK, BL6 5QR

MARYAN, MRS. JOAN ESTHER
[pen.] Joan Esther Maryan; [b.] 26 December 1924, Pottespury, Buck's; [p.] Mr. and Mrs. William and Edna Cooper; [m.] Mr. James Albert Maryan, 26 January 1946; [ch.] Paul, Susan, Mark, Emelie, Robert, Grandchildren - David, Danial Gemma, Thomas, Jessica (Charlotte, Mellisa, Philip, Rachael, Catheryne; [ed.] St. Mary's Convent, Np'ton, Technical Art School, Np'ton. "Parks School; [occ.] Denver, Colorado U.S.A. SwitchBoard Operator, retired ATS Ambulance Driver, 4 1/2 yrs. Sales Ass. Avon Cosmetics U.S.A.; [memb.] Life Member A.T.S. and British Rail, spouce of late employee, Life Member of the Ladies' Club A.T.S.; [hon.] Medals Awarded active service 1941 to 1945 with 93123 Joan Esther Cooper, home address "Roade Main Garage Ltd, Roade, Np, Tonshire; [oth. writ.] Poems written "Winter Time", "Summertime", "Tomorrow", "Day by Day", "Rocky Mountains", "Colorado", "Strangers in The Night", "Dead of Night", "The Way of Life" "Precious Years"; [pers.] I've painted in oil many pictures, rolled them up and given them to people who have been kind to my family and me: James never read my poems, I wish he could have seen the world through my eyes: It's a wonderful World.; [a.] Northampton, Northamptonshire, UK, NN4 8AY

MATHESON, LINDA
[b.] 21 April 1944, Dunfermline; [p.] John and Jean Dickson; [m.] Douglas Matheson, 19 September 1964; [ch.] Kevin Matheson; [ed.] Queen Anne Secondary High School, Dunfermline, Lauder Technical College, D'line; [occ.] Not working was a school secretary; [hon.] None apart from R.S.A. shorthand and typing qualifications.; [oth. writ.] Two other poems published - "Dunfermline Abbey" and "Holiday Home - The East Neuk of Fife."-Arrival Press, Peterborough.; [pers.] I try to convey in my poetry the ordinary, simple things of everyday life. The wonders of nature and people. I started to write after reading Derek Tangye's Books. He influenced me in his writings.; [a.] Dunfermline, Fife, UK, KY12 8PH

MATTHEWS, JOAN YVONNE
[b.] 3 November 1940, Birmingham; [p.] Edward and Violet Crook; [m.] Derek George Matthews, 29 March 1958; [ch.] Jacqueline, Annette and Philip, Grandchildren, Katie, Lauren, Jay and Liam, Joseph and Jessica; [ed.] Sec/Mod/School; [occ.] (Retired sales consultant); [memb.] Local Womens Institute and Patron of Local Operatic Society; [hon.] Diplomas in: Art and Design and Handwriting and Election, Painting titled = 'Tree Secrets' was displayed in = Glyn Vivian Art Gallery at Swansea in 1952; [oth. writ.] Poems in numerous anthologies, over 40% have been accepted for publication. (By different publishers); [pers.] I write what I feel deep inside. Sometimes I convey a message in my poetry. I realize that I have my own style of writing.; [a.] Swansea, Glamorgan, UK, SA7 9RZ

MAUBEC, PATRICIA ANNE
[b.] 29 June 1942, Bombay, India; [p.] Lewis Twinn, Barbara Twinn; [m.] Serge Jean Maubec M.B.E., 2 April 1980 (2nd Marriage); [ch.] Sara Jane, David James (1st Marr); [ed.] St. Joseph's Marist Convent, Barnstaple, Devon. Pitman's Secretarial College, Southampton Row, London; [occ.] Wife and Keeper of House!; [hon.] G.C.E. Certs: - Eng. Language, Eng. Literature, Art. Other Certs: - Music, Speech and Drama, Ballet; [oth. writ.] Poetry and short stories for enjoyment; [a.] Forest, Guersey, CI, UK, GY8 0AJ

MAVERS, WILLIAM A.
[b.] 23 November 1969, Glasgow; [p.] Betty; [ed.] Barrgarran Primary School and Park Mains High School (both situated in Erskine); [occ.]

Poet and Musician; [oth. writ.] 'Sometimes', 'Reflections', 'The Long Night', 'Moments', 'Women', 'Tomorrow Never Comes', 'Whispered Words Of Love', 'After All This Time', 'All We Have Has Been Written', 'The Wizard Of The Wings'; [pers.] Most of my writings are influenced by the single most important thing in my life...'Love'. After all it's what makes this world go around. You know sometimes we cannot express ourselves through our actions and that is when the Power of the written word can come into its own. I am a firm believer that words speak louder than actions and not the other way around as some would have us believe.; [a.] Erskine, Renfrewshire, UK, PA8 6DS

MAXWELL-CHARTERS, THOMAS COLIN
[pen.] Colin Maxwell-Charters; [b.] 25 September 1942, Carlisle; [p.] Thomas Charters, Isabel Charters; [ed.] Carlisle Art College, Goldsmiths' College, Leicester University; [occ.] None due to blindness and arthritis; [memb.] Glasgow Blind Writers' Group, The British Haiku Society; [hon.] Studied art in Paris and Amsterdam; [oth. writ.] Senryu published in BHS journal "Blithe Spirit", Short stories recorded by Calibre; [pers.] Hold no prejudice of any kind. Writing style is terse. Captivated by Japanese poetry.; [a.] Dumfries, Dumfriesshire, UK, DG1 3EZ

MAYLOR, CHRISTINA
[b.] 21 December 1976, Liverpool; [p.] Joyce J. Maylor; [ed.] Liverpool John Moores University; [occ.] Student Teacher; [memb.] National Union of Teachers and Anti Child Prostitution Campaign; [pers.] This poem is based on somebody who ridiculed me about my dyslexia. And how "dyslexics are a waste of space".; [a.] Lydiate, Merseyside, UK, L31 0DA

MAYNARD, MR. ROYSTON
[pen.] R. A. Maynard; [b.] 20 August 1959, St. Kitts, WI; [p.] Verna Maynard and Eugene Bussue; [ch.] Royston Jr., Francesca, Georgia, Eugene, Rachael, Angel; [ed.] Kentwood Comprehensive; [occ.] Martial Arts Instructor; [hon.] 4th Degree Black Belt Instructor. Master and founder of 'Taeguk' self defence martial art.; [pers.] I feel, "The blessing of the holy spirit gives me inspiration and the grace of God guides my pen, to give thanks with reverence for gifts bestowed.";
[a.] Friern Barnet, London, UK, N11 3ER

MCALICE, LINDSAY ALEXANDRA
[b.] 3 April 1977, Billinge; [p.] Peter McAlice and Sandra McAlice; [ed.] (Nine G.C.S.E's and currently studying biology and psychology 'A' - Levels); [occ.] (Hoping to join the Royal Navy as an officer 1997); [memb.] The British Horse Society; [pers.] I feel poetry is inspired by three gifts; emotion, feeling and pleasure, without these factors a poem is nothing more than structured words on a page and true meaning can never really be found.; [a.] Ashton-in-Makerfield, Wigan, Gtr Manchester, UK, WN4 9JY

MCAULIFFE, CLAIRE
[b.] 26 January 1974, London; [p.] Pauline and David McAuliffe; [m.] David Bignell, 14 September 1996; [ed.] Presdales School; [occ.] Secretary; [memb.] Deegan Academy of Irish Dance School; [pers.] This poem is dedicated to the one I love.; [a.] Hertford, Herts, UK, SA13 7SL

MCCAIRNS, CHRIS
[pen.] James Kenna; [b.] 7 March 1988, Doncaster; [m.] Susan, 19 August 1937; [ed.] Stonyhurst College Lancs; [occ.] Pilot; [oth. writ.] Short stories; [a.] Somerset, UK, BA8 0DA

MCCAMBRIDGE, JAMES
[pen.] Marks Walters R.D. Gunmige; [b.] 19 June 1950, Bootle; [p.] R. Luthy and James McCambridge; [ed.] St. Georges R.C. PRY School, St. Thomas Aquinas S60 Mod, Udult Education College, Huyton Technical College; [occ.] Wood Machinist Actor of Walk on Parts; [memb.] The Folio Society, A Leading Casting Agency, Ama-

teur Dramatic Society, Local Modeling Agency; [hon.] C.SE English Lit, Lang, History Geography O'Level English Lang, O'Level Lit, O'Level History, Maths, Science, Psychology Geography; [oth. writ.] Short stories, children's stories, magazine reporting poems submitted to local publishers.; [pers.] In my writing I search for romance and realism, that's a diamond precious and rare I am in love with early classic writers like Dickens, and Austin, G. Elliot. Early Romantic Poets.; [a.] Liverpool, Lancashire, UK, L9 3AB

MCCANN, KEVIN
[b.] 18 October 1950, Lough Gall; [p.] Terence McCann, Cathleen McCann; [occ.] Carer; [pers.] I strive to enable others to be more aware as to the natural and physical environment in my writing. I am greatly influenced by the area where I live, also the local community. 89, Cloven Eden Road, Cloven Eden, Lough Gall; [a.] Armagh, Armagh, UK, BT61 8LB

MCCARTHY, ANDY
[b.] 20 May 1946, Ireland; [m.] 1969; [ch.] 5; [occ.] Artist/Writer; [oth. writ.] None so far, currently working to complete my first collection of poetry. This is my first time submitting work to a publisher.; [pers.] The poems I am working on at the moment are part of a celebration of my 50th year I have just had. A very successful exhibition of my paintings to mark this special year.; [a.] Limerick, Ireland

MCCOOMBS, JEAN
[pen.] Jean McCoombs; [b.] 13 August 1941, Forestgate, East London; [p.] Alice and Gordon Fitzgerald; [m.] Terence McCoombs, 17 October 1964; [ch.] James John, Wendy Jean; [ed.] St. Francis and St. Angelas Ursuline Convent; [occ.] Housewife; [oth. writ.] Several other poems scribbled since the age of nineteen I composed 'Sweeney' because my son played the part in his school play.; [pers.] My poems cover a wide range of subjects. Mainly about things occurring in my personal life of happenings in the world at large. Patience influenced me greatly. By making me become 'socially aware'; [a.] Romford, Essex, UK, RM3 7QJ

MCCORMACK, SUZANNE
[pen.] Suzanne McCormack; [b.] 18 May 1974, Tyrone, NI; [p.] Terry and Rosemary McCormack; [ed.] St. Mary's Primary School, Pomeroy Co. Tyrone N. Ireland, Our Lady's High School Cookstown Co. Tyrone N. Ireland; [occ.] Clerical Ass. Endsleigh Insurance; [oth. writ.] Nothing has been published before; [pers.] Ireland's beautiful scenery is my inspiration.; [a.] Cheltenham, Glos, UK, GL51 8PG

MCDERMOTT, PAUL
[b.] 24 November 1977, Liverpool; [p.] Linda and Harry; [ed.] Maghull High School, Hugh Baird College, Bootle; [occ.] I have just left college and currently work in a wholesalers in Liverpool called Parfetts; [oth. writ.] I have been writing stories and poetry all my life, but until now I have never had it published, when you wrote to me and offered to publish my poem, it was like a dream come true.; [pers.] The constant encouragement by my family and friends help make it possible to write poetry. My poems always reflect something that concerns me. Peace was written about a contrast between war and peace.; [a.] Liverpool, Merseyside, UK

MCDONNELL, JOHN
[pen.] Sein M. Donanaill; [b.] 24 April 1939, Tralee, Eire; [p.] Father - was Soldier, Mother Farmers; [m.] Farmers, June 1961; [ch.] Five; [ed.] National School; [occ.] Shoe Maker, Lock Smith; [oth. writ.] Bride of Youth, Berlin Wall, Ethiopia, A Splendid Day, Genius Man - The Scientist 'Yedda' of Oneness, Early Dawn; [pers.] Fill the hills I daffodils introine in depth the long days sun. For spring is here and life renews. When young fine trees will wave their beechy bows. "O Live".

MCEVOY, JUDY
[b.] 8 August 1941, Bradford; [p.] Mary and Ernest Halliwell; [m.] Stephen McEvoy, 25 March 1961; [ed.] Secondary School; [occ.] Retired (Ex Building Society Clerk); [oth. writ.] Numerous unpublished poems of various themes, spiritual, dramatic romantic and amusing (Comedy); [pers.] My poems are reflections of my observations of life and death.; [a.] Bradford, West Yorkshire, UK, BD13 2NX

MCEWEN, STUART
[b.] 16 September 1930, Denton, Manchester; [p.] James Robert McEwen, Lizzie McEwen; [ed.] Audenshaw Grammar, Stockport College of Technology; [occ.] Retired Chemist; [memb.] Institute of Science Technology, Society of Authors, Denton Art Society, Local Probus and Bowls Clubs; [oth. writ.] Thesis on relations between science and religion, published by Manchester College Oxford, public performances of two plays.; [pers.] I believe that genuine co-operation between people, aided by scientific progress, can steadily improve the standard of life, and its quality.; [a.] Denton, Lancashire, UK, M34 2AB

MCFADDEN, NOREEN M.
[b.] 20 September 1965, Glasgow; [p.] Mary M. Fadden, Michael M. Fadden; [ed.] Educated locally, Primary School, Secondary School 20 levels in Arithmetic and Secretarial Studies; [occ.] Post person; [oth. writ.] Poem called Freedom in local book called Tears and Laughter funded locally, also Simple Eyes That See published in Anchor Poetry.; [pers.] By getting my poetry published is my way of expressing my views in this ever changing world, and knowing at the end of my time I have inspired good people to carry on fighting for justice in all walks of life.; [a.] Gorbals, Glasgow, UK, G5 9NF

MCFARLAND, JILLIAN
[b.] 24 August 1978, Strabane, Co. Tyrone; [p.] Ken and Doris McFarland; [ed.] Portadown College, now studying English and French at Trinity College, Dublin; [occ.] Student at Trinity College, Dublin; [a.] Tandragee, Armagh, UK, BT62 2BE

MCGIFFEN, MARGARET
[pen.] Jec; [b.] 24 October 1947, Dundee; [p.] William and Annie Cunningham; [m.] Clive Angus McGiffen, 22 October 1983; [ch.] M31 F24 F12; [ed.] Secondary School Linlathen High School, Dundee; [occ.] Civil servant (Mod); [oth. writ.] Childrens Story; [pers.] Life is but a dream, seconds away from eternity.; [a.] Scunthorpe, North Lincs, UK, DN20 9QA

MCGLADE, SHIRLEY ALISON
[pen.] Sam, Arni; [b.] 27 April 1962, Alton; [p.] Mr. A. Bampton and Mrs V. J. Bampton; [ed.] Bishop Rheindorp, Larch Avenue, Guild Ford Surrey. Durham, Mr. Bevan Teacher.; [occ.] Care, Nurse. Catering Manager.; [oth. writ.] The Tramp, Childhood Memories. Spring, True Friendship, Missing You: The Forgotten Garden: Many published.; [pers.] To Carole, poem written especially: To say thank you for being around, over the years. To keep always in your memories. Love also to Eric, and kids, may every day be happy, and full of smiles. I love you all. Sam.; [a.] Guildford, Surrey, UK, GU3 1JQ

MCGREGOR, PETER GAVIN
[pen.] "Nautes"; [b.] 19 December 1931, Glasgow; [p.] William and Jean McGregor; [m.] Elsie Russell McGregor, 9 December 1955; [ch.] Gordon and David; [ed.] Moorpark Primary, Renfrew High, Paisley Technical College, Stow College and Kingston, Polytechnic; [occ.] Retired Seamen's Missionary; [memb.] Stobhill Kidney Patients Association, National Kidney Federation, Seamen's Christian Friend Society; [hon.] Lupton and Pearman Award for Kidney Patients -1996; [oth. writ.] Various articles in "Living

Links" magazine, journal of the Seamen's Christian Friend Society; [pers.] Greatly influenced by Biblical study and Evangelical Teaching. Enjoy reading sea stories and Biographies.; [a.] Renfrew, Scotland, PA4 0BX

MCGUINNESS, MRS. KATHLEEN
[b.] 2 January 1923, Newhaven, Sx; [p.] Eleanor, William; [m.] Thomas McGuinness, 6 April 1944; [ch.] Thomas Maureen; [ed.] Newhaven Girls School Sussex; [occ.] Retired Nurse; [a.] Eastbourne, East Sussex, UK, BN23 6SQ

MCGUIRK, JOHNNEY
[b.] 28 July 1961, Dublin; [p.] Christy and Kay McGuirk; [m.] Emer, 23 September 1993; [ch.] Sarah; [ed.] Second Level; [pers.] A child is powerless, but only for a short while, take time look close, see their power and strength, help build it not take it away.; [a.] Swords, Dublin, Eire

MCKELL, LISA MARIE
[b.] 4 March 1976, Alexandria; [p.] Margaret and John McKell; [ed.] Hermitage Academy, Clydebank College; [occ.] Senior Care Assistant Mardon House Residential Home; [hon.] Duke of Edinburgh; [oth. writ.] Several poems published in other books.; [pers.] Poetry is a fantastic way of being able to put your feelings on paper and I feel most privileged to be able to share my feelings with others.; [a.] Helensburgh, Argyll and Bute, UK, G86 7LJ

MEADOWS, AGNES
[pen.] Agnes Meadows; [b.] 18 March 1947, Cologne, W Germany; [p.] Charles and Margot Meadows; [ed.] Tum Hood Grammar, Eastham College of further Education; [occ.] Fundraising consultant and arts management; [hon.] Certificate of Proficiency in Journalism, Member of the Institute of Fundraising managers; [oth. writ.] Journalist on an East London newspaper, then freelanced for magazines in Mexico and sometimes in London. Wrote and narrated 4 shows for Indian classical dance companies. Poetry readings in N. London. 2nd prize in the Library of Avalon Poetry Comp. 1995 for "Sennen"; [pers.] Poetry, like life, should be filled with passion, for horizons to strive to reach, and glimpse of worlds other than your own.; [a.] London, UK, EC1R 4SY

MEAGHER, PILS
[pen.] Pils Meagher; [b.] 24 June 1976, St. Josephs, Clonmel; [p.] Thomas (Deceased) and Margeret; [ed.] Ardfinnan N.S. Cahir Vocational; [occ.] Unemployed Musician and Poet; [hon.] This is the first time I have submitted my poetry to the public and I am delighted you like it. I have "contributed a verse to the Play of Life" to loosely quote Whitman; [oth. writ.] I have over 80 songs and hope to pursue a career in music. I have roughly 120 poems. I have been writing poetry since I was 16. My longest is an 18 page journey through a personal breakdown.; [pers.] I find poetry to be a great release. The most of my work is dark introspective commentary on my life and the world around me. My poetry is a collection of life's occurrences full of memoirs and aspirations.; [a.] Ardfinnan, Clonmel, Tipperary, UK

MEDLOCK, MRS. MARGERY
[b.] 27 November 1924, Newcastle, Tyne; [p.] Frederick Charles and Ellen Curry; [m.] Laurence Hornsby Medlock, 7 October 1950; [ch.] Stuart Anthony B. A., Heather Jayne B. Ed.; [ed.] Oxbridge Lane Girls School - Stockton Private Tuition Shorthand-Office Experiences. At 18 yrs. Joined Wrns 1943-1946-1947-1949 Ended Engagement as p/o Wren, The Citadel, Admiralty.; [occ.] Retired (Amateur Artist and Writer) Sold is paintings; [memb.] Ex-Wrens Association (Darlington Branch), Beamish Hall Arts Group (Now Petrod); [hon.] Silver cup awarded for art display judged by Art Master St. Hild's Art College Durham University Presented by Lady

Steel.; [oth. writ.] Short Stories for my Grand-Daughter - Published - small booklet "History of Beamish Hall". Couple of articles for magazines.; [pers.] I have often thought that the charm of life has disappeared in this world of "Anything Goes" and falling standards of Discipline and goodmanners. How pleasant to switch to TV and see a programme that is gracious rather than characters showing anger and verbal abuse. (In the guise of Drama).; [a.] Darlington, Durham, UK, DL3 7PY

MELDON, URSULA
[b.] 12 February 1921, Nr Bodmin, Cornwall; [p.] Major Leonard D'Arcy, Fox and Mary; [m.] Desmond Meldon, 31 January 1948, at Gloucester; [ch.] One - Helen; [ed.] Lausanne - Gumley House Richmond - Finishing School Brussels 6 years Army - Became Lecturer at A.T.S. Signals School. From the Signals School - I was chosen to go totally at B.A.F. HQ - Bari - there was still fighting at cassino; [occ.] Retired - but busy with lyrics and printing; [memb.] Can't afford on my pension; [hon.] Had several when I was young for lyrics - times literary - also time and tide - many solo invited art exhibitions.; [oth. writ.] A lyric accepted last month by the arrival press - entitled... "A Cornish Childhood"; [pers.] I'm totally overcome - and a million thanks.; [a.] Saint Just, Cornwall, UK, TR19 7JJ

MELLON, CECILY
[b.] 18 April 1941, Dublin; [p.] Dr. Cecil Moore, Mrs. May Moore; [m.] Andrew Mellon, 12 March 1983; [ch.] Rose-May, Douglas; [ed.] Alexandra School, Dublin Alexandra College, University of Dublin and Art College (N.C.A.D.) Dublin; [occ.] Secondary School Teacher, Ballymahon Convent, Goldsmith Country, Longford; [memb.] Chairperson, Athlane Riding Club A.I.R.C.; [oth. writ.] I only started writing poetry - two years ago and have harders of them in books at home - hard written in exercise books. Maybe two hundred poems. I never tried to publish any.; [pers.] I write from my heart for pleasure. I write to record what I see around me in an unspoiled countryside. Influenced by Oliver Goldsmith and William Butler Yeats.; [a.] Kenagh, Longford, UK

METALLINOU, ILIANA
[b.] 24 February 1954, Corfu; [m.] Victor Savvanis, 18 May 1980; [ch.] Elisabeth, Vasilis; [ed.] Corfu High School, Bell School of Languages-Cambridge, Chiswick Polytechnic-West London, Open University (Arts one year), ICS (Spanish, cartooning); [occ.] Teacher of English as a foreign language, run my own school; [memb.] Corfu Studies Society, Corfu Music Society; [hon.] Cambridge Certificate of Proficiency in English, Pitman Certif. in advanced English for overseas candidates, General Certif. of education examination in English Language.; [pers.] We can always live under a rainbow, as long as we are willing to see it.; [a.] Corfu, 49100

METCALF, SARA JANE
[b.] 22 December 1980, Inverness; [p.] James and Linda Metcalf; [ed.] Still attending school in 5th year as St. Leonards Secondary School; [memb.] Member of the Scottish Youth Theatre; [hon.] 4th year award for Design and Technology and (SCE), Certificate and a Music Module Certificate as well.; [pers.] I taught myself how to play the keyboard. But still need to learn more. I like making my own music up and I like making up songs to. I'm also very keen on acting, and enjoy making up poems as well.; [a.] Glasgow, Scotland, G33 4LY

MEYERN, ELAINE
[b.] 28 September 1951, London; [p.] Florance and Arther; [m.] David Peter, 15 July 1972; [ch.] Scott and Carley; [ed.] Comprehensive, Girls, London, Later years Bexley College; [occ.] Mother, wife nature student; [memb.] P.T.A. Tap dancer; [hon.] NVQ Admin Plus Various

Skills; [oth. writ.] A previous poem published; [pers.] I express my feelings about people and life in rhyme, I love poetry both reading and writing.; [a.] Bexley, Kent, UK, DA5 3ES

MICHAELS, MR. DEAN
[pen.] Sometimes P. J. Crawford, (Peter James); [b.] 11 January 1971, Walthamstow, London; [p.] Mary and Peter Ellis (Divorced); [m.] Miss Christine Munday - Girl friend; [ch.] She has two, Hayley and Elisha; [ed.] Went to Woy Woy High School in N.S.W. Australia. Left at 14 years of age to work, save and travel which I do as constantly as possible.; [occ.] Residential Social Worker (Rehabilitating 6 Ex mentally ill patients from long stay wards); [memb.] UK Bungee Club at present going for my Hangliding Pilots License; [hon.] Never listened to people in the past in regards to over publishing my work so I have never been granted an honour or an award in fact I was surprised as well as shocked I received your excellent letter.; [oth. writ.] Several hundred poems of different forms (been writing ever since I was about 6) one song and one short horror story. (At present contemplating another.); [pers.] If possible I would like to dedicate this work to one Mrs. Margaret Jones who I'll always be grateful to. Thanks for all your help Marg. Philosophical statement: "We're here for a good time, not a long time."; [a.] Dagenham, Essex, UK, RM8 2TB

MIDDLETON, GEOFF
[b.] 21 March 1947, Leeds; [p.] Mary Agnes Middleton, George Kay Middleton; [m.] Susan Elizabeth, 6 October 1984; [ch.] Louise, Sonia, Ian; [ed.] Ingram Road Primary and Matthew Murray Comprehensive, Leeds; [occ.] Gardener; [memb.] Wortey Parish Church Dramatic Society; [oth. writ.] Other poems in family cards (unpublished), pantomime scripts, of which two have been performed by above amateur dramatic society.; [a.] Leeds, West Yorkshire, UK, LS12 4TQ

MILEHAM, LEAH ELIZABETH
[b.] 29 March 1944, Seaham; [p.] Andrew D. and Edith Nicholson; [m.] Christopher Charles, 26 September 1964; [ch.] Heather, Christopher John; [ed.] Secondary Modern; [occ.] Housewife retired registered general nurse; [memb.] Royal College of Nursing Wild Fowl and Wetlands Assc. Creative writing group at Seaham Library (started June 1996); [oth. writ.] Nothing published; assortment of short stories and poems written for creative writing group.; [pers.] I have always wanted to write and be published. Only now can I devote the time to give to my work. Encouraged by my creative writing friends.; [a.] Seaham, Durham, UK, SR7 0LU

MILES, PEARL SHIRLEY
[b.] 2 July 1960, Worcester; [p.] Cyril and Pamela Nicholas; [m.] Brian Charles Miles, 2 July 1992; [ed.] Somers Park Primary, Dyson Perrins C of E School; [occ.] Housewife; [oth. writ.] None to date; [pers.] Written from the heart "The Rose" is a reminder of the sadness and grief I have. After 7 years of trying for a child my dream came true. Then 6 months into the pregnancy I had a fall and shortly after I lost the twins on the 7th/8th Nov. 94. I placed a red rose beside them to show the love, the pain and the loss I carry within me.; [a.] Malvern, Worcestershire, UK, WR14 1TS

MILLER, ELLEN
[pen.] E. Miller; [b.] 22 May 1982, London, England; [p.] Miss Patricia Miller, Mr. Leslie Elias; [ed.] Still currently at school in The Hersham Pr1 Centre; [oth. writ.] Many poems have been written at home but before this I have never done anything with them; [pers.] To everyone who helped me succeed thanks. And to those who didn't well ha. I'm glad I had the chance to come all this way with my own work.; [a.] Walton, Surrey, UK, LT12 3RG

MILLO, MICHAEL JOHN
[b.] 20 July 1944, Kilwinning, Scotland; [p.] Anne and Mick Millo; [m.] Sheila Diane, 1 July 1972; [ed.] Bishop Challoner Grammar School and "Battle Court" Military Crammer; [occ.] Head of Commercial Activities at the National Army Museum; [memb.] M.G. Car Club; [hon.] B.A. Classical Studies, Dip Eur Hum. - Diploma in European Humanities; [oth. writ.] Poems - yet unpublished; [a.] Bromley, Kent, UK

MILLS, SONIA
[b.] 2 December 1936, Horsham, Sussex; [p.] Ralph and Billie Tarratt; [m.] Arthur Mills, 25 July 1959; [ch.] David and Julie Mills; [ed.] Various Boarding and Grammar Schools ending with Winchester High; [occ.] Part-time Secretary; [oth. writ.] Short stories and poems for own pleasure. But never submitted anything to a publisher before.; [pers.] This poem was written to express children's feelings (both from personal and my grandchildren's experiences) about how their emotions and loyalties are torn when their parents part. Their heartache is seldom fully understood and considered by adults.; [a.] Ipswich, Suffolk, UK, IP3 9DQ

MILLS, TRACEY
[pen.] Tracey-Anne Mills; [b.] 13 October 1963, Bath; [p.] Terrence Cole, Diane Cole; [ch.] Abigail Louise; [ed.] Diocesan Girls School, Bath; [memb.] International Institute of Beauty Therapists; [hon.] 1 HBC Beauty Therapy; [pers.] My poetry is written on personal feelings and experiences.; [a.] Coleraine, Wiltshire, UK, SN14 8EW

MILLWARD, RICKIE LEE
[b.] 20 April 1983, California, USA; [p.] Colin Harwood and Marina Millward; [ed.] Sydenham Girls School year 9 Student; [occ.] At secondary school; [oth. writ.] I am 13 years old and I have been writing poetry for the last 4-5 years. This is the first time I have entered a competition.; [pers.] I write my poetry, when and as the mood takes me. My poetry is always personal and based on everyday experiences.; [a.] London, UK, SE16 4LQ

MITCHELL, NIGEL TROY
[b.] November 24, 1964, Redruth; [p.] Frank Mitchell, Terena Mitchell; [ed.] Camborne Comprehensive School; [occ.] Lorry Driver/Cutter West Country Metals Ltd; [pers.] I write my poetry on things that spark my imagination, be it love, life or nature. I have been writing them since I was thirteen, this is my first contest, and my first publication.; [a.] Camborne, Cornwall, TR14 7HQ

MIZEN, MARGARET
[b.] 13 December 1943, Bristol; [p.] Irene Lambert, William Lambert; [m.] Mervyn Mizen, 24 June 1972; [ch.] Sharon Louise - Tracey Anne; [ed.] Bristol Central Commercial School; [occ.] Housewife; [pers.] This is my first poem, my mother died last year at the grand age of 94 and these thoughts are based on her life.; [a.] Bristol, UK, BS14 9TW

MOBBERLEY, DAVID
[b.] 12 July 1948, Birmingham; [p.] Edward and Mildred Mobberley; [m.] Divorced; [ch.] Darren; [ed.] Brandwood School - Kings Heath; [occ.] Postman; [memb.] Longbow Society, Lisa Stansfield Fan Club; [oth. writ.] three books of verse, numerous anthologies and magazines world-wide; [pers.] Life is the preparation of the soul for everlasting journey.; [a.] Birmingham, West Midlands, UK, B14 6EG

MOFFAT, ELIZABETH
[pen.] A. C. Jordan; [b.] March 5, 1980, Dumfries; [p.] Audrey Moffat and James Moffat; [ed.] Dalbeattie High School; [oth. writ.] A few poems and several short stories unpublished; [a.] Dalbeattie, DG5 4DZ

MONAGHAN, NICHOLAS SIMON
[b.] 4 June 1976, Pontefract; [p.] Patrick Monaghan, Lynne Monaghan; [ed.] Carleton High School, Pontefract; [a.] Castleford, Yorkshire, UK, WF10 3DE

MONTEGRIFFO, DONNA LORRAINE
[b.] 4 May 1950, Kent; [p.] Eileen and George Hall; [m.] Andres Mauricio Montegriffo, 7 July 1976; [ch.] Michael and Peter, (stepchildren) Natalyn-Marisa; [ed.] Bexleymeath High School for Girls.; [occ.] Business Administrator; [memb.] Tennis and Bowls Club; [hon.] Several awards in guiding; [oth. writ.] Several short stories and poems.; [pers.] I hope to highlight the trauma of silent suffering through writing from encounters of heart felt experiences among friends and family.; [a.] Gibraltar

MOODY, ELLEN G.
[pen.] Pruellen; [b.] 4 July 1923, Forest Gate Essex; [p.] Harold Gurl and Annie E. Gurl; [m.] Percy Moody, 20 October 1951; [ch.] Annette Lucille; [ed.] Ardleigh Green Senior School, Hornchurch Essex, City Day Continuation School London; [occ.] Retired civil servant; [hon.] City school essay prize, R.S.P.C.A. London Essay Prize, English R.S.A. State 1 Credit, English R.S.A. Stage II Pass; [oth. writ.] Poems published in Church and local magazines.; [pers.] My dream would be to emulate the style and brilliance of John Betjeman.; [a.] Peterborough, Cambs, UK, PE7 3SX

MOODY, JOYCE
[b.] 8 February 1946, Chepstow; [p.] Mr. and Mrs. Bissett; [m.] David Moody, 2 January 1965; [ch.] Dean and Julia; [ed.] Abergavenny, Secondary Modern School; [occ.] Component Cutter, Factory Work for Sony's

MOON, NANCY
[b.] 7 November 1945, Guernsey; [p.] Roy Le Page, Marjory Le Page; [m.] Frank Moon, 17 October 1963; [ch.] Frank, Sarah; [occ.] Housewife; [pers.] I began writing poetry at first as if someone was holding the pen, to my amazement it just seemed to fall out onto the page and has not stopped I think my mother's love and great insight into people has been the foundation of my writing.; [a.] Saint Peter Port, Guernsey, UK, GY1 1ZA

MOORE, BRETT
[b.] 17 August 1961, Cheltenham; [p.] Margaret Moore; [m.] Divorced; [ch.] Aidan Lloyd, Aaron James; [ed.] Christ Church Technical High School, Inlingua Teachers Training School; [occ.] Machine Setter; [memb.] Gloucestershire Wildlife Trust; [oth. writ.] Several poems unpublished; [pers.] I try to reflect my personal experiences and wishes for the world as honestly as possible.; [a.] Cheltenham, Gloucestershire, UK, GL50 3LA

MOORE, COLIN
[b.] 1 April 1965, Glasgow; [p.] David and Mary Moore; [ed.] Greenfaulds High School, Falkirk College of Technology; [occ.] Lead Technician; [memb.] Fishery Management, Chairman/Director of U.C.A.P.A Ltd; [hon.] City and Guilds in Communication, City and Guilds Advanced - Plumbing; [oth. writ.] Synthetic nymphs for River and Stream. A guide to the life cycles of nymphs and larvae in the River Clyde. Synths - How and When to Fish them for the overworked doctors who work with a constant convoy or belt of patients.; [a.] Cumbernauld, North Lanarkshire, UK, G67 4AB

MOORE, KATHLEEN
[b.] 6 December 1954, Glasgow; [p.] Elizabeth Boyd and Robert Boyd; [ed.] Our Lady of Lourdes Sec. School, Jordanhill College; [occ.] Unemployed (due to chronic illness); [memb.] Local art group; [hon.] Diploma of Community Education; [oth. writ.] This is my first attempt at competition or publication; [pers.] I endeavour to embody the gamut of human emotions in my writing.; [a.] Glasgow, Lanarkshire, UK, G53 7EN

MOORHOUSE, JEAN
[b.] April 4, 1938, Salford; [p.] Olga and Bill High; [m.] Divorced; [ch.] Deborah, Robert, Bruce and Amanda; [ed.] Broughton High School Girls; [occ.] Retired; [oth. writ.] First attempt; [pers.] Romantic dreamer locked in the past.

Disenchanted with present day selfish society. Long for old style community spirit.; [a.] Sketran, Banff. Scotland. AB45 3DA

MOORHOUSE, OLGA M.
[b.] 23 March 1929, Accrington, Lancs; [p.] William, Agnes Taylor; [m.] John Moorhouse, 29 December 1948; [ch.] Austen John; [ed.] St. Oswalds R.C. Primary Accrington, St. Agnes R.C. Secondary Accrington; [occ.] Retired; [memb.] All Saints Choir Ashton-on-Mersey, Ashton-on-Mersey-Sale Golf Club, Past Member Halle Choir 1969-1976; [hon.] Lady Captain Ashton-on-Mersey Golf Club 1976; [oth. writ.] None published; [pers.] Poetry is my outlet, in times of worry, concern and happiness.; [a.] Sale, Cheshire, UK, M33 5BA

MORAN, JAYNE
[b.] 10 August 1976, Co. Louth, Eire; [p.] Patsy Moran, Jo Moran; [ed.] Mt. Sackville, Co. Dublin Our Lady's School, Wicklow; [occ.] Works Abroad; [oth. writ.] School Magazine and Annual; [pers.] I get such satisfaction from writing poetry and feel that if more people did, there would be a lot more smiling faces in this world.

MORLEY, R.
[pen.] Rona Dorothy Grace; [b.] 11 April 1921, Upton, St. Leonards; [p.] Clara Morris and Henry Ballinger; [m.] Upton St. Leonard, Gloucester; [ed.] Upton St. Leonard's Village School; [oth. writ.] Name and place of birth of self and parents sufficient. Jewels of the imagination.; [a.] Leyton, London, UK, E10

MORRIS, CORINNE J.
[pen.] Coco; [b.] 4 September 1979, Birmingham; [p.] Joe and Etheline Morris; [ed.] Attended Holly Lodge High School in Smethwick, and I am now currently attending Sutton Coldfield and Sign Language. College studying T.V. and Video Production; [a.] Smetwick, Warley, West Mids, UK, B67 7PA

MORRISH, KENNETH WALTER
[pen.] Ken Morrish; [b.] 9 May 1921, Nr. Bableigh; [p.] Sidney and Annie Morrish; [m.] Lydia Mary Hoyle, 21 April 1943; [ed.] Local Village School; [occ.] Farming; [hon.] Took part in Dave Allens Program; [oth. writ.] Spring Devon; [pers.] Went to school at 4 yrs old took my dinner and left at 14 yrs old went home to work on the farm where I still live.; [a.] Devon, UK, EX32 0NI

MORRISON, SANDRA
[pen.] G. N. Ray; [b.] 28 September 1957, Salford, England; [p.] Norman Marsh, Joan Marsh; [m.] Simon Andrew Morrison, 17 September 1993; [ch.] Philip Robert; [ed.] Broughton High, (1974) Salford University (1996); [occ.] Clerical Officer Salford City Council; [hon.] BTEC UNC/NVQ4-Business and Finance; [oth. writ.] Story told through poetry when read consecutively and Three Childrens' Stories, Lyrics.; [pers.] To write for enjoyment and utilise my imagination to its maximum and best exploiting the philosophical, empathetic and compassionates and understanding side of my personality. Writing verse allows me to communicate effectively to many.; [a.] Worsley, Greater Manchester, UK, M28 25X

MOSS, MARGARET ELIZABETH
[b.] 16 December 1967, Wolverhampton; [m.] K. Moss, 23 July 1996; [occ.] Care worker; [oth. writ.] Fools For A Jester

MOSS, MICHAEL JOHN
[b.] 1 January 1939, New Rossington, Yorkshire; [p.] Kenneth and Alice Moss; [m.] Muriel Moss, 18 August 1963; [ch.] Susan and Karl; [ed.] Maltby Grammar School 1951, served 25 yrs. Royal Navy 1955-1979, College of Estate Management 1985; [occ.] Retired; [memb.] Langstone Christian Fellowship; [oth. writ.] Considerable number of poems (mostly religious/social nature); [pers.] I write what I feel deep down to make others aware of the value of themselves, the world and their fellow human beings.; [a.] Portsmouth, Hampshire, UK, PO2 0RP

MOWER, EMILY
[b.] 9 February 1982, Bury St Edmunds; [p.] Elizabeth Anne Mower and William Michael Mower; [occ.] Still at school - stowua and high school; [pers.] Hate is a form of fear, to hate something is to fear it greatly; [a.] Old Newton, Near Stowmarket, Suffolk, UK, IP14 4HG

MOY, LISA ANNE
[b.] 25 February 1981, Hexham; [p.] Ernest Moy, Joan Moy; [ed.] Hexham East First School, Hexham Middle School, Hexham Queen Elizabeth high school; [occ.] Still attending school; [memb.] Girls group from 1990-1995, Youth Initiative; [hon.] At the age of 7 in 1989 I passed the preliminary selection committee of Cadbury's National Exhibition of Children's Art.; [oth. writ.] "The Wizzy Dizzy Waltzer"; [pers.] I like to write poems as it can be a good way to express your feelings. And it also lets others experience them as well. I am influenced by what goes on in the outside of my doors.; [a.] Hexham, Northumberland, UK, NE46 1DN

MPAULO, JACQUELINE RUKUBA
[pen.] Jacqui-R; [b.] 1 November 1965, Kampala; [p.] Lorna Belford Coon, Martin Rukuba; [m.] Sam Edwin Mpaulo, 30 April 1992; [ch.] Samantha Jacqueline Mpaulo, Gavin Bernard Mpaulo; [ed.] Mackie Academy, Scotland, University of Botswana, Uganda Management Institute; [occ.] Assistant Manager News Africa Magazine; [memb.] Uganda Journalists Association; [oth. writ.] On Refugees, Abused Children, Child Prostitutes in Uganda, Unpublished; Three Poems Published in Ufahamu (Journal of the African Activist Association 1992); [pers.] Through my poetry I am able to reflect on the diversity of humankind that mine eyes have seen...and in its suffering...I am able to cleanse my soul in the words I write...; [a.] Kampala, Uganda

MUIRHEAD, MRS. M.
[b.] 21 January 1937, Dumbarton; [p.] Mathew Kelly Wallace, Alice Sinclair; [m.] Raymond Henry Muirhead, 29 October 1958; [ch.] Kenneth Raymond Muirhead, Brian John Muirhead; [ed.] Began school at the age of 4 years while in care of the church during the war later attended Boroughmuir Senior Secondary School; [occ.] Severely Disabled Housewife; [hon.] Received a Bursary after primary education, Gold Federation Certificate for Burns Poetry, many class prizes. Compelled to give up schooling when parents separated.; [oth. writ.] Began writing about 1 year ago to encourage other disabled people. Entering the competitions after friends persuaded me to submit entries. Since have written books on Child Safety for local police and am now writing second book.; [pers.] Took up writing as I had decided to teach myself to type to prevent further loss of power form hands. As I needed something to type, began to write.; [a.] Edinburgh, Scotland, EH13 9NB

MULLEN, STEPHEN
[b.] 29 March 1968, Halifax; [p.] John, Pauline Mullen; [m.] Linda Mullen, 7 September 1996; [ed.] Halifax Catholic High School; [occ.] Caretaker (Ex Soldier); [memb.] A life member of the Regimental Association, The Duke of Wellington's Regiment; [oth. writ.] None published; [pers.] I write of love and life, and to do this you must try both. I have great respect for all first World War poets.; [a.] Brighouse, West Yorkshire, UK, MD6 4EQ

MUMBY, MISS EMMA JANE
[b.] 24 August 1979, Bradford, West Yorkshire; [p.] Mr. John Mumby and Mrs. Lesley Mumby; [ed.] Sierra Bernia - Spain Fielden Park College; [occ.] Student; [oth. writ.] One poem published in Spanish publication.; [pers.] I wrote (The Speed) after the death of a close friend, and helped me to grieve freely.; [a.] Manchester, Lancashire, UK, M21 7JG

MUNRO, ANDREW F.
[pen.] Andrew Andrew; [b.] 23 July 1954; [p.] George and Betty Munro; [m.] Widower (Renee); [ch.] Stepson Michael Bilkus; [ed.] Comprehensive School Kenfig Hill South Wales.; [occ.] Painter/Decorator; [memb.] Blackpool Christian Fellowship. (B.C.F); [hon.] 9 'O' Levels. 2 'A' Levels (Taken At night School); [oth. writ.] 1. Passionate in Time 2. Messengers From The North West 3. We Are His Hands 4. Broken Promises 2 - 3 - 4 are Christian Publication.; [pers.] I only started writing after my wife (Renee) died, in order to explain my feelings in grief. Then when I started going to church, (B.C.F) and found the Lord, I found I was writing more but with Jesus in mind.; [a.] Blackpool, Lancashire, UK, FY2 0XL

MURDOCH, GILL
[b.] 9 January 1971, Edinburgh; [p.] Keith Murdoch, Marisa Lincoln; [ed.] Craigmount High School Stevenson College (Edinburgh); [occ.] GP information services officer; [memb.] Royal Scott Leisure Club, Westfield Dance Studio; [oth. writ.] "Forgive Me Baby" published in earth works editor (Glenn Jones); [pers.] We are all made of the same flesh and blood, therefore we should not hurt each other.; [a.] Edinburgh, Lothian, UK, EH4 5NP

MURFITT, DAVID
[pen.] David Betty; [b.] 23 October 1943, Enneth; [p.] Claude Murfitt and Grace Murfitt; [m.] Betty Joy Murfitt, 27 February 1965; [ch.] Denise, Elizabeth, Mary Griffin, Kevin, William, David Murfitt, Andrew, David Murfitt; [a.] Wisbech, Cambs, UK, PE14 0AY

MURPHY, CAROLINE
[b.] 27 July 1982, Co. Limerick; [p.] Liam Murphy, Nora Murphy; [ed.] Kilcornan National School, Colaiste Mhuire, Askeaton; [occ.] Student; [memb.] Local Youth Club; [oth. writ.] Several poems and writings unpublished.; [pers.] I observe life in great detail and my poetry depicts every day life as seen from my perspective.; [a.] Askeaton, Limerick, UK

MURPHY, CHRISTOPHER
[b.] 18 December 1984, Norwich; [p.] Peter and Carole Murphy; [ed.] West Earlham First School moved up to West Earlham middle then up to Blackdale Middle; [memb.] School captain of football team. Member of the Salvation Army; [hon.] I have a lot of awards and certificate for sports. Eg. Cross Country, Football Man of Match twice, Athletics; [oth. writ.] Stories which I have written and have yet to have published.; [pers.] I enjoy writing stories and poems and also drowning pictures and carbon characters.; [a.] Norwich, Norfolk, UK, NR5 8SA

MURPHY, CHRISTOPHER
[b.] 3 July 1964, Derby; [p.] James and Patricia Murphy; [m.] Linda Carolan; [ed.] St. Ralph Sherwin, Duffield Rd., Derby, High Park College, Buxton; [occ.] Psychiatric Nurse; [oth. writ.] "The Shadow Dancers", "Carnival of Fears", "The Lost Prayer"; [pers.] I'd rather have a full bottle in front of me, than a full frontal labotomy.; [a.] Aughton, Lancashire, UK, L39 9EE

MURPHY, GED
[pen.] Ged Murphy; [b.] 21 February 1962, Wexford, Republic of Ireland; [p.] David Joseph Murphy, Mary Murphy; [m.] Nicola Murphy, 13 June 1992; [ch.] Alexandra Murphy, Melissa Murphy; [ed.] Christian Brothers School Wexford, Rep. of Ireland, Saint Andrews/Salford Manchester; [occ.] Representative London Taxi International; [hon.] Sales Techniques for Sales Representatives (at unipart house Oxford); [oth. writ.] 8 poems not published; [pers.]"Grandad's Farewell" was to comfort a few, but now has touched so many.; [a.] Middleton, Manchester, UK, M24 1JW

MURPHY, MRS. P. A.
[pen.] Patricia Ann; [b.] 12 March 1934, Bucks; [p.] Lily and Frank Matthews; [m.] Edward Murphy, 15 October 1955; [ch.] Keith, Brian, Steven, Glaine, Denise; [ed.] Slough High School; [occ.] Retired District, Nurse; [oth. writ.] "To Be A Mother" published in a local newspaper.; [pers.] I like to write about subjects prose or poetry about which I have strong feelings.; [a.] Bicester, Oxfordshire, UK, OX6 8FR

MURRAY, JOANNE P.
[pen.] Joanne P. Murray; [b.] 23 February 1980, Dublin; [p.] Peter and Noeline Murray; [ed.] Primary Ed. at Mount Amville P. School went at 12 years of age to Notre Dame des Missions Secondary Churchtown) 14 where 1 completed Junior Cert examination, now studying for leaving cert; [occ.] Student; [memb.] Member of Notre Dame Prize Winning Senior Choir which takes up a lot of my time; also a student of singing, piano and both descent and treble recorder for which I am currently sitting exams.; [hon.] Won 2nd prize for a poem about Easter, the following year when I was 2 I won 1st prize with a poem about "New Life" This was published in the Catholic Herald Standard and the Irish Catholic in June 1992. Won a medal for Descent Recorder; [oth. writ.] "Easte" (a poem about easte!) 'New Life' a poem about all the happenings in Spring for birth to "sometimes" death. I prefer to write about nature. If something suddenly hits me it sometimes inspires me as where my lovely Coez, Cindy died - that was very sad.; [pers.] I love nature and especially birdwatching which I get a lot of practice at in my large garden and at our house in the Hills of Donegal. I also love animals in general and have a Shih-tzu called Chloe, and are rescued cat called "Zazza" as he was always crying! And Mitzy a long haired grey cat; [a.] Dundrum, Dublin 14

MURRAY, ROBERTA ANNE
[b.] 18 March 1937, Gt Harwood; [p.] Mr. and Mrs. Robert James Murray; [ed.] Notre Dame Grammar School Blackburn from 5-16 yrs followed by Nurse Training at 18 yrs; [occ.] Retired Senior Nurse; [hon.] Registered G. N. and Reg. nurse mentally handicapped teaching diploma for teaching of mentally handicapped. Certificates for Elocution (in my teens); [oth. writ.] A few but only in a file, compiled for myself; [pers.] This is my very first effort at publication.; [a.] Rishton, Lancs, UK, BB1 4JY

MURRAY, WISDEAN F.
[b.] 8 December 1910, Rothesay; [p.] George and Jean Murray; [m.] Mary M. Smith, 19 February 1935; [ch.] Grace (Now Mrs. MacLennan); [ed.] Bonar-Bridge H.G. School St. Margaret's School, Cardiff Rothesay Academy Bennett College, Sheffield; [occ.] Teacher (Speech/Drama); [memb.] Fellow Cl Inst of Marketing London College Speech (Music) Director of Masque Theatre School; [hon.] M.B.E. (to Marketing and allow attitudes in Elaneal Industry) L.L.C.M. (Speech/Drama) F. Cl. Inst of Marketing; [oth. writ.] Play and sketch scripts for theatrical use.; [pers.] I adore simplicity in all forms, and tend to encourage care and kindness to all, irrespective of creed or colour.; [a.] Glasgow, Strathclyde, UK, G76 7PU

MUSSON, SARAH
[b.] 11 October 1976, Harborough, Magna; [p.] Rosalie Musson, Clifford Musson; [ed.] Bishop Wulstan RC High, Rugby High, Portsmouth University; [memb.] Portsmouth University Drama Society; [hon.] Media Studies BA (Hons); [oth. writ.] Another poem published in a local anthology of poets.; [pers.] Poetry is something very beautiful and very personal. It's a part of you on paper - it's emotion on paper.; [a.] Rugby, Warwickshire, UK, CV23 0TT

MYLONAS, MRS. ELENI
[b.] 5 May 1967, London; [p.] Memnon and Despina Ioannou; [m.] Alexander Mylonas, 6 April 1986; [ch.] Loucas and Memnon Mylonas; [ed.] London, England, Advanced Level Studies: English Literature, Sociology, Art, Business Studies; [occ.] Writer; [oth. writ.] Novels romantic fiction (publishers - avon books) titles: Attraction of Opposites, Trust and Betrayal, Pasts of Distinction, Precarious Predicaments, A Woman's Instinct.; [pers.] My inspiration is my dear husband Alec and the intense love that we share, for this has caused me to question many elements of life, for when one discovers something so special, one must treasure it always.; [a.] Nicosia, Cyprus

NAFEES, BEENISH
[b.] 11 November 1978, Pakistan; [p.] Mr. Nafees A. Siddiqui, Shaheda Siddiqui; [ed.] Queen's College, London A-Levels; [occ.] Student; [memb.] Old Queen's Society; [hon.] Queen's College Associateship was awarded in 1996. Deputy Senior Student of Queen's College; [pers.] Hope is perhaps the only continuous feeling in one's life. I try to express that potential of humanity, rekindling that hope in the hearts of mankind.; [a.] London, UK, W1M 7PP

NANU, IRINA-ROXANA
[b.] 16 January 1981, Bucharest; [p.] Dan Nanu, Julietta Nanu; [ed.] Gh. Lazar "National College, I'd like to sturdy (at University) Romanic Languages, Law, History and Biology; [occ.] Pupil (in College); [memb.] Member of the Romanian Archive Society". I'm not on my way to become a "Mensa" member; [hon.] Several prizes in history, biology (National Olympiades), several scholarships; [oth. writ.] Several history articles, which were published in anthologies, several articles about the unsolved mysteries of the world published in a school magazine.; [pers.] I try to reflect the real world we're living in. I have been influenced by our National Romantic Poet - Mihai Eminescu and by Oscar Wilde, my favorite poet.; [a.] Bucharest, Romania, 70711

NASH, MISS MICHALA LEE
[b.] 20 November 1971, Ponty Pridd, Mid-Glam; [p.] Mr. Edwin Nash and Mrs. Kay Nash; [m.] Mr. Wayne Parry (Fiance); [ed.] Educated at Treorchy Comprehensive School, Treorchy Mid-Glamorgan; [occ.] Psychiatric Care Assistant; [pers.] Dedicated to Mom and Dad who brought me into the world and to ones at Dunblane whose lives were tragically taken out.; [a.] Ton Pentre, Mid-Glam, UK, CF41 7AN

NEILSON, IAN ALAN
[b.] 9 April 1920, Scotland; [p.] Alan Neilson and Edith Neilson (Both Dec'd); [m.] Mary Elizabeth Neilson, 2 April 1955; [ed.] City of Norwich School, R.A.F College 1936-1939. R.A.F. 1936-1950; [occ.] Retired Farmer; [memb.] R.A.F. Club, Desert Air Force Assn., C.L.A. Assn.; [hon.] B.E.M (mil.), M.I.D (2); [oth. writ.] "El Alamein" to Halton magazine. "The Last Farewell" to the Eagle of the Glider Pilot Regt. Assn.; [pers.] I enjoy reading all poetry esp. Robert Burns, Thomas Hood, Robert L. Stevenson, Henry Longfellow.; [a.] Norwich, Norfolk, UK, NR16 1ES

NI CHOCHLAIN, FIONA
[b.] 22 January 1968, Dublin; [p.] Citi Ni Chochlain, Liam O. Cochlain; [ed.] Mount Anville Secondary School, St. Nicholas Montessori College; [occ.] Co-Owner of a Montessori School in Templeogue, Dublin; [memb.] Stillorgan Musical Company, Temple Tennis Club; [oth. writ.] First time to have anything published.; [pers.] Nature is a constant source of wonder and inspiration to me!; [a.] Templeogue, Dublin, UK, D6W

NICHOLLS, JULIAN
[b.] 7 May 1943, Penzance; [p.] A. W. and B. J. Nicholls; [m.] Jeanne, 1983; [ch.] Simon and Alison; [ed.] Secondary School; [occ.] Ex British Rail and Trinity House Corporation; [memb.] Royal British Legion, Llanelli R.F.C. Harborne Village Club and Institute.; [oth. writ.] "Penzance Boy" (Unpublished) a walk to Paschewdaele (unpublished) numerous poems four of which have been published.; [pers.] An exiled Cornishman who hopes to return to Cornwall soon. Has a great love of the sea having spent a number years seagoing also an interest in the first World War especially the Battles of Ypres.; [a.] Birmingham, West Midlands, UK, B17 9AH

NOLAN-SYNNOTT, CELINE A.
[pen.] C.A.N.S.; [p.] Mary C. Madden and Daniel O. Nolan; [m.] Garrett Nolan-Synnott, 17 June 1988; [ch.] Lucas G. Nolan-Synnott; [ed.] Our lady of the Assumption - College of Marketing and Design, Bonton St. College, University of Ireland, Teacher of Marketing Design; [occ.] Graphic Designer Dedicated Mother and Wife; [memb.] C.A.R.I. Foundation (Children at Risk in Ireland) Founder Director/Member Harolds Cross Musical Society; [hon.] Honours Medalist London Academy of Drama and Music - Irish College of Music Drama Examinations/medals, T.E.F.L. Teacher of English Media/Graphic Artist; [oth. writ.] Several poems presently writing a novel - articles for trade magazines.; [pers.] Poetry is expression from the soul. Enabling otherwise silent people, a voice. In my experience it has opened many hearts and bonded friendships.; [a.] Celbridge, Kiloare, Ireland

NOONAN, DAWN E.
[b.] 21 September 1957, Bracknell; [p.] John Best, Jean Best; [m.] Glenn Noonan (Deceased), 9 June 1984; [ed.] Earth Hill School Langley College; [occ.] Microfilm Jacketer; [hon.] City and Guilds of ladies hairdressing; [oth. writ.] I have had two poems published in 2 anthologies (1996); [pers.] I have written poetry since a child. A hobby I enjoy very much. Since the loss of my husband I have found a release for many emotions in my poems.; [a.] Bracknell, Berkshire, UK, RG12 9GH

NORRIS, EVELYN
[b.] 4 March 1933, Gateshead; [p.] Lily and Arthur Burgess; [m.] Edward Norris, 28 October 1950; [ch.] 6 Barbara, Michael, Lyn, Jenny, Thelma, Pauline; [ed.] Kelvin Grove Girls School Gateshead; [occ.] Office work for B.M.F. (British Motorcyclists Federation); [oth. writ.] Several unpublished poems written for fun; [pers.] I try never to be bored, and to use my imagination, to give pleasure to my family and friends.; [a.] New Malden, Surrey, UK, KT3 6QN

NURDIN, ERIC
[b.] 12 June 1938, Wigan; [m.] Margaret Derbyshire, 30 June 1962; [ch.] Stephen and Mark; [ed.] Secondary Modern; [occ.] Took early retirement after 30 years in a food factory; [oth. writ.] Short story published in a Northern Sunday Newspaper; [pers.] Relative newcomer to writing following a busy working life. Writing poetry comes easier than ideas for story writing. I haven't as yet discovered any true vocational direction to concentrate on.; [a.] Wigan, Lancs, UK, WN1 3XZ

O'BRIEN, DENNIS P.
[pen.] Ginger; [b.] 7 June 1929, Abercregan; [p.] Annie Maude and Thomas O'Brien; [m.] Etty O'Brien, 20 December 1952; [ch.] Christine, Patricia, Dennis John; [ed.] Cymmer Comprehensive School Nr Port-Talbot; [occ.] Bricklayer, retired; [oth. writ.] "Village Memories", "The Joy", "Short Winded", "Deep Sense Of Humour", "The Hangers On", "All Glued Up", "Imagination", "The Garden Wall", "Me And You", "The Humm", these are some of the poems that I have written, but have not been published; [pers.] My main ambition is to make people happy, despite my past experiences, especially in my writing.; [a.] Port Talbot, West Glamorgan, UK, SA13 3LE

O'SHEA, EVELINE PATRICIA
[pen.] Sister Ann-Marie; [b.] Ireland; [p.] Anne and Daniel O'Shea; [ed.] Convent School Tipperary, B.ED. Southampton, B.D. London, M.ED Exeter; [occ.] Primary School Teacher (Guernsey); [memb.] Member of Religious Community (Sisters of Mercy); [oth. writ.] Collection of humorous poems published in religious magazine; [pers.] I try to communicate feelings and emotions which are part of our common experiences.; [a.] Guernsey, Channel Islands, UK, GY1 1JH

OAKMAN, ANNE
[b.] 6 January 1978, Bletchley; [p.] Oliver Oakman, Margaret Oakman; [ed.] Aylesbury High School Maths, Physics and English Literature Agleves A-levels French A/S-Level; [occ.] Student at St. Andrews University Studying English Literature and Philosophy; [memb.] St. Andrews University Chorus Violin Player; [hon.] Books, Challenge '94; [oth. writ.] First published poem; [pers.] Writing and reading what others have written is the greatest pleasure I know.; [a.] St. Andrews, Fife, UK, KY16 9XW

OBASI, MARIA
[b.] 14 September 1983, London; [p.] John Obasi, Martha Obasi; [ed.] St. Thomas RC Secondary School; [memb.] France World (Pen-Pal Club), School Netball Club; [pers.] I hope to show truth in my work. I love poems about real life.; [a.] Woodgreen, London, UK, N22 6QU

OGENDAHL, ANNE
[b.] 6 January 1954, Denmark; [p.] Johannes and Bende Ogendahl; [m.] Erling Jan Sorensen (Fiance); [ed.] Copenhagen Commercial College (in English Commercial Correspondence and Literature); [occ.] Freelance copywriter; [hon.] 1996 International Songwriters Association (Limerick City, Ireland) Award for Achievement and Excellence in the field of Country Music, lyric writing of outstanding quality; [oth. writ.] 5 books in Danish (2 children's books and 3 humour books for adults), various short stories in Danish magazines, 2 poems in 'Hvedekorn' Danish poetry magazine; [pers.] Many of my poems reflect my interest in the questions of life and death in relation to time and space.; [a.] Vanlose, Copenhagen, Denmark, 2720

OGLES, LESLIE
[b.] 9 April 1951, London; [p.] James Ogles and Jennie Ogles; [m.] Dawn Ogles (Nee Hately), 15 September 1973; [ch.] Joanne Louise Ogles, Lorna Jayne Ogles; [ed.] Abbey Wood Comprehensive School; [occ.] Bus Driver; [oth. writ.] Various poems and humoureus essays (often inspired by events and family and friends); [pers.] I have various ideas at different stages of developments for short stories, plays and even a "sitcom". My ultimate aim is to of course write a novel. ("Lead the way..." was inspired by the recent sudden death of my mother).; [a.] London, UK, SE28 8NS

OGUN, DARE
[b.] 22 October, Owo, Nigeria; [p.] Caroline Bisi Ogun; [ed.] Imade College Owo University of Ife Nigeria; [occ.] Graphic Artist and Fashion Designer; [oth. writ.] Jesus in Colours - an anthology, when he divined - a short story; [pers.] I eagerly await my death hour and since death, the ripper has no form nor visage, and stalks on us all, I consider him an award.; [a.] London, UK, SE8 3AJ

OKAFOR, AMAZIGOM O. C.
[pen.] Ama Okafor; [b.] 25 August 1984, UCH, London; [p.] Mr. Nkemdilim and Mrs. Ngozika Okafor; [ed.] Stroud Green Pre-school, St. Aidan's Primary School, The Henrietta Barnett School for girls (current school); [memb.] Girl's Brigade, School Orchestra (violinist), Netball, Tennis, Hockey, Athletics, Football, School Choir, Basketball; [hon.] Associated Board for the Royal Schools of Music Awards - Grade 1 Violin pass, grade 2 violin - distinction - now studying grade 4, grade 1 piano - merit, studying grade 3, current

school Council Rep., Former School Charity Rep. Outstanding Athlete Award, Primary School Gold Certificate, Swimming Certificates, Girl's Brigade Certificates, and Barnet Science Challenge Certificate; [oth. writ.] Various poems and stories in class - Adolf Hitler, Vegetarianism and Meateating, Candy Land, The Wood, and others.; [pers.] 'Poetry is very much an enjoyable hobby for me, and I derive a lot of knowledge from it.' For the rest of the 'honors and awards' section, see the piece of paper attached to this form.; [a.] London, UK, N4 3RZ

OKAFOR, NWABUOGOCHUKWU N.
[pen.] Ogo Okafor; [b.] 21 March 1986, Royal Free Hospital, London; [p.] Mr. Nkemdilim and Mrs. Nigozika Okafor; [ed.] Stroud Green Pre-School, St Aidans Primary School, (Current School).; [memb.] Girl's Brigade, School - Orchestra, (Violinist), School Dance - Club Basket ball, Athletics, Netball, Football and School - Choir.; [hon.] Swimming Certificates (Junior Grade), School Gold Certificate and Former School Council Rep.; [oth. writ.] The tiny Ghosts, it's not fair, fake relationships, the magic wand, rain forests, Ho! Ho! Ho!, Floating, the cock shoe, tennis and red rose.; [pers.] "I love writing especially poems, and would like to write poems and stories for children as part of my hobby.";
[a.] London, UK, N4 3RZ

OKAFOR, OBIAGERI NWANNEKA
[b.] 13 July 1976, London; [p.] Benedette Okafor; [occ.] Student; [oth. writ.] I write short dramas which are not published. I wrote a few other poems too. All not published.; [pers.] I write on emotions and feelings and I very much like my work to look Shakespearean. I work very hard to produce the best I can because I believe that the highest reward is not what you get for your deed but what you become by it.; [a.] Tottenham, Haringey, UK, N15 4QT

ONIONS
[pen.] Betty; [b.] 5 November 1936, West Midland; [p.] Mr. and Mrs. Alfred Bray; [m.] Widow 1983, 5 November 1955; [ch.] Carol Ann and Paul Stephen; [ed.] Secondary Modern School for Girls; [occ.] Retired Handicapped (Care Assistant Worker); [memb.] Readers Digest Gothic Writing Poetry Local Library; [pers.] It takes 33 muscles to smile and sixty six to present- why overwork your muscles, make two people smile on a day.; [a.] Wilsford, Linconshire, UK

ORMROD, CHRISTINE
[b.] 30 January 1945, Bolton; [m.] Ronald, 4 April 1964; [ch.] Martin Phillip, Stephanie, Jane; [ed.] Secondary Modern School; [occ.] Security Officer; [memb.] Member of Bolton Writers Circle now Disbanded; [hon.] G.C.E. 'O' Level in English Literature taken at the age of 37; [oth. writ.] 3 poems published in books but no money received also in earlier years had a few poems published in Bolton evening news; [pers.] I find my own mood dictates my poetry most, although I have written personal poems for friends on a variety of subjects. I can recollect reading a book found in our box room at the age of about 8. I think I was hooked on poetry from then on. But only started writing in my early 20's.; [a.] Bolton, Lancashire, UK, BL3 4EW

ORRIDGE, ROLAND
[b.] 4 December 1919, Shirebrook, Derbyshire; [p.] John and Rose Edith Orridge; [m.] Constance Orridge (Nee Croucher), 7 February 1944; [ch.] Patricia Ann; [ed.] Dunscroft Boys Elementary School, S. Yorks; [occ.] Retired; [oth. writ.] "Thru the Itchens and Worthies"; [a.] Burnham-on-Crouch, Essex, UK, CM0 8LR

OSBALDESTON, PAULA
[pen.] Paula Osbaldeston; [b.] 27 February 1964, Manchester; [p.] Brenda Kelly and Dennis Kelly; [m.] Anthony F. Osbaldeston, 8 August 1987; [ch.] Sou-Ryan Francis/Daughter-Jordan Kelly;

[ed.] Failsworth Comprehensive Secondary School Oldum College of Technology - Art/Display/Design; [occ.] Housewife/Computer/Course/would be author; [hon.] Northwest Regional Certificate in Display/General Art and Design; [oth. writ.] Runner-up in children's story competition.; [pers.] I take great pleasure in writing, and hope to give others pleasure in reading it. My greatest influences are my children, and life itself.; [a.] Failsworth, Manchester, UK, M35 0WX

OSBORNE, PENNY
[b.] 24 September 1940, Leamington Spa; [p.] Harold Ward, Doris Ward; [m.] Ken Osborne, 15 June 1963; [ch.] Daniel, Darren, Andrew, Martin, Wayne, Kerry, Jason and Debbie; [ed.] Campion Secondary Modern; [occ.] Housewife; [memb.] British Printing Society; [hon.] Lady Printers of the Year 1985 (joint award with colleague); [oth. writ.] Several poems; [pers.] I believe that God is good and the devil a liar I write to uplift, encourage and inspire.; [a.] Royal Leamington Spa, Warwickshire, UK, CV32 5NG

OWENS, CLAIRE
[b.] 6 May 1978, Lanark; [p.] George and Joan Owens; [ed.] 1983-1990 Law Primary School, 1990-1996 Carluke High School, 1996-1998 Motherwell College Studying Childcare and Educations.; [pers.] Never underestimate your abilities and always strive to achieve your expectations.; [a.] Carluke, Lanarkshire, UK, ML8 5JG

OZKAN, OZLEM
[b.] 11 September 1983, Turkey; [p.] Mr. and Mrs. Ozkan; [ed.] Student At "Langham School"; [oth. writ.] Short stories; [pers.] I love reading and writing.; [a.] Tooterham, UK, NI5 4LL

PACKHAM, MISS ANNA
[b.] 27 April 1980, Guernsey; [p.] Mr. and Mrs Packham; [ed.] Blancmelande Girls College, and Grammar School, Guernsey; [occ.] Student at Grammar School; [hon.] Home Economics and Technology Cup., Science and Technology Cup., Science Cup., Duke of Edinburgh Bronze Award; [oth. writ.] One poem written for English Coursework; [pers.] For me poetry is like a river because it flows from the heart expressing deep emotion and meaning.; [a.] Guernsey, Channel Islands, UK, GY3 5DS

PAGE, MISS C.
[b.] 12 September 1974, Dartford; [p.] Gill and George Page; [ed.] Dartford Girls Grammar, Harlow College/Middlesex University (joint course); [occ.] Unemployed but I enjoy writing as much a I can; [hon.] HND Journalism, BA Writing and Publishing with a Minor in Politics; [oth. writ.] This is the first thing I have had published but I have written many things, such as a school pantomime which was all in rhyme; [pers.] I do not usually write poems in this style so it is a great boost for me to be good. I hope to write more and get more things published in the future; [a.] Rye, East Sussex, UK, TN31 7HJ

PAIN, GEORGE
[pen.] George Edward Pain; [b.] 29 October 1956, Sunderland; [p.] Audrey and Wallace Pain; [ed.] Grammar School, C.C.A.T.; [memb.] Mensa, Cambridge Union Society; [oth. writ.] Songetry, Six Sorgettes and an ode.; [pers.] I have tried to concentrate my creative endeavors on the task of creating a new poetic entry I.E. the songette.; [a.] Hull, UK, HU9 2AG

PAINE, MARGARET LUCY
[m.] Jim; [ch.] James and Stephen; [occ.] State Enrolled Nurse Working with elderly people; [pers.] I enjoy writing poetry and short stories, my work enables me to observe people in different situations and am able to take inspiration from this. "Hope" was written in memory of my late father.

PANK, MRS. KAY
[b.] 10 March 1948, London; [p.] Mr. J. W. Corby (Deceased), Mrs. S. M. Corby; [m.] Roy

Pank, 15 December 1969; [ed.] Kingsbury County, Grammar School NW9, Harrow Technical College; [occ.] Artist; [memb.] Royston Art Society; [hon.] Series of illustrations for local paper; [oth. writ.] Poems - some of which were published in the local paper.; [pers.] My poems reflect a conflict of emotions. Certain events will 'trigger' random thoughts that need to be coordinated.; [a.] Royston, Herts, UK, SG8 9BB

PANTLING, MISS CLARE LISA
[pen.] Miss Clare Lisa Pantling; [b.] 27 May 1977, Carshalton; [p.] Robert and Sandra Pantling; [ed.] Glenthorne High School for girls; [occ.] Unemployed; [hon.] I won a one star amateur Athletic Award; [oth. writ.] I've written some other poems but never have I sent any off.; [pers.] I've always worked to become a famous writer and at the moment I'm writing two books at the same time, it's very easy since I have loads of time on my hands, but I must admit it's very hard work. I write poems only so other people can enjoy them. My dream is to be a famous writer and to see it to suition.; [a.] Sutton, Surrey, UK, SM2 6TP

PAREKH, BHAV-NEETA
[b.] 12 September 1978, Wolverhampton; [p.] Mr. Kishan and Mrs. Shakuntla Parekh; [ed.] Colton Hills School, Wulfrun College; [pers.] I love every form of self-expression. Whether it be film, poetry or art, it is the most satisfying and enriching occurrence we will ever possess.; [a.] Wolverhampton, West Midlands, UK, WV11 1BZ

PARK, COLIN
[b.] 6 October 1946, Jesmond; [p.] Stanley Park, Mary Park; [m.] Brita Malmheden-Park, 17 April 1976; [ch.] Hanna Park, Jennifer Park; [ed.] Whitley Bay Grammar School, Coventry College of Education, University of Leicester, University of Birmingham; [occ.] English Teacher (VIth form Colleges) Gothenburg Education Authority; [memb.] Morgan owners group-Sweden, British Club-Gothenburg; [hon.] English Literature, Bachelor of Philosophy (Education): Applied Linguistics; [oth. writ.] Poems published in English school's poetry anthology; Translation work for the United Nations (Swedish to English); [pers.] I strive to portray meaningful human situations as I see them today and have great respect for the talents of contemporary poet/song writers-in particular, John Lennon and Paul McCartney.; [a.] Bramhult, Sweden, S507 33

PARKES, DENNIS
[b.] 4 March 1919, Springfield Dudley; [p.] James and Edith Elizabeth; [ed.] Compulsory State Education 5-14 yrs short term teen age College Night School; [occ.] O.A.P. now my important school days started just after Great War 1914-1918; [oth. writ.] Poems published Arrival Press (Peterborough) (P.I.B.I. Huntingdon now poetry in Print) (Hilton House) publishers (Norwich).; [pers.] Many jobs - factories, Blacksmith, railways, stone mines, Lorry driver etc. Road works, Lorry driving sets you round many things. I think compulsory state of education is the backbone of England, schools are fountains of education. Happy is the man who findeth wisdom.

PARKINSON, ROSINA E.
[b.] 23 December 1914, Brierley Hill; [p.] Joseph Price, Laura Price; [m.] Walter Parkinson (Deceased), 27 December 1937; [ch.] Jennifer Madeleine, Rosina Josephine, Victoria Bernadette, Sandra Judith; [ed.] Moor Street School; [occ.] Retired (previously a nurse, housewife and mother, play group leader); [memb.] Brierley Hill and District Society of Artists, Writers Group, Robin Woods Centre; [oth. writ.] Several poems published in local magazines.; [pers.] Over the years my poems and writings have reflected my interest in environmental conservation and ecology.; [a.] Stourbridge, West Midlands, UK, DY8 4TQ

PARSONS, DANIEL
[pen.] Monsoon Project; [b.] 15 August 1979, Watford; [p.] Maria Parsons, Colin Parsons; [ed.] St. Wilfrids 6th Form (Crawley); [occ.] Student; [oth. writ.] Articles for a school magazine; [pers.] Many of my poems are actually lyrics to songs that I write and play. In my writing I try to reflect my own personal feelings, and thoughts on modern life and its values.; [a.] Crawley, West Sussex, UK, RH10 3DB

PASHA, YASMIN
[b.] 14 March 1979, Carshalton; [p.] Yamin Pasha and Naheed Pasha; [ed.] GCSE's 1995 4A's (English language, double Science, History) 5A's (English Literature, German, Business Stud., Art, CDT and B (Maths) - Coombe Girl's School, Studying for 'A' levels in Biology, Chemistry and Physics; [occ.] Full time student at Wimbledon High, Mansel RD, Wimbledon SW19 4AB, going to read medicine next year.; [memb.] I am a member of Mensa and the Wimbledon Squash and Badminton Club; [hon.] I have received a special school prize for "Outstanding Achievement" in my G.C.S.Es; [oth. writ.] My event article about the Duke of Edinburgh's Silver Expedition was published in the school magazine.; [pers.] When I am moved or inspired by a real life situation I try to express this through my poetry and writing; I would also like to challenge the common misconception that modern scientists are not articulate enough to string two words together.; [a.] London, Surrey, UK, SW19 3DX

PATERSON, JILLIAN
[pen.] Bridgette Brackston; [b.] 9 January 1980, Dundee; [p.] Tom Paterson and Gina Paterson; [ed.] Rockwell High School; [occ.] School girl; [memb.] Taek Won Do, Girls Football Team, School Theatre Group; [hon.] International Black Belt, National Referee and Empire, Runner up for Pushkin Essay Prize, Modern Studied Individual Study Award 1995; [pers.] My poetry is based on true, honest and realistic feelings and is inspired by such poets as Iain Crichton Smith and Emily Dickenson.; [a.] Dundee, Scotland, DD3 6QH

PATTINSON, GILLIAN
[pen.] Trigger Mann; [b.] 5 November 1970, Wigton; [p.] Jack and Mary Pattinson; [m.] Kevin Holden; [ch.] Nikki, Lisa-Marie, Siann; [ed.] Nelson Thomlinson Comprehensive School; [occ.] Mother; [oth. writ.] Several Poems none of which I have sent to be published; [a.] Wigton, Cumbria, UK, CA7 9BP

PAUL, RUPAK KUMAR
[pen.] R. K. Paul; [b.] 29 October 1972, Barnet, London; [p.] Robin Paul, Mira Paul; [ed.] Christ's College Comprehensive, Warwick University, Leeds University; [occ.] Automotive Engineering Student, Leeds University; [memb.] Alfa Romeo Owners Club, BMW Drivers Club, Leeds University Union Motor Club, Leeds Science Fiction Society; [hon.] Maths, Physics, Chemistry, English A-levels, B Eng (hons) degree in Mechanical Engineering; [oth. writ.] Currently writing long novel and book on BMW 'Small Six Engines' (mechanical poetry, if you like). None published yet.; [pers.] I strive to diminish the apparently perceived gap between the arts and the sciences, creativity and engineering, humanity and machines...my writing often reflects the experiences of a lonesome drifter. I generally am inspired by great science fiction writers such as Aldous Huxley and Sir Isaac Asimou.; [a.] Finchley, Gt. London, UK, N3 2QP

PAWAR, MISS BINA
[b.] 3 May 1977, Barnet; [p.] Prem Pawar, Mala Pawar; [ed.] Copthall Girls School, Queen Elizabeth Girls School, Westminster University; [occ.] Studying Artificial Intelligence F/T; [memb.] East African Association and Anti Racist Alliance (ARA); [hon.] A levels Art and Business studies; [oth. writ.] Several poems and short stories published in local newspaper and magazines for teenage youth eg "More!", "Buss"!; [pers.] I feel life itself is just an illusion it may appear to be simple for some but for me personally it's never solid, it's crazy and hard and I reflect that in all my writings therefore life has inspired me a lot!; [a.] Finchley, Barnet, UK, N3 2AB

PEACOCK, SANDRA HELEN
[pen.] Helen Thomas; [b.] 2 June 1941; [p.] Dorothy Woodall, George Woodall; [m.] Stuart Peacock; [ch.] One; [ed.] Wilmslow School, Stockport Technical College, Halifax College of Further Education; [occ.] Company Director; [memb.] Special Constabulary; [oth. writ.] Two poems published in 1974; [pers.] Remember, we only rent the earth, and the Landlord is watching you.; [a.] Beaumaris, Gwynedd, UK, LL58 8UN

PEEL, DORIS MAY
[b.] Pensioner, Warwickshire; [p.] Deceased; [m.] Deceased, 10 August 1946; [ch.] George, Ted, Kathryn; [ed.] Comprehensive; [occ.] Retired; [memb.] Kenton Methodist Church Choir; [oth. writ.] Long-Way Home, first book, published 1995, also, poems in Poetry Festival, The Golden Realm of Poetry, poems printed in Kenton Methodist Church Magazine also an article.; [pers.] I like to share my poetry otherwise there is no point in writing.; [a.] Kenton, Middx, UK, HA3 9AS

PELIDIS, MARY
[pen.] Mary Pelidis; [b.] 4 February 1948, Gwelo, Rhodesia; [p.] Michael and Zaharoula; [ed.] Bulawayo Teachers College (Rhodesia); [occ.] T.O.E.F.L in Language Schools; [memb.] Sacristan's Guild of St. Paul's Anglican Church Athens; [oth. writ.] Poetry of a lighter/humorous nature.; [pers.] Give pleasure to both the reader and the listener by reciting not only my own poetry but that of the great "spirits" of this Art; [a.] Kaisariani, Athens, Greece

PERKINS, MAX
[b.] 16 February 1922, Canada; [p.] Lorimer Perkins; [m.] Margurite Perkins, 12 September 1947; [ch.] 4 Sons, 1 Daughter; [ed.] 1 year University 10 years Military Flying; [occ.] Retired; [memb.] "Adeiron Society for Practice of Philosophy" University of Calgary 2500 University Dr. NW T2N 1N4; [hon.] None known King's commendation for war service mid.; [oth. writ.] Various poems some couplings have lost or let go of various thoughts in rhyme over the years; [pers.] I try to record thoughts of things, seen, heard or that come to mind, May - be back in Canada by the time published; [a.] Worcester Park, Surrey, UK, KT4 8TF

PETERS, JANE NATASHA
[b.] 7 May 1980, Bath; [p.] Rob Peters, Karen Peters; [ed.] Ralph Allen School currently at: City of Bath College; [occ.] Part time waitress, hoping to become a physical education teacher; [memb.] City of Bath Athletic Club; [pers.] I have always been interested in poetry since I was very young, I strive to reflect my life and feelings in my writing. I have been greatly influenced by the greatest lyric poet W. B. Yeats.; [a.] Bath, NE Somerset, UK, BA2 2UE

PETERS, NATASHA
[b.] 25 October 1981, London; [p.] Judith Peters; [ed.] I am currently a year 10 student for my GCSE's at ADT College in Putney London; [memb.] The Press Pack Hola-la (penpal club) from the post office, From Newsround and the Radio Times.; [hon.] BT Challenge certificate of Achievement, UK Junior Mathematical Challenge 1995 Bronze certificate and the RSA Spell test Certificate; [oth. writ.] I have written various short stories and poems which have won prizes in competitions - but these are currently unpublished.; [pers.] I believe that every day is a gifted opportunity to laugh, to learn, to achieve, to make some happy, to be happy.; [a.] London, UK, W12 0PB

PETTY, LYNN
[b.] 9 May 1956, London; [p.] Charles and Caroline Petty; [ch.] Katie Leanne; [occ.] Company Secretary; [hon.] Currently Studying, BA Arts and Languages; [oth. writ.] Personal Pleasure Only; [pers.] Writing allows one to express their true self, who, would otherwise, remain silent.; [a.] Romford, Essex, UK, RM7 9PD

PHEE, GAIL M.
[b.] 15 June 1961, Glasgow; [p.] James Pike, Margaret Pike; [m.] Robert Phee, 20 January 1996; [ch.] Leanne, Donna, Craig; [ed.] Our Lady's High School Cumberland, Cumberland College of Commerce, University of Life; [occ.] Hygiene Assistant; [oth. writ.] Poetry privately gifted to friends and family; [pers.] I am influenced by my own personal experiences and share the pain and joy through my words.; [a.] Glasgow, Strathclyde, UK, G53 7JL

PHELAN, MICHELLE
[pen.] Corey; [b.] 23 May 1981, Kildare; [p.] Kieran and Elizabeth Phelan; [ed.] Presentation Secondary School Kildare; [memb.] Killcullen Canoeing Club, Bishopsland Youth Club; [pers.] I give much thought to death. Where will I go? Will my mind live on in blackness? Do I cease to exist altogether? What is the purpose of life? Why must we face life knowing of certain death?; [a.] Kildare, Co. Kildare

PHILLIPS, MARCIA
[b.] Exeter; [m.] Owen Phillips; [ch.] Barry, Kim (Girl), Gillian; [ed.] Mount St. Mary's Convent School, Exeter; [occ.] Ex-Nurse now severely disabled; [memb.] The Ehlers-Danlos Syndrome (Connective Tissue Disorder) Support Group; [oth. writ.] One small book of poems, namely, "Share my World", and a Book of Poems for Children, "In the Land of Children", collected and printed by friends, to raise money for the support group of my syndrome.; [pers.] I dedicate my winning poem to my four grandchildren, who fill my world with sunshine, and if I, with my poems, can bring light and enjoyment into the lives of others, then I am happy.; [a.] Exeter, Devon, UK, EX4 8NZ

PILCHER, SHERI ROSE
[b.] 15 March 1978, London; [p.] Maralyn and Bill Pilcher; [ed.] Brampton Manor and Barking Abbey Comprehensive School; [occ.] Business Enterprise undergraduate at Staffordshire Uni.; [a.] Eastham, London, UK, E6 3NB

PINNOCK, CLIFTON L.
[m.] August 1975; [ch.] Three; [occ.] Science Technician; [memb.] Open University Poetry Society; [oth. writ.] Poems on nature, love, spiritual matters and social aspects.; [pers.] I am an Afro-Caribbean and a Christian. I enjoy reading poetry and writing poems, particularly poems about nature and poems on religious themes. I would like to express my sense of fulfillment by sharing through my poems.; [a.] Birmingham, Staffs, UK, B43 7EJ

PIZZOCHERO, ELISABETTA
[pen.] Pizzochero; [b.] 29 November 1964, Genova; [p.] Fulvio Pizzochero, Adrian Fantini; [ed.] S. Dorotea High School, University of Genoa; [occ.] Italian Teacher, American International School in Genoa; [pers.] My poems usually reflect a bitter reality but there is always room for love and hope. I have been greatly influenced by the Italian Ermetic poets such as Eugenio Montale.; [a.] Genova, Italy, 16143

PLATT, LESLIE GEORGE
[b.] 30 May 1933, Exeter; [p.] Deceased; [m.] Hannah Theresa, 26 December 1955; [ch.] Three (all male); [ed.] Intermediate in Art and Crafts National Diploma in design. Newport and Swansea Art Colleges; [occ.] Retired; [memb.] NIL; [hon.] N.D.D. (Stained Glass Design); [oth. writ.] 1. "Memories" of An Evacuee (to be submitted for publication), 2. A "Two Part" series in the local press, celebrating some 50 years as an Evacuee to Wales. (Prime space), 3. Some Religious Articles.; [pers.] When I talk about myself, I find, that I am speaking on the merit and importance of others.; [a.] Swansea, West Glamorgan, UK, SA5 5DH

POLKEY, MARGARET JEANNE
[pen.] Margaret Jeanne Polkey; [b.] 18 January 1932, Barry; [p.] James and Dorothy Baker; [m.] William, 24 December 1976; [ch.] 3; [ed.] Sec/Modern; [occ.] Retired; [oth. writ.] None as yet but will continue to strive for inspiration; poem dedicated to my husband; [pers.] This poem sums up the love I felt for my husband when we first met and the love I still feel for him my favourite poets are Robert Burns and Tennyson; [a.] Barry, S. Glam, UK, CF62 9AY

POOLE, PAULINE JANICE
[pen.] Jan Poole; [b.] 29 February 1960, Lewisham; [p.] Geoffrey Basil Walker, Florence Walker; [m.] Graham Poole, 26 April 1980; [ch.] Carlene Elizabeth, Mark Alexander; [occ.] Lunchtime Supervisor Anglican "Lay" Minister; [oth. writ.] Poems/Prose published in "Midlands Verse 1992" Local Church Magazines and others; [pers.] A pen draws the depth of our souls, and the world lives on.; [a.] Sutton Coldfield, W. Mids, UK, B75 6BN

PORTER, JOAN
[pen.] Joan Porter; [b.] 22 February 1927, Newcastle; [p.] Robert Porter, Lilly Porter; [ed.] Hookergate Grammar School, College of Commerce Newcastle, Faculty of Astrological Studies; [occ.] Astrologer; [memb.] B.A.P.S.; [hon.] Diploma Faculty Astrological Studies and Diploma Mayo School Astrology; [oth. writ.] None - apart from writing thousands of daily and monthly horoscopes for radio and magazines.; [pers.] I am constantly attempting to understand the meaning of life and am deeply interested in alchemy and the possibility of the immortality of the soul.; [a.] Chopwell, Newcastle, Tyne and Wear, UK, NE17 7HE

POULSEN, JANET
[b.] July 3, 1945, Oxford; [p.] Mrs. Phyl, Mr. E. Seamons (Deceased); [m.] Married in July 1972, divorced twenty years later; [ed.] Tewin Water School for the Partially Deaf, Weiwyn Herts; [occ.] On Incapacity Benefit due to profound deafness and Meniere's disease and Tinnitus; [memb.] Various Associations for Hearing Disability, Tinnitus Association; [oth. writ.] When I was young. Published in Rhyme. Reason Editor Kerrie Pateman Page 72. Rushton Village Church Page 16 Anchor Poets from the South.; [pers.] I believe in peace, and in all that is good in people. I worked for as long as I was able, and now have time to think of all the things I could have learnt at school but didn't bother to do so.; [a.] Blandford Forum, Dorset, DT11 7RJ

PRESTON, LESLEY
[b.] 7 July 1968, Shipley; [p.] Harry Preston and Winifred Preston; [ed.] Nabwood Grammar; [occ.] Machine Setter; [memb.] Windhill Christian Fellowship; [pers.] This poem was written for my cousin in Australia but I also believe it reflects God's love for us. A perfect love.; [a.] Shipley, West Yorkshire, BO17 7PQ

PRICE, CHRISTOPHER NOEL
[pen.] Noel Christie; [b.] 24 September 1923, Cashel; [p.] Richard Price, Mary Price; [m.] Bernadette Connery, 15 November 1954; [ch.] Mary, Richard, Bernadette, Christine, Caroline, Terry, James, Jacqueline, Ryan Christopher; [ed.] National School Cashel, Christian Brothers Cashel; [occ.] Musician; [memb.] Cashel Pipe Band, Cashel Brass Band, Mick Dellahunty Dance Band, Cashel Operatic and Pantomime Society; [hon.] "Shadows in the Moonlight" Played on the B.B.C. Cashel-Nat Ri, The old Candle-light played on Tipperary Mid. West Radio; [oth. writ.] "Listen as Angels Sing", "One Hour With Me", several songs featured with Cashel Panomime Society.; [pers.] Words are but voices of the mind, actions are a living proof.; [a.] Cashel, Tipperary, Ireland

PRICE, GRAHAM WILLIAM
[pen.] Cudmore; [b.] 13 January 1933, South Wales; [p.] George and Gladys Price; [m.] Pamela Yvonne; [ch.] Lawton; [ed.] Cowbridge Grammar School, Swansea University, London School of Economics and Political Science; [occ.] Managing Director Cudmore Associates; [memb.] Cardiff Country Club, Cardiff Ruaby Club Welsh Academicals; [hon.] BSC (Econ) Hons. Post Graduate Diploma Business Studies, Ford Trust Scholar University Colours Boxing; [oth. writ.] 1. Co-Author Superfit for Business, 2. Computopia in Across the Universe; [pers.] I carefully study the impact of computer/telecommunication technology or social mores.; [a.] Ross-on-Wye, Herefordshire, UK, HR9 6DD

PRICE, MICHAEL
[b.] 20 April 1958, Snow Lake, Canada; [p.] Derek and Vicki Price; [m.] Lyn Price, 25 June 1983; [ed.] Kings College, Worcester, Newbury Technical College, Newbury; [occ.] Sales Manager, Finance Company; [memb.] Mensa; [hon.] Several Awards for Public Speaking; [oth. writ.] Poems published in various books and local papers, books include "The Way We Were" and "First Time Out"; [pers.] If all you see is practicality, you will never experience the bliss, and the pain, of poetry.; [a.] Hungerford, Berks, UK, RG17 9QA

PRIOR, TINA
[b.] 16 March 1976, March, Cambs; [p.] Brian and Gloria Prior; [ed.] Cromwell Community College, Chatteris.; [occ.] Chef; [hon.] Project Trident Gold Award.; [oth. writ.] Several poems published in local anthologies.; [pers.] English was never my strong point at school. I tried too hard. Writing comes from the heart, not the head.; [a.] Chatteris, Cambs, UK, PE16 6SX

PROUT, STEPHEN
[b.] 26 November 1968, London; [p.] Malcolm and Jill; [m.] Denise, 13 July 1996; [ed.] Leon School, Bletchley, Milton Keynes; [occ.] Accountant; [memb.] Member of Association of Accounting Technicians; [oth. writ.] Articles for Union Magazine; [pers.] Being an accountant is not all figures, figures, figures you know - I would like the opportunity to forward other work.; [a.] Milton Keynes, Bucks, UK, MK14 6BJ

PUMMELL, LEONORA JANE
[pen.] Jessika Jones; [b.] 19 June 1974, Harrogate; [p.] Fay Pummell, Derek Pummell; [ed.] Belmont-Birklands School, Harrogate, St. Aidan's and St. John Fisher's Associated Sixth Form, Harrogate; [occ.] Unemployed; [memb.] The Guild of International Songwriters and Composers, Independent Film Workshop; [pers.] When I write, it is a reflection on my state of mind at the time and if I were to pick up a pen and write at this moment a different style would occur.; [a.] Harrogate, North Yorkshire, UK, HG1 4QF

QUANT, ALMA
[b.] 8 July 1934, Newark-on-Trent, Notts; [p.] John and Ivy Quant; [m.] Divorced, 29 March 1958; [ch.] 2, Boy Mitchell, Girl Lynnette now 3 grandchildren and 1 great grandchildren; [ed.] I had little education and always in B. Class Newark - Mount School - (C of E); [occ.] All life - (working time) nurse/welfare officer in civil life and military; been sick - in hospital 1 year in Germany will not return to work - Osteoporum; [memb.] None in writing world- sports clubs, German clubs, cooking clubs, before illness; [hon.] Only for hobbies learning German and the people sports, cooking; [oth. writ.] Many at home only - letter writing is my hobby and fantasy. For me writing is an escape from this hectic world and pain.; [a.] Detmold, Germany, 32758

QUARTERMAN, ELIZABETH ANN
[b.] 9 July 1963, London; [ed.] St. Mary and St. Joseph School Sidcupikent, Charing Cross and Westminster Medical School; [occ.] Obstetrician; [pers.] "We are God's work of art, created in Christ Jesus to live the good life as from the beginning he meant us to live it". (St. Paul, Ephesians 2:10)

QUIBELL, DOROTHY
[b.] Rotherham; [occ.] Retired; [oth. writ.] One poem previously printed. Try to reflect a touch of humour.

QUINN, JULIE ANNE
[pen.] Amber Avalon; [b.] 16 October 1964, Halifax; [p.] Glynis, John Brian Quinn; [m.] Andrew Mark Carson who I love to bits living together thirteen years.; [ch.] Christopher Carson/James Carson; [ed.] Olevel, Batley Art College to Study Design. I didn't go back for my exam results, I guess I should, shouldn't I!; [occ.] Made redundant due to form going down. I'll find something else.; [memb.] Since a young child I've always known that I was and still am sphylic, I see ghosts and my dreams come true as well as my visions, "Although I cannot control them I wait for them to happen and write it all down."; [hon.] This to me is an Honour! As a young child I was visited by three fall Angels, they told me not to be afraid and to just listen to what they have to say. I now have a very strong feeling to spread the word!; [oth. writ.] Poems-" Living In The Nineties", "Evergreen", "Hot Summer's Day", "See His Face", "My Three Tall Angels",these are some of the unpublished poems: I have hundreds.; [pers.] I'm yet an unknown author of poetry, my aim is to have a best selling 'true' novel published within two years; I can dream! And try! I've written and illustrated three young children's books, I've yet to try and get them published, as well as a large book of my poems for grown ups.; [a.] Huddersfield, UK, HD3 4QT

RABBAGE, ANN
[pen.] Rebecca Beer; [b.] 4 April 1932, Exeter; [p.] Win Passmore, Reg Passmore; [m.] Walt Rabbage, 15 January 1985; [ch.] Lyndar Lesley, Nigel and Elaine; [ed.] Convent Ilfracoombe, St. Hilda's and Edfertun House Exeter; [occ.] Housewife, trained Window Dresser and later nursed Langdon Hosp. 18 years.; [hon.] Owing to family crisis I left school begun school cert. but daughter Lesley Kermond managed Gilton College Cambridge from Exeter Tec. College. B.A. 1972 also Mastery Arts -London School Economics 1986; [oth. writ.] Several short stories and a collection of poems (started writing at the age of twelve) now able to devote more time to it.; [pers.] Having loved poetry all my life, Lord Byron my idol in my youth. To me poetry is beauty, it puts the soul back into today's sad and middle world.; [a.] Dawlish, Devon, UK, EX7 9NF

RADESTOCK, SHEILA JANE
[b.] 27 May 1937, Hoylake, Wirral; [p.] Harold and Florence Marriott; [m.] Edward Radestock, 27 March 1973; [ch.] Georgina, Andrew, Claire and Granddaughter Emma; [ed.] Hoylake Parade School; [occ.] Housewife; [oth. writ.] Poems - "Lost Memories", "Eternal Love", "Birth, A Mothers Love"; [pers.] I dedicate my poem to my beloved father and mother who taught me to have compassion for others without regard to race or religion "There but for the grace of God go I" sadly my mother died in July 1996. But I know they would have been so proud.; [a.] Hoylake, Wirral, Merseyside, UK, L47 2DB

RAFEEQ, ASIMA
[pen.] Bic Medium; [b.] 16 July 1981, Stoke-on-Trent; [p.] Mohammed Rafeeq, Khailda Rafeeq; [ed.] My last year at Birches Head High School, I am planning to go to college to study law and English and maybe art; [oth. writ.] I am writing a story about myself, It is called "My Diary", it will include everything what I have done in past recent years.; [pers.] I strive to reflect the goodness of mankind in my writing. I have been greatly influenced by the imaginative poets.; [a.] Stoke-on-Trent, UK, ST1 4PS

RAGHEI, AMENA
[pen.] Me; [b.] 5 March 1976, Washington, D.C.; [p.] Janet Bikowski and Hadi Raghei; [ed.] Primary and middle education at the Arabic School in Vienna, High School at Vienna International School, Vienna, Austria; [occ.] Student at University of Vienna (Psychology Major/English Minor); [hon.] Received Honorable Mention in Emerson College Creative Writing Competition, June 1994. There were 25 Honorable mentions out of 540 entries.; [oth. writ.] Some of my poems were printed in my high school paper.; [pers.] I cannot say just where my life has led me. Perhaps I have not lived long enough to tell, perhaps I simply have not died to know.; [a.] Vienna, Austria, A 1190

RAINEY, RACHEL
[b.] 6 March 1967, Killyleagh; [p.] Ivy Morrison, James Morrison; [m.] Henry Stephen Rainey; [ch.] Robert Thomas, Phillip James; [occ.] Civil Servant; [oth. writ.] Several poems published in poetry now anthologies.; [pers.] I hope my poetry conveys feelings and emotions which the reader can identify with. Wordsworth has been the greatest poetic inspiration to me.; [a.] Killyleagh, Down, N Ireland, BT30 9PT

RANDALL, GILLIAN
[b.] 12 June 1944, Worthing; [m.] Brian Randall, 2 October 1975; [ch.] Daniel Alexander and Gemma Leanne; [ed.] Ickenham Technical College, Middlesex; [occ.] Sales Advisor; [memb.] No club membership - but member of congregation of Jehovah's Witnesses; [hon.] Aged '5' won my first poetry prize - aged '11' - Essay award for County. As adult - several awards for different poems.; [oth. writ.] Poetry in school and local magazines printed - and a few newspaper articles - plus one poem enacted by local theatre group in variety show.; [pers.] I really enjoy writing personal odes for people when having special events in their lives - giving a little joy is a real bonus on both sides.; [a.] Wells, Somerset, UK, BA5 1TT

RAVENSCROFT, FRANK
[b.] 17 June 1922, Preston; [p.] William and Alice Ravenscroft; [m.] Olga Claire Ravenscroft (Deceased), 11 May 1946; [ch.] Barbara, Bryan, Robert, Frances, Jacqueline; [occ.] Retired Computer Service Engineering Manager; [oth. writ.] Numerous poems and works of prose, novels and manuscripts for TV and stage, illustrated children's books. None published to date.; [pers.] My writings reflect my environment and life in general - sentiment and reality.; [a.] Leyland, Preston, Lancashire, UK

RAVEY, BARRY LESLIE
[pen.] Barry Leslie Ravey; [b.] 10 September 1946, Chesterfield; [p.] Leslie Ravey, Dorothy Ravey; [m.] Wife - Marie Anne Ravey, 29 October 1977; [ch.] Wayne, Tina, Joanne, Laura, Ronald; [ed.] The Manor Central School Comprehensive, Saltergate, Chesterfield Derbyshire; [occ.] Caretaker, Winwick Road Collegiate Institute, Warrington; [oth. writ.] Several poems published in H.M. forces magazines in Germany whilst serving in Royal Engineers from 1964 to 1983, (regular army); [pers.] I just enjoy writing poems, mainly to bring enjoyment and laughter and sometimes serious feelings and emotion into people's lives. I was influenced earlier in my life by my father, Leslie.; [a.] Warrington, Cheshire, UK, WA2 9PD

RAWSON, MICHAEL
[b.] 21 February 1969, Hereford; [p.] W. E. and E. M. Rawson; [ch.] Daniel, Kane and Theo; [ed.] Bishop De Hereford's Bluecoat School; [occ.] Valet; [memb.] MENSA; [oth. writ.] I write songs and poems purely for my own pleasure but have often dreamed of so doing for a living.; [pers.] My hope is that by writing from the heart, my work glorifies God and speaks to all who read it.; [a.] Hereford, Herefordshire, UK, HR4 9TY

RAY, JULIA A.
[b.] 17 March 1941, Nantwich; [p.] Edward and Annie Griffiths; [m.] Trevor Ray; [ch.] Rosalind, James, Lorraine and Andrea; [ed.] Bunbury Girls School, Cheshire; [occ.] Assistant Secretary, Leading Health Care Charity; [oth. writ.] Currently completing "Anthony" based on events of lives of grandchildren.; [a.] Wrexham, Flintshire, UK, LL12 9EE

RAYNER, MELANIE
[b.] 10 November 1979, Barnet; [p.] Janet and Gerald Rayner; [ed.] Hillside School, Borehomwood Oaklands College; [occ.] A level student, part time weekend job at local Tesco; [memb.] Hillside V19's Girls Basketball Team; [oth. writ.] I had another poem published when I was 14 in the "Hertfordshire Young Writers Regional Anthology."; [pers.] My poetry reflects my own personal feelings. In my recent poem "Granddad" I wrote down my memories and feelings of my Granddad and how much I miss him.; [a.] Borehamwood, Hertfordshire, UK, WD6 5LQ

RAZAQ, MR. YASAR
[b.] 6 January 1977, Walthamstow; [p.] Mr. Abdul Razaq, Miss Irshad Razaq; [m.] Miss Sarwat Darr, August of next year (97); [ed.] Warwick Boys School, sir George Monour College; [occ.] Student and Manager/Business Director for A and R Tailors Ltd.; [memb.] Wing Chung King Fuu (a form of martial arts); [oth. writ.] I have many other writings, none of which have been published. I write many poems to my wife to be.; [pers.] My poetry describes my feelings about life. I write about love, hate, life, death etc. however most of my poetry is about love, and my wife to be gives me all the inspiration I need.; [a.] Walthamstow, London, UK, E17 9JG

READER, DEBBIE
[b.] 21 July 1973, Wimbledon; [p.] Pat and Ken Reader; [pers.] I wrote this poem for my boyfriend Gary Worsford at the beginning of our relationship, and with his love and understanding I am growing more secure and confident every day, thanks Gary, I love you.; [a.] Moroen, Surrey, UK, SM4 4JW

REECE, HELEN
[b.] 7 January 1954, Eccles, Manchester; [ed.] Sale Grammar School, University of York BA Hons Music; [occ.] Director of Music Hinchingbrooke School; [memb.] Cambridge University Musical Society (CUMS); [pers.] I am primarily a Musician - composer, pianist, singer. However, I have also been expressing my feelings through poetry since I was eight years old. I drive to work along the stretch of the AI described in my poem and I have felt deeply moved by the transformation of the countryside into a village four-lane motor way.; [a.] Sawtry, Cambs, UK

REED, CAROLINE
[b.] 17 August 1980, Ascot; [p.] Sally Reed and Tony Reed; [ed.] The Woodroffe School, (Lyme Regis, Dorset); [occ.] Full time student; [memb.] Taoist arts, organization, DCC Life Class, Lyme Regis Film Society; [oth. writ.] None other published; [pers.] Poetry relieves the feelings, touches the senses and involves the mind.; [a.] Dalwood, Devon, UK, EX13 7EG

REES, RACHEL L.
[pen.] Rachel L. Rees; [b.] 25 November 1981, Carmarthen; [p.] Malcolm Rees and Susan Rees; [ch.] Gerwin and Kelly.; [ed.] Currently studying for G.C.S. E's in: English, Eng. Lit. Maths. Science. Business Studies, History, R.E. Tex-

tiles.; [occ.] Still in school (secondary); [memb.] International Library of Poetry; [hon.] Of course my poem being published in "Jewels of The Imagination" but also awards for other poems and certain achievements in school, such as effort grades, awards for different sports representing the school and also good grades in Exams!!!; [oth. writ.] Several poems at new to public in newspapers, churches, schools and on special occasions i.e.- Christmas I always give out my own poems and writings to special people, and have recently started to give my own poetry book.; [pers.] Many people have influenced me in my life. I feel strongly about racism so people like Martin Luther King,Jr. have helped to bring my feelings out in writing. The world and people around me helped to express my thoughts so people can listen and understand what I am saying.; [a.] Milford Haven, Pembrokeshire, UK, SA73 3NW

REEVE, JEAN
[pen.] Louise Roach; [b.] 23 August 1948, Greenwich, London; [p.] Mr. and Mrs. Roach; [ch.] 2 boys aged 20 and 24; [ed.] Secondary - started work at 16 at Junior S/H Typier worked my way up to Secretary; [occ.] Student with a part-time job; [oth. writ.] One Christian Poem published in a Christian poetry book. Acted out one poem I wrote while doing a drama course - it was a funny poem.; [pers.] We've only got one life - don't blow it, there are no second chances. Nobody's perfect, we all make mistakes, especially me!; [a.] Lowestaft, Suffolk, UK, NR32 2DQ

REEVE, JOYCE D. M.
[b.] 28/9/19, Norwich; [p.] James Edward Reeve & Ethel Annie Nee Leftley; [ed.] Blyth Secondary School, Norwich; After Retirement, I have achieved the following 1) LTCL (Piano Teaching) 2) "A" level Art & Design [occ.] Retired BT Higher Evecutive Officer/Piano Teacher (Private); [memb.] Music-EPTA (European piano teachers assn), ISM (International Society of Musicians), Art-Peterborough Art Society (Committee Member), Huntingdonshire Art Society, Society of Amateur Artists, Poetry Club, Mountain Ash; [hon.] International Society of Poets - Editor's Choice Award 1996, Poetry Club - recommended for chartered poet-1996, commendation-Illustrated Poet of the Year-1996; [oth. writ.] Several poems published locally in magazines. [pers.] I write about current situations and historic subjects which have influenced them. I believe there is much we can learn from past experiences. I am optimistic about the often hidden human goodness in ordinary people.; [a.] Peterborough, Cambridgeshire PE4 7RY

REID, ALLAN
[b.] 15 October 1958, Buckie; [p.] Alexander and Norma Reid; [m.] Irene, 3 April 1981; [ch.] Kerry and Allan; [ed.] Buckie High School; [occ.] Nightshift worker in local factory. (Was in the Gordon Highlanders for 13 years); [oth. writ.] Have written over 200 poems, wrote to Yonkly magazine for a year and have entered only one other competition.; [pers.] I don't read other peoples poetry and write for the pleasure and nothing else. My wife and kids read my poems before I put them away into an old briefcase. I write in different styles and class myself as an abstract poet. I will be buying the book in the near future.; [a.] Portknockie, Buckie, Banffshire, UK

REID, JAMES
[pen.] James Reid; [b.] 29 January 1950, Johnstone; [p.] George and Eliz Reid; [m.] Ann Reid, 13 October 1971; [ch.] Richard, Colin, Annette, Janice; [ed.] Faifley Primary School, Clydebank High School, Clydebank College; [occ.] Engineer; [memb.] Former S.F.A. Referee (grade five), A.E.E.U. Crucible Snooker Club; [oth. writ.] Several poems published in local magazine poems read on nearby radio station, playette performed; [a.] Clydebank, West Dunbartonshire, UK, G81 4JX

REID, WAYNE R. J.
[pen.] Ribsy; [b.] 11 May 1965, Romford; [p.] Alice; [m.] Tara Shrimpton (Fiancee); [ch.] Sian, Christina, Jordan; [ed.] Harrow Lodge, Hornchurch Barking College, Romford; [occ.] Nightshift Foreman; [oth. writ.] Catalogue of over 140 original songs and poems; [pers.] I write because I can, it would be nice to think it made a difference.; [a.] Romford, Essex, UK, RM7 0DU

RENWICK, LEONARD GEORGE
[b.] 14 February 1927, London; [p.] Frederick George Renwick and Lilian Charlotte Renwick; [m.] Patricia Susan Renwick, 20 June 1953; [ch.] Jane Markscheffel; [ed.] Galleywall Road School, Bermondsey, London; [occ.] Garage Proprietor, (Retired); [memb.] Billericay Arts, Association Writers Workshop, Vice President and Member of Billericay Rugby Football Club; [hon.] Chairman and Later President (3 yrs.) of Romford and District Chamber of Commerce; [oth. writ.] Several poems, short stories and a novel, so far not entered for publication.; [pers.] I hope that one day my work will give as much pleasure in the reading as it has given me in the writing.; [a.] Basildon, Essex, UK, SS16 5RB

REYNOLDS, MRS. JEANNETTE
[pen.] Jeannette Downing; [b.] 27 June 1955, Birmingham; [p.] Raymond and Lillian Downing; [m.] Michael Reynolds, 4 August 1973; [ch.] Marc Jennifer Cherie; [ed.] Moseley Modern Secondary School Birmingham; [memb.] Hostess to French Students, Volunteer Assistant to Pre School children, Volunteer Helper, YMCA, Club Country-Western line dancing; [hon.] Swimming Certificate; general certificate of Secondary Education; [oth. writ.] Several poems, published in local paper; [pers.] The poem I wrote "Our Rose Garden" is dedicated to my father, whom I loved deeply and was never to busy to talk and listen to me I would be very happy to see people be kind and talk and listen to each other. It loses nothing and means a lot, especially listen to what children have to say, not just adults; happiness for me as a child was being listened to.; [a.] Redditch, Worcs, UK, B98 9HU

RICE, MARGARET A.
[pen.] Maggie; [b.] 21 February 1944, Somerset; [p.] Kenneth and Jean Maxwell; [m.] Raymond D. Rice, 6 August 1966; [ch.] Andrew and Nicola Rice; [ed.] Bishop Fons Grammars Taunton School, Rachel McMillan Training College London, University of Illinois USA; [occ.] Lecturer in early years education; [memb.] National Children's Bureau, London; [hon.] Master's degree in Early Childhood Education 1971, USA; [oth. writ.] Educational articles and papers. NCB Partnership Paper. 1985.; [pers.] I have been writing poems since the early 60's. I made a decision in 1993 to spend more time on my 'creative' side and make time to 'sketch', write children's stories and share my poems.; [a.] Tiverton, Devon, UK, EX16 4HZ

RICHARDS, JEAN ALICE REBECCA
[b.] 13 May 1930, London; [p.] Harriet Emma and Edward Joseph Richards; [ed.] Wales and London; [occ.] Retired (Banking); [memb.] I.Q. Bankers Association (Now Retired); [pers.] In my lifetime, I may not accomplish renown or acclaim, but what a wonderful "feel good factor" inside myself to be able to create again.; [a.] Cardigan, Dyfed, Wales, UK, SA43 3AX

RICHARDSON, NICOLA JAYNE
[pen.] Nicola Jayne Richardson; [b.] 23 December 1962, Kendal, Cumbria; [p.] Ralph, Marjore Parr; [m.] Philip Richardson R.A.F, 22 May 1992; [ch.] Michael (15), Danie (12), Chloe (3); [ed.] Lakes School Windermere Lancaster College (Hairdressing) Carlisle College (Psychology); [occ.] Shop Assistant Sports Shop; [oth. writ.] I have had several other poems published in various anthologies.; [pers.] People should respect the earth.; [a.] Brampton, Cumbria, UK, CA8 1BT

RIELLY, MICHAEL JOHN
[pen.] Scottish Mick; [b.] 27 December 1958, Glasgow; [occ.] Early Retirement through illness.

RILEY, DOUGLAS
[b.] 1 October 1942, Aberdeen; [p.] Janice Riley, Philip Riley; [m.] Elizabeth Alexandria; [ch.] Gordon Douglas and Elaine Elizabeth; [ed.] Aberdeen College and "The University of Life."; [occ.] PSU Driver and Traveller Among Folk.; [pers.] Momentary jewels I see, within Nature's, wider, cluttered sphere. Awakens my mind, and pen - hopefully - for all to eternity.; [a.] Aberdeen, Aberdeenshire, UK, AB25 2RS

RIMINGTON, ADRIAN B.
[b.] 21 November 1956, Chesterfield; [p.] Albert Rimington, Muriel Rimington; [ed.] Middlecroft County Secondary, University of Life; [occ.] Retired Ex-financial Consultant; [memb.] Church of England, Full Gospel Business Men's Fellowship International, Christian Research Association; [hon.] Dip. M.A.M.S.A Managing and Marketing Sales Association; [oth. writ.] "The Anthology of a Busy Life" slim volume awaiting publication.; [pers.] Do what you enjoy or love, and should you get paid, then that is even better!; [a.] Chesterfield, Derbyshire, UK, S40 4XD

RING, IRENE
[b.] 11 June 1926, Owinby; [p.] Mr. and Mrs. Brooks; [m.] 1943; [ch.] Maureen, Adrin; [ed.] Mkt. Rasen Secondary Modern; [memb.] Garden Club, Charity work for local Hospice and Cancer; [oth. writ.] Our World, The Time of Year, About God, 2 Prayers; I am now writing a story about my village.; [pers.] I love doing poetry; it is a great hobby. I also do flower arrangements for weddings and other things.; [a.] Lincoln, Lincolnshire, LN4 1NN

ROBERTS, ALISON MICHELE
[pen.] Ali Roberts; [b.] 4 March 1967, Shrewsbury; [p.] Michael George, Susan George; [m.] Alan Douglas Roberts, 23 September 1989; [ch.] Daniel Edward, William Charles; [ed.] Harlescott County School Shrewsbury, Shropshire; [occ.] Housewife and full-time mother; [memb.] Marilyn Lives Society, A club dedicated to the memory of Marilyn Monroe; [oth. writ.] I have had two other poems. I enjoy writing short stories. I am currently working on a fictional story about Marilyn Monroe, of whom I am a big fan; [pers.] I do not believe there is a good or a bad poem. They are as good or bad as the reader thinks they are. I personally like simple, easy to understand rhyming poetry.; [a.] Amesbury, Wiltshire, UK, SP4 7QE

ROBERTS, JOHN ADAM
[pen.] Adam Roberts; [b.] 5 February 1964, Clapham, London; [p.] Mrs. E. V. Roberts, J. S. Roberts; [ed.] Welshpool High School, Powys Wales. Morley College, Lambeth London. Roehampton Institute, Wandsworth, London; [occ.] Psychology Undergraduate Yr. 1; [memb.] Pending member of student psychological society.; [hon.] Access distinction (London Open College Federation) in psychology anthropology; [oth. writ.] Personal unpublished poetry portfolio; [pers.] You're only here once and not for a trial run, so get in there and succeed!; [a.] Tooting, Wandsworth, London, UK, SW17 9NE

ROBERTSON, GORDON S.
[b.] 27 June 1969, Falkirk; [p.] David Robertson, Jean Robertson; [ed.] Graeme High School, Falkirk Falkirk College of Technology; [occ.] Insurance Clerk; [oth. writ.] Published by poetry now.; [pers.] In life, always remember: The menu is not the meal.; [a.] Glasgow, UK, GS1 1QB

ROBINSON, CYRIL
[b.] 12 April 1926, Preston, Lancs; [p.] Thomas and Helen Robinson; [m.] Eileen, Mary Robinson, 22 December 1947; [ch.] Ann - Julie, Thomas, Sylvia, Daniel, Mary; [ed.] Scholar of Theology 9 papers; [occ.] Retired; [hon.] Med-

als Awarded for service at sea in the MN. Ten papers of a twelve paper scholar of theology degree at Wycliffe College Toronto; [oth. writ.] My Everest as yet unpublished only completed this year." Frighten The Bear Away Daddy"; [pers.] My Everest is an autobiography it tells about my life on the form running away to sea being struck down by polio. Emigrating to Canada, becoming an Anglican I was unable to complete the degree because of illness, infections, epitites. The degree course was discontinued and I was unable to complete. I came back to England in 1967 and became a Probation Officer. Later I was offered the position of senior youth leader at the Mayflower Family started by David Shepherd now Bishop of Liverpool. The Mayflower is in the East end of London. I was only fourteen when I ran away to sea. The war had just started. I was in the Malta Convoys as well as the Atlantic and other squares of war. I was only 11 when my father died my mother died shortly after I was born. I have no conscious memory of my mother. I was put on a farm when my father died and had to work from 6 AM to eleven for a summer.; [a.] Preston, Lancashire, UK, PR2 1US

ROBINSON, DAVID
[b.] 2 January 1995, Newcastle upon Tyne; [p.] Raymond and Mary Robinson; [m.] Ann Bernadette Robinson, 21 July 1990; [ch.] Gordon, Katherine, John, Billyray, Charlotte-Lea; [ed.] Basic Secondary Modern Education Albert Road and Longfield Road Secondary Modern School Darlington; [occ.] Forklift Driver "Gallaher Ltd" Tobaccos Factory; [memb.] Kell's and District Racing Pigeon Society; [oth. writ.] Pigeon "Ode" published in local pigeon paper "Dicky's Homing Dreams"; [pers.] As a working class man I escape the monotony of work by making up poems usually of work mates or people I meet in my social circles; [a.] Ballymena, Antrim, UK, BT42 3JD

ROBINSON, OLIVE MARGERET
[pen.] Maggie Robbin, Olive Margaret; [b.] 19 August 1928, Frizington; [p.] Frederick Stanley and Maggie Jenkinson; [m.] Deceased 19 August 1958, 19 August 1948; [ch.] Two sons and one daughter; [ed.] Frisington Council School, Cumbria; [occ.] Am a nature writer self taught!; [hon.] 2 awards for poetry mention I local cress etc. I've read a poem out an radio occ. I've had one or two read out for me!; [oth. writ.] I wrote for 'Partia Trust' in the '80s in their magazine called 'Futer Friends' I've had articles published on comments etc. in different papers and magazines. Occ. poem in the London edition of the 'O.F.N.' also in 'Egremont Today'; [pers.] Life is a journey of discovery! Of loving, trusting, and losing. Of joy, sorrow, and despair, of renewal and of 'Wonder'.; [a.] Whitehaven, Cumbria, UK, CA28 7HA

ROBINSON, PATRICK
[b.] 16 February 1968, Dublin, Eire; [ed.] Christian Brothers College, Woodbrook, Co. Dublin, Ireland; [occ.] Cavalry Soldier, British Army; [hon.] 5 Medals and a GOC's Commendation for Bravery; [oth. writ.] About 200 unpublished; [pers.] My writings realize the beauty of life and give the naive a glimpse into the horrors of military conflict.; [a.] Parkstone/Poole, Dorset, UK, BH12 3HX

ROBINSON, RACHELL
[b.] 4 June 1972, Derbyshire; [p.] Derek and Brenda Walton; [m.] Michael Robinson, 14 July 1990; [ed.] Ladymanners Secondary School, Bakewell, Derbyshire; [occ.] Caterer and Freelance Writer; [oth. writ.] Two unpublished dramatic novels, article for "Cat World" magazine, twenty installments of a historical novel in "The Gibraltar Chronicle", scripts for local radio, sports reports for "The Gibraltar Chronicle".; [pers.] Writing must be the ideal occupation. In what other career can one disappear into a

completely different lifetime? I hope that my writing provides the reader with a temporary escape into a better world.; [a.] Plymouth, Devon, UK, PL5 4HH

ROBINSON, THELMA MARGARET
[b.] 1 May 1956, Sunderland; [p.] John and Thelma Walsh; [m.] John Robinson, 12 March 1977; [ch.] 1 boy and 1 girl; [ed.] St. Thomas Aquinas, Secondary Modern, Sunderland; [occ.] Assembler for Electronics Company; [memb.] Guro Travel Club, Book Club; [oth. writ.] A few poems written for my own pleasure, none ever submitted for publication; [pers.] My writing is a form of therapy, helping me to put my problems in perspective.; [a.] Washington, Tyne and Wear, UK, NE38 9BH

ROBSON, JOAN
[b.] 27 August 1935, Westiminster; [p.] Harold Wombell, Nellie Wombell; [m.] Kenneth Dow Robson, 21 October 1961; [ed.] Western Road County Secondary School, Mitcham; [occ.] Retired P.A.; [memb.] Wild Life Conservation Societies, Animal Rescue Societies. Woodfield Entertainers; [hon.] RSA English and Shorthand; [oth. writ.] Many poems unsubmitted for publication.; [pers.] A concern that mankind has not yet accepted the importance of the conservation of the link between all forms of life.; [a.] Leatherhead, Surrey, UK, KT22 7BW

RODSAETHER, FREDRIK CHRISTIE
[pen.] Fredrik Christie Rodsaether; [b.] 12 June 1971, Bergen; [p.] Ketil Rodsaether, Marianne Christie; [ch.] Junie Bohmann Rodsaether; [occ.] Songwriter in "The Siwrl"; [pers.] I write to remember who I was. Inspired by the works of poets such as Oscar Wilde.; [a.] Oslo, Norway, N 0661

ROJAS-MITRE, MARGOT
[pen.] M. Mitre; [b.] 22 February 1950, Bolivia; [p.] Enrique Rojas, Pastora Rojas; [ed.] Ingavi College, High Business Institute and Secretarial; [occ.] Cashier; [oth. writ.] Several poems plus a manuscript for a book.; [pers.] The best way to express life is by one's writing. Only the thought counts and nothing else.; [a.] London, UK, NW10 9UG

ROSCOE, MAUREEN
[b.] 22 April 1941, Liverpool; [p.] Samuel and Cathrine Crossley; [m.] Fredrick Roscoe, March 1976; [ch.] Kaven, David, Jonathan; [ed.] St. Philomena's School, Aintree Hospital Nurse, Training School Liverpool; [occ.] Housewife; [hon.] Awarded The Chest Disease Prize 1970; [a.] Liverpool, Lancashire, UK, L10 4YF

ROSE, WILLIAM GARDINER
[b.] 1 February 1967, Shropshire; [p.] Rolland, Lynda Coomansingh; [ed.] The Corbet School Baschurch Shrewsbury Art School (1985) Sunderland University (Scientific and Natural History Illustration); [occ.] Scientific Illustrator; [pers.] A great deal of my work is inspired by the change in seasons and the intense beauty of natural subjects. As a small child I read Keats and Wordsworth, so my love of nature probably stems from these poets.; [a.] Shrewsbury, Shropshire, UK, SY4 3QX

ROSS, LOUISE
[b.] 2 August 1983, Maldon, Essex; [p.] Richard Ross, Angela Ross; [p.] Plume School Maldon; [memb.] Extra Curriculum School Music Club; [hon.] Expressive Arts 1995, Personal and Social Education 1996; [pers.] I enjoy both writing and reading poetry as I find it expressive and therapeutic.; [a.] Maldon, Essex, UK, CM9 4SJ

ROWE, DAWN
[b.] 17 October 1925, Bristol; [p.] Harold and Helen Thomas (Deceased); [m.] Widow, 29 March 1947; [ch.] Four girls, one boy; [ed.] Girls High School Bristol and W.A.A.F. 1943-1947, recently two courses Glos College; [occ.] Retired; [memb.] R.A.F.A. Asst. Welfare Officer -

Glos U.R.A. (University Third Age); [hon.] Entitled to Service Medal; [oth. writ.] Several poems for my own pleasure, not published; [pers.] As a soldier in communications receiving a commendation medal words writing and learning have always dominated my life - my father was employed in print after leaving first world war; [a.] Cheltenham, Gloucestershire, UK

ROWE, MRS. MARY
[b.] 26 July 1947, Charsfield, Suffolk; [p.] Henrietta and Charles Crane; [m.] Graham Rowe, 22 July 1972; [ch.] Two: Julie and Andrew; [ed.] Local school then Wickham Market Primary; [occ.] Housewife; [pers.] Writing poetry is my way of relaxing; [a.] Suffolk, UK, IP13 7PT

RUDD, JOHN
[b.] 12 January 1923, Whitehaven; [occ.] Pensioner

RUDDY, SIMON PETER
[b.] 1 October 1973, Salford; [p.] Peter Ruddy, Susan Ruddy; [ed.] Hope High School, Eccles VI Form College University of Teesside; [occ.] Student; [hon.] BSC Hows Criminology; [pers.] If my writing can bring pleasure to one person, then it can be considered successful.; [a.] Salford, Greater Manchester, UK, M6 8BF

RUDGE, KELLY
[b.] 5 June 1980, Wolverhamtpton; [p.] Ron Rudge, Alma Rudge; [ch.] Wednesfield High School; [ed.] Year 12 (sixth form) student; [occ.] Martial Arts Club; [memb.] Attitude Towards Work at School 1993-1994, Award for English and Science 1995-1996; [pers.] I have only recently started to write poetry and I feel my writing perhaps relates to feelings that people may need to express.; [a.] Wolverhampton, West Midlands, UK, WV12 5UG

SACHDEV, RAM
[b.] 22 March 1981, London; [p.] Mrs. Satvir Sachdev; [ed.] Eton College; [occ.] Student; [memb.] Wentworth Golf and Tennis Club, Surrey Poets, The Short Stories Club, Surrey Drama; [hon.] Surrey Poet of the Year Award, Short Story of the Month Award, Young Poets Award, Macbeth Prize; [oth. writ.] Several poems published in Club Magazine, short stories in local magazines and newspapers.; [pers.] You can only succeed in life if you believe in yourself, nothing else matters.; [a.] Wentworth, Surrey, UK, GU25 4NE

SAINSBURY, PETER ANTHONY
[pen.] Tony Sainsbury; [b.] 19 August 1958, Risca, Gwent; [p.] Enid and Peter Sainsbury; [m.] Divorced; [ch.] Sophie - 6, Ben - 4; [ed.] Pontymister Secondary Modern School, Gwent School of Nursing (Qualified as an enrolled nurse in 1979); [occ.] Unemployed due to long-term illness (anxiety/depression); [oth. writ.] Two other poems published in a charity book, for the Alzheimers Disease Society.; [pers.] For some years now I have suffered from an illness that renders me anxious, prone to depression and lacking in self-confidence. Throughout this time however, I have always been able to respond to and utilize, humour. "Good times" is therefore a reflection of both sides of my personality — in darkness can also be found light.; [a.] Risca, Gwent, UK, NP1 6QJ

SAMMUT, JO DEGUARA
[pen.] Jo Sammut; [b.] 6 February 1945, Mellieha, Malta; [p.] Joseph and Carmela Sammut; [m.] Emanwel, 31 May 1964; [ch.] Karen - Isabelle, Rita, Victoria; [ed.] Primary and 2 Years Secondary St. Paul's Bay, Primary School, St. Theresa Grammar School For Girls M Dina, Malta.; [occ.] Housewife, and taking care of elderly mother-in-law.; [oth. writ.] Short stories not published.; [pers.] I reckon if a person is good to others, he/she will be happy and make everyone else around happy.; [a.] St. Paul's Bay, Malta, SPB 09

SAMPSON, MARK
[b.] 16 November 1964, Burham, Kent; [p.] Peter Sampson, Iris Sampson; [ed.] Lewes Priory School; [occ.] Civil Servant and History Student; [memb.] PTC Union, Romney Hythe and Dymchurch Railway Association, Harvey Hopper; [oth. writ.] Poems published in local Bonfire Society Programme and in Fanzines Run by supporters of Brighton and Hove Albion.; [pers.] I try to write poems about the world I see around me.; [a.] Lewes, East Sussex, UK, BN7 1XN

SAMUEL, MICHAEL
[b.] 13 August 1968, High Wycombe; [p.] Mr. and Mrs. Samuel; [ed.] Hatlers Lane Secondary School, Bucks College; [occ.] A student of English at a University in Aberystwyth; [memb.] The Working Tite Arts Magazine, the English Society; [hon.] Access Pass in Humanities; [oth. writ.] Published short story in the High Wycombe 'Star', poems in the University of Works Art Magazine, and many unpublished poems, short stories, and a novel or tune; [pers.] The beautiful idea of a pastoral setting presented by Stienbeck in 'Canning Row' most vividly revealed to me the beauty that social exclusion clinics use by sweetly juxtaposing contrasting images. He showed that true beauty, in that eternal essence, is the imagination. I have tried to imitate this in poetry.; [a.] Highwycombe, Bucks, UK, HP13 6XZ

SANDERSON, MRS. C. G.
[b.] 16 June 1957, Cardiff; [p.] Delores and Douglas Pepper; [m.] Steven James Sanderson, 12 May 1990; [ch.] Jessica Elizabeth, Emily Annabelle; [ed.] Fitzalan High School; [occ.] Full-time mum and housewife; [oth. writ.] For years I have scribbled down verses - putting them into a box! This is the very first time I have ever dared to enter a competition.; [pers.] What I see with my eyes are my thoughts on paper. It truly saddens and concerns me the way things are going in the world. I just pray it gets better - for my children's sake.; [a.] Lisburn, Northern Ireland, BT28 3SE

SANDERSON, JOHN
[b.] 3 November 1938, Blackpool, Lancs; [p.] Deceased; [m.] Joan Sanderson, 3 June 1994; [ch.] Jonathan, Abigail and Naomi; [ed.] Blackpool Grammar School and University Scholarship (PEMB CAMB); [occ.] Retired; [memb.] Ex NUJ and Ex (Chartered Institute of Secretaries); [hon.] Scholarship and awards during my time spent in central and local government administration; [oth. writ.] Various poems published in anthologies and press articles (ex-free-lance journalist); [pers.] I write on all manner of topics and it is special to me that others can identity with my emotions and thoughts whether humourous or philosophical.; [a.] Blackpool, Lancashire, UK, FY4 4HT

SANDERSON, MATT
[b.] 10 March 1975; [occ.] Pipeline worker, traveler; [pers.] And God bless E.E. Cummings and I raise a glass to Brendan Behan and if you love the life you live, live the live you love; [a.] Northallerton, N. Yorks, UK, DL7 0DQ

SANDHU, PARJIT
[pen.] Sandhu Parjit Kaur; [b.] 9 March, Wolverhampton; [occ.] Student; [hon.] Sponsored Readathon received Gold medal and did sponsored walks; [oth. writ.] Only write poems of my own which are unpublished.; [pers.] Writing poems about the sea world is a dream I find deeply fulfilling and I am grateful to share my dream with others.; [a.] Wolverhampton, England, UK, WV2 3HL

SANDHU, SATVEER
[pen.] Satty; [b.] 30 December 1981, England; [p.] Mr. Manjit Sandhu, Mrs. Harpal Sandhu; [ed.] 4th year at High School; [occ.] Student; [oth. writ.] Several other poems; [pers.] I became interested in poetry after taking out a poetry book from my local library, which inspired me to write my own poems.; [a.] Ilford, Essex, UK, IG3 9PE

SAUNDERS, PAUL
[b.] 5 March 1964, Hextable, Kent; [p.] Roger Saunders, Jean Saunders; [m.] Alison Saunders, 2 June 1995; [ed.] Hextable Comprehensive, the Open University, University of London; [occ.] Coordinator, Voluntary Organization in Mental Health; [memb.] British Psychological Society, Weald of Kent Preservation Society; [hon.] B.A. (Hons) Psychology, MSC Mental Health Studies; [oth. writ.] Self-published two short poetry books, poem featured in the Anthology of Contemporary Poets book 1992, also articles for local newspapers.; [pers.] I try to write poetry that is both accessible and enjoyable for people who wouldn't regard themselves as poetry lovers.; [a.] Hextable, Kent, UK, BR8 7RD

SAVEKER, CATHRYN
[b.] 12 August 1959, Birmingham; [p.] Pamela Hebden, Brian Bebden; [m.] Martin Saveker, 22 November 1986; [ch.] Rebecca and Thomas; [ed.] John Wilmott Grammar School, Sutton Coldfield.; [occ.] Retired from Military Service in 1985 Riding Teacher. Operate livery yard on our farm.; [memb.] British Horse Society; [oth. writ.] Have numerous poems which I have never attempted to publish. Have just completed fantasy/adventure novel. Am currently writing more poems and am putting together a back designed to help sufferers of 'M.F.' - on illness which I battled for 3 years and from which I have now recovered.; [pers.] I strive to comment on the trials and and wonders of life in my writing. I greatly admire the works of William Blake.; [a.] Middleton, Staffordshire, UK, B78 2BT

SCAMBLER, SUZANNE
[b.] 23 March 1977, England; [ed.] London Studio Centre; [occ.] Performing Arts Student; [hon.] Various awards for Dance and Drama, Singing; [oth. writ.] I've written and performed my poems which I wrote in hospital; [pers.] I have been battling against a long illness and have found great comfort in poetry.; [a.] Harpenden, Herts, UK, AL5 3LN

SCHARNHORST, MAVIS
[pers.] I would like to dedicate this poem to the Rev. Stephen Grey of St. Michael's Church Bamford as it is based on a true happening in 1996.; [a.] Bury, Lancashire, UK

SCHOFIELD, CHERYL B.
[pen.] Chez; [b.] 8 September 1964, Castleford; [p.] Alma Hill, Eric Hill; [m.] Divorced; [ch.] William Hayon, Laura Lee; [ed.] Castleford High School; [oth. writ.] Several poems and short stories; [pers.] My poems reflect my autumnal feelings. I believe a lot can be expressed through poetry.; [a.] Castleford, West Yorkshire, UK, WF10 3BN

SCHOFIELD, EVELYN
[b.] 6 May 1944, Crieff; [p.] Helen Sharp, Arthur Sharp; [m.] Kenneth Douglas Schofield, 12 June 1968; [ch.] Susan Lesley and Evonne Kristeen; [ed.] Crieff Junior School, Morrison's Academy for Girls, Crieff Further Education Centre; [occ.] Housewife; [memb.] Foxhills Gold and Country Club, Post House Forte Health Club, Guildford; [oth. writ.] None as yet as I have only been writing for a short time; [pers.] I have been interested in poetry both reading and reciting from my early years. From Burns to Wordsworth, they have been my inspiration.; [a.] Woking, Surrey, UK, GU21 5TA

SCOTT, FRED
[b.] 26 April 1908, Fatfield; [p.] John James Scott; [m.] Margaret Jane Scott; [ch.] Six; [ed.] Local School; [occ.] Mine overman; [memb.] Kings College 3 years, N.A.C.O.D.S. 20 years; [hon.] Fire and Rescue Brigade for thirteen years, took part in Boldon Fire, William Pit Whitehaven Easington Pit Disaster, Weetslade Pit Disaster; [oth. writ.] Letters to various people about the state of the health service and the DRS and all the solicitors aiding and abetting the government in such a huge way; it's erroneous in point of law; [pers.] The poetry is the God's honest truth about the DRS' negligence. He refused me attention. My Lord Jesus Christ himself gave me back my life. He showed me down the corridor of life, in all these disasters his unseen hand was there with me.; [a.] Newcastle, Northumberland, UK, NE15 8LY

SCOTT, WALTER
[pen.] Walter Scott; [b.] 17 June 1911, Royton, Lancs; [p.] Annie and William Scott; [m.] Emily Scott (Deceased), 29 December 1936; [ch.] Mavis and John; [ed.] Sts Aidans and Oswald R.C. School, Royton; [occ.] Retired; [memb.] Military only. Royal Signal Assc., life member since 11-1-46; [hon.] No civil, Campaign and war medals only; [oth. writ.] "Porridge International", Spike Millican Comp, British Isles, Finals 24-1-84, first attempt. "The Last Farewell", Poetry in the British Isles. Passages of Time Current Finals 96/97; [pers.] My first poem, 1984, written as a challenge to the one written by Spike Milligan in National Newspapers, Comp. I write on impulse on current events mostly many poems written - only three submitted for publication.; [a.] Shaw, Lancs, UK, OL2 7AJ

SCOTT-ALLEN, JOAN
[pen.] Joan Vass; [b.] 4 December 1924, Wimbledon; [p.] Vic and Win Vass; [ch.] Seven, 1 adopted; [ed.] Ashford Middx Comprehensive School; [occ.] Retired; [oth. writ.] Poems published/ L Dearsley/D Stores. Story of life with handicapped womans own 5 chapter world war II from unpublished book "Up She goes". By Portsmooth News for completed books written and 12 yrs. am looking for an agent! Various articles published; [pers.] I am almost self taught a wealth of experiences that hopefully will touch the readers and subsequently make a better world. Spent 4 yrs in WW2 doing a fish inheard of subsequently raised 8 children, a variety of jobs and experiences, finished by life's work as mortally handicapped nurse.; [a.] Fareham, Hampshire, UK, PO14 1HY

SEALEY, GWYNETH
[b.] 28 April 1924, Skewen; [p.] Elizabeth Rees and Water Rees; [m.] Robert Sealey, 17 December 1949; [ch.] Mark, Andrea, Micheal, Margaret and Helena; [ed.] Goed Franc Elementary; [occ.] Retired; [oth. writ.] Short story Parish mag! Read on television competition. Published in book form 1985.; [pers.] My interest is in people, especially the young. I write mainly about what I have learned on this journey through life.; [a.] Cardiff, S Glamorgan, UK, CF3 7HE

SEAMAN, PETER HAMILTON
[b.] 11 October 1945, Headingley; [p.] Thomas Headland and Eleanor Robertson; [m.] Margaret Woods, divorced 1967-1991; [ch.] Paul Desmond, Tracey Rebecca, Tanya Michelle; [ed.] Musician - grade 8 piano, classical guitar, theory and history of music; [occ.] Music tutor - keyboards, piano, guitar, organ - Wirral Grammar School; [oth. writ.] Children's musical stories, "The Stories from Kennel Loice", 5 songs recorded, Christmas Cantata for choir/orchestra, Missa Brevis, Essay on the Trinity; [a.] Wallassy, Merseyside, L44 5RA

SECHER, HANNE
[b.] 14 July 1957, Elsinore, Denmark; [m.] Dr. Henning Noer; [ed.] University of Copenhagen, University of AARHUS; [occ.] Biologist; [hon.] Biology; [oth. writ.] Mostly scientific papers.; [pers.] I think it is very important to ask many questions, and to search for answers with an open and reflective mind.; [a.] Morke, Denmark, 8544

SEDDON, STEFAN
[b.] 5 March 1974, Dulwich; [p.] Gary Seddon, Janet Seddon; [ed.] Dartford Grammar School; [occ.] Metropolitan Police Traffic Warden; [memb.] Labour Party, British UFO Research Association, Territorial Army; [oth. writ.] One

short poem published in "Fast Return" a sci-fi fanzine; [pers.] I hope through my writing to bring poetry back to the masses. I feel a lot of modern poetry is a crime to the art and alienates the people who read it.; [a.] Greenhithe, Kent, UK, DA9 9QP

SEGUNA, OMAR
[b.] 25 July 1977, Cospicua; [p.] George Seguna, Rito nee Flask; [ed.] University of Malta; [memb.] "Ghagda tal-Malti", consisting of local writers and students of the Maltese Language, and Amnesty International; [hon.] A regular contributor in Maltese journals and newspapers.; [oth. writ.] Collections of poems, plays, pamphlets, novels and short stories; [pers.] I strive for a world without suffering and violence, and where harmony and brotherhood for all mankind will prevail. People from all over the world will love one another.; [a.] Cospicua, Malta, CSPO 5

SEMMENS, GWYNIRIS
[b.] 11 January 1922, South Wales; [p.] William Lugg, Margaret Lugg; [m.] Stanley Semmens, 31 March 1956; [ch.] June, Linda, Stephen; [ed.] Bronllwyn School Gelli; [occ.] Housewife; [memb.] Old Cornwall Society, Age Concern, Pendeen Songsters; [hon.] 1996 Cornish Gorsedd Kewny Cup, Reading on Radio Cornwall, several highly commended certificates; [oth. writ.] Stories published in magazine, Childrens Stories, plays enacted at Methodist Chapel; [pers.] I try to communicate sympathy or happiness to my fellow man. I like helping people.; [a.] Trewelard, Cornwall, UK, TR19 7DN

SEMPLE, HILARY
[b.] Johannesburg; [occ.] Lecturer in English Literature: University of the Witwatersrand; [oth. writ.] Academic

SEWARD, RITA
[b.] 22 April 1950, London; [p.] Joseph Perfect, Mary Perfect; [m.] Michael Seward, 1 January 1972; [ch.] Martin, Mark and James; [ed.] Shearwater, Secondary School; [occ.] Mother and wife; [oth. writ.] Six poems published in "Poetry Now" anthologies.; [pers.] I write what I feel in my heart and see with my eyes, most of which is free for us all.; [a.] Camberley, Surrey, UK, GU17 9BU

SEXTON, TOM
[pen.] Tom; [b.] 27 September 1917, Isleworth, Middlesex; [p.] Edward Thomas Sexton, Ada Sexton; [m.] May Sexton, 4 November 1939; [ch.] Three; [ed.] Public school, The Blue School, The Square, Isleworth; [occ.] OAP; [memb.] Veteran of the D' Day Landings in the year of 1944 a soldier I had to be; [oth. writ.] Poems published two up till now one the title yes is 'Daydreams' the second was 'Hounslow Town' the best

SEYMOUR, PAUL R.
[pen.] Paul Bearer; [b.] 2 July 1959, Erith, Kent; [p.] David and Jean (Both Deceased); [m.] Joanne, 28 July 1984; [ch.] Niggy and Mischief (Both cats!); [ed.] What education?; [occ.] Self Employed, Computer Support Specialist; [memb.] Human Race (Under sufference!); [hon.] Some "minor" awards for poetry. Qualified Funeral Director (undertaker to you).; [oth. writ.] Various, none made it "Big Time" so far. Poems from the graveyard.; [pers.] Ex-undertaker (8 years), sick sense of humour, love computers, want to be very, very rich! Desperately wants to be famous, all help welcome!; [a.] Erith, Kent, UK, DA8 1NY

SHAFIQUE, SOBIA
[b.] 23 May 1984, Slough; [ed.] Godolphin First/Middle, Herschel Grammar; [occ.] A student at Herschel Grammar School; [pers.] I dedicate this poem to my Grandmother who died suffering from breast cancer.; [a.] Slough, Berkshire, UK, SL1 3EB

SHAKEL, PERCY
[b.] 7 September 1907, Marchweil; [p.] James and Anne Shakel; [m.] Olga Rose, 28 January 1935;

[ed.] Russel School, near Wrexham. Crippled at 10 years of age and have never done any school since. I taught myself at home.; [occ.] Farming, now retired.; [memb.] Founder of the Chester Canine Society, also used to train dogs for obedience and good manners.; [pers.] I study nature and have had a lot to do with horses and ponies.; [a.] Chester, Cheshire CH3 7AN

SHAW, DEREK
[pen.] "Derek"; [b.] 23 April 1943, Bacup; [p.] Robert and Evelyn; [m.] Lynne, 30 November 1963; [ch.] Karen, Glen, Nicola; [ed.] Blackthorn S.M.S. Bacup; [occ.] Retired following a heart attack; [oth. writ.] In August this year I was selected to have my entry "Please Can I Go to the Football Match" published by a leading publisher. I am at present writing a volume on a comedy character I have created; [pers.] I only took up writing 2 yrs ago, people seemed to like my poems and asked me to write for them. I love to see people smile at my poetry and it gives me an enormous amount of satisfaction, when I see my poems framed.; [a.] Rossendale, Lancashire, UK, BB4 7AE

SHAW, JOHN ANTONY
[b.] 20 October 1955, Haydock; [p.] Robert and Winnifred Shaw; [ed.] Windermere Rd, Sec. Mod. Leigh, Lancs, Leigh Grammar School, Padgate College; [occ.] I am disabled; [memb.] "Making Space" organization for suffering of Schizophrenia and their families; [oth. writ.] "No Breakfast Today, Lads" - a novella. "Henmione" - a novella "Cathansis" - a poetry anthology (all three unpublished as yet!); [pers.] I suffer from bi-polar disorder. I seek to promote awareness of mental health problems generally through my art; [a.] Athenton, Lancashire, UK, M46 0RB

SHAW, MELANIE
[b.] 3 November 1971, Nottingham; [hon.] Given Editor's Choice Award 1996 for my poem 'Mother Nature'; [oth. writ.] Poem 'Mother Nature' published in anthology 'Voices On The Wind'; [a.] Nottingham, UK, NG2 2HQ

SHEEHAN, ANTHONY P.
[b.] 15 July 1931, Romford; [p.] William and Mary Sheehan; [m.] Rosemary Barker, 22 June 1957; [ch.] Jacqueline Mary, Lynda Jane; [ed.] St Peter's School (Private) Southbourne; [occ.] Retired Accountant Services Manager; [memb.] Conservative Club, Dlloyd Leisure Club, Old Boys Society, interested in linguistics; [oth. writ.] I have always written for pleasure without thought of publication. I enjoy writing French poetry.; [pers.] Catholic approach to all writings. Creativity causes, produces all my writings including subject matter.; [a.] Bournemouth, Dorset, UK, BH7 6QR

SHELDON, JOAN
[b.] 15 May 1939, Warrington; [ch.] Five; [occ.] Housewife; [oth. writ.] None I have sent anywhere before. I write them then leave them. I have written my life story but not known any knowledge of what to do with it.; [pers.] I am a believer in the Lord Jesus Christ, and I believe these poems came from him, a gift he passed on to me, he inspired me.; [a.] Warrington, Cheshire, UK, WA2 9ES

SHEPHERD, JOHN EDWIN
[pen.] John E. Shepherd; [b.] 1 February 1947, Birmingham; [m.] Dorothy Shepherd, 7 September 1968; [ch.] Gareth 22 yrs, Helen 17 yrs; [ed.] Sudell Road Secondary School Darwen Lancs; [occ.] Student Support-Worker Blackburn College; [oth. writ.] Articles published in local wildlife magazines.; [pers.] Poetry is a new and exciting experience for me. I strive to write for people's enjoyment and entertainment and to write from experience and from life.; [a.] Darwen, Lancashire, UK, BB3 2PY

SHEPHERD, ROGER
[b.] 3 March 1943, Yorkshire; [ed.] Surrey - Bisley; [occ.] Teacher, "The Infinite Way"; [hon.] City and Guilds 7037/7036 Teaching

Learning Skills, City Guilds I.T. Computer Technology 1 and 2 level; [oth. writ.] Book - "In The Beginning I Was Born" publishes to be sought poems - "I Love Many Towards My Work, You May Read More If You Like"; [pers.] I am a teacher for mankind. These reflections are in many books, for my spirit within, is to guide me - Spiritual philosophy unfolds in me by Joel S. Goldsmith; [a.] Boxhill-on-Sea, East Sussex, UK, TN40 1DS

SHERWOOD, MRS. CATHARINE FRANCES
[b.] 24 April 1951, Bell End; [p.] Maud and Frank Nock; [m.] Laurence John Sherwood, 14 April 1973; [ed.] Powke Lane School and Sivister's Ln High School for Girls; [occ.] Housewife; [a.] Warley, West Midlands, UK, B65 9LH

SHIPLEY, NIGEL
[b.] 9 June 1978, Scunthorpe; [p.] Roy and Hazel Shipley; [ed.] North Axholme Comprehensive John Leggott College; [occ.] Having a year out before university.; [oth. writ.] Lots of poems and plays but this is my first published piece.; [pers.] Equality regardless of sexuality, race, gender. I try to use poetry and other mediums to make people think about their actions and the effect they have on others.; [a.] Scunthorpe, North Lincolnshire, UK, DN17 4DY

SHUREY, RICHARD
[b.] 22 September 1951, Llwynapia; [p.] Ken Shurey, Clara Shurey; [m.] Christine Shurey, 6 May 1972; [ch.] Neil, Kevin, Catherine Shurey; [ed.] Pentre Grammar School; [hon.] Won First Prize in School Home Safety Competition; [oth. writ.] This is my first poem published; [pers.] I wish to proclaim the love of God and I hope many people will come to experience the love of God in their own personal lives; [a.] Tonypondy, Rhondda Cynon Taff, UK, CF40 1JR

SIMS, PEGGY
[b.] 16 February 1929, Sligo, Republic of Ireland; [p.] Jack Sims, 9 October 1968; [ch.] Nil; [ed.] Leaving Certificate (Hons); [occ.] Retired Nurse; [memb.] Roscommon Abbey Writers Group, Roscommon Co., Roscommon, Republic of Ireland; [oth. writ.] Published in anthologies, magazines and papers.; [pers.] I try to portray the value of simple ordinary scraps and life as it is, rather than what we would like.

SINCLAIR, EMMA
[pen.] K10; [b.] 15 July 1976, London; [m.] Jonny Jacobs (Partner); [ed.] Haberdashys Askes, Elstree Leeds University; [occ.] Student; [hon.] French and Spanish (J. Hons); [pers.] I saw the poems in 20 minutes, I didn't think it would be published. Yay! Long live Latin America.; [a.] London, UK, N2 0RE

SLADE, CAROLE
[b.] 10 October 1944, Melksham; [p.] Deceased; [m.] Alan, 20 March 1965; [ch.] Three children; [ed.] Secondary Modern School; [occ.] Housewife; [memb.] I am a member of the U.R.C. Church, I was ordained as an elder in the church but at present I am not holding office.

SLOAN, JOHN ANTHONY
[b.] 16 October 1947, Kilbirnie; [p.] Matthew Sloan, Alice Sloan; [m.] Isabel Sloan, 25 July 1970; [ch.] Mark Sloan; [ed.] St. Bridgets Secondary School, Kilbirnie, Ayrshire; [occ.] Trucks Assembly, Volvo Trucks, Irvine; [pers.] "I could not let the death of an industry which served an entire community for generations and which I loved dearly be entirely forgotten, I just had to say goodbye"; [a.] Kilbirnie, Ayrshire, UK, KA25 7JB

SMEDLEY, CAROLINE
[b.] 17 February 1966, Kingslyn, Norfolk; [p.] Brian and Catherine Beatrice Smedley; [ch.] Johnathon Brian; [ed.] Churchfields Secondary; [occ.] Mother; [memb.] British Red Cross Society; [hon.] English Literature; [oth. writ.] The same poem has been put onto a cross-stitch design and published in 'Cross-Stitch' Magazine;

[pers.] I enjoy writing, it gives me great pleasure. I hope to pass this interest on to my son, one day.; [a.] Cricklade, Wiltshire, UK, SN6 6HL

SMITH, ANDREW
[b.] 25 December 1965, Leicester; [p.] Brian Smith and Betty Smith; [ed.] Longslade College; [pers.] If you have a passion for the subject matter, it reflects in the written word.; [a.] Sileby, Leics, UK, LE12 7LG

SMITH, ANGELINA
[b.] 11 August 1980, Swansea; [p.] Rosemary and Gareth Smith; [ed.] Studying at Tycoch College Swansea; [occ.] Student; [oth. writ.] First Time; [pers.] As my belief is that there is so much racism in the world, I decided to write my views in my poem.; [a.] Swansea, West Glamorgan, UK, SA5 5JS

SMITH, AVRIL
[b.] 1 April 1955, London, UK; [p.] Mr. and Mrs. Smith; [ed.] Fitzwimarc Sec Mod Rayleigh Essex; [occ.] Tupperware Rep.; [oth. writ.] 5 novels, numerous poems unpublished; [pers.] Would very much like the rest of my poetry and at least one of my novels published. Wish to work as a writer of some description. Poetry is my great love; my father wrote poems (deceased).; [a.] Thundersley, Essex, UK, SS7 3UU

SMITH, MRS. IRENE A. R.
[pen.] Jaimi; [b.] 18 December 1938, Aberdeen; [p.] William and Elizabeth; [m.] Ronald, 11 November 1965; [ch.] Beverley, Irene, Adrienne and Kevin; [ed.] Secondary school; [occ.] Retired; [hon.] City and Guilds for Domestic Science; [oth. writ.] Poems printed in - Island Moods and Reflections, Poets in Scotland, Sunlight and Shadows, and Passages of Time; [pers.] I have seven lovely grandchildren and a large extended family. This will be the fifth poem I've had printed.; [a.] Aberdeen, Grampian, UK, AB21 9XS

SMITH, MRS. J. M.
[b.] 19 September 1920, Norwich; [p.] Sidney and Christianna Ingate; [m.] Norman John Smith, 22 August 1950; [ch.] Michael; [ed.] Church of England; [occ.] Housewife (past Youth Leader for 17 years).; [memb.] WRVS; [hon.] Intermediate Trinity College of music exams passed with honours.; [oth. writ.] 'To My Son', 'The Wedding Day', 'A Prayer For Every Day', 'At The End Of The Day', 'Where Does The River Flow To', 'In Days Of Yore'; [pers.] To think of the lovely things in life, quiet moments to reflect on past, happy memories to listen to music for relaxation, time to garden, and always to find time to help others less fortunate than myself.; [a.] Norwich, Norfolk, UK, NR6 5LX

SMITH, JANET
[b.] 7 September 1959, London; [p.] Frederick and Pat Trench; [m.] Alan Smith, 19 April 1980; [ch.] Sarah Louise, Emily Ruth; [ed.] St. Thomas more Buxton; [pers.] I have enjoyed poetry from an early age. I write my poetry to channel and express feelings, discoveries and emotions; [a.] Chesterfield, Derbyshire, UK, S41 0NH

SMITH, JASON
[pen.] Jason Roberts-Smith; [b.] 12 June 1972, Stoke-on-Trent; [p.] Leslie Smith and Jacqueline Smith; [ed.] Brownhills High School, Leek College of Further Education and School of Art; [occ.] Unemployed; [hon.] Centra Award for Photograph; [oth. writ.] I am currently finishing a novel of contemporary fiction and hoping to publish it.; [pers.] My writing is influenced by the good and bad in people. I am a big fan of contemporary fiction.; [a.] Tunstall, Staffordshire, UK, ST6 6BU

SMITH, JOAN
[pen.] Joan Orth; [b.] 22 July 1935, London; [p.] Emily Orth, Ronald Orth; [m.] James Smith, 7 February 1953; [ch.] Five daughters, 2 sons; [ed.] Charlton Secondary School for Girls; [occ.] Retired; [oth. writ.] One poem published in 1996 Summer Poetry Review; [a.] London, UK, SE2 9QJ

SMITH, JOAN
[pen.] Lara; [b.] Birmingham; [p.] Margaret Snape, Walter Snape; [m.] Leslie Smith; [ch.] Pamela, Michael, Sandy; [ed.] Kings Norton Grammar; [occ.] Housewife/Career; [pers.] My poems I dedicate to Colin, a wonderful caring man. A shining light in dark times, he touched my lost emotions and inspired my imagery.; [a.] Teignmouth, Devon, UK, TQ14 8RU

SMITH, KEVEN
[pen.] Keven George; [b.] 15 September 1958, Leics; [p.] Barry and Pat Smith; [m.] Divorced; [ch.] Liam Ashley, Kelly Marie; [ed.] Rawlins Community College Quorn Leics; [occ.] Production Engineer; [oth. writ.] Several poems and children's stories never submitted for publishing.; [pers.] I hope people will use their imagination to find the picture in my poetry. I let the reader have their own conclusion. I don't direct. I just compose.; [a.] Loughborough, Leicestershire, UK, LE12 7TF

SMITH, KIM FRANCES
[b.] 9 May 1958, Leeds; [p.] Marlene Watson, Derek Watson; [m.] Graham Smith, 24 June 1995; [ch.] Daniel George, Rebecca; [occ.] Owner 'Snuggle Bunnies' Babywear and Nursery Centre; [memb.] White Rose Boating Club; [a.] Leeds, Yorkshire, UK, LS26 0NY

SMITH, M. J.
[b.] 30 May 1965, Cardiff; [p.] Elizabeth, Leonard; [occ.] Fire Fighter - London Fire Brigade; [oth. writ.] Although I've been writing poetry on and off now since the age of 15 yrs, this is my first entry to any competition.; [pers.] Positive thought with just intentions attracts good vibrations from everywhere, and helps to bring about favorable conclusions. (In recognition of my guardian angel.); [a.] Windsor, Berks, UK, SL4 5AX

SMITH, MICHAEL
[b.] 3 January 1931, Newcastle upon Tyne; [p.] Michael and Ellen; [m.] Maureen, 24 August 1957; [ch.] Michael, Kevin, Clare; [ed.] St. Cuthbert's Grammar School, New Castle upon Tyne; [occ.] Retired; [memb.] MITD, Secretary of West Window a Creative Writing year for Handicapped and/or disabled; [hon.] Queens police long service, a four conduct medal; [oth. writ.] Articles/poems, local and national press and mags, autobiography - due to be published anthology of work; [pers.] Influences by 33 1/2 years police service and 7 years in inbuster before being forced into retirement by 4 strokes.

SMITH, PHILIP
[pen.] Raven; [b.] 17 January 1973, Gloucester; [p.] Robin and Ruth Smith; [ed.] Newent Comprehensive School after Redmarley Primary School; [memb.] Redmarley United Football Club, The Ledbury Academy of Tae Kwon-Do; [oth. writ.] A finished manuscript but nothing published as yet.; [pers.] We are all outsiders in a world that promises everything. What we actually get however, is hell, disguised as heaven, damnation in the form of paradise. Many, if not all are fooled by this deception. We didn't make this place...we just live here.; [a.] Relmarley, Gloucestershire, UK, GL19 3NB

SMITH, RACHEL E.
[b.] 4 December 1982, Grimsby; [p.] Richard Smith, Elizabeth Smith; [ed.] Currently studying at Bentley Wood High School; [memb.] Regular attendance of Kenton Baptist Church, Suzanne's Riding School, 1st Kenton Girls Brigade; [oth. writ.] Poems and short stories mainly related to school work. One story was published in an amateur magazine; [pers.] Poetry is a beautiful way of expressing thoughts and feelings. It is enjoyable for both the author and those who read it. It is one of the many gifts that God has given us.; [a.] Harrow Weald, Middlesex, UK, HA3 6RZ

SMITH, TERESA JEANNE
[b.] 20 May 1948, Croydon; [p.] Robert Furtado C.B. and Marcelle Furtado; [m.] Dr. Geoffrey Smith, 16 February 1978; [ed.] Croydon High School GPDST, Baston School Hayes, Kent, The Middlesex Hospital Nurses Training School; [occ.] Housewife - previously nursing officer in the Royal Air Force; [oth. writ.] Several poems published in anthologies by Triumph House, Poetry Now, Anchor Books; [pers.] My outlook on life has been influenced by time spent living in Afghanistan and living and working as a nurse in England, Germany and the Arabian Gulf; [a.] Uckfield, East Sussex, UK, TN22 1BJ

SMITH, THOMAS
[b.] 7 November 1980, Leadgate; [p.] Frank Smith, Pauline Smith; [ed.] St. Bedes, Comprehensive Lanchester; [occ.] Student; [memb.] Belle Vue Sports Centre, under 16's Football Club; [pers.] I wrote this poem in the memory of my mum who died when I was four years old.; [a.] Consett, Durham, UK, DH8 6HB

SMITH, TOM
[b.] 4 July 1946, Edinburgh, Scotland; [p.] Alexander and Janet; [m.] Yvonne, 6 June 1987; [ed.] Secondary Clare Modern - and others including change in Singapore as my father was a member of the Royal Air Force (Eng-Lit., Eng-Lang) GCE 'O' Level Self-Sgt. Ramc. Rtd. after 25 years S.E.N.; [occ.] Driver, Transport division - Social Services, Warwick County Council; [memb.] Royal College of Nursing UKCC, (State Enrolled Nurse); [hon.] Long Service and Good Conduct Medal Royal Society of Arts, for Technical Drawing; [oth. writ.] Keen on spontaneous jotting of poetry since 1980 and have a book full, which are mainly reflections on my life and life in general. I am a bit of a romantic and compassionate person who likes to read keep fit - enjoy - tennis, golf, and other sports.; [pers.] I believe in Christians attitudes and wish everyone could take the example Jesus gave us, to heart - it would be a far better world. Favorite quote - origin Chinese - "No man is at all hours wise".; [a.] Nr. Daventry, Northants, UK, NN11 6DP

SMITH, TRACY LEE
[b.] 21 December 1976, Dublin, Ireland; [pers.] Since a small child, I have been an avid wrestling fan and this poem was written about a professional wrestler whom I admire.

SMITH-WARREN, MRS. LINDA P.
[b.] 31 March 1954, Newport, Mon; [p.] Robert and Betty Newberry; [m.] John B. Smith-Warren, 10 April 1972; [ch.] Michelle, Barry and Gayna; [ed.] Duffryn High School; [occ.] Disabled Housewife; [memb.] Competitor's companion; [hon.] Touch typing and short hand passed with merits; [oth. writ.] Including this poem I have had 40 poems published in anthologies, also one in a magazine, I have also had an article published in a magazine about poetry; [pers.] I write about life in general, including about disabilities created from arthritis which I suffer myself.; [a.] MacDuff, Aberdeenshire, UK, AB44 1UX

SMYTH, JILL
[b.] 7 October 1950, Birmingham; [p.] Francis and Doris Cooper; [m.] Bill Smyth, 30 December 1995; [ch.] Stuart and David Bailey, Christine Turner; [occ.] Ward receptionist; [pers.] A tribute to my father, 1904-1990. A proud man who lost all dignity, but not love.; [a.] Minehead, Somerset TA24 UN

SMYTH, S. ALEXANDER
[pen.] Sandy; [b.] 22 July 1972, London; [p.] Mr. Anthony John Smyth, Mrs. Audrey Smyth; [ed.] St. John's School Leather head GCSE French B, English C, Eng. Lit C, Maths C, Latin C A-Level Maths D Kingston University B. Sc Maths and Computing; [occ.] Analyst Programmer; [memb.] Sutton and Cheam Chess Club, Guitar Society;

[hon.] Grade 8 piano and guitar B. Sc Maths and Computing, Postgraduate certificate in numerical analysis with Computational Modelling; [pers.] Everyone should try writing poetry; the end result is always satisfying.; [a.] Epsom, Surrey, UK, KT19 8RV

SPARROW, ROY M.
[b.] 29 March 1945, Chester; [p.] Stanley Sparrow, Lily Lavinna Ethel Sparrow; [m.] Ruth Elizabeth Sparrow, 9 May 1994; [ch.] Cheryl Ann, Amanda Jane; [ed.] College Secondary Modern School Chester; [occ.] Training and Health and Safety Advisor; [memb.] Royal Signals Association, Royal British Legion, Institute of Occupational Safety and Health; [hon.] N.E.B.O.S.H. Food Hygiene (Advanced); [oth. writ.] Children's stories as yet unpublished.; [pers.] Our life on this earth is so short that I try to incorporate love, kindness, happiness and all things good into my writing.; [a.] Sheffield, South Yorkshire, UK, S31 8QL

SPENCER, VICTORINE ZAHALLA
[pen.] McAllister; [b.] 31 July 1929, British Guyana; [p.] Nathar and Ada McAllister; [ch.] Rodney, Hamlets Debbie; [ed.] I left school before my 12th birthday, I had not a mother, since she died when I was only 6 years old. My stepmother never cared about educating us.; [occ.] I am now donor as you may have noticed by my date of birth; [memb.] I am a Latter Day Saint for the past 15 years.; [hon.] I have none but do work at other things including writing; [oth. writ.] Yes, I do have six poems published, in anthologies before my big illness I told about. I also write stories and plays but because I have no help to bring them up to date I put them away and hope for the best.; [pers.] Yes as for me, life was a hassle from the start. But I struggled from the start. But I struggled to keep my head above water, one of my aims was to reach out and help my fellow men in what small way I could and as J. Kennedy died I wrote my first poem to his wife soon it went to now.; [a.] London, UK, 6EZ

ST. JOHN-BYLES, VEE ASQUITH
[pen.] Laura St. John-Byles; [b.] 20 November 1951, Stratford; [p.] John Andrews and Norma Andrews; [m.] Paul St. John-Byles, 18 September 1996; [ch.] Lee-Asquith, Steven Asquith, Mark Byles and Simon Byles; [ed.] St. Martins Comprehensive, Brentwood, Brentwood County High School and University of North London; [occ.] Ex. Senior Social Worker; [memb.] Local writer's groups; [hon.] BA Hons (Sociology) and Certificate of Qualification in Social Work (C.Q.S.W.); [oth. writ.] Submissions of various poems to papers and magazines, private family recitals or on family celebration cards!!; [pers.] I find that inspiration is found through observation and utilization of all one's senses, thus everything I write comes from what I feel, see, hear, smell or touch. These are powerful tools indeed!; [a.] Bude, Cornwall, UK, EX23 9LZ

STAFFORD, EVE
[pen.] E. V.; [b.] 12 October 1947, Middlesex; [p.] Eileen and Charles Kimmer (Deceased); [ch.] Vanessa, Amanda and Yolanda; [ed.] Vynes Grammar School, Ickerham Middx., Walfort College of Art 1990/1991; [occ.] Artist/Clairvoyant Housewife; [memb.] Welsh Academy; [hon.] Editors Choice Award from the National Library of Poetry 1993 (USA); [oth. writ.] Many poems and 2 short stories. Poem "Ode to the Ladies of the Right" published in Sunday Sport Newspaper 1992, Poem "Deterioration" published by the National Library of Poetry 1993. (USA); [pers.] A sufferer of M.E. (Myalgic Encephalomyalitis) for some years, I had to adjust to a quiet way of life. I took up writing and painting and trained as a spiritualist medium. Much of my work is based on true life but equally some is spiritually inspired.; [a.] Nantyglo, Gwent, UK, NP3 4LJ

STANFORTH, MICHAEL JR.
[b.] 20 February 1955, Whitby; [p.] Michael, Elsie Stanforth; [m.] Karen, 8 September 1979; [ch.] Melanie Dion, Megan, Warren Jason; [occ.] Self Employed Window Cleaner and Mobile Disc Jockey; [memb.] Whitby Bowling Club, Whitby Friendship Amateur Rowing Club. International Songwriters Association; [oth. writ.] Local reports on activities in the town's paper. "Dream of Dreams" published in an anthology called "The Big Sleep".; [pers.] My mind is crammedfull of thoughts and ideas. It is an honour to come from the birth place of the first English poet, songwriter "Caedmon".; [a.] Whitby, North Yorkshire, UK, YO21 1NA

STANTON, PETER DAVID
[pen.] Peter Stanton; [b.] 6 March 1970, Chesterfield; [p.] Margaret Elizabeth and Raymond Stanton; [ed.] Steve Marsh Guitar School, Chesterfield (on and off since 7 yrs. old), 1981-1983 Hasland Hall School, 1983-1986 Chesterfield Boys School, 1986-1993 Chesterfield College (part time), 1994-1996 Homerton School of Health Studies, Peterborough (full time), 1996-present Derby University (part time); [occ.] Estimator's Assistant, Barnale Construction, Walsall; [memb.] Chesterfield Classical Guitar Society; [hon.] BTEC HNC Building Studies, Grade 7 in Classical Guitar (Guild Hall School of Music and Drama); [oth. writ.] Songwriting; [pers.] Words of meaning come from my thoughts surrounded by feelings about experiences in our lives which I hope when shared will help us learn to cope, understand and love.; [a.] Chesterfield, Derbyshire, UK, S41 0NQ

STAPLETON, LENA
[b.] 27 May 1945, Bath, England; [m.] Tobias Stapleton, 27 May 1967; [ch.] Six; [ed.] Primary Level; [occ.] Housewife; [pers.] I often write poems but never send them in. This will be my first one published; [a.] Crosshaven, Cork, Ireland

STARR, JAMES MOLINEAUX
[b.] 28 August 1946, Manchester; [p.] Paul Starr, Florence Starr; [m.] Angela Mary Starr, 4 December 1971; [ch.] Marie Starr, Jean Starr; [ed.] Oldwood Secondary School, Woodhouse Park Wythenshawe Manchester; [occ.] Unemployed; [oth. writ.] Published poems, All Over Again - published in the book The Way It Is - Anchor Books 1994, Golden Days - published in the book Pleasure and Pain Arrival Press 1994; [pers.] To date I have written over 300 poems covering many topics, some inspired by actual events, some fictitious. I write for fun and enjoyment.; [a.] Wythenshawe, Greater Manchester, UK, M22 1SB

STEVENS, BRIAN MICHAEL ROBERT
[b.] July 2, 1937, Holloway, New Foundland; [p.] Robert Stevens and Annie Amy Stevens; [m.] Pamela Margaret (nee Dupen) Cherry, September 5, 1959; [ch.] Mark and Ian; [ed.] L.V. School Slough (1942-1943), (1943-1947) (Evacuated), Derbyshire Notts Board, (1947-1948), St. Joseph (RC) Junior Laton London - Elem, (1948-1952), St. Georges (RC) Secondary - Walthampston E17; [occ.] Disabled - Registered (1984) Blind, [memb.] H.A.C. Blind (were Winchwler) Club, Subscriber to "Doors", (In and out of Dorset), Hexagon Center (March 1987-1995) (February) for Disabled - Chandler's Ford, Eastleigh (twice a week), Talking Newspaper Monthly Magazines (Submit Taple of my own - and old masters work); [oth. writ.] One poem published in "door 51" 6 months previous and 15-18 poems published in 1985-1986 in "Winchester Extra", (Free Newspaper) when there was a "Poets Corner".; [pers.] Generally work with the seasons, (or ahead of them) influenced by surrounded in Mid County, also by like of writings by Hardy, Housman, Glare, Dobson. Hold an old fashioned sense of values. Out of step with modern world? Transfer Variety of Thoughts to paper and type.; [a.] Alresford Winchester, Hants

STEVENS, MISS ZOE
[b.] 11 July 1982, Shrewsbury; [p.] Derek Stevens, Susan Stevens; [ed.] Wrockwardine Wood School; [memb.] Drama Center, Wrockwardine Wood School; [oth. writ.] Two more poems published in Anchor Books.; [a.] Telford, Shropshire, UK, TF2 0DU

STEVENSON, ANN
[pen.] Ann McAllister; [b.] 5 May 1942, Port Glasgow; [p.] Sally McAllister; [m.] Edward Stevenson, 1 July 1961; [ch.] 7, 4 girls 3 sons 6 grandchildren; [ed.] St. Columbus High School Greenock; [occ.] Housewife, (Retired Hairdresser); [memb.] Hairdressers Federation (retired); [hon.] Certificate of Advanced Hairdressing; [pers.] I was inspired by the Holy Spirit so I wrote this poem for people to get an insight into alcoholic or drug addict inner pain. Therefore we must pray for them instead of condemning them and their families too.; [a.] Gourock, Inverclyde, UK, PA19 1TE

STEVENSON, MRS. GILLIAN DAWN
[b.] 4 August 1959, London; [p.] Barbara Presland, Henry Presland; [m.] James Albert Stevenson, 29 September 1979; [ch.] Cheryl Ann, Louise Stevenson; [ed.] Sarah Bonnell School; [occ.] Sales Adviser; [pers.] I try to reflect in my writings the trials and tribulations of life, reflecting my heartfelt feeling for myself and those who enter and touch my life.; [a.] London, UK, EI5 4NW

STEVENSON, JESSIE KENNEDY
[pen.] J. K. Dunnett; [b.] 27 May 1935, Caithness; [p.] David Dunnett and Margaret Dunnett; [m.] James T. Stevenson, 1 March 1962; [ch.] Three; [ed.] Wick High School.; [occ.] Medical Secretary (Practice Manager)

STEWART, GWENDOLINE ROSEMARY
[pen.] Gwendoline Rose; [b.] 7 May 1935, Nuneaton, Warks; [p.] Rose Hannah and Robert Shepherd; [m.] David John Stewart, 19 September 1992; [ed.] Swinnerton Sec Modern Chilvers, Coton Warwickshire Adult Education, Vegetarian Cookery - Dressmaking; [occ.] Retired Florist; [memb.] N.A.F.A.S. Flower Guild, Gardening Club; [hon.] 1st City and Guilds (Floristry), Floor Management (Retail), show awards (Flower Arrangements and Alpines); [oth. writ.] Christmas poems published in local evening paper.; [pers.] Life and all that's around inspires me, and I find different values in all poetry.; [a.] Nuneaton, Warwickshire, UK, CV10 0EN

STEWART, JAMES SCOTT SHEDDEN
[pen.] 'Scoosh'; [b.] 1 April 1969, Ayrshire Central Hospital; [p.] Mr. Hamilton Stewart, Mrs. Joyce Shedden-Stewart; [ed.] Ravenspark Academy, Irvine Ayr College, Ayr, Glasgow Caledonian University, Glasgow; [occ.] Student of Physics (3rd Year) Glasgow Caledonian University; [memb.] Glasgow Caledonian University Boxing Club (Founder Member), Kilmarnock and Dalry Boxing Clubs; [hon.] O-N-D Building and Surveying, HNC Applied Science; [oth. writ.] Several other unpublished poems.; [a.] Irvine, Ayrshire, UK, KA12 9DD

STOCKBRIDGE, ZITA
[b.] 9 March 1982, Sidcup, Kent; [p.] P. C. Stockbridge, T. J. Stockbridge; [ed.] The Grammar School for Girls Wilmington Kent; [memb.] Newsround Press/Packer; [a.] Bexley, Kent, UK, DA5 3DZ

STOCKTON, SANDRA DENISE
[pen.] Sandra D. Stockton; [b.] 23/8/49, Birmingham; [p.] Gordon & Irene Stockton; [ed.] Handsworth Wood School for girls. B'Ham; [occ.] Secretary for Midland Red West LTD.; [hon.] Piano, Birmingham College of Music; [oth. writ.] Several poems awaiting publication, currently working on a book about caring for a loved one with "Alzeimers Disease", Inspirational verse- "Trust" published in Voices on the Wind, 1996; [pers.] I believe a lot can be achieved in life if you have faith and believe, and I try to reflect this in my writing which uplifts me, and I hope it does the same for the reader. [a.] Kidderminster, Worcestershire DY11 5BJ

STONE, DONALD
[pen.] Don Stone; [b.] 15 April 1926, Leeds 9; [p.] Albert, Jeanie Stone; [m.] D.V.D., 1956; [ch.] Anne Maria, Michael D. I.; [ed.] Elementary education, left at 14 yrs. old, Ellerby Lane School, Leeds 9; [occ.] Retired; [oth. writ.] Loves Needs, published, several unpublished works; [pers.] Every poet needs inspiration and encouragement for their work. So I therefore dedicate my efforts to my daughter Anne Maria, with love and gratitude.; [a.] Leeds, West Yorkshire, UK, LS14 RBQ

STONE, MR. D.
[pen.] Don Stone; [b.] April 15, 1926, Leeds; [p.] Albert F. Stone and Jeannie Stone; [m.] Divorced - Jean, April 2, 1956; [ch.] Anne Maria and Michael David Ian; [ed.] Ellerby Lane Elementary Leeds; [occ.] Retired - Ex Painter and Decorator, Wartime-merchant Navy; [hon.] Wartime Medal 1939-1945; [oth. writ.] Several unpublished poems.; [pers.] Life is a school of learning, study wisely. Even mistakes are beneficial providing we don't repeat them.; [a.] Leeds, W. Yorks, LS14 2BQ

STONES, MALCOLM
[b.] 3 October 1934, Wombwell, Yorks; [p.] John William Stones, Louisa Stones; [m.] Sylvia Margaret Stones, 3 December 1960; [ch.] Malcolm David and Shirley Ann; [ed.] College; [occ.] Systems Development Manager; [oth. writ.] A Dolphin's Story (short story), Blue The Robot (short story), Mystic Africa (medium length story), numerous poems; [pers.] My poems are personal or topical. An essential ingredients is humour. I also write short/medium length stories. "A Dolphin's Story" was submitted to "Sea World", California, USA who expressed interest. Not yet published.; [a.] Haddenham, Buckinghamshire, UK, HP17 8HG

STOPHER, LESLIE JOHN
[b.] 31 August 1920, London; [p.] Deceased; [m.] Deceased - 12 April 1994, 7 August 1943; [ch.] Roger, Lesley and Lynn; [ed.] Normal - in Norfolk, Birmingham - and in the Army; [occ.] Retired from swimming teacher; [memb.] Life memberships of Cornwall Region Surf Life Saving Assn. Southern Region (Dorset) SLSA. Perranporth SLS Club, Weymouth Long Distance Swimming Club; [hon.] The Queens Commendation 1960 for Brave Conduct - during 2 royal humane parchment - 2 vellum, rescues as a Cornish Life Guard (7 years) Royal Life Saving Society = Service Cross - 1981 highest award at the time - President of New Quay Cornwall S.C. A.SA Advanced Teachers Cert. (Swimming); [oth. writ.] New Poets 1959 - "Could I Wish for More"; [pers.] I have written several dance numbers - words and music, also several marches, my poems come from my heart. In the Army - 1934 - 1947. The Lancashire Fusiliers Army Swimming Instr. 1966 -1985.; [a.] Perranporth, Cornwall, UK, TR6 0EE

STOREY, JEFF
[b.] 14 November 1958, Hartlepool; [p.] William Storey, Evelyn Bruce; [m.] Julie Susan Storey, 11 September 1985; [ch.] Adam Storey (20 October 1996); [ed.] Blackhall Secondary School and Acrerigg Secondary (Peterlee); [occ.] On work placement with IODA (Individual and Organizational Development and Assessment), Supported by a re-employment project, OPVS, run by East Dwham Partnership; [hon.] Winner in the Echo and Sunderland Family Health Services Authority's "Write a Healthy Poem" contest 13-9-92; [oth. writ.] Several poems published in local magazines and newspapers.; [pers.] My poetry is a mixture of personal experiences, observations, politics and sociological aspects. It is a diary of who I am at the time, therefore every poem or group of poems is different.; [a.] Peterlee, Durham, UK, SR8 5LS

STRONG, RICHARD S.
[b.] 16 March 1963, South Shields; [p.] Bob and Audrey Strong; [m.] Veronica Muckble; [ed.] Whitburn and Boldon Comprehensive, Life - 33 years; [occ.] Storeman - Onwa UK.; [memb.] Sergeant - Territorial Army - Royal Artillery.; [oth. writ.] A large collection of as yet unpublished work!; [pers.] Only by opening your eyes, can you see! Only by standing-up can you be counted! Tiny snow flakes form glaciers!; [a.] South Shields, Tyne and Wear, UK, NE34 8TG

SUMNER, ALLAN
[b.] 23 February 1930, Salford, Surrey; [p.] Deceased; [m.] Margaret Mary, 12 August 1950; [ch.] Five; [ed.] King School Kew Surrey, Church - School. Left age 13 yrs.; [occ.] Retired; [oth. writ.] Dozens of poems waiting hopefully for publication on all subjects. I have so many I don't know which to enter. Maybe all.; [pers.] My writing is based on personal experience, short, sweet and brief and simple to read.; [a.] Totnes, Devon, UK, TQ9 5FQ

SUPAN, JOSIPA
[b.] May 26, 1979, Zagreb; [p.] Branko & Blanka; [ed.] Finished primary school and bilingual french high school that I am still attending, French, English and Spanish language schools; [occ.] Student; [memb.] Member of a literary and poetry group INA, A member of French Open Society Alliance Frangaise; [hon.] An award by Croatian Literary Society for the topic of victims of Bleiburg; An international award by Alliance Frangaise for one of the 16 best essays in Croatia in French; newspaper awards for poetry; [oth. writ.] Mostly essays published in catholic magazine "Mi" for young people, poems published in national newspapers like "Vencernji List" and "Vjesnik", stories published in children's magazines; [pers.] Love is agony and ecstasy in the same emotion, as much as it is a crazy joy it is equally justified pain. Nevertheless, we all want it so hard, we allow it to make ways of our dreams, our lives, throughout it we search for the proof of belonging to somebody and our reflection of emotions in someone we love. [a.] Zagreb, Zagreback Zupanija, 10000

SUTHERLAND, SAMANTHA
[b.] 28 April 1967, Reading; [p.] Derek Coates, Jan Coates; [m.] Mark Sutherland, 1 September 1990; [ch.] Jack, Hollie, Emma and Megan; [ed.] Smithdon High School; [occ.] Home Maker; [oth. writ.] Joint writer and artist of regular cartoon series in local parish magazine.; [a.] Camberley, Surrey, UK, GU15 4AL

SWIFT, CHRISTINE
[b.] 23 December 1948, Hillingdon; [p.] Mr. and Mrs. G. Brind; [m.] Divorced; [ch.] Paul, Kerry, Andrew; [ed.] Secondary Modern Swakeleys Girls School, Long Lane, Ickenham, Middx; [occ.] Knitting Machinist and Mother; [hon.] Awards for various things Inc: 1st prize in local show for machine knitting, vegs, fruit, and also 1st prize in the novices class in the "Middlesex Wine Festival"; [oth. writ.] Not tried to have my poems or writing published before.; [pers.] I have been greatly inspired by being in love again with Mr. Dennis Pepper. I met him, 30 years ago. We met again after 28 years, now it's come full circle; [a.] West Drayton, Middlesex, UK, UB7 8LQ

SZEREMETA, ANNA
[b.] 13 September 1959, Nottingham; [p.] Gluseppe Giacone, Mirella Giacone; [m.] 28 April 1979; [ed.] Arthur Mee Girls School Nottingham, South Nottinghamshire College further Education; [occ.] Soft Furnishings (Interior Design Ideas); [hon.] 1st in poem competition at school, 1st in the Micheal Willets Award for Chalk Drawing entitled 'My England'; [oth. writ.] 'The Stirring', 'Lonely Foxclove', 'Belvedere', 'Lazy Summer Morn' (none of the above have been published.); [pers.] I have always had a love of words, and how they relate one to another on paper. I try to use words in the way an artist would use his palette. I find people and situations most interesting. I would like to think I'm a realist - this I try to reflect in my work.; [a.] West Brideford, Nottingham, UK, NG2 6GG

TABOR, CATHERINE JOY
[pen.] Cay Tabor; [b.] 17 June 1971, Sidcup; [p.] Brenda Colley, John Tabor; [m.] Fiance - Keith Jeffrey; [ch.] One son Henry John Edward Jeffrey; [occ.] Mother; [pers.] I wrote my poem for my fiance the day after my son was born. Harry was born 7 weeks early and although at the time my baby was very poorly, this was my way of celebrating his birth and thanking the neonatal unit in Queen Marys hospital, family and friends for the care and love they showed in his first weeks with us.; [a.] Orpington, Kent, UK, BR5 4LL

TAFT, ILONA
[b.] 15 April 1982, Bromsgrove; [p.] Martin Taft, Christine Taft; [ed.] Currently studying GCSE's at Invicta Grammar School for Girls; [oth. writ.] Poem - Out in the Open, published - May, 1996, Book - Young Writers Carousel Kent.; [a.] Maidstone, Kent, UK, ME14 5QZ

TALBOT, ROSEMARY
[b.] 16 July 1932, Bagshot, Surrey; [p.] Geck James Talbot, Violet Talbot; [m.] Divorced; [ch.] Robert E. Agar, John S. Agar, Alexis P. Webb; [ed.] Branksome Hill Rd School, Sandhurst Berks, 60 and Atworth; [occ.] Retired; [memb.] 40 S Club Sandhurst, Royal British Legion Corsham Wilts; [oth. writ.] Unpublished book of poems, some have been recited to club members and in church.; [pers.] My mother taught me to love and appreciate poetry, I write from the heart, I also paint watercolors and read a great deal.; [a.] Mensham, Wiltshire, UK, SN12 8JQ

TALIB, QAISER MAHMOOD
[b.] 24 September 1977, Birmingham; [p.] Nishat Zacheor (Mother), Talib Hussain (Father); [ed.] Moseley Secondary School, Birmingham GCSE's, 8, including A's in Engl., Language and Lit., 'A' levels - C, 2 D's (Eng/Bus, and History); [occ.] Unemployed; [hon.] I wish.; [oth. writ.] Have done work experience at Wolverhampton Star and Express, Jan 1996. Had an article published on the Polaris Missile at a local museum.; [pers.] Fave quotes ol-my Hero — James Dean, JD - I want to grow so tall so that nobody can reach me. Not to prove anything but just to go where you ought to go, when you dedicate your whole life and all you are to one thing.; [a.] Birmingham, Warks, UK, B11 3LE

TANDY, CHRISTINE ELIZABETH
[b.] 29 September 1948, Caerphilly; [p.] Vera Patchell, Edward Patchell; [m.] Terence Tandy, 5 August 1972; [ed.] Caerphilly Girl's Grammar School, Dudley College of Education Birmingham University; [occ.] Retired School Teacher; [memb.] Bewdley Choral Society, various history groups; [hon.] Various; [oth. writ.] Selection of poems to be published in 1997. Various articles for magazines, children's poems.; [pers.] I have always enjoyed the poetry of the "war poets" probably because I heard such a lot about war heroism from my grandmother. I also enjoy light-hearted poetry.; [a.] Bewdley, Worcestershire, UK, DY12 1DB

TANNER, STEVEN
[b.] 10 February 1978, Canterbury; [p.] Kay Tanner and Ron Tanner; [ed.] Abbey Secondary School and 6th form College; [occ.] Trainee Golf Professional; [memb.] Maidstone Golf Club, Canterbury Snookee Club; [hon.] 8 GCSE Passes, 2 A-Levels, 2 As-Levels - Inc English Lit.; [oth. writ.] Many poems published in different anthologies like 'Poets in the South-East' and 'Who Dares Wings', currently working on own poem book; [pers.] I strive to become a more professional poet to give readers the pleasure and great satisfaction, because after all, it is you,

the readers, that keep the world of poetry alive!; [a.] Faversham, Kent, UK, ME13 7DP

TANTI HUGHES, MRS. JONQUIL R.
[b.] 23 June 1938, Grantown-on-Spey, Scotland; [p.] Edward Francis, Dorothy Francis (Nee Stuart); [m.] Edward Paul Tanti, 27 September 1993; [ed.] Aberlour High School, St. Andrews University - M.A., Victoria University of Manchester - Post Grad. Diploma in Social Work, London University - P.G.C.E.; [memb.] Member British Legion (Malta Branch), Malta Union Club (Vice Chairperson), British Resident's Association, George Cross Island Association, St. Andrew's Society; [oth. writ.] Letters on topical issues to local newspapers, various articles in the Malta Union Club Magazine, including one on my collection of early tins.; [pers.] All my poems reflect various aspects of my personal, spiritual or psychic experience, many of which are in the 'inspirational' genre. The published poem is the best example of this, and as such was written very quickly, with little or no correction.; [a.] Msida, Malta, MSD 05

TAPPIN, SARAH
[b.] 5 March 1978, Oxford; [p.] Philip and Paula Tappin; [ed.] Wheatley Park Comprehensive School; [occ.] Customer Care Co Ordinator; [pers.] All we think we know is never as much as we really do.; [a.] Oxford, Oxon, UK, OX3 8BH

TAYLOR, JOHN
[b.] 22 September 1964, Glasgow; [p.] Catherine and Douglas Hutchison; [ed.] Barrhead High School, Reid Kerr College, Caledonian University, Glasgow; [occ.] Student Nurse; [oth. writ.] Personal poems only which have never been published.; [pers.] I hope my words are encouraging and wish to thank My Grandparents - Chris and Jack Elliott, and my nieces Joanne and Isla for giving me the Enthusiasm.; [a.] Glasgow, Strathclyde, UK

TAYLOR, MR. LACHLAN
[pen.] "Lachlan Taylor"; [b.] 26 June 1922, Falkirk; [p.] William and Margaret Taylor (Dec.); [m.] Anne McFarlane Henry (Dec.), 4 March 1967; [ed.] Comprehensive, left at fourteen, obtained day school lower certificate; [occ.] Pensioner; [hon.] 2nd World War Medals; [oth. writ.] Have 24 poems in anthologys, have 2 in poetry magazines; this accomplished in seven years, when I first sent in 9 poems for a competition; [pers.] Have always loved writing poetry and reading others' poetry. Shelley, Shakespeare and Burns amongst my favorite poets. My own poems I don't think are for intellectuals.; [a.] Falkirk, Stirlingshire, UK, FK5 4JT

TAYLOR, ROBIN
[b.] 25 December 1945, Bearsted, Kent; [p.] Joan Burles, Karl McGregor; [ed.] Kingston College (Jamaica), Wentworth High School (Jamaica), Netteswell Secondary and Modern, Sandon House School,; [occ.] Unemployed; [oth. writ.] Have written other poems, and sayings, and a short story, all of which I'm hoping to eventually get published. Am presently working on a book, and a script.; [pers.] My aim is to be open-minded enough, to be aware of life, rather than take it for granted, and so to reflect it in my poems. My philosophical statement is..if it wasn't for people, the world would be a better place to live.; [a.] Margate, Kent, UK, CT9 3XU

TEEK, SARA
[b.] 8 February 1951, Iver Heath, Bucks; [p.] Cecily Teek and Jack Teek; [ed.] Convent boarding school, Slough College of Technology; [occ.] Retired; [memb.] Associateship of London Academy of Music, Dramatic Art. Member Uxbridge Young Farmers 1967-81. Member Gerrards Cross Centre Players 1975-present; [hon.] A.L.A.M. (Speech) 1972 5 "O" levels and business studies; [oth. writ.] Play "Biding Time" 1994; [pers.] I love fairness. I strive to fight

against prejudice and oppression, championing the human rights of myself and others. I have a love of life. Joie de Vivre.; [a.] Hillingdon, Middx, UK, UB8 3UE

TELFORD, MERVIN SIMEON
[b.] 1 February 1961, London; [p.] Eva Hanuschke Telford, Naki Aten Telford; [ch.] Leon, Nakayi, Channe, Tashinga; [ed.] Fort Luton Secondary School, The Military, self taught artist and poet.; [occ.] Physical Training Instructor, Artist/Sculptor, Illustrator; [oth. writ.] Poems and short stories.; [pers.] I endeavor to see the beauty and be conscious of the mystery that is often unnoticed along life's path.; [a.] London, Tottenham, UK, N15 6ES

TEMPLETON, ELLEN MAISLE
[b.] 11 July 1975, Grantham; [p.] Nanette J. Templeton; [ed.] No education since the age of ten, due to ill health.; [occ.] Un-employed; [oth. writ.] A selection of poetry, poem published in the Silver Lining Appeal, the kidney patients' magazine and one in a local newspaper.; [pers.] I have been inspired to write poetry since I became ill, aged ten, with kidney failure, being on dialysis and having a transplant when I was fifteen.; [a.] Grantham, Lincolnshire, UK, NG32 1QP

TENNENT, MRS. IRIS
[b.] 16 July 1928, Levenshulme, M/C; [p.] Elizabeth Needham and Robert Lowe; [m.] James Young Tennent, 16 April 1949; [ch.] Stephen James, David Young, Paul Martin, Mark Scott; [ed.] Chapel Street School, Chapel Street, Levenshulme, Manchester; [occ.] Retired from Screen Printer Textiles; [oth. writ.] Poems and short stories, none published; [pers.] This poem is dedicated to my eldest son Stephen and his wife Alison. They gave their jobs up six years ago to go to "Romania" to care for the children in the orphanages; [a.] Earby, Lancashire, UK, BB8 6QS

THOMAS, IBIKUNLE
[b.] March 1963, Lagos, Nigeria; [p.] Tinvola Thomas and Olabisi Thomas; [ed.] University of Lagos, Nigeria B.Sc. (hons.) Sociology. Due to start post graduate course in Public Relations in September 1997 (University of Stirling, Scotland); [hon.] Certificate of Merit for Organizational Ability - as President of Sociological Students Association, University of Lagos, Nigeria (1984/85); [oth. writ.] I like writing poems, songs, and articles on diverse themes. I am currently writing my 1st novel.; [pers.] "The Fight" is dedicated to my parents as they celebrate the golden jubilee anniversary of their wedding.; [a.] Bow, London, UK, E3 3BQ

THOMAS, MISS EMMA JANE
[b.] 4 May 1978, Abertridwr; [p.] Ian John Thomas, Rosemaire Lily Sharn, Angelyn Thomas; [ed.] Bedwas Comprehensive School University of Wales Newport; [hon.] 'A' Level English Literature, 'A' Level Religious studies plus ten G.C.S.E's and Complete youth and award scheme; [oth. writ.] Currently Studying B.A. Hons Primary Education with Qualified Teacher Status.; [pers.] Through the poem 'Oh Sinful Eden' I wanted to emphasize the importance of life in this world with a religious connection; [a.] Bedwas, Gwent, UK, NP1 8AE

THOMAS, JOSEPHINE
[b.] 2 January 1935, Kingston on Thames; [p.] Adopted; [m.] Ivor Evans Thomas, Widow; [ch.] Dane-Tudor, Serena-Iris; [ed.] Private; [occ.] Sculptor; [memb.] Friends of the Earth and local choir; [oth. writ.] Poetry Now 1992, South West and Aspects of Love, Arrival Press also Rich Pickings (Poetry Now); [pers.] Forgiveness sets you free. Special thoughts to my mother and father and my adopted family.; [a.] Helston, Cornwall, UK, TR12 6LY

THOMAS, MARGARET ALICE
[b.] 19 September 1920, Clifton Reynes; [p.] Maud Mary and Charles Sizer; [m.] Gwilym Tho-

mas, 16 February 1952; [ch.] Four daughters; [ed.] Olney Council School and Olney Secondary Modern; [occ.] Retired Housewife; [hon.] Editor's Choice Award; [oth. writ.] The New Britain

THOMAS, REBECCA HORSFALL
[b.] 20 December 1972, Episkopi; [p.] Bill Horsfall Sue Horsfall; [ed.] All Hallows Ind. School, Old Hall Ind. School; [occ.] Police Officer; [pers.] "Regret nothing, Reveal in life"; [a.] Nuneaton, Warwickshire, UK, CV10 9NW

THOMAS, SHARON
[pen.] Sharon Thomas; [b.] 17 December 1972, Wrexham; [p.] Alan Thomas, Kathleen Thomas; [ed.] Ysgol Bryn Alyn, Gwersyllt, Wrexham; [occ.] Quality Control Technician, Sutures Ltd., Ruabon, Wrexham; [pers.] I have a strong interest in the unknown and have tried to express my innermost feelings through my writing.; [a.] Wrexham, UK, LL14 1NW

THOMPSON, JAMES
[b.] 10 September 1975, Doncaster; [ed.] Queen Elizabeth Grammar School, Wakefield; [occ.] Student at Lyon University, France; [hon.] World Black Mamba Champion, County Togga Champion, Head Au Mur Silver Medalist; [oth. writ.] Moonstorm Rising, novel, hope to be published; [pers.] Just because you're paranoid, it doesn't mean they're not out to get you!

THOMPSON, SARAH JANE ISABELLA
[pen.] Sarah Thompson; [b.] 30 March 1986, Newtownards; [p.] Shaw Thompson and Evelyn Thompson; [ed.] Kinallen Primary School; [occ.] School Girl; [memb.] Dromara Youth Club; [hon.] Bronze Medal Banbridge Speech and Drama Festival/5000M B.T. Swimathon Award/Best 1st year cup in Junior Girls Brigade/Trinity College London Initial Grade with Merit in Pianoforte.; [oth. writ.] 1st Placed Victorian Project/Runner-up Missionary Project/ various poems and short stories.; [pers.] I have received much encouragement from my teachers at Kinallen primary school.; [a.] Dromore, Down, UK, BT25 2NW

THOMSON, ALISTER H.
[b.] 9 July 1928, Rogart; [p.] (Deceased) Angus and Jenny Thomson; [m.] (Deceased) Liz Thomson, 14 December 1968; [ed.] Rogart Public School, Sutherland Technical School Golspie; [occ.] Retired; [memb.] Bon Line Club, Indoor and Outdoor, British Legion, Post Office Veterans; [oth. writ.] Several poems published. (Arrival Press) and (Poetry Now) 2 published Int. Library of Poetry; [pers.] Attempt to write on what I feel and on life as I see it.; [a.] Inverness, Inverness-shire, UK, IV1 2DS

THOMSON, DENIZE
[pen.] Fuggle; [b.] 23 February 1952, Sunderland; [p.] Wallace A., Martha A. Fuggle; [m.] Peter; [ch.] Debra, Donna, Twins, Peter, Patrick; [occ.] Housewife, Poet; [oth. writ.] Poems published in anthologies; [pers.] Miles of love leads us to a path of fate.; [a.] City of Sunderland, UK, SR6 0EJ

THOMSON, MARGARET JEAN
[pen.] Greta; [b.] May 20, 1933, Rumbling Bridge, Kinross-shire; [p.] Alexander and Rosaline Wood (Nee Gray); [m.] James Spalding Thomson (Deceased March 1990), April 31, 1952; [ch.] 5 girls and 1 boy; [ed.] Crook of Devon, Fossoway, Kinross-shire-Primary, Kinross-Secondary; [occ.] Retired; [pers.] I have only recently been writing poetry mostly reflecting the peace of my surroundings. This has helped me greatly, adjust to my life without my husband. Ease the pain of my loss.; [a.] Morar by Mallaig, Inverness-shire, Scotland, PH40 4PB

THORNTON, CYRIL OSCAR
[pen.] Peter Brayson Thornton; [b.] 23 November 1916, Delhi (British India); [p.] Alfred Cecil Thornton/Nora May Thornton nee Brayson; [m.] Mary Audrey Joyce Thornton nee Halliday, 4 October 1941; [ch.] Gillian Eve, Christine Ann, Audrey Marilyn, Roger Alfred Charles,

Peter Valfre, Beverly May; [ed.] Public School; [occ.] Retired Civil Servant and Businessman - Amateur Poet and playwright; [memb.] Army and Navy Club London Writer/Publisher/Producer, member of Performing Right Society Ltd and Mechanical Copyright Protection Society Ltd; [hon.] Military Cross Mention in Despatches; [oth. writ.] Several poems/Film Documentary/Radio Plays; [pers.] Do what you can when you can to increase the sum of human happiness; [a.] Uckfield, East Sussex, UK, TN22 2BA

THORNTON, GAIL
[b.] 1 May 1980, Birmingham; [p.] Kevin Thornton, Brenda Thornton; [ed.] Saltley Secondary School, Joseph Chamberlaing, Sixth Form Collage; [occ.] Student; [pers.] In my poetry I try to ask the questions which seem to have no answers. It is when we are able to find the answers that the true "meaning" of life is known.; [a.] Birmingham, Warwickshire, UK, B9 5UU

THORNTON, KATHLEEN
[pen.] Kathleen Thornton; [b.] 29 August 1936, Alyth; [p.] Eliza Buick, Walter T. Buick; [m.] William C. H. Thornton, 4 April 1958; [ed.] Alyth Junior Secondary; [occ.] Nursing Officer (retired); [memb.] Royal College Nursing, Perthshire Art Association, Retirement Health Service Fellowship; [oth. writ.] Recently a poem published by Anchor Books and several more in near future.; [pers.] Favorite hymn is 'All Things, Bright and Beautiful'; [a.] Perth, Perthshire, UK, PH1 1JR

TIBBITS, LUCY
[b.] 18 January 1978, Leamington Spa; [p.] Jean and Anthony, brother Richard; [ed.] GCSE's, A-Level Literature and Art, Foundation Course studying Fine Art; Interior Design diploma; [occ.] Interior Designer; [hon.] Won and was placed in Stratford Festival Children's Poetry Competition on several occasions.; [a.] Stratford-on-Avon, Warwickshire, CV37 9FD

TIDWELL, NEVILLE
[b.] 25 October 1932, Rushington, Lincs; [p.] Edwin James Tidwell, Violet Tidwell; [m.] Joan Tidwell (Deceased) 10 February 1965; [ch.] David James, Lurena; [ed.] Course Grammar, Cambridge University and Oxford University; [occ.] University Senior Lecturer; [memb.] Society for Old Testament-Study; [hon.] MA (Cantab et Oxon), BD (Oxon), Barwell Scholar, Selwyn College, Cambridge; [oth. writ.] Contributions to books and journals as specialist fields of research, poems local magazines.; [pers.] Influenced by metaphysical and Romantic poets and Robert Browning and Gerald Manky Hopkins. Poetry reflects on the relationship between nature and culture.; [a.] Alsager, Cheshire, UK, ST7 2NR

TOKARSKI, MARGARET JANE JADWIGA
[b.] 11 March 1963, Saint Albans; [pers.] Life is like a book - except in a book you know how many chapters there are and you can read the ending.; [a.] Milton Keynes, Buckinghamshire, UK

TOLLEY, CONSTANCE MAY
[b.] 21 April 1936, Corley Moore, Warwickshire; [occ.] Retired; [hon.] Not for writing poetry. I have never before, this year 1996, written poetry in my life.; [oth. writ.] Svengali, Pain, Despair, The Child In The Snow; [pers.] A few scribbled words, on a Christmas card, to my sister and husband, created the birth of this poem. I dedicate this completed work back to you - Donna and Viv.; [a.] Birmingham, West Midlands, UK, B31 2XG

TOMSETT, TERENCE M. P.
[b.] 8 March 1939, Balham, London; [p.] Jack (Dec.), Sheila; [m.] Divorced; [ch.] Tina 36, Terry 25 yrs. old; [ed.] Sec. Med.; [occ.] Master Builder; [memb.] Flying Group, Golf Club, Karate Club; [oth. writ.] Several poems and short sto-

ries, nothing ever submitted for publication. I did, however, send a poem to H.M. The Queen and received a reply of great delight from her, this was 1976.; [pers.] I am very concerned about our society, crime does seem to pay and it's time draconian measures returned to put criminality down.; [a.] Hertford, Herts, UK, SG14 2EJ

TOOK, DAVID MCCARTNEY
[b.] 25 August 1962, Greenock; [p.] Anne (Harrison) Took, William Took; [m.] Jacqueline Took (Gibbons), 21 October 1995; [ch.] Brian, Michelle, Joseph, Hayley, Becki; [ed.] Notre Dame High School, James Watt College, Paisley College of Technology; [occ.] Unemployed, previously, House Supervisor (Whitbread); [hon.] Licenciateship in Shipbuilding and Engineering, ASNT Level 2 Radiography, ASNT Level 1 Dye Pen Inspection, CSWIP Mag Par Inspection; [oth. writ.] A Flight Of Fantasy, Our Little Secret, I Know, Free Me, Forgiven, Dreaming (none published); [pers.] To my family - in life there is love and pain, it is the pain of loving you all, that keeps me alive. Make life worth living and you'll stay alive forever.; [a.] Barrow in Furness, Cumbria, UK, LA14 4BD

TOWNLEY, CATHERINE
[b.] 27 March 1962, Cheshire; [p.] Alan Knott, Shirley Knott; [m.] Divorce; [ch.] Sarah, Rachel, Stephen; [ed.] Secondary School Stockport College, Manchester University; [occ.] Nursing Superintendent; [memb.] UKCC; [hon.] Diploma in Professional Nursing Studies; [oth. writ.] Poems and short novels unpublished; [pers.] My poetry reflects this ever changing society and often affords me the escapism from it - which we all need!; [a.] Stockport, Cheshire, UK, SK8 7AG

TOWNSEND, ANN PATRICIA
[pen.] Apt; [b.] 14 November 1934, Derby; [p.] Jack and Theadora Buxton; [m.] Robert Townsend, 9 November 1955; [ch.] Edwin Geoffrey, Judith, Beryl; [ed.] Moravian School Oakbrook Derby - Educated World War II mainly on Tennyson; [occ.] Retired but still writing; [memb.] Church of England High Church Section (Catholic); [oth. writ.] Poems on events as they happen and held in book form - warning to children printed in most papers national and local after mass murders.; [pers.] Life is what each and every one of us make of our lives. Poetry is the art of a few - that should be passed for all to share.; [a.] Sheffield, Derbyshire, UK, S30 2ZA

TRAVERS, EDWARD
[b.] 7 November 1947, Dublin; [p.] Thomas and Mary; [m.] Antoinette, 19 March 1973; [ch.] Julie-Ann, Louise, Gillian; [ed.] DE, La Salle School Ballyfermot, Dublin 20; [occ.] Taxi Driver; [memb.] The Planetary Society, Astronomy Ireland; [oth. writ.] Poem (Evo) published in Quiet Moments.; [a.] Lucan, Dublin, Ireland

TREACY, PATRICK
[b.] 26 April 1956, Enniskillen; [p.] Patrick and Sheila Treacy; [ed.] St. Michaels Grammar Enniskillen, Queens University Belfast, Royal College of Surgeons, Dublin; [occ.] Doctor; [memb.] British Medical Association, Royal Dublin Society; [hon.] AER Lingus Young Scientists Award, Norman Rae Gold Medal R.C.S.I., BSC (Hons) Q.U.B., Mb.Bch (R.C.S.I.), DRCOG, DCH, DTM (R.C.S.I.); [oth. writ.] Column writer "Fermanagh Herald", Irish Medical Times, column writer "Doctors Post"; [a.] Garrison, Fermanagh, UK, BT93 4AF

TREHEARN, JASON LEWIS
[b.] 12 October 1971, Ipswich; [p.] Derek Trehearn, Ann Trehearn; [ed.] Northgate High School; [occ.] Clerical Assistant; [memb.] Trinity Football Club; [hon.] GCSE English; [pers.] If only one of my poems relates to just one person, then I have been successful.; [a.] Ipswich, Suffolk, UK, IP4 2RP

TRENTHAM, MRS. JEAN MARY
[pen.] Laura Cleghorn; [b.] 12 November 1943, Chelmsford; [p.] Thomas Cleghorn, (Tom Clegg stage name), Lyn Cleghorn; [m.] M. Brian Trentham, 2 February 1963; [ch.] Mark Christopher, Yvonne Anne, Marie-Louise, Pauline Michelle; [ed.] Epping Comprehensive, Petersborough Regional College; [occ.] Housewife (Retired draughts person and illustrator); [oth. writ.] Several short stories (children) and many poems (none published). I have also written about my father (who has been a great influence on my life) as seen through the eyes of a child.; [pers.] I was introduced to poetry at a very early age by my father, and have been influenced by him ever since. He also has written an autobiography which is excellent, and needs to be published.; [a.] Chatters, Cambridgeshire, UK, PE16 6RX

TRUSSLER, LINDA
[pen.] Linda Blake-Trussler; [b.] 3 August 1949, London; [p.] Elsie Blake, Albert Blake; [m.] Arthur Trussler, 25 April 1970; [ch.] Asa Blake-Trussler, Alexander Lewis Blake-Trussler; [ed.] Elms, Acton, London evening study only.; [occ.] Personal Secretary Derby City General Hospital; [oth. writ.] I have written approx. 40 poems - including - "Our Home", "Music", "The Supernatural", "Are We Alone?", "Someone Else", "Love", "Human Dreams and Wishes", "Natures Voice", "Laughter", and many more.; [pers.] I put down in rhyme how I see everyday life - how I see the world we live in - what there is around us - how other people appear to us - how lucky some of us are - how unlucky some of us are.; [a.] Derby, Derbyshire, UK, DE3 5 LJ

TSANG, ANGELA
[b.] 19 February 1984, Lowestoft, England; [p.] Mr. and Mrs. M. Tsang; [ed.] Fen Park Primary And Kirley Middle School, Lowestoft; [occ.] School girl; [memb.] Martial Arts, Brownies, Hockey and Netball Clubs; [hon.] Governor's Cup for Progress, a year award for a good progress; [oth. writ.] My mum was born in China and speaks Mandarin while my dad was born in Hong Kong and speaks Cantonese. They were married in Hong Kong and my brother and I were both born in England here in East Anglia.; [pers.] I have had a poem published in "Hear my Voice", poetry written by Suffolk School children of all ages in form 4-12 and from all over the country and this has encouraged me to continue to try to write poetry. I enjoy writing English; [a.] Lowestoft, Suffolk, UK, NR33 0BT

TWELVES, P. A.
[pen.] 'Darkie'; [b.] 15 March 1947, Spalding, Lincs.; [p.] John Robert and Eileen Mary Twelves; [m.] Divorced; [ch.] Two; [ed.] Sir John Gleed School, Spalding, Lincolnshire; [occ.] In college gaining my level 3 NVQ in Administration; [oth. writ.] I have written many poems and a short story - I have never attempted publication, because my poems are a reflection of a very unhappy time in my life and I didn't think any-one would 'feel' them.; [pers.] I was doubtful about entering my poem - it was my first and my favorite, selfishly I wasn't sure about its worth as poetry.; [a.] Werrington, Peterborough, Cambs, UK, PE4 6NN

TYE, BETTY
[b.] 20 March 1939, Enfield; [p.] Edward Bright and Dora Bright; [m.] Trevor Tye, 23 June 1962; [ch.] Adrian Trevor and Beverly Katharine; [ed.] Edmonton Technical School, Private Piano Lessons and Secretarial Education; [occ.] Part time Legal Secretary/Pianist; [memb.] Furzefield Swimming Club; [hon.] Cumulative Certificate and Book Prize from the London College of Music. Festival Medals A.L.C.M.; [pers.] I dedicate "Joys of a Pianist" to my wonderful parents for their encouragement and support and to a great music teacher and friend, Monica. I really enjoy poetry and am now in the process of working on further poems.; [a.] Chestnut, Hertfordshire, UK, EN7 5JU

TYLER, CYNTHIA
[m.] Widow; [ch.] Two sons - Sonny and Leo; [pers.] In memory of Leo Tyler tragically killed in a car accident March 1995. Words are all I have left to say I love and miss him so.; [a.] Wisbech, Cambs, UK, PE13 5AQ

TYLER, RICHARD
[b.] 28 September 1973, Lewisham; [p.] Mr. V. Tyley, Mrs. W. Tyley; [ed.] BA (Hons) Humanities 2, 11 (96), T.E.F.L. Qualification (July 95) Luton University; [occ.] PGCE (Upper Primary) De Montfort University, Milton Keynes; [memb.] Kent AC (Cross-Country) Tequila Club (Hanstead, London); [hon.] Humanities; [oth. writ.] Pernambular bu lu lu, yet to be published, describes the futility of celebrating a patriarchal year 2000. The cosmic mother earth at least pure, sexy love should really dictate the 3rd millennium.; [pers.] I know the new century dictates events to most people but it means nothing to me. Sex means much more, sex and pure passion.; [a.] Lewisham, London, UK, SE6 2LA

VASSALLO, BERNADETTE
[b.] 21 June 1996, Malta; [p.] Dr. and Mrs. L. A. Vassallo (Father Deceased); [ed.] Primary - St. Joseph Court School, Sliera, Molk, Secondary - Continental School, Jeddah Saudi Arabia, 6th form, New Hall School, Boreham, Essex, University of Malta, Talqrogg, Msida, Malta obtained a Bachelors of Arb. degree in English and Communication Studies,; [occ.] Postgraduate student in Media Studies, Education and Associate English as a foreign language teacher; [memb.] 1) Amnesty International Malta, 2) Junior Chamber Malta, 3) AISEC; [hon.] 1) Bachelors of Art Degree in English and Communications, 2) E.C.I.S. Award for International Understanding (1986), 3) Public of Edirburgh Bronze Award; [oth. writ.] Various travel features published in Maltese local publications for student and youth travel. A series of unpublished personal poems and personal writings written between 1988 to date. A few feature articles on Amnesty International.; [pers.] To be born, to live, to die are the three things, which we have roamed about, to do the best of.; [a.] St. Julians, Malta, SLM 13

VEITCH, JUNE MARY
[pen.] Gus; [b.] 9 May 1938, Plymouth; [occ.] Mr. and Mrs. F. G. Butler; [m.] Terry, 2 June 1962; [ch.] Jacqueline Roger; [ed.] Sec. School; [occ.] Housewife; [oth. writ.] Also included other details. (Pathfield to Dartmoor) poem included. "Window of Life" published in Jewels of the Imagination. Boat voyage started poetry July 1996. Self Taught Artist, Barbarian Theme, and Dartmoor. Paintings (Board and Canvas). Given to raise funds.; [pers.] Rediscovered hidden talent lain dormaint over the years. I now appreciate poetry and art which have opened my eyes to discover the innermost feelings of other poets.; [a.] Plymouth, Devon, UK, PL7 1RX

VELLA, MS. THERESA
[b.] 30 September 1957, Manikata, Malta; [p.] Anthony (Late) and Liberata Vella; [ed.] Maria Regina Grammar School/B. Educ. (Hons) (1976-81) at the University of Malta; [occ.] Teacher of French and Geography in a secondary school; [oth. writ.] Several poems published in local newsletters and newspapers, both in English and Maltese. Inclusion of a poem in anthology "Voices On The Wind" (1996); [pers.] Catching the moment and forgetting about it is sowing the seed in the peat of time. The sunshine of love then makes each poem break out, transforming the day's barrenness into the music of the heart.; [a.] Manikata, Malta, SPB 07

VERRAN, MRS. LUCY FLORENCE
[b.] 11 January 1917, Maida Vale, London; [p.] Florence Elenoar Broome, Frederick Broome; [m.] Oliver Vincen Verran (Deceased), January 1933; [ch.] John, Melvin, and twins Margaret and David; [ed.] Church of England Elementary

School in a small village in Buckinghamshire - name - "Mursley"; [occ.] Retired - I shall be 80 years old on Jan. 11th 1997; [pers.] Many thanks for your so kind interest in my poetry! I I am keenly interested in nature and a lover of animals. I am also a sincere Christian and have so much to thank God for!; [a.] Whitleigh, Plymouth, Devon, UK, PL5 4EA

VINNICOMBE, SUSAN
[b.] 10 June 1959, Exeter, Devon; [p.] Raymond V. Phillis Gill; [m.] Divorced; [ch.] Three; [ed.] Priory High School Exeter; [occ.] Chiropodist; [oth. writ.] I have an exercise book full of poems but I have never shown them to anyone, up until sending you "I am me".; [pers.] The poems I have written are mostly about my own personal emotions at the time. Writing feelings down on paper help me deal with situations.; [a.] Newton Abbot, Devon, UK, TQ12 6SR

VIRR, FAVIL
[b.] 16 August 1978, India; [p.] Valerie Virr and Maurice Virr; [ed.] Cardinal Newman School, Newman Sixth Form College; [memb.] Previously belonged to Helter Skelter Dance Company; [oth. writ.] Written several other poems and short stories - not published. Also display booklet promoting Newman Sixth Form College.; [pers.] My predominant ambition throughout my writing is to move and inspire all, to touch upon some aspect of your own lives which may be reflected in my work.; [a.] Brighton, East Sussex, UK

WADE, GILLIAN M.
[pen.] Helen Rhodes; [b.] 14 April 1958, Keighley, West Yorks; [p.] Mr. J. B. Haggas, M. E. Rhodes; [m.] Peter Wade, 1 December 1984; [ch.] Helen Frances Wade, Katherine Elizabeth Wade; [ed.] Greenhead Grammar School, Keighley. Margaret McMillan College of Ed.; [occ.] Teacher of Dyslexic Children, Kinklees Metropolitan Education Authority; [memb.] B.D.A. (British Dyslexia Association); [hon.] Cert. Ed. (English and Education). B.D.A. Diploma; [oth. writ.] Working on a few ideas for poetry, short stories, writing on special needs and children's books; [pers.] I particularly enjoy poetry and would enjoy the opportunity of writing songs.; [a.] Leeds, West Yorkshire, UK, LS20 9EW

WAGSTAFF, RACHEL
[b.] 5 February 1980, Beckenham, UK; [ed.] St. David's College, old palace school; [occ.] Student; [memb.] Norwich City F.C.; [oth. writ.] Two other poems published.; [pers.] At present, I am hoping to read philosophy at university. I write a lot in my spare time, and this is one of my earlier poems, dedicated to my little brother Thomas.; [a.] Croydon, Surrey, UK, CR0 8BX

WAITE, STEPHEN M.
[pen.] Stephen M. Waite; [b.] 23 May 1954, Bradford, West Yorkshire; [p.] Jean and George Waite; [m.] Maureen; [ed.] Belle Vue Grammar, Bradford, West Yorkshire; [occ.] Oil Company Buyer; [memb.] Institute of Purchasing and Supply. American Institute of Photography. Mensa Royal Shakespeare Company.; [oth. writ.] Various writings published as poetry and as song lyrics.; [pers.] Everything written, as in life, is about light and shade. I strive to achieve an even balance.; [a.] Gorleston, Norfolk, UK, NR31 6RT

WALKER, ALISON
[b.] 25 May 1960, Mexborough; [p.] James Drummond, Nancy Drummond; [m.] Cristopher Walker, 23 March 1986; [ch.] Stuart, Daniel; [ed.] Swinton Comprehensive School; [occ.] Mother and Housewife; [oth. writ.] Various Poetry Now publications; [pers.] I hope to bring pleasure to other people through my writings.; [a.] Upton, West Yorkshire, UK, WF9 1EY

WALKER, JANICE
[pen.] Sonny; [b.] 11 January 1959, Victoria Hos., Worksop; [p.] William and Constance

Walker; [ed.] Hallcroft Secondary; [occ.] Previously nursed, worked for famous Mp. now caring for severely disabled girl; [hon.] English Lit C.S.E, Art C.S.E; [oth. writ.] Two poems published in other anthologies. One short story in magazine. Now writing short story called the "Freezeaer" two poems going through to semifinal.; [pers.] I find great pleasure in writing poetry, its almost like an addiction. I have a fascination about the sea and sky and often use these themes in my poetry. I aim to write lyrics for a famous singer, one day, maybe I'm dreaming, but this is my goal. To all my family and friends `I Love You All'.; [a.] Worksop, Notts, UK, S80 1SD

WALKER, JOSEPH
[b.] 28 May 1947, Stepney; [p.] Late-Charlotte and Henry John; [m.] Linda, 1967; [ch.] Three; [ed.] Secondary Modern Mansford -Bethnal Green E2; [occ.] London Licensed Taxi Driver; [hon.] Editor's Choice award from you. 3rd place winner in "A Passage in Time"; [oth. writ.] Show Me the Sign, I'm Looking for the Piano; [pers.] There is too much sadness in this world, if I can emit happiness through my poems to all you people out there then I know I'm doing something right.; [a.] London, Bethnal Green, UK, E2 0DS

WALKER, MARGARET
[b.] 19 November 1937, Hitchin; [p.] Robert Monk, Bertha Monk; [m.] John Walker, 20 September 1996; [ed.] Hitchin Girls Grammar School, Loughborough University, School of Librarianship, The Open University; [occ.] Retired Librarian; [pers.] Having suffered from Agoraphobia for three months earlier this year, I have tried to draw on this experience in my poem.; [a.] Hitchin, Herefordshire, UK, SG4 9LF

WALLACE, BARBARA
[pen.] Barbara Wallace; [b.] 11 August 1941, Langton Green, Kent; [p.] Enid Reed, Arthur Reed; [m.] David Edward Wallace (Deceased), 15 March 1972; [ch.] Hannah Marie; [ed.] Rye Grammar School, East Sussex; [occ.] Clerk/Typist with a removal firm; [oth. writ.] Other poems but not published, written for pleasure.; [pers.] I like to show feeling in my work. Many years ago I enjoyed poetry at school but never in my wildest dreams did I imagine I would get one published.; [a.] Barming, Maidstone, Kent, UK, ME16 9BE

WALLER, WILLIAM G.
[pen.] Bill; [b.] 8 June 1915, Portsmouth; [p.] William Charles and Sarah Elizabeth; [m.] Margaret (Peg) Baster, 29 December 1938; [ch.] Terence Christopher and Margaret Jane; [ed.] Barton Peveril Grammar School. Eastleigh, Hants University of Southampton; [occ.] Retired Heamaster; [memb.] Radio Amateur Invalid and Blind Club, President Romsey Blind Club, Head Teacher Association; [hon.] Bachelor of Arts (Hons b.a. London Diploma in Education (Cambridge External) CKY and Guilds Radio Amateur G8YWA.; [oth. writ.] Sunshine and Shadow - collection of poems pub. 1990.; [pers.] Registered blind. All poems composed on pocket tape recorder. All profit from Sunshine and Shadow donated to various charities. Founder Head of Romsey School; [a.] Romsey, Hampshire, UK, SO51 7QE

WALLIS, GEORGINA ETHEL
[pen.] Gina Wallis; [b.] 18 October 1919, Greenwich; [p.] Walter and Ethel Wallis; [ed.] High School and Pitmans College; [occ.] Retired from Civil Service (Ministry of Defence); [oth. writ.] Poems and stories, some with historical background, none have been published.; [pers.] Was in the Red Cross and A.R.P. then volunteered for A.T.S. and served as a plotter on combined operations (plotting convoys etc); [a.] Romford, Essex, UK, RM3 8YR

WALSH, LISA
[b.] 16 September 1972, Isle of Wight; [p.] Sarah Bunting, Michael Garland; [ed.] Carisbrooke High School, Newport, Isle of Wight; [occ.] Dental Practice Manager; [pers.] I try to write about personal emotions which everyone will know and understand, and my inspiration has come from another island poet, Lynn New.; [a.] Yarmouth, Isle of Wight, UK, PO41 0SX

WALSH, PAT M.
[b.] London; [p.] Australian; [ed.] Convent; [occ.] Retired Nurse; [memb.] U3A (University of 3rd age) (Drama-French), Local Hospice, "Friends" of local theatre; [hon.] Commendation for poem from Hilton House Publishers - National Poet of Year 1996; [oth. writ.] 8 poems already published - two more to be published soon.; [pers.] Only started writing poetry 1985. Carrying on family tradition of writing as father (who died 1952) was an author.; [a.] Weston-super-Mare, N. Somerset, UK, BS23 2PF

WALSH, SARAH
[b.] 9 June 1982, St. Finbars, Cork; [p.] Marie and Patrick Walsh; [m.] Parents - 1 March 1980; [ed.] Currently Attending Carrigaline Community School (Secondary) 2nd Year; [occ.] Being 14 and trying to get through life, enjoying it.; [hon.] Well I was first in my entrance exam in English out of a 180 pupils. Entrance into Secondary. I had a newspaper published just once with Niamh O' Mahony - Best Friend Always.; [oth. writ.] I write personal poems, I prefer to keep them personal. I wrote a book, but only let friends read. My long essays in primary school made teachers cry (14-15 pages); [pers.] "We are all equal, all of us are trying to play the game of life. No one is better than anyone else, so don't act like you are". My poem is dedicated to Niamh O' Mahony. I was influenced by life's trials.; [a.] Carrigaline, Cork, UK

WANDER, DEBBIE
[b.] 6 April 1957, Plymouth, Devon; [p.] Don MacKay, Monica MacKay; [ch.] Bert, Bill and Ed; [occ.] Nurse Aromatherapist, Reflexologies, Spiritual Healer; [pers.] May we never cease to appreciate the colours and the splendour of another's tapestry as they weave, or stop searching for the brightness in another's soul.; [a.] Paignton, Devon, UK, TQ3 3YB

WARNER, DOROTHY ROWCROFT
[pen.] D. R. Payn Le Sueur; [b.] Victoria Vancouver Island, British Columbia, Canada; [p.] Arthur William and Ruby Frances (nee Rowcroft) Payn Le Sueur; [ch.] Son: Lt. Col. Michael Richard Goodliff; [ed.] St. George's School for Girls, Victoria, and Monterey, Oak Bay, Victoria; [occ.] Various outdoors, also designing, sketching, sewing, needlepoint, etc., reading, correspondence-writing and, recently, poetry; [pers.] Keep going!; [a.] Warnham, West Sussex, UK, RH12 3RF

WARREN, JAMES HENRY
[b.] 13 March 1926, Liverpool; [p.] Walter (Died 1928), Lilian (Died 1988); [m.] Violet (Died 1984), 27 December 1948; [ch.] Daughter Jane; [ed.] 1930-1940 Linacre School Liverpool Highland Light Infantry 1944-1946. Discharged, head wound from German tank shell; [occ.] Retired; [memb.] United Kingdom Association, Professional Teacher of Dancing; [oth. writ.] I submitted a poem in 1980 to an army magazine titled "The Sound of Silence", it was so silent, no one knew it was there. 1996 - "A Raindrop Life", published in Voices on the Wind; [pers.] Word processors are re-incarnated women. They are beautiful contraptions, designed to send strong men to early graves, and sane men into lunatic asylums.; [a.] Wigan, Lancashire, UK, WN5 9EJ

WATKINS, JOHN STIRLING
[b.] 21 July 1943, Co Durham; [ch.] Kieran and Patrick; [ed.] St. Mary's College, Middlesbrough, Newcastle University; [occ.]

Physician; [oth. writ.] Poetry with satirical or spiritual theme (unpublished); [pers.] Favourite writers are Edmund Spenser, William Shakespeare, Edward Albee, and Douglas Dunn.; [a.] Exeter, Devon, UK, EX2 4PP

WATORSKI, ANIELA
[pen.] Ski; [b.] 17 July 1970, Canterbury, Kent; [p.] Mary and Dick Watorski; [ed.] Harriett Comprehensive School London R.D. Basingstoke, Hants; [occ.] Currently travelling Australia since September 1996; [oth. writ.] I have always enjoyed poetry and write my own occasionally for pleasure as gifts.; [pers.] I just want to thank my parents for all their love and support. To you both I am eternally grateful.; [a.] Ramsgate, Kent, UK, CT11 9PL

WATSON, TIM
[b.] 11 January 1931, Singapore; [p.] Tom Watson, Joan Coope; [m.] Roselyn Craven, 6 November 1965; [ch.] Peter Robert, Melanie Jane; [ed.] The King's School, Canterbury, Western Australia Institute of Technology, Bath University; [occ.] Retired Physics Teacher; [memb.] Institute of Physics; [oth. writ.] Articles about physics education and the mechanics of rowing, including the Greek trireme. Poem "Prisoners" published in "A Moment in Time".; [a.] Worcester, UK, WR5 2AB

WATTS, MICHAEL ALAN
[pen.] Mike Watts; [b.] December 1, 1937, Marton-in-Cleveland; [p.] Lt. Col. Alan Watts, Marion Watts; [m.] Philippa Watts, September 15, 1962; [ch.] 2 and one Grandchild; [ed.] Denstone College, Uttoxeter Staffs; [occ.] Chartered Accountant and Composer; [memb.] Institute of Chartered Accountants, Chartered Institute of Taxation, Licentiate Trinity College of Music London, Associate Member British Guild of Composers, Society for Promotion of New Music, Astrological Society.; [hon.] Only qualifications and a Number of Music Competition first prizes.; [oth. writ.] "Five Crystals" (includes this entry, no. 2) "Mike's Doodlebug" (poems and short stories) from the ridiculous to paranormal), "Black Ether" (Horror), Sketches for the Ansaphone, "The Isle of the Dead" (after Arnold Böcklin and Rachmaninov). My timely encounter with the late Sir Arnold Bax (Composer).; [pers.] I am not interested in fiction. My subject is reaching into the mind, searching the crystal, seeking truth and answers through prayer, the paranormal. And as a contrast, happy madness and the ridiculous (read "My New Gong").; [a.] Bournemouth, Dorset, BH1 1JA

WEALE, COLIN IVOR
[b.] 18 March 1958, Herefordshire; [p.] S. J. Weale and E. M. Weale; [ed.] Redhill Comprehensive, Hereford Technical College; [occ.] Industrial Refrigeration; [memb.] Bureu of Freelance Photographers, Vice-Chairman of 'Heli-Bull', Charity Fund Raising Group; [hon.] O level English and Art, C and G Mechanical Engineering; [oth. writ.] First publication. Many poems have been written. Currently working on a novel for future publication.; [pers.] Poem dedicated to the memory of my mother and grandmother. 'There is good in everyone, seek and you shall find': my mother's philosophy.; [a.] Hereford, Herefordshire, UK, HR2 8HW

WEATHERS, HELEN
[pen.] Anna Rose Bailey; [b.] 27 August 1948, Aberdeen; [p.] William Keith, Margaret Keith; [m.] Eric Weathers, 8 August 1970; [ch.] Leigh-Anne, Gordon; [ed.] Aberdeen High School for Girls, Aberdeen College of Education; [occ.] Teacher; [memb.] Mensa; [hon.] Scottish International SWBA (Bowls) 1990; [oth. writ.] This will be my 4th published this year. Others published by Poetry Guild and Poetry Now; [pers.] Life is now. Make the most of it. Leave your mark, not a blot.; [a.] Elgin, Moray, UK, IV30 3AW

WEBB, ANN LORETTA
[pen.] Ann Loretta Harrison-Webb; [b.] 6 April 1935, Horsforth, Nr Leeds; [p.] Deceased; [m.] Kenneth Webb (Ex-printer), 7 June 1976; [ed.] Secondary Modern and College Commerce, College of Drama (Speech Training); [occ.] Retired; [hon.] For Ballroom, and Latin American Dancing only and Scottish Country Dancing; [oth. writ.] 1 volume of poems entitled "Poems of an Insomniac"! 1 volume of the children's poems called "Miss Molly the Jolly Dolly"; [pers.] I firmly believe in making friends (not enemies)! Also in the use of kindness and understanding in all relationships. Plus that good health is all-important and movement to music helps me to keep well.; [a.] Bradford, West Yorkshire, UK, BD10 9LF

WEBSTER, MRS. JEAN
[b.] 23 April 1927, Stafford; [p.] Mr. and Mrs. T. A. Rhodes; [m.] Divorced, 10 June 1950; [ch.] Two; [ed.] High School; [occ.] Artist - Flower Paintings; [memb.] Art School; [oth. writ.] Children's stories including P.D.S.A.; [a.] Truro, Cornwall, UK, TR4 8BD

WEIGHT, HAZEL
[b.] 21 January 1925, London, SW; [p.] Capt. Eldred Dickinson, Gladys Dickinson; [m.] Donald Weight, 17 December 1949 - Reigate; [ch.] Francis John, Stuart, Carol, Josephine; [ed.] Private tutor (wartime), due to illness, encouraged by Wea Tutor Mrs. E. M. Smith of Rewley House, Oxford; [occ.] Retired; [memb.] Bucks, Berks and Oxon, Naturalist Trust; [oth. writ.] Poems in magazines and anthologies and I am currently working on a book of green poems and Haiku, also a book of children's poems.; [pers.] I believe that the natural world has an all important part to play in our mental and spiritual well-being.; [a.] Chalfont St Giles, Bucks, UK, HP8 4EN

WELLINGS, JENNIFER C.
[b.] 29/12/41, Huddersfield Yorks; [p.] John & Lily Simpson; [m.] David G. Wellings, 11th August 1962; [ch.] two; [ed.] Manchester High School; [occ.] Housewife & Sunday school teacher; [oth. writ.] Book of childrens poetry (unpublished) various poetry some published in anthologies; [a.] Peterboro, Cambs.

WELLS, ASHLEY
[pen.] Ashley Wells; [b.] 13 April 1982, Arbroath; [p.] Freda, Martyn Wells; [occ.] Full time education; [memb.] Fan Club of Sean O'Farrell and Shown Cuddy; [pers.] I would like to see peace in Ireland so all Irish people could live their own lives again.; [a.] Arbroath, Scotland, DD11 3SE

WELLS, COLIN
[pen.] C..; [b.] 19 October 1967, Leicester; [p.] Victor and Joan Wells; [ch.] Stefan; [ed.] Mary Lindwood School (Leics); [occ.] Crown Court Security Officer; [hon.] Gulf Medal and Rosette - 1991; [oth. writ.] Various for family and friends none published; [pers.] I started to write poetry whilst serving in the Gulf Conflict in 1991 and now try and reflect the world as I see it.; [a.] Leicester, Leicestershire, UK

WEST, ALAN CHARLES
[b.] 19 February 1961, London; [p.] James West, Sylvia West; [ed.] Willesden High School (comprehensive); [occ.] Clerical Officer for local health authority; [oth. writ.] A collection of poems and song lyrics written for my own pleasure, none of which I have ever offered for publication.; [pers.] I have been writing poetry and song lyrics since around 1978. I write from personal experience, emotions and imagination. My main influence has been singer/songwriter Marc Almond.; [a.] Chiswick, London, UK, W4 4ED

WEST, STEVE
[b.] 3 August 1953, Leicester; [m.] Mrs. Jo West, 28 May 1983; [ch.] Keira Rebecca West, Alan Owen West; [ed.] Linwood Boys Sec Mod Leicester; [occ.] News Agent; [oth. writ.] Lots of

poems and philosophical pieces all sitting at home doing nothing! Friends and relatives trying to get me to get them published but total lack of confidence in myself!; [pers.] I try to write what most people inwardly think. I want people to identify with what I write, not to read poetry and think, 'what is this poem going on about?' I think some poets override simple language and lose the focus of their points, which should be to let the reader easily understand them and not to struggle with the language.; [a.] Barwell, Leicestershire, UK, LE9 8DQ

WESTON, CARRIE-ANNE
[b.] 30 April 1981, Maidstone; [p.] Angela Bronchett, Ion Weston; [ed.] Chalton Court School (still studying); [occ.] Student studying for GCSE's; [oth. writ.] Two poems published in Chalton Court Newspaper; [pers.] I wish to thank Matthew King for showing me I have talent, cheers.; [a.] Maidstone, Kent, UK, ME15 9LE

WESTON, EILEEN HELEN
[b.] 17 February 1925, Grimsby; [p.] Leonard Froud, Frances Helen Froud; [m.] Reuben Weston, 23 April 1949; [ed.] Louth Grammar School, Bridgwater Grammar School, S.E.N. University College Hosp., London; [occ.] Retired; [memb.] The Lace Guild G. Britain, The Late Society (Bobbin Lacemaker); [oth. writ.] Article in Lincolnshire Life. Items in Lace Guild and Lace Society publications. 1st and 2nd prizes in local village show for poetry. Article in "Last Journal of the Queen's Own Hussars" - re: my grandfather's experiences in the Boer War.; [a.] Dinas Powys, Vale of Glamorgan, UK, CF64 4SA

WESTON, WAYNE
[b.] 15 September 1996, Ashton-under-Lyne; [p.] Don and Claire Weston; [ed.] All Saints High School, Dukinfield; [occ.] Office Clerk; [oth. writ.] Nothing published, have sent several articles on music and film to various newspapers and magazines, no luck yet still trying, would love to write on a freelance basis.; [pers.] Poem comments on the two most unnecessary and degenerative social evils - sycophancy and megalomania in the workplace - was originally written as a song, main influences, Bob Dylan and Neil Young.; [a.] Dukinfield, Cheshire, UK, SK16 5JU

WHARF, RUTH
[pen.] Ruth Wharf-Gardner; [b.] 31 July 1946, Morden, Surrey; [p.] Charles and Maud Marshall; [m.] Stanley Wharf, 12 May 1995; [ch.] John, Paul, David, Tanya; [ed.] Convent of the Holy Family, London; [occ.] Psychiatric Nurse; [memb.] London Dramatic Society; [hon.] Awards in counselling; [oth. writ.] A number of poems as yet unsubmitted plus a hymn which has been set to music and is sung daily in a church in Cyprus.; [pers.] When writing serious poetry, my innermost feelings come into being and I try to put these feelings into words.; [a.] Fleet, Hampshire, UK, GU13 0LP

WHARNSBY, MRS. S.
[b.] 5 November 1951, Romford; [p.] Mr. and Mrs. J. McGillivary; [m.] D. A. Wharnsby, 8 May 1971; [ch.] Mark; [occ.] Management Accounts; [oth. writ.] None, this was the first; [pers.] Written after the passing away of my Mum, Janet McGillivary.

WHIDDETT, PERCY WILLIAM
[pen.] John Whiddett; [b.] 15 January 1927; [p.] Percy Whiddett, Jessie Whiddett; [m.] Beryl Elizabeth Whiddett Nee Jarvis, 27 January 1951; [ch.] Paul John, Rosalind Mary; [ed.] Pembury Village School until 14 years of age; [occ.] Retired; [oth. writ.] One previous poem in a Christian magazine. "Living Waters" and a hymn for local church.; [pers.] "Soldiers for Christ" was written when I was asked to write a poem for a family service. The thoughts expressed are from childhood memories and a very real experience spanning 50 years.; [a.] Pembury, Kent, UK, TN2 4EP

WHITE, HAYLEY ELIZABETH
[b.] 23 October 1969, Edmonton; [p.] John M. White, Pauline W. White; [ch.] Lydia, Rose, Gwendoline; [ed.] Queen Eleanor Comprehensive; [occ.] Chemistry Technician; [pers.] To John G. Taylor, my poetic inspiration with love.; [a.] Waltham Cross, Hertfordshire, UK, EN8 7SR

WHITE, SAM
[pen.] Azaria; [b.] 24 January 1981, Birmingham; [p.] Diane Hadley, Michael Hadley; [ed.] Moat Farm Junior School. Langley High School; [occ.] Student at Langley High School; [hon.] Various swimming and dancing medals and trophies; [pers.] My poems are influenced by my spiritual awareness and moods. I strive to find the meaning of life. However I was influenced by my Mom to write disguise.; [a.] Oldbury, West Midlands, UK, B68 9NJ

WHITEWOOD, MARK
[b.] 15 August 1953, Coventry; [p.] Ellen Loovaine and George Henri Whitewood; [m.] Gail Whitewood, 19 July 1995; [ch.] Warwick Henry, Leanne Rachel, Mia Elizabeth; [ed.] The Woodlands School, Trinity College; [occ.] Business Advisor; [memb.] Association Independent Entrepreneurs, Pabulum IBC Team; [hon.] City and Guilds 147 151, B.A. (Hons), M.A., D.B.A.; [pers.] We should all strive to use our minds, as well as machines; [a.] Coventry, West Midlands, UK, CV5 8HU

WHITFIELD, WINIFRED
[pen.] Winn Whitfield; [b.] 16 March 1907, St. Helens; [p.] William Hankinson, Ainnie; [m.] George Whitfield, 1923; [ch.] Two girls; [ed.] Private school, Thenonto, a church school, trained to be a supervisor and head cook for Pilkingtons; [occ.] Pensioner; [oth. writ.] I have always written (since childhood) but never done anything about it, wrote a book about St Helens and other jottings I picked out, school on the hill out. I liked the sound of it; getting old, but love my prose.; [a.] St. Helens, Merseyside, UK, WA10 3SW

WHITNEY, ROSALIND
[m.] Byron Bevan Whitney; [ch.] Ashley, Greg, Philip; [ed.] Neath Girls Grammar School; [occ.] Retired Civil Servant; [memb.] Amnesty International; [pers.] Poetry is a powerful vehicle of expression which can soothe, comfort and inspire others. I thank my family for their love and support.; [a.] Neath, West Glam, UK

WICKREMESINGHE, NALINI
[b.] Colombo, Sri Lanka; [p.] Don Richard and Ruby Wijewardene; [m.] Esmond Wickremesinghe; [ch.] Four sons and one daughter; [occ.] Company Director, associated with publishing, books, television, radio; [hon.] Presidents Arts Council of Sri Lanka 1985 - 1988; [oth. writ.] Early poems, articles published in newspapers; [pers.] Deeply interested in the arts, environment and politics. Writing poetry is a pastime; [a.] Colombo, Colombo 3, Sri Lanka

WILDMAN, SUZETTE
[pen.] Bic; [b.] 13 March 1971, London, England; [p.] Joan Williams and Jesmond Wildman; [ch.] Tara (7), Myles (3); [ed.] St. Martin - in the Fields High School Goldsmiths College, London University, Adult Correspondence College; [occ.] Pre - Licensed, Psychotherapist; [memb.] British Association Psychotherapists, British Eszema Society, Member of Victim Support and Rape Crisis Centre; [oth. writ.] I have written several poems and songs and I am in process of writing a book!; [pers.] I strive to reflect a compilation of my feelings about issues and life in general. Through my writing I want to express a depth of spiritual alliance with my readers, enabling them to touch a chord of exploratory fact and feeling. I admire the works of Shakespeare and early English poets, however I am greatly influenced to express through writing what I feel as an outlet of emotions by someone very special

who shares my life: my mentor, my support, my friend Vincent F. Abraham. Thank you!; [a.] East Dulwich, London, UK, SE15 3LU

WILKES, JAMES
[pen.] James R. Wilkes; [b.] 5 March 1978, Croydon; [p.] Margaret Wilkes, Brian Wilkes; [ed.] St. Andrews Cofe High School, NVQ In Child Care; [occ.] Trainee Nursery Nurse; [memb.] Sunday School Teacher, Assistant Beauer Scout Leader, Scout Helper; [pers.] I base my poems on past experience true to real life mainly in hospital.; [a.] Thornton Heath, Surrey, UK, CR7 8AY

WILKS, NORA
[pen.] Nora Houlihan Wilks; [b.] 8 May 1927, Tralee, Eire; [p.] Frank and Honora Houlihan; [m.] Donald Wilks, 4 April 1953; [ch.] Two sons (John and Peter); [ed.] Presentation Convent, Tralee, Co Kerry, Eire; [occ.] Retired; [memb.] Tralee Writers; [oth. writ.] Short stories and poems published in local magazine, short story published in Irish National Magazine and poem published in U.K. anthology of poems.; [pers.] Now that I have retired, I am fulfilling my life's ambition to write short stories and poems.; [a.] Tralee, Kerry, Eire

WILLIAMS, ALAN JAMES
[pen.] Alan Williams; [b.] 6 February 1943, Manchester; [p.] Ethel and James (Both Deceased); [m.] 23 September 1972, (Now divorced 3 years); [ch.] Helen; [ed.] Worsley Technical College; [occ.] Poet; [memb.] Manchester Chamber of Commerce and Industry; [hon.] O.N.C. Mechanical Engineering G.C.E. 'O' levels - Maths, English Language, Geography and Engineering Drawing, Eccles and Dist. League - Bowler of the year 1980. Several Brewers buy my printed and framed poems, to hang on pub walls.; [oth. writ.] Specialized personal poems - printed and framed. Specific theme poems for pubs etc., standard poems for pubs-both printed and framed. Poems applicable to high St. Businesses. Poems written for company advertising purposes, orthodox poems on all subjects.; [pers.] At the end of the day, there'll come a time, when life will depart, from this body of mine. As I leave, I'd like to think, I've helped you all, enjoy a drink. I have been greatly influenced by the writing of Roy Orbison.; [a.] Eccles, Gt. Manchester, UK

WILLIAMS, CHRIS
[b.] 5 January 1981, Cardiff; [p.] Richard and Lorraine Williams; [ed.] St. Cenydd Comprehensive; [occ.] In school; [oth. writ.] Several unpublished poems and short stories.; [pers.] Life is like the road the traveler follows, it goes from place to place, but doesn't lead anywhere.; [a.] Caerphilly, County Borough, UK, CF83 2UG

WILLIAMS, CLAUDINE GALLAWAY
[b.] 28 November 1977, London; [ed.] St. Marylebone Secondary School; [occ.] A - Level student currently in my last year; [oth. writ.] One of five winners in a JAL Japanese Haiku competition for world children 1990, from JAL foundation and Japanese Airlines; [pers.] I've enjoyed writing poems for as long as I can remember, so it is very satisfying to gain recognition from a poetry organization. This is also the first time I have written a poem in a dramatic narrative style; [a.] Islington, London, UK

WILLIAMS, ELWYN
[b.] 21 June 1929, Bangor, North Wales; [p.] John Williams, Elizabeth Williams; [m.] Mary Williams, 21 March 1959; [ch.] Clive Williams, Peter Williams; [ed.] Friars Grammar School, North Wales. Liverpool College of Art; [occ.] Retired Head of Education Services, Manchester Art Galleries; [memb.] Founder Member, Mountaineering Club of North Wales; [hon.] National Diploma in Design (N.D.D.) Art Teacher's Diploma (A.T.D.), Appointed First Chairman of Moderators to Supervise Art Examinations in

Secondary Schools Throughout Northern England. Responsible for 90,000+ candidates in 1987. I was sent several times to Northern Ireland to help develop art examinations in the province.; [oth. writ.] Practicing artist. Many works held in private collections throughout England and some held in private collections in Ireland, the U.S.A., and Australia. I have lectured at several universities and art galleries in the United Kingdom, including the National Gallery, London; [pers.] Probably best to leave my drawings and poems to speak for themselves.; [a.] Tarleton, Lancashire, UK, PR4 6US

WILLIAMS, GARETH JAMES
[b.] 7 July 1976, Wembley, Middx; [p.] Robert Williams, Pamella Jones; [ed.] Gunnersbury Catholic School, Brentford, L1 Po Chun United World College, Hong Kong, School of Oriental and African Studies, London; [occ.] Chinese and History Student; [oth. writ.] Many unpublished poems; [pers.] I attempt to capture my own experiences from an outside perspective in such a way so as to mirror my view of human kind, the way we are, the way we live, the way we feel.; [a.] Harrow, Middx, UK, HA2 7DD

WILLIAMS, JOHN HENRY
[pen.] Henry Clifton - (1971); [b.] 8 December 1928, Worcester - (9B); [p.] Robert Felix Williams and Ruby Evelyn (Nee Langston); [m.] Marjorie Violet (Nee Shellam), 6 December 1952; [ch.] Four - three alive (all boys); [ed.] Martley Chantry for Sons, Self great witley - with some R.I.B. plus Hereford Technical College plus Young Farmers Excursions; [occ.] Agricultural Engineer - Blacksmith/Farrier - Etc, etc, etc., etc.; [memb.] None now - all because of a lot of local ill will should be worth a fortune. But things are not quite right - not yet settled - hence - enclosed poems.; [oth. writ.] Just three poems. IE Regency Press 1971; [pers.] Some of us catch for all sorts of ill regard - I happen to be just one of those; I am fund owner etc. I am classified as an Ex Bankrupt. Case no. 11 Worcester Country Court 1967. Not a very just case.; [a.] Great Witley, Worcester, UK, WR6 6JU

WILLIAMS, JOHN STEVEN
[pen.] Steve Williams; [b.] 19 April 1969, Gravesend; [p.] Albert Williams, Kathleen Williams; [m.] Margaret Williams, 30 November 1991; [ch.] Lynn Aiken; [ed.] Southfields Secondary Gravesend; [oth. writ.] This is my first poem that I have entered into competition; [pers.] Poetry is a form of self expression where feelings are shared in a way that brings strangers together and loved ones closer.; [a.] Ashford, Kent, UK, TN24 0PL

WILLIAMS, JULIAN GAIUS
[b.] 18 June 1959, Carmarthen; [p.] D. K. and M. P. Williams; [ed.] Amman Valley Comprehensive School; [occ.] Unemployed; [memb.] Contributor to a newsletter, 'Connect' in Shansea "Gwalia" Housing Association; [hon.] The captain's prize for poetry on ship, "S.S. Weanda', 1971, W.J. E.C., G.C.E., 'O' Level in English Language (Grade "B"), Grades 1, 2, 3 Royal School of Music (Piano) also interviewed on television, by Bob Humphries on B.B.C. Wales 'Week in, Week Out'; [oth. writ.] For a short story congratulatory and complimentary letter reply from 'Daily Mirror', 5 poems published in my school magazine and essay on science-fiction between 1971-1975, letter published in Melody Maker, novella submitted to B.B.C. competition and professor at Cardiff University.; [pers.] In my poems and essays I express feeling, concepts, imagination, impressive expression, description, philosophy, romance, originality, inspiration, ingenious ideas, meaning, ecstatic and euphoric writing, interesting, enjoyable narrative, information, emotion and essential ideas for plot or theme of writing and vocabulary. Poem 'Peter Pan in Stages' broadcast on Radio Caroline in 1974; [a.] Ammanford, Dyfed, UK

WILLIAMS, LARA MICHELLE
[b.] 20 July 1980, Brierley Hill; [p.] Patricia Williams, David Cox; [ed.] Cradley C.E. School, Cradley High, Crestwood School, Halesowen College; [occ.] Student, studying B Tec National Diploma Early Childhood Studies; [memb.] First Act (Drama); [hon.] 5. 9. CSE's. 2 UKA Alliance Certificates; [oth. writ.] 1 poem in local magazine; [pers.] My poem hopefully highlights abuse in the home and is also dedicated to my family, and friends, and doctors and nurses who have cared for me over the years.; [a.] Brierley Hill, Westmidlands, UK, DY5 4NB

WILLIAMS, VALERIE
[pen.] Valerie Preece; [b.] 29 June 1947, Hereford; [p.] Doreen Preece, Harold Preece; [m.] Divorced; [ch.] Debbie, Karen, Ian; [ed.] Secondary Modern; [occ.] Nursing Assistant; [oth. writ.] Poem to be published in November by the Poetry Guild "Monarch of The Glen", two essays printed in local newspapers; [pers.] I feel that poetry is a state of mind, an extension of the author. I am deeply moved by good verse.; [a.] Hereford, Herefordshire, UK, HR1 1PG

WILLIAMSON, ANNE
[b.] 10 March 1939, Gateshead; [p.] Ralph Richardson, Sarah Richardson; [pers.] I write purely and simply for pleasure in the hope that someone, somewhere will experience this same emotion on reading one of my poems.; [a.] Gateshead, Tyne and Wear, UK, NE8 3JY

WILLIAMSON, DERRICK
[b.] 4 April 1933, Sydenham; [p.] Amy; [m.] Sheila-Ann, 31 August 1973; [ch.] David; [ed.] Forest Hill School; [occ.] Counselling Psychologist; [memb.] International Association of Hypno-Analysts; [hon.] M.A., Psychology of Therapy and Counselling; [oth. writ.] Poem published in Counselling Magazine; [pers.] The more I listen, the greater the depth of emotion is given to my understanding.; [a.] Lincoln, Lincolnshire, UK, LN2 4TW

WILLIAMSON, DOREEN MARY
[pen.] Dawn Williams; [b.] 3 June 1926, Whitstable, Kent; [p.] Florence and Micheal Cashman; [m.] Lancelot Williamson - deceased 1974, 25 December 1953; [ch.] Russel and Deborah; [ed.] Endowed Girls School Whitstable; [occ.] Retired; [memb.] The Surrey Spiritual Healers Association; [oth. writ.] Poems printed in church magazines and newsletters.; [per.] I try to set an example to others, especially my grandchildren, and hope to bring people love, comfort and relaxation through my writings.; [a.] Tooting, London, UK, SW17 9TA

WILLIAMSON, W.
[pen.] Bally Billy; [b.] 30 August 1931, Madras, India; [p.] Mr. and Mrs. Williamson; [ed.] Passed Junior Cambridge Examination at Barnes High School (boarding school), Deolali Bombay State, India; [occ.] Retired; [oth. writ.] The best things in life are free, they are there for you and me, if you don't have a dime, you can still have a good time. 'Cause the best things in life are free.; [pers.] Life is an echo, it all comes back, the good, the false, and the true. So give the world the best you have and the best will return to you.; [a.] Hayes, Middx, UK, UB10 0DN

WILLIS, ALBERT G.
[b.] 15 March 1917, Droitwich, Worcs; [p.] Jesse and Dora; [m.] Emily Nora Tivy, 16 April 1941; [ch.] One foster-son; [ed.] Worcester Royal Grammar School, School of Accountancy - Examinations of the Chartered Institute of Secretaries; [occ.] Retired - Local Government Officer; [memb.] Various clubs and societies over the years; [hon.] Service Medal and Bar awarded by the Order of St. John of Jerusalem for 20 plus years voluntary service in the St. John Ambulance Brigade; [oth. writ.] Poem "Some Thoughts on Alzheimer's Disease" published in A Passage

of Time, April 1996. Various articles published in local church magazines, in-house and in-hospital periodic reviews. Also numismatic/metal articles published in both U.K. and U.S. hobby magazines. Have recently returned to my home town after an absence of almost 40 years - the constant background noise of the nearby Motorway has replaced the sound of the nightingales all those years ago.; [a.] Droitwich, Worcestershire, UK, WR9 7DL

WILSON, ARCHIE
[b.] May 23, 1947, Lowestoft; [p.] Archie And Rosina Wilson; [m.] Irene Wilson; [ch.] Darren, Jenny Wilson; [ed.] Kirkley RD Comprehensive Lowestof, Ipswich Civic College; [occ.] Logistics Manager; [memb.] Director Eqous Theater Company, Member Widmer End Players; [oth. writ.] Stories in writings magazines poetry in local newspaper. Theatre critic for local paper.; [pers.] I write to entertain from personal experience and to demonstrate the beauty of the English Language.; [a.] High Wycombe, Burks, HP15 6BU

WILSON, BARBARA
[b.] 9 June 1971, Dungannon, NI; [p.] Thomas Wilson, Barbara Ann Wilson; [ed.] Jordans Town School (for the blind), Royal National College University of Ulster, Coleraine; [occ.] Journalist; [oth. writ.] Poems and articles published in local community newspaper; [pers.] I write what I see and feel in my imagination whether it be a true response to the wider world. I believe one single poem can mean many different things to each reader.; [a.] Dungannon, Tyrone, UK, BT71 7SU

WILSON, ELIZABETH
[b.] 10 March 1954, Liverpool; [p.] Robert Wilson, Elizabeth Muriel Wilson; [ed.] Cuddington County Primary School, Hartford Girls' School, Cheshire School of Art; [occ.] Portrait Artist; [memb.] Political Animal Lobby Honorary Member; [hon.] MENSA Certificate of Merit; [oth. writ.] Various poems accepted for publication in seven anthologies.; [pers.] Although many of my poems are modern in style, without rhyme, I tend to lean mainly towards the traditional, romantic. I am, therefore, delighted that an increasing number of anthologies are embracing such poetry, concluding that threads of Wordsworth and Keaths may still be found in today's tapestry of poets.; [a.] Chester, Cheshire, UK

WILSON, JULIA
[pen.] Ellen Hillary-Fawcett; [b.] 9 November 1947, Buddle House Farm, Richmond, North Yorks; [p.] Thomas and Eva Jane Fawcett; [m.] William Wilson, 15 January 1973; [ch.] Esther Jane and Hannah Lucy Wilson; [ed.] Marske (Swaledale) C.E. Junior School, Richmond (N. Yorkshire), County Modern Scarborough College of Technology; [occ.] Process Operator for a pharmaceutical company; [pers.] Poetry is a form of expressing emotions that would otherwise be kept hidden. It is a balm for the soul.; [a.] Barnard Castle, Durham, UK, DL12 9AS

WILSON, MICHELLE G.
[b.] 24 April 1976; [p.] Janet and Michael Wilson; [ed.] Won Scholarship to Queen Ethelburga's girl's school, Leeds University.; [occ.] At Leeds University reading English Literature.; [memb.] Creative Writing Society of Leeds, National Ballet and Leeds Squash and Tennis Club.; [hon.] Albert Schwgtzer Essay Title, Yorkshire Television Award for Drama, Gold Duke of Edinburgh; [oth. writ.] Poems and news articles published in university paper, articles in the 'Yorkshire Post Newspaper'.; [pers.] "Wherever there is creativity truth flowers, truth is a flowering of creativity".; [a.] Leeds, Yorkshire, UK, LS16 5PG

WINGROVE, JOY J.
[b.] 10 February 1936, Sheffield; [p.] Ethel Leech and Percy Moor; [m.] Charles, 2 October 1982; [ch.] Robert and Lorraine; [ed.] Dronfield Gram-

mar School, Derbyshire; [occ.] Nurse; [memb.] Royal College of Nursing; [hon.] SRN, RMN, OHNC Nursing Qualifications; [oth. writ.] Poetry and short stories.; [pers.] Would like to have published a book of children's poems, (still written); loves all kinds of poetry.; [a.] Lincoln, Lincs, UK, LN6 9HX

WINSTANLEY, ANNE
[pen.] Gilly; [b.] 19 August 1954, Bristol; [p.] Valerie Mary Kendall; [ch.] Safron, Sian, Shela; [ed.] Stockwell Hill Secondary, Soundwell College; [occ.] Accounts Clerk and Health Care Assistant; [memb.] Royal Life Saving Society; [oth. writ.] I have never until now sent in anything for publication.; [pers.] My writings are based on personal experiences and life around me, to leave as a gift to my three daughters.; [a.] Bristol, UK, BS15 1RZ

WINTERBURN, JOHN
[b.] 27 September 1933, Great Yarmouth; [p.] Alfred and Margaret Winterburn (Both Deceased); [m.] Mary Rowland, 18 April 1959; [ch.] Helen Clare, Rachael Ann; [ed.] Great Yarmouth Technical High School, Great Yarmouth and Lowestoft College of Further Education; [occ.] Retired M.D., Own hosiery and knitwear factory; [memb.] Gorleston E.B.A. "Brownston Hall", Hopton, E.B.A.; [hon.] Past (hon.) Member of the Institute of Industrial Managers M.I.I.M., Handwriting Waterman Pen Co. Award - Best in all East Anglia - when teenager.; [oth. writ.] Compulsive diarist, other unpublished poems.; [pers.] Immensely influenced by "The Immortal Bard"; [a.] North Walsham, Norfolk, UK, NR28 9XR

WOOD, BRIAN
[b.] 5 June 1956, Stockport; [p.] Audrey Wood and Harold Wood (Both Deceased); [m.] Divorced; [ed.] Raddish Vale Comprehenshive Stockport College; [occ.] Sales Manager and Freelance Writer/Promoter; [memb.] Blackburn Civic Society, Run/Own "Magic Village Promotions and Publications"; [hon.] Multi-award nominated poet. Included in over 10 anthologies in 1996 alone. Contribute to Lancashire Evening Telegraph, Citizen News Papers, etc.; [oth. writ.] Ex RBC News Headlines. Industrial journals, music dress, contributor to several news papers, lyricist publishing own book "Poems of Love, Life and Death" in 1997. Organizing Blackburn Poetry Festival 1997; [pers.] I try and capture and incorporate and program Surrealism allied to a literary desire for the reader to repeatedly re-read my work - gaining an extra 'something' each time. Greatness and entertainment are intimate bedfellows.; [a.] Blackburn, Lancashire, UK, BB2 6BH

WOOD, DENISE
[pen.] Denise King; [b.] 25 September 1953, Dublin; [p.] Christopher and Eileen King; [m.] 11 March 1972; [ch.] Three; [ed.] Dominican Convent Primary, Dominican Convent Secondary; [hon.] 1st Prize Cookery Award, R.S.A. Typing; [oth. writ.] I was inspired by Frank O'Connor and William Wordsworth among others.; [pers.] The one who cares, can find Peace with their soul.; [a.] Rotherham, S. Yorks, UK, S63 7AE

WOODBRIDGE, MRS. BARBARA
[pen.] Barbara Woodbridge; [b.] 20 June 1945, Southall, Middlesex; [p.] Deceased; [m.] Mr. Peter Woobridge, 30 August 1969; [ed.] Dormers Wells Secondary Modern School for Girls; [occ.] Receptionist/Typist; [oth. writ.] Several rhymes written during a temporary period after being made redundant, before finding a permanent position.; [pers.] After losing both parents at a very early age and working hard all my life, I have always tried to see the lighter side of life and take much pleasure in reading rhymes, poetry, singing and dancing and listening to music.; [a.] Ashford, Middlesex, UK, TW14 8RT

WOODCOCK, TERENCE VICTOR
[pen.] T.V. Woodcock; [b.] 26 December 1936, West Bromwich; [p.] Mary and William Woodcock; [m.] Mary, 7 September 1963; [ch.] Anthony and Emma; [ed.] Charlemont Infants/Junior School, Chronehills Secondary Technical School, West Bromwich Technical College, Dudley Technical College; [occ.] Retired Electrical Engineer; [memb.] The Institution of Electronics and Electrical Incorporated Engineers, I Eng. M.I.E.I.E.; [hon.] City and Guilds Higher National Certificate in Electrical Engineering; [oth. writ.] Children's poems and nursery rhymes, poems, popular songs, hymns, Christmas songs, satirical sketches about the people I used to work with, and songs written for my children when young.; [pers.] To have imagination is a great gift from God - to waste this gift by not exercising it, is sacrilege.; [a.] Pershore, Worcestershire, UK, WR10 1PB

WOODS, KARL
[b.] 13 June 1976, Sevenoaks; [p.] Sylvia Arnold; [ch.] Michael Fletcher; [ed.] Astor School, Dover Wolverhampton University; [occ.] Student; [memb.] Greenpeace, Amnesty International; [hon.] Business Studies, Sociology; [oth. writ.] Poems and articles for school/University magazines. Currently re-writing my first book.; [pers.] Dedicated to my sister and my friends. You bring out the best in me.; [a.] Deal, Kent, UK, CT14 7XA

WOOLLACOTT, TREVOR FRANCIS
[b.] 16 September 1965, Winchester; [p.] Harry Ivor Woollacott, Noreen Woollacott; [ed.] Priory Comprehensive, Broadoak Sixth Form Centre; [occ.] Revenue Officer; [memb.] Manchester United Supporter's Club, (Bridgwater and South West), Registered Blood Donor; [oth. writ.] "Reflections" (published in previous anthology "Quiet Moments"); [pers.] Life is seldom, if ever, as we would wish. Consequently, the price of escapism is isolation.; [a.] Weston super Mare, North Somerset, UK, BS22 0NY

WOOSTER, TERESA ANN
[b.] 6 May 1973, Edgware; [p.] Robert Wooster, Jennifer Wooster; [ch.] Jasmin Eva and Kyle Kristian; [ed.] Greenhill College, West Herts College; [occ.] Mother and Artist; [oth. writ.] I have a number of unpublished poems, which consist of personal experiences and emotions.; [pers.] With my poetry I hope to touch the heart of people's dreams and share an understanding of their feelings.; [a.] Pinner, Middlesex, UK, HA5 5NU

WORTHINGTON, COLIN
[b.] 21 May 1948, Edinburgh; [m.] Fiona Gallagher; [ch.] Sara and James; [occ.] Manager of Local Football Club, Meadow Star FC, and Poet.; [memb.] First Friday Poetry Reading Club (Edinburgh); [oth. writ.] Apart from having many poems published in assorted anthologies and poetry magazines, my first full volume of work published by Minerva Press "Cracked but not Broken" ISBN 1-85863-938-7; [pers.] If I have created something from deep inside that brings a smile to your lips or a thought to your head, then I have been completely rewarded.; [a.] Edinburgh, UK

WRIGHT, ARNOLD
[b.] 1 August 1920, Spennymoor; [p.] Orphan - since 1929; [m.] Silvia A. Wright, 14 June 1956; [ch.] Three: Paul, Bernard, James; [ed.] No formal education, trained to become a professional opera singer with life's experience; [occ.] Retired; [oth. writ.] Radio scripts and broadcasting in Canada. RAF Panto scripts and shows, magazine articles.; [pers.] Before I die 'The wisdom and wit of an aging twit' a love song of sixty or so poems. Politically pithy - humouress - very sad and loving, hoping for a wider audience, on video - with song.; [a.] Brighton, Sussex, UK, BN2 2BF

WRIGHT, DAWN
17 May 1970, Sleaford; [p.] Vivienne Wright; [ch.] Daniel Robin Arliss; [ed.] Kirton Primary School; [occ.] Housewife, part time cleaner; [memb.] Y.O.C. group leader (Junior Membership of RSPB) for Boston and surrounding areas; [hon.] St. Johns Ambulance First Aid Course - pass - certificate; [oth. writ.] Lift off was a personal development project lasting 3 yrs. I attended one of the courses and wrote a poem on personal development, opinions. Read out to audience of 200, approx. Personal pleasure, is children's stories at moment, plus poetry. [pers.] I've long been interested in writing poetry, and will study soon too, in the hope of one day having a book published. I base some of my writing on my interest in children and wild life. My drive/ambition for improvement is one of the inspirations for my poem, Time...did, can, will...change. [a.] Boston, Lincolnshire PE20 2LT

WRIGHT, JOY
[b.] 13 September 1918, Eastleigh; [p.] L. Byrne and F. Byrne; [m.] Francel S. Wright, January 1947; [ch.] Penelope and Lawrence Wright; [ed.] Secondary Modern School Eastleigh; [occ.] Housewife; [memb.] Amateur Dramatic Society Grammar School Parents Ass. Avdenshaw Manchester, Gurnard Ladies Choir, Gurnard Isle of Wright, Cowes Dramatic and Operatic Society; [hon.] English Language - Credit German Grade I Credit; [oth. writ.] Many poems and stories over the years - not tried to publish, several articles in local paper.; [pers.] My poem 'Lady and Her Dog' was inspired by a statue I have on my window sill. Most of my poems are reflections on life and observations of the countryside and people.; [a.] Cowes, Isle of Wight, UK, PO31 7NN

WRIGHT, LAURA NEE MAROCCO
[b.] 26 December 1925, Trieste; [p.] Dead; [m.] Douglas James Wright, 5 September 1948; [ed.] High School for Teachers Certificate, M.A. Ca Foscari University, Venice, (Foreign Languages and Literature); [occ.] Writing (After a career as English Professor from 1950 to 1980 and several years as Head Mistress in high schools); [memb.] Anglo-Italian Association (member), British Film Club (member), Friends of the Local Dialect (founder member), Societa Artistico-Letteraria (Artistic and Literary Association) (Vice President and Head of Theatre Section.); [hon.] Play writing: Four regional first prizes and a national second prize. Poetry: Trophies from Australia and a regional first prize. Prose: Regional first and second prizes for long novels plus mentions.; [oth. writ.] From 1981 to 1995: Thirteen plays performed in Trieste and other towns as well as abroad. A collection of poems in Italian. Title: Nine Pennies. (Nove Soldi) A collection of long novels. Title: The Echoes of Deep Silence. (Gli echi del profondo silenzio). Poems and prose published in the cultural pages of newspapers and magazines and included in anthologies: 1) Venezia Giulia Writers, 2) Tales Told by Our People, 3) In the Forge of Words, 4) Trieste Poets. Plays, poems, prose and interviews also broadcast by R.A.I. Telequattro and other private broadcasting stations.; [pers.] Sound, words and suggestions are means to underline the soul's message intended as the link between micro- and macro-cosmos.; [a.] Trieste, Friuli-Venezia Giulia, Italy, 34136

WYATT, SUZANNE
[b.] 19 November 1984, Cheadle, Stoke-on-Trent; [p.] Mr. Philip William and Mrs. Eileen Wyatt; [ed.] St. Giles RC Primary School and now Painsley R.C. High School Pupil; [occ.] Student; [oth. writ.] St. Giles Anthology of Poetry/unpublished.; [pers.] Inspired by poetry of environmental issues and my own imagination.; [a.] Cheadle, Stoke-on-Trent, UK, ST10 1PT

WYLES, CORAL ROSE
[b.] 18/10/48, Romford; [p.] Daphne & Ron Archer; [m.] John, 18/3/67; [ch.] Celest, Samantha & Elizabeth; [occ.] Compiling my own book of poetry, and writing childrens stories which I hope to have published soon; [ded.] His faith has never faltered mine has all but disappeared, he urged me to keep writing, I withdrew into my fears. But, braver pens than I have bared all to go on so my poem's dedicated to my love, my life, my John.; [a.] Kingsclere, Berks, RG20 5T6

YALE, MARGARET MARY
[b.] 27 May 1925, Bloxwich; [p.] Abraham and Mary Bannister; [m.] Jeffrey T. Yale, 12 August 1950; [ed.] St. Peters RC School Bloxwich W. Mids.; [occ.] Retired Tailoress; [oth. writ.] Inspirational poems written by me just for personal pleasure.; [pers.] Inspiration to write poetry first came to me whilst recovering from a serious illness; it gave me time to reflect on life and to put my feelings into words.; [a.] Birmingham, Warwickshire, UK, B42 1QF

YATES, MRS. JOAN
[b.] Rochdale; [m.] Trevor Yates; [ch.] One girl, One boy; [occ.] Quality Control Tester; [a.] Rochdale, Lancs, UK, OL12 9HL

YATES, NICOLA DAWN
[pen.] Niki Yates; [b.] 20 June 1946, Birmingham, UK; [p.] Una and Neville Yates; [m.] Divorced; [ch.] Peter and Nicholas (Strauss); [ed.] Edgbaston High School, Wispers School (Sussex), Open University; [occ.] Independent, Distributor with Forever Living Products; [memb.] St. Mary's Church, Rotterdam, Open Univ. Graduates Assoc., Open Univ. Psychological Soc., British Psychological Soc.; [hon.] BSC (honors open); [oth. writ.] Poem pub. Oupoets Mag.; [pers.] My poetry is written out of my love for people and relationships, that the benefits I have received may be rendered again, line for line, deed for deed to somebody; [a.] Schiedam, The Netherlands, 3121 TC

YATES, PATRICIA
[pen.] Patricia Yates; [b.] 6 December 1960, Liverpool; [p.] Henry Bentley, Patricia Bentley; [m.] John Yates, 25 June 1983; [ch.] John, Carl and Paul; [ed.] St. Anne's R.C. Secondary Modern; [occ.] Housewife; [pers.] I try to reflect in my poetry the importance and appreciation of everyday life. I try to find some goodness in every aspect of life.; [a.] Liverpool, Merseyside, UK, L14 3LW

YOUNG, KENNETH
[b.] 3 January 1923, Prestwich, Manchester; [p.] Joseph Chadwick Young, Ida Gertrude (nee Bury); [ed.] Stand Grammar, Whitefield Manchester Univ. (Classics), London Univ. (Philosophy), McMaster Univ, Ontario (Philosophy), Univ. of Pennsylvania (Thilos.); [hon.] B.A. (Manchester), B.A. (London), M.A., (Penn.); [oth. writ.] Translation of "West Over Sea" by Jon Leisfall (Norwegian M.P.) for Findhorn Foundation.; [pers.] My top priority is rescuing this planet from the rocketing population and spiralling motor traffic, and resisting the hostility of entrenched orthodoxies to honest inquiry.; [a.] Tomintoul, Banffshire, UK, AB37 9EX

YOUNG, MRS. B. D.
[pen.] Barbara Dearness; [b.] 20 January 1907, Leith, Scotland; [m.] George Young (Deceased) 2 March 1932; [ch.] Two; [ed.] Perth, Academy General Education; [occ.] Retired Nurse; [memb.] Red-Cross Club; [oth. writ.] Have been interested in national poet, Robert Burns.; [a.] Perth, Perthshire, UK, PH2 8JQ

ZABIELA, NOOSHA
[b.] 15 June 1980, Jersey, C.I.; [p.] Mrs. Sandra Le Moine and Keith Zabiela; [ed.] First Tower Primary School, Grainville Secondary School; [occ.] Secretary of her Grandfather's Sign Writing Business; [hon.] Headmaster's Prize on leaving First Tower Primary School.; [pers.] This poem is dedicated to Angela Butel. I would also to thank my mother for entering this poem towards the competition.; [a.] St. Helier, Jersey Channel Islands, UK, JE2 3JH

ZORICA, GEORGIE
[pen.] Geofil Lyubov-Zoriastro; [b.] 25 April 1935, Slavonski Brod, Yogoslavia; [p.] Marko and Juliana Lyuboevich-Zorica; [m.] Vida (Nee Bosniakovich) Zorica, 7 August 1965 (Melb. Australia); [ch.] Son Marko L. Zorica; [ed.] In linguistics and metaphysics, mostly self-educated in Switzerland, Australia and Britain (specialized in Religion - Zoroastrianism in particular); [occ.] Unemployed; [memb.] Labour Party, Fabian Society, and SCRSS, Society for Co-Operation in Russian Studies; [hon.] Several medals in various olympic wrestling championships and competitions!; [oth. writ.] Several poems in English, only one published. Many essays, articles and letters, some letters published in English newspapers, also several articles published in Yugoslavian magazines. Now, I am preparing a book "Truth the Holy Truth", or "Angelic Verses Satanished", An Alternative Religious (and Secular) History, from Abraham to Zoroaster-the Bible to Zend-Avesta, or v.v.!!; [pers.] I am trying to bring the light of the dawn of new spiritual consciousness to humanity..For it is, "blinded by (the Mammon), God of this materialistic Dark Age" (Cor 4:4), multiplied exceedingly, and it's now lemming-like, heading for the nearest precipice, to throw itself into the darkest abyss of the bottomless Hell?!; [a.] Tulse Hl, Lambeth, London, UK, SW2 2HD

524

Index
of
Poets